FUNK & WAGNALLS
NEW ENCYCLOPEDIA

fw

VOLUME 18
NORWICH to
PEYOTE

FUNK & WAGNALLS NEW ENCYCLOPEDIA

JOSEPH LAFFAN MORSE, Sc.B., LL.B., L.H.D., LL.D.
Editor in Chief, Funk & Wagnalls Encyclopedias, 1946–69
WILLIAM H. HENDELSON, Editorial Director,
and successor Editor in Chief

Funk & Wagnalls, Inc., New York

Funk & Wagnalls
New Encyclopedia
© 1972
By Funk & Wagnalls, Inc.

Library of Congress Catalog
Card Number 72-170933

Copyright Under the Articles of the Copyright Convention of the Pan-American Republics and the United States

**PRINTED IN THE UNITED STATES OF AMERICA
ALL RIGHTS RESERVED**

ggb

FUNK & WAGNALLS
NEW ENCYCLOPEDIA

LIST OF ABBREVIATIONS USED IN THE TEXT*

abbr.	abbreviated	fr.	from	O.T.	Old Testament
AC; a-c	alternating current	Fr.	French	oz.	ounce
A.D.	*anno Domini* (Medieval Lat., in the year of the Lord)	ft.	foot	P.M.	*post meridiem* (Lat., after noon)
		g	gram		
		Gael.	Gaelic	Pol.	Polish
		gal.	gallon	pop.	population
alt.	altitude	Ger.	German	Port.	Portuguese
A.M.	*ante meridiem* (Lat., before noon)	Gr.	Greek	prelim.	preliminary
		Heb.	Hebrew	pron.	pronounced
AM	amplitude modulation	Hind.	Hindustani	q.v.	*quod vide* (Lat., which see)**
amu	atomic mass unit	h.p.	horsepower		
anc.	ancient	hr.	hour	r.	reigned
Ar.	Arabic	Hung.	Hungarian	R.	River
AS.	Anglo-Saxon	Hz	hertz or cycles per second	rev.	revised, revision
A.S.S.R.	Autonomous Soviet Socialist Republic			R.R.	railroad
		I.	Island	Rum.	Rumanian
at.no.	atomic number	i.e.	*id est* (Lat., that is)	Russ.	Russian
at.wt.	atomic weight	in.	inch	Ry.	railway
b.	born	Ind.	Indian	S.	south; southern
bbl	barrel	Ir.	Irish	sec.	second
B.C.	before Christ	It.	Italian	S.F.S.R.	Soviet Federated Socialist Republic
bd.ft.	board feet	K.	Kelvin		
bev	billion electron volts	kg	kilogram	Skr.	Sanskrit
		km	kilometer	Sp.	Spanish
b.p.	boiling point	kw	kilowatt	sp.gr.	specific gravity
B.T.U.	British Thermal Unit	kw hour	kilowatt hour	sq.	square
		lat.	latitude	sq.mi.	square mile
bu.	bushel	Lat.	Latin	S.S.R.	Soviet Socialist Republic
Bulg.	Bulgarian	lb.	pound		
C.	centigrade	long.	longitude	St.; Ste.	Saint
cent.	century	m	meter	Sum.	Sumerian
Chin.	Chinese	M.	Middle	Sw.	Swedish
cm	centimeter	mev	million electron volts	temp.	temperature
Co.	County			trans.	translation
colloq.	colloquial	mg	milligram	Turk.	Turkish
cu.	cubic	mi.	mile	U.A.R.	United Arab Republic
Czech.	Czechoslovakian	min.	minute		
d.	died	M.L.	Medieval Latin	U.K.	United Kingdom
Dan.	Danish	mm	millimeter	U.N.	United Nations
DC; d-c	direct current	mod.	modern	U.S.	United States
Du.	Dutch	m.p.	melting point	U.S.A.	United States of America
E.	east; eastern	m.p.h.	miles per hour		
ed.	edition; editor	Mt(s).	Mount, Mountain	U.S.S.R.	Union of Soviet Socialist Republics
Egypt.	Egyptian	N.	north; northern		
Eng.	English	N.T.	New Testament		
est.	estimated	OE.	Old English	var.	variant
ev	electron volt	OF.	Old French	vol.	volume
F.	Fahrenheit	OHG.	Old High German	vs.	versus or against
fl.	flourished	ON.	Old Norse	W.	west; western
FM	frequency modulation	ONF.	Old Norman French	yd.	yard

* For a more extensive listing of abbreviations, widely used by authoritative sources in many fields, *see* ABBREVIATION. Charts of pertinent abbreviations also accompany the articles BIBLE, CANON OF THE; DEGREE, ACADEMIC; ELEMENTS, CHEMICAL; MATHEMATICAL SYMBOLS; WEIGHTS AND MEASURES. Accent marks and special letters are explained in the article DIACRITIC MARK.

** The abbreviation (q.v.) stands for the Latin words "quod vide," meaning "which see." The placement of this abbreviation after a word—or a name or term—indicates that the word itself is the title of a separate article in the encyclopedia. By looking up the article on this word, or the entries on each word in a series that is followed by the plural form (qq.v.) of the abbreviation, the reader will find specific information about the words used as well as additional data about the main topic of the article he is reading.

FUNK & WAGNALLS
NEW ENCYCLOPEDIA

NORWICH, city in Connecticut, and county seat of New London Co., on the Thames R., 50 miles S.E. of Hartford. Industries are textiles, apparel, paper, fabricated metals, leather, insulated wire, and engraving. The Slater Memorial Museum and its annex, the Converse Art Gallery, are in Norwich. The city is the birthplace of Benedict Arnold (q.v.), whose house has been preserved. Settled in 1659, Norwich was incorporated as a town in 1685 and as a city in 1784. The town and city were consolidated in 1951. Pop. (1960) 38,506; (1970) 41,433.

NORWICH, Great Britain, county borough of Norfolk Co., England, 114 miles N.E. of London. A cathedral, almost wholly Norman in style, was begun in 1096; it is surmounted by a Norman tower and a decorated spire 315 ft. tall. Norwich is known for its textile fabrics. Its principal industrial products are shoes, leather goods, chocolate, silk, pharmaceuticals, and electrical equipment. Pop. (1969 est.) 118,800.

NORWICH TERRIER, or CANTAB TERRIER, type of small terrier (q.v.) popular in Great Britain in the last two decades of the 19th century and introduced into the United States about 1920. The dog is useful for hunting rabbits and other small game, and is popular as a pet. The Norwich terrier is from 10 to 12 in. high at the withers and weighs from 10 to 12 lb. It has dark, bright, and expressive eyes; a strong jaw; a short, strong neck; short and powerful legs; and a medium-sized tail. The hair of the coat is hard and wiry, usually red in color, but sometimes either black and tan or grizzle. The dog is a hardy, active little animal, and is noted for its loyalty.

NORWOOD, city of Ohio, in Hamilton Co., near Cincinnati, of which it is a suburb. It manufactures motor vehicles, electrical apparatus, tools, office fixtures, soap products, and playing cards. Norwood is the site of the Playing Card Museum, where there is a display of cards showing the development from the first-known type to those used in modern times. Settled early in the 19th century, the community, originally called Sharpsburg, was incorporated as a village in 1888 and as a city in 1903. Pop. (1960) 34,580; (1970) 30,420.

NOSE, organ of smell (q.v.), and also part of the apparatus of respiration (q.v.) and voice; *see* VOICE AND SPEECH. Considered anatomically, it may be divided into an external part—the visible projecting portion, to which the term "nose" is popularly restricted—and an internal part, consisting of two chief cavities, or nasal fossae, separated from each other by a vertical septum, and subdivided by spongy or turbinated bones projecting from the outer wall into three passages or meatuses, with which various sinuses in the ethmoid, sphenoid, frontal, and superior maxillary bones communicate by narrow apertures.

The margins of the nostrils are usually lined with a number of stiff hairs (vibrissae) which project across the openings and serve to arrest the passage of foreign substances, such as dust and small insects, which might otherwise be drawn up with the current of air intended for respiration. The skeleton or framework of the nose is partly composed of the bones forming the top and sides of the bridge, and partly of cartilages, there being on either side an upper lateral and a lower lateral cartilage, to the latter of which are attached three or four small cartilaginous plates, termed sesamoid cartilages; there is also the cartilage of the septum which separates the nostrils, and in association posteriorly with the perpendicular plate of the ethmoid and with the vomer, forms a complete partition between the right and left nasal fossae.

The nasal fossae, which constitute the internal part of the nose, are lofty and of considerable depth. They open in front through the nostrils and behind terminate in a vertical slit on either side of the upper part of the pharynx,

NOSTRADAMUS

Structure of External Nose

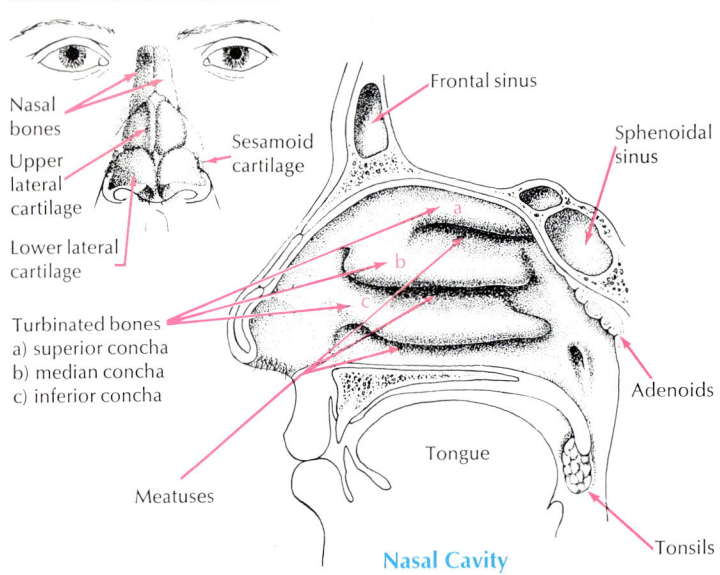

Nasal bones
Upper lateral cartilage
Lower lateral cartilage
Turbinated bones
a) superior concha
b) median concha
c) inferior concha
Sesamoid cartilage
Frontal sinus
Sphenoidal sinus
Adenoids
Tongue
Meatuses
Tonsils

Nasal Cavity

Structure of the human nose, showing the relative positions of the nasal bones and cartilage, the sinuses, and the turbinated bones and meatuses inside the nasal cavity.

above the soft palate (q.v.), and near the orifices of the Eustachian tubes, leading to the tympanic cavity of the ear (q.v.).

The mucous membrane lining the nose varies in its structure in different parts of the organ. In the olfactory region the mucous membrane is very thick and colored by a brown pigment. The olfactory nerve, or nerve of smell, terminates in the nasal cavity in several small branches; these ramify in the soft mucous membrane, and end in tiny varicose fibers which in turn terminate in elongated epithelial cells projecting into the free surface of the nose.

For diseases of the nose, see COLD, COMMON; HAY FEVER.

NOSTRADAMUS, assumed Latin name of MICHEL DE NOTREDAME (1503–66), French physician and astrologer, born in Saint Remi, Provence, and educated at Avignon and Montpellier. He achieved distinction for his treatment of those stricken with the plague (q.v.), during outbreaks of the disease in southern France. He was also called to Aix and Lyons in 1545 during a plague epidemic in those cities. Nostradamus subsequently attracted widespread attention by his claim that he could predict the future, and in 1555 he published a famous collection of prophecies, in rhymed quatrains, called *Centuries*. Catherine de Médicis (q.v.), Queen of France invited him to court to cast the horoscopes of her sons, and upon the accession of Charles IX (q.v.) he was appointed court physician. The name "Nostradamus" is now used to designate any person who professes to be a seer.

NOTATION, in science or art, any system of marks or symbols used to represent entities, processes, facts, or relationships in an abbreviated or nonverbal form; see LANGUAGE. See also for example, the articles CHEMISTRY: *Chemical Symbolism and Equations;* MUSICAL NOTATION. In the arts notation is also used in choreography (see DANCE) and in plotting camera or acting movement. Special symbolic vocabularies are also useful with certain games, such as chess (q.v); for diagrammatic offensive or defensive study by teams in many sports; and for military strategy. Shorthand (q.v.), too, is a form of notation.

For the history of mathematical notation, see NUMERALS. This article considers various forms of mathematical notation for ordinary numbers using either the familiar Arabic numerals or analogous symbols. See MATHEMATICS.

The universal system of mathematical notation is the decimal system (q.v.), which is a base-ten, positional system; that is, ten symbols (0, 1, 2, 3, 4, 5, 6, 7, 8, 9) are used to represent numbers, and the quantity represented by a digit depends on its position in the number. Thus, the number 3,098,323 is an abbreviation for $3 \times 10^6 + 0 \times 10^5 + 9 \times 10^4 + 8 \times 10^3 + 3 \times 10^2 + 2 \times 10 + 3$ units. The first 3 (reading from right to left) represents three units; the second 3, three hundred units; the third 3, three million units.

Any whole number greater than 1, in fact, can be used as the base for numerical notation. Some primitive tribes used systems based on the numbers, 3, 4, or 5. The Babylonians and others used the sexagesimal system, based on the number 6; the Romans used, although not completely, the duodecimal system based on the number 12; the Maya used the vigesimal system based on the number 20. The binary system, based on the number 2, was used by some primitive tribes and is of increasing importance in present-day computer systems.

The number of symbols or digits needed to represent a number is the number of units in the base. Thus, two digits, 0, 1, suffice to represent a number in the binary system; six digits, 0, 1, 2, 3, 4, 5, are needed to represent a number in the sexagesimal system; and twelve digits, 0, 1, 2, 3, 4, 5, 6, 7, 8, 9, t (ten), e (eleven), are needed to represent a number in the duodecimal system. The number 30155 in the sexagesimal system is the number $3 \times 6^4 + 0 \times 6^3 + 1 \times 6^2 + 5 \times 6 + 5 = 3959$ in the decimal system; the number 2et in the duodecimal system is the number $2 \times 12^2 + 11 \times 12 + 10 = 430$ in the decimal system. To write a given base-ten number n as a base-b number, divide (in the decimal system) n by b, divide the quotient by b, the new quotient n by b, and so on until the quotient 0 is obtained. The successive remainders are the digits in the base-b expression for n. For example, to express 3959 (base ten) in the base six, we write

```
6 ) 3959
  ) 659   5
  ) 109   5
  )  18   1
  )   3   0
  )   0   3
```

from which, as above, $3959_{10} = 30155_6$; the base is frequently written as a subscript of the number.

The larger the base, the more symbols are required, but fewer digits are needed to express a given number. The number 12 is convenient as a base because it is exactly divisible by 2, 3, 4, and 6; for this reason, many mathematicians have advocated its adoption in place of the base ten.

The first twenty numbers in the binary notation are 1, 10, 11, 100, 101, 110, 111, 1000, 1001, 1010, 1011, 1100, 1101, 1110, 1111, 10000, 10001, 10010, 10011, 10100. The binary system became a virtual necessity with the development of digital electronic computers in the 1940's because its two digits, 0, 1, could be made to correspond to the "off" and "on" positions of a switch, or to the "open" and "closed" relays and circuits; see COMPUTER. See also SYMBOLS, MATHEMATICAL. J.Si.

NOTRE DAME (Fr., "Our Lady"), Virgin Mary; see MARY, SAINT. The term has served as the name for Roman Catholic churches and for Roman Catholic abbeys, shrines, and educational institutions dedicated to the Virgin. Several religious orders bear the name as well; most are devoted to educational work; see ORDERS, RELIGIOUS. The most famous of the churches is the Cathedral of Notre Dame in Paris, begun about 1160. It is one of the finest existing examples of Gothic architecture (q.v.). See also CATHEDRAL.

NOTRE DAME, UNIVERSITY OF, Roman Catholic institution of higher education for men, founded in 1842 by the Congregation of Holy Cross and governed by a predominantly lay board of trustees. The university is situated in Notre Dame, a suburb of South Bend, Ind. The university comprises colleges of arts and letters, law, science, engineering, and business administration, and a graduate school. The degrees of bachelor, master, and doctor are conferred. In 1967 a new curriculum was organized leading to the degree of master in business administration. The Laetare Medal, granted to American Catholic laymen and women for distinction in beneficent human endeavor, was inaugurated by the university in 1883. Notre Dame is well known for its football team, which for many years headed the list of American teams in an unbroken record of intercollegiate football victories. In 1968 the university libraries housed more than 863,000 bound volumes. The art gallery has a wide range of works, including a Dr. Thomas Dooley memorial collection. In 1968 the enrollment totaled 7841 students, the faculty numbered 968, and the endowment was about $62,000,000.

NOTTINGHAM, Great Britain, county borough of Nottinghamshire, England, on the Trent R., about 125 miles N.W. of London. The principal manufactures are lace, hosiery, textile and tobacco products, and bicycles. Nottingham Castle, built after the Norman invasion of England in 1066, and rebuilt in 1674, is now used as an art museum. Pop. (1969 est.) 303,090.

NOTTINGHAMSHIRE, Great Britain inland county of England, bounded on the N. by Yorkshire, on the E. by Lincolnshire, on the S. by Leicestershire, and on the W. by Derbyshire. Manufacturing and coal mining are the main industries. Area, 827 sq.mi.; pop. (1969 est.) 969,730.

NOUAKCHOTT, town and capital of Mauritania, 3 mi. from the Atlantic Ocean, and about 150 miles N.E. of Saint-Louis. It is a trading center

NOUN

for livestock, fish, millet, and gum and is a coastal road hub on the Trans-Mauritania Highway. A desert-trail terminus before independence, Nouakchott was made capital of the new republic in 1958. It is the site of the National School of Administration (1966). The town was founded as a coastal fort in 1903. Pop. (1965 est.) 15,000.

NOUN (fr. Lat. *nomen,* "name"), in grammar, a word or name denoting a thing, place, person, idea, quality, or action, used in a sentence as the subject or object of a verb, or as the object of a preposition. The noun is one of the eight basic parts of speech; see GRAMMAR. Although the noun is generally distinct from the verb and the pronoun in function and inflection (q.v.), noun and pronoun frequently show similarities, and noun and verb sometimes take the same form, as in the Hottentot and Polynesian languages. Verbal nouns also occur in the Semitic and Indo-European languages (qq.v.) in the form of infinitives that are nouns in form and verbs in function. Because of the similarity of function of nouns and pronouns, in many Indo-European languages pronominal inflection has been extended to pronouns.

Nouns may be inflected to indicate gender, case, and number. In modern English, gender has been eliminated, and only three cases occur: nominative, genitive (or possessive), and objective. English nouns have two forms to indicate numbers: singular and plural. The plural is usually formed by adding an s or es to the singular form of a noun. A number of exceptions to this rule exist, however, such as "teeth," the plural of "tooth," and "children", the plural of "child".

Nouns in modern English are divided into two main classes called proper and common, the latter being further divided into abstract and collective categories. Proper nouns, always capitalized, denote individuals and personifications, as in "John" and "Liberty"; common nouns denote concrete material things, as in "table" and "horse"; abstract nouns denote qualities, as in "goodness" and "pleasure"; and collective nouns denote masses of units, as in "army" and "majority", and may usually be the subject of both the singular and plural forms of a verb.

NOVA (Lat. *novus,* "new"), in astronomy, faint star that at an unpredictable time and place suddenly becomes exceedingly bright, reaching its maximum intensity in a few days, then declining to its original or lesser brightness over a period of months or years. Many novae at their maximum brightness are about 160,000 times as bright as in their normal state. For a few days very bright novae may appear as the brightest objects in the sky, except for the moon and the sun; other novae are too dim to be seen with the naked eye and can be observed only with a telescope.

Novae are designated by the constellation to which they belong and the year of their outburst. Since systematic astronomic records have been kept, novae such as Nova T. Coronae Borealis have been observed to repeat the outburst of brightness. Some of the novae that have been observed in the galactic system are Kepler's star in Ophiuchus (1604), Nova Cygni (1876), Nova Aurigae (1891), and Nova Persei (1901). The brightest nova on record appeared in the constellation Cassiopeia (q.v.) in 1572. Over a hundred novae have been identified in the great spiral nebula in Andromeda (q.v.). In addition to the normal novae found in the galactic system of which the earth is a part, extraordinarily bright novae, called supernovae, appear on an average of once every hundred years. Supernovae often attain a brightness about one hundred million times that of the sun (q.v.).

No completely satisfactory theory has been evolved to account for the appearance of novae. According to present-day evidence, these stars expand from internal pressures until a sudden explosion occurs, releasing vast amounts of radiant energy. A recent theory, postulated by the American physicist Lyle B. Borst (q.v.), holds that such explosions are caused by thermonuclear reactions, in which radioactive beryllium (q.v.) is formed by nuclear fusion; see NUCLEAR WEAPONS. Following the explosion, the star contracts and returns to a steady state. See STARS: *Variable Stars.*

NOVA IGUAÇU, city of Brazil, in Rio de Janeiro State, 18 miles N.W. of downtown Rio de Janeiro. Industries include paper milling, gem cutting, coffee and fruit processing, vegetable canning, metalworking, and the manufacture of chemicals, rubber products, and pharmaceuticals. Pop. (1960) 134,708.

NOVALIS, pen name of BARON FRIEDRICH VON HARDENBERG (q.v.).

NOVA LISBOA, formerly HUAMBO, city in Angola, and capital of Huambo District, on the Cuvo R., about 300 miles S.E. of Luanda. It lies at an altitude of 5500 ft. and is a shipping and processing center for an agricultural area. The repair shops of the Benguela Railway are in the city. Nova Lisboa received its present name in 1928. Pop. (1960) 70,629.

NOVARA, city in Italy, and capital of Novara Province, 60 miles N. of Turin. It is an agricultural marketing center, principally for rice. Industries

NOVA SCOTIA

include publishing and the manufacture of metal products, chemicals, textiles, toys, and food products. Novara was founded by Ligurians and became a Roman colony. A free town during the Middle Ages, it later came under control of the Duchy of Milan and then passed to the House of Savoy in 1734. Pop. (1961) 86,190.

NOVA SCOTIA, easternmost of the Maritime Provinces of Canada, bounded on the N.W. by New Brunswick and the Bay of Fundy (see FUNDY, BAY OF), on the N. by Northumberland Strait and the Gulf of Saint Lawrence (see SAINT LAWRENCE, GULF OF), and on E., S., and S.W. by the Atlantic Ocean. The province consists of two portions: Nova Scotia proper, a large peninsula linked to New Brunswick by the narrow Isthmus of Chignecto, and Cape Breton Island (q.v.), separated from the peninsula by the Strait of Canso; see CANSO, STRAIT OF. Sable Island (q.v.), administratively part of Nova Scotia, is a low, sandy island situated 100 mi. off the E. coast. The area of Nova Scotia is 21,425 sq.mi.

THE LAND

The peninsula has a very irregular coastline (about 1200 mi. long) with excellent harbors, particularly on the Atlantic side. No part of Nova Scotia is farther than 50 mi. from the sea. Nova Scotia is a detached portion of the Appalachian Mt. system of North America. Although a level coastal plain occurs along Northumberland Strait, most of the peninsula is a rough or rolling highland, called the Atlantic Upland, which ranges between 500 and 1000 ft. in elevation. The highest point (1747 ft.) in the province is in the Cape Breton Highlands on Cape Breton Island. Along the Bay of Fundy is a long, straight ridge of traprock called North Mt. Between North Mt. and the main part of the Atlantic Upland lies the fertile Annapolis-Cornwallis valley, which is famous for its apples.

Rivers and Lakes. Nova Scotia has many small rivers and lakes. Most of the rivers are short and flow either S.E. to the Atlantic Ocean or N.W. to the Bay of Fundy or Northumberland Strait. A notable exception is the Annapolis R., which flows into the Bay of Fundy from the N.E. The Bay of Fundy is noted for high tides; the difference between high and low water averages 40 ft. or more. At the head of Cobequid Bay, an extension of the Bay of Fundy, the tidal range averages more than 50 ft. Cape Breton Island is al-

The busy waterfront area of Halifax, the largest city and capital of Nova Scotia.   Canadian Consulate General

NOVA SCOTIA

INDEX TO MAP OF NOVA SCOTIA

Cities and Towns

Advocate Harbour ... C 2	Lawrencetown .... B 3	Stellarton .... E 2	Gaspereau (lake) ...... C 3
Aldershot .... C 2	Little Brook .... B 3	Stewiacke .... D 2	George (bay) .... F 2
Amherst .... C 2	Liverpool .... C 3	Sydney .... G 1	George (cape) .... F 2
Annapolis Royal ..... B 3	Lockport .... B 4	Sydney Mines .... G 1	Grand Pré Nat'l
Antigonish .... E 2	Londonderry .... D 2	Tatamagouche .... D 2	Hist. Pk. .... C 2
Arichat .... G 2	Louisburg .... G 2	Terence Bay .... D 3	Great Pubnico (lake) .. B 4
Armdale .... D 3	Louisdale .... G 2	Thorburn .... E 2	Haute (isl.) .... B 2
Aylesford .... C 2	Lower West Pubnico . A 4	Three Mile Plains .... C 3	Jordan (bay) .... B 4
Baddeck .... G 1	Lunenburg .... C 3	Trenton .... E 2	Kejimkujik (lake) ..... B 3
Barrington .... B 4	Mabou .... F 1	Truro .... D 2	Kejimkujik Nat'l Park . B 3
Bear River .... B 3	Maccan .... C 2	Tusket .... B 4	La Have (isls.) .... C 3
Bedford .... D 3	Mahone Bay .... C 3	Upper Stewiacke ..... E 2	La Have (river) .... C 3
Berwick .... C 2	Margaree .... F 1	Waterville .... C 2	Liverpool (bay) .... C 3
Boylston .... F 2	Margaree Forks ..... G 1	Waverley .... D 3	Long (isl.) .... A 3
Bridgetown .... B 3	Meteghan .... A 3	Wedgeport .... A 4	Madame (isl.) .... G 2
Bridgewater .... C 3	Middle Musquodoboit E 2	Westville .... E 2	Mahone (bay) .... C 3
Brookfield .... D 2	Middleton .... B 3	Weymouth .... B 3	McNutt (isl.) .... B 4
Brooklyn .... C 3	Milford Station ...... D 2	Windsor .... C 2	Medway (river) ...... B 3
Canning .... C 2	Milton .... C 3	Wolfville .... C 2	Mersey (river) .... B 3
Canso .... G 2	Moser River .... E 3	Yarmouth .... A 4	Minas (basin) .... C 2
Cape North .... G 1	Mulgrave .... F 2		Minas (channel) ..... C 2
Chester .... C 3	Musquodoboit	**Physical Features**	Mira (bay) .... H 1
Chéticamp .... F 1	Harbour .... D 3		Mira (river) .... G 2
Church Point .... B 3	New Germany .... C 3	Ainslie (lake) .... F 1	Molega (lake) .... C 3
Clark's Harbour ..... B 4	New Glasgow .... E 2	Amet (sound) .... D 2	Mouton (isl.) .... C 4
Clementsvale .... B 3	New Waterford ..... H 1	Andrew (isl.) .... G 2	North (cape) .... G 1
Dartmouth .... D 3	Nictaux Falls .... C 3	Annapolis (river) ... B 3	Northumberland (str.) . D 1
Debert .... D 2	Noel .... D 2	Aspy (bay) .... G 1	Nuttby (mt.) .... D 2
Digby .... B 3	North Dartmouth ... D 3	Boularderie (isl.) .. G 1	Panuke (lake) .... C 3
Dominion .... G 1	North Sydney .... G 1	Bras d'Or (lake) .... G 1	Pictou (isl.) .... E 2
Donkin .... H 1	Oxford .... D 2	Breton (cape) .... H 2	Ponhook (lake) ...... C 3
Ecum Secum .... E 2	Parrsboro .... C 2	Brier (isl.) .... A 3	Port Royal Nat'l
Elmsdale .... D 3	Petit-Étang .... F 1	Canso (strait) ...... F 2	Hist. Pk. .... B 3
Enfield .... D 3	Pictou .... E 2	Cape Breton (isl) .. G 1	Roseway (river) .... B 3
Florence .... G 1	Port Hawkesbury ... F 2	Cape Breton Highlands	Rossignol (lake) .... B 3
Gabarouse .... G 2	Port Hood .... F 1	Nat'l Park .... G 1	Sable (cape) .... B 4
Glace Bay .... H 1	Port Mouton .... B 4	Cape Sable (isl.) ... B 4	Sable (isl.) .... H 4
Goldboro .... F 2	Pugwash .... D 2	Carleton (river) .... B 4	Saint Ann's (bay) .. G 1
Grand-Étang .... G 1	Reserve Mines ..... G 1	Chedabucto (bay) .. F 2	Saint Lawrence (gulf) . E 1
Guysborough .... F 2	River Hébert .... C 2	Chiguecto (bay) .... C 2	Saint Margaret's
Halifax (cap.) .... D 3	River John .... D 2	Chignecto (cape) ... B 2	(bay) .... D 3
Hantsport .... C 2	Riverport .... C 3	Cobequid (bay) ..... D 2	Saint Mary's (bay) . A 3
Herring Cove .... D 3	Sackville .... D 3	Country (harbor) ... F 2	Saint Paul (isl.) .... G 1
Hopewell .... E 2	Saint Ann's .... G 1	Digby Neck (penin.) . A 3	Scatari (isl.) .... H 1
Ingonish .... G 1	Saint Peter's .... G 2	Fisher (lake) .... B 3	Sherbrooke (lake) ... C 3
Inverness .... F 1	Sheet Harbour ..... E 3	Fort Anne Nat'l	Shubenacadie (lake) .. D 3
Joggins .... C 2	Shelburne .... B 4	Hist. Pk. .... B 3	Split (cape) .... C 2
Kentville .... C 2	Sherbrooke .... E 2	Fortress of Louisburg	Tancook (isl.) .... C 3
Kingston .... C 3	Ship Harbour .... E 3	Nat'l Hist. Park ... H 2	Tor (bay) .... F 2
	Shubenacadie .... D 2	Fundy (bay) .... B 2	Verte (bay) .... D 1
	Springhill .... D 2	Gabarus (bay) ...... G 2	West (point) .... G 4

most bisected from N.E. to S.W. by the saltwater Bras d'Or Lake (q.v.), the only large lake in the province.

Climate. The climate of the province is predominantly cool and humid. Nova Scotia does not have great extremes of temperature because of the moderating influence of the surrounding seas. The dominant climate factor is the Labrador Current (q.v.). Winters are not severe, but spring is delayed by the presence of ice and icy water offshore. Summers are pleasantly cool; mild weather continues into the fall during a period of Indian summer. The average annual temperature over most of the peninsula is about 44° F. At Halifax the July and January average temperatures are 65° F. and 26° F., respectively. Recorded extremes of temperature are 99° F. and −21° F. The growing season varies from about 160 days in the S. to 135 days in the N.

The province has a mean annual precipitation of between 47 and 54 in., about one sixth of which occurs in the form of snow. In general the coast remains ice-free throughout the winter.

Plants. Much of Nova Scotia is covered by mixed forests consisting of such hardwoods as oak, maple, and birch and such softwoods as pine, balsam fir, and spruce. The province is noted for the number and profusion of its wild flowers.

Animals. The large mammals of Nova Scotia are the deer, bear, and moose. Smaller animals include the fox, wildcat, muskrat, beaver, otter, porcupine, mink, raccoon, and weasel. Among the game birds are the pheasant, ruffed grouse, and Hungarian partridge. The inland waters contain salmon and trout; lobster, scallops, haddock, cod, herring, and various other varieties of edible fish are abundant offshore.

Parks and Other Places of Interest. Cape Breton Highlands National Park, comprising 367 sq.mi. of the most rugged part of Cape Breton Island, includes coastal and highland scenery. The province also contains several national historic parks. Halifax Citadel is an outstanding example of military engineering of the late 18th and early 19th centuries. The Fortress of Louisbourg, which figured in several critical bat-

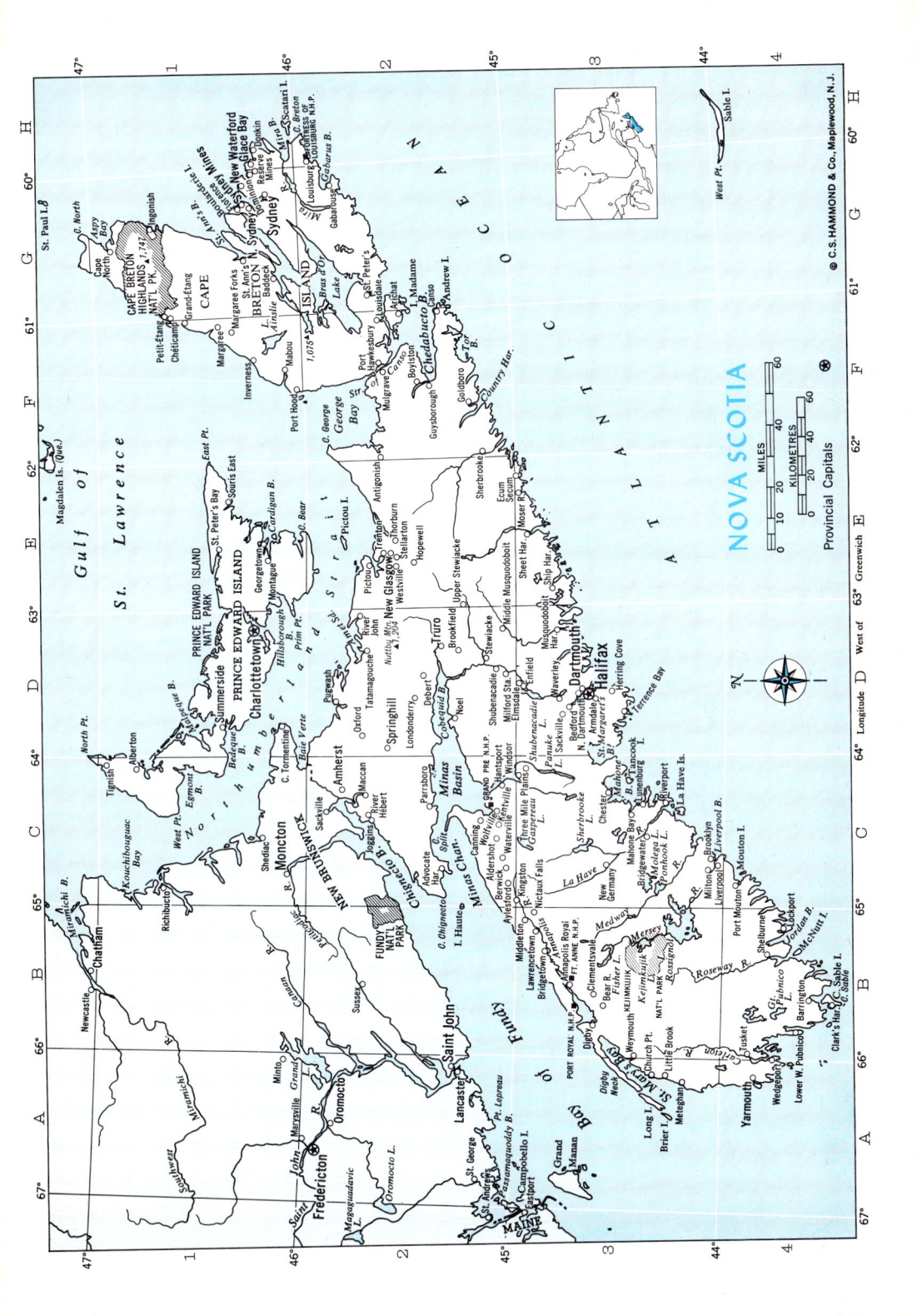

NOVA SCOTIA

NOVA SCOTIA

tles between the French and British during the 18th century, contains ruins of an old, walled French city. Port Royal, Fort Anne National Historic Park, and Grand Pré Memorial Park are the sites of former Acadian settlements. Every year a Gaelic festival, known as the Gaelic Mod, is held at Saint Ann's and a festival featuring highland games takes place at Antigonish.

THE PEOPLE
According to the latest official census (1966) the population of Nova Scotia is 756,039 (1969 est., 764,000). Farm population declined by more than 20 percent in the period between 1961 and 1966, and urban population increased by 10 percent in the same period. The population of Nova Scotia is about 58 percent urban. Most Nova Scotians are of British descent; in the early 1960's about 12 percent were of French-Canadian descent and 6 percent were of German descent. The remaining population included some 3250 American Indians, mainly Micmac, and almost 12,000 Negroes. Descendants of New Englanders who arrived before the American Revolution live in the Annapolis-Cornwallis valley and along the s. shore.

The province has three principal cities, Halifax, Sydney (qq.v.), and Dartmouth. Halifax, the capital and chief seaport, was founded in 1749 as a counterpoise to the French town and fort of Louisbourg. Sydney, an industrial and commercial city on Cape Breton Island, was founded in 1785. Clustered around Sydney in the coal-mining region are the towns of Glace Bay (q.v.), Sydney Mines, North Sydney, and New Waterford. Dartmouth, a coastal town across from Halifax, is an industrial center. Other important towns on the mainland include Truro (q.v.), Amherst, New Glasgow, Yarmouth, Springhill, Stellarton, and Kentville.

Education and Cultural Facilities. Education is compulsory for all children beginning at the age of six; the period of compulsory education extends to the age of fourteen in rural areas and to sixteen in urban areas. Public schools are nondenominational and free. Secondary education is provided in academic and vocational high schools, and special schools are maintained for the handicapped.

ELEMENTARY AND SECONDARY SCHOOLS. According to the latest available government statistics, in the late 1960's Nova Scotia had 837 public, federal, and private elementary and secondary schools (except private kindergartens), which were attended by some 207,900 students annually; full-time teachers totaled 8520. The province also had eight federal schools for Indians, with thirty-three teachers and 818 students. Each year more than 2000 students attended special schools for the blind and deaf, schools of nursing, and technical institutions.

COLLEGES AND UNIVERSITIES. In the late 1960's Nova Scotia had sixteen institutions of higher education with a combined annual enrollment of 10,000 students, according to the latest available government statistics. The degree-conferring institutions include Acadia University in Wolfville; Dalhousie University, University of King's College, Mount Saint Vincent University, Nova Scotia Technical College, and Saint Mary's University, all in Halifax; Saint Francis Xavier University in Antigonish; and Collège Sainte-Anne in Church Point.

LIBRARIES AND MUSEUMS. In the mid-1960's Nova Scotia had fourteen public libraries, nine university libraries, and sixty-seven school libraries. Museums (all located in Halifax), include the Army Museum, the Maritime Museum of Canada, the Nova Scotia Museum of Science, and the Historical Museum housed in the Public Archives of Nova Scotia; Historical museums are also located in Annapolis Royal and Louisbourg. The Alexander Graham Bell Museum is located in Baddeck, Cape Breton Island.

THE ECONOMY
The economic activities of Nova Scotia are diversified. The most important primary industry is fishing, which has surpassed mining in recent years as the major industry. Agriculture and forestry also contribute substantially to the wealth of the province. The most important source of electric energy in Nova Scotia is thermal-electric power, with coal as the fuel. According to the latest government statistics the installed generating capacity in the late 1960's was 696,000 kw annually, with 544,000 kw, or nearly 78 percent, derived from thermal sources. The undeveloped waterpower resources are estimated at about 165,000 kw.

Manufacturing. The manufacturing industries of Nova Scotia annually engaged more than 32,000 production workers in the mid-1960's, according to the latest government statistics; more than 25 percent were employed in the metropolitan area of Halifax. The largest groups were employed in the food and beverage industries, in the manufacture of transportation equipment, and in the paper and allied industries. The annual value of shipments for all industry groups in the late-1960's approached $719,-000,000; the food and beverage industries accounted for about $180,000,000, the manufacture of transportation equipment totaled some $70,000,000, and paper and allied industries accounted for nearly $50,000,000.

Nova Scotia. Plate 1. Sunrise over the harbor of Halifax, the capital of Nova Scotia and the principal Atlantic seaport of Canada.

Canadian Consulate

Nova Scotia. Plate 2. *Above: Halifax Citadel, one of numerous historic forts in Halifax, which at one time was a strongly fortified British garrison town. Below, left: The Fortress of Louisbourg, on Cape Breton Island, built by the French about 1713 and extensively restored in the 1960's. Below, right: A fishing boat in the waters off Nova Scotia. Fishing is the leading industry of the easternmost Maritime Province of Canada.*

Canadian Consulate

NOVA SCOTIA

Agriculture. Farming operations in Nova Scotia in the late 1960's accounted for cash receipts totaling almost $40,000,000 annually, according to the latest government statistics. Apples, grains, hay, and potatoes are the principal crops. Dairy products, beef cattle, eggs and poultry, hogs, and sheep are also important sources of farm income.

In the late 1960's the province had about 118,000 cattle and calves, 70,000 hogs, and 2,700,000 poultry. Dairy farming is concentrated in central Nova Scotia and on Cape Breton Island near Sydney. The Annapolis-Cornwallis valley is the oldest commercial apple-producing region in Canada; annual crops exceeding 3,000,000 bu. are common. Many other tree fruits and berries also are produced in the valley. Poultry and egg production has increased rapidly in recent years. In the mid-1960's farms in Nova Scotia numbered about 9700, totaling about 1,900,000 acres and averaging about 192 acres each. The abandonment of land and a decline in farm population are long-standing problems.

Fishing. The leading industry in the province is fishing. In 1967 Nova Scotia led the nation in the landed value of fisheries, with about $50,000,000 according to latest government statistics. Lobsters are the most important of the catch, which includes cod, flounder, sole, haddock, halibut, herring, scallops, and swordfish. More than 14,000 fishermen are employed and the value of all fishing products in 1967 was estimated by the government to be about $100,000,000. Digby, Lunenburg (q.v.), Liverpool, Shelburne, and Yarmouth are the leading fishing ports.

Mining. The mining industry ranks second in importance in Nova Scotia. The value of mineral production approached $80,000,000 annually in the late 1960's, of which coal accounted for more than $50,000,000, according to the latest government statistics. The province ranked first in national production of barite, coal, and gypsum, and second in the output of salt. Nova Scotia produces more than one third of all the coal mined in Canada, but production has declined in recent years owing to high costs of production and increasing competition from the petroleum industry. Nearly all the coal produced in the province comes from Cape Breton Island or from near the New Brunswick border. The most important nonmetallic mineral product of Nova Scotia is gypsum, which is mined in Windsor. Salt is mined in Malagash and is produced also by the evaporation of seawater. Other minerals of commercial importance are copper, lead, and zinc. Sand and gravel are also valuable.

Forestry. Nova Scotia is covered by about 20,000 sq.mi. of forest land, of which more than 75 percent is privately owned. The stand of timber is estimated at nearly 10,000,000 cu.ft., about two thirds of which is softwoods. According to the latest government statistics, the volume of wood cut annually in the mid-1960's totaled more than 100,000,000 cu.ft.; the annual value of all shipments of sawmills was more than $16,000,000, when production totaled about 200,000,000 bd.ft.

Tourism. Nova Scotia is visited by some 1,000,000 tourists annually. Among the main attractions within the province are the provincial and national parks, which cover more than 800 acres, the historic parks, and the numerous beaches along the coast.

Transportation. Nova Scotia is served by more than 1300 mi. of railroad. The province has more than 15,000 mi. of road, of which about one quarter is paved. A causeway provides a road link between Nova Scotia proper and Cape Breton Island. Ferries operate between Yarmouth and Bar Harbor, Maine; and during the summer season between Yarmouth and Boston, Mass.; between Digby and Saint John, New Brunswick; and between North Sydney and Port-aux-Basques and Argentia, both in Newfoundland. Halifax, the largest ice-free port in Canada, handles a great deal of extra traffic in the winter. It ranks seventh in Canada in the tonnage of cargo loaded and unloaded. Nova Scotia has twenty-two aircraft landing areas and is served by several airlines.

Communications. The province is served by 6 daily newspapers, more than 30 weekly newspapers, and 18 periodicals. Nova Scotia has 18 radio stations, 2 of which are part of the Canadian Broadcasting Corporation (C.B.C.). Television stations of the C.B.C. are located in Halifax and Sydney, and a commercial television station is located in Halifax.

GOVERNMENT

Nova Scotia is one of the four original provinces of the Confederation of Canada, which was formed according to the terms of the British North America Act of 1867. The province is represented in the Canadian parliament by ten senators and eleven members of the House of Commons.

The nominal chief executive of Nova Scotia is the lieutenant governor, who is appointed by the Canadian federal government. Actual power is in the hands of the executive council, a cabinet formed by the party having a majority of the seats in the legislature. The legislature is the unicameral house of assembly, which consists of

NOVA SCOTIA

forty-six members elected for a maximum term of five years by universal suffrage.

All judicial offices are appointive. The provincial government appoints the judges of magistrates' courts. Appointments to all higher courts, including the supreme court and the county courts, are made by the Federal government.

Local Government. The province of Nova Scotia consists of three cities, operating under special charters and special legislation; thirty-nine towns, operating under the Town Incorporation Act; and eighteen counties, which are organized as twenty-four rural municipalities and supervised by the department of municipal affairs.

Voting Qualifications. Canadian citizens or other British subjects, twenty-one years of age and complying with certain residential requirements of the province and electoral district, may vote in Federal and provincial elections.

HISTORY

The peninsula was discovered in 1497 by the Italian navigator John Cabot (*see under* CABOT), sailing under the English flag. The first settlements were made by French colonists, who called the region Acadia (q.v.), or Acadie, and founded Port Royal in 1605. England refused to recognize French claims and in 1621 the Scottish-born poet and courtier Sir William Alexander (q.v.) was given a royal grant that included Acadia, called Nova Scotia ("New Scotland") by the English. The region was the subject of considerable Anglo-French dispute during the 17th century. New England colonists made many attempts to obtain possession of the region and in 1710, during the War of the Spanish Succession, British forces captured Port Royal; see SPANISH SUCCESSION, WAR OF THE. By the Peace of Utrecht, which ended the war, France, in 1713, gave up all claim to the peninsula. Nearly all the settlers, however, were French-Catholic Acadians who supported many French attempts to regain possession of Nova Scotia. In 1755 the Acadians were forcibly deported, as commemorated in the poem "Evangeline" by the American author Henry Wadsworth Longfellow (q.v.). Settlers from New England were brought to Nova Scotia to replace the Acadians. Some home rule was granted by the terms of the constitution of 1758.

Cape Breton Island was ceded by France to Great Britain in 1763, following the Seven Years' War (q.v.). After the beginning of the American Revolution (q.v.), about 35,000 American colonists who were loyal to Great Britain emigrated to Nova Scotia. Successive waves of emigration were chiefly from Scotland, notably from the Highland region. In addition, between the American Revolution and about 1815, several thousand Negroes were brought to Nova Scotia from the United States and the West Indies and settled around Halifax. During the early years of the 19th century the Napoleonic Wars (q.v.) in Europe brought great prosperity to the lumber and shipbuilding industries of Nova Scotia; for a time the colony also enjoyed a large share of the West Indian trade formerly dominated by the New England colonies.

During the War of 1812 (q.v.) Nova Scotia was the chief British base in North America. The colony was given responsible government in 1848 after reiterated demands to the British government by the colonists. In 1867 Nova Scotia and Cape Breton Island became a province of Canada. After formation of the province a business decline and the lure of good land in western Canada started a period of depression and emigration, which has to some degree continued to the present. Following World War II (q.v.), however, considerable economic progress was made.

The Liberal Party was in power during most of the provincial history of Nova Scotia. The Progressive-Conservative Party won the election of 1956 and in the late 1960's still held power. Other parties from time to time won some legislative seats but never gained a majority in the legislature.   DOMINION BUREAU OF STATISTICS

NOVATO, city of California, in Marin Co., near the w. shore of San Pablo Bay, about 8 miles N. of San Rafael. Novato is in a fruit- and truck-farming and dairy region. Hamilton Air Force Base is nearby. Pop. (1960) 17,881; (1970) 31,006.

NOVAYA ZEMLYA, archipelago of the Soviet Union, part of the Russian S.F.S.R., in the Arctic Ocean. It is comprised of two large islands, separated by a narrow strait, Matochkin Shar, and many small islands located N. of the Arctic Circle. The archipelago separates the Barents Sea on the w. from the Kara Sea on the E. It is about 600 mi. long and from 35 to 90 mi. wide. Novaya Zemlya was discovered as early as the 10th century. In 1594 the Dutch navigator Willem Barents (q.v.) explored the archipelago.

NOVEL, fictional prose narrative in which characters and situations are depicted within the framework of a plot. It constitutes the third stage in the development of imaginative fiction, following the epic (*see* EPIC POETRY) and the romance (q.v.).

The term "novel" (Lat. *novellus,* dim. of *novus,* "new") appears to have been applied during the early Renaissance (q.v.) to any new story. In the 12th and 13th centuries it was a common designation among the Provençal poets of France for a realistic tale of intrigue told in verse form; see PROVENÇAL LANGUAGE AND LITERATURE. The term "novella" was popularized by the Italian author Giovanni Boccaccio as the title of a short anecdotal narrative in prose. When his Italian tales were translated into English the term itself passed into the English language. The earliest ascertained use of the term "novel" in English literature occurs in *The Palace of Pleasure* (1566), a group of tales translated by William Painter (1540?–94) principally from the works of Boccaccio and the Piedmontese writer Matteo Bandello.

ORIGINS OF THE NOVEL
Prose narratives were composed throughout the ancient world, and many tales that subsequently became a part of the European literary tradition originated in Egypt. In India the novel probably began with *Daśakumāracarita* ("Adventures of the Ten Princes") by Dandin, a Sanskrit writer of the late 6th century A.D. The Chinese novel did not begin to develop until the time of the Yüan (Mongol) Dynasty (1260–1368); it is replete with dramatic incidents but deficient in characterization. In Japan the first novel of consequence is the *Genji Monagatari* ("The Tale of Genji", 11th cent.; Eng. trans., 1935), by the Baroness Murasaki Shibiku (fl. 11th cent.). This work is a long love story containing much valuable information on Japanese court society about 1000 A.D. After an extended period of decline, Japanese fiction underwent a renaissance in the 17th century, as exemplified especially in the works of the novelist Kyokutei Bakin (1767–1848), whose *Hakkenden* ("Tale of Eight Dogs") is perhaps the most famous of all Japanese novels. Novels had a considerable vogue among the Greeks in the early centuries of the Christian Era. Worthy of mention are the romance *Æthiopica* by Heliodorus of Emesa (now Homs), Syria; the *Ephesiaca* (containing the essential features of the story of Romeo and Juliet by the 16th-century writer William Shakespeare) by Xenophon of Ephesus, Asia Minor; and *Daphnis and Chloë*, the most exquisite of the pastoral romances, generally attributed to the Greek writer Longus. The chief examples of novels written in the Latin language at this time are the *Metamorphoses* or *The Golden Ass* by Lucius Apuleius, a native of Numidia in northern Africa, and the *Satyricon*, generally considered to be the work of the Roman writer Gaius Petronius Arbiter (fl. 1st cent. A.D.).

Middle Ages and Renaissance. The long narrative verse tale, the equally voluminous prose romance, and the Old French *fabliau*, a metrical anecdote frequently cynical in tone and coarse in subject matter, all flourished in Europe during the Middle Ages (q.v.) and contributed to the subsequent development of the novel. This development was notably advanced in Spain during the 16th century by the so-called *picaresque,* or rogue, story, in which the protagonist is a merry scapegrace or vagabond who goes through a series of realistic and exciting adventures; see PICARESQUE NOVEL. Although Englishmen of the age of Elizabeth I (q.v.), Queen of England, were well acquainted with the latest innovations in the art of fiction on the Continent, literary activity in England during this period occurred almost exclusively in the drama. Experiments with the novel form included *Arcadia* (1580–81) by the English writer Sir Philip Sidney, an attempt to combine the idyllic pastoral tale of the type of *Daphnis and Chloë* with the medieval romance of chivalry (q.v.), and to give them the structure of Heliodorus' *Æthiopica*. Other important Elizabethan novels are *Euphues, the Anatomy of Wit* (1579) and *Euphues and his England* (1580) by John Lyly; *Perimedes the Blacke-Smith* (1588) and *Menaphon* (1589) by Robert Greene; *Rosalynde, Euphues Golden Legacie* (1590) and *Euphues Shadow, the Battaile of the Sences* (1592) by Thomas Lodge; and *The Unfortunate Traveller, or The Life of Jack Wilton* (1594) by Thomas Nash. The only novel of consequence in English literature from the Elizabethan age to the Restoration (q.v.) is the *Argenis* (1621) by the Scottish satirist John Barclay, composed originally in Latin and later translated into French and English. This work, cast in the form of a political allegory, is important as a link between the romance of antiquity and the French *roman de longue haleine* ("long-winded novel"). The best examples of this type of novel are two works by Magdeleine de Scudéry, *Grand Cyrus* (1649–53) and *Clélie* (1656), each in ten volumes. Other French novels of the period include *Roman Comique* ("Comic Novel", 1651–57) by Paul Scarron, and *La Princesse de Montpensier* ("The Princess of Montpensier", 1662), *Zayde* (1670), and *La Princesse de Clèves* ("The Princess of Cleves", 1678) by the Comtesse de La Fayette.

DEVELOPMENT OF GENRES
As the novel became increasingly popular during the 18th and 19th centuries, a number of different types of novels were developed. Some of these became immensely popular for a time and subsequently lost favor. Others, such as the historical novel, continue to be written in the 20th century.

Early English Realistic Novel. One of the earliest English novels to give a realistic picture of

NOVEL

the life of the lower classes in mid-17th-century London is *The English Rogue* (part one, 1665–71) by Richard Head (1637–86). Another realistic novel of the period is *Oroonoko* ("The Royal Slave", about 1678) by Mrs. Aphra Behn. The realism of the novel, further developed in the allegorical narrative *Pilgrim's Progress* (1678) by John Bunyan, was brought to a new intensity by Daniel Defoe in his *Robinson Crusoe* (1719). The technique of novel writing was notably advanced by Samuel Richardson in *Pamela: or Virtue Rewarded* (1740), *Clarissa: or the History of a Young Lady* (1747–48), and *Sir Charles Grandison* (1753), and by Henry Fielding in *Joseph Andrews* (1742), *Tom Jones* (1749), and *Amelia* (1751). Fielding, unlike Richardson, did not use the somewhat cumbersome epistolary method to tell his story, but let his characters speak directly. His narrative, too, though interspersed with extraneous episodes and digressions, is for the most part in the third person. Another exponent of the realistic novel was Tobias George Smollett, who in *The Adventures of Roderick Random* (1748), *The Adventures of Peregrine Pickle* (1751), and *The Expedition of Humphry Clinker* (1770), furnished a vivid picture of manners in the lower-class society of his time. The salient characteristics of Smollett's work, an easy style and occasional shocking audacity, were taken up and exaggerated by Laurence Sterne in his *Life and Opinions of Tristram Shandy* (1760). About this time Oliver Goldsmith wrote *The Vicar of Wakefield* (1766), the source of many subsequent idyls of village life.

Didactic Novel. In the next generation a number of writers, influenced by the pedagogic and political ideas of *Émile, ou Traité de L'Éducation* ("Emile, or Treatise of Education", 1762) by the French philosopher Jean Jacques Rousseau, made the novel a vehicle for theories of education and politics. Among these writers, who are the originators of the didactic novel was the British political philosopher William Godwin (*Caleb Williams*, 1794; and *St. Leon*, 1799).

Novel of Manners. The novel of manners, concerned with the speech and behavior of the characters as social types formed by peculiar cultural conditions, is well represented in the works of Fanny Burney (*Evelina*, 1778; *Cecilia*, 1782) and Maria Edgeworth (*Castle Rackrent*, 1800; *The Absentee*, 1812). This type of novel reached its highest development, however, in the urbane stories of Jane Austen (*Sense and Sensibility*, 1811; *Pride and Prejudice*, 1813; *Emma*, 1816). A 20th-century example of the novel of manners is *The Forsyte Saga* (1922) by John Galsworthy.

Gothic and Romantic Novel. One manifestation of the romantic spirit was the so-called Gothic novel. Such novels were tales of terror and the supernatural, marked by the literary use of ghostly apparitions, preternatural manifestations, and the extended descriptions of ruins (particularly as seen by moonlight) and of nature in its wild and terrifying aspects (such as mountainous regions, waterfalls, thunderstorms, and avalanches). The first Gothic novel was *The Castle of Otranto* (1764) by the British statesman and amateur antiquary Horace Walpole. Other notable British exponents of the genre were Ann Radcliffe (*The Mysteries of Udolpho*, 1794), William Beckford (*Vathek: An Arabian Tale*, 1782), Matthew Gregory Lewis (*Ambrosio, or the Monk*, 1796), and Mary Wollstonecraft Shelley (*Frankenstein*, 1818). In the United States the Gothic novel was represented in the work of Charles Brockden Brown (*Wieland: or, The Transformation*, 1798), who influenced the American authors Edgar Allan Poe and Nathaniel Hawthorne. Many elements of the modern mystery story (q.v.) stem from the Gothic novel.

The German poet and dramatist Johann Wolfgang von Goethe made a notable contribution to the development of the novel with his *Die Leiden des Jungen Werthers* ("The Sorrows of Young Werther", 1773–78), which created the vogue of the hero concerned almost exclusively with his own feelings. This work had great influence on the literature of Western Europe and gave much impetus to the romantic movement which was then developing; see ROMANTICISM.

Historical Novel. The Gothic novel, relying on the historical background of the Middle Ages, was a step toward fictional works in which history was the chief interest. Written within this trend were the *Waverley* novels by Sir Walter Scott, an acknowledged master of British historical fiction, who produced about thirty volumes giving a broad panoramic view of English and Scottish history from the closing decades of the 11th century to the turn of the 19th. Among his British followers were William Harrison Ainsworth (*Rookwood*, 1834) and, indirectly, the Scottish novelist Robert Louis Stevenson, known for his novels of adventure (*Treasure Island*, 1883; *Kidnapped*, 1886). Scott also influenced many novelists abroad, notably Alessandro Francesco Tommaso Antonio Manzoni in Italy, Gustav Freytag in Germany, Alexandre Dumas, *père*, Victor Marie Hugo in France, and James Fenimore Cooper in the U.S. Among the historical novels written during the 20th century are the many popular works of Kenneth Roberts, and

Gone With the Wind (1936) by the American novelist Margaret Mitchell.

THE MODERN NOVEL

Although the genres discussed above continue to be used, the most important works of prose fiction in the 20th century are generally considered to be those derived from three 19th-century forms: the realistic novel, the psychological novel, and the sociological novel. These forms are closely related, and all make use of the techniques of dialogue, characterization, and description developed in earlier novels.

Realistic Novel. In France, the prolific author Honoré de Balzac maintained that the novel should be documentary in its reliance on experience and observation. His complex *La Comédie Humaine* ("The Human Comedy", 1842–48) consists of forty-seven volumes in which every phase of French society is depicted with extreme realism and devotion to detail, profoundly influencing the works of subsequent novelists. An exponent of the new realism in fiction was the British novelist Charles Dickens, who, in such works as *Oliver Twist* (1837–39), *Nicholas Nickleby* (1838–39), and *Hard Times* (1854), graphically portrayed the life of the middle and lower classes of London. Another eminent British novelist, William Makepeace Thackeray, wrote of the manners of the middle and upper classes with exquisite humor and irony in *Vanity Fair* (1847–48) and *Henry Esmond* (1852). The social criticism exemplified in the works of Dickens and Thackeray was repudiated by the British novelist Anthony Trollope, who accused his fellow novelists of creating vices in society merely for the purpose of attacking them. Trollope's view of life is presented in six separate novels known as the Barsetshire Chronicles (1853–67), including *The Warden* and *Barchester Towers*. Realistic detail and richly humorous dialogue characterize the novels of the American writer Samuel Langhorne Clemens, known as Mark Twain (*The Adventures of Huckleberry Finn*, 1884).

Psychological Novel. The later novels of Dickens (*David Copperfield*, 1850; *Great Expectations*, 1860; *Our Mutual Friend*, 1864) display an increasing depth in the analysis of their central characters, making them in many respects the first important psychological novels. Such analysis was also developed to a considerable degree by the British novelists Charlotte Brontë (*Jane Eyre*, 1847) and her sister Emily Brontë (*Wuthering Heights*, 1847), whose writings, with their mysterious settings and passionate themes, were greatly influenced by the Gothic novel. Other important contributions to the development of the psychological novel were made by George Eliot (*Middlemarch*, 1872) and George Meredith (*The Egoist*, 1879).

Many psychological novels examine the conflicts of a character with the world about him, a theme that was developed in such works as Goethe's *Wahlverwandtschaften* ("Elective Affinities", 1809) and *Le Rouge et le Noir* ("The Red and the Black", 1831) by the French writer Stendhal (pen name of Marie Henri Beyle). Other novels deal with the internal conflicts of an individual, often in terms of an obsessive passion or idea, as in *Moby Dick* (1851) by the American novelist Herman Melville. The most notable exponent of this type of novel was the Russian writer Fëdor Mikhailovich Dostoevski. In such works as *Crime and Punishment* (1869), *The Idiot* (1868–69), *The Possessed* (1871), and *The Brothers Karamazov* (1880), he achieved a depth of analysis and philosophical interpretation never surpassed by later writers. Dostoevski's novels are frequently concerned with profound ethical, political, and religious ideas, depicted in a setting of obsessive personal relationships. A concern with philosophical ideas also marks the works of such Russian novelists as Ivan Aleksandrovich Goncharov (*Oblomov*, 1858) and Ivan Sergeevich Turgenev (*Fathers and Sons*, 1862). Several French novelists portrayed the development of an individual through a detailed analysis of his external surroundings, as in the novels of Gustave Flaubert (*Madame Bovary*, 1857; *The Sentimental Education*, 1874) and Edmond Louis Antoine de Goncourt and Jules Alfred Huot de Goncourt (*Charles Demailly*, 1860). This type of analysis received its fullest development in France in *The Remembrance of Things Past* (1913–1928) by Marcel Proust. One of the most ambitious literary efforts ever undertaken, this series of novels studies the nature of memory and obsessive love in the context of a varied and complex social situation.

The enigmatic nature of social relationships, and their effect on the individual personality, are minutely analyzed in the novels of the American authors Henry James (*The Portrait of A Lady*, 1881; *The Bostonians*, 1886; *The Wings of the Dove*, 1902; *The Golden Bowl*, 1904) and Edith Newbold Wharton (*Ethan Frome*, 1911). Joseph Conrad, a Polish-born British novelist noted for his command of English prose, depicted the moral conflicts of individuals involved in problematic situations; his major novels (*Lord Jim*, 1900; *Nostromo*, 1904; *Under Western Eyes*, 1911; *Victory*, 1915) have often been compared with the works of Dostoevski.

NOVEL

Several British novelists became increasingly concerned with all aspects of an individual's life, notably in the novels of D. H. Lawrence who was one of the first novelists to deal explicitly with sexual relationships (*Women in Love*, 1921; *Sons and Lovers*, 1923). The analysis of an individual's inner consciousness became highly developed in the works of Virginia Woolf (*Jacob's Room*, 1922; *To the Lighthouse*, 1927), reaching its culmination in the works of James Joyce, whose *Ulysses* (1922) and *Finnegans Wake* (1939) virtually exhausted the possibilities of the novel as a means of portraying the characteristics of a single individual.

Subsequent psychological novelists frequently depicted their protagonists as the representatives of philosophical ideas, as in the novels of the French writers André Gide (*Pastoral Symphony*, 1919), François Mauriac (*Thérèse*, 1928), André Malraux (*Man's Fate*, 1933), Jean-Paul Sartre (*Nausea*, 1938), and Albert Camus (*The Stranger*, 1942; *The Plague*, 1947). Symbolic representations of the problems of modern life are combined with psychological analysis in the novels of the German authors Thomas Mann (*The Magic Mountain*, 1924; *Doctor Faustus*, 1947) and Hermann Hesse (*Der Steppenwolf*, "The Steppenwolf", 1927; *Goldmund*, 1959), and, most notably, in the haunting, dreamlike narratives of the Austrian novelist Franz Kafka (*The Trial*, 1924; *The Castle*, 1926; *Amerika*, 1927). In the works of the Russian-born American novelist Vladimir Nabokov (*Lolita*, 1955; *Pale Fire*, 1962; *Ada*, 1969), an explicit portrayal of philosophical themes is rejected in favor of a minute analysis of character, and numerous devices of structure and language are used, somewhat as in the novels of Joyce, to provide entertainment in themselves, apart from the requirements of character or plot. Other efforts to extend the range of the psychological novel have been made by the French author Alain Robbe-Grillet (1922–), the principal exponent of the so-called new novel, in which characters are portrayed almost entirely through their relationships to external objects. His novels, which have been greatly influenced by his work in motion pictures, include *Jealousy* (1957) and *La Maison de Rendez-vous* ("The House of Rendezvous", 1965).

Sociological Novel. Like the psychological novel, the sociological novel, which is realistic in content and treatment, uses psychological analysis and combines elements of the novel of manners and the didactic novel. Much sociological fiction illustrates the philosophical doctrine of determinism (q.v.), a theory by which conduct is made to depend wholly on the factors of heredity and environment, the concept of man as a free moral agent being disavowed. Political, economic, and military events, moreover, frequently form essential elements in the personal relationships with which the sociological novel deals. Usually such events are specific to a particular historical period or geographical area, and in this respect the sociological novel differs from the novel of psychological analysis, which tends to emphasize the universal problems of the human personality, apart from specific conditions of place or time.

Elements of the sociological novel are found in many of the novels of Dickens, with their emphasis on the social problems of 19th century England. The first and greatest example of the genre, however, is usually thought to be *War and Peace* (1863–69) by the Russian novelist, philosopher, and social reformer Count Lev Nikolaevich Tolstoi. Tolstoi also dealt with personal problems in a sociological context in the novels *Anna Karenina* (1875–77) and *Resurrection* (1899–1900). His influence on subsequent writers was enormous, particularly in Russia, where such writers as Maksim Gorki (*The Mother*, 1907), Mikhail Alexsandrovich Sholokhov (*And Quiet Flows the Don*, 1934), and Boris Leonidovich Pasternak (*Doctor Zhivago*, 1956) continued to deal with the interrelationships of personal problems and political events.

In France the movements known as naturalism and realism (qq.v.), stressing uncompromising portrayals of the problems of everyday life, found expression in the novels of Émile Zola (*Nana*, 1880; *Germinal*, 1885; *The Human Beast*, 1890) and Guy de Maupassant (*A Woman's Life*, 1883; *Strong as Death*, 1889). The Italian novelist Alberto Moravia, author of *Two Women* (1958), and the German novelist Günter Grass, known for his *Local Anesthetic* (1969) are also naturalists. The works of the British writers Samuel Butler (*The Way of All Flesh*, 1903), Thomas Hardy (*The Return of the Native*, 1878; *The Mayor of Casterbridge*, 1886; *Tess of the D'Urbervilles*, 1891; *Jude the Obscure*, 1895), and H. G. Wells (*Mr. Britling Sees It Through*, 1916) portray a variety of British settings and social problems. Also in Great Britain the novelist and scientist C(harles) P(ercy) Snow (1905–) undertook a series of novels collectively entitled *Strangers and Brothers* (1940–70) dealing with numerous scientific and political questions as they influenced life in his country over a period of several decades.

In the U.S. many novelists have dealt with the reactions of individuals to specific political and economic conditions at particular periods in American history. Among the most widely read of such socially conscious novelists are Edward Bellamy (*Looking Backward,* 1888), Frank Norris (*McTeague,* 1899; *The Octopus,* 1901), Stephen Crane (*The Red Badge of Courage,* 1895), Theodore Dreiser (*Sister Carrie,* 1900; *An American Tragedy,* 1925), Sherwood Anderson (*Poor White,* 1920), Upton Beall Sinclair (*The Jungle,* 1906), Sinclair Lewis (*Main Street,* 1920; *Babbitt,* 1922), John Dos Passos (*U.S.A.,* 1937), Erskine Caldwell (*Tobacco Road,* 1932), James Thomas Farrell (*Young Lonigan,* 1932), John Ernst Steinbeck (*The Grapes of Wrath,* 1939), and Richard Wright (*Native Son,* 1940). Greater depth in the portrayal of character, and a more original use of language, are found in the novels of F(rancis) Scott Fitzgerald (*This Side of Paradise,* 1920; *The Great Gatsby,* 1925; *Tender is the Night,* 1934), Ernest Hemingway (*The Sun Also Rises,* 1926; *A Farewell to Arms,* 1929; *For Whom the Bell Tolls,* 1940), William Faulkner (*The Sound and the Fury,* 1929; *Light in August,* 1932; *The Mansion,* 1959), and Thomas Wolfe (*Look Homeward, Angel,* 1929). After World War II a number of American novels continued to explore the problems of the individual in a specific social setting. Notable contemporary novelists include John Cheever (*The Wapshot Chronicle,* 1957), James Baldwin (*Giovanni's Room,* 1958), and John Updike (*The Centaur,* 1963). In addition, the American authors Norman Mailer (*The Naked and the Dead,* 1948; *Armies of the Night,* 1968) and Truman Capote (*Other Voices, Other Rooms,* 1948; *In Cold Blood,* 1965), produced a type of novel drawn directly from actual experience. Referred to by Capote as the "nonfiction novel", this type of work was exemplified by his *In Cold Blood.*

See also separate entries on most of the authors referred to throughout this article, whose life dates are not mentioned, and articles on the literature of the various nations of the world, such as AMERICAN LITERATURE.

NOVEMBER, eleventh month of the Gregorian calendar, having thirty days. Among the Romans it was the ninth month of a year composed of ten months. November consisted of twenty-nine days until the Roman statesman and general Gaius Julius Caesar (q.v.) gave it thirty-one in his Julian-reform calendar. *See also* CALENDAR.

NOVENA, (Lat. *novēnus,* "nine each"), in the Roman Catholic Church, devotion consisting of a prayer asking some special grace (q.v.), said on nine successive days or on one day in each of nine successive weeks, as on nine Tuesdays. In an emergency the prayers may be said nine times on the same day. According to the revision of concessions of indulgences (*see* INDULGENCE) in 1968, a partial indulgence is attached to three novenas only, when made publicly: for the feasts of the Nativity, of Pentecost, and of the Immaculate Conception (qq.v.). The idea of novenas may have come from the nine days spent in prayer by the Apostles (*see* APOSTLE) between the Ascension and Pentecost.

NOVGOROD, city of the Soviet Union, in the Russian S.F.S.R., and capital of the Novgorod Oblast, on the Volkhov R., 110 miles S.E. of Leningrad. Among its industrial products are woodworks, china, and processed foods. One of the oldest Russian cities, Novgorod was a commercial and cultural center in medieval Europe. The city was the capital of the independent republic of Sovereign Great Novgorod in 1136, and a trading center during the 13th century. It is rich in architectural relics of the 11th through the 17th centuries for which it has become known as a "Museum City". During World War II it was occupied by German forces, 1941–44. Pop. (1970) 128,000.

NOVI SAD, city in Yugoslavia, and capital of Vojvodina Autonomous Province, on the Danube R., 45 miles N.W. of Belgrade. It is the commercial center of an important agricultural area. Industries include the manufacturing of electrochemical equipment, industrial porcelain, candy, and agricultural machinery. It also has factories engaged in the manufacture of electrical equipment, textiles, chemicals, and pottery. Founded in 1670, the city was the cultural center of the Serbian people in the 18th and 19th centuries. It was incorporated into Yugoslavia in 1918. Pop. (1961) 102,469.

NOVOCAINE *or* **PROCAINE,** synthetic anesthetic alkaloid, $C_{13}H_{20}O_2N_2HCl$, derived from anesthesin. Novocaine was first synthesized in 1905 by the German chemist Alfred Einhorn. It has an anesthetic action similar to but far less toxic than that of cocaine (q.v.). Fatal doses of novocaine must be six to seven times as large as the dosage of cocaine required to produce death. Novocaine occurs in colorless crystals; it is soluble in water and alcohol, slightly soluble in chloroform, and insoluble in ether. It can withstand boiling without deterioration and melts at 156° C. (313° F.). It is widely used in regional anesthesia but is ineffective in producing anesthesia of mucous membranes. Novocaine is used in dentistry, surgery, and obstetrics, and is sometimes administered to relieve pain of the lower back. It is also used in rectal suppositories. In the compound known as procaine penicillin, the anesthetic effect of the novocaine permits painless administration of massive doses of penicillin so that one injection of the compound will remain effective for several days. Some individuals are hypersensitive to novocaine and develop hives when the drug is injected subcutaneously. More serious aftereffects, such as nausea, vomiting, decrease of pulse rate, and even convulsions, may occur if the drug is injected into the blood stream.

NOVOCHERKASSK, city of the Soviet Union, in the Russian S.F.S.R., on the Aksai R., a tributary of the Don R., about 25 miles N.E. of Rostov. The chief manufactures are machinery, explosives, and locomotives. Founded in 1805 by the Don Cossacks (see COSSACKS), it was the last stronghold of the counterrevolution (1917–1920). Pop. (1970) 162,000.

NOVOKUZNETSK, formerly STALINSK, city of the Soviet Union, in the Russian S.F.S.R., on the Tom' R., about 200 miles S.E. of Novosibirsk. A major industrial center of the mineral-rich Kuznetsk Basin (q.v.), it is at the head of navigation of the Tom' and has railroad connections with several major lines. The city is one of the chief iron and steel centers of the Soviet Union and is the site of diversified industrial establishments, including coking and chemical works, aluminum plants, and factories engaged in the manufacture of machinery and building materials. Educational institutions include a metallurgical school and a teachers college.

The present-day city comprises the former communities of Kuznetsk and Novo Kuznetsk. Kuznetsk developed around an old fortress established (about 1618) on the E. bank of the Tom' R. An industrial center, known as Novo Kuznetsk, was established on the opposite side of the river in the 1930's. In 1932, with the completion of the iron and steel works, the two communities were combined and reconstituted as the city of Stalinsk. The city received its present name in the early 1960's. Pop. (1970) 499,000.

NOVOROSSIYSK, city and port of the Soviet Union, in the Russian S.F.S.R., on the E. coast of the Black Sea, about 60 mi. S.W. of Krasnodar. The city is an important petroleum port and cement-manufacturing center. The city is on the site of a 13th-century Genoese colony and an Ottoman Turkish fort that was built in 1722 and captured by the Russians in the early 19th century. The modern city was built in 1838. Novorossiysk saw fighting in the aftermath of the Russian Revolution of 1917. It was occupied by the Germans in World War II. Pop. (1970) 133,000.

NOVOSIBIRSK, formerly NOVONIKOLAEVSK, city of the Soviet Union, in the Russian S.F.S.R., and capital of Novosibirsk Oblast, on the Ob' R.,

about 150 miles S.E. of Tomsk. It is an industrial and transport center. Machine manufacturing includes diesel trucks, agricultural and mining machinery, heavy machine tools, and hydraulic presses. The city produces cold-rolled steel for the automobile and tractor industries. Shipbuilding, cotton milling, saw milling, plastics, abrasives, bicycles, and food processing are the other industries. Pop. (1970) 1,161,000.

NOYES, Alfred (1880–1958), British poet, born in Staffordshire, and educated at the University of Oxford. He visited the United States in 1913 as lecturer at the Lowell Institute in Boston and in the following year accepted an appointment as professor of modern English literature at Princeton University; he taught there until his resignation in 1923. His first volume of poetry, *The Loom of Years*, was published in 1902, and his popularity increased with the publication of *The Flower of Old Japan* (1903). In *Forty Singing Seamen* (1907) and *Drake* (1908) his poems centered around the sea. Many of his ballads, such as "The Highwayman" and "The Barrel-Organ", have become well known. He also wrote verse dramas, of which *Robin Hood* (1927) is the best known; novels, including *The Winepress* (1913); an epic trilogy entitled *The Torch Bearers* (1922, 1925, 1930); and a volume of verse called *Shadows on the Down*. His autobiography, *Two Worlds for Memory*, was published in 1953.

NOYES, John Humphrey (1811–86), American social reformer, founder of the Oneida Community (q.v.), born in Brattleboro, Vt., and educated at Dartmouth College and Yale Divinity School. In 1833 he was licensed as a Congregational minister but the following year lost his license because of his "perfectionist" doctrine; see PERFECTIONISTS. The doctrine attributed a dual sexual nature to God and taught that no one was bound by any moral code because Jesus Christ saved men from sin. Noyes experimented with communal living, and to that end established his Perfectionist Community in 1836 in Putney, Vt. In 1846 public condemnation of his tenet of "complex marriage", the practice of free sexual sharing within a community, forced him to disband his community; two years later he reestablished it in Oneida, N.Y. Financially a successful community, it gave up its social structure and became a corporation in 1881, becoming known for its manufacture of silverware. Faced with adultery charges, Noyes fled to Canada in 1880. He wrote a number of religious treatises, including *Bible Communism* (1848) and *Scientific Propagation* (about 1873).

NUBIA, in modern times a region in N.E. Africa roughly occupying both sides of the Nile R. val-

NUCLEAR ENERGY

ley between what are now Aswân in the Arab Republic of Egypt and Khartoum in the Republic of the Sudan. The area of the region in the N.E. part of the Republic of the Sudan is called the Nubian Desert. In ancient times Nubia was called Cush and ruled by Egypt for some 1800 years. In the 8th century B.C. the Nubians achieved independence and subjugated Egypt. After maintaining some degree of independence for more than 2000 years, Nubia was conquered by the Arabs in the 14th century and by Egypt in 1820. In the late 19th century the region was controlled by the Muslim revolutionary leader known as the Mahdi (q.v.).

NUCLEAR ENERGY, energy released in an atomic explosion, in a nuclear-power plant, or in any reaction involving the nuclei of atoms; see ATOM AND ATOMIC THEORY. Because the source of this energy is the nucleus (q.v.) of the atom, the term "nuclear energy" is the proper scientific designation, but in popular usage "atomic energy" and "nuclear energy" are used interchangeably.

Chemical energy, as opposed to nuclear energy, has its origin in processes that involve electrons in the outer part of the atom. Chemical processes generally produce energy changes measured in a few electron volts (ev) whereas the splitting of a uranium nucleus releases almost 200 million electron volts (mev) of energy. Thus the power potential of nuclear energy is vastly greater than the limited sources of energy that man taps in chemical processes, such as the burning of coal or other combustibles.

Atomic research began at the end of the 19th century with the discovery of X rays by the German physicist Wilhelm Roentgen (q.v.) and the investigations of radioactivity (q.v.) by the French physicist Antoine Henri Becquerel (*see under* BECQUEREL). In 1905 the theoretical physicist Albert Einstein (q.v.) published his special theory of relativity (q.v.), from which came the equation $E = mc^2$ expressing the relation between mass and energy. The elucidation of the nature of the atom and the nucleus by the British physicist Ernest Rutherford, the Danish physicist Niels Bohr (qq.v.), and their co-workers followed.

It was recognized very quickly that the atom and particularly its core, or nucleus, contained vast amounts of energy. The release of this energy, however, had been observed only as spontaneous emissions from radioactive substances. Rutherford's classic experiment (1919), in which he achieved atomic disintegration by bombarding nitrogen atoms with alpha particles, and subsequent experiments using artificially accelerated particles as bombarding projectiles paved the way for the discovery of the neutron (q.v.) and the production of artificial radioactivity. These two events were milestones on the road to the large-scale release of nuclear energy.

The discovery of the neutron by the British physicist Sir James Chadwick (q.v.) made it almost certain that physicists eventually would split the uranium atom. Yet, a misinterpretation

Differences in hydrogen atoms. All hydrogen isotopes have one electron and one proton; deuterium also contains a neutron; tritium has a second neutron, making it radioactive. Oak Ridge Institute of Nuclear Studies

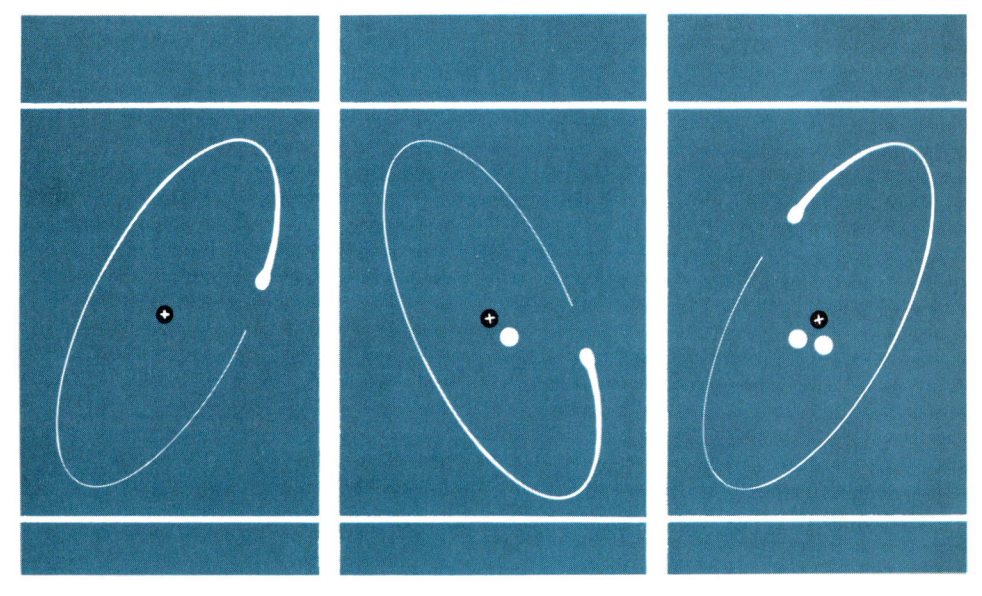

25

NUCLEAR ENERGY

of experiments performed in 1934 by the Italian physicist Enrico Fermi (q.v.) postponed this achievement. Upon bombarding a sample of uranium with neutrons, Fermi observed types of radioactivity in the irradiated sample that he could not identify with any of the heavy radioactive elements. These short-lived radioactive substances puzzled Fermi, who finally concluded that he had created new atoms lying beyond uranium (transuranium elements) in the periodic table and that were heavier than uranium. Thus, Fermi postulated the synthesis of elements 93 and 94 as produced by the capture of neutrons in uranium. Not until years later was it recognized that the radioactive products of Fermi's experiment were two fragments of the uranium atom, which had been split by the addition of a neutron to its nucleus.

Fermi's announcement of his synthesis of transuranium elements stimulated research in many countries. For four years scientists, following the wrong trail, found what appeared to be species of elements even beyond element 94. Two German chemists, Otto Hahn (q.v.) and Fritz Strassmann (1902–), reported in 1939 that they had bombarded purified uranium with neutrons and then analyzed the irradiated sample. They discovered radiochemical evidence of the presence of barium (element 56), which is a medium-weight element. Faced with the paradoxical production of barium as a result of the bombardment of uranium, they postulated that an atom of uranium might split up into two atoms, one of barium and the other of technetium (element 43). But they were reluctant to conclude that anything so implausible-sounding as the splitting of a massive uranium atom into two nearly equal parts had occurred.

Nuclear Fission. During the winter of 1938–39, the Austrian physicist Lise Meitner (q.v.), a former colleague of the two German chemists, who was then a refugee from Germany, received news in Sweden of the Hahn-Strassmann experiments. Together with her nephew, the Danish physicist Otto Robert Frisch (1904–), she developed a theory to explain the splitting, or fission, of uranium. According to this theory, the nucleus of the uranium atom is thrown into violent oscillation as a result of capturing a neutron; under certain conditions the atom distorts into a dumbbell shape. Then the uranium nucleus snaps into two fragments, which fly apart with a speed of 10,000 miles per second. The fission fragments yield up their energy rapidly by throwing adjoining atoms into excited motion; thus, the release of nuclear energy manifests itself as heat.

Chain Reaction. The fission of the uranium atom also releases neutrons. These are produced very quickly from the highly unstable fission fragments. These fission neutrons are of the greatest significance because they are the basis of a self-sustaining reaction. When an atom of uranium splits, two or three neutrons are given off. In a mass of uranium the possibility exists that some of the neutrons will strike the nuclei of other uranium atoms and cause additional fissions. The succession of such self-perpetuating fissions is called a chain reaction.

Fissionable Materials. If some neutrons are released inside a very large mass of pure uranium, no chain reaction will take place. This lack of reaction stems from the existence of two different kinds of uranium atoms, or isotopes, within the mass; see ISOTOPE. The most abundant isotope is uranium-238, which constitutes 99.3 percent of naturally occurring uranium. The scarce isotope is uranium-235. It is chemically identical to the heavier isotope uranium-238, but differs physically in possessing three fewer neutrons in its nucleus. Because of this difference, uranium-235 is much more easily fissioned than uranium-238. Indeed, the neutrons that are released in fission split uranium-235 readily, but very few of them are energetic enough to split uranium-238. Uranium-235 is

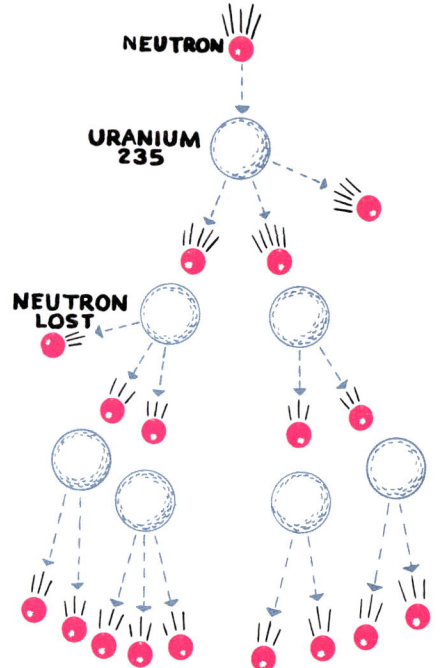

Neutrons released by fission of one atom produce additional fissions, causing a self-sustaining chain reaction.
U.S. Atomic Energy Commission

NUCLEAR ENERGY

called a fissionable or fissile material because a mass of it will sustain a chain reaction.

Although uranium-238 is not classed as a fissile material, it is used as a source of such material. If placed within a chain-reacting system, some of the neutrons are absorbed in the uranium-238 and convert it to uranium-239 by a simple capture process. Rapid radioactive decay, whereby a beta particle is emitted, converts this isotope of uranium into an isotope of element 93, neptunium-239. Another beta disintegration changes neptunium-239 into an isotope of element 94, plutonium-239. Because the latter fissions in much the same manner as uranium-235, it is also classed as a fissile material. In the same general manner thorium-232 may be transformed into uranium-233, which is also a fissile material. For this reason both thorium and uranium-238 are called fertile materials, that is, substances capable of being transformed into fissile materials.

Atomic Bomb. During World War II the United States government launched a $2,000,000,000 effort, called the Manhattan Project, to produce an atomic bomb (A-bomb). The initiative for this work was taken by a small group of atomic scientists who explored the feasibility of the concept. Cooperating with U.S. scientists were British scientists and other foreign-born scientists, such as Fermi and the Hungarians Leo Szilard, Eugene P. Wigner, and Edward Teller (qq.v.).

Initial success with a chain-reacting system was achieved on Dec. 2, 1942, on the campus of the University of Chicago, where tons of graphite and uranium and uranium oxide were assembled into the first nuclear reactor by a group of scientists led by Fermi. Removal of cadmium-plated, neutron-absorbing control rods from within the reactor started up the first self-sustaining neutron reaction. This experiment also proved that the release of nuclear energy could be controlled. These accomplishments signaled the beginning of the Atomic Age.

In order to make an A-bomb, it was necessary to produce sizable amounts of fissile material. Huge production facilities were designed for the continuous separation of the isotope uranium-235 from natural uranium. The separation had never before been undertaken on such a colossal scale. To insure success, a variety of parallel projects were established to produce weapon-grade uranium-235. Starting with a feed material containing only 0.7 percent of the desired uranium-235, it was hoped that the end product would consist of more than 90 percent pure uranium-235. See DIFFUSION.

At the same time the scientists decided to produce an alternative bomb material, plutonium. For this purpose controlled chain reactions were investigated, and experimental low-power piles were built as powerful neutron sources. It was hoped that natural uranium could be irradiated inside such nuclear reactors to produce useful amounts of plutonium-239.

The controlled chain reaction produced very large amounts of heat, which had to be conducted away from the reactor core to keep the core from melting. This problem was solved by pumping coolants through tubes, or channels, in the reactor core. Three enormous reactors eventually were constructed on the banks of the Columbia R. in the State of Washington at a total cost of $450,000,000. Cold water from the river was circulated through the reactors to keep them cool. These plants were the forerunners of nuclear reactors used for the production of electrical power, although at that time the heat produced in the process was disposed of as an undesirable by-product.

As a result of these parallel projects for the production of fissile uranium and plutonium, pound quantities of weapon-grade bomb material became available in mid-1945. Anticipating this success, scientists had organized an intensive project at Los Alamos, N.Mex., to determine how such material might be used to produce a nuclear explosion. The weapons laboratory was under the direction of the American physicist J. Robert Oppenheimer (q.v.).

The first A-bomb was detonated in the desert near Alamogordo, N.Mex., on July 16, 1945, by an implosion technique; see NUCLEAR WEAPONS. The first military use of atomic explosives occurred on Aug. 6, 1945, when an A-bomb was exploded over the Japanese city of Hiroshima. Four years later the Soviet Union successfully tested its first nuclear bomb, thus ending the American monopoly in atomic weapons.

The U.S., Great Britain, and the Soviet Union, striving to construct more powerful and more diversified atomic weapons, launched a series of bomb tests. By 1955 more than one hundred nuclear tests had taken place. As a result, a variety of nuclear weapons emerged, among them A-bombs that were much more efficient in the consumption of nuclear material. At the same time, the physical size (that is, the weight and volume) of these weapons was reduced from the massive 1945 bombs to packages that could be fitted into an artillery shell or adapted as a warhead for a ballistic missile. Additional types of A-bombs were developed for use as torpedoes, land mines, and depth charges.

NUCLEAR ENERGY

Improvements in the design of production plants and vast acceleration of world production of uranium created an immense increase in the stockpile of fissile material. The production of natural uranium by non-Communist countries, measured in tons of uranium oxide (U_3O_8), has been estimated at 18,000 tons per year. Assuming, roughly, that it takes one ton of natural uranium to produce one bomb, it is apparent that present-day bombs in stockpiles number in the thousands, or even tens of thousands. (It should be noted, however, that a large portion of the uranium that is now produced is used for fuel for nuclear-power reactors, not as bomb material.) Supplies of weapons material were great enough in 1964 for the U.S. to begin cutting plutonium production. Between 1964 and 1968 seven of the Atomic Energy Commission's fourteen production reactors were shut down.

While fission weapons were being perfected, the hydrogen bomb (H-bomb) also became a reality. This revolutionary development was foreseen as a possibility even before the creation of the A-bomb.

Thermonuclear Fusion. Astrophysicists had long believed that the stars derive their energy from nuclear sources, for if the source of stellar energy were chemical it would have been exhausted long ago. The first scientist to describe the nuclear reaction responsible for the production of energy in the stars was the American physicist Hans Albrecht Bethe (q.v.), who received the Nobel Prize in physics in 1967 for his work. By virtue of his theoretical studies (1938) and subsequent research, it is known that deep inside a star, such as the sun, is a mass of highly compressed hydrogen. The interior temperature of the sun is about 15,000,000° C. Under conditions of high temperature and pressure, the atoms of hydrogen make countless collisions every second. A few of these impacts are such that atoms of hydrogen ultimately fuse together to form atoms of the next most complex element, helium. This thermonuclear (heat-induced) reaction, or fusion process, releases nuclear energy in the form of heat; see ATOM AND ATOMIC THEORY: *Thermonuclear Fusion.* See also NUCLEAR WEAPONS: *Thermonuclear, or Fusion, Weapons;* RADIOACTIVE FALLOUT.

PEACETIME APPLICATIONS OF NUCLEAR ENERGY

Just as nuclear energy can be used as an explosive, the self-same energy can be harnessed for peacetime applications. The energy of the uranium atom may be utilized in controlled form for the production of electrical energy. Moreover, the variety of radioactive isotopes produced with nuclear reactors and particle accelerators may be used in science, medicine, and industry; see ACCELERATORS, PARTICLE.

It was with this in mind that President Dwight D. Eisenhower (q.v.) proposed the "atoms for peace" program, in an address to the United Nations on Dec. 8, 1953, suggesting that the nations pool their individual resources in the development of the peacetime uses of the atom. As a result of his proposal seventy-two nations agreed to an international conference, which was convened in Geneva, Switzerland, in August, 1955. This conference, followed by two more in September, 1958, and September, 1964, saw the exchange of scientific and technical information on many phases of nuclear energy. The International Atomic Energy Agency (q.v.) was founded in 1957 as a result of President Eisenhower's "atoms for peace" program. The

The nuclear ship Savannah, *the world's first nuclear-powered merchant ship, designed and built for the U.S. Department of Commerce.* Maritime Administration

NUCLEAR ENERGY

Drawing of the High Flux Isotope Reactor Facility at Oak Ridge National Laboratory.

agency's members include all the major nuclear powers with the exception of Communist China. This organization has two major objectives: the use of nuclear energy as a key to industrial development, particularly in the underdeveloped countries of the world; and safeguarding the peaceful uses of nuclear energy to prevent their being diverted to a military purpose. In pursuit of the second objective, the agency is promoting agreements that provide for international inspection of nuclear-reactor facilities used for peaceful purposes throughout the world.

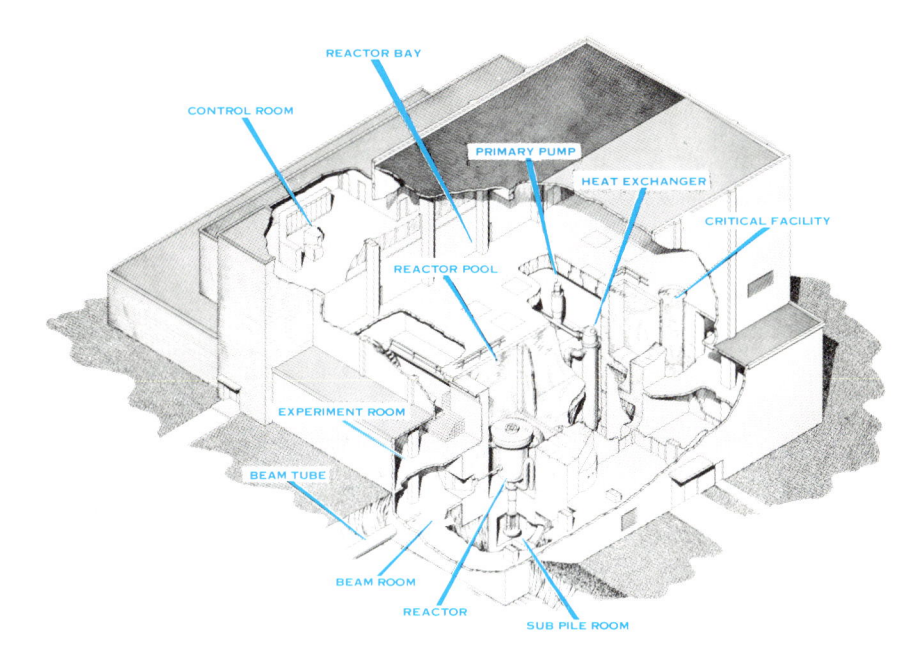

Radioisotopes. Information on the uses of radioisotopes is openly available, and even the radioisotopes are shared. The applications of radioactivity began long before World War II, and the free publication of data about radioisotopes has encouraged the widespread use of the material. Furthermore, radioisotopes have had little classified military use and thus the flow of information about their peaceful applications has not been impeded. The atom has been put to thousands of uses in agriculture, medicine, industry, and many fields of scientific research. For example, the study of the absorption of fertilizers by plants has been accelerated by "tagging" experimental batches of chemical nutrients with such radioactive atoms as radiophosphorus. After the "labeled" fertilizer is deposited close to the roots of the plants under investigation, periodic checks are made of the radioactive emanations from various parts of the plant. Because minute traces of a radioactive substance may be easily detected with a Geiger counter, it is possible for scientists to trace the course of a chemical through the structure of plants. Radioisotopes used in this manner are often referred to as tracers (q.v.). Much valuable knowledge about the mechanism of plant growth has been gained, and the information has already been put to practical advantage in the production of food crops.

On a more basic research level, scientists are using radioisotopes to inquire into such fundamental processes as cell physiology (*see* PHYSIOLOGY: *Physiology of the Cell*), plant growth, and photosynthesis (q.v.), the mechanism by which a plant makes use of sunlight to form the carbohydrates essential to its existence. The use of tracers enables the scientist to investigate the inner workings of cellular processes.

By "labeling" insects and crop pests with a radioactive material, investigators can determine the flight range and migration habits of those bothersome organisms. The specific effect of various insecticides can be evaluated by "labeling" the insecticide. Thus radioisotopes serve as a valuable tool in enhancing man's food supply.

In the field of medicine the applications of radioisotopes are as limitless as the ingenuity of

NUCLEAR ENERGY

the researchers permits. Many body processes too complex to be followed with ordinary techniques can be traced by injecting "tagged" atoms into the body or into test animals. The uptake, course, and ultimate fate of many drugs within the body may thus be studied.

In addition, industry has found a great variety of uses for tracer atoms. Because of the extreme sensitivity of the tracer method, it is possible to study in hours many industrial processes that otherwise would require months of study. For example, by incorporating a radioactive material in a machine part such as a piston, it is possible to analyze the degree of frictional wear by measuring the invisible fragments of metal that are carried away by the lubricant. In the same way the efficiency of lubricants, the rate of rubber-tire wear, or any frictional process may be investigated. In many out-of-the-way places long-lived, reliable power sources are needed. They may be used, for example, to power isolated meteorological equipment located in arctic regions, navigational buoys and lighthouses, and space satellites and lunar probes. Radioisotopes are ideally suited for these applications because they release heat while they decay, and the heat can easily be converted into electricity.

Each specific contribution of radioactive isotopes to man's welfare seems rather small, but myriad applications yield such varied information that the ultimate value of radioisotopes to mankind is incalculable.

Nuclear Power. A pound of uranium has the heat-power content of 2,300,000 lb. of coal or

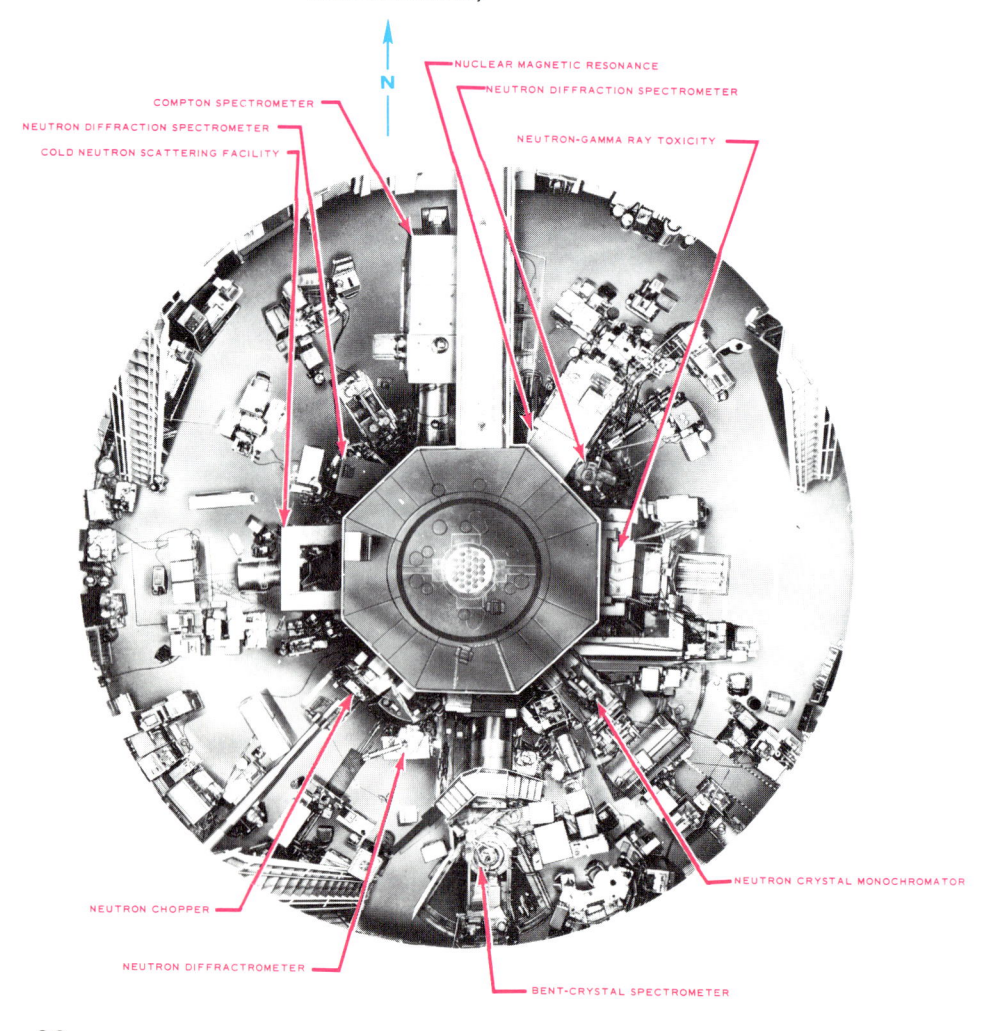

Equipment used in a nuclear laboratory fans out on all sides from a typical research reactor.
Argonne National Laboratory

In neutron physics, reactor shields necessary for research facilities and for nuclear-power applications, for instance, in nuclear submarines, are tested in experiments such as the manganese salt bath. The reactor is seen glowing at the left in the picture; the sphere to the right contains fissionable materials such as uranium-233 and uranium-238, and the salt solution.

Oak Ridge National Laboratory

Nuclear Energy. Plate 1.

National Institutes of Health

Above: An experimental cardiac pacemaker is powered by a minute thermoelectric generator, fueled by plutonium-238. If proved successful, the pacemaker would require surgical replacement only about once every ten years. Right: The spectacular heat glow, caused by the radioactive decay of a pellet of curium-242, depicts a powerful isotopic power source. As in the case of other transuranium elements, curium undergoes fission spontaneously and is an important heat source, providing small packets of power for long periods of time.

Oak Ridge National Laboratory

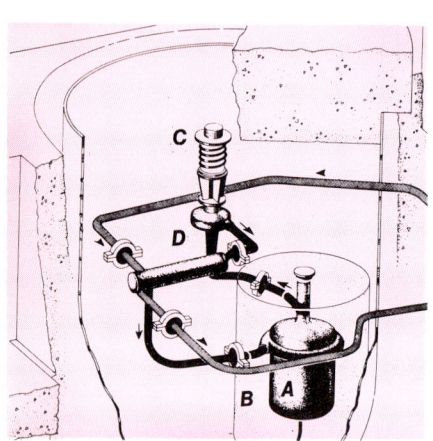

Nuclear Energy. Plate 2. The molten-salt reactor (top) is a complex system designed for low-cost electric-power production by nuclear fission. The simplified line drawing (above) shows: (A) reactor vessel, where the fuel (highly radioactive fluoride salts of uranium, lithium, beryllium, and zirconium) is circulated at 1200° F. to produce 10,000 kw in heat by fission; (B) thermal shield; (C) fuel pump; (D) heat exchanger, where the heat is removed for power production. Controlled thermonuclear fusion has been achieved experimentally with the use of complex devices such as the DCX-2 system (right), developed at the Oak Ridge National Laboratory. The DCX-2 is capable of creating a dense plasma of heavy hydrogen at temperatures of over 100,000,000° C.

Oak Ridge National Laboratory

NUCLEAR ENERGY

250,000 gal. of petroleum. To utilize even a portion of the energy contained in the uranium, however, requires some of the most complicated and expensive equipment ever produced by modern technology. Nevertheless, the development of large, centrally located nuclear-power plants has reached the point at which nuclear fuels have become economically competitive with coal, oil, or natural-gas power plants. The conventional "fossil" fuels will probably never be replaced entirely by nuclear fuels. For one thing, the competition from nuclear energy has stimulated research on more efficient use of the fossil fuels, making their use less expensive than before; and for many applications nuclear energy simply is not feasible. A nuclear-powered automobile, locomotive, or home-heating system would be prohibitively massive and costly. The procedures and complex control equipment that protect a nuclear reactor against accidents or the leakage of radioactive material are impractical for small power units. In addition, the dangers of radioactive contamination that may follow an accident involving a nuclear-powered airplane or locomotive, although not great, must also be considered.

Nuclear Propulsion. Unlike fossil fuels, which require oxygen to support combustion, nuclear fuels are self-sufficient. This makes uranium an ideal fuel for submarine-propulsion equipment. A nuclear-powered submarine can operate for months on a single charge of uranium fuel, enormously extending the time it can remain underwater and its range of action. For these reasons, the navies of both the U.S. and the Soviet Union have built more than 100 nuclear-powered submarines. The first U.S. nuclear submarine, the U.S.S. *Nautilus,* was launched in 1954. The U.S. Navy launched its first nuclear-powered aircraft carrier, *Enterprise,* in 1960; see AIRCRAFT CARRIER. The first nuclear-powered merchant ship, the N.S. *Savannah,* was launched in 1959. The Soviet Union has launched a nuclear-powered icebreaker, the *Lenin.* Another area in which nuclear power is expected to play an important role is in space. Small reactors, as well as isotope sources, have operated reliably in satellites. Reactor-power systems have been designed for possible use in lunar colonies and space stations. Nuclear rockets are potentially capable of providing greater thrust than conventional liquid- or solid-fueled rockets and are expected to be used for space missions. *See* NUCLEAR POWER: *Fission Power.*

Research Reactors. Nuclear reactors can be used to probe the atom in somewhat the same way as particle accelerators are used. Research reactors produce copious quantities of neutrons that can be used to make radioisotopes or to probe the structures of targets at which the neutrons are directed. Many large universities and government and industrial laboratories make use of reactors for medical, industrial, and fundamental scientific research. The High Flux Isotope Reactor, completed in 1965 at the Oak Ridge National Laboratory, Oak Ridge, Tenn., produces relatively large amounts of the transuranium elements and isotopes. The Brookhaven Medical Research Reactor, completed in 1959 at Brookhaven National Laboratory (q.v.), is the center of a laboratory for medical research with neutrons and radioisotopes.

Neutrons have been used experimentally to treat certain kinds of cancer. The neutrons are directed against chemicals that have been absorbed by the cancerous cells. The atoms of the absorbed chemical are made to fission by the neutrons, which in turn irradiate and destroy the cancerous cells from within.

Neutron activation analysis makes it possible to locate previously undetectable amounts of an impurity in a substance. The substance is irradiated in a reactor, then placed in a sensitive detecting apparatus. The detector sorts out atoms of the impurity, each of which has a distinctive radioactive "fingerprint". Neutron activation analysis has been used in archeology and crime detection.

The technique of neutron radiography makes use of the penetrating power of neutrons to produce X-ray-like photographs through substances that are opaque to ordinary X rays.

Hydrogen-Fusion Power. Nuclear power obtained from the fission of uranium and plutonium will continue to be used for the foreseeable future. However, though uranium is available in many parts of the world, the supply of high-quality ore that can be purified economically using present-day methods is severely restricted. The breeder reactor (see NUCLEAR POWER: *Nuclear-Power Reactors*) will tap almost all the fission energy of the uranium available, rather than the few percent now used. Nevertheless, someday another source of energy will be required. One possible source of energy is the thermonuclear fusion of hydrogen. Controlling the fusion of hydrogen is an immense challenge to nuclear scientists. Scientists must confine a reaction in which hydrogen gas is heated to temperatures measured in millions of degrees centigrade. No substance could possibly withstand such temperatures, and even if it could the heat would dissipate quickly. For these reasons it will be necessary to confine the heated

NUCLEAR PHYSICS

hydrogen in a "magnetic bottle" in which magnetic and electric forces contain the plasma.

The development of a practical thermonuclear reactor is being pressed in the U.S., the U.S.S.R., Great Britain, Western Europe, and Japan. So far, success in reaching and holding the necessary temperatures and in containing the gas has been slight. But if the problems can be solved, mankind will have an inexhaustible source of power. Hydrogen, the fuel of the fusion process, is as plentiful as the water in the oceans. R.E.L.

NUCLEAR PHYSICS. See ATOM AND ATOMIC THEORY; NUCLEUS; NUCLEAR ENERGY; QUANTUM MECHANICS; QANTUM THEORY.

NUCLEAR POWER, economically useful power derived from the release of nuclear energy in controlled nuclear reactions; see NUCLEAR ENERGY. Modern civilization has been built largely by the exploitation of heat energy produced by burning fossil fuels, that is, coal and petroleum. The age of steam power was ushered in with the use of coal as fuel for steam engines. This solid fuel was supplemented subsequently by the liquid fuels, oil and gasoline, which are utilized in internal-combustion engines. The fossil fuels, which may also be classed as chemical fuels, are natural resources that are exhausted with use. In the mid-20th century man liberated the energy in the nucleus of the atom, thus providing the possibility of a practically inexhaustible fuel supply.

Chemical fuels produce heat while combining with oxygen during the combustion process. Nuclear fuels, principally uranium, produce heat without combustion in devices called nuclear reactors. Even a small amount of a chemical fuel, such as a teaspoon of gasoline, ignites readily, but to produce heat in a nuclear reactor a certain minimal amount (critical mass) of nuclear fuel is required. Nuclear reactors are devices that produce a controlled chain reaction in a nuclear fuel. A nuclear chain reaction is a self-sustaining sequence of fissions in uranium (or plutonium, q.v.) atoms, which release neutrons that, in turn, cause neighboring uranium (or plutonium) atoms to fission. On the average, 2.5 neutrons are emitted per fission, only one of which is needed to sustain the chain reaction. Some of the emitted neutrons not involved in the chain reaction escape from the reactor, and others are absorbed inside the reactor in nonfission processes.

Development of Nuclear Fission. The first nuclear reactors were built during World War II. Known initially as atomic piles, these reactors were built not to produce power but to serve as a source of neutrons in the production of plutonium. Plutonium was utilized as a fissile substitute for uranium-235, the scarce isotope of natural uranium that is capable of sustaining a nuclear chain reaction. Uranium-235 constitutes only 0.7 percent of naturally occurring uranium; almost all of the remaining 99.3 percent is composed of the nonfissile isotope uranium-238. See NUCLEAR WEAPONS; URANIUM.

CHAIN REACTION. At the beginning of World War II, nuclear scientists, led by the Italian physicist Enrico Fermi (q.v.), sought a means of achieving a controlled chain reaction using natural uranium as the nuclear fuel. One of their principal problems in designing a chain-reacting assembly was that neutrons released in the fission of uranium-235 atoms could not build up a chain reaction in a mass of natural uranium, no matter how large. Fission neutrons are extremely energetic (that is, fast) and must be slowed down (or moderated) if they are to be captured most effectively by uranium nuclei. Fast neutrons lose some of their energy as they collide elastically with surrounding matter, in a manner similar to that in which billiard balls lose energy when they strike each other. In a mass of natural uranium, many collisisions are required before the neutrons are moderated sufficiently, and the neutrons run considerable risk of bumping into atoms that will absorb them unproductively. Fermi and his associates built an assembly incorporating graphite, a substance that could moderate the neutrons with fewer collisions. In this assembly, graphite blocks were interspersed with lumps of uranium metal and uranium oxide in an arrangement that permitted fission neutrons to be moderated before they could be lost.

The first successful chain reaction was achieved on Dec. 2, 1942, in a graphite-uranium reactor built in a squash court under the west stands of the athletic field at the University of Chicago. Even though this reactor, called Chicago Pile Number One, operated for only a few weeks, this event signaled the beginning of the atomic age. In 1943 the reactor was rebuilt at a site southwest of Chicago, where it operated until 1954.

PLUTONIUM-PRODUCING REACTORS. The first experimental nuclear reactors operated at low power levels and released only small amounts of heat inside the reactor core. Control of the fission process was accomplished by sliding in or out of the core a long rod of a neutron-absorbing element such as cadmium or boron. Pulling the control rod out of the core initiated operation of the reactor by allowing the number of neu-

NUCLEAR POWER

trons to build up inside the core. Pushing the rod back into the core caused more neutrons to be absorbed and thus depressed the chain reaction.

Although many of the neutrons in this type of reactor are captured by uranium-235, some neutrons are absorbed by uranium-238. This results in the formation of the heavier isotope, uranium-239, which disintegrates, eventually to form the fissile isotope plutonium-239. Thus, even in reactors operating at low power levels, some plutonium is produced. To increase the production of plutonium while maintaining the chain reaction, the supply of fission neutrons must be greatly increased; this requires a massive reactor operating at high power levels.

Because plutonium-producing reactors evolve large quantities of heat, reactor experts introduced a coolant into the reactor to conduct the heat away from the uranium-fuel elements. Three huge reactors of this type were built during World War II on the banks of the Columbia R. in the State of Washington. Cold water from the river was pumped through channels in the graphite structures, thus cooling the tons of heated uranium rods.

Radiation Hazard. The hazards of radiation are such that protective measures must be employed throughout the operation of a reactor. SHIELDING. The core of a nuclear reactor becomes highly radioactive; hence a protective barrier must be used to prevent or reduce the escape of penetrating neutrons and gamma rays; see RADIOACTIVITY. To prevent escape of fission products from the fuel, the uranium-fuel rods are encased in a thin jacket, often made of aluminum or zirconium. Shielding against the escape of radiation from the massive reactor is accomplished by enclosing the device inside a bulky mantle of concrete, often 7 ft. or more thick.

The introduction of shielding material requires the use of mechanical aids to carry out operations at a distance. Because the fuel elements must be periodically replaced, elaborate remote-control devices are employed to remove uranium elements from the reactor core and to introduce fresh fuel rods. Fuel elements must be replaced when only a small percentage of the fissile atoms has been used up. Because of contamination resulting from fission products, which depress the chain reaction, much of the valuable uranium fuel remains unconsumed. For this reason the discharged fuel rods are processed chemically to recover the uranium. Before conventional chemical processing is attempted, each uranium rod, being extremely radioactive, must be allowed to dissipate its radioactivity for several months. This ties up the inventory of valuable uranium and thereby increases the costs of nuclear power. Scientists are developing new high-temperature, remote-control reprocessing methods that can be carried on behind heavy shielding. These methods, if successful, will greatly reduce the required cooling-off period.

WASTE DISPOSAL. Millions of gallons of contaminated chemical solutions accumulate in the processing of waste products from nuclear reactors. The disposal of these radioactive wastes is a difficult problem, but one on which progress is being made. As large quantities of the dangerous radioactive wastes are troublesome and expensive to transport, one phase of the problem involves evaporation of the liquids to reduce the quantity of wastes. Another phase is the disposal of the remaining materials in such manner as to avoid contamination of man's environment. One of the principal difficulties is that some of the radioactive isotopes in the fission products persist for decades and even centuries. Consequently, any effort to solve the problem must take into consideration not only protection of the present-day population but also the safety of future generations.

Disposal of the fission wastes at sea is not a fully satisfactory method of solving the problem because of the tendency of marine organisms to accumulate some of the radioisotopes within their bodies. Moreover, too little is known about the mixing of surface and deep water in the oceans to permit optimism about the ultimate dilution of wastes disposed of in this manner. At present the most promising approach to the problem of the ultimate disposal of radioactive wastes involves, first, calcining the liquid wastes by roasting at high temperature until the radioactivity is immobilized in an artificial bricklike material; and, second, storing these calcined "pots" in abandoned salt mines. Salt mines remain dry for thousands of years; one would expect that immobilized radioactive material, once placed in a salt mine, would remain there forever. Experiments to test disposal of radioactive wastes in salt mines in Carey, Kans., are being undertaken by the Atomic Energy Commission's Oak Ridge National Laboratory, at Oak Ridge, Tenn.

Future research will probably solve the waste-disposal problem, but it must be stressed that a significant nuclear-power industry would produce staggering amounts of radioactivity, equivalent annually to the radioactivity resulting from thousands of atomic-bomb explosions.

Role of Fission Power. The world supply of fossil fuels is not without limit. Although coal is

NUCLEAR POWER

the most abundant of the fossil fuels, much of the remaining supply is in thin veins deep within the earth, and the cost of removing it is increasing. The world consumption of other fossil fuels, especially natural gas and premium grades of petroleum, is also increasing greatly. In an industrialized society like that of the United States, the demand for electric power doubles every ten years. The source for most of this power is the fossil fuels, especially coal. Even though new coal beds and oil fields are being discovered, world power consumption is increasing at a greater rate than the discovery of new energy sources. The fact that coal, oil, and natural gas are sources of valuable synthetic materials such as pharmaceuticals and plastics is another reason for conserving existing supplies of fossil fuels.

For all these reasons, a shortage of premium fossil fuels is probable. In the more distant future, the supplies of coal will be exhausted, first in the resource-poor continents, then in resource-rich North America. Scientists have therefore focused their attention on the development of nuclear fuels as a replacement for the fossil fuels. One advantage of nuclear energy in an industrialized society is that nuclear reactors do not give off smoke and dust particles that pollute the atmosphere.

Uranium was once thought to be a rare mineral, but worldwide exploration, stimulated by the nuclear-arms race, uncovered many new deposits of uranium-bearing ores. Many of the ores yield only 0.1 percent pure uranium, in contrast to the 60 percent yields obtained initially from pitchblende deposits in the then Belgian Congo. Improvements in ore-processing and chemical-engineering techniques, however, have made it possible to exploit even very low-grade uranium ores. These improvements have vastly increased the total supply of uranium. In terms of energy content, the estimated world

The world's first nuclear reactor, at the University of Chicago, produced thermal power of about 200 watts. Today, reactors produce more than a million thermal kilowatts. Argonne National Laboratory

reserves of uranium already exceed by many times the known supplies of fossil fuels. To the uranium deposits must be added thorium deposits. Thorium can be converted into uranium-233, a valuable reactor fuel. India possesses large reserves of thorium ore and is pursuing a long-range nuclear-research program designed to make use of its thorium deposits.

Every ton of granite contains about 12 grams of uranium and thorium. This material, if completely extracted from the granite, would yield far more energy than that required to separate the granite into its component minerals. It thus seems possible that the uranium and thorium in granite could be used ultimately as a limitless source of energy. Realization of this possibility, however, depends on using the thorium or uranium in the so-called breeder reactor (for which, see below).

Nuclear-Power Reactors. A single pound of uranium contains as much heat energy as 2,300,000 lb. of coal. An amount of fissile material no larger than a golf ball contains as much heat energy as 250,000 gal. of gasoline. These figures imply that the fissile material is an extremely compact source of power. This is not entirely the case. Before the self-sustaining chain reaction can take place, enough fuel must be contained in a reactor to form a critical mass, which can range from a few pounds of uranium

NUCLEAR POWER

highly enriched with uranium-235 to thousands of pounds of natural uranium. Control rods (see *Plutonium-Producing Reactors,* above) are required to shut down the chain reaction and to keep the nuclear reaction going at a constant rate as the fuel is consumed. Other basic parts of a nuclear reactor, all of which add to its weight and size, include a reflector, which surrounds the core and prevents the leakage of neutrons; the coolant, a fluid or gas that removes the heat produced by the fission reaction; the reactor vessel, which contains all the reactor components, usually under pressure; thermal and radiation shielding; and a neutron moderator, a material that helps the fission process by slowing down the neutrons. In water-moderated reactors the moderator and coolant are the same substance, that is, water. Some reactors, called fast reactors (see below), do not have a moderator. Finally, to prevent the escape of fission products if the fuel accidentally becomes overheated and melts, the entire reactor is surrounded by a massive steel and concrete shell.

Several types of nuclear-power reactors have been constructed, each having particular advantages. Great Britain, faced with continually increasing fuel costs, was the first country to make a large-scale commitment to nuclear-power generation. Great Britain needed reactors that could produce plutonium for military purposes as well as commercial power. Because it did not have large-scale facilities for producing enriched uranium, as did the United States, Britain chose a gas-cooled, graphite-moderated reactor design. In this type of reactor, a gas (carbon dioxide) is pumped under pressure through a matrix consisting of graphite (the moderator) and many tons of natural uranium-fuel elements. The carbon dioxide absorbs heat as it passes through the reactor. It then flows through heat exchangers and the heat is transferred to water, which turns into steam. The steam then passes through a conventional steam-driven turbogenerator to generate electricity. The Calder Hall reactors, which began operation in October, 1956, constituted the first full-scale nuclear-power station ever constructed. By the late 1960's, some twenty-five reactors of this design had been built in Great Britain. Their combined generating capacity in 1966 exceeded the combined capacity of all other nuclear-power stations in the world. The first British nuclear-power program called for 5,000,000 kw of generating capacity by the late 1960's. Under a second program, in which an advanced gas-cooled reactor design was to use fuel slightly enriched with uranium-235, Britain planned to have an additional 8,000,000 kw capacity by 1975.

France has also concentrated on gas-cooled reactor designs. The first French nuclear-power station, at Marcoule, began operation in 1958. In Canada, which has inconveniently located fossil-fuel deposits but large reserves of uranium, the reactors are moderated and cooled by heavy water and the fuel used is natural uranium. Canada's first nuclear-power station was built at Rolphton, Ontario, in 1962. The first power reactor to use heavy water as a moderator and coolant, it is the prototype for larger Canadian nuclear-power stations.

In the U.S., the Atomic Energy Commission (q.v.), or A.E.C. has examined a great many nuclear-reactor design concepts for possible use by the electric utility industry. Because the U.S. produces sufficient quantities of uranium-235, the program has from the beginning made use of enriched rather than natural uranium fuel. By the mid-1960's, two concepts had been developed sufficiently for wide-scale exploitation by private industry, the boiling water reactor (B.W.R.) and the pressurized water reactor (P.W.R.). Both types use pure water as the coolant-moderator. In both types, water in a closed vessel is heated by the fission reaction and used to make steam. In the B.W.R. the water boils within the reactor vessel, whereas in the P.W.R. the water, being under higher pressure, cannot boil. Steam from the B.W.R. can be used to drive a turbogenerator directly or it can pass through a heat exchanger where it transfers its heat to steam flowing in another piping system. This secondary steam then drives the turbogenerator. In the P.W.R. heated water under pressure passes to a heat exchanger where steam is generated.

Both reactor designs were developed from separate experiments conducted for the A.E.C. at the National Reactor Testing Station, near Arco, Idaho, beginning in 1953. In 1955 an experimental B.W.R. supplied electricity to Arco, the first time nuclear energy had been used to light a town. The first plant to be completed in the A.E.C. power-reactor demonstration program was the Experimental B.W.R. at Argonne National Laboratory, Argonne, Ill. This was in 1956. The first full-scale nuclear-power station built in the U.S. was the P.W.R. built at Shippingport, Pa., in 1957. Both B.W.R. and P.W.R. power stations have increased their capacity from tens to hundreds of thousands of kilowatts of electricity. During 1966 and 1967, for the first time, public utilities in the U.S. placed orders

37

NUCLEAR POWER

for nuclear-power stations having a greater total generating capacity than fossil-fuel power stations ordered during the same period.

The Soviet Union is pursuing a diversified nuclear-power program similar in many respects to that of the U.S. The first Soviet power reactor was a small experimental power station (the AM-1), which went into operation near Moscow in 1954. Nuclear-power programs also exist in many other countries, some of the countries having purchased reactors from Great Britain, Canada, the U.S., or the Soviet Union. Countries that have built or bought nuclear-power stations include Belgium, Czechoslovakia, East Germany, India, Italy, Japan, Norway, Pakistan, Spain, Sweden, Switzerland, and West Germany.

PORTABLE POWER STATIONS. Small "packaged" power reactors have been developed by the A.E.C. for the United States Army to supply emergency power in areas with power shortages. Current versions of these power stations were mostly smaller versions of the commercial P.W.R. units. As the technology of these packaged power stations improves, drastic reductions in size should be possible, resulting ultimately in a power station weighing less than 100,000 lb. One design, the PM No. 1, has operated for extended periods at a radar station near Sundance, Wyo. Another power station, the PM-3A, in 1966 operated continuously at McMurdo Sound, Antarctica, for nearly 3400 hr. A floating barge containing a nuclear-power station large enough to supply electricity for a community of 10,000 to 20,000 persons was completed in 1966.

BREEDER REACTORS. The fissile portion of natural uranium consists of the scarce isotope uranium-235. The remaining uranium-238, about 99 percent of the natural uranium, must be converted into plutonium before it can be used as fuel. All reactors that contain some uranium-238, therefore, convert some uranium atoms into plutonium, some more efficiently than others. To avoid running out of nuclear fuel eventually, however, it is necessary to convert at least as many uranium atoms into plutonium as are consumed in the fission reaction. A nuclear reactor that accomplishes this at the same time that it is producing power is called a breeder reactor. In a uranium breeder reactor, the uranium-238 is the ultimate fuel, the plutonium itself being burned. The successful breeder would make available for energy the vast resources of low-grade uranium (and possibly thorium) ores that would be much too costly to use if only the rare uranium-235 were burned.

The breeder reactor now being developed most intensively in the U.S., Great Britain, France, and the Soviet Union is the liquid-metal-cooled, fast breeder reactor, although other breeder concepts are also being developed. The fast breeder reactor has no moderator to slow down neutrons. Instead, high-speed neutrons emitted from a compact fuel core are absorbed by a blanket of uranium-238 that surrounds the core. In this process some of the uranium-238 atoms are converted into plutonium. The plutonium can then be used as a substitute for uranium-235 in a conventional nuclear-power station or in a breeder reactor. The fast breeder reactor is cooled by a liquid metal, usually sodium, which does not moderate neutrons. When liquid sodium and water mix, an explosive chemical reaction takes place. Therefore, the heat-exchanger equipment used to transfer the heat from sodium to water is more complicated and expensive than the heat exchangers used with other types of reactors.

Complicated problems made it probable that large-scale breeder reactors would not be commercially feasible and usable by utility companies before 1980. However, an experimental breeder reactor developed for the A.E.C. in Idaho, the Experimental Breeder Reactor No. 1, produced the first usable electricity from nuclear energy on Dec. 20, 1951.

PROPULSION REACTORS. Although large in size, nuclear reactors are well suited for certain types of propulsion equipment, particularly for ships. The world's first nuclear-powered submarine, the U.S.S. *Nautilus,* was launched in 1954. By the end of 1966, Congress had authorized the construction of 104 nuclear-powered submarines, including 41 capable of carrying and launching Polaris missiles and 1 deep-submergence research vessel. Six nuclear-powered surface ships had been authorized, that is, 2 aircraft carriers, 1 cruiser, and 3 frigates.

Ship-propulsion reactors are of the pressurized-water type and have enriched uranium-fuel cores. Improved cores were expected to enable the ships to travel for long periods without refueling. The *Nautilus* traveled 62,000 mi. on its first core and more than 91,000 mi. on its second. Newer cores under development were expected to propel submarines about 400,000 mi. without refueling. Cores used in aircraft-carrier propulsion reactors were expected to last about thirteen years. Nuclear reactors also power British and Russian naval vessels; the U.S. merchant ship, N.S. *Savannah*; and the Russian icebreaker, *Lenin.* Other countries, including France and Japan, were also conducting research on nuclear ship propulsion in the late

NUCLEAR POWER

A technician weighs a specimen of plutonium in an experimental nuclear fuel development facility at Argonne National Laboratory. Argonne National Laboratory

1960's. See also NUCLEAR ENERGY: *Nuclear Propulsion.*

Between 1946 and 1961, the U.S. undertook the development of an aircraft nuclear-propulsion power plant. Adapting a powerful reactor for use in an aircraft proved to be extremely difficult. The reactor required between 50 and 100 tons of shielding; it had to operate at bright-red heat; and it had to be small enough to fit inside a large airplane. Because of these problems, and also because of the successful development of intercontinental ballistic missiles, the project was dropped in 1961.

The results of experiments for a nuclear-powered rocket were more encouraging. In a nuclear rocket, the energy supplied by combustion is replaced by the energy produced by nuclear fission. A single propellant, hydrogen, rather than a propellant and an oxidizer, passes through the reactor and is heated. The hydrogen expands greatly and is discharged through the rocket exhaust, propelling the rocket forward. Hydrogen is the lightest chemical and the most efficient propellant. Using a nuclear reactor as the source of heat, hydrogen has a specific impulse twice as great as the most efficient chemical rockets. The A.E.C. and the National Aeronautics and Space Administration (q.v.), or NASA, have begun a joint program to develop an engine, the Nuclear Engine for Rocket Vehicle Application (NERVA), as the upper stage for a space vehicle. It was expected that NERVA would develop power equivalent to about 5,000,000 thermal kw and produce 250,000 lb. of thrust for about 60 min. See ROCKET.

The A.E.C. Systems for Nuclear Auxiliary Power (SNAP) program has developed two kinds of small nuclear-power plants for use in space. One type uses radioisotopes to produce electricity over a long period of time. The first practical power plant of this design was installed in a navy navigational satellite that was launched into orbit in 1961. Powered by plutonium-238, the power plant continued to function for more than six years. A power plant of similar design was left on the moon by Apollo astronauts in July, 1969.

The other SNAP concept is a small, compact nuclear reactor. The first such reactor was launched in 1965 and supplied 500 watts of power in orbit for 43 days before a malfunction in the satellite-control system forced the reactor to shut down; a similar design operated continuously on earth for a year. Larger SNAP reactors with power outputs as high as 50 kw were being developed in the late 1960's. In the future such a reactor might be used for nuclear-electric propulsion (ion propulsion) systems.

The primary components of an experimental breeder reactor are: (A) reactor vessel; (B) vessel cover; (C) fuel storage basket; (D) fuel transfer arm; (E) sodium coolant pump; and (F) primary heat exchanger. "Breeding" is necessary for utilization of 99 percent of all uranium.
Argonne National Laboratory

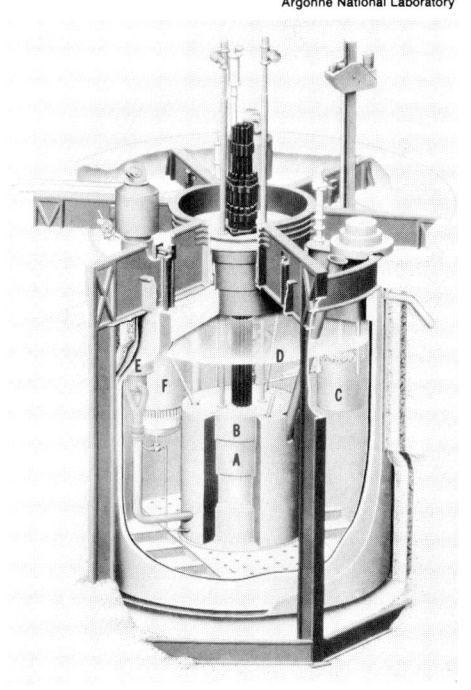

NUCLEAR POWER

Industry in the U.S. has given some thought to the development of nuclear-powered locomotives, but nuclear reactors appear unsuitable for this purpose. Such a propulsion system would be very heavy and uneconomical to construct and operate in the relatively small size required for a locomotive. A possible radiation hazard might also arise if the locomotive should be involved in a wreck. Similar considerations rule out nuclear-powered automobiles and trucks. Although small nuclear-powered engines seem impractical for everyday use on earth, it is possible that power-storage devices such as fuel cells, charged from central-station nuclear plants, may prove practicable, thus employing nuclear energy indirectly to meet almost every power requirement.

Peaceful Uses of Nuclear Explosives. That nuclear explosives could be used for peaceful purposes, such as excavating deep holes, was first proposed in the late 1940's. The idea was raised again during the Suez Canal crisis of 1956 as a method of excavating a sea-level canal through Israel. In 1957 the A.E.C. established the Plowshare program to investigate possible peaceful uses of nuclear explosives. Information from U.S. nuclear and thermonuclear weapons tests was made available to Plowshare scientists. A series of underground tests that began in December, 1961, has provided further information on the possible use of nuclear and thermonuclear excavations. Nuclear explosives could result in considerable savings in time and money for projects requiring large excavations. Possible projects include a sea-level canal across Central America, conversion of tar-bearing sands to crude oil using thermonuclear heat, mining of inaccessible mineral deposits, excavation of storage reservoirs for natural gas, the development of artificial lakes and seas in desert regions together with hydroelectric-power projects, and the excavation of new harbors. For scientists, a nuclear explosion provides an intense source of high pressures and temperatures, fundamental particles such as neutrons and neutrinos, and most forms of electromagnetic radiation. New elements and isotopes that do not occur naturally on earth have been created in nuclear explosions. *See also* TRANSURANIUM ELEMENTS.

Water Desalinization. Dual-purpose nuclear reactors can be constructed that will develop electric power and at the same time desalinate water. Large quantities of steam are required to drive the turbogenerators installed in a nuclear-power station. The steam cools as it passes through the turbines, finally reaching a temperature that is ideal for distilling pure water from saline water. The construction of a large, dual-purpose reactor may be feasible near the sea where the electricity requirements alone are not great enough to justify the construction of a nuclear-power station. The A.E.C. was conducting desalinization studies jointly with the United States Department of the Interior, and an experimental dual-purpose nuclear reactor was being considered for construction off the coast of California in the late 1960's. Studies indicated that similar dual-purpose reactors might be feasible in Israel, Mexico, and other coastal desert areas. *See also* WATER: *Water Desalinization.*

Fusion Power. The possibility that power might eventually be derived from nuclear fusion was suggested by several lines of investigation. FUSION IN STARS. For billions of years the countless millions of stars in the universe have been radiating vast amounts of energy derived from thermonuclear reactions. Such nuclear reactions, which occur at temperatures of millions of degrees, involve the fusion of nuclei with the attendant release of nuclear energy; *see* NUCLEAR ENERGY: *Nuclear Fusion.* Since the 1930's scientists have developed theories to explain the origin of stellar energy.

Because hydrogen is the most abundant element in the universe, it is natural to consider it as a source of cosmic energy. Several physicists, among them the American Nobel laureate Hans Albrecht Bethe (q.v.), proposed a series of thermonuclear reactions to explain the evolution of energy in the sun. According to their views, deep inside the sun the hydrogen nuclei, stripped of their electrons, are greatly compressed, weighing ten times more than a comparable amount of lead. This mass of hydrogen is at a temperature of about 15,000,000° C. At such temperatures and pressures the hydrogen nuclei make innumerable collisions every second. A few of these collisions result in the synthesis, or fusion, of the hydrogen nuclei to form heavier helium nuclei. In the process heat energy is released. Although the actual amount of heat released in a unit volume of the sun's core is rather small, the sun is so perfectly insulated by its outer mantle that this heat is sufficient to keep the interior temperature close to 15,000,000° C.

MAN-MADE FUSION. The thermonuclear reaction in the sun proceeds very slowly because the type of hydrogen that takes part in the fusion process is the light hydrogen isotope hydrogen-1, also known as protium. Experiments with cyclotrons showed that the heavier isotopes of hydrogen react more rapidly. Double-weight hydrogen, or deuterium (q.v.), and triple-weight

A small pilot reactor, used experimentally to gather information for the design of large-scale power reactors.
Argonne National Laboratory

hydrogen, or tritium (q.v.) are used in the hydrogen bomb; see NUCLEAR WEAPONS: *Hydrogen Bomb.*

Even using the heavy isotopes of hydrogen, temperatures of the order of 100,000,000° C. are necessary to produce a controlled fusion reaction; see *Hydrogen Plasma,* below.

At these temperatures, gases, in sufficient density, would damage the containing vessel. If these gases were to strike the walls of the vessel, moreover, another difficulty would be encountered. Because the atomic nuclei and electrons in high-temperature gases move so fast, all of them, unless prevented from doing so, would strike the walls within a millionth of a second. They would, as a result, lose all their kinetic energy; see KINETIC THEORY. Therefore, one problem in developing a practical fusion reactor is to discover a method of confining the hydrogen at the very high temperatures necessary for fusion. Another problem is how to attain the temperature required to initiate fusion.

HYDROGEN PLASMA. At the high temperatures noted, hydrogen atoms are stripped of their electrons, forming a mixture of bare hydrogen nuclei and electrons. Such a mixture is called a plasma.

The kinetic energy of plasma particles usually is expressed in electron volts (ev), a unit of energy equal to the energy acquired by an electron when it is accelerated through a potential difference of 1 volt (q.v.). An ion having 1 ev of energy has an associated temperature of 11,400° C.

Fusion reactions in a hydrogen plasma occur at an appreciable rate when the plasma particles attain about 10,000 ev, associated with temperatures in the range of 100,000,000° C. Thus, to achieve controlled fusion reactions, man must produce temperatures far higher than those in the interior of the sun.

All approaches to the creation of a dense plasma of heavy hydrogen at fusion temperatures (100,000,000° C.) use magnetic lines of force to contain the hot plasma. The hydrogen ions, being electrically charged, are wound into tight spirals by a strong magnetic field, and thus their tendency to hit the walls is greatly reduced. Various configurations of magnetic fields have been tried. A frequently used configuration has been the magnetic "mirror", consisting of a cylindrical region of relatively weak magnetic field "corked" at both ends by regions of strong magnetic field. High-energy, heavy-hydrogen ions injected into the mirror accumulate in much the same way in which protons are trapped in the Van Allen radiation belts by the magnetic field of the earth. Experiments of this sort in the U.S. and the U.S.S.R. have resulted in plasmas as hot as 1,000,000,000° C. for many seconds; however, the plasmas have been at least a million times too tenuous to support appreciable fusion. Moreover, when attempts are made to increase the density, the plasma becomes violently unstable and strikes the walls of the containing vessel.

Other methods for confining and heating the plasma include the "pinch", in which an intense discharge through a gas is constricted and confined by its own magnetic field; and the "stellarator", which uses a toroidal or pretzel-shaped externally produced magnetic field for confinement.

All attempts to establish a very hot, stable,

NUCLEAR WEAPONS

dense plasma have encountered the same basic difficulty: the plasma becomes unstable when it approaches the densities necessary for fusion. The outlook for achieving controlled fusion is therefore fairly pessimistic. However, the incentive to achieve success remains very great inasmuch as the fuel for a fusion reactor, heavy hydrogen, is present to the extent of 1 part in 5000 of ordinary hydrogen and is therefore extremely abundant in the oceans. A glass of ordinary water contains enough heavy hydrogen to provide energy equivalent to that of 20 gal. of gasoline.

LIMITLESS FUEL. Should fusion power prove feasible, mankind would have an essentially limitless fuel (heavy hydrogen), which would, compared to fission fuels, yield energy with relatively little radioactivity; moreover, a fusion reactor would undoubtedly be intrinsically safer than a fission reactor. On the other hand, even if controlled fusion proves impossible, fission based on breeder reactors still affords mankind a limitless, although less convenient, fuel supply in the residual uranium and thorium of the crust of the earth.

See also ATOM AND ATOMIC THEORY.   A.M.W.

NUCLEAR WEAPONS, explosive devices, designed to release nuclear energy (q.v.) on a large scale, used in military applications. The first atomic bomb (or A-bomb), which was tested on July 16, 1945, at Alamogordo, N.Mex., represented a completely new type of explosion. All explosions prior to that time derived their power from chemical sources, specifically, from the rapid burning or decomposition of some chemical compound; see EXPLOSIVES. Such chemical processes release only the energy of the outermost electrons in the atom; see ATOM AND ATOMIC THEORY.

Nuclear explosives, on the other hand, involve energy sources within the infinitesimal core, or nucleus (q.v.), of the atom. The first A-bomb gained its power from the splitting, or fission, of all the nucleus of the heavy atom; see URANIUM. A small sphere about the size of a baseball produced an explosion equal to that of many thousands of tons of TNT.

Subsequently, other types of bomb were developed to tap the energy of light elements, such as hydrogen. In these bombs the source of energy is the fusion process, in which nuclei of the isotopes (see ISOTOPE) of hydrogen combine to form a heavier helium nucleus. See *Thermonuclear, or Fusion, Weapons*, below.

Weapon research since 1945 has resulted in the production of bombs that range in power from a fraction of a kiloton (1000 tons of TNT equivalent) to many megatons (1,000,000 tons of TNT equivalent). The Soviet Union claims to have developed a bomb with a power equivalent to 100 megatons of TNT; it is known that one of over 50 megatons has been tested. Furthermore, the physical size of the bomb has been drastically reduced, permitting the development of nuclear artillery shells and small missiles that can be fired from portable launchers in the field. Although nuclear bombs were originally developed as strategic weapons to be carried by large bombers, nuclear weapons are now available for a variety of both strategic and tactical applications. Not only can they be delivered by different types of aircraft, but rocket missiles of a great range of sizes are now capable of carrying nuclear warheads. Such missiles can be launched from the ground, from the air, or from underwater. The nuclear weapon has thus become very versatile, both in power and in the manner of its use. Because of the necessity for a certain minimum mass, however, as explained below, it is doubtful whether very small nuclear weapons, for example, hand grenades, are feasible.

Fission Weapons. Three areas of investigation were important in the development of fission weapons.

ENERGY LIBERATION IN FISSION. In 1905 the American theoretical physicist Albert Einstein (q.v.) published his special theory of relativity (q.v.). According to this theory, the relation between mass and energy is expressed by the equation $E = mc^2$, which states that a given mass (m) is associated with an amount of energy (E) equal to this mass multiplied by the square of the velocity of light (c). A very small amount of matter is equivalent to a vast amount of energy. For example, if 1 lb. of matter could be converted completely into energy, the energy released would be equivalent to that of 10,000,000 tons of TNT.

In 1939, as a result of experiments by the German chemists Otto Hahn (q.v.) and Fritz Strassmann (1902–), who split the uranium atom into two roughly equal parts by bombardment with neutrons (see NEUTRON), the Austrian physicist Lise Meitner (q.v.), with her nephew, the Danish physicist Otto Robert Frisch (1904–), explained the process of nuclear fission, making the release of atomic energy within reach.

THE CHAIN REACTION. When the uranium nucleus fissions, it breaks up into a pair of nuclear fragments and releases energy. At the same time, the nucleus emits very quickly a number of fast neutrons, the same type of particles that initiated the fission of the uranium nucleus. It is this

NUCLEAR WEAPONS

fact that makes it possible to achieve a self-sustaining or perpetuating series of nuclear fissions; the neutrons emitted in fission produce a chain reaction, with continuous release of energy.

The light isotope of uranium, uranium-235, is easily split by the fission neutrons and, upon fission, emits an average of about 2.5 neutrons. One neutron per generation of nuclear fissions is necessary to sustain the chain of reactions. Others may be lost by escape from the mass of chain-reacting material, or be absorbed in impurities or in the heavy uranium isotope, uranium-238, if it is present. Any substance capable of sustaining a fission chain reaction is known as a fissile material. *See* NUCLEAR ENERGY: *Fissionable Materials.*

CRITICAL MASS. A small sphere of pure fissile material, such as uranium-235, about the size of a golf ball, would not sustain a chain reaction. Too many neutrons escape through the surface area, which is relatively large compared with its volume, and thus are lost to the chain reaction. In a mass of uranium-235 about the size of a baseball, however, the number of neutrons lost through the surface is compensated for by the neutrons generated in additional fissions taking place within the sphere. The minimum amount of fissile material (of a given shape) required to maintain the chain reaction is known as the critical mass. Increasing the size of the sphere produces a supercritical assembly, in which the successive generations of fissions increase very rapidly, leading to a possible explosion as a result of the extremely rapid release of a large amount of energy. In an atomic bomb, therefore, a mass of fissile material greater than the critical size must be assembled instantaneously and held together for about a millionth of a second to permit the chain reaction to propagate before the bomb explodes. A heavy material, called a tamper, surrounds the fissile mass and prevents its premature disruption. The tamper also reduces the number of neutrons that escape from the fissile mass.

If every atom in 1 lb. of uranium were to split, the energy produced would equal the explosive power of 9000 tons of TNT. In this hypothetical case, the efficiency of the process would be 100 percent. In the first A-bomb tests, such efficiency was not approached. Moreover, a 1-lb. mass is too small for a critical assembly.

DETONATION OF ATOMIC BOMBS. Various schemes have been devised to activate the atomic bomb. The simplest system is the gun-type weapon, in which a projectile made of fissile material is fired at a target of the same material so that the two weld together into a supercritical assembly. The atomic bomb exploded by the United States over Hiroshima, Japan, on Aug. 6, 1945, was a gun-type weapon. It had the energy equivalent of about 20 kilotons of TNT.

A more complex method, known as implosion, is utilized in a spherically shaped weapon. The outer part of the sphere consists of a layer of closely fitted and specially shaped devices, called lenses, consisting of high explosive and

The U.S.S. Nautilus, the world's first nuclear-powered submarine, built in 1955, foreshadowed the Polaris and Poseidon missile-carrying submarines of the 1960's and early 1970's.

designed to concentrate the blast toward the center of the bomb. Each segment of the high explosive is equipped with a detonator, which in turn is wired to all other segments. An electrical impulse explodes all the chunks of high explosive simultaneously, resulting in a detonation wave that converges toward the core of the

43

NUCLEAR WEAPONS

weapon. At the core is a sphere of fissile material, which is compressed by the powerful, inwardly directed pressure, or implosion. The density of the metal is increased, and a supercritical assembly is produced. The Alamogordo test bomb, as well as the one dropped by the U.S. on Nagasaki, Japan, on Aug. 9, 1945, were of the implosion type. Each was equivalent to about 20 kilotons of TNT.

Regardless of the method used to attain a supercritical assembly, the chain reaction proceeds for about a millionth of a second; during this process vast amounts of heat energy are liberated. The extremely fast release of a very large amount of energy in a relatively small volume causes the temperature to rise to tens of millions of degrees. The resulting rapid expansion and vaporization of the bomb material causes a powerful explosion to occur.

Production of Fissile Material. Much experimentation was necessary to make the production of fissile material practical.

SEPARATION OF URANIUM ISOTOPES. The fissile uranium-235 isotope of uranium accounts for only 0.7 percent of natural uranium; the remainder is composed of the heavier uranium-238. No chemical methods suffice to separate uranium-235 from ordinary uranium, because both uranium isotopes are chemically identical. A number of techniques were devised to separate the two, all of which depend in principle upon the slight difference in weight between the two types of uranium atoms.

A huge gaseous-diffusion plant was built during World War II in Oak Ridge, Tenn., at a cost of $550,000,000. This plant was expanded into a $1,000,000,000 installation after the war, and two similar plants were built near Paducah, Ky., and Portsmouth, Ohio. The feed material for this type of plant consists of a uranium-hexafluoride gas, which is extremely corrosive. The gas is pumped against barriers that have many millions of tiny holes, through which the lighter molecules, which contain uranium-235 atoms, diffuse at a slightly greater rate than the heavier molecules, containing uranium-238; see DIFFUSION. After the gas has been cycled through thousands of barriers, known as stages, it is highly enriched in the lighter isotope of uranium. The final product is weapon-grade uranium containing more than 90 percent uranium-235. In the late 1960's weapon-grade uranium cost $5500 per pound in contrast to the price of natural uranium, which was $12 per pound.

PRODUCING PLUTONIUM. Although the heavy uranium isotope uranium-238 will not sustain a chain reaction, it can be converted into a fissile material by bombarding it with neutrons and transforming it into a new species of element. When the uranium-238 atom captures a neutron in its nucleus, it is transformed into the heavier isotope uranium-239. This nuclear species quickly disintegrates to form neptunium-239, an isotope of element 93; see NEPTUNIUM. Another disintegration transmutes this isotope into an isotope of element 94, called plutonium-239. Plutonium-239, like uranium-235, undergoes fission after the absorption of a neutron and can be used as a bomb material. Producing plutonium-239 in large quantities requires an intense source of neutrons; the source is provided by the controlled chain reaction in a nuclear reactor. See NUCLEAR POWER.

During World War II nuclear reactors were designed for the specific purpose of providing neutrons to produce plutonium. The U.S. Atomic Energy Commission now has huge plutonium-production reactors in Hanford, Wash., and near Aiken, S.C., capable of manufacturing large quantities of plutonium each year.

Thermonuclear, or Fusion, Weapons. Even before the first atomic bomb was developed, scientists realized that a type of nuclear reaction different from the fission process was theoretically possible as a source of nuclear energy. Instead of using the energy released as a result of a chain reaction in fissile material, nuclear weapons could utilize the energy liberated in the fusion of light elements. This process is the opposite of fission, since it involves the fusing together of the nuclei of isotopes of light atoms such as hydrogen. It is for this reason that the weapons based on nuclear-fusion reactions are often called hydrogen bombs, or H-bombs. Of the three isotopes of hydrogen the two heaviest species, deuterium and tritium (qq.v.), combine most readily to form helium. Although the energy released in the fusion process is less per nuclear reaction than in fission, 1 lb. of the lighter material contains many more atoms; thus, energy liberated from 1 lb of hydrogen-isotope fuel is equivalent to that of about 26,000 tons of TNT, or almost three times as much as from uranium. This estimate, however, is based upon complete fusion of all hydrogen atoms. Fusion reactions occur only at temperatures of several millions of degrees, the rate increasing enormously with increasing temperature; such reactions consequently are known as thermonuclear (heat-induced) reactions. Strictly speaking, the term thermonuclear implies that the nuclei have a range (or distribution) of energies characteristic of the temperature. This distribution of energies plays an important role in making

NUCLEAR WEAPONS

rapid fusion reactions possible by an increase in temperature. *See* ATOM AND ATOMIC THEORY: *Thermonuclear Fusion.*

Development of the hydrogen bomb was impossible before the perfection of A-bombs, for only the latter could yield the tremendous heat necessary to achieve fusion of hydrogen atoms. Thus, atomic scientists regarded the A-bomb as the trigger of the projected thermonuclear device.

THERMONUCLEAR TESTS. Following dvelopmental tests in the spring of 1951 at the U.S. Eniwetok Proving Grounds in the Marshall Islands during Operation Greenhouse, a full-scale, successful experiment was conducted on Nov. 1, 1952, with a fusion-type device. This test, called Mike, which was part of Operation Ivy, produced an explosion with power equivalent to several million tons of TNT (that is, several megatons). The Soviet Union detonated a thermonuclear weapon in the megaton range in August, 1953. On March 1, 1954, the U.S. exploded a fusion bomb with a power of 15 megatons, a weapon nearly 1000 times the force of the first atomic bomb used in World War II. It created a glowing fireball, more than 3 mi. in diameter, and a huge mushroom cloud, which quickly rose into the stratosphere.

The March 1, 1954, explosion led to worldwide recognition of the nature of radioactive fallout (q.v.). The fallout of radioactive debris from the huge bomb cloud also revealed much about the nature of the thermonuclear bomb. Had the bomb been a weapon consisting of an A-bomb trigger and a core of hydrogen isotopes, the only persistent radioactivity from the explosion would have been the result of the fission debris from the trigger and from the radioactivity induced by neutrons in coral and seawater. Some of the radioactive debris, however, fell on the *Lucky Dragon,* a Japanese vessel engaged in tuna fishing about 100 mi. from the test site. This radioactive dust was later analyzed by Japanese scientists. The results demonstrated that the bomb that dusted the *Lucky Dragon* with fallout was more than just an H-bomb.

Fission-Fusion-Fission Bomb. The thermonuclear bomb exploded in 1954 was a three-stage weapon. The first stage consisted of a big A-bomb, which acted as a trigger. The second stage was the H-bomb phase resulting from the fusion of deuterium and tritium within the bomb. In this process helium and high-energy neutrons are formed. The third stage resulted from the impact of these high-speed neutrons on the outer jacket of the bomb, which consisted of natural uranium, or uranium-238. No chain reaction was produced, but the fusion neutrons had sufficient energy to cause fission of the uranium nuclei and thus added to the explosive yield and also to the radioactivity of the bomb residues.

Effects of Nuclear Weapons. The effects of nuclear weapons were carefully observed.

BLAST EFFECTS. As is the case with explosions caused by conventional weapons, most of the damage to buildings and other structures from a nuclear explosion results, directly or indirectly, from the effects of blast. The very rapid expansion of the bomb materials produces a high-pressure pulse or shock wave that moves rapidly outward from the exploding bomb. In air, this shock wave is called a blast wave because it is equivalent to and is accompanied by powerful winds of much greater than hurricane force. Damage to structures is caused both by the high excess pressure (or overpressure) of air at the front of the blast wave and by the extremely strong winds that persist after the wave front has passed. The degree of blast damage suffered on the ground depends on the TNT equivalent

A mushroom cloud rises above the test site after the first U.S. firing of an atomic artillery shell on May 25, 1953, at Frenchman Flat, Nevada. U.S. Army

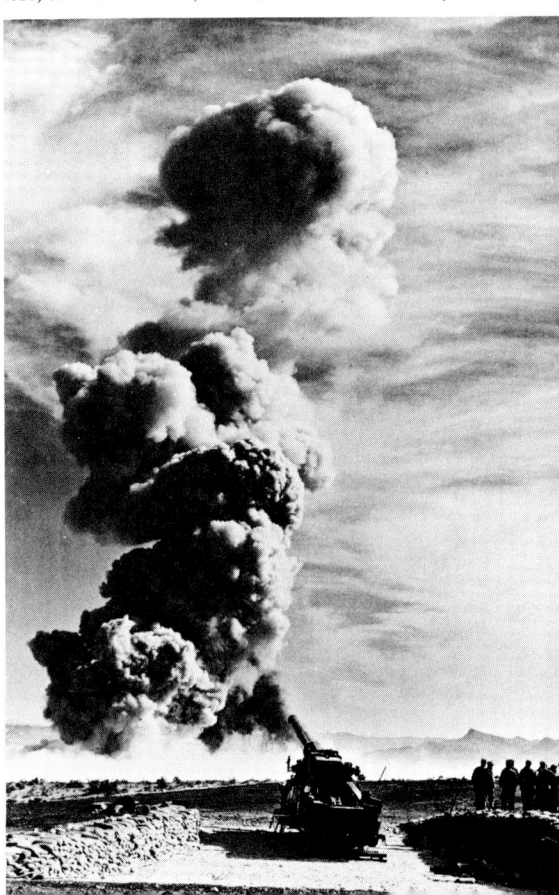

NUCLEAR WEAPONS

of the explosion; the altitude at which the bomb is exploded, referred to as the height of burst; and the distance of the structure from ground zero, that is, the point directly under the exploding bomb. For the 20-kiloton A-bombs detonated over Japan, the height of burst was about 1800 ft., because it was estimated that this height would produce a maximum area of damage to the existing structures. If the TNT equivalent had been larger, a greater height of burst would have been chosen. On the other hand, in order to destroy more of the stronger targets, the explosion altitude should have been lower.

Assuming a height of burst that will maximize the damage area, a 10-kiloton bomb will cause severe damage to wood-frame houses, such as are common in the U.S., to a distance of over 1 mi. from ground zero, and moderate damage as far as 1½ mi. (A severely damaged house probably would be beyond repair.) The damage radius increases with the power of the bomb, approximately in proportion to its cube root. If exploded at the optimum height, therefore, a 10-negaton weapon, which is 1000 times as powerful as a 10-kiloton weapon, will increase the distance tenfold, that is, out to 11 mi. for severe damage and 15 mi. for moderate damage of a frame house. Light damage, for example, broken windows, blown-in doors, and broken plaster, will extend to greater distances. For stronger structures the damage distances are, of course, less.

FLASH BURNS AND FIRES. The very high temperatures attained in a nuclear explosion result in the formation of an extremely hot incandescent mass of gas called a fireball. For a 10-kiloton explosion in the air, the fireball will attain a maximum diameter of about 1000 ft.; for a 10-megaton weapon the fireball may be 3 mi. across. A flash of thermal (or heat) radiation is emitted from the fireball and spreads out over a large area, but with steadily decreasing intensity. The amount of heat energy received at a certain distance from the nuclear explosion depends on the power of the weapon and the state of the atmosphere. If the visibility is poor or the explosion takes place above clouds, the effectiveness of the heat flash is decreased. The thermal radiation falling upon exposed skin can cause what are called flash burns. A 10-kiloton explosion in the air can produce moderate (second-degree) flash burns, which require some medical attention, as far as 1½ mi. from ground zero; for a 10-megaton bomb, the corresponding distance would be over 20 mi. Milder burns of bare skin would be experienced even farther out. Most ordinary clothing provides protection from the heat radiation, as does almost any opaque object. Flash burns occur only when the bare skin is directly exposed, or if the clothing is too thin to absorb the thermal radiation.

The heat radiation can initiate fires in dry, flammable materials, for example, paper and some fabrics, and such fires may spread if conditions are suitable. The evidence from the A-bomb explosions over Japan indicates that many fires, especially in the area near ground zero, originated from secondary causes, such as electrical short circuits, broken gas lines, and upset furnaces and boilers in industrial plants. The blast damage produced debris that helped to maintain the fires and denied access to fire-fighting equipment. Thus, much of the fire damage in Japan was a secondary effect of the blast wave.

Under some conditions, such as existed at Hiroshima but not at Nagasaki, many individual fires can combine to produce a fire storm similar to those that accompany some large forest fires. The heat of the fire causes a strong updraft, which produces strong winds drawn in toward the center of the burning area. These winds fan the flame and convert the area into a holocaust in which everything flammable is destroyed. Inasmuch as the flames are drawn inward, however, the area over which such a fire spreads may be limited.

PENETRATING RADIATION. Besides heat and blast, the exploding nuclear bomb has a unique effect, that is, it releases penetrating nuclear radiation, which is quite different from thermal (or heat) radiation; see RADIOACTIVITY. When absorbed by the body, nuclear radiation can cause serious injury. For an explosion high in the air, the injury range for these radiations is less than for blast and fire damage or flash burns. In Japan, however, many individuals who were protected from blast and burns succumbed later to radiation injury.

Nuclear radiation from an explosion may be divided into two categories, namely, prompt radiation and residual radiation. The prompt radiation consists of an instantaneous burst of neutrons and gamma rays, which travel over an area of several square miles. Gamma rays are identical in effect to X rays; see XRAY. Both neutrons and gamma rays have the ability to penetrate solid matter, so that substantial thicknesses of materials are required to attenuate them to harmless proportions.

The residual nuclear radiation, generally known as fallout, can be a hazard over very large areas that are completely free from other effects of a nuclear explosion. In bombs that gain their energy from fission of uranium-235 or plutonium-239, two radioactive nuclei are produced for every fissile nucleus split. These fission products account for the persistent radioactivity in bomb debris, because many of the atoms have half-lives measured in hours, days, months, or years; see HALF-LIFE.

Two distinct categories of fallout, namely, early and delayed, are known. If a nuclear explosion occurs near the surface, earth or water is taken up into a mushroom-shaped cloud and becomes contaminated with the radioactive weapon residues. The contaminated material begins to descend within a few minutes and may continue for about twenty-four hours, covering an area of thousands of square miles downwind from the explosion. This constitutes the early fallout, which is an immediate hazard to human beings. No early fallout is associated with nuclear explosions high in the air, such as occurred over Japan.

If a nuclear bomb is exploded well above the ground, the radioactive residues rise to a great height in the mushroom cloud and descend gradually, during a period of weeks or months, over a large area. This is called the delayed fallout and does not constitute an immediate hazard.

Human experience with radioactive fallout has been minimal. The principal known case histories have been derived from the accidental exposure of natives and fishermen to the fallout from the 15-megaton explosion that occurred on March 1, 1954. The nature of radioactivity, however, and the immense areas contaminable by a single bomb undoubtedly make radioactive fallout potentially one of the most lethal effects of nuclear weapons.

CLEAN H-BOMBS. On the average, about 50 percent of the power of an H-bomb results from thermonuclear-fusion reactions and the other 50 percent from fission that occurs in the A-bomb trigger and in the uranium jacket. A clean H-bomb is defined as one in which a significantly smaller proportion than 50 percent of the energy arises from fission. Because fusion does not produce any radioactive products directly, the fallout from a clean weapon is less than that from a normal or average H-bomb of the same total power. If an H-bomb were made with no uranium jacket but with a fission trigger, it would be relatively clean. Perhaps as little as 5 percent of the total explosive force might result from fission; the weapon would thus be 95 percent clean. An H-bomb with no uranium jacket and no fission trigger, if it could be realized, might be regarded as 100 percent clean. This would be the so-called neutron bomb. Although no radioactive fission products would result, the large number of neutrons released in the thermonuclear reactions would induce radioactivity in materials, especially earth and water, in the vicinity of the explosion. The neutrons could also cause radiation injury to exposed individuals. Blast and heat effects attendant on the explosion of a neutron bomb would undoubtedly be significant.

See also DISARMAMENT; INTERNATIONAL CONTROL OF ATOMIC ENERGY; WARFARE.   S.G.

NUCLEIC ACIDS, extremely complex molecules produced by living cells and viruses. Their name came from the fact that they were first obtained from the nuclei of living cells. Certain nucleic acids, however, are found not in the cell nucleus but in cell cytoplasm. Nucleic acids have at least two functions: to pass on hereditary characteristics from one generation to the next, and to trigger the manufacture of specific proteins. How nucleic acids accomplish these functions is the object of some of the most intense and promising research currently carried on. The nucleic acids are the fundamental substances of living things, believed by researchers to have been first formed about 3,000,000,000 years ago, when the most elementary forms of life began on earth. The origin of the so-called genetic code (q.v.) they carry has been accepted by researchers as being very close in time to the origin of life itself. Biochemists have succeeded in deciphering the code; that is, determining how the sequence of nucleic acids dictates the structure of proteins.

The two classes of nucleic acids are the deoxyribonucleic acids (DNA) and the ribonucleic acids (RNA). The backbones of both DNA and RNA molecules are shaped like helical strands. Their molecular weights (see MOLECULE) are in the millions. To the backbones are connected a great number of smaller molecules (side groups) of four different types; see CHEMICAL COMPOUNDS, SYNTHETIC: *Plastics and Elastomers*. The sequence of these molecules on the strand determines the code of the particular nucleic acid. This code, in turn, signals the cell how to reproduce either a duplicate of itself or the proteins it requires for survival.

All living cells contain the genetic material DNA. The cells of bacteria may have but one strand of DNA, but such a strand contains all the information needed by the cell in order to reproduce an identical offspring. The cells of mammals contain scores of DNA strands grouped together in chromosomes. In short, the structure of a DNA molecule or combination of

NUCLEIC ACIDS

DNA molecules determines the shape, form, and function of the offspring, whether the offspring is a virus, a bacterium, a plant, or a human being.

The pioneering research that revealed the general structure of DNA was performed by Francis H. C. Crick, James Dewey Watson, and Maurice H. F. Wilkins (qq.v.). Wilkins obtained an X-ray diffraction picture of the DNA mole-

The British biophysicist Dr. Maurice H. F. Wilkins studies a model of a DNA molecular structure. Dr. Wilkins won a Nobel Prize for discoveries concerning the molecular structure of nucleic acids. UPI

cule in 1951. Based on this picture, Crick and Watson were able to construct a model of the DNA molecule that was completed in 1953. For their work, these scientists received the 1962 Nobel Prize in medicine and physiology. Arthur Kornberg (q.v.) synthesized DNA from "off-the-shelf" substances, for which he was awarded, with Severo Ochoa (q.v.), the 1959 Nobel Prize in medicine and physiology. The DNA that he synthesized, although structurally similar to natural DNA, was not biologically active and could not reproduce itself. In 1967, however, Kornberg and a team of researchers at Stanford University succeeded in producing biologically active DNA from relatively simple chemicals. when mixed with bacterial cells, this DNA forced the cells to produce living viruses; see VIRUS.

Certain kinds of RNA have a slightly different function from that of DNA. They take part in the actual synthesis of the proteins a cell produces. This is of particular interest to virologists because many viruses reproduce by "forcing" the host cells to manfuacture more viruses. The virus injects its own RNA into the host cell, and, for reasons not yet fully explained, the host cell obeys the code of the invading RNA rather than that of its own RNA. Thus the cell produces proteins that are, in fact, viruses instead of the proteins required for cell function. The host cell is destroyed in the process and the newly formed viruses are free to inject their RNA molecules into other host cells.

The structure of two types of RNA and their function in protein production have been determined, one type by a team of Cornell University and the United States Department of Agriculture investigators led by Robert W. Holley (q.v.) of Cornell, and the other type by James T. Madison (1933–) and George A. Everett (1924–) of the Department of Agriculture. Important research into the interpretation of the genetic code and its role in protein synthesis was also performed by the Indian-born chemist Har Gobind Khorana at the University of Wisconsin Enzyme Institute and the American biochemist Marshall W(arren) Nirenberg (qq.v.) of the National Heart Institute. Sol Spiegelman (1914–) and Ichiro Haruna at the University of Illinois have synthesized one type of RNA. *See also* HEREDITY.

S.Z.L.

NUCLEUS, in atomic structure, the positively charged central mass of an atom about which the orbital electrons revolve; *see* ATOM AND ATOMIC THEORY; ELECTRON. The nucleus is composed of nucleons, that is, protons and neutrons, and its mass accounts for nearly the entire mass of the atom; *see* NEUTRON; PROTON. Because the diameter of the nucleus as compared with the diameter of the entire atom is extremely small (atomic diameters are approximately 10^{-8} cm, and nuclear diameters are roughly 10^{-12} cm), nuclei are extremely dense. A number of models of nuclear structure have been postulated to account for the properties of the nucleus as a whole. Although each model is supported by some experimental observations, none has been successful in accounting for all properties. The *liquid-drop model* was the first to gain wide support. This model treats the nucleus as though it were a drop of dense fluid with uniform composition. The *nuclear-shell model,* advanced in the late 1940's and still widely employed, assumes that each component of the nucleus (nucleon) moved about independently, but under the influence of all other nucleons; the nucleons are assumed to be arranged in shells in analogy with the atomic electrons. The *collective model,* first advanced in the 1950's, combines many of the aspects of the two previous models and accounts for apparently distorted nuclei.

The least stable arrangement of nuclei is one in which an odd number of neutrons and an odd number of protons are present; all except four isotopes containing nuclei of this kind are radioactive; *see* Isotope; Radioactivity. The presence of a large excess of neutrons over protons detracts from the stability of a nucleus; nuclei in all isotopes of elements above bismuth in the periodic table contain this type of arrangement and they are all radioactive; *see* Periodic Law. The greatest number of known stable (nonradioactive) nuclei contain an even number of protons and an even number of neutrons.

According to an early conception, nuclei consisted of protons and electrons that were bound together largely by the electrostatic attraction between oppositely charged particles. The electrostatic force theory was discarded when it was demonstrated that nuclei contain neutrons and that electrons are outside the nucleus. In a nucleus composed of neutrons and protons, the only charged particles are the positively charged protons, and hence they would be expected to repel each other. According to the most widely accepted current theory, nuclear particles are held together by "exchange forces," in which pions (*see* Meson), common to both neutrons and protons, are continuously exchanged between them. The binding of protons and neutrons by mesons is similar to the binding of two atoms in a molecule through the sharing or exchange of a common pair of electrons; *see* Valence.

Nuclear masses can be accurately determined by use of the mass spectrograph; *see* Spectrograph, Mass. The masses of the constituent particles, the neutrons and protons, are well known. If the sum of the masses of the individual neutron and protons of a nucleus is compared with the measured mass of the nucleus, the mass of the nucleus is found to be smaller than that of its component parts. The difference between these values has been transformed into energy, called binding energy, in the nuclear-building process. *See* Nuclear Energy. R.Ho.

NUCLEUS, in biology. *See* Cell.

NUDISM, manner and cult of life in the nude. Specifically, nudism is practiced for the physical benefit derived from exposure of the body to healthful qualities of sunlight and fresh air; in a wider sense, however, it is a philosophy and a way of life. The proponents of nudism maintain that when clothing is not absolutely necessitated by the rigors of the weather it should be abandoned, as it serves to focus erotic attention upon the body, thereby exciting an unhealthy sexual prurience. The shame customarily associated with nakedness in modern civilized society results, according to nudists, from centuries of cultural conditioning against complete exposure of the body in public. Nudism, by correcting in its practitioners this false sense of shame, enhances their self-assurance and furnishes them with a new appreciation of the essential beauty and dignity of the human body.

Archeological evidence indicates that nudism, in the form of sunbathing, was practiced in antiquity by the Babylonians, Assyrians, Greeks, and Romans. In modern times the rise of nudism is indentified with the *Nacktkultur* ("culture of nakedness") movement in Germany. The advocates of this movement emphasized its value in relation to preventive hygiene, claiming for their practices a highly tonic effect upon both body and mind. With the advent of National Socialism in Germany, however, the movement declined as a result of strong government restrictions. Nudist societies are maintained in most European countries, and are particularly prevalent in Norway, Sweden, and Finland. Although nudism has made no great progress in North America, the American Sunbathing Society, with headquarters at May's Landing. N.J., has branch organizations throughout the United States.

NUESTRA SEÑORA DE LA ASUNCIÓN. *See* Asunción.

NUEVO LAREDO, city of Mexico, in Tamaulipas State, on the Rio Grande, 140 miles N.E. of Monterrey, and opposite Laredo, Texas. Connected to Laredo by the International Bridge and by rail, it is a major port of entry and a tourist center, as well as a market for cattle, cotton, grains, and sugarcane raised in the area. Industries include textile and flour milling, cotton ginning, fruit canning, sawmilling, coffee and vegetable-oil processing, and printing. The city was founded in the mid-1700's and was considered a part of Laredo until 1848, when the east bank of the river was ceded to the United States. Pop. (1960) 112,280.

NUFFIELD RADIO ASTRONOMY LABORATORIES. *See* Jodrell Bank Observatory.

NULLIFICATION, in the history of American political theory, the alleged right of a State to suspend operation of a Federal law within its boundaries. The right of nullification was asserted on the basis of a belief that States are the ultimate sources of sovereignty, and that the Federal government is simply a league of freely

NULLIFICATION

associated States, the authority of which the State is free to recognize or ignore in accordance with its best interests. This belief stemmed from the beginning of the republic, when the States, jealous of their sovereignty and fearful of tyranny, agreed to yield certain of their powers to the United States, as specifically set forth in the Constitution of the United States (q.v.) only after the looser Articles of Confederation (q.v.) had proved ineffective. The principle of nullification was supported by many of the founding fathers. In 1798 and 1799, the Kentucky and Virginia resolutions (q.v.), drafted by American statesmen James Madison and Thomas Jefferson (qq.v.), respectively, affirmed the validity of nullification and warned against Federal usurpation of State sovereignty. New England States nullified an unpopular embargo (q.v.) in 1809–10; and fifteen years later, Georgia nullified Federal laws relating to American Indians; see EMBARGO ACT.

As the development of industry and more intensive settlement linked the different parts of the country more closely together, nullification was opposed by advocates of the primacy of the Federal government. One of the foremost of these, United States Senator Daniel Webster (q.v.), in his most famous speech before the U.S. Senate, warned Senator Robert Young Hayne (q.v.) of South Carolina in 1830 that nullification would cause the Union to fall apart and that the American flag, "stained with the blood of fratricidal war", would wave over "the dismembered fragments of our once glorious empire". Soon after, in 1832, South Carolina called a State convention that declared "null, void, and no law" the high protective tariff (q.v.) of that year; see TARIFFS, UNITED STATES. President Andrew Jackson (q.v.) threatened to send troops to enforce the tariff in the port of Charleston. Senator John Caldwell Calhoun of South Carolina, one of the leading advocates of nullification, joined with Senator Henry Clay (qq.v.) of Virginia to reconcile the claims of South Carolina with those of the Federal government. As a result, a compromise tariff was passed, the South Carolina convention repealed the ordinance of nullification, and both sides of the controversy claimed a victory.

A final resolution of the question of nullification was thus postponed until 1861, when South Carolina, followed by other Southern States, seceded from the Union and precipitated the Civil War; see CIVIL WAR, THE AMERICAN. Although at the cost of the "blood of fratricidal war" predicted by Webster, this great conflict confirmed the primacy of the Federal government in the authority granted it by the Constitution, and no subsequent attempts have been made by any States to nullify Federal laws. Nevertheless, the question of distribution of powers between the States and the Federal government remains a live issue. The current proponents of "States' rights" (q.v.), still principally from the South, expound a point of view that, in opposing extensions of Federal power, has descended lineally from the original nullification theories of Jefferson and Calhoun. See also UNITED STATES OF AMERICA: History.

NULLITY OF MARRIAGE. See ANNULMENT OF MARRIAGE.

NUMAZU, city and port of Japan, in Shizuoka Prefecture, on the island of Honshu, at the mouth of the Kano R., on Suruga Bay, 28 miles N.E. of Shizuoka. It is an important road hub and a rail junction on the Tokaido Line; connections are made here for the Izu Peninsula resort towns and for Mt. Fuji. A market center in an area of sericulture and agricultural production, the city trades in silk, fish, and vegetables and manufactures machinery and textiles. It is an old settlement; a castle existed here from 1479 to 1868. Seaside resorts lie east and south of the city, including the emperor's villa. Numazu Park is a scenic spot on the bay. Numazu became a city in 1923. Pop. (1965) 159,880.

NUMBER, word or symbol used to designate quantities or, by extension, entities having quantitylike properties.

Rational Numbers. The simplest numbers are the natural numbers, 1, 2, 3, . . . , used in counting; they are also called the whole numbers, positive integers, or positive rational integers. The natural numbers are closed with respect to addition and multiplication; that is, the sum and product of two natural numbers are always natural numbers. Because the quotient of two natural numbers is not always a natural number, it is convenient to introduce the positive fractions to represent the quotient of any two natural numbers. The natural number n is identified with the fraction $n/1$. Furthermore, because the difference of two positive fractions is not always a positive fraction, it is expeditious to introduce the negative fractions (including the negative integers) and the number zero (0). The positive and negative integers and fractions, and the number 0, comprise the rational number system. see RATIONAL NUMBERS.

The sum, difference, product, or quotient of two rational numbers is always a rational number. Division of any number by zero, however, is not allowed; see ZERO. It can be shown that every rational number can be represented as a

NUMBERS

repeating or periodic decimal, that is, as a number in the decimal notation, which after a certain point consists of the infinite repetition of a finite block of digits. Conversely, every repeating decimal represents a rational number. Thus, 617/50 = 12.34000 . . . , and 2317/990 = 2.304040. . . . The first expression is usually written as 12.34, omitting the infinite repetition of the block consisting of the single digit 0. The second expression is frequently written as 2.3$\overline{40}$ or 2.3$\underline{40}$ or 2.34$\dot{0}$ to indicate that the block of two digits, 4 and 0, is repeated infinitely. The first type of expression is called a finite or terminating decimal, and the second type of expression is called an infinite periodic or repeating decimal ("infinite" is frequently omitted).

Irrational Numbers. The development of geometry (q.v.) indicated the need for more numbers; the length of the diagonal of a square with sides one unit long cannot be expressed as a rational number. Similarly, the ratio of the circumference to the diameter of a circle is not a rational number. These and other needs led to the introduction of the irrational numbers. A decimal expansion that is not either of the two types described above represents an irrational number. For example, $\sqrt{2}$ = 1.4142135623 . . . and π = 3.1415926535 . . . are irrational numbers, and their decimal expansions are necessarily nonterminating and nonperiodic. The totality of the rational and irrational numbers makes up the so-called real number system. See also NUMERALS.

Imaginary Numbers. The product of a real number multiplied by itself is 0 or positive; the equation $x^2 = -1$ has no solutions in the real number system. If such a solution is desired, new numbers must be invented. Let $i = \sqrt{-1}$ be a new number representing a solution of the preceding equation. All numbers of the form $a + bi$, in which a and b are real numbers, belong to the complex number system. If b is not 0, the complex number is called an imaginary number; if b is not 0 but a is 0, the complex number is called a pure imaginary; if b is 0, the complex number is a real number. See IMAGINARY NUMBERS.

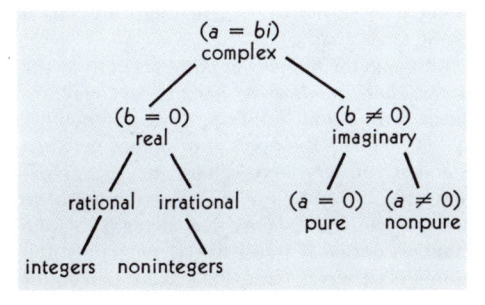

Imaginary numbers (the term must not be used in a literal sense but in the technical sense just described) are extremely useful in the theory of alternating currents and many other branches of physics and natural science.

The relationships of the various types of numbers are illustrated in the so-called number family tree. See table at bottom of left column.

Complex Numbers. In 1799 the German mathematician Karl Friedrich Gauss (q.v.) proved that every algebraic equation of degree n having the form

$$x^n + a_1 x^{n-1} + \ldots + a_{n-1} x + a_n = 0,$$

in which $a_1, a_2, \ldots, a_n$ are arbitrary complex numbers, is satisfied by at least one complex root; see EQUATIONS, THEORY OF.

Whereas real numbers represent points on a line, complex numbers can be placed in correspondence with the points on a plane. To represent the complex number $a + bi$ geometrically, the x-axis is used as the axis of the real number a, and the y-axis serves as the axis of the pure imaginary bi; the complex number, therefore, corresponds to the point P with the rectangular coordinates a and b; see ANALYTIC GEOMETRY. The line, or vector (q.v.), joining the origin with the point $P(a, b)$ is the diagonal of a rectangle with the sides a and bi. If the complex number $a + bi$ is multiplied by -1, the vector OP is rotated through 180°, and the point P falls in the third quadrant; a rotation of 90°, therefore, represents multiplication of the complex number by i, as $-1 = 1^{-2}$, and $i(a + bi)$ represents a point in the second quadrant if $a + bi$ represents a point in the first quadrant.

Mystical and magical qualities have been ascribed to numbers both in antiquity and in modern times. The pseudo science of numerology attempts to interpret the occult by means of the symbolism of numbers, which is based on the Pythagorean doctrine that all things are numbers and consist of geometrical figures in various patterns. See PYTHAGORAS. J.Si.

NUMBERS, book of the Old Testament (see BIBLE), in the King James Version, THE FOURTH BOOK OF MOSES, CALLED NUMBERS. The English title is derived from the title of the book in the Vulgate (q.v.), *Numeri* (Lat., "Numbers"). *Numeri* is in turn a translation of the title of the book in the Greek-language version called the Septuagint. The Jews, who have named each of the five books comprising the Pentateuch (q.v.) after the first word or first significant word of the Hebrew text, entitle Numbers *Be-Midbar* (Heb., "in the wilderness"). The book continues the account of the origins and early history of the

```
              (a = bi)
              complex
             /        \
        (b = 0)      (b ≠ 0)
         real       imaginary
        /    \       /      \
  rational  irrational (a = 0) (a ≠ 0)
     /    \           pure   nonpure
integers  nonintegers
```

51

NUMBERS, THEORY OF

Jewish people begun in the books of Genesis and Exodus (qq.v.).

"In the wilderness" is by far a more appropriate title than "Numbers" (the latter refers to the census, or numbering, of the Israelite tribes recorded in the opening chapters), for the book is concerned chiefly with the desert wanderings of the Israelites, under the leadership of the lawgiver and prophet Moses (q.v.), from their final days at Mount Sinai until their arrival, nearly forty years later, at the plains of Moab, close to the Promised Land of Canaan (qq.v.). The book may be divided into three sections: (1), the final days at Mount Sinai (1:1–10:10); (2), a period of approximately thirty-eight years of wandering in the desert south of the Promised Land (10:11–20:13 or, as some scholars prefer, 10:11–21:13); and (3), the final approach to the border of Canaan from the east.

The first section deals almost exclusively with statistical and legal matters. The second section begins with an account of the Israelites' departure from Sinai. It relates, among other stories, that of the sedition of Aaron (q.v.) and Miriam, the brother and sister of Moses (chapter 12); and that of the sending out of Israelite spies into Canaan, their conflicting reports, and the Israelites' condemnation to forty years in the wilderness (chapters 13–14). Chapter 17 tells of the miraculous budding of Aaron's rod, a sign that the Levites (q.v.) are the Lord's elect.

The third section of Numbers tells of the Israelites' unsuccessful attempt to enter Canaan through the land of Edom (q.v.), and of Aaron's death (20:14–29); relates the selection of the Hebrew leader Joshua (q.v.) as successor to Moses (27:12–23); and tells (chapter 32) of the distribution of land east of the Jordan R. to the tribes of Gad and Reuben (qq.v.). A résumé of the stages of Israel's journey from Egypt to the border of Canaan (33:1–49) is followed by a description of the ideal boundaries of Canaan; and provisions for the apportionment of the land, the establishment of Levitical cities and cities of refuge for murderers, and rules for marriage to keep the lands of Israel intact (chapters 34–36) close the book. Notable throughout is the emphasis on matters of interest to the priests of Israel, indicating the probable main source of its subject matter, the so-called P source, dating from about the 6th century B.C. For a discussion of the documentary hypothesis, see BIBLE; GENESIS.

NUMBERS, THEORY OF, branch of mathematics that deals with the properties and relationships of numbers; see NUMBER. According to this broad definition, the theory of numbers includes most of mathematics, particularly mathematical analysis. Generally, however, the theory of numbers is confined to the study of integers, or occasionally to some other set of numbers having properties similar to the set of all integers, that is, whole numbers as opposed to fractions.

Nature of Integers. If a, b, c are integers such that $a = bc$, a is called a multiple of b or of c, and b or c is called a divisor or factor of a. If c is not ± 1, b is called a proper divisor of a. An even integer is a multiple of 2, for example, $-4, 0, 2, 10$; an odd integer is an integer that is not even, that has the remainder 1 when divided by 2, for example, $-5, 1, 3, 9$. A perfect number is a positive integer that is equal to the sum of all its positive, proper divisors; for example, 6, which equals $1 + 2 + 3$, and 28, which equals $1 + 2 + 4 + 7 + 14$ are perfect numbers. A positive number that is not perfect is imperfect and is deficient or abundant according to whether the sum of its positive, proper divisors is smaller or larger than the number itself. Thus, 9, with proper divisors 1, 3, is deficient; 12, with proper divisors 1, 2, 3, 4, 6, is abundant.

Primes. A lot of the theory of numbers is devoted to the study of primes. A number p, not ± 1, is a prime if its only divisors are $\pm 1, \pm p$. A number a is composite, if $a = bc$, in which neither b nor c is ± 1. The first ten positive primes are 2, 3, 5, 7, 11, 13, 17, 19, 23, 29; the first ten positive composite numbers are 4, 6, 8, 9, 10, 12, 14, 15, 16, 18. A composite number can be factored into a product of primes in only one way, apart from the order of the factors; thus, $9 = 3 \times 3$; $10 = 2 \times 5$; $12 = 2 \times 2 \times 3$.

The ninth book of the *Elements* by the Greek mathematician Euclid (q.v.) contains the proof of the proposition that the number of primes is infinite, that is, no largest prime exists. The proof is remarkably simple: let p be a prime and $q = 1 \times 2 \times 3 \times \ldots \times p + 1$, that is, one more than the product of all the integers from 1 through p. The integer q is larger than p and is not divisible by any integer from 2 through p, inclusive. Any one of its positive divisors, other than 1, and any one of its prime divisors, therefore, must be larger than p. It follows that there must be a prime larger than p.

Although the number of primes is infinite, the primes become relatively scarce as one proceeds further and further out into the number system. Indeed, the number of primes between 1 and n, for very large values of n, is approximtely n divided by the natural logarithm of n; see LOGARITHMS. Twenty-five percent of the numbers between 1 and 100, 17 percent of the numbers between 1 and 1000, and 7 percent of

NUMERALS

the numbers between 1 and 1,000,000 are primes.

Two primes that differ by 2 (for example, 5, 7; 17, 19; 101, 103) are called twin primes. It is not known whether the number of twin primes is infinite. Another conjecture is that every even number greater than 2 can be expressed as the sum of two primes; thus, $4 = 2 + 2$; $6 = 3 + 3$; $8 = 3 + 5$; $10 = 5 + 5$; $20 = 3 + 17$; $100 = 3 + 97$; however, a general proof is still lacking.

The greatest common divisor (g.c.d.) of two integers a and b is the largest positive integer that divides both a and b exactly. Euclid gave a method for finding the g.c.d. of two integers. If the g.c.d. of two integers is 1, the two numbers are said to be relatively prime, or one integer is said to be prime to the other. If $p, q, \ldots, u$ are the distinct prime divisors of a positive integer n, the number of positive integers not exceeding and prime to n is given by the formula

$$\phi(n) = n \left(1 - \frac{1}{p}\right)\left(1 - \frac{1}{q}\right) \cdots \left(1 - \frac{1}{u}\right).$$

If a, b, m are integers (m, positive) such that $a - b$ is a multiple of m, then a is congruent to b with respect to the modulus m, which is written

$$a \equiv b \pmod{m}.$$

This expression itself is called a congruence; congruences behave in many respects like equations. The theory of congruences is very important in number theory; for example, congruence theory can be used to solve problems known as Chinese remainders. An illustrative problem of this type is: Find the first two positive integers having the remainders 2, 3, 2, when divided by 3, 5, 7, respectively. The answer, 23 and 128, was given by the Chinese mathematician Sun-Tsŭ in the 1st century A.D. *See also* DIOPHANTINE ANALYSIS; FERMAT'S LAST THEOREM; INDETERMINATE EQUATION. J.Si.

NUMERALS, signs or symbols for graphic representation of numbers. The earliest forms of number notation were simply groups of straight lines, either vertical or horizontal, each line corresponding to the number one. Such a system is inconvenient when dealing with large numbers, and as early as 3400 B.C. in Egypt and 3000 B.C. in Mesopotamia a special symbol was adopted for the number 10. The addition of this second number symbol made it possible to express the number 11 with two instead of eleven individual symbols and the number 99 with eighteen instead of ninety-nine individual symbols. Later numeral systems introduced extra symbols for a number between 1 and 10, usually either 4 or 5, and additional symbols for numbers greater than 10. In Babylonian cuneiform notation the numeral used for 1 was also used for 60 and for powers of 60; the value of the numeral was indicated by its context. This was a logical arrangement from the mathematical point of view because $60^0 = 1$, $60^1 = 60$, and $60^2 = 3600$. The Eygptian hieroglyphic system used special symbols for 10, 100, 1000, and 10,000.

The ancient Greeks had two parallel systems of numerals. The earlier of these was based on the initial letters of the names of numbers: the number 5 was indicated by the letter "pi"; 10 by the letter "delta"; 100 by the antique form of the letter H; 1000 by the letter "chi"; and 10,000 by the letter "mu". The later system, which was first introduced about the 3rd century B.C., employed all the letters of the Greek alphabet plus three letters borrowed from the Phoenician as number symbols. The first nine letters of the alphabet were used for the numbers 1 to 9; the second nine letters for the decades from 10 to 90; and the last nine letters for the hundreds from 100 to 900. Thousands were indicated by placing a bar to the left of the appropriate numeral, and tens of thousands by placing the appropriate letter over the letter M. The late Greek system had the advantage that large numbers could be expressed with a minimum of symbols, but it had also the disadvantage of requiring the user to memorize a total of twenty-seven symbols.

Roman Numerals. The system of number symbols created by the Romans had the merit of expressing all numbers from 1 to 1,000,000 with a total of seven symbols: I for 1, V for 5, X for 10, L for 50, C for 100, D for 500, M for 1000, M for 1,000,000. A small bar placed over the numeral multiplies the numeral by 1000. Thus, theoretically, it is possible by using an infinite number of bars to express the numbers from 1 to infinity. In practice, however, one bar is usually used; two are rarely used and more than two are almost never used. The simplicity of Roman numerals was such that almost anyone could learn to use them, and today, more than 2000 years after their introduction, these numerals are still in limited usage. The Roman system had one drawback, however, in that it was not suitable for rapid written calculations. The processes of arithmetic are possible using this notation, but are extremely difficult.

Arabic Numerals. The common system of number notation in use in most parts of the world today is the so-called Arabic system. This system was actually first developed by the Hindus and was in use in India in the 3rd century B.C. At that time the numerals 1, 4, and 6 were

53

NUMEROLOGY

written in substantially the same form used today. The Hindu numeral system was probably introduced into the Arab world about the 7th or 8th century A.D. The first recorded use of the system in Europe was in the year 976.

The important innovation in the Arabic system was the use of positional notation, in which individual number symbols assume different values according to their position in the written numeral. Positional notation is made possible by the use of a symbol for zero (q.v.). The symbol 0 makes it possible to differentiate between 11, 101, and 1001 without the use of additional symbols, and all numbers can be expressed in terms of ten symbols, the numerals from 1 to 9 plus 0. Positional notation also greatly simplifies all forms of written numerical calculation. See NOTATION.   J.Si.

NUMEROLOGY. See NUMBER.

NUMIDIA, ancient Roman name for that part of N. Africa roughly equivalent to modern Algeria. Numidia was inhabited by two tribes noted for their horsemanship. In the second Punic War (218–201 B.C.) between Carthage and Rome the western tribe of Numidians supported Hannibal (q.v.), the leader of Carthage; see PUNIC WARS. Masinissa (238?–149 B.C.), king of the eastern Numidians, joined the Romans. With the victory of Rome, all of Numidia was united under Masinissa's rule. The most famous of his successors were Jugurtha (q.v.) and Juba I (d. 46 B.C.). After the victory of the Roman statesman and general Gaius Julius Caesar (q.v.) over Juba in the African war, Numidia became (46 B.C.) a Roman province called Africa Nova. In 30 B.C. the Roman emperor Augustus (q.v.) restored the western part of Numidia to Juba II (d. 19 A.D.); and five years later the eastern part was united with Africa Vetus to form the province of Africa. Under the Roman emperor Lucius Septimius Severus (q.v.), Numidia once more became a separate province. The country was conquered successively by the Vandals (q.v.) in the 5th century, and by the Arabs in the 8th century; it remained under Arab control until the conquest of Algeria by the French in the 19th century.

NUMISMATICS (Gr. *nomisma*, "coin"), study or collection of coins, medals, paper money, and objects similar to these in form or purpose. Coins, especially those of antiquity, are the principal subject of inquiry in numismatics. This article deals entirely with coins; for discussion of other subjects of numismatics, see MEDAL; MONEY.

Coins are pieces of metal stamped with an emblem, portrait, inscription, or any other device showing that they were made under official

Ancient coins. Obverse sides shown in left column, reverse sides, in right column. Top to bottom: Lydian; Athenian; Egyptian; Macedonian; Syrian; Roman; Roman.
Chase Manhattan Bank

auspices, and have intrinsic or exchange value as money. The metals in which coins are usually minted are gold, silver, copper, and bronze and other alloys, such as electrum (q.v.), a mixture of gold and silver; lead, iron, platinum, nickel, and aluminum have also been used at various times.

In the terminology of numismatics, the side of the coin on which the main device is struck is called the obverse, while the other side is known as the reverse. The identifying portrait, figure, or scene on either side is called the type. A secondary device in the field is called the symbol, and the principal inscription on either side is called the legend. The place where the coin is made is called the mint.

The study of ancient coins yields considerable information about political, commercial, and economic history and the art and culture of antiquity. Thus, ancient Roman coins found in India and ancient Arab coins discovered in Scandinavia indicate the extent of international trade between the Roman Empire and India and between the Muslim world and northern Europe. The complete chronological series of ancient Greek coins can be utilized by scholars in determining the dating of much of Greek art, as the coins exhibit the same technique, style, and subject matter of contemporary sculpture and other objects. Coins are also one of the principal sources of knowledge concerning such ancient peoples as the Iberians (q.v.), who left few other remains.

For collectors, the value of a coin depends on its rarity, its condition, and the demand for it. Some specialized collectors concentrate on only one specimen of a coin; others, on obtaining coins produced in a particular period or year. One of the rarest United States coins is a $5 gold piece minted in 1822; it is said to have a value of about $50,000. Famous collections of coins can be seen at the British Museum in London, at the Smithsonian Institution in Washington, D.C., and at the American Numismatic Society and the Chase Manhattan Bank Money Museum, both in New York City.

Greek Coinage. The earliest Greek coins, struck about 640 to 630 B.C. in the ancient country of Lydia in Asia Minor (qq.v.), are made of electrum. In the beginning the obverses were marked with sunken parallel lines or striations and the reverses with a rough punch mark, which is a small counterstamp. Soon simple types, such as animal representations and heads of divinities, were stamped on the obverses, while punch marks were retained for the reverses. The punch mark gradually became larger and more elaborate with the use of geometric patterns and finally became an incuse, or stamped, square. The early coins of the Greek colonies of Magna Graecia in southern Italy have no punch marks; the same type appears in relief on the obverse and in intaglio (q.v.) on the reverse. By the end of the 6th century B.C. most coinage had types on both sides, usually referring to the patron divinity of the city. Thus the coins of Athens show the head of the goddess Athena (q.v.) on the obverse and an owl, the bird of Athena, on the reverse. These early coins are either uninscribed or bear abbreviated inscriptions identifying the mints, the places where the coins were made. Various weight standards were in use, notably the Aeginetan standard, which was the most popular, and the Attic-Euboeic, which supplanted the Aeginetan. The most common denominations were the *stater* and the *drachma* with their multiples and divisions.

The finest Greek coins were issued in the period from the end of the Greco-Persian Wars in 478 B.C. to the accession of the Macedonian king Alexander the Great (see ALEXANDER III) in 336 B.C. Symbols were common, and the names of the minting authorities were usually inscribed in full. Well-known artists often executed the designs, and their names sometimes appeared on the coins. The silver coinage of Athens had a wider circulation than any other coinage in the Mediterranean region and was imitated in Syria and Egypt. In Asia Minor during this period an electrum coinage was issued at Cyzicus. At the same time, gold coins called *darics* and silver coins called *sigloi*, bearing a representation of the king of Persia, were produced at Persian mints. Coinage was also issued on a large scale by Phoenician cities such as Sidon, where the standard unit was called the *shekel*; see PHOENICIA.

In Greece between 359 and 336 B.C., during the reign of the Macedonian king Philip II (q.v.), the first important gold coinage in the world was issued, and copper coins came into common circulation, replacing the minute silver coins previously used for small change. In the vast coinages issued under Philip II and his successor, Alexander III, the head of a divinity such as Zeus (q.v.) or Heracles (see HERCULES) appears as the obverse type. Both monarchs had their names inscribed on the coins, and Alexander also added the word *Basileus* (Gr., "king"). Portraits were used on the money of the successors of Alexander, and, in the three centuries following his death in 323 B.C., the coins of the rulers of Macedonia, Syria, Egypt, and Bactria (q.v.) provide the art historian with an unparalleled

NUMISMATICS

series of royal likenesses. During this period many coins were dated either by the regnal years of the king or by eras, of which the most important was the dynasty of kings called the Seleucidae (q.v.), their reign dating from the battle of Gaza in 312 B.C. Under Roman domination Greek towns were allowed to operate their local mints and to issue bronze coins. The special privilege of striking large silver coins, called *tetradrachmae* or four drachma pieces, was granted to a few cities, notably Antioch in Syria, Caesarea in Cappadocia, and Alexandria in Egypt. These coins generally bear the head of the reigning Roman emperor on the obverse and a type of local significance on the reverse. Most local mints were closed about the year 268 A.D., but the mint at Alexandria was permitted to continue in operation until approximately 294 A.D.

Roman Exchange. The earliest Roman coinage, dating from the early 3rd century B.C., was of bronze and consisted of a standard unit of currency called the *as* and its subdivisions: the *semis* ($\frac{1}{2}$ as), the *triens* ($\frac{1}{3}$ as), the *quadrans* ($\frac{1}{4}$ as), the *sextans* ($\frac{1}{6}$ as), the *uncia* ($\frac{1}{12}$ as), and occasionally the *semuncia* ($\frac{1}{24}$ as). Silver coins patterned on Greek models were adopted by the Romans in the 3rd century B.C. and reflected in the Romano-Campanian series. In the late 3rd century a silver coinage representing multiple values of the as was issued. These silver coins, known as the *denarius, quinarius,* and *sesterce* or *sestertius,* were the equivalents respectively of 10 asses, 5 asses, and 2½ asses. The three denominations bear the head of the goddess Roma on the obverse and a sign indicating the value of the coin; the name Roma and figures of deities or heroes appear on the reverse.

In the 2nd century B.C. the currency was reorganized, and the relation between silver and copper coins was changed so that the denarius equaled 16 asses instead of 10. The right of coinage was exercised by a board of three moneyers, or coin makers, who now placed their names, initials, or monograms on the coins. About 150 B.C. the types on the silver coins began to be highly varied, each moneyer selecting his own designs to record family traditions, religious cults, or historical events. The Roman statesman and general Gaius Julius Caesar (q.v.) was the first to place his portrait on a Roman coin in 44 B.C.

The last important change in the coinage of the Roman Republic took place in 89 B.C. when the as was reduced to the value of half an uncia, or $\frac{1}{24}$ of its original value; the silver coins remained unchanged. Gold pieces had been is-

Early coins. Top to bottom: Byzantine; Italian; English; Venetian; Bermudian; colonial New England; early United States. Chase Manhattan Bank

sued irregularly since the 3rd century B.C., and in the last hundred years of the Republic, ending in 27 B.C., gold coins called *denarii aurei* were common.

The coinage of the Roman Empire began with the reign of the first Roman emperor Augustus (q.v.) from 27 B.C. to 14 A.D. The coins were made out of gold or silver or from aes, a combination of copper and orichalum, or brass. The aes coinage from this time until the 3rd century A.D. bears the letters SC, standing for *senatus consulto* (Lat., "by order of the Senate"), which originally had a reference to the reverse type and later became merely a denominational mark. The obverse of imperial coins generally bears the head of the emperor with his name and titles; the reverse is stamped with any of a number of types, such as a deity, personification, group, or monument, with explanatory inscriptions or a continuation of the imperial titles of the obverse. The aes coins were, in order of value, the *quadrans* (¼ as), *semis* (½ as), *as*, *dupondius* (2 asses), and *sestertius* (4 asses). Two coins were minted in silver: the *quinarius* (2 sestertii) and the *denarius* (4 sestertii); and two coins were of gold: the *quinarius aureus* (12½ silver denarii) and the *denarius aureus* (25 silver denarii).

Until the end of the 2nd century A.D. Roman coinage was of fine quality in design and technique. Subsequently, however, the coins became debased. The silver coins were made of alloys with a high copper, tin, or lead content, and the denarius was often copper merely coated with silver. The large aes coins, such as the sestertius, dupondius, and as, were no longer issued. In the late 3rd century A.D. a monetary reform by the emperor Diocletian (q.v.) reestablished the gold, silver, and copper coinage. During the reign of the emperor Constantine I (q.v.), a new gold unit called the *solidus* was put into circulation, with the *semissis* (½ solidus) and later the *triens* (⅓ solidus). Silver coins, the *miliarense* and the *siliqua*, also appeared; in copper the *follis* and its fractions were coined. These coins, which generally bear portraits, remained in circulation until the end of the Western Roman Empire in 476 A.D.

Byzantine Coinage. In the Eastern Roman or Byzantine Empire (q.v.) the coinage consisted of the gold solidus and its fractions, occasional silver issues, and the copper follis with its fractions, the latter being a reform introduced by the Eastern Roman emperor Anastasius I (q.v.). The portrait of the reigning emperor appeared as the usual type on the obverse until the reign of the Byzantine emperor Justinian II (669–711), when it occupied the reverse. The first appearance of a portrait of Christ on the coinage also appeared under Justinian's rule. After the iconoclastic controversy was ended in the 9th century (*see* ICONOCLASM), a Christian figure occupied at least one side of the coin. On the reverse the earlier coins bear such types as a figure personifying victory, and the later examples bear images of Christ or the Virgin Mary (q.v.). In the inscriptions, Latin was gradually superseded by Greek and disappeared entirely at the end of the 11th century. The latest Byzantine coins are from the emperor John VIII Palaeologus (q.v.) and are of silver. In 1453, Constantinople (now İstanbul) was captured by the Turks. No coins of the last Byzantine emperor, Constantine XI Palaeologus (1404–53), have as yet been identified.

Coins of the Middle Ages. In Western Europe the coins of the separate states founded on the ruins of the Roman Empire retained the form and style of late Roman coins. Latin was the universal language for inscriptions. The principal coins in circulation in the early Middle Ages were the silver denarius and its half, the *obol*. The coins issued by authority of the Ostrogothic, Visigothic, and Vandal kingdoms (*see* GOTHS; VANDALS) of Italy, Spain, and North Africa were usually of silver and copper, and sometimes of gold. The Visigothic coinage in Spain began at the end of the 6th century and continued until the Arab conquest in the 8th century, when an Arab coinage was begun. The numerous Arab coins of the late 7th century bear bilingual Latin and Arabic inscriptions. Coinage was common throughout the other parts of the vast Muslim world. As images were in general proscribed by Islam, types were usually confined to legends in Arabic.

In England, coinage began in the 7th century, the two principal coins being the silver *sceat* and the copper *styca*. Many early examples have runic letters (*see* RUNES) accompanying the Latin inscription.

In the Frankish kingdom (*see* FRANKS), the Merovingian (q.v.) kings issued gold solidi and trientes beginning in the 6th century. Early in the 8th century, the Carolingian (q.v.) kings issued mostly epigraphic and some portrait coins, chiefly the silver denarius and the gold triens. This coinage spread from the Frankish kingdom and became the standard currency of most of Western Europe. Subsequently a vast number of denominations and issues were produced by local feudal authorities, both lay and ecclesiastical. The finest coins of the Middle Ages were the gold solidi and half-solidi issued by Freder-

NUMISMATICS

ick II (q.v.), Holy Roman Emperor. These bear a portrait bust of the emperor on the obverse and an eagle on the reverse.

In 1252 an important gold coin called the *florin* was introduced in Florence, Italy. Because of the commercial greatness of the city, the florin subsequently circulated throughout Europe and was widely imitated. The imitations included the Dutch *gulden,* and the Venetian *ducat* or *sequin;* the latter became a world currency and was continued in use until the 19th century.

Coins of the 14th century, often richly ornamented, include the French silver *tournois* and gold *mouton,* the German silver *groschen,* and the English *noble* or *rose noble.*

Renaissance Coinage. Coinage was generally not uniform at this time as a great variety of issues were minted by the innumerable states, kingdoms, and principalities. The German *taler,* first issued in 1486, became the principal European coin and influenced the form of other coins including the English *crown,* the French *écu,* and the Italian *scudo.* Italian Renaissance (q.v.) coins of the 15th and 16th centuries were often designed by well-known artists, among them the master goldsmith Benvenuto Cellini (q.v.).

American Issues. The earliest coinage of the New World was issued in Mexico in 1522. The earliest English coinage in the Western Hemisphere, issued from 1616 to 1624 by the English settlers of Bermuda, consisted of copper *shillings,* and *sixpence, threepence,* and *twopence* pieces. These bear a representation of a hog, and are therefore known as hog money. In 1652 the Massachusetts colonists issued the first coinage struck by any of the American colonies, a series of shillings, sixpences, and threepences, all of which were coined until 1686. The first regular U.S. coinage did not begin until 1793. See DOLLAR.

Coins of the Orient. In the Orient, coinage originated in China at some uncertain time between the 12th and 8th centuries B.C. The earliest coins were in the form of small bronze knives and spades, indicating that such utilitarian objects had served previously as articles of barter. Round coins were issued in the 6th century B.C. In the 4th century A.D. the definitive form of a round coin with a square hole in the center was established. This form had a strong influence on all the coinages of the Far East until the end of the 19th century.

The Japanese learned the art of coinage from the Chinese. The first coins were of bronze and were issued in the 8th century A.D. Gold and silver coins came into general use in the 16th century.

India, Siam, Korea, and other countries of the Far East had native coinages of considerable antiquity, but since the late 19th century the minting of silver and copper coins modeled on Occidental examples has been universal.

THE AMERICAN NUMISMATIC SOCIETY

NUN, member of a religious order for women, living in a convent under vows of poverty, chastity, and obedience; see ORDERS, RELIGIOUS; SISTERHOODS. Female monasticism (q.v.) occurs notably in Roman Catholicism, although it is not limited to that church or to Christianity. In Roman Catholicism the orders vary in the stipulations of the vows, some being permanent and others only for fixed periods of time. The orders vary somewhat in dress, purpose, and rule, but all follow generally the same basic principles. The nuns are devoted to a purely contemplative life or to a life of charity, including teaching and nursing. The heads of convents are variously called abbesses, prioresses, and mothers superior, and a nun generally is addressed as "Sister".

NÚÑEZ CABEZA DE VACA, Álvar. See CABEZA DE VACA, ÁLVAR NÚÑEZ.

NUNNERIES. See SISTERHOODS.

NUREMBERG or **NÜRNBERG,** city of West Germany, in Bavaria State, on the Regnitz R., about 100 miles N.W. of Munich. It is a commercial and industrial center, served by railroads and the Ludwig Canal, which connects the Danube and Main rivers. Toys are the best-known manufacture; various types of machinery, electrical equipment, optical goods, beer, food and bakery products (*Lebkuchen*), and novelties in metal, carved wood, and ivory, known collectively as Nuremberg wares, are other important products.

Nuremberg was first mentioned in a document dating from 1050. After a period of rule by various German nobles, it was made a free imperial town in 1219. It subsequently became noted for its manufactures, particularly of wooden wares. During the 15th and 16th centuries the city was a center of culture. Among the celebrated artists who worked there in the 15th century was the German painter and engraver Albrecht Dürer (q.v.). The meistersinger (q.v.), members of German guilds formed in the 14th century to cultivate music and poetry, included the German poet and dramatist Hans Sachs (q.v.) and were the subject of the opera *Die Meistersinger von Nürnberg* (1867) by the German composer Richard Wagner (q.v.). In 1806 the city was annexed to the Kingdom of Bavaria. Beginning in 1933 it was the site of the annual

The square is Nuremberg's marketplace, providing almost everything from fresh fruits and vegetables to flowers. UPI

September convention of the National Socialist Party; see NATIONAL SOCIALISM. As a production center for heavy engines, especially for aircraft, it was extensively bombed by Allied air forces during World War II. Following the war the city was incorporated in the United States zone of occupation and was the site of the trials of German war criminals by an international tribunal of Allied jurists; see WAR-CRIMES TRIALS.

The medieval walled city at the center of Nuremberg was severely damaged during World War II. Much of it, however, including an 11th-century castle, was restored, and masterpieces by the German artists Dürer and Hans Holbein (q.v.) among others, were preserved. Pop. (1968 est.) 466,668.

NUREMBERG TRIALS. See WAR-CRIMES TRIALS: *Nuremberg Trials.*

NUREYEV, Rudolf (Hametovich) (1938–), Russian-born ballet dancer, born in Irkutsk. His first public performance was at the age of seven, when he performed folk dances for wounded Soviet soldiers during World War II. After the war he danced in the corps de ballet of the Ufa Opera, in the Soviet city of Ufa. In 1955 Nureyev was accepted in the advanced class of the Leningrad Ballet School, and three years later, after winning a national classical ballet competition, became soloist with the Kirov Ballet in Leningrad. In June, 1961, while the Kirov troupe was in Paris on a European tour, Nureyev defected and was granted asylum by the French government. One week after his defection he joined the Grand Ballet de Marquis de Cuevas, a leading French company. His debut with that company in the role of the prince in *The Sleeping Beauty* was an enormous success. He made his London debut in 1961 and the following year became permanently associated with the Royal Ballet of London. In 1962 he made his American debut with the Ruth Page Chicago Opera Ballet, in New York City. Later that year he performed in *Prince Igor* with the Chicago company in its home city. The first of his many appearances with the British ballerina Margot Fonteyn (q.v.) was in the 1962 production of *Giselle,* after which the dancers became the foremost ballet duo of the time.

Nureyev is noted for the effortlessness and grace of his leaps and other technical feats, for his dramatic abilities, and for his compelling stage presence. His autobiography, *Nureyev,* was published in 1963.

NURSERY SCHOOL AND DAY NURSERY, institutions for the care and development of children of prekindergarten age. Originally, many of the day nurseries offered only custodial care,

59

NURSERY SCHOOL AND DAY NURSERY

whereas the nursery schools offered educational activities as well. Now, in many instances, both are planned to offer valuable educational experiences. A remaining major difference, however, is the time schedule on which they operate. A day nursery is likely to open earlier and close later than a nursery to enable working mothers to transport the children to and from the nursery before and after attending work.

Origins. Nursery schools developed within the day-nursery movement, which arose in Europe early in the 19th century as a reflection of the increasing employment of women in industry. The absence of large numbers of mothers from their homes during the day led to widespread neglect of children and stimulated various charitable agencies to seek means of caring for the children.

The early leader of this movement was the French philanthropist Jean Baptiste Firmin Marbeau (1798–1875), whose studies proved that the high rate of infant mortality in France was largely due to the absence of working mothers, and who in 1846 founded the Crèche (Fr., "cradle") Society of France, with the aim of fostering child care. Within a relatively short period, day nurseries had been established in many parts of France and several other European countries had followed suit. Many of these nurseries were wholly or partly supported by local and national governments. A large number of the nurseries were set up in factories, enabling mothers of nursing children to take brief periods from their work in order to tend to the needs of their offspring.

Development. In the United States, the first day nursery was opened in 1854 by the Nursery and Child's Hospital of New York City. Nurseries were established in various areas during the latter half of the 19th century; most of them were charitable, though a few operated on a commercial basis. Both in Europe and in the U.S., the day-nursery movement received great impetus during World War I, when shortages of manpower caused the industrial employment of unprecedented numbers of women. In England, France, Germany, and Italy, nurseries were established even in munitions plants, under direct government sponsorship. Although the number of nurseries in the U.S. also rose precipitately this rise was accomplished without government aid of any kind. During the years following World War I, however, Federal, State, and local governments gradually began to exercise a measure of control over the nurseries, chiefly by licensing them and by inspecting and regulating the conditions within the nurseries.

The development of nursery schools occurred after World War I, beginning in England and rapidly spreading to other countries as scientific studies of children revealed the importance of the early years of a child in the formation of character. The first nursery schools in the U.S. were started under the auspices of colleges and universities, and served as laboratories for child study, teacher education, studies in home economics, and parent education. For some years, the chief distinction between the day nursery and the nursery school, besides the difference in activities offered to preschool children, was that the former were mainly charitable institutions designed to aid needy families, whereas nursery schools were for the most part commercial enterprises catering to those who could afford their services. More recently, the distinction has gradually been narrowed in most countries, as day nurseries have begun to employ trained personnel capable of giving educational guidance to their charges.

The outbreak of World War II was quickly followed by an increase in the number of day nurseries in almost all countries, as women were again called upon to replace men in the factories. On this occasion the U.S. government immediately came to the support of the nursery schools, allocating $6,000,000 in July, 1942, for a nursery-school program for the children of working mothers. Many States and local communities supplemented this Federal aid. By the end of hostilities, in August, 1945, more than 100,000 children were being cared for in centers receiving Federal subsidies. Soon afterward, the Federal government drastically curtailed its expenditures for this purpose and later abolished them, causing a sharp drop in the number of nursery schools in operation. The expectation that most employed mothers would leave their jobs at the end of the war was only partly fulfilled, however, and the postwar years witnessed the development of a widespread movement, headed by sociologists, social workers, teachers, and other interested groups, which sought renewed government aid to meet the need for a comprehensive day-care program.

Head Start. The government program Head Start, began under the Economic Opportunity Act of 1964, in a nationwide effort to provide preschool children from economically and culturally disadvantaged backgrounds, and their families, the educational, medical, psychological, and social services they may lack.

These Head Start programs are of two types. Summer Head Start operates for the most part during school vacation and is for children who are eligible for kindergarten or first grade and who will be attending school for the first time in the fall; Full Year Head Start may operate for a period of up to twelve months. Children from this program usually move into kindergarten or first grade. When a program is operated for more than six hours a day it is considered a Head Start day-care program, because it is then supplementing parental care beyond the desirable duration of an educational or enrichment program. See also KINDERGARTEN; PRESCHOOL EDUCATION. L.L.

NURSING, PRACTICAL, practice of nursing on a level of responsibility just below that of the professional nurse; see NURSING, PROFESSIONAL. Under the supervision of a physician or a registered professional nurse, the licensed practical nurse gives nursing care in situations relatively free of clinical complexity, when the state of the patient is stable. In more complex cases, or when the behavioral state of the patient requires more specific care, the practical nurse acts as an assistant to the professional nurse.

In the United States, prospective practical nurses prepare for their profession, generally on the completion of high school and usually after passing a qualifying examination, by enrolling in one of about 1200 schools of nursing, community colleges, and vocational education programs licensed by the States. Full-time attendance includes classroom study, clinical practice, and experience with patients in hospitals or other institutions. Completion of such a course, nine months to two years in length, prepares the student for a State board of nursing examination; after passing the test the applicant receives a license to practice.

NURSING, PROFESSIONAL, profession practiced primarily by women but also by men that provides care to the sick and disabled and teaches the principles of maintaining health and preventing disease to patients in their homes and in institutions.

The obligations of the professional nurse range from the simple to the complex; their extent depends somewhat on her desire and willingness to extend her activity into specialized areas and to acquaint herself with new and sometimes evolving techniques.

Duties. Among the simpler duties of the professional nurse are those of bathing and feeding the patient, bedmaking, and administering prescribed drugs. More complex duties involving professional understanding are estimating and charting the condition of the patient as revealed by pallor, pulse, and respiration and the evaluation of the effect of drugs and their side-effects.

NURSING, PROFESSIONAL

Standard duties include the management of equipment for oxygen therapy, for intravenous feeding, for blood transfusions, and for evaluating the patient's vital signs as, for example, by reading the oscilloscope to follow the patient's heart action. She may also instruct the diabetic patient how to give himself insulin injections or a mother in the details of care for a newborn baby. She will be called on periodically to evaluate social and family factors and cope with the emotional and physical needs of patients in difficult situations.

Functions. In more specialized areas the professional nurse may learn to monitor such specialized equipment as the respirator or iron lung used for cases of bulbar poliomyelitis or the so-called kidney machine used for clearing the blood in renal disease. As a dental nurse, she may learn to develop x-ray films. As a surgical nurse, she may sterilize instruments and other apparatus; in the recovery room, she will position and turn the patient and be prepared to give supportive measures until the physician arrives. Work in the intensive-care ward, with its recurring emergencies, will tax all her skills. If she functions as a school nurse, she may conduct physical examinations, refer appropriate cases for eye examinations, dental care, or chest x-rays, and explain the importance of vaccination and inoculation to parents.

To enable her to concentrate on her specialized work, the professional nurse may be relieved of routine duties by the practical nurse or by the nurse's aide. The latter may undertake to feed, wash, and move the patient, serve as a diet assistant, and do routine clerical work, including simple reports. Many girls serve as nursing aides as a preliminary to a professional nursing career; see NURSING, PRACTICAL.

Nursing Education. In 1970 about 1300 schools of nursing in the U.S. met the legal standards set by the States in which they operate; two years of study was the minimum. Entrance requirements to nursing schools are good health, graduation from high school in the upper median, good judgment, a sense of responsibility, and the ability to master the required techniques. Three types of nursing schools prepare students for the licensure examination: schools owned and operated by hospitals that grant a diploma; junior and community colleges that administer two-year programs leading to the associate of arts degree; and collegiate schools of nursing administered by senior colleges and by universities that confer the Bachelor of Science degree. Both the baccalaureate and associate degree programs utilize

Above: Nurses shown at the National Institutes of Health, Bethesda, Md., attend a clinic on radiation. *Right:* Nurses caring for a patient at Quito Hospital, Ecuador.

World Health Organization

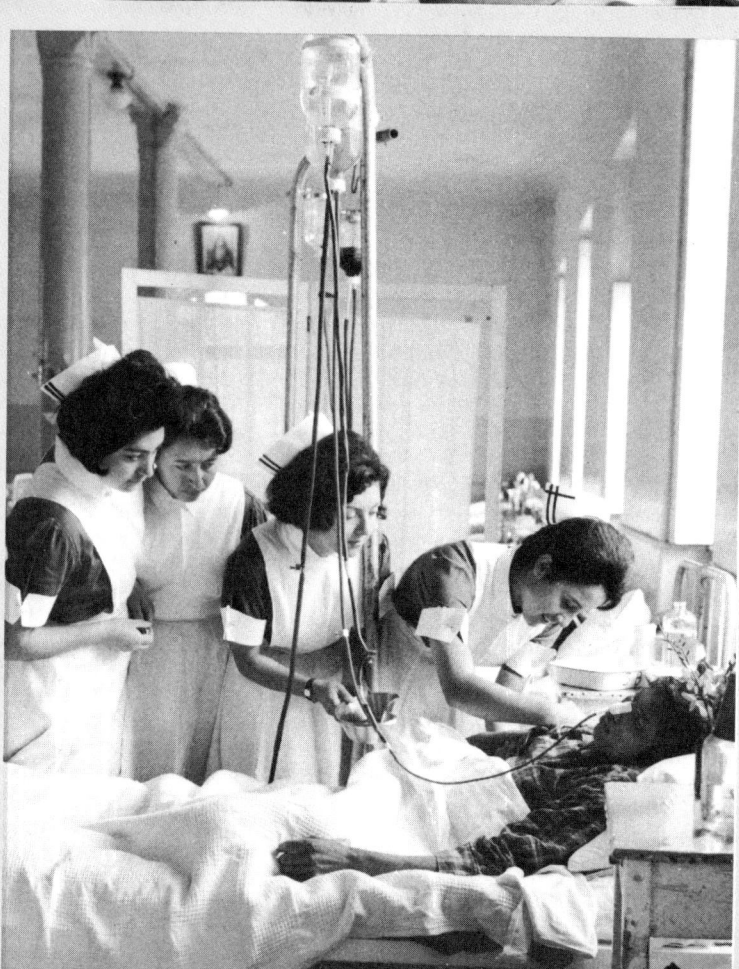

community health agencies and hospitals to provide students the necessary clinical nursing experience. In addition to nursing theory and its application to the care of patients, all curriculums provide general education courses, with emphasis on the natural and social sciences.

HISTORY OF NURSING

Over the centuries, nursing has evolved from a simple profession to a rigorous and highly specialized discipline.

Early History. Among the early Romans, the nurse was one of a number of medical and physical attendants, including the bonesetter, the barber, the bath attendant, the masseur, the drug seller, and the midwife, each of whom exercised a special medical or paramedical skill. In the Middle Ages, some Christian monasteries were opened to the sick; a few orders of nuns established convents for their special care. The period between the 12th and 15th centuries witnessed the development of hospitals in Europe (see HOSPITAL); the movement was especially strong in England, where Saint Bartholomew's Hospital was established in 1123 and Saint Thomas' was founded in 1213. The hospitalers recruited women as helpers. Toward the end of the 12th century Saint Hildegard (q.v.), founder of the convent of Rupertsberg, organized a school to train nurses for service in hospitals. Many great sisterhoods devoted to this work, founded in Italy and Spain in the 14th century, survive today. In 1634, Saint Vincent de Paul (q.v.) founded the first French organization for the relief of the suffering at Bresse; first known as Servants of the Poor, it was later called Sisters of Charity. The modern system of training nurses evolved from these simple beginnings.

Modern Nursing. In 1840 the British philanthropist Elizabeth Fry (1780–1845) organized the Protestant Nursing Sisters to care for London outcasts. In the 1850's the British nurse Florence Nightingale (q.v.) advanced the movement for the more efficient training of nurses, raising it from a disregarded and ill-regulated occupation to a profession served by women specially qualified and trained. In 1872 the New England Hospital for Women and Children in Boston first offered a graded course in nursing; in New York City, the training school of Bellevue Hospital, the first American school organized on the Florence Nightingale plan, graduated its first class in 1875.

In 1907 the American Hospital Association established the three categories of attendant nurse, bedside nurse, and teaching or executive nurse; in 1922 the Rockefeller Foundation (see ROCKEFELLER UNIVERSITY) recommended training

A group of students in nursing and midwifery at a health center in Libreville, Gabon.
World Health Organization

periods from eight to twenty-eight months for these groups and a postgraduate course of eight months for teachers, administrators, and public health nurses. In 1923 the American social worker, Josephine Goldmark (1877–1950) prepared a report for the Committee for the Study of Nursing Education that established criteria for accrediting nursing schools. A 1947 report entitled "Nursing for the Future," financed by the Carnegie Foundation for the Advancement of Teaching (q.v.) and written by the American social scientist Esther Lucille Brown, forecast the evolution of clinical nursing as a specialty. In 1970 the National Commission for the Study of Nursing Education, established by the surgeon general of the United States, suggested that nursing be made an independent calling and advocated closer collaboration with the medical profession.

Nursing Service. In addition to staff and administrative positions in hospitals and institutions, opportunities for nurses include military and Federal Civil Service positions, private-duty nursing, public-health service, teaching, research, and industrial and school nursing. The Committee on Professional Registries of the American Nurses' Association (A.N.A.) supervises a placement service for the private practice of nursing through its 865 affiliated district nurses associations located in fifty-four States and territories of the U.S. These registries meet standards set by the State associations, which follow guidelines established by the A.N.A. The

NUT

American Red Cross maintains a roster of nurses for local, State, and national emergencies; the World Health Organization and the Peace Corps (qq.v.) employs nurses for service abroad.

A.R.W.

NUT, term commonly and loosely applied to any dry, hard-shelled fruit or seed having a rind that can be easily separated from the internal, edible kernel. In botanical terminology, the term "nut" is restricted to an indehiscent, one-seeded fruit, which has developed from a compound ovary and has external walls hardened to a woody consistency. Such so-called true nuts may be edible or inedible; common examples are acorns, beechnuts, chestnuts, and hazelnuts. Examples of fruits or seeds that are incorrectly and popularly termed nuts include: almonds and walnuts, which are drupes (see FRUIT) with the fleshy outer layer removed; peanuts, which are seeds contained in pods; and horse chestnuts and Brazil nuts, which are seeds contained in capsules. See also separate articles about most of the nuts mentioned above.

NUTCRACKER, common name for any bird in the genus *Nucifraga* of the Crow family, found in the coniferous forests of the colder regions of the Northern Hemisphere. The birds are so called because of their long, heavy bills which they use to crack nuts. They also eat insects, and the eggs and young of other birds. The best-known species are the European nutcracker, *N. caryocatactes*, about 13½ in. long, and Clark's nutcracker, *N. columbiana*, about 12½ in. long, found in western North America. Clark's nutcracker, which is light gray in general body color, with black and white wings and tail, inhabits high mountains just below the timber line. It is noted for its unusual flying habits, often dropping from a high peak with its wings closed and plummeting several hundred feet before suddenly opening them in flight.

NUTHATCH, common name for any of fifteen species of passerine birds that constitute the sub-family Sittinae of the family Sittidae, and are widely distributed in the Northern Hemisphere. The birds, which rarely exceed 5½ in. in length, are bluish gray in general body color. They have long, straight, sturdy bills, long wings, and short tails. Nuthatches are noted for their curious arboreal habits. Deriving their sole support from their powerful feet and long claws, they often move about head downward on the vertical surface of a tree trunk, digging into cervices in the bark for adult insects, larvae, or eggs. The birds also feed on grain and nuts, breaking them by pecking at the hard outer coatings with their bills. Nuthatches have a characteristic, high-pitched, nasal cry. They nest in natural crevices or in nesting holes in trees abandoned by other birds, especially woodpeckers. The nest is lined with pieces of bark, rabbit hair, grass, and feathers. Usually four to ten creamy-white eggs, speckled with brown, gray, or purple, are deposited in a clutch.

The four North American species are all contained within the genus *Sitta*. The most common species, *S. carolinensis,* the white-breasted nuthatch, is found throughout the United States east of the Rocky Mts. and is abundant in winter as well as summer. It is about 5½ in. long, and is grayish blue above and white below, with patches of brown on the lower abdomen. The adult male is characterized by a black crown. The pygmy nuthatch, *S. pygmaea,* of the western U.S., is one of the smaller species, being about 4 in. long.

NUTLEY, town of New Jersey, in Essex Co., 5 miles N. of Newark. It is a residential suburban area that has manufactures of textiles, pharmaceuticals, and metal products. The Enclosure, a wooded public park, was the center of a colony of writers and artists after the American Civil War. The location was settled about 1680, and the town was incorporated in 1902. Pop. (1960) 29,513; (1970) 32,099.

NUTMEG, common name applied to a family, Myristicaceae, of evergreen shrubs and trees, especially to plants of the genus *Myristica*. The family, which comprises about eight genera and

Nutmeg, Myristica

NUTRITION, HUMAN

one hundred species, is native to the Moluccas in Indonesia; the nutmeg has also been widely cultivated in southern Asia, the West Indies, and Brazil for its seeds, which yield various spices, and for its timber. Plants in the family are dioecious, with inconspicuous flowers. The fruit is a yellow drupe having a diameter of about 2 in., popularly called the nutmeg apple, which splits into two equal halves, thereby revealing the seed surrounded by a fleshy outer coating. In plants of the genus *Myristica,* which contains about eighty species, this seed is dried to form the culinary spice popularly known as nutmeg; the fleshy coating is peeled off and also dried, to form the spice known as mace. The commonest nutmeg tree is *M. fragrans,* which grows to a height of about 50 ft.

NUTRIA. See Coypu; Fur.

NUTRITION, HUMAN, science that deals with nutrients and other substances in food; with their action and interaction; and with the processes by which the organism ingests, digests, absorbs, transports, utilizes, and excretes food substances to achieve growth and maintain health. The 20th century concept that the health and well-being of a person depend upon the kinds and amounts of food he eats is based on discoveries in the biological and physical sciences and the development of methods and instruments for the measurement of nutrients.

Classes of Nutrients. Food constituents are classified into five major groups of nutrients: carbohydrate (q.v.), fats (see Fats and Fixed Oils), proteins (q.v.), minerals, and vitamins (q.v.). Because water is essential, it may also be classed as a nutrient. The human body is composed of these same materials and carries on all its functions through chemical interactions involving the individual nutrients; see Food.

Each nutrient group consists of a number of individual nutrients. Carbohydrates, obtained from plant foods in the form of starches and sugars, combine with oxygen and release energy; providing 4 calories per g. of carbohydrate, they are a major dietary source of calories. When the intake of carbohydrates and other sources of calories is greater than required by expenditure of energy, the excess is converted to fat and stored in the body. Fats, which occur in both plants and animals and are composed of fatty acids and glycerol, are called glycerides and may be simple or highly complex substances. Because the body cannot construct linoleic and arachidonic acid, these essential polyunsaturated fatty acids must be supplied preformed in food. Fats may be stored in the body or be completely oxidized to carbon dioxide and water for excretion by the lungs and kidneys; in the oxidative process, energy at the rate of 9 calories per g. of fat is produced.

Functions of Nutrients. The primary function of protein is to build body tissue and to synthesize enzymes, some hormones, and other substances that regulate body processes. Proteins, obtained from both plant and animal sources, are numerous; they are composed of some twenty organic acids containing nitrogen and called amino acids; eight of these are essential, since the body cannot synthesize them and they must be supplied preformed in foods. Animal proteins are a better source of the essential amino acids than plant proteins. Since the demand for energy takes precedence over other body functions, protein producing 4 calories per g. will be degraded to provide calories if there is an inadequate intake of fats and carbohydrates.

Inorganic mineral nutrients are required in the structural composition of hard and soft body tissues; they also participate in such processes as the action of enzyme systems, the contraction of muscles, nerve reactions, and the clotting of blood; see Blood: *Coagulation;* Nervous System. These mineral nutrients, all of which must be supplied in the diet, are of two classes: the so-called major elements, represented by such minerals as calcium, phosphorus, potassium, sodium and sulfur, and the trace elements (q.v.) such as cobalt, copper, magnesium, manganese, zinc, and possibly molybdenum. Vitamins, also essential to the diet, fall into two groups: the fat-soluble and the water-soluble. Excess amounts of fat-soluble vitamins may be stored in the body, but water-soluble vitamins not utilized in metabolic functions are readily excreted. Unlike other nutrient constituents, individual vitamins have no similarity of chemical structure or of specific function in the metabolic process; they are components of enzyme systems whose function is mainly catalytic; see Metabolism; Catalysis.

Water is also an essential nutrient. Perhaps two thirds of the body—bones, soft tissues, and body fluids—is water. Essential for the circulation of blood, water also transfers nutrients to cells, excretes waste, and controls body temperature. Some water is produced by oxidation of fats, carbohydrates, and proteins in the metabolic process. Most of the daily loss of water, however, through urine, feces, expired air, evaporation from skin, sweat, nasal secretion, tears, and milk during lactation, must be replaced by water from foods and beverages.

Nutrients in Metabolism. The nutrients are interdependent and interact with each other in

NUTRITION, HUMAN

the processes of metabolism. In digestion (q.v.), the proteins, carbohydrates, and fats in food are broken down into simpler forms so that these nutrients can pass across the intestinal membranes for absorption into the bloodstream and transport to various body cells. Here they undergo various metabolic processes that include synthesis into structural tissues and the regulatory systems, oxidation for production of energy, and degradation to soluble end-products for excretion by the kidneys. The individual nutrients are all interdependent and interact with each other in these processes. Since the body is a dynamic organism, there is a continuous interchange of constituents within cells. These constituents, for example, participate in the never-ending replacement of red blood cells (see BLOOD: *Blood Formation*), that have an average life of 120 days; new cells are continuously being created in the bone marrow.

Applied Nutrition. The daily amounts of each nutrient required for all body processes vary among individuals according to age, sex, rate of growth, activity, and hereditary differences. The average daily requirements for groups of the same age, sex, and activity have been determined and prepared for the use of physicians, nutritionists, and dietitians. Applied nutrition also takes account of the factors that influence choices of food; these include income, the availability of food, cultural and traditional patterns, and degree of understanding of nutrition.

Nutritional Status. Since nutrition influences growth, development, and functioning, inadequate intake of one or more nutrients manifests itself in a variety of measurable changes, some of which may appear in a short period of time, while others may be delayed. Lack of certain vitamins produces specific diseases such as beriberi, pellagra, rickets, scurvy, (qq.v.), and xerophthalmia; see DEFICIENCY DISEASES. Inadequate intakes of iron lead to iron-deficiency anemia (see ANEMIA), while lack of iodine is the cause of endemic goiter; see GOITER. Extreme cases of deficiency diseases are comparatively rare in the United States; more common are anemia caused by inadequate intake of iron and folic acid, and deficiencies resulting from medical disorders and parasitic infections; see PARASITE. Malnutrition in milder forms appears among persons whose meals are poorly chosen, and among the poor who do not have enough food.

Nutritional status can be determined by the following methods: (1) observation and clinical examination of such external surfaces as skin, eyes, scalp, and mouth, and of such organs near the surface of the body as the thyroid gland; (2) measurements of skin thickness and of such factors as height and weight in relation to age; (3) biochemical measurements of the amounts of proteins, certain vitamins, and minerals that appear in blood, urine, and tissue; and (4) dietary studies to determine the composition of diet and the inclusion therein of required nutrients.

W.J.D. & E.N.T.

NU, U. See BURMA, UNION OF: *History*.

NUX VOMICA, name given to the seed of *Strychnos nux-vomica*, a tree native to the Coromandel Coast of India, Ceylon, and other parts of southeast Asia. The seeds contain two alkaloids closely related to each other that act as powerful poisons on the animal body, causing violent tetanic convulsions and death. These alkaloids are named strychnine (q.v.) and brucine. See STRYCHNOS.

NYASA, LAKE. See MALAWI, LAKE.

NYASALAND. See MALAWI.

NYÍREGYHÁZA, town of Hungary, 29 miles N.E. of Debrecen. It has tobacco interests, a livestock industry, and manufactures of soap, candles, machines, and cement. It is the seat of a Greek-Catholic bishop. Pop. (1962 est.) 59,000.

NYLON, term applied to a synthetic resin widely used for textile fibers, characterized by great strength, toughness, and elasticity, and processed also in the form of bristles and molded articles. Nylon was developed in 1935 by scientists of E.I. du Pont de Nemours & Co. (*see under* DU PONT), headed by the American chemist Wallace Hume Carothers (1896–1937). It is usually made by polymerizing adipic acid and hexamethylenediamine, an amine derivative; see POLYMER. Adipic acid is derived from phenol; hexamethylenediamine is made by treating adipic acid catalytically with ammonia and hydrogenating the product; see HYDROGENATION. The widely circulated slogan that nylon is made from coal, air, and water refers to the processes by which phenol may be obtained from coal, the hydrogen from water, and nitrogen from air. Nylon is insoluble in water and in ordinary organic solvents; it dissolves in phenol, cresol, and formic acid, and melts at 263° C. (505° F.).

In making textile fibers, small chips of the nylon polymer, which is obtained as a tough, ivorylike material, are melted and forced through holes in a metal disk called a spinneret. The filaments are congealed by a blast of air and are then drawn to about four times their original lengths. The diameter of the filaments is controlled by changing the rate at which the molten nylon is pumped into the spinneret and the rate at which the filaments are drawn away. Filaments much finer than those of ordinary textile

NYLON PRODUCTION

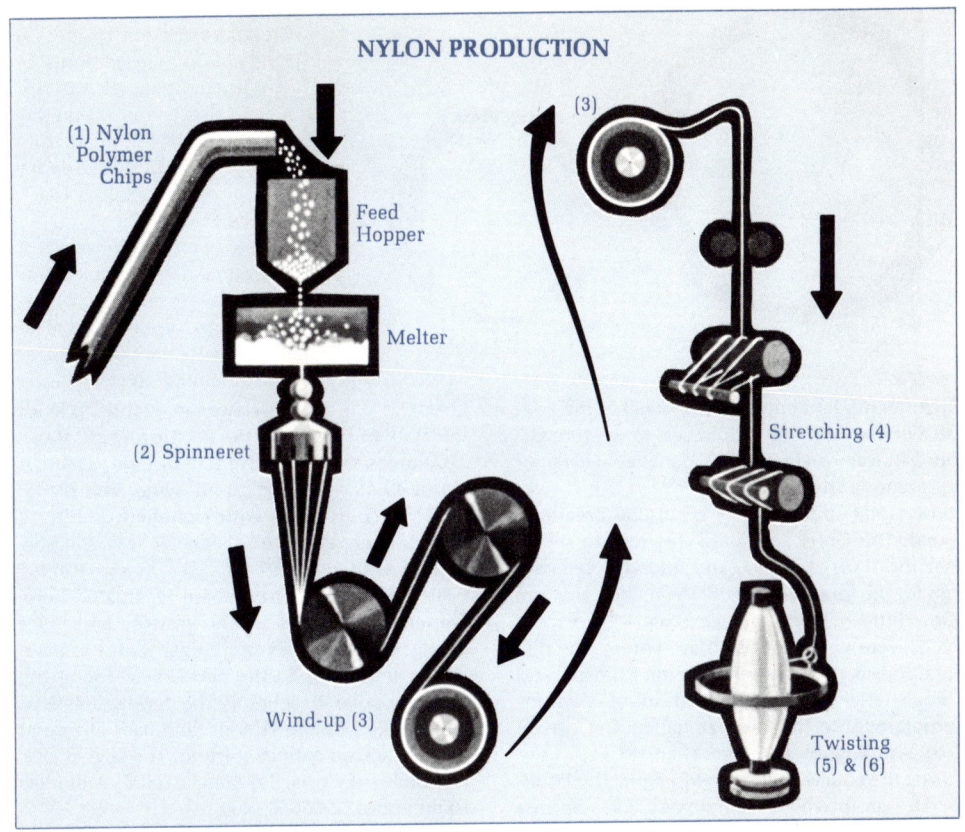

Production of nylon: (1) Nylon polymer chips flow to a feed hopper and are melted; (2) Melted chips are pumped into a spinneret and extruded to form continuous solid monofilaments; (3) Filaments are taken up on a bobbin; (4) Nylon is stretched; (5 and 6) Assembled continuous filaments are twisted into yarn and wound onto bobbins. Man-Made Fiber Producers Assn., Inc.

fibers can be made from nylon. Nylon fibers have the appearance and luster of silk; their tensile strength is higher than that of wool, silk, rayon, or cotton. Dyes are applied either to the molten mass of nylon or to the yarn or finished fabric. Acetate rayon dyes are usually used for dyeing nylon.

Nylons made from acids and amines other than adipic acid and hexamethylenediamine have somewhat different properties but resemble generally the nylon described above.

Uses. Nylon is used in the manufacture of fabrics that have the appearance or light weight of silk. It has almost replaced silk in the manufacture of hosiery and is popular for other articles of clothing, such as night garments, underwear, blouses, shirts, and raincoats. Nylon fabrics are water-resistant; they dry quickly when laundered and usually require no ironing. Among the many other articles for which nylon fibers are used are parachutes and insect screening. In addition to its wide application as a textile fiber, nylon is used in making medical sutures, strings for tennis rackets, brush bristles, rope, and fishing nets and lines. Molded nylon is also used for many articles, including insulating material, combs, dishware, and machinery parts.

NYMPHAEACEAE. See WATER LILY.

NYMPHS, in Greek and Roman mythology, lesser divinities or spirits of nature, dwelling in groves and fountains, forests, meadows, streams, and the sea. They are usually described as young and beautiful maidens, fond of music and dancing. The nymphs were distinguished according to the various parts of nature they represented, and included the Oceanids, or daughters of Oceanus (q.v.), the ocean that flows around the earth; the Nereids (q.v.), or daughters of the sea god Nereus (q.v.), nymphs of the Mediterranean Sea; the Potameides, or river nymphs; the Naiads, or nymphs of springs and fresh-water streams; the Oreads, or nymphs of mountains and grottoes; and the Dryads (qq.v.), nymphs of the forests.

Oo

O, fifteenth letter and fourth vowel in the English alphabet and other alphabets of western Europe. It was originally a Phoenician character representing the Semitic letter *'ayn,* which was consonantal and stood for a guttural breathing sound. The Greeks adopted this sign to represent the short *o* vowel, and added a separate sign for the long sound of *o;* the names *omicron* (Gr., "little o") and *omega* ("big o"), respectively, were given later to these letters. The distinction was not continued by the Romans, and a single letter, standing for both sounds, was incorporated into the Latin alphabet. The capital O of the English alphabet changed very little during the course of its development. The Phoenician sign in which it originated was approximately circular; in the Greek and Latin alphabets it gradually assumed the oval shape that is its usual form at the present time. In English the letter o represents two principal sounds: long *o,* as in the words old, no, and bone; and short *o,* as in nod, hot, and golf. The letter also stands for the sounds heard in shorn, wolf, son, and do. The long *o* sound is indicated by a variety of spellings, as in the words oh, sew, dough, tow, and foe.

As an abbreviation the capital O is used for the month of October, for the States of Ohio and Oregon, and for ocean. Lowercase o is used as an abbreviation for words such as occidental, oriental, old, order, and octave. As a symbol the capital O is used in chemistry for oxygen, in logic for the particular negative proposition (some A is not B), is mathematics for zero, in medicine for a major blood type, and in psychology for a person who is both the observer and subject of an introspective demonstration or experiment. O, either capital or lowercase, stands for the fourteenth or fifteenth in an order, class, group, or series. O is also used in compound adjectives and nouns to denote circular or oval forms, as in O-shaped.   M.P.

OAHU, one of the Hawaiian Islands, part of the State of Hawaii, in the Pacific Ocean, about 2100 miles S.E. of San Francisco, Calif. Oahu is about 40 mi. long and 26 mi. wide. The island, which is coextensive with Honolulu County, is the commercial center of Hawaii and is important to United States defenses in the Pacific. Pearl Harbor (q.v.) naval base is situated here. The chief industries are the growing and processing of pineapples and sugar cane; tourism also is important to the economy. Among the many popular beaches is the renowned Waikiki, backed by the famous landmark Diamond Head (q.v.), an extinct volcano. The largest city, Honolulu (q.v.), is the State capital. Area, 589 sq.mi.; pop. (1960) 500,409.

OAK, common name applied to trees and shrubs belonging to the genus *Quercus* of the Beech family. The genus, which contains about 300 species, is native to the North Temperate Zone, and is widely cultivated for its timber and bark and for shade and ornament. Oak trees are generally deciduous, but are sometimes evergreen in the warmer, southerly portions of their range. These evergreen oaks are commonly called "live oaks". Oak leaves are simple and alternate, and vary in shape among different species. The inconspicuous male and female flowers are borne on the same plant. The staminate flowers are borne in spikes or catkins; the pistillate flowers are usually solitary. The fruit is an acorn, or nut, having characteristic elliptical shape, capped by a persistent, scaly involucre which forms a cup. Oak trees are noted for their great longevity, and the word oak has proverbially been associated with strength. The wood is hard, durable, and elastic, and was formerly used, throughout history, extensively in the construction of homes and ships. Although still employed for these purposes, oakwood is now chiefly used in the manufacture of furniture, panelings, and wooden floors. In Europe, British oak, *Q. robur,* and in the United States, white oak, *Q. alba,* and red oak, *Q. borealis,* are used for these purposes. The cork oak, *Q. suber,* is the chief source of commercial cork (q.v.). Tannin, used in leather-tanning and dyeing industries, is derived from the bark of various oak trees; see TANNINS. The acorns of such oaks as the valonia oak, *Q. aegilops,* found in southern Europe and Asia Minor, also contain large quantities of chemicals used in leather processing. The bark of the black oak, *Q. velutina,* called quercitron, yields a yellow dye. Acorns are also used as food for swine.

Among other trees called oaks are the Australian trees constituting the genus *Casuarina,* and the silk oaks of the genus *Grevillea* (q.v.).

OAKLAND, city in California, and county seat of Alameda Co., on the mainland shore of San Francisco Bay, linked with San Francisco by the 8¼-mi. Oakland–San Francisco Bay Bridge. The city is served by three railroads, and leading scheduled airlines and chartered airlines operate out of Metropolitan Oakland International Airport. The city is a focal point of the California freeway system and the center for the Bay Area Rapid Transit System, which is scheduled for completion in 1972. As a world port, the city has extensive shipping facilities, including the Port of Oakland, the largest containerized cargo terminal in the Western United States, with more than 2 mi. of berthing space. In the heart of the city is Lake Merritt, a 160-acre body of salt water, surrounded by Lakeside Park, which contains recreational facilities for children, a Natural Science Center, and specialized gardens. On the west side of the lake is the Kaiser Industrial Complex, a $50,000,000 office building constructed in 1955 and a $30,000,000 addition scheduled for completion in 1970. New public buildings include the State Office Building, the Hall of Justice, the County Administration Building, and the Alameda County Health Building. The Oakland–Alameda County Coliseum Complex comprises a stadium, a fully enclosed sports arena, and extensive exhibit space. The Coliseum is the home of major-league teams in baseball, hockey, football, basketball, and soccer.

Cultural facilities include the new Oakland Museum, with collections of art, cultural history, and natural sciences, and several theater groups. Institutions of higher education include Mills College (women, 1852), College of the Holy Names (1868), Peralta Junior College

White oak, Quercus alba. The Wye Oak, near Wye Mills, Md., is believed to be one of the largest white oaks in the U.S. It is approximately 95 ft. high, with a branch spread of 165 ft. Maryland Dept. of Information

OAK LAWN

(1927), and California College of Arts and Crafts (1907). Oakland has a council-manager form of government, with an elected mayor.

Commerce and Industry. Oakland is experiencing rapid growth as an industrial center. Industries in the city include food processing, printing and publishing, and the manufacture of automobiles and trucks, office equipment, tin and glass containers, calculating and data processing machines, fabricated metal products, chemicals, paints, and floor coverings. The city is the site of a U.S. Army base and a U.S. Navy hospital.

History. Oakland was founded on a Spanish grant in 1850. It was incorporated as a town in 1852 and as a city in 1854, and it was made county seat in 1873.

Population. Between 1910 and 1950 the population of Oakland increased from 150,174 to 384,575. In 1960 the population was 367,548, and in 1970 it was 361,561.

OAK LAWN, village of Illinois, in Cook Co., adjoining Chicago on the w. Lying in an area of truck farms and nurseries, it manufactures electronic equipment, mechanical devices, furniture, building materials, and starch. The village was incorporated in 1909. Pop. (1960) 27,471; (1970) 60,305.

OAKLEY, Annie (1860–1926), real name PHOEBE ANNE OAKLEY MOZEE, American markswoman and performer, born in a pioneer log cabin in Darke County, Ohio. Associated with Buffalo Bill's Wild West Show (see CODY, WILLIAM FREDERICK) from 1885 to 1902, she was the sensation of America and Europe because of her almost uncanny accuracy with a rifle, a weapon she began to use at the age of six to help provide food for her family. As a young woman she was one of the best-known market hunters in the country. As a performer with a rifle she could hit a playing card thrown into the air a dozen times before it finally touched the ground.

OAK PARK, city of Michigan, in Oakland Co., adjoining Detroit on the N. and 10 miles N.W. of the city center. Oak Park produces tools and dies, metal products, electronic and communications equipment, fiber and food products, canvas, aircraft and space equipment, and machinery. It was incorporated as a village in 1927 and as a city in 1945. Pop. (1970) 36,762.

OAK PARK, village of Illinois, in Cook Co., near the Des Plaines R., about 9 miles w. of Chicago, of which it is a suburb. Oak Park is one of the largest villages in the nation. The American novelist Ernest Hemingway (q.v.) was born in Oak Park, and the American architect Frank Lloyd Wright (q.v.), who resided here, designed several of its structures, including Unity Church. The village was first settled in 1830. Pop. (1960) 61,093; (1970) 62,511.

OAK RIDGE, city of Tennessee, in Anderson Co., 20 miles N.W. of Knoxville, occupying about 9 sq.mi. of the 93-sq.mi. government reservation known as the Oak Ridge Area. The Oak Ridge Institute of Nuclear Studies, the Oak Ridge National Laboratory, and government uranium processing plants are located in Oak Ridge. The town was organized in 1942 to provide a residence community for personnel working in the various Oak Ridge plants of the atomic-energy project; see ATOMIC ENERGY COMMISSION; NUCLEAR ENERGY. Government ownership of property, houses, and shops in the city was terminated in 1955. Large-scale improvements have converted the temporary town into a permanent community, which was incorporated as a city in 1959. The population reached a peak of 75,000 during World War II. Pop. (1960) 27,169; (1970) 28,319.

OAKVILLE, port and city of Canada, in Ontario Province, in Halton Co., on Lake Ontario, 20 miles s.w. of Toronto. Industries include oil refining, boatbuilding, woodworking, textile milling, printing, auto assembly, and the manufacture of chemicals, auto parts, lumber, metal and foundry products, paint, plastics, industrial equipment, porcelain, and electric equipment. Oakville provided the setting for the "Jalna" novels of the Canadian writer Mazo de la Roche (q.v.). It is the site of a museum. In 1962 the city annexed the entire surrounding township of Trafalgar. Pop. (1966), 52,793.

OATES, Titus (1649–1705), English conspirator, the principal informer in the so-called Popish plot in England, born in Oakham, and educated at the University of Cambridge. Taking advantage of the hostility of the public toward Catholics, in 1678 Oates embellished details of a fictitious plot by Roman Catholics to murder the Protestant monarch, Charles II (q.v.), King of England, and to enthrone Charles' brother, a Roman Catholic, later James II (q.v.), King of England.

As a result of the perjured testimony of Oates and his followers about thirty-five people lost their lives between 1678 and 1681, while Oates himself for a time received a large pension, and lived in Whitehall Palace. A reaction set in against Oates and in 1684 he was imprisoned. In 1685 with the accession of James II, Oates was found guilty of perjury and sentenced to life imprisonment. After the Glorious Revolution (q.v.) in 1688 he was freed by William III (q.v.), King of England.

OATS, common name applied to the seeds or entire plants of herbs belonging to the genus *Avena* of the Grass family; *see* GRASSES. The genus, which contains about fifty species, is native to the cooler temperate regions of the world. Several species, especially the common oat, *A. sativa,* are widely cultivated for their grain, which is used as feed for cattle and horses and in the production of cereals for human consumption; the stems and leaves are used for hay, silage, and pasturage. Other important species of oats besides the common oat are the wild oat, *A. fatua,* wild red oat, *A. sterilis,* and side oat, *A. orientalis.* These oats are important rotation crops; some of them are grown from fall seedings in various areas as winter crops to prevent soil erosion.

The low cost of oats, which are high in protein (q.v.) and Vitamin B_1 (*see* VITAMIN), has made them popular breakfast cereals. In Scotland, oats have been highly esteemed as a staple food for many decades. In recent years, oats have been used in the preparation of processed food products and industrial products. Among the processed food products are various breakfast cereals that can be served with little cooking, and others requiring no cooking that are served cold. Avenex is an oat flour used as a stabilizer in the preparation of ice cream, chocolate, peanut butter, and lard, and as a preservative inner coating for paper bags used to package salted nuts, coffee, and potato chips. The most important industrial product from oats is furfural, a chemical derived from oat hulls, and used as a solvent in various refining industries and for other manufacturing purposes.

World production of oats in the late 1960's averaged over 56,000,000 tons annually; one fourth of this total was produced in the United States.

OB', river of the Soviet Union, rising in N.W. Siberia, on the N. slopes of the Altay Mts., near the border with Mongolia. The Ob', about 2500 mi. long, flows generally N.W. where it receives its chief tributary, the 1844-mi. Irtysh R., turns to the N., and empties into the Gulf of Ob' an arm of the Arctic Ocean. The river drains an area of more than 1,000,000 sq.mi. An important water route for the region, the Ob' is used principally to transport lumber and grain, although navigation is impeded by ice in winter. A few industrial cities and a hydroelectric plant have been built on the banks of the river near its source. The combined Ob'-Irtysh system, the longest river system of Asia, is about 3460 mi. long.

OBADIAH, book of the Old Testament (*see* BIBLE), in the King James Version, OBADIAH; in the Douay Version, used by Roman Catholics, it is entitled The Prophecy of Abdias (a Latin transliteration of the Hebrew name Obadiah). It is the shortest book in the Old Testament (twenty-one verses), and is one of twelve short prophetic books known, primarily because of the brevity of each, as the Minor Prophets (*see* BIBLE, CANON OF THE). Tradition attributes it to the Hebrew prophet Obadiah (q.v.), but many modern scholars question the unity of the book and ascribe it to more than one author, one of whom may have been the prophet Obadiah. It is generally agreed that the book dates from postexilic times: verses 11–14 most probably refer to the destruction of Jerusalem in 587 B.C. (*see* BABYLONIAN CAPTIVITY; JEWS: *The Kingdom*). Many dates have been suggested, however, for other passages, some of them as early as the 9th century and others as late as the 4th century B.C.

The first part of Obadiah (1–14) foretells the fall of Judah's traditional enemy Edom (qq.v.). The specific grievance against Edom expressed in the book doubtless was provoked by the hostility of the Edomites at the time of the capture of Jerusalem. Apparently, the Edomites assisted in the destruction of the city, and in the capture of Israelite refugees. The remainder of the book (15–21) is eschatological in nature (*see* ESCHATOLOGY). A "day of the Lord" (15) is prophesied, at which time, in addition to Edom, the neighboring nations will be punished for their behavior toward Israel. Thereafter, Israel will possess all of Palestine (q.v.) and "the kingdom shall be the Lord's" (21).

OBADIAH (Heb., "servant of Yahweh"), Hebrew prophet (fl. 6th cent. B.C.), and author of the book of the Old Testament that bears his name (*see* book of OBADIAH). Aside from his writings, nothing is known of Obadiah.

OBEID, EL, city in the Sudan, and capital of Kordofan Province, 220 miles S.W. of Khartoum. Gum arabic and oilseeds are the chief articles of trade. The city is a commercial center, a rail terminus, and a junction of roads and camel caravan routes. In 1883 a force of Egyptians was destroyed near El Obeid by a large army of the Mahdi (q.v.), the Muslim agitator Mohammed Ahmed. Pop. (1964 est.) 60,000.

OBELISK, in architecture, four-sided tapering shaft terminating in a pyramidal or conical top. In ancient Egypt, pairs of these monuments, each hewn from a single piece of red granite and set on a cubical base, often flanked temple entrances. Associated with sun worship, these monoliths were especially numerous at Heliopolis (q.v.), the City of the Sun, in Egypt. The pointed tops were frequently sheathed in brass or gold; sculptured dedicatory or commemora-

OBELISK

One of the two obelisks popularly called Cleopatra's Needles is now in Central Park, New York City.
Metropolitan Museum of Art

tive hieroglyphs about the Egyptian Pharaohs usually ran down the sides of the shaft. Obelisks were produced throughout ancient Egyptian history, the dwarf specimens generally dating from the earliest and latest periods, and the giant specimens from the Middle Kingdom; see EGYPT: *History*. Roman emperors transported many back to Rome as trophies of conquest, and a number were carved imitatively in Italy as memorial monuments. The two obelisks popularly called Cleopatra's Needles stood at Heliopolis from the 15th century B.C. until the 1st century B.C., when they were moved by the Roman emperor Augustus (q.v.) to Alexandria; in 1878 one was transported to, and erected on the Thames Embankment, London, and in 1880 the other, a gift of Ismail Pasha (q.v.), Khedive of Egypt, was brought to America and set up in Central Park, New York City. The latter is 69 ft. 6 in. high and 7 ft. 9 in. thick at the base, and weighs 200 tons. The 76-ft. high Obelisk of Luxor, which stands in the Place de la Concorde in Paris, dates from the 21st century B.C. and was presented to the king of France by the viceroy of Egypt in 1831.

The obelisk form is still used in monuments and decorations and as an architectural adjunct. It was a popular feature in baroque (q.v.) and neoclassical tombs, and has been used everywhere in the Western world as an ornamental element in parks, gardens, and cemeteries. It has often been added to fountains, balustrades, and gables; see ARCHITECTURE. The Bunker Hill Monument in Boston, Mass., and the Washington Monument (qq.v.) in Washington, D.C., are built in the shape of obelisks; as opposed to the traditional obelisk, which is constructed of a single piece of solid rock, these monuments are not monolithic.

OBERAMMERGAU, village of West Germany, in Bavaria State, on the Ammer R., 45 miles S.W. of Munich. Wood carvings are manufactured in the village. Situated in the Bavarian Alps, Oberammergau is a popular tourist resort. Here the famous Passion Play (q.v.), that originated in 1634, is performed. It was first presented by the townspeople in gratitude for the end of a plague epidemic. Except for the years 1870, 1920, and 1940, when war or unstable postwar conditions prevailed, the play has been performed every tenth year since 1680 in keeping with a vow made by the 17th-century villagers. The day-long performances attended by thousands are held in the open-air, and the actors belong to the village. Pop. (1961) 4660.

OBERHAUSEN, city of West Germany, in North Rhine-Westphalia State, near the right

OBESITY

bank of the Rhine R., 35 miles N. of Cologne. Oberhausen is in the center of the Ruhr industrial region and has extensive iron foundries, railway shops, chemical works. Glass and various iron, steel, and tin wares, including wire and wire rope for cables, are manufactured here. In the vicinity are important coal, zinc, and iron mines. Pop. (1966 est.) 255,825.

OBERLIN COLLEGE, coeducational privately controlled nondenominational institution of higher learning, situated in Oberlin, Ohio, founded in 1833, and known as Oberlin Collegiate Institute until 1850, when its present name was adopted. Oberlin was the first coeducational college in the United States; see COEDUCATION. Two years after its founding the college admitted students "without respect to color", becoming the first U.S. college to do so; prior to the Civil War it was known as a center for antislavery activities. Charles Grandison Finney (1792–1875), professor of theology and president of Oberlin from 1851 to 1866, first promulgated at the college his doctrine of evangelical Calvinism which later became known as Oberlin Theology. The divisions of the institution include the college of arts and sciences and the conservatory of music, for which the college is particularly well known. The degrees of bachelor and master are granted in liberal arts and sciences and in music. A master of arts degree in teaching is also conferred. In 1968 the college library housed more than 725,000 bound volumes. In 1968 the student enrollment totaled 2622, the faculty numbered 234, and the endowment was about $66,667,000.

OBERON, king of the elves or fairies, and the husband of Titania, the fairy queen. Oberon is first mentioned as "Roi du Royaume de la Féerie" (fairy king) in the 13th-century French poem *Huon de Bordeaux* ("Huon of Bordeaux"). The name first appeared in English in the translation (1534?) by English author John Bourchier, 2nd Baron Berners (1467–1533), and was adopted in many ballads, and also in the play, *The Scottish History of James IV* (1592), by the English writer Robert Greene (q.v.). Oberon's popularity stems largely from his characterization in the play *A Midsummer Night's Dream* by the English dramatist William Shakespeare.

OBESITY, *or* CORPULENCE, *or* OVERWEIGHT, body condition characterized by storage of excessive amounts of fat in adipose tissue beneath the skin and within other organs, including muscles. All mammals store body fat; in normal women 25 percent, and in normal men 15 percent, of body weight is stored as fat. Medically, obesity is defined as an accumulated level of body fat above which health is impaired.

Deposition of fat, which has twice the potential energy of carbohydrate or protein, is a way of storing energy for retrieval in time of future need. Growing animals anticipate surges of growth by laying down extra energy as fat; preadolescent plumpness in children is characteristic, as is the stored body fat upon which animals draw during hibernation. Certain mammalian species have unusual distributions of fat appropriate to their needs. Camels and Brahma cattle, which live in warm climates and cannot sustain a blanket of insulating fat over their bodies, store a large proportion of body fat in humps on their backs and necks as a reservoir of energy.

The Last Supper scene from the famous Oberammergau Passion Play. The play, depicting the life of Christ, has been presented in Oberammergau almost every decade since 1634. UPI

OBESITY

Similarly, some Hottentot women living in a warm climate tend to store excess body fat over their buttocks. By contrast, marine animals such as the sea lion and the seal, which live in a cold environment, deposit stored fat subcutaneously as a blanket of insulating material.

Desirable weights, derived from the data of insurance companies, reflect experience with different degrees of overweight, which in turn reflect the proportion of stored body fat. Persons who are 30 percent or more overweight run measurably increased risks of disease, notably diabetes, cardiovascular and gallbladder disease, and arthritis, and often encounter complications in surgery. This associative evidence does not establish the fact that obesity causes these diseases and does not necessarily justify a conclusion that correction of obesity lessens the risk of disease. Nevertheless, it is clear that extreme obesity is associated with an increased threat to health.

Causes and Treatment. The causes of obesity are generally misapprehended. Disturbances of the endocrine system (q.v.) are rarely encountered. Although obesity appears to run in families, it is not regarded as an hereditary trait; more probably, familial obesity is an expression of learned transmission patterns of eating and inactivity. The belief that certain foods are especially fattening is equally erroneous. Each of the three major foodstuffs—fat, carbohydrate, and protein—is readily converted into body fat when energy intake is in excess of need. While any one can become overweight by overeating, persons also become overweight by reducing their expenditure of energy, a condition that often occurs in persons who are sedentary, bedridden, or crippled.

Treatment of existing obesity requires two approaches. The first demands limitation of energy intake to force the body to draw on its stores of fat for its day-to-day requirements, thus causing loss of weight. The second depends upon increasing the expenditure of energy by exercise, by diminishing the amount of sleeping time, or by exposure to cold, all of which exact a price and contribute to a negative balance of energy. Obese tissue accumulated over the years must be dissipated gradually at a maximal rate of one pound a week, which requires a daily deficit of 500 calories, if damage to health is to be avoided. For this reason, starvation, a current fad, is a danger that may conceivably lead to death. No drug may be used safely to accelerate this process. Advertised commercial formulations do no more than eliminate salt and water from the body, reducing weight, but doing nothing to lessen excess deposits of adipose tissue. Hormones are equally useless, as are drugs claimed to diminish appetite. Massage and mechanical devices are ineffective in so-called spot reducing.

The human figure is a subtle blend of adipose tissue overlying muscular support. Exercise will enlarge and firm these muscles, resulting in maximal improvement of figure. For persons with an excess amount of weight accumulated over the years, a program of reduction under expert supervision has been recommended by physicians. G.V.M.

OBOE, musical instrument, soprano member of the oboe family of instruments, constructed of wood with a conical bore and a double-reed mouthpiece, and producing a penetrating, rather nasal sound; see REED, in music. The oboe is constructed in three pieces that fit together with the mouthpiece at the smaller end and fingerholes and stops along its length. Its range comprises two octaves (q.v.) plus a sixth (see INTERVAL). The A tone of the oboe is used to fix the pitch for all other instruments of the orchestra. The alto oboe is called an English horn; the bass of the family is called a bassoon (q.v.).

The immediate predecessor of the oboe, the shawm, appeared during the Renaissance and was built in many ranges from soprano to bass. The oboe d'amore and oboe di caccia, or hunting oboe, were popular members of the shawm family during the 16th and 17th centuries. Used extensively in France, the oboe became known as the *hautbois* in contradistinction to the deeper-toned *grosbois,* or bassoon. The present form of the instrument dates from the mid-19th century, when many improvements in construction were effected.

O'BOYLE, Patrick Aloysius, Cardinal (1897–   ), Roman Catholic ecclesiastic, born in Scranton, Pa. He was graduated from the University of Scranton in 1917 and was ordained a priest in 1921. O'Boyle undertook postgraduate studies at the New York School of Social Work, graduating in 1931. For four years he served on the faculty of the School of Social Service at Fordham University. He led the war relief program of the National Catholic Welfare Conference from 1943 to 1947. In 1948 he was consecrated archbishop of Washington, D.C., and in 1967 was elevated to the cardinalate by Pope Paul VI (see under PAUL).

OBREGÓN, Álvaro (1880–1928), Mexican soldier and political leader, born near Alamos, Sonora State. In 1912 he organized a force of about 400 Indians. As commander of this force he entered the service of Francisco Madero (q.v.), president of Mexico, and crushed a revolt. After the death of Madero in 1913, Obregón supported the Mexican political leader Venustiano Carranza (q.v.). During the ensuing two years, Obregón helped defeat the various rebel forces led by the Mexican statesman Victoriano Huerta, and the Mexican revolutionaries Francisco Villa (qq.v.), better known as Pancho Villa, and Emiliano Zapata (1877?–1919); in a battle against Villa, Obregón lost his right arm. Upon the election of Carranza to the presidency in 1915, Obregón was appointed commander in chief of the Mexican army. In 1920 he led a successful revolt against Carranza, and soon afterward was elected president. He instituted a number of labor, agrarian, and educational reforms, and in 1923 secured the formal recognition of his government by the United States. Between 1924 and 1928 he was politically inactive. He was reelected president in 1928, but was assassinated before he could take office.

OBSERVATORY, building or series of buildings especially constructed for use in making astronomical observations. Modern observatories customarily house telescopes (see TELESCOPE), although the term is also sometimes applied to buildings used for observing magnetic or meteorological phenomena. The earliest known astronomical observatories were built by the Chinese and the Babylonians about 2300 B.C. These observatories were probably little more than high platforms giving an unobstructed view of the sky. About 300 B.C. the most famous observatory of classical times was built in Alexandria, Egypt. Although no details concerning this observatory remain, it was probably equipped with instruments such as astrolabes by which the celestial latitude and longitude (q.v.) of a star or planet could be measured. The Alexandria observatory was in continuous operation for about 500 years.

After the beginning of the Christian era, the Arabs established a number of observatories at Damascus, Baghdad, and at Mokatta near Cairo in Egypt. The last-named was built about 1000 A.D. The first observatory in Europe was set up in Nuremberg in 1471. A century later, the largest and most completely equipped of the early European observatories was built by the Danish astronomer Tycho Brahe (q.v.) on the island of Ven. Brahe's observatory, in which he lived and worked with his students from 1576 to 1596, was equipped with a large quadrant used in making accurate measurements of the altitudes of celestial bodies. These observations were used by the

Palomar Observatory, with the 200-in. Hale reflecting telescope pointing north.
Mount Wilson & Palomar Observatories

A view of the Yerkes Observatory, located at Williams Bay, Wis., near the Illinois State line. Yerkes Observatory

German astronomer Johannes Kepler (q.v.) in the development of his theory of the solar system.

After the invention of the telescope about 1609, a number of new observatories were built in various European cities. Among the most famous of these were the French National Observatory at Paris, established in 1667, and the British Royal Observatory, often called the Greenwich Observatory (q.v.), founded in 1675. Both of these observatories are still in existence. The first observatory to be constructed in the United States was built at Chapel Hill, N.C., in 1831. The Naval Observatory (q.v.) at Washington, D.C., was established in 1843–44. Other famous U.S. observatories which are described in separate articles are the Lick Observatory, the Mount Wilson Observatory, the Palomar Observatory, and the Yerkes Observatory.

Classification of Observatories. Astronomical observatories are classified into several types. Government observatories are usually occupied with continuous observation of the stars and planets for the preparation of navigational tables and the determination of standard times; see NAVIGATION. Observatories connected with educational institutions are used chiefly for training students in the techniques of astronomical observation. Certain university observatories and other observatories not connected with institutions are dedicated to purely observational problems such as the discovery of comets and the discovery and measurement of variable stars. Many of the larger observatories are entirely devoted to the problems of astrophysics (see SPECTRUM: *Astrophysical Applications*), or the physics of the stars. In addition some observatories have separate apparatus which is used for the study of solar phenomena; a few observatories make only solar observations.

In the 1950's a new type of observatory was established for the study of radio emanations from the sun and stars. Research in this field, called radio astronomy (q.v.) is conducted with instruments known as radio telescopes.

A number of amateur astronomers build their own observatories in or near their homes. Such observatories usually contain telescopes and other equipment often constructed by the owners themselves. These observatories supplement the work of professional observatories, in fact, by keeping track and making measurements of variable stars, meteors, and comets, which are too numerous to be constantly watched by professional astronomers.

High-Altitude and Orbital Observatories. A relatively new field of astronomical technology is concerned with study of the universe from a point high above the earth, using equipment carried by balloons, rockets, and orbiting observatories; see BALLOON; ROCKET; SATELLITE; ARTIFICIAL. Carrying telescopes, cameras, and instruments for spectral analysis, these vehicles provide a means of studying the stars and planets free of distortion from the earth's atmosphere (q.v.); see SPECTRUM.

The first observatory, the satellite Cosmos 215, was launched by the Soviet Union in March, 1968. It was equipped with eight telescopes for studying ultraviolet radiation from outer space and one for X-rays, and had limited success in its six-week life. On Dec. 7, 1968, the U.S. launched a 4400-lb. Orbiting Astronomical Observatory (OAO-II), a 10 ft. by 21 ft. satellite, equipped with spectrometers, designed to study ultraviolet radiation from young stars and to photograph planets and interstellar matter. Moving in an orbit 480 mi. above the earth, OAO-II in twenty-three days gathered twenty times as much spectral data as had been collected previously over fifteen years by sounding-rocket flights.

See also ASTRONOMY; RADAR ASTRONOMY; TELESCOPE.

OBSIDIAN. *See* RHYOLITE.

OBSTETRICS, branch of medical science and practice concerned with the study and care of women during pregnancy, parturition, and the puerperium, or postpartum period. Most obstetricians also practice gynecology (q.v.), that branch of medicine (q.v.) related to the diagnosis and treatment of disorders of the female reproductive organs. As a branch of medical study obstetrics is concerned with the anatomy and physiology of the female organs of reproduction (q.v.), conception and pregnancy, and labor, normal or abnormal, including delivery, that is usually vaginal, often requiring forceps, but sometimes by Caesarean section (q.v.). It is also concerned with the return of the reproductive organs to their normal state.

History. Originally the art of assisting in childbirth was called midwifery. A woman giving birth (q.v.) was aided by another woman, called a midwife, who was qualified only by her practical experience. During the 16th century, however, physicians began to supervise childbirth.

The writings of the ancient Greek physician Hippocrates (q.v.) contain the earliest attempt to formulate a practice of obstetrics. In 98 A.D. the Greek physician Soranus (fl. 2nd cent. A.D.) published a work "on the diseases of women", which shows a considerable advance in the knowledge of the anatomy of the female organs. In the 4th century a remarkable book was published by the Greek medical writer Moschion, *Peri tōn Gunaikeiōn Pathōn,* which is sometimes called the first obstetric work published. It is based on Soranus, and shows a sound anatomical knowledge. From this time until the beginning of the 16th century it may be said that obstetrics made no progress.

In 1668 the French surgeon François Mauriceau (1637–1709) published his *Treatise,* which ran through seven editions, and was for long the standard work on the subject. It was translated into English by the English physician Hugh Chamberlen (1630?–1720?) in 1672, and it seems to be about this time that men began generally to engage in the practice of what was then called midwifery. The Chamberlens and others took it up in England; while the Duchesse de La Vallière, (1644–1710), the mistress of Louis XIV (q.v.), King of France, by employing Julian Clement, a surgeon of high eminence, in her first confinement in 1663, did much to establish the practice in France.

About the end of the 16th or beginning of the 17th century, the forceps was invented by the English obstetrician Peter Chamberlen (1572–1626). The original instrument was modified by the French obstetrician André Levret (1703–80); subsequently its construction was elaborated by the French surgeon Stéphane Tarnier (1828–97).

In 1847 the British physician Sir James Simpson (1811–70) first employed chloroform anesthesia to relieve the pain of labor, and this marks one of the most beneficent advances in the history of obstetrics. Introduction of an anesthesia in 1915, "Twilight Sleep", was thought to have solved the problem of painless labor, but an extensive trial proved it unsatisfactory. Obstetrical analgesia, so called because the woman remains conscious and is able to co-operate, was developed by the American physician James Tayloe Gwathmey (1863–1944) and the American surgeon Asa B. Davis (1861–1930). It was first employed in the Lying-In Hospital in New York, and proved to be an advance over any other method known.

Until about 1870 the great scourge of maternity hospitals, and also a frequent cause of disaster in private practice, was the prevalence of outbreaks of puerperal fever (q.v.) because of infection; *see* SEMMELWEIS, IGNAZ PHILIPP. In that year the teaching of the British surgeon Joseph Lister (q.v.) began to influence obstetric practice, and gradually the use of sterile techniques (asepsis) became the rule in maternity hospitals, markedly reducing the incidence of infection.

Recent developments in obstetrics include antibiotic and sulfonamide therapy, that have further reduced the incidence of infection and complications associated with childbirth. Hemorrhages, formerly responsible for many deaths in childbirth, are now controlled by the use of blood transfusions. The discovery of various human-blood types, such as the Rh factor (q.v.), made possible the control of fetal mortality arising from Rh incompatibilities. Among present-day efforts to minimize the pain of childbirth is a program of prenatal training for the type of delivery known popularly as natural childbirth. This program consists of educational lectures on the physiological process involved in birth, and of exercises designed to promote relaxation and applied during labor. By the successful application of natural-childbirth techniques the patient may undergo labor and delivery without the need of analgesia medication.

See also EMBRYOLOGY; GESTATION; MULTIPLE BIRTH. L.J.V.

OCALA, city in Florida, and county seat of Marion Co., about 34 miles s. of Gainesville. A marketing center, the city has light manufacturing. It is the site of Central Florida Junior College, established in 1957. A resort city, Ocala was incorporated in 1868. Pop. (1960) 13,598; (1970) 22,583.

OCARINA, small, egg-shaped musical instrument, perhaps originating in Italy in the early 19th century. In the course of the 19th century the ocarina gained great popularity among street players. The modern ocarina is made of hollow metal, earthenware, or plastic with fingerholes and a protruding spout which serves as a mouthpiece. It produces a whistlelike tone, the pitch of which is controlled by the number of holes which are left open. The ocarina is a type of "globular flute"; in America, in colloquial usage, it is called a "sweet potato", which it resembles in size and shape.

O'CASEY, Sean (1890–1964), Irish playwright, born in Dublin. As a youth he lived in the slums of Dublin and worked as an unskilled laborer. In 1916 he participated in the Easter Rebellion (q.v.), a Dublin uprising against British rule. In 1926 he left Ireland, where his plays had been badly received and went to live in England. O'Casey was the outstanding Irish dramatist of the second quarter of the 20th century. His plays are characterized by a lyrical prose style, realistic and tensely dramatic situations, a deep sense of the tragedy of commonplace lives, rich humor, and a hatred of political oppression. Many of his dramas were first produced at the noted Abbey Theatre (q.v.) in Dublin. Among his plays are *The Shadow of a Gunman* (1923), *Juno and the Paycock* (1924), *The Plough and the Stars* (1926), *Red Roses for Me* (1942), *Cock-a-doodle Dandy* (1949), and *The Drums of Father Ned* (1960). He also wrote six autobiographical works between 1939 and 1954 in which he discussed his personal life, the movements in which he engaged, and political and literary personages he knew. These works were collected and published in two volumes entitled *Mirror in My House* in 1956. A collection of essays, *Under a Colored Cap*, was published in 1963. See IRISH LITERATURE: *Irish Literary Revival*.

OCCASIONALISM, term employed to designate the philosophical system devised by the followers of the 17th-century French philosopher René Descartes (q.v.) who, in attempting to explain the interrelationship between mind and body, concluded that God is the only cause. The occasionalists begin with the assumption that certain actions or modifications of the body are preceded, accompanied, or followed by changes in the mind. This assumed relationship presents no difficulty to the popular conception of mind and body, according to which each entity is supposed to act directly upon the other; philosophers, however, asserting that cause and effect must be similar, could not conceive the possibility of any direct mutual interaction between substances as dissimilar as mind and body. According to the occasionalists the action of the mind is not, and cannot be, the cause of the corresponding action of the body. They maintain that whenever any action of the mind takes place, God directly produces in connection with that action, and by reason of it, a corresponding action of the body; the converse process is likewise true. This theory did not solve the problem, for if the mind cannot act upon the body (matter), then God, conceived as mind, cannot act upon matter. Thus if God is conceived as other than mind, then He cannot act upon mind. A proposed solution of this problem was furnished by exponents of radical empiricism such as the American philosopher and psychologist William James (*see under* JAMES); *see* EMPIRICISM. They dispose of the dualism (q.v.) of the occasionalists by denying the fundamental difference between mind and matter.

OCCULTISM (Lat. *occulere*, "to hide"), belief in hidden or mysterious powers not explained by known scientific principles of nature, and the attempt to bring these powers within

Sean O'Casey   UPI

human control by scientific methods. The medieval concept of occult properties included only those properties that may be revealed by experimentation. The alchemists, astrologers, seers, and others who practiced this "science" of experimentation were a small group, usually in conflict with orthodox theology. Consequently their work was considered mysterious, and the term "occultism" gradually came to denote the study of supernatural forces. Nevertheless, all the so-called natural sciences stemmed from occultism, and early scientists were frequently called magicians and sorcerers because of the mystery attributed to their investigations by most of their contemporaries. Modern occultism is generally considered to have begun with the concept of animal magnetism, first developed by the Austrian physician Franz Anton Mesmer (q.v.) in the late 18th century; see MESMERISM. Mesmer believed that certain individuals possess occult powers, comparable to the magnetic powers of the magnet, that can be used to invoke the supernatural. In the mid-19th century occultism took the form of spiritualism (q.v.), a belief that the spirits of the dead may manifest themselves through the agency of living persons called mediums. After the turn of the century occultism included serious investigations of forms of extrasensory perception (ESP) such as mental telepathy that, although still not within the usual area of scientific research, are considered by some to be valid natural phenomena explicable by accepted scientific methods. See CLAIRVOYANCE; HYPNOSIS; PSYCHICAL RESEARCH.

OCCUPATIONAL DISEASES, in medicine, illnesses resulting from hazards in specific working conditions, and generally caused by poisons, chemicals, irritants, fumes, radiation, exposure to specific infections, or an unhealthful environment. In law the meaning of the term is limited to diseases that are specifically recognized as compensable under workmen's compensation (q.v.) laws or court decisions.

The ancients recognized particular diseases as incident to such employment as lead or quicksilver mining, but these diseases were regarded as ills of slaves, and as of no general interest. Even the guild (q.v.) of the Middle Ages did little to protect its members from the hygienic hazards incident to the stone and metal trades. This characteristic indifference to the health of the worker persisted after the establishment of the factory system; see FACTORIES AND THE FACTORY SYSTEM. In the United States and most countries of western Europe during the 19th century a few factory laws were enacted, but these affected only the employment of women and children, forbidding night work and barring their employment in certain exceptionally hazardous or unhealthful occupations; see CHILD LABOR; WOMEN, EMPLOYMENT OF. With the development of preventive medicine in the last two decades of the century, social agencies initiated a movement aimed at extending protection to all workers by establishing minimum hygienic standards of heating, ventilation, and sanitary facilities, and elminating or controlling hazardous processes. This movement made little headway at first; after 1910 various States of the U.S. enacted workmen's compensation laws, factory inspection acts, and other legislation aimed at eliminating dangerous conditions in industrial plants and providing compensation for employees suffering from occupational diseases on the same basis as compensation for industrial accidents.

Various methods of classifying occupational diseases have been advocated, but no single method has been generally adopted. The diseases may be divided into diseases caused by airborne agents, contact agents, abnormal physical surroundings, and psychogenic factors. Airborne agents include smoke fogs, dusts, gases, or sprays carrying toxic material such as mercury, lead, carbon bisulfide, phosphorus gases, and arsenic dust. They also include clouds of such chemically inert material as coal dust, sand, asbestos, and other abrasives which, by mechanical irritation, cause the various forms of pneumoconiosis or black lung disease, such as anthracosis and silicosis, as well as increasing susceptibility to tuberculosis and cancer (qq.v.). Bacterial diseases prevalent in certain trades, such as anthrax, formerly called woolsorters' disease, also belong in this category. Contact agents include chemical irritants which cause various forms of dermatitis (q.v.) and cancer of the skin. Abnormal physical surroundings cause such ailments as the bends (q.v.), from variations of air pressure; radiation burns from X rays or radioactive materials; heat exhaustion and heat stroke; and glass blowers' cataract. Psychogenic factors cause such ailments as neuromuscular fatigue and migraine. L.J.V.

OCCUPATIONAL THERAPY, paramedical treatment of planned activity administered by an occupational therapist under the direction of a physician to promote the recovery of persons stricken with mental illness or physical disability, sometimes following accidents. Originally regarded as a way of filling the time of convalescent patients, it has now become a program of work specifically selected for its physical, emotional, mental, and vocational value.

OCCUPATIONAL THERAPY

The therapist's work is based on the physician's statement of the patient's diagnosis, prognosis, personality, and physical and emotional limitations, as well as the objectives sought. Often, the therapist engages in a form of vocational rehabilitation (see REHABILITATION, VOCATIONAL) in choosing activities that will teach new basic skills of daily living to those who never acquired them or who have lost them, as in the case of amputees or those otherwise recently crippled. Additionally, in dealing with patients who have never been employed, who have held jobs requiring no skills, or who must change their type of work because of their acquired disability, the therapist may also engage in prevocational testing and guidance.

The trained therapist is versed in such activities as gardening, weaving, hand industries, music, various types of recreation and education, creative handcraft such as clay modeling and leather tooling, and manual arts. After determining the patient's willingness to involve himself and his capacity and interest in a given field, the therapist will employ one or more of these activities to create the desired result in a variety of ways. Whether he is dealing with the physically or emotionally ill, the chronic patient, normal adults, the aged, or children, the therapist works in two areas: the functional and the psychological or psychiatric.

Functional Therapy. Functional therapy operates within the limits of the patient's physical tolerance to develop or reestablish nervous and muscular coordination, to extend the motion of joints, and to strengthen muscles. Functional therapy is especially important for those who have lost the use of a limb through amputation and must be taught to use artificial members. It is also important for those who have suffered attacks of arthritis, cerebral palsy, poliomyelitis, or neurological disabilities. While such therapy may not restore total function, even a degree of restoration will often help the patient to be able to work again.

Psychological and Psychiatric Therapy. The services of a psychologist are of value to the ill or disabled patient whose attitude is one of depression that leads him to regard himself as useless. Such therapy, in providing mental stimulus and exercise, can do much to restore a normal outlook and prepare him to accept retraining in some skill within even his limited capacity. The psychiatrist is called upon to deal with cases of more severe depression where a patient's outlook cannot be improved by routine psychological therapy, where he cannot adjust to hospital life, where his disability seems overwhelming, and where his condition is such that he must be followed, supported, and reassured when he begins to engage in some form of productive work; see PSYCHOTHERAPY. Such therapy can also serve in diagnosis by observation of the patient's reaction to a normal work situation, which may suggest additional forms of treatment that may move him further along the road to recovery.

OCEAN AND OCEANOGRAPHY, great body of salt water comprising all the oceans and seas that cover nearly three fourths of the surface of the earth, and the scientific study of the physical, chemical, and biological aspects of the so-called world ocean. The major goals of oceanography are the understanding of the geologic and geochemical processes involved in the evolution and alteration of the ocean and its basin, to evaluate the interaction of the ocean and the atmosphere (q.v.) so that greater knowledge of climatic variations can be attained, and to describe the factors controlling biological productivity in the sea; see BIOLOGY; CLIMATE; GEOLOGY.

Ocean Basin Structure. The oceans cover 71 percent of the surface of the earth, or about 361,000,000 sq.km., or 139,382,100 sq.mi. The average depth of the ocean is about 4 km or 2½ mi. Major features of the ocean basins include the continental shelves, which are shallow regions adjacent to the continents, generally less than 200 m in depth; these merge into the continental slope and continental rise, which are regions of steeper slope descending to the ocean floor, large regions of which are extremely flat; see CONTINENT. In the central parts of the oceans exist the mid-ocean ridges, which are mountainous regions with active volcanoes and a high concentration of earthquakes; see EARTHQUAKE; VOLCANO. The discovery and description of these ridges has played an important part in the formulation of current theories of motion in the earth's crust, including ideas of ocean-floor spreading, continental drift, and mountain building. The Mid-Atlantic Ridge extends from the Norwegian Sea through Iceland and the Azores, which are volcanic islands, to the south Atlantic, where it is equidistant from the African and South American coasts. The ridge continues into the Indian Ocean, with a branch that reaches into the Gulf of Aden and the Red Sea, then passes between Australia and Antarctica and into the eastern South Pacific. The East Pacific Rise extends north to the Gulf of California; the Easter Islands and the Galápagos are volcanic islands that are part of this submarine mountain chain. The ridge system seems to merge into the continents in several areas, such

OCEAN AND OCEANOGRAPHY

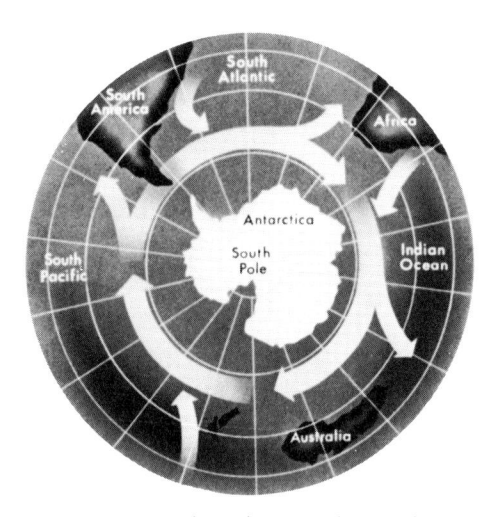

Diagram showing how the Antarctic gyre (current wheel) links all the oceans together.
By permission of Scholastic Magazines, Inc.

as the Red Sea and the Gulf of California, and such areas are regions of great geologic activity, characterized by volcanoes, or earthquakes and faults, such as the San Andreas falult in southern California; *see* FAULT.

The mid-ocean ridges are a key feature in the current ideas of ocean-floor spreading, for it is from these ridges that the ocean floor is thought to grow, at a rate of up to 4 or 5 cm per year. Volcanic material from within the earth is added to the crust as the ocean floors spread, but the reasons for this phenomenon are not fully known; it is not known yet whether internal forces are pulling the earth's crust apart or whether the ridges are pushing the crust apart. It appears, however, that in some regions of the world, the continents are moving apart as the ocean floors spread from the ridges. The shapes of the west African and South American coastlines are considered good evidence in favor of the continental drift theory. In other regions, the moving crust is being forced under the continents in regions known as trenches, which are great ocean depths most commonly found around the edge of the Pacific. Trenches are found adjacent to the Aleutian Islands, Japan, the Philippines, Tonga and Kermadec islands, and the west coast of South America. The trenches commonly reach depths of more than 7 km (4.34 mi.), the deepest known point is about 10.9 km (6.76 mi.), in the Mariana Trench, east of the Philippines. Trenches are also characterized by volcanic and seismic activity, indicative of motions and stresses within the earth's crust; *see* SEISMOLOGY.

The structure and topography of the ocean floor is studied through the use of sonar (q.v.) and seismic techniques. Depths are found by measuring the time for a sound wave to travel from the surface of the ocean to bottom, and to return; *see* SOUNDING. Often several returns are recorded, indicating several layers of sediment below the surface of the ocean floor. More ex-

The flow of surface currents around the ocean. These currents are caused by winds and are of great importance in navigation. By permission of Scholastic Magazines, Inc.

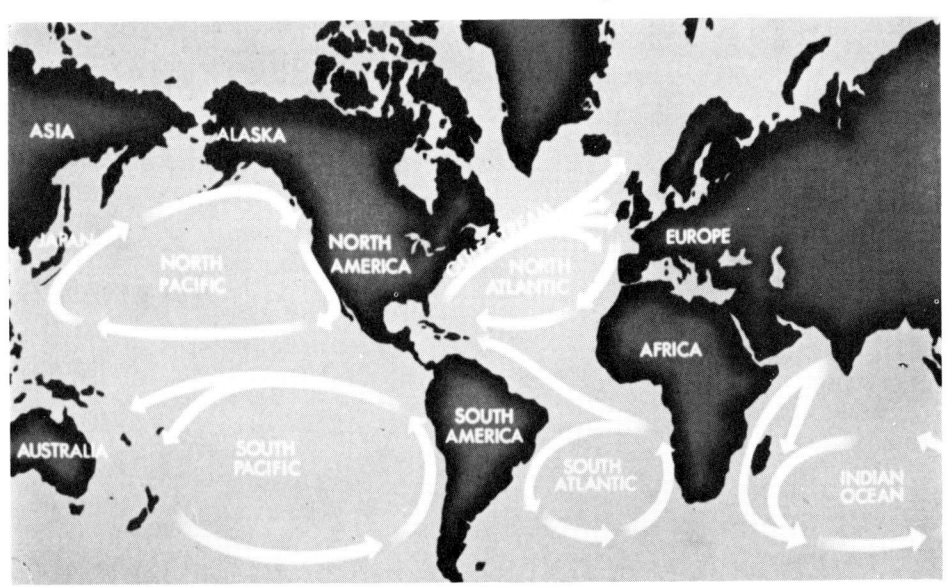

The Oceanographer *entering the harbor at Monaco during a 1967 global scientific expedition. The ship is one of the largest and most modern oceanographic research vessels ever constructed by the U.S.*
Environmental Science Services Admin.

tensive studies of the structure beneath the ocean floor are carried out by one ship firing an explosive in the water, and another recording the reception of sound waves on sensitive instruments. Some of the waves travel directly to the ship, others travel to the ocean floor, are refracted within the layers of sediment, and then travel to the other ship. The strength of the explosive and the distance between the ships determines the amount of detail of the sub-bottom structure made available, but in this way the thickness of the sediments can be determined and some conclusions drawn about the nature of the ocean bottom and its substructure. The ocean floor is covered by an average of ½ km of sediment, but the thickness varies up to about 7 km (4.34 mi.) in the Argentine Basin in the South Atlantic. Some regions, particularly the central parts of the mid-ocean ridges, have very little, if any, sediment on them; dredging in these areas has only brought up volcanic rocks.

The sediments themselves are studied by dredging and taking core samples of the ocean floor. Since 1968, deep-sea drilling (q.v.), conducted by the National Science Foundation research ship *Glomar Challenger*, has obtained entire sedimentary columns from the ocean floor in a large number of places; see DEEP-SEA EXPLORATION. These sediments have been found to consist of detrital and organic components, and their compositions vary with depth, distance from continents, and local factors such as submarine volcanoes, or high biological productivity. Clay minerals, being formed by the weathering of continental rocks and carried out to sea by rivers and wind, are abundant in the deep sea. Thick deposits of such detrital material often exist near mouths of rivers, and on continental shelves; fine particles of clay are spread through the ocean and accumulate slowly on the deep-ocean floor. Also accumulating in the sediments of many regions are the hard remains of small organisms such as the calcium carbonate shells of foraminifera (q.v.), and the siliceous shells of marine protozoans such as radiolaria, and diatomaceous algae; see DIATOMS; PROTOZOA. These microscopic shells of animals and plants, when found in the sediments, are extremely useful in determining the time of deposition of the sediment and the environment at the time the organism was living. Much is known about the ecology and evolution (qq.v.) of these organisms, and their samples are of great assistance for studying past climates. One of the great puzzles of earth science is that the oldest sediment obtained from the ocean, as determined by its paleontology (q.v.), or study of fossil life, is about 130,000,000 years

Oceanography. Plate 1. Two striking underwater studies. The sargassum fish (above) is a small, beautifully shaped and colored fish of genus Histrio. It follows masses of the brown algae, genus Sargassum, floating in the open sea, as in the Sargasso Sea in the North Atlantic. The marine crustacean (below), seen breaking apart floating microorganisms, called diatoms, is found in all oceans of the world.

Pictures Plates 1 and 2. Dr. Roman Vishniac

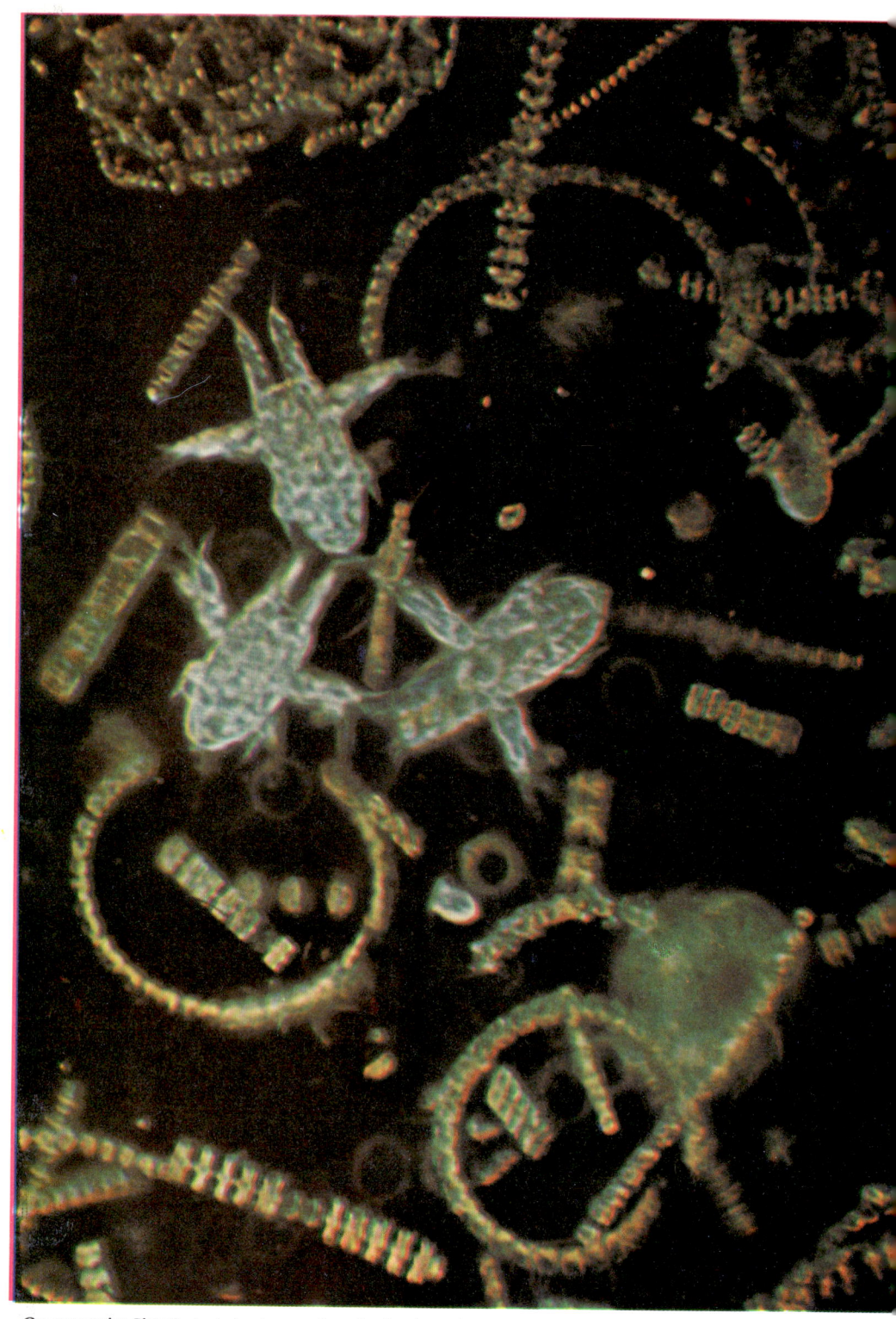

Oceanography. Plate 2. *A photomicrograph study of a drop of seawater reveals the variety of microscopic animal and plant life called plankton. Algae, bacteria, and diatoms that make up the plankton, are found drifting in the oceans of the world. A quart of seawater may contain as many as 1,000,000 such organisms.*

OCEAN AND OCEANOGRAPHY

old. Because the earth is generally estimated to be about 4,500,000,000 years old, the ocean basins as we know them today are comparatively young features of the earth's surface.

Composition of Seawater. Seawater is a dilute solution of several salts, and the salinity of seawater is expressed in terms of total dissolved salts in parts per thousand parts of water. Salinity varies from nearly zero in continental waters to about 44 parts per 1000 in the Red Sea, which is a region of high evaporation. In the main ocean salinity averages about 35 parts per 1000, varying between 34 and 36 parts per 1000. The major cations, or positive ions (see ION), present, and their approximate abundance per 1000 parts of water are: sodium, 10.5; magnesium, 1.3; calcium, 0.4; and potassium 0.4 parts. The major anions, or negative ions, are chloride, 19 parts per 1000, and sulfate, 2.6 parts. These ions constitute the major portion of the dissolved species in seawater, with bromide ions, bicarbonate, silica, various trace elements (q.v.), and inorganic and organic nutrients making up the remainder. The ratios of the major ions vary very little throughout the ocean and only their total concentration changes. The major nutrients, though not very abundant in comparison to the major ions, are extremely important in the biological productivity of the sea. Trace metals are of specific importance for certain organisms, but carbon, nitrogen, phosphorous, and oxygen are almost universally important to marine life. Carbon is found mainly as bicarbonate, HCO_3^-; nitrogen as nitrate, NO_3^-; and phosphorous as phosphate, $PO_4^=$.

The temperature (q.v.) of ocean water ranges from 26° to 27° C. in tropical surface water to as low as −1.4° C., the freezing point (q.v.) of seawater, in polar regions. Surface temperatures generally decrease with increasing latitude, with seasonal variations in temperature being less than about 7° to 8° C. Deep-water temperatures are generally between 2° and 5° C. In the upper 100 m, the water is as warm as at the surface; from 100 m to approximately 1000 m, the temperature drops rapidly to about 5° to 6° C., and below this the temperature gradually drops about another 4°. The region of rapid temperature change is known as the thermocline.

Ocean Currents. The surface currents of the ocean, as seen in Fig. 1, are characterized by large gyres, or currents that are kept in motion by prevailing winds (see WIND), but the direction of which is altered by the rotation of the earth; see CORIOLIS FORCE. The best known of these currents is probably the Gulf Stream (q.v.) in the North Atlantic; the Kuroshio Current (q.v.) in the North Pacific is a similar current, and both serve to warm the climates of the eastern edges of the two oceans. In regions where the prevailing winds blow offshore, such as the west coast of Mexico and the coast of Peru and Chile, surface waters move away from the continents and they are replaced by colder, deeper water, a process known as upwelling, from as much as 300 m down. This deep water is rich in nutrients and these regions have high biological productivity and provide excellent fishing. Deep water is rich in nutrients because decomposition of organic matter exceeds production in deeper water; plant growth occurs only where photosynthetic organisms have access to

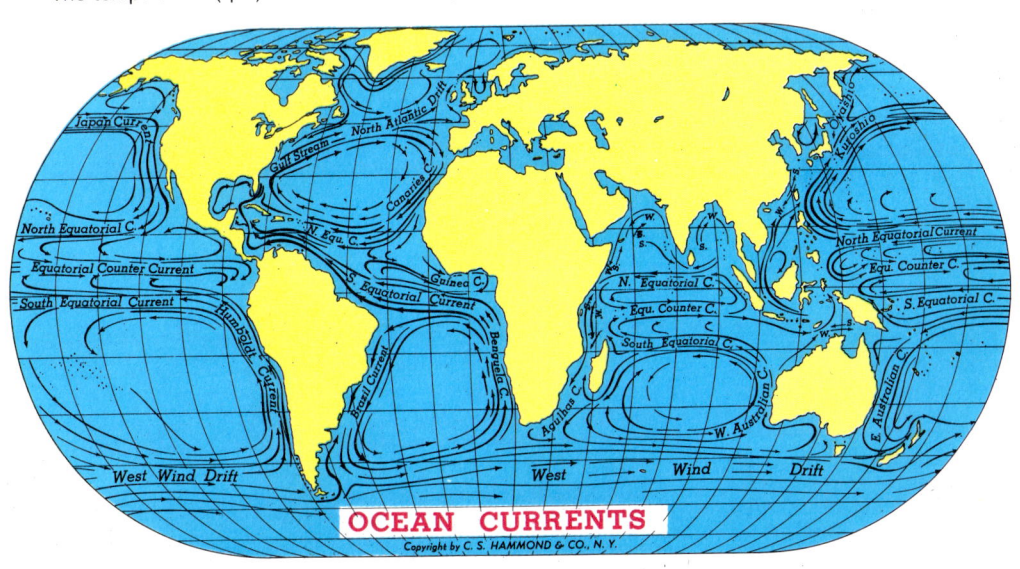

OCEAN CURRENTS
Copyright by C. S. HAMMOND & CO., N.Y.

OCEAN AND OCEANOGRAPHY

light; see PHOTOSYNTHESIS. When organisms die, their remains sink and are oxidized and consumed in the deeper water, thus returning the valuable nutrients to the cycle. The regions of high productivity are generally regions of strong vertical mixing in the upper regions of the ocean. In addition to the western edges of the continents, the entire region around Antarctica is one of high productivity because the surface water there sinks after being chilled, causing deeper water to replace it.

Although the surface circulation of the ocean is a function of winds and the rotation of the earth, the deeper circulation in the oceans is a function of density (q.v.) differences between adjacent water masses, and is known as thermohaline circulation. Salinity and temperature are the determinants of density, and any process which changes the salinity or temperature affects the density. Evaporation increases the salinity, hence the density, and causes the water to become heavier than the water around it, so it will sink. Cooling of seawater also increases its density. Because ice discriminates against sea salts, partial freezing increases the salinity of the remaining cold water, forming a mass of very dense water. This process is occurring in the Weddell Sea, off Antarctica, and is responsible for forming a large part of the deep water of the oceans. Water sinks in the Weddell Sea to form what is known as the Antarctic Bottom water, which flows gradually northward into the Atlantic and eastward into the Indian and Pacific oceans. In the North Atlantic, saline water cools and sinks to a moderate level to form the North Atlantic Deep water, which flows slowly southward; this water mass is less dense than the Antarctic Bottom water, and hence flows at less depth. Whereas speeds of surface currents can reach as high as 250 cm per sec., or 5.5 m.p.h., a maximum for the Gulf Stream, speeds of deep currents vary from 2 to 10 cm per sec., or less. Once a water mass sinks below the surface, it loses contact with the atmosphere (q.v.), and can no longer exchange gases with it. Oxygen, dissolved in the water, is used up in the oxidization of dead organic matter, and it is slowly depleted as the water mass remains below the surface. Thus, the oxygen content gives the oceanographer a qualitative idea of the "age" of the water mass, that is, the time it has been away from the surface. Radioactive carbon 14 (C^{14}) is produced in the atmosphere and enters the ocean in the form of carbon dioxide gas, which equilibrates, or keeps in balance, with the bicarbonate ion of seawater. Carbon 14 has a half-life (q.v.) of about 5700 years, and decays with time, so its activity in a deep-water mass is largely a measure of the time since that water mass was at the surface.

The general pattern of deep-ocean circulation that is apparent from these measurements is that the deep-water masses formed in the North Atlantic and off Antarctica mix and flow together through the Indian and Pacific oceans, and that the oldest water found is in the deep North Pacific, which has an age of up to 1500 years.

Resources. The oceans are being looked to as a major source of food for the future. It has been pointed out that there are regions of high productivity in the oceans, but there also exist larger regions of low productivity. Production is the amount of organic matter fixed, or changed into stable compounds, by photosynthetic organisms in a given unit of time. Estimates of the yearly world ocean production of organic matter, fixed from inorganic carbon and nutrients, amount to about 130,000,000,000 metric tons. This process begins with phytoplankton, which are photosynthetic plants that turn carbon into organic matter with the aid of sunlight; zooplankton and fish feed on phytoplankton, and each member of the chain has its own predator; see PLANKTON. Most of this organic matter is recycled and reused, so that the standing crop of organic material is only a small fraction of this

Oceanographers lowering a coring apparatus from the side of a research vessel. The apparatus is designed to take samples of the ocean bottom.
Lamont Geographical Observatory, Columbia University

Oceanography. Plate 3. The recent advances in orbital photography have made possible the development of spacecraft oceanography as a new phase of fishery science. This photograph of the southern tip of Florida and the Florida Keys (toward bottom of picture), taken by orbiting astronauts, assists in the study of pink-shrimp nursery grounds. The deep blue to the right of the Keys is the main flow of the warm Florida Current, flowing north from the Gulf of Mexico. Eddies from the current flow through the Keys, distributing shrimp larvae into shallow nursery waters.

U.S. Department of Agriculture

Oceanography. Plate 4. Two views of a typical underwater landscape in the warm tropical seas photographed by John F. Wehmiller of Columbia University. Left: In a small depression in a coral reef can be observed a large so-called brain coral, about 3 ft. across, with its surface covered by ridges and furrows. Also visible are several smaller heads of coral, a sponge, and a sandy floor. Below: The close-up photograph depicts a large sea-fan coral, about 3 ft. high, and several sponges.

annual total. The harvestable amount of organic matter is a function of technology, tastes, needs, and the ability of the system to sustain this harvest. Presently, yearly harvests amount to about 52,500,000 metric tons of fish, 1,500,000 metric tons of large whales, and about 700,000 metric tons of seaweed. Estimates of the maximum harvestable amounts on a sustained-yield basis amount to about 150,000,000 to 200,000,000 metric tons per year. Thus, predictions are that the sea can yield only about 3 to 4 times the present amount of organic food resources. The decline of the whaling industry in recent years is a strong case against rapid and unwise exploitation of oceanic food resources; see WHALING. Food from the sea will be a good source of protein (q.v.), but cannot meet the total world demand for calories in the future. The present yield of about 60,000,000 tons supplies about 60×10^{12} kilocalories, or about 2 percent of the calories needed by the present world population. These 60,000,000 tons yield about 12,000,000 tons of protein, which is nearly 30 percent of the needs of the world at the present time; see CALORIE; FOOD; NUTRITION.

The mineral resources of the sea have only recently begun to be known to man. The sea is so enormous that the supply of several valuable metals is abundant, but it is difficult, if not impossible, to extract these materials. The sea is estimated, for example, to contain 10,000,000,000 tons of gold, yet the concentration of the metal is so low that it is impossible to recover this resource. Today the major minerals being obtained from seawater are magnesium, bromine, and sodium chloride, or common salt. The ocean floor yields sand, gravel, and oyster shells for construction purposes, and small quantities of diamonds are found in some submarine gravel bars. Phosphorite is a phosphorous mineral known to be available on the sea floor, which has potential use as an agricultural fertilizer (q.v.). Much interest has been expressed recently in manganese nodules, which are spherical concretions on the sea floor containing about 20 percent manganese, 10 percent iron, 0.3 percent copper, 0.3 percent nickel, and 0.3 percent cobalt. These are all valuable minerals that have not been obtained yet to any great extent from the sea floor.

Offshore oil and gas wells are presently supplying about 17 percent of the world petroleum (q.v.) production. Most of these wells are in the shallow waters of the continental shelves, but deep-sea drilling techniques are expected to discover petroleum on the outer continental margins. Many of the geologic structures under the sea floor which are reservoirs for petroleum also contain significant sulfur (q.v.) deposits; this mineral is now being extracted from some of these deposits.

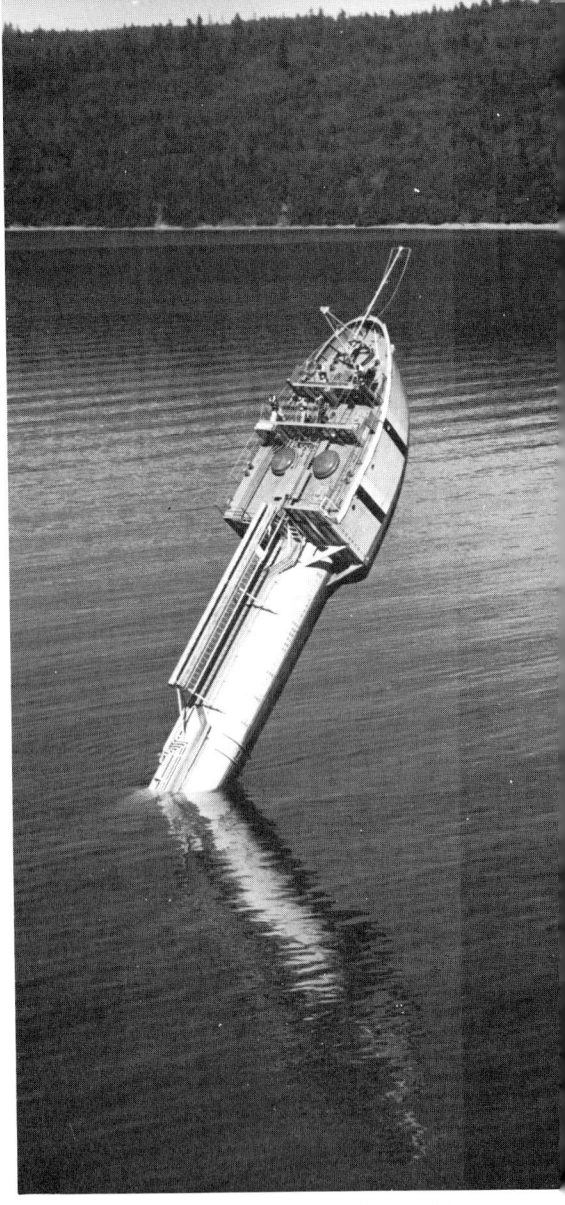

The "FLIP SHIP" or Floating Instrument Platform. Flip, when floated, turns up, like a bottle, as a 55-ft. instrument platform to study the ocean. The ship, 355-ft. long and weighing 600 tons, is a valuable tool to oceanographers. U.S. Navy

Pollution. The sea is expected to yield still larger quantities of valuable resources to man in the future. The water itself is being utilized on a small scale at present through desalinization, and as man has become more dependent on the resources of the sea, the concern for the preservation of the integrity of the ocean has grown

OCEAN GROVE

also. The contaminative effect of increasing technological development and industrialization has already been known to disrupt and destroy the fragile coastal ecology by indiscriminate discharge of industrial and municipal waste products into the sea. The pollution of the marine environment by petroleum and chemical spillage, sewage disposal into the oceans or into the streams leading into them, insecticides and pesticides in marine fish and birds, increasing levels of lead in the surface waters, and the disposal of hot water from power plants into the sea, with disastrous consequences for the marine life, have all helped to focus the attention of the international community on the need for controlled use of resources and planned disposal of waste products. *See also* Conservation; Water Pollution.

J.F.W. & E.B.S.

OCEAN GROVE, unincorporated community of New Jersey, in Monmouth County, part of Neptune Township, on the Atlantic Ocean, immediately s. of Asbury Park, from which it is separated by Wesley Lake. The community was founded in 1869 as a site for Methodist camp meetings. It is still a religious resort, with a 10,000-seat auditorium in which services are held. More than 40,000 people visit Ocean Grove during the summer, mainly to attend services. In accordance with an early law, the streets of Ocean Grove are chained on Sundays to prevent vehicular traffic. Pop. (permanent) about 5000.

OCEANIA, name sometimes used to designate the division of the globe comprising all the islands in the Pacific Ocean. The subdivisions of Oceania are Melanesia, Micronesia, and Polynesia (qq.v.), which are grouped together in accordance with the physical and cultural characteristics of the natives, and the Malay Archipelago (q.v.). Australia and New Zealand are occasionally included.

OCEANIA, FRENCH. *See* Polynesia, French.

OCEAN ISLAND, formerly BANABA, island in the Pacific Ocean, one of the Gilbert and Ellice Islands (q.v.), a British colony, near the equator, between the Gilbert Islands and Nauru. Ocean Island is the only island in the colony that is not a coral atoll. It contains rich deposits of high-grade phosphate that have been worked since about 1920. Ocean Island was discovered in 1804 and annexed to the Gilbert and Ellice Islands in 1900. It was the administrative center of the colony before World War II. During the war the Banabans, a people indigenous to the island, were removed to a Japanese labor camp on another island. After the war the Banabans were persuaded by the British to relocate to one of the Fiji Islands, and were given mining royalties. In 1969, however, the Banabans were agitating for their return to Ocean Island. Area, 2 sq.mi.; pop. (1968) 2192.

OCEANSIDE, city of California, in San Diego Co., on the Pacific Ocean, at the mouth of the San Luis Rey R., 35 miles N. of San Diego. A beach resort, it is in an area producing limes and other citrus fruits, avocados, and truck-farm products. Radios, machine products, and ice are manufactured. Oceanside is the site of Mira Costa College (1934; junior college). The restored San Luis Rey Mission (1798) is 4 miles to the N.E. and Palomar Observatory is nearby. Founded in 1883, the city was incorporated in 1888. Pop. (1960) 24,971; (1970) 40,494.

OCEANSIDE, unincorporated community of New York, in Nassau Co., on Long Island, part of the town of Hempstead, about 20 miles S.E. of central New York City. The community manufactures chemicals, machine products, industrial equipment, electrical devices, and paper products. Oceanside was settled in 1758 and called Christian Hook. The name was changed to Oceanville in 1864 and to Oceanside in 1889. Pop. (1960) 30,488; (1970) 35,028.

OCEANUS, in Greek mythology, one of the Titans (q.v.), the son of Uranus, and Gaea (qq.v.). Together with his wife the Titaness Tethys (q.v.) he ruled over Ocean, a great river encircling the earth, which was believed to be a flat circle. The nymphs of this great river, the Oceanids, were their daughters, and the gods of all the streams on earth were their sons. In later legends, when Zeus, chief of the Olympian gods, and his brothers Poseidon and Hades (qq.v.) overthrew the Titans and assumed their power, Poseidon and his wife Amphitrite (q.v.) succeeded Oceanus and Tethys as rulers of the waters; *see also* Olympus.

OCELOT, *or* TIGER CAT, *or* SPOTTED CAT, *or* LEOPARD CAT, wild carnivorous mammal, *Felis*

Ocelot, Felis pardalis   New York Zoological Society

pardalis, of the Cat family, found from Texas to Peru. The ocelot, which resembles the domestic cat in form, attains a length of about 3 ft. The back of the animal is tinted with olive tan or chestnut, marked with stripes and spots of black. The belly is usually white, marked with black. Ocelots inhabit forests, and are expert at climbing trees. At night they search for their food, which consists of birds and small mammals. Two kittens are normally produced in a litter.

OCHOA, Severo (1905–), Spanish-American biochemist, born in Luarca, Spain, and educated at the University of Madrid. After graduate work in Glasgow, Berlin, and Heidelberg, he taught at the universities of Madrid, Heidelberg, and Oxford. In 1940 he settled in the United States, becoming a citizen in 1956. Ochoa joined the faculty of the College of Medicine of New York University in 1942 and in 1954 he was named chairman of the department of biochemistry. Ochoa shared the 1959 Nobel Prize in medicine and physiology with the American biochemist Arthur Kornberg (q.v.) for their independent research on ribonucleic acid (RNA) and deoxyribonucleic acid (DNA), substances that exist in the nuclei of all living cells and control heredity. Ochoa had synthesized RNA in 1955. *See* NUCLEIC ACIDS.

OCHS, Adolph Simon (1858–1935), American newspaper publisher, born in Cincinnati, Ohio, and educated in the primary schools of Knoxville, Tenn. He was a newsboy and printer's apprentice (1869–73), a compositor (1873–77), and in 1877 became a staff member of the Chattanooga *Dispatch* and then its editor in chief. The following year he became publisher of the Chattanooga *Times*, which he made one of the outstanding newspapers of the South. In 1896 Ochs gained control of the forty-five year old New York *Times*, then bankrupt. As its publisher he followed a policy of thorough, nonpartisan, and unsensational coverage of news, in contrast to the "yellow journalism" prevailing at the time, and by his journalistic method developed the New York *Times* into one of the leading newspapers in the world. He also was responsible for introducing rotogravure printing of newspaper photographs to journalism. From 1902 to 1912 he was the owner of the Philadelphia *Times* and the Philadelphia *Public Ledger*; he consolidated the two newspapers, retaining the latter name, and in 1913 sold the newspaper to American publisher Cyrus Hermann Kotzchmar Curtis (q.v.). Ochs involved himself in various philanthropic enterprises and he underwrote (1925) the publication of *Dictionary of American Biography* (20 vol., 1928–37), with a contribution of $500,000. He was a member of the executive committee and a director of the Associated Press news agency from 1900 until his death. *See* NEWSPAPERS.

OCKHAM, William of *or* **OCCAM, William of,** known as DOCTOR INVINCIBILIS (Lat., "unconquerable doctor") and VENERABILIS INCEPTOR (Lat., "worthy initiator") (1285?–1349?), English philosopher and Scholastic theologian, born in Ockham, Surrey, England. He entered the Franciscan order and studied and taught at the University of Oxford from 1309 to 1319. Denounced by Pope John XXII (*see under* JOHN) for dangerous teachings, he was held in house detention for four years (1324–28) at the papal palace in Avignon, France, while the orthodoxy of his writings was being examined. Siding with the Franciscan general against the Pope in a dispute over Franciscan poverty (*see* FRATICELLI), Ockham fled to Munich in 1328 to seek the protection of Louis IV (q.v.), Holy Roman Emperor, who had rejected papal authority over political matters. Excommunicated by the pope, Ockham wrote against the papacy and defended the emperor until the latter's death in 1347. The philosopher died of the plague while seeking reconciliation with Pope Clement VI (r. 1342–52). Ockham won fame as a rigorous logician who applied logic to show that many truths held by Christian philosophers (for example, God is one, omnipotent, Creator of all things; and the human soul is immortal) could not be proved by philosophical or natural reason but only by divine revelation. His name is applied to the principle of economy in formal logic, which is known as Ockham's razor. He founded the Nominalist (q.v.) school, which became the leading rival of the Thomistic and Scotistic schools. *See* SCHOLASTICISM. W.N.C.

OCMULGEE NATIONAL MONUMENT, region of historic interest in Georgia, adjoining the city of Macon, preserving some of the most important prehistoric remains of the Mound Builders (q.v.) in the Southeast. Within the area are the remains of many centuries of Indian occupation, representing settlements of successive tribes of Indians believed to have lived there as far back as 8000 B.C. Earthwork fortifications are found there as well as burial and ceremonial mounds. A museum in the area contains relics including bones, tools, weapons and other artifacts. The monument, covering 683.48 acres, was established in 1936. It is administered by the National Park Service (q.v.).

O'CONNELL, Daniel (1775–1847), Irish national leader, called "the Liberator", born near

Cahirciveen, County Kerry, and educated in France. He returned to Ireland, studied law, and was admitted to the bar in Dublin in 1798. He soon gained a reputation as a leading constitutional and criminal lawyer. At the same time his interest in the Irish national problem led him to begin a career of political activity. O'Connell led a group of lawyers in reviving (1805) the Irish Catholic Committee, which grew into a strong movement containing almost all Catholic Irishmen including the priesthood. Operating solely within constitutional limits, by 1813, the committee succeeded in making the British Parliament agree to seat Irish Catholics if the Church would give Parliament the right to veto the choice of Catholic bishops. When O'Connell opposed this compromise, his movement lost momentum and collapsed. He revived it in 1823 by organizing the Catholic Association, which was run on a democratic basis. Elected to Parliament in 1828 from County Clare, O'Connell refused to serve until the anti-Catholic oath had been repealed. This refusal stimulated such formidable agitation that the Catholic Emancipation Act (q.v.) was passed the following year, abolishing all obstacles to Catholic representation in Parliament. O'Connell was reelected, and he entered the House of Commons for County Clare in 1829, retaining his seat until his death. In England, O'Connell helped to pass the Reform Bill of 1832 and often allied himself with the Whig Party (q.v.) in Parliament; see REFORM BILLS.

As head of the Catholic Association, O'Connell received a large yearly income from voluntary contributions by the Irish people, who supported him in a series of demonstrations in favor of Irish home rule. In 1841 O'Connell became the first Catholic lord mayor of Dublin to hold that office since the reign of James II (q.v.), King of England. Beginning in that year, meetings were held throughout the country to extend the home-rule movement. The movement assumed such huge proportions that O'Connell and several other leaders were arrested in 1843 and convicted of seditious conspiracy in 1844. O'Connell's conviction was subsequently reversed by the House of Lords, and he resumed his career. At this time a great famine descended upon Ireland, and younger elements in O'Connell's party began to advocate revolutionary doctrines which he had always opposed. Their arguments in favor of violent opposition to British rule led to an open split in Irish ranks in 1846. O'Connell, distressed by this disaffection and in ill health, moved to Genoa, Italy, where he died. See also IRELAND: History.

O'CONNELL, William Henry Cardinal (1859–1944), American prelate, born in Lowell, Mass. He was educated at Boston College and at the North American College in Rome, where he was appointed rector in 1895. In 1901 he was consecrated bishop of Portland, Maine. In 1905 O'Connell was sent as papal envoy to the ruler of Japan. The following year he was made coadjutor to the archbishop of Boston. In 1907 he succeeded to the archiepiscopal see of Boston and in 1911 was created cardinal.

O'CONNOR, Thomas Power, called TAY PAY (1848–1929), Irish journalist and nationalist leader, born in Athlone, County Westmeath, and educated at Queen's College, Galway. While working as a free-lance newspaperman, O'Connor wrote *Life of Lord Beaconsfield* (1876), an acrid biography of the British statesman Benjamin Disraeli, 1st Earl of Beaconsfield (*see under* DISRAELI). In 1880 he was elected to the British Parliament and there supported the nationalist leader Charles Stewart Parnell (q.v.). O'Connor's long, unbroken tenure in Parliament secured him the popular title, "Father of the House of Commons". He became president of the Irish Nationalist League in 1883 and made the first of several tours to the United States in 1881 to raise funds for support of the nationalist movement. O'Connor founded several radical Irish newspapers, including the *Star* and the *Sun*, and a literary publication, *T.P.'s Weekly* (1902). He wrote many articles, short stories, and two longer works, *The Parnell Movement* (1886) and *Memoirs of an Old Parliamentarian* (1929).

OCTANE NUMBER. See GASOLINE.

OCTAVE, in music, interval consisting of eight notes embracing eight diatonic intervals; see INTERVAL; SCALE. It is the interval common to all scales in the history of Western music. The term octave is also applied to the eighth note of the scale. This meaning was introduced about 550 B.C. by the Greek mathematician and philosopher Pythagoras (q.v.), who discovered the octave to be that tone (q.v.) that is produced by twice the vibration frequency of the first note of the scale. The frequency ratio of the octave to the tonic or key note is thus 2:1. See also MUSIC.

OCTAVIA (d. 11 B.C.), Roman matron, daughter of the Roman general Gaius Octavius (d. 59 B.C.), grandniece of the Roman general Gaius Julius Caesar (q.v.), and sister of Octavian, later the Roman emperor Augustus (q.v.). Octavia was distinguished for her beauty and her virtue. In 40 B.C., upon the death of her first husband, the consul Gaius Claudius Marcellus (fl. 1st cent. B.C.), she consented to marry the Roman soldier Mark Antony (*see* ANTONIUS, MARCUS), to make secure the reconciliation between him and her brother. When Antony deserted her for the Egyptian queen Cleopatra (see under CLEOPATRA), Octavia remained loyal to her husband, even aiding him with reinforcements on occasion. Octavian was indignant at the treatment she received and wished her to leave her husband's house. When war broke out between Octavian and Antony in 32 B.C., the latter crowned his insults by sending Octavia a notice of divorce. After Mark Antony's death in 30 B.C., Octavia brought up not only her own children but also Antony's children by his first wife Fulvia (d. 40 B.C.) and by Cleopatra. Octavia herself had five children: two daughters by Antony, and a son and two daughters by her first husband. Her son, Marcus Claudius Marcellus (43–23 B.C.), was adopted by Augustus and apparently intended to succeed the latter as emperor, but died at the age of twenty. Among the descendants of Octavia's two daughters, Antonia Major (fl. 1st cent. A.D.) and Antonia Minor (36 B.C.–37 A.D.), were four rulers of the Roman Empire: the empress Livia Drusilla (56 B.C.–29 A.D.) and the emperors Claudius I, Nero, and Caligula (qq.v.).

See also ROME, HISTORY OF: *Internal Conflict.*

OCTAVIA (42?–62 A.D.), Roman Empress, the daughter of the Roman emperor Claudius (q.v.) and his third wife Valeria Messalina (d. 48 A.D.). In 53 Octavia married emperor Nero (q.v.), who later deserted her at the request of his mistress Poppaea Sabina (d. 65 A.D.). Through the jealousy of Poppaea, whom Nero had married, a charge of adultery was brought against Octavia; she was sent to the island of Pandataria and there killed. She is the heroine of a Roman historical play that has been attributed to Roman statesman and dramatist Lucius Annaeus Seneca (see under SENECA).

OCTAVIAN. See AUGUSTUS.

OCTOBER, tenth month of the Gregorian calendar (q.v.), containing thirty-one days. October was the eighth month of the ancient Roman calendar as evidenced by the name October (Lat. *octo,* eight). Columbus Day occurs on October 12 and is observed as a holiday in most States and territories of the United States. Halloween occurs on Oct. 31 and is observed in the U.S. and other countries with masquerading, bonfires, and games.

OCTOPUS, or DEVILFISH, or POULP, or POLYPUS, common name for any of the eight-armed, dibranchiate, cephalopod mollusks (see MOLLUSCA) constituting the order Octopoda, especially those in the genus *Octopus.* The octopus has a large, soft, elliptical body containing a pair of huge eyes with oblong pupils, and a large,

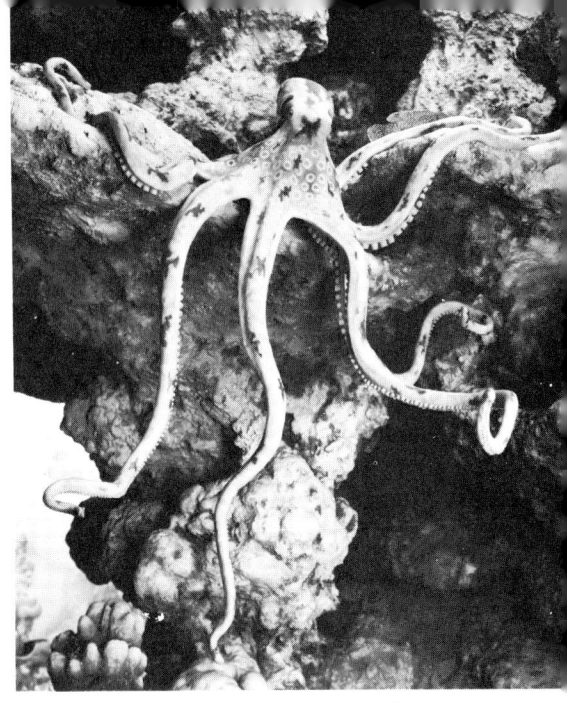

Octopus of the family Octopodidae. Sucker disks are on the underside of its tentacles.
American Museum of Natural History

horny beak. The body is attached to a membranous foot, from which the arms radiate. The creature spends most of its life in caves or crevices among the rocks or coral (q.v.) deposits of the ocean bottom, creeping over the bottom by means of two rows of suckers on each arm. The octopus also uses its suckers to grasp its prey, which consists chiefly of crabs; see CRAB. The octopus occasionally leaves its lair at night, propelling itself backward through the water by means of water that it ejects through the swimming funnel or siphon, a tube opening into and through the foot from the body. Like the squid and the cuttlefish (qq.v.), the octopus is capable of ejecting a murky fluid, commonly called "ink", through its siphon to darken the water about it, screening it from enemies. Contrary to popular belief, most octopuses are small creatures, less than 1 ft. in diameter from the tip of one arm to the tip of the opposite arm. Several species, however, are larger; *O. vulgaris,* of the Mediterranean Sea and the European Atlantic coast, attains a diameter of about 7 ft., and *O. punctatus,* of the American Pacific coast, attains a diameter of about 14 ft. Large octopuses are used as food by the peoples of the Mediterranean and Pacific regions. See CEPHALOPODA.

ODD FELLOWS, INDEPENDENT ORDER OF, secret, fraternal benefit society, organized in Great Britain in the 18th century, and introduced into the United States in 1819. *See* FRATER-

ODE

NAL ORDERS. The exact origin of the order is not known. A number of Odd Fellows lodges existed in Great Britain in 1780; these were united as the Patriotic Order shortly thereafter. The Patriotic Order eventually became the Independent Order of Odd Fellows, Manchester Unity, and the principal British fraternal order.

The first Odd Fellows lodge in the U.S. stemming from the Manchester group was Washington Lodge No. 1, established in Baltimore, Md., April 26, 1819. Another lodge was formed in Boston, Mass., in 1820, and a third in Philadelphia, Pa., in 1821. The Grand Lodge of the United States was established in Baltimore, Feb. 22, 1821, and served as the governing body for lodges in New York, Pennsylvania, Massachusetts, and Maryland. The Grand Lodge was chartered by the Manchester Unity in 1826 and maintained its affiliation until 1842, when it separated from the British organization and became the Independent Order of Odd Fellows. Until 1852, membership in the American order was restricted to men, but in that year the Rebekah degree of membership, open to both sexes, was established. In the latter half of the 19th century the American order established branches in all the States of the U.S. and in many foreign countries.

Originally, the main object of the Odd Fellows in the U.S. was "to relieve the brethren, bury the dead, and care for the widow and the orphan". Gradually, their purposes have been broadened to include the "elevation of the character of man" as a religious person with a belief in God (as a supreme power) and the principles of friendship, love, and truth. The order maintains homes for the aged, the poor, and for widows and orphans in several States, and provides its members with financial aid in cases of sickness or death. National headquarters is in Baltimore, Md. In 1971 the total membership of the order was about 1,384,000.

ODE, originally, poem arranged to be sung to the accompaniment of a musical instrument, such as the lyre (q.v.). Among the ancient Greeks, lyric odes fell into two broad categories, those to be sung by a single voice and those to be sung by a group, or choir. The simpler form of the Greek ode, for a single voice, was cultivated by Sappho, Alcaeus, Anacreon, and other early poets who wrote in the Aeolic or Ionic dialect of the Greek language (q.v.). The choral ode, composed to be sung by a group, was invented by the Greek people known as the Dorians (q.v.); see CHORUS. An important innovation was produced by Alcman of Sparta when he divided the chorus into two parts, one called the strophe, or turn, and the other known as the antistrophe, or counterturn; the two groups of performers turn, respectively and successively, to the right and to the left, the one group turning to face and answer the other. Stesichorus of Sicily added a third part called the epode, or aftersong, which was sung by the entire chorus after their movements to the right and to the left. The choral ode, consisting of the strophe, the antistrophe, and the epode, was adapted by Simonides of Ceos to the warlike Dorian music. He was followed by Pindar, the greatest lyric poet of Greece. Extant portions of Pindar's work include, besides several fragments, forty-five epinician or victory odes, composed for the victors at the four great Panhellenic festivals, the Olympian, Pythian, Isthmian, and Nemean games. The poems of Bacchylides, which were discovered on papyri in 1896, include thirteen epinician odes and six dithyrambs, or odes connected originally with the worship of Dionysus (q.v.), god of nature and of wine. Each ode of Pindar and Bacchylides has its own complicated metrical structure corresponding to its music. The simpler Greek measures of the odes for a single voice were imitated by the Roman lyric poets Gaius Valerius Catullus and Horace, who used the ode as a purely literary form which, if read aloud, was declaimed rather than sung. Horace modeled his odes on those of Alcaeus particularly, and Catullus was influenced by Sappho. The Romans made no attempt to imitate the elaborate measures of the odes of Pindar and Bacchylides.

The modern ode, dating from the Renaissance (q.v.), is written as pure poetry, without musical accompaniment; it is exalted in tone, more impersonal than the ordinary lyric, and it deals progressively with a single dignified theme. The earliest English odes are the *Epithalamion* and the *Prothalamion* of Edmund Spenser. Among other English writers of odes are Ben Jonson, Richard Crashaw, John Milton, Abraham Cowley, Andrew Marvell, John Dryden, William Collins, and Thomas Gray. Cowley sought to imitate the structure and content of the Pindaric ode; he failed to understand the fundamental division into strophe, antistrophe, and epode, but he impressed his conception of the ode as a lofty and tempestuous composition on later English literature. Gray had a better understanding of Pindaric structure; he divided his *Progress of Poesy* into three stanzas, each stanza being subdivided into strophe, antistrophe, and epode. The English ode, however, as usually composed, is merely a succession of stanzas in lines of varying length and meter. Of musical settings for odes the most famous are the twenty-eight by Henry Purcell and the four by George Frederick Handel.

Among the great English odes of the 19th century are William Wordsworth's *To Duty* and *Intimations of Immortality;* Samuel Taylor Coleridge's *To France;* Percy Bysshe Shelley's *To the West Wind, To Liberty, To Naples,* and *To a Skylark;* John Keats' *To a Nightingale, To Autumn,* and *On a Grecian Urn;* Alfred, Lord Tennyson's *On the Death of the Duke of Wellington;* and Algernon Charles Swinburne's *To Victor Hugo.* Among American odes is James Russell Lowell's *Commemoration Ode,* Allen Tate's *Ode to the Confederate Dead.*

See individual articles on the poets mentioned in this article.

ODENSE, city and port in Denmark, and capital of Odense Administrative Division, on the island of Fyn, about 85 miles S.W. of Copenhagen. The third largest city in Denmark, Odense is a major commercial and transportation center, linked by a deepwater canal with Odense Fjord. Principal industries include machinery, metal products, glass, processed foods, and textiles. The city, which dates from the 10th century, contains the Cathedral of Saint Canute, built in the 13th century, the best example of Gothic architecture in Denmark. The Church of Our Lady was constructed in the 12th century. Odense is the birthplace of Danish writer Hans Christian Andersen (q.v.). Pop. (1965) 107,531.

ODER, one of the principal rivers of eastern and central Europe. It rises 10 miles N.E. of Olomouc, Czechoslovakia, and flows generally N.E. into Poland, where it is the second-longest river. The Oder continues generally N. past Raciborz, Opole, Wrocław, and Kostrzyn into the Baltic Sea at Szczecin. The river is 563 mi. long and navigable from Raciborz. It is connected by canal with the Spree, Havel, and Elbe rivers in East Germany.

Before World War II the Oder flowed through German territory; with the defeat of Germany in 1945 a provisional German-Polish border was set along a line formed by the Oder and Neisse rivers. The government of West Germany delayed recognizing the new border and the subsequent loss of about 40,000 sq.mi. of land until 1970. See GERMANY: *History;* POLAND: *History.*

ODESSA, city in Texas, and county seat of Ector Co., 160 miles S.W. of Abilene. An oil and livestock center, it is the principal communications hub of a large area. Major oil fields lie to the S.; industries include oil and gas refining, and the manufacture of petrochemicals and oilfield equipment. The city is the site of Odessa College (1946; junior college) and the Ector County Coliseum. Founded in 1881, Odessa was settled by Russo-Germans in 1886 and incorporated in 1927. The oil boom began in 1929. Pop. (1960) 80,338; (1970) 78,380.

ODESSA, city and port of the Soviet Union, in the Ukranian S.S.R., and capital of Odessa Oblast, on the Black Sea, 275 miles S. of Kiev. Major industries include automobile assembly, petroleum refining, food processing, and the production of heavy machinery, chemicals, and clothing. The city is a cultural as well as an industrial center; institutes of higher learning include a university, polytechnic and medical schools, a marine academy, and a conservatory of music. Odessa is one of the chief ports of the U.S.S.R. and the largest Ukrainian resort. The city descends in terraces from a high central plateau to the sea; it is laid out in tree-lined rectangles.

Odessa was the site of an ancient Greek settlement that had ceased to exist by the 4th century A.D. No further effort was made to exploit the site until the 14th century, when a Tatar chief built a fort there. Ottoman Turks captured it in the 16th century, and in 1795 the town, which had developed around the fort, was taken by the Russians, who built a port and naval base there. During the Crimean War (q.v.) Odessa was bombarded by combined French and British naval forces. In 1876–77 it successfully fought off a Turkish attack. Odessa was the site of a workers' revolution in 1905, supported by the crew of the Russian battleship *Potemkin.* During World War II, Odessa was captured by the Germans on Oct. 16, 1941, after two months of heroic resistance, and retaken by the Soviet army on April 10, 1944. Pop. (1970) 892,000.

ODETS, Clifford (1906–63), American playwright, born in Philadelphia, Pa., and reared in New York City. He left school at the age of fifteen to become an actor. He later participated in Theatre Guild productions and in 1931 was one of the founders of the Group Theatre in New York City. Most of his plays were produced by the Group Theatre, including *Waiting for Lefty* (1935, a one-act play which established his fame), *Awake And Sing* (1935), and *Till the Day I Die* (1935). After the unsuccessful production of his *Paradise Lost* (1935), Odets went to Hollywood, Calif., where he wrote the motion-picture scenario of *The General Died at Dawn* (1936). Returning to New York after two years, he wrote more plays for the Group Theatre, including *Golden Boy* (1937), *Silent Partner* (1938), *Rocket to the Moon* (1938), *Night Music* (1940), and *Clash by Night* (1941), all concerned with the frustration of individual potentialities by

ODIN

Clifford Odets

economic insecurity and the materialistic ideals of middle-class society. Odets subsequently spent several years in Hollywood and wrote many motion-picture scenarios, including *None But the Lonely Heart* (1943) and *The Story on Page One* (1959). He also wrote the plays *The Big Knife* (1949) and *The Country Girl* (1950).

ODIN (ON. *Odhinn,* AS. *Woden,* OHG. *Wōdan, Woutan*), in Norse mythology, king of the gods. His two black ravens, Huginn (Thought) and Muninn (Memory), flew forth daily to gather tidings of all that was being done throughout the world. As god of war, Odin held court in Valhalla (q.v.), where all brave warriors went after death in battle. His greatest treasures were his eight-footed steed Sleipner, his spear Gungner, and his ring Draupner. Odin was also the god of wisdom, poetry, and magic, and he sacrificed an eye for the privilege of drinking from Mimir, the fountain of wisdom. Odin's three wives were earth goddesses, and his eldest son was Thor (q.v.), the god of thunder.

ODONTOLITE. See IVORY.

ODYSSEUS. See ULYSSES.

ODYSSEY, epic poem by the ancient Greek poet Homer (q.v.), recounting the wanderings of the Greek hero Odysseus (*see* ULYSSES) at the close of the Trojan War (q.v.). Like Homer's *Iliad* (q.v.), the *Odyssey* is regarded as one of the greatest literary works ever produced. Particularly noteworthy in the *Odyssey* are the majesty of language, the descriptions of Odysseus' desperate efforts to return to his home in Ithaca, and the detailed delineation of the hero's character.

The Homeric narrative begins with the victorious Greeks setting sail for their homes after sacking Troy. For nine days Odysseus' ships are driven by a storm, but on the tenth day they reach the land of the Lotus-eaters in Africa, where some of the companions of Odysseus eat fruit of the lotus (q.v.) and wish to remain in the land forever. Their leader compels them to leave, however, and sailing north again, they reach the land of the Cyclopes (*see* CYCLOPS), where they are captured by the one-eyed giant Polyphemus (q.v.). Odysseus blinds the giant and escapes to the island of Aeolus (q.v.), ruler of the winds, who gives him a favorable breeze and binds the remaining unfavorable winds in a bag. Odysseus' companions, in search of treasure, open the bag. At once the ships are swept back to the island, from which Odysseus and his crew are now sternly excluded. They reach the land of the Laestrygons, a race of cannibals, who destroy all the ships except one, in which Odysseus escapes. The hero next lands on the island of Aeaea, the home of the sorceress Circe (q.v.). With the help of the god Hermes (q.v.), Odysseus escapes her enchantments and is hospitably entertained. After a year he departs and with directions from Circe goes to the entrance of the underworld to receive the prophecy of his future from the seer Teiresias (q.v.). Teiresias discloses to Odysseus the implacable enmity of Poseidon, whose son, Polyphemus, Odysseus had blinded, but assures him that he will reach Ithaca in safety if he does not meddle with the herds of the sun-god Helios (q.v.).

Odysseus passes the perilous island of the Sirens (q.v.) in safety, but when he sails between the monsters Scylla and Charybdis (*see* SCYLLA AND CHARYBDIS), Scylla devours six of his companions. He next comes to the island of Helios, where his crew, in spite of Teiresias' warning, kills some of the cattle of the sun-god. Helios immediately seeks vengeance. The ship is struck by a thunderbolt and all the crew is drowned except Odysseus, who clings to the mast and is finally washed ashore on the island of Ogygie, the abode of the nymph Calypso (q.v.). Calypso holds Odysseus captive for seven years. Although she offers him immortality if he will remain with her, his love for his wife Penelope and his son Telemachus (qq.v.) and his longing for home are too deep. At the entreaty of his special guardian, the goddess Athena, (q.v.), Zeus sends Hermes, messenger of the gods, to command his release. Sailing eastward on a raft that he built on Ogygie, Odysseus is seen by the implacable Poseidon, who rouses against him a terrible storm that wrecks his raft. With the aid of the goddess Ino, Odysseus safely reaches the land of the Phaeacians. Naked and worn by fatigue, he falls asleep, but is found by the princess Nausicaä (q.v.); she receives him kindly and brings him to the city. Entering the palace under Athena's protection, he is entertained by the king, who promises him safe convoy to his home. Aboard ship he falls asleep. When he reaches Ithaca he is placed on shore with the rich presents of the Phaeacians while still unconscious.

Disguised as a beggar, he goes to the hut of the swineherd Eumaeus, and there meets and reveals himself to his son Telemachus. The next day he is brought by Eumaeus to the palace, where he is recognized only by his old dog Argos and is harshly treated by his wife's suitors, who during his long absence have been living riotously on his estate. After an interview with the unsuspecting Penelope, to whom he foretells her husband's return, he is recognized by his old nurse, Euryclea, whom he swears to silence. The next day all the suitors fail to string the great bow of Odysseus, a task designed for them by Penelope. The hero, still disguised as a beggar, takes the bow, easily strings it, and shoots an arrow through a row of twelve rings. After this feat he slays all the suitors. The *Odyssey* ends with his reconciliation with Penelope.

The story of the *Odyssey* has served as a model for many literary works, most notably in the novel *Ulysses* (1922) by the Irish novelist and poet James Joyce (q.v.).

OEDIPUS, in Greek mythology, King of Thebes, the son of Laius and Jocasta (qq.v.), King and Queen of Thebes. Laius was warned by an oracle that he would be killed by his own son. Determined to avert this fate, he bound together the feet of his newborn child and left him to die on a lonely mountain. The infant was rescued by a shepherd, however, and given to Polybus, King of Corinth, who named the child Oedipus ("Swollen-foot") and raised him as his own child. The boy did not know that he was adopted, and when an oracle proclaimed that he would kill his father he left Corinth. In the course of his wanderings he met and killed Laius, believing that the king and his followers were a band of robbers, and thus unwittingly fulfilled the prophecy.

Lonely and homeless, Oedipus arrived at Thebes, which was beset by a dreadful monster called the Sphinx (q.v.). The frightful creature frequented the roads to the city, killing and devouring all travelers who could not answer a riddle that she put to them. When Oedipus successfully solved her riddle, the Sphinx killed herself. Believing that King Laius had been slain by unknown robbers, and grateful to Oedipus for ridding them of the Sphinx, the Thebans rewarded Oedipus by making him their king and giving him Queen Jocasta as his wife. For many years the couple lived in happiness, not knowing that they were really mother and son. Then a terrible plague descended on the land and the oracle proclaimed that Laius' murderer must be punished. Oedipus soon discovered that he had unknowingly killed his father. In grief and despair at her incestuous life, Jocasta killed herself and when Oedipus realized that she was dead and that their children were accursed, he put out his eyes and resigned the throne. He lived in Thebes for several years, but was finally banished. Accompanied by his daughter Antigone (q.v.) he wandered for many years. He finally arrived at Colonus, a shrine near Athens sacred to the powerful goddesses called the Eumenides (q.v.). At this shrine for supplicants Oedipus died, after the god Apollo (q.v.) had promised him that the place of his death would remain sacred and would bring great benefit to the city of Athens, which had given shelter to the wanderer.

OEDIPUS COMPLEX. See PSYCHOANALYSIS: *Theory of Psychoanalysis: Instinctual Drives.*

OEHLENSCHLÄGER, Adam Gottlob (1779–1850), Danish poet and dramatist, born in Vesterbro, Copenhagen. After unsuccessful attempts at a career first in business and then as a comic actor, he turned to literature in 1802. His poetry and dramatic works were influenced by those of the Romantic movement in Germany and by the Old Norse sagas. His first published volume of verse was *Digte* (1803), and within the next two years he established a national reputation. He traveled throughout Europe from 1805 to 1809, returning to Denmark to become professor of aesthetics at the University of Copenhagen. Oehlenschläger was the leader of the Romantic movement in Danish literature. Most of his plays are based on Scandinavian history or Norse mythology. They include the lyric drama *Sanct-Hansaften-Spil* ("Saint John's Eve Play", 1803) and the historical tragedies *Hakon Jarl* ("Earl Hakon", 1807), *Baldur hin Gode* ("Baldur the Good", 1808), and *Axel and Valborg* (1809; Eng. trans., 1851). Other important works are the tragedy *Correggio* (1811; Eng. trans., 1846) and the fantasy in verse *Aladdin of the Wonderful Lamp* (1820; Eng. trans., 1857).

OENOMAUS. See PELOPS.

OERSTED, Hans Christian, *or* ORSTED, HANS CHRISTIAN (1777–1851), Danish physicist and

OFFALY

chemist, born in Rudköbing, and educated at the University of Copenhagen. He was appointed professor of physics at the University of Copenhagen in 1806. In 1819 he discovered that a magnetic needle is deflected at right angles to a wire carrying an electric current, and thus he initiated the study of electromagnetism; see ELECTRICITY: *History*. In 1825 Oersted became the first to isolate the element aluminum (q.v.). His *Manual of Mechanical Physics* appeared in 1844.

OFFALY, county of the Republic of Ireland, in Leinster Province, situated in the central plain of the republic, and bounded on the w. by the Shannon R. Peat is produced; hops, barley, potatoes, and turnips are grown; and livestock is raised. Manufacturing establishments include textile mills, distilleries, and shoe factories. Most of the county is level; the Bog of Allen covers the s.w. and the Slieve Mts. rise to 1700 ft. in the N.E. The county town is Tullamore, and the width of the county is crossed by the Grand Canal. Danish raths, or hill fortresses, and remains of ancient churches and monasteries are among the points of interest. The county was part of the Kingdom of Offaly in ancient Ireland. It became County King's in 1568 and was renamed in 1921. Area, 771 sq.mi.; pop. (1966) 51,717.

OFFENBACH, town of West Germany, in Hesse State, on the Main R., 3 miles E. of Frankfurt-am-Main. Offenbach is known for the manufacture of leather goods; industrial establishments include machine shops, tanneries, and plants producing chemicals. Among points of interest is a Renaissance palace. Pop. (1967 est.) 116,575.

OFFENBACH, Jacques (1819–80), French composer, born in Cologne, Germany, and educated at the Paris Conservatory. In 1837 he became cellist in the orchestra of the Paris Opéra-Comique, and in 1849 was made conductor at the Théâtre Français. His first complete opera, *Pepito*, was performed at the Opéra-Comique in 1853. From 1855 to 1861 he managed a theater named the Bouffes-Parisiens, where he produced a large number of one-act operas of his own composition. The success of this venture so enhanced his reputation that more of his longer operas were performed at the Opéra-Comique and at the Paris Opéra. From 1873 to 1875 Offenbach managed the Théâtre de la Gaieté in Paris. By 1875 he had composed ninety operettas, for many of which the French playwright and novelist Ludovic Halévy had written librettos; see under HALÉVY. Among these operettas were *Orphée aux Enfers* ("Orpheus in Hades", 1858), *La Vie Parisienne* (1866), and *La Grande Duchesse de Gérolstein* (1867). His masterpiece, the four-act opera *Les Contes d'Hoffmann* ("The Tales of Hoffmann", 1880), which contains the popular "Barcarolle", was not performed until 1881, after Offenbach's death. The composer's works were very popular in his time, but with the exception of *Orpheus in Hades* and *Tales of Hoffmann* they are rarely performed today. His musical style is prevailingly light, witty, and gay, and his operettas are masterpieces of satire.

OFFICE MACHINES, instruments and devices designed to relieve the work load of the modern business office by performing repetitive or routine tasks. The high frequency with which routine clerical functions must be repeated has made the development of such machines economically feasible.

Office machinery can be categorized in terms of the clerical requirements which the machine fulfills. Machines are made to prepare and duplicate written documents, to record, process, and store data (*see* DATA PROCESSING), to assist in oral communications, to handle and count money, to keep numerical records, and to facilitate the handling of records, mail, and paper in bulk.

Preparation of Documents. Office documents usually consist of handwritten or mechanically produced records containing numeric and alphabetic information, or punched cards, punched-paper tapes, drums, and disks used as inputs for electronic data-processing equipment and computers; *see* COMPUTER.

The autographic register is a device used for producing commercial documents such as sales slips, bills, statements, and receipts. It consists of a small case containing a supply of continuous printed forms on which information is entered by hand. When completed, the original form is pulled or ejected from the machine, the next form moving automatically into place. The information is also entered on the supplementary forms by means of carbon paper, and these copies are retained within the case for record.

The typewriter (q.v.) is now used universally to prepare letters and many other business documents rapidly in a legible form. The check-writing machine is used to enter on checks the date, amount, and authorized signature. Most checkwriting machines print this information in serrated characters that perforate or emboss the paper of which the check is made, at the same time forcing acid-proof ink into the fibers of the paper to prevent forgery (q.v.).

The keypunch machine records information by punching a series of round or rectangular holes in the columns of a punch card. The machine is activated by key strokes on a keyboard

OFFICE MACHINES

that is similar in layout to the keyboard of a typewriter, except for additional keys that control the movement of the cards through the machine. The groups of punched holes indicate characters consisting of the integers 0 through 9, the letters of the alphabet, and punctuation marks. Each punch card contains 80 or 90 columns, and only one character can be punched in each column. Statements, checks, and inventory records can be entered on punch cards where the material printed on the card corresponds to the punched entry.

The key verifier is a machine that checks the accuracy of the information recorded on the punch card. It is a key-activated machine, physically similar to the keypunch machine, on which the same entries are repeated by a second operator. If the second set of punches matches the original set, the card is passed.

The punched-paper-tape machine records information on a reel of paper tape using a special code based on the position of holes punched in a row along the width of the tape. The tape moves forward automatically row by row so that one character of information is recorded on each row. The characters that can be coded on the tape are the same as those coded on punch cards.

Both punch-card and punched-paper-tape machines can be easily connected to specially equipped calculating machines, typewriters, cash registers, and bookkeeping machines; see BOOKKEEPING; CASH REGISTER. In such cases, while the originating machine is preparing the document, the information is simultaneously recorded on the punch card or punched-paper tape, which can then be used as the in-put to a computer. For handling large amounts of data, such as income tax, personnel, or inventory records, the punched-paper tape has largely been replaced today by magnetic tape, drums, and disks attached directly to a computer.

Duplication of Drawings and Documents. The techniques of duplication are some of the most highly mechanized of business procedures. A few copies of a typed document can be produced easily by inserting sheets of carbon paper and onionskin paper into the typewriter. Photographic processes are commonly used to duplicate drawings and illustrations, although many typed and written documents are now stored on microfilm or duplicated on high-speed contact printers. Some of the photographic processes produce a negative (an image with light-to-dark reversal), and others produce a positive. All photocopying processes rely on the exposure of a chemically treated light-sensitive paper or film, followed usually by automatic developing and fixing; see PHOTOGRAPHY.

Blueprint or dyeline images are used for copies of such line drawings as tracings or charts. Blueprint paper is exposed to light through a transparent original drawing. The negative image on the paper is developed in a chemical solution and washed in clear water. Dyeline paper is treated the same way, but does not require washing; whiteprint copies are therefore somewhat stronger than blueprints.

Modern dictating machines are used by executives and secretaries to speed the flow of business communications.
IBM Corp.

OFFICE MACHINES

In the dry-line process, known also as the diazo process, the positive image is developed with ammonia fumes, thus avoiding the use of any liquid chemical and eliminating paper shrinkage; see DIAZO COMPOUNDS.

Duplication of Typed Matter. Reproductions made by camera processes, such as the photostat and microfilm, are used to produce exact copies of materials other than line drawings. Besides photographic processes, five general processes are used in the office for duplicating typed matter. These are the hectographic, mimeographic methods, and embossed-plate processes, offset printing, or offset lithography, and xerography. Letterpress, gravure, rotary press, and other stereotype print processes are used only for commercial communication on a very large scale; see PRINTING TECHNIQUES.

Hectographic processes use a master copy typed in a heavy soluble ink; the image is lifted by dissolution in a spirit solvent or in gelatin. As the name suggests, hectograph copiers can produce about 100 clear transcripts.

In the spirit-solvent process, usually known as "ditto" process, the master is a reversed impression prepared by backing up the master sheet with a sheet of heavily inked hectograph carbon paper. The master is wrapped around the drum of the duplicating machine, on which the copy paper is moistened slightly with a spirit solvent. The machine then rolls the moistened paper against the master, dissolving the impression onto the paper. The gelatin process is now rarely used.

Mimeographs, or stencil duplicators, use a master copy cut into a thin stencil material. The stencil is then mounted on a perforated drum; a viscous ink is forced through the perforations, through the typed impressions, and onto the copy paper.

The dermatype stencil, in use since 1912, is made of porous open-weave paper coated with a coagulated protein. Pressure on the stencil parts the coating but leaves the paper intact to support the open centers of loop letters. The typewriter, stylus, or some implement capable of penetrating the coating without tearing the paper is used to prepare, or "cut" the stencil.

Hectograph and mimeograph machines can be hand-operated or electrically driven; the latter are capable of turning out copies at about 2 sheets per sec. A hectograph master impression can be used for 100 to 200 copies, a mimeograph stencil for as many as 5000 copies. If more than 5000 copies are required from a single master, processes such as embossed-plate printing are used.

The addressing machine is the archetype of embossed-plate processes. In this process names, addresses, and other pertinent data are embossed on a metal plate by a machine known as graphotype. The addressing machine presses the plates down through an inked ribbon to make the impression on envelopes, mailing strip lists, or letters. Today, the metal embossed plate has to a great extent been replaced by plastic plates similar to those used for personal credit cards. Modern addressing machines are equipped with controls for selecting and printing only certain plates, or making several impressions of any one of them, in accordance with coded directives indicated by tabs on the plates. The initial arrangement of the plates is preserved, each plate emerging from the machine in its original order.

The complete text of a letter can be embossed on letter-sized plates for duplication on page forms. This method of duplicating letters and other page-sized documents is normally not available in the business office itself, but is used in letter shops, direct-mail promotion agencies, and other special communications organizations.

Offset lithographic printing uses a metal, plastic, or fiberboard master plate. The metal plate is prepared photographically, which accounts for the frequently used term "photo-offset"; the plate can be made to include halftone material. Certain types of non-metallic plates

Duplicating stencil masters can be made in just 4 seconds on the infrared copying machine. The master stencil can reproduce more than 1000 copies.
Minnesota Mining & Manufacturing Co.

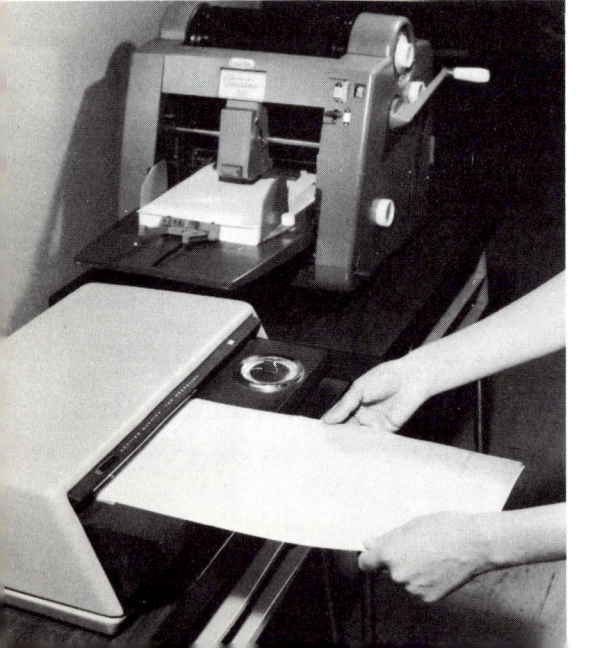

OFFICE MACHINES

can be prepared on specially equipped typewriters or Varitypers, that provide various sizes and styles of type, or with special pencils. Illustrative and graphic matter on these masters is limited generally to line drawings.

The prepared plate is placed on an offset press. Ink deposited on the plate by a roller clings to the type or other matter but is spurned by the material with which the plate is coated. The ink image is then offset onto a smooth rubber blanket which in turn deposits it on the paper. As many as 50,000 or more copies can be made from a single offset plate, and this process has become steadily popular since the late 1960's for large-scale duplication.

Office copiers are the most widely used method today of duplicating letters, correspondence, reports, forms, and other printed or handwritten documents. They are grouped into so-called wet or dry machines, depending on whether or not they use liquid chemicals, but the wet process has now been almost entirely replaced by the dry process. Dry processes include thermography, in which heat is used to transfer the image from the original document to a specially treated paper duplicate; and an electrostatic, or xerographic, process which may or may not require a specially treated paper to transfer the image. In this process, the image to be copied is optically projected onto a positively charged metal plate coated with a material that responds to light of different intensities by losing a varying portion of its charge. A negatively charged pigmented powder is dusted over the metal plate. The powder adheres to those areas which have retained the positive charge, thus making visible the image to be reproduced. A sheet of paper is then pressed against the metal plate and quickly passed through a baking or fixing chamber in which the powder is bonded to the paper. See XEROGRAPHY.

Machines that facilitate written communications include also the telautograph machine, which transmits handwriting. In addition, machines such as teletypewriters and teleprinters transmit typed data, and facsimile equipment transmit pictorial information over long distances through telephone hookups. See TELEGRAPH.

Oral Communications. The spoken word is transmitted by a large variety of intercommunicating devices supplemented by paging and answering systems. Most of these devices make use of the technologies of radio electronics and telephony; see ELECTRONICS; RADIO; TELEPHONE.

The telephone is, of course, the most common communications aid. It is used to reach people both within the business organization and outside it.

The businessman today may use, in addition, wired sound systems to communicate with his associates. These systems include microphones at the pickup point and amplifiers and loud speakers at each terminal point.

PAGING SYSTEMS. For locating people in a building or plant, several types of paging and answering systems are used. Some are simple wired sound devices with powerful loudspeakers that can be heard over a large area. Others use coded signal bells, lights, or small receivers which beep when a radio signal is transmitted from a central station in the office building. The person paged then reports by the nearest telephone.

DICTATING MACHINES. Dictating machines are a special category of oral-communications equipment. Most modern dictating machines are small, highly specialized recording and playback systems, in which the signals from a microhone are amplified and recorded either magnetically, on wire or tape, or electro-acoustically as tracks on a plastic belt, disc, or cylinder. The stenographer's set is equipped to play the recording back under manual or pedal control. See SOUND RECORDING.

Stenotype machines have a small keyboard on which several keys can be pressed down simultaneously. The keys represent sounds rather than letters. The stenotypist strikes groups of keys, comparable to chords on the piano keyboard, in order to register the sounds of words. Because cursive shorthand and recording dictating machines are adequate for taking business dictation, the stenotype machine finds its widest use in court and similar proceedings which must be recorded with utmost accuracy and at very high speed.

Handling of Money. The intimate and essential association of the commercial world with credit and monetary exchange has brought about the development of much machinery to handle both money itself and the numerical records associated with commercial transactions.

REGISTERS. The cash register, invented originally to discourage dishonesty and pilferage, keeps a record of sales. On each sale a modern cash register is capable of recording the type of merchandise, the total price, discounts, taxes, special classifying information, time and date of sale, identifying codes for the salesperson and department, and in some models, the amount of change due. The machine is basically a listing-adding machine equipped to open a cash drawer automatically.

COIN HANDLING MACHINES. Coin-counting ma-

101

OFFICE MACHINES

chines originally were used almost exclusively in banks, but their use has spread into business and industry. The coin counter moves coins past several sets of progressively larger slots or holes, and the coins slip through the first hole big enough to pass them. Most machines are equipped to test the coins for weight and composition and to reject counterfeit coins. Increasingly important today are automatic bank-note counters, and electronic check-processing machines that read characters recorded in magnetic ink on the check.

POSTAGE METERS. Handling of postage has become mechanized in almost all offices, large and small, by the use of postage-permit meters, which print any amount of postage up to the total capacity of the machine. The postage deliverable is paid for in advance at the Post Office, which adjusts the machine accordingly. As the postage is applied to letters or, in the case of packages, to strips of gummed tape, the cost is automatically deducted. Most machines are equipped to print a small advertisement or announcement alongside the stamp.

CLOCK OPERATED SYSTEMS. The general problem of security for money and goods has led to the development of a large family of clock-operated mechanisms which can be used variously to register the identity of a person who unlocks a door; to operate security and alarm systems that require cyclical resetting by watchmen; to endorse, certify, or cancel checks; and to stamp payroll-record cards with the time of arrival and departure of an employee or with the time at which he started and finished each of his assigned jobs.

Handling Numerical Records. The invention of counting and computing mechanisms made possible the development of numerous machines to assist in the handling of numerical records. Of these, the adding machine is the archetype.

ADDING MACHINES. In general, an adding machine works by the controlled turning of gears known as accumulating gears, the first representing units, the next tens, the next hundreds, and so on. Each gear turns the gear to its left once every 10 revolutions. Thus the tens gear advances $\frac{1}{10}$ of a revolution each time the units gear rotates completely, and in turn moves the hundreds gear $\frac{1}{10}$ of a revolution each time it makes one complete rotation. The mechanism driving the accumulating gears is controlled by stops operated from the keyboard.

Many adding machines today are electrically operated, but crank-operated machines are still used for low-volume work. Machines are either key-set or key-driven. In the key-set type the operator sets up a number on the keyboard and then operates a crank or motor bar to enter the number in the machine. In the key-driven machine the pressure on each key performs the work and no crank or motor bar is needed.

Key-driven machines are nonlisting, that is, they produce no printed record. Most key-set machines print transactions on a roller-fed strip of paper. Some machines have tabulating carriages like book-keeping machines, so that ledger cards or statements can be inserted.

On most modern adding machines, subtraction is performed automatically; the subtract control either reverses the accumulating gears or causes a complement of the number in the keyboard to be added in the gears. On machines not equipped to subtract automatically, the operator can subtract by adding the complement of the subtrahend.

CALCULATING MACHINES. Calculators are adding machines that also can multiply and divide automatically. Most calculators are key-set, nonlisting machines which perform multiplication and division by repeated addition and subtraction. In the early 1960's calculators which perform these operations electronically were introduced. Electronic calculators operate on similar principles to the computer. Quick, quiet, and easy to use, they provide their answers either on a cathode-ray tube or on printed tape, depending on the model. Electronic calculators can also incorporate small computing programs which may be inserted in magnetic-tape casettes; these programs can be used automatically to compute discounts, compound interest, or perform short scientific calculations in technical offices.

Most calculators have at least two sets of dials on the carriage. The total, or product, dials show the sum in addition, the product in multiplication, the minuend (and remainder) in subtraction, and the dividend (and remainder) in division. The other set generally shows the multiplier and quotient. Some machines have a separate set of dials for the multiplier; others have check or register dials that indicate the amount entered in the keyboard. Some calculators have a small ten-key keyboard for entering multiplier or divisor; others use one keyboard for all number entries.

All electronic calculators have a single keyboard usually arranged in rows and columns. Operations such as add, subtract, multiply, divide, total, store, recall, and so on are then performed by depressing the corresponding operation key.

A computer programmer removes a reel of magnetic tape containing computer programs from a file library.
Leo Choplin – Black Star

BOOKKEEPING AND BILLING MACHINES. Bookkeeping machines are essentially compound adding mechanisms built with a wide carriage to receive such documents as ledger cards and statements. These machines are equipped to record the transactions and contain several tallying registers. Separate registers accumulate the totals for each vertical and horizontal column. Thus a bank ledger may have one column to pick up the old balance, another column in which deposits are entered, two columns in which the amounts of checks are subtracted, a fifth column in which the new balance is posted (thus clearing the horizontal tally register), and one or more nonadding columns for information to guide the bookkeeper in analyzing the account. Each of the columns (excluding the nonadding columns) is vertically summed for proof and total of the daily transactions.

Some types of billing and bookkeeping machines are merely tabulating typewriters with a primitive adding mechanism which does not accumulate horizontally and vertically at the same time. The term "billing machine" was applied originally to a typewriter designed to post on continuous-form bills of the fanfold, interfold, or roll variety. Because this type of machine provides no check against the operator's accuracy, it is gradually dropping out of use.

Tabulating Equipment. Before the invention of the electronic computer, a series of machines was developed to process information recorded on punched cards. These electromechanical machines, often referred to as E.A.M. equipment, include card sorters, interpreters, reproducing punches, collators, and accounting machines; *see* ACCOUNTING; AUTOMATION.

The card sorter arranges a number of punched cards into a desired numerical or alphabetical order. The cards are aligned, fed into a hopper, and passed through a READ station which sorts them into stacks according to the holes punched on the card.

The interpreter prints along the top edge of each card the integers and letters recorded in the card as a series of punched holes. All or part of the information recorded on the cards may be printed.

The reproducing punch duplicates a stack of cards, or gang punches additional information into them. A card is placed in a READ hopper and a stack of blank cards are placed in a PUNCH hopper. The READ mechanism reads the information recorded on the card and the PUNCH mechanism punches this information into a blank card. In gang punching a punched card is placed on top of the stack of blank cards, and the cards are placed in the card hopper of the PUNCH mechanism, which punches the additional information into the stack.

The collator merges two stacks of punched cards from separate hoppers into one stack according to an ascending or descending sequence of numbers.

The accounting machine reads, adds, subtracts, compares, and selects the information recorded on a stack of punched cards and prints

OFFICE MACHINES

summarizing reports from this information on continuous paper forms. The operation of the accounting machine is controlled by a pre-wired control panel. These electro-mechanical machines and cards have today been generally replaced by electronic computers and input devices, except in some specific instances such as bill and credit-card sorting.

Electronic Computer. This is essentially a high-speed calculating device, possessing an internal memory, and capable of being operated by internally stored instructions. The computer consists of a central processing unit containing storage locations and an operating program, an arithmetic unit that performs the required calculations, and a control system that enables the computer to perform many different kinds of operations. In addition to the central processing unit, different input-output devices enable data to be entered into or taken out of the computer. These devices include punch-card- and punched-paper-tape readers, punch-card- and punched-paper-tape punches, printers, and magnetic-tape and magnetic-disc units that are capable of both reading and writing information on magnetic tape and magnetic discs.

Record Handling. To facilitate record keeping, an office today has many systems and machines based on the simple principle of the alphabetically or categorically indexed file. The so-called credit register is a compact record-keeping device that has been partly or completely mechanized in many offices.

Most large business systems today, however, store data on microfilm or as magnetic recordings on tapes, drums, or discs. The latter method is most frequently used in conjunction with electronic computing systems; the former is used mostly for compact storage of seldom-used records. Punched or tabulating cards are used for records which must be processed by tabulating systems and as index cards for massive records of other kinds.

Handling of Mail and Paper. A large range of paper-handling machines are used in offices today, principally to cut paper into pieces of specific size, to punch holes of various shapes and positions in sheets of paper, to collate and arrange paper in specified order, and to bind sheets of paper. Some machines fold pieces of paper and insert them neatly into envelopes. Other machines seal the envelopes and others open standard-sized envelopes by shaking their contents into one end and cutting off the other end. Time stamps automatically mark received mail with the time of receipt. Other machines are used for sealing packages with gummed paper tape or with wax. Because of the enormous amount of paper that passes through a large modern business office, machines have been developed to destroy paper, by chopping or mashing it, and to bale it neatly for sale or disposal as waste.

OFFICE OF PRICE ADMINISTRATION, Agency of the United States government in World War II, created as the Office of Price Administration and Civilian Supply by a Presidential order issued in April, 1941. This agency, known as the O.P.A., was charged with forestalling inflation by stabilizing rents and prices and by preventing speculation, hoarding, profiteering, and price manipulation. The name of the agency was changed to Office of Price Administration in August, 1941, by a Presidential order which also transferred the functions relating to civilian supply to another government agency. Subsequently, the powers of the O.P.A. were expanded by several Congressional enactments to include the rationing of scarce commodities to consumers, and the determination of maximum prices for goods and residential rents. The O.P.A. was notably successful during World War II, but soon after the conclusion of hostilities in 1945 it became the center of a bitter controversy, as many groups of producers demanded the abolition of all price controls and a number of groups of consumers fought for their retention. In December, 1946, the O.P.A. was incorporated into the newly established Office of Temporary Controls.

OFFSET PRINTING. See Printing Techniques: *Offset Printing.*

O'FLAHERTY, Liam (1896–), Irish novelist, born in the Arran Islands, County Galway, and educated at University College, Dublin. He was one of the leading Irish novelists of the second quarter of the 20th century. His works are characterized by naturalistic realism and powerful drama. Among his books are *Thy Neighbor's Wife* (1924), *The Informer* (1925, subsequently made into a motion picture of the same name), *Mr. Gilhooley* (1926), *Land* (1946), *Two Lovely Beasts and Other Stories* (1950), *Insurrection* (1951), and *The Stories of Liam O'Flaherty* (1956). *Two Years* (1930) and *Shame the Devil* (1934) are autobiographical works.

OGASAWARA. See Bonin Islands.

OGBOMOSHO, city of Nigeria, in the Western State, 55 miles N.E. of Ibadan. Ogbomosho is a road hub in an area that produces cotton, tobacco, corn, cassava, and various vegetables. Cotton, tobacco, and shea nuts are processed. A teachers' college is located in Ogbomosho. Pop. (1969 est.) 370,963.

OGDEN, city in Utah, and county seat of Weber Co., at the confluence of the Ogden and Weber rivers, 32 miles N. of Salt Lake City. It is the industrial and distribution center for a fertile agricultural area and has large railroad shops, meat-packing plants, flour mills, canneries, creameries, powdered-milk plants, an oil refinery, and factories manufacturing iron castings and clothing. Ogden is the second-largest city in the State, and has the main railroad station between the Rocky Mts. and the Pacific coast. Ogden is the site of Weber State College, established in 1889, and of a regional headquarters of the United States Forest Service. The city is at the foot of the Wasatch Mts., at an elevation of 4300 ft. above sea level. Towering above it is Mt. Ogden (9575 ft.). The site of the present city was settled by the Mormons in 1847, and in 1851 the settlement was incorporated. Pop. (1960) 70,197; (1970) 69,478.

OGDENSBURG, city and port of entry of New York, in Saint Lawrence Co., at the confluence of the Saint Lawrence and Oswegatchie rivers, 35 miles s.w. of Massena. It is the trade center of an agricultural and timber area. Manufactures include office equipment and processed dairy food. Ogdensburg is a summer resort, the headquarters of the St. Lawrence customs district, and the site of the Remington Art Memorial, which contains collections of Indian relics, and paintings and bronzes by the 19th-century American artist Frederic Remington (q.v.).

A fort was established by the French on the site of the present city in 1749, and it was taken by the British about 1760. The British abandoned the fort in 1796. During the so-called Patriots' War in 1837 the city was a base for Americans aiding rebellious Canadians in an attempt to drive the British from Canada. Ogdensburg was incorporated as a village in 1817 and as a city in 1868. On Aug. 18, 1940, it was the site of the Ogdensburg Declaration, in which President Franklin Delano Roosevelt (q.v.), together with the Canadian prime minister, William Lyon Mackenzie King (q.v.), announced the establishment of the Permanent Joint Board on Defense; the board continues to function as an organ for discussion of security problems shared by the United States and Canada. Pop. (1960) 16,122; (1970) 14,554.

OGLETHORPE, James Edward (1696–1785), British philanthropist and colonist, born in London, England, and educated at the University of Oxford. He was elected to the House of Commons in 1722 and subsequently became interested in prison reform, particularly in alleviating the condition of those imprisoned for debt. He formulated a plan for the resettlement of debtors in America and in 1732 was granted a royal charter for the purpose of realizing this plan. With a band of 116 emigrants, Oglethorpe landed at the present site of Charleston, S.C.,

James Edward Oglethorpe

early in 1733, and on Feb. 12, 1733, he founded the colony of Savannah, in what is now the State of Georgia. He acted as administrator of the colony for ten years and in 1742 defeated a Spanish force that had invaded the colony from Florida. In 1743 Oglethorpe returned to England, where he was commissioned a general in 1765. In his later years he associated with the literary circle led by the British critic Samuel Johnson (q.v.).

OGPU. See G.P.U.

O'HARA, John Henry (1905–70), American writer, born in Pottsville, Pa. After graduating from preparatory school in 1924, O'Hara traveled around the United States, eventually settling in New York City, where he wrote for various magazines and newspapers. He began publishing short stories in *The New Yorker* magazine in 1928. His first novel, *Appointment in Samarra* (1934), was warmly received by the critics and the public. Introducing the themes that ran through much of his later work, it described in revealing detail the lives and aspirations of the upper class in a fictional Pennsylvania town called Gibbsville, concentrating on their drives toward money, sex, and status. His next novel, *Butterfield 8* (1935), like all his works a popular success, is a tragic story of life on the sordid fringes of New York City café society and the underworld.

A collection of short stories, *Pal Joey* (1940),

O'HIGGINS

written in the form of letters from a cynical night-club singer, was made into a musical comedy by O'Hara and the theatrical director George Abbott, the composer Richard Rodgers, and the lyricist Lorenz Hart (qq.v.). *Pal Joey* was a failure in its first New York City production (1940), but a revival twelve years later was widely acclaimed.

During the 1940's O'Hara wrote mostly slick short stories in which he demonstrated his ability with dialogue and his flair for catching the essence of his characters and of his era. In 1949 he returned his attention to the wealthy people of Gibbsville in the novel *A Rage to Live*. O'Hara produced twenty-four books, an average of more than one book a year, in the 1950's and 1960's. For the novel *10 North Frederick* (1955) O'Hara received a National Book Award for fiction. *And Other Stories* (1968) and *The O'Hara Generation* are the last of his books published in his lifetime; a completed novel, *The Ewings*, remained unpublished at his death.

O'HIGGINS, Bernardo (1778–1842), Chilean soldier and statesman, born in Chillán. After spending several years studying in England and Spain, O'Higgins returned to Chile in 1802. He took part in the nationalist revolution against Spain in 1810 and was made commander of the patriot army in 1813. Defeated by royalist troops at Rancagua in 1814, O'Higgins fled across the Andes with most of his followers. There he joined the Argentine revolutionist José de San Martín (q.v.), with whom he returned to defeat the Spanish at Chacabuco in 1817. He was made supreme director of Chile in 1817, and he proclaimed Chilean independence in 1818. O'Higgins angered the aristocracy by proposing democratic reforms, and he was deposed in 1823. He spent the rest of his life in exile in Peru.

OHIO, one of the North-Central States of the United States, bounded on the N. by Michigan and Lake Erie, on the E. by Pennsylvania and the Ohio River (q.v.), on the S. by the Ohio R., and on the W. by Indiana. Ohio is generally square in shape, measuring at its greatest extent about 225 mi. from E. to W. and about 215 mi. from N. to S.

THE LAND

The terrain of Ohio consists predominantly of rolling hills and glaciated, undulating plains, the only level portion being a strip of ancient lake bottom in the N., adjacent to Lake Erie. South of the lake plain and E. of a line extending generally southwestward from Trumbull County, the terrain falls within the Allegheny Plateau. The plateau region is hilly, with elevations ranging from 500 ft. along the Ohio R. to 100 ft. in the W. Except where dissected by deep river valleys,

Area (35th State in rank)	41,222 sq. mi.
Land	41,018 sq. mi.
Inland water	204 sq. mi.
Population	(1970, 6th in rank) 10,652,017
	(1960, 5th in rank) 9,706,397
	(1950) 7,946,627
Altitude	433 ft. to 1550 ft.
Capital	Columbus (1970) 539,677
Largest city	Cleveland (1970) 750,903
Entered Union (17th State)	March 1, 1803
Nickname	The Buckeye State
Motto	With God, All Things Are Possible
Tree	buckeye
Flower	scarlet carnation
Bird	cardinal

the terrain of the plains region, to the W. of the Allegheny Plateau, is gently undulating. Campbell Hill (1550 ft.), in Logan County, is the highest point in the State. The lowest point, along the Ohio R. in Hamilton County, is about 433 ft. above sea level. The average elevation of the State is 850 ft.

Rivers and Lakes. Ohio has two drainage systems, the basin of the Ohio R. and the basin of Lake Erie. The Ohio R. forms the entire border with West Virginia and Kentucky. The streams of the Ohio basin are the Muskingum, Great Miami, Scioto, Mahoning, and Hocking rivers. Among the chief rivers flowing into Lake Erie are the Maumee, Sandusky, Cuyahoga, Huron, and Portage. Most of the natural lakes within the State are small. Among many reservoirs are Grand Lake on the Saint Marys R., Indian Lake on a tributary of the Great Miami R., Dillon Reservoir on the Muskingum R., Mosquito Creek Reservoir, and a series of reservoirs including the Atwood, Dover, Leesville, Tappan, Clendening, Piedmont, and Berlin on the Tuscawaras R. and its tributaries.

Climate. Ohio has an essentially continental climate, characterized by moderate extremes of heat and cold and wetness and dryness. Summers are moderately warm and humid, winters are reasonably cold, and autumns are cool and dry. The highest temperature recorded in the State was 113° F. (at Wilmington); the lowest, −39° F (at Milligan). Precipitation averages 28 in. annually, with the S.W. receiving the most and the lakeshore the least. Average snowfall ranges from 60 in. in the lake area to 16 in. or less along

Climate	Cincinnati	Cleveland	Columbus
Normal temperatures (in ° F.)			
January maximum	41.3	34.8	37.8
January minimum	26.1	20.3	22.0
July maximum	87.5	82.8	86.6
July minimum	66.3	60.2	62.9
Annual	55.2	49.2	52.0
Normal precipitation (in inches)			
Wettest month	4.18	3.52	4.16
Driest month	2.24	2.33	2.11
Annual	39.51	35.35	36.67
Latest frost	April 15	April 21	April 17
Earliest frost	Oct. 25	Nov. 2	Oct. 30
Mean number of days between latest and earliest frosts	192	195	196

OHIO

INDEX TO MAP OF OHIO

Cities and Towns

Aberdeen E6
Ada C8
Addyston B9
Adena J5
Akron ⊙ G3
Alger C4
Alliance H4
Amberley C9
Amherst F3
Andover J3
Ansonia A5
Antwerp A3
Arcanum A6
Archbold B2
Arlington C4
Arlington Heights C9
Ashland ⊙ F4
Ashley E5
Ashtabula ⊙ J2
Athens ⊙ F7
Attica E3
Aurora H3
Austinburg J2
Austintown J3
Avon F2
Avon Lake F2
Ayersville B3
Bainbridge D7
Ballville D3
Baltimore E6
Barberton H3
Barnesville J6
Barton J5
Batavia ⊙ B7
Bay Village G2
Beach City G4
Beachwood H2
Bedford H3
Bedford Heights H3
Bellaire K6
Bellbrook C6
Belle Center D4
Bellefontaine ⊙ C5
Bellevue E3
Bellville E4
Beloit J4
Belpre G7
Berea G10
Bergholz J4
Bethel B8
Bethesda J5
Beverly G6

Bexley E7
Blanchester B7
Blue Ash C4
Bluffton C4
Boardman J3
Bolivar G4
Botkins B5
Bowling Green ⊙ C3
Bradford B5
Bradner C3
Bratenahl H10
Brecksville H3
Bremen F6
Brewster G4
Bridgeport J5
Bridgetown B9
Brilliant J5
Brimfield H3
Bristolville J3
Broadview Heights H10
Brookfield J3
Brooklyn H10
Brooklyn Heights H10
Brook Park G2
Brookside J6
Brookville B6
Brunswick G3
Bryan ⊙ A3
Buckeye Lake F6
Bucyrus ⊙ E4
Burlington H3
Burton J3
Butler F4
Byesville H6
Cadiz ⊙ J5
Caldwell ⊙ G3
Calcutta J5
Cambridge ⊙ H5
Camden A6
Campbell J3
Canal Fulton G4
Canal Winchester E6
Canfield J3
Canton ⊙ H4
Cardington E5
Carey D4
Carrollton ⊙ H4
Castalia E3
Cedarville C6
Celina ⊙ A4
Centerburg E5
Centerville B6
Chagrin Falls H3
Chardon ⊙ H2
Chauncey F7
Chesapeake F9
Chesterland H2
Cheviot B9

Chillicothe ⊙ E7
Cincinnati ⊙ B9
Circleville ⊙ D6
Cleveland ⊙ H9
Cleveland Heights H9
Cleves A9
Clinton G4
Clyde E3
Coal Grove F9
Coldwater A5
Columbiana J4
Columbus (capital) ⊙ E6
Columbus Grove B4
Conneaut J2
Continental B3
Convoy A4
Cortland J3
Coshocton ⊙ G5
Covedale B10
Covington B5
Craig Beach J3
Crestline E4
Creston G3
Cridersville B4
Crooksville G6
Crystal Lakes C6
Cuyahoga Falls G3
Dalton G4
Danville F5
Dayton ⊙ B6
Deer Park B3
Defiance ⊙ B3
Degraff C5
Delaware ⊙ D5
Delphos B4
Delta B2
Dennison H4
Deshler C3
Devola H7
Dillonvale J5
Dover G4
Doylestown G4
Dresden G5
Dunkirk C4
East Canton H4
East Cleveland J9
East Liverpool J4
East Palestine J4
East Sparta H4
Eaton ⊙ A6
Eaton Estates A3
Edgerton A3
Edgewood J2
Elida B4
Elmore D3

Elmwood Place B9
Elyria ⊙ F3
Englewood B6
Enon C6
Euclid H9
Evendale B9
Fairborn C6
Fairfax C9
Fairfield A7
Fairlawn G3
Fairport Harbor H2
Fairview Park G9
Fayette B2
Findlay ⊙ D5
Flushing J5
Forest C4
Forest Park C10
Forestville C9
Fort McKinley B6
Fort Recovery A5
Fort Shawnee B4
Fostoria D3
Frankfort D7
Franklin B6
Franklin Furnace E8
Frazeysburg F5
Fredericktown E5
Fremont ⊙ D3
Gahanna E4
Galion E4
Gallipolis ⊙ F8
Gambier F5
Garfield Heights H3
Garrettsville H3
Gates Mills H3
Geneva J2
Genoa D2
Georgetown ⊙ C8
Germantown B6
Gibsonburg D3
Girard J3
Glendale C9
Glouster F6
Gnadenhutten G5
Golf Manor B7
Goshen B7
Grafton F3
Grandview D6
Granville E5
Greenfield D7
Greenhills B9
Green Springs E3
Greentown G4
Greenville ⊙ H4
Greenwich E3

Groesbeck B9
Grove City D6
Groveport E6
Hamden F7
Hamilton ⊙ A9
Harrison H4
Hartville A9
Heath F5
Hebron A3
Hicksville A3
Highland Heights G3
Hilliard D5
Hillsboro ⊙ C7
Hiram H3
Holgate C2
Holland B3
Hopedale J5
Hubbard B6
Huber Heights B6
Hudson B4
Huron E3
Independence H9
Indian Hill E8
Ironton ⊙ F5
Jackson ⊙ E7
Jackson Center B5
Jamestown C6
Jefferson ⊙ J2
Jeffersonville C6
Jewett H5
Johnstown E5
Kent H3
Kenton ⊙ C4
Kettering B6
Kingston E7
Kingsville J2
Kirtland H2
Lagrange F3
Lakemore H3
Lakeview C4
Lakewood G2
Lancaster ⊙ E6
Lansing J5
Leavittsburg J3
Lebanon ⊙ B7
Leesburg C7
Leetonia J4
Leipsic C3
Lewisburg A6
Lexington E4
Liberty Center B3
Lima ⊙ B4
Lincoln Heights C9
Lisbon ⊙ J4
Lockland C9
Lodi F3

Logan ⊙ F6
London ⊙ C6
Lorain F3
Loudonville F4
Louisville H4
Loveland D9
Lowellville J3
Luckey D3
Lynchburg C7
Lyndhurst J10
Macedonia B9
Mack C9
Madeira H2
Madison H2
Magnolia G6
Malta G6
Malvern H4
Manchester D8
Mansfield ⊙ E4
Mantua H3
Maple Heights A5
Maria Stein A5
Mariemont C9
Marietta ⊙ G7
Marion ⊙ D4
Martins Ferry J5
Marysville ⊙ D5
Mason B7
Massillon H4
Masury J3
Maumee C2
Mayfield J9
Mayfield Heights J9
McArthur ⊙ F7
McComb C3
McConnelsville ⊙ G6
McDonald J3
Mechanicsburg C5
Medina ⊙ F3
Mentor H2
Mentor-on-the-Lake G2
Miamisburg B6
Middleburg Heights G10
Middlefield H3
Middleport F7
Middletown A6
Midland C7
Milan E3
Milford D9
Millersburg ⊙ F4
Mineral Ridge J3
Minerva H4
Minerva Park E5
Mingo Junction J5
Minster B5
Mogadore H3

Continued on page 110

⊙ County seat.

107

OHIO

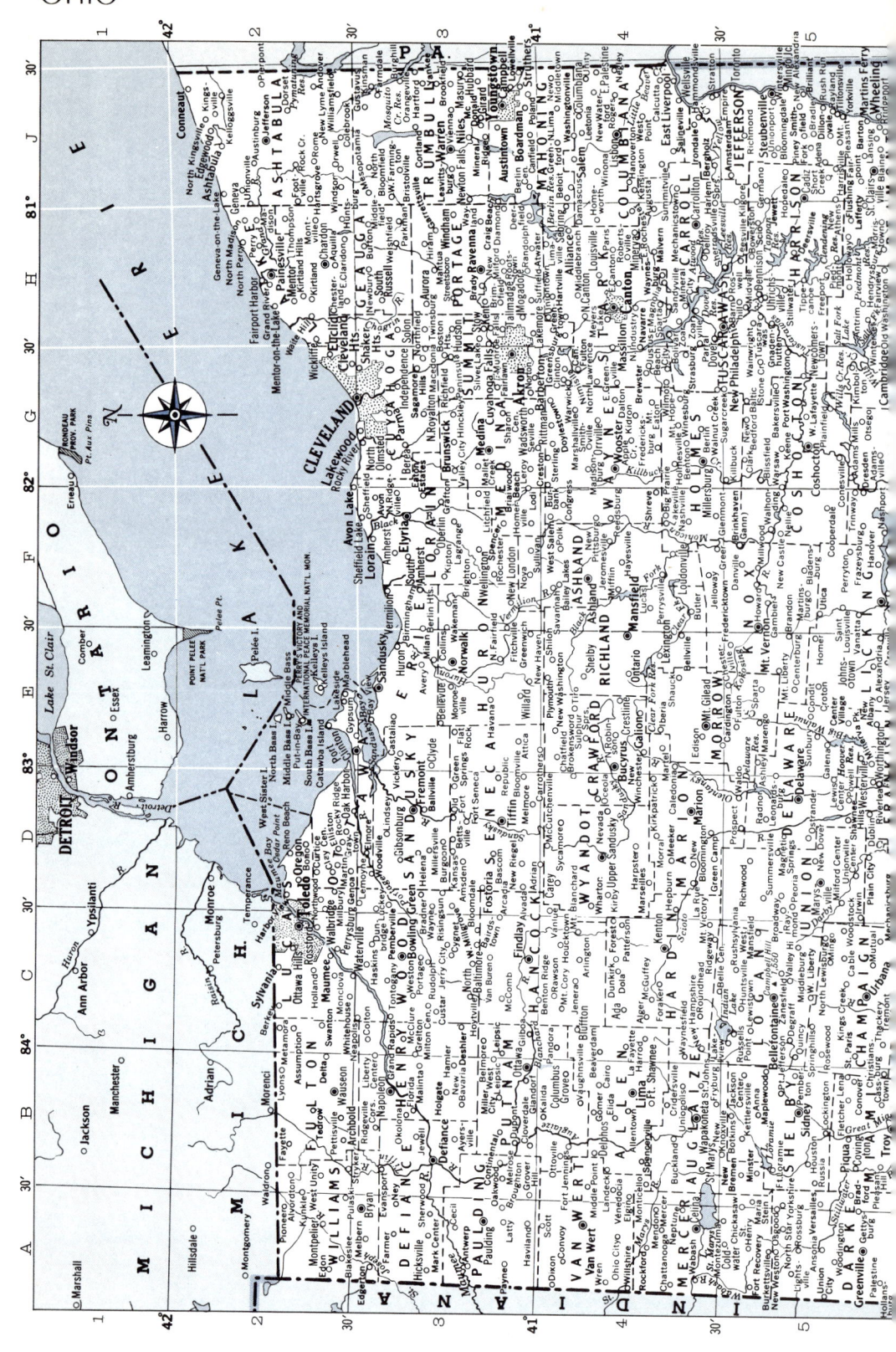

OHIO

OHIO

Index to Map of Ohio — Continued from page 107

Monroe ....B 7	Parma Heights ....G 9	Springdale ....B 9	Williamsburg ....B 7
Monroeville ....E 3	Pataskala ....E 5	Springfield ⊙ ....C 6	Willoughby ....J 8
Montgomery ....C 9	Paulding ⊙ ....A 3	Steubenville ⊙ .....J 5	Willoughby Hills ....J 9
Montpelier ....A 2	Payne ....A 3	Stow ....H 3	Willowick ....J 8
Moraine ....B 6	Peebles ....D 8	Strasburg ....G 4	Wilmington ⊙ ....C 7
Moreland Hills ......J 9	Pemberville ....C 3	Streetsboro ....H 3	Windham ....H 3
Morrow ....B 7	Pepper Pike ....J 9	Strongsville ....G 10	Wintersville ....J 5
Mount Gilead ⊙ ....E 4	Perry ....H 2	Struthers ....J 3	Woodlawn ....C 9
Mount Healthy ......B 9	Perrysburg ....C 2	Stryker ....B 3	Woodsfield ⊙ ....H 6
Mount Orab ....C 7	Piketon ....E 7	Sugarcreek ....G 5	Woodville ....D 3
Mount Sterling ......D 6	Pioneer ....A 2	Sunbury ....E 5	Wooster ⊙ ....G 4
Mount Vernon ⊙ ...E 5	Piqua ....B 5	Swanton ....C 2	Worthington ....E 5
Munroe Falls ....H 3	Plain City ....D 5	Sycamore ....D 4	Wyoming ....C 9
Napoleon ⊙ ....B 3	Pleasant Hill ....B 5	Sylvania ....C 2	Xenia ⊙ ....C 6
Navarre ....H 4	Plymouth ....E 4	Tallmadge ....H 3	Yellow Springs ......C 6
Neffs ....J 5	Poland ....J 3	Terrace Park ....D 9	Yorkville ....J 5
Nelsonville ....F 7	Pomeroy ....G 7	The Plains ....F 7	Youngstown ⊙ ....J 3
Nevada ....D 4	Port Clinton ⊙ .....E 2	Tiffin ⊙ ....D 3	Zanesville ⊙ ....G 6
Newark ⊙ ....F 5	Portsmouth ....D 8	Tiltonsville ....J 5	
New Boston ....E 8	Powhatan Point ......J 6	Tipp City ....B 6	**Physical Features**
New Bremen ....B 5	Prospect ....D 5	Toledo ⊙ ....D 2	
Newburgh Heights ..H 9	Radnor ....D 5	Toronto ....J 5	Auglaize (river) ......B 4
New Carlisle ....C 6	Randolph ....H 3	Trenton ....B 7	Black (river) ....F 3
Newcomerstown ....G 5	Ravenna ⊙ ....H 3	Trotwood ....B 6	Blanchard (river) ....C 4
New Concord ....G 6	Reading ....C 9	Troy ⊙ ....B 5	Blennerhassett
New Lebanon ....B 6	Reno Beach ....D 2	Twinsburg ....J 10	(isl.) ....G 7
New Lexington ⊙ ..F 6	Reynoldsburg ....E 6	Uhrichsville ....H 5	Buckeye (lake) ......F 6
New London ....F 3	Richfield ....G 3	Union ....B 6	Campbell (hill) ......C 5
New Madison ....A 6	Richmond Heights ...H 9	Union City ....A 5	Chagrin (river) ......J 8
New Matamoras .....H 6	Richwood ....D 5	University Heights ..H 9	Cuyahoga (river) ....H 10
New Miami ....A 7	Ripley ....C 8	Upper Arlington .....D 6	Delaware (res.) .....E 5
New Middletown ...J 4	Rittman ....G 4	Upper Sandusky ⊙ ..D 4	Erie (lake) ....H 1
New Paris ....A 6	Rockford ....A 4	Urbana ⊙ ....C 5	Grand (river) ....H 2
New Philadelphia ⊙ G 5	Rocky River ....G 9	Utica ....F 5	Great Miami
Newport ....H 7	Rosemount ....D 8	Vandalia ....B 6	(river) ....A 7
New Richmond ......B 8	Roseville ....F 6	Van Wert ⊙ ....A 4	Hocking (river) ......F 7
New Straitsville .....F 6	Rossford ....C 2	Venice ....B 9	Huron (river) ....E 3
Newton Falls ....J 3	Rossmoyne ....C 9	Vermilion ....F 3	Indian (lake) ....C 5
Newtown ....C 10	Russells Point ....C 5	Versailles ....A 5	International Peace
New Washington ....E 4	Sabina ....C 7	Vienna ....J 3	Memorial Nat'l
Niles ....J 3	Sagamore Hills .....J 10	Wadsworth ....G 3	Mon. ....E 2
North Baltimore .....C 3	Saint Bernard ....B 9	Walbridge ....C 2	Kelleys (isl.) ....E 2
North Canton ....H 4	Saint Clairsville ⊙ ..J 5	Walton Hills ....H 10	Kokosing (river) .....E 5
North College	Saint Henry ....A 5	Wapakoneta ⊙ ......B 4	Little Miami (river) ..C 9
Hill ....B 9	Saint Marys ....B 4	Warren ⊙ ....J 3	Little Muskingum
Northfield ....J 10	Saint Paris ....C 5	Warrensville	(riv.) ....H 6
North Hampton .....C 5	Salem ....J 4	Heights ....H 9	Loramie (lake) ......B 5
North Industry ......H 4	Salineville ....J 4	Washington	Mad (river) ....C 6
North Kingsville ....J 2	Sandusky ⊙ ....E 3	Court House ⊙ ...D 6	Maumee (bay) ......D 2
North Olmsted ......G 9	Scio ....H 5	Waterville ....C 3	Maumee (river) .....A 3
North Randall ....H 9	Sebring ....H 4	Wauseon ⊙ ....B 2	Middle Bass (isl.) ...E 2
North Ridgeville ....F 3	Seven Hills ....G 3	Waverly ⊙ ....D 7	Mohican (river) .....F 4
North Royalston ...H 10	Seville ....G 3	Waynesburg ....H 4	Mound City Group
Northwood ....D 2	Shadyside ....J 6	Waynesville ....B 6	Nat'l Mon. ....E 7
North Zanesville ....G 6	Shaker Heights ......H 9	Wellington ....F 3	Muskingum (river) ..G 6
Norton ....G 4	Sharonville ....C 9	Wellston ....F 7	Ohio (river) ....B 8
Norwalk ⊙ ....E 3	Sheffield ....F 3	Wellsville ....J 4	Olentangy (river) ...D 4
Norwood ....C 9	Sheffield Lake ....F 3	West Alexandria .....A 6	Perrys Victory Nat'l
Oak Harbor ....D 2	Shelby ....E 4	West Carrollton .....B 6	Mon. ....E 2
Oak Hill ....E 8	Shreve ....F 4	Westerville ....D 5	Portage (river) ......D 3
Oakwood ....B 6	Sidney ⊙ ....B 5	West Jefferson ......D 6	Pymatuning (res.) ...J 2
Oakwood ....H 9	Silver Lake ....G 3	West Lafayette ......G 5	Rocky (river) ....G 9
Oberlin ....F 3	Silverton ....C 9	Westlake ....G 9	Rocky Fork (lake) ...D 7
Obetz ....E 6	Smithfield ....J 5	West Liberty ....C 5	Saint Joseph
Olmsted Falls ....G 9	Smithville ....G 4	West Milton ....B 6	(river) ....A 3
Ontario ....E 4	Solon ....J 9	Weston ....C 3	Saint Marys (lake) ..A 4
Orange ....J 9	Somerset ....F 6	West Portsmouth ....D 8	Sandusky (bay) .....E 3
Oregon ....D 2	Somerville ....F 4	West Salem ....F 4	Sandusky (river) ....D 3
Orrville ....G 4	South Amherst ......F 3	West Union ⊙ ....C 8	Scioto (river) ....D 8
Orwell ....J 2	South Euclid ....H 9	West Unity ....B 2	South Bass (isl.) ....E 2
Ottawa ⊙ ....B 3	South Lebanon .....B 7	Westview ....G 10	Stillwater (river) ....B 5
Ottawa Hills ....C 2	South Point ....E 9	Wheelersburg ....E 8	Tiffin (river) ....B 3
Ottoville ....B 4	South Russell ....H 9	Whitehall ....E 6	Tuscarawas (river) ..H 5
Oxford ....A 6	South Zanesville ....F 6	Whitehouse ....C 2	Vermilion (river) ....F 3
Painesville ⊙ ....H 2	Spencerville ....B 4	Wickliffe ....J 9	Wabash (river) .....A 5
Parma ....H 9	Springboro ....B 6	Willard ....E 3	

the Ohio R. The average annual number of days with measurable precipitation ranges from 106 at Portsmouth to 132 at Cincinnati, 135 at Columbus, and 153 at Cleveland. Windstorms are associated with heavy thunderstorms or line squalls, and three or four tornadoes occur each year.

Plants and Animals. Among the more abundant plants of Ohio are the black-eyed Susan, alfalfa, buttercup, camomile, celandine, dandelion, evening primrose, ground ivy, honeysuckle, mint, mustard, aster, goldenrod, sunflower, and Queen Anne's lace. Shrubs commonly found are the black raspberry, high

The civic center of Columbus, the capital of Ohio.

blackberry, bittersweet, sumac, witchhazel, hawthorn, pussy willow, blue dogwood, and silky dogwood. Trees include white and red oak, hard and soft maple, black walnut, basswood, tulip poplar, beech, hickory, sycamore, willow, birch, cottonwood, and white ash.

Animals found in Ohio include the muskrat, mink, raccoon, red fox, gray fox, opossum, white-tailed deer, several species of squirrels, and the eastern cottontail rabbit. Common birds are the cardinal, green heron, herring gull, bobwhite quail, mourning dove, yellow-billed cuckoo, several woodpeckers, ruby-throated hummingbird, several species of wrens, barn swallow, robin, eastern bluebird, starling, eastern meadowlark, and goldfinch. More than 170 species of fish, including bluegill, catfish, varieties of bass, and muskellunge, populate the rivers and lakes of the State.

Parks, Forests, and Other Places of Interest. Ohio has two national monuments, the Mound City Group National Monument and Perry's Victory and International Peace Memorial National Monument (qq.v.). Wayne National Forest occupies more than 100,000 acres near Athens in the S.E. part of the State. Among forests and parks maintained by the State are Shawnee State Forest, near Portsmouth; Scioto Trail State Forest, near Chillicothe; Pymatuning Reservoir State Park, near Andover; Portage Lakes State Park, near Akron; Grand Lake State Park, near Saint Marys; and Roosevelt Lake State Park, near Friendship. Fort Ancient State Memorial, in Warren Co., contains prehistoric Indian earthworks, burial mounds, and the remains of village sites.

Among the historic sites in Ohio are Fort Meigs, Fort Miami, and the site of the Battle of Fallen Timbers, all reminders of the Indian wars; the birthplace of the inventor Thomas A. Edison (q.v.) at Milan; and, near New Philadelphia, the rebuilt Moravian Church of Schoenbrunn, which was destroyed during the American Revolution.

Sports. Lake Erie on the N. and numerous reservoirs and lakes provide Ohio with good fishing. Among species found are black and white bass, walleye and northern pike, crappie, bluegill, perch, channel catfish, carp, and, in limited waters, trout. Muskellunge have been planted. Game animals and birds hunted include white-tailed deer, fox and gray squirrels, cottontail rabbit, ring-necked pheasant, bobwhite quail, ruffed grouse, Hungarian partridge, and wild turkey. Skiing is a recently developed sport in Ohio. Several resorts have been established, including Boston Hills, at Peninsula; Clear Fork, at Butler; and Snow Trails, at Mansfield.

THE PEOPLE

According to the 1970 decennial census, the population of Ohio was 10,652,017, an increase of 9.7 percent over the 1960 population. The urban segment comprised 8,025,697 persons, 75.3 percent of the total, compared with 73.4 percent in 1960. The rural segment comprised 2,626,320 persons, 24.7 percent of the total, compared with 26.6 percent in 1960. Ethnically, the

OHIO

1970 population was distributed as follows: white persons, 9,646,997, nonwhites, 1,005,020, including 970,477 Negroes, 5555 Japanese, 5305 Chinese, 6654 Indians, 3490 Filipinos, and 13,539 others. The percentage of native-born residents was 95.9; of foreign-born, 4.1. The major countries of origin of the foreign-born, in order of rank, were Germany, Great Britain, and Poland. The 1970 population density averaged 260.0 per sq.mi., compared with 236.6 in 1960.

The chief cities are Columbus, the capital and second-largest city, a railroad, manufacturing, and agricultural marketing center, the site of Ohio State University; Cleveland, the largest city, a port on Lake Erie and a major industrial and educational center; Cincinnati, the third-largest, a transportation, manufacturing, and cultural center; Toledo, the fourth-largest, a port on Lake Erie, a shipping and rail terminal and manufacturing center; and Akron, world center of the rubber industry. In addition to these, four cities (Dayton, Youngstown, Canton, and Parma) have populations over 100,000.

Education. The public-school system of Ohio was established in 1785. Education is compulsory for all children between the ages of seven and eighteen.

ELEMENTARY AND SECONDARY SCHOOLS. In 1968 public elementary schools numbered approximately 3189, and public secondary schools, 1055. Enrollment was about 1,698,000 in elementary and about 727,000 in secondary schools. Teachers in private schools numbered about 12,925 in the mid-1960's.

UNIVERSITIES AND COLLEGES. In the mid-1960's university and college enrollment in Ohio was about 290,000. In 1966 the State had eighty institutions of higher education, sixty-seven of which were private. State institutions include Ohio State University, the University of Cincinnati (qq.v.), Central State University, Miami University, Ohio University, Bowling Green University, Cleveland and Kent State universities, and the universities of Akron and Toledo. Private institutions include Antioch College, Case Institute of Technology, Hebrew Union College-Jewish Institute of Religion, Oberlin College, Wittenberg University (qq.v.), Baldwin-Wallace College, Cleveland-Marshall Law School, Defiance College, Denison University, Hiram College, John Carroll University, Kenyon College, Lake Erie College, Marietta College, Ohio Wesleyan University, the University of Dayton, Urbana College, Western College for Women, and Western Reserve University.

LIBRARIES AND MUSEUMS. Among the large libraries of Ohio are the public libraries of Akron (500,000 volumes), Cleveland (more than 3,000,000), Columbus (680,000), Dayton and Montgomery County (850,000), Cincinnati and Hamilton County (more than 2,000,000), and Toledo (850,000). The State Library of Ohio, in Columbus, has some 900,000 volumes, periodicals, and documents on local history and genealogy. Cultural institutions include the Cincinnati Art Museum and the Taft Museum, both in Cincinnati; the Cleveland Museum of Art, with a 50,000-volume library; the Cleveland Museum of Natural History, which includes a planetarium and observatory; and the Salvador Dali Museum, all in Cleveland; and the Museum and Library of the Ohio Historical Society, in Columbus. Of special interst is the Air Force Museum, in Dayton, with items pertaining to military aviation history. The National Professional Football Hall of Fame is in Canton.

THE ECONOMY

Ohio is an industrial State. About 82 percent of all personal income is derived from private nonfarm sources, more than 16 percent from governmental sources (including social security and military benefits), and about 1 percent from agriculture. The major portion of wage income is paid by manufacturing; other large amounts are paid, in descending order, by wholesale and retail trade, national and local governments, and services. About 38 percent of nonfarm workers are employed in manufacturing.

The Tyler-Davidson Fountain, located on Government Square in downtown Cincinnati, Ohio.
Cincinnati Chamber of Commerce

Manufacturing. According to the most recent Census of Manufactures (1968), production workers in Ohio totaled 1,020,000. The largest groups were employed in the manufacture of nonelectrical machinery, in the primary-metals industries, and in the manufacture of transportation equipment and fabricated metal products. Almost one fourth were employed in the Standard Metropolitan Statistical Area (q.v.) of Cleveland, and three fifths of these worked in the city itself. Other manufacturing centers were Cincinnati, Dayton, and Youngstown. The adjusted value added by manufacture (see VALUE) in the largest industries in 1967 totaled $3,294,500,000 for nonelectrical machinery, $2,757,000,000 for primary-metals industries, $2,634,500,000 for transportation equipment, and $2,099,700,000 for fabricated metal products. According to the most recent published figures, the value added by all manufacturing in Ohio in 1968 was $22,312,000,000.

Agriculture. The diversified agriculture of Ohio is concentrated on the production of dairy products, cattle, hogs, and soybeans. Among major crops, besides soybeans, are corn, hay, wheat, tomatoes, and red-clover seeds. Farms numbered 111,000 in 1970, totaling some 17,400,000 acres and averaging 157 acres each. Cash income from crops, livestock, and government payments in 1968 was $1,318,292,000.

Mining. The mineral resources of Ohio include coal, stone, cement, and lime. In the mid-1960's, according to the latest available statistics, mineral production was valued at $455,000,000 annually, representing about 2.2 percent of the U.S. total. In quantity of production Ohio ranked first in clays and lime, third in oven coke, and fourth in salt and sand and gravel. Mineral production was reported in eighty-six counties; the leaders were Belmont, Harrison, and Sandusky counties. Major deposits of coal are located in Belmont and Harrison counties; of lime, in Sandusky County; and of salt, in Summit and Wayne counties. Cement production was reported in eight counties, notably Greene, Muskingum, and Lawrence counties. Fire clays were produced in fifteen counties, with Tuscarawas County leading; and miscellaneous clays were produced in thirty-eight counties, with Cuyahoga County the leading producer. Franklin and Hamilton counties led the sixty-eight counties reporting sand and gravel production. The proved reserves of crude oil in 1970 were 127,367,000 bbl.

Forestry. The forest land of Ohio consists predominantly of hardwoods. The forest land, primarily under private ownership, comprises some 5,000,000 acres. It produces a net annual cut of sawtimber of some 267,000,000 bd.ft.

Tourism. The third-largest industry of Ohio is tourism. In the mid-1960's some 28,000,000 persons visited the State each year, spending an estimated $2,000,000,000. The major attractions were in the N. part of the State, including Cedar Point, an amusement park on Lake Erie, and East Harbor State Park.

Transportation. The first railroad in Ohio was the Erie & Kalamazoo Railroad, inaugurated on Oct. 3, 1836, and now a part of the Penn-Central

An Ohio cornfield. A great agricultural State, Ohio is one of the major States in the production of corn, soybeans, and hay. Ohio Development and Publicity Commission

A finished tire is removed from a vulcanizing mold. Ohio is the foremost producer of automobile tires in the U.S. U.S. Rubber Co.

OHIO

Co. The State is served by twelve other Class 1 railroads, including the C & O/B & O and the Norfolk & Western with a total of about 8585 mi. of track. Rural and municipal roads totaled 107,753 mi. in 1967. Highways of the Federally aided Interstate Highway System totaled 1530 mi. in 1968; Federally aided primary and secondary roads totaled 29,760 mi. Airports numbered about 445 in 1969, and 21 airlines (9 of which were major carriers) provided trunk and local service. The major lake ports are Ashtabula, Cleveland, Conneaut, Lorain, Sandusky, and Toledo. The Ohio R., with its tributary the Muskingum R., forms the principal commercial waterway.

Communications. The first newspaper in Ohio was the *Centinel of the North-Western Territory*, founded in Cincinnati in 1793. The State in 1967 had ninety-six daily newspapers, seventeen Sunday papers, 254 weeklies, and eight Negro papers, five daily and three weekly. Among the leading papers were the Cleveland *Plain Dealer* and *Press*, the Cincinnati *Enquirer* and *Post & Times Star*, the Columbus *Dispatch* and *Citizen-Journal*, and the Toledo *Blade* and *Times*. Of some 110 AM and 125 FM (twenty-four educational) radio stations operating in 1967, among the earliest were WHK in Cleveland and WING in Dayton, both established in 1921. Television stations totaled thirty-nine of which eight were devoted to educational programming.

GOVERNMENT

Ohio is governed under the constitution of 1851, as revised and amended. Executive authority is vested in a governor, a lieutenant governor, an attorney general, and a secretary of state, all elected for four-year terms, and other elected and appointed officials. Legislative authority is exercised by the Senate, with thirty-three members elected for four-year terms; and the House of Representatives, with ninety-nine members elected for two-year terms. The legislature meets biennially in odd-numbered years. The judicial system consists of a seven-member supreme court, courts of appeals, and lesser courts, including courts of common pleas and probate and juvenile courts. The State is divided into eighty-eight counties.

Ohio is represented in the United States Congress by two Senators and twenty-four Representatives.

Voting Qualifications. Suffrage is extended generally to U.S. citizens eighteen years of age who meet the residence requirements (one year in the State and forty days in the county and election precinct).

HISTORY

The first European to explore the territory of present-day Ohio was, probably, the French explorer Robert Cavelier, Sieur de La Salle (q.v.), who claimed to have discovered and ascended the Ohio R. in 1669. When, in 1682, La Salle claimed the entire valley of the Mississippi R. for France, the region between the Great Lakes (to Lake Erie) and the Ohio R. was considered a French possession. French claims were not acknowledged by continuous British colonies, particularly Virginia, which claimed all the territory north of the Ohio R. and west of the Mississippi. After about 1730, traders from Pennsylvania and Virginia entered the area, and in 1749 George II (q.v.), King of Great Britain, awarded a royal grant to the Ohio Company (q.v.), organized by Virginia planters and London merchants, to settle and trade in the valley of the Ohio. The French governor of Canada, in the same year, sent an officer, Pierre Joseph de Céloron de Blainville (1693–1759), to bury lead markers in the name of France along the river banks. Settlements established by the Ohio Company inevitably caused French resentment, and in 1756 clashes between the French, their Indian allies, and the British precipitated the French and Indian War (q.v.). By the terms of the Treaty of Paris in 1763, the victorious British acquired undisputed title to the territory; see PARIS, TREATY OF The Indian allies of France, however, refused to acknowledge British supremacy; they revolted in 1763 in the so-called Conspiracy of Pontiac (see PONTIAC). The Indian war was ended by treaty in 1765.

Conflicting Claims. In 1774, Great Britain made the territory part of Canada. Resentment of the American colonies at the annexation of land claimed by them was one of the causes of the American Revolution. During the war the American frontier leader George Rogers Clark (see under CLARK) invaded and held the region from 1779 to 1783. In the latter year Great Britain ceded its rights to the area, known as the Northwest Territory (q.v.), to the United States. By 1786 all the States had ceded their separate claims in the Northwest Territory to the Federal government, except Connecticut, which retained its claim to the Western Reserve (q.v.) until 1800, and Virginia, which retained its claim to the Virginia Military District, between the Little Miami and Scioto rivers, until 1852. The United States Congress in 1785 enacted the Land Ordinance, establishing conditions for sale of land in the territory, and in 1787 passed the Northwest Ordinance, providing for administration of the territory. The Ohio Company of As-

A view of the Ohio River from the Indiana shoreline.
Standard Oil Co. (N.J.)

sociates was organized in 1786 by veteran officers and soldiers to facilitate land sales.

Early Settlement. The first authorized permanent settlement was founded in 1788 at Marietta the building of which was supervised by American Revolutionary officer and pioneer Rufus Putnam (1738–1824), one of the founders of the Ohio Company of Associates (q.v.). Cincinnati was established in 1789, and in 1798 Cleveland was founded in the Western Reserve. Indians, alarmed at the increasing number of settlers, rose in a series of frontier wars; in 1795 the Indians, defeated by American forces, ceded rights to most of present-day Ohio. Territorial government, under a Federal governor, was instituted in 1799. Ohio was separated from the remainder of the Northwest Territory in 1800, and in 1803 it became the first State of the territory to be admitted to the Union. The capital was first established at Chillicothe and, after several moves, was fixed at Columbus in 1816.

Ohio became continually more prosperous and populous after achieving Statehood; its population, about 42,000 in 1800, increased to more than 230,000 by 1810. The invention of the steamboat made Cincinnati a great river port; and the completion of the Erie Canal (q.v.) from Lake Erie to the Hudson R. in 1825, and of the Ohio and Erie Canals from Portsmouth to Cleveland in 1835 gave the State a shipping route to the Atlantic Ocean inaugurating an era of prosperity. During this period the Mormons (q.v.) under Joseph Smith (q.v.) came to Kirtland, and until 1838 Ohio was the center of Mormonism.

The State was strongly antislavery from its inception, and its cities became famous stops on the Underground Railroad (q.v.) for escaping slaves. During the American Civil War Ohio furnished large contributions of money and troops to the Union forces. Although no major battles were fought in Ohio, in 1863 Morgan's Raid, a series of attacks by Confederate troops under General John H. Morgan (q.v.), caused severe damage in southern Ohio.

After the Civil War. Manufacturing gradually replaced agriculture as the leading Ohio industry. Ohio politics were gradually dominated by the industrialists, notably by George B. Cox (1853–1916), political leader of Cincinnati, and Marcus Alonzo Hanna (q.v.) in Cleveland. Corruption in Ohio politics was notorious until the 1890's, when Ohio citizens demanded reform measures. In 1912, in a constitutional convention, thirty-four amendments were adopted, including provision for initiative and for referendum and recall. Also among the amendments was the authorization of measures to prevent floods in southern Ohio. Floods devastated the Ohio valley several times, notably in 1913, 1915, and 1937.

Since the Civil War and the organization of modern political parties, the Ohio electorate has voted for candidates of the Republican Party in Presidential elections, except in 1912, 1916, 1932, 1936, 1940, 1948, and 1964, when Democratic candidates carried the State. In 1968

OHIO

Ohio gave the Republican candidate, Richard M. Nixon (q.v.), 1,791,014 votes and the Democratic candidate, Hubert H. Humphrey (q.v.), 1,700,586 votes. Eight Presidents of the U.S. have been born in or have been residents of Ohio: William Henry Harrison, Ulysses S. Grant, Rutherford Birchard Hayes, James Abram Garfield, Benjamin Harrison, William McKinley, William Howard Taft, and Warren Gamaliel Harding (qq.v.).

OHIO, river of the United States, formed by the confluence of the Allegheny and Monongahela rivers at Pittsburgh, Pa. It is 981 mi. long and a principal tributary of the Mississippi River (q.v.). The Ohio flows N.W. out of Pittsburgh and then generally S.W., forming the boundaries between Ohio and West Virginia, Ohio and Kentucky, Indiana and Kentucky, and Illinois and Kentucky; it joins the Mississippi R. at Cairo, Ill. The chief tributaries of the Ohio include the Tennessee, Wabash, and Kentucky rivers. Among the cities on the Ohio are Cincinnati, Ohio, Evansville, Ind., Wheeling, W.Va., and Louisville, Ky. The Ohio R. is navigable throughout its course.

OHIO COMPANY, name of two companies organized in the 18th century for the colonization of the Ohio country. The first company was organized in 1749. George II (q.v.), King of Great Britain, granted the company 500,000 acres of land around the forks of the Ohio R. The colonizing efforts of the company were seen by the French as a challenge to their claim on the region, and the rivalry helped to cause the French and Indian War (q.v.). In 1770 the Ohio Company merged with the Vandalia Company.

The second company, the Ohio Company of Associates, was formed in 1786. In 1787 a large tract of land was purchased, and in the following year Marietta (q.v.) was founded by colonists sent out by the company.

OHIO STATE UNIVERSITY, THE, coeducational State-controlled land-grant (see LAND-GRANT COLLEGES) institution of higher learning, situated in Columbus, Ohio, with branches in Lima, Mansfield, Marion, and Newark. The university was chartered in 1870 and opened for instruction three years later; until 1878 it was known as Ohio Agricultural and Mechanical College. The divisions of the university include the colleges of arts and sciences, a federation that includes the colleges of the arts, biological sciences, humanities, mathematical and physical sciences, and social and behavioral sciences; the colleges of administrative sciences, agriculture and home economics, dentistry, education, engineering, law, medicine, optometry, pharmacy, veterinary medicine; and the graduate school and university college. In addition the schools of allied medical professions, architecture, home economics, journalism, music, natural resources, nursing, physical education, and social work are affiliated with the appropriate colleges. The degrees of bachelor, master, doctor, and various professional degrees are granted. In 1968 the university libraries housed about 2,200,000 bound volumes. Student enrollment in 1968 totaled 45,262, the faculty numbered about 4200, and the endowment was approximately $22,365,000.

OHM. See ELECTRICAL UNITS: *Resistance, Capacitance, Inductance.*

OHM, Georg Simon (1787–1854), German physicist, born in Erlangen, and educated at the University of Erlangen. From 1833 to 1849 he was director of the Polytechnic Institute of Nuremberg, and from 1852 until his death he was professor of experimental physics at the University of Munich. Ohm investigated many problems in physics, but he is best known for his research on electrical currents. His formulation of the relationship between current, electromotive force, and resistance, known as Ohm's law, is the basic law of current flow. The unit of electrical resistance was named the ohm in his honor; see ELECTRIC CIRCUIT. Ohm was awarded the Copley medal of the Royal Society of London for Improving Natural Knowledge in 1841 and was made a foreign member of the society the following year. His books include *The Galvanic Current Investigated Mathematically* (1827; Eng. trans., 1891).

OHM'S LAW. See ELECTRIC CIRCUIT.

OIL. See ESSENTIAL OIL; FATS AND FIXED OILS; LUBRICANTS; PETROLEUM.

OILBIRD, or FATBIRD or GUÁCHARO, bird, *Steatornis,* only surviving species of a family, Steatornithidae, in the Goatsucker order. Young oilbirds are valued as food and for their fat, which is extracted and used as a butter substitute. The oilbird resembles the goatsucker but has a stronger beak and eats palm nuts rather than insects. It is about 12 in. long. The mottled plumage is reddish-brown and gray, barred with black and dotted with white. The oilbird is found in deep caverns in northern South America and Trinidad, and is especially abundant near Cumana, Venezuela. The bird emerges from these caverns at night to seek its food.

OIL CITY, city of Pennsylvania, in Venango Co., on the Allegheny R., about 45 miles N.E. of New Castle. Situated in the oil-producing section of the State, Oil City is a refining and distribution center. The city manufactures oil-field equipment, machinery, paint, glass, and metal products. The city was founded about 1860, after oil had been discovered at Titusville, some 15 mi. away, by Edwin Laurentine Drake; *see* PE-TROLEUM: *History.* The city quickly became a center of the new industry. It was incorporated as a borough in 1862 and as a city in 1871. Bituminous coal is mined. Pop (1960) 17,692; (1970) 15,033.

OIL PAINTING, art of applying oil paint to a suitable ground for the purpose of making pictures. The paint consists of powdered pigment ground to a colloidal paste in a drying oil, that is, an oil which upon exposure to air reacts with oxygen to become, by polymerization of its molecules (*see* POLYMER), a horny solid that binds and protects the particles of pigment embedded in it. The ground on which the paint is laid consists of a support, either a panel of wood or composition or, more frequently, a linen, cotton, or jute cloth stretched tightly on a frame. The support is protected by a coating of glue size and is thinly covered with a preparation to which the paint will adhere. Both the grain of the cloth and the tooth (roughness or smoothness) of the preparation, as well as its absorbency to oil, are important factors in determining the ease with which the painter works and the character of the surface of the finished painting.

The preparation of paint and canvas is more a matter of skill and knowledge than of elaborate equipment, and although most artists purchase commercially prepared painting materials, many prefer to make their own. The pigments, colored powders which must be lightproof, insoluble, and chemically inert, are mixed to a stiff paste with drying oil, usually linseed oil, although poppy or walnut oil may be used also, and varnish may be added. This mixture is then rubbed smooth with a glass muller on a flat plate of unpolished glass, more pigment or oil being added until the proper buttery consistency is obtained. The paint is then packaged in tubes.

Present-day pigments are fairly standardized. Lead carbonate, titanium oxide, and zinc oxide are used for whites. For yellows, oranges, and reds, cadmium sulfides and alizarin crimson are used. Blues and greens are made of various salts of cobalt, aluminum, sulfur, iron, and nickel. The earth colors, including reds, ochers, and browns, are derived from natural clays and oxides. The blacks are made from forms of carbon.

The painting ground may be white, but in usual practice it is given a toning coat of pearl gray, tan, or pink. The picture is sketched on this in pencil or charcoal or begun directly in paint. The paint is applied with brushes, a flexible spatula called a pallette knife, or more rarely, with the fingers. According to the usually accepted procedure, the light shades are applied thick and the darks thin. The work proceeds in a series of sittings, beginning with broad areas of color which are refined and corrected as the work continues. Several layers of paint are needed to obtain richness and variety of surface. As a general rule, in the initial stages of a painting, the paint is kept thinner and leaner than in the later stages. The picture is begun with turpentine alone used as a diluent; admixtures of oil or varnish are reserved for the later and finishing sessions. The paint usually dries fast enough to be worked over the next day.

The finished picture must be varnished to protect the surface from dirt and to restore depth of tone to the darker passages, which, with the drying of the oil, turn lighter and lose their dark accents and richness of color. The varnish usually is prepared from resins such as gum mastic or dammar dissolved in spirits of turpentine. Because all varnishes eventually darken and become discolored, the present-day painter tries to select one that can be removed and replaced. The varnish never should be applied until the picture is thoroughly dry, at least a year after it is painted; otherwise the varnish will combine with the paint and cannot be removed without damaging the surface of the painting.

Oil painting is a fairly recent development. Traditionally it is said to have been invented by the Flemish painters Jan and Hubert van Eyck (*see under* EYCK), but recent scholarship has indicated that the art was known long before their time. Because of the ease with which oil paint could be used and the variety of effects that could be obtained, it found wide acceptance among artists as a supplement to the media in use at that time. *See* ENCAUSTIC PAINTING, FRESCO; TEMPERA PAINTING; WATER-COLOR PAINTING. The water media, tempera, and glue and wax emulsions dry almost immediately and change tone in drying, so that the shades of color when dry are difficult to match with fresh wet paint. Usually all tones to be used in these media must be mixed in advance and kept until the picture is finished. Blendings and gradations of tones are difficult, and corrections by overpainting are nearly impossible.

Oil painting, on the other hand, dries more slowly, and the colors change relatively little in drying. Tones are easy to match and corrections

OIL PAINTING

by overpainting are easy to make. The painter is not limited to linear brush strokes or to prearranged linear composition, and he has freedom in color, improvisation, and chiaroscuro (q.v.) impossible without the use of oils.

The oil painting of van Eyck has little in common with oil painting as it is practiced in modern times. Van Ecyk followed quite strictly the methods of the tempera tradition. On a panel covered with gesso, that is, a mixture of glue and whiting applied hot and sanded smooth when dry, he began with a drawing in ink nearly as detailed and elaborate as the finished picture was to be. Upon this he painted in several layers of transparent glaze. The light portions of the van Eyck paintings are thin, the white of the gesso panel showing through, and the darks are built up with layer upon layer of color, with gradations of tone that are impossible to obtain with modern oil paints. The details are almost microscopically fine. The precise composition of van Eyck's painting medium is not known to us. His secret was brought to Italy by the Venetian painter Antonello da Messina (1430?–79). There, during the 16th, 17th, and 18th centuries, the oil technique was elaborately developed by Italian painters such as Il Giorgione, Titian, Paolo Veronese, Il Tintoretto, and Giovanni Battista Tiepolo (qq.v.). The great innovation of the Venetians was painting on canvas. The earlier schools had always painted on panels of wood covered with canvas and gesso. The Venetians eliminated the unwieldy wooden panel and devised a flexible canvas ground. Because the latter was not limited in size, as wooden panels are, and also could be rolled up for shipping, it broadened the demand for large paintings. The Venetian masters, with the help of trained assistants and production-line methods, were able to turn out heroically proportioned pictures in enormous quantities. Large canvases required a freer style of painting than was permitted by the linear restrictions of the tempera style. To solve this problem, the Venetians began the picture on a toned ground and executed the painting in a monochrome of gray, white, brown, or black, using a fast-drying glue or tempera medium. This monochrome underpainting, which was executed in the studio from drawings made in advance rather than from models or from nature, did not need to be highly finished. It served to establish the composition of the picture, systematize the lighting of the objects in it, and set up the pattern of light and dark areas by which the modeling of the object was obtained. The dried underpainting was refined and oil paint applied in more or less transparent layers.

In subsequent times underpainting in tempera largely was abandoned, although until the middle of the 19th century some form of underpainting was in use. The usual practice of painters during the 18th and 19th centuries was to begin their pictures in oil tones of black and gray. When dry the pictures were repainted in colored paint to correspond to the colors of nature; part of the gray underpainting was left to provide the cold blue tones needed in flesh or shadows.

The exact formulas of the oil preparations and tempera media used by the old masters are for all practical purposes unknown. Further, it is nearly impossible to reconstruct the formulas by chemical analysis. The kinds of pigments used by the old masters are well known, however. Many of the pigments have proved to have been subject to fading, and the range of colors was quite limited, having contained no bright yellows or oranges and no safe brilliant green.

Along with new developments in chemistry during the 19th century, many new and brilliant pigments came into use. Some of these proved to be unreliable, but others, such as cobalt blue, the cadmium reds and yellows, and viridian, proved to be safe. The most significant technical advance of the 19th century in oil painting was the invention of the collapsible metal tube for packaging paints. Formerly, oil paint had to be made by the artist in his studio and used there. Landscapes had to be painted in the studio from sketches, from memory, or from imagination. After the introduction of the tube, portable painting kits became available and the art of oil painting was carried out of doors. Subsequently, direct painting without previous sketches or preparation, such as was practiced by the impressionists, became common among oil painters.

In the next important development manufacturers, to make paint in commercial quantities, added preservatives such as wax or various emulsifiers to the paint to keep it fresh until opened. The additives changed the character of the paint, in particular, by rendering the denser pigments less opaque. Impasto, the thick application of pigments to canvas, then came into vogue among artists. The practice of underpainting disappeared almost entirely.

The impressionist technique of composing with small dots of bright colors and of applying bright colors to the shadows, instead of the standard grays, browns, and blacks of earlier times, profoundly influenced the treatment of light in modern painting; see IMPRESSIONISM (in painting). With increased interest in nonobjective painting, that is, painting that does not strive for realistic representations (see ABSTRACT AND NONOBJECTIVE ART), painters have experimented considerably with new textures, for example, by adding sand to paint, as did the French painter Georges Braque (q.v.); or painting in Ripolin, a form of commercial enamel, as did the Spanish-French cubist painter Juan Gris (q.v.); or building up paint textures with plaster of Paris, sprayed-on nylon, and the like. Such innovations are as generally accepted in the medium of oil painting as is the tight and precise technique of the Spanish painter Salvador Dali (q.v.) or the almost wash-drawing style of the American painter Reginald Marsh (1898–1954). Oil paint, by the variety of the effects it can produce and by the ease with which it can be manipulated, has been one of the most effective means of expression of the visual artist. M.G.

OISE, river of France, rising in the Ardennes region of S. Belgium, flowing generally S.W. through the French departments of Nord, Aisne, Oise, and Val d'Oise, and Yvelines, and joining the Seine R. about 6 mi. below Pontoise. It is 186 mi. long. In World War I French troops, during March and April, 1918, were heavily attacked on the Oise, the Germans forcing them back at Chauny and capturing Landricourt and Coucy-le-Château. In June the last great German effort was made in this area. The German supreme war effort, however, had been spent and their battle line was now 50 mi. longer, a serious matter for their dwindling troops. With the aid of the American troops, now arriving, the Allies began their offensive in October, 1918, and drove back the Germans trying to hold their position along the Oise.

OITA, city and port in Japan, and capital of Oita Prefecture, on Kyushu Island, on the S. shore of Beppu Bay, 65 miles S.E. of Yawata. It is a manufacturing center noted for livestock and raw silk. From the 13th century Oita was the seat of the Otomo daimyos, the most powerful of the Kyushu lords. It was at Oita, formerly called Funai, that the Portuguese navigator Fernão Mendes Pinto (about 1514–83) landed in 1543 and introduced firearms to the Japanese. The Jesuits established a mission at Oita soon after. Pop. (1968 est.) 243,000.

OJIBWA or **OJIBWAY**, also called CHIPPEWA, largest and most important North American Indian tribe of the Algonquian (q.v.) linguistic family. They inhabited an extensive territory between Lake Huron and the Turtle Mts. in North Dakota, and reaching into southern Canada. According to Ojibwa tradition, the tribe originally emigrated from the region of the Saint Lawrence R. in the east, in company with the related Ottawa and Potawatomi (qq.v.). The three tribes separated at what is now Mackinaw City, Mich., the Ojibwa spreading westward along both shores of Lake Superior, while the two other tribes went southward. The Ojibwa tribe was scattered over a vast area. It comprised a large number of bands divided into permanent clans said to have numbered more than twenty. Originally, the clans were divided into five phratries, or groups, from which the later number developed. One of the clans claimed the hereditary chieftainship of the entire tribe; another claimed precedence in the councils of war.

The Ojibwa followed an economy based chiefly on hunting, fishing, farming, and the gathering of wild fruits and seeds, particularly the abundant wild rice of the lake region; they also made sugar from maple syrup. Their houses were built on pole frames in wigwam shape and were usually covered with birch bark. Birchbark sheets were also used for keeping simple pictographic records of tribal affairs. Ojibwa mythology was elaborate; the chief religious and superstitious rites centered about the Medewiwin, or grand medicine society.

Although the Ojibwa were one of the largest Indian tribes north of Mexico, they did not have extensive relations with the early European explorers and settlers. They became known to Europeans in the mid-17th century, when they were confined within a narrow area along the shore of Lake Superior by the hostile incursions of the Sioux and Fox (qq.v.). They acquired firearms from the French about 1690, drove off their enemies, and subsequently greatly expanded their territory. The Ojibwa supported the French against the English in the various wars fought in North America, namely King William's War, Queen Anne's War, King George's War, and the French and Indian War (qq.v.). In the American Revolution and the War of 1812, they sided with the British against the Americans. In 1815 they joined with the other belligerent tribes in signing a treaty of peace with the United States government. Under the terms of subsequent treaties, they sold the greater part of their former territories. At the present time the Ojibwa live on a number of reservations in Michigan, Minnesota, Wisconsin, North Dakota, and Montana. They number about 21,750.

OKA, river of the Soviet Union, the Russian S.F.S.R. It rises S. of Orel, and flows 918 miles N. and N.E. through highly populated agricultural and industrial areas, to Gor'kiy. There it joins the Volga R., of which it is the chief western affluent.

OKAYAMA, city and port in Japan, and capital of Okayama Prefecture, on Honshu Island, 70 miles w. of Osaka. It manufactures porcelain ware, textiles, and rush mats. Points of interest include ruins of a feudal castle, the 22-acre, 18th-century park Koraku-en, and a medical university. Pop. (1968 est.) 322,000.

OKAZAKI, city of Japan, in Aichi Prefecture, on the island of Honshu, on the Yahagi R., 20 miles s.e. of Nagoya. A road junction on the Tokaido rail line, it is also the center of a cotton-spinning and weaving industry. In Okazaki Park is the feudal castle that was the birthplace of Iyeyasu (1542–1616), founder of the Tokugawa shogunate; see JAPAN: *History: The Tokugawa Shogunate*. Pop. (1965) 194,408.

OKEECHOBEE, lake of south-central Florida, on the N. edge of the Everglades (q.v.). The second-largest freshwater lake wholly within the United States, Okeechobee is about 35 mi. long and 30 mi. wide, and has an area of about 700 sq.mi.

O'KEEFFE, Georgia (1887–   ), American painter, born in Sun Prairie, Wis., and educated at the Art Institute of Chicago and Columbia University. She taught art in Texas from 1913 to 1918, and the Art Students League of New York City began to exhibit her work in 1916. The following year the American photographer, editor, and art-gallery director Alfred Stieglitz (q.v.), whom she married in 1924, showed her work at his celebrated New York City gallery, "291"; he exhibited her work annually until the year of his death, 1946.

"Cow's Skull: Red, White, and Blue", an oil painting completed by Georgia O'Keeffe in 1931.
Metropolitan Museum of Art – Alfred Stieglitz Collection

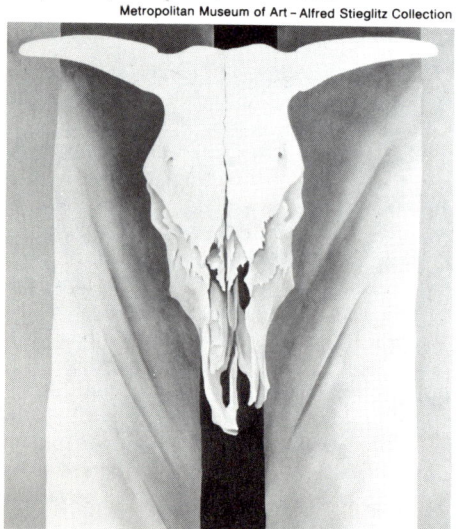

Georgia O'Keeffe is famous for the purity, harmony, and singular femininity of her style. She is best known for her vivid close-ups of individual flowers and for her New Mexican desert landscapes. Although she handles her subject matter representationally, she employs elements of surrealistic composition and abstract design. Miss O'Keeffe received the 1970 Gold Medal Award for art of the National Institute of Arts and Letters (q.v.), and her paintings are included in museum and private collections throughout the United States.

OKEFENOKEE SWAMP, large swamp in s.e. Georgia and n.e. Florida. It is drained by the Saint Marys and Suwannee rivers. It is made up of islands, lakes, brush vines, and cypress forests, and contains a great variety of animals, birds, and fish. Okefenokee Swamp is about 45 mi. long and covers an area of about 660 sq.mi.; much of it lies within the Okefenokee National Wildlife Refuge.

O'KELLY, Seán Thomas (1882–1966), Irish journalist and political leader, second president of Eire (now the Republic of Ireland), born in Dublin where he was educated. He was a frequent contributor to Irish and American newspapers on the subject of Irish politics, and, to disseminate his views on Irish independence, he founded and edited in Dublin the newspaper *The Nation.* For many years O'Kelly was vice-president of the Fianna Fáil, or Republican Party, and he was one of the founders of the Sinn Fein (q.v.). O'Kelly was elected a deputy to the first Dáil Éireann, the parliament of Ireland in 1919, when he also became an envoy to France and Italy. From 1924 to 1926 O'Kelly was his country's envoy to the United States. He was minister of finance from 1939 until 1945, when he was elected president of Eire. O'Kelly was re-elected in 1952 and served until 1959.

OKINAWA, island of the s.w. Pacific Ocean, under United Nations trusteeship and United States administration, largest of the Ryukyu Islands, 330 miles s. of the Japanese island of Kyushu. The chief industries are agriculture, fishing, lumbering, food processing, and the manufacture of textiles, Panama hats, and pottery. United States military bases also contribute to the economy. Extending generally n.e. to s.w., the island is 60 mi. long and 9 mi. wide. The entire coast is fringed with coral reefs. The terrain of the northern two thirds of Okinawa is mountainous and forested. The southern third is hilly, rolling country and contains most of the Okinawan population. Naha (q.v.) is the largest and most important city and the major port of Okinawa, and it is the capital of the Ryukyu Islands.

OKLAHOMA

History. Until the 14th century, Okinawa was an independent kingdom; but paid tribute to China between the 14th and 19th centuries. Japan annexed Okinawa in 1879. Little commercial development was undertaken by the Japanese, who fortified the island and, between the two World Wars, built large airfields in the southern third, particularly around Naha. Until 1945, Okinawa was the seat of Okinawa Prefecture, Japan. On April 1, 1945, during World War II, the United States Tenth Army landed on the W. coast of Okinawa, thus beginning the last great amphibious operation of the war. The Japanese resisted with tenacity, and the battle became one of the most bitter of the Pacific campaigns. Of the 36 Allied ships sunk during the campaign, 26 were destroyed by Japanese kamikaze (suicide) pilots. On June 21, after 82 days of fighting, organized Japanese resistance ceased. Japanese deaths amounted to 110,071; American losses were 12,281. The Japanese lost 7830 airplanes, the American forces, 763. The Okinawan airfields were quickly reconstructed and developed by the U.S. Army, and the U.S. Air Force used them to launch daily bombing attacks against the Japanese main islands beginning in late June; see WORLD WAR II: *Battles for Iwo Jima and Okinawa*. Although Okinawa has been under U.S. control since the surrender of Japan in August, 1945, negotiations were concluded in November, 1969, to return it to Japan in 1972. Area, 467 sq.mi.; pop. (1965) 758,777.

OKLAHOMA, West South-Central State of the United States, bounded on the N. by Colorado and Kansas, on the E. by Missouri and Arkansas, on the S. by the Red R., and on the W. by Texas and New Mexico. Oklahoma is roughly rectangular in shape, with a narrow panhandle extending westward in the N. The main part of the State measures about 305 mi. from E. to W. and 205 mi. from N. to S.; the panhandle is about 165 mi. from E. to W. and 34 mi. from N. to S.

Area (18th State in rank)	69,919 sq. mi.
Land	69,031 sq. mi.
Inland water	888 sq. mi.
Population	(1970, 27th in rank) 2,559,253
	(1960, 27th in rank) 2,328,284
	(1950) 2,233,351
Altitude	287 ft. to 4973 ft.
Capital and largest city	Oklahoma City (1970) 359,671
Entered Union (46th State)	Nov. 16, 1907
Nickname	The Sooner State
Motto	Labor Omnia Vincit
	(Labor Conquers All Things)
Song	"Oklahoma"
Tree	redbud
Flower	mistletoe
Bird	scissor-tailed flycatcher

THE LAND

The topography of Oklahoma includes isolated groups of mountainous wooded highlands and treeless plains and prairies. The highest elevation, 4973 ft., is at Black Mesa at the N.W. tip of the panhandle. The lowest point, 287 ft., is on the Little R. in McCurtain County. The average elevation of the State is 1300 ft. The highland areas of Oklahoma include the Ozark Plateau in the N.E., the Ouachita Mts. in the S.E., the Wichita Mts. in the S.W., and the Great Plains, which form a lofty tableland in the N.W. A level to gently rolling plain lies S. of the Ouachita Mts.; the region W. of the Ozark Plateau consists of prairies traversed by deep-cutting streams.

Rivers and Lakes. The important rivers of Oklahoma are the Arkansas, which flows S.E. across the N.E. corner of the State; the Cimarron, Salt Fork, Canadian, and North Canadian rivers, which join the Arkansas R.; and the Red R., which forms the border with Texas in the S. The natural lakes of Oklahoma are small; however, the State has numerous large reservoirs. Among the largest are Lake Texoma, partly in Texas, formed by Denison Dam on the Red R.; Eufaula Reservoir on the Canadian R.; Fort Gibson Reservoir and Lake o' the Cherokees on the Neosho R.; Keystone, Short Mt., and Webbers Falls reservoirs on the Arkansas R.; Tenkiller Ferry Reservoir on the Illinois R.; and Oologah Reservoir on the Verdigris R.

Climate. The climate of Oklahoma is mostly continental in type, with pronounced daily and seasonal temperature changes. Summers are long and sometimes very hot, but mitigated by low humidity and southerly breezes. Winters are cold but relatively short. The highest temperature recorded in the State was 120° F. (at Tishomingo); the lowest, −27° F. (at Watts). Rainfall is heaviest in late spring and early summer and is usually adequate. Annual average snowfall ranges from 2 in. in the S.E. to 25 in. in parts of the Panhandle; it rarely remains on the ground longer than a few days. The average annual number of days with measurable precipitation is 82 at Oklahoma City and 90 at Tulsa. In the E. part of the State, ten to fifteen thunderstorms occur per year, sometimes accompanied by hail; and tornadoes occur on an average of five per year.

Climate	Oklahoma City	Tulsa
Normal temperatures (in ° F.)		
January maximum	45.9	45.9
January minimum	28.1	26.5
July maximum	92.8	92.9
July minimum	72.2	71.4
Annual	60.3	59.7
Normal precipitation (in inches)		
Wettest month	5.19	5.26
Driest month	1.31	1.62
Annual	30.82	37.08
Latest frost	March 28	March 31
Earliest frost	Nov. 7	Nov. 2
Mean number of days between latest and earliest frost	223	216

121

OKLAHOMA

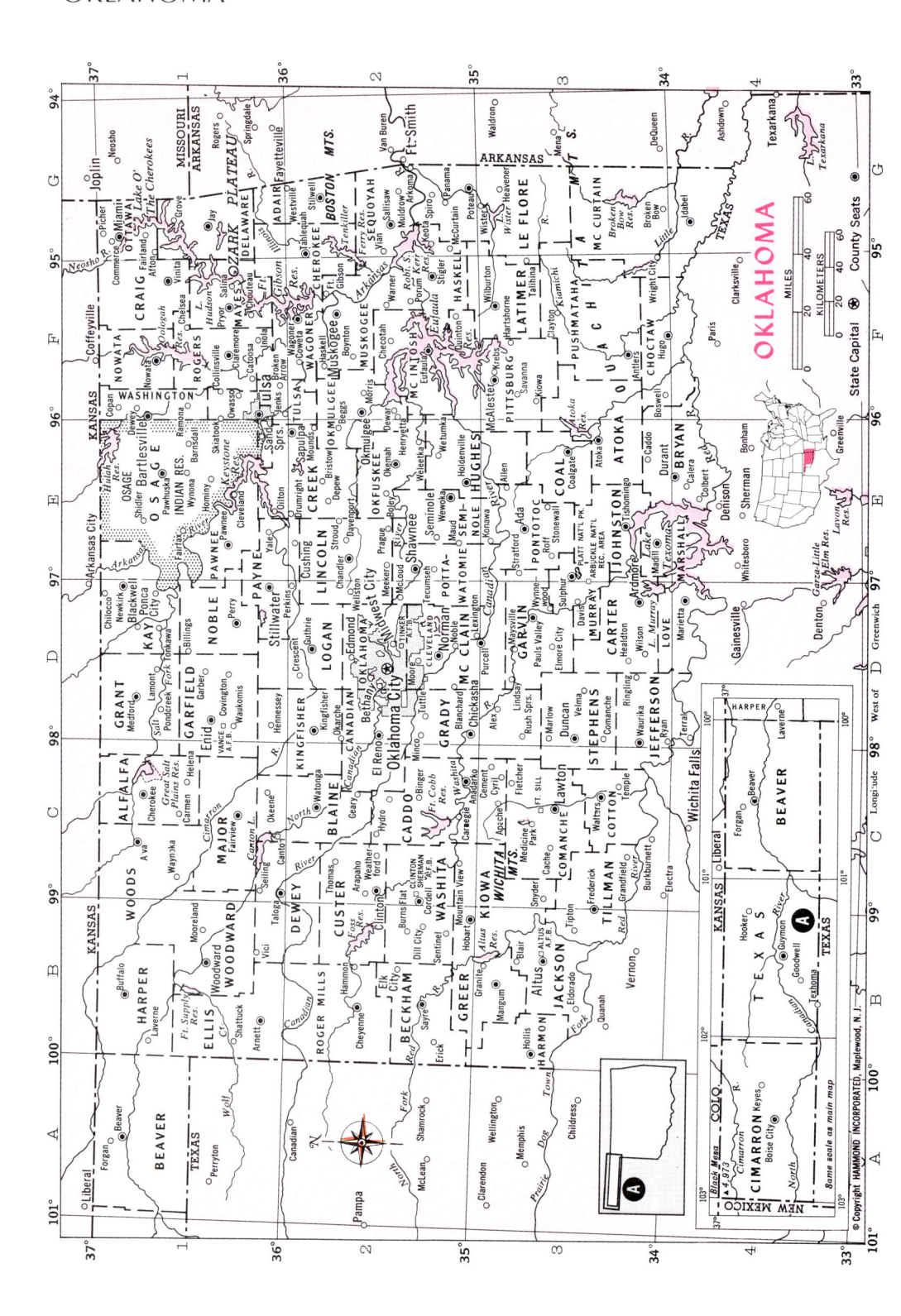

OKLAHOMA

INDEX TO MAP OF OKLAHOMA

Cities and Towns

Ada ⊙	E 3
Afton	F 1
Alex	D 3
Allen	E 3
Altus ⊙	B 3
Alva ⊙	C 1
Anadarko ⊙	C 2
Antlers ⊙	F 3
Apache	C 3
Arapaho ⊙	C 2
Ardmore ⊙	E 3
Arkoma	G 2
Arnett ⊙	B 1
Atoka ⊙	E 3
Barnsdall	E 1
Bartlesville ⊙	E 1
Beaver ⊙	A 1, C 4
Beggs	F 2
Bethany	D 2
Billings	D 1
Binger	C 2
Blackwell	D 1
Blair	B 3
Blanchard	D 2
Boise City ⊙	A 4
Boley	E 2
Boswell	F 3
Boynton	F 2
Bristow	E 2
Broken Arrow	F 1
Broken Bow	G 3
Buffalo ⊙	B 1
Burns Flat	B 2
Cache	C 3
Caddo	E 3
Calera	E 4
Canton	C 1
Carmen	C 1
Carnegie	C 2
Catoosa	F 1
Cement	C 3
Chandler ⊙	D 2
Checotah	F 2
Chelsea	F 1
Cherokee ⊙	C 1
Cheyenne ⊙	B 2
Chickasha ⊙	D 2
Chilocco	D 1
Chouteau	F 1
Claremore ⊙	F 1
Clayton	F 3
Cleveland	E 1
Clinton	B 2
Coalgate ⊙	E 3
Colbert	E 4
Collinsville	F 1
Comanche	D 3
Commerce	F 1
Copan	F 1
Cordell ⊙	C 2
Covington	D 1
Coweta	F 2
Crescent	D 2
Cushing	E 2
Cyril	C 3
Davenport	E 2
Davis	D 3
Depew	E 2
Dewar	F 2
Dewey	F 1
Dill City	B 2
Drumright	E 2
Duncan ⊙	D 3
Durant ⊙	E 3
Edmond	D 2
El Reno ⊙	C 2
Eldorado	B 3
Elk City	B 2
Elmore City	D 3
Enid ⊙	D 1
Erick	B 2
Eufaula ⊙	F 2
Fairfax	E 1
Fairland	G 1
Fairview ⊙	C 1
Fletcher	C 3
Forgan	A 1, C 4
Fort Gibson	F 2
Frederick ⊙	C 3
Garber	D 1
Geary	C 2
Goodwell	B 4
Grandfield	C 3
Granite	B 3
Grove ⊙	G 1
Guthrie ⊙	D 2
Guymon ⊙	B 4
Haileyville	F 3
Hammon	B 2
Hartshorne	F 3
Haskell	F 2
Healdton	D 3
Heavener	G 3
Helena	C 1
Hennessey	D 1
Henryetta	E 2
Hinton	C 2
Hobart ⊙	B 2
Holdenville ⊙	E 2
Hollis ⊙	B 3
Hominy	E 1
Hooker	B 4
Hugo ⊙	F 3
Hydro	C 2
Idabel ⊙	G 4
Inola	F 1
Jay ⊙	G 1
Jenks	F 2
Keota	G 2
Keyes	A 4
Kingfisher ⊙	D 2
Kiowa	F 3
Konawa	E 3
Krebs	F 3
Lamont	D 1
Laverne	A 1, C 4
Lawton ⊙	C 3
Lexington	D 2
Lindsay	D 3
Madill ⊙	E 3
Mangum ⊙	B 3
Marietta ⊙	D 4
Marlow	D 3
Maud	E 2
Maysville	D 3
McAlester ⊙	F 3
McLoud	E 2
Medford ⊙	D 1
Medicine Park	C 3
Meeker	E 2
Miami ⊙	G 1
Midwest City	D 2
Minco	C 2
Moore	D 2
Mooreland	B 1
Morris	E 2
Mounds	E 2
Mountain View	C 2
Muldrow	G 2
Muskogee ⊙	F 2
Newkirk ⊙	D 1
Noble	D 2
Norman ⊙	D 2
Nowata ⊙	F 1
Oilton	E 1
Okarche	D 2
Okeene	D 2
Okemah ⊙	E 2
Oklahoma City (cap.)	D 2
Okmulgee ⊙	E 2
Owasso	F 1
Panama	G 2
Pauls Valley ⊙	D 3
Pawhuska ⊙	E 1
Pawnee ⊙	E 1
Perkins	D 2
Perry ⊙	D 1
Picher	F 1
Ponca City	D 1
Pondcreek	D 1
Porum	F 2
Poteau ⊙	G 2
Prague	E 2
Pryor ⊙	F 1
Purcell ⊙	D 3
Quinton	F 2
Ramona	E 1
Ringling	D 3
Roff	D 3
Rush Springs	D 3
Ryan	D 3
Salina	F 1
Sallisaw ⊙	G 2
Sand Springs	E 1
Sapulpa ⊙	E 2
Savanna	F 3
Sayre ⊙	B 2
Seiling	C 1
Seminole	E 2
Sentinel	B 2
Shattuck	B 1
Shawnee ⊙	E 2
Shidler	E 1
Skiatook	E 1
Snyder	C 3
Spiro	F 2
Stigler ⊙	F 2
Stillwater ⊙	D 1
Stilwell ⊙	G 2
Stonewall	E 3
Stratford	E 3
Stroud	E 2
Sulphur ⊙	E 3
Tahlequah ⊙	G 2
Talihina	F 3
Taloga ⊙	B 1
Tecumseh ⊙	E 2
Temple	C 3
Terral	D 4
Texhoma	B 4
Thomas	C 2
Tipton	B 3
Tishomingo ⊙	E 3
Tonkawa	D 1
Tulsa ⊙	F 1
Tuttle	D 2
Velma	D 3
Vian	G 2
Vici	B 1
Vinita ⊙	F 1
Wagoner ⊙	F 2
Walters ⊙	C 3
Warner	F 2
Watonga ⊙	C 2
Waukomis	D 1
Waurika ⊙	D 3
Waynoka	C 1
Weatherford	C 2
Weleetka	E 2
Wellston	D 2
Westville	G 2
Wetumka	E 2
Wewoka ⊙	E 2
Wilburton ⊙	F 3
Wilson	D 3
Wister	G 3
Woodward ⊙	B 1
Wright City	F 3
Wynnewood	D 3
Wynona	E 1
Yale	E 1

Physical Features

Altus (res.)	B 3
Altus A.F.B.	B 3
Arbuckle Nat'l Rec. Area	E 3
Arkansas (river)	F 2
Atoka (res.)	F 3
Black Mesa (mt.)	A 4
Boston (mts.)	G 2
Broken Bow (res.)	G 3
Canadian (river)	D 3
Canton (lake)	C 1
Cherokees (lake)	G 1
Cimarron (river)	C 1
Clinton Sherman A.F.B.	C 2
Eufaula (res.)	F 2
Fort Cobb (res.)	C 2
Fort Gibson (res.)	F 1
Fort Sill	C 3
Fort Supply (res.)	B 1
Foss (res.)	B 2
Great Salt Plains (res.)	C 1
Hudson (lake)	F 1
Hulah (res.)	E 1
Illinois (river)	G 1
Keystone (res.)	E 1
Kiamichi (river)	F 3
Lake O' The Cherokees (lake)	G 1
Little (river)	G 3
Murray (lake)	D 3
Neosho (river)	F 1
North Canadian (river)	C 2
North Fork Red (river)	A 2
Oologah (res.)	F 1
Osage Indian Res.	E 1
Ouachita (mts.)	F 3
Ozark (plateau)	G 1
Platt Nat'l Park	E 3
Prairie Dog Town Fork (riv.)	A 3
Red (river)	E 4
Robert S. Kerr (res.)	F 2
Salt Fork, Arkansas (riv.)	D 1
Tenkiller Ferry (res.)	G 2
Texoma (lake)	E 3
Tinker A.F.B.	D 2
Vance A.F.B.	C 1
Washita (river)	C 2
Wichita (mts.)	C 3
Wister (lake)	G 3
Wolf (creek)	A 1

⊙ County seat.

Plants and Animals. Forest trees in E. Oklahoma include pines, oaks, elms, hickories, ashes, and cottonwood. Walnut and cedar trees and native grasses, sagebrush, and yucca grow in other areas of the State. Animals of the woodland areas include the white-tailed deer, wildcat, beaver, raccoon, mink, and opossum. Wildlife of the plains includes black-tailed jackrabbit, pocket gopher, coyote, and black-tailed prairie dog.

Parks, Forests, and Other Places of Interest. The one national park in Oklahoma is Platt National Park (q.v.) near Sulphur, containing many cold mineral springs. Part of Ouachita National Forest is in Oklahoma, the remainder in Arkansas; it contains mountains, lakes, mineral springs, and game refuges. The Arbuckle National Recreation Area (q.v.) surrounds Arbuckle Reservoir. The State parks have historic associations as well as extensive recreational facilities.

The "Statue of a Cowboy" in front of the State capitol is a tribute to the settlers of the State.   Philip Gendreau

Among them are Beaver's Bend State Park, near Broken Bow; Lake Murray State Park, near Ardmore; Quartz Mt. State Park, near Altus; Robbers' Cave State Park, near Wilburton; Roman Nose State Park near Watonga; Sequoyah State Park, near Muskogee; and Lake Texoma State Park, on the Texas border. Various places of interest in Oklahoma reflect the Indian and pioneer heritage of the State. Dances, ceremonies, and festivals are held yearly by Indians in many areas, notably the Cherokee Sacred Fire Ceremony, near Gore, and the Osage dances in Pawhuska. A Chisholm Trail and Pioneer Day celebration is held each year at El Reno. In Fort Sill, near Lawton, is the guardhouse, now a museum, in which the Apache Indian chief Geronimo (q.v.) was confined for a time. Other attractions of the State include the petrified woods and dinosaur fossils in Cimarron County; an ancient cypress tree more than 56 ft. in circumference near Broken Bow; and the Will Rogers Memorial near Claremore.

Sports. With a number of rivers and some well-developed lakes, Oklahoma provides year-round fishing. Species found include black and white bass, bluegill, crappie, channel and blue catfish, bullhead, and rainbow trout. Game animals and birds hunted are white-tailed deer, antelope, gray and fox squirrels, cottontail rabbit, jackrabbit, wild turkey, ring-necked pheasant, and bobwhite and scaled quail.

THE PEOPLE

According to the 1970 decennial census, the population of Oklahoma was 2,559,253, an increase of 9.9 percent over the 1960 population. The urban segment comprised 1,740,137 persons, 68 percent of the total, compared with 62.9 percent in 1960. The rural segment comprised 819,092 persons, 34 percent of the total, compared with 37.1 percent in 1960. Ethnically, the 1970 population was distributed as follows: white persons, 2,280,362, nonwhites, 278,867, including 171,892 Negroes, 98,468 Indians, 1408 Japanese, and others. The percentage of native-born residents was 99.1; of foreign-born, 0.9. The 1970 population density averaged 37.2 per sq.mi., compared with 33.8 in 1960.

The chief cities, in order of population, are Oklahoma City, the capital, and the industrial and financial center of the State; Tulsa, center for oil production and agricultural trading; Lawton, a center of agricultural industries; Norman, heart of an agricultural area and site of the University of Oklahoma; Midwest City, a manufacturing center; Enid, a rail hub and commercial center for a wheat- and cattle-growing and oil-producing area; and Muskogee, a manufacturing center.

Extensive lands in Oklahoma are set aside for Indian tribes, including the Cheyenne, Arapaho, Kiowa, Comanche, Apache, Caddo, Delaware, Wichita, Kaw, Otoe, Missouri, Pawnee, Ponca, Tonkawa, Iowa, Kickapoo, Potawatomi, Sac, Fox, and Osage. In addition, members of the Five Civilized Tribes—Cherokee, Chickasaw, Choctaw, Creek, and Seminole—occupy some 768,000 acres in the State.

Education. The public-school system of Oklahoma was established in 1890. Education is free and compulsory for all children between the ages of seven and eighteen.

ELEMENTARY AND SECONDARY SCHOOLS. In the mid-1960's public elementary schools numbered about 1675 and public secondary schools, about 925. Enrollment was about 347,000 in elementary and about 251,000 in secondary schools. Teachers in the public-school system numbered about 13,375 in elementary and about 11,325 in secondary schools. In the mid-1960's private institutions included about 95 elementary schools with some 18,300 students, and about 30 secondary schools with some 4100 students. Teachers in private schools numbered about 975.

UNIVERSITIES AND COLLEGES. In the mid-1960's Oklahoma had thirty-four institutions of higher learning, eleven of which were privately supported. University and college enrollment was about 85,375. State institutions include the Uni-

OKLAHOMA

versity of Oklahoma (q.v.), Cameron State College, Langston University, Northeastern Oklahoma Agricultural and Mechanical College, Northeast State College, Northwest State College, Oklahoma State University of Agriculture and Applied Science, Southeastern State College, and Southwestern State College. Private institutions include Bethany-Nazarene College, Oklahoma Baptist University, Oklahoma Christian College, Oklahoma City University, Philips University, and the University of Tulsa.

CULTURAL INSTITUTIONS. Museums include the Southern Plains Museum and the adjoining National Hall of Fame for Famous American Indians, in Anadarko; the Woolaroc Museum, in Bartlesville; the Museum of the Great Plains, in Lawton; the Oklahoma Historical Society and the Oklahoma Art Center, both in Oklahoma City; and the Gilcrease Museum and Philbrook Art Center, in Tulsa.

THE ECONOMY

Oklahoma has a diversified economy. About 66 percent of all personal income is derived from private nonfarm sources, more than 28 percent from governmental sources (including social security and military benefits), and about 4.5 percent from agriculture. The major portion of wage income is paid, in descending order, by national and local governments, manufacturing, wholesale and retail trade, services, and mining. Almost 25 percent of nonfarm workers are employed in governmental activities, and more than 5 percent in mining, including petroleum extraction. Wholesale and retail trade employ 22 percent of workers. Oklahoma is visited each year by some 24,000,000 tourists, who spend about $204,000,000.

At the disposal of electric utilities and industrial plants in the State, according to the latest available statistics (1966), were some 335,000 kw of developed waterpower; an estimated 866,000 kw remained for future development.

Manufacturing. According to the most recent Census of Manufactures (1967), production workers in Oklahoma totaled 78,900. The largest groups were employed in the manufacture of nonelectrical machinery, fabricated metal products, and transportation equipment. About 35 percent were employed in the Standard Metropolitan Statistical Area (q.v.) of Tulsa, and half of these worked in the city itself. The other manufacturing center was Oklahoma City. The value added by manufacture (see VALUE) in the largest industries totaled $190,900,000 for nonelectrical machinery, $164,600,000 for fabricated metal products, and $156,900,000 for transporation equipment. Food processing, although ranking

Price Tower, Bartlesville, Okla. Designed by Frank Lloyd Wright in 1956, it has been cited for embodying trends toward future architecture. Eastman Kodak Co.

125

Oklahoma. Plate 1. Above: View of Tulsa, called the "oil capital of the world", the center of a vast oil-producing region. Below: The State capitol, at Oklahoma City, is unique in having oil-drilling equipment on its grounds.

Pictures Plates 1 and 2.
Oklahoma Planning & Resources Board

Oklahoma. Plate 2. Right: The Prayer Tower, focal point of the Oral Roberts University campus in Tulsa was designed by the American architect Frank W. Wallace (1923–   ). The coeducational institution, connected with the Pentecostal-Holiness Church, was founded in 1965 and includes a theological seminary. Below: View of the Wichita Mts., in southwestern Oklahoma.

The annual wheat harvest, with big "gleaner" combines moving across the fields. Wheat is Oklahoma's major crop.   UPI

fourth in employment, ranked second in value added, at $177,700,000. According to the most recent published figures, the value added by all manufacturing in Oklahoma in 1968 was 1,509,000,000.

Agriculture. The agriculture of Oklahoma is diversified, with concentration on the production of cattle, wheat, dairy products, and peanuts. Another major crop is hay. In the late-1960's, according to latest available statistics, Oklahoma ranked fourth in wheat and sorghum grain. In 1970 farms numbered about 90,000, totaling some 37,200,000 acres and averaging 413 acres each. Cash income from crops, livestock, and government payments in 1968 was $954,397,000.

Mining. The mineral resources of Oklahoma include petroleum, natural gas, natural-gas liquids, and cement. In the mid-1960's, according to the latest available statistics, mineral production was valued at $881,000,000, representing about 4.3 percent of the U.S. total. In quantity of production, Oklahoma ranked second in tripoli and helium, third in natural gas and natural-gas liquids, and fourth in petroleum. Mineral production was reported in seventy-six counties, the leaders being Stephens, Garvin, Osage, Carter, Texas, Kingfisher, Beaver, Creek, McClain, and Seminole counties. Petroleum was produced in sixty-six counties, the leaders being Stephens, Osage, Carter, Garvin, and Creek counties. Cement was produced in Pontotoc, Mayes, and Rogers counties. The proved reserves of crude oil in 1970 were 1,389,983,000 bbl., and indicated additional reserves were 503,602,000 bbl.

Forestry. The forest land of Oklahoma is divided between hardwoods and softwoods. The forest land, primarily under private ownership, comprises some 5,000,000 acres. It produces a net annual cut of sawtimber of some 124,000,000 bd. ft.

Transportation. The first railroad in Oklahoma was the Missouri-Kansas-Texas, inaugurated on June 6, 1870. The State is served by five other Class I railroads, including the Atchison, Topeka & Santa Fe System, the Saint Louis–San Francisco, and the Chicago, Rock Island & Pacific, with a total of about 5100 mi. of track. Rural and municipal roads totaled 106,769 mi. in 1967. Highways of the Federally aided Interstate Highway System totaled 798 mi. in 1968; Federally aided primary and secondary roads totaled 22,081 mi. Airports numbered about 195 in the mid-1960's, and six airlines provided trunk and local service in 1967. The Arkansas-Verdigris R. system forms a commercially navigable waterway.

Communications. The first newspaper in Oklahoma was the *Cherokee Advocate*, founded at Tahlequah in 1844 and printed in Cherokee and English. The State in 1967 had fifty-three daily newspapers, forty-two Sunday papers, 213 weeklies, and four Negro papers, one daily and three weekly. Of some sixty AM and twenty-five FM (four educational) radio stations operating in 1967, among the earliest was WKY (1920) in Oklahoma City. Sixteen television stations were in operation, of which three were devoted to educational programming.

GOVERNMENT

Oklahoma is governed under the constitution of 1907, as amended. Executive authority is vested in a governor, a lieutenant governor, an attorney general, and a secretary of state, all elected for four-year terms, and other elected and appointed officials. Legislative authority is exercised by the Senate, with forty-eight members elected for four-year terms; and the House of

OKLAHOMA CITY

Representatives with ninety-nine members elected for two-year terms. The legislature meets annually. The judicial system includes a nine-member supreme court, a court of criminal appeals, district and superior courts, and various special and lesser courts. The State is divided into seventy-seven counties.

Oklahoma is represented in the United States Congress by two Senators and six Representatives.

Voting Qualifications. Suffrage is extended generally to U.S. citizens eighteen years of age who meet the residence requirements (six months in the State, six months in the county, and thirty days in the election district).

HISTORY

The Spanish explorer Francisco Vásquez Coronado (q.v.) was the first European to enter Oklahoma, in 1541. French traders and trappers visited the region in the 16th and 17th centuries. In 1803, as a result of the Louisiana Purchase (q.v.), all of Oklahoma except the extreme western panhandle portion of the present State became a part of the United States. In 1817 the Federal government began sending the large Indian populations of Alabama, Georgia, Florida, and Mississippi to the region. Oklahoma was divided among the Five Civilized Nations, consisting of the Creek, Cherokee, Chickasaw, Choctaw (qq.v.), and Seminole Indian tribes. In 1834 the region was established as the Indian Territory (q.v.), and the tribal authority of the Indian nations within the territory was assured.

During the Civil War, the Indians of the territory, many of whom owned slaves, sided with the Confederacy. After the war, by a series of treaties from 1866 to 1883, the Indian nations were forced to cede the western half of the territory to the U.S. as a home for other Indian tribes. Great tracts of land still remained unoccupied, and although white men were forbidden by law to settle on these lands, colonization schemes were developed by various groups; as a result, President Rutherford B. Hayes (q.v.) issued proclamations in 1879 and 1880 forbidding settlement in the territory. Violations occurred frequently, and agitation for the opening of the lands to white men increased to a point at which Congress in 1885 authorized the President to open negotiations with the Creek and Seminole tribes for the purpose of opening the unoccupied tracts for settlement. The negotiations were successfully concluded in 1889, and at noon on April 22 the land was opened to the public. A race for the best lands and town sites ensued as nearly 50,000 persons flooded the Territory the first day. Tent towns were laid out, farms sprang up, and the population of the area increased at an extraordinary rate.

On March 2, 1890, the Federal government established the Territory of Oklahoma, which consisted of lands in the southern part of the region and the western portion of the Indian Territory, in addition to the panhandle strip north of Texas. Additional lands were opened to settlement in 1891, 1892, 1893, 1895, 1901, and 1906. The Territory of Oklahoma sought Statehood as early as 1891. Indian Territory did not seriously try to gain Statehood until 1905. In 1906, after prolonged debate in Congress, a bill was passed providing that both territories be admitted to the Union as one State, if such union were approved by each territory. On Nov. 16, 1907, the combined territories entered the Union as the 46th State.

From 1908 through 1964 the Democratic candidate for President carried Oklahoma, except for the elections of 1920, 1928, 1952, 1956, and 1960, when the Republican candidate received the majority of votes. In 1968 the State gave the Republican candidate, Richard M. Nixon (q.v.), 449,697 votes and the Democratic candidate Hubert H. Humphrey (q.v.), 306,658 votes.

OKLAHOMA CITY, city and capital of Oklahoma, and county seat of Oklahoma Co., on the North Canadian R., near the center of the State, about 100 miles s.w. of Tulsa. It is the largest city in population in Oklahoma and the leading commercial, manufacturing, and financial center. Educational institutions in the city and vicinity include Oklahoma City University (Methodist), established in 1904, the University of Oklahoma School of Medicine (see OKLAHOMA, UNIVERSITY OF), Oklahoma City Law School, Oklahoma Christian College, Oklahoma State University Technical Institute, Southwestern College, and Midwest Christian College. The State Capitol, surrounded by a landscaped area of 100 acres, is of white limestone in Roman Corinthian design. Oklahoma City is governed under the council-city manager system.

Commerce and Industry. Oklahoma City is one of the principal markets for cotton and livestock in the United States, the chief distributing and shipping point of the State, and the headquarters of an extensive area of natural-gas and oil production. Numerous producing oil wells are within the city limits. The city has large wholesale and retail firms, insurance offices, and a branch of the Federal Reserve Bank. Industries include meat-packing plants, flour and feed mills, cotton gins, cotton and cottonseed-oil mills, machine shops, ironworks, printing and publishing plants, and factories manufac-

OKLAHOMA, UNIVERSITY OF

turing airplanes, steel, oil-field equipment, storage tanks and batteries, asphalt, and furniture. A number of new firms manufacture electronic equipment.

History. The site of the present city was no-man's land and was opened to white settlement by Presidental proclamation in the famous Run of April 22, 1889. By nightfall of that day a tent colony of 10,000 settlers had been established. Oklahoma City was chartered in 1890 and made the State capital in 1910.

Population. Between 1910 and 1950 the population of Oklahoma City increased from 64,205 to 243,504. In 1960 it was 324,253, and in 1970 it was 366,481.

OKLAHOMA, UNIVERSITY OF, coeducational State-supported institution of higher learning, located in Norman, Okla. Founded in 1890 by act of the first Oklahoma Territorial legislature, the university opened for instruction two years later. Divisions of the university are a graduate college; university college; colleges of arts and sciences, business administration, education, engineering, fine arts, law, library science, pharmacy, and social work; an extension division; and, at Oklahoma City, schools of medicine and nursing. The university maintains a biological station at Lake Texoma on the Oklahoma-Texas border. The degrees of bachelor, master, and doctor are conferred. In 1968 the college libraries housed more than 1,019,000 bound volumes. In 1968 total enrollment was 19,930, the faculty numbered about 2000, and the endowment of the university was approximately $13,477,000.

OKMULGEE, city in Oklahoma, and county seat of Okmulgee Co., about 38 miles s. of Tulsa. The city has oil and gas wells, coal mines, and varied manufacturing. From 1868 to 1907, this area was the chief center of the Creek Indians. A museum, originally a Creek council house, is nearby. The city was settled in 1872. Pop. (1960) 15,951; (1970) 15,180.

OKRA or **GUMBO,** common name applied to an annual herb, *Hibiscus esculentis,* belonging to the Mallow family; see HIBISCUS. The okra, which is native to Africa, is extensively cultivated in the southern United States and the West Indies for its long, many-seeded pod that, when still young and green, is used to thicken soups and stews and as a cooked vegetable itself. The okra bears large, yellow flowers, similar in structure to typical *Hibiscus* flowers, and is occasionally planted in flower gardens in warm regions of the U.S.

OKUMA, Marquis Shigenobu (1838–1922), Japanese statesman, born in Saga. While still a young man he began to oppose Japanese feudalism and championed constitutional government. Okuma became minister of finance in 1869, and during the following twelve years modernized the fiscal structure of Japan. In 1882 he founded both the Kaishinto ("Progressive Party") and what is now Waseda University in Tokyo. He served as foreign minister in 1888–89 and 1896–97 and as prime minister in 1898 and from 1914 to 1916. During Okuma's second premiership Japan joined the Allies in World War I, flourished economically, and issued the Twenty-One Demands to China (q.v.), which exacted Japanese territorial, industrial, and transportation privileges in that country. See JAPAN: *History.*

OLAF or **OLAV,** name of a number of European kings. Brief accounts of less important rulers are included in this article under the names of the countries which they ruled. The more important monarchs are described in separate biographical articles, to which the reader is referred below.

DENMARK

Olaf I, nicknamed HUNGER (d. 1095), King of Denmark (1086–95). His epithet derives from famines afflicting the Danes during his reign.

Okra, Hibiscus, esculentis

Olaf II (1370–87), King of Denmark (1376–87) and as Olaf IV, King of Norway (1380–87), the son of Haakon VI Magnusson (1339–80), King of Norway and Margaret (q.v.), Queen of Denmark. His mother ruled as regent of each realm during Olaf's minority; he never personally exercised royal power.

DUBLIN AND NORTHUMBRIA

Olaf Godfreyson (d. 941), King of Dublin (934–41) and King of Northumbria (940–41). Olaf shared his rule of Northumbria with his cousin Olaf Sitricson (see below).

Olaf Sitricson, known in sagas as OLAF THE RED (d. 981?), King of Northumbria (940–44, 949–52) and King of Dublin (944–49, 952–80). In 940–41 Olaf ruled Northumbria jointly with his cousin Olaf Godfreyson. He was expelled from his English domain in 944. Thereupon he went to Ireland. He reigned in Dublin until 949, when he regained the Northumbrian throne. After his second expulsion from England in 952, he governed his Irish kingdom until his defeat by fellow Danes at Tara in 980. Soon afterward he died in exile at Iona in the Hebrides Islands.

NORWAY

Olaf I (969–1000). See OLAF I, King of Norway.

Olaf II (995?–1030). See OLAF II, King of Norway.

Olaf III, known as OLAF HARALDSSON and OLAF KYRRE ("the Quiet") (d. 1093), King of Norway (1066–93), the son of King Harold III (see under HAROLD). Olaf brought the Norse fleet to Norway after the death of his father at Stamford Bridge in England in 1066. He ruled jointly with his brother Magnus II Haraldsson (see under MAGNUS) from 1066 to 1069 and after the death of his brother, ruled alone. His reign was noted for peace and for the continued Christianization of Norway.

Olaf IV, known as OLAF MAGNUSSON (1100?–15), King of Norway (1103–15), the son of King Magnus III (see under MAGNUS). He reigned jointly with his older brothers, Eystein Magnusson (1089–1122) and Sigurd I (1089?–1130). Because his brothers are considered to have been the real rulers, Olaf is not always assigned a numeral among the Norwegian kings of his name.

Olaf IV (1370–87). See Olaf II, under *Denmark*, above.

Olaf V, real name ALEXANDER EDWARD CHRISTIAN FREDERIK OF GLÜCKSBURG (1903–), King of Norway (1957–), the son of King Haakon VII (see under HAAKON), born in Sandringham, England. He went to Great Britain with his father and the Norwegian government after the German invasion of Norway in 1940, during World War II. Olaf was commander in chief of the Norwegian armed forces in 1944–45; he returned to Norway after the defeat of Germany in 1945.

SWEDEN

Olaf, called the LAP KING (d. 1024?), King of Sweden (993–1024). Little is known about him except that he was converted to Christianity and thus became the first Christian king of Sweden.

OLAF I, known as OLAF TRYGGVESSON (about 963–1000), King of Norway (995–1000). The great-grandson of Harold I, King of Norway (see under HAROLD), he spent his early years in exile with his parents in Russia, England, and Ireland. Olaf participated in piratical raids on French, English, and Irish coasts from about 990 to 994. About 993 he was converted to Christianity. In 995 he sailed to Norway, deposed the pagan ruler, Earl Haakon (937?–95), became king, and made Trondheim his capital. Olaf hoped to convert Norway to Christianity and to unite Scandinavia into one realm under his rule. He was partly successful in the first project, but failed in the second when the Norwegians were overwhelmed by the Danes and Swedes in a naval battle (near what is now Rügen Island, East Germany) in the Baltic Sea. Following his defeat Olaf committed suicide by leaping into the sea. Norse literature contains many legends about his heroism and popularity. He was succeeded by the joint rulers Eric (d. 1024?) and his brother Earl Sweyn (d. 1017), sons of Earl Haakon.

OLAF II, known as OLAF HARALDSSON and SAINT OLAF (about 995–1030), King of Norway (1015–28), a descendant of Harold I, King of Norway (see under HAROLD). In his youth he fought with Ethelred II (q.v.), King of England, against Denmark. During his reign Olaf tried to complete the conversion of the Norwegians to Christianity and to unify the country. He made royal officials of many men of humble birth. As a result the jealous nobility welcomed the invasion of Norway by Canute II (q.v.), King of England and Denmark in 1028. Olaf, deserted by his nobles, fled to Russia. In 1030, in an attempt to regain the throne, he was killed in the Battle of Stiklestad. He was succeeded by Canute's son Sweyn (r. 1028–35). Olaf is remembered as the champion of national unification and as the saintly hero who continued the Christianization of Norway. He was canonized in 1164 and made the patron saint of Norway; his feast day is July 29. In 1847 the Order of Saint Olaf was instituted in his memory by King Oscar I (q.v.).

OLATHE, city in Kansas, and county seat of Johnson Co., about 19 miles s.w. of Kansas City.

OLBERS

A trading center, the city has varied manufacturing, including cowboy boots and farm machinery. Pop. (1960) 10,987; (1970) 17,917.

OLBERS, Heinrich Wilhelm Matthäus (1758–1840), German physician and astronomer, born in Abergen (now part of Bremen), and educated at the University of Göttingen. He practiced medicine at Bremen but is known for his astronomical studies. In 1779 he devised a method, still employed by astronomers, for calculating the orbits of comets. In 1815 he discovered a comet that was named after him. In 1781 he identified Uranus as a planet rather than as a comet, as had previously been assumed. Olbers discovered the planetoids Pallas in 1802 and Vesta (qq.v.) in 1807. He also first proposed the hypothesis, later called Olbers' hypothesis, that all planetoids are fragments of a disrupted planet that formerly revolved around the sun.

OLD AGE. See GERIATRICS; GERONTOLOGY; LONGEVITY.

OLD-AGE PENSIONS, provision of annuities for the aged. Old-age pensions, granted by a government to its employees, first appeared in France in the early 19th century and in Great Britain in 1834, and were instituted in newly unified Germany in 1873. The establishment of pensions spread to many other European countries in the first decade of the 20th century.

In the United States, the railroads remained until 1913 the only important employer group to provide old-age pensions for their employees. Today three principal sources of old-age pensions exist in the U.S. The most important is the social-security system established by the Social Security Act of 1935; see SOCIAL SECURITY. Under this law, employers and employees contribute to a government fund used to provide monthly allowances to employees past the age of sixty-five; reduced benefits are available starting at the age of sixty-two, or for widows at the age of sixty. The second type of old-age pension is one provided directly by many employers, sometimes with the assistance of employee contributions, to people who have been employed by them for specified minimum periods of time; it includes pensions provided by both private employers and government agencies.

Third, the increasing tendency of trade unions to demand improved financial provision for retiring workers in their labor contracts has been an important factor in the enrichment of these programs. Collectively bargained plans are often administered jointly by trustees selected by the employers and unions, implemented with funds contributed by the employers and administered by the unions or by a trustee.

It is often possible for retired employees to receive financial support from two or more sources. Almost all employees, including domestic workers, and the self-employed are now covered by social security. Special provisions in the Federal tax laws permit self-employed persons to establish private pension plans for themselves and their employees, with tax advantages similar to those given to approved corporate pension plans. A frequent supplement to old-age pensions is provided by the veterans' pensions which are issued to certain classes of war veterans; (see under VETERANS ADMINISTRATION).

A.Tr.

OLD BAILEY, name of a street in London, England, that is the site of the Central Criminal Court. Prior to 1834 Old Bailey was the name of a historic criminal-court, at the same location, the jurisdiction of which was at that time assumed by the Central Criminal Court. Old Bailey was the scene of many famous criminal trials; it is graphically described in *A Tale of Two Cities* (1859), by the British novelist Charles Dickens (q.v.). Central Criminal Court is still popularly called Old Bailey.

OLDCASTLE, Sir John (1377?–1417), titled BARON COBHAM after his marriage to Lady Joan Cobham in 1408, English leader of the Lollards (q.v.) and religious martyr, born probably in Almeley, Herfordshire. In 1401, while serving in the campaign of King Henry IV (q.v.) to put down the Welsh rebel Owen Glendower (q.v.), he became a close friend of Henry, Prince of Wales, later Henry V (q.v.) King of England. Oldcastle served in the House of Commons in 1404 and in the House of Lords after 1409. Meanwhile, in defiance of royal decrees, he joined the Lollards. In 1413, the year of Prince Henry's accession to the throne, Oldcastle was convicted and condemned to death as a heretic. Henry V granted his old friend a forty-day respite in the hope that he would recant. Oldcastle escaped from imprisonment in the Tower of London (q.v.), and early in 1414 led an abortive revolt of the Lollards against the throne. For almost four years thereafter he continued his Lollardian activities as a fugitive in Herfordshire. Captured on Dec. 14, 1417, Oldcastle was executed the same day by hanging and was burned on the scaffold.

A character bearing the name Oldcastle appears as one of the comrades of Prince Hal in the anonymous Elizabethan play *The Famous Victories of Henry V.* In the original version of *Henry IV,* an adaptation of that play by William Shakespeare (q.v.), Oldcastle's name was attached to a similar character; the latter was renamed Sir John Falstaff in the printed version of 1598.

OLD CATHOLICS, Christian denomination organized in Munich, Germany, in 1871 by Roman Catholics who protested the dogma, proclaimed the previous year by Vatican Council I, of the personal infallibility of the pope in all *ex cathedra* pronouncements; see INFALLIBILITY; VATICAN COUNCILS. The Munich protest, by forty-four professors under the leadership of the German theologians and historians Johann Joseph Ignaz von Döllinger (q.v.) and Johannes Friedrich (1836–1917), was directed against the binding authority of the Vatican Council. To this protest a number of professors at Bonn, Breslau (now Wrocław, Poland), Freiburg, and Giessen declared their adhesion. At Cologne in 1873 the German theologian Joseph Hubert Reinkens (1821–96) was elected bishop of the Old Catholics in the ancient fashion, by "clergy and people", that is, by all the Old Catholic priests and by representatives of the Old Catholic congregations. He was consecrated at Rotterdam by the bishop of Deventer, the Netherlands, and acknowledged by the German states of Prussia, Baden, and Hesse. Döllinger refused to become involved in organized schism and eventually broke with the movement, but he never returned to the Roman Catholic Church.

Old Catholic practices differ somewhat from those of Roman Catholicism. The Mass (q.v.) is said in the vernacular. Priests are allowed to marry. Intercommunion with the Anglican Communion (q.v.) was accomplished at a conference in Bonn in July, 1931, the concordat being ratified later by the Vienna congress of the Old Catholic Church and by the convocations of Canterbury and York of the Church of England (q.v.). The Eastern Orthodox churches rejected Old-Catholic overtures for intercommunion. According to the most recent figures, the Old Catholics number fewer than 250,000.

OLDENBURG, city of West Germany, in Lower Saxony State, on the Hunte R., 25 miles N.W. of Bremen. Industries of Oldenburg include agricultural machinery, textiles, and processed food. The city is a road and railroad junction and is linked by inland waterways to the Ruhr R. Among the places of interest in Oldenburg are Lamberti Church, which was built in 1270, and the Landesbibliotek, a library founded in 1792.

First mentioned about 1108, Oldenburg was chartered as a town in 1345 and was the seat of the counts of Oldenburg until 1667 when control of the county passed to Denmark. From 1777 to 1918 the city was the capital of the dukes of Oldenburg, and from 1918 to 1945 it

Old English sheepdog   Evelyn M. Shafer

was capital of the former Oldenburg State. Pop. (1968 est.) 130,711.

OLD ENGLISH. See ENGLISH LANGUAGE: *History*.

OLD ENGLISH SHEEPDOG, breed of medium-sized working dog used primarily for guarding herds of sheep or cattle. The breed is believed to have developed in western England in the 17th century. The animal was used in England at the beginning of the 18th century for assisting drovers in driving sheep and cattle to market, and was then known as the "drover's dog". The old English sheepdog can also be trained as a retriever and as a draft animal, and because of its even temper it is a good companion for children. The male varies in height from about 21 to 25 in. at the shoulder; the height of the bitch is somewhat less. The animal has a square-shaped skull, dark eyes, a tapering nose with a blunt end, medium-sized ears lying flat to the sides of the head, straight forelegs and muscular hind legs, and moves with a characteristic rolling gait. Many of the breed have no tail; some have tails that are between 1½ and 2 in. in length. The coat is profuse, usually either gray or bluish grey and sometimes with white markings; it is occasionally so shaggy that its hair conceals the eyes.

OLD GLORY. See FLAG OF THE UNITED STATES.

OLDHAM, Great Britain, county borough of Lancashire, England, 7 miles N.E. of Manchester. It is in a coal-mining area; the city is a cotton-milling center and also has engineering plants and leather tanneries. Oldham was incorporated as a town in 1849 and made the county borough in 1888. Pop. (1969 est.) 108,280.

OLD RED SANDSTONE. See DEVONIAN PERIOD.

OLDS, Ransom Eli (1864–1950), American automobile manufacturer, born in Geneva, Ohio. Olds, a mechanic, began to experiment with horseless carriages in the 1880's. In 1885 he built

OLD SAYBROOK

a successful steam-propelled three-wheeled vehicle. Ten years later he constructed a four-wheeled automobile powered by a gasoline engine. He founded the Olds Motor Works, the first automobile factory and the first to use an assembly line, in 1897. About 12,000 Oldsmobiles were produced between 1902 and 1904, when Olds sold his interest in the company. From 1904 to 1924 Olds was president, and from 1924 to 1936 chairman of the board, of the Reo Motor Car Company. This company produced the Reo, a popular automobile of the 1920's, its name an acronym formed from the initials of the manufacturer. After 1936 Olds was engaged in various business enterprises, including the production of power lawn mowers and a mortgage and loan company.

OLD SAYBROOK, town of Connecticut, in Middlesex Co., on Long Island Sound, at the mouth of the Connecticut R., 28 miles E. of New Haven. The principal industries are agriculture, fishing, boat building, and the manufacture of hardware and processed food. The town is chiefly a residential community and a summer resort. Nearby is the town of Old Lyme, a noted art center. Old Saybrook, one of the oldest settlements in Connecticut, contains several fine colonial buildings, and at Saybrook Point is an old cemetery where one of the original settlers of Old Saybrook is buried.

The site of the present town was a Dutch trading post as early as 1623. The first permanent settlement in the area was established in 1635 by a group of English colonists under the leadership of the colonial governor John Winthrop (q.v.), the younger. In 1644 the Saybrook Colony became a part of the Connecticut Colony. The Collegiate School of America, from which Yale University (q.v.) developed, was founded there in 1701. In the early days of the settlement it was an important center of trade with the West Indies and was noted for its shad-fishing industry. The American inventor David Bushnell (see under BUSHNELL) built the first submarine ever used in warfare in Saybrook in 1776. Saybrook and Old Saybrook were separated in 1852 and the town of Old Saybrook was incorporated in 1854. In 1947, to prevent confusion of names, the town of Saybrook was renamed Deep River. Old Saybrook now includes several unincorporated communities and the borough of Fenwick. Pop. (1960) 5274; (1970) 8468.

OLD STURBRIDGE. See STURBRIDGE.

OLD TESTAMENT. See BIBLE: *The Growth of the Bible: The Old Testament.*

OLD VIC THEATRE, theater in London, England; since 1963, headquarters for the government-financed National Theatre of Great Britain. Called the Royal Coburg Theatre when it opened in 1818, it was for many years a popular site for the production of melodrama, the most widely performed theatrical fare of the 19th century. In 1833 it was renamed the Royal Victoria Theatre. In 1880, in a badly deteriorated condition, the building was bought by the British social reformer Emma Cons (1838-1912) for the presentation of lectures, concerts, and other offerings for the moral and spiritual enlightenment of the neighborhood. It was then known as the Royal Victorian Music Hall, and later, popularly, as the Old Vic. In 1898 Miss Cons was joined in the management of the music hall by her niece, Lilian Mary Baylis (1874-1937).

In 1914, under Miss Baylis' management, the theater was organized as a nonprofit institution, devoted to the production in repertory of the plays of William Shakespeare and of opera performed in the English language. By 1923 the Old Vic had produced all of Shakespeare's plays, the first theater in the world to accomplish this feat. From 1946 to 1951 the Old Vic Theatre School, connected with the Old Vic Theatre, flourished under the French director Michel Saint-Denis (1897-   ). The Old Vic Theatre building itself, severely damaged by bombs during World War II, was rebuilt and reopened in 1950. The repertory company, which first appeared in 1946 and subsequently performed in many countries of the world, has at one time or another included virtually all of the leading actors of the British theater, among them, Sir John Gielgud, Sir Laurence Olivier, Sir Michael Redgrave, and Sir Ralph Richardson (qq.v.).

In 1943 the Old Vic sent a company to perform at the Theatre Royal in Bristol, England. In 1946 the Bristol Old Vic was established as a permanent repertory company. When the National Theatre of Great Britain took over the London Old Vic in 1963, the Bristol group continued as a separate organization. The Bristol Old Vic, one of six theatrical companies subsidized by the arts council of Great Britain, maintains a theater school as well as a repertory company.

OLEAN, city of New York, in Cattaraugus Co., on the Allegheny R., at the mouth of Olean Creek, 70 miles S.E. of Buffalo. It is served only by railroad freight service. The city is surrounded by an area producing oil and is an oil-storage and refining center. Other industries are electroplating, tool and die works, and the manufacture of floor and wall tiles, cutlery, furniture, compressors and turbines, industrial machinery, and electrical components. Olean was first settled in 1804 as a lumbering center. It was chartered as a city in 1893. The city was an embarkation point for westward bound settlers who sailed down the Allegheny R. to the Ohio R. Pop. (1960) 21,868; (1970) 19,169.

OLEANDER, genus of plants of the Dogbane family. The species are evergreen shrubs with leathery leaves, which are opposite or in threes; the flowers are in terminal branching cymes. The common oleander, *Nerium oleander,* is known also as rose laurel, and is a native of the Mediterranean region and has exceedingly poisonous sap.

OLEOMARGARINE. *See* MARGARINE.

OLIBANUM *or* **FRANKINCENSE,** gum resin derived from several species of Oriental trees of the genus *Boswellia,* growing in northeastern Africa and Arabia. For commerce it is hardened into semitransparent, yellowish tears and masses. Bitter in taste, olibanum is hard and brittle, but is often pulverized. It is of little commercial importance today, but is used widely in ceremonial incense (q.v.) for churches and temples. *See also* FRANKINCENSE.

OLIGARCHY, in political philosophy, form of government in which the supreme power is vested in a few persons. Political writers of ancient Greece used the term to designate the debased form of an aristocracy (q.v.), or government by the best citizens. In an oligarchy, the government is in the control of a faction of persons who are intent upon their own interests to the exclusion of the welfare of the people. *See* GOVERNMENT.

OLIGOCENE EPOCH, division of geologic time in the Tertiary Period of the Cenozoic Era (q.v.). It followed the Eocene Epoch and preceded the Miocene Epoch (qq.v.), beginning about 40,000,000 years ago and lasting for about 15,000,000 years.

No great upheavals of the earth's crust occurred during Oligocene times, and most of the rocks belonging to this epoch were originally marine sediments. Oligocene deposits are found along the Atlantic seacoast in South Carolina and Florida and along the coast of the Gulf of Mexico. Other Oligocene formations, not of marine origin, occur in Oregon, Wyoming, and the Dakotas. The Bad Lands and Black Hills regions are particularly rich in the remains of fossil mammals that lived in Oligocene times. In Europe, rocks of Oligocene origin are found in France, Germany, and Switzerland. Deposits left by the sea and by freshwater streams during the Oligocene Epoch are characteristic of the Alps and the Carpathian Mts., both of which were low plains at the time.

Flora and Fauna. The climate of the Oligocene Epoch in the area now occupied by the continental United States was subtropical; palm trees and other subtropical species flourished as far north as the present Canadian border. The climate farther to the north was correspondingly temperate; dense deciduous forests covered many parts of Alaska, Siberia, Greenland, and Spitsbergen. Beginning in this epoch, however, the climate gradually became cooler and the temperate and tropical vegetation groups gradually moved farther south.

The fauna of the Oligocene included modern types of reptiles such as alligators, which, during this period, lived as far north as Wyoming and the Dakotas. Mammals were represented by various primitive types of horses and rhinoceroses. One Oligocene rhinoceros, the *Baluchitherium,* is believed to be the largest land mammal that ever existed. This animal, remains of which have been found in southern Asia, was about 13 ft. in height, 25 ft. in length, and had a skull 5 ft. long. Another Oligocene group related to both the horse and the rhinoceros was the titanotheres, which resembled rhinoceroses but had two, rather than one, bony horns on the nose. No descendants of the group are extant. Other Oligocene animals included primitive dogs and cats and early primates. *See* GEOLOGY, HISTORICAL; PALEONTOLOGY.

OLIGOPOLIES. *See* MONOPOLY AND COMPETITION.

OLINDA, city and port of Brazil, in Pernambuco State, on the Atlantic Ocean, 4 miles N. of Recife, with which it is linked by road and streetcar. A leading beach resort and art center in an area of sugar plantations, the city processes sugar and manufactures cigars and textiles. Olinda, long the most important city in northern Brazil, was prominent in early colonial history, traces of which are found in the old churches and buildings. The monasteries of São Francisco and São Bento have art collections, and the regional museum, State museum, and sugar museum are of interest. The fort of São Francisco, called the "Cheese Fort"; the Prefeitura, or government house of the captains general; and the Joaquim Nabuco Institute are also in the city. Founded in 1535, Olinda was the capital of a Portuguese colonial captaincy until it was succeeded by Recife; from 1630 to 1654 it was under Dutch rule. Pop. (1960) 100,545.

OLIVE, common name for plants of the genus *Olea,* type genus of the family Oleaceae in the order Gentianales. The Olive family is characterized by usually opposite leaves and four-parted flowers; the fruits may be berries, drupes, or

Olive groves in southern Spain. Olive oil is an important export commodity for Spain.
Spanish National Tourist Office

capsules. In addition to the typical genus, the most important genera are *Fraxinus,* ash; *Syringa,* lilac; *Ligustrum,* privet; *Jasminum,* and *Forsythia.* The name olive is particularly applied to the plants, fruit, and wood of *Olea europaea,* varieties of which have been cultivated since the early days of civilization in Asia Minor and southeastern Europe for the fruit and the oil expressed from the fruit; see ESSENTIAL OIL. It is native to Syria and in its wild state is a low, thorny shrub with opposite, simple, entire leaves, small white axillary flowers, and a drupaceous fruit with a thin, hard pericarp. In cultivation the plant is a tree, seldom exceeding 30 ft. in height; the fruit is oval, purple when ripe, and rich in oil. Many varieties of the species are cultivated in the regions surrounding the Mediterranean Sea, the subtropical regions of South America, and California. In these regions the best grades of fruit are harvested, when green, for pickling in brine or, when ripe, for preserving. The balance of the crop is pressed for olive oil, which is an important export commodity of Greece, Italy, Portugal, and Spain.

In its native habitat of ancient Syria, the possession of a strain of cultivated olive, which yielded much more oil and commercial wealth than the wild variety, was regarded as a symbol of cultural and economic advancement; the offer of an olive branch, from which such trees were cultivated, was regarded as a symbol of friendship and came to be accepted as a token of peace. Among the ancient Greeks, the olive was regarded as the gift of the goddess Pallas Athena (see ATHENA), to whom it was sacred; and a crown of olive branches was a symbol of the highest honor bestowed by the state. Olive oil later came to be regarded more as a necessary substitute for butter and other animal oils than as a luxury.

The wood of the olive is hard, often variegated, and is valued for cabinetwork. Other species of the genus are important timber trees of Australia and are known collectively as *maire.* The hard wood of *O. laurifolia* is the black ironwood of Natal Province, South Africa; see IRONWOOD.

OLIVES, MOUNT OF, or MOUNT OLIVET, limestone ridge in Jordan, lying just to the E. of Jerusalem (q.v.). The ridge, reaching about 2700 ft. at its highest point, is separated from Jerusalem only by the narrow Kidron Valley. It takes its familiar name from a grove of olive trees that stood on its western flank. The ridge has three summits: the northernmost is often called Mt. Scopus; see HEBREW UNIVERSITY. On the central summit is a village that was once called Olivet and is now named Tur (Ar., "the mount"). Around this central summit, which is the Mount of Olives properly so called, many events of Christian history took place. At the top stands a Muslim chapel, on the supposed site of the Ascension (q.v.) of Jesus Christ (q.v.), as described in Acts 1:2–12. On the slope is the site at which, according to tradition, Jesus wept over Jerusalem (Luke 19:41–44) during His triumphal entry into the city; see PALM SUNDAY. High on the slope are a Carmelite (see CARMELITES) church and convent near the site of a church built by Saint Helena (q.v.); other structures nearby are identified with various ecclesiastical traditions. See BETHANY; GETHSEMANE.

OLIVETANS, religious order (see ORDERS, RELIGIOUS) of the Roman Catholic Church; its full title is the Congregation of Our Lady of Mt. Olivet. It was founded in 1313 by Blessed Bernard Tolomei (1272–1348), professor of philosophy at the University of Siena. The order was approved by Pope Clement VI (1291–1352) in 1344. The Olivetans joined the Benedictine Confederation in 1959 and hence are known as Olivetan Benedictines. In the United States they are represented in the States of New York and Louisiana.

OLIVIER, Sir Laurence Kerr (1907–), British theatrical and motion-picture actor, producer and director, born in Dorking, Surrey. At the age of fifteen he made his first stage appearance in a special performance of *The Taming of the Shrew,* by William Shakespeare, at Stratford-on-Avon, birthplace of the playwright. He was a member of the Birmingham Repertory Company of Birmingham, England, from 1926 until 1928. Olivier made his American theatrical debut in New York City in 1929. In 1930 and 1931 he appeared in *Private Lives,* by the English playwright Noel Coward (q.v.), in London and New York City. In 1937 and 1938 he was a member of the Old Vic Shakespearian repertory company in London; see OLD VIC THEATRE. Olivier became codirector of the Old Vic in 1944 and in 1946 he appeared with the company in America.

In 1938 he made his first important film, *Wuthering Heights.* In 1946 a film version of Shakespeare's play *Henry V* was released; it had been produced and directed by and starred Olivier. He produced, directed, and starred in film versions of Shakespeare's *Hamlet* (1950), for which he received an award from the Academy of Motion Picture Arts and Sciences as best actor of the year, and *Richard III* (1956), and he performed the title role in a film version of *Othello* (1966). Among the other films in which he appeared are *Rebecca* (1940), *Pride and Prejudice* (1940), *Carrie* (1952), *The Entertainer* (1960) and *The Shoes of the Fisherman* (1968).

In the theater Olivier played classical roles from Greek tragedy to Restoration comedy, as well as a wide variety of roles in contemporary plays. A theatrical producer and director as well as actor, Olivier was named head of the newly created National Theatre of Great Britain in 1962. He was Knighted in 1947.

OLIVINE, mineral composed of magnesium and iron silicate, $(Mg,Fe)_2SiO_4$. It crystallizes in the orthorhombic system and usually occurs in the form of granular masses. The color ranges from olive green or grayish green to brown. Olivine has a hardness ranging from 6.5 to 7 and a sp.gr. ranging from 3.27 to 3.37. It exhibits conchoidal fracture, has a glassy luster, and is transparent or translucent. Found principally in ferromanganese igneous rocks, such as basalt and peridotite, it occurs in the lavas of Mt. Vesuvius near Naples, Italy, in Norway, Germany, and Arizona. A rock called dunite is composed almost entirely of olivine. A transparent, green variety of olivine, called peridot, and a greenish-yellow variety of olivine, called chrysolite, are used to some extent as gem-stones.

OLMSTED, Frederick Law (1822–1903), American landscape architect, born in Hartford, Conn., and educated at Yale College (now Yale University). He traveled throughout Europe and the United States, studying landscape gardening and agricultural methods. In 1857 he was appointed superintendent of Central Park, in New York City, the first great metropolitan park in the U.S. In collaboration with the American landscape architect Calvert Vaux (1824–95) he designed new plans for the park, which had a strong influence on park design throughout the country; see LANDSCAPE ARCHITECTURE. Subsequently, he planned a large number of city parks, including Morningside, Prospect, and Riverside parks, New York City; Jackson and Washington parks, Chicago; and the grounds of the Capitol, Washington, D.C. He was the first commissioner of Yosemite National Park, Calif. Olmsted was one of the first landscape architects in America to preserve the natural features of the terrain and to add naturalistic elements when lacking.

OLMÜTZ. See OLOMOUC.

OLOMOUC, city of Czechoslovakia, in Severomoravský Region, on the Morava R., 40 miles N.E. of Brno. The trade and industrial center of the fertile Hana region specializing in dairying and barley, the city has iron- and steelworks, breweries, and saltworks and manufactures smoked meats, malt, sugar, chocolate, candy, cement, and machinery. It is a historic Moravian city and contains the Palacký University, the 12th-century Saint Wenceslaus Cathedral, the 13th-century town hall, an archbishop's palace, and other baroque buildings of the 16th and 17th centuries. Founded in 1050, Olomouc was a joint capital of Moravia with Brno until 1640 and alternated after that. In 1242 the Mongols were defeated here, and the city was devastated by the Swedes in 1642. Important treaties effecting European boundary changes were

OLSZTYN

signed in Olomouc in 1478 and 1850. While under Austrian rule, in the 19th century, it was called Olmütz. Pop. (1966 est.) 77,000.

OLSZTYN, city in Poland, and capital of Olsztyn Province, on the Łyna R., about 80 miles S.E. of Gdańsk. An important railroad and industrial center, the city has a large trade in livestock, grain, and leather and has plants engaged in sawmilling and papermaking and in the production of stoves. Olsztyn was founded about the middle of the 14th century. With the surrounding region, it became a Polish possession in 1466 and passed to Prussian sovereignty in 1772. The city subsequently became part of the Prussian province of East Prussia and known by its German name of Allenstein. Following World War II it was transferred to Polish control under the provisions of the Potsdam Conference (q.v.). Pop. (1968) 89,700.

OLYMPIA, city and capital of the State of Washington, and county seat of Thurston Co., at the southern end of Puget Sound, 60 miles S.W. of Seattle. Transportation facilities include railroads, coastal and overseas ships, and a municipal airport. Among the industrial establishments in the city are breweries, canneries, sawmills, and factories manufacturing veneer and plywood. The Olympia oyster, a small oyster indigenous to the southern waters of Puget Sound, is a famous product of the city. Traffic of the port

An aerial view of Olympia, the capital of the State of Washington, with its government buildings in the foreground and Puget Sound in the background.
Cowley Photos

of Olympia is largely in lumber and lumber products, floated logs, and oysters.

Olympia is situated amid low hills, with the Olympic Mts. towering on the northern horizon and Mt. Rainier on the E. The group of State buildings, including the capitol and the Temple of Justice, stand on a promontory above the sound and are constructed of white stone in a classic design. The city is headquarters of the Olympic National Forest and the terminus of the Olympic Highway.

The site of the city was first settled in 1846 and in 1850 was laid out. It became the capital of Washington Territory in 1853, was chartered as a city in 1859, and was made the State capital in 1889. Pop. (1960) 18,273; (1970) 23,111.

OLYMPIA, site of the Olympian games (q.v.), celebrated every four years by the ancient Greeks. Olympia was situated in a valley in Elis, in western Peloponnesus, through which runs the Alpheus R. It was not a town, but only a sanctuary with buildings connected with games and the worship of the gods. Olympia was a national shrine of the Greeks and contained many treasures of Greek art such as temples, monuments, altars, theaters, statues, and votive offerings of brass and marble. The *Altis,* or sacred precinct, enclosed a level space about 660 ft. long by nearly 580 ft. broad. In this space were the chief centers of religious worship, the votive buildings, and the buildings connected with the administration of the games. The most celebrated temple was the *Olympieum,* dedicated to Olympian Zeus (q.v.), father of the gods. In

OLYMPIAN GAMES

this temple was a colossal statue of Zeus made of ivory and gold, the masterpiece of the Athenian sculptor Phidias (q.v.). Next to the *Olympieum* ranked the *Heraeum,* dedicated to Hera (q.v.), the wife of Zeus. In this temple, probably the oldest Doric building known, stood the table on which were placed the garlands prepared for the victors in the games. The votive buildings included a row of twelve treasure houses and the *Philippeum,* a circular Ionic building dedicated by Philip II (q.v.), King of Macedonia, to himself. Outside of the *Altis,* to the east, were the *Stadium* and the *Hippodrome,* where the contests took place, and on the west were the *Palaestra,* or wrestling school, and the *Gymnasium,* where all competitors were obliged to train for at least one month. Explorations conducted from 1875 to 1881, under the auspices of the German government, threw much light upon the plans of the buildings. Many valuable objects were discovered, the most important of which was a statue of Hermes (q.v.), the messenger of the gods, by the Greek sculptor Praxiteles (q.v.).

OLYMPIAD, in Greek chronology, interval of four years between two successive celebrations of the Olympian games (q.v.). The use of Olympiads as a convenient system of chronological reckoning appears chiefly in literature, beginning about 300 B.C. in the writings of the Greek historian Timaeus (about 356–about 260 B.C.). Although the Olympian games were celebrated in much earlier times, the first Olympiad dates from 776 B.C., the year in which the first official list of victors was kept.

OLYMPIAN GAMES, most famous of the four great national festivals of the ancient Greeks, the other three being the Isthmian, Pythian (qq.v.), and the Nemean games; *see* GAMES, ANCIENT. The Olympian games were celebrated every four years in the sanctuary of Zeus at Olympia, in the western part of the Peloponnesus, Greece; the time of the festival varied from the beginning of August to the middle of September. At first the athletic contests occupied only a single day, but in later times five or six days were required to present all of the sports attractions. The origin of the games goes back to remote antiquity. The official list of victors in the athletic competitions began in the year 776 B.C. with an athlete named Coroebus, who won the foot race. The list is not generally regarded as authoritative, however, for any period prior to the 5th century B.C. According to the accepted belief, the earliest and for long the only contest was the *stadion,* or short-distance foot race, run over a course of about 630 ft. In 724 B.C. the *diaulos,* or race covering two stadia, was introduced; and at the next celebration of the Olympian games the *dolichos,* a long race of about 15,120 ft., was instituted. At that time also, the contestants discarded the loincloth and appeared naked, a custom that prevailed from then on. In 708 B.C. both wrestling and the *pentathlon* (in which each athlete participated in five different events, such as throwing the discus, throwing the javelin, foot racing, jumping, and wrestling) were introduced, in 688 B.C. boxing, and in 680 B.C. the race for four-horse chariots. Two more contests were added in 648 B.C., the horseback race and the *pancratium,* a combination of boxing and wrestling. In 632 B.C. contests for boys were established, which from 616 B.C. were standardized in separate events of boxing, wrestling, and running. The foot race for men in armor was added in 520 B.C., and during the 4th and 3rd centuries B.C. other novelties, particularly in horse racing, were from time to time attempted. A contest of trumpeters and heralds was inaugurated in 396 B.C., the successful contestant being permitted to demonstrate his skill in announcing the victors in the athletic competitions. During the greater part of their history the Olympian games were held at Elis, although the city of Pisa, in the territory of which Olympia was situated, frequently disputed this honor, until early in the 6th century, when Pisa was destroyed by Elis and Sparta.

Preparations. The chief officials of the Olympian games were the Hellenodikai, whose number varied from one or two to twelve, though the usual number seems to have been ten. Early in the year of the games envoys from Elis were sent throughout the Greek world to invite the city-states to join in paying tribute to Zeus. At first the games had merely a local character, but they soon became national in scope. The city-states thereupon dispatched *theoriae,* or sacred deputations, to bring their offerings to Zeus and to vie with one another in the splendor of their equipment and the proficiency of their athletic feats. The competitions were open only to men of Greek descent who were free from the taint of impiety, bloodguiltiness, or grave infraction of the laws. All contestants were required to train assiduously for ten months before the games were held. The last thirty days the athletes were obliged to spend at Elis under the close supervision of the Hellenodikai, although this condition may have applied only to novices. Withdrawal from the list of entrants before the game was punished with heavy fines.

Athletic Events. The order of the events is not precisely known, but the first athletic contest

OLYMPIAN GAMES

was almost certainly the stadion. The first day of the festival was devoted to sacrifices, especially to Zeus. At this time both the officials and contestants took a solemn oath, the former to judge fairly, the latter that they had faithfully observed the prescribed conditions of their training period and would compete with fairness. The second day began, in all probability, with foot races, for which the spectators gathered in the stadion, an oblong plain enclosed by sloping banks of earth. The course was marked at both ends by a marble sill about 80 ft. long and 18 in. wide and containing two grooves to give the runners a foothold in starting. The terminus was always at the same end, but the starting point varied for the single and double courses. Another group of contests was formed by wrestling, boxing, and the pancratium. In the first of these sports the object was to throw the antagonist to the ground three times; the struggle was never continued on the ground. Boxing became more and more brutal throughout the course of the Olympian games; at first the pugilists wound straps of soft leather over their fingers as a means of deadening the blows, but in later times hard leather, sometimes weighted with metal, was used. The highest praise, however, was reserved for athletes who achieved their success through a defense so perfect that they were able to exhaust their opponents without striking a blow or receiving a cut. In the pancratium, the most rigorous of the sports, both wrestling and boxing were employed, the contest being continued until one or the other of the participants acknowledged his defeat.

The horse races were run in the hippodrome. This sport, in which each entrant owned his horse, was confined to the wealthy, but was nevertheless a very popular attraction. The successful racer was accorded high honors in his native city-state. After the horse racing came the pentathlon (q.v.). The exact sequence of the events in this competition, and the method employed to determine the winner, are unknown. In the throwing of the discus, the object used was a plate of bronze, probably lens-shaped. In the throwing of the javelin, the implement was hurled with the aid of a strap, which was wound about the shaft, thereby producing a rotary motion that secured greater distance and accuracy. The jumping event was always judged for distance, not for height.

The last event of the Olympian games was frequently the race in armor, the distance being twice the length of the stadion. At first the runners wore the full panoply of a hoplite, or completely equipped infantry soldier, but later they carried only the shield. On the last day of the festival the victors were awarded crowns of wild olive from the sacred olive tree, which constituted the only official prize, and were banqueted by the State of Elis at the Prytaneion, or public hall consecrated to Hestia, goddess of the hearth. The victor returned home in triumph, in a chariot at the head of a chanting procession. He was celebrated in the panegyrics of poets, and in many cities lived for the remainder of his life at public expense.

Decline. The Olympian games reached their highest development during the 5th and 4th centuries B.C. Gradually, however, the festival took on a professional character, and in Roman times, although the spectators were as numerous and the splendor as great as in the earlier period, the competitors were virtually all professional athletes, against whose irregular mode of life physicians and moralists alike directed their censure. Yet the games continued until 394 A.D., when they were finally suppressed by the Roman emperor Theodosius I (q.v.), on the ground that they violated the spirit of Christianity. For an account of the modern games, see OLYMPIC GAMES. See also ATHLETICS.

OLYMPIC GAMES, designation applied to an international athletic competition, held quadrennially and restricted to amateurs. A modified revival of the Olympian Games (q.v.), one of the great festivals of ancient Greece, the Olympic Games were inaugurated, in 1896, largely as a result of the efforts of the French sportsman and educator Baron Pierre de Coubertin (1863-1937). The initial moves of his revival campaign, which included wide circulation of a colorful account of the ancient festival, gained little popular support. In 1894, however, with the help of a few individuals, he succeeded in establishing the International Olympic Committee. This committee enlisted the aid of sports organizations and individuals of various countries, chiefly European at first. It also drafted plans and policy for the projected Games, and selected Athens as an appropriate site of the first Olympic Games. A basic feature of Olympic policy has been that amateur athletes of all nations are eligible to participate in the Games. In addition, the various events are regarded as competitions among athletes as individuals rather than as representatives of nations. To a large degree the last-named feature of Olympic policy has been obscured in recent years through the emphasis given by news media to the over-all performance of the participating countries. On the whole, however, the Games have remained free of commercial and political influences.

The first woman in the history of the modern Olympic Games to light the Olympic fire runs up the ninety steps toward the Olympic torch during the opening ceremony of the 1968 games at Mexico City. UPI

History. The first modern Games, held in April, 1896, attracted athletes from the United States, Great Britain, and eleven other nations. Only forty-two events in nine sports were scheduled for these games, held in a stadium erected for that purpose. Among the events were six track contests, namely, the marathon, four runs (100, 400, 800, and 1500 meters), and the 110-meters hurdle; and six field contests, namely, the pole vault, high jump, broad jump, sixteen-pound shot put, discus, and hop, step, and jump. Contestants from the U.S. were victorious in nine of the track and field events. The marathon race, commemorating a heroic running feat of ancient Greek times, was won by a Greek contestant; see MARATHON.

The second Olympic Games (1900) took place in Paris. Saint Louis, Mo., was the site of the Games in 1904. A special Olympic competition, not of the regular cycle, was held in Athens in 1906. Subsequent sites were London (1908), Stockholm (1912), Antwerp (1920), Paris (1924), Amsterdam (1928), Los Angeles (1932), Berlin (1936), London (1948), Helsinki (1952), Melbourne (1956), Rome (1960), Tokyo (1964), and Mexico City (1968). The Olympic Games scheduled for Berlin in 1916 were canceled because of World War I, and those scheduled for 1940 and 1944 were canceled because of World War II. The Games of the twentieth Olympiad, 1972, will be staged in Munich, Germany.

Following the Games of 1904, which had little international significance because the contestants were mainly from the U.S., more and more nations have entered teams in the Olympic Games. In the 1936 Games forty-nine nations were represented. Athletes from 114 nations competed in the Olympic Games of 1964. The total number of participating athletes has also grown greatly, increasing from the relative few who competed at Athens in 1896 to over 6000 in 1968. Since the inception of the Games, more than 50,000 athletes have competed in the various contests. A similar development has marked the competitive struggle in many countries among qualified athletes for membership on the Olympic teams. The Olympic tryouts, elimination games conducted for aspirants quadrennially under the auspices of the various national Olympic Committees, are outstanding occasions in the realm of amateur athletics, particularly in the U.S.

Later Developments. Since the first Olympic Games of the modern cycle several significant developments have occurred. One major feature has been the marked increase of Olympic competition among women, notably since 1924. Secondly, there has been a steady increase in the number of sports and events open to competition at the Olympic Games. Winter sports, including hockey, figure skating, and skiing, became a part of the Olympic program in 1924. Ex-

OLYMPIC GAMES

OLYMPIC GAMES OF 1968

MEDALS WON BY COMPETING NATIONS

Country	Gold Medals (1st place)	Silver Medals (2nd place)	Bronze Medals (3rd place)	Total Medals
United States	45	28	34	107
U.S.S.R.	29	31	31	91
Hungary	10	10	12	32
Japan	11	7	7	25
East Germany	9	9	7	25
West Germany	5	10	10	25
Poland	5	2	11	18
Australia	5	7	5	17
Italy	3	4	9	16
France	7	3	5	15
Rumania	4	6	5	15
Czechoslovakia	7	2	4	13
Great Britain	5	5	3	13
Kenya	3	4	2	9
Mexico	3	3	3	9
Bulgaria	2	4	3	9
Yugoslavia	3	3	2	8
Denmark	1	4	3	8
Netherlands	3	3	1	7
Iran	2	1	2	5
Canada	1	3	1	5
Switzerland	0	1	4	5
Sweden	2	1	1	4
Finland	1	2	1	4
Cuba	0	4	0	4
Austria	0	2	2	4
Mongolia	0	1	3	4
New Zealand	1	0	2	3
Brazil	0	1	2	3
Turkey	2	0	0	2
Ethiopia	1	1	0	2
Norway	1	1	0	2
Pakistan	1	0	0	1
Venezuela	1	0	0	1
Cameroons	0	1	0	1
Jamaica	0	1	0	1
Greece	0	0	1	1
India	0	0	1	1
Taiwan	0	0	1	1

cluding the winter Games, the number of sports on the program of the 1968 Olympics totaled nineteen, namely basketball, boxing, canoeing, cycling, equestrian, fencing, field hockey, gymnastics, modern pentathlon (riding, cross-country running, swimming, shooting, and fencing), rowing, shooting, soccer, swimming, track and field, volleyball, water polo, weight lifting, wrestling, and yachting. Three additional sports will be included in the 1972 Games in Munich, namely archery, field-handball, and judo.

A third development has been the progressively superior performance by successive generations of Olympic athletes. For example, the winning time for the 100-meters run in the Olympics of 1896 was 12 sec.; the time for the same event in 1968 was 9.9 sec., an Olympic record. The winning distance for the discus throw in 1896 was 95 ft. 7½ in.; the winning distances in 1948, 1952, 1956, and 1960 were respectively 173 ft. 2 in., 180 ft. 6⅛ in., 184 ft. 10½ in., and 194 ft. 2 in. In the Games of 1968 a United States athlete threw the discus 64.78 meters to set a new Olympic and world record. Old or original marks have been similarly bettered in many other events. Finally, popular interest in the Olympic Games has kept abreast of the growth of the institution itself.

Scoring. Olympic Games scores, all unofficial, are computed according to one of three systems. In the point system of scoring, 10 points are credited for first place in the various events, 5 points for second place, 4 points for third place, 3 points for fourth place, 2 points for fifth place, and 1 point for sixth place. This system has been criticized as favoring populous nations entering teams in a large number of relatively obscure events. Another scoring system lists the number of gold medals, that is, first places, won by each nation. The third method is a so-called weighted system which calculates the ratio of gold medals to every million persons, permitting a relatively fair comparison of the performances of large and small nations.

See also WINTER OLYMPICS and individual articles on sports mentioned above.   A.B.

OLYMPIC NATIONAL PARK, region of natural interest in N.W. Washington, containing the Olympic Mts., one of the finest remaining areas of virgin forest in the Pacific Northwest, and a variety of unusual wildlife. Mount Olympus, the highest peak of the mountains, reaches an altitude of 7954 ft. above sea level. On the slopes of Mt. Olympus and several of the other high peaks are numerous glaciers and glacial streams and lakes. Stands of Douglas fir, western hemlock, western red cedar, Sitka spruce, western white pine, and white fir extend up the sides of the mountains, from 1500 ft. to 3500 ft. Beyond, the forests gradually lessen in density to the 5000-ft. elevations, where they give way to alpine meadows. In the lower valleys of the western slopes, where the rainfall averages 142 in. annually, are the noted rain forests, resembling jungles, with thick undergrowth and deep carpets of moss. The most-noted species of wildlife in the park is the Roosevelt elk, now nearly extinct in other regions. Other wildlife includes black-tailed deer, Rocky Mountain goats, black bears, cougars, coyotes, beavers, minks, raccoons, otters, wolves, eagles, hawks, ravens, and grouse. The park, covering 896,599.10 acres, was authorized as Mt. Olympus National Monument in 1909 and established as a national park in 1938. It is administered by the National Park Service (q.v.).

OLYMPUS, highest mountain in Greece, 9550 ft. above sea level, on the boundary between Thessalia and Macedonia, near the Aegean Sea. In early Greek mythology it was believed to be the home of the gods. On its summit were the palaces of the gods, which had been built by Hephaestus (q.v.), god of metalwork. The entrance to Olympus was through a gate of clouds, protected by the goddesses known as the Seasons. Zeus (q.v.), king of the gods, had his throne on Olympus, and here the gods feasted on nectar and ambrosia, and were serenaded by the sweet songs of the Muses (q.v.). The twelve major Olympian deities were Zeus and his wife Hera; his brothers Poseidon, god of the sea, and Hades, god of the underworld; his sister Hestia, goddess of the hearth; and his children, Athena, goddess of wisdom, Ares, god of war, Apollo, god of the sun, Artemis, goddess of the moon and of the hunt, Aphrodite, goddess of love, Hermes (qq.v.), messenger of the gods, and Hephaestus. Later Greek writers transferred the home of these Olympian deities from Olympus to a heavenly region free from snow and storm and filled with dazzling light.

OLYNTHUS, city of ancient Greece, in Macedonia, on the Chalcidice Peninsula (now Khalkidhiki), at the head of the Toronaic Gulf. Founded by the Chalcidians from Euboea (q.v.), the city first became prominent as the result of its leading role during the revolt of the Chalcidians against Athens in the late 5th century B.C. For some time Olynthus was the head of a powerful confederacy, called the Chalcidic League, but the city was subdued by Sparta in 379 B.C. and totally destroyed by Philip II (q.v.), King of Macedonia, in 348 B.C. The Olynthiac orations, three speeches delivered by the famous Greek orator Demosthenes (q.v.) in 348 B.C., when Philip seized the city, requested the Athenians to aid the citizens of Olynthus.

OMAGUA, South American Indian tribe of the Tupi-Guarani (q.v.) linguistic family, living in northeastern Peru and western Brazil. Their economy is based on agriculture, hunting, and fishing. At the time of the Spanish conquest in South America in the 16th century, an erroneous report credited the Omagua with having rich stores of gold, and in 1536, 1541, and 1560 unsuccessful attempts were made by the Spanish to conquer their lands. In the 17th century Jesuit missionaries established forty villages of Omagua converts along the Amazon River (q.v.); they prospered despite frequent attacks by Portuguese slave hunters. After the expulsion of the Jesuits from the Spanish colonies in 1767 the mission settlements broke up and the Omagua returned to their former way of life.

OMAHA, North American Indian tribe of the Siouan stock (q.v.), closely related to the Kansa, Osage, Quapaw (qq.v.), and Ponca tribes, and formerly inhabiting an extensive territory on the west side of the Missouri R., between the Platte and Niobrara rivers, within the present boundaries of Nebraska. They followed an economy based on the cultivation of corn and vegetables and the hunting of buffalo. Their dwellings were generally earth-covered lodges, but they also built bark lodges and carried skin tepees with them on their hunting expeditions. In 1802 the Omaha were greatly reduced in number by an epidemic of smallpox. Subsequently, they were even further reduced by incessant warfare with the Sioux (q.v.), which was terminated through the intervention of the United States government. In 1854 the tribe ceded a large part of their territory to the U.S.; the remainder was retained as a reservation, part of which was later sold to the government as a reservation for the Winnebago (q.v.) tribe. In 1882 the Omaha were granted the right to hold land individually. The tribe numbers about 1800. *See* AMERICAN INDIANS: *Indians of the United States and Canada: The Plains Area.*

OMAHA, city and port of entry in Nebraska, and county seat of Douglas Co., the largest city in population in the State, on the Missouri R., opposite Council Bluffs, Iowa. Ten railroads serve the city, and the Omaha Municipal Airport is the central airport on the New York-San Francisco air route and the terminus of the Omaha-Kansas City route. The city is the site of the University of Nebraska (q.v.) at Omaha, the University of Nebraska College of Medicine and the Presbyterian Theological Seminary. One of the outstanding buildings in Omaha is the Joslyn Memorial, a cultural center and concert hall. The city is governed under the mayoral system.

Commerce and Industry. Omaha is the industrial and commercial center of Nebraska. Industries in the city include the manufacture of locomotives, paints and varnishes, machinery, linseed oil, and food products. The city is a market for the grain of the surrounding area and an important livestock and meat-packing market.

History. Omaha was first settled in 1846–47 and was laid out as a town in 1854. Its site, close to the geographical center of the United States, soon made it an important transportation and trading center. Before the completion of the Union Pacific Railroad in 1869, Omaha was the most northerly outfitting point for overland wagon trains to the West. Until 1867, when Nebraska became a State, Omaha was the capital of the Territory of Nebraska. On March 23, 1913, the city was devastated by a tornado during which 142 persons were killed.

Population. Between 1910 and 1950 the population of Omaha increased from 124,096 to 251,117. In 1960 the population was 301,598, and in 1970 it was 347,328.

OMAN

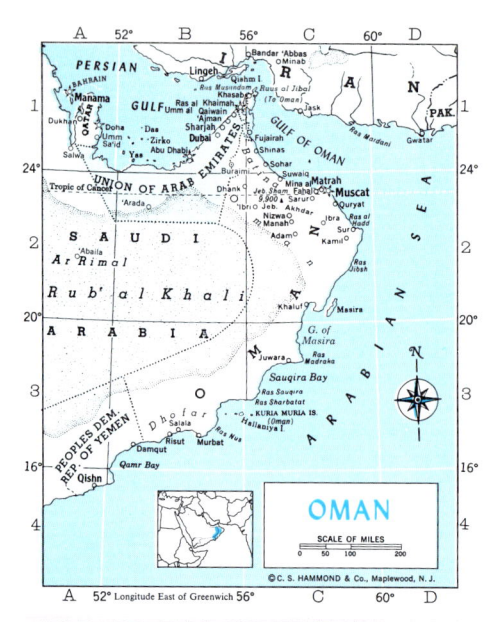

INDEX TO MAP OF OMAN

Cities and Towns

Adam	C 2
Dhank	B 2
Ibra	C 2
'Ibri	B 2
Juwara	C 3
Kamil	C 2
Khaluf	C 2
Khasab	B 1
Manah	C 2
Matrah	C 2
Mina al Fahal	C 2
Murbat	B 3
Muscat (cap.)	C 2
Nizwa	C 2
Quryat	C 2
Risut	B 3
Salala	B 3
Sarur	C 2
Shinas	C 1
Sohar	C 1
Sur	C 2
Suwaiq	C 2

Physical Features

Akhdar, Jebel (mt. range)	C 2
Batina (reg.)	C 1
Dhofar (reg.)	B 3
Hadd, Ras al (cape)	C 2
Jibsh, Ras (cape)	C 2
Madraka, Ras (cape)	C 3
Masira (gulf)	C 3
Musandam, Ras (cape)	B 1
Oman (reg.)	C 2
Ruus al Jibal (dist.)	C 1
Sauqira (bay)	C 3
Sham, Jebel (mt.)	C 2
Sharbatat, Ras (cape)	C 3

OMAN, formerly MUSCAT AND OMAN, independent hereditary sultanate, or monarchy, extending about 1000 mi. along the S.E. coast of the Arabian Peninsula, bordered on the N. by the Gulf of Oman, on the E. and S. by the Arabian Sea, on the S.W. by the Peoples Democratic Republic of Yemen, on the W. by the Rub 'al Khali (Empty Quarter) of Saudi Arabia, and on the N.W. by the Union of Arab Emirates. Oman falls naturally into four physical divisions: a coastal plain; a mountain range running approximately from the N.W. to the S.E.; an interior plateau; and, in the southwest, a semicircular plain which extends to the foot of a steep line of hills. Areas of cultivation are in the Jebel Akhdar, or Green Mts., where some heights exceed 9000 ft.; Batina, the coastal plain N.W. of Muscat; and the province of Dhofar along the S.W. coast. Dates are the principal agricultural product.

The area of the sultanate is estimated at 82,000 sq.mi. (the inland boundaries are undemarcated). The total population, primarily Arab, is about 750,000 (1968 est.). The capital and chief port is Muscat (pop., about 6000). Matrah (pop., about 14,000) is the largest city.

Revenue is derived primarily from custom duties and payments by oil companies. Oil was discovered in 1964 and production was begun in 1967; the yield is about 350,000 barrels per day. Annual revenue in the late 1960's was about $2,400,000. The principal exports include oil, dates, pomegranates, dried limes, and dried fish. Imports include grains, sugar, cement, vehicles, and cotton goods. The unit of currency in Oman is the Riyal Saidi (1 Riyal Saidi equals U.S. $2.40; 1970).

History. British influence in the area began in 1798, when the East India Company (q.v.) obtained commercial rights from the sultan to the exclusion of the French and the Dutch. From 1900 to 1959, the dynasty was split: an imam who had the allegiance of the inland tribes was supported by Egypt (then United Arab Republic) and Saudi Arabia, while the ruling sultan was supported by Great Britain. In 1959 the sultan's forces defeated those of the imam and the imam was forced to flee into exile. In January, 1968, the British declared that they would withdraw completely from the area east of the Suez Canal by the end of 1971. The ruling sultan Said Bin Taimur (1910–), acceded to the throne in 1932, was overthrown by his son Qabus bin Said (1952–) in a palace coup in July, 1970. The new ruler promised to reverse the policies of stern autocracy and isolation that had been instituted by his father. He announced that in the future the income from oil would be used to create a better life for the people. He also changed the name of the sultanate from Muscat and Oman to Oman to symbolize the unity of the country.

OMAR KHAYYÁM (fl. 11th cent.), Persian poet, mathematician, and astronomer, born in Nishapur (now in Iran). As astronomer to the royal court, he was engaged with several other scientists to reform the calendar. Their work resulted in the adoption of a new era, the Jalalian, or Seljuk. This mode of reckoning dated from March 15, 1079. As a writer on algebra, geometry, and other mathematical subjects Omar stands out as one of the most notable mathematicians of his time. He is, however, most famous as the author of the *Rubáiyát*, or quatrains. The British poet and translator Edward FitzGerald (q.v.) was the first to introduce Omar to the West through a version of 100 of the quatrains. The version is a paraphrase, often very close,

A painting showing Omar Khayyám, the great Persian mathematician, astronomer, and poet working out the calendar, 1074 A.D.   Bettmann Archive

which has caught the spirit of the original. About 1000 of these epigrammatic four-line stanzas are found, in different works and manuscripts, ascribed to Omar.

OMDURMAN, city of the Republic of the Sudan, opposite Khartoum, near the junction of the White and Blue Nile rivers. It is a marketing center for the surrounding agricultural area with trade in cotton, grain, and handicrafts. On Sept. 2, 1898, the forces of Mohammed Ahmed, referred to by some as the Mahdi (q.v.) were defeated decisively at Omdurman by Anglo-Egyptian troops; see KHARTOUM; SUDAN, REPUBLIC OF THE: *History.* Pop. (1966 est.) 198,000.

OMIYA, city of Japan, in Saitama Prefecture, on the island of Honshu, N. of Urawa and 17 miles N.W. of Tokyo. A rail junction on the Tohoku Line, the city is the trade center of an agricultural area producing rice, silk, and wheat and has workshops of the National Railways. It is the site of the Hikawa Shrine, founded in the 5th century B.C. Omiya Park has sports facilities. Pop. (1965) 215,644.

OMMIADS. See CALIPH: *The Umayyad Caliphs.*

OMSK, city of the Soviet Union, in the Russian S.F.S.R., and capital of Omsk Oblast, at the confluence of the Om and Irtysh rivers, about 400 miles W. of Novosibirsk. It is a major commercial center of the steppe belt, on the Trans-Siberian Railway and with steamer connection down the Irtysh R. In the city are grain mills, oil refineries, and plants manufacturing textiles, agricultural machinery, and railroad equipment. During the Russian Revolution (q.v.) the city was the scene of severe fighting and for a while was declared the capital of Russia by Aleksandr Vasilievich Kolchak (q.v.), the leader of the counter-revolutionary forces. In 1919, with the establishment of the Soviet government, Omsk temporarily became the Siberian capital. The city has a regional museum, the Siberian Agricultural Academy, medical and veterinary institutes, and the Central Pushkin Library. Founded in 1716 as a fort for protection against Kirghiz marauders, Omsk became a town in 1804 and expanded rapidly after it was made a station of the Trans-Siberian Railway. The novelist Fëdor Mikhailovich Dostoevski (q.v.) was confined here (1849–54) in a fortress near the city; he described it in his *Memoirs from the House of the Dead.* Pop. (1970) 821,000.

ONEGA, LAKE, lake of the Soviet Union, in the Russian S.F.S.R. After Lake Ladoga, which lies to the S.W., it is the largest lake in Europe, about 60 mi. at its greatest breadth and about 150 mi. in length; its maximum depth is about 360 ft. It is about 768 sq.mi. in area. The lake is fed by numerous rivers but its only outlet is the river Svir', which flows into Lake Ladoga. *See* LADOGA, LAKE.

ONEIDA, North American Indian tribe belonging linguistically to the Iroquoian family and forming part of the Iroquois (qq.v.) confederacy. The name by which the tribe is known is a corruption of an Indian word meaning standing rock and referring to a boulder sacred to the tribe and situated near the site of their ancient village on Lake Oneida, New York. Their territory included the region surrounding the lake and later extended south to the Susquehanna R. The tribe was friendly toward the French colonists and Jesuit missionaries, although most members of the confederacy were hostile to the outsiders. During the American Revolution the Oneida sided with the colonists and were obliged to take refuge within the American settlements when their fellow tribes took the side of the British. After the war most of the Oneida returned to their former territory, but many moved to Canada and settled in the region of the Thames R., Ontario, where their descendants still remain. Between 1820 and 1835, most of the Oneida who had returned to their homes in New York State sold their land and moved to a reservation at the head of Green Bay, Wis. In a recent year the Oneida numbered about 3500 in Wisconsin and about 350 in New York.

ONEIDA, city of New York, in Madison Co., about 13 miles s.w. of Rome. Manufactures include plastic, paper, and wood products, and silverware. In 1848, the American social reformer John Humphrey Noyes (q.v.) established the Oneida Community (q.v.). Pop. (1960) 11,677; (1970) 11,658.

ONEIDA COMMUNITY, communistic society established at Oneida, N.Y., in 1848, and dissolved about 1880. The community was founded originally at Putney, Vt., by the American religious leader John Humphrey Noyes (q.v.) in 1838. The members of the community, who were called Perfectionists (q.v.), believed that freedom from sin could be obtained on earth by communion with God, followed by a renunciation of personal property and of binding personal relationships, including marriage. After being expelled from Putney, where the group's practices had aroused opposition, the members settled at Oneida and established several successful manufacturing enterprises there. All properties, including farms and industries, were held in common; the community government was conducted by committees that met weekly in public sessions. Cohabitation was permitted, but conception was directed, theoretically, by the community leaders, who attempted to impose eugenic principles in order to produce healthy and intelligent offspring. Children were reared by the community, which in many cases provided them with professional and technical training.

Because of outside antagonism to the system of "complex marriage" maintained by the community, the system was abandoned in 1879. Soon afterward, the members also abolished their communal-property system. A joint-stock company, known as Oneida Community, Limited, was formed to carry on the various manufacturing establishments. The company still exists; but it has gradually narrowed its activities from the manufacture of steel traps and silk and the canning of fruits and vegetables to the manufacture of fine plated and sterling silverware, for which it is now known.

See COMMUNISM: *History: Early American Experiments in Communism.*

ONEIDA, LAKE, lake in New York State, on the boundaries of Madison, Oswego, Oneida, and Onondaga counties. It is about 22 mi. long and has a maximum width of 5 mi. The Oneida and Fish rivers are the chief affluents. A canal connects it with Lake Ontario on the N. and with the New York State Barge Canal on the E.

O'NEILL, Eugene Gladstone (1888–1953), American dramatist, son of the Irish-American actor James O'Neill (1847–1920), born in New York City. He accompanied his father on theatrical tours during his youth, attended Princeton University for one year (1906–07), and worked subsequently as a clerk in New York City. From 1909 to 1912 he prospected for gold in Honduras, served as assistant manager of a theatrical

Eugene O'Neill   Random House

troupe organized by his father, went to South America and South Africa as an ordinary seaman, toured as an actor with the troupe managed by his father, and worked as a newspaper reporter in New London, Conn. Having contracted a mild case of tuberculosis, in 1912 he became a patient in a sanatorium; there he wrote his first plays. In 1914–15, after leaving the sanatorium, he studied the techniques of playwriting at Harvard University under the American author and educator George Pierce Baker (q.v.).

During most of the next ten years O'Neill lived in Provincetown, Mass., and New York City, where he was associated both as a dramatist and as a manager with The Provincetown Players (q.v.). This experimental theatrical group staged a number of his one-act plays, beginning with *Bound East for Cardiff* (1916), and several long plays, including *The Hairy Ape* (1922). *Beyond the Horizon* (1920; Pulitzer Prize, 1921), a domestic tragedy in three acts, was produced successfully on the Broadway stage, as was *The Emperor Jones* (1920), a study of the disintegration of the mind of a dictator under the influence of fear. In the nine-act play *Strange Interlude* (1927; Pulitzer Prize, 1928) O'Neill sought to portray the way in which hidden psychological processes impinge upon outward actions. O'Neill's most ambitious work, the trilogy *Mourning Becomes Electra* (1931), was an attempt to recreate the power and profundity of the ancient Greek tragedies by setting the themes and plot of the *Oresteia* by the ancient Greek dramatist Aeschylus (q.v.) in 19th-century New England. *Ah, Wilderness* (1932), written in a relatively light vein, was highly successful.

O'Neill's other dramas include *Moon of the Caribees* (1918), *Anna Christie* (1921; Pulitzer Prize, 1922), *All God's Chillum Got Wings* (1924), *Desire Under the Elms* (1924), *The Great God Brown* (1926), *Lazarus Laughed* (1926), *Marco Millions* (1928), *Dynamo* (1929), and *Days Without End* (1934).

From 1934 until his death O'Neill suffered from poor health. During this entire period he worked intermittently on a long cycle of plays dealing with the history of an American family but completed only *A Touch of the Poet* (produced posthumously, 1957). After 1939 he wrote three other plays unrelated to the cycle: *The Iceman Cometh* (1946), which portrays a group of characters unable to live without illusions, and two tragedies dealing with his family, *Long Day's Journey Into Night* (produced posthumously, 1956) and *A Moon for the Misbegotten* (produced posthumously, 1957). O'Neill was awarded the 1936 Nobel Prize in literature.

Many of O'Neill's dramas are marked by new theatrical techniques and symbolic devices that express religious and philosophical ideas and give his characters psychological depth. He employed the sound of tom-toms gradually increasing in volume to mark an increase in tension, masks to indicate shadings of personality, lengthy asides in which his characters voice their hidden thoughts, and choruses used as in ancient Greek tragedies to comment on the action of a play.

O'Neill is considered the most important American dramatist. Throughout his career he attempted to deal with fundamental human problems seriously and with integrity. His best works convey forcibly his vision of modern man, a victim of circumstances who cannot believe in God, destiny, or free will and who therefore blames impersonal causes for his misery and punishes himself for his own sin and guilt. Despite the seriousness and theatrical brilliance of many of O'Neill's plays, much of his symbolism is obscure, and his innovations in stagecraft often do not achieve the desired effects. In addition, the language of his characters has been criticized for lapses into banality or bathos at many of the most compelling moments of his plays. By bringing psychological realism, philosophical depth, and poetic symbolism into the American theater, however, O'Neill's work raised the standards of most later American dramatists. See DRAMA: *National Drama: United States.*

O'NEILL, Hugh, 3rd Baron of Dungannon and 2nd Earl of Tyrone (1540?–1616), Irish revolutionist. He succeeded as chieftain of the O'Neills in 1593, and having secured a pledge of support from Spain, raised an army to fight the English power in Ireland. His initial successes led to a truce with the English in 1599, but hostilities were soon renewed and, in 1601, as he was marching to meet the Spanish army that had landed in Ireland, he was defeated by an English force at Kinsale. In 1603 he was forced to make a formal submission. He was pardoned by James I (q.v.), King of England, but in 1607, suspecting the English of duplicity, O'Neill fled to Rome, where he lived for the rest of his life. See IRELAND: *History.*

ONEONTA, city of New York, in Otsego Co., about 50 miles N.E. of Binghamton, in the W. foothills of the Catskill Mountains (q.v.). Manufactures include clothing, machinery, aluminum, and wood products. It is the site of Hartwick College, founded in 1928, and the College at Oneonta of the State University of New York. Gilbert Lake State Park is nearby. Pop. (1960) 13,412; (1970) 16,030.

ONION, common name applied to any biennial herb of the genus *Allium,* belonging to the Lily family, but usually restricted to *A. cepa,* native to Asia, and cultivated in temperate and subtropical regions for thousands of years. The true onion is a bulb-bearing plant with long, hollow leaves with thickened bases that make up most of the bulb. It contains sulfurous, volatile oils which give it a pungent taste. The white or pink flowers, which are borne in umbels, have six sepals, six petals, six stamens, and a solitary pistil. In the varieties known as top onions, the flowers are supplanted by small bulblets which may be grown to obtain new plants. The fruit is a loculicidal capsule. Onion bulbs and stems are eaten raw or cooked, and are used as seasoning in cookery. Onions raised in warm areas are planted as winter crops, and are milder in taste and odor than onions planted in cooler regions. Yellow Bermuda and white Spanish on-

ONITSHA

ions are among the mildest cultivated onions. Production of onions in the United States in the late 1960's exceeded 1,441,000 tons a year. The onion grows well in rich, moist soil; when the crop ripens, the bulbs are pulled and spread thinly on a dry surface in the open air until dry. They are stored in slotted or open-mesh bags to keep them dry enough to prevent sprouting.

Wild Onion, Allium cernuum

Other plants in the genus *Allium* also called onions include: the wild onion, *A. cernuum;* the shallot, *A. ascalonicum;* and the green onion or common leek, *A. porrum.* Both the shallot and the green onion, which have small bulbs, are also known as scallions. Compare GARLIC.

ONITSHA, city of Nigeria, in the East-Central State, on the Niger R., 50 miles s.w. of Enugu. Besides trading in palm products, corn, nuts, vegetables, and fruits, the city manufactures petroleum products, tires, bearings, nails, and is a source of mineral water. A teachers' college for women and a leper colony are in Onitsha; the city is also the residence of the Obi of Onitsha, an Ibo leader. In 1966 it was connected to Asaba by the longest road bridge in the country. Pop. (1969 est.) 189,067.

ONNES, Heike Kamerlingh. See KAMERLINGH ONNES, HEIKE.

ONONDAGA, North American Indian tribe belonging linguistically to the Iroquoian family (q.v.), and by alliance to the Iroquois (q.v.) confederacy. The territory they occupied centered about Onondaga Lake in central New York State and extended north to Lake Ontario and south to the Susquehanna R. Their principal village, which contained 140 houses in the 17th century, was called Onondaga or Onondaga Castle. This village served as the capital of the Iroquois confederacy, and the Onondaga were the official guardians of the council fire of the league. The tribe ranked as the chief member of the confederacy, although the Mohawk (q.v.) and the Seneca, living on the frontier of the league territory, were more warlike and became more prominent in Iroquoian relations with European settlers and other tribes. During the American Revolution the Onondaga sided with the British, and after the war most of the tribe emigrated to a reservation on the Grand R., in Canada, where their descendants still live. The rest of the tribe were placed on reservations in the region of their former territory in Onondaga County, N.Y.

ONSAGER, Lars (1903–), American chemist, born in Oslo, Norway, and educated at the Norwegian Technical University, Trondheim, and the Federal Institute of Technology, Zürich, Switzerland. In 1928 he came to the United States to teach at Johns Hopkins University. From 1928 to 1933 he taught also at Brown University, and after 1933 he was associated with the department of chemistry at Yale University. At Brown, in 1931, he was working on irreversible processes when he formulated what has been called the fourth law of thermodynamics, a series of equations showing various reciprocal relationships, as between heat and voltage in an electrical circuit; see THERMODYNAMICS. For this work Onsager was awarded the 1968 Nobel Prize in chemistry. Onsager became a U.S. citizen in 1945.

ONTARIO, city of California, in San Bernardino Co., about 35 miles E. of Los Angeles. It is served by railroad and maintains an international airport. Ontario is surrounded by a fertile fruit-producing area and the industries in the city include fruit processing as well as the manufacture of aircraft and clothing. Ontario was founded in 1882 by settlers from Ontario Province, Canada, and was incorporated in 1891. Population (1960) 46,617; (1970) 64,118.

ONTARIO, province of Canada, bounded on the N. by Hudson and James bays, on the E. by Québec Province, on the S. by the State of New York, lakes Ontario, Erie, Huron, and Superior, and the State of Minnesota, and on the W. and N.W. by Manitoba. The province has an area of 412,582 sq.mi., of which nearly 17 percent is

Ottawa, Ontario, the capital of Canada, with its Gothic-style parliament buildings.
National Film Board of Canada

water area; the latter includes the Canadian portion of the Great Lakes (q.v.).

Most of the s. boundary of Ontario is formed by the Great Lakes and connecting waterways, including, from E. to W., the Saint Lawrence R., the Thousand Islands, Lake Ontario, Niagara R., Lake Erie, the Detroit R., Lake Saint Clair, the Saint Clair R., Lake Huron, North Channel, Lake Superior, Rainy Lake, Rainy R., and Lake of the Woods.

THE LAND

In general, Ontario may be divided into two broad regions, namely, N. Ontario, which constitutes the vast bulk of the province, and s., or peninsular, Ontario, which is approximately the region lying between lakes Ontario, Erie, and Huron. The dividing line between the two regions extends from Mattawa on the Ottawa R. through Lake Nipissing and along the French R. to Georgian Bay. Northern Ontario comprises more than five sixths of the area of the province but has less than 15 percent of the population; s. Ontario has about 85 percent of the population and less than one sixth of the area.

More than half of N. Ontario is a low, rolling, rocky plateau with many lakes. It is part of the extensive Canadian Shield (q.v.), which is covered with thin soil and thousands of lakes. The watershed between Hudson Bay and the Great Lakes is very close to Lake Superior; the highest point in Ontario is Tip Top Hill (2120 ft.), which overlooks Lake Superior. The clay belt, a region with clay soils of some agricultural value, extends N.W. from the central portion of the Ontario-Québec border for about 500 mi. Farther N. the land slopes toward Hudson Bay in a plain, or Hudson Bay lowlands, which is from 100 to 200 mi. wide in a N.W. to S.E. direction.

The Canadian Shield extends through s. Ontario to about the N.E. shore of Lake Ontario but does not include the easternmost tip of the province. To the s. and W. of the shield, s. Ontario is a level or gently rolling plain. The only outstanding feature is the Niagara escarpment, from 200 to 300 ft. high, which extends from Niagara Falls generally W. and N.W. for a distance of about 300 mi.

Rivers and Lakes. Northern Ontario is drained mainly by rivers flowing into Hudson Bay. The Severn, Attawapiskat, Albany, and Moose are the largest rivers. The Ottawa R. is a major tributary of the St. Lawrence. In s. Ontario, the Grand R. and the Thames R. flow into Lake Erie and Lake St. Clair, respectively. In addition to the Great Lakes, the principal lakes in the province are Lake Simcoe, which is linked to Lake Ontario by a chain of rivers, lakes, and canals called

149

ONTARIO

INDEX TO MAP OF ONTARIO

Cities and Towns

Acton	B 3	Coniston	B 1	Kingston	D 2
Ajax	B 1	Copper Cliff	B 1	Kingsville	A 4
Alexandria	E 2	Cornwall	E 2	Kiosk	C 1
Alliston	A 3	Deep River	D 1	Kirkland Lake	E 3
Almonte	D 2	Deer Lake	B 3	Kitchener	B 3
Amherstburg	A 3	Delhi	B 3	Lakefield	C 2
Angus	B 2	Deseronto	D 2	Lambeth	B 3
Armstrong Station	D 2	Dresden	A 3	Lansdowne House	D 3
Arnprior	D 2	Dryden	D 3	Leamington	A 3
Arthur	B 3	Dundas	C 3	Levack	B 1
Atikokan	D 3	Dunnville	B 2	Lindsay	C 2
Attawapiskat	E 3	Durham	C 3	Lions Head	B 2
Auden	D 3	Eganville	A 1	Listowel	B 3
Aurora	C 3	Elliot Lake	B 1	Little Current	C 2
Aylmer	B 3	Elmira	B 3	Lively	B 1
Bancroft	C 2	Espanola	A 3	London	B 3
Barrie	D 2	Essex	D 3	Mac Tier	C 2
Barry's Bay	C 2	Exeter	B 3	Madawaska	E 1
Bay Ridges	A 3	Favourable Lake	C 2	Madoc	D 2
Beaverton	C 1	Fenelon Falls	B 3	Manitouwadge	E 3
Belle River	E 3	Fergus	B 3	Manitowaning	D 3
Belleville	A 2	Ferris	B 3	Marathon	D 3
Blenheim	A 2	Forest	B 3	Markdale	E 2
Blind River	B 1	Fort Albany	E 3	Marmora	C 3
Bobcaygeon	C 2	Fort Erie	D 2	Massey	B 2
Bonfield	C 3	Fort Frances	E 3	McKellar	C 3
Bowmanville	B 2	Frankford	E 2	Meaford	D 2
Bracebridge	B 2	Fraserdale	B 2	Midland	B 2
Bradford	C 1	French River	E 2	Millbrook	C 3
Bramalea	D 3	Galt	C 3	Milton	B 3
Brampton	B 3	Gananoque	C 3	Milverton	B 3
Brantford	C 3	Gateway	B 3	Minden	C 3
Bridgeport	B 3	Georgetown	B 3	Mississauga	C 3
Brighton	D 2	Geraldton	E 3	Mitchell	B 3
Brockville	E 2	Glencoe	B 3	Moosonee	E 3
Burk's Falls	C 3	Goderich	B 2	Morrisburg	D 3
Burlington	A 2	Gore Bay	B 2	Mount Forest	B 3
Byng Inlet	C 3	Gravenhurst	C 3	Napanee	C 3
Caledonia	B 3	Grimsby	B 3	New Liskeard	E 2
Callander	C 1	Guelph	B 3	Newmarket	B 3
Campbellford	D 2	Hagersville	B 3	Niagara Falls	E 3
Cannington	C 2	Haileybury	E 3	Nipigon	B 3
Cardinal	E 2	Haliburton	C 2	Nobel	B 2
Carleton Place	B 2	Hamilton	C 3	Noelville	B 2
Casselman	E 2	Hanover	A 3	North Bay	C 1, E 3
Chalk River	D 1	Harriston	B 3	Norwich	B 3
Chapleau	E 3	Harrow	D 2	Norwood	C 3
Chatham	A 3	Havelock	C 2	Oakville	C 3
Chesley	B 2	Hawkesbury	B 3	Orangeville	A 3
Chesterville	B 2	Hearst	E 2	Orillia	C 3
Clinton	B 3	Huntsville	B 3	Oshawa (nat'l cap.)	E 2
Cobalt	D 2	Ingersoll	B 3	Ottawa (nat'l cap.)	E 2
Cobourg	C 3	Iroquois	E 3	Owen Sound	B 2
Cochrane	E 3	Kapuskasing	D 2	Palmerston	A 1
Colborne	B 2	Kemptville	E 2	Paris	B 3
Collingwood	B 2	Kenora	D 2	Parkhill	D 3
		Killaloe Station	B 2	Parry Sound	C 2
		Kincardine			

Pembroke	D 2	Tilbury	E 3
Penetanguishene	B 2	Tillsonburg	C 3
Perth	D 2	Timmins	B 2
Petawawa	C 2	Tobermory	A 2
Peterborough	A 3	Toronto	A 2
Petrolia	D 2	Trenton	D 2
Pickle Crow	B 3	Trout Lake	D 2
Picton	D 2	Tweed	C 2
Point Edward	A 3	Uxbridge	E 2
Porcupine	E 3	Vankleek Hill	C 2
Port Colborne	B 3	Verner	B 1
Port Dover	B 3	Victoria Harbour	C 1
Port Elgin	B 2	Walkerton	B 2
Port Hope	C 2	Wallaceburg	C 2
Port Perry	B 1	Warren	B 3
Port Rowan	B 3	Waterford	B 3
Port Stanley	C 2	Waterloo	C 3
Powassan	C 1	Wawa	B 3
Prescott	E 2	Welland	C 3
Preston	A 3	West Lorne	B 3
Providence Bay	D 3	Wheatley	C 3
Red Lake	B 2	Whitby	B 2
Renfrew	C 2	Whitney	E 2
Richmond	C 3	Wiarton	B 3
Richmond Hill	E 2	Windsor	C 3
Ridgetown	B 3	Wingham	B 3
Rockland	C 3	Woodstock	
Saint Catharine's			
Saint Mary's		**Physical Features**	
Saint Thomas			
Sandy Lake		Abitibi (river)	E 3
(Favourable Lake)	D 3	Albany (river)	D 3
Sarnia	A 3	Algonquin Prov. Park	C 2
Sault Sainte Marie	D 3	Amherst (isl.)	D 2
Schreiber	C 3	Balsam (lake)	C 2
Seaforth	B 3	Bays (lake)	C 2
Sharbot Lake	E 3	Black (river)	C 2
Shelburne	D 2	Bruce (penin.)	B 2
Simcoe	B 3	Burnt (river)	A 2
Sioux Lookout	C 3	Cabot Head (prom.)	A 3
Smiths Falls	B 2	Christian (isl.)	C 2
South River	E 2	Cockburn (isl.)	A 2
Southampton	C 3	Croker (cape)	B 2
Spanish	B 2	Duck (isls.)	A 1
Stayner	B 2	Erie (lake)	B 2
Stittsville	C 3	Fitzwilliam (isl.)	B 2
Stoney Creek	B 3	Georgian (bay)	C 3
Stratford	C 3	Georgian Bay Isls.	B 2
Strathroy	B 3	Nat'l Park	B 2
Sturgeon Falls	C 1	Grand (river)	E 3
Sudbury	B 1, E 3	Hudson (bay)	A 2
Sundridge	C 2	Huron (lake)	E 3
Sutton West	E 2	Inverhuron Prov. Park	B 2
Tecumseh	A 1	James (bay)	E 3
Thessalon	B 2	Joseph (lake)	C 2
Thornbury	D 3	Kawartha (lakes)	C 2
Thorold	C 3	Lake of the Woods	D 3
Thunder Bay		(lake)	

Lake Superior Prov. Park	E 3
Long (point)	C 3
Madawaska (river)	B 2
Magnetawan (river)	B 2
Main (channel)	A 2
Manitoulin (isl.)	B 2
Mazinaw (lake)	D 2
Mississippi (lake)	C 2
Muskoka (lake)	D 2
Nipigon (lake)	C 3
Nipissing (lake)	C 1
North (channel)	B 2
Nottawasaga (bay)	C 2
Ontario (lake)	D 2
Opeongo (lake)	B 2
Ottawa (river)	A 2
Owen (sound)	B 2
Panache (lake)	D 2
Parry (isl.)	B 3
Pelee (point)	B 3
Petawawa (river)	C 2
Petre (point)	E 2
Pinery Prov. Park	B 3
Pins (point)	B 3
Point Pelee Nat'l Park	A 4
Polar Bear Prov. Park	E 3
Presqu'ile Prov. Park	D 3
Prince Edward (pen.)	D 3
Quetico Prov. Park	D 3
Rice (lake)	C 2
Rideau (lakes)	D 2
Rideau (river)	E 2
Rondeau Prov. Park	B 3
Rosseau (lake)	C 2
Saint Clair (lake)	A 3
Saint Clair (river)	A 3
Saint Joseph (lake)	C 3
Saint Lawrence (river)	E 2
Saint Lawrence Isls. Nat'l Park	D 2
Saugeen (river)	C 2
Scugog (lake)	C 2
Seul (lake)	C 3
Severn (river)	B 1
Simcoe (lake)	B 3
Spanish (river)	E 3
Superior (lake)	A 2
Sydenham (river)	E 3
Thames (river)	B 3
Wanapitei (river)	C 2
Welland (canal)	E 3
Weslemkoon (lake)	C 2
Winisk (river)	B 2
Wolfe (isl.)	D 3
Woods (lake)	

150

ONTARIO

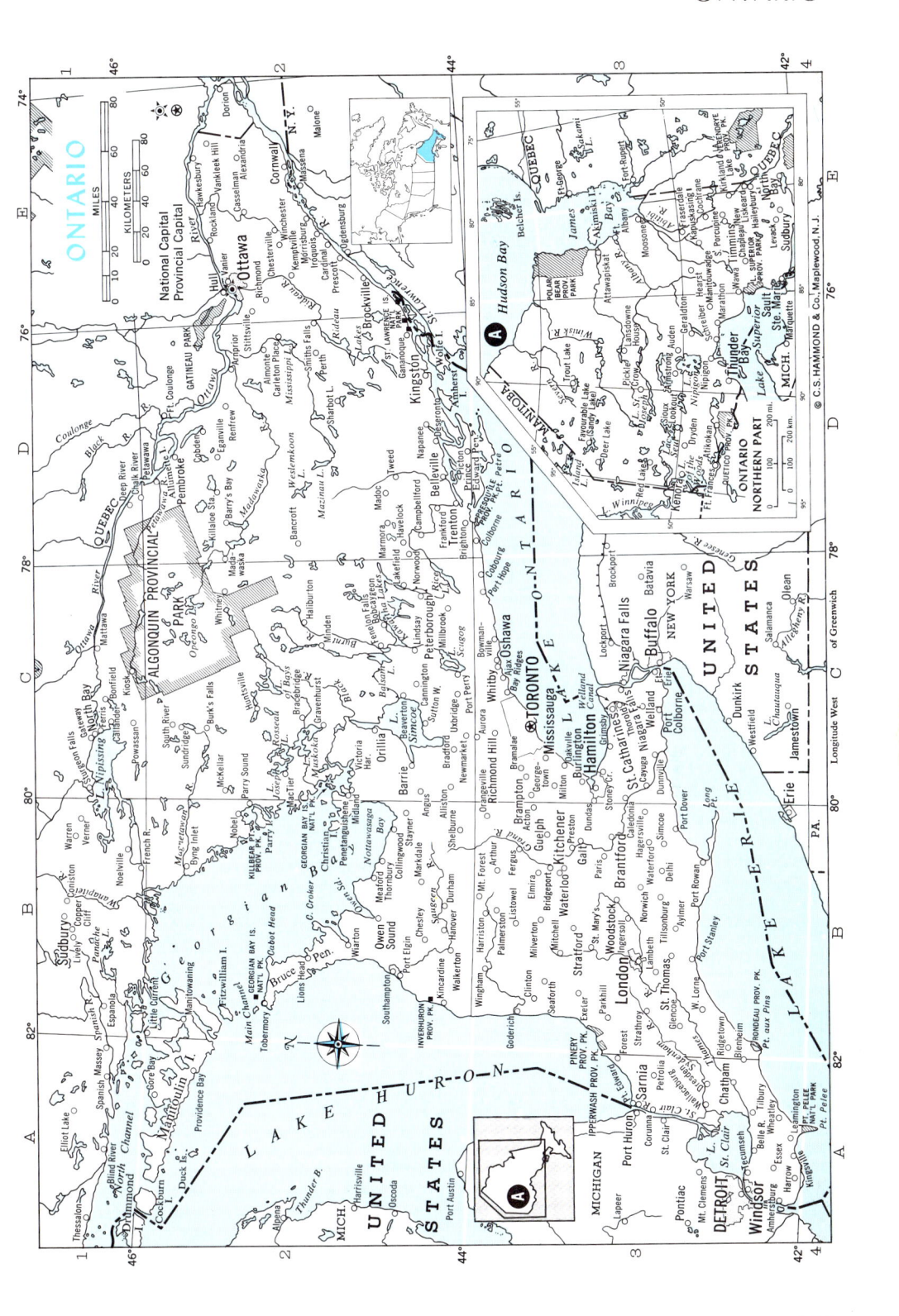

ONTARIO

the Trent Canal system; and Lake Nipissing, Lake Abitibi, Lake Timiskaming, Lake Nipigon, and Lake of the Woods.

Climate. Extending for about 1000 mi. in both an E. and W. and a N. and S. direction, Ontario has wide climatic variations. Thus the Hudson Bay shore of Ontario has a subarctic climate, whereas the Lake Erie shore has one of the warmest climates in Canada. Temperature extremes for the province as a whole range from $-53°$ to $105°$ F. Winters are longer and colder to the N. and W. Average January temperatures are $24°$ F. at Toronto in the S.; $12°$ F. at Ottawa in the E.; $8°$ F. at Fort William in the W.; $0°$ F. at Cochrane in the clay belt; and about $-15°$ F. along the Hudson Bay shore. July averages show less variation. The average July temperature at Toronto is $71°$ F.; at Ottawa, $69°$ F.; at Fort William and Cochrane, $63°$ F.; and along the Hudson Bay shore, about $50°$ F. Temperatures in peninsular Ontario are modified by the Great Lakes.

Precipitation varies from about 35 in. annually in the S.E. to about 24 in. annually in the N.W. The proportion of precipitation that occurs as snow increases toward the N. and W. The heaviest total snowfall, about 120 in. (10 in. of snow equal about 1 in. of rain), occurs near Georgian Bay. Snowfall diminishes to about 40 in. in the extreme S. because of the warmer climate and to about 60 in. in the N. because of the relatively dry climate. Drought is sometimes a problem in the W. part of S. Ontario, where moderate rainfall is combined with an unusually warm climate.

Plants. Much of N. Ontario is covered with coniferous forests consisting of black spruce, white spruce, jack pine, balsam fir, tamarack, and cedar mixed with such hardy deciduous trees as birch and poplar. To the S. the proportion of deciduous trees in the forest increases; the most common deciduous trees are maple, oak, beech, ash, and basswood. Along the shore of Hudson Bay the vegetation consists of tundra, which is a mixture of mosses, lichens, grasses, and low shrubs. The Hudson Bay lowlands is a transition zone in which stunted, scattered trees of the coniferous forest are mixed with kinds of tundra ground cover. Most of the forest in S. Ontario has been cleared for farmland, but extensive reforestation policies have been carried out since the establishment of Conservation Authorities in 1946.

Animals. Ontario has a wide variety of big-game animals, fur-bearing animals, migratory waterfowl, and game fish. In the N. are found moose, woodland caribou, black bears, timber wolves, foxes, martens, weasels, beavers, and muskrats. The lakes and rivers of the Canadian Shield and the Great Lakes contain whitefish, pike, bass, maskinonge, pickerel, and various kinds of trout and other fish. These bodies of water also support large populations of native and migratory ducks, geese, and herons. In the S. are white-tailed deer, raccoons, squirrels, chipmunks, rabbits, and groundhogs, as well as pheasant, and a wide variety of smaller birds.

Parks and Other Places of Interest. Ontario has four large provincial parks, more than ninety small ones, and a few small national parks and historic sites. The largest provincial parks are Algonquin Park, which is between the Ottawa R. and Georgian Bay; Quetico Park, which lies along the boundary with Minnesota in the W.; and Lake Superior and Sibley parks, on the E. and N. shores, respectively, of Lake Superior. The system of parklands covers about 5850 sq.mi. More than forty areas have been established as Wilderness Areas, ranging in size from less than 1 sq.mi. to the 225-sq.mi. area of treeless tundra bordering on Hudson Bay and the 938-sq.mi. Pukaskwa area on the N. shore of Lake Superior. An area of 4500 sq.mi. extending across the N. shore of Georgian Bay to Lake Nipissing is being developed as a recreational reserve.

The national parks are Georgian Bay Islands, off the tip of Bruce Peninsula; St. Lawrence Islands, at the outlet of Lake Ontario; and Point Pelée, which projects far into Lake Erie. Historic parks include Fort Henry at Kingston, Fort Wellington at Prescott, Fort York at Toronto, Fort Malden at Amherstburg, Old Fort Erie at Fort Erie, and Woodside at Kitchener. Among the best-known vacation areas and points of interest is Niagara Falls (q.v.), which is located on the boundary with New York. On the S. edge of the Canadian Shield are many well-known resort areas, including the Muskoka Lakes and Lake Simcoe, N. of Toronto, North Bay on Lake Nipissing, the Rideau Lakes N.W. of the St. Lawrence R., and Manitoulin Island in Lake Huron.

The city of Hamilton has two botanical gardens, the Royal Botanical Gardens and Gaga Park; impressive floral plantings are found in the parks along the Niagara R., particularly in Victoria Park at Niagara Falls. The Stratford Shakespearean Festival attracts many summer visitors to Stratford.

THE PEOPLE

According to the latest official census (1966), the population of Ontario was 6,960,870 (1969 est., 7,425,000). Ontario receives more than 67,000 foreign immigrants every year, as well as many thousands of people from other parts of the country.

Children ride in an ox-drawn cart during a festival at Upper Canada Village near Morrisburg, Ontario.

The population of the province is very unevenly distributed. Southern Ontario, an area of about 50,000 sq.mi., has an average density of a little more than 120 inhabitants per sq.mi.; N. Ontario, an area of about 300,000 sq.mi., has an average population density of approximately 2.5 per sq.mi.

The people of Ontario are of the following national or racial origin: British, 59.5 percent; French, 10.4 percent; German, 6.4 percent; other European, 20.1 percent; native Indian and Eskimo, 0.8 percent; and other, 2.8 percent.

About 78 percent of the population of Ontario consists of native-born Canadians. Of the foreign-born about 45 percent were born in Great Britain or the U.S.

Ontario is highly urbanized; approximately 83 percent of the people live in towns and cities. One third of the entire population of the province lives in the metropolitan area of Toronto (q.v.). The largest metropolitan centers are Toronto, the provincial capital; Ottawa, the dominion capital; Hamilton, an important transportation center; Windsor, an industrial city and railroad terminus; and London (qq.v.), an industrial city. Other leading cities and industrial centers are Saint Catharines, Oshawa (qq.v.), and Kitchener; Sudbury is an important mining center; and Sault-Sainte-Marie (q.v.) is a railroad center, port of entry, and noted summer resort.

Education and Cultural Facilities. Education in Ontario is free and compulsory for all children between the ages of eight and sixteen. The public-school system is under the supervision of the provincial department of education and is nondenominational; however, Roman Catholic schools, known as separate schools, may receive a share of the school funds proportional to the number of Roman Catholic taxpayers in the locality.

ELEMENTARY AND SECONDARY SCHOOLS. According to the latest available government statistics, in the late 1960's Ontario had about 5830 public, Federal, and private elementary and secondary schools (except private kindergartens), which were attended annually by 1,914,000 students; full-time teachers totaled 78,110. The province also had schools for the blind, the deaf, and schools of nursing which had a total annual enrollment of more than 10,000 students. About 100 Federal schools for Indians were annually attended by about 6500 students in the mid-1960's, according to the latest available government statistics.

COLLEGES AND UNIVERSITIES. In the late 1960's Ontario had 68 institutions of higher learning, including 17 which grant degrees. Full-time undergraduate enrollment for all of the institutions totaled about 70,000 annually. The degree-granting institutions include the University of Toronto; Carleton University and the University of Ottawa in Ottawa; Queen's University and Royal Military College of Canada in Kingston; University of Western Ontario in London; Waterloo Lutheran University and Waterloo University; Brock University at St. Catharines; the University of Guelph at Guelph; Lakehead University at Port Arthur; Laurentian University of Sudbury; McMaster University at Hamilton; Trent University at Peterborough; and the University of Windsor; see OTTAWA, UNIVERSITY OF; TORONTO, UNIVERSITY OF; and WESTERN ONTARIO, UNIVERSITY OF.

LIBRARIES AND MUSEUMS. Ontario has a well-devel-

Ontario accounts for more than one-quarter of Canada's mineral output. The province produces a wide range of minerals, including uranium, cobalt, nickel, and gold.
National Film Board of Canada

oped public library system serving most towns and cities and some outlying areas. Special government, university, and research libraries in Ottawa and Toronto also exist. The principal museums and art galleries are the National Museum of Canada and the National Gallery of Canada, both in Ottawa, the Royal Ontario Museum in Toronto, and art galleries in Toronto, Hamilton, and London. The Royal Botanical Gardens are in Hamilton.

THE ECONOMY

Manufacturing is the principal economic activity of Ontario. Also important to the economy of the province are the mining and forestry industries and agriculture. Ontario is well endowed with good sites for hydroelectric-power development and nearly all these sites are utilized. According to latest government statistics, the total annual hydroelectric generating capacity in the late 1960's was 6,337,000 kw; thermal-power capacity was 3,922,836 kw.

Manufacturing. Ontario is the center of manufacturing activity in Canada; in terms of value more than half of Canadian manufactures are produced in the province. Centrally located in Canada, the province is close to the great manufacturing belt of the U.S.

Ontario annually employed about 775,000 production workers in the mid-1960's, according to the latest available government statistics; more than 35 percent were employed in the census metropolitan area of Toronto. Other manufacturing centers are Hamilton, Kitchener, Windsor, London, and Ottawa. The largest employers are the transportation-equipment, the food and beverage, the primary-metal, and the fabricated-metal industries. The annual value of shipments of all industry groups approached $18,000,000; the transportation-equipment industry accounted for more than $3,000,000; the food and beverage industries totaled about $2,700,000; primary-metal manufactures were valued at about $1,700,000; and metal-fabricating industries accounted for about $1,500,000.

Agriculture. Ontario leads all the Canadian provinces in value of farm production; in 1969, according to latest available government statistics, annual cash receipts from the sale of farm products totaled about $446,193,000. Farms numbered about 110,000, totaling some 18,000,000 acres, and averaging about 163 acres each. Agriculture is diversified. Cash receipts from livestock and products, including poultry, eggs, and dairy products, make up about 70 percent of the total. The balance is mainly from field crops. Ontario ranked first in the late 1960's among the provinces in annual output of mixed grains (about 51,000,000 bu.), soybeans (9,000,000 bu.), beans (1,600,000 bu.), and tame hay (8,000,000 tons), and ranked second in sugar beets (287,000 tons), and third in oats (58,700,000 bu.). Ontario is the largest national vegetable and fruit producer and is the leading producer of dairy products. In the late 1960's livestock included over 900,000 milk cows, 710,000 calves; other cattle totaled about 1,600,000. Ontario also had more than 25,500,000 hens and chickens, 2,000,000 hogs, and 250,000 sheep and lambs.

Fishing. The fishing industry is of relatively little importance in Ontario; it consists almost entirely in the taking of perch, pickerel, smelt, and whitefish from the Great Lakes. According to the latest available government statistics, in the mid-1960's the annual catch totaled about 50,000,000 lb. and the total value of all products of the fisheries totaled about $6,500,000. About 3000 people are employed annually in the fishing industry.

Mining. For more than half a century Ontario has been the leading mineral-producing province in Canada. The estimated annual value of all mineral production in Ontario in the late 1960's, according to the latest available government statistics, was more than $1,190,000,000. The leading metallics and their approximate values included nickel ($350,000,000), copper ($255,000,000), iron ore ($95,000,000), zinc

ONTARIO

($80,000,000), gold ($55,000,000), and uranium ($40,000,000). The most important nonmetallics included salt ($20,000,000), nepheline syenite ($4,000,000), elemental sulfur ($1,800,000), and gypsum ($1,500,000).

The most important single mining region is the Sudbury Basin, which provides more than half of the total mineral production of Ontario by value. Copper, iron ore, nickel, and platinum metals are mined there. North of Sudbury, between Lake Timiskaming and the N. edge of the Canadian Shield, cobalt, gold, and silver are extracted in a number of mining towns including Cobalt, Kirkland Lake, and Timmins. Ontario has several important iron-ore regions, notably the Michipicoten Range, a continuation of the famous iron-bearing ranges of Minnesota and Wisconsin, and Steep Rock Lake w. of Fort William, both in N.W. Ontario; and Marmora in central Ontario N. of Belleville. Uranium is produced in the Elliot Lake region N. of Lake Huron. Of the nonmetallic minerals, natural gas, gypsum, petroleum, and salt are produced in the s., and asbestos and nepheline syenite are produced in the Canadian Shield area. Structural materials, such as cement, clay, gravel and sand, lime, and stone, are produced mostly in the s.

Forestry. Ontario has about 270,000 sq.mi. of forest land, of which about 165,000 sq.mi. are classified as productive and are primarily under public ownership. The stand of timber is more than 111,000,000,000 cu.ft., some three fifths of which is softwoods. According to the latest available government statistics, in the mid-1960's the annual cut approached 570,000,000 cu.ft.; the annual total value of shipments from primary mills was about $700,000,000.

Tourism. The economy of Ontario profits from tourism. The province is visited by more than 23,000,000 persons each year who spend about $1,500,000,000. Main attractions for tourists are Niagara Falls, the numerous parks, the Thousand Islands, and Fort Henry.

Transportation. Southern Ontario has a dense network of roads and railroads and many ports on the Great Lakes and the St. Lawrence R.; this transportation network is connected at all convenient points with that of the neighboring U.S. In contrast, N. Ontario has only one E. and W. road and is traversed by few railroad lines. Road and railroad construction is difficult in the terrain of the Canadian Shield, with its solid-rock hills and many swamps, bogs, lakes, and rivers to be crossed or avoided. Aside from minerals and lumber, the region originates little freight traffic; local passenger traffic also is small.

Ontario has about 10,000 mi. of railroads. Hamilton, Toronto, Ottawa, and London are major railroad centers. The railroads crossing the extreme s. part of the province carry much traffic between Detroit and Buffalo, for the shortest route between these cities is across Ontario. In addition, the province has about 78,000 mi. of roads, 74,000 mi. of which are surfaced. Recent developments are the extension of the system of four-lane divided highways in s. Ontario, particularly in the Toronto area. Ontario has about 38 percent of the motor vehicles registered in Canada. The province is well served by airlines and has connections with

Aircraft built at the Downsview, Ontario, plant of the de Havilland Aircraft of Canada Ltd., are exported throughout the world.
National Film Board of Canada

ONTARIO

major cities in North America and overseas. The international airport at Toronto is one of the largest and busiest airports in Canada.

SAINT LAWRENCE SEAWAY. The St. Lawrence Seaway, with a minimum depth of 27 ft., provides water transport from Lake Erie to Montréal, making navigation by oceangoing vessels possible as far inland as the head of Lake Superior. The entire Ontario shore of Lake Ontario, therefore, is accessible to large vessels. Harbors, docks, and loading facilities at Prescott, Toronto, and Hamilton, as well as at Sarnia (q.v.), Sault-Ste.-Marie, and Port Arthur (q.v.), have undergone expansion since the opening of the seaway in 1959, and construction was in progress in the late 1960's on the channel to bypass the city of Welland. According to latest available government statistics, traffic passing through the seaway in the late 1960's totaled almost 61,000,000 cargo tons, an increase of more than 80 percent over the 1960 figure.

Communications. According to the latest available government statistics, in the mid-1960's Ontario was served by nineteen television stations, four of which were privately owned, and one that broadcasted in French. The province has about eighty radio stations, and an additional four stations which broadcast in French. About fifty daily newspapers are published, one of which is in the French language; of the more than 290 weekly newspapers published, six are in the French language. More than forty-two telephones are in use per 100 population.

GOVERNMENT

The government of the province of Ontario was established according to the terms of the British North America Act (q.v.) of 1867, under which Nova Scotia, New Brunswick, Québec (Lower Canada), and Ontario (Upper Canada) became the original provinces of the Dominion of Canada. Ontario has a unicameral legislature, called the legislative assembly, of 108 seats. Members are elected by popular vote for terms not to exceed five years. The executive council is a cabinet formed by the dominant party in the legislative assembly. The lieutenant governor, the nominal head of government, is appointed by the Federal government of Canada.

The highest provincial court is the supreme court of Ontario, consisting of the court of appeal and the high court of justice. County or district courts, division courts, magistrates' courts, and police courts, as well as special courts, exist. Appeals may be carried to the Supreme Court of Canada. Judges of the magistrates' courts and lower courts are appointed by the provincial government; judges of higher courts are appointed by the Federal government.

Local Government. The province is divided into counties or unions of counties and subdivided into townships and urban municipalities of various sizes. Supervisory control of municipalities is exercised by a department of municipal affairs and the Ontario municipal board. Toronto is a metropolitan municipality, created in 1954 as a federation of the city of Toronto and twelve outlying municipalities. The municipality is governed by a metropolitan council consisting of the mayor and eleven senior members of the city council, and, from the local councils, the mayors, thirteen controllers, and two aldermen.

Voting Qualifications. In general the franchise is enjoyed by every person who is a Canadian citizen or a British subject and is twenty-one years of age or older.

HISTORY

The first white man to visit parts of what is now Ontario was the French explorer Étienne Brulé (q.v.), who ascended the Ottawa R. in 1610–11 and again in 1615 with the French explorer Samuel de Champlain (q.v.); in the latter year they penetrated to Georgian Bay. A Jesuit mission was established among the Huron (q.v.) Indians soon afterward; it was destroyed when the Huron were attacked by the Iroquois in 1649. The French constructed a number of forts and trading posts but made no attempts to colonize the region. The earliest English settlement was Moose Factory, a Hudson Bay post established in 1671. Rivalry, often bloody, developed between the British and French over the lucrative fur trade. Under the terms of the Treaty of Paris in 1763 at the conclusion of the French and Indian War (q.v.) between France and Great Britain, the region was established as British territory. In 1774 the area which is now Ontario, as well as much territory now part of the United States, was attached to the British colony of Québec.

After the American Revolution (q.v.) thousands of Tories, who called themselves United Empire Loyalists, settled in the southern part of the region; they were followed by other Americans who wanted to buy good land cheaply. The region was under French civil law during this period and had no representative government. The English-speaking pioneers expressed dissatisfaction with the governmental and legal system; as a result of their insistence the Ontario region was established in 1791 as a separate colony called Upper Canada, and Québec became Lower Canada. The small degree of local autonomy granted to Upper Canada did not satisfy the inhabitants, however, and in 1837 the Upper Canadians rose in rebellion. Upper Canada and Lower Canada were reunited in 1841 by the British authorities in the hope that the merger would lead eventually to the Anglicization of the French Catholic population of Lower Canada. This hope was not realized, however, and a paralyzing political deadlock ensued. In 1867, on the eve of confederation, Upper Canada and Lower Canada were again separated, with Upper Canada becoming the province of Ontario.

By the beginning of World War I the great waves of migration to Ontario were over, the good agricultural land was fully occupied, the tremendous mineral wealth of the Canadian Shield was known, and manufacturing was a thriving industry. During the first half of the 20th century Ontario was governed most of the time by the Progressive-Conservative Party. The Liberal Party was usually the second-strongest party in the province. The United Farmer Party governed the province from 1919 to 1923, and the Cooperative Commonwealth Federation, now the New Democratic Party, received a large portion of the vote in 1943. Three political parties are active in Ontario, namely the Progressive-Conservative Party, the Liberal Party, and the New Democratic Party. In all the elections since 1948 the Progressive-Conservatives have won an overwhelming majority of the seats in the Ontario legislature.

DOMINION BUREAU OF STATISTICS

Farms in the Lake Huron district of Ontario. Ontario leads all other Canadian provinces in value of farm production. National Film Board of Canada

ONTARIO, LAKE, lake of North America, easternmost and smallest of the five Great Lakes. It receives at its s.w. corner the waters of the upper lakes by the Niagara R., and at its N.E. corner it issues into the Saint Lawrence. It is about 247 ft. above sea level, has a maximum depth of about 778 ft., a maximum width of 53 mi., and is 193 mi. long. It is 7540 sq.mi. in area.

On the shores of the lake are many convenient harbors and thriving ports, chief among which are Kingston, Port Hope, Cobourg, Toronto, and Hamilton in Canada, and Oswego, Sackets Harbor, and Rochester in New York. Many lighthouses along the coasts facilitate navigation, and the lake is connected to Lake Erie by the Welland Canal, with the Hudson R. by the New York State Barge Canal, and with the Ottawa R. by the Rideau Canal. See GREAT LAKES.

ONTOLOGY. See METAPHYSICS.

ONYX, quartz mineral composed of alternating bands of chalcedony and opal (qq.v.). The bands, straight, parallel and usually colored black and white in alternating layers, are used as a gemstone, often for cameos. Compare AGATE.

OPAL, noncrystalline gem mineral consisting of hydrated silica in the gel state. Opal has a hardness of between 5.5 and 6.5, and a sp.gr. of 1.9 to 2.3. The fracture of the mineral is conchoidal and its luster varies from glassy to dull. In color the opal also shows extreme variations from white to black, and in transparency from transparent to opaque.

OP ART

One of the chief characteristics of the opal is the brilliant play of colors which may be seen in superior stones. These colors result from the cracking of the original stone as it hardens and the deposition of additional opal in the cracks. The indices of refraction of the original stone and the additional deposits are frequently different and result in light interference causing a play of colors. Opal has been used as a gemstone for many centuries in spite of a superstition that the gem brings bad luck to its owners.

A large number of different types of opal are known, but usually only the transparent or translucent varieties are used as gems. Gem opals include white opals; black opals; fire opals, which are yellow to red in color; girasol, which has a bluish-white opalescence; harlequin opals, which show uniform patches of contrasting colors; and lechosa opals which have a deep-green play of color within the stone. Other types of opal include moss opal, which has inclusions of foreign material resembling moss; hydrophane, a porous, white opal which is cloudy when dry and transparent when the pores are filled with water; and hyalite, a colorless, glasslike, and transparent form of opal. Diatomaceous earth, sometimes called tripolite, is a chalky form sometimes used for polishing and other industrial purposes.

Opals are found chiefly in Australia, Czechoslovakia, Honduras, Mexico, and Nevada.

OP ART, shortened form of OPTICAL ART, style of painting involving the creation of certain optical illusions, for example, images that are not present, colors that have not been painted, or formations that seem to shift and change. The op artist, familiar with the intricate mechanics of sight, purposely uses color and pattern to tease or deceive the eye. Typical op-art canvases show common geometrical forms, as squares, circles, lines, or dots. At first they seem no more than neatly designed arrangements. Upon continued viewing, however, the patterns change, shifting, projecting, receding, radiating. Looking at one spot on the canvas, the viewer, with peripheral vision, may "see" a color, shape, or movement nearby; an illusion, it disappears when the eyes attempt to focus directly upon it. Another op-art phenomenon is the experiencing of afterimages and, in some instances, dizziness.

The term "op art" was first used to describe works shown at the Museum of Modern Art, New York City, in a 1965 exhibition, "The Responsive Eye". Among those included in "The Responsive Eye" were such established artists as the Americans Josef Albers (1888–), Morris

"Baroque Experiment: Fred Maddox", painted by Jeffrey Steele in 1964. The king-size oil painting is an example of the optically illusory effects that mark the style of Op Art. UPI

Louis (1912–62), and Ad Reinhardt (1913–67), none of whom considered themselves op artists; the Israeli Yaacov Gipstein (1928–), who paints under the name Agam; the Americans Richard Joseph Anuszkiewicz (1930–) and Lawrence Poons (1937–); the Briton Bridget Riley (1931–); and the Frenchman Victor Vasarely (1908–).

Op art at first caught the public fancy partly because it is fascinating and partly because it reflects the tremendous contemporary interest in hallucinatory visual effects produced by the so-called psychedelic drugs. Also it vividly illustrates the theory that life is never static but in a continuous state of change and motion. By 1970, however, pure op art had virtually disappeared from the galleries. It has been appropriated instead by the makers of posters and fabrics, and has been employed in virtually every other area of graphic design. In addition, many serious painters continue to experiment with the purely perceptual effect of line, shape, and color.

OPELIKA, city in Alabama, and county seat of Lee Co., about 26 miles N.W. of Columbus, Ga., near the Chattahoochee R. Primarily a marketing center, the city has varied manufacturing, including textiles, cottonseed products, lumber, and fertilizer. Opelika was settled in 1836, incorporated as a town in 1854, and as a city in 1899. Pop. (1960) 15,678; (1970) 19,027.

OPELOUSAS, city in Louisiana, and parish seat of Saint Landry Parish, about 22 miles N. of Lafayette. Primarily a shipping center, the city has light manufacturing. Founded about 1765 by French traders, it is one of the oldest cities in the State. Pop. (1960) 17,417; (1970) 20,121.

OPEN DOOR, in modern diplomacy, doctrine or policy advocating equal trading rights in the nation to which it is applied for all other nations. The open-door doctrine was first enunciated by the United States with respect to China at the end of the 19th century. Russia, Germany, France, and Great Britain had at that time already obtained control of important areas of China, and it appeared that the country would soon be divided into spheres of influence into which other trading nations would have no access. The U.S. was unwilling to compete for territory, but desired access to China for trading purposes. Accordingly, on Sept. 6, 1899, Secretary of State John Milton Hay (q.v.) sent notes to Great Britain, France, Germany, Russia, Italy, and Japan, asking them for formal declarations to the effect that they would not interfere with the rights of other nations in any treaty port, or with the vested interests of other nations in territories under their control. Recognizing that they themselves could lose more than they would gain by restrictive and mutually exclusive arrangements, all of the recipients of the note indicated their willingness to make such declarations. On July 3, 1900, therefore, Secretary Hay sent another note to eleven nations, defining the American position and requesting adherence to principles of "equal and impartial trade with all parts of the Chinese Empire" and preservation of "Chinese territorial and administrative" integrity. All eleven nations answered with formal approval of these principles.

The open-door doctrine was not successful in preventing extension of monopolistic Russian control of Manchurian ports and other facilities in 1902 and again in 1946, or of monopolistic Japanese control in the same area prior to World War I and again in the 1930's. It expressed, however, the real interests of the western European powers and of the U.S., and it served as an indicator of their Chinese policies for almost half a century. France, Great Britain, and Belgium used the policy in territories under their control on the west coast of Africa, and France observed it in Morocco during the time that country was under French control.

OPEN-HEARTH PROCESS. See IRON AND STEEL MANUFACTURE: *Open-Hearth Process.*

OPEN SHOP, in labor relations, business establishment or factory in which workers may be employed without regard to their membership or nonmembership in a trade union. The abolition of the open shop is usually one of the primary demands made by labor unions when they engage in collective bargaining with employers because the freedom of employers to hire and retain nonunion help generally has the effect of making all attempts at unionization ineffective. The alternatives to the open shop are the closed shop and the union shop; *see* CLOSED-SHOP AGREEMENT; UNION-SHOP AGREEMENT.

OPERA, drama in which all or part of the dialogue is sung and in which there are instrumental overtures, interludes, and accompaniments. Other types of musical theater that are closely related to opera include musical comedy and operetta (qq.v.).

16th and 17th Century Origins. Opera began in Italy, in the late 16th and early 17th centuries. Its precedents included many Italian madrigals (*see* MADRIGAL) of the time, in which scenes involving dialogue, but no staged action, were set to music. Opera itself was developed by a group of musicians and scholars who called themselves the Camerata (It., "salon"). The Camerata had two chief goals: to revive the musical style used in ancient Greek drama and to develop an alternative to the highly contrapuntal music of the late Renaissance; *see* MUSIC: *The Renaissance*). Specifically, they wanted composers to pay close attention to the texts on which their music was based, to set these texts in a simple manner, and to make the music reflect, phrase by phrase, the meaning of the text. These goals were probably characteristic of ancient Greek music, although detailed information about Greek music was not available to the Camerata and is still not available today; *see* MUSIC: *Antiquity.*

The Camerata developed a style of vocal music called monody (Gr., "solo song"). It consisted of simple melodic lines with contours and rhythms that followed the spoken inflections and rhythms of the text. The melody was accompanied by a series of chords on a harpsichord or other instrument. Two members of the Camerata, Giulio Caccini (1550?–1618) and Jacopo Peri (1561–1633), realized that monody could be used for soliloquies and dialogues in a staged drama. In 1597 Peri made use of this insight by writing the first opera, *Dafne*. In 1600 an opera called *Euridice* was performed in Florence, incorporating music by both Peri and Caccini.

The first composer of genius to apply himself

OPERA

Detail of the score of the first publicly-produced opera (1600), Euridice. Bettmann Archive

to opera was the Italian Claudio Monteverdi. His operas made use not only of the word-centered monodic style but of songs, duets, choruses, and instrumental sections. The non-monodic pieces had a coherent shape based on purely musical relationships. Monteverdi thus demonstrated that a wide variety of musical procedures and styles could be used in opera to enhance the drama.

Opera spread quickly throughout Italy. The principal Italian opera center during the middle and late 17th century was Venice. The next most important was Rome. In Rome a clear differentiation was made for the first time between the singing styles of aria and recitative (qq.v.). Monody, the style of which was close to recitative, died out. The chief Roman composers were Stefano Landi (about 1590–about 1655) and Luigi Rossi (1597–1653). Venetian audiences liked lavish stage settings and spectacular visual effects, such as storms and descents of the gods from heaven. The leading early composers in Venice were Pier Francesco Cavalli (1602–76) and Marc'Antonio Cesti (1623–69).

Neopolitan Style. A new kind of opera grew in Naples in the late 17th century by Alessandro Scarlatti. Neapolitan audiences liked solo singing, and Neapolitan composers began to further differentiate between various kinds of singing. They developed two kinds of recitative: *recitativo secco* (It., "dry recitative"), which was accompanied only by a harpsichord and a bass instrument, and *recitativo accompagnato* (It., "accompanied recitative"), which was used for tense situations and accompanied by the orchestra. The Neapolitans also introduced arioso, a style that combined arialike melodic contours with the conversational rhythms of a recitative.

By the beginning of the 18th century, the Neapolitan style, with its emphasis on tuneful and entertaining music, had been taken up by composers in most parts of Europe. The only country where this did not happen was France. There, an Italian-born composer, Jean-Baptiste Lully, founded a French school of opera. Lully's patron was Louis XIV (q.v.), King of France, and the pomp and splendor of the French court finds echoes in the massive, slow-moving choral and instrumental episodes of Lully's operas. Ballet was more prominent in Lully's French operas than in Italian operas. His librettos were based on classical French tragedy; see FRENCH LITERATURE: *The Classic Period in French Literature.* The melodic lines followed the distinctive inflections and rhythms of the French language. Another of Lully's contributions was the establishment of the first standardized overture type, known as the French overture; see OVERTURE.

Wide Popularity. In the late 17th and early 18th centuries, a German style of opera existed along with the Italian in Germany. The most important German operatic center was Hamburg, where an opera house was opened in 1678. Reinhard Keiser (1674–1739) composed more than one hundred works there. After Keiser's death Italian composers and singers dominated all the opera houses in Germany.

Italian opera was extremely popular in England. Nevertheless, two operas by English composers were frequently performed there in the years around 1700: *Venus and Adonis* by John Blow (1649–1708) and *Dido and Aeneas* by Henry Purcell. These works were an outgrowth of the English stage genre, the masque (q.v.). They incorporated French and Italian elements, particularly the instrumental writing of Lully and the emotional recitatives and arias of the Italians. The German-born composer George Frederick Handel had his greatest successes in England. He wrote forty operas in the Italian style there during the 1720's and 1730's, after which he gave up opera and turned to the oratorio (q.v.).

By the 18th century opera had moved away from the ideals of the Camerata and adopted a large number of artificialities. Many Italian boys, for instance, were castrated so that their voices would not change but would remain in a high range. The combination of the voice of a boy and the chest development of a man resulted in a piercing quality and agile technique that was extremely popular. Singers of this type, who played the roles of women were called castrati.

The final scene of Wolfgang Amadeus Mozart's famous opera, Cosí fan Tutte, *as performed by the Metropolitan Opera in New York City.* Louis Mélancon

They, along with all other singers, were valued more for their beautiful voices and virtuoso singing techniques than for their acting abilities. Exhibitions of bel canto (It., "beautiful singing") thus became the principal goal of opera, and operas came to consist of little more than a series of spectacular arias. The arias themselves followed a single formal scheme, A-B-A, called da capo.

Preclassic and Classic Periods. Several composers in the mid-18th century tried to change operatic practices. They used forms other than the da capo for arias. They also made greater use of choral and instrumental music. The most important of the composers who introduced these reforms was the German-born Christoph Willibald Gluck. A parallel 18th-century development that helped to reform operatic practices was the growth of comic opera. Comic opera was known under various names: in England it was called ballad opera; in France, opéra comique; in Germany, Singspiel; and in Italy, opera buffa. All these types were lighter in style than the traditional *opera seria* (It., "serious opera"). Some of the dialogue was spoken rather than sung. The plots concerned everyday people and places rather than mythological characters. These traits are clearly seen in the

The death scene of Tosca, *written by Giacomo Puccini in 1900, is in the style of the Italian opera seria, which usually has a tragic mood.* John G. Ross - UPI

Act I of Richard Wagner's Lohengrin, *from a performance by the Metropolitan Opera in New York City.*
Louis Mélancon

work of the first Italian master of comic opera, Giovanni Battista Pergolesi. Because comic operas emphasized naturalness and good acting, they showed composers of serious opera some of the ways by which their own works could be made more realistic. The composer whose operas best embodied the ideals of the reform movement was the Austrian Wolfgang Amadeus Mozart.

Romantic Period. France, Italy, and Germany were the nations leading in opera during the 19th century. During the first half of the century, the most important center was Paris. Parisian audiences liked spectacular stage sets and crowd scenes as well as ballets and choruses. The type of opera that incorporates all these elements is called grand opera, and the composers who established the grand-opera style were Gasparo Spontini (1774–1851) and Giacomo Meyerbeer. In the three French operas of Louis Hector Berlioz the splendor of the grand-opera style is focused on the creation of genuine drama. The comic-opera styles that flourished in Paris were called opéra comique and opéra bouffe. As in the 18th century, comic operas continued to have smaller casts than serious opera, used a simpler musical idiom, and had spoken dialogue instead of recitative. Jacques Offenbach was the most prominent composer of French comic operas. After mid-century the scenic splendor and large choruses and orchestras of grand opera began to merge with the appealing melodies and human characterizations of comic opera. Examples of the merged style were *Faust* by Charles François Gounod, *Carmen* by Georges Bizet, and the operas of Jules Émile Frédéric Massenet.

In Italy during the 19th century, opera was valued above all other musical genres. As in the 18th century, the sheer beauty of fine solo singing continued to be an important consideration. French influences, however, caused Italian composers to write more music for the orchestra and chorus and for ensembles of soloists. The principal Italian composer in the first half of the century was Gioacchino Antonio Rossini. The operas of Gaetano Donizetti and Vincenzo Bellini were also extremely popular. Italian opera in the second half of the century was dominated by Giuseppe Verdi. Verdi's early operas followed the 18th-century tradition, with separate arias, ensembles, and choruses. His last works, however, disguised or eliminated the divisions between numbers so that a continuous flow of music resulted. In this and other ways he was responding to influences from Germany.

Germany, which was the cradle of Romanticism (q.v.), developed a distinctive type of opera, called Romantic opera. It emphasized the unfamiliar and remote. Plots were often based on historical or legendary subjects. Forest scenes, village festivals, and folklike melodies were used. *Fidelio,* the only opera of the German master, Ludwig van Beethoven, contains some of the emphasis on frightening situations that characterizes Romantic opera. The type, however, was more truly established by *Der Freischütz* ("The Free Shooter") by Karl Maria Friedrich Ernst von Weber. During the first half of the 19th century, Weber's example was followed by many minor composers including Heinrich Marschner (1795–1861) and Albert Lortzing (1801–51).

Operatic Equipment. Above: Hair pieces for both male and female characters are created, styled, and stored in the wig room of the Metropolitan Opera Company. Right: Large scenic backdrops or sets are hung to their full length and painted in "alleys" on three different levels at the Metropolitan Opera. UPI

German opera in the second half of the century was dominated by Richard Wagner. The earliest works were in the Romantic tradition. Gradually, however, Wagner began to develop a new type, which he called *Musikdrama* (Ger., "music drama"). In music drama, the earlier German tendency to unify all literary, visual, and musical elements was fully realized. Wagner even went so far as to write his own librettos and to have an opera house of his own design built at Bayreuth (q.v.).

The musical characteristics for which Wagner is known include the use of *Leitmotiven* (Ger., "leading motives"). A leitmotif is a short segment of melody and harmony which represents a person, object, or idea. The use of leitmotifs in the orchestral or vocal parts enabled Wagner to indicate the thoughts and feelings of his characters even when their dialogue concerned other matters. It proved to be a useful dramatic device and was adopted by many opera composers throughout the world.

The Late-19th and 20th Centuries. French and German opera styles were the basis of Russian opera that emerged in the mid-19th cen-

Stairways, lobbies, and balconies are lined up with first nighters as the Metropolitan Opera opens another season at Lincoln Center, New York City. UPI

tury. Pëtr Ilich Tchaikovsky wrote operas in the French grand-opera tradition. National Russian elements, such as folk tunes and peasant scenes, appeared in the operas of Mikhail Ivanovich Glinka, the founder of Russian national opera, Aleksandr Porfirevich Borodin, Modest Petrovich Musorgski, and Nikolai Andreevich Rimski-Korsakov (qq.v.). The 20th-century operas of Sergei Prokofiev and Dimitri Dimitrievich Shostakovich have also incorporated folk elements.

In Czechoslovakia, German and folk influences predominated in the operas of Bedřich Smetana and Leoš Janáček.

Opera in the United States during the 19th century was dominated by German styles; see AMERICAN MUSIC: *The 19th Century*. William Henry Fry (1815–64) wrote the first American Opera, *Leonora*. Among East-coast composers, Charles Wakefield Cadman, in the early 20th century, wrote two operas based on American Indian subjects and melodies.

Italian opera composers after Verdi tended to heighten the emotional element in opera, producing sentimentality and sensationalism. The style that emphasized sensationalism is often called *verismo* (It., "realism"), a term that refers to the presence in the opera plots of everyday people acting under the impact of violent impulses. The operas of Ruggiero Leoncavallo and Pietro Mascagni are typical examples. Sentimentality is one of the chief characteristics of operas by Giacomo Puccini. The many successful stage works of Italian-American Gian-Carlo Menotti are in the Verdi-Puccini tradition.

German opera after Wagner was dominated by Richard Strauss. In many ways Strauss followed Wagner's example, although he never used plots or characters to promote philosophical beliefs, as Wagner did. Many other German composers followed Wagner's example more closely, notably the composer and teacher Engelbert Humperdinck. French opera in the tradition of Bizet and Massenet was maintained by Gustave Charpentier and others.

The earliest distinctively 20th-century artistic innovation to be applied to opera was impressionism (q.v.). It was used by the French composer Claude Debussy in his only opera, *Pelléas et Mélisande*. Among the non-French composers who made use of impressionism was the Italian Ildebrando Pizetti (1880–1968). Atonality and the twelve-tone method (see MUSIC: *The 20th Century*) were used in operas by the Austrian Arnold Schönberg and his pupil Alban Berg. These operas also incorporated a novel singing style called *Sprechstimme* or *Sprechgesang* (Ger., "speech voice" or "speech song"), in which the performer glides from note to note in a manner midway between speech and song. The 20th-century style called neoclassicism is represented by the operas of the Italian Ferruccio Benvenuto Busoni, the Russian-born Igor Fëdorovich Stravinsky, the German Paul Hindemith, the American Virgil Thomson, and others.

Opera. Plate 1. Above: Joy Davidson, American mezzo-soprano, sings the title role of Carmen, by Georges Bizet, in a New York City Opera Company production. Below: In the Triumphal Scene of Giuseppe Verdi's Aïda, the returning hero Radames is welcomed by the king, shown in a production by the Metropolitan Opera Company in New York City.

Opera. Plate 2. Left: Beverly Sills sings the role of Elizabeth I in Roberto Devereaux, an opera by Gaetano Donizetti based on the historic events surrounding the execution of the 2nd earl of Essex, who had fallen from the queen's favor. Below: American bass Norman Treigle sings the title role in Mefistofele, by Arrigo Boito, leading a fiendish chorus in the Witches' Sabbath scene. Both productions were staged by the New York City Opera Company.

Beth Bergman

Contemporary composers in all parts of the world have incorporated folk and popular styles in their operatic works. The Bohemian-American Ernst Krenek wrote several operas in the 1920's and 1930's incorporating jazz elements. The French composer Darius Milhaud has used jazz as well as Brazilian folk tunes and rhythms. The Spanish composers Isaac Albéniz and Manuel de Falla have used Spanish folk music. In the U.S. George Gershwin, Leonard Bernstein, and Douglas Stuart Moore (1893–1969) have used American subjects as well as folk and popular idioms. In Great Britain, Benjamin Britten has not used folk material but Shakespearean and other British subjects written in a manner pleasing to English audiences.

Other composers who have successfully applied 20th-century idioms to the composition and staging of operas include the Italians Luigi Dallapiccola (1904–) and Gian Francesco Malipiero (1882–); the Germans Boris Blacher (1903–), Werner Egk (1901–) and Hans Werner Henze (1926–); the Argentine Alberto Evaristo Ginastera (1916–); the German-American Kurt Weill; and the Czech-American Hugo Weisgall (1912–).

See separate articles on those composers whose birth and death dates are not given.

J.V.

OPERETTA, in music, play with music. In the 18th century, the term meant a short opera (q.v.), but in the 19th and 20th centuries it came to mean a play with music of light character and popular appeal; see also VAUDEVILLE. The French operetta developed in small theaters such as the Bouffes Parisiens, founded by the composer Jacques Offenbach (q.v.). The form, originally a one-act piece, later grew into a three-act or four-act play that approached the Opéra comique; see COMIC OPERA. For this type of work, Offenbach and his countryman Charles Lecocq (1832–1918), composer of La Fille de Madame Angot (1872), used the term opéra bouffe.

The roots of the Viennese operetta lay in the singspiel and the local farce. Franz von Suppé (1819–95) excelled in this form, producing such works as Light Cavalry (1866), The Beautiful Galatea (1865), and Boccaccio (1879). With Johann Strauss the Younger (see under STRAUSS), the operetta of Vienna reached international repute. His younger contemporary Karl Millöcker (1842–99) produced The Beggar Student (1882) to acclaim in Great Britain and the United States. The waltz (q.v.) was an essential element in the operetta of the younger Strauss, and with The Gypsy Baron (1885) he introduced a significant quality of sentimentality and operatic seriousness, which became an important musical facet of the typical Viennese second act finale. Important Viennese composers of operettas were Franz Léhar (q.v.), Robert Stolz (1880–), Oskar Straus (1870–1954), composer of The Chocolate Soldier (New York, 1909), and Emmerich Kalman (1882–1953), composer of Countess Maritza (1924). Stolz was especially known for his work on White Horse Inn (New York City, 1936).

The English operetta developed from the short ballad opera to more extended works, of which Clari, or the Maid of Milan (1823), by Henry Rowley Bishop (q.v.) is the best known; it is now remembered for the tune "Home, Sweet Home". The development reached a climax in the light operas of Sir Arthur Seymour Sullivan and Sir William Schwenck Gilbert (qq.v.), perhaps the most popular of which are HMS Pinafore (1878) and The Mikado (1885). The operetta Bittersweet (1929) by Sir Nöel Coward (q.v.) is a late example of the genre.

The outstanding American operetta composer was the Irish-born Victor Herbert (q.v.), whose forty operettas included The Red Mill (1906) and Naughty Marietta (1910). Among other noted Americans in this field were Henry Louis Reginald de Koven, the Czech-born Rudolf Friml, and the Hungarian-born Sigmund Romberg (qq.v.). American operettas that achieved considerable success include de Koven's Robin Hood (1890), Friml's Rose Marie (1924) and The Vagabond King (1925), and Romberg's The Student Prince (1924) and The Desert Song (1926). After 1930 the operetta form was largely superseded, at least in the U.S., by that of the musical comedy or musical play; see MUSICAL.

J.V.

OPIUM, milky exudation from the unripe capsules of the opium poppy, Papaver somniferum, of the family Papaveraceae. Produced chiefly in China, India, Iran, Turkey, the Soviet Union, and the Balkan countries, opium is imported into Europe and the United States chiefly from the Balkan countries and the Middle East; China absorbs most of the surplus of India and Iran. In its commercial form, opium is a chestnut or reddish-brown globular mass, sticky and rather soft, but hardening from within with age. It has a heavy narcotic odor and in taste is disagreeable and bitter. Chemically, it is a mixture of various organic acids, chiefly meconic acid, with alkaloids, mainly codeine, morphine (qq.v.), and narcotine. These alkaloids are valuable in medicine for their sedative and narcotic properties, as is the gum itself, which is also smoked as an intoxicant. Opium also contains fats, resins, sugars, albumin, and water.

OPIUM WAR

Most of the opium produced is used illicitly as an intoxicant. It produces pleasant dreams, profound sleep, and, in sufficiently large doses, can cause death. Antidotes for opium are strong tea and other stimulants, and sharp electrical shocks. The legitimate world demand for opium amounts to about 600 tons a year, but about six times that amount is distributed through illegal trade. Morphine and codeine are derived from opium.

The first steps toward worldwide control of opium traffic were taken at the Hague International Opium Convention in 1912. Further agreements were reached under the auspices of the League of Nations, and beginning in 1946 all earlier agreements came under the jurisdiction of the United Nations Commission on Narcotic Drugs. A protocol agreement was signed in 1953 by fifty nations, but several countries in the Middle East and Far East have continued the production of opium.

See DRUGS, ADDICTION TO; NARCOTICS.

OPIUM WAR, war between Great Britain and China, 1839–42, resulting from the attempt of the Chinese government to prevent the importation of opium from India. By the Treaty of Nanking, which ended the war, China opened certain ports to British trade and ceded Hong Kong to Great Britain.

OPOLE (Ger. *Oppeln*), city and port in Poland, and capital of Opole Province, on the Odra R., 50 miles S.E. of Wrocław. A rail junction and grain-trade center, it lies in a quartz-quarrying region and manufactures machinery, textiles, cement, lime, lumber and wood products, tile, and flour. Capital of a duchy from 1163 to 1532, Opole passed to the Hapsburgs and, in 1742, to Prussia. As a part of Germany, the city was capital of the Prussian province of Upper Silesia from 1919 to 1945. Pop. (1964 est.) 68,800.

OPORTO, city in Portugal, and capital of Douro Litoral Province, on the Douro R., which reaches the Atlantic Ocean 3 mi. to the W. and, about 170 miles N.E. of Lisbon. Oporto is the second-largest city in Portugal. Because of the sandbars that obstruct the mouth of the Douro R., an Atlantic harbor has been constructed at Leixões, 4 mi. farther N. The chief industries are the manufacture of leather goods, clothing, and woolen, cotton, and silk fabrics. Oporto is the principal place of export for port wine. The city is the site of a Gothic cathedral; an 18th-century tower, the Torre dos Clérigos ("Tower of the Clergy"); and the Dom Luis Bridge. The University of Oporto, founded in 1911, is also in the city. Pop. (1966) 321,900.

OPOSSUM, common name of the marsupial animals in the family Didelphidae, which is made up of twelve genera and about sixty-five species. Opossums, found only in the Western Hemisphere, range in size from 6 to 30 in., including the long, naked, prehensile tail, which is from 2 to 10 in. long. The common Virginia opossum, *Didelphis marsupialis,* is the largest of the opossums, measuring 30 in., of which one third is the tail. The front feet have five toes with claws; on the hind feet the outer four toes bear claws and the inmost is opposable, like a thumb, and nailless. The Virginia opossum is covered with long, sleek white hair and an undercoating of soft, woolly fur. It has a pointed, slender face and large, broad, naked ears. An opossum has fifty teeth. Most species are omnivorous, usually preferring a diet of insects and already dead animals. They are nocturnal, sleeping in a burrow during the day and hunting food at night; most are arboreal. The Yapok, *Chironectes,* of South America is aquatic, having webbed hind feet for swimming. One of the best-known characteristics of opossums, their habit of feigning death when they are surprised, has given rise to the expression "playing possum"

Most species have the abdominal pouch char-

Virginia opossum, Didelphis marsupialis. *Female opossum and young.*
Gordon S. Smith – National Audubon Society

acteristic of marsupials (q.v.); however, in some South American species this pouch is rudimentary or absent. A female opossum may have as many as nineteen nipples within the pouch, but twelve to fourteen is the usual number. Of the four to twenty-four young that may be born in a litter only eight or nine usually survive. The gestation period is about thirteen days, and the newborn opossums, less than ½ in. long and weighing about ⅓ gram, are quite undeveloped. They must spend about two months in the mother's pouch attached to the nipples before they are able to move about.

The Virginia opossum, found throughout eastern United States and occasionally in the western States is edible and considered a delicacy in the South; it is hunted with the aid of dogs and, when treed, is captured with a forked stick. Opossum fur formerly had commercial value but is of little use now. The name opossum is frequently shortened to possum.

OPPENHEIMER, J. Robert (1904–67), American physicist, born in New York City, and educated at Harvard University and the universities

Dr. J. Robert Oppenheimer, in 1948, as chairman of the General Advisory Committee of the Atomic Energy Commission. UPI

of Cambridge and Göttingen. After serving as a National Research fellow at the California Institute of Technology (1927–28) and with the International Education Board (1928–29), he was assistant professor of physics (1929–31), associate professor (1931–36), and full professor (1936–47) at the University of California and at the California Institute. During a leave of absence (1943–45) he served as director of the atomic-bomb project at Los Alamos. N.Mex. In 1947 he became director of the Institute for Advanced Study in Princeton, N.J., serving until the year before his death. He was chairman of the General Advisory Committee of the Atomic Energy Commission (q.v.) from 1947 to 1952. In 1954 he was suspended as an A.E.C. consultant on charges that association with Communists had made him a poor security risk. Subsequently efforts were made to clear him of this accusation, and in 1963 the A.E.C. conferred on him its highest honor, the Enrico Fermi Award. Oppenheimer is also noted for his contributions relating to the quantum theory, cosmic rays, and theory of relativity. His writings include *Science and the Common Understanding* (1954) and the posthumously published *Lectures on Electrodynamics* (1970).

OPPER, Frederick Burr (1857–1937), American illustrator and cartoonist, born in Madison, Ohio. He first contributed to humerous magazines and later was on the staff of the New York *Journal*. He was associated with the weekly *Puck* from 1880 to 1899. Noted for his sharp, witty drawings, he illustrated books by the American humorist Edgar Wilson Nye (1850–96) and by the American writer Samuel Langhorne Clemens and the *Mr. Dooley* series by the American humorist Finley Peter Dunne (qq.v.). Opper created the comic-strip characters Happy Hooligan and Alphonse and Gaston.

OPPIAN, name of two Greek didactic poets of antiquity. **1.** A poet, born in Cilicia, who flourished in the 2nd century. He composed a work in five books on fishing, entitled *Halieutica*, which is extant. The poem, written in an ornate and artificial style, was dedicated to the Roman emperor Marcus Aurelius and his son the Roman emperor Lucius Commodus (qq.v.). **2.** The author of a poem in four books on hunting, entitled *Cynegetica* and probably composed early in the 3rd century. This poet speaks of his home as Apamea, in Syria. The metrical structure of the poem, which is extant, is inferior to that of *Halieutica*.

OPTICS, branch of physical science dealing with the propagation and behavior of light (q.v.). In a general sense, light is that part of the electromagnetic spectrum that extends from the X-ray region to the microwave range and includes the radiant energy that produces the sensation of vision; *see* ELECTROMAGNETIC RADIATIONS; SPECTRUM; X RAY. The study of optics is divided into geometrical optics and physical optics, and these branches are discussed below.

OPTICS

NATURE OF LIGHT

Radiant energy (q.v.) has a dual nature and obeys laws that may be explained in terms of a stream of particles or packets of energy called photons, or in terms of a train of transverse waves; see PHOTON; RADIATION; WAVE MOTION. The concept of photons is used to explain the interactions of light and matter that result in a change in the form of energy, as in the case of the photoelectric cell or fluorescence and phosphorescence (qq.v.). The concept of transverse waves is usually used to explain the propagation of light through various substances and some of the phenomena of image formation. Geometrically, a simple transverse wave may be described by points that oscillate in the same plane back and forth across an axis perpendicular to the direction of oscillation such that at any instant of time the envelope of these points is, for example, a sine function that intersects the axis; see GEOMETRY; TRIGONOMETRY. The wave front progresses and the radiant energy travels along this axis. The oscillating point may be considered to describe the vibration of the electric component or vector (q.v.) of the light wave. The magnetic component vibrates in a direction perpendicular to that of the electric vector and to the axis. The magnetic component is ineffective and may be ignored in the study of visible light. The number of complete oscillations or vibrations (see VIBRATION) per second of a point on the light wave is known as the frequency (q.v.). The wavelength is the linear distance parallel to the axis between two points in the same phase or occupying similar positions on the wave, for example, the distance from maximum to maximum in the case of a sine function representation. Differences in wavelength manifest themselves as differences in color (q.v.) in the visible spectrum. The visible range extends from about 400 nanometers (violet) to 700 nanometers (red), a nanometer being equal to a billionth of a meter. White light is a mixture of the visible wavelengths. There are no sharp boundaries between wavelength regions, but 10 nanometers may be taken as the low wavelength limit for ultraviolet radiation. Infrared radiation, which includes heat energy, includes the wavelengths from about 700 nanometers to approximately 1 mm; see INFRARED.

Propagation. The velocity of an electromagnetic wave is the product of the frequency and the wavelength. In a vacuum this velocity is the same for all wavelengths. The velocity of light in material substances is, with few exceptions, less than in a vacuum. Also, in material substances this velocity is different for different wavelengths, as a result of dispersion. The ratio of the velocity of light in vacuum to the velocity of a particular wavelength of light in a substance is known as the index of refraction of that substance for the given wavelength. The index of refraction of a vacuum is equal to 1 and that of air is 1.00029, but for most applications it is also taken to be 1. If the medium through which the light is traveling is absorbing, such as a thin layer of metal, the index of refraction of that medium is written as a complex number or the sum of a real number and a so-called imaginary number. Mathematical treatment of these complex numbers yields physically meaningful results. The imaginary part of the complex index of refraction leads to the factor that describes the attenuation of the light due to absorption. The real number, sometimes called the propagation constant, results in a factor that describes the state of oscillation or phase of the wave and becomes identical to the index of refraction when there is no absorption; see ABSORPTION; PHASE RULE. In a medium with normal dispersion, the propagation constant increases as the wavelength decreases. The opposite dependence is called anomalous dispersion. If a material has a preferential absorption for a small band of wavelengths, then the propagation constant can vary rapidly from the normal dependence on wavelength to the anomalous behavior from one side of the wavelength band to the other.

The laws of reflection and refraction of light are usually derived using the wave theory of light introduced by the Dutch mathematician, astronomer, and physical scientist Christian Huygens (q.v.). Huygens' principle states that every point on an initial wave front may be considered as the source of small, secondary spherical wavelets that spread out in all directions from their centers with the same velocity, frequency, and wavelength as the parent wave front. When the wavelets encounter another medium or object, each point on the boundary becomes a source of two new sets of waves. The reflected set travels back into the first medium and the refracted set enters the second medium. It is sometimes simpler and sufficient to represent the propagation of light by rays rather than by waves. The ray is the flow line, or direction of travel, of radiant energy, and the assumption is made that light does not bend around corners. Geometrical optics ignores the wave theory of light and traces rays through an optical system by applying the laws of reflection and refraction.

GEOMETRICAL OPTICS

This is an area of optical science which deals

OPTICS

with the application of laws of reflection and refraction of light in the design of lenses (see *Lenses,* below) and other optical components of instruments. If a light ray that is traveling through one homogeneous medium is incident on the surface of a second homogeneous medium, part of the light is reflected and part may enter the second medium as the refracted ray and may or may not undergo absorption in the second medium.

Reflection and Refraction. The amount of light reflected depends upon the ratio of the refractive indexes for the two media. The plane of incidence contains the incident ray and the normal (line perpendicular) to the surface at the point of incidence (see fig. 1). The angle of inci-

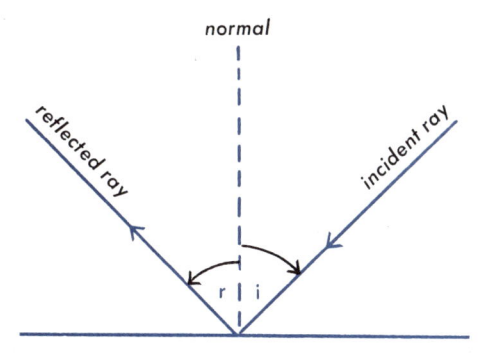

r = angle of reflection   i = angle of incidence

Fig. 1. *Fundamental laws of reflection*

dence (reflection or refraction) is the angle between the incident (reflected or refracted) ray and this normal. The laws of reflection state that the angle of incidence is equal to the angle of reflection and that the incident ray, the reflected ray, and the normal to the surface at the point of incidence all lie in the same plane. If the surface of the second medium is smooth or polished it may act as a mirror (q.v.) and produce a reflected image. If the mirror is flat or plane, the image of the object appears to lie behind the mirror at a distance equal to the distance between the object and the surface of the mirror. The light source in fig. 2 is the object A, and a point on A sends out rays in all directions. The two rays that strike the mirror at B and C, for example, are reflected as the rays BD and CE. To an observer in front of the mirror, these rays appear to come from the point F behind the mirror. It follows from the laws of reflection that CF and BF form the same angle with the surface of the mirror as do AC and AB, respectively. If the surface of the second medium is rough, then normals to various points of the surface lie

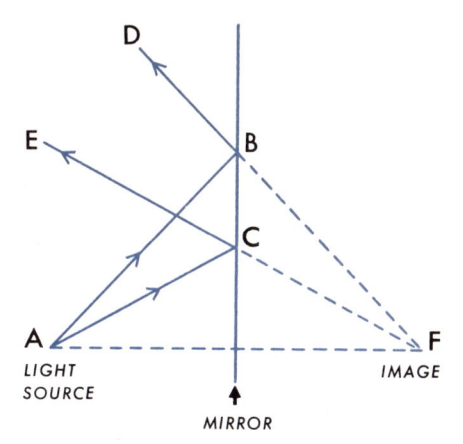

Fig. 2. *Reflection from a plane mirror*

in random directions. In that case, rays that may lie in the same plane when they emerge from a point source nevertheless lie in random planes of incidence, and therefore of reflection, and are scattered and cannot form an image.

SNELL'S LAW. This important law, named after the Dutch mathematician Willebrod von Roijen Snell (1591–1626), states that the product of the refractive index and the sine of the angle of incidence of a ray in one medium is equal to the product of the refractive index and the sine of the angle of refraction in a successive medium. Also, the incident ray, the refracted ray, and the normal to the boundary at the point of incidence all lie in the same plane. Generally, the refractive index of a denser transparent substance is higher than that of a less dense material, that is, the velocity of light is lower in the denser substance. If a ray is incident obliquely, then a ray entering a medium with higher refractive index is bent toward the normal, and a ray entering a medium of lower refractive index is deviated away from the normal. Rays incident along the normal are reflected and refracted along the normal. In making calculations, the optical path, which is defined as the product of the distance a ray travels in a given medium and the refractive index of that medium, is the important consideration. To an observer in a less dense medium such as air, an object in a denser medium appears to lie closer to the boundary than is the actual case. A common example, that of an object lying under water and the observer above water, is shown in fig. 3. Oblique rays are chosen only for ease of illustration. The ray DB from the object at D is bent away from the normal to A. The object, therefore, appears to lie at C where the line ABC intersects a line normal to the surface of the water and passing through D.

171

OPTICS

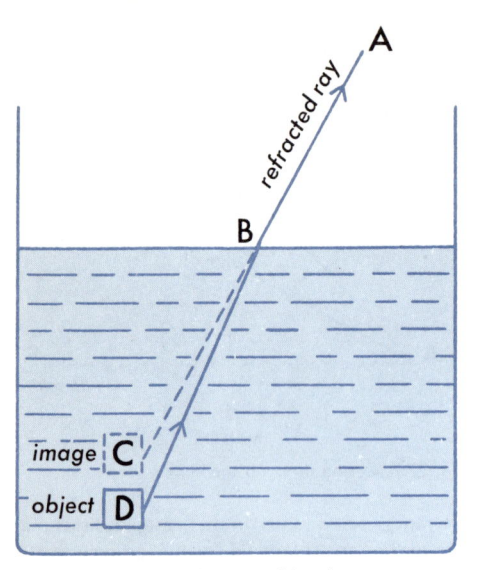

Fig. 3. *As a result of refraction, object in water appears closer to the water's surface.*

The path of light passing through several media with parallel boundaries is shown in fig. 4. The refractive index of water is lower than that of glass. Since the refractive index of the first and last medium is the same, the ray emerges parallel to the incident ray AB, but it is displaced.

PRISM. If light passes through a prism, a transparent object with flat, polished surfaces at angles to each other, the exit ray is no longer parallel to the incident ray. Because the refractive index of a substance varies for the different wavelengths, a prism can spread out the various wavelengths of light contained in an incident beam and form a spectrum. In fig. 5, the angle CBD between the path of the incident ray and the path of the emergent ray is the angle of deviation. If the angle the incident ray makes with the normal is equal to the angle made by the emergent ray, the deviation is at a minimum. A measurement of the angle of minimum deviation and the angle between the faces of the prism allows the refractive index of the prism to be calculated.

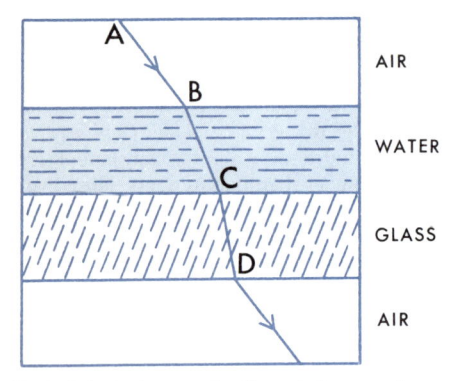

Fig. 4. *Refracted ray passing through three media*

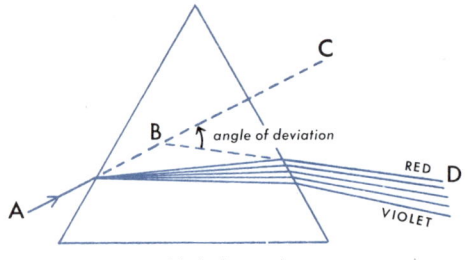

Fig. 5. *Refraction of light by a prism*

CRITICAL ANGLE. A ray is bent away from the normal when it enters a less dense medium, and the deviation from the normal increases as the angle of incidence increases, there is an angle of incidence, known as the critical angle, such that the refracted ray makes an angle of 90° with the normal to the surface, and travels along the boundary between the two media. If the angle of incidence is increased beyond the critical angle, the light rays will be totally reflected back into the incident medium. Total reflection cannot occur if light is traveling from a less dense to a denser medium. The three drawings in fig. 6 show ordinary refraction, refraction at the critical angle, and total reflection. In recent years, a new, practical application of total reflection has been found in the use of fiber optics. If light enters a solid glass or plastic tube obliquely, the light can be totally reflected at the boundary of the tube and, after a number of successive total reflections, emerge from the other end of the tube. Glass fibers can be drawn to a very small diameter, coated with a material of lower refractive index, and then assembled into flexible bundles or fused into plates of fibers and used to transmit images. The flexible bundles, which can be used to provide illumination as well as to transmit images, are a valuable addition to medical examination and research since they can be inserted into various openings.

Spherical and Aspherical Surfaces. Traditionally, most of the terminology of geometrical optics was developed with reference to spherical reflecting and refracting surfaces. Aspherical surfaces, however, are sometimes used. The optic axis is a reference line that is an axis of symmetry. If the optical component is spherical, the optic axis passes through the center of a lens or mirror and through the center of curvature.

OPTICS

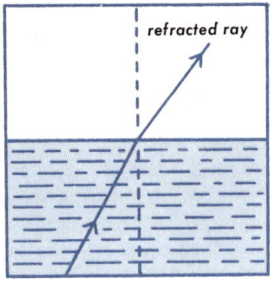

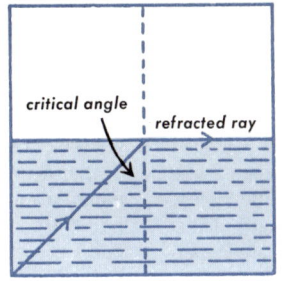

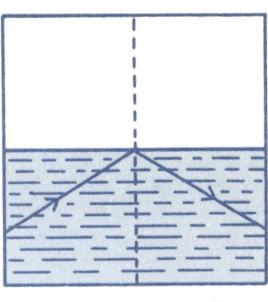

ORDINARY REFRACTION | REFRACTION AT CRITICAL ANGLE | TOTAL REFLECTION

Fig. 6. *Critical angle of refraction*

Light rays from a very distant source are considered to travel parallel to one another. If rays parallel to the optic axis are incident on a spherical surface, they are reflected or refracted so that they intersect or appear to intersect at a point on the optic axis. The distance between this point and the vertex of a mirror or a thin lens is the focal length. If a lens is thick, calculations are referred to planes called principal planes rather than to the surface of the lens. A lens may have two focal lengths, depending upon which surface (if the surfaces are not alike) the light strikes first. If an object is at the focal point, the rays emerging from it are made parallel to the optic axis after reflection or refraction. If rays from an object are converged by a lens or mirror so that they actually intersect in front of a mirror or behind a lens, the image is real and inverted, or upside down. If the rays diverge after reflection or refraction so that the light only appears to converge, the image is virtual and erect. The ratio of the height of the image to the height of the object is the lateral magnification.

If it is understood that distances measured from the surface of a lens or mirror in the direction in which light is traveling are positive and distances measured in the opposite direction negative, then if u is the object distance, v the image distance and f is the focal length of a mirror or of a thin lens, then the equation

$$\frac{1}{v} + \frac{1}{u} = \frac{1}{f}$$

applies to spherical mirrors and the equation

$$\frac{1}{v} - \frac{1}{u} = \frac{1}{f}$$

applies to spherical lenses. If a simple lens has surfaces with radii r_1 and r_2 and the ratio of its refractive index to that of the medium surrounding it is n, then

$$\frac{1}{f} = (n-1)\left(\frac{1}{r_1} - \frac{1}{r_2}\right).$$

The focal length of a spherical mirror is equal to half the radius of curvature. As is shown in fig. 7, rays parallel to the optic axis incident on a concave mirror with its center of curvature at C are reflected so that they intersect at B, halfway between A and C. If the object distance is greater than the distance AC, the image is real, inverted, and diminished. If the object lies be-

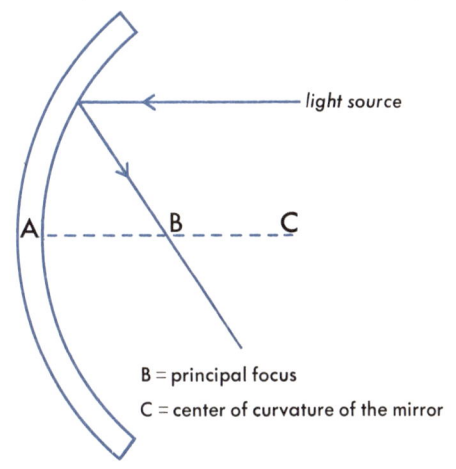

B = principal focus
C = center of curvature of the mirror

Fig. 7. *Reflection from a concave spherical mirror*

tween the center of curvature and the focal point, the image is real, inverted, and enlarged. If the object is located between the surface of the mirror and the focus, the image is virtual, upright, and enlarged. Convex mirrors form only virtual, erect, and diminished images.

Lenses. Lenses made with surfaces of small radii have the shorter focal lengths. A lens with two convex surfaces will always refract rays parallel to the optic axis so that they converge to a focus on the side of the lens opposite to the object. A concave lens surface will deviate incident rays parallel to the axis away from the axis so that even if the second surface of the lens is convex, the rays diverge and only appear to come to a focus on the same side of the lens as

OPTICS

the object. Concave lenses form only virtual, erect, and diminished images. If the object distance is greater than the focal length, a converging lens forms a real and inverted image. If the object is sufficiently far away, the image is smaller than the object. If the object is placed sufficiently close to the focus, this real image becomes larger than the object. If the object distance is smaller than the focal length of this lens, the image is virtual, erect, and larger than the object. The observer is then using the lens as a magnifier or simple microscope (q.v.). The angle subtended at the eye by this virtual enlarged image is greater than would be the angle subtended by the object if it were at the normal viewing distance. The ratio of these two angles is the magnifying power of the lens. A lens with a shorter focal length would cause the angle subtended by the virtual image to increase and thus cause the magnifying power to increase. The magnifying power of an instrument is a measure of its ability to bring the object apparently closer to the eye. This is distinct from the lateral magnification of a camera (see PHOTOGRAPHY: *Cameras*) or telescope (q.v.), for example, where the ratio of the actual dimensions of a real image to those of the object increases as the focal length increases. *See also* LENS.

The amount of light a lens can admit increases with its diameter. Because the area occupied by an image is proportional to the square of the focal length of the lens, the light intensity over the image area is directly proportional to the diameter of the lens and inversely proportional to the square of the focal length. The image produced by a lens of a 1-in. diameter and 8-in. focal length would be one fourth as bright as the image formed by a lens of 1-in. diameter and 4-in. focal length. The ratio of the focal length to the effective diameter of a lens is its focal ratio or the so-called f-number. The reciprocal of this ratio is called the relative aperture. Lenses having the same relative aperture have the same light-gathering power, regardless of the actual diameters and focal lengths.

Aberration. Geometrical optics predicts that rays of light emanating from a point are imaged by spherical optical elements as a small blur. The outer parts of a spherical surface have a different focal length than does the central area, and this defect would cause a point to be imaged as a small circle (q.v.). The difference in focal length for the various parts of the spherical section is called spherical aberration. If, instead of being a portion of a sphere, a concave mirror is a section of a paraboloid (*see* PARABOLA) of revolution, parallel rays incident on all areas of the surface are reflected to a point without spherical aberration. Combinations of convex and concave lenses can be used to help correct for spherical aberration, but this defect cannot be eliminated from a single spherical lens for a real object and image.

The manifestation of differences in lateral magnification for rays coming from an object point not on the optic axis is called coma. If coma is present, light from a point is spread out into a family of circles that fit into a cone, and in a plane perpendicular to the optic axis, the image pattern is comet-shaped. Coma may be eliminated for a single object-image point pair, but not for all such points, by a suitable choice of surfaces. Corresponding or conjugate object and image points, free from both spherical aberration and coma, are known as aplanatic points, and a lens having such a pair of points is called an aplanatic lens. Astigmatism is the defect which spreads the light coming from an off-axis object point along the direction of the optic axis. If the object is a vertical line, the cross-section of the refracted beam is an ellipse (q.v.) which collapses first into a horizontal line, spreads out again, and later becomes a vertical line. If a flat object has any extent, the surface of best focus is curved, or curvature of field results. Distortion arises from a variation of magnification with axial distance, and is not caused by a lack of sharpness in the image. Because the index of refraction varies with wavelength, the focal length of a lens also varies, and causes longitudinal or axial chromatic aberration. Magnification also depends upon wavelength, and formation of different image sizes by various wavelengths is known as lateral chromatic aberration. Converging and diverging lenses grouped together, and combinations of glasses with different dispersions, help to minimize chromatic aberration. Mirrors are free of this defect. In general, achromatic lens combinations are corrected for chromatic aberration for two or three colors.

PHYSICAL OPTICS

This branch of optical science consists of the study of polarization of light, interference and diffraction, and the spectral emission, composition, and absorption of light.

Polarization of Light. The atoms in an ordinary light source emit pulses of radiation of extremely short duration. Each pulse from a single atom is a nearly monochromatic (consisting of a single wavelength) wave train. The electric vector corresponding to the wave does not rotate about the axis across which it oscillates as the wave travels through space, but keeps the same angle, or azimuth, with respect to the direction of travel. The initial azimuth can have any value. When a large number of atoms are emitting light, these azimuths are randomly distributed, the properties of the light beam are the same in all directions, and the light is said to be unpolarized. If the electric vectors for each wave all have the same azimuth angle (or all the transverse waves lie in the same plane), the light is plane, or linearly, polarized. The equations that describe the behavior of electromagnetic waves discuss two sets of waves, one with the electric vector vibrating perpendicular to the plane of incidence and the other with the electric vector vibrating parallel to the plane of incidence, and all light can be considered as having a component of its electric vector vibrating in each of these planes. A certain synchronism or phase difference may persist in time between the two vibrations of the component, or the phase differences may be random. If light is linearly polarized, for example, this phase difference becomes zero or 180°. If the phase relationship is random, but more of one component is present, the light is partially polarized. When light is scattered by dust particles, for instance, the light scattered 90° to the original path of the beam is plane polarized, and this is the reason skylight from the zenith is markedly polarized. At angles other than zero or 90° of incidence, the reflectance at the boundary between two media is not the same for these two components of vibrations. Less of the component that vibrates parallel to the plane of incidence is reflected. If light is incident on a nonabsorbing medium at the so-called Brewster's angle, named after the British physicist David Brewster (1781–1868), the reflectance of the component vibrating parallel to the plane of incidence is zero. At this angle of incidence, the reflected ray would be perpendicular to the refracted ray, and the tangent of this angle of incidence is equal to the refractive index of the second medium if the first medium is air.

Certain substances are anisotropic, or display properties with different values when measured along axes in different directions, and the velocity of light in them depends on the direction in which the light is traveling. Some crystals are birefringent, or exhibit double refraction; *see* CRYSTAL. Unless light is traveling parallel to an axis of symmetry with respect to the structure of the crystals (the optic axis of the crystal), it is separated into two parts that travel with different velocities. A uniaxial crystal has one axis. The component with the electric vector vibrating in a plane containing the optic axis is the ordinary ray; its velocity is the same in all directions through the crystal, and Snell's law of refraction holds. The component vibrating perpendicular to the plane of the optic axis forms the extraordinary ray, and the velocity of this ray depends on the direction through the crystal. If the ordinary ray travels faster than the extraordinary ray, the birefringence is positive; otherwise it is negative.

If a crystal is biaxial, there is no component for which the velocity is independent of the direction of travel. Birefringent materials can be cut and shaped to introduce specific phase differences between two sets of polarized waves, to separate them, or to analyze the state of polarization of any incident light. A polarizer transmits only one component of vibration either by reflecting away the other by means of properly cut prism combinations or by absorbing the second component. A material that preferentially absorbs one component of vibration exhibits dichroism, and Polaroid is an example of this. Polaroid consists of many small dichroic crystals embedded in plastic and identically oriented. If light is unpolarized, Polaroid absorbs approximately half of it. Because light reflected from a large flat surface such as water or a wet road is partially polarized, properly oriented Polaroid can absorb more than half of this reflected glare light. This explains the effectiveness of Polaroid sunglasses. The so-called analyzer may be physically the same as a polarizer. If a polarizer and analyzer are crossed, the analyzer is oriented to allow transmission of vibrations lying in a plane perpendicular to those transmitted by the polarizer, and blocks or extinguishes the light passed by the polarizer. Substances that are optically active rotate the plane of linearly polarized light. Either a crystal or a solution of sugar, for example, may be optically active. If a solution of sugar is placed between a crossed polarizer and analyzer, the light is able to pass through. The amount of rotation of the analyzer required to restore extinction of the light permits the determination of the concentration of the solution. An instrument based on this principle is the polarimeter.

Some substances, such as glass and plastic, that are not normally doubly refracting may become so if subjected to stress. If such stressed materials are placed between a polarizer and analyzer, the bright and dark areas that are seen give information about the strains. The technology of photoelasticity is based upon double refraction produced by stresses.

Birefringence can also be introduced in otherwise homogeneous materials by magnetic and

OPTICS

electric fields. The Faraday effect, named after the British physicist and chemist Michael Faraday (q.v.), refers to the fact that a strong magnetic field parallel to the direction of propagation of the light can induce optical activity. An electric field across a liquid may cause it to become doubly refracting, the phenomenon being known as the Kerr effect, after the British physicist John Kerr (1824–1907). If an appropriate material is placed between a crossed polarizer and analyzer, light is transmitted depending upon whether the electric field is on or off. This can act as a very rapid light switch or modulator.

Interference and Diffraction. When two light beams cross, they may interfere or interact in such a way that the resultant intensity pattern is affected; see INTERFERENCE. The degree of coherence, or waves in phase and of one wavelength, is related to the ability of waves to produce a steady state that depends upon the phase relationships of successive wave fronts remaining constant with time. If the phase relationship changes rapidly and randomly, two beams are incoherent. If two wave trains are coherent and if the maximum of one wave coincides with the maximum of another, the two waves combine to produce a greater intensity in that place than if the two beams were present but not coherent. If coherence exists and the maximum of one wave coincides with the minimum of another wave, the two waves will cancel each other in part or completely, thus decreasing the intensity. A dark and bright pattern consisting of interference fringes may be formed. To produce a steady interference pattern the two wave trains must be polarized in the same plane. Atoms in an ordinary light source radiate independently, so a large light source usually emits incoherent radiation. To obtain coherent light from such a source, a small portion of the light is selected by means of a pinhole or slit. If this portion is then again split by double slits, double mirrors, or double prisms, and the two parts made to travel definite but different paths before they are combined again, an interference pattern results. Devices which do this are called interferometers, and find use in measuring such things as diameters of stars, distances or thicknesses, and deviations of an optical surface from the required shape in terms of wavelengths of light; see INTERFEROMETER. Such an interference pattern was first demonstrated by the British physicist Thomas Young (q.v.) in the experiment illustrated in fig. 8. Light that had passed through one pinhole illuminated an opaque surface that contained two pinholes. The light that passed through the two pinholes formed a pattern of alternately bright and dark circular fringes on a screen. Wavelets are drawn in the illustration to show that at points such as A, C, and E (intersection of solid line with solid line) the waves from the two pinholes arrive in phase, and combine

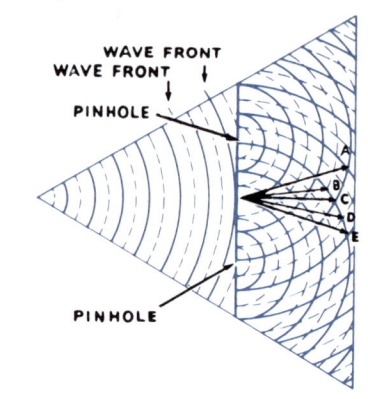

Fig. 8. *Interference of light caused by passage through two pinholes.*

to increase the intensity. At other points such as B and D (intersection of solid line with dashed line), the waves are 180° out of phase, and cancel each other.

Light reflected at each surface of a very thin transparent film on a smooth surface can interfere. The rainbow colors of a film of oil on water are a result of interference, and they demonstrate the importance of the ratio of film thickness to wavelength. A single film or several films of different material can be used to increase or decrease the reflectance of a surface. Dichroic beam splitters are stacks of films of more than one material, controlled in thickness so that one band of wavelengths is reflected and another band of wavelengths is transmitted. An interference filter made of such films transmits a very narrow band of wavelengths and reflects the remainder. The shape of the surface of an optical element can be checked by touching it to a master lens, or flat, and observing the fringe pattern formed because of the thin layer of air remaining between the two surfaces.

Light incident on the edge of an obstacle is bent or diffracted, and the obstacle does not form a sharp geometric shadow. The points on the edge of the obstacle act as a source of coherent waves, and interference fringes, called a diffraction pattern, are formed. The shape of the edge of the obstacle is not exactly reproduced because part of the wave front is cut off. Because light passes through a finite aperture when it goes through a lens, there is a diffraction pattern around the image of an object. If

OPTICS

the object is very small, the diffraction pattern appears as a series of concentric bright and dark rings around a central disk called the Airy disk, after the British astronomer George Biddell Airy (1801–92). This is true for an aberration-free lens. If two particles are so close together that the two diffraction patterns overlap and the bright rings of one pattern fall on the dark rings of the second pattern, the two particles appear to merge, or cannot be resolved. A theory of the German physicist and optician Ernst Karl Abbe (1840–1905) first explained image formation by a microscope on the basis of the interference of diffraction patterns of various points on the object.

Fourier analysis is a mathematical treatment, named after the French mathematician Jean Baptiste Fourier (q.v.), that assigns a frequency spectrum to an object, and permits the calculation of the diffraction pattern of an object at some plane intermediate between the object plane and image plane, allowing the calculation of the appearance of the image. Such an analysis is possible because a complex wave can be considered as consisting of a combination of simple waves. Optical systems are sometimes evaluated by choosing an object of known Fourier components and then evaluating the Fourier components present in the image. Such procedures measure the optical transfer function. Extrapolations of these techniques sometimes allow extraction of information from poor images. Statistical theories have also been included in analyses of the recording of images.

A diffraction grating consists of several thousand slits equal in width and equally spaced (formed by ruling lines on glass or metal with a fine diamond point). Each slit gives rise to a diffraction pattern, and the many diffraction patterns interfere. If white light is incident, a continuous spectrum is formed. Prisms and gratings are used in instruments such as monochromators, spectrographs, or spectrophotometers to provide nearly monochromatic light or to analyze the wavelengths present in the incident light; see SPECTROGRAPH, MASS; SPECTROHELIOGRAPH. See also DIFFRACTION GRATING.

Stimulated Emission. The atoms in common light sources, such as the incandescent lamp, fluorescent lamp, and neon lamp (q.v.) produce light by spontaneous emission, and the radiation is incoherent. If a sufficient number of atoms have absorbed energy so that they are excited into appropriate states of higher energy, stimulated emission can occur. Light of a certain wavelength can produce additional light that has the same phase and direction as the original wavelength, and it will be coherent. Stimulated emission amplifies the amount of radiation having a given wavelength, and this radiation has a very narrow beam spread and a long coherence path. The material that is excited may be a gas or solid, but it must be contained or shaped to form an interferometer in which the wavelength being amplified is reflected back and forth many times. A small fraction is transmitted by one of the mirrors of the interferometers. Maser is an acronym for microwave amplification by stimulated emission of radiation; see ELECTRONICS. If optical frequencies are being amplified by stimulated emission, the term laser (q.v.) is commonly used. Energizing a very large number of atoms to be in the appropriate upper state is called pumping. Pumping may be optical or electrical. Since lasers can be made to emit pulses of very high energy that have a very narrow beam spread, laser light sent to the moon and reflected back to the earth can be detected. The intense narrow beam of the laser has found practical application in surgery, and in the cutting of metals.

The Hungarian-born British physicist and electrical engineer Dennis Gabor first noted that if the diffraction pattern of an object could be recorded and the phase information also retained, the image of the object could be reconstructed by coherent illumination of the recorded diffraction pattern. Illumination of the diffraction pattern with a wavelength longer than that used to produce the diffraction pattern would result in magnification. Because the absolute phase of light wave cannot be directly detected physically, it was necessary to provide a reference beam coherent with the beam illuminating the object to interfere with the diffraction pattern and provide phase information. Before the development of the laser, the Gabor scheme was limited by the lack of sufficiently intense coherent light sources.

A hologram is a photographic record of the interference between a reference beam and the diffraction pattern of the object. Light from a single laser is separated into two beams. The reference beam illuminates the photographic plate, perhaps via a lens and mirror, and the second beam illuminates the object, which forms a diffraction pattern on the photographic plate. If the processed hologram is illuminated by coherent light, not necessarily of the same wavelength that was used to make the hologram, the image of the object is reconstructed, and a three dimensional image of the object can be obtained. Holograms of a theoretical object can be produced by computing machines, and the

OPTIMISM

image of these reconstructed; see PHOTOGRAPHY: *20th Century: Holography*.

Intense, coherent laser beams permit the study of new optical effects that are produced by the interaction of certain substances with electric fields, and that depend on the square or third power of the field strength. This is called nonlinear optics, and the interactions being studied affect the refractive index of the substances. The Kerr effect, mentioned earlier, belongs to this group of phenomena. Harmonic generation of light has been observed; see HARMONICS. Infrared laser light of wavelength 1.06 microns, for example, can be changed to green light with a wavelength of 0.53 microns in a crystal of barium sodium niobate. Broadly tunable sources of coherent light in the visible and near infrared ranges can be produced by pumping with light of shorter wavelengths. A lithium niobate crystal can be made to fluoresce in red, yellow, and green by pumping it with laser light having a wavelength of 488 nanometers. Certain scattering phenomena can be stimulated by a single laser to produce a source of intense, pulsed, monochromatic wavelengths at a wide variety of wavelengths. One of the features of high power optical experiments is a self-focusing effect that produces very short-lived filaments as small as 5 microns in diameter. A large area of application of nonlinear optical effects is the development of efficient broad-band modulators for communication systems; see MODULATION. H.J.

OPTIMISM, doctrine that the existing order of things is, as a whole, the most perfect or the best that could have been created, or that can be conceived. Some advocates of optimism maintain the position that although God was not bound to create the most perfect order of things, yet the existing order is de facto the best; others contend that the perfection and wisdom of God necessarily require that His creation should be the most perfect. The German philosopher Baron Gottfried Wilhelm von Leibniz (q.v.) dealt with the optimistic theory as a philosophical system in his *Essais de Théodicée* ("Essays on Theodicy", 1710). The work was ridiculed by the French author and philosopher Voltaire (q.v.) in his philosophical novel *Candide* (1759). The doctrine upholding the opposite point of view is called pessimism (q.v.).

OPUNTIA. See PRICKLY PEAR.

ORACLE, response delivered by a deity or supernatural being to a worshiper or inquirer; also, the place where the response was delivered. The responses were supposed to be given by divine inspiration and were manifested through the medium of man; through their effect on certain objects, as in the tinkling, at the ancient Greek town of Dodona, of a cauldron when hit by a chain impelled by the wind; or by the actions of sacred animals. Oracles date from the greatest antiquity. Among the ancient Egyptians all the temples were probably oracular; see EGYPTIAN RELIGION. In later days one of the most renowned oracles was that of Amon (q.v.), in the oasis of Siwa, Egypt. Oracles were used by the Hebrews, as in the consultation of the Urim and Thummin (q.v.) by the high priest (q.v.). The oracles in Phoenicia (q.v.) were associated with the deities Baalzebub and other Baalim; see BAAL. Oracles were also common throughout Babylonia and Chaldea; see BABYLONIAN RELIGION. The most renowned Greek oracle was that of Apollo at Delphi (qq.v.). In Asia Minor the most celebrated was the one at Didyma, near Miletus (q.v.). See DIVINATION.

ORADEA (Hung. *Nagyvarad*), city in Rumania, and capital of Crișana Region, on the Crișul Repede R., near the Hungarian border, about 80 miles N.W. of Cluj. It is a railway junction, the commercial center of an important grape-growing area, and an industrial center with factories for food-processing, textile, shoe, clothing, glass, tool, and agricultural machinery. Among the noteworthy features in the city are several churches, notably the parish church containing the remains of Ladislaus I, King of Hungary (1040?–95), who made the city a Roman Catholic bishopric in 1080. Oradea was ceded by Hungary to Rumania following World War I. Occupied by Hungarian forces during World War II, it again passed to Rumanian control after 1945. Pop. (1966) 124,026.

ORAN, city and port of Algeria, on the Mediterranean Sea, 261 miles S.W. of Algiers. Oran, the second largest city in Algeria, is the exporting center for wine, alcohol, wheat, meat, wool, hides, and iron ore. Food processing and the manufacture of shoes, cigarettes, textiles, and glass are the chief industries. Oran was built by the Moors. The French took possession of it in 1831 and held it until Algeria gained its independence in 1962. Pop. (1966) 327,493.

ORANGE, fruit of several trees of the genus *Citrus*, especially the sweet orange, *C. sinensis*; the sour orange, *C. aurantium*; and the mandarin orange, or tangerine, *C. reticulata*. The fruit is technically an hesperidium, a kind of berry; it consists of several easily separated carpels, each containing several seeds and many juice cells, covered by a leathery exocarp, or skin, containing numerous oil glands. Orange trees are evergreens, seldom exceeding 30 ft. in height; the leaves are oval and glossy and the flowers are white and fragrant. Three different essential oils are obtained from oranges: oil of orange, or oil of orange peel, obtained from the rind of the fruit and used principally as a flavoring agent; oil of petitgrain, obtained from the leaves and twigs and used in perfumery; and oil of neroli, obtained from the blossoms and used in flavorings and perfumes. See CURAÇAO.

Oranges, of great commercial importance, are cultivated in warm regions though native to southeastern Asia; the sour orange was introduced to cultivation in the countries of the Mediterranean region by the Arabs about the 10th century, and the sweet orange was introduced by Genoese traders in the 15th century.

In the United States the principal orange-producing States are Florida (the orange blossom is the official State flower of Florida), California, Texas, and Arizona. In 1970 the yield of oranges in the U.S. exceeded 5,500,000 tons. The principal varieties of the sweet orange cultivated by orange growers of eastern U.S. are the Hamlin and Parson Brown, both early-maturing, seedy varieties with thin, russet skin and juicy pulp. Both eastern and western growers cultivate the Valencia, a late variety that is commercially "seedless," having two to five seeds. The principal crops of the western growers consist of the Valencia and the Bahia or Washington navel orange, imported from Bahia, Brazil, in 1870, and developed in Washington, D.C., by the United States Department of Agriculture. The navel orange is a seedless orange, with medium-thick rind, in which a second small, or abortive, orange grows. A variety of the Washington navel orange is the principal orange product of Texas. The bitter orange is cultivated to a limited extent for marmalade and to provide root stock for less vigorous strains. About 30 percent of the total crop of oranges is sold as whole fruit; the remainder is used in preparing frozen and canned orange juice, extracts, and preserves.

ORANGE, city of California, in Orange Co., about 30 miles S.E. of Los Angeles. It is in the midst of the citrus-fruit region of the State. Industrial establishments include citrus packing houses and factories manufacturing chemicals, plastics, and insulated wire. Orange was founded as Richfield in 1868, given its present name in 1875, and incorporated in 1888. It is the site of Chapman College, founded in 1861. Pop. (1960) 26,444; (1970) 77,374.

ORANGE, community in New Jersey. See ORANGES, THE.

ORANGE, city and port of entry in Texas, and county seat of Orange Co., at the head of deep-water navigation on the Sabine R., 22 miles E. of Beaumont. Orange lies in an area of many irrigation canals and is connected to the Gulf of Mexico by the Sabine-Neches Waterway. The surrounding region has oil and gas fields and produces rice, cattle, sulfur, timber, and truck-farm products. Industries include shipbuilding, lumber and rice milling, and the manufacture of steel products, chemicals, food products, plastic, paper, and wood products, cement, nylon, appliances, and beverages. The area was reputedly a lair of the pirate Jean Laffite (q.v.) in the early 1800's. Huntley, Green's Bluff, Jefferson, and Madison were all early names of the community. The city was founded in 1836, incorporated in 1858, and rebuilt after a hurricane in 1865. Pop. (1960) 25,605; (1970) 24,457.

ORANGE, river of southern Africa, rising on the w. slope of the Drakensburg range in Lesotho. It flows generally S.W. through Lesotho and enters the Republic of South Africa, where, turning N.W., it forms the boundary between the provinces of the Orange Free State and the Cape of Good Hope. The Orange continues on a W. course through the northern part of the Cape of Good Hope, finally forming the border between that province and the South African administered territory of South-West Africa. The Orange empties into the Atlantic Ocean at Alexander Bay. The Orange R. is about 1300 mi. long; its chief tributary is the Vaal R.

ORANGE, Prince of. See WILLIAM I, known as William the Silent; WILLIAM III, King of England.

ORANGEBURG, city in South Carolina, and county seat of Orangeburg Co., on the Edisto R., about 75 miles N.W. of Charleston. It is in an agricultural area. Industries include the manufacture of tools, plywood, clothing, office machines, chemicals, and meat packing. Claflin University (1869), South Carolina State College (1896), and Edisto Memorial Gardens, for flower research, are situated here. Pop. (1960) 13,852; (1970) 13,252.

ORANGE FREE STATE, province of the Republic of South Africa, separated from Transvaal Province on the N. by the Vaal R., and bordered on the E. and S.E. by Natal Province and Lesotho, and on the S. and S.W. by the Cape of Good Hope Province. The Orange R. forms the S. border. The capital and largest city is Bloemfontein (q.v.). The province is largely a plateau, lying between 4000 and 5000 ft. above sea level. Mountains in the E. descend gradually to great plains, with very few trees except along the rivers. The Orange Free State is primarily pastoral, and cattle, horses, goats, and sheep are raised in huge herds. Farming districts are chiefly in the E.;

crops include wheat, corn, oats, potatoes, tobacco, apples, and plums, and kafir. Gold, diamonds, and coal are mined in the province. Industries include the processing of oil from coal and the manufacture of fertilizer, agricultural tools, blankets and woolens, clothing, hosiery, cement, and pharmaceuticals. A government-owned railroad extends for some 1660 mi. through the province. Education is free and compulsory for children between the ages of seven and sixteen. The University College (founded 1855), which was granted independent status in 1949 as The University of the Orange Free State, is at Bloemfontein. English and Afrikaans (q.v.) are both official languages.

History. The first European settlements in the region were made between 1810 and 1820. In 1836 the great emigration, called the "great trek", of Boers (q.v.) from the Cape Colony, where they were dissatisfied with British government, occurred to this area. The Boers created a republic which, in 1848, was annexed by force by the British, who named it the Orange River Sovereignty. Six years later Great Britain relinquished the territory, which then became known as the independent Orange River Free State. In 1899 the state joined with the Transvaal in the South African War (q.v.) against Great Britain. In 1900 the area was occupied and annexed by Great Britain as the Orange River Colony. During the settlement of peace terms in 1902, the state acknowledged British sovereignty. In 1907 the colony was granted responsible government similar to that of the Transvaal. In 1910, as the Province of the Orange Free State, the region was incorporated into the Union of South Africa (since 1961, the Republic of South Africa). Area, 49,866 sq.mi.; pop. (1960) 1,386,547.

ORANGEMEN, members of the Orange Society, formed by Protestants in County Armagh, Ireland, after the Battle of the Boyne in 1690, which was fought between Protestant and Roman Catholic forces. The name of the society is based upon the Protestant support of William III (q.v.), the former Prince of Orange, who succeeded to the English throne in 1689 after Protestants succeeded in ousting the Roman Catholic Stuart king, James II (q.v.). The society grew rapidly, establishing many lodges in both England and North America. By 1797, it had about 200,000 members. The Orangemen were, however, charged with anti-Catholic bigotry and were forced by Parliament to suspend their activities in Ireland from 1813 to 1828. When the British prime minister William Ewart Gladstone (q.v.) declared in favor of Irish home rule in 1885, the Orange order became a center of resistance and gained many new members, especially in Ulster. By the mid-20th century, the Orangemen had become influential among farmers, skilled workers, and professional men and had lodges for women as well. The society is now regarded as principally a fraternal order. The most important holiday of the society is celebrated on July 12, the anniversary of the Battle of the Boyne; see BOYNE, BATTLE OF THE.

ORANGES, THE, suburban community of New Jersey, in Essex Co., about 5 miles N.W. of Newark; it comprises Orange, East Orange, West Orange, and South Orange. The city of Orange has plants for the manufacture of textiles, pharmaceuticals, and business machines. It was settled about 1675 and incorporated as a city in 1872. Pop. (1960) 35,789; (1970) 32,566.

East Orange is a prominent insurance center. The chief industries are the manufacture of dynamos, electric motors, automotive equipment, and sewer pipes and pipe fittings. The city is the site of Upsala College (Lutheran; founded in 1893). Originally a part of Orange, East Orange was separated from it in 1862 and chartered as a city in 1899. Pop. (1960) 77,259; (1970) 75,471.

The chief industrial product in West Orange is electrical equipment. Other products include machinery, metal products, tiles, and clothing. The American inventor Thomas Alva Edison (q.v.) established his home and experimental laboratories here in 1887; the Edison home is one of the principal landmarks. Originally a part of Orange, West Orange was separated from it in 1862 and incorporated as a town in 1900. Pop. (1960) 39,894; (1970) 43,715.

South Orange is a residential village and the seat of Seton Hall University (q.v.). It was incorporated in 1869. Pop. (1960) 16,175; (1970) 16,971.

ORANGUTAN or **ORANGOUTAN,** or ORANG-UTAN (Malay *orang*, "man"; *hutan*, "forest"), anthropoid ape, *Pongo pygmaeus*, found in the moist forests of Borneo and Sumatra, and characterized by reddish-brown hair which attains a length of over a foot on the arms and thighs. The orangutan, which attains a standing height of about 4½ ft., lacks hair on its face, ears, hands, and feet. The animal's head is large with a high forehead, small ears, a manlike nose, and a receding chin. Natives call the beast the "man of the woods". The orangutan has a thick neck, a robust body with a corpulent abdomen, long arms, and short, bowed legs. It lives alone, with a mate, or in small groups, and leads an arboreal existence, swinging from branch to branch during the day, feeding on leaves and fruit, and constructing platforms of branches and leaves

ORATORY, CONGREGATION OF THE

Orangutan, Pongo pygmaeus
Arthur W. Ambler – National Audubon Society

high in the trees as a resting place. The beast never attacks man and is docile in captivity unless provoked, when it can be extremely dangerous. It can be tamed and trained but is not as intelligent as the chimpanzee. See APE.

ORATORIO, large-scale musical composition for voices and instruments, of a dramatic or contemplative nature, and usually about a religious subject. Although the libretto may contain dramatic incidents, similar to that of the opera (q.v.), oratorios are usually performed in concert without scenery or costumes.

The history of the oratorio began in the mid-16th century, when the Italian priest Filippo de'Neri (1515–95) organized devotional services in the oratory, or prayer hall, of a church in Rome. The services included sermons, prayers, hymn singing, and devotional music. After opera spread from Florence to Rome in the early 17th century, some of its characteristics, including the recitativelike vocal style called monody (see OPERA), and the use of a dramatic libretto, were incorporated into music written for the oratory services. Works of this type were called oratorios. Some of the early oratorios were performed like operas, with the use of scenery, costumes, and staged action. Soon, however, a narrator (testo) sang descriptions of settings and actions. By the mid-17th century, the oratorio was easily distinguishable from opera in its use of a testo, its lack of staged action, its generally contemplative tone, and its emphasis on music for chorus rather than for solo voices. The early composers of oratorios included the Italian Giacomo Carissimi, his student, the Frenchman Marc-Antoine Charpentier (1634–1704), and the Italian opera composers Alessandro Stradella (1645?–82) and Alessandro Scarlatti. In Germany oratorios were composed by Heinrich Schütz and Johann Sebastian Bach among many others. The German-born British composer, George Frederick Handel (q.v.), created the British oratorio.

During the later 18th and 19th centuries, most major composers wrote oratorios with musical styles borrowed from their operas, symphonies, and other secular music. These composers included the Germans Franz Joseph Haydn and Felix Mendelssohn, the Hungarian Franz Liszt, the Briton Edward Elgar, and the Frenchmen Hector Berlioz, Charles François Gounod, and César Franck. Oratorios were very popular in the United States, especially those by 19th-century composers in New England, most notably Horatio Parker. See also AMERICAN MUSIC: *The 19th Century.*

The composition of oratorios has decreased markedly in the 20th century. The most notable examples have been written by the Briton William Walton, the French-born Arthur Honegger, the Russian-born Igor Stravinsky, the German-born Paul Hindemith and Arnold Schoenberg, and the Hungarian Zoltán Kodály.

See separate articles for those composers whose birth and death dates are not given.

ORATORY, CONGREGATION OF THE, either of two Roman Catholic religious associations.

The first is the oratory founded in Rome in 1575 by the Italian priest San Filippo de Neri (1515–95). Its rules were codified under the Italian prelate Baronius (q.v.) and approved by Pope Paul V (*see under* PAUL) in 1612. Its essential constitution is that of a body of priests living in community but without monastic vows. The British religious leader Cardinal John Henry Newman (q.v.) introduced the Oratorians to England in 1849. The houses are independent. In 1942, however, they formed a confederation known as the Institute of the Oratory of Saint Philip Neri. They are represented by several houses in the United States.

The other oratory was founded along the same lines in France by the French religious leader Cardinal Pierre de Berulle (1575–1629) in 1611. It is a distinct institution with its own superior general. Suppressed during the French Revolution (q.v.), it was reconstituted in 1852 as the Oratory of Jesus and Mary.

ORCAGNA

ORCAGNA, real name ANDREA DI CIONE (1308?–68?), Italian painter, sculptor, mosaicist, and architect, born in Florence. In 1343 he became a member of the painters' guild of Medici e Speziali. A follower of the painting tradition of the Florentine artist Giotto (q.v.), Orcagna was regarded as one of the leading masters of the period. He often collaborated with his three brothers, all of whom were, like him, influenced by Giotto. The only painting known to be an entirely independent work by Orcagna is an altarpiece, "Christ Enthroned with Saints", created for the Strozzi Chapel in Santa Maria Novella, Florence, in 1357. In this work the firmly-drawn figures stand out in bold relief from the background. The same chapel contains frescoes by Orcagna. In 1355 Orcagna began work on the famed sculptured tabernacle at the Church of Or San Michele, Florence, intermittently visiting Orvieto to direct the construction of, and also execute mosaics for, the cathedral there. From 1364 to 1367 he was occupied with the construction of the Cathedral of Santa Maria del Fiore in Florence. He became a member of the sculptors' guild in 1352 and carved many fine works that anticipated the style of the Renaissance.

ORCHARD, area of land on which fruit trees are cultivated. Fruit cultivation began in the United States in colonial days as an adjunct of common farming. The ground surface of farm orchards, generally covered with grasses, was valued primarily for its utility in grazing small livestock such as sheep, and the fruit was chiefly used for home consumption. The development of scientific methods of fruitgrowing, storage, and transportation led, in the 19th century, to the emergence of orchards as primary commercial crop sources.

Climate is the critical factor determining which fruits may be grown in a given area; citrus fruits and most commercially cultivated nuts are grown in warm regions and protected by artificial heat against unseasonable frosts. The quality of the yield is dependent on soil conditions. Fertility of the surface layer is necessary, but adequate depth and drainage of the surface layer are of greater importance. Trees separated by only a few hundred feet, but growing in soils with different drainage conditions, may vary in yield by ratios of 3 or 4 to 1. Most fruit trees are planted in rows spaced 20 ft. apart in both directions; in apple orchards, however, this distance is increased to 40 ft. In orchards composed of dwarf trees, the intervening space is reduced. Many trees bear fruit in greater abundance when fertilized by pollen from other varieties of the same species; some varieties of apple, cherry, and plum bear practically none unless cross-pollinated. A common way of effecting cross-pollination is to intersperse several varieties throughout the orchard; pollen from each tree is dispersed at random and usually fertilizes fruits on a tree of a different variety.

Maintenance of orchard soil at maximum efficiency requires careful attention to soil moisture and supply of nitrogen. In late summer and early fall, maturation of fruit and development of resistance to low temperatures are hastened by reduction of nitrogen and moisture supply. This reduction is best accomplished by the growth of surface crops, such as legumes or cereal grains, which further serve to replenish the supply of humus and nitrogen when mowed in late fall. Irrigation is commonly employed in fruitgrowing in dry areas of northwestern U.S. and parts of California.

Heavy pruning, especially of young trees, was formerly performed to concentrate growth in branches which could be reached easily. This practice has been modified because of the discovery that heavy trimming delays bearing by several years. Young trees are now pruned sufficiently to retain their shape. Weak, diseased, or shading wood is always removed and, as the trees mature, crowding or crossing branches are eliminated. Additional pruning of mature trees is necessary to confine them to their allotted space and to keep fruitbearing branches within practical picking distance. A few fruits, especially peaches and apricots, require extensive pruning to force proliferation of shoots and to increase the size of fruit. Individual growers usually prune mature fruit trees severely, despite consequent reduction of total yield, because quality is usually sufficiently improved to justify the total cost, and because pruned trees produce hardier buds.

Distribution. The major fruit crop of the U.S. is the apple crop; apples are grown commercially in most parts of the country, the chief centers being the Great Lakes region, New England, and the Northwest. Apples also form the major Canadian fruit crop, being grown in Ontario, the chief fruit region of Canada, and in British Columbia and Nova Scotia. The chief grape-producing areas in the U.S. are California, the Great Lakes region, the Hudson R. valley, and the Gulf States. The commercial production of pears is chiefly confined to the Pacific coast States, Michigan, and New York; apricot growing is chiefly confined to California; and plum raising is chiefly confined to California, Oregon, and Washington. Citrus fruits are grown princi-

ORCHESTRA

pally in California, Florida, and Texas, California producing most of the lemons and oranges and Florida and Texas most of the grapefruit. The chief center of sweet-cherry production is along the Pacific coast; cherries are also grown in New York, Michigan, and Wisconsin.

Semitropical fruits other than citrus fruits, such as olives, dates, and avocados, are produced in small quantities in California, Arizona, and Florida; they are also imported from Mediterranean countries, chiefly France and Italy. Tropical fruits are not extensively cultivated in the U.S. Small quantities of nuts are grown in the U.S.; pecans are grown in southern U.S. from Florida to Texas; walnuts are chiefly raised in California and Oregon; almonds are chiefly cultivated in California; filberts are raised in Washington and Oregon; and chestnuts are grown in a few isolated areas of the U.S.

See FRUIT.

ORCHESTRA, large group of performers playing various musical instruments. The word "orchestra" originally signified the section in ancient Greek theaters between the stage and the audience that was used by dancers and instrumentalists. In a modern theater that part of the auditorium reserved for musicians is called the orchestra pit, and the term "orchestra" is often also used to designate the part of the ground floor used for audience seating.

The number of players in a modern orchestra varies from about two dozen to well over one hundred. The group is led, or guided, in its performance by a conductor; see CONDUCTING. The instruments are divided into four sections: string (first and second violin, viola, cello, double bass, and harp), woodwind (piccolo, flute, oboe, English horn, clarinet, bass clarinet, bassoon, and double bassoon), brass (French horn, trumpet, trombone, and tuba), and percussion (piano, drum, and special percussion instruments such as cymbals, the triangle, and blocks of wood); see MUSICAL INSTRUMENTS.

Arrangement of the Orchestra. The seating arrangement of an orchestra is determined by the conductor. The string section, forming $\frac{1}{2}$ to $\frac{2}{3}$ of the orchestra, is usually placed with the first and second violins facing the conductor on his left and the violas and cellos on his right. The leader of the string section, called the first violinist, is titled the concert master and sits nearest the conductor. The woodwind and brass sections constitute 10 to 20 percent each of the orchestra. They are typically placed in front of the conductor so that their various timbres can reinforce the strings and provide areas of special color within a composition. The percussion instruments, comprising about 10 percent of the orchestra and used primarily to accentuate the rhythmic movement, are placed farthest back or at the extreme ends of the orchestra pit.

Types of Orchestras. Several types of instrumental ensembles exist in modern music. The symphony orchestra, described above, executes

A view of a modern orchestra, shown with its string section nearest to the conductor, the brasses and woodwinds behind them, the percussion instruments to the far right and the choir in the rear.

Agence France Presse

ORCHESTRA

the larger forms of instrumental music, for example a symphony or a concerto (qq.v.); itself regarded as the "performer", the symphony orchestra is commonly arranged prominently on the stage. The operatic orchestra and the ballet orchestra, usually similar in size and structure to the symphony orchestra, perform in conjunction with vocal and dance companies. A chamber orchestra by design consists of fewer than a dozen instruments, most often within the string or woodwind families; see CHAMBER MUSIC. The jazz orchestra, developed during the 1930's and 1940's, uses traditional instruments specially conducive to this popular form of improvisatory music; see JAZZ: *Eelements of Jazz: Texture*. A modern-day band (q.v.) is usually distinguished by its lack of string instruments and is typically used for popular or marching music. A very small jazz or dance band is commonly called a combo.

History. The invention of many of the instruments of the modern orchestra, as well as the realization of the various capabilities of each, is of fairly recent origin. During the Middle Ages and the Renaissance (qq.v.) vocal music was dominant although instruments sometimes followed the voice parts at the discretion of the performers. In specifically instrumental compositions, such as dance music and music for outdoor processions, the instruments to be used were seldom specified by the composer, again being left to selection by the performers.

The Venetian composer Giovanni Gabrieli (1554?–1612) in his *Sacrae Symphoniae* (1597) is thought to have been the earliest to assign parts to specific instruments. The distinctive characteristics of particular instruments were first exploited by another Italian composer Claudio Monteverdi (q.v.). Later in the 17th century a major contribution toward technical discipline in orchestral playing was made by the French composer Jean Baptiste Lully (q.v.). His orchestra was established at the court of Louis XIV (q.v.), King of France, and was known as *Les Vingt-quatre Violons du Roi* (Fr., "the king's twenty-four violins"); it exemplified the trend away from ensembles of wind instruments to groups composed predominantly of strings.

Until the late 18th century the size of orchestras tended to remain between twenty and thirty players. The German organist Johann Sebastian Bach (*see under* BACH), employed after 1723 as musical director in Leipzig, had an orchestra of some twenty players; about half of these played string instruments as in a modern orchestra. The Austrian symphonist Franz Joseph Haydn (q.v.) usually wrote for an orchestra of about twenty or twenty-five players. Orchestras during the lifetime of the German composer Ludwig van Beethoven (q.v.) contained thirty to forty players. Thereafter, as 19th-century composers sought new and dramatic ways to express themselves in music, orchestras became larger. The massive sonorities produced by large ensembles began to be valued over the delicate orchestral clarity that had prevailed during the 18th century. By the early 20th century orchestras of about one hundred players were considered optimal.

Orchestras. Today most of the major cities have large symphony orchestras. The oldest symphony orchestra in the United States is the New York Philharmonic, established as the Philharmonic Society of New York at New York City in 1842. A founder and one of the initial conductors of the orchestra was Ureli Corelli Hill (1802?–75). The group is presently located at the Lincoln Center for the Performing Arts and is now directed by French-born Pierre Boulez (qq.v.). Another long-established U.S. orchestra is the Boston Symphony Orchestra, founded in 1881 at Boston, Mass., by the American banker Henry Lee Higginson (1834–1919). The first conductor of the Boston Symphony Orchestra was the British Sir George Henschel (1850–1934); its current leader is German-born William Steinberg (1899–   ). The oldest symphony orchestra in Canada is L'Orchestre Symphonique de Québec, founded in 1902. The Toronto Symphony Orchestra, another leading Canadian group, was founded in 1922 and is presently directed by Czechoslovakian Karel Ancerl (1908–   ). An internationally famous Latin American orchestra is the National Orchestra of Mexico, founded in 1928 by its long-time conductor Carlos Chávez (q.v.). Important European symphony orchestras include the Philharmonisches Orchester, founded 1882, Berlin; the Concertgebouw Orchestra, founded 1883, Amsterdam; the Orchestre de la Suisse Romande, founded 1918, Geneva; and the London Philharmonic Orchestra, founded 1932, London.

See also MUSIC; ORCHESTRATION.

ORCHESTRATION, *or* INSTRUMENTATION, in music, combining of instruments in the composition of orchestral music. The technique of orchestration originated during the late 16th century, when composers began to assign specific instruments to specific parts of the musical composition. In the 18th century the makeup of orchestras became standardized, and composers began to explore the possibilities of the massed and solo timbres that were available to them. *See* ORCHESTRA.

The Early 18th-Century Orchestra. This consisted of string instruments (first and second violins, violas, cellos, and double basses) and woodwinds (a pair of oboes and/or flutes and a bassoon). Composers wrote three parts for the strings, two in a treble range played by the violins, and one in a bass range played by the cellos and double basses. The viola rarely had a part of its own but merely doubled, or followed, one of the other three parts. The woodwind instruments also mostly doubled or reinforced the string parts, blending with them and giving richness to the orchestral sound. The clarinet and the French horn were added to the orchestra about the middle of the 18th century. The horn played occasional solos and added volume and richness to the orchestral sound. Trumpets and tympani were often used for brilliance in fast movements and at climaxes. Trombones and percussion instruments other than the tympani were not used in operatic orchestras until the late 18th century and did not become common in symphony orchestras until well into the 19th century.

The Late 18th-Century. Composers as the Austrians Franz Joseph Haydn and Wolfgang Amadeus Mozart (qq.v.) wrote music in four and five parts, often using the winds in independent solo and ensemble roles rather than merely as supports for the strings. The trend in composition, therefore, was away from a homogeneous three-part texture to a four- or five-part texture in which the winds provided many different hues and flashes of color.

The 19th Century. At this time the tone of the viola began to be appreciated. The German symphonist Ludwig van Beethoven (q.v.) was among the first composers to give violas prominent parts. He was also among the first to exploit the French horn as a solo instrument. Other important innovators in orchestration included the French composer Louis Hector Berlioz and the German composer Richard Wagner (qq.v.). They used improved wind instruments in increasingly varied ways, both in massive and delicate sonorities. Composers also discovered that two or more instruments playing the same pitch can yield a tone quality entirely unlike that of any of the component instruments playing alone. Largely as a result of the increased individuality given each instrument of the orchestra, the orchestral music of the late 19th century became quite complex, especially in the tone poems of the German composer Richard Strauss and the symphonies of the Austrian composer and conductor, Gustav Mahler (qq.v.).

Orchestration in the 20th Century. Instrumental potentialities were still further exploited. Such French composers as Claude Achille Debussy and Maurice Ravel (qq.v.) emphasized the sensuous and pictorial color effects available to the modern orchestra; see SYMPHONIC POEM. The Russian-American composer Igor Fëdorovich Stravinsky (q.v.), one of the masters of modern orchestration, often broke with classical tradition, giving the melody to the brass section and transferring the percussive function to the strings.

Orchestration in modern popular music is closely associated with the history of jazz (q.v.). The instruments of the jazz ensemble were divided into three broad types: rhythm (banjo or guitar, string bass, piano, and drums); reed (clarinet and saxophone), and brass (cornet, trumpet, and trombone). The rhythm instruments provided an insistent, throbbing accompaniment to the melodic line carried by the reeds and brasses. In recent dance music, orchestra leaders have employed so-called arrangers to compose sets of free variations on popular melodies and provide the instrumentation specifically adapted to the resources of a particular orchestra.

ORCHID, common name applied to perennial epiphytes and herbs constituting the family Orchidaceae of the order Orchidales. The family, which contains about 550 genera and more than 15,000 species, is cosmopolitan, and the larger

Orchid, Vanda caerulea   Bermuda News Bureau

tropical members are widely cultivated for the decorative flowers. Orchids of the genus *Vanilla* (q.v.) bear pods which yield the vanilla flavoring of commerce. Orchid flowers are very irregular and frequently grotesque in appearance. They have three petal-like sepals and three petals, only two of which are alike; the third petal, known as the *labellum,* may have any of a num-

ORDEAL

ber of shapes; in the butterfly orchid the labellum resembles a butterfly. Stigma, style, and stamens are united into a column unique to orchids. The fruit is a dry capsule or pod.

For further information on familiar cultivated orchids, see CATTLEYA; EPIDENDRUM; LADY'S-SLIPPER.

ORDEAL, practice of referring disputed questions to the judgment of God, determined either by lot or by the success of certain experiments.

Throughout Europe the ordeal existed in various forms under the sanction of law and was closely related to the oath. The most prevalent kinds of ordeal were those of fire, water, and the wager of battle. Fire ordeal was allowed only to persons of high rank. The accused had to carry a piece of red-hot iron in his hand for some distance or to walk barefoot and blindfolded across a 9-ft. space of red-hot plowshares. The hand or foot was bound up and inspected three days afterward. If the accused had escaped unhurt, he was pronounced innocent; if otherwise, he was guilty. Water ordeal was the usual mode of trial allowed to bondsmen and rustics, and was of two kinds, the ordeal of boiling water and of cold water. The ordeal of boiling water, according to the laws of Athelstan (q.v.), the first King of England, consisted of lifting a stone out of boiling water, where the hand had to be inserted as deep as the wrist; the triple ordeal deepened the water to the elbow. The person allowed the ordeal of cold water, the usual mode of trial for witchcraft (q.v.), was flung into a pool. If he floated he was guilty; if he sank he was acquitted. In the wager of battle the defeated party, if he craved his life, was allowed to live as a "recreant", that is, on retracting the perjury to which he had sworn.

In the ordeal of the bier, a suspected murderer was required to touch the body of the murdered man and was pronounced guilty if the blood flowed from the murdered man's wounds. The ordeal of the eucharist was in use among the clergy: the accused party took the sacrament in attestation of innocence. A similar ordeal was that of the corsned, or consecrated bread and cheese: if the accused swallowed it freely he was pronounced innocent; if it stuck in his throat he was presumed to be guilty.

In England the ordeal seems to have been continuous till the middle of the 13th century. On the Continent it was, generally speaking, abolished earlier, although as late as 1498 a Franciscan friar proposed that he and the Italian reformer Girolamo Savonarola (q.v.) undergo an ordeal by fire as a test of the truth of the doctrines preached by the latter.

ORDER OF DEMOLAY, organization for boys, fourteen to twenty-one years old, founded in Kansas City, Mo., in 1919 by Frank S. Land (1850–1959). Named after the martyred grand master of the Knights Templars (q.v.), Jacques de Molay (1243?–1314), the order aims to build good citizens and provides social, civic, and athletic activities. Each chapter is sponsored by a Masonic group; see FREEMASONS. To join, a boy must be of good character, believe in God, and be recommended by two members or a Master Mason. Active membership in the United States is 161,000; abroad, 5000.

ORDERS, HOLY, in the Roman Catholic and Eastern Orthodox churches and in the Church of England and other Anglican churches, the sacrament (q.v.) by which a bishop, priest, or deacon is ordained. The sacrament, administered by a bishop, is conferred through the placing of hands on the candidate and the pronouncement of a prescribed formula of words.

The term "Holy Orders" also refers to a hierarchical ranking or grading system within the Roman Catholic and Eastern Orthodox churches and the Anglican churches; each grade or order has certain ecclesiastical powers. The Western rite of the Roman Catholic Church recognizes three major orders (priest, deacon, and subdeacon) and four minor orders (acolyte, exorcist, reader, and porter); the Eastern rite acknowledges two major orders (priest and deacon) and two minor orders (subdeacon and reader). The Eastern Orthodox Church has three major (bishop, priest, and deacon) and two minor (subdeacon and reader) orders. The Anglican churches recognize only the major orders of bishop, priest, and deacon. The Roman Catholic Church does not regard the rank of bishop as a separate order, but as the completion and extension of the priesthood.

Most Protestant denominations recognize the equal priesthood of all the faithful, and deny that Christ instituted a sacrament of orders that created a separate and specific priesthood. Hierarchical distinctions within a denomination are usually of an administrative nature.

See also BISHOP; PRIEST.

ORDERS, RELIGIOUS, religious bodies, especially of the Christian Church, whose members live under a distinctive rule, or discipline. The members of the greater number of Christian religious orders are ordained priests, although lay brothers and women are admitted to several and a few are only for women. See AUGUSTINIANS; BENEDICTINES; CARMELITES; CISTERCIAN; DOMINICANS; FRANCISCANS; JESUITS; KNIGHTS OF SAINT JOHN OF JERUSALEM; KNIGHTS TEMPLARS; MERCY, SISTERS OF;

PAULISTS; TRAPPISTS. *See also* FRIAR; MENDICANT FRIARS; MONASTICISM; NUN.

ORDOVICIAN PERIOD, division of geologic time in the Paleozoic Era, following the Cambrian Period and preceding the Silurian Period (qq.v.). The Ordovician Period began about 500,000,000 years ago and lasted about 60,000,000 years.

The typical rock strata of the Ordovician system are found in New York State and, consequently, the names of many of the geologic subdivisions are localities in the State.

The Ordovician rocks are chiefly limestones, with the exception of the upper and lower series, which may be very shaly. Belts of Ordovician rocks are found around the New York Adirondacks; from central New York westward to Wisconsin and Minnesota; along the line of the Appalachians on the eastern and sometimes on the western slope from Vermont to Alabama; around the V-shaped Archean or Laurentian of Canada; and in Ohio, Kentucky, Indiana, and Tennessee. Ordovician rocks are also known in the Uinta, Wasatch, and Rocky mountains. The Taconic disturbance, a period of mountain building in northeastern North America began toward the end of the Ordovician Period.

Fauna. During the Ordovician Period, about 60 percent of the North American continent and much of northern Europe were submerged, as evidenced by the largely marine fossils. Prominent among these are a few primitive, fishlike vertebrates and colonial graptolites, the latter of which were something like modern hydrozoans. *See* GEOLOGY, HISTORICAL; PALEONTOLOGY.

ORDZHONIKIDZE, city of the Soviet Union, in the Russian S.F.S.R., and capital of the North Ossetian A.S.S.R., on the Terek R., at the northern foot of the Caucasus Mts., 375 miles S.E. of Rostov. It is a rail-spur terminus, at the northern end of the Georgian Military Road to Tbilisi. An industrial center, the city smelts zinc, lead, and silver and has railroad shops, metalworking and fruit-canning plants, and factories manufacturing apparel, wines, porcelain, glass, and wood products. The Gizel'don hydroelectric plant lies 12 miles to the S.W. The city has a university (with teachers', agricultural, and medical faculties), a drama theater, a regional museum, and a metals institute. Founded as the fortress of Vladikavkaz in 1783, the city has been the capital of the Terek Region (1863), of the Mountain A.S.S.R. (1921-24), of the North Caucasus Territory, and of the North Ossetian A.S.S.R. since 1936. It was called Ordzhonikidze from 1933 to 1944 and Dzaudzhikau from 1944 to 1954. Pop. (1970) 236,000.

ORE. *See* MINING.

OREADS, in Greek mythology, nymphs (q.v.) of grottoes and mountains. One of the most famous Oreads was Echo, who was deprived by the goddess Hera (qq.v.) of the power of speech and could only repeat the last words that were said to her.

ÖREBRO, city and port of Sweden, and capital of Örebro County, at W. end of Hjalmaren Lake, about 100 miles W. of Stockholm. The major industry of the city is the manufacture of shoes. Minerals obtained from the neighboring zinc, copper, and iron mines are conveyed to Göteborg and Stockholm by means of the extensive system of canals that connects the lakes of the interior with the maritime ports. Örebro is one of the oldest settlements in Sweden. The modern city, rebuilt after the fire of 1854, has a number of medieval structures. At the Diet of Örebro, held in 1529, Lutheranism was established as the state religion of Sweden. Pop. (1966 est.) 86,003.

OREGON, one of the Pacific States of the United States, bounded on the N. by Washington, on the E. by Idaho, on the S. by Nevada and California, and on the W. by the Pacific Ocean. Oregon is roughly square in shape, measuring about 300 mi. from E. to W. and 260 mi. from N. to S.

Area (10th State in rank)	96,981 sq. mi.
Land	96,315 sq. mi.
Inland water	666 sq. mi.
Population	(1970, 31st in rank) 2,091,385
	(1960, 32nd in rank) 1,768,687
	(1950) 1,521,341
Altitude	sea level to 11,235 ft.
Capital	Salem (1970) 68,296
Largest city	Portland (1970) 382,619
Entered Union (33rd State)	Feb. 14, 1859
Nickname	The Beaver State
Motto	The Union
Song	"Oregon, My Oregon"
Tree	Douglas fir
Flower	Oregon grape
Bird	western meadowlark

THE LAND

Topographically, Oregon consists of two distinct regions, the larger of which occupies about two thirds of the area of the State. This region, part of the Great Basin (q.v.), is a generally arid tableland with rugged mountainous outcroppings and an average elevation of 5000 ft. It is bounded on the W. by the Cascade Range (q.v.), which extends the length of the State parallel with the coast. Mount Hood (11,235 ft.), the highest summit of the Cascades, is the highest point in Oregon. The lowest point is sea level, and the average elevation is 3300 ft. A lesser mountain system, the Coast Range, traverses the second topographical area of the State, which extends from the Cascades to the coast. Maximum elevations of this system rarely exceed

OREGON

INDEX TO MAP OF OREGON

Cities and Towns

Agate Beach .... A 2	Hines .... D 3	Salem ⊙ (cap.) . B 2, A 2	Grande Ronde (river) .. E 2
Albany ⊙ .... B 2	Hood River ⊙ ..... C 2	Sandy .... B 2	Harney (basin) ...... D 3
Altamont .... C 3	Huntington .... E 2	Scappoose .... B 2	Harney (lake) ...... D 3
Amity .... B 2	Independence ...... B 2	Seaside .... B 2	Hart (lake) .... D 3
Arlington .... C 2	Jacksonville .... B 3	Sheridan .... B 2	Hells (canyon) ..... E 2
Ashland .... B 3	Jefferson .... B 2	Silverton .... A 2	High (desert) ...... C 3
Astoria ⊙ .... B 1	John Day .... D 2	Sisters .... C 2	High Mtn. Sheep
Athena .... D 2	Jordan Valley ..... E 3	Springfield .... B 2	(res.) .... E 2
Baker ⊙ .... E 2	Joseph .... E 2	Stayton .... B 2	Hills Creek (res.) ... B 3
Bandon .... A 3	Junction City ...... B 2	Sutherlin .... B 3	Hood (mt.) .... C 2
Bates .... D 2	Keizer .... A 2	Sweet Home .... B 2	Jefferson (mt.) ..... C 2
Bay City .... B 2	Kerby .... B 3	The Dalles ⊙ ..... C 2	John Day (lake) .... D 2
Beaverton .... A 2	Klamath Falls ⊙ ... C 3	Tigard .... A 2	John Day (river) ... D 2
Bend ⊙ .... C 2	La Grande ⊙ ...... E 2	Tillamook ⊙ ...... B 2	Kincheloe (point) ... A 2
Bly .... C 3	La Pine .... C 3	Toledo .... B 2	Klamath (river) .... B 3
Brookings .... A 3	Lake Oswego ...... A 2	Union .... E 2	Lookout (cape) ..... A 2
Brownsville .... B 2	Lakeview ⊙ .... C 3	Vale .... E 2	Lookout Point (res.) . B 3
Burns ⊙ .... D 3	Lebanon .... B 2	Valsetz .... B 2	Lost (river) .... C 3
Canby .... A 2	Lincoln City .... A 2	Vernonia .... B 2	Malheur (lake) ..... D 3
Canyon City ⊙ .... D 2	Madras ⊙ .... C 2	Waldport .... A 2	Malheur (river) ..... E 3
Canyonville .... B 3	Malin .... C 3	Wallowa .... E 2	McLoughlin House
Carlton .... B 2	Mapleton .... B 2	Warm Springs ...... C 2	Nat'l Hist. Site .... A 2
Cascade Locks ..... B 2	Maupin .... C 2	Warrenton .... A 1	McNary (dam) ..... D 2
Central Point ...... B 3	McMinnville ⊙ .... B 2	Wasco .... C 2	Middle Fork Willamette
Chiloquin .... C 3	Medford ⊙ .... B 3	West Linn .... A 2	(river) .... B 3
Clatskanie .... B 1	Merrill .... C 3	Weston .... D 2	Molalla (river) ..... A 2
Condon ⊙ .... C 2	Metzger .... A 2	Willamina .... B 2	Nehalem (river) .... B 2
Coos Bay .... A 3	Mill City .... B 2	Winston .... B 3	North Fork John Day
Coquille ⊙ .... A 3	Milton-Freewater ... D 2	Woodburn .... A 2	(river) .... D 2
Corvallis ⊙ ...... B 2	Milwaukie .... A 2	Wood Village ...... A 1	North Umpqua (river) . B 3
Cottage Grove .... B 3	Molalla .... A 2		Oregon Caves Nat'l
Creswell .... B 3	Monmouth .... B 2	**Physical Features**	Mon. .... B 3
Dallas ⊙ .... B 2	Moro ⊙ .... C 2	Albert (lake) .... C 3	Owyhee (lake) ..... E 3
Drain .... B 3	Mount Angel ...... A 2	Alvord (desert) ..... D 3	Owyhee (river) ..... E 3
Dufur .... C 2	Mount Vernon ..... D 2	Alvord (lake) ...... D 3	Portland Int'l Airport . A 1
Eagle Point .... B 3	Myrtle Creek ...... B 3	Antelope (res.) ..... E 3	Powder (river) ..... E 2
Eastside .... A 3	Myrtle Point ...... A 3	Blanco (cape) ...... A 3	Prineville (res.) .... C 2
Elgin .... D 2	Netarts .... B 2	Blue (mts.) .... D 2	Pudding (river) ..... A 2
Elmira .... B 2	Newberg .... A 2	Bluejoint (lake) .... D 3	Rouge (river) ...... B 3
Enterprise ⊙ ..... E 2	Newport ⊙ .... A 2	Bonneville (dam) ... B 2	Silver (creek) ...... D 3
Estacada .... B 2	North Bend .... A 3	Butte (creek) ...... A 2	Silver (lake) .... C 3
Eugene ⊙ .... B 2	Nyssa .... E 3	Cascade (mt. range) . B 3	Silver (lake) .... D 3
Falls City .... B 2	Oakland .... B 3	Coast (mt. range) ... B 3	Silvies (river) ...... D 3
Florence .... A 3	Oakridge .... B 3	Columbia (river) ... B 1	Snake (river) ...... E 2
Forest Grove ...... A 2	Ontario .... E 3	Crane Prairie (res.) . C 3	Sprague (river) ..... C 3
Fossil .... C 2	Oregon City ⊙ . B 2, A 2	Crater (lake) .... C 3	Steens (mts.) .... D 3
Garibaldi .... B 2	Pacific City .... B 2	Crater Lake Nat'l	Strawberry (mt.) .... D 2
Gearhart .... B 1	Pendleton ⊙ ...... D 2	Park .... B 3	Summer (lake) ..... C 3
Gladstone .... A 2	Philomath .... B 2	Crescent (lake) ..... C 3	Thielson (mt.) ...... C 3
Glendale .... B 3	Pilot Rock .... D 2	Crooked (river) .... C 2	Three Sisters (mt.) .. C 2
Gold Beach ⊙ .... A 3	Port Orford .... A 3	Crump (lake) ...... D 3	Umatilla (river) .... D 2
Grants Pass ⊙ .... B 3	Portland ⊙ .... B 2, A 1	Deschutes (river) ... C 2	Umatilla Ind. Res. .. D 2
Gresham .... A 2	Powers .... A 3	Detroit (res.) ...... B 2	Umpqua (river) .... B 3
Halfway .... E 2	Prairie City .... D 2	Donner und Blitzen	Upper Klamath (lake) . B 3
Harrisburg .... B 2	Prineville ⊙ ...... C 2	(river) .... D 3	Waldo (lake) ...... B 3
Hayesville .... A 2	Prospect .... B 3	Drews (res.) .... C 3	Wallowa (mts.) ..... E 2
Heppner ⊙ .... D 2	Rainier .... B 1	Fern Ridge (res.) ... B 2	Wallula (lake) ..... D 1
Hermiston .... D 2	Redmond .... C 2	Flagstaff (lake) .... D 3	Warm Springs (res.) . D 3
Hillsboro ⊙ ... B 2, A 1	Reedsport .... A 3	Fort Clatsop Nat'l	Warm Springs Ind. Res. C 2
	Riddle .... B 3	Mem. .... A 1	Warner (valley) .... D 3
⊙ County seat.	Roseburg ⊙ .... B 3	Gerber (res.) .... C 3	Wickiup (res.) ...... C 3
	Saint Helens ⊙ .... B 2	Goose (lake) .... C 3	Willamette (river) ... B 2

4000 ft. Most of the region between the Coast Range and the Cascades is occupied by the valley of the Willamette River (q.v.), the most fertile portion of Oregon. East of the Cascades is an area of nearly level basins and valleys bordered by long, gently sloping alluvial fans. In the N.E. corner of the State are the Wallowa and Blue mountains. The coastline of Oregon, about 300 mi. in length, is generally regular.

Rivers and Lakes. The Columbia River (q.v.), which forms three fourths of the Oregon-Washington boundary, is the principal river of the State. Its mouth, the only deepwater harbor between San Francisco, Calif., and Cape Flattery, Wash., is navigable for 95 mi.; its upper course is a source of hydroelectric power. The Bonneville Dam, which crosses the river in Multnomah County, is so constructed as to permit salmon to move upstream to spawn. Other major dams on the Columbia are The Dalles and the John Day and McNary dams. Other important rivers, all of which flow into the Columbia, are the Willamette, John Day, and Deschutes rivers, and the Snake R., which forms more than half of the border with Idaho.

The State has many natural lakes, mainly situated in the s. of the tableland region. Notable is Crater Lake, 6161 ft. above sea level, which lies in the crater of an extinct volcano and is remarkable for the intense blue of the water. Other lakes in the region include Klamath Lakes, Summer Lake, Lake Abert, and the connected Harney and Malheur lakes. Some of these lakes are often dry.

Climate. Oregon has a mild but varied climate. In coastal areas the mean temperature of the

OREGON

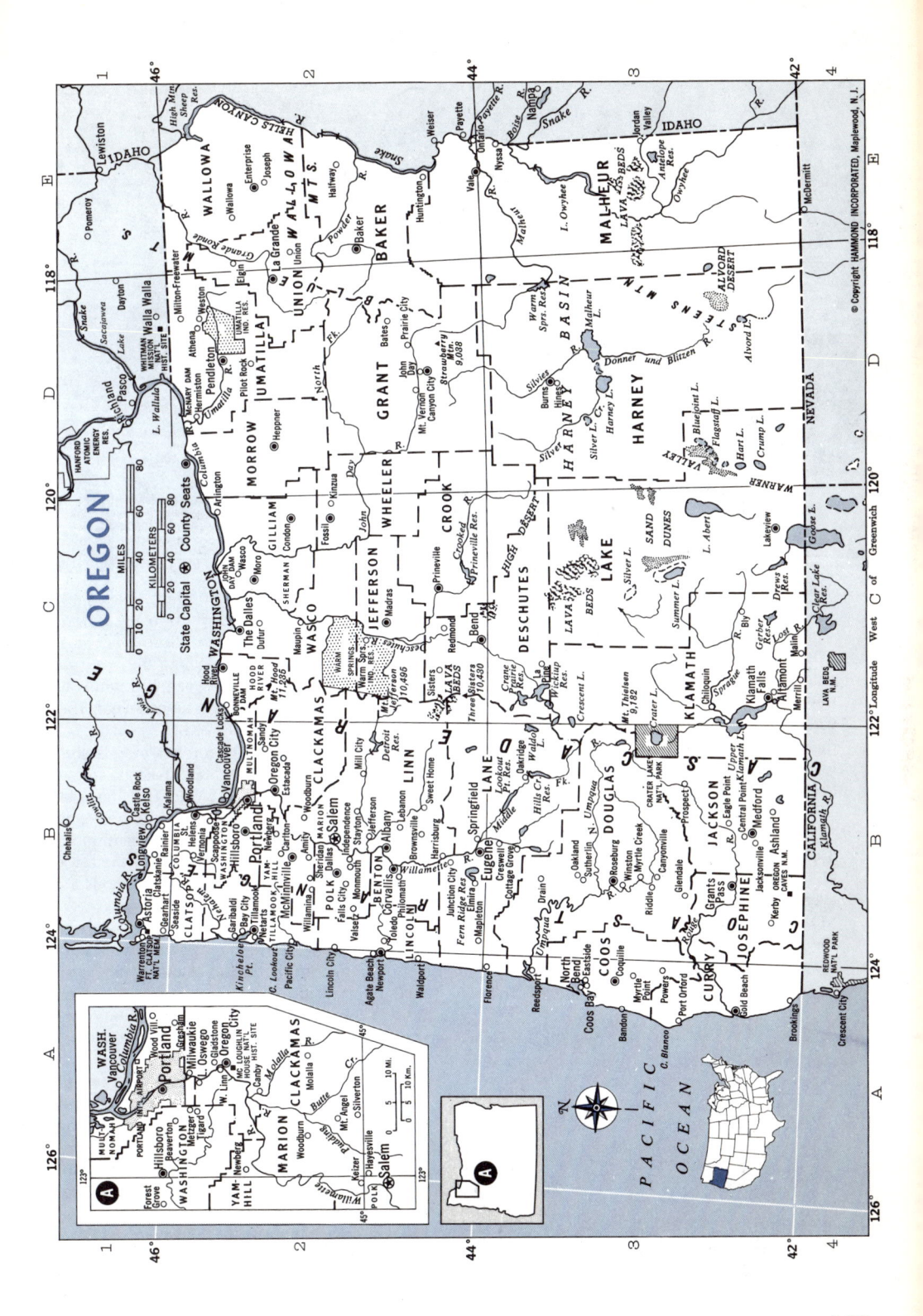

Majestic Mt. Hood, the highest point in Oregon, is reflected in the clear waters of Frog Lake in Mount Hood National Forest in northern Oregon.
Oregon State Highway Commission

coldest month is only 15° F. lower than that of the warmest month. East of the Cascade Mts. variations are greater in the interior valleys. The mean temperature range in the Willamette valley is 38° F. in January and 66° F. in July. The highest temperature recorded in the State was 119° F. (at Pendleton); the lowest, −54° F. (at Seneca). The average annual rainfall varies from 8 in. in plateau regions to 200 in. on the upper w. slopes of the Coast Range; along the coast it averages 70 to 90 in. Snowfall ranges from 300 to 550 in. annually in the Cascades to 1 to 3 in. on the coast; in inland valleys it averages 10 to 15 in., and in the plateau region it ranges from 15 to 60 in. The average annual number of days with measurable precipitation ranges from 101 at Pendleton and 102 at Medford to 152 at Portland and 199 at Astoria. Thunderstorms are most frequent in the mountains, where they cause a number of forest fires each year, and winds of hurricane force occur several times a year. Tornadoes are rare and short-lived.

Plants and Animals. Oregon has more standing timber than any other State. Forests, chiefly in the w., cover nearly 50 percent of the total land area. Conifers, mostly firs, pines, and spruces, are predominant. In the w. section four fifths of the trees are Douglas firs. In the E. the ponderosa pine is predominant. Redwoods are found in the s.w. Wild flowers include lily, orchid, trillium, bitterroot, and violet species.

The fauna of Oregon includes the black-tailed deer, pronghorn antelope, wapiti (elk), gray wolf, puma, black bear, coyote, raccoon, beaver, muskrat, and several species of rabbits and squirrels. The lakes and rivers teem with salmon, trout, smelts, and other fish.

Parks, Forests, and Other Places of Interest. The one national park in Oregon is Crater Lake National Park (q.v.), near Fort Klamath. Oregon Caves National Monument (q.v.), near Oregon Caves, is a limestone cavern with formations of great variety and beauty. The Fort Clatsop National Memorial (q.v.), near Astoria, is the site of the winter encampment of the Lewis and Clark Expedition (q.v.) of 1804–06. Oregon has fourteen national forests covering about 15,500,000

Climate	Medford	Pendleton	Portland
Normal temperatures (in °F.)			
January maximum	42.4	39.3	44.9
January minimum	28.4	25.1	35.5
July maximum	88.3	89.3	79.2
July minimum	55.7	57.8	57.9
Annual	52.6	52.8	54.6
Normal precipitation (in inches)			
Wettest month	3.38	1.49	7.42
Driest month	.18	.22	.39
Annual	19.78	12.38	42.37
Latest frost	April 25	April 27	Feb. 25
Earliest frost	Oct. 20	Oct. 8	Dec. 1
Mean number of days between latest and earliest frosts	178	163	279

acres: Deschutes, near Redmond; Fremont, near Bly; Klamath, near Medford (partly in California); Malheur, near Burns; Mount Hood, near Portland; Ochoco, near Bend; Rogue River, near Medford; Siskiyou, near Brookings; Siuslaw, near Corvallis; Umatilla, near Pendleton; Umpqua, near Canyonville; Wallowa-Whitman National Forests, near Enterprise; and Willamette, near Eugene. Among the parks maintained by the State are Battle Mt. State Park and Emigrant Springs State Park, both near Pendleton; and John Day State Park, near Dayville.

Sports. With the Pacific Ocean along its entire w. border and many rivers and lakes, Oregon offers a wide variety of fishing. Five species of Pacific salmon are found in coastal waters. Freshwater species include seven varieties of trout, Rocky Mountain whitefish, black, warmouth, and kelp bass, crappie, yellow perch, and bluegill. Saltwater fish are sea perch, ling cod, flounder, and red snapper. Striped bass and shad, native to the Atlantic coast, have been planted on the w. coast. Large game animals hunted are white-tailed, mule, and Coast deer, Roosevelt and Rocky Mountain elk, antelope, and mountain goat (by residents only). Small game includes cottontail rabbit, jackrabbit, snowshoe hare, ring-necked pheasant, ruffed, sage, and blue grouse, and California and mountain quail. The winter-sports season in the higher elevations and E. of the Cascade Range runs from November to May. Among popular ski areas are the Hoodoo Ski Bowl, near Bend; the Mt. Hood Ski Bowl, near Portland; and Willamette Pass, near Eugene. The Cascade Mts. offer excellent climbing. Of interest to the experienced are Three Sisters Mt. (10,354 ft.), Mt. Jefferson (10,522 ft.), and Mt. Hood. In Crater Lake National Park are many mountain trails for novices, among them Discovery Point Trail, overlooking Crater Lake.

THE PEOPLE

According to the 1970 decennial census, the population of Oregon was 2,091,385, an increase of 18.2 percent over the 1960 population. The urban segment comprised 1,402,704 persons, 67.1 percent of the total, compared to 62.2 percent in 1960. The rural segment comprised 688,681 persons, 32.9 percent of the total, compared with 37.8 percent in 1960. Ethnically, the 1970 population was distributed as follows: white persons, 2,032,079, nonwhites, 59,306, including 26,308 Negroes, 13,510 Indians, 6843 Japanese, 4814 Chinese, 1633 Filipinos, and 6198 others. The percentage of native-born residents was 96; of foreign-born, 4. The major countries of origin of the foreign-born, in order of rank, were Canada, Great Britain, and Germany. The 1970 population density averaged 21.7 per sq.mi., compared with 18.4 in 1960.

The chief cities are Salem, the capital and third-largest city, an agricultural processing and marketing center; Portland, the largest city, a port on the Willamette R., an agricultural trading and manufacturing center; Eugene, the second-largest, a lumbering and shipping center, site of the University of Oregon; and Medford, the fourth-largest, a resort and center of a lumbering and farming area.

The largest Indian reservation in Oregon, both in size and population, is Warm Springs, occupied by the Walla Walla and Wasco tribes. Others are Umatilla, for the Walla Walla and Cayuse; Celillo Village, for the Walla Walla; and Burns, for the Paiute.

Education. The public-school system of Oregon was established in 1849. Education is free and compulsory for all children between the ages of seven and eighteen.

ELEMENTARY AND SECONDARY SCHOOLS. In the mid-1960's public elementary schools numbered about 1000 and public secondary schools, about 300. Enrollment was about 291,000 in elementary and about 183,000 in secondary schools. Teachers in the public-school system numbered about 12,350 in elementary and about 9375 in secondary schools. In the mid-1960's private institutions included about 150 elementary schools with some 30,400 students, and more than 40

The 19th-century explorer and fur trader Dr. John McLoughlin, "Father of Oregon", overlooks the Willamette River from his vantage point near U.S. Highway 99E at Oregon City. Oregon State Highway Commission

OREGON

secondary schools with some 7400 students. Teachers in private schools numbered about 1450 in 1966.

UNIVERSITIES AND COLLEGES. In the mid-1960's Oregon had thirty-three institutions of higher education, nineteen of which were private. University and college enrollment was about 67,700. Public institutions include the University of Oregon, Eastern Oregon College, Oregon State University, Portland State College, Southern Oregon College, and Southwestern Oregon Community College. Private institutions include Lewis and Clark College, Maryhurst College, Multnomah College, Pacific University, Reed College, the University of Portland, and Willamette University.

LIBRARIES AND MUSEUMS. The Oregon State Library, in Salem, has about 700,000 volumes and a collection of State archives. Cultural institutions include, in Eugene, the Museum of Natural History, and the University of Oregon Museum of Art, which has an unusual collection of Oriental art; and, in Portland, the Oregon Historical Society, the Portland Art Museum, and the Oregon Museum of Science and Industry.

THE ECONOMY

Oregon has a diversified economy. Almost 75 percent of all personal income is derived from private nonfarm sources, almost 22 percent from governmental sources (including social security and military benefits), and about 3 percent from agriculture. The major portion of wage income is paid, in descending order, by manufacturing, national and local governments, wholesale and retail trade, and services. About 25 percent of nonfarm workers are employed in manufacturing, about 22 percent in wholesale and retail trade, and about 20 percent in governmental activities. Oregon is visited each year by some 6,600,000 tourists, who spend about $468,000,000.

Oregon has large waterpower resources. At the disposal of electric utilities and industrial plants in the State, according to the latest available statistics (1966), were some 3,012,000 kw of developed waterpower; an estimated 5,767,000 kw remained for future development.

Manufacturing. According to the most recent Census of Manufactures (1967), production workers in Oregon totaled 131,400. The largest groups were employed in the processing of lumber and wood products and in food processing. About 40 percent were employed in the Standard Metropolitan Statistical Area (q.v.) of Portland, and half of these worked in the city itself. Other manufacturing centers were Eugene and Salem. The value added by manufacture (see VALUE) in the largest industries totaled $775,400,000 for lumber and $296,600,000 for food and kindred products. The manufacture of transportation equipment, although ranking third in employment, ranked fifth in value added, at $102,600,000. According to the most recent published figures, the value added by all manufacturing in Oregon in 1968 was $2,460,000,000.

Agriculture. Almost any crop grown in the Temperate Zone can be cultivated in Oregon, particularly in the w. part of the State. Thus, there is equal emphasis on the production of crops and livestock, and principal commodities include cattle, dairy products, wheat, and pears. The State also produces hay and potatoes. In the late-1960's, according to latest available statistics, Oregon ranked high among the States producing cherries, hops, prunes, strawberries, and walnuts. Farms numbered about 39,500 in 1970, totaling some 20,900,000 acres and averaging 529

The golden statue "The Pioneer" can be seen atop Oregon's white marble capitol in Salem, overlooking a green mall and other modern buildings in the capitol group.
Oregon State Highway Commission

Logs going into a mill at Bend, Oreg. Oregon is the leading State in timber production.
American Forest Products Industries, Inc.

acres each. Cash income from crops, livestock, and government payments in 1968 was $535,405,000.

Fishing. Oregon is one of the Pacific Coast States; its fisheries provide crab, flounder, halibut, herring, mackerel, sardine, salmon, shrimp, and tuna. The catch varies from year to year; in the mid-1960's it exceeded 57,000,000 lb., valued at $7,000,000.

Mining. Oregon has great mineral resources, particularly in the s.w. part. These include sand and gravel, stone, cement, and nickel. In the mid-1960's, according to the latest available statistics, mineral production was valued at $64,000,000 annually, representing less than 1 percent of all U.S. mineral production. In quantity of production, Oregon ranked first in nickel and second in pumice. Mineral production was reported in all counties; the leaders were Douglas, Clackamas, Multnomah, and Lane counties. Major deposits of pumice were located in Deschutes and Gilliam counties, and deposits of nickel in Douglas and Curry counties. Sand and gravel was produced in Multnomah, Lane, Douglas, and Morrow counties; and cement production was reported in Baker, Clackamas, and Jackson counties.

Forestry. Timber industries are among the major industrial activities of Oregon. The State has some 26,500,000 acres of commercial forest land, predominantly softwoods, and a third of it under private ownership. It produces a net annual cut of sawtimber of some 10,750,000 bd.ft.

Transportation. The first railroads in Oregon were the Union Transportation Co. and the Portage Railroad, both inaugurated in 1859 and both now part of the Union Pacific Railroad. In addition to the Union Pacific, the State is served by four other Class 1 railroads, including the Southern Pacific Co., with a total of about 3155 mi. of track. Rural and municipal roads totaled 85,590 mi. in 1967. Highways of the Federally aided Interstate Highway System totaled 734 mi. in 1968; Federally aided primary and secondary roads totaled 12,296 mi. Airports numbered about 180 in the mid-1960's, and seven airlines provided trunk and local service in 1967.

Communications. The first newspaper in Oregon was the *Oregon Spectator*, founded in Oregon City in 1846. The State in 1967 had twenty-one daily newspapers, five Sunday papers, 109 weeklies, and one Negro daily. Among the leading papers were the Portland *Oregonian* and *Oregon Journal* and the Salem *Capital Journal* and *Oregon Statesman*. Of about eighty AM and fifteen FM (six educational) radio stations operating in 1967, among the earliest were KAST in Astoria and KMED in Medford, both established in 1922. Fifteen television stations were in operation, two of which were devoted to educational programming.

GOVERNMENT

Oregon is governed under the constitution of 1859, as amended. Executive authority is vested in a governor, an attorney general, and a secretary of state, all elected for four-year terms, and other elected and appointed officials. Legisla-

193

OREGON

tive authority is exercised by the Senate, with thirty members elected for four-year terms; and the House of Representatives, with sixty members elected for two-year terms. The legislature meets biennially in odd-numbered years. The judicial system includes a seven-member supreme court, circuit courts, and various local and special courts.

Oregon is represented in the United States Congress by two Senators and four Representatives.

Local Government. The State is divided into thirty-six counties, each governed by a three-member, elective county court.

Voting Qualifications. Suffrage is extended generally to U.S. citizens eighteen years of age who have resided six months in the State.

HISTORY

In 1542–43 a Spanish navigator, Bartolomé Ferrelo, sailed from Mexico to a point near southern Oregon. In 1602–03 his exploit was duplicated by another Spanish mariner, Sebastián Vizcaíno (1550?–1615). In the meantime, in 1579, the English navigator Sir Francis Drake (q.v.) sailed along the Pacific coast, possibly as far north as Oregon. Other Spanish explorers made voyages to Oregon coastal waters during the 17th and 18th centuries. In 1775 the Spanish navigator Bruno Heceta sailed to the mouth of the Columbia R. In 1778 the British sea captain James Cook (q.v.) saw the Oregon coast near the mouth of the Alsea R. Within the next decade various British and American vessels frequented the northern Pacific coast. In 1788 occurred the first known landing of white men on the Oregon coast, by seamen of the American vessel *Lady Washington,* commanded by Captain Robert Gray (q.v.). On a second voyage, in 1792, Captain Gray discovered the great river, which he named the Columbia, after his ship; the United States later claimed the entire region drained by the Columbia, basing its claim on Gray's voyage. George Vancouver (q.v.), a British captain, was at this time exploring Puget Sound. Fur traders entered the region in 1793. The immense wilderness, inhabited only by Indian tribes, was explored in 1804–05 by the Americans Meriwether Lewis and William Clark (*see* LEWIS AND CLARK EXPEDITION).

Oregon's Fur Trade. A trading post in the Columbia R. region was established in 1811 by the Pacific Fur Company of John Jacob Astor (*see under* ASTOR) at Astoria. After the declaration of the War of 1812 between Great Britain and the U.S., Astoria was sold to the British North West Company and renamed Fort George.

Negotiations in 1818 led to the establishment of the 49th parallel as the boundary between the U.S. and British possessions as far west as the Rocky Mts.; *see* NORTHWEST BOUNDARY DISPUTE. Because an agreement could not be reached regarding the boundary west of the Rocky Mts. and north of the 42nd parallel, the two countries agreed to a ten-year period of joint occupancy. In 1819 Spain, which also had laid claim to the Oregon country, relinquished its claims to all Pacific coast territory north of the 42nd parallel; and in 1824 and 1825, by treaties with the U.S. and Great Britain, Russia relinquished claim to territory south of the parallel 54°40'. The Anglo-American convention was extended in 1827.

The rich Oregon fur trade was controlled by the British Hudson's Bay Company, which had absorbed the North West Company. During the 1840's organized American immigration to the Oregon territory began, and the "Oregon question" became a matter of concern.

A Question of Sovereignty. By 1843 Americans were demanding that Great Britain relinquish all jurisdiction south of 54°40' latitude; in 1844 the Democratic Party slogan, on which James Knox Polk (q.v.) was elected President of the U.S., was "Fifty-four forty, or fight". At length, in 1846, the two countries agreed, in the Oregon Treaty, on the 49th parallel as the boundary from the Rockies to the coast, and a line along the mid-channel between Vancouver Island and the mainland to the Pacific Ocean. In 1848 Oregon was established as a Territory; as originally established, it covered all the area between the 42nd and 49th parallels, from the Rocky Mts. to the Pacific Ocean, and included present-day Washington and parts of Idaho, Montana, and Wyoming. Many Oregon settlers left for California after the discovery of gold there in 1849, but the depopulation was more than compensated for after the passage by Congress of the Donation Land Act in 1850, giving large tracts of land free to settlers in Oregon. The increase of population and prosperity prompted the settlers to hold a convention in 1857 and request Statehood, which was granted in 1859. Indian rebellions and wars became increasingly serious after the American Civil War (1861–65). The Modoc War (1864–73) and the Shoshone War (1866–68) were marked by fierce battles and widespread destruction. Many Indian engagements were fought in the 1870's, when the tribes were being forced to move to reservations.

Progressive Growth. With the completion of the Union Pacific Railroad in 1869, population and economic activity began to grow in the

Oregon Indians in colorful tribal costumes help get the annual Pendleton Round-Up underway. Held in September, it draws cowboys from throughout the nation for various competitions.   Oregon State Highway Commission

State. In the three decades between 1870 and 1900 the population increased from 90,923 to 413,536. Oregon was among the first States to enact many presently accepted devices of government, such as the initiative and referendum (1902), the direct primary (1904), recall (1908), and woman's suffrage (1912).

In Presidential elections the majority of the Oregon electorate has voted for candidates of the Republican Party, except in the elections of 1868, 1912, 1932, 1936, 1940, 1944, and 1964, when Democratic candidates received the majority of votes cast in the State. In 1968 Oregon gave the Republican candidate, Richard M. Nixon (q.v.), 408,433 votes and the Democratic candidate, Hubert H. Humphrey (q.v.), 358,865 votes.   F.D.H.

OREGON, former name of a river of the United States. *See* COLUMBIA.

OREGON CAVES NATIONAL MONUMENT, area of natural interest in Josephine County, S.W. Oregon, in the Siskiyou Mts., about 6 miles N. of the California boundary. The monument contains a group of limestone caverns noted for their beautiful rock formations. The most famous of the caves is Paradise Lost, a chamber 60 ft. in height, with stalactites in the shape of flowers. The monument, covering 480 acres, was established in 1909. It is administered by the National Park Service (q.v.).

OREGON GRAPE, common name applied to an evergreen shrub, *Mahonia aquifolium*, belonging to the Barberry family. The shrub, which is native to western North America, is the State flower of Oregon. It grows to a height of more than 3 ft., and bears large, glossy, pinnate leaves with spiny, dark-green leaflets. The yellow flowers, which are borne in racemes, have nine sepals, six petals, six stamens, and a solitary pistil. The fruit is an attractive, bluish-black berry. The plant is cultivated as a hedge shrub in the United States.

OREGON QUESTION. *See* NORTHWEST BOUNDARY DISPUTE; OREGON: *History*.

OREGON TRAIL, overland pioneer route to the northwestern United States. About 2000 mi. long, the trail extended from Independence, Mo., to the Columbia R. in Oregon. The first part of the route followed the Platte R. for 540 mi. through what is now Nebraska to Fort Laramie in present-day Wyoming. The trail continued along the North Platte and Sweetwater rivers to South Pass in the Wind River Range of the Rocky Mts. From there the main trail went south to Fort Bridger, Wyo., before turning into the Bear R. valley and north to Fort Hall in present-day Idaho. A more direct route from the South Pass to the Bear R. was Sublette's Cutoff, which was fifty-three mi. shorter but more arid than the main trail. In Idaho the Oregon Trail followed the Snake R. to the Salmon Falls and then went north past Fort Boise (now Boise). The route entered what is now Oregon, passed through the Grande Ronde R. valley, crossed the Blue Mts., and followed the Umatilla R. to the Columbia R.

Originally, like many of the main roads of the country, sections of the Oregon Trail had been crossed by the Indians and trappers. As early as 1742–43, part of the trail in Wyoming had been

OREL

blazed by the Canadian explorer Pierre Gaultier de Varennes, Sieur de la Vérendrye (q.v.); the Lewis and Clark Expedition (q.v.), undertaken between 1804 and 1806, made more of it known. The German-American fur trader and financier John Jacob Astor (*see under* ASTOR), in establishing his trading posts, dispatched a party overland in 1811-12 to follow in the trail of these explorers. Later, mountain men such as the American explorer James Bridger (q.v.), who founded Fort Bridger, in 1843, contributed their knowledge of the trail, and often acted as guides. The first emigrant wagon train, headed by the American pioneer-physician Elijah White (1806-79), reached Oregon in 1842. The trip took the early pioneers some five or six months, a journey fraught with much hardship resulting from poor equipment, illness, and attack by the Indians, for whom the growing number of pioneers on the trail was an ever-constant threat. At first, the termination point of the Oregon Trail was Astoria, Oreg.; later, it was extended into southern Oregon to the fertile and valuable land in the Willamette Valley.

OREL, city of the Soviet Union, in the Russian S.S.R., and capital of Orel Oblast, on the Oka R., 222 miles S.W. of Moscow. The city is a road and railroad junction and a center of agricultural trade. Engineering, including the manufacture of machinery and tools, is the most important industry. Brewing, shoemaking, flour milling, and meat packing are other industries. The city was founded in the 16th century. Orel was the birthplace of the 19th-century Russian novelist Ivan Sergeevich Turgenev (q.v.), and his house is now a museum. Pop. (1970) 232,000.

ORELLANA, Francisco de (1500?-45), Spanish explorer and soldier, born in Trujillo. He went to Peru in 1535. In 1540 he accompanied the Spanish explorer Gonzalo Pizarro (q.v.) as second in command on an expedition across the Andes Mts. into the country to the east, which was reported to abound in gold, silver, and cinnamon. After many misfortunes the expedition reached the Napo R. The supplies being exhausted, Orellana was ordered in 1541 to sail down the Napo R. with fifty men in search of provisions and signs of treasure. He descended the stream to its junction with the Amazon River (q.v.), in present-day northeastern Peru, but instead of returning proceeded down the river to the Atlantic Ocean. The voyage to the mouth of the Amazon lasted nearly eight months. From the mouth of the river he sailed to Spain, relating descriptions of a marvelous race of female warriors whom he named after the classical Amazons (q.v.). Orellana was granted permission by the Spanish government to explore the land he had discovered and set forth in 1544 with an expedition. He died in the new territory within a year.

OREM, city of Utah, in Utah Co., about 7 miles N. of Provo. The city is a canning center for the surrounding irrigated agricultural area. Steel is produced nearby. Pop. (1960) 18,394; (1970) 25,729.

ORENBURG, formerly CHKALOV, city of the Soviet Union, in the Russian S.F.S.R., and capital of Orenburg Oblast, on the Ural R. at its confluence with the Sakmara R., about 400 miles S. of Perm'. An important industrial center, Orenburg contains railway repair shops, petroleum refineries, and factories for the production of machinery, metal goods, textiles, leather goods, and processed foods. The city derived its name of Orenburg from an earlier settlement that had occupied a site at which the Ural joined the Or R. It was established at its present site in 1743. During the revolution of 1917 the city was the scene of considerable fighting. In 1938 the name of the city was changed to Chkalov in honor of Valeriy Chkalov (1904-1938), an aviator who made a nonstop flight from Moscow to Vancouver, Wash., in 1937. The name of the city was changed back to Orenburg in 1957. Pop. (1970) 345,000.

ORENSE, city of Spain, in the region of Galicia, and capital of Orense Province, on the Mino R., about 80 miles S.E. of La Coruña. The city, at the center of an agricultural region, has some light industry. The hot sulfurous springs have been used since Roman times. Orense has a handsome bridge and a Gothic cathedral, both dating from the 13th century. The city reached its peak as capital of the Suevi (q.v.) kingdom in the 6th and 7th centuries. Pop. (1966) 71,768.

ORESTES, in Greek mythology, son of Agamemnon, King of Mycenae, and Clytemnestra (qq.v.). He was still a boy when his mother and her lover Aegisthus (q.v.) murdered Agamemnon. Orestes' older sister, Electra (q.v.), fearing for the boy's life, sent him to live with their uncle, Strophius, King of Phocis. There he grew up with Pylades, son of Strophius, who became his lifelong companion. When he reached maturity Orestes realized that he had a sacred duty to avenge the death of his father, but the crime of matricide was abhorrent to him. He consulted the oracle at Delphi (q.v.) and was advised to kill the two who had murdered his father. With Pylades he returned to Mycenae and avenged Agamemnon's death. Pursued by the avenging goddesses the Erinyes (q.v.), Orestes wandered through many lands. Finally, at the command of the god Apollo, he went to Athens to plead his cause before the goddess Athena (qq.v.) and a council of nobles, the Areopagus (q.v.). Orestes declared himself guilty of matricide, but stated that he had been cleansed of guilt through suffering. The court, accepting the plea, acquitted Orestes.

According to the dramas of the Greek playwright Euripides (q.v.), some of the Erinyes refused to accept the verdict and continued to pursue Orestes. In despair he again consulted the Delphic oracle. He was advised to go to the land of the Taurians (modern Crimea) and steal the sacred image of Artemis (q.v.) from the temple of the goddess. With Pylades he went to the temple and discovered that the priestess was his sister Iphigenia (q.v.), whom he had thought to be dead. With her help they stole the sacred statue and returned with it to Mycenae. Thereafter the Erinyes let Orestes live in peace. See ATREUS, HOUSE OF.

ØRESUND, ("the sound"), strait connecting the strait of Kattegat on the N. with the Baltic Sea on the S., and separating Sweden on the E. from the Danish island of Sjaelland on the W. Øresund forms part of the usual shipping passage between the North and Baltic seas. It is 65 mi. long, varies in width from about 30 mi. to 2½ mi., and has a minimum depth of 23 ft. The most important seaports on the strait are Copenhagen, Denmark, and Malmö, Sweden.

ORGAN, musical instrument in which compressed air is directed into tuned pipes to produce sound. The mechanism of the organ consists of three parts: the sound-producing apparatus, which includes the pipes; the wind supply; and the controls, which include one or more keyboards.

The Pipes. Organ pipes are made of various woods and metals and in various sizes and shapes. They can produce many tone qualities in a wide range of pitches. The high- to low-sounding pipes that produce the same tone quality are grouped in a set called a rank or a stop. In churches and auditoriums, a few ranks of pipes are usually arranged in a decorative pattern and exposed to view.

Two kinds of pipes are used: the flue and the reed type. A flue pipe operates like an ordinary whistle. Air enters from the bottom and begins to vibrate as it passes over the edge of an opening in the side of the pipe. This vibration causes all the air in the pipe to vibrate, producing a musical tone. Some flue pipes, especially those made of wood, have a flutelike quality. Others produce tones somewhat similar to those of string instruments. Many differences in tone quality can be achieved through differences in construction; for example, the top of the pipe may be either open or stopped, and the sides may be either straight or tapered.

A reed pipe consists of a small flattened metal tube containing a metal tongue; this tube is connected to a large pipe called a resonator. The musical tone is produced when air enters the first tube and causes the tongue to vibrate, leading to further vibrations in the air column of the resonator. Many reed tones are somewhat similar to the tones of such wind instruments as the trumpet, trombone, clarinet, and bassoon.

One of the characteristics of organ pipes is the production of a steady tone with no changes in volume. To make the music louder or softer, the player must add pipes to those already sounding or cut off the air flow to some of the sounding pipes. This procedure does not permit smooth changes from loud to soft; furthermore, adding or subtracting pipes always alters the tone quality to some extent. To allow for gradual changes, some ranks of pipes in a modern organ are placed in a chamber, called a swell box, which has an opening covered by slats as in a Venetian blind. A continuous change from loud to soft can be made by opening and closing the slats.

Wind Supply. The wind for a rank of organ pipes is supplied from a closed box, called a

This modern organ, designed and built in Holland, is based on the principles of the European baroque organs of three centuries ago. British-born organist E. Power Biggs (1906–), well known for his interpretation of Johann Sebastian Bach's organ pieces, is shown at an organ of Harvard University.

ORGAN

wind chest, on which the pipes are mounted and which is usually hidden from view. Air enters the wind chest at a constant pressure (about 1½–2 ounces per square inch).

Controls. In small organs the pipes, wind supply, and controls are contained in the same unit. Controls for larger organs are usually grouped in a separate unit called a console. The console of a modern organ contains one or more keyboards, sometimes as many as seven, as well as a pedal keyboard placed under the others. Another important part of the control system contains the rows of knobs or switches called stops; they are placed between the keyboards and on panels extending above and to the sides. The organist uses a stop knob to bring a particular rank of pipes under the control of a particular keyboard. When he has several keyboards he can easily control many different ranks of pipes. An echo, or antiphonal, organ at the back of an auditorium may be linked to one keyboard, several ranks of unenclosed pipes to another, and several ranks of pipes in a swell box to yet another. Because no standard specifications exist for the design and arrangement of pipes and controls, each pipe organ is unique. Thus, an organist must study each organ he plays and experiment with the various combinations of tone qualities it can produce.

History. The earliest type of organ was the hydraulis, first developed by the Greek inventor Ctesibius (300?–250? B.C.). The wind mechanism of the hydraulis consisted of a large container partially filled with water. Air was pumped into the container, pushing against the water until the pressure was great enough to cause some of the air to escape through valves and into a wind chest. The hydraulis was used in ancient Rome and at least until the 13th century of the Christian era. During the 10th century a hydraulis was built in Winchester, England, with 400 pipes and four keyboards played by two organists. Seventy men were needed to work the bellows that supplied air to the wind chests. The sound was clangorous and unpleasant, because the tone quality was produced by all the ranks of pipes in the instrument. No way had yet been found to engage certain individual ranks and leave others silent.

During the 14th century smaller organs with a delicate tone quality were developed. The smallest instruments, called portative organs or, in Italy, *organetti,* could be carried from room to room or in processions. Somewhat larger, nonportable instruments, called positive organs, were also developed. By the 15th century pedal keyboards were in use, and a stop mechanism had been developed, enabling the player to engage individual ranks of pipes. Often, however, the stop mechanism was so cumbersome that a second player was needed to operate it.

During the 17th and 18th centuries the tone qualities of organ pipes were greatly refined. Organ builders began to construct instruments in which the individual ranks could be either sharply contrasted or sounded together harmoniously. This development enabled organists to give each voice-part of a polyphonic composition its own tone color, thereby clarifying the complexities of music by such composers as the German organist Johann Sebastian Bach (*see under* BACH).

The stop mechanism of 18th-century organs remained fairly cumbersome, largely because music of the time did not call for complex changes in tone color during the course of a piece. During the 19th and early 20th centuries, organ builders attempted to duplicate the instrumental qualities and dynamic range of an orchestra. With the application of electricity to the stop mechanism, organs became larger and increasingly complex.

Among notable 19th-century composers for the organ were the Hungarian Franz Liszt, the German Felix Mendelssohn, and the French composer Camille Saint-Säens (qq.v.). The latter, in his Symphony No. 3 in C, the "Organ Symphony", used the organ as part of a large orchestral ensemble.

Electronic Organs. In many modern organs the sound is produced not by pipes but by such electronic devices as vacuum tubes (q.v.). Although most electronic organs have been designed to duplicate the tone qualities of a pipe organ, such instruments are frequently criticized for their pinched and artificial sound. During the late 1960's, however, the particular tone quality of electronic organs became important in a type of popular music known as "rock". The reason for the importance lies in the nature of rock bands, which make extensive use of electrical amplification. Within a context of electrically modified sound, the distinctive qualities of the electronic organ become both appropriate and desirable.

Reed Organs. Keyboard instruments in which the wind supply is directed toward free metal reeds are called reed organs. One of the most popular types of reed organ is the melodeon, developed in the United States about 1825. Another type, the harmonium, was developed in Germany about 1810. J.V.

ORGANIC CHEMISTRY. See CHEMISTRY: *Major Divisions of Chemistry: Organic Chemistry.*

ORGANIZATION OF AMERICAN STATES

ORGANIZATION FOR ECONOMIC COOPERATION AND DEVELOPMENT, known as O.E.C.D., international body comprised of twenty-one countries, eighteen of which are in Europe, participating in a permanent cooperation designed to harmonize the policies of the member nations. The O.E.C.D. makes available all information relevant to the formulation of national policy in every major field of economic activity. Its principal goals are: (1) to promote employment, economic growth, and a rising standard of living in member countries, while maintaining stability; (2) to contribute to sound economic expansion of both member and nonmember nations in the process of development; and (3) to further the expansion of world trade on a multilateral, nondiscriminatory basis in accord with international obligations. Policies are formulated and ideas shared at meetings held throughout the year.

This form of cooperation, rooted in the growing interdependence of national economies, began on April 16, 1948, when a group of sixteen European countries founded the Organization for European Economic Cooperation (O.E.E.C.) to allocate aid under the European Recovery Program (q.v.) and to work together for postwar recovery. The O.E.C.D., succeeding the O.E.E.C., was established on Sept. 30, 1961, in order to broaden the scope of cooperation.

The twenty nations that signed the Convention of the O.E.C.D. on Dec. 14, 1960, were Austria, Belgium, Canada, Denmark, France, Great Britain, Greece, Iceland, Ireland, Italy, Luxembourg, the Netherlands, Norway, Portugal, Spain, Sweden, Switzerland, Turkey, the United States, and West Germany. Japan, the twenty-first country to join, became a full member on April 28, 1964. Yugoslavia, although not a full member, takes part on an equal basis with member countries in some of the O.E.C.D. activities and is an observer at others. Finland, which earlier sent observers to certain O.E.C.D. meetings, became a full member in 1969.

ORGANIZATION OF AFRICAN UNITY (Fr. *Organisation de l'Unité Africaine*), pan-African regional organization, often referred to as O.A.U. Its purposes are to promote African unity and solidarity, to coordinate political, economic, cultural, health, scientific and defense policies, to develop a better life for the peoples of Africa, to defend the independence and territorial integrity of member nations, and to eliminate colonialism on the continent. The assembly, consisting of heads of state of the member nations or their representatives, is the policy-making body of the organization. Decisions made in periodic conferences of foreign ministers are subject to approval by the assembly. Peace-keeping efforts are made through the Commission of Mediation, Counciliation, and Arbitration and through ad hoc committees. The commission attempted without success to deal with two of the most disruptive African civil wars in recent years, those in the Republic of Zaire and Nigeria (qq.v.). Financial and other support for African peoples and governments opposing colonial rule is channeled through a so-called liberation committee. Technical research in improved methods of agriculture is conducted through a scientific and research commission.

The O.A.U. was founded in 1963 by thirty independent African nations at a conference in Addis Ababa called by the emperor of Ethiopia Haile Selassie (q.v.). Forty-one African nations were members in 1972. Not members are the Republic of South Africa, which was excluded because of its racial policies, Rhodesia, and the Spanish and Portuguese overseas territories or possessions.

ORGANIZATION OF AMERICAN STATES, known as O.A.S., regional alliance comprising the United States and twenty-four nations of Latin America. It was established April 30, 1948, by twenty-one nations at the ninth of the Inter-American Conferences (q.v.), held at Bogotá, Colombia. The organization is an outgrowth of the International Union of American Republics, created in 1890 at the First International Conference of American States, held in Washington, D.C. The Pan American Union (q.v.), which became the most important organ of the earlier organization, is now the general secretariat of the O.A.S., with headquarters in Washington.

The basic purposes of the O.A.S., as described in the charter, are "(1) to strengthen the peace and security of the continent; (2) to prevent possible causes of difficulties and to ensure the pacific settlement of disputes that may arise among the Member States; (3) to provide for common action on the part of those States in the event of aggression; (4) to seek the solution of political, juridical, and economic problems that may arise among them; and (5) to promote, by cooperative action, their economic, social, and cultural development".

Within two decades after its adoption the charter of the O.A.S. proved to be too limited in scope and structure to deal effectively with pressing socioeconomic problems arising from change and growth in the Western Hemisphere. In order to strengthen the structure of the organization the Protocol of Amendment to the

ORGAN PIPE CACTUS NATIONAL MONUMENT

Charter of the O.A.S., known as the Protocol of Buenos Aires, was signed on Feb. 27, 1967. The amendments become effective upon ratification of the protocol by two thirds of the member nations (twelve states of the sixteen needed had ratified the amendments by 1970). The most important amendments are designed to raise living standards, to ensure social justice, and to achieve economic development and integration among the nations of the Western Hemisphere.

Under the amendments the O.A.S. will function through eight major organs, replacing the six organs of the original charter. They are: (1) the General Assembly, which will meet annually (replacing the Inter-American Conference); (2) the Meeting of Consultation of Ministers of Foreign Affairs; (3) the councils of the organization (the Permanent Council, the Inter-American Economic and Social Council, and the Inter-American Council for Education, Science, and Culture); (4) the Inter-American Juridical Committee; (5) the Inter-American Commission on Human Rights; (6) the General Secretariat; (7) the specialized conferences, called to deal with specific instances of international cooperation or technical problems; and (8) the specialized organizations, established among member nations to deal with specific needs in specific areas, such as health, history and geography, or problems of children.

The twenty-four member nations of the O.A.S. are Argentina, Barbados (admitted in 1967), Bolivia, Brazil, Chile, Colombia, Costa Rica, Cuba, the Dominican Republic, Ecuador, El Salvador, Guatemala, Haiti, Honduras, Jamaica (admitted in 1969), Mexico, Nicaragua, Panama, Paraguay, Peru, Trinidad and Tobago (admitted in 1967), Uruguay, and Venezuela, as well as the U.S. The Communist-oriented government of Cuba, however, has been excluded from active participation. Each member nation shares the expenses of the O.A.S. in proportion to its contribution to the United Nations.

See also ALLIANCE FOR PROGRESS and articles listed under INTER-AMERICAN.

ORGAN PIPE CACTUS NATIONAL MONUMENT, region of natural interest in s.w. Arizona, on the Mexican border, preserving several rare forms of flora and fauna. The monument was named for the organ-pipe cactus, or *Pachycereus marginatus,* the second-largest species of cactus native to the United States, which grows in abundance here. Also found in this arid desert region are the giant saguaro cactus, *Carnegiea gigantea,* which reaches a height of 60 ft. or more, the mesquite (q.v.) and ocotillo trees, and the poisonous lizard known as the Gila monster (q.v.). The monument, covering 330,874.25 acres, was established in 1937. It is administered by the National Park Service (q.v.).

ORIGANUM. See MARJORAM.

ORIGEN, or ORIGENES, surnamed ADAMANTIUS (185?–254? A.D.), celebrated Christian writer, teacher, and theologian of antiquity, born in Alexandria, Egypt, of Christian parents. His father, Leonides (d. 202), suffered a martyr's death during the persecutions under Roman Emperor Lucius Septimius Severus (q.v.). Origen studied with the Greek theologian Clement of Alexandria (q.v.) and at the age of eighteen was appointed to succeed Clement as head of the Alexandrian catechetical school. He taught both pagans and Christians in his popular classes at Alexandria for about twenty-eight years. During this period he composed the chief of his dogmatic treatises (*see* DOGMA) and began his many works of textual and exegetical criticism; *see* BIBLE, INTERPRETATIONS OF THE; BIBLE SCHOLARSHIP: *Textual Criticism.* His labors were occasionally interrupted by journeys to Rome, Arabia, Antioch (now Antâkya, Turkey), Greece, and Palestine.

Career. Visiting in Palestine in 216 Origen, a layman, had been invited by the bishop of Jerusalem and the bishop of Caesarea (q.v.) to lecture in the churches on the Scriptures. About 230 A.D. the same bishops ordained him a presbyter without consulting Origen's own bishop, Demetrius of Alexandria (126–231). Out of personal jealousy and for other reasons, Demetrius had long been hostile to Origen, and these events heightened his antagonism. By the decision of a synod (*see* COUNCIL) held at Alexandria under Demetrius, Origen was forbidden to teach in that city. A second Alexandrian synod, consisting of bishops only, deprived him of the office of presbyter. This decision was based on opposition to certain of Origen's doctrinal teachings and practices. The churches of Palestine, Phoenicia, Arabia, and Achaea (an ancient district of Greece) declined to concur in the sentence.

Origen then (about 232 A.D.) settled at Caesarea, his home for the next twenty years. He founded there a school of literature, philosophy, and theology. During the persecutions (250) of the Christians under Emperor Decius (q.v.), Origen was imprisoned and tortured. He was released on the death of the emperor in 251, but, weakened by his injuries, he died about three years later.

Writings. Origen was probably the most accomplished Biblical scholar of the early Church. He was a voluminous writer, the total of his works being estimated at 6000. These works included letters, treatises in dogmatic and practical theology, apologetics, exegeses, and textual criticism. Among the writings that have survived is a long apologetic work, *Contre Celsum* ("Against Celsus"), considered the most important Greek apology extant. Another notable work is a theological treatise preserved, in a somewhat altered form, in a Latin version made by the Roman theologian Tyrannius Rufinus (345?–410) in the 4th century A.D. under the title *De Principiis* (Lat., "On First Principles"). Origen's accomplishments as an exegete and student of the text of the Old Testament were outstanding. The exegetical works have been preserved mostly in Latin translations. In his Hexapla, Origen presented the Old Testament in the original Hebrew, a Greek transliteration of it, and four previously translated Greek versions of the Septuagint, all arranged in six parallel columns; this arrangement provided the title of the work, from the Greek for "six". A large portion of the Hexapla was preserved in the numerous excerpts made by scholars of the 4th century.

Evaluation. Origen is regarded as the father of the allegorical method of scriptural interpretation. He taught the principle of the threefold sense, corresponding to the threefold division of man into body, spirit, and soul (q.v.), which was then a common concept. Like his teacher Clement, Origen was a Platonist (*see* PLATO) and endeavored to combine Greek philosophy and the Christian religion. He developed the idea of Christ (*see* JESUS CHRIST) as the Logos, or Incarnate Word, who is with the Father from eternity, but he taught also that the Son was subordinate to the Father in power and dignity; *see* CHRISTOLOGY; TRINITY. This latter doctrine and others, such as that of the preexistence of the soul, were severely criticized by many of his contemporaries and by later writers. Origen's disciples and followers were long regarded as heretics, and theories developed from his doctrines became the subject of considerable theological controversy during the Middle Ages; *see* HERESY.

ORIGINAL SIN, in Christian doctrine, first sin (q.v.) committed by Adam (*see* ADAM AND EVE) as related to or manifested in its consequences to his posterity, the human race. *See* AUGUSTINE, SAINT; EVIL, ORIGIN OF.

ORINOCO, one of the longest rivers of South America, about 1700 mi. long. The source of the Orinoco is in the Guiana Highlands, on the slopes of the Sierra Parima, in extreme S.E. Venezuela, on the border of Brazil. It flows N.W. to a point about 25 miles E. of La Esmeralda where it divides. One arm, the Brazo Casiquiare R., goes S. and after a course of 180 mi. enters the Río Negro, a tributary of the Amazon R. The main branch continues N.W. to the town of San Fernando de Atabapo, where it receives the Guaviare R. and flowing generally N., forms the border between Venezuela and Colombia. After passing over the Maipures and Atures rapids and receiving the Meta R. on the left, it meets the Apure R. The Orinoco R. then turns N.E. and traverses the llanos or plains of Venezuela before emptying into the Atlantic Ocean. Its waters, an average of 4 mi. wide, are augmented from the right by several rivers, including the Caura and the Caroní. The delta of the river, with an area of 8000 sq.mi., begins about 120 mi. from the Atlantic. The total area of the drainage basin is approximately 450,000 sq.mi. The Orinoco is navigable for ocean-going ships for 260 mi., from the mouth to the city of Ciudad Bolívar, the major commercial and communications center for the drainage basin. It is navigable for smaller craft for a distance of about 1000 mi.

The Orinoco was sighted in 1498 by the Italian navigator Christopher Columbus (q.v.), and was first explored in 1530–31 to the confluence with the Meta R. Members of an expedition led by the American physician and explorer Herbert Spencer Dickey (1876–1948) claimed to have reached the headwaters of the Orinoco in 1931. Several Brazilian and Venezuelan expeditions made in 1944 and in the 1950's further penetrated the region to the site that is now accepted as the headwaters of the Orinoco.

ORIOLE, common name applied to approximately thirty-four species of passerine birds of the family Oriolidae, especially those in the genus *Oriolus*, confined entirely to the Old World. The members of the family are generally of a bright-yellow or golden color, which is set off by the black of the wings. Thirty-one species are enumerated under the genus. The best known is the golden oriole, *O. oriolus*. The adult male is about 9 in. long and in general color is a rich golden yellow. The bill is dull orange red with a black streak reaching from its base to the eye, the iris of which is blood red. The wings are black, with markings and a conspicuous wing spot of yellow. The two middle feathers of the tail are black, shaded to olive at the base, the very tips yellow, the basal half of the others black, the distal half yellow. The legs, feet, and claws are dark brown. In certain areas of central and southern Europe the bird is common in summer; it is common in Iran, and ranges through central Asia as far as to Irkutsk, in southern Soviet Union. It winters in South Af-

Golden oriole, Oriolus oriolus

Eric Hosking – National Audubon Society

rica. The orioles of North America belong to the family Icteridae, commonly known as Blackbird family (*see* BLACKBIRD), which includes the Baltimore oriole; *see* BALTIMORE BIRD.

ORION, constellation located on the celestial equator east of Taurus (q.v.). It is an oblong configuration with three stars in line near its center. It is represented on pictorial charts as the figure of Orion (q.v.), the hunter in Greek mythology, standing with uplifted club. Three bright stars represent his belt and three fainter stars aligned south of the belt represent his sword. Alpha (α) Orionis, or Betelgeuse (q.v.) is located in the left corner of the oblong, corresponding to Orion's shoulder. Beta (β) Orionis, or Rigel, is diagonally opposite Betelgeuse. A nebula (q.v.) surrounding the three stars marking Orion's sword is one of the most conspicuous bright nebulae in the heavens.

ORION, in Greek mythology, handsome giant and mighty hunter, the son of Poseidon (q.v.), god of the sea, and of Euryale, the Gorgon (q.v.). Orion fell in love with Merope, the daughter of Oenopion, King of Chios, and sought her in marriage. He cleared her father's island kingdom of wild beasts, and brought the spoils of the chase as presents to his beloved. Oenopion, however, constantly deferred his consent to the marriage, and Orion attempted to gain possession of the maiden by violence. Incensed at his behavior, her father, with the aid of the god Dionysus (q.v.), threw him into a deep sleep and blinded him. Orion then consulted an oracle, who told him he could regain his sight by going to the east and letting the rays of the rising sun fall on his eyes. Orion followed this advice, going as far east as Lemnos, where his sight was restored. Determining to punish Oenopion, he went back to Chios. The king had fled, however, so Orion went on to Crete. There he lived for a while as the huntsman of the goddess Artemis (q.v.). The goddess eventually killed him, either because she was jealous of his affection for Aurora, goddess of the dawn, or because she was tricked into slaying him by her brother Apollo (q.v.). After Orion's death, Artemis made him a constellation, which shows him with a girdle of three stars, wearing the skin of a lion, and carrying a club.

ORISKANY, BATTLE OF, military engagement of the American Revolution (q.v.). It was fought near Oriskany, N.Y., on Aug. 6, 1777, between a force of Loyalists led by the British colonial administrator Sir John Johnson (1742–1830) and the Mohawk Indian chief Joseph Brant (q.v.) both under the command of British officer Barry St. Leger (1737–89), on the one hand, and Americans under General Nicholas Herkimer (q.v.) on the other. General Herkimer was mortally wounded in the battle, and more than a third of the forces on each side were killed or wounded. The British were forced to retreat thus ending hopes for a British victory at Saratoga. A monument erected in 1880 marks the site of the battleground, which is now a public park.

ORISSA, State of the Republic of India, bordered on the N. by Bihar State and West Bengal State, on the E. by the Bay of Bengal, on the S. by Andhra Pradesh State, and on the W. by Madhya Pradesh State. The 200-mi. long coastline is largely smooth and unindented and lacks good ports. The coastal strip is narrow, level, and extremely fertile. Most of the population is engaged in raising rice. Other agricultural products are pulses, cotton, tobacco, sugarcane, and turmeric. Among the livestock raised are buffalo and other cattle, sheep, and goats. The State has a large export trade in fish. Industries include the production of pig iron and steel, the manufacture of textiles, cement, paper, glass, aluminum, flour, and soap, and the processing of sugar and oil. Cottage industries, or homemade crafts, in the State include handloom weaving and the making of baskets, wooden articles, hats, nets, and silver filigree works. The capital of Orissa is Bhubaneswar.

Orissa came under British control in 1803. In 1912 it was united as a province with Bihar, but it became a separate province in 1936. In 1949 it became a State, with the addition of some small native States. The boundaries were unchanged with the States Reorganization Act of 1956.

Area, 60,164 sq.mi.; pop. (1965 est.) 19,300,000.

ORIZABA. *See* CITALTÉPETL.

ORIZABA, city of Mexico, in Veracruz State, 68 miles s.w. of Veracruz City. It lies in a fertile garden region of sugar plantations, 4030 ft. above the sea. It is a tourist resort and an industrial city, containing textile mills, breweries, and sugar refineries. Pop. (1969 est.) 100,000.

ORKNEY ISLANDS, Great Britain, group of islands, islets, and skerries of Scotland, comprising the county of Orkney, separated from the mainland of Scotland by the Pentland Firth. Fewer than thirty of the islands are inhabited. All together the Orkney Islands have a coastline of some 600 mi. and an aggregate area of 376 sq.mi.; the largest of the islands are Pomona or Mainland, Hoy, Sanday, Westray, South Ronaldsay, Rousay, Stronsay, Eday, and Shapinsay. The surface is generally low and treeless. The mean annual temperature is 45°, the rainfall 34.3 in. Agriculture and fishing are the principal industries. Kirkwall, the capital (on Pomona), and Stromness are the only towns. The standing stones of Stenness and the prehistoric chambered burial mound of Maeshowe are the chief places of interest. Pop. (1967 est.) 17,878.

ORLANDO, city in Florida, and county seat of Orange Co., 125 miles s. of Jacksonville. It is the largest inland city of Florida, a noted winter resort, and the center and shipping point of an agricultural area producing citrus fruits and vegetables. Among the industrial establishments in the city are extensive fruit and vegetable packing and canning plants. In the vicinity are Orlando Air Force Base and Cape Kennedy. Within the city are numerous freshwater lakes, and the surrounding region contains a total of 1000 lakes. Orlando contains many parks, noted for their semitropical foliage and flowers; the city is the site of Orlando Junior College (1941). Rollins College, established in 1885, is at Winter Park, 5 miles N.E. of the city. Also nearby is Walt Disney World, a vast amusement park. Orlando was settled in 1843 and incorporated in 1875. Pop. (1960) 88,135; (1970) 99,006.

ORLANDO, Vittorio Emanuele (1860–1952), Italian statesman, born in Palermo, and educated at the University of Palermo. He served as minister of education from 1903 to 1905, minister of justice from 1907 to 1909 and again from 1914 to 1916, and minister of the interior from 1916 to 1917. He favored the entry of Italy into World War I on the side of the Allies and in 1917 was elected prime minister. Orlando headed the Italian delegation to the Paris Peace Conference in 1919. His failure to obtain the territorial concessions that had been secretly promised to Italy by the Allies in 1915 under the Treaty of London caused the downfall of his ministry in June, 1919. Six months later he was elected president of the chamber of deputies. He was at first a supporter of the fascist government established by the Italian dictator Benito Mussolini (q.v.) in 1922, but after the slaying of the Socialist leader Giacomo Matteotti (1885–1924) by the fascists in 1925 he withdrew his support (*see* FASCISM). Three years later Orlando resigned from the chamber. From 1944 to 1946 he was again president of the chamber of deputies and served thereafter in the constituent assembly. Orlando's writings include more than 100 works on juridical subjects.

ORLÉANS, city in France, and capital of Loire Department, on the Loire R., 77 miles s.w. of Paris. It is a road, rail, and commercial center. Important industries include the processing of foodstuffs and the manufacture of textiles and farm machinery. Public edifices include a cathedral that was destroyed by the French Protestants, or Huguenots (q.v.), in 1567, and rebuilt by Henry IV (q.v.), King of France, and his successors; and various Renaissance structures including a fine-arts museum. These buildings and the rich history of Orléans combine to make the city a popular tourist resort.

Orléans Cathedral, Orléans, France, as seen during the 1920's. The cathedral was rebuilt by King Henry IV and his successors, beginning in 1601, after its destruction at the hands of the Huguenots in 1567.

ORLÉANS

Orléans is on the site of Cenabum, the Gallic town burned in 52 B.C. by the Roman statesman and general Gaius Julius Caesar (q.v.) to avenge the murder of Roman traders. It was rebuilt by the Roman emperor Lucius Domitius Aurelian (q.v.) and named Aurelianum, whence its modern name. In the 6th and early 7th centuries Orléans was the capital of the Frankish kingdom, after which it became a favored residence of the kings of France. In 1428–29 the city was besieged by the English during the Hundred Years War (q.v.), but was liberated by the French heroine Joan of Arc (q.v.), called therefore the Maid of Orléans. The town was the headquarters for the Huguenots (q.v.) during their wars. In the Franco-German War it was occupied by the Germans in 1870, and during World War II much damaged by bombings. Pop. (1968) 100,134.

ORLÉANS, name of a cadet or younger branch of the Valois and Bourbon (qq.v.) dynastic houses of France. The name was derived from the Duchy of Orléans surrounding the city of Orléans. In 1344 the Valois king Philip VI (q.v.) created the title duc d'Orléans for his son Philippe (1336–75) who died without issue. Louis I, Duc d'Orléans (1372–1407), was given the title in 1392 by his brother Charles VI, King of France (see under CHARLES). Louis was subsequently assassinated by John, Duke of Burgundy (1371–1419); the murder touched off a civil war between the Burgundy and Orléans houses. Louis was succeeded in the dukedom by his son Charles d'Orléans (see below), and in 1498 by his grandson Louis, who became king as Louis XII (q.v.), whereupon the title reverted to the crown. Subsequent Valois dukes included Charles d'Orléans (1522–45), a son of King Francis I (q.v.). The Valois dynasty ended in 1589; it was succeeded by the Bourbon house which in 1626 revived the title.

In that year King Louis XIII (q.v.) recreated the title for his brother Gaston Jean Baptiste d'Orléans (see below); upon Gaston's death the title passed to Louis' son Philippe I, Duc d'Orléans (1640–1701), who is regarded as the founder of the Bourbon-Orléans House. Philippe's son Philippe II (see below) became duke in 1701; he was succeeded as duke in 1723 by his son Louis (1703–52), in 1752 by his grandson Louis Philippe d'Orléans (1725–85), and in 1785 by his great-grandson Louis Philippe Joseph d'Orléans (see below). A lineal descendent Louis Philippe Albert d'Orléans, Comte de Paris (1838–94); inherited but did not bear the title. The latter's son Louis Philippe Robert (1869–1926) assumed the title in 1894 as a pretender to the throne.

Charles d'Orléans (1391–1465). He commanded at the Battle of Agincourt (q.v.) in 1415, but was taken prisoner and carried to England, where he employed himself in hunting and writing verses. He was ransomed in 1440 and was returned to France.

Gaston Jean Baptiste d'Orléans (1608–60). He troubled France with incessant and bloody, but fruitless, intrigues against the French cardinal and statesman Duc de Richelieu (q.v.). During the minority of Louis XIV (q.v.) he placed himself at the head of the Fronde, the movement in opposition to the administration of the French cardinal and statesman Jules Mazarin (q.v.), but soon betrayed his friends and came to terms with the court. After Mazarin's final triumph, Orléans was confined to his castle at Blois.

Philippe II d'Orléans (1674–1723). He became regent of France on the death (1715) of Louis XIV (q.v.), King of France. The chief events of his regency are the Quadruple Alliance (q.v.) of 1719 and the downfall of the Spanish cardinal and statesman Giulio Alberoni (1664–1752). His confidence in the banking schemes of Scottish financier and speculator John Law (q.v.) seriously involved the country.

Louis Philippe Joseph d'Orléans (1747–93). He adopted the name "Philippe-Egalité" during the French Revolution (q.v.) and succeeded to the title on his father's death (1785). As the States-General drew near he distributed books and papers throughout France advocating liberal ideas. In June, 1789, he led the forty-seven nobles who seceded from their own order to join the third estate. He was elected a deputy for Paris to the Convention and voted for the death of Louis XVI (q.v.). In 1793, during the Reign of Terror that accompanied the French Revolution, he was guillotined. His son Louis Philippe (q.v.) became king of France in 1830.

ORLÉANS, ISLE OF, island of Canada, in the Saint Lawrence R., in the province of Québec, the southern extremity being about 5 miles N.E. of the city of Québec. It is about 20 mi. long and has an area of 69 sq.mi. Potatoes, strawberries, cheese, and poultry are the chief products. The island, which contains several villages, is a popular summer resort. The British army officer James Wolfe (q.v.) camped here during the siege of Québec in 1759.

ORLÉANS, THE MAID OF. See JOAN OF ARC, SAINT.

ORMANDY, Eugene (1899–   ), American conductor, born in Budapest, Hungary. A child prodigy on the violin, he entered the State Academy of Music in Budapest at the age of five and later studied at the University of Budapest. Ormandy toured Hungary and central Europe as a child violinist prior to World War I. He left a teaching post in Budapest to settle in the United States in 1921, becoming an American citizen in 1927. From 1921 until 1928 Ormandy conducted the Capitol Theater orchestra in New York City. During the 1920's and early 1930's he frequently conducted radio orchestras. From 1931 until 1936 Ormandy conducted the Minneapolis Symphony Orchestra. He joined the Philadelphia Orchestra in 1936, becoming permanent conductor and music director in 1938. While maintaining that position, Ormandy has also been guest conductor of many leading orchestras and gained worldwide reputation.

ORMOC, city and port of the Philippines, in Leyte Province, on Leyte Island, on Ormoc Bay, an arm of the Camotes Sea, 32 miles s.w. of Tacloban. A port and market center in an area producing chiefly rice and sugar, the city has milling industries. It was one of the chief ports of supply for the Japanese during World War II until it was captured by American troops in 1944. The city was renamed MacArthur after 1950 in honor of the American general Douglas MacArthur (q.v.), who helped to liberate the country. The earlier name was later restored. Pop. (1960) 62,764.

ORMONDE, titles of earls, marquises, and dukes held in the Irish peerage by members of the Butler family; that of duke existing also in the English peerage after 1682. James Butler (1305–37) was created 1st earl of Ormonde after his marriage (1327) to Eleanor de Bohun (fl. 14th cent.), granddaughter of Edward I (q.v.), King of England. Among the more important members of the Butler family who subsequently held the titles were the following.

James Butler, 12th Earl and 1st Duke of Ormonde (1610–88), Irish statesman and soldier, born in London. After 1640 he supported the English statesman Sir Thomas Wentworth, 1st Earl of Strafford (q.v.), in his campaigns against the Irish who were rebelling against English domination. In 1642 Ormonde was created a marquis and two years later became lord lieutenant of Ireland. In 1649 he concluded a peace granting the Irish free exercise of the Catholic religion. With the conquest of Ireland in 1650 (*see* GREAT REBELLION), Ormonde fled to France. After the Restoration (q.v.) he returned, and in 1661 he received the title duke of Ormonde in the Irish peerage and again was named lord lieutenant of Ireland. In the latter position he encouraged learning and manufacturing in Ireland. In 1669, having lost the king's favor, he was dismissed and became chancellor of the University of Oxford. Shortly afterward an attempt was made on his life by Thomas Blood (q.v.), an Irish adventurer. Ormonde was restored as lord lieutenant in 1677 and served until 1682, when he was raised to the English peerage as duke of Ormonde.

James Butler, 2nd Duke of Ormonde (1665–1745), son of Thomas Butler, Earl of Ossory (1634–80), and grandson of the 1st Duke, born in Dublin, and educated in France and at the University of Oxford. He served in the armies of William III (q.v.), who was declared king of England by Parliament, at the Battle of the Boyne (q.v.) and subsequently in wars on the Continent. After the accession of Anne (q.v.) as queen of England in 1702 he served with the English forces in Spain; *see* SPANISH SUCCESSION, WARS OF THE. He was lord lieutenant of Ireland from 1702 to 1705 and again in 1710–11, and subsequently succeeded John Churchill (q.v.), 1st Duke of Marlborough, as commander in chief of the combined armies of England and Holland, holding the latter post until 1714. Strongly sympathetic towards the Jacobites (q.v.), Butler was forced to flee to France. He took part in the unsuccessful Jacobite invasion of England from Spain in 1715, and thenceforth lived at the Spanish court.

ORNITHOLOGY, scientific study of birds. *See* BIRD.

ORONTES (Ar. '*Asi,* Turk. *Asi*), river in s.w. Asia, forming part of the border between Lebanon and Syria, and between Syria and Turkey. It rises near the city of Ba'albek, Lebanon, and flows in a northerly direction between the Lebanon and Anti-Lebanon mountains into Syria. It flows N. to the city of Antioch (now Antâkya), Turkey, and then W. to the Mediterranean Sea, through a total course of 250 mi. The damming of the Orontes R. in Syria provides irrigation water for the rich river valley. In ancient times the valley of the Orontes R. formed a corridor between Asia Minor and Egypt.

OROZCO, José Clemente (1883–1949), Mexican painter, born in Zapotlán del Rey, Jalisco State, and educated at the National Autonomous University of Mexico. In 1922 he became one of the leaders of the Syndicate of Painters and Sculptors that sought to revive the art of fresco painting, under the patronage of the Mexican government. Orozco's most important early work was a series of frescoes for the National Preparatory School in Mexico City, commemorating the revolutionary uprisings of peasants and workers in Mexico. Between 1927 and 1934 he worked in the United States. There, he executed a set of murals entitled "The Dispossessed" at the New School for Social Research

ORPHAN

Scene from "The Dispossessed", a set of murals painted by José Clemente Orozco, at the New School for Social Research in New York City.
New School For Social Research

in New York City. In Pomona College, Claremont, Calif., he painted a fresco on the theme of the Greek hero Prometheus (q.v.). His mural panels for the Baker Library at Dartmouth College, Hanover, N.H., depict the history of America in the "Coming of Quetzalcoatl", the "Return of Quetzalcoatl", and "Modern Industrial Man". In the 1930's he painted his great murals in Mexico City and Guadalajara, and in the 1940's he explored on canvas the unique style that he already had conveyed in his murals. In his later years, Orozco's simple dramatic style became more expressionistic (*see* EXPRESSIONISM); his subject matter remained the suffering of man. Orozco contributed to the revival of fresco technique, design, and subject matter, and is regarded as one of the foremost mural painters in the Western Hemisphere. Representative work executed by Orozco can be found at the Museum of Modern Art, New York City.

ORPHAN, in law, minor who has lost one or both parents. In ancient times the care of orphans was a purely private matter. The responsibility of the community for the care of orphans was recognized by the early Christians, and collections to raise funds were taken among the members of congregations. Later church charity provided for the establishment of orphan asylums as well as for the care of orphans in monasteries. The duty of the state to provide for orphans was first recognized in the early 17th century, in England, where they were frequently placed in institutions known as workhouses. The abuses of the workhouse system led in the 18th century to the establishment by the government of separate residential schools, called barrack schools, for the housing and instruction of orphans, and to a substantial growth in the number of orphan asylums founded by private groups. In recent years the emphasis has shifted to care in foster homes and to provision by the state for financial assistance in the form of pensions paid to widowed mothers.

In other countries, including the United States, orphans are also recognized as wards of the state, and governmental provision is made for their care. In the U.S. both State and Federal legislation provide for aid to orphans in various forms, including their total support when necessary in such institutions as orphanages and foster homes. Liability for the care of an orphan with one surviving parent is, as a general rule, included in the various State statutes regulating the responsibilities of parents for the care of their children. In addition, in needy cases, monthly money allotments are given to the parent to aid in the support of the child. The amount of such aid varies from State to State. Under the Federal Social Security Act of 1935 and amendments, the Federal government contributes one half of whatever rate a State pays dependent children. *See* MATERNAL AND CHILD WELFARE; ORPHANAGE; SOCIAL SECURITY.

ORPHANAGE, institution for the care of orphaned, and also dependent or neglected, children, who have passed infancy but are not yet able to support themselves. An orphanage is distinguished from a foundling hospital in that the latter cares only for infants. Most orphanages admit children who are not orphans. Physically or mentally handicapped children and delinquent children were at one time reared in orphanages, but separate institutions are now maintained for them in most civilized countries.

The first institutions for the care of children were foundling homes established by the Roman Catholic Church during the Middle Ages as a deterrent to infanticide by destitute parents. Orphanages developed in Great Britain and the United States principally during the 19th and early 20th centuries; they became favorite objects of philanthropy as a result of growing concern at the ill-treatment of children exposed by such books as *Oliver Twist* (1837–39) by the British novelist Charles Dickens (q.v.).

Orphanages in the U.S. are maintained by religious organizations, by social or fraternal organizations, by private endowment, and by government institutions. In recent years, governmental authorities have tended to favor foster home care with State assistance over institutional care, as a result of growing criticism of the effects of institutional regimentation on the personalities of children. This criticism also led to the establishment of research bodies, such as the Child Welfare League of America, to find means for eliminating the harmful effects of institutional life. As a result, a tendency has arisen toward organization of orphanages on a so-called cottage system, in which children live together in small groups under the care of a house mother. In these groups ordinary clothing is worn rather than uniforms, and efforts are made to integrate the lives of the children with the life of the community. All Jewish institutions and most Protestant institutions, for example, make provision for the education of their charges in public schools in which they can meet and associate with other children. In addition, increasing emphasis is given to securing qualified supervisory personnel; and increasingly high salaries are offered by most institutions to attract people with medical, psychiatric, dietary, and social-work training. *See* ORPHAN.

ORPHEUS, in Greek mythology, poet and musician, the son of the Muse Calliope (*see* MUSES) and Apollo (q.v.), god of music, or Oeagrus, King of Thrace. He was given the lyre by Apollo, and became such an excellent musician that he had no rival among mortals. When Orpheus played and sang, he moved everything animate and inanimate. His music enchanted the trees and rocks and tamed wild beasts, and even the rivers turned in their course to follow him. As a young man he sailed with the Argonauts (q.v.) in search of the Golden Fleece (q.v.), and when the heroes grew weary of rowing, he would strike his lyre and inspire them to fresh effort. He saved the crew, too, from the Sirens (q.v.). Hearing their irresistibly sweet song, the heroes forgot everything and turned the ship toward the shore where the Sirens sat. There the Argonauts would have perished had Orpheus not drowned out the Sirens' song with an even sweeter song of his own, thereby allowing the sailors to put the ship back on course.

Orpheus is best known for his ill-fated marriage to the lovely nymph Eurydice (q.v.). Soon after the wedding the bride was stung by a viper and died. Overwhelmed with grief, Orpheus determined to go to the underworld and try to bring her back, something no mortal had ever done. When he played on his lyre, all the vast multitude of the dead were charmed to stillness. Hades (q.v.), the ruler of the underworld, was so moved by his playing that he gave Eurydice back to Orpheus on the one condition that he would not look back until they reached the upperworld. Orpheus could not control his eagerness, however, and as he gained the light of day he looked back a moment too soon, and Eurydice vanished. In his despair, Orpheus forsook the company of men and wandered in the wilds, playing for the rocks and trees and rivers. Finally a fierce band of Thracian women, who were followers of the god Dionysus (q.v.), came upon the gentle musician and killed him. When they threw his severed head in the river Hebrus, it continued to call for Eurydice, and was finally carried to the shore of Lesbos, where the Muses buried it. After Orpheus' death his lyre became the constellation Lyra. For the importance of Orpheus in Greek religious history *see* ORPHISM.

ORPHISM, in classical religion, mystic cult of ancient Greece, believed to have been drawn from the writings of the legendary poet and musician Orpheus (q.v.). Fragmentary poetic passages, including inscriptions on gold tablets found in the graves of Orphic followers from the 6th century B.C., indicate that Orphism was based on a cosmogony, which centered on the myth of the god Dionysus Zagreus, the son of the deities Zeus (q.v.) and Persephone (q.v.). Furious because Zeus wished to make his son ruler of the universe, the jealous Titans (q.v.) dismembered and devoured the young god. Athena (q.v.), goddess of wisdom, was able to rescue his heart, which she brought to Zeus, who swallowed it and gave birth to a new Dionysus (q.v.). Zeus then punished the Titans by destroying them with his lightning and from their ashes created man. As a result, man had a dual nature: his earthly body was the heritage of the earth-born Titans; his soul came from the divinity of Dionysus, whose remains had been mingled with that of the Titans.

According to the tenets of Orphism, man should endeavour to rid himself of the Titanic or evil element in his nature and should seek to preserve the Dionysiac or divine nature of his being. The triumph of the Dionysiac element would be assured by following the Orphic rites of purification and asceticism. Through a long series of reincarnated lives man would prepare himself for the afterlife. If he had lived in evil, he would be punished for his wickedness, but if he had lived in holiness, after death his soul would be completely liberated from Titanic elements and reunited with the divinity. See MYSTERIES, CLASSIC.

ORR, John Boyd. See BOYD ORR, JOHN, 1ST BARON BOYD ORR.

ORRISROOT. See IRIS.

ORSK, city of the Soviet Union, in the Russian S.F.S.R., on the Ural R. at its confluence with the Or' R., 115 miles S.E. of Orenburg. A rail junction, Orsk is the center of the mineral-rich Orsk-Khalilovo industrial district, where coal, nickel, iron, copper, gold, silver, sulfur, chromite, titanium, cryolite, and clay are mined. The city has plants processing iron and steel, nickel, aluminum, oil, alcohol, and flour; engineering works; and meat-packing and fruit-canning factories. It also manufactures machinery, locomotives, petroleum products, and agricultural equipment. Built on the site of the original fortress of Orenburg (founded in 1735 and moved to its present location in 1743), the frontier station was made a city in 1866 and became known for its cattle market. Industrialization was begun in the late 1930's and developed during World War II. Pop. (1970) 225,000.

ORTEGA Y GASSFT, José (1883–1955), Spanish writer and philosopher, born in Madrid, and educated at the universities of Madrid and Marburg. In 1910 he was appointed professor of metaphysics at the University of Madrid. His articles, lectures, and essays on philosophical and political issues contributed to a Spanish intellectual renaissance in the first decades of the 20th century and to the fall of the Spanish monarchy in 1931. He was a member from 1931 to 1933 of the Cortes (Spanish parliament) that promulgated the republican constitution. After the outbreak of the Spanish Civil War in 1936 he lived abroad, returning to Spain in the late 1940's. His solution for the problems of modern civilization is stated in *The Revolt of the Masses* (1930; Eng. trans., 1932). In the work that earned him an international reputation, he decries the destructive influence of mass-minded, and therefore mediocre, men who, if not directed by the intellectually and morally superior minority, encourage the rise of totalitarianism. His many writings include *The Modern Theme* (1923; Eng. trans., 1933), *Invertebrate Spain* (1921; Eng. trans., 1937), *The Dehumanization of Art* (1925; Eng. trans., 1948), and the posthumously published *Some Lessons in Metaphysics* (1970; Eng. trans., 1970).

ORTHOCLASE. See FELDSPAR.

ORTHODONTICS. See DENTISTRY.

ORTHODOX CHURCH, *or* HOLY ORTHODOX CATHOLIC APOSTOLIC EASTERN CHURCH, body of Christians who use the Byzantine rite (*see* LITURGY) in their various native languages, accept the Christian faith as it was formulated in the 1st millennium A.D., and reject the supremacy of the pope. They agree in accepting the authority of the first seven ecumenical councils (*see* COUNCIL), but reject later councils held by the Western Church. The schism between East and West was the result of a long process of theological estrangement and separate historical development; *see also* EASTERN CHURCH. It became final when the Roman Catholic Church (q.v.), by unilateral decision, added the word *Filioque* (q.v.; "[and] from the Son") to the text of the original creed defined by the early councils. This event took place early in the 11th century and led to the famous mutual excommunication of 1054. Patriarch Photius (q.v.) had earlier objected to the addition and the doctrine it implied. Other doctrinal, disciplinary, and liturgical issues were also involved, such as the preservation in the Christian East of married clergy; *see* CELIBACY.

The Orthodox Church, with a world membership of about 138,000,000, ranks third in numbers among the divisions of Christendom. It claims to be the organic continuation of the true church founded by the Apostles (*see* APOSTLE), but is open to the contemporary ecumenical dialogue; *see* ECUMENICAL MOVEMENT. According to numerous contemporary statements by the Orthodox Church, it considers that Christian unity can be restored only through a joint commitment to the one true faith, and not by submitting to an external criterion, such as the Roman see.

All the local Orthodox churches (Alexandria in the United Arab Republic, Antioch in Syria, Jerusalem, Russia, Serbia, Bulgaria, Rumania, Georgia S.S.R. in the Soviet Union, Greece, Poland, Albania, and Czechoslovakia) recognize the honorary primacy of the patriarch of Constantinople (İstanbul, Turkey). By far the largest of these local churches is the Church of Russia, in the Soviet Union. Missionary dioceses are established in Japan, Alaska, and east Africa.

More than 2,000,000 Orthodox Christians live in the United States. They are presently divided into ethnic dioceses (Greek, Russian, Serbian, and others), but their cooperation is increasing through the activities of a Standing Conference of Bishops. A united Orthodox Church of America is likely to emerge in the future.

See CHRISTIAN CHURCH, HISTORY OF THE; CHRISTIANITY; EASTERN RITE, CHURCHES OF THE. J.M.

ORTHOGRAPHY. See SPELLING.

ORTHOPEDICS, branch of surgery devoted to the diagnosis and treatment of illnesses, injuries, deformities, and malformations of the musculoskeletal system, including bones, joints, ligaments, muscles, and tendons. The orthopedist thus deals with traumatic injuries to bones, such as fractures and dislocations; disturbances in joints, such as sprains, torn cartilages or strained ligaments, and inflammations of muscle or connective tissues, such as bursitis, myositis, and tendonitis; and he corrects back problems, such as strains, ruptured discs, or curvatures; foot problems, such as flat feet or high arches; and neck disorders, such as strains or arthritis. Orthopedic surgeons employ mechanical appliances, such as braces, splints, and casts, and in surgical procedures use extensively hardware such as screws, pins, nails, and bolts and nuts, particularly in repairing broken bones. In the 20th century the science and mechanics of orthopedics have developed greatly, keeping pace with the advance in general surgery and pathology. Open operations are performed freely; many deformities are cured by operative means alone; improved X-ray techniques have made the diagnosis of bone and joint lesions more exact and the results of treatment more satisfactory. The transplantation of bone, fascia, muscle, and tendon for the restoration of function to, or the replacement of, destroyed tissue and even the use of newly devised metal prostheses to replace arthritic joints are now commonplace achievements. L.J.V.

ORTHOPTERA, large and important group of insects including the grasshopper or true locust, katydid, cricket, cockroach, walking stick, leaf-insect, and mantis (qq.v.). The mouthparts are fitted for biting, and the metamorphoses are incomplete. The young, when first hatched, closely resemble the adult insects except in size and the absence of wings. The eggs are few in number and as a rule are laid in specialized egg cases, although some orthoptera deposit eggs without such cases; a few members scatter their eggs. About 23,000 species exist; but, in spite of the comparatively small number of eggs, many of the species are tenacious of life and apparently very prolific, and swarm in enormous numbers of individuals, as in the case of the destructive migratory locusts. The ability to produce sounds of a more or less musical character by rubbing one part of the body upon another is highly developed. Only the male of families that jump, the Saltatoria, has this ability, the object of which is to attract the female. The runners, Cursoria, and graspers, Raptoria, make no sound. In these groups, especially in the tropical forms, the wings seem to be of little use as organs of flight, but they are of striking value in ornamentation and in concealment. This is especially true with the Phasmidae, the walking sticks, and Mantidae, the praying mantis. Even the eggs resemble the seeds of plants.

ORURO, city in Bolivia, and capital of Oruro Department, on a plateau about 12,000 ft. above sea level, 120 miles S.E. of La Paz. Oruro is the third largest city in Bolivia. It is a major railroad junction and an important commercial center in the heart of a tin-mining region. Industries include tin smelting and the manufacture of shoes and clothing. The city was settled in 1595 by Spaniards interested in its silver deposits and it flourished as a silver-mining center in colonial times. Pop. (1967 est.) 91,911.

ORVIETO, city of Italy, in Umbria Region, in Terni Province, 78 miles N.W. of Rome. Set high on an isolated plateau of tufa rock, more than 1000 ft. above sea level, Orvieto is the marketing and industrial center of a rich agricultural region; agricultural machinery, wrought iron, and handicrafts are manufactured here. The city is also known for its white wine. Orvieto occupies the site of the Etruscan town of Volsinii. A beautiful cathedral, construction of which was begun about 1290 and continued into the 14th century contains frescoes by the Italian painters Fra Angelico and Luca Signorelli (qq.v.). The former papal palace, completed early in the 14th century, is now a museum. Pop. (1961) 9,617.

ORWELL, George, real name ERIC BLAIR (1903–50), British writer, born in Motihari, India, and educated at Eton College. He served with the Indian Imperial Police in Burma from 1922 to 1927, when he returned to Europe. In poor health, and striving to become a writer, he lived for several years in poverty, first in Paris and then in London. His first works entitled *Down and Out in Paris and London* (1933) and *Burmese Days* (1934) are largely autobiographical. In 1936 Orwell went to Spain and joined the Republican forces in the Spanish Civil War. He described his war experiences in *Homage to Catalonia* (1938). In the most significant phase of his literary career, Orwell's political convictions underwent a profound change. Becoming increasingly anti-Stalinist and antitotalitarian, he

OSAGE

developed an overriding concern for the future of individual liberty. His condemnation of a regimented society is expressed in the allegorical fable *Animal Farm* (1945) and in the satirical novel *Nineteen Eighty-Four* (1949). The latter work presents a terrifying picture of life in a completely authoritarian society.

Among Orwell's other writings are *Keep the Aspidistra Flying* (1936), *Coming Up for Air* (1939), *Critical Essays* (1946), and *The Collected Essays, Journalism and Letters of George Orwell* (4 vol., 1968).

OSAGE, North American Indian tribe of Siouan stock (q.v.), formerly holding an extensive territory between the Missouri and Arkansas rivers. Their culture was typical of that of the Plains Indians (q.v.). Their first contact with white men occurred in the 17th century, when they were discovered by French explorers near the Osage R. in present-day Missouri. The Osage subsequently allied themselves with the French in warfare against other tribes, particularly the Illinois (q.v.). Between 1808 and 1870 the Osage sold most of their land to the United States. In 1870 they entered their present reservation in northeastern Oklahoma, securing favorable terms in land leases and interest derived from trust funds held for them by the U.S. government. Subsequently, oil was discovered on their lands, and with the royalties on the oil wells to supplement their incomes they became the wealthiest Indian community in the nation. Their population was estimated at 5500 in the early 19th century; in the early 1960's they numbered about 3000.

OSAGE, river of Missouri, rising in Vernon Co. The river flows S.E. and E. past the power plant at Osceola, then N.E., forming the 130-mi. Lake of the Ozarks, which is impounded by the Bagnell Dam and is the center of a popular resort area. The Osage R. then joins the Missouri R. 10 miles S.E. of Jefferson City, Mo. Including its main headstream, the Marais des Cygnes R., the length of the Osage is 500 mi.

OSAGE ORANGE *or* **BOWWOOD,** common name for a thorny American tree, *Maclura pomifera,* in the Mulberry (q.v.) family, Moraceae. It is so called because its bright-orange wood was used by the Osage Indians for bows and because its green nonedible fruit resembles an orange in shape and size. The tree has been known to rise to a height of 60 ft., and is widely cultivated in the warmer parts of the eastern United States as an ornamental or hedge tree, although it is native to southern and central U.S. Its wood is used for railway sleepers, fence posts, fuel, and for the extraction of a yellow dye.

OSAKA, city and port in Japan, and capital of Osaka Prefecture, on Honshu Island, on Osaka

The Burmese pavilion at Expo 1970, held in Osaka. In the background is the modern pavilion of the Japanese electric power industry. UPI

OSCILLOGRAPH

Bay, at the mouth of the Yodo R., about 25 miles s.w. of Kyoto. By incorporation of the suburbs, Osaka has become the second largest city in Japan, both in area and population. It ranks among the three largest ports in the nation and accommodates major oceangoing vessels. The airport of Osaka is the key point in the air routes of Japan. Osaka is a major industrial city of Japan and an important financial and commercial center. Industries include the manufacture of steel, machinery, textiles, ships, automobiles, electrical equipment, and cement. The city is intersected by many canals spanned by bridges. Osaka has several parks, the largest of which is Tennoji Park, containing botanical gardens. The city is famous as the home of Japanese drama (q.v.), particularly *Bunraku* or puppet theater. Among the institutions of higher education are Osaka University and Osaka City University. Osaka was the site of an international exposition in 1970.

The city dates from about 300 A.D., when, as Naniwa, it was the capital of Japan. Under the orders of Japanese general and statesman Toyotomi Hideyoshi (1536–98), who made Osaka his feudal capital in 1583, Toyotomi Castle, which still dominates the city, was completed in 1585. During his administration Osaka first became a flourishing center of commerce. Osaka was incorporated as a city in 1889. Two years later some 10,000 lives were lost in an earthquake. The city also was extensively damaged by fires in 1909 and 1912. Pop. (1968 est.) 3,078,000.

OSBORN, Henry Fairfield (1857–1935), American paleontologist, born in Fairfield, Conn., and educated at Princeton University. He was professor of comparative anatomy at Princeton from 1883 to 1890, when he joined the faculty of Columbia University, serving as professor of biology (1891–96), professor of zoology (1896–1910), and dean of the faculty of pure science (1892–95). In 1891 Osborn was appointed curator of vertebrate paleontology at The American Museum of Natural History (q.v.), and served from 1908 to 1933 as president of the board of trustees of the museum, for which he developed one of the major collections of vertebrate fossils in the world; see PALEONTOLOGY. From 1924 until his death he was senior geologist of the United States Geological Survey. Osborn was one of the leading paleontologists of the 20th century. Among his writings are *The Age of Mammals* (1910) and *Origin and Evolution of Life* (1917).

OSCAR I (1799–1859), King of Sweden and Norway (1844–59), second of the Bernadotte monarchs, son and successor of Charles XIV John (q.v.), born in Paris, France. In 1810 Oscar was made duke of Södermanland when his father was elected crown prince of Sweden. In 1823 he united the Bernadotte and Bonaparte families by marrying Joséphine de Beauharnais (1807–76), the granddaughter of Joséphine de Beauharnais (*see under* BEAUHARNAIS), wife of Napoleon I (q.v.), Emperor of France. Oscar I is noted for the economic and social reforms that he instituted upon accession to the throne.

OSCAR II (1829–1907), King of Sweden (1872–1907) and King of Norway (1872–1905), third son of King Oscar I, and brother of King Charles XV (qq.v.), born in Stockholm. The chief event of his reign was his sophisticated response to increasing tension between Sweden and Norway; in 1905 he decided to relinquish the throne of Norway, thus severing the union between the two countries that had existed since the Napoleonic era. Oscar II encouraged industrial progress in Sweden. He was a naval authority and a writer; in addition, his expertise in international affairs made him an obvious choice as arbitrator of several international disputes.

OSCEOLA (1800?–38), Seminole Indian leader, born near the Chattahoochee R., Georgia. His father was a British trader and his mother was the daughter of a Creek chief. His mother took him to live in northern Florida while he was still very young, and there he became a leader of the Seminoles, heading the opposition to the cession of tribal territories to the United States.

Osceola was the recognized leader of the faction of Seminoles that strongly objected to negotiating with the U.S. government in 1835 for the westward migration of the tribe. As a result of his opposition Osceola was briefly imprisoned. A few months after his release he killed the Indian agent and began attacks on the Americans that precipitated large-scale warfare between the Seminoles and the U.S. In 1837 he was seized while conferring under a flag of truce with the American military commander and was imprisoned first at Saint Augustine, Fla., and then at Fort Moultrie, S.C., where he died. *See* SEMINOLE WARS.

OSCILLATION. *See* VIBRATION. *See also* RADIO; SOUND.

OSCILLOGRAPH, instrument that records, on paper or film, wave patterns that are equivalent to the oscillations of an electric voltage, or that converts mechanical oscillations into an equivalent electric current before recording them on paper or film in the form of wave patterns. The electromechanical type of oscillograph consists in principle of a galvanometer (*see* ELECTRIC METERS) to which is attached an apparatus that rec-

211

OSCILLOSCOPE

ords the movements of the galvanometer coil. The recording apparatus may consist of a mirror that reflects a beam of light from the moving coil upon a photographic film moving at a fixed rate, or it may be a lightweight pen or stylus connected to the coil that writes on a moving paper chart. The recordings are called oscillograms. Electromechanical oscillographs are limited to recording oscillations having not much more than 500 Hz. One well-known type of electromechanical oscillograph is the electrocardiograph, which records the electric currents produced by a beating heart (q.v.). See OSCILLOSCOPE.

OSCILLOSCOPE, electronic instrument that records as a trace of light on the face of a cathode-ray tube changes in the voltage of an electric or electronic circuit; see ELECTRONICS: *Cathode-Ray Tube* for principles of operation. Oscilloscopes are widely used throughout industry and in scientific laboratories to test and adjust electronic equipment and to follow extremely rapid oscillations in electric voltages, the oscilloscope is capable of following changes that occur within several billionths of a second. By attaching special converters to an oscilloscope it is possible to convert mechanical vibrations, sound waves, and other forms of oscillatory motion into electrical impulses that can be followed on the face of the cathode-ray tube.

OSHAWA, city and port of Canada, in Ontario Province, on Lake Ontario, 34 miles N.E. of Toronto. The city has automobile factories and woolens, iron and steel products, and leather goods are manufactured. Pop. (1966) 78,082.

OSHKOSH, city in Wisconsin, and county seat of Winnebago Co., on the western shore of Lake Winnebago, at the mouth of the Fox R., 75 miles N.W. of Milwaukee. Transportation facilities include railroads, river steamers, and a municipal airport. Oshkosh is the center of a farming, dairying, and lumbering region. The principal industries are woodworking, the manufacture of metal wares, textiles, and electronics equipment, and the processing of food and beverages. The city is the site of a branch of Wisconsin State University (q.v.). It is a popular summer resort and winter sports center. The site of the present city was an important trading station for French fur trappers in the 18th century. It was first permanently settled in 1836 and became a city in 1853. It was named in honor of a chief of the Menominee (q.v.) Indians. Pop. (1960) 45,110; (1970) 53,221.

OSHOGBO, city of Nigeria, in the Western State, 50 miles N.E. of Ibadan. Oshogbo is serviced by a railroad, and is a major center of cocoa processing; other industries include palm and tobacco processing and cotton weaving. The surrounding area produces cotton, vegetables, corn, and cassava. Feldspar deposits have been found. Pop. (1969 est.) 242,336.

OSIER WILLOW. See WILLOW.

OSIJEK, city of Yugoslavia, in the constituent Republic of Croatia, capital of Osijek Oblast, on the Drave R., 130 miles E. of Zagreb. It is a port and an industrial center with oil refineries, flour and sugar mills, and factories producing chemicals, furniture, and matches. The city was built on the site of an ancient Roman colony called Mursa and was first mentioned as Osijek in the 12th century. Pop. (1961) 73,125.

OSIRIS, in the religion of ancient Egypt, one of the principal deities. Originally the local god of Abydos and Busiris, Osiris, who represented the male productive force in nature (*see* PHALLICISM), became identified with the setting sun. Thus he was regarded as the ruler of the realm of the dead in the mysterious region below the western horizon. Osiris was the brother and husband of Isis (q.v.), goddess of the earth and of the moon, who represented the female productive force in nature. According to legend Osiris, as king of Egypt, found his people plunged in barbarism and taught them law, agriculture, religion, and other blessings of civilization. He was murdered by his evil brother Set, who tore the body to pieces and scattered the fragments. Isis found and buried his scattered remains, however, and each burial place was thereafter revered as sacred ground. Their son Horus (q.v.), sired by a temporarily regenerated Osiris, avenged his father's death by killing Set and then ascended the throne. Osiris lived on in the underworld as the ruler of the dead, but he was also, through Horus, regarded as the source of renewed life. See EGYPTIAN RELIGION.

OSKALOOSA, city in Iowa, and county seat of Mahaska Co., about 22 miles N.W. of Ottumwa. Manufactures include farm equipment, wood and metal products, and clothing. It is the site of William Penn College, founded in 1873. Settled in 1844, the city was incorporated in 1853. Pop. (1960) 11,053; (1970) 11,224.

OSLER, Sir William (1849–1919), Canadian physician, born in Tecumseh, Ontario, and educated at Trinity College and McGill University in Montréal, University College in London, and the universities of Berlin and Vienna. He was professor of physiology and pathology at McGill University from 1875 to 1884, professor of clinical medicine at the University of Pennsylvania from 1884 to 1889, professor of medicine at Johns Hopkins University from 1889 to 1904, and

The harbor of Oslo with the city hall in the background, left.   Norwegian Official Photo

Gulstonian lecturer at the Royal College of Physicians, London, in 1885. In 1905 he was appointed regius professor of medicine at the University of Oxford. A physician of the first rank and a stimulating teacher, he was knighted in 1911. During 1914–15 Osler was engaged in supervising the general medical preparedness of the British forces of World War I (q.v.), and he helped to organize and equip the Queen's Canadian Military Hospital. As a result of his years at Johns Hopkins, he was of particular importance in the development of the practice of internal medicine in the United States. Osler wrote *The Principles and Practice of Medicine* (1892), *A Way of Life* (1914), and *A Concise History of Medicine* (1919).

OSLO, city, seaport, and capital of Norway, on the Skagerrak Strait, at the head of the Oslo Fjord. Oslo is the commercial and cultural center of Norway. The most important manufactures include electrical equipment, chemicals, clothing, and processed food. The city is modern in design and architecture and is noted for many museums and public statues and a lack of slums. Points of interest include Akershus fortress (built about 1300), the City Museum (occupying an 18th-century manor house), the University of Oslo (1811), the royal palace (1848), and the Storting (Parliament) building.

History. The first settlement was established as Oslo by Harold III, King of Norway (*see under* HAROLD), in 1048. King Haakon V (*see under* HAAKON) made the city the royal residence about 1300, and during the following century it flourished as a port. After Oslo was destroyed by fire in 1624, it was rebuilt by Christian IV (q.v.) and renamed Christiania (or Kristiana). In 1716 it was occupied by Charles XII (q.v.), King of Sweden. The city enjoyed an artistic and economic renaissance during the 19th century, and it again became the capital of independent Norway in 1905. Christiania reassumed the official name Oslo in 1925. Pop. (1968 est.) 484,275.

OSMAN *or* **OTHMAN** (1259–1326), founder of the Ottoman Empire (q.v.), born in Bithynia (now part of Turkey). With the decline of the empire of the Seljuks (q.v.), he seized a portion of Bithynia. He then conquered the territory of Nicaea, and gradually subdued a great part of Asia Minor. He thus established the Osmanli, or Ottoman, Empire.

See CALIPHS: *The Ottomans and the Modern Empire;* TURKEY: *History.*

OSMIRIDIUM. See IRIDIUM; OSMIUM.

OSMIUM, metallic element, member of the platinum group, with at.no. 76, at.wt. 190.2, b.p. over 4000° C. (7232° F.), m.p. about 3030° C. (5486° F.), sp.gr. 22.6$^{20°}$, and symbol Os. It was discovered in 1803 by the British chemist Smithson Tennant (1761–1815). The metal occurs native in platinum ores and as an alloy, osmiridium, with iridium. Osmium has the greatest density of any known substance. It is a bluish-white, brittle metal, with a hardness of 7. It is not attacked by ordinary acids, but dissolves in aqua regia or fuming nitric acid. It forms salts in which it has valences of 2, 3, 4, 6, and 8. The chief use of the metal is in the alloy osmiridium; *see* IRIDIUM. It is also used, alloyed with platinum, for standard weights and measures.

OSMOSIS

OSMOSIS, in botany and chemistry, the flow of one constituent of a solution through a membrane while the other constituents are blocked and unable to pass through the membrane. Experimentation is necessary to determine which membranes permit selective flow, or osmosis, because not all membranes act in this way. Many membranes allow all or none of the constituents of a solution to pass through; only a few allow a selective flow. In a classic demonstration of osmosis, a vertical tube containing a solution of sugar is placed, with its lower end closed off by a semipermeable membrane, in a container of water. As the water passes through the membrane into the tube, the level of the sugar solution in the tube rises visibly. A semipermeable membrane that may be used for such a demonstration is the membrane found just inside the shell of an egg, that is, the film that keeps the white of the egg from direct contact with the shell. In this demonstration, the water moves in both directions through the membrane; the flow is greater from the vessel of pure water, however, because the concentration of water is greater there, that is, there are fewer impurities in this solution than in the sugar solution. If osmosis is allowed to continue, the level of liquid in the tube of sugar solution will rise until the flow of water from the tube of sugar solution, under the influence of hydrostatic pressure, just equals the flow of water into the tube. Thereafter no further rise in level will occur. The hydrostatic pressure establishing this equality of flow is called osmotic pressure. It is osmotic pressure, for example, that sends water from the roots to the topmost branches of a tree. A variety of physical and chemical principles is involved in the phenomena of osmosis in animals and plants. T.W.D.

OSNABRÜCK, city of West Germany, in Lower Saxony State, on the Hase R., 58 miles N.E. of Dortmund. It is an industrial center, producing railroad equipment, steel cables, automobile bodies, textiles, paper, and processed food. The city has a rebuilt 8th-century cathedral and a Gothic town hall, where one of the treaties of the Peace of Westphalia was signed in 1648; see WESTPHALIA, PEACE OF. About 65 percent of Osnabrück was destroyed in World War II but rebuilt. Pop. (1966) 142,587.

OSORNO, city in Chile, and capital of Osorno Province, on the Rahue R., at its confluence with the Damas R., in the heart of the Chilean lake district, 500 miles S.W. of Santiago. A road hub on the main railroad line, it is a tourist center and gateway to the numerous lake and mountain resorts to the E. and S.E. and to the Argentine national parks across the Andes Mts. Called the "Pearl of the South", Osorno is the trading center of agricultural valleys in which wheat, oats, livestock, and timber are raised. Industries in the city include meat processing, flour milling, sawmilling, brewing, and the manufacture of agricultural equipment and dairy products. Osorno was founded in 1553, on the site of the native village of Chauracahuin, by the Spanish conquistadores under Pedro de Valdivia (q.v.) and was originally called Santa Marina de Gaete. Actually settled in 1558 and named San Mateo de Osorno, the city was destroyed by Araucanian Indians in 1602. It was resettled from 1776 to 1796 on the orders of Ambrosio O'Higgins (1720?–1801), Irish soldier of fortune and father of Bernardo O'Higgins (q.v.). In the late 1800's an influx of German settlers spurred the growth of Osorno, and in 1895 the railroad reached the city. Pop. (1960) 55,091.

OSPREY or **FISH HAWK,** common name applied to a cosmopolitan hawk, *Pandion haliaëtus*; see HAWK. The bird, which is about 2 ft. long, is dark brown above and white below. The undersurface of the female is streaked with brown. The osprey, when seeking food, hovers over a body of water, and dives beneath the surface to capture fish in its talons. Ospreys build large, basketlike nests of sticks in trees, sometimes close to human habitations, and breed in the same nests for many years. The characteristic cry of the osprey is a thin, shrill whistle. The rarity of this species is thought to be due to the increasing use of pesticides by man.

OSSETS, people descended from the Alans (q.v.) or Alani, speaking Ossetic, a language of the Iranian branch of the subfamily of Indo-Iranian languages (q.v.) and inhabiting Ossetia, a region of the Soviet Union in the central Caucasus. They are also variously known as Osetes, Ossetes, Ossetas, Ossetines, and Ossetians. Ossetia comprises the South Ossetian Autonomous Oblast, created in 1922, and lying within the boundaries of the Georgian S.S.R.; and the North Ossetian A.S.S.R., created in 1936, and a part of the Russian S.F.S.R. Christianity was introduced among the Ossets in the 12th century; subsequently, a large number of them adopted Islam (q.v.). They were conquered by the Russians in 1802. At the present time the North Ossets export timber and cultivate a number of crops and vegetables, principally corn. They also engage in dairy farming. The South Ossets, fewer in number than the northern, are chiefly pastoral, herding sheep and goats in the east and cattle in the west. Peasant industries include the manufacture of leather goods, fur caps, daggers, and metalware. The two chief dialect groups of the Ossetic language are the Digor in the north and the Iron in the south. Since the Ossets received political and cultural autonomy, the Latin alphabet has been adopted for the writing of the Ossetic language, formerly written in the Armenian alphabet. The population of the North Ossetian A.S.S.R. is (1970) 553,000; the population of the South Ossetian Autonomous Oblast is (1970) 100,000.

OSSIAN or **OISIN**, legendary Gaelic poet, supposedly the son of Finn Mac Cool, a 3rd-century literary hero. Ossian is known primarily through the works of the Scottish poet James Macpherson (q.v.), who published *Fingal*, an epic poem in six books, in 1761, and *Temora* in 1763. These works purported to be translations of poems composed by Ossian; today most experts believe that they are probably original compositions. See IRISH LITERATURE: *Irish Literature in Gaelic: Middle Irish Period: Fenian Cycle*.

OSSIETZKY, Carl von (1889–1938), German journalist and pacifist, born in Hamburg. As a young man he was a member of the German peace society of the Austrian pacifist Alfred Hermann Fried (q.v.), but served as a conscript in the German army throughout World War I. In Berlin after the war he was an associate editor of the daily *Volkszeitung*, which he left in 1927 to become editor of the left-wing weekly *Weltbühne*. His outspoken antimilitarist articles led to his trial and conviction in 1931 for allegedly divulging military secrets, but he was released in a general amnesty in December, 1932. Two months later he was arrested as an enemy of the new National Socialist regime and imprisoned. Within four years he contracted tuberculosis and was transferred to a hospital, but remained in custody. When Ossietzky was awarded the 1935 Nobel Peace Prize, the German dictator Adolf Hitler (q.v.) took offense and German citizens were thereafter forbidden to accept any Nobel prizes.

OSSINING, village of New York, in Westchester Co., on the Hudson R., 5 miles N. of Tarrytown. Manufactures include transportation equipment, processed food, and clothing. The village is the site of the 38 mi.-long Croton Aqueduct arch, begun in 1837 and completed in 1842, and Sing Sing Prison, built between 1825 and 1828 and known until about 1920 as a maximum-security prison. The village was settled about 1750, incorporated as Sing Sing in 1813, and named Ossining in 1901. Pop. (1960) 18,662; (1970) 21,659.

OSTADE, Adriaen van (1610–85), Dutch painter and engraver, born in Haarlem. He studied with the Dutch artist Frans Hals and later came under the influence of the great Dutch master Rembrandt (qq.v.). Ostade painted many small genre pictures, lively and vigorous and full of subtle effects of light and shade. His subject matter was tavern scenes, peasants drinking and smoking, itinerant musicians, village festivities, and quaint village characters. He also executed fifty etchings depicting peasant life.

OSTEND or **OOSTENDE**, town and port of Belgium, in West Flanders Province, on the North Sea Canal, 14 miles W. of Bruges. It is the second-largest Belgian port and has important fishing and shipbuilding industries. Ostend, now a popular seaside resort, was founded as a fishing village in the 9th century. A wall was built around it in 1445, and it was fortified by Prince William I (q.v.) of Orange in 1583. Ostend was the last Dutch stronghold in Belgium. Between 1601 and 1604 the town heroically resisted a Spanish siege, in which 40,000 Spanish were killed, and the Flemish surrendered only after the town had been reduced to ruins. The Ostend Manifesto (q.v.) was drawn up in Ostend in 1854. During World War II the Germans used the town as an important submarine base until the British sealed the harbor by sinking a ship at its entrance. Pop. (1967 est.) 57,765.

OSTEND MANIFESTO, title of a document drawn up by the American statesmen James Buchanan (q.v.), later the fifteenth President; John Young Mason (1799–1859), and Pierre Soulé (1801–70), the ministers to Great Britain, France, and Spain, respectively, at Ostend, Belgium, on Oct. 9, 1854. Shortly prior to that date, Soulé had entered into negotiations with the Spanish government for the purchase of Cuba by the United States. His diplomatic blunders incurred the censure of his superiors, who ordered him to consult with the other envoys named above. The result of this conference was the Ostend Manifesto, which urged Spain to sell Cuba to the U.S. and implied that the U.S. would use force if Spain refused. Publication of the manifesto caused a sensation among antislavery forces in the U.S., who feared that the acquisition of Cuba, where slavery was a well-established institution, would strengthen the proslavery forces. The controversy soon abated, however, and new grounds for North-South conflict were avoided, when the government of the U.S. repudiated the manifesto.

OSTEOMYELITIS, term applied to any inflammation of bone or bone marrow, usually caused by infection by such microorganisms as *Staphylococcus aureus*, various streptococci, tuberculosis, and a host of others, as well as several fun-

OSTEOPATHY

gus organisms. The microorganisms generally reach the bone through the blood stream from infection elsewhere. Occasionally osteomyelitis occurs by direct infection after surgery or after a compound fracture, or as a result of trauma. Staphylococcal osteomyelitis most often occurs in boys from two to twelve years old; it may, however, occur in persons of any age or either sex, especially if systemic infection has been immediately preceded by a blow to a bone. Other forms of osteomyelitis may occur in any patient, often in elderly ones, particularly diabetics or people with poor circulation where osteomyelitis may complicate an ulcer on a toe or foot.

Osteomyelitis, especially bacterial, may occur as an acute disease. Common symptoms include chills followed by fever, with exquisite pain and swelling above the site of inflammation. Because osteomyelitis usually first appears near a joint at the end of a long bone in the lower limb, the condition is often mistaken for arthritis. The inflammation begins in the marrow cavity and causes softening and erosion of the long bones, often with the formation of pus-containing abscesses, and soon spreads over the entire bone, with consequent death of the hard portions of the bone. If the pus is not drained quickly, the pressure caused by accumulation within a limited space results in the extrusion of pus from the weakened outer surface of the bone into the region below the fibrous membrane covering the bone (peristeum), causing the membrane to be stripped away and spontaneous drainage through the skin to occur, with formation of chronic draining sinuses. Further extension of the suppurative process results in metastasis (q.v.) to other bones, and sometimes in death.

Chronic osteomyelitis, as is often seen in tuberculosis, fungus infections, or in patients with bacterial infections from other organisms, tends to run a slower and less dramatic course, with less severe pain and less fever, often eventuating in bony destruction, which on X ray may even resemble a bone tumor, and the development of chronic draining sinuses. Acute osteomyelitis (staphylococcal osteomyelitis used to be the commonest form) is treated by injections of antibiotics such as penicillin, and by concurrent surgery to open the affected bone and drain the pus and dead tissue. Incomplete drainage results in chronic inflammation of the bone. Since the advent of potent antibiotic drugs, acute osteomyelitis has become rare.

L.J.V.

OSTEOPATHY, system of complete medical practice based on the principle that health depends on the maintenance of proper mechanical relationships among the various parts of the body. According to osteopathic theory, defects in the musculoskeletal system, that is, in the muscles and the bones, influence the natural function of internal organs. To correct structural abnormalities, manipulative therapy, treatment with the hands or by mechanical means, is used. The osteopathic physician, or osteopath, also utilizes all other accepted therapeutic agencies, such as drugs, surgery, and X ray, in the diagnosis and treatment of disease and injury. Ostepathic medicine holds that true health involves complete physical, mental, and social well-being, rather than merely the absence of disease. The osteopath, therefore, must treat the whole patient, considering such factors as nutrition and mental habits, in addition to the physical symptoms.

The fundamental principles of osteopathic medicine were formulated in 1874 by the American physician Andrew Taylor Still (1828–1917). Still organized the first osteopathic school at Kirksville, Mo., in 1892. Six accredited osteopathic colleges now exist in the United States, a new institution, affiliated with Michigan State University, having been opened in 1969.

The modern osteopathic physician must have at least three, and preferably four, years of premedical study at an accredited college or university; four years of training at an osteopathic college; and one year of internship. Graduates of an osteopathic college receive the degree D.O., that is, doctor of osteopathy. Doctors wishing to specialize must take up to an additional five years of residency training, depending on the field they plan to enter. The overwhelming majority of today's osteopathic graduates, however, enter general practice.

Osteopathic physicians are licensed in all States and participate in all Federal health programs including Medicare and Medicaid (q.v.).

AMERICAN OSTEOPATHIC ASSOCIATION

OSTIA, ancient city of Italy, in Latium, at the mouth of the Tiber R., about 46 miles s.w. of Rome. Ostia was famed for its marshes, the salt from which was conveyed over the Salarian Way, and it was the port to which grain from Sicily and Sardinia was delivered. The city was reputedly founded about 640 B.C. by the fourth legendary king of Rome, Ancus Marcius (q.v.). Ostia was long the chief base of the Roman navy until the harbor finally became filled with silt. In the 1st century A.D., the Roman emperor Claudius (q.v.) dug a new harbor 2 miles N. of Ostia, and connected it to the Tiber R. by a canal. The development of a new town, commonly called Portus, around the new harbor diminished the commercial importance of Ostia. At the height of prosperity in the 2nd and 3rd centuries, Ostia had a population of about 75,000 but began to decline soon thereafter. It was destroyed by the Saracens (q.v.) in the 9th century and revived during the Middle Ages. The ruins, systematically excavated since 1854, are second in importance only to those of Pompeii (q.v.). Comprising a number of public buildings, temples, shrines, and tombs, these ruins provide invaluable data concerning the nature of a prosperous ancient seaport.

OSTRACISM, in Greek antiquity, political procedure providing for the temporary banishment of any citizen whose presence appeared to threaten public welfare. The law of ostracism is thought to have been first promulgated in Athens by the statesman Cleisthenes (*see under* CLEISTHENES) in 510 B.C. The first recorded enforcement was the ostracism of friends and relatives of the Athenian tyrant Hipparchus (about 555–514 B.C.) from 487 to 485 B.C. Every year the Athenian assembly by a show of hands decided upon imposing ostracism. If the assembly decided in the affirmative, a date for public voting was set and the citizens, voting by tribes, deposited their ballots in boxes in the marketplace. On a fragment of pottery, or ostracon, each voter wrote the name of the person whom he wished to be exiled. The man who received the most votes out of a required minimum of 6000 total ballots cast had to leave Athens within ten days and remain away for ten years. Ostracism did not inflict any stigma upon the victim, and neither his property nor his civil rights were in any way disturbed. The ostracized man might be recalled by vote of the assembly. Among the prominent statesmen who suffered ostracism were Aristides, Themistocles, and Cimon (qq.v.). More than 500 ostraca bearing the name of Themistocles, ostracized in 471 B.C., have been discovered. Hyperbolus (d. 411 B.C.), a minor Athenian demagogue, was the last person ostracized (417 B.C.); the vote had been intended to decide between the Athenian statesmen Nicias (470?–413 B.C) and Alcibiades (q.v.), who combined their forces against the much less influential Hyperbolus. This occurrence resulted in the abandonment of the system. More than 1500 ostraca have been found in recent years in the vicinity of the Athenian Acropolis and marketplace, including many that bear the names of statesmen known from literary sources to have been ostracized.

OSTRAVA, city in Czechoslovakia, and capital of Severomoravský Region, on the Oder R., at the confluence of the Ostravice R., 170 miles E. of Prague. The fourth-largest city in the country, it is a transportation hub and a leading metallurgical center in the most densely industrial section of Czechoslovakia. Situated in the Ostrava-Karviná coalfield, it is composed of Moravská Ostrava, a combination of previously independent industrial centers, Slezská Ostrava, and several other recently developed cities. Ostrava has iron- and steel-rolling mills, boiler and power plants, and railroad shops. Aluminum alloys, chemicals, drugs, synthetic gases, plastics, petroleum products, building materials, apparel, ceramics, furniture, and food products are manufactured. A mining school is located in the city. Large-scale industrial development began in the 20th century. Pop. (1966 est.) 265,000.

OSTRICH, common name applied to a large, flightless bird, *Struthio camelus,* of the order Struthioniformes, native to Africa. Ostriches are the largest and strongest of living birds, attaining a height from crown to foot of about 8 ft. and a weight of up to 300 lb. They have long necks and small heads, with large eyes and short, broad beaks. They spread their small wings when running, and have long, powerful legs which are used for defense. The feet have only two toes, the outer of which is rudimentary. Male ostriches are black in color, with white wings and tail. The white feathers of the male, which are large and soft, are the ostrich

African ostrich, Struthio camelus   Hellmuth Pollaczek

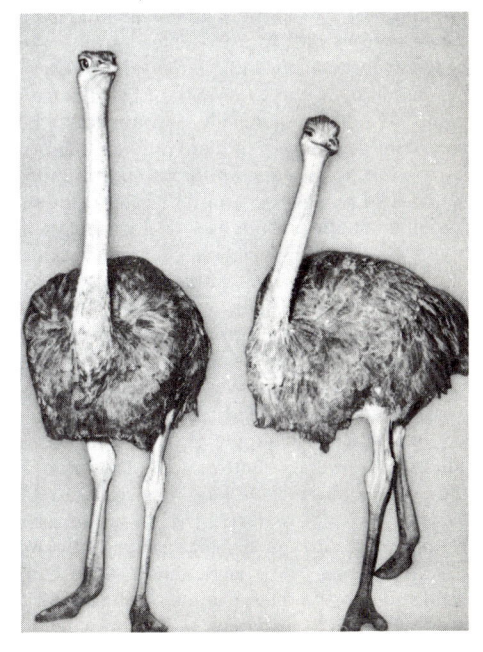

plumes of commercial value. The female is a dull grayish brown.

Ostriches are rapid runners, and can attain a running speed of about 40 m.p.h. The males are polygamous and travel about in hot, sandy areas with three or four females, or in groups of four or five males accompanied by mates and young. The females lay their yellowish white eggs together in a single large depression in the sand. The eggs weigh about 3 lb. each and have a volume of about 3 pints. To guard the eggs against destruction the male sits on them at night, while the females incubate them in turn during the day.

In the last half of the 19th century ostrich farming, or the breeding of domesticated ostriches for their plumes, was carried on extensively in South Africa, Algeria, Australia, France, and the United States. Ostrich plumes were used in hatmaking and dressmaking. Toward the end of the 19th century, annual world income from ostrich farming amounted to about $10,000,000. Today, ostrich farming is an extremely small-scale industry, the demand for ostrich plumes being almost negligible.

Five sub-species of ostrich inhabit various parts of Africa. The so-called American ostrich is actually a rhea (q.v.).

OSTROGOTHS. See GOTHS: *Ostrogoths.*

OSTWALD, Wilhelm (1853–1932), German physical chemist, born in Riga, Latvia (now Latvian S.S.R.), and educated at the University of Dorpat (now Tartu State University). In 1881 he was appointed professor in the Riga Polytechnic Institute and from 1887 to 1906 served as professor of physical chemistry and director of the chemical laboratory at the University of Leipzig, Germany. Ostwald is generally considered to be one of the founders of modern physical chemistry and is especially known for his contributions to the field of electrochemistry (q.v.), including important studies of the electrical conductivity and electrolytic dissociation of organic acids. He invented a viscometer that is still used for measuring the viscosity of solutions. In 1900 he discovered a method of preparing nitric acid by oxidizing ammonia. This method was used by Germany during World War I for manufacturing explosives after the Allied blockade had cut off the regular German supply of nitrates, and it is still used in several countries under the name of the Ostwald process. Ostwald received the 1909 Nobel Prize in chemistry. His works include *Natural Philosophy* (1902; Eng. trans., 1910) and *Colour Science* (1923; Eng. trans., 1931). Ostwald's son, the German chemist Wolfgang Ostwald (1883–1943), also became a famous scientist and is generally regarded as the founder of colloid chemistry. See CHEMISTRY: *Physical Chemistry;* COLLOIDAL DISPERSION.

OSTYAK *or* **OSTIAK,** western Siberian tribe speaking Ostyak, a language of the Ugric branch of the Finno-Ugric languages (q.v.), and inhabiting the upland valleys of the Ural Mts. principally the basin of the Ob' R. The name is also applied to a group of tribes of different languages, the so-called Ostyak-Samoyeds (see SAMOYEDS), who inhabit the region between the Urals and the Yenisei R. Ostyaks generally are short and spare in body, with white skin and brown eyes and hair. They live chiefly by hunting and fishing. Their handicrafts include carving in wood, bone, and birch bark. In a recent year the Ostyaks and Ostyak-Samoyeds numbered more than 20,000; members of the Ostyak-speaking tribe numbered about 1500.

OSWALD, Lee Harvey. See KENNEDY, JOHN FITZGERALD; WARREN REPORT.

OSWEGO, city and port of entry in New York, and county seat of Oswego Co., at the confluence of the Oswego R. and Lake Ontario, 34 miles N.W. of Syracuse. An important city on the New York State Barge Canal System (q.v.), it has a 1,000,000-bu. capacity grain elevator. Manufactures include textiles, clothing, oil-well supplies, chemicals, and cement. The city is the site of State University of New York College at Oswego. Oswego was founded by the British in 1722, and it became an important fur-trading post. Fort Ontario, a State historic site since 1951, was built here in 1755; it was held by the French from 1756 to 1759, when it was retaken by the British. Oswego was incorporated as a village in 1828, and as a city in 1848. Pop. (1960) 22,155; (1970) 23,844.

OTHMAN. See OSMAN.

OTIS, Elisha Graves (1811–61), American inventor and manufacturer, born in Halifax, Vt. He was a pioneer in the construction and manufacture of steam-powered elevators and elevator devices. In 1854, at an exposition in New York City, he demonstrated his most important invention, an automatic safety device for stopping an elevator should the supporting cables break; see ELEVATOR. Four years later he designed and installed the first passenger elevators in the United States; this achievement heralded the age of the skyscraper. Shortly before his death he patented a steam-driven elevator, which became the basis of the internationally known Otis Elevator Company.

OTIS, James (1725–83), American colonial leader, born in West Barnstable, Mass., and educated at Harvard College (now Harvard Univer-

James Otis

sity). He entered the legal profession in Boston in 1748 and served as advocate general of the Boston vice-admiralty court from 1756 to 1761. He resigned from that office to appear as counsel for the merchants of Boston, in opposition to the issuance of writs of assistance enabling the royal customs collectors to search the establishments of merchants suspected of possessing contraband and thereby violating the Molasses Act of 1733. In a famous address to the court, in February, 1761, Otis declared that any act passed by Parliament contrary to the natural rights of the American colonists was invalid. Although he failed to prevent the issuance of the writs, he was recognized thereafter as the leader of radical colonial opponents to British measures. He was elected to the Massachusetts General Court (legislature) in 1761 and three years later became the head of the Massachusetts branch of the Committees of Correspondence (q.v.). In 1764 he also prepared a cogent plea for free speech and against taxation by Parliament: *The Rights of the British Colonies Asserted and Proved.* Otis' ideas were incorporated in the documents of the Stamp Act Congress (q.v.) in 1765. Otis also condemned the Townshend Acts (q.v.) of 1767 as driving the colonists to revolt. In 1769 he was physically attacked by a conservative customs collector who opposed his published statements; his injuries were so severe that he was compelled to withdraw from public life.

OTITIS. See EAR: *Ear Diseases.*

OTRANTE, Joseph Fouché, Duc d'. See FOUCHÉ, JOSEPH, DUC D'OTRANTE.

OTSU, city in Japan, and capital of Shiga Prefecture, on Honshu Island, on Lake Biwa, 5 miles E. of Kyoto. It lies in a rich farming region and is a resort center; it is known for the manufacture of fibers and textiles. Points of interest include the 7th-century Buddhist temple, Mii-dera, and the biological laboratory of Kyoto University. For periods during the 2nd and 7th centuries A.D. Otsu was the site of the imperial court. Pop. (1966 est.) 117,000.

OTTAWA, North American Indian tribe belonging to the Algonquian (q.v.) linguistic family, and formerly living in the region of the upper Ottawa R., Canada. In culture, the Ottawa were similar to the several other tribes inhabiting the same area; *see* AMERICAN INDIANS: *Eastern Woodland Area.* They carried on an extensive intertribal trade along the water routes. The Ottawa had rules of moral conduct, embodied in twenty-one precepts, that strikingly resemble the code of the Biblical Ten Commandments.

About 1650 the Ottawa were driven out of their territory by the Iroquois (q.v.) and took refuge on Manitoulin Island in Lake Huron, Canada. They later moved to the southern shore of Lake Superior, but were obliged to return to Manitoulin Island when they were attacked by the Sioux (q.v.). Subsequently they extended their territory until they controlled all of lower Michigan, parts of Ohio and Illinois, and an area on the Canadian side of Lake Huron. During the colonial period the Ottawa fought on the side of the French, and one of their chiefs, Pontiac (q.v.), achieved wide renown as a leader in warfare against the British. During the American Revolution and the War of 1812, the tribe was allied with the British against the Americans. In 1870 several bands of Ottawa moved to the Indian Territory (q.v.), in what is now the State of Oklahoma, and soon lost their tribal identity. The majority of the Ottawa remained in Michigan, first on reservations, and then in scattered communities where many still reside; about 250 Ottawa also live today in Oklahoma.

OTTAWA, river in Canada, the principal tributary of the Saint Lawrence R. It rises 160 miles N. of Ottawa, on the Laurentian divide, and flows generally S.E. until after a course of about 685 mi., most of it along the boundary between the

OTTAWA

provinces of Ontario and Québec, it falls into the St. Lawrence by two mouths that form the island of Montréal. During its course the Ottawa R. is fed by many important tributaries, such as the Madawa and Rideau on the right and the Gatineau and the Rivière-du-Lièvre on the left. These, with the Ottawa itself, form the means of transit for a large lumber trade. The Ottawa is connected with Lake Ontario at Kingston by the Rideau Canal and is navigable for 250 mi.

OTTAWA, city in Illinois, and county seat of LaSalle Co., about 13 miles E. of LaSalle. The city is in an agricultural region that produces grains, legumes, livestock, poultry, and dairy products. Ottawa's deposits of silica, sand and clay provide some of the materials for its manufacturing industry that includes ceramic products, asphalt, cement, zinc, and farm machinery. Bituminous coal is mined in the area. In 1858 the first Lincoln-Douglas debate was held here. It was one of a series of debates held between Abraham Lincoln and Stephen A. Douglas (qq.v.) in a contest in 1858 for the seat of Senator from Illinois. Several State parks are nearby. Pop. (1960) 19,408; (1970) 18,716. See ILLINOIS: *Parks, Forests, and Other Places of Interest.*

OTTAWA, city in Kansas, and county seat of Franklin Co., on the Marais des Cygnes R., about 38 miles S.E. of Topeka. The city has varied manufacturing. It is the site of Ottawa University, founded in 1865. Founded in 1864, the city was incorporated in 1866. Pop. (1960) 10,673; (1970) 11,036.

OTTAWA, city and capital of Canada, in Ontario Province, and county seat of Carleton County, at the confluence of the Ottawa and Rideau rivers, 100 miles S.W. of Montréal. Manufactures include paper, furniture, watches, clothing, and processed food. At the western end of the city the Ottawa R. forms the rapids known as Chaudière Falls, the major source of hydroelectric power for the factories of the city. The Rideau Canal, extending from Ottawa to Kingston on Lake Ontario, divides the city into the Upper Town, which is predominantly British, and the Lower Town, predominantly French. The streets of Ottawa are wide and laid out regularly in a gridiron pattern; the city contains about 1500 acres of park. The chief architectural features are the Gothic-style Parliament and departmental buildings, occupying three sides of a quadrangle on Parliament Hill, 125 ft. above the Ottawa R. Other notable buildings include the Roman Catholic Cathedral of Notre Dame, the Anglican Christ Church Cathedral, the official residence of the governor-general, known as Rideau Hall, the National Victoria Museum, the Carnegie Library, and the National Art Gallery. Among the notable educational institutions are the University of Ottawa (q.v.), Carleton University (1942), and the Ontario Institute of Technology.

History. The city was founded in 1827 by Colonel John By (1781–1836), a British-born Canadian engineer who supervised the building of the Rideau Canal, completed in 1832. The settlement, named Bytown, grew rapidly as a result of the development of the lumber trade. It was incorporated as a city under its present name in 1854 and four years later was selected by Victoria (q.v.), Queen of Great Britain, as the capital of Canada; in 1867 it became the capital of the new dominion of Canada. Pop. (1966) 290,741.

OTTAWA, UNIVERSITY OF, coeducational institution of higher learning, located in Ottawa, Ontario Province, Canada. The institution was founded as the College of Saint Joseph in 1848, renamed the College of Bytown in 1849, and was granted a civil charter as a university in 1866. In 1889 Pope Leo XIII (*see under* LEO) conferred upon it the rank of university. In 1933 its power to grant degrees in all branches of learning was confirmed by the provincial legislature. The university includes faculties of medicine, theology, canon law, law, philosophy, social sciences, pure and applied science, arts, psychology and education, and schools of library science, physical education, hospital administration, nursing, and social welfare. Languages of instruction are French and English. Five arts colleges are affiliated with the university. These colleges provide curricula roughly comparable to those of secondary school and two years of college in the United States and lead to a degree of *baccalauréat des arts*. Until recently the arts degree was usually required before one could enroll in a French-language division of a Canadian university. In 1965 the formerly Roman Catholic university was secularized to enable it to receive provincial aid. The faculties of theology and canon law, however, remained under the control of the Church and became Saint Paul University, which is now federated with the University of Ottawa. The degrees of bachelor, master, and doctor are granted. The university libraries contain 340,000 bound volumes. In addition, students have access to the 550,000 bound volumes in the Parliament library. In 1966–67 student enrollment numbered about 12,000, and the faculty, about 775.

OTTER, any aquatic carnivore of the genus *Lutra*, belonging to the family Mustelidae, which also includes the badger and the weasel

River otters, Lutra canadensis   William Vandivert

(qq.v.). In the common species, *L. lutra,* distributed through Europe and Asia, the body may attain a length of 2½ ft., and the tail half as much; the head is broad and flat, with short, rounded ears; the blunt snout bears lateral slitlike nostrils. The ears and nostrils can be closed when the animal is diving. The long body is covered with chestnut fur, the legs are short, but strong, and the feet are clawed as well as webbed. The otter lives in a hole by the edge of the water, and feeds especially on fish, but also on small mammals, birds, frogs, and crayfish. A similar species, *L. canadensis,* is found in North America. The otters of North America were once abundant, but owing to the value of their fur and the subsequent trapping, they are now comparatively rare, except in the Hudson Bay region. See SEA OTTER.

OTTERHOUND, special breed of dog descended from the old Southern Hound and the Welsh Harrier of Great Britain. It has large broad feet, a rough, grizzly coat varying in color, good sight, and a keen scent. It is a powerful swimmer, has great endurance, and is of a savage disposition. The average height is 24 to 26 in. and weight 50 to 75 lb.

OTTO (1848–1916), King of Bavaria (1886–1913), the son of Maximilian II, King of Bavaria (1811–64), born in Munich. Otto, who succeeded his elder brother Louis II, King of Bavaria (*see under* LOUIS), had been insane since 1873 and was under restraint at his accession. He was king only in name and reigned through the regency of his uncle Luitpold, Prince Regent of Bavaria (1821–1912), until 1912 and of his cousin Louis, later Louis III, King of Bavaria (*see under* LOUIS), thereafter. Otto was deposed in 1913 and was succeeded by his cousin.

OTTO I *or* **OTHO,** full name OTTO FRIEDRICH LUDWIG (1815–67), King of Greece (1832–62), the second son of Louis I, King of Bavaria (*see under* LOUIS), born in Salzburg, Austria, and was educated in Munich. When Greece freed itself from Turkish domination in the War of Independence of 1832, he was chosen by the London Conference as sovereign of the new Greek monarchy. He ruled under a regency of three Bavarian advisers until 1835. Otto became increasingly unpopular with the Greeks because of his German ministers, heavy taxes, his religion, the intervention of his German wife in governmental affairs, and his delay in granting a constitution. In 1843 Bavarian troops were withdrawn from Greece, and a Greek uprising forced him to appoint Greek ministers and to authorize a constitution. Otto's prestige fell rapidly as the British and French blockaded the port of Piraiévs and Greece became involved in the Crimean War (q.v.), which lasted from 1854 to 1856. In 1862 Otto was deposed by a revolutionary government, and he returned to Bavaria.

OTTO *or* **OTHO,** name of four Holy Roman emperors.

Otto I, called OTTO THE GREAT (912–73), Emperor (962–73), King of Germany (936–73), the son of Henry I (q.v.), King of Germany. After subduing an uprising of nobles incited by his brother, Otto consolidated his kingdom by granting duchies to faithful relatives and followers. In 951 he marched to Italy to assist Adelaide, Queen of Lombardy (931?–99), against **Berengar II,** King of Italy (d. 966). Otto defeated Berengar and married Adelaide, thereby becoming ruler of northern Italy. When he returned to Germany, he again crushed a rebellion of nobles and halted a Hungarian invasion in 955. In 962

OTTO

he was crowned Holy Roman emperor. In 963 he deposed Pope John XII (*see under* JOHN) and had Leo VIII (d. 965) elected in his stead. Otto sought to make the church subordinate to the authority of the empire, but assisted in spreading Christianity throughout his domain. He negotiated unsuccessfully with Byzantine emperor Nicephorus II Phocas (913?–69) for an alliance between the Byzantine and Holy Roman empires, but was able to arrange a marriage between his son Otto II and Theophano (955?–91), daughter of the Byzantine emperor Romanus II (939–63).

Otto II (955–83), Emperor (967–83), King of Germany (961–83), the son of Otto I, with whom he ruled jointly from 967 to 973. In 976 he suppressed a rebellion led by his cousin Henry II, Duke of Bavaria (951–95). Two years later, having been attacked by Lothair, King of France (941–86), Otto drove the French out of Lorraine, but was unsuccessful in besieging Paris. Later Lothair renounced Lorraine and peace was established. Otto next invaded southern Italy, gaining possession of Naples, Salerno, and Taranto, but was overwhelmingly defeated by the Greeks and Saracens at Cotrone in 982. His wife, Theophano, brought Byzantine refinement and culture into the German court.

Otto III (980–1002), Emperor (980–1002), son of Otto II, born in Kessel, Germany. He reigned under the coregency of his mother, Theophano, and his grandmother, Adelaide, from 983 to 991 and then under the regency of a council from 991 to 996. In 996 Otto assumed control, and having been crowned king of the Lombards, he went to Rome and established his cousin Bruno as Pope Gregory V (d. 999). After Gregory's death Otto made his own former tutor, Gerbert, pope as Sylvester II (*see under* SYLVESTER). Otto remained in Rome until his death, striving to make the city the capital of the Holy Roman Empire and to restore many of the customs of the ancient Roman Empire.

Otto IV, known as OTTO OF BRUNSWICK (1175?–1218), Emperor (1198–1215), the son of Henry the Lion, Duke of Saxony and of Bavaria, and the grandson of Henry II (qq.v.), King of England. He was educated at the court in England and was supported by the Guelphs (*see* GUELPHS AND GHIBELLINES) as successor to the imperial crown in opposition to Philip, Duke of Swabia (1176?–1208). Otto fought Philip for ten years and was crowned in 1209, a year after Philip's assassination. When Otto seized papal territory in 1210, he was excommunicated by Pope Innocent III (*see under* INNOCENT). A year later his deposition was declared by a council of German princes, who invited Frederick, King of Sicily, later Frederick II (q.v.), Holy Roman Emperor, to take the throne. Otto, favored by John (q.v.), King of England, continued to fight against Frederick and against Philip II (q.v.), King of France, who was supported by the pope. In 1215, after being defeated by the French army at Bouvines in 1214, Otto retired to his estates in Brunswick, where he remained until his death.

OTTOMAN EMPIRE, empire founded in the 14th century by Osman (q.v.), leader of the Ottoman Turks. Osman was succeeded by a series of the most warlike princes in history. They greatly extended the bounds of the Turkish dominion and about 1357 crossed the Hellespont into Europe. In 1361 Murad I, Sultan of Turkey (*see under* MURAD), made Adrianople (present-day Edirne) the seat of the Turkish Empire. The dominions of the Greeks were gradually reduced, and after a long siege Muhammad II (1430–81), Sultan of Turkey, took Constantinople (now İstanbul) in 1453. See TURKEY: *History.*

OTTUMWA, city in Iowa, county seat of Wapello Co., on the Des Moines R., 75 miles N.W. of Burlington. Ottumwa is in the heart of the Iowa bituminous coalfields. Extensive dams furnish waterpower; the industrial establishments of the city include brass foundries, meat-packing houses, and plants manufacturing agricultural implements, electronic parts, mining and construction tools, and bricks and tiles. The site of a junior college, Ottumwa was settled in 1843, incorporated in 1851, and chartered as a city in 1857. Pop. (1960) 33,871; (1970) 29,610.

OTUS *and* **EPHIALTES,** in Greek mythology, two giants, the twin sons of Poseidon (q.v.), god of the sea, and of Iphimedia. Known as the Aloadae or sons of Aloeus after the husband of their mother, they were renowned for their strength and daring, and at the age of nine they declared war upon the Olympian gods. In order to reach the home of the gods, they piled Mt. Ossa upon Olympus (q.v.), and Pelion upon Ossa. The goddess Artemis (q.v.) tricked them into inadvertently slaying each other while hunting a white hind. After death they were punished for their arrogance in Tartarus (q.v.). According to another legend, the twins imprisoned Ares (q.v.), god of war, for thirteen months.

OTWAY, Thomas (1652–85), English dramatist, born in Trotton, and educated at the University of Oxford. In 1672, after one unsuccessful appearance as an actor, he began to write plays in verse. His first play, the tragedy *Alcibiades*, was produced in 1675, and the tragedy *Don Carlos,* produced the following year, established his reputation as a dramatist. Otway served as an officer with an English regiment in Flanders in 1678; he wrote his most famous plays after returning to London in 1679. One of the most successful dramatists of his time, he nevertheless, died in poverty.

Otway's most important works are the tragedies *The Orphan* (1680) and *Venice Preserved* (1682). Both plays were immediately successful and were performed regularly for more than 200 years. Otway gave his characters considerable emotional depth and intensity; his intricate plots are skillfully contrived, and his verse is natural and often extremely moving.

OUACHITA, river in Arkansas and Louisiana, rising in the Ouachita Mts. in Arkansas, and flowing S.E. into Louisiana. After a course of about 605 mi. it joins the Red R., above the junction of the Red R. and the Mississippi. From Jonesville, La., to the Red R., it is known locally as the Black R.

OUAGADOUGOU, or WAGADUGU, city and capital of Upper Volta, and of capital Centre Department, about 475 miles N.W. of Accra. It is a major trade and road center, and a terminus of the 687-mi. railroad to Abidjan, Ivory Coast, on the Atlantic Ocean. The surrounding area produces livestock, grains, cotton, vegetables, and shea nuts and has granite and lignite deposits. Industries in the city include processing of vegetable oil and shea-nut butter, cotton ginning, textile weaving, brewing, and the manufacture of apparel, rugs, soap, soft drinks, handicrafts (bronze and copperware), and animal by-products. The city has a branch of the Institut Français d'Afrique Noire (with a museum), a sports stadium, and the palace of a Mossi chief. Center of an independent Mossi kingdom, Ouagadougou became capital of a French protectorate in 1897 and of a territory in 1919. From 1937 to 1947 the city was administrative center of the Upper Ivory Coast Region of the Ivory Coast colony. Pop. (1963 est.) 63,000.

OUIDA, pen name of MARIE LOUISE DE LA RAMÉE (q.v.).

OUJDA, city in Morocco, and capital of Oujda Province, 180 miles N.E. of Fez, near the Algerian border. The city, a rail and road junction, is a major center for trade in local wine, citrus fruit, grapes, wheat, barley, vegetables, tobacco, sheep, wool, and esparto grass. Lead, coal, and manganese mines are adjacent. Oujda is the site of Abd el-Moumen College and a municipal stadium. Founded in the late 10th century and ruled by several Arab and Berber dynasties, the city was captured by the French in 1844 and again in 1859, and was occupied by them from 1907 to 1956. The name is also spelled Oudjda. Pop. (1960) 128,645.

OULU, city in Finland, and capital of the Oulu Department, on the Gulf of Bothnia, about 330 miles N. of Helsinki. The principal industries are flour milling, food processing, and the manufacture of leather goods. It is the site of the University of Oulu, established in 1958. Oulu was founded in 1375 by the Swedes as a fortified center against the Russians. It was incorporated in 1610 and during the 19th century became a prosperous commercial center. Pop. (1968) 83,190.

OUNCE. See WEIGHTS AND MEASURES.

OUNCE or **SNOW LEOPARD,** wild, carnivorous mammal, *Uncia uncia,* of the Cat family, found in the mountains of central Asia. The animal, which attains a body length of about 4 ft.,

Ounce, Uncia uncia, known as a snow leopard.
R. Van Nostrand — National Audubon Society

is white and bluish gray in color, spotted with black. The large eyes are usually bluish gray. The ounce subsists on mountain animals, such as mountain sheep and ibexes and also hares and rodents. The ounce is not ferocious, but it is seldom seen by man in the wild because of its inaccessible haunts and nocturnal habits.

OUTDOOR RECREATION, BUREAU OF, agency of the United States Department of the Interior, established in 1962 as a Federal agency to meet current and future outdoor recreation needs. Two major responsibilities of the bureau are to keep up to date the nationwide Outdoor Recreation Plan, prepared in 1968, and to administer the Land and Water Conservation Fund, established in 1965; see CONSERVATION. The latter provides funds for the acquisition and development of Federal, State, and local recreation lands, areas, and facilities. See NATIONAL PARK SERVICE.

Other responsibilities are to assess present and future outdoor recreation resources and needs; assist Federal, State, local, and private efforts; and support research related to outdoor recreation programs. The director of the bureau serves as executive director of the President's Council on Recreation and Natural Beauty, established in 1966.

The bureau's Division of Water Resources Studies assesses the needs for water-oriented recreation, formulates recreation action plans, and devises solutions to special problems such as water pollution (q.v.) and conflicting land use. It also reviews reports of Federal and Federally licensed water projects. Headquarters of the bureau, which has six regional offices, is in Washington, D.C.

OUTREMONT, city of Canada, in Québec Province, in Hochelaga Co., on Montréal Island, on the N.W. side of Mount Royal Park, 3 miles S.W. of downtown Montréal. The city has railroad yards, and it manufactures cheese and other food products. It is the site of the Collège Stanislas (1938) and the Collège Jésus-Marie (1933). The city was founded in the early 19th century as Côte-Sainte-Catherine by members of the Roman Catholic order of Sulpicians; the name was changed in 1875. It was incorporated as a town in 1895 and as a city in 1915. Pop. (1966) 30,881.

OVARY, in anatomy, organs of female animals and human beings producing reproductive cells, called eggs or ova. The ovaries are analogous to the testes in the male. They are two oblong, flattened, ductless glands about one and one-half inches long in the human subject, on either side of the uterus (q.v.), to which they are connected by ligaments and by the Fallopian tubes (q.v.). The ovary is composed of two portions, an external or cortical portion, and a deep, medullary portion. The cortical portion in the adult contains an enormous number of follicles or sacs varying greatly in size. They are the Graafian follicles and contain the ova, the female element of reproduction (q.v.); see REPRODUCTIVE SYSTEM: *Gonads.* The ovary secretes hormones (q.v.) which, with secretions from the pituitary gland (q.v.), contribute to feminine secondary, sexual characteristics. Such hormones also regulate menstruation (q.v.). The union of the ovum with the male sperm cell results in fertilization (q.v.).

The ovary may be the site of several diseased conditions. It can be the seat of acute and chronic inflammation. This may arise from injuries during labor, operations in the pelvic area, or gonorrheal infection spreading from the vagina. The ovary also may be the seat of neoplasms, or new growths, of several varieties. Some represent fluidic enlargements of one or more Graafian follicles and attain an enormous size, sometimes weighing 100 lb. or more. These are known as ovarian cysts; see CYST. Other growths, of a rather solid nature, are known as dermoid cysts. These enlargements, usually benign, occasionally prove to be malignant.

The treatment of ovarian disease by ovariotomy, removal of the affected organ, is one of the triumphs of modern surgery. Formerly, relief in cystoma was only obtained by periodic tapping, that is, withdrawing some of the fluid by means of a medical instrument. An operation to remove an ovarian cystoma was first performed by the American surgeon Ephraim McDowell (1771–1830) of Kentucky in 1809 and was established in Great Britain as a regular operation by Charles Clay of Manchester, who operated on his first case in 1842.

OVARY, in botany. See FRUIT; OVULE.

OVERBURY, Sir Thomas (1581–1613), English courtier, born in Compton Scorpion. In 1601, at Edinburgh, he met Robert Carr (d. 1645), who became Viscount Rochester, the Scottish favorite of James I (q.v.), King of England. The two became friends, and Overbury was, through Carr's influence, knighted in 1608. He incurred the anger of Frances Howard, Countess of Essex, Carr's mistress, by opposing their marriage, and on a trivial pretext was confined to the Tower of London, where he was poisoned at her instigation. Overbury holds a minor place in English literature, his work including *A Wife* (1614) and *Characters* (1614).

OVERLAND, city of Missouri, in Saint Louis Co., 10 miles N.W. of downtown Saint Louis. The Army Records Center and Publications Center are situated here. The city was incorporated in 1939. Pop. (1960) 22,763; (1970) 24,949.

OVERLAND PARK, city of Kansas, in Johnson Co., 6 miles S.W. of Kansas City. Manufactured here are farm machinery, aluminum products, and electronic parts; the area has dairy farms. The city was incorporated in 1960. Pop. (1960) 21,110; (1970) 76,623.

OVERTURE, in music, instrumental introduction to an opera (q.v.) or other musical or nonmusical dramatic work. Some independent instrumental compositions of the 19th and 20th centuries have also been called overtures by their composers. The first operas, dating from the early 17th century, had no overtures but were introduced by vocalists who summarized the action to follow. Instrumental introductions became common by the mid-17th century, when two standard overture forms developed. The French overture, created by the Italian-French composer Jean-Baptiste Lully (q.v.), was in two parts, the first slow and stately, the second fast with many contrapuntal details; see COUNTERPOINT. Later in the 17th century the Italian composer Alessandro Scarlatti (q.v.) introduced an Italian overture, which consisted of three sections: fast, slow, and fast. It was one of the forerunners of the independent instrumental genre, the symphony (q.v.).

Until the late 18th century, overtures were seldom related to the operas that followed them. The overtures were usually hastily written at the last minute, and audiences rarely listened to them, preferring instead to talk or even eat while the music was being played. The Italian opera reformer Christoph Willibald Gluck (q.v.) was among the first composers to reject these practices. Gluck's overtures often set the emotional tone of the opera to follow and incorporated melodies from it. The influence of Gluck's ideas on the Austrian composer Wolfgang Amadeus Mozart (q.v.) is evident in Mozart's opera *Don Giovanni* (1787), wherein music from late scenes is first heard in the overture. The extensive use of music from the opera itself can be found in the first three *Leonore* overtures by the German composer Ludwig van Beethoven (q.v.). The overture had, by the 19th century, developed into a single movement, similar to the first movement of the sonata or symphony. Many brilliant overtures were written by the Italian composer Gioacchino Antonio Rossini (q.v.); they include the popular *William Tell* overture (1829). The form was further extended by the German composer Richard Wagner (q.v.); the overtures to his operas review the dramatic action of the plot and incorporate themes from the music of the drama. In Wagner's operas the overture became an extended prelude that led without a break into the music of the first act. Most subsequent composers of opera discarded the overture entirely, although it continued to be used for the operetta and the musical comedy (qq.v.).

Outstanding examples of the overture to nonmusical dramatic works are Beethoven's overture to *Coriolan* by the Austrian playwright Heinrich Josef von Collin (1771–1811) and the overture to *A Midsummer Night's Dream* of William Shakespeare by the German composer Felix Mendelssohn (*see under* MENDELSSOHN).

OVERWEIGHT. See OBESITY.

OVID, in full PUBLIUS OVIDIUS NASO (43 B.C.–17? A.D.), Roman poet, born in Sulmo (now Sulmona), near Rome, Italy. Educated for the bar, he became highly proficient in the art of declamation, but his genius was essentially poetical, and he devoted most of his time and energy to writing verse. After inheriting his father's

Ovid, Roman poet, is best known for his masterpiece, the Metamorphoses, *written in fifteen books.*
Bettmann Archive

property, Ovid went to Athens to complete his education. He later traveled in Asia and Sicily with his friend the poet Aemilus Macer (d. 16 B.C.). By the age of thirty, Ovid had been married three times and divorced twice, and he may have carried on an intrigue with the woman whom he celebrated in his poetry as Corinna. His private life was that of a gay, well-to-do, and somewhat licentious man of letters. At Rome, where he resided until his fiftieth year, he was assiduously courted by the distinguished and fashionable society of the city, including the emperor Augustus (q.v.) and the imperial family. In 8 A.D. Ovid was banished to Tomi (now Constanța, Rumania). According to Ovid, one reason for his banishment was the publication of *Ars Amatoria,* a poem on the art of making love. More probably the poem, which had been in circulation for almost ten years, served merely as a pretext. A second reason, never disclosed by Ovid, may have been his knowledge of a

OVID

scandal involving the emperor's granddaughter Julia (q.v.). Ovid did not lose his citizenship, or give up hope of repatriation, as revealed in the many poems written to his friends during his exile at Tomi, but his entreaties and those of his friends were unavailing. He died at Tomi, an honored citizen of the town.

Early Works. The poetry of Ovid falls into three divisions, the works of his youth, of his middle age, and of his years of exile at Tomi. In the first period, Ovid continued the elegiac tradition of the poets Sextus Propertius and Albius Tibullus (qq.v.), both of whom he knew and admired. The *Amores,* originally in five books, but revised and abridged to three, are erotic poems centering about Corinna, but they display little real feeling and are characterized by artificiality and cleverness. Other works of this period reveal Ovid as a didactic poet imparting instruction on love. Among these poems are *Medicamina Faciei,* a fragment on cosmetics; the *Ars Amandi,* or *Ars Amatoria,* in three books; and a kind of recantation in one book, the *Remedia Amoris. Medea,* a tragedy highly praised by ancient critics, has not been preserved. Ovid's interest in mythology first becomes apparent in his *Heroides,* or *Epistulae Heroidum,* twenty-one fictional love letters, mostly from mythological heroines to their lovers.

Middle Period. In his middle period Ovid wrote the *Metamorphoses,* in fifteen books. The work deals with all the transformations recorded in mythology and legend from the creation of the world down to the time of the Roman statesman and general Gaius Julius Caesar (q.v.), whose change into a star marks the last of the series. Deservedly famous as a handbook of Greek mythology, it is composed in a witty and, at times, almost burlesque spirit. The other work of the middle period is the *Fasti,* a poetic calendar describing the various Roman festivals and the legends connected with each. Of the projected twelve books, one for each month of the year, only the first six are extant, and it is believed that these are probably all that Ovid completed.

Works in Exile. The works composed during the period of Ovid's exile are pervaded by melancholy and despair. These works include five books of elegies, namely the *Tristia,* which are descriptive of his unhappy existence at Tomi and contain numerous appeals to the clemency of Augustus; the *Epistulae ex Ponto,* poetic letters similar in theme to the *Tristia;* the *Ibis,* a short invective invoking destruction on a personal enemy; and the *Halieutica,* a poem extant only in fragments, about the fish of the Euxine (now the Black Sea). The *Nux* and the *Consolatio ad Liviam* are usually considered spurious. With the exception of the *Metamorphoses* and the fragmentary *Halieutica,* both of which are in the dactylic hexameter meter, all the poetry of Ovid is composed in the elegiac couplet, a meter which he brought to its highest degree of perfection; see VERSIFICATION.

Criticism. Ovid was one of the most influential of Roman poets during the Middle Ages and the Renaissance. Lodovico Ariosto and Giovanni Boccaccio, in Italy, and Geoffrey Chaucer and John Gower (qq.v.), in England, found in his mythological narratives a rich quarry of romantic tales. Edmund Spenser, William Shakespeare, John Milton (qq.v.), and many other English poets were indebted to him. Although Ovid was at times superficial, he was a born storyteller, and his ingenuity, cleverness, and gaiety have endeared him to generations of modern readers.

See LATIN LITERATURE: *The Golden Age: The Augustan Period.*

OVIEDO, city in Spain, and capital of Oviedo Province, about 15 miles S.W. of Gijón. It is a transportation and industrial center of the surrounding agricultural and mining region. The principal manufactures include firearms, gunpowder, and textiles. Oviedo is famed as the site of several medieval churches and a cathedral. Begun in 1388, the cathedral contains the royal Asturian tombs. The city is also the site of the University of Oviedo, established in 1604.

Oviedo was founded about the middle of the 8th century. It reached the height of its importance during the 9th century, when it was the capital of the kingdom of Asturias. Pop. (1965) 132,646.

OVULATION. See MENSTRUATION; REPRODUCTION; REPRODUCTIVE SYSTEM: *Gonads.*

OVULE, in botany, name applied to immature seeds, which are produced within the ovary of a flower. In flowering plants, the history of the ovule is generally as follows.

At the site of the future seed (q.v.), an outgrowth, the nucellus or megasporangium, develops; this becomes covered by two integuments which grow up from its base, but which leave an opening at the top called the micropyle. Within the nucellus is the megaspore mother cell. It divides into two and then into four; one of these megaspores then typically divides into eight nuclei to become the embryo sac or female gametophyte; it is called the embryo sac because the embryo will develop in it.

The young male plants, or male gametophytes, are popularly referred to as pollen grains; these are contained in modified leaves called stamens. When a pollen grain is placed on the stigma, it sends out a tube which grows down to the ovary and eventually enters the ovule. Two sperms are then discharged into the embryo sac; one of these fuses with the egg nucleus at the micropylar end of the embryo sac, and this fertilized egg then develops into the

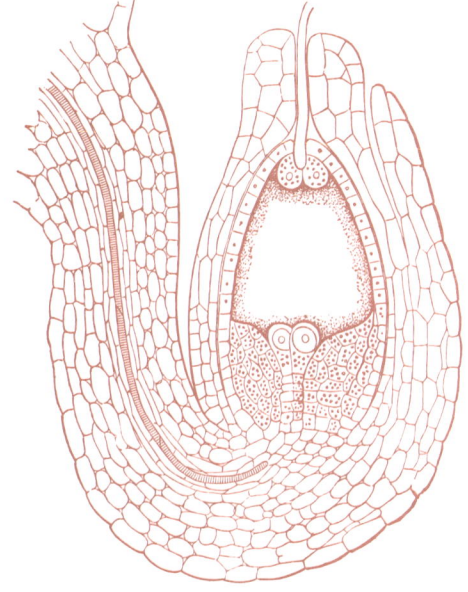

Section of an ovule, showing the entry of the pollen tube into the embryo sac.

embryo of the seed. The other sperm fuses with two nuclei near the middle of the embryo sac; the resulting triple-fusion nucleus develops into the endosperm, which usually remains as the food storage tissue of the seed. *See* FERTILIZATION; FLOWER; PLANT BREEDING; POLLINATION.

OVUM. *See* EGG.

OWATONNA, city in Minnesota, and county seat of Steele Co., about 63 miles S. of Minneapolis. A marketing center for dairy products, it has printing and engraving plants, and metal products are made. Rich in mineral water, Owatonna was Minnesota's first health resort. It is the site of the National Farmers' Bank, designed by the American architect Louis Henri Sullivan (q.v.); built in 1908, it is one of the best examples of modern architecture in the State. Pop. (1960) 13,409; (1970) 15,341.

OWEN, name of a British social reformer and an American legislator and diplomat who were father and son.

Robert Owen (1771–1858), British social reformer, born in Newtown, Wales. He had little opportunity for schooling and began work in a textile shop at the age of ten. His progress was rapid and he was manager of one of the largest cotton mills in Manchester, England, at nineteen. In 1794 he helped establish an independent company, and in 1799 he and his associates purchased the spinning mills in New Lanark, Scotland. There Owen put into effect the social theories for which he later became famous. About 2000 people were connected with his mills, 500 of them children from Scottish poorhouses. The great majority lived in the same squalor that characterized all industrial communities of that period. Believing that character is formed by early environment and training, Owen paid particular attention to the establishment of schools in his community, including the first nursery school in Great Britain. He also instituted improvements in housing and sanitation and opened a store at which goods could be bought for little more than cost.

The New Lanark experiment was highly successful in both its business and social aspects, and it drew visitors from all over Europe. Encouraged by this success, Owen began a campaign in 1815 for legislation prohibiting employment before the age of ten and night work before eighteen, and establishing a ten-and-one-half hour maximum working day for children under eighteen. This effort met with only limited success, and the bill that finally passed Parliament included few of Owen's proposals. Owen became disillusioned with reform schemes and began to campaign for immediate changes to transform the social structure of Great Britain. He urged the establishment of co-operative communities, in which the members would conduct their own agriculture and industry, living communally and sharing the product of their labor. This suggestion was strongly opposed by other businessmen, and Owen determined to put it into practice in the United States. In 1825, he purchased 30,000 acres of land in Indiana and founded a community called New Harmony (q.v.). An unbalanced selection of personnel, among whom several necessary occupations were inadequately represented, caused the dissolution of the community in 1828, and Owen returned home. Other Owenite communities, established in Great Britain, were somewhat successful. In London Owen found himself the leader by popular acclaim of a new and powerful labor movement, and he began a campaign for the establishment by unions of their own industries.

The National Equitable Labor Exchange was founded in 1832 to market the products of these industries; a National Operative Builders Union

OWEN

was set up to take over the construction industry. Governmental opposition was so intense, however, that Owen was forced to dissolve the movement in 1834, and he withdrew from active participation in labor affairs.

During the rest of his life, Owen devoted himself to the promotion of his theories. Owen is noted both for his contributions to educational practice, based on his belief in the importance of early training, and for his socialist ideas and experiments. At the present time Owen's influence is more apparent in the cooperative movement (q.v.), which began at Rochdale, England, than in modern socialist movements. See ROCHDALE SOCIETY OF EQUITABLE PIONEERS; SOCIALISM.

Robert Dale Owen (1801–77), American legislator and diplomat, son of Robert Owen, born in Glasgow, Scotland, and educated at the New Lanark school run by his father and in Switzerland. Owen accompanied his father on a trip to the United States in 1825 to help in the founding of the short-lived colony at New Harmony (q.v.), Ind. He remained in the U.S., settling first in New York City in 1829 and becoming a cofounder of the socialistic newspaper *Free Enquirer.* In 1832 he returned to Indiana and was elected to the State legislature as a Democrat three years later. He was elected to Congress in 1842 and again in 1844. In 1853, he was appointed United States minister to Naples, Italy. After his return to the U.S. in 1858, he took an active part in the campaigns of the abolitionists (q.v.). Owen's writings include *The Wrong of Slavery* (1864) and an autobiography, *Threading My Way* (1874).

OWENS, Jesse, real name JAMES CLEVELAND OWENS (1913–), American athlete, born in Decatur, Ala., and educated at Ohio State University. He competed in interscholastic track meets while attending secondary school, excelling in the running broad jump, the 100-yd. dash, and the 220-yd. dash and setting new records for these events in 1933. As a member of the Ohio State University track squad in 1935, he established a new world record (26 ft. 8¼ in.) for the running broad jump; the next year he set a new world record (10.2 sec.) for the 100-m dash.

A member of the United States track team in the Olympic Games (q.v.) of 1936, held in Berlin, Germany, Owens became the first American and the second athlete in history to win three Olympic events: he won the 100-m dash in 10.3 sec., equaling the Olympic record; he set a new Olympic and world record by finishing the 200-m dash in 20.7 sec.; and he won the running broad jump with a leap of 26 ft. 5⅜ in., setting a new Olympic record. He was also a member of the U.S. 400-m relay team that year, which set a new Olympic and world record of 39.8 sec. Despite his outstanding performance, however, the German dictator Adolf Hitler (q.v.) refused to acknowledge the victories of Owens on account of his being a Negro.

Owens played an active role in youth athletic programs and in 1952 became secretary of the Illinois Athletic Commission. His autobiography *The Jesse Owens Story* was published in 1970.

OWENSBORO, city in Kentucky, and county seat of Daviess Co., on the Ohio R., 50 miles s.w. of Brandenburg. It is one of the largest leaf and strip tobacco markets in the United States. Industries include meat packing, flour milling, distilling, canning, and the manufacture of radio tubes, tobacco products, steel, and chemicals. The city is the site of Kentucky Wesleyan College, founded in 1858, and Brescia College, founded in 1874. The city was settled about 1800 and incorporated in 1866. Pop. (1960) 42,471; (1970) 50,329.

OWL, common name for any of 133 species of birds constituting the order Strigiformes. The head is large and broad, the cranial bones highly pneumatic, and the facial region flattened; the short, hooked beak is strong and sharp. The large eyes are directed forward, and only slightly

Jesse Owens, in 1934 as an Ohio State trackman, broad jumps a distance of 26 ft. 1½ in. to win an N.C.A.A. meet. UPI

Screech owl, Otus asio   UPI

movable; the upper eyelid is large, and both eyelids are fringed with barbed plumelets, and have a thin, bare margin; the third eyelid, or nictitating membrane, is conspicuous. The iris is unusually broad, and is capable of being greatly expanded and contracted.

Owls range over the whole globe except in the Antarctic Region and on some oceanic islands. They are generally nocturnal, with noiseless, buoyant flight, and acute senses of eyesight and hearing. They are either solitary or live in pairs, and although often regarded with superstitious aversion, are usually harmless birds. Their food consists of small mammals, birds, and insects, especially nocturnal lepidoptera; some species prey on fish, either habitually or occasionally. If found abroad during the day they are persecuted by smaller birds, being bewildered and rendered helpless by the unaccustomed glare of daylight. When surprised, owls hiss like a cat and make a clicking noise with their bills; some have a harsh shrieking cry, others give a melodic hoot.

The long-eared and short-eared owls of America, Europe, and Asia, *Otus asio* and *O. accipitrinus*, have peculiarly developed ears, that open upward on one side and downward on the other. The specialization of the ear is carried to its greatest known limit in Tengmalm's owl, *Nyctala tengmalmi,* that has developed a different bone structure on each side of the head. Of American species belonging to this family, one of the most noteworthy is the burrowing owl, *Speotyto cunicularia.* Found in western North America and southern Florida, it shares the burrows of several species of mammals, while on the pampas of South America it lives in the holes of the viscacha, armadillos, and large lizards, or makes a hole for itself, that is often in-

OXENSTIERNA

vaded by rattlesnakes. Among the best known owls of North America are the screech owl, *Otus asio,* the barred owl, *Strix varia,* and the great horned owl, *Bubo Virginianus;* see GREAT HORNED OWL.

The tawny owl, *Strix aluco,* is a common British species. It has a hooting call that is easily recognized at night. The diurnal snowy owl, *Nyctea scandiaca,* known as the harfang in Sweden, is a circumpolar bird, breeding chiefly within the Arctic Circle, and common in parts of Greenland and Iceland, the Soviet Union, and North America. Barn owls form a family of their own, Tytonidae, while all other owls are in the family Strigidae.

OWOSSO, city of Michigan, in Shiawassee Co., about 27 miles N.E. of Lansing. The city has varied manufacturing. Governor Thomas Edmund Dewey (q.v.) of New York was born here. Pop. (1960) 17,006; (1970) 17,179.

OX. See CATTLE.

OXENSTIERNA, Count Axel Gustafsson (1583–1654), Swedish statesman, born near Enköping, and educated at the universities of Rostock, Jena, and Wittenberg in Germany. In 1612 he was appointed chancellor of Sweden by Gustavus II (q.v.), King of Sweden. He negotiated peace settlements with Denmark in 1613, with Russia in 1617, and with Poland in 1623, and was appointed governor-general of the province of Prussia in 1626. Following the death of the king, Oxenstierna became the most powerful statesman in Swedish history, when in January, 1633, the diet designated him legate plenipotentiary in Germany, with absolute power over the vast territories conquered by the Swedish armies. In the same year he organized the Protestant princes of Germany into a mutual-assistance organization known as the Evangelical League. In 1636 he negotiated the Treaty of Wismar with France, whereby Sweden, whose resources had been severely strained as a result of her recurring wars, gained the promise of aid from France while making no major concessions or sacrifices. Another of his brilliant achievements was the planning of the Danish War of 1643–45, which resulted in the Peace of Bromsebro, whereby Denmark, the hereditary enemy of Sweden, was stripped of her power. During the regency of the young Christina, Queen of Sweden (1626–89), Oxenstierna wielded almost absolute power in the foreign and domestic policies of his country. After her accession in 1644, however, disputes with the queen led to the decline of his power. He was created a count in 1645. See SWEDEN: *History: The Expansion of Sweden.*

OXFORD

OXFORD, Great Britain, county borough of Oxfordshire, England, at the confluence of the Cherwell and Isis rivers, so called as a tributary of the Thames, about 55 miles N.W. of London. The chief industry of the city is automobile manufacturing. It is the site of the University of Oxford, one of the oldest and best known universities in the world; see OXFORD, UNIVERSITY OF.

The city is also a famous tourist attraction. The center of the town is at a place called "Carfax" (derived from *quadrifurcus,* "fourforked"), from which four main streets run to the four points of the compass. The main street is High Street (the "High"), a part of London Road with Carfax at one end and Magdalen Bridge at the other. Also in the city are the churches of Saint Michael, dating from the 11th century, and Saint Mary the Virgin, from the 13th century; the Bodleian Library (q.v.); and the Sheldonian Theatre, built (1669) at his expense by Gilbert Sheldon (1598–1677), Archbishop of Canterbury.

The first recorded mention of Oxford dates to the early 10th century when it was a trading center. In the 10th and 11th centuries it was attacked by the Danes. By the 13th century, with the establishment of the university, it was an educational center. In the 14th century it was a headquarters for the religious reform movement of the English theologian John Wycliffe (q.v.). Oxford was later made a High Church and from 1642 to 1645, it was the capital of Charles I (q.v.), King of England. During the Great Rebellion (q.v.) Oxford was a center for the Royalists. Pop. (1969 est.) 109,720.

OXFORD AND ASQUITH, 1st Earl of. See ASQUITH, HERBERT HENRY, 1ST EARL OF OXFORD AND ASQUITH.

OXFORD MOVEMENT, known also as TRACTARIANISM, religious revival emphasizing the catholic, that is, apostolic and universal, origins of the Church of England (q.v.); see APOSTLE; REVIVALS, RELIGIOUS. Adherents of the movement held that the apostolic succession, that is, the valid transmission of apostolic authority to administer sacraments (see SACRAMENT) was not broken by the English Reformation (see REFORMATION: *National Movements*) and that the Church of England constitutes a branch of the holy catholic church, of which the Roman Catholic and the Greek Orthodox churches also are branches. The chief leaders of the movement were the British theologians John Keble, Cardinal John Henry Newman, and Edward Bouverie Pusey (qq.v.), all of whom were connected with the University of Oxford.

Beginnings. The Anglican clergyman and scholar Keble initiated the movement with a sermon, "On the National Apostasy", at Oxford on July 14, 1833. Citing a recent statute abolishing ten bishoprics in Ireland, Keble warned the Church of England against the threat of domination by secular authorities and accused contemporary churchmen of national apostasy (see APOSTATE) in abandoning the principles of 16th- and 17th-century Anglican theologians.

Later that month a group of religious leaders who agreed with Keble's thesis met and pledged their support of the principles embodied in the *Book of Common Prayer* (q.v.) and of the doctrine of apostolic succession.

The Tracts. Beginning in September, 1833, Keble and several of his associates, chief among them Newman, Richard Hurrell Froude (1803–36), and Isaac Williams (1802–65), elaborated their religious views in a series of ninety pamphlets entitled *Tracts for the Times,* from which the term Tractarianism is derived. Newman also contributed greatly to the movement through persuasive weekly sermons delivered over a period of eight years. the movement received additional impetus through the adherence in 1834 of Pusey, whose prestige was so great that its members became known popularly as Puseyites.

The Tractarians held that the Church of England, as part of the catholic church created by divine authority, was more than a merely human institution. They claimed further that Anglican bishops were the rightful successors of the Apostles according to canon law (q.v.). The Tractarians considered that the Church of England represented the *via media* (Lat., "middle way") between Roman Catholicism and Protestantism, both of which they regarded as abhorrent, and held that the church could be saved only through a return to its catholic origins.

Opposition to the Oxford movement became intense after the publication in 1838–39 of the *Literary Remains of Richard Hurrell Froude,* edited by Newman and Keble. This work alarmed and antagonized many Anglican bishops because of its sympathetic attitude toward Roman Catholicism and its attacks on the leaders of the Reformation. Thenceforth the bishops opposed the Oxford movement with increasing vigor.

Tract 90, issued by Newman in February, 1841, brought the conflict with the authorities of the church to a climax. In the tract Newman attempted to prove that the Anglican Thirty-nine Articles of Religion (see ARTICLES, THE THIRTY-NINE) were not inconsistent with the dogma of the Roman Catholic Church (q.v.). The leaders of the Church of England condemned the tract formally on March 15, and on the insistence of the

OXFORD, UNIVERSITY OF

bishop of Oxford publication of the *Tracts for the Times* was discontinued.

Consequences. Several hundred clergymen thereupon left the Church of England and became members of the Roman Catholic Church, joined, in 1845, by Newman himself.

The supporters of the Oxford movement who remained within the Church of England were known thereafter as Anglo-Catholics. After 1860 emphasis shifted from questions of doctrine to those of ceremony, giving rise to the movement known as ritualism (q.v.), which sometimes is confused with the Oxford movement.

Tractarianism made important contributions to the Church of England. It restored the dignity of the church and its ministers, revived interest in theology and church history, strengthened appreciation of catholic liturgy, and inspired new artistic achievements in ecclesiastical music and architecture. In addition, the movement led to the organization of religious sisterhoods (q.v.) and stimulated a fresh awareness of the social responsibility of Christians, as evidenced, for example, by the establishment of Anglican missions in city slums.

OXFORDSHIRE, or OXON, Great Britain, county of England, bounded on the N. by Warwickshire and Northamptonshire, on the E. by Buckinghamshire, on the S. by Berkshire, and on the W. by Gloucestershire. It is watered by the Thames River (q.v.), with its tributaries the Windrush, Evenlode, Cherwell, and Thame. The Oxford and Birmingham Canal affords access to the midland coal fields. The soil is fertile, and the state of agriculture advanced, producing barley, oats, and wheat; livestock, cattle, sheep, and pigs are raised. Ironstone is worked near Banbury (q.v.). The manufactures include blankets, paper, and gloves. The county borough and largest city is Oxford (q.v.). Area, 751 sq.mi.; pop. (1969 est.) 374,610.

OXFORD, UNIVERSITY OF, oldest institution of higher learning in England, situated in Oxford, Oxfordshire. Although the origin of the university is obscure, continental scholars are known to have lectured in Oxford as early as 1117, possibly attracted by the nearness of the palace of the scholarly King Henry I (q.v.). About 1167 the expulsion of foreigners from the University of Paris, resulting from the quarrel between King Henry II and Thomas à Becket (qq.v.), Archbishop of Canterbury, caused a migration of English students to Oxford.

Origin. By 1185 Oxford was already a center of learning, possessing organized faculties granting regular degrees, and in the reign of Richard I (q.v.) scholars were maintained there by the royal bounty. Before the end of the 12th century the existing schools at Oxford came to be considered a *studium generale*, at which students and doctors from all the great universities of Europe congregated. In 1214, by order of the papal legate, a chancellor of the university was chosen to preside over a self-governing guild of masters. Like the University of Paris, Oxford was divided into nations, or groups of students from general regions: the North, including Scottish students; and the South, including Irish and Welsh students. The faculty of arts was of chief importance, overshadowing those of law, medicine, and theology.

Separate colleges were gradually established, composed of voluntary associations of students who joined together in renting houses, instead of living separately at their own expense in the town. These voluntary student associations then obtained licenses from the university. The development of the colleges was further strengthened by the arrival, in the mid-13th century, of the mendicant orders of Dominicans, Franciscans, Carmelites, and Augustinians (qq.v.), which acquired property in the town, built houses, and soon gained influence among the students. About the same time, colleges began to be established by private benefaction; the earliest of these colleges were University College (1249), founded as Durham Hall through a bequest of the English ecclesiastic William of Durham (d. 1249); Balliol College (between 1263 and 1269), founded by the Scottish baron John de Baliol (*see under* BALIOL) and his wife Devorguila (d. 1290); and Merton College (1264), founded by Walter de Merton, bishop of Rochester (d. 1277). The last-named college was the first of its kind in the modern sense of the term, and served as a model for subsequent colleges at both Oxford and Cambridge. Thereafter more and more students became members of individual colleges, in which instruction was given within the college walls, and a comparable decrease took place in the number of students living alone in the town, or in religious houses or independent student halls.

Impact of the Renaissance. The new learning of the Renaissance (q.v.; *see also* HUMANISM) was warmly received at Oxford, and the earliest students of Greek in England were Oxford scholars. Notable among these students were the Dutch humanist Desiderius Erasmus, and such Englishmen as the humanist Thomas Linacre, the theologian John Colet, the statesman Sir Thomas More (qq.v.), and the scholar of Greek William Grocyn (1446?–1519). During the Reformation (q.v.) the severing of ties with the Roman Cath-

231

Aerial view of the University of Oxford, Oxford, England. The Gothic spires completely dominate the surrounding landscape. British Information Services

olic Church put an end to the scholastic methods of teaching at Oxford and Cambridge, and both universities suffered loss of land and revenues. In 1571, during the reign of Elizabeth I, an act was passed incorporating and reorganizing the university, and in 1636, during the reign of Charles I, the statutes of the university were codified by William Laud (qq.v.), Archbishop of Canterbury, who was then chancellor of Oxford; these two sets of codes remained the official governing statutes of the university until the middle of the 19th century. Oxford was a center of the Royalist Party during the Great Rebellion (q.v.), from 1642 to 1645, although the town of Oxford favored the Parliamentary cause. The soldier and statesman Oliver Cromwell (see under CROMWELL) was chancellor of the university from 1651 to 1657, after the town was taken by the Parliamentarians, and was responsible for preventing both Oxford and Cambridge from being closed down by the Puritans (q.v.), who distrusted university education on the grounds that it was dangerous to religious belief. During the 18th century the university was largely Jacobin (see JACOBITES) in sentiment, while the town took the part of the Hannoverians, but after 1785, in the reign of George III (q.v.), Oxford took little part in politics. In the latter half of the 18th century, academic conditions, which had been neglected since the Great Rebellion, improved. During the 19th century written examinations for admission replaced oral tests; the university also became more liberal in regard to admission of religious dissenters. The first of the four colleges for women, all established before the beginning of the 20th century, was founded in 1879.

Structure. The University of Oxford is a federation of colleges, each with its own internal organization and laws, united under the university itself, which maintains separate officials and legislative bodies. The chief officer of the university is the chancellor, its nominal head, elected for life by members of the Convocation (see below), who are graduates of the university holding the degree of M.A.; the chancellor is generally a peer of the realm. The actual head of the university is the vice-chancellor, nominated annually by the chancellor from among the heads of the colleges. Two proctors, charged with the responsibility of disciplinary measures regarding the junior members of the university (the undergraduates), are elected annually from two colleges, with the various colleges electing in rotation.

The business of the university is transacted by four bodies: the Ancient House of Congregation, consisting of masters of arts of not less than two years' standing, heads of colleges, deans of degrees of colleges, professors, examiners, and other lesser officials, which exercises authority as a body conferring ordinary degrees; the Congregation of the University, constituted by act of Parliament in 1854 and consisting of university officers, professors, and other members of the teaching staff, which discusses and votes on proposed statutes submitted by the Hebdomadal Council (the most influential body of the university in regard to practical administration; see below); the Convocation, consisting basically of all M.A.'s of the university; and the Hebdomadal Council, a body of practical educators which promulgates legislation and guides university policy and is composed of the vice-chancellor, the retiring vice-chancellor, the proctors, and eighteen other members elected by the Congregation of the University.

Each college is organized under a head (variously called warden, provost, principal, president, or master, in different colleges) and is composed of fellows, tutors, and scholars, or undergraduates. The officer charged with the internal discipline is usually known as the dean. All members of a college above the undergraduates are known collectively and colloquially as "dons". Each undergraduate is assigned a tutor, who is responsible for the undergraduate during his residence at the college and for his academic work. Formal teaching is chiefly by means of lectures, which are given by professors and lecturers of the university and by college teaching staffs.

Degrees and Special Fields. Examinations are conducted and degrees granted by the university itself. Two examinations for the degree of bachelor of arts are required: the first, known as the first public examination, is taken after one or two years, according to whether or not the candidate seeks honors in his subject; and the second, taken two years later, is known as honour schools. The degree of master of arts requires no further study or examination but is granted to the recipient of a B.A. after three or four years and the payment of certain fees. The university also grants the degrees of bachelor and doctor in divinity, law, medicine, letters, science, music, and other fields. In contrast to Cambridge, which became noted for its concentration in the fields of mathematics and science, Oxford long maintained a close adherence to traditional classical education. In recent years, however, its curricula have been expanded to include a larger variety of subjects, particularly modern languages and economics, and emphasis has been placed upon scientific and medical research.

The number of students registered at Oxford in 1967–68 totaled 10,202; the faculty numbered about 1300. Oxford has a famous library (see BODLEIAN LIBRARY), founded in 1602 by the English diplomat Sir Thomas Bodley (1545–1613), containing 2,850,000 bound volumes and 50,000 manuscripts. The combined university libraries hold about 3,700,000 bound volumes. The university has its own press, Clarendon Press. The colleges and their dates of foundation are listed on the accompanying table.

College	Founded	College	Founded
All Souls	1438	Pembroke	1624
Balliol	1263	Queen's	1340
Brasenose	1509	St. Anne's	1952
Christ Church	1546	St. Antony's	1950
Corpus Christi	1517	St. Catherine's	1962
Exeter	1314	St. Cross	1965
Hertford	1874	St. Edmund Hall	1270
Jesus	1571	St. Hilda's	1893
Keble	1868	St. Hugh's	1886
Lady Margaret Hall	1878	St. John's	1555
		St. Peter's	1929
Linacre	1965	Somerville	1879
Lincoln	1427	Trinity	1554
Magdalen	1458	University	1249
Merton	1264	Wadham	1612
New College	1379	Wolfson	1965
Nuffield	1937	Worcester	1714
Oriel	1326		

OXIDATION, in chemistry, term used to signify reaction of an element or compound with oxygen (q.v.) to form oxides, that is, compounds containing oxygen. The term is also applicable to certain other reactions. When iron rusts, for example, it combines with oxygen from the air to form ferric oxide. Another example is the burning of methane gas, CH_4, to give oxides of carbon and hydrogen. The reactions of iron and of methane with oxygen are in many ways similar to their reactions with chlorine, except that in the latter case chlorides, $FeCl_3$, CCl_4, and HCl, are formed instead of oxides. The electron theory of atomic structure pictures the iron atoms in reaction with oxygen or with chlorine as losing electrons, which are transferred in the one case to oxygen and in the other to chlorine; see ATOM AND ATOMIC THEORY. The loss of electrons, therefore, whether by iron or another substance, is what is meant by oxidation. In this sense, such reactions with chlorine are regarded as oxidation, even though no oxygen is involved. See also ELECTRON.

The oxygen and chlorine, on accepting electrons from iron, become negative oxygen ions and chlorine ions respectively (see ION; IONIZATION) and are said to be reduced. Because electrons are lost by iron only when an agent is present to combine with them, the two proc-

OXIDE

esses, that is, oxidation or loss of electrons, and reduction or gain of electrons, always proceed together. Sometimes oxidation-reduction reactions are given the shortened name, redoxes. Important oxidizing agents or electron-acceptors, in addition to such nonmetallic elements as oxygen and chlorine, include compounds such as hydrogen peroxide, nitric acid, concentrated sulfuric acid, chlorates, dichromates, and permanganates. T.W.D.

OXIDE. See OXYGEN.

OXNARD, city of California, in Ventura Co., 66 miles N.W. of Los Angeles. The principal industries are fruit and vegetable packing, canning, and freezing and the manufacture of agricultural implements, cement and glass products, and aircraft equipment. Nearby is Port Mugu Naval Air Missiles Test Center. Founded in 1897, the city was incorporated in 1903. Pop. (1960) 40,265; (1970) 71,225.

OXUS, ancient name of a river of Asia. See AMU-DAR'YA.

OXYGEN, gaseous element with at.no. 8, at.wt. 15.9994, b.p. −182.97° C. (−297.35° F.), m.p. −218.76° C. (−361.77° F.), sp.gr. 1.4291, and symbol O. Oxygen was discovered in 1774 by the British chemist Joseph Priestley and, independently, by the Swedish chemist Karl Wilhelm Scheele (qq.v.); it was shown to be an elemental gas by the French chemist Antoine Laurent Lavoisier (q.v.) in his classic experiments on combustion; see CHEMISTRY: *History.* Oxygen is the most abundant of all the elements. It is present in the atmosphere to the extent of 21 percent by volume or 23.15 percent by weight; in the oceans to the extent of 85.8 percent (88.8 percent of pure water is oxygen); and as a constituent of most rocks and minerals, constituting 46.7 percent of the solid crust of the earth. Oxygen comprises 60 percent of the human body. It is a constituent of all living tissues; almost all plants and animals require oxygen, in the free or combined state, to maintain life; see RESPIRATION.

Properties. Oxygen is a colorless, odorless, tasteless, slightly magnetic, nontoxic gas. It can be condensed to a pale blue liquid that is strongly magnetic. Pale blue solid oxygen is produced by compression of the liquid. Three allotropic forms of oxygen are known to exist: ordinary oxygen, containing two atoms per molecule, formula O_2; ozone (q.v.), containing three atoms per molecule, formula O_3; and a pale blue, nonmagnetic form, O_4, containing four atoms per molecule, which readily breaks down again into ordinary oxygen. Three stable isotopes of oxygen are known. Oxygen-16 (atomic mass 16) is the most abundant isotope; it comprises 99.76 percent of ordinary oxygen. For the use of oxygen-16 in determination of atomic weights, see ATOM AND ATOMIC THEORY.

Oxygen is prepared in the laboratory from salts, such as potassium chlorate, barium peroxide, and sodium peroxide. The most important industrial methods for the preparation of oxygen are the electrolysis of water and the fractional distillation of liquid air. In the latter method air is liquefied and allowed to evaporate. The nitrogen in the liquid air is more volatile and boils off first, leaving the oxygen. Oxygen is stored and shipped in either liquid or gaseous form.

Oxygen is a component of a great number of organic and inorganic compounds, in which it has a valence of two. It forms compounds, called oxides, with all elements except the inert gases. The rate of the reaction, called oxidation, varies with different elements. Ordinary combustion, or burning, is a very rapid form of oxidation. In spontaneous combustion, the heat evolved by the oxidation reaction is sufficiently great to raise the temperature of the substance to the point that flames result. For example, phosphorus combines so vigorously with oxygen that the heat liberated in the reaction causes the phosphorus to melt and burn. Certain very finely divided powders present so much surface area to the air that they burst into flame by spontaneous combustion; they are called pyrophoric substances. Elements such as sulfur, hydrogen, sodium, and magnesium combine with oxygen less energetically and burn only after ignition. Some elements, such as copper and mercury, form oxides slowly, even when heated. Inactive metals, such as platinum, iridium, and gold, form oxides only through indirect methods. For discussion of oxides of elements see separate articles on each of the elements.

Uses. Large amounts of oxygen are used in high-temperature welding torches, in which a mixture of oxygen and another gas produces a flame of much higher temperature than is obtained by burning gases in air. Oxygen is administered medicinally to patients whose respiratory functioning is impaired. It is also supplied to persons in aircraft flying at high altitudes where concentration of oxygen is insufficient to support normal respiratory processes. Oxygen-enriched air is used in open-hearth furnaces for steel manufacture; see IRON AND STEEL MANUFACTURE: *Open-Hearth Process.*

In the late 1960's, the annual production of purified oxygen in the United States totaled

OYSTER

about 1,750,000 tons, most of which is employed in the preparation of a mixture of carbon monoxide and hydrogen called synthesis gas, used for the synthesis of methanol and ammonia. High-purity oxygen is used also in the metal-fabrication industries, and in liquid form is of great importance as a propellant for guided missiles and rockets; see ASTRONAUTICS; GUIDED MISSILE; ROCKET. S.Z.L.

OYO, city of Nigeria, in the Western State, 35 miles N. of Ibadan. A textile center with cotton-weaving and tobacco-processing industries, the city trades in tobacco, cocoa, cotton, grains, palm products, and cassava. Tin and gold are found in the vicinity. The city is the residence of the Alafin of Oyo, a political leader of the Yoruba people, who established a state here in 1780. Pop. (1969 est.) 130,290.

OYSTER, marine, bivalve mollusks of the family Ostreidae. Several of the more than fifty living species of oysters are used extensively for food. Certain inedible species, known commonly as pearl oysters, produce commercially valuable pearls. Pearl oysters belong to a separate family, the Pteriidae; see MOLLUSCA; PEARL.

Structure. Oysters attach themselves to rocks or lie on the sea bottom. They are unable to move, but are often dislodged from their resting place by waves. The shell of the oyster is irregularly oval in shape; it consists of a left and right valve joined together at the narrow anterior end by an elastic ligament which acts as a hinge; see BIVALVE. Attached to both valves is a strong muscle called the adductor, which keeps the shell tightly closed. When the adductor relaxes, the elastic ligament pulls the valves apart. The left valve, upon which the oyster rests, is deeper and thicker than the upper right valve. Except for the dark, pigmented areas where the shell is connected to the adductor, the inner surfaces of the valves are porcelainlike white. Two folds of fleshy membrane, called the mantle, cover the soft body of the oyster and adhere closely to the inner surfaces of the shell. The mantle secretes the organic and inorganic substances that make up the shell.

At the anterior end of the body, between two pairs of thin lips, or palps, is an opening that constitutes the mouth of the oyster. The oyster has two pairs of sickle-shaped respiratory organs, the gills, which are covered with hairlike structures known as cilia. A short gullet connects the mouth to the stomach. The body also contains the digestive, reproductive, circulatory, excretory, and nervous systems.

The oyster feeds on microscopic organisms brought into the shell with the current produced by the movement of the cilia. Small particles caught on the surface of the gills are pushed toward the labial palps, which sort them out before they reach the mouth.

Anatomy of the oyster. The right valve was removed and the left mantle (l.m.) was curled up to expose the organs under it: m., mouth; l.p., labial palps; per., pericardium; g., gills; ad.m., adductor muscle; t., tentacles; sh., shell; an., anus; r., rectum; r.m., right mantle; h., heart.

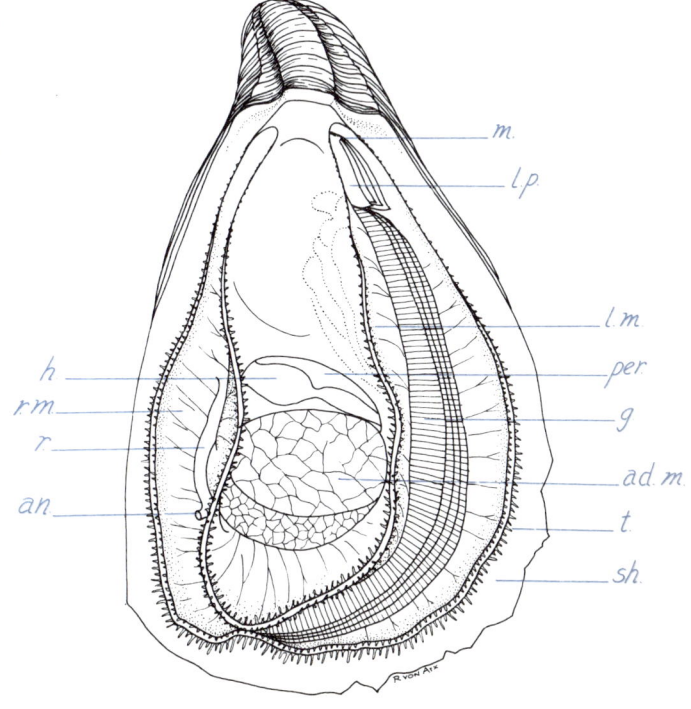

235

OYSTER

Reproduction. Oysters have varying life processes. The European oyster, *Ostrea edulis,* and the Olympia oyster, *O. lurida,* of the American Pacific coast, are hermaphrodites, that is, their reproductive organs contain both eggs and sperm. The eggs are fertilized within the body and are retained in the gills until shell-bearing larvae are formed. In the American blue point oyster, *Ostrea virginica,* of the Atlantic coast, and the Portuguese oyster, *O. angulata,* the sexes are separate. Females produce many millions of eggs which are discharged into the water, where fertilization occurs. The larvae develop within six hours, swim actively for about two or three weeks, and then settle on stones or shells, where they mature.

Maturity is attained by the end of the first year and the oyster continues to breed for the rest of its life. The reproductive season varies according to the latitude of the habitat. For example, blue point oysters breed in northern latitudes from the end of May until September, and in southern waters from March to December.

Distribution. Oysters are found throughout the world. They usually form large beds, which extend in warm waters from the tidal zone to a depth of from 80 to 100 ft. Beds of American blue point oysters are found along the eastern coast from the Gulf of St. Lawrence to the shores of the Gulf of Mexico. Chesapeake Bay is the largest oyster-producing body of water in the world, though many of its oyster beds have been depleted through overfishing or pollution. There are also large beds of edible oysters in Japan and Australia. The Japanese oyster, *Ostrea laperousii,* was successfully introduced to the Pacific coast of North America and to Australia. The chief species native to Australia is *O. commercialis.* The native American Olympia oyster, which is much smaller and has a thinner shell than other edible species, is found on the west coast of North America from Canada to Mexico. Several species of edible oysters inhabit the coastal regions of Central and South America.

Oyster culture is practiced in many countries. Young oysters, called seed oysters, are placed on suitable bottoms provided with artificial collectors, such as tile or shells, which serve as a resting place for the oysters until they grow to marketable size. The most elaborate system of cultivation is practiced in Japan, France, and the Netherlands.   P.S.G. & K.A.C.

OYSTER CATCHER, common name for any of six species of shore birds constituting the family Haematopodidae, which is closely allied to the plovers (*see* PLOVER), and distinguished chiefly by the long, vertically flattened bill, legs of moderate length, and feet with only three toes. The

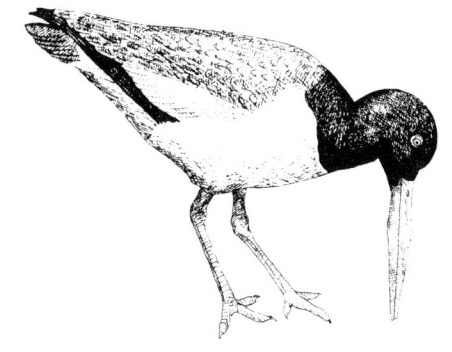

Oyster catcher, Haematopus palliatus

common American species is *Haematopus palliatus,* found in the south Atlantic States. The bird is 19 in. long, has a bright red bill, is black on the upper parts with a white underside; it feeds on shore mollusks and marine worms.

OYSTER PLANT. *See* SALSIFY.

OZARK MOUNTAINS, heavily timbered plateau, lying between the Arkansas and Missouri rivers, and stretching s.w. from Jefferson City, Mo., through Missouri and Arkansas into Oklahoma and Kansas. The average height is about 2000 ft., and the Boston Mts. are the highest section.

OZONE (Gr. *ozein,* "to smell"), allotropic form of oxygen (q.v.) having three atoms in each molecule, formula O_3. Ozone is pale blue in color and possesses a penetrating odor; it has b.p. $-111.9°$ C. ($-169.52°$ F.), m.p. $-192.5°$ C. ($-314.5°$ F.), and sp.gr. $2.144_0°$. Liquid ozone is a deep blue, strongly magnetic liquid. Minute amounts of ozone are present in the atmosphere, particularly in the upper regions. Ozone is formed when an electric spark is passed through oxygen, and causes a detectable odor near electrical machinery. The commercial method of preparation consists of passing cold, dry oxygen through a silent electrical discharge. Ozone is much more active chemically than ordinary oxygen and is a better oxidizing agent. It is used in purifying water, sterilizing air, and bleaching certain foods.

Pp

P, sixteenth letter and twelfth consonant of the English alphabet. The modern form of the letter first appeared in the Latin alphabet as an adaptation of the Greek letter *pi*, which was in turn derived from the Phoenician *pe*. The Phoenician letter originated in an Egyptian hieratic character based upon an Egyptian hieroglyph representing a shutter. The historical development of the letter may be summarized as follows:

Roman	Early Greek	Phoenician	Egyptian Hieratic	Egyptian Hieroglyphic
P	⌐ or ⌐	⌐	〜	▭

The English initial *p* sound is pronounced by closely compressing the lips and then strongly emitting the breath so as to separate them. The sound is technically called voiceless or mute and is related to the voiced *b*. Most English words beginning with the *p* sound are of Greek, Latin, or French origin. In a number of English words, p stands for the *b* sound in cognate Indo-European languages, as in the word pool, which is translated as *bala* in Lithuanian. In cognate words, English p generally corresponds to German pf and f, Latin b, and Greek b. The letter p is often silent in English words of Greek derivation, particularly when it is part of initial combinations such as pn, ps, and pt. Examples include pneumonia, psychic, and ptarmigan. The digraph ph, corresponding to the Greek *phi*, is pronounced *f*, as in pharmacy and phonetic.

As an abbreviation, the capital P is used for titles, such as Pope; for Pacific, patrol, and port; and for the pawn in chess. The capital or lowercase P is used for pastor, priest, president, and proconsul. Lowercase p may stand for page, penny, peseta, peso, or population; in music it denotes *piano*, or "softly."

As a symbol, capital P is used in chemistry for phosphorus, in electricity for power, in physics for pressure, and in logic for predicate. In either capital or lowercase form, P is a symbol for the fifteenth or, when J is included, sixteenth in a series, class, order, or group. In physics, *p* in lowercase italics denotes proton and vapor pressure. M.P.

PACARAIMA, SIERRA, range of mountains 300 mi. long separating Venezuela from Brazil. It reaches a height of 9219 ft. at Mt. Roraima.

PACHUCA, officially PACHUCA DE SOTO, city in Mexico, and capital of Hidalgo State, 55 miles N.E. of Mexico City. The rich silver mines of the district are said to have been worked by the Aztecs (q.v.) before the Spanish conquest. Industries include silver and gold refining, tanneries, pulque distilleries, soapworks, soft-drink factories, and iron foundries. Pop. (1960) 69,432.

PACIFERON. *See* IMMUNITY.

PACIFICA, city of California, in San Mateo Co., on the Pacific Ocean, 10 miles s. of San Francisco. A fishing and bathing resort, the city was formerly a major area for the production of artichokes; nurseries are now prevalent. Electronic equipment, meat products, and cement are manufactured. The city is the site of the Sanchez adobe house (1840's) and museum, and Sharp Park State Beach is nearby. Pacifica was formed in 1957 by the amalgamation of Rockaway Beach, Sharp Park, Edgemar, Linda Mar, Pacific Manor, Pedro Point, Vallemar, Salada Beach, Fairway Park, and Westview, all unincorporated villages or developments. Pop. (1960) 20,995; (1970) 36,020.

PACIFIC GROVE, city of California, in Monterey Co., on Monterey Bay, about 16 miles w. of Salinas. The Hopkins Marine Laboratory of Stanford University is located here. The city was founded in 1874 and incorporated in 1889. Pop. (1960) 12,121; (1970) 13,505.

PACIFIC ISLANDS, TRUST TERRITORY OF, territory of about 2100 islands and atolls in the Pacific Ocean which, in 1946, was placed under the trusteeship of the United Nations and is ad-

Vasco Núñez de Balboa, discoverer of the Pacific Ocean, claimed it for the monarchs of Spain.
American Museum of Photography

ministered by the United States government. The islands, which were taken from Japan during World War II (q.v.), include the Caroline, Mariana, and Marshall islands (qq.v.); Guam (q.v.), however, in the Marianas, is a Territory of the U.S. Pop. (1970) 90,940. *See* TRUSTEESHIP COUNCIL.

PACIFIC OCEAN, vast body of water lying between North and South America on the east and Australia, the Malay Archipelago, and Asia on the west. The name Pacific was given to it by the Portuguese navigator Ferdinand Magellan (q.v.). On the north it connects with the Arctic Ocean, by the Bering Strait, and southward it merges into the great expanse of water formerly called the Southern Ocean; the parallel of 40° S. lat. was commonly taken as the limit in this direction. Present-day geographers consider the southern boundary to be Antarctica. The Pacific is the largest and deepest of the oceans. Exclusive of dependent seas, it has an area of 64,186,300 sq.mi., greater than the entire land surface of the globe. The greatest length of the ocean, from north to south, is about 8300 nautical mi., and the greatest breadth, along the parallel of 5° N. lat. is about 9300 nautical miles.

The mean depth of the Pacific is about 14,000 ft. Its western basin is the more diversified, shallow water and immense depths occurring irregularly; the greatest depth yet found (36,198 ft.) is in the Mariana Trench, off the island of Guam, where in 1960 a depth of 35,800 ft. was reached by the bathyscaphe *Trieste*; *see* DEEP-SEA EXPLORATION.

The Pacific Ocean contains more than 30,000 islands, only a few of them being found N. of the equator. Most of the islands are referred to by the name Oceania, the three chief groupings of which are Polynesia, Micronesia, and Melanesia. Polynesia encompasses islands of the central Pacific, including Hawaii, Easter Island, New Zealand, and the Ellice, Cook, and Marquesas islands. Among the widely scattered islands of Micronesia, in the western Pacific, are the Caroline, Gilbert, Mariana, and Marshall islands. Melanesia, the area s. of Micronesia, stretches in an arc E. and N. off Australia and encompasses the Bismarck Archipelago, New Guinea, the Solomons, and other groups. In addition to these three main groups, the Pacific contains the Galápagos, Aleutian, Japan, and Indonesian island groups, and Okinawa, Taiwan, and Wake Island. *See* separate articles on the islands and groups mentioned above; *see also* OCEAN AND OCEANOGRAPHY.

PACIFIC OCEAN

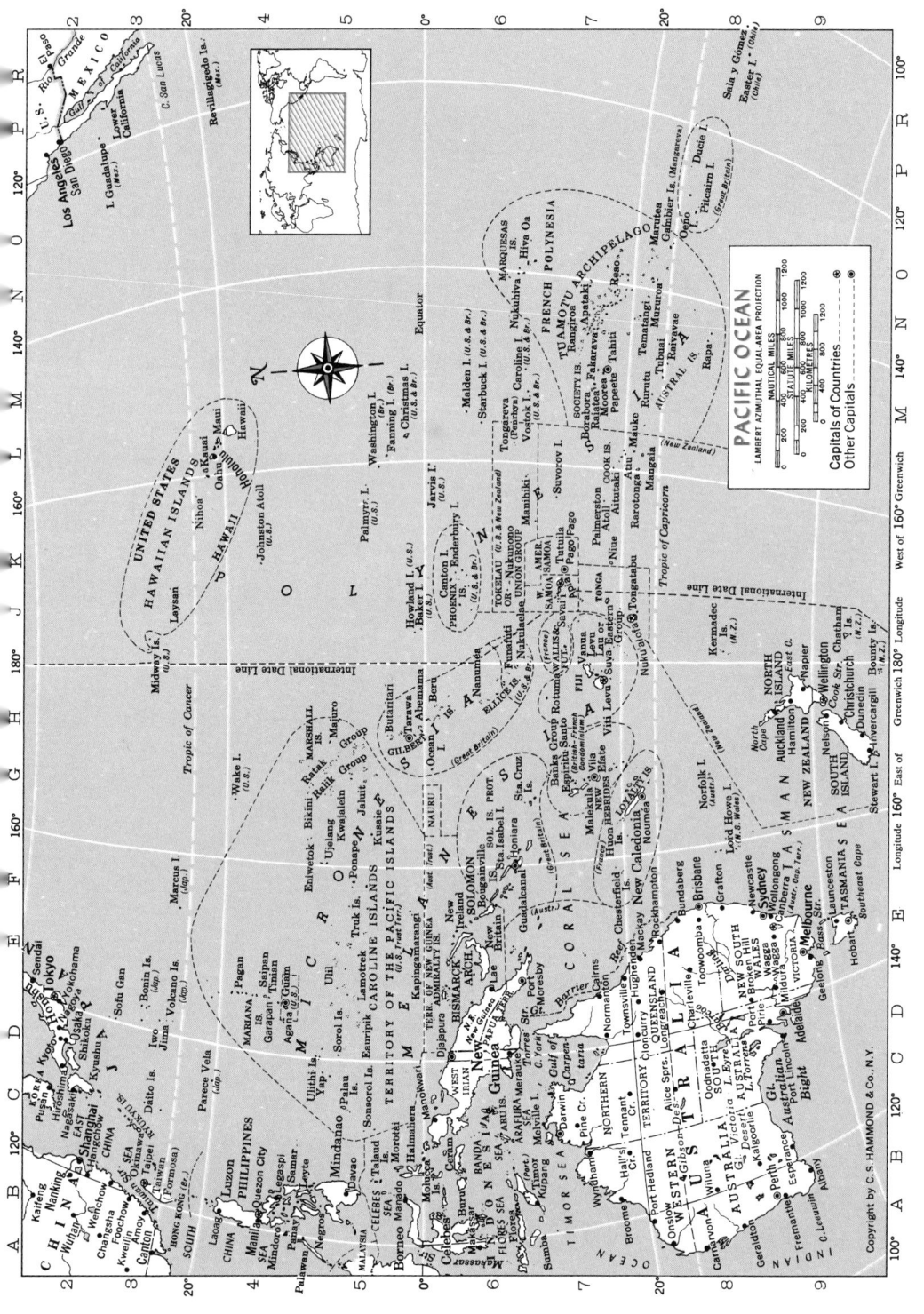

For index to map, see next page.

239

PACIFIC OCEAN

INDEX TO MAP OF PACIFIC OCEAN

Abemama (isl.), Gilb. & Ell. Is. .. H5
Adelaide, Australia .. D9
Admiralty (isls.), Terr. New Guinea .. E6
Agaña (cap.), Guam .. E4
Aitutaki (atoll), Cook Is. .. K7
Albany, Australia .. B9
Alice Springs, Australia .. D8
American Samoa .. K7
Apataki (isl.), Fr. Polynesia .. M7
Apia (cap.), W. Samoa .. J7
Arafura (sea) .. D6
Atiu (isl.), Cook Is. .. J5
Auckland, N.Z. .. E9
Austral (isls.), Fr. Polynesia .. H9
Australia .. D8
Australian Capital Territory, Australia .. F9
Baker (isl.) .. J5
Bass (str.), Australia .. E9
Bikini (atoll), Pacific Is. .. G4
Bismarck (arch.), Terr. New Guinea .. E6
Borabora (isl.), Fr. Polynesia .. L7
Bougainville (isl.), Terr. New Guinea .. F6
Bounty (isls.), N.Z. .. H10
Brisbane, Australia .. F8
Broken Hill, Australia .. E9
Cairns, Australia .. E7
Canberra (cap.), Australia .. F9
Canton (isl.), Gilb. and Ell. Is. .. J6
Caroline (isl.) .. L6
Caroline (isls.) .. E5
Carpentaria (gulf), Australia .. D7
Chatham (isls.), N.Z. .. J10
Christchurch, N.Z. .. H10
Christmas (isl.), Gilb. and Ell. Is. .. L5
Cook (isls.) .. K7
Cook (str.), N.Z. .. H7
Coral (sea) .. F7
Darling (riv.) .. E8
Darwin, Australia .. D7

Ducie (isl.) .. O8
Dunedin, N.Z. .. H10
Eastern (isl.), Chile .. P8
Eastern (Lau)(isls.), Fiji .. J7
Eauripik (atoll), Pacific Is. .. F5
Efate (isl.), New Hebrides .. G7
Ellice (isls.), Gilb. and Ell. Is. .. H6
Enderbury (isl.), Gilb. and Ell. Is. .. K6
Eniwetok (atoll), Pacific Is. .. G4
Espiritu Santo (isl.), New Hebrides .. G7
Eyre (lake), Australia .. D8
Fakarava (isls.), Fr. Polynesia .. M7
Fanning (isl.), Gilb. and Ell. Is. .. L5
Fiji .. H7
Fremantle, Australia .. B9
Funafuti (atoll), Gilb. and Ell. Is. .. J6
Gambier (isls.), Fr. Polynesia .. N8
Garapan (cap.) .. E4
Geelong, Australia .. E9
Gilbert (isls.), Gilb. and Ell. Is. .. H5
Gilbert and Ellice (isls.) .. H5
Great Australian (bight), Australia .. C9
Great Barrier (reef), Australia .. E7
Guadalcanal (isl.), Br. Solomon Is. .. F6
Guam (isl.) .. E8
Hamilton, N.Z. .. H9
Hawaii (isl.), U.S. .. L4
Hawaiian (isls.), U.S. .. K3
Hiva Oa (isl.), Fr. Polynesia .. N6
Hobart, Australia .. H10
Honiara (cap.), Br. Solomon Is. .. G6
Honolulu (cap.), Hawaii .. L3
Hoorn (isls.), Wallis and Futuna .. J7
Howland (isl.) .. J5
Invercargill, N.Z. .. H10
Jaluit (atoll), Pacific Is. .. G5

Jarvis (isl.) .. K6
Johnston (atoll) .. K4
Kalgoorlie, Australia .. C8
Kapingamarangi (isl.), Pacific Is. .. F5
Kauai (isl.), Hawaii .. L3
Kermadec (isls.), N.Z. .. J8
Kusaie (isl.), Pacific Is. .. G5
Kwajalein (atoll), Pac. Is. .. G5
Lae, Terr. New Guinea .. E6
Lamotrek (atoll), Pacific Is. .. E5
Lau (Eastern)(isls.), Fiji .. J7
Laysan (isl.), Hawaii .. J3
Lord Howe (isl.), Australia .. G9
Loyalty (isls.), New Caledonia .. G8
Majuro (atoll), Pacific Is. .. H5
Malden (isl.) .. L6
Malekula (isl.), New Hebrides .. G7
Mangaia (isl.), Cook Is. .. L8
Mangareva (Gambier) (isls.), Fr. Polynesia .. N8
Manihiki (atoll), Cook Is. .. K7
Mariana (isls.) .. E4
Marquesas (isls.), Fr. Polynesia .. N6
Marshall (isls.) .. H4
Marutea (isl.), Fr. Polynesia .. N8
Maui (isl.), Hawaii .. L3
Mauke (isl.), Cook Is. .. L8
Melanesia (reg.) .. G6
Melbourne, Australia .. E9
Melville (isl.), Australia .. D7
Micronesia (reg.) .. G5
Midway (isls.) .. H3
Moorea (isl.), Fr. Polynesia .. L7
Mururoa (isl.), Fr. Polynesia .. N8
Nanumea (atoll), Gilb. and Ell. Is. .. H6
Napier, N.Z. .. H9
Nauru .. G6
Nelson, N.Z. .. H10
New Britain (isl.), Terr. New Guinea .. F6

New Caledonia (isl.) .. G8
Newcastle, Australia .. F9
New Guinea (isl.) .. D6
New Guinea, Territory of .. E6
New Hebrides (isls.) .. G7
New Ireland (isl.), Terr. New Guinea .. F6
New South Wales (state), Australia .. E9
New Zealand .. G9
Nihoa (isl.), Hawaii .. K3
Niihau (isl.), Hawaii .. K3
Niue (isl.) .. K7
Norfolk Island (terr.), Australia .. G8
North (cape), N.Z. .. H9
North (isl.), N.Z. .. H9
Northern Territory, Australia .. D7
Nouméa (cap.), New Caledonia .. G8
Nuku'alofa (cap.), Tonga .. J8
Nukuhiva (isl.), Fr. Polynesia .. L8
Nuku'aelae (atoll), Gilb. and Ell. Is. .. J6
Nukunono (atoll), Tokelau Is. .. K6
Oahu (isl.), Hawaii .. K3
Ocean (isl.), Gilb. and Ell. Is. .. H6
Oeno (isl.) .. N8
Pacific Islands, Territory of the .. F5
Pagan (isl.), Pacific Is. .. E4
Pago Pago (cap.), American Samoa .. K7
Palau (isls.), Pacific Is. .. D5
Palmerston (atoll), Cook Is. .. K7
Palmyra (isl.) .. K5
Pappete (cap.), Fr. Polynesia .. L7
Papua .. E6
Penrhyn (Tongareva) (atoll), Cook Is. .. L6
Perth, Australia .. B8
Phoenix (isls.), Gilb. and Ell. Is. .. J6
Pitcairn (isl.) .. O8
Ponape (isl.), Pacific Is. .. F5

Port Moresby (cap.), Papua .. E7
Queensland (state), Australia .. E8
Raiatea (isl.), Fr. Polynesia .. L7
Raivavae (isl.), Fr. Polynesia .. M8
Ralik (isls.) .. G4
Rangiroa (atoll), Fr. Polynesia .. M7
Rapa (isl.), Fr. Polynesia .. M8
Rarotonga (isl.), Cook Is. .. K8
Ratak (isls.) .. G4
Reao (atoll), Fr. Polynesia .. N7
Rockhampton, Australia .. F8
Rotuma (isl.), Fiji .. H7
Rurutu (isl.), Fr. Polynesia .. L8
Saipan (isl.) .. E4
Sala y Gómez (isl.), Chile .. P8
Santa Cruz (isls.), Br. Solomon Is. .. G6
Santa Isabel (isl.), Br. Solomon Is. .. G6
Savai'i (isl.), W. Samoa .. J7
Society (isls.), Fr. Polynesia .. L7
Solomon (isls.) .. F6
Solomon Islands Protectorate, British .. G6
Sonsoro (isls.), Pacific Is. .. D5
Sorol (isls.) .. E5
South (isl.), N.Z. .. G10
South Australia (state), Australia .. D8
Starbuck (isl.) .. L6
Stewart (isl.), N.Z. .. G10
Suva (cap.), Fiji .. H7
Suvorov (atoll), Cook Is. .. K7
Sydney, Australia .. F9
Tahiti (isl.), Fr. Polynesia .. M7
Tarawa (atoll), Gilb. and Ell. Is. .. H5

Tasman (sea) .. G9
Tasmania (state), Australia .. F10
Tematangi (isl.), Fr. Polynesia .. M8
Timor (sea) .. B7
Tinian (isl.), Pacific Is. .. E4
Tokelau (isls.) .. J6
Tonga .. J7
Tongareva (atoll), Cook Is. .. L6
Tongatapu (isl.), Tonga .. J8
Torrens (lake), Australia .. D9
Torres (str.) .. E6
Townsville, Australia .. E7
Truk (isls.), Pacific Is. .. F5
Tuamotu (arch.), Fr. Polynesia .. M7
Tubuai (isl.), Fr. Polynesia .. M8
Tutuila (isl.), American Samoa .. K7
Ujelang (isl.), Pacific Is. .. G5
Ulil (isl.), Pacific Is. .. E5
Ulithi (atoll), Pacific Is. .. D4
Union (Tokelau) (isls.) .. J6
Vanua Leva (isl.), Fiji .. J7
Victoria (state), Australia .. E9
Vila (cap.), New Hebrides .. G7
Viti Levu (isl.), Fiji .. H7
Vostok (isl.) .. L7
Wake (isl.) .. G4
Washington (isl.), Gilb. and Ell. Is. .. L5
Wellington (cap.), N.Z. .. H10
Western Australia (state), Australia .. C8
Western Samoa .. J7
Wollongong, Australia .. F9
Yap (isl.), Pacific Is. .. D5
York (cape), Australia .. E7

In the trade-wind belts of the Pacific the winds are generally uniform except when such belts approach the western coasts, where they are modified by monsoon influences. In Polynesia hurricanes called typhoons are of frequent occurrence. North and south of the Tropical Zone the winds exhibit little regularity, though a westerly direction is most frequent. The currents of the Pacific Ocean are less marked in character than those of the Atlantic. Their movement and direction generally follow prevailing winds.

For information concerning animal and plant life in the Pacific Ocean see ANIMALS, GEOGRAPHICAL DISTRIBUTION OF; PLANTS, GEOGRAPHICAL DISTRIBUTION OF.

See also OCEANS AND OCEANOGRAPHY.

PACIFISM, opposition to war (q.v.) and other violence, expressed either in an organized political movement or as an individual ideology. Pacifism varies from a form that is absolute and doctrinal to a relative and more practical form. Absolute pacifists are against all wars and against violence in whatever form it may take; relative pacifists are selective of the wars and violence they oppose. Most absolute pacifists stress the immorality of the taking of one man's life by another man. The philosophy of pacifism has been propounded throughout history on grounds of morality, divine will, or economic and social utility; the term itself, however, did not become current until early in the 20th century.

Goals and Approaches. In attempting to prevent war, pacifists must achieve four principal goals. A climate of feeling favorable to peace must be established; the potential causes of conflict, inherent in such factors as economic competition, the quest for power, and fear of foreign domination, must be eliminated or minimized; means for the settlement of disputes must be provided, as in mediation, arbitration, and trial procedures; and, finally, means must be provided to insure observance of the settlements that are made.

Several distinctive approaches to achieving these goals have been advanced. The first is the absolute pacifism of some religious sects, such as the Mennonite Church (q.v.) and the Society of Friends, members of which believe they can convert aggressors to peaceful ways by setting an example of loving, nonviolent behavior; see FRIENDS, SOCIETY OF. This is the attitude expressed in the New Testament Sermon on the Mount, but it is much older than Christianity, permeating the teaching of Buddha, Confucius (qq.v.), and other Eastern philosophers. Absolute pacifism assumes both that its practitioners will be able to maintain moral courage when faced with aggression and provocation, and that their opponents will be affected by a constant return of good for bad. Such pacifism has never been entirely successful, however. Although the early Christians maintained this attitude through several generations, their uncompromising opposition to the use of force disappeared after the Church became allied with the Roman state in the 4th century. A contemporary proponent of this philosophy usually claims the status of conscientious objector (q.v.) when faced with military service.

Less absolute pacifists advocate other codes of behavior. For example, a second approach bars the use of force and urges moral persuasion, but also envisages passive resistance such as the resistance offered to British rule in 20th-century India and the civil disobedience (q.v.) of American civil-rights activists. Critics of this view contend that resistance in any form destroys the possibility of convincing an aggressor of his victim's friendliness, and that even passive resistance provokes frustration, resentment, and further oppression. The same arguments are usually applied to a third theory, which favors active resistance, including nonviolent acts of sabotage and agitation against an invader. See also CIVIL RIGHTS AND CIVIL LIBERTIES.

Several approaches to the problem of peace involve a readiness to use force in certain circumstances, usually characterized as defensive. One approach permits armed defense against attack, but not assistance to other nations being attacked. Proponents of another theory, that of collective security, urge a defensive combination of peace-loving nations against violators of the peace. If such a policy is not to result merely in a system of rival alliances, it must be implemented by international machinery able to make and enforce settlements. Advocates of collective security accordingly support all international organizations such as the Permanent Court of Arbitration, the League of Nations, and the United Nations (qq.v.).

The least passive of the pacifist philosophies, which accepts the use of force as necessary to the establishment of peace, is that of revolutionary socialism, which claims that the capitalist system will never permit the development of a workable international security organization because it promotes international rivalry. The revolutionary socialists assert that only socialism (q.v.) can eliminate the economic rivalries that breed war, and thus make possible an effective international government; see also COMMUNISM.

PACIFISM

History. Although organized peace movements did not appear until the 19th century, the modern search for a means of preventing war began with the rise of national states at the end of the Middle Ages (q.v.). In the 14th century, the Italian poet Dante Alighieri (q.v.) proposed a world empire to abolish war; in the 15th century George of Poděbrad, King of Bohemia (1420–71), proposed an international parliament; in the 16th century, Henry IV (q.v.), King of France, made a similar suggestion; in the 17th century, the English Quaker William Penn (q.v.) wrote *An Essay towards the Present and Future Peace of Europe* (1694); and in the 18th century, the French writer Charles Irénée Castel (1658–1743), who was known as the Abbé de Saint-Pierre, influenced readers of his time with his proposals for securing "perpetual peace".

The first peace society in history was organized in New York in 1815 by the American merchant David Low Dodge (1774–1852); another was organized in Massachusetts in the same year by the theologian Noah Worcester (1758–1837); and both were incorporated into the American Peace Society founded by the pacifist William Ladd (1778–1841) in 1828. Other peace societies were established in European countries later in the century; and, in 1848, the American linguist Elihu Burritt (1810–79) founded the League of Universal Brotherhood, which established branches in the United States, Great Britain, France, and Holland. These early idealistic groups formulated no specific plans to prevent war, however. The American peace movement lost momentum during the Civil War, when many of its adherents maintained that preservation of the Union and the abolition of slavery (q.v.) were to be achieved at any cost; *see* CIVIL WAR, THE AMERICAN.

Many new groups were organized toward the end of the 19th century, including the International Workingmen's Association (q.v.), which advocated workers' strikes to prevent wars, and the International Peace Bureau (q.v.), comprised of national peace councils and committees from various countries. Frequent meetings and congresses and the announcement of such awards as the Nobel Peace Prize (*see* NOBEL PRIZES) stimulated public interest in the peace movement. The formation of an international postal union in 1874 was considered an important milestone in practical cooperation between nations. Nevertheless, wars multiplied in frequency and intensity during the same period. The South African War, the Spanish-American War, and finally World War I (qq.v.) all but destroyed the peace movement.

Following World War I, efforts of pacifists were in part directed toward achieving collective security through the League of Nations. This organization was loosely constructed, however, providing no really effective means of preventing war. By 1941 most of the nations of the world were involved in World War II (q.v.). This was followed in turn by the establishment of the United Nations, with its more elaborate machinery for keeping the peace.

Many other international peace organizations also continue to exist. The greatest impetus to pacifism in modern times was the development and use of nuclear weapons at the close of World War II. Faced with the possibility of total nuclear war, many previously uncommitted individuals and pacifists throughout the world began to organize and work for a ban against the production of nuclear weapons, for the cessation of the testing of such weapons, and for the disarmament of those nations already possessing them. *See* DISARMAMENT; INTERNATIONAL CONTROL OF ATOMIC WEAPONS; NUCLEAR WEAPONS.

Another development has been the popularization of the concept that some wars, such as World War II, may be justified, while other wars are unjustifiable. During the 1960's, numerous organizations and individuals, including many persons not strictly pacifists in the sense of being opposed to all wars, began increasingly to oppose American military activities in Southeast Asia. *See* UNITED STATES OF AMERICA, THE: *History*.

PACKAGING, industrial and marketing technique for containing, protecting, identifying, and facilitating the sale and distribution of agricultural, industrial, and consumer products. Virtually all manufactured and processed goods require packaging during some phase of their production and distribution.

The package must maintain the purity and freshness of its contents and protect them from the outside environment; if the contents are harmful, corrosive, or poisonous, the package must also protect the outside environment. The package must identify the contents and its quantity, and it must facilitate distribution. The package may contribute to the convenient use of its contents by special dispensing or closure features.

Packaging Materials. The basic materials of packages today include paper, paperboard, cellophane, steel, aluminum, glass, wood, textiles, and plastics. These materials are processed or fabricated into flexible, semirigid, or rigid containers. Conventional package forms include wraps, bags, pouches, cartons, set-up boxes, cans, bottles, pails, drums, barrels, and bulk containers. All packages must be sealed in some way, and many require an opening for dispensing the contents. Identification is usually accomplished by direct imprinting or by an applied lable. The Fair Packaging and Labeling Act, a Federal law enacted in 1966, vests regulatory authority in the Food and Drug Administration, with respect to foods, drugs, and cosmetics, and in the Federal Trade Commission, with respect to other commodities.

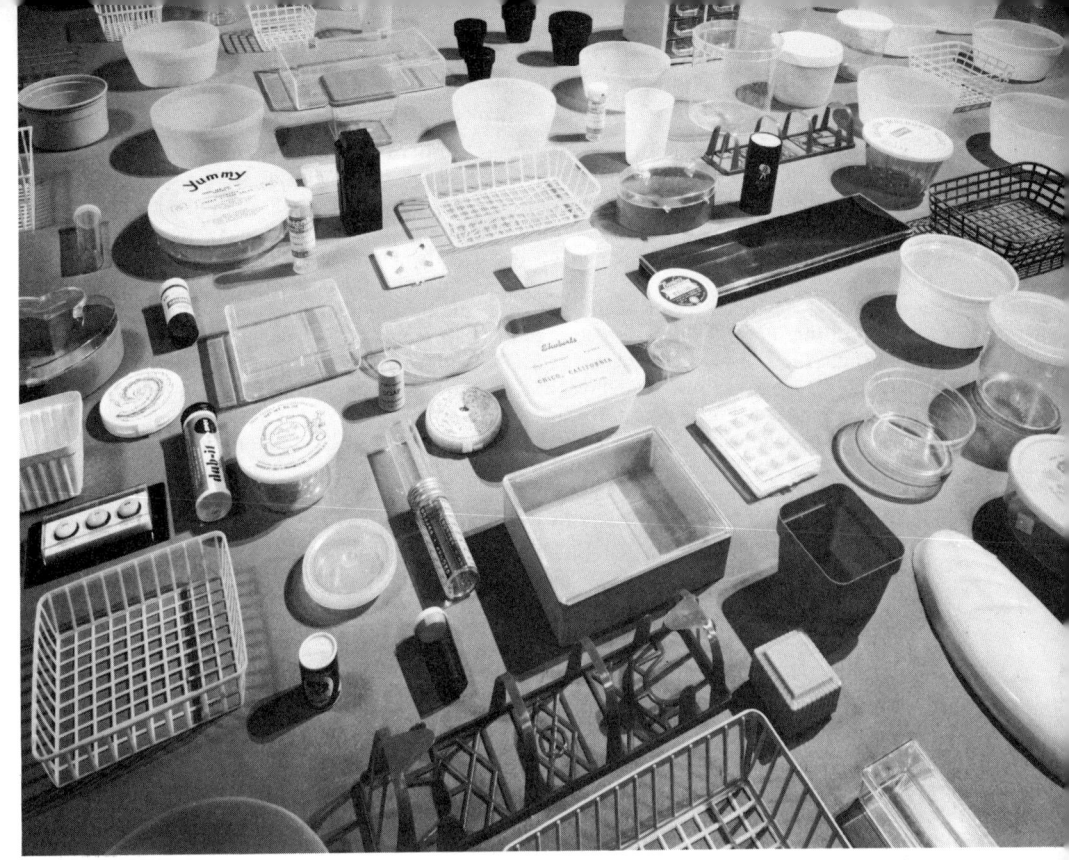

Of the artifacts created by man the package is among the oldest. Any object that was stored or transported needed to be packaged. Originally, leaves, hollowed-out tree limbs, gourds, skins, reed baskets, and earthenware vessels were used as containers. As civilization developed and became more complex, containers were developed to meet specific needs. Glass bottles were used in Egypt more than 2000 years before the Christian era. A jar containing an ointment, with the name of the maker engraved on the lead cover, has been found, a "labeled" package made in ancient Rome.

In 1746 the first package for a branded product appeared when a Briton, a Dr. James, sold his "Fever-Powder" in a pasteboard box. A few years later Yardley's of London began selling their lavender water in bottles, and Crosse and Blackwell began selling olive oil and mustard in jars. Also in England, A. F. Pears launched what was to become one of the most consistently prosperous industries in the world when he established the first packaged-soap business.

Modern Packaging Methods. The birth of the modern packaging industry occurred in 1810 when two inventors, Auguste de Heine and Peter Durand, took out patents on iron and tin containers, called cans, for preserving foods. *See* CANNING. During the 19th and early 20th centuries, advances in container fabrication re-

Containers in a wide array of materials and shapes have been devised by the packaging industry.
Dow Chemical Co.

Innovations in the traditional tin can (now made of a variety of materials) include containers with hand-opened tabs on the top and, illustrated here, plastic strips that can be peeled off.
American Can Co.

PACKING INDUSTRY

sulted in the development of most of the standard metal and paper containers in use today. The development of mechanical printing processes, photoengraving, and process color printing made it possible to decorate the containers with a variety of colorful designs.

Concurrently, significant changes took place in merchandising. In 1899 the National Biscuit Company introduced its successful Uneeda Biscuit package. This package is generally considered to have signaled the end of the cracker-barrel, bulk-merchandising procedures of the country-store era. The volume and variety of self-service products available to consumers continues to expand. Today is the era of the convenience package, including home permanents, cook-in-bag foods, spray-on bandages, blister-packaged hardware supplies, and easy-opening beer and soft-drink containers.

It has been estimated that a linear foot of shelf space in a modern supermarket is worth $150 in newspaper advertising. Each package in a major chain of supermarkets may be displayed before 1,000,000,000 shoppers in one year. The package must be designed to attract the attention of the shopper in about one fifth of a second, which is the amount of time the average shopper surveys any particular package in a market. Surveys show that between 50 and 70 percent of buying decisions are made on impulse at the moment of selection. These factors underlie the need for manufacturers to appeal to impulse buying by planning well-designed packages.

The reported cost of packaging containers shipped in 1939 was about $2,000,000,000. In 1947 the cost was about $5,400,000,000. Twenty years later it exceeded $16,000,000,000. The total value of packaging material used at the retail or store level, including packaging costs, is double this amount.

See also INDUSTRIAL DESIGN.   D.A.

PACKING INDUSTRY, large industry concerned with the slaughtering and processing of cattle, sheep, and hogs. It is one of the most important industries in the United States, having large centers in Chicago, Kansas City, Milwaukee, and other cities of the Middle West. The packing industry has tended to decentralize in recent years, however, and slaughtered livestock are now generally moved directly from farms, ranches, and feedlots to meat-packers. The cattle-slaughtering sector of the U.S., in particular, has moved westward toward higher concentrations in the Western Corn Belt and Great Plains, where beef is shipped to wholesalers and retailers primarily in the form of carcasses or fresh wholesale cuts. Hog slaughtering is still carried on chiefly in large plants, where the hogs are processed into numerous cuts and products.

The term "meat-packing", which was originally applied to the curing and packing of the flesh of the hog, has been extended to include all operations connected with the utilization and transformation, into merchantable form, of the different parts of animals slaughtered for food.

In accordance with the Humane Slaughter Act of 1958, all livestock are now made insensible and immobilized before they are killed. For cattle, a captive bolt, a type of gun designed for stunning, is generally used. Hogs often are immobilized painlessly through gassing. *See* ANESTHESIA; CRUELTY TO ANIMALS; VIVISECTION.

Many parts of the slaughtered animals are shipped for consumption as fresh meat, while other parts, especially of the hog, are cured and smoked. The fatty portions are converted into lard and commercial grease by so-called rendering processes. Bones are converted into glue, fertilizer (qq.v.), animal feeds, and other usable products, including pharmaceuticals; hoofs and horns are used or sold for other purposes.

Refrigeration and Transportation. The meat of slaughtered livestock, after thorough chilling, is shipped in refrigerator cars or refrigerated motor carriers to cities. In the cities the meat is placed in cold-storage warehouses owned by the packing companies, and from these it is delivered to dealers. Truck and rail transportation are sometimes combined in so-called piggyback shipments. Before cold storage of meat was introduced in the U.S., it was customary to ship the living animals to the eastern parts of the country. *See* REFRIGERATION.

Cattle Slaughtering. In recent years labor-saving devices have been widely adopted in the dressing and processing of cattle. A continuous rail system is generally used today, whereby cattle are chained by one leg and hoisted to a movable pulley on an overhead rail and are then slaughtered; from this position blood leaves the body so quickly that death occurs almost instantly, and for purposes of kosher (q.v.) ritual this method of slaughtering is defined as humane even without prior stunning. The carcasses then move slowly along a continuously moving rail to stations where each required process is completed, including skinning, disembowelling, and beheading. Before going into refrigeration, the carcasses are cut down the backbone and split into sides. Beef is usually shipped to wholesalers and retailers as sides or quarters, but carcasses are more and more today being further divided into wholesale or primal cuts, such as chucks, rounds, and loins; a few plants with fast distribution reduce the carcass to retail consumer cuts at the packing plant.

Hog Slaughtering. Hog slaughtering always has involved more complete processing at the packing plant than cattle slaughtering. The carcasses of slaughtered hogs also move on continuous rail or chain systems. Most often the hog carcass is first conveyed through scalding vats or troughs to dehairing machines. Hogs generally are not beheaded or dismembered in any way during the slaughtering and dressing process, which includes eviscerating, washing, and trimming. Later, however, hogs nearly always are almost completely cut up, in separate rooms, into primal cuts such as loins, legs, and picnic hams or shoulders. Certain cuts, including loins, are sold fresh, without processing, but most cuts go through one or more processing operations. Although some plants still soak particular cuts in barrels filled with brine, it has generally been necessary to shorten the curing process. On cuts like hams, a curing solution is usually pumped internally. Other cuts such as bellies, which are used for bacon, are mechanically saturated with curing solution through hollow needles. Many cuts are also smoked thoroughly or more lightly, depending on the product desired, at the packing plant. Nearly all packing plants that slaughter hogs also produce a complete line of sausage and variety meats, including frankfurters, link sausages, luncheon meat, and all types of dried, cured sausage.

Legislation. Although inspection by the Federal government of meat used in the packing industry was provided for in earlier acts of Congress (1890–91 and 1895), it was not until 1906 that comprehensive legislation was introduced. By the act of 1906 all cattle, sheep, goats, and hogs became subject to ante-mortem and post-mortem examination when the meat was to be used in interstate or foreign commerce; later the act was extended to include reindeer (q.v.). By this legislation about 60 percent of the total meat supply of the U.S. was brought under inspection. The Packers and Stockyards Act of 1921 added further control, directed against trust activities. The recent Wholesome Meat Act of 1958 requires all meat-packers to meet Federal inspection requirements, and agreements to that effect have been made between the various States and the Federal government.

See also CATTLE; HOG; MEAT; SHEEP.   W.F.W.

PADANG, city of Indonesia, on the w. coast of the island of Sumatra, at the base of the Padang highlands, 4 miles N. of the port of Telukbajur (formerly Emmahaven). It is the shipping center of a region noted for the production of coal, rubber, copra, coffee, spices, tobacco, resins, cinchona bark, rattan, and tea. The city has an airport and is the site of Panchasila University. Dutch traders established a trading post at Padang about 1680. It was largely under British control between 1781 and 1819, when the Dutch regained possession. The Japanese occupied the city during World War II. Pop. (1961) 143,699.

PADDLEFISH, either of two species, *Psephurus gladius* of the Yangtze valley in China and *Polyodon spathula* of the Mississippi valley in the United States. These form the family Polyodontidae. Paddlefish are scaleless and have a paddlelike extension on the snout. The mouth, located beneath the paddle, is very large. The American species reaches a weight of 160 lb. and a length of about 6 ft.; the Chinese paddlefish is about twice this size. Although the paddlefish is not popular as a food, the eggs make good caviar.

PADDLE-WHEEL BOAT. *See* SHIPS AND SHIPBUILDING: *Steamships.*

PADEREWSKI, Ignace Jan (1860–1941), Polish pianist, composer, and statesman, born in Podolia, and educated at the Warsaw Conservatory and in Berlin and Vienna. Shortly after making debuts in Vienna in 1887 and in Paris in 1889, he established himself as the most popular concert pianist since Franz Liszt (q.v.), and was especially known for his interpretations of the music of the Polish composer Frédéric François Chopin (q.v.). Paderewski made the first of his many tours of the United States in 1891. His compositions include the opera *Manru* (1901), a symphony, concertos, and orchestral and piano pieces, among which is his popular *Minuet in G*. Between 1910 and 1920 Paderewski devoted himself to the cause of Polish independence; he aided in organizing a committee for the assistance of victims of World War I in Poland and made concert tours in the U.S. to raise funds for Polish relief. After the war he was elected prime minister and foreign minister in the Polish republic and he held office from January to November, 1919; *see* POLAND: *History.*

PADRE ISLAND NATIONAL SEASHORE, conservation and recreation area of Texas, 67.5 mi. long, comprising the center section of Padre Island, a barrier island 113 mi. long in the Gulf of Mexico. *See* NATIONAL PARK SERVICE.

PADUA (It. *Padova;* anc. *Patavium*), city of Italy, in Veneto Region, and capital of Padua Province, on the Bacchiglione R., 22 miles W. of Venice. An industrial center, the city has plants

245

producing machinery, automotive parts, furniture, and plastics. The production of liquors and foodstuffs such as sugar, pasta, and canned vegetables is important also. Padua is a picturesque city with arcaded streets which lead into open squares. The University of Padua (q.v.) is one of the oldest universities in Europe. Padua's most celebrated church is the Basilica Sant' Antonio, begun in the 13th century and built in Romanesque-Gothic style; it contains the tomb of Saint Anthony of Padua. In the piazza in front of the church stands the equestrian monument to the Venetian condottiere Erasmo Gattamelata (1370?–1443) by the Italian sculptor Donatello (q.v.). The Scrovegni Chapel is famous for its interior with frescoes by the Florentine artist Giotto (q.v.). Other frescoes are in the Palazzo della Ragione; the Palazzo in addition is known for its great hall, which is nearly 259 ft. long. The Civic Museum contains antiquities, coins, and a fine art gallery. The botanical garden dates from 1545.

Padua was one of the wealthiest cities of N. Italy in late Roman times. Although destroyed by the Lombards in 601, Padua recovered quickly and flourished as an independent commune. In 1405 Padua was taken by Venice. For the later history of the city, see VENICE. Padua suffered considerable damage from bombing in World War II. Pop. (1967 est.) 221,447.

PADUA, UNIVERSITY OF, coeducational autonomous institution of higher learning, located in Padua, Italy, and supported by the national government. The university was founded in 1222 by a group of dissident scholars from the University of Bologna. The University of Padua is organized into the following faculties: jurisprudence, political science, economics and commerce, philosophy and letters, education, medicine and surgery, science, pharmacy, engineering, architecture, and agriculture. The degree of *laurea*, entitling the recipient to the honorific *dottore*, is awarded by all faculties after a four- to six-year course of study. The *laurea* is approximately equivalent to an American degree of master. Post-*laurea* studies are offered by most faculties and lead to a higher specialized diploma after an additional period of study, normally two years in length. The library contains about 415,000 bound volumes, 2600 manuscripts, and 1600 incunabula. In 1968–69 student enrollment was about 21,000; the faculty numbered about 1000.

PADUCAH, city in Kentucky, and county seat of McCracken Co., on the Ohio R., 48 mi. above its mouth, and 226 miles S.W. of Louisville. It carries on a large trade by river and railroad. An Atomic Energy Commission Plant provides jobs for the people of the city. Industries include uranium separation and the manufacture of hosiery, motorboats, textiles, wire, shoes, radio components, and automobile radiators. Paducah was settled in 1821, incorporated as a town in 1831 and as a city in 1856. Pop. (1960) 34,479; (1970) 31,627.

PAEAN, ancient Greek god who acted as a healer. Paean appears in the works of Homer (q.v.) and other early poets as a personal god, a divine physician who was invoked to cure disease and also to avert threatened destruction from other causes. The name later became an epithet of Apollo (q.v.), god of medicine. The term became the name for a recognized division of Greek choral lyric poetry, a song of triumph or thanksgiving, usually addressed to Apollo the Healer. Paeans were composed by the ancient lyric poets, especially Bacchylides and Pindar (qq.v.). Prayers or hymns accompanying the libation at a sacrifice or sung to the gods with the libation at a marriage feast were also known as paeans. In modern usage, a paean is an exultant song, outburst, or speech of appreciation.

PAESTUM, ancient city of Italy, in Campania Region, on the Gulf of Salerno, 24 miles S.E. of the modern city of Salerno. Founded by Greek colonists from Sybaris between 650 and 600 B.C., the city was originally called Poseidonia. It was subdued by the Romans, who established a colony there about 273 B.C. During the 1st century B.C., Paestum was famous for its roses, mentioned by several Roman poets, including Vergil (q.v.). The town was sacked by the Saracens in the 9th century A.D. and finally abandoned in the 16th century. Paestum is famed today for the fine ruins of three large Doric temples, namely the Temple of Poseidon (q.v.), god of the sea; the Basilica; and the Temple of Ceres (q.v.), the Roman deity corresponding to Demeter (q.v.), Greek goddess of agriculture. The Temple of Poseidon is one of the most perfectly preserved of ancient Greek temples.

PÁEZ, José Antonio (1790–1873), Venezuelan revolutionist and political leader, born in Acarigua. He was a commander of the Venezuelan revolutionary armies during the war of independence (1810–22), and inflicted a series of defeats upon the Spanish which forced them to leave Venezuela in 1822. In the same year he was involved in the negotiations whereby Venezuela was incorporated into the federated state of Great Colombia, which had been established in 1819 by Simón Bolívar (q.v.). Páez fomented a revolt against Bolívar and in 1830 set up an independent Venezuelan government with himself as president and dictator; Páez retained these posts until 1846. In 1847 he led a revolt against his elected successor, José Tadeo Monagas (1784–1868); the uprising was quickly suppressed, and Paéz was captured and imprisoned for three years. He lived in exile, chiefly in the United States, from 1850 to 1858, and then returned to Venezuela. In 1861 he reestablished himself as dictator, but was forced to resign two years later because of popular pressure for a constitutional government. He spent the rest of his life in the U.S.

PAGANINI, Nicolò (1782–1840), Italian composer and violin virtuoso, born in Genoa, where he studied with local musicians. He made his first public appearance as a violinist at the age of nine and toured several towns in Lombardy at thirteen. Until 1813, however, he did not actively pursue the career of a virtuoso performer. He preferred to enjoy himself in romantic liaisons, gambling, and, from 1805 to 1813, in the social pleasures of a position as musical director at the court of the sister of Napoleon I (q.v.), Emperor of France, Maria Anna Elisa Bacciocchi, Princess of Lucca (1777–1830). In 1813 Paganini left Lucca and began touring Italy, where his technical ability as a violinist attracted wide attention. He extended his tours to Vienna, Austria, in 1828, and to Paris, France, and London, England, in 1831. In Paris he met the Hungarian pianist and composer Franz Liszt (q.v.), who was inspired to develop the techniques of piano playing as Paganini had developed those for the violin. The violinist went into partial retirement in 1834. His playing astonished the listeners of his day, many of whom believed he was in touch with supernatural powers. He could perform complex works using only one of the four strings of the violin, and play chords of two and three notes, creating the illusion that more than one violin was being played. His own works include twenty-four caprices for violin solo (1801–07), eight concertos, and many sonatas.

Nicolò Paganini, a drawing by the 19th-century French artist Jean Auguste Dominque Ingres.

PAGE, Walter Hines (1855–1918), American journalist, publisher, and diplomat, born in Cary, N.C., and educated at Randolph-Macon College and Johns Hopkins University. As a journalist, he crusaded for reforms in the South. From 1887 to 1895 he was on the staff of the *Forum,* a monthly periodical published in New York City. He then joined the *Atlantic Monthly,* of which he was editor in chief in 1898–99. In 1899 with the American publisher Frank Nelson Doubleday (1862–1934), he founded the publishing firm of Doubleday, Page & Company. They established the *World's Work,* a monthly magazine of general commentary, in 1900, and Page was its editor until 1913. In that year he was appointed ambassador to Great Britain by President Woodrow Wilson (q.v.). After the outbreak of World War I in 1914, Page strongly argued that the United States should enter the war on the side of the Allies. Because President Wilson intended to maintain neutrality, Page threatened resignation before the American declaration of war in April, 1917. Page was the author of *The Rebuilding of Old Commonwealths* (1902); an autobiography *A Publisher's Confession* (1905); and, under the pen name Nicholas Worth, a·novel, *The Southerner* (1909).

PAGODA. See CHINESE ART: *Architecture;* INDIAN ART AND ARCHITECTURE: *Architecture;* JAPANESE ART AND ARCHITECTURE: *Architecture.*

PAGO-PAGO, village, port, and capital of the United States territory of American Samoa, on the S.E. coast of Tutulia. It became an American naval and coaling station in 1878, and has been under the protection of the U.S. since 1900. It is the only port for large vessels in American Samoa. Pop. (1960) 1251; (1970) 2451.

PAHLAVI or **PAHLEVI,** family name of two rulers of Iran, formerly Persia.

PAINE

Riza Shah Pahlavi (1877–1944), Shah of Persia (1925–35), Shah of Iran (1935–41), born in Savad Kouh, Mazandern Province. He entered the Persian army as a youth, and in 1921 was commander of a Persian Cossack force. A large part of Persia was then controlled by Soviet troops whom Pahlavi expelled. By a coup d'etat he established a new government in which he was minister of war and commander in chief of the armed forces. In 1923 he became premier, and two years later, when the Majles, or National Assembly, deposed the reigning shah, Ahmed Shah (1898–1930), Pahlavi was elected shah. In 1935 he officially changed the name of the country from Persia to Iran. His reign was notable for the introduction of Western customs and for his attempts to improve the transportation system and the financial structure of Iran. In 1941, during World War II, Great Britain and the U.S.S.R. occupied Iran and forced Pahlavi to abdicate in favor of his son, Mohammed Riza Pahlavi. See IRAN: *History;* PERSIA.

Mohammed Riza Pahlavi (1919–   ), Shah of Iran (1941–   ), son of Riza Shah Pahlavi, born in Tehran, and educated in Switzerland and at the Tehran Military College. In September, 1941, during World War II, he became shah upon the abdication of his father. The new shah supported the Allies during the remainder of the war. In the postwar period his reign was marked by political turbulence generated in particular by the emergence of powerful communist and nationalist movements. He was wounded slightly during an assassination attempt in 1949. In August, 1953, he briefly fled the country following an attempted coup d'etat by the newly deposed Premier Mohammed Mossadegh (q.v.). The outstanding achievement of the shah's reign has been agrarian reform. In 1951 he began distributing the royal lands to tenant farmers, and in 1962 he ordered large private landholdings broken up to allow peasant ownership.

Although the shah ruled as a constitutional monarch, he delayed accepting the crown of Iran until he felt his country had made significant social and economic progress. The coronation took place in October, 1967. The shah's eldest son and heir apparent, Prince Riza Pahlavi, was born in 1960.

PAINE, Robert Treat (1731–1814), American jurist and revolutionary leader, born in Boston, Mass., and educated at Harvard College (now Harvard University). He entered the ministry and in 1755, during the French and Indian War, acted as a chaplain. Later he studied law and was admitted (1759) to the bar. In the fall of 1770 he prosecuted the British soldiers on trial for murder for their part in the Boston Massacre (q.v.). He was elected (1773) to the Massachusetts General Court. After its dissolution by the royal governor in 1774 it was succeeded by the Provincial Congress, in which Paine served as a delegate in 1774–75 and as speaker of the lower house in 1777. From 1774 to 1778 he was also a delegate from Massachusetts to the Continental Congress and n that capacity was one of the signers of the Declaration of Independence (q.v.). He served from 1777 to 1790 as the first attorney general of Massachusetts, helped draft (1780) the present State constitution, and participated in founding (1780) the American Academy of Arts and Sciences (q.v.). He served as a State supreme court judge from 1790 to 1804.

PAINE, Thomas (1737–1809), Anglo-American political philosopher, born in Thetford, Norfolk, England. In 1774, with introductions from Benjamin Franklin (q.v.), representative of the American colonies in Great Britain, Paine sailed for Philadelphia. On Jan. 1, 1776, appeared his pamphlet *Common Sense* (q.v.), which argued for complete American independence. He wrote a series of pamphlets, *The American Crisis,* that George Washington (q.v.) ordered to be read to his men to help improve their morale. These pamphlets were widely read throughout the colonies during the American Revolution. In 1778 Congress appointed him secretary of the committee of foreign affairs. He lost the post

Thomas Paine

during a political dispute and was appointed clerk of the Pennsylvania legislature, and in 1785 received from Congress $3000, and from New York a confiscated royalist farm at New Rochelle. In 1787 he returned to Great Britain, where in 1791-92 he published *The Rights of Man*, the most famous of all the replies to *Reflections upon the French Revolution* by British statesman and orator Edmund Burke (q.v.). A million and a half copies were sold in England alone; the British government indicted the author for treason and Paine fled to France. There he was elected by Pas-de-Calais Department as a deputy to the National Convention; he voted with the Girondists (q.v.). He offended the faction of Maximilien de Robespierre (q.v.), a leading member of the Committee of Public Safety (q.v.) in the French Revolution, and in 1794 was imprisoned. Just before his arrest he wrote Part I of *The Age of Reason*, against atheism and against Christianity, and in favor of deism. Part II appeared in 1795, and a portion of Part III in 1807. The book alienated George Washington and most of his old friends. After an imprisonment of eleven months Paine was released and restored to his seat in the National Convention. He became disgusted with French politics, and involved himself chiefly with the study of finance, until 1802 when he returned to America in a ship placed at his service by President Thomas Jefferson (q.v.). Paine's book *The Age of Reason* influenced Biblical criticism in the 19th century.

PAINESVILLE, city in Ohio, and county seat of Lake Co., on the Grand R., about 28 miles N.E. of central Cleveland. Manufactures include machinery, chemicals, and synthetic fibers. It is the site of Lake Erie College, founded in 1856. The city was laid out about 1805 and incorporated in 1832. Pop. (1960) 16,116; (1970) 16,536.

PAINLEVÉ, Paul Prudent (1863-1933), French statesman and mathematician, born in Paris, and educated at the École Normale Supérieure. He taught mathematics at the École Normale and the Sorbonne between 1892 and 1903, when he was appointed professor of general mathematics at the University of Paris. His career as a statesman began in 1906 with his election as an independent socialist to the Chamber of Deputies. During World War I he served from 1915 to 1916 as minister of public instruction and inventions, and in 1917 as minister of war and premier of France, holding these two offices concurrently. In March, 1917, he appointed General Henri Philippe Pétain (q.v.) commander in chief of the French army, and in October he took part in international discussions preliminary to the conference at Versailles; see VERSAILLES, TREATY OF. The following month he resigned from the cabinet after being criticized for tolerating defeatism in the French conduct of the war. In 1924 he returned to government service as president of the Chamber of Deputies, and the next year, succeeding Édouard Herriot (q.v.), again became premier. In the cabinets of 1926 and 1928 he served as minister of war, and was minister of aviation from 1930 to 1931 and from 1932 to 1933. Among his mathematical works are *Leçons sur la Théorie Analytique des Équations Differentielles* ("Lessons on the Analytical Theory of Differential Equations", 1897).

PAINTED CUP *or* **INDIAN PAINTBRUSH,** common name applied to annual, biennial, and perennial herbs constituting the genus *Castilleja* of the Figwort family. The genus, which contains about fifty species, is native to the cooler portions of North America and Asia. Because painted cups are parasitic on the roots of other plants, they have not been naturalized and have rarely been cultivated away from their native habitat. The plants have long, hairy, unbranched stems with alternate leaves. The uppermost leaves, or bracts, are brilliantly colored and much showier than the inconspicuous interspersed flowers. The flowers, which are borne in spikes, have a two-lobed calyx, a two-lobed corolla, four stamens, and a solitary pistil. The corolla, which is usually yellow, is encased within the calyx, and is usually indiscernible. The fruit is a two-celled capsule. The common painted cup, *C. linariaefolia*, is the State flower of Wyoming. The calyx of this plant is greenish white, but the bracts are intense vermilion. The scarlet paintbrush, *C. coccinea*, is a common wild plant of the eastern United States. Common Indian paintbrush, *C. septentrionalis*, is a hardy herb found in Canada and in the mountainous regions of northern U.S. from New England to the Rocky Mts.; its calyx is greenish white tinted with purplish red.

PAINTED DESERT, in Arizona, plateau region of colored rock extending S.E. from the Grand Canyon to the Petrified Forest National Park, along the N.E. bank of the Little Colorado R.

PAINTING, in art, changing the color and texture of a surface by the application of pigment. The art of painting developed from the primitive cave decorations of prehistoric times to the highly sophisticated and varied processes used today. Painting is accomplished in any combination of the entire range of colors and black, white, and gray on a suitable surface, such as cloth (especially linen or canvas), wood, metal, plaster, or clay (fired or unfired); the work thus accomplished may be representational, inspirational, or purely decorative. For explanations of the various types of painting, see such separate articles as FRESCO; MINIATURE PAINTING; MURAL PAINTING; OIL PAINTING; TEMPERA PAINTING; and WATERCOLOR PAINTING. Information about the art of important cultures appears in the sections on painting in such articles as BYZANTINE ART; ISLAMIC ART AND ARCHITECTURE; and RENAISSANCE ART AND ARCHITECTURE. The art of different countries is discussed in entries such as ITALIAN ART AND ARCHITECTURE and PERSIAN ART AND ARCHITECTURE and also in the sections on culture in modern country articles. Schools of painting are usually the topic of separate articles, for example, BARBIZON SCHOOL; FLORENTINE PAINTING AND SCULPTURE; and HUDSON RIVER SCHOOL. Various movements in modern art are discussed also in separate entries, as ABSTRACT AND NONOBJECTIVE ART; CUBISM; and IMPRESSIONISM. Other related articles include AESTHETICS; ART; CHIAROSCURO; DRAWING; and GLASS, PAINTED AND STAINED. See also separate articles on individual painters.

PAINTING, ENCAUSTIC, method of painting practiced by the ancients, especially by the Greeks, in which the colors were mixed with wax and resin and softened by aid of fire. Apart from some portraits, no important specimens of Greek encaustic paintings are known to be extant, and it is an art the secret of which is largely lost. Several processes of encaustic painting were used by the Greeks and Romans. In the process most commonly practiced the mixtures of color and wax were spread within determined outlines by means of a metal spatula known as a *cestrum*. The *cestrum* had one flat end and one pointed end. In a type of encaustic painting known as *cestrotum*, a design was burned into horn or ivory with the heated pointed end of the *cestrum*, after which the mixtures of color and wax were introduced into the incisions.

Encaustic painting retained its integrity of color longer than any other medium known to ancient painters. The "Battle of Marathon" painted by the Greek artist Polygnotus in the 5th century B.C., was preserved in Athens for more than 900 years. Some of the mural paintings found in and about the ruins of the ancient Roman city of Pompeii are encaustic paintings; several encaustic paintings found in the suburbs of Pompeii are preserved in the Metropolitan Museum of Art, New York City. During the 19th century, efforts were made by various artists to revive encaustic painting, but they were largely unsuccessful. An encaustic method originated by the German artist Fernbach (1793–1851) was used to decorate the Hohenstaufer Hall of the Royal Palace in Munich. Diego Rivera (q.v.) used this method in his work on the Anfiteatro Bolivar in Mexico City, 1922.

PAINTS, colors or pigments, dry or mixed with oil, and used as decorative or protective coatings for various surfaces; see COLOR. The principal white pigments are white lead, zinc oxide, lithopone, and titanium oxide. The desired color is usually obtained by using natural earth colors. In making paint, the pigments and a small quantity of oil are thoroughly mixed by machinery into a paste. To this paste is added linseed oil, turpentine, liquid drier, coloring pigments, and sometimes plasticizers to give flexibility to the film. Enamel paints consist of zinc oxide and lithopone in brown linseed oil and high-grade varnish (q.v.); see ENAMEL. Luminous paints contain various phosphorescent sulfides of barium, strontium, and calcium; see FLUORESCENCE AND PHOSPHORESCENCE. Water colors for artists are finished either in dry cake or moist condition. In both cases they contain the finest pigments ground in gum arabic or dextrin. For the moist form glycerin (q.v.) is added.

Among the new types of paint are various synthetic resins and the water-thinned latex paints, introduced in 1949; see PLASTICS; RESINS. Most of the latex paints are limited to interior use, and are increasingly popular because of the lack of odor and the ease of application. See CHEMICAL COMPOUNDS, SYNTHETIC: *Paints and Coatings.*

PAISLEY, Great Britain, borough in Renfrew County, Scotland, on the White Cart Water, 7 mi. s.w. of Glasgow. Paisley shawls, so celebrated between 1805 and the middle of the 19th century, are no longer made. Paisley is a thread-manufacturing center. Industries include wool and silk milling, bleaching, printing, and tanning, and the manufacturing of soap and chemicals. Pop. (1969 est.) 95,182.

PAKISTAN, republic, in the northern part of the Indian subcontinent and belonging to the Commonwealth of Nations (q.v.). The republic comprises the provinces of East Pakistan and West Pakistan, which are separated by more than 1000 mi. of territory belonging to the Republic of India, and the federal capital area which includes the former capital city, Karachi (q.v.); see INDIA; INDIA, REPUBLIC OF. Rawalpindi (q.v.) is now the capital of Pakistan.

East Pakistan, the smaller of the two provinces, has an area of 55,126 sq.mi.; it lies in the N.E. part of the subcontinent and is bordered on the N. and W. by the Republic of India, on the E. by Burma and the Republic of India and on the

PAKISTAN

s. by the Bay of Bengal. It extends from lat. 21° N. to lat. 27° N. and from long. 88° E. to long. 92°30′ E.

West Pakistan has an area of 310,403 sq.mi.; it lies in the N.W. part of the Indian subcontinent and is bounded on the N. and N.W. by Afghanistan, on the N.E. by Jammu and Kashmir, on the E. and S.E. by the Republic of India, on the S. by the Arabian Sea, and on the W. by Iran. It extends from lat. 24° N. to lat. 37° N. and from long. 62° E. to long. 75°30′ E. The status of Jannu and Kashmir (q.v.) is a matter of bitter dispute between India and Pakistan.

The two provinces of Pakistan have a coastline totaling 950 mi. in length; the total area of the country is 365,529 sq.mi., not including Jammu and Kashmir and the enclave of Junagadh, all claimed by Pakistan.

THE LAND

The two provinces of Pakistan exhibit strikingly different physical characteristics. West Pakistan is a dry region characterized by great extremes of altitude and temperature; East Pakistan is a low-lying, water-logged area with a relatively narrow range of climatic variation.

The topography of West Pakistan is dominated by the Indus River (q.v.), which enters the province in the N.E. and flows S. into the Arabian Sea. The Indus forms in general the line of demarcation between the two main land forms of the province, namely, the Indus plain, which extends principally along the E. side of the river, and the Baluchistan highlands, which lie to the W. The province has two lesser land forms, the coastal plain, which is a narrow strip of land bordering the Arabian Sea, and the Kharan basin, which is W. of the Baluchistan highlands.

The Indus plain in Pakistan varies in width from 50 to 200 mi.; from N. to S. it includes portions of three main regions, namely, the Punjab plains, the Sind, and the Great Indian Desert. The Punjab region is drained by the Sutlej, Ravi, Chenab, and Jhelum rivers, which are tributaries of the Indus; these rivers supply the irrigation system which waters the Indus plain.

The Baluchistan highlands contain a series of mountain ranges that are offshoots of the Himalaya; among these are the Hindu Kush, the Safed Koh Range (qq.v.), the Sulaiman Range, and the Kirthar Range. The highest peak in the highlands is Tirich Mir (25,263 ft.) in the Hindu Kush. The Safed Koh Range, which rises to 15,620 ft., is pierced by the famed Khyber Pass (q.v.) on the Pakistan-Afghanistan border.

The Badshahi Mosque, in Lahore, West Pakistan, built by the 17th-century Mogul emperor Aurangzeb. UPI

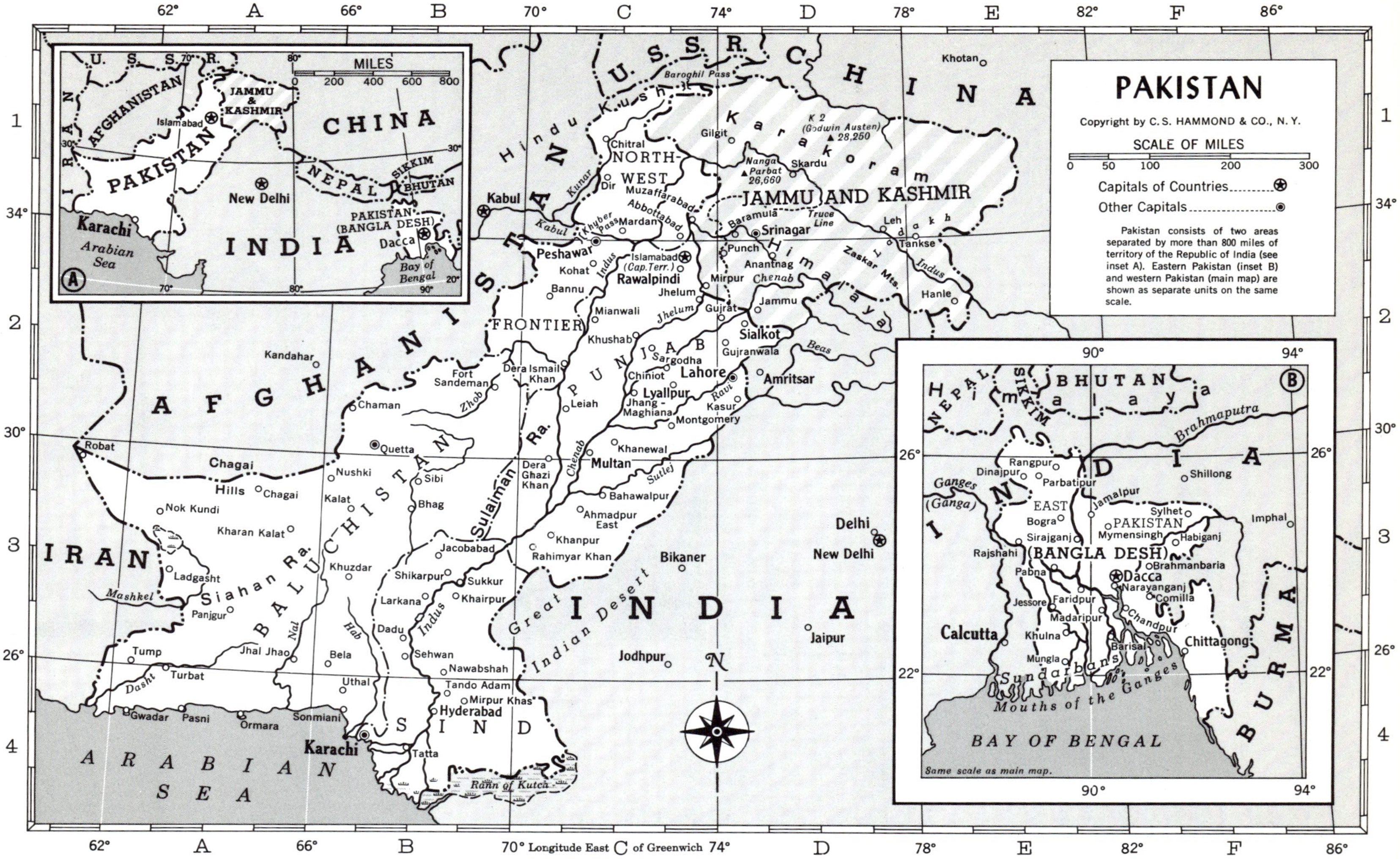
PAKISTAN
Copyright by C.S. HAMMOND & CO., N.Y.
SCALE OF MILES
0 50 100 200 300
Capitals of Countries
Other Capitals
Pakistan consists of two areas separated by more than 800 miles of territory of the Republic of India (see inset A). Eastern Pakistan (inset B) and western Pakistan (main map) are shown as separate units on the same scale.
U. S. S. R.
CHINA
AFGHANISTAN
IRAN
INDIA
ARABIAN SEA
JAMMU AND KASHMIR
NORTH-WEST FRONTIER
PUNJAB
BALUCHISTAN
SIND
Hindu Kush
Karakoram
Himalaya
Baroghil Pass
Khyber Pass
Truce Line
Zaskar Mts.
Sulaiman Ra.
Siahan Ra.
Chagai Hills
Great Indian Desert
Rann of Kutch
K 2 (Godwin Austen) 28,250
Nanga Parbat 26,660
Khotan
Gilgit
Skardu
Chitral
Dir
Muzaffarabad
Abbottabad
Mardan
Baramula
Srinagar
Leh
Ladakh
Tankse
Hanle
Kabul
Peshawar
Kohat
Islamabad (Cap.Terr.)
Rawalpindi
Punch
Anantnag
Mirpur
Jhelum
Gujrat
Jammu
Bannu
Mianwali
Khushab
Sargodha
Sialkot
Gujranwala
Amritsar
Lahore
Chiniot
Lyallpur
Jhang-Maghiana
Kasur
Montgomery
Leiah
Dera Ismail Khan
Kandahar
Fort Sandeman
Chaman
Quetta
Robat
Nushki
Sibi
Kalat
Bhag
Chagai
Nok Kundi
Kharan Kalat
Ladgasht
Panjgur
Khuzdar
Dera Ghazi Khan
Multan
Khanewal
Bahawalpur
Ahmadpur East
Khanpur
Rahimyar Khan
Jacobabad
Shikarpur
Sukkur
Khairpur
Larkana
Dadu
Sehwan
Nawabshah
Tando Adam
Mirpur Khas
Hyderabad
Tatta
Karachi
Bela
Uthal
Sonmiani
Ormara
Pasni
Gwadar
Tump
Turbat
Jhal Jhao
Bikaner
Jodhpur
Jaipur
Delhi
New Delhi
Indus
Kabul
Kunar
Jhelum
Chenab
Ravi
Beas
Sutlej
Zhob
Nal
Hab
Mashkel
Dasht
N
70° Longitude East of Greenwich 74°
MILES
0 200 400 600 800
NEPAL
SIKKIM
BHUTAN
PAKISTAN (BANGLA DESH)
Dacca
Bay of Bengal
Arabian Sea
A
B
Himalaya
Brahmaputra
Ganges (Ganga)
EAST PAKISTAN (BANGLA DESH)
BURMA
Rangpur
Dinajpur
Parbatipur
Shillong
Imphal
Jamalpur
Sylhet
Mymensingh
Habiganj
Bogra
Sirajganj
Rajshahi
Brahmanbaria
Pabna
Dacca
Narayanganj
Comilla
Jessore
Faridpur
Madaripur
Chandpur
Calcutta
Khulna
Barisal
Chittagong
Mungla
Sundarbans
Mouths of the Ganges
BAY OF BENGAL
Same scale as main map.

PAKISTAN

INDEX TO MAP OF PAKISTAN AND BANGLA DESH

BANGLA DESH

Cities and Towns

Barisal	F 3
Bogra	E 3
Brahmanbaria	F 3
Chandpur	F 3
Chittagong	F 3
Comilla	F 3
Dacca (cap.)	F 3
Dinajpur	E 3
Faridpur	E 3
Habiganj	F 3
Jamalpur	F 3
Jessore	E 3
Khulna	E 3
Madaripur	E 3
Mungla	E 3
Mymensingh	F 3
Narayanganj	F 3
Pabna	E 3
Parbatipur	E 3
Rajshahi	E 3
Rangpur	E 3
Sirajganj	E 3
Sylhet	F 3

Physical Features

Bengal (bay)	F 4
Bengal (region)	E 3
Ganges (Ganga) (river)	E 3
Mouths of the Ganges (delta)	E 4
Sundarbans (delta)	E 4

PAKISTAN

Provinces

Baluchistan	A 3
Capital Territory	C 2
Northwest Frontier	C 1
Punjab	C 2
Sind	B 4

Cities and Towns

Abbottabad	C 1
Ahmadpur East	C 3
Bahawalpur	C 3
Bela	B 3
Bhag	B 3
Chagai	A 3
Chaman	B 2
Chiniot	C 2
Chitral	C 1
Dadu	B 3
Dera Ghazi Khan	C 3
Dera Ismail Khan	C 2
Dir	C 1
Fort Sandeman	B 2
Gujranwala	D 2
Gujrat	D 2
Gwadar	A 4
Hyderabad	B 4
Islamabad (cap.)	C 2
Jhal Jhao	A 3
Jhang Maghiana	C 2
Jhelum	C 2
Kalat	B 3
Karachi	B 4
Kasur	D 2
Khairpur	B 3
Khanewal	C 2
Khanpur	C 3
Kharan Kalat	A 3
Khushab	C 2
Khuzdar	B 3
Kohat	C 2
Ladgasht	A 3
Lahore	C 2
Larkana	B 3
Leiah	C 2
Lyallpur	C 2
Mardan	C 1
Mianwali	C 2
Mirpur	D 2
Mirpur Khas	B 4
Montgomery	C 2
Multan	C 3
Nawabshah	B 3
Nok Kundi	A 3
Nushki	B 3
Ormara	A 4
Panjgur	A 3
Pasni	A 4
Peshawar	C 2
Quetta	B 3
Rahimyar Khan	C 3
Rawalpindi	C 2
Robat	A 3
Sargodha	C 2
Sehwan	B 3
Shikarpur	B 3
Sialkot	D 2
Sibi	B 3
Sonmiani	B 4
Sukkur	B 3
Tando Adam	B 4
Tatta	B 4
Tump	A 3
Turbat	A 4
Uthal	B 4

Physical Features

Arabian (sea)	A 4
Baroghil (pass)	C 1
Chagai (hills)	A 3
Chenab (river)	C 3
Dasht (river)	A 4
Hab (river)	B 3
Hindu Kush (mts.)	C 1
Indus (river)	B 3
Jhelum (river)	C 2
Khyber (pass)	C 1
Kunar (river)	C 1
Kutch, Rann of (salt lake)	B 4
Nal (river)	A 3
Rann of Kutch (salt lake)	B 4
Ravi (river)	D 2
Siahan (mts.)	A 3
Sulaiman (mts.)	B 3
Sutlej (river)	C 3
West Pakistan (region)	C 2
Zhob (river)	B 2

East Pakistan encompasses the lowlands of the Indo-Gangetic Plain which terminates in the alluvial plain of two great rivers, the Ganges and the Brahmaputra (qq.v.); the Ganges flows into the province from the N.W. and the Brahmaputra from the N.E. The southern part of the delta is occupied by the Sunderbans, a region of marshes and swamps which extends W. into India.

Climate. The climate of West Pakistan varies widely from place to place. In the mountain regions of the N. and W., temperatures fall to freezing levels during the winter; in the Indus plain area temperatures range between 90° F. and 120° F. in summer. Throughout most of West Pakistan rainfall is scarce, ranging from 15 to 25 in. annually.

In East Pakistan the climate is normally hot and wet. Temperatures vary from 67° F. to 102° F.; rainfall annually varies from 70 to 170 in. and averages about 100 in. Much of the rainfall takes place during the monsoon, a rainy season named for a wind which blows from the S.W. from April to October.

Natural Resources. The resources of Pakistan are primarily agricultural. The mineral resources of the country, which are located mainly in West Pakistan, include salt, chromite, coal, gypsum, limestone, iron ore, sulfur, clay, petroleum, and natural gas.

Plants and Animals. Plant life is varied and abundant in East Pakistan, mainly because the rainfall in that province is copious. In both provinces the mountain regions, notably the Himalaya, bear a varied vegetation depending on the altitude. Arctic flora grow on the higher slopes. Dense forests of spruce, evergreen oak, chir or cheer pine, and a cedar known as the deodar are found at lower altitudes. Numerous species of tropical and subtropical plant life thrive at the base of the mountains. The Ganges-Brahmaputra delta region of East Pakistan contains mangroves, bamboo trees, a hardwood timber tree called the sal, and dipterocarps, a family of trees yielding timber, oils, and resins.

The animal life of Pakistan also shows striking differences in the two parts of the country. In West Pakistan, deer, boar, bear, crocodile, and waterfowl abound. The chief animal species in East Pakistan are elephants, tigers, and wild hogs, as well as various species of poisonous and nonpoisonous snakes. In the freshwater and saltwater areas of both provinces fish of many varieties are to be found.

Waterpower. Hydroelectric-power production in Pakistan is confined largely to West Pakistan, which contains many swift-flowing rivers. The two largest hydroelectric projects in the country are the Warsak project on the Kabul R. and the Karnafuli project in East Pakistan. The annual total of electric energy produced in Pakistan was about 3,500,000,000 kw hours in the late 1960's, according to latest available statistics. In 1965 an agreement with Canada provided for the construction of a 137,000-kw nuclear power plant in Karachi.

THE PEOPLE

The ethnological background of the population is extremely varied, largely because the country

253

The people of Pakistan. Above: Pakistanis work on an irrigation project on the Indus River. Left: Women and children wait in line at Dacca, East Pakistan, for milk rations provided by the government with the assistance of the United Nations Children's Fund.

United Nations

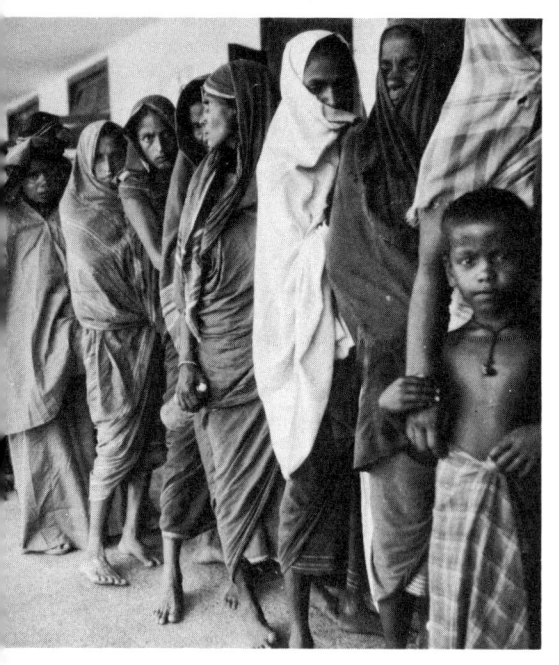

lies in an area that was invaded repeatedly during its long history. The people of West Pakistan are from such ethnic stocks as the Dravidians, Indo-Aryans, Greeks, Scythians, Huns, Arabs, Mongols, Persians, and Afghans. The population of East Pakistan, which is less varied in its racial background than that of West Pakistan, is made up largely of Bengalis, a people of mixed Aryan, Mongolian, and Dravidian extraction.

Population. The population of Pakistan (census 1961) was 93,831,982; the United Nations estimated (1970) 114,190,000. The overall population density is about 289 persons per sq.mi.: 922 persons per sq.mi. in East Pakistan and 138 persons per sq.mi. in West Pakistan. About 51 percent of the population lives in East Pakistan. The urban population expanded from 5.1 percent of the total population in 1901 to 13.1 percent in the census of 1961.

Political Divisions. The chief political divisions of Pakistan are the provinces of East Pakistan and West Pakistan and the federal Karachi area, which is located geographically in West Pakistan and includes the former capital city of Karachi and 566 sq.mi. of territory adjoining the city.

For administrative purposes, West Pakistan is divided into ten divisions in which governmental authority is represented by commissioners. These divisions are comprised of smaller units, namely districts and agencies. The province was created on Oct. 14, 1955, through the amalgamation of Punjab, the North-West Frontier Province, Sind, Baluchistan, Bahawalpur, Khairpur, the Baluchistan States Union, and the frontier areas under the administration of Baluchistan and the North-West Frontier Province. The capital city of West Pakistan is Lahore (q.v.).

PAKISTAN

East Pakistan is divided into three administrative units, namely Dacca, Chittagong, and Rajshahi, which are subdivided into seventeen districts. The province was formed concurrently with the founding of Pakistan in 1947; it comprises the E. portion of the former British Indian province of Bengal and the major portion of the Sylhet District of Assam (q.v.). The capital of East Pakistan Province is Dacca (q.v.).

Principal Cities. The principal cities of West Pakistan, and their populations, according to the 1961 census, are Karachi (1,912,598); Lahore, a rail junction (1,296,477); Hyderabad, the rail center, (434,537); Lyallpur, center of the cotton industry (425,248); Multan (358,201); the industrial city Rawalpindi (340,175); and Peshawar (218,691), the hub of trade with Afghanistan (q.v.). The leading cities of East Pakistan are Dacca (556,712), the port Chittagong (364,205), Narayanganj (162,054), and Khulna (127,970).

Religion. The leading religion of Pakistan is Islam (q.v.), which is the faith of about 88 percent of the population. Hinduism and Christianity (qq.v.) form the leading minority religions; other religious groups include the Sikhs (q.v.), Buddhists (see BUDDHISM), and the Parsees (q.v.). The constitution, although defining Pakistan as an Islamic nation, guarantees freedom of religion for all faiths and sects.

Languages. The constitution recognizes two official languages, Bengali and Urdu, and provides that English shall be used for official purposes until 1972; see BENGALI LANGUAGE AND LITERATURE; HINDUSTANI LANGUAGE. Urdu is the language of most of West Pakistan, and Bengali that of East Pakistan; in both provinces English is spoken and written widely and is used in many schools and institutions of higher learning. In West Pakistan a number of other languages and dialects are spoken, notably Punjabi, Sindhi, Pushtu, Baluchi, and Persian.

Education. In 1961, only 15.9 percent of the total population of Pakistan was literate: 17.6 percent in East Pakistan and 13.6 percent in West Pakistan. Education is not compulsory. Girls attend separate schools at both the primary and secondary levels.

ELEMENTARY AND SECONDARY SCHOOLS. In the mid-1960's more than 55,000 primary schools were annually attended by about 6,900,000 pupils, and about 7000 secondary schools had an enrollment of approximately 2,600,000.

SPECIALIZED SCHOOLS. In the same period more than 130 teacher-training schools and colleges and technical schools had an annual enrollment of about 28,000.

UNIVERSITIES AND COLLEGES. Total enrollment at the ten universities in Pakistan was about 28,000; about 248,000 students attended colleges of arts and sciences, and medical and agricultural colleges, which numbered more than 300.

Culture. As a Muslim nation, Pakistan is strongly influenced by the culture and traditions of Islam. Hindu and British influences, however, are widespread.

LIBRARIES AND MUSEUMS. Karachi is the seat of the most important libraries in Pakistan; these include the Liaquat National Library, the Central Secretariat Library, and the National Archives.

In an outdoor school operated by a community-development project, the pupils sit on mats and only the teacher has a desk.
Jack Ling – UNICEF

Students work in a laboratory at the Karachi Polytechnic Institute, a project financed by the United Nations Special Fund.
P. Almasy – UNESCO

The National Museum of Pakistan, in Karachi, contains important materials from the Indus Valley civilizations, as well as Buddhist and Islamic artifacts. The University Museum at Dacca specializes in Bengali collections.

ARCHEOLOGY. Several important sites of the Indus Valley civilization, which thrived from three to four millennia before Christ, have been excavated. Among the most notable are Mohenjo Daro and Harappa. These excavations, begun in 1922, reveal the existence of highly organized cities constructed of burnt red brick, with grain storage, water supply, and drainage systems. The achievements in art and science of the pre-Aryan Indus Valley civilization compare favorably with those of the contemporary civilization of Mesopotamia.

THE ECONOMY

Agriculture remains the chief economic activity of Pakistan. Commerce and industry have expanded since independence, but inflation has become a mounting problem. Central economic planning was instituted in 1951.

In the late 1960's the ordinary budget showed revenues of about $1,582,000,000 and equal expenditures. The capital budget, for economic development, showed revenues of approximately $1,128,000,000 and approximately the same expenditures.

Agriculture. About 63,650,000 acres, or 26.6 percent of the total land area, is under cultivation. Agriculture engages about 85 percent of the population and provides 45 percent of the national income and 86 percent of export earnings. About 85 percent of the land under cultivation is devoted to food crops for local consumption. Although food production has remained constant in recent years, the growing population has forced Pakistan to become a major importer of wheat and rice.

In the late 1960's the leading crops, together with the approximate annual production in tons, were sugar cane (30,500,000), rice (14,095,000) and wheat (7,123,000). Other major crops were jute, corn, cotton, and tea. The livestock population included about 34,000,000 head of cattle, 10,300,000 sheep, 10,100,000 goats, 925,000 asses, and 500,000 horses.

Forest and Fishing Industries. About 5 percent (6,000,000 acres) of the total land area is forest. Pulp and bamboo are important products in East Pakistan.

Fishing resources, although underdeveloped, are extensive. In the late 1960's the annual catch was about 550,000 tons, of which more than 75 percent was of freshwater origin. Fish is a staple item in the diet of East Pakistan.

Mining. In the late 1960's the most important minerals, with average annual production figures in tons when available, were gypsum, rock salt (330,000), limestone (3,150,000), and chromite (50,000). Crude petroleum production reached about 136,000,000 gal.; production of natural gas was about 69,200,000 cu.ft.

Manufacturing. The manufacturing capacity of both East and West Pakistan is still small, but production has been steadily expanding. In the late 1960's, industry accounted for about 12 percent of the annual gross national product, as compared with 1.5 percent in 1950.

In the mid-1960's more than 4500 factories were operating in Pakistan, each employing an average of twenty workers. About 75 percent of total production is in the food-processing and textile sectors. Important products include cotton textiles, jute manufactures, cement, fertilizers, steel, sugar, and chemicals.

Currency and Banking. The basic monetary unit is the Pakistani rupee (1 rupee equals U.S.$.21; 1970). The main elements of the banking system are the State Bank of Pakistan, a number of large commercial banks, called scheduled banks, and several nonscheduled banks. The State Bank, established in 1948, issues banknotes, manages the currency and credit systems, the public debt, and exchange controls, and supervises the operations of the commercial banks.

PAKISTAN

Commerce and Trade. The foreign trade of Pakistan consists largely in the exporting of raw material and the importing of manufactured products. In the late 1960's, the annual totals of imports and exports were about $890,000 and $685,000,000 respectively. The principal imports, in descending order of value, are machinery, iron and steel, grains, transport equipment, electrical goods, drugs, medicines, and chemicals. Principal exports are raw jute, jute manufactures, raw cotton, cotton manufactures, raw wool, hides and skins, and tea.

Transportation. The wide geographical separation of the two provinces and the lack of modern transportation facilities are major hindrances to the development of Pakistan. The terrain of both East Pakistan and West Pakistan presents formidable obstacles to internal overland transportation. The two Pakistani provinces are connected by a railroad and various roads which traverse Indian territory, but for reasons of speed or economy, communication between the provinces takes place mainly by ship and by airplane.

The country has about 26,000 mi. of roads, of which more than 90 percent are in West Pakistan. In the late 1960's, according to latest available statistics, about 175,000 motor vehicles were registered in Pakistan. The railroad network totals more than 7000 mi., of which about 5300 mi. are in West Pakistan. The merchant fleet comprises more than 500,000 deadweight tonnage and includes about 50 oceangoing vessels. Karachi, the principal port, handles about 3,672,000 tons of shipping annually.

Pakistan has two domestic airlines, Pakistan International Airlines and Pakistan Aviation, Ltd.; in addition, several foreign international airlines make regular stops at Karachi.

Communications. In the mid-1960's about 135,000 telephones and 550,000 licensed radios were in use. Television broadcasting was begun in Lahore and Dacca in 1964 and in Karachi in 1966. Newspapers are mainly printed in Urdu, Bengali, and English. Pakistan has a considerable number of daily newspapers, most of them with small circulations. The major dailies are concentrated in the Punjab area and in the city of Karachi.

GOVERNMENT

Pakistan is governed under a constitution that was proclaimed on March 1, 1962. The head of the state is the president, who must be a Muslim at least thirty-five years of age. He is elected to a five-year term by about 80,000 electors, called basic democrats, who are members of local government councils elected by popular vote on

Jute is carried to market by farmers near Dacca, East Pakistan. The country is among the world's largest producers of jute. UPI

the basis of adult suffrage. The president is subject to impeachment by a majority of three quarters of the national assembly; to discourage frivolous proceedings, the movers of the impeachment will lose their seats if the motion is not supported by at least a simple majority. The president and the speaker of the assembly must be from different provinces of Pakistan. The president has the power to appoint the ministers heading the departments of the government.

Health and Welfare. Sanitation conditions throughout Pakistan remain poor; major health problems are malaria, tuberculosis, and intestinal diseases. In 1956, a National Council of Social Welfare was established, but progress in this field has been minimal.

PAKISTAN

Legislature. The unicameral national assembly of 313 seats consists of 138 members from West Pakistan and 162 from East Pakistan, plus 13 seats reserved for women. The members from the two provinces are chosen by the basic democrats; the women are chosen by the provincial legislatures. Legislation must conform to Muslim principles and requires the approval of the president; his veto may be overridden by a two-thirds vote.

Political Parties. The Muslim League, the group that brought Pakistan to independence, is the main political force in the country. From 1958 to 1962 all political parties were suspended by President Mohammed Ayub Khan (1907–). After 1962, opposition groups were allowed to form but none has risen to challenge Muslim League supremacy. The chief minor parties are the National Democratic Front, the Awami League, and the Pakistan People's Party.

Local Government. Each province has a legislature of 150 members, also selected by the basic democrats. The ministers of the provinces are appointed by the provincial governors, with the consent of the president.

Judiciary. The judicial system is patterned after that of Great Britain. The supreme court of Pakistan has original, appellate, and advisory jurisdictions; the justices are appointed by the president. Each province has its own high court, the justices of which are also named by the president. District and sessions courts in each province have original jurisdiction and some appellate jurisdiction.

Defense. The Pakistani army, a volunteer force, has a total strength of about 250,000. Naval personnel includes more than 9000 officers and men, and the air force has about 15,000 personnel.

HISTORY

For the history of the territory before Aug. 15, 1947, see INDIA: *History.*

Hindu-Muslim Strife. At the inception of the new state of Pakistan Mohammed Ali Jinnah (q.v.) became the first governor-general. Although independence was celebrated with rejoicing in both Pakistan and the Union of India, strife between the newly created dominions began almost immediately thereafter. The first great conflict centered on the persecution of religious minorities when predominantly Hindu areas were awarded to Pakistan, or when predominantly Muslim areas were awarded to India. About half the population of Lahore, then the largest city in Pakistan, were Hindus or Sikhs, nearly all of whom emigrated to India. At the same time Muslims from East Punjab began moving into Pakistan. Rioting and bloodshed between the two great religious groups became common. The influx of Muslim refugees into West Punjab became a major concern, and on Aug. 27, 1948, the dominion government invoked emergency powers, ordering its various provinces and states to take assigned numbers of refugees. By Feb. 26, 1949, about 5,100,000 Muslims from India had emigrated to West Punjab, and about 3,565,000 Pakistani Hindus had been resettled in the Union of India.

A second grave problem arose in princely states ruled by Muslims or Hindus in which the majority of the population followed a religion different from that of the ruler. In Kashmir (see JAMMU AND KASHMIR) the Hindu maharajah Sir Hari Singh (1895–1961) agreed to join the Union of India in late 1947 against the will of his predominantly Muslim subjects. Both Pakistan and India sent in troops, and in 1948 India referred the dispute to the United Nations Security Council. On April 21, 1948, the council agreed to hold a plebiscite in Kashmir to determine the ultimate disposition of that state.

Trade Problems. Economic problems provided another source of conflict between the two dominions. Pakistani-Indian conferences were held in 1947 concerning Indian processing of Pakistani jute. The negotiations were ineffective after Pakistan initiated export duties on jute, which were necessary as a primary source of revenue. In 1948 Pakistan began to invite foreign investors to aid in the development of its natural resources. With Pakistan and India holding irreconcilable viewpoints regarding the proposed plebiscite, U.N. attempts to arbitrate the Kashmir dispute met with systematic failure during 1949 and 1950. On April 2, 1951, Pakistan approved a new U.N. plan to end the dispute. India rejected certain features of the plan, however, further aggravating the protracted crisis. Pakistani-Indian relations improved somewhat during 1951 as a result of full resumption in February of trade between the two countries. On Oct. 16 Prime Minister Liaquat Ali Khan (1895–1951) was assassinated by a political fanatic. Khwaja Nazimuddin (1894–1964), the governor-general, was named to succeed him in office.

The economic situation deteriorated during 1953. The lack of sufficient foreign exchange necessitated barter agreements, such as one signed in March with Communist China, whereby Pakistan would receive coal in exchange for its cotton. The imminent threat of famine, coupled with Muslim factional disputes, caused the downfall of the Nazimuddin government on April 17. Mohammed Ali (1909–63), am-

At a religious observance held in Karachi, seaport in southwestern Pakistan, during the month of Muharram, first month of the Islamic year, members of the Shi'ite sect walk barefoot through burning coals. This and other acts of penance are performed in commemoration of the martyrdom of Hussein, grandson of the Prophet, thirteen centuries ago. UPI

bassador to the United States, became prime minister. The new government planned drastic cuts in expenditures in a desperate attempt to improve the economic situation.

On Sept. 8, 1954, Pakistan became a signatory of the Southeast Asia Treaty, a U.S.-sponsored document providing for the collective defense of southeast Asia and the southwest Pacific, excluding Taiwan; see SOUTHEAST ASIA TREATY ORGANIZATION.

Unification. The Pakistani governor-general dissolved the constituent assembly on Oct. 24. In the new constituent assembly elected on June 21, 1955, the Muslim League won 35 of the 80 seats, and the two Bengali (East Pakistan) parties known as the United Front and the Awami (People's) League together won 38 seats. The election ended the one-party rule of the Muslim League, which had been in power since the inception of Pakistan as an independent nation. Prime Minister Mohammed Ali resigned on Aug. 7. He was succeeded by the former finance minister Chaudhri Mohammed Ali (1905–   ), who also succeeded him as head of the Muslim League.

The various provinces and States of West Pakistan were merged on Oct. 14 into a single political and administrative unit. The move brought protests from Afghanistan, which had long advocated independent status for some 7,000,000 Pathan tribesmen inhabiting West Pakistan. Afghanistan severed diplomatic relations with Pakistan on Oct. 18. Under the terms of a constitution adopted on March 2, 1956, Pakistan ended its status as a dominion and became an independent Islamic republic. The country retained its membership in the Commonwealth of Nations, however. The new constitution guaranteed religious freedom and granted suffrage to women.

Changing Leadership. In March, 1956, the former governor-general Iskander Mirza (1899–1969) was elected provisional president. Prime Minister Chaudhri Mohammed Ali remained in office until September, 1956, when he was succeeded by Huseyn Shaheed Suhrawardy (1893–1963), leader of the Awami League in East Pakistan.

In October, the Kashmiri Constituent Assembly adopted a constitution proclaiming that Kashmir was irrevocably a part of the Indian Union. The following month Pakistan protested to the U.N. Security Council against the accession of Kashmir to India without a plebiscite. In January, 1957, the Security Council, supporting Pakistan, approved a resolution calling for a plebiscite in Kashmir to determine its futute status.

In June, 1957, diplomatic relations between Afghanistan and Pakistan were restored. Suhrawardy resigned the following October and was succeeded as prime minister by Ismail Ibrahim

259

PAKISTAN

Chundrigar (1897–1960), leader of the Muslim League, who formed a coalition with the Republican Party. The coalition ended in December, 1957. Sir Firozkhan Noon (1893–   ), a leader of the Republican Party, thereupon became prime minister.

On Oct. 7, 1958, following a dispute among members of the cabinet, President Mirza declared martial law, dismissed the government, and annulled the constitution. All political parties were banned. Mirza surrendered his position on Oct. 27 to the commander in chief of the army, General Mohammed Ayub Khan (1907–   ), who thereafter ruled almost absolutely until March, 1969.

A land-redistribution program was initiated by the government in September. Individual ownership was restricted to 500 acres of irrigated or 1000 acres of unirrigated land.

Mohammed Ayub Khan was sworn in as the first elected president in February, 1960, after being overwhelmingly endorsed in a secret ballot by elected representatives of village councils. He immediately announced plans to draw up a new constitution. The second five-year plan for economic development took effect on July 1. In August the seat of government was transferred from Karachi to Rawalpindi pending construction of a new capital to be called Islamabad.

Ties with the Soviet Union and China. Pakistan accepted in August a Soviet offer to explore the oil and mineral resources of the country. Further Soviet offers of economic assistance were disclosed in January, 1961. On Jan. 27 the Warsak dam on the Kabul R. was inaugurated. Largely Canadian financed, it would supply irrigation water for about 120,000 acres. A government ordinance of March 2 restricted the contracting of polygamous marriages. A renewal of the dispute concerning the Pathan tribesmen of West Pakistan again led Afghanistan, on Sept. 6, to break off diplomatic relations with Pakistan and to close the frontier. A new constitution for Pakistan was announced on March 1, 1962 (see *Government,* above). Pakistan again brought the Kashmir issue before the U.N. Security Council on April 27; India maintained that the accession of Kashmir was conclusive and not subject to a plebiscite. On April 28, some 80,000 electors voted for members of the national assembly in the first nationwide election.

Ministerial talks in 1963 to prepare for a high-level Indian-Pakistani conference on the Kashmir question collapsed. Pakistani displeasure over U.S. military aid to India following the outbreak of fighting between India and Communist China resulted in a deterioration of Pakistani-U.S. relations. Pakistan turned increasingly to countries sharing its mistrust of India. Pakistan and Communist China signed a trade agreement on Jan. 5 and a provisional border agreement for the demarcation of a 300-mi. strip of frontier between the two countries on March 2. Disaster hit East Pakistan on May 28–29, when about 22,000 persons were killed by a cyclone. Communist China abandoned its neutral position on the Kashmir question in February, 1964, to support the Pakistani position. In meetings in July, the two countries took further steps toward improving their relations.

War with India. In January, 1965, President Ayub Khan was reelected to a five-year term. During the first half of the year border incidents between Pakistan and India increased, culminating in an outbreak of open fighting in August, 1965. During the next six months fighting continued on a limited scale with neither side gaining appreciable headway. Through the efforts of the Soviet Union a peace conference was arranged in Tashkent, U.S.S.R., in January, 1966. After prolonged negotiations both sides agreed to sign a declaration providing for a withdrawal to positions held prior to the outbreak of hostilities. The truce, placed under U.N. supervision, continued through 1967 with only minor violations.

Domestic Unrest. Students in West Pakistan began to demonstrate for university reform in October, 1968. Encouraged by the opposition Pakistan People's Party, led by Zulfikar Ali Bhutto (1928–   ), a former foreign minister, the students soon widened their protest to include an attack on the Ayub government itself and the 1962 constitution. In February, 1969, thousands of workers joined the students in a general strike called throughout East and West Pakistan. In the clashes between strikers and police that followed nearly 100 people were killed. Ayub's attempts to conciliate his political opponents failed, and later that month he announced that he would not be a candidate in the presidential election scheduled for March, 1970.

On March 25, 1969, Ayub resigned in favor of the army commander in chief Agha Mohammed Yahya Khan (1917–   ), who decreed martial law, abrogated the constitution, and dissolved the local assemblies. The disturbances largely ceased, and Yahya set late 1970 as the date for the first direct elections to the national assembly. In the new assembly, East Pakistan would have 162 delegates, West Pakistan, 138 delegates, and of the 13 women in the assembly, 7 would be from East Pakistan.

A devastating cyclone struck East Pakistan on Nov. 12, 1970; an estimated 500,000 persons were killed and millions were made homeless. International relief efforts aided the survivors, but the Pakistani government was widely criticized for its slow reaction. Despite the disaster, the assembly elections took place as scheduled on Dec. 7, 1970. In East Pakistan the Awami League, headed by Sheikh Mujibur Rahman (1922–), won 151 seats; in West Pakistan Bhutto's Pakistan People's Party won 81 seats. Rahman immediately announced demands for further autonomy for East Pakistan; and Bhutto threatened to boycott the assembly. Subsequently Yahya postponed convening the assembly. A protest strike, called to reinforce demands for independence of East Pakistan, resulted in martial law and the dispatch of federal troops to quell the revolt in what the Bengalis proclaimed as the independent state of Bangla Desh ("Bengal Nation"). The Bengalis, poorly armed and suffering heavy losses, received much international sympathy for their struggle. After arresting Rahman in March, 1971, and much hard fighting, the federal government announced in mid-April that the separatist movement had been subdued. Throughout the year, the Bengalis continued their militant opposition, however, resorting to guerrilla tactics. Reports by East Pakistan refugees, migrating to India by the hundreds of thousands, about atrocities committed by West Pakistan soldiers, led to growing tension between the two countries and ultimately in an Indian invasion of East Pakistan. Pakistan acceded to Indian demands, and Yahya resigned the presidency and was succeeded by Bhutto, who freed Rahman, and who, in turn, established a Bangla Desh government in January, 1972.

PALAEOLOGUS, name of an illustrious Byzantine family that formed the last dynasty of the Byzantine Empire (q.v.), from 1261 to 1453. Michael VIII (1234–82), first of eight emperors from this family, was a soldier and administrator who tried to heal the breach between the Eastern and Western churches. The last member of the family was Constantine Palaeologus (1404–53), the last Byzantine emperor, whom the Ottoman Turks killed during the capture of Constantinople (now İstanbul, Turkey) in 1453.

PALAMAS, Kostes (1859–1943), Greek poet, born in Pátrai, and educated at Missolonghi and the University of Athens. He wrote in demotic speech, the vernacular as compared to the literary language; see GREEK LITERATURE: *The Modern Period*. His first important work was *Tragoudia tes Patridos Mou* ("Songs of My Fatherland", 1886), his expression of an aim to revive Greek literary eminence. Other works include *The Twelve Books of the Gypsy* (1907; Eng. trans., 1964), and *The King's Flute* (Eng. trans., 1966).

PALATE, roof of the mouth, consisting of two portions, the hard palate in front and the soft palate behind. The hard palate is formed of periosteum covered by mucous membrane (qq.v.) and arches over to meet the gums in front and on either side. The soft palate is a movable fold of mucous membrane enclosing muscular fibers; its sides blend with the pharynx, while its lower border is free. It is suspended from the rear of the hard palate so as to form an incomplete wall or division between the mouth and

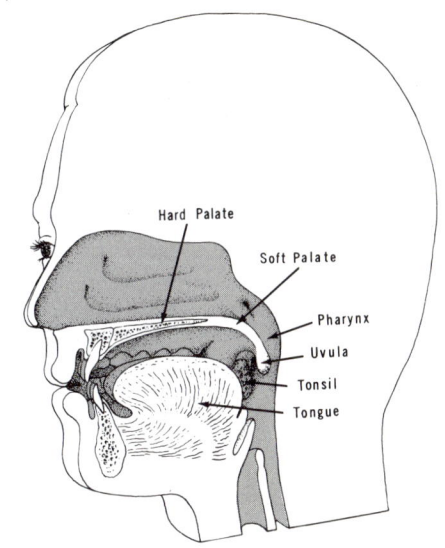

Diagram of the palate and related structures.

the pharynx that, in swallowing, is raised to close the entrance to the nasal passages.

A small cone-shaped structure, the uvula, hangs from the lower border of the soft palate. The space left between the arches of the palate on the two sides is called the isthmus of the fauces. It is bounded above by the free margin of the palate, below by the tongue (q.v.), and on each side by the pillars of the soft palate and tonsils; see TONSIL.

Just as the upper lip may be split through imperfect development, a condition known as harelip (q.v.), so also may there be a more or less decided split of the palate. In this inborn deformity, which is inherited in only one-quarter of the cases, the bones of the hard palate fail to join as the fetus develops. The cleft is readily closed by surgery, preferably at an early age before the child begins to talk.

PALATINATE

Enlargement or relaxation of the uvula is not uncommon; it may irritate the larynx (q.v.) and cause a tickling cough and expectoration. The palate may also suffer from ulceration and perforation. The rashes of certain infectious diseases appear on the mucous membrane of the palate and cheeks before appearing on the skin.

PALATINATE, in German history, name of two imperial regions not related geographically, the western Rhenish or Lower Palatinate (Ger. *Rheinpfalz* or *Niederpfalz*) and the Upper Palatinate (Ger. *Oberpfalz*) of N.E. Bavaria (q.v.). The Rhenish Palatinate, which historically comprised territory for the most part w. of the Rhine R. in central Germany, was, in 1947, incorporated into the West German State of Rhineland-Palatinate (q.v.). The Upper, or Bavarian, Palatinate is the region w. of Bohemia and N. of the Danube R. The name palatinate derives from the ancient and medieval office of Count Palatine, a nobleman who held judicial powers and had charge of the various imperial castles where German emperors stayed while traveling; hence the term became associated with the districts where the count palatines were sovereign representatives. The two palatinates became politically united at the end of the 18th century. See GERMANY: *History*; GOLDEN BULL; HOLY ROMAN EMPIRE.

PALATINE, village of Illinois, in Cook Co., about 28 miles N.W. of central Chicago. Situated in a farm area, the village has varied manufacturing. It is the site of William Rainey Harper College, founded in 1965. Palatine was founded in 1855 and incorporated in 1869. Pop. (1960) 11,504; (1970) 25,904.

PALATINE HILL, one of the seven hills of Rome, according to tradition the site of the earliest Roman settlement. On its N.W. slope was the Lupercal, a cave in which Romulus and his twin brother Remus (qq.v.) are said to have been suckled by a she-wolf. On this hill, according to legend, Romulus founded the city of Rome. During the Roman Republic, temples and some of the finest private houses in Rome stood on the summit of the Palatine or on its slopes, and under the empire, the hill became the site of imperial residences. The emperor Nero (q.v.) included the entire hill within the precincts of his *aurea domus* (Golden House), erected after the disastrous fire of 64 A.D. From the time of Roman Emperor Marcus Aurelius Alexander Severus (208?–235), the Palatine Hill ceased to be an official residence of the emperors.

PALAU ISLANDS. See CAROLINE ISLANDS.

PALAWAN, island and province of the Philippines, in the extreme s.w. of the island group, between the Sulu and South China seas. The island is about 280 mi. long and 25 mi. wide with a mountain chain running through the center culminating in Mt. Mantalingajan, 6843 ft. The province includes a number of smaller islands. Coconut, sugar, rice, lumber, and livestock are produced. Area of island, 4550 sq.mi.; pop. (1960) 162,669.

PALEMBANG, city and port in Indonesia, and capital of South Sumatra Province, on the island of Sumatra, on the Musi R., about 250 miles N.E. of Djakarta. It is a trade center for the surrounding oil and rubber producing area, and there are refineries in the suburbs of Plaja and Sungaigerong. In Palembang are shipyards and iron foundries. Palembang was the capital of the Hindu-Sumatran 8th-century kingdom of Sri Vijaya. Pop. (1961) 474,971.

PALENQUE, ancient city of Mexico, in Chiapas State, near the village of Palenque. The city, dating from the Maya civilization, was buried in a dense tropical forest. The ruins consist of terraces on top of pyramids of cut stone, surmounted by stone buildings with mansard roofs. Most of the buildings are only one story high; some may have had four. Walls have figures in relief, or figures and hieroglyphs in stucco, with remains of brilliant colors. The principal structure, known as the Palace, 228 ft. long, stands on a truncated pyramid. There is an arched bridge and a subterranean waterway.

PALEOCENE EPOCH, earliest division of geologic time in the Tertiary Period of the Cenozoic Era (q.v.). It followed the Cretaceous Period and preceded the Eocene Epoch (qq.v.), beginning about 70,000,000 years ago and continuing for about 10,000,000 years. It was a transitional period, and some geologists include it in the Eocene Epoch. Mountain building was accelerated as the Cretaceous Period ended, and the present-day Rocky Mts. and the South American Andes Mts. had been formed by the end of the Paleocene Epoch. During this period parts of Europe and North America rose above the waters that submerged them in Cretaceous and Eocene times, and the climate was cooler than in the surrounding periods. The rocks of the Paleocene Epoch are sandstones, shales, and limestone. The thickest of these rock formations are found in Wyoming.

Fauna. Life forms during the epoch included the earliest types of mammals, among them marsupials, primitive hoofed animals (condylarths), and archaic flesh eaters (creodonts). Remains of primitive insect eaters and ancestral types of monkeys have been found. The dinosaurs had disappeared, but a few reptiles persisted, and insects were widespread. *See* Geology, Historical; Paleontology.

PALEOGRAPHY, in its widest sense, science that deals with the writing of ancient times and that of the Middle Ages, whether on materials regarded as destructible or indestructible; in its restricted sense, paleography denotes only the study of writing on such destructible materials as wax, papyrus (q.v.), parchment and vellum (q.v.), and paper. The study of inscriptions engraved on stone or metal is called the science of epigraphy. Latin paleography owes its origin to the study of diplomatics, or ancient legal documents, and in turn led to the study of ancient Greek writing, through the investigation of the manuscripts of the Greek Church fathers of the early Christian era.

Ancient Writing Materials. Ancient writing materials included leaves, bark, clay, and leaden tablets, but the most commonly used were the wax tablet, the papyrus roll, and later the parchment book. Wax tablets were convenient for letters, accounts, and writing of a temporary nature. Papyrus sheets, made into rolls from 20 to 30 ft. in length, provided the most common writing material of classical antiquity, being in constant use from about 500 B.C. to 300 A.D., and even later for nonliterary purposes. The papyrus roll had several disadvantages; because it had to be rerolled after each reading, it was extremely awkward to use for reference, and often from excessive wear the beginning and end of a roll would be torn or mutilated. This mutilation caused the lacunae, or gaps, which sometimes appear in the works of classical authors.

Parchment, known to have been employed for literary works at Rome as early as the 1st century A.D. and used by the Greeks much earlier, became increasingly popular, and by the 4th century, Greek and Latin literature was generally transferred from the papyrus roll to the parchment codex, made into book form in imitation of the wax tablet. The codex was much more suitable for long works and lent itself more readily to convenient reference. Some pagan works, however, were not transcribed, and many losses occurred in this period, especially among the works of Greek writers. The pages of the early codices were large, and the practice of writing in columns, usually two, but sometimes three or four, was taken over from the papyri; poetry was transcribed with each verse written continuously across the page.

Ancient Writing Styles. In both the papyrus rolls and the parchment books which supplanted them, the regular practice was not to separate words, although in some writing, both inscriptions and literary works, dots or points were used as divisions. Word division did not become common until about the 9th century, when many wrong divisions were made; for instance, *opsonatu redeo,* a phrase in the *Menoechmi* of the Roman comic dramatist Titus Maccius Plautus (q.v.), was divided as *opso nature deo* and then corrupted into *ipso naturae deo.*

The two styles of penmanship in antiquity are known as the formal literary, or book, hand and the more rapid cursive hand, which was employed for nonliterary, everyday purposes. The extant manuscripts of the classical authors exhibit either the ancient book hands or various scripts that developed later, in the Middle Ages, under cursive influence.

All Greek and Roman manuscripts, ancient and medieval, are classified either as majuscule, that is, written in large letters, or as minuscule, written in small letters. Majuscule writing is subdivided into (1) capitals, either square capitals, carefully formed with angles to resemble inscriptions carved on stone, or rustic capitals, drawn with somewhat greater freedom with oblique and short cross strokes; and (2) uncials, modified capitals, in which curves are favored and angles avoided as much as possible; originally, the shape of both types of majuscule letters was dictated by the materials used, capitals having been incised on hard stone on which a chisel could not easily make curves, and uncials having been written on such nonresistant surfaces as papyrus. Minuscules, or small letters, resulted from the rapid and inartistic writing of majuscules under cursive influence; the letters became changed in form and reduced in size, but minuscule writing is in most instances distinct from cursive writing.

Greek Writing. The science of paleography as applied to the study of Greek writing on papyrus is of modern date. Previous to the discoveries of the past one hundred years (*see* Papyri, Discoveries of), Greek papyri were customarily classified according to the style of writing, as the literary, or book, hand or the cursive hand. Although these styles are sharply differentiated, there is no set form for either one. Writing on vellum may be classed as uncial or minuscule, and this distinction can be sharply drawn in the Middle Ages, when the literary hands were settled. The uncial of the medieval period is a lineal descendant of the literary style in the papyri, but the medieval minuscule is a new style, based on the cursive but molded into an exact form and becoming finally the regular hand for literary purposes.

Our knowledge of early Greek writing is de-

PALEOGRAPHY

pendent upon the evidence of inscriptions, the study of which is the science of Greek epigraphy. The earliest literary papyrus, that of the *Persae* by the Greek poet Timotheus (446?–357? B.C.), is written in capital letters very similar to those of inscriptions. By the 3rd century B.C. the book hand had become uncial, and a handsome broad uncial continued in use on papyri until the 6th or 7th century A.D. Three periods in the history of Greek writing on papyrus may be recognized: the Ptolemaic, from 330 to 27 B.C., marked by freedom and breadth of style; the Roman, from 27 B.C. to 305 A.D., marked by roundness and curved, flowing strokes; and the Byzantine, from 360 A.D. to the Arab conquest of Egypt in 640, marked by a large, handsome style.

The oldest vellum manuscripts are the great uncial codices of the Bible, the *Codex Vaticanus* and the *Codex Sinaiticus,* both probably of the 4th century A.D.; these manuscripts have essentially the uncial characters of the papyrus rolls. About the 7th century a slanting uncial became popular; this type of uncial became pointed, with a strong contrast between heavy and light strokes, and is known as the Slavonic uncial, because it formed the basis of the Slavic alphabet. When the Greek uncial was taken over in the 9th century by the Slavs, the Greeks developed for their formal book hand a minuscule writing based upon cursive. Manuscripts written in Greek minuscules are very numerous. They are classified as the *vetustissimi,* from the 9th to the middle of the 10th century, distinguished for their purity and simplicity; the *vetusti,* from the middle of the 10th to the middle of the 13th century, in which contractions and abbreviations become more frequent; the *recentiores,* from the middle of the 13th to the middle of the 15th century, written with great carelessness, as were the contemporary Gothic scripts of western Europe; and the *novelli,* comprising the manuscripts written after the fall of Constantinople in 1453.

Latin Writing. The study of the history of Latin paleography begins with majuscule writing as found in the earliest Latin manuscripts extant, such as the Vergil (q.v.) manuscripts of the 4th and 5th centuries A.D., which are written in square or rustic capitals. As a literary hand, uncial writing extends from the 5th to the 8th century; uncial was predominantly the writing used for Biblical and patristic works and seems to have been developed by the Christians, perhaps formalized by the early copyists of the Bible under the influence of Greek uncials. The cursive hand in general use influenced the literary majuscule hand, so that a style designated as half-uncial became a popular book hand, and this, being a clear and beautiful script, had an important effect upon some of the medieval book hands. The contest between formal majuscule and cursive minuscule ended, however, in the victory of the latter. After the 7th century, the various book hands were all minuscule, developed by scribes from the cursive with an admixture of uncial or half-uncial forms. The earliest examples of the cursive style are the wall inscriptions and wax tablets of the ancient city of Pompeii, written before 79 A.D. The minuscule scripts that developed from cursive becam the so-called national hands of the Middle Ages, each assuming an individuality according to the locality in which it prevailed.

Development of Styles. The important national hands are seven in number. The Beneventan, or Lombardic, script is the writing of southern Italy, as practiced in the monasteries of Monte Cassino and La Cava from the 9th to the 13th century. The Visigothic was employed for books and documents of Spain from the 8th to the 12th century. The Insular scripts, those of Ireland and England from the 7th to the 11th century, differ from the Continental forms of writing in that they were not derived from the cursive style, but from the half-uncial, which had been taken to Ireland by missionaries in the 4th and 5th centuries. Manuscripts written in the Insular scripts are noted for their calligraphic forms and their ornamentation.

The script written in France during the 7th and 8th centuries is called Merovingian (q.v.), or pre-Carolingian; this hand never reached the calligraphic form, which marked the highest development of the other national hands, for it was supplanted by the round minuscules of the Carolingian (q.v.) reform. The reform of writing which marked the reign of the emperor Charlemagne (q.v.) had its origin in the monasteries of France, where much attention was given to the copying of earlier manuscripts. The scribes wrote in a plain, simple, and beautiful script that was strongly influenced by the earlier half-uncial characters. A new hand was the result, which is known as the Carolingian minuscule, and which became the literary hand of the Frankish Empire.

In the 11th century the Carolingian began to assume an individual form in the various nations of western Europe. This period was the starting point of the history of modern hands, which are traced to the Roman alphabet. In the 12th century appeared the so-called Gothic writing, a modification of the Carolingian minuscule with angles replacing the curves. Exces-

PALEONTOLOGY

sive angularity and compression, and the use of numerous contractions and abbreviations, made the Gothic script difficult to read, and it was often artistically awkward as well as illegible. A renaissance of the Carolingian style took place in Italy in the 14th century, developing a very regular and beautiful style, which led to the Humanistic script of the 15th century. The Humanistic hand served as the model for the typesetters of Italy, and so preserved the clear and simple Roman letters that go back through the Carolingian script to the half-uncials of the earlier period. These minuscule letters were the ancestors of the lowercase letters of the modern Roman type; the Gothic script was used for the lowercase of German type.

Research Problems. The difficulty of deciphering medieval manuscripts arises largely from the contractions, abbreviations, and ligatures, which were employed to economize labor and parchment. In the early manuscripts, written in capitals and uncials, abbreviations were rarely used, but they became more frequent in the 6th and 7th centuries. More than 5000 contractions of Latin words were used in France between the 7th and the 16th centuries; in England more than 1000 are found in official Latin documents of the Tudor (q.v.) period alone. Fortunately, the Carolingian scribes, who copied many of the best medieval manuscripts of Latin authors, employed abbreviations somewhat sparingly. In Gothic writing, abbreviations of every kind appeared with the greatest frequency.

See also WRITING. G.E.D.

PALEOLITHIC, designating the earliest era in the history of mankind, which comprises the three periods of Lower Paleolithic, Middle Paleolithic, and Upper Paleolithic, and followed by the Mesolithic. The era was characterized by progress from use of crude stone tools to finer stone tools, the first bone tools, cave paintings, and sculptured figurines. *See* ARCHEOLOGY.

PALEONTOLOGY, study of fossil animal and plant life that existed in remote geological times. The study of such remains is important not only in tracing the evolutionary history of organisms that now exist but also in the determination of the relative ages of geological deposits.

The term "fossil" is applied to actual remains of living organisms preserved and protected from decay by enclosure in the crust of the earth. Commonly only the harder and more resistant parts of organisms, such as bones, shells, and teeth of animals and woody tissue of plants, were preserved in this manner. In some cases the original materials underwent little change in shape after they were embedded in mineral deposits, but the original substance of the organism was petrified (turned into stone). Petrification took place in either of two ways. The open spaces of porous materials such as bone and some types of shell were filled with mineral solutions that dried and hardened, leaving a stonelike fossil that is heavier and more compact than the original material. Calcium carbonate and silica are the most common mineral materials that formed this type of fossil. In some instances, organic material was completely replaced chemically by an inorganic material, usually silica. In such fossils no trace of the original

A fossilized worm trail embedded in sedimentary rock. The worm fed and traveled by swallowing mud and extruding it. UPI

organic matter remains, but the entire structure of the organism was preserved, including the microscopic details of individual cells. The fossil forests of the western United States are well-known examples of this form of petrification.

Outlines of softer and more delicate animal and plant tissues were frequently preserved in the form of carbon prints in stone when the tissues were subjected to heat while in contact with a stone surface. Natural molds were formed when an animal or plant was enclosed in a sedimentary deposit that later hardened. Water seeping through the stone dissolved the original material, leaving a natural mold. Sometimes these molds were later filled with mineral

PALEONTOLOGY

material, forming replicas of the original organisms. The footprints and body prints that prehistoric animals left on soft surfaces such as mud flats are also sometimes preserved in stone, as are fossil animal droppings.

The true nature of fossils was not generally understood until about the beginning of the 19th century, when the basic principles of modern geology were established. From about the year 1500, scholars engaged in a bitter controversy over the origin of fossils. One group held the modern view that fossils are the remains of prehistoric plants and animals, but this group was opposed by another, which declared that they are either freaks of nature or creations of the devil. In the 18th century, many believed that all fossils are relics of the Biblical flood, and that fossils of such diverse animals as mastodons and salamanders were the remains of men who perished in that disaster.

PALEOZOIC LIFE

The fossils of ancient animals and plants are usually incomplete, but paleontologists, aided by their knowledge of living forms and of comparative anatomy, are usually able to reconstruct the form of an organism as it appeared in life.

Cambrian Period. Very few fossils belonging to the Precambrian Era of geological history are known, and the first abundant fossil deposits appear in the rocks of the Cambrian Period at the beginning of the Paleozoic Era. The first abundant fossils date from approximately 600,000,000 years ago. The reason for the scarcity of earlier fossils is not fully understood, but some geologists believe that in Precambrian times most species of animals were soft-bodied, and that shells and other hard body parts adapted to preservation first developed in the Cambrian Period.

At the beginning of the Paleozoic Era, animal life was entirely confined to the seas. With the exception of the vertebrates, all the phyla of the animal kingdom existed in Cambrian times, and the first vertebrates, which were primitive fishes, appeared in the Ordovician Period, which followed the Cambrian. The characteristic animals of the Cambrian Period were the trilobites, a primitive form of crustaceans, which reached their fullest development in this period and became extinct in Permian times. Among the mollusks, the earliest snails appeared in this period, as did the cephalopods. Other groups represented in the Cambrian Period were brachiopods, bryozoans, and foraminifers. The flora of the Cambrian was entirely confined to such low forms as seaweeds in the oceans and lichens on land.

Ordovician Period. The most characteristic animals of this period were the graptolites, which were small, colonial coelenterates. The first vertebrates and the earliest corals emerged during the Ordovician Period. The largest animal of that time was a cephalopod mollusk that had a shell about 10 ft. in length. The flora of this period resembled that of the Cambrian Period.

Silurian Period. The most important evolutionary development of this period was the first air-breathing animal, a scorpion, fossils of which have been found in Scandinavia and Great Britain. The remaining fauna of the period resembled that of earlier Paleozoic times. The first fossil records of vascular plants, that is, land plants with conducting tissue, appear in the Silurian Period. They were simple plants without differentiation into stem and leaf.

Devonian Period. The dominant forms of animal life in this period were fishes of various types, including sharks, lungfishes, armored fishes, and primitive forms of ganoid fishes that are believed to have been the evolutionary ancestors of the amphibia. Fossil remains found in Pennsylvania and Greenland indicate that early forms of amphibia may have existed during the period. Lower animal forms included corals, starfishes, sponges, and trilobites. The earliest known insect was found in Devonian rock.

The Devonian is the first period from which

Close-up photograph of a fossilized brachiopod, a clamlike creature measuring about ½ in. in diameter.
UPI

PALEONTOLOGY

any considerable number of fossilized plants has been preserved. During this period the first woody plants developed, and before the period had closed, the land-growing forms included seed ferns, ferns, scouring rushes, and scale trees, the modern relatives of which are club mosses. Although the present-day equivalents of these groups are mostly small plants, they developed into treelike forms in the Devonian Period. Fossil evidence indicates that forests existed in Devonian times, and petrified stumps of certain of the larger Devonian plants are two ft. in diameter.

Mississippian (Lower Carboniferous) Period. The seas of this period contained a variety of echinoderms and foraminifers, as well as most of the forms of animal life appearing in the Devonian. A group of sharks, the Cestraciontes or shell crushers, were predominant among the larger marine animals. The predominant group of land animals was the Stegocephalia, an order of primitive, lizardlike amphibians that developed from the lungfishes. During the Mississippian Period the various forms of land plants became diversified and grew larger, particularly those which grew in low-lying swampy areas.

Pennsylvania (Upper Carboniferous) Period. This period saw the evolution of the first reptiles, a group that developed from the amphibia and that was completely independent of a water environment. Other land animals included spiders, snails, scorpions, more than 800 species of cockroaches, and the largest insect ever evolved, a species resembling the dragonfly, with a wingspread of about 29 in. The largest plants were the scale trees, the tapered trunks of which were as much as 6 ft. in diameter at the base and 100 ft. high. Cordaites, which had pithy stems surrounded by a woody shell, was more slender but even taller. The first true conifers also developed during the Pennsylvania Period.

Permian Period. The chief features of the animal life of the Permian Period were the disappearance of many forms of marine animals and the rapid spread and evolution of the reptiles. In general the Permian reptiles were of two types: lizardlike reptiles that lived wholly on land, and sluggish, semiaquatic types. A comparatively small group of reptiles that evolved in this period, the Theriodontia, was the group from which mammals later developed. Among the plants the scale trees became more rare, and the predominant vegetation was composed of ferns and conifers.

MESOZOIC LIFE

The Mesozoic Era as a whole is often called the Age of Reptiles because the reptile phylum was dominant throughout the entire age.

Triassic Period. The most notable of the Mesozoic reptiles were the dinosaurs, which first evolved in Triassic times. The Triassic dinosaurs were not as large as their descendants in later Mesozoic times, and were comparatively slender animals that ran on their hind feet, balancing their bodies with heavy, fleshy tails. They seldom exceeded 15 ft. in length. Other reptilian forms of the Triassic Period included such aquatic reptiles as the ichthyosaurs, and a group of flying reptiles, the pterosaurs. During this period the first mammals appeared. The fossil remains of these animals are fragmentary, but they were apparently small in size and reptilian in appearance. Among the other land animals were insects and snails. In the sea, the first ancestors of the modern bony fishes, Teleostei, made their appearance. The plant life of the Triassic seas included a large variety of marine algae. On land, the dominant vegetation was composed of evergreens, such as ginkgos, conifers, and palms. Small scouring rushes and ferns still existed, but the larger members of these groups had become extinct.

Jurassic Period. In the Jurassic Period the evolution of the dinosaurs produced four distinct types or tribes: heavy four-footed sauropods, such as *Brontosaurus;* two-footed carnivorous dinosaurs, such as *Tyrannosaurus;* two-footed vegetarian dinosaurs, such as *Trachodon;* and four-footed armored dinosaurs, such as *Stegosaurus.* The winged reptiles were represented by the pterodactyls, which, during this period, ranged in size from extremely small species to others that had wingspreads of 4 ft. Marine reptiles included plesiosaurs, a group that had broad, flat bodies like those of turtles, with long necks and large flippers for swimming; icthyosaurs, which had scaly bodies; and primitive crocodiles. During the Jurassic the first true bird, *Archaeopteryx,* evolved from the reptiles. Although this animal, which was about the size of a modern crow, had feathers, its toothed jaw and the structure of its wings clearly indicate its reptilian origin. The mammals of the Jurassic Period comprised four orders, all of which were smaller than small modern dogs. In this period the evolution of the insects resulted in the development of a number of the modern orders, including moths, flies, beetles, grasshoppers, and termites. Shellfish included lobsters, shrimps, and ammonites, as well as the extinct group of belemnites that resembled squids and had cigar-shaped internal shells. The flora of the Jurassic Period was dominated by cycads. Fossils

PALEONTOLOGY

of most species of Jurassic plants are widely distributed in the temperate zones and polar regions, indicating that the Jurassic climate was uniformly mild.

Cretaceous Period. The reptiles were still the dominant form of animal life in the Cretaceous Period. The four tribes of dinosaurs found in the Jurassic also lived during this period, and in addition a fifth tribe, horned dinosaurs like *Triceratops*, appeared. The largest of the pterodactyls, *Pteranodon*, lived in this period. This flying reptile, which had a wingspread of 24 ft., is the largest flying animal known. The pliosaurs also increased in size during Cretaceous times and reached a maximum length of 50 ft. Among the other reptiles of the period were the first snakes and lizards. Several types of Cretaceous birds are known, among them *Hesperornis*, a diving bird about 6 ft. in length, which had only vestigial wings and was unable to fly. Mammals of the period included the first marsupials, which strongly resembled the modern opossum, and the first placental mammals, which belonged to the group of insectivores. Among the shellfish, the first crabs developed at this time. A number of the modern varieties of fishes also evolved during the Cretaceous Period.

The most important evolutionary advance in the plant kingdom during this period was the development of deciduous woody plants, which first appeared in early Cretaceous rock formations. Figs, magnolias, sassafras, and poplars were among the earliest to evolve, and by the end of the period many of the modern varieties of trees and shrubs had made their appearance, and represented more than ninety percent of the known plants of the period. Mid-Cretaceous fossils include remains of beech, holly, laurel, maple, oak, plane tree, and walnut. Some paleontologists believe that these deciduous woody plants first evolved in Jurassic times but grew only in upland areas where conditions were unfavorable for their preservation as fossils.

CENOZOIC LIFE

The first portion of the Cenozoic Era represents a transition in the animal kingdom from the Age of Reptiles to the Age of Mammals. The large dinosaurs and other reptiles that had dominated the life of the Mesozoic Era disappeared abruptly, and the only important members of the group appearing among the fossils of early Cenozoic times were crocodiles, turtles, lizards, and snakes, all essentially similar to the modern representatives of these groups. With the decline of the reptiles the mammals suddenly increased in number and variety of types.

Paleocene Epoch. Seven groups of Paleocene mammals are known, all of which appear to have developed in northern Asia and to have migrated to other parts of the world. These primitive mammals had many features in common. All were small, with no species exceeding the size of a small modern bear. All were four-footed, having five toes on each foot and walking on the soles of the feet. Almost all the Paleocene mammals had slim heads with narrow muzzles and small brain cases. The predominant

A primitive ant embedded in amber some 100,000,000 years ago. The discovery, by Mr. and Mrs. Edmund Frey of Mountainside, N.J., sheds new light on the evolution of social insects from primitive wasps. UPI

mammals of the period were members of three groups that are now extinct. These were the creodonts, which were the ancestors of the modern carnivores; the amblypods, which were small, heavy-bodied animals; and the condylarths, which were light-bodied herbivorous animals with small brains. The Paleocene groups that have survived are the marsupials, the insectivores, the primates, and the rodents, all of which were represented during this period by small, primitive species.

Eocene Epoch. In the Eocene Epoch, a number of direct evolutionary ancestors of modern animals appeared. Among these animals, all of which were small in stature, were horses, rhinoceroses, camels, rodents, and monkeys. The creodonts and amblypods continued to develop during the epoch, but the condylarths became extinct before its close. The first aquatic mammals, the ancestors of the modern whales, also appeared in Eocene times, as did such modern birds as eagles, pelicans, quail, and vultures. The flora of the early Cenozoic Era did not differ substantially from that of the late Mesozoic. In these times, however, and continuing to the present, the changes in vegetation have been chiefly in the migration of vegetation types in response to changes in climate.

Oligocene Epoch. In this epoch most of the archaic mammals that characterized the earlier portion of the Cenozoic Era disappeared and in their place appeared representatives of a large number of the modern mammalian groups. The creodonts became extinct, and the first true carnivores, resembling dogs and cats, evolved. Other animals of the period included beavers, camels, mice, rabbits, rhinoceroses, and squirrels. The first anthropoid apes also lived during this time but became extinct in North America during the epoch. Two extinct groups of animals flourished during the Oligocene Epoch: the titanotheres, related to the rhinoceros and the horse; and the oreodonts, small, doglike, grazing animals.

Miocene Epoch. The development of the mammal during the Miocene Epoch was conditioned by an important evolutionary development in the plant kingdom, the first appearance of the grasses. These plants, which were ideally suited for forage, encouraged the growth and development of grazing animals such as horses, camels, and rhinoceroses, which were abundant during the epoch. During the period the mastodon evolved, and in Europe and Asia a gorilla-like ape, *Dryopithecus*, was common. Various types of carnivores, including cats and wolflike dogs, ranged over many parts of the world.

Pliocene and Pleistocene Epoch. The paleontology of the Pliocene Epoch does not differ in any marked extent from that of the Miocene, although the period is regarded by many zoologists as the climax of the Age of Mammals. The Pleistocene Epoch in both Europe and North America was marked by the abundance of large mammals, most of which were essentially modern in type. Among them were buffaloes, elephants, mammoths, and mastodons; the latter two became extinct before the close of the epoch. In Europe antelopes, lions, and hippopotamuses also appeared. Carnivores included badgers, foxes, lynxes, otters, pumas, and skunks, as well as such now-extinct species as the giant saber-toothed tiger. In North America the first bears made their appearance, apparently as migrants from Asia. Other migrants included armadillo and ground sloth, which came to North America from South America, and the musk ox, which ranged southward from the arctic regions. An important development of the Pleistocene Epoch was the emergence of the first primitive man; see MAN, ANCIENT.

See separate articles on each of the geological periods and on most of the animal and plant groups mentioned above. *See also* ANIMALS, MIGRATION OF; EVOLUTION: *Paleontology;* FOSSIL; GEOLOGY, HISTORICAL.   S.C.

PALEOZOIC ERA, one of the major divisions of geological history, in which the earliest fossiliferous rocks, or rocks containing the earliest evidences of life, were formed. It was preceded by the Pre-cambrian Era and followed by the Mesozoic Era (qq.v.). The Paleozoic Era began about 600,000,000 years ago and lasted about 375,000,000 years. The stratigraphic systems included in this era were laid down in the Cambrian, Ordovician, Silurian, Devonian, Carboniferous, and Permian Periods (qq.v.). See GEOLOGY, HISTORICAL.

PALERMO (anc. *Panormus*), city and seaport in Italy, and capital of Palermo Province, on the N.W. coast of Sicily, on the Tyrrhenian Sea, about 125 miles w. of Messina. Palermo is a trading center for products of w. and central Sicily, including citrus fruits, sumac, wine, tartar, grain, oils, manna, and sulfur. It is also an industrial center with plants engaged in food processing, steelmaking, shipbuilding, and the manufacture of furniture, leather products, glass, chemicals, cement, textiles, and paper. Many of the oldest buildings in the city date from the period when Sicily was a Norman kingdom and show Arab, Byzantine, Norman, and Spanish influences. Outstanding examples are the cathedral (built 1169–85), the Palatine Chapel (1140), and the

Shoppers inspect the offerings of sidewalk flower vendors in Palermo.   Standard Oil Co., N.J.

Church of San Giovanni degli Eremiti (1132).

Palermo was founded as Panormus by the Phoenicians and was a Carthaginian colony until taken by the Romans (254 B.C.). It subsequently passed into the hands of the Goths (440 A.D.), the Byzantines (535), the Saracens (830), the Normans (1072), and the Holy Roman emperors (1194). In 1282 it was the scene of the massacre of the ruling Frenchmen, which was known as the Sicilian Vespers (q.v.). For subsequent history, see SICILY: *History*. Pop. (1968 est.) 652,380.

PALESTINE, city in Texas, and county seat of Anderson Co., about 90 miles E. of Waco. In a rich oil and gas area, it is primarily a marketing center. Tile and glass are manufactured. It is also the site of the Palestine Salt Dome, a deep deposit of rock salt some 30,000 ft. in diameter. Settled in 1846, Palestine was incorporated in 1871. Pop. (1960) 13,974; (1970) 14,525.

PALESTINE (Heb. *Pelishti*, "Philistine"), designation, since ancient times, for a region, of varying extent in western Asia bordering the eastern Mediterranean Sea; and also, in the 20th century, for a territory under the mandate of Great Britain from 1920 to 1948; see MANDATES. For the history of the region since the termination of this mandate, see ISRAEL; JORDAN, HASHEMITE KINGDOM OF. At a very early date the name Palestine was applied to the portion of the Mediterranean coast, occupied by Philistines (q.v.), a martial people who emigrated either from the island of Crete or from the S. coast of Asia Minor; later, however, the term came to include the land of the Israelites; see JEWS. In 1920 the British acquired Palestine, which then included Transjordan (now Jordan), as a mandate of the League of Nations (q.v.). In 1923 the independence of Transjordan was proclaimed subject to British obligations. The mandated territory after 1923 was bounded on the N. by Lebanon and Syria, on the E. by the Dead Sea and the Jordan R., on the S. by the Egyptian province of Sinai, and on the W. by the Mediterranean Sea. The area of the Palestinian mandate excluding Transjordan was 10,429 sq.mi. comprising 10,157 sq.mi. of land and 272 sq.mi. of inland water.

THE LAND

The distinctive physiography of Palestine is due to the deep depression through which the Jordan River (q.v.) flows. This depression is the result of a geological cataclysm by which the entire plateau E. of the Mediterranean Sea was split from N. to S. as far as the Red Sea. In Palestine the earth's crust immediately W. of the fault broke and fell precipitously toward the deep valley formed by the upheaval. Throughout almost the whole course of the Jordan R. this valley is now lower than the level of the Mediterranean Sea. Thus the Waters of Merom (Lake Hula) are about 7 ft. above sea level; but Lake Tiberias (q.v.; Sea of Galilee) about some 10 mi. farther S., has a surface elevation 682 ft. below sea level; and the Dead Sea, 65 mi. south of Lake Tiberias, has a surface elevation of 1292 ft. below sea level.

PALESTINE

The land surface of Palestine falls generally into four parallel zones: namely, the seacoast plain, the hills and mountains w. of the Jordan R., the valley of the Jordan, and the plateau region E. of the great depression. The hilly range w. of the Jordan R. is broken and irregular, and may be divided into several distinct regions. In the extreme s. is the Negev (q.v.), a desert steppe region or tableland, 1500 to 2000 ft. above sea level, intersected by wadis, or ravines, running E. toward the Mediterranean Sea. The largest of these ravines is the Wadi Beer Sheva, which passes ancient Beersheba (q.v.) and enters the Mediterranean as Wadi Habesor a few miles s. of ancient Gaza (q.v.). The N. part of the Negev is higher than the s. (about 2500 ft. above sea level), and marks the beginning of the highland or mountain region of the ancient Kingdom of Judah. The greatest elevation of the Judean Range is reached near the subdistrict of Hebron (3370 ft.). Toward Jerusalem (q.v.) the altitude diminishes in places to about 2400 ft., but becomes higher again to the north. The crest of the Judean highland averages nearly 15 mi. in width, the descent from it to the Dead Sea, about 10 or 15 mi. away, being rapid and terminating in steep cliffs. The whole region bordering on the Dead Sea is wild, barren, and rocky. It was known in Biblical times as the Wilderness of Judea, or Jeshimon (the desert waste). West of the Judean highland the country sinks gradually toward the coastal plain. From the coastal plain several large valleys lead up into the interior highlands.

The central highland of Palestine continues N. of Jerusalem for more than 40 mi. The descent to the valley of the Jordan is in places very abrupt, though traversed by a number of passable valleys, one of which, the Wadi Fara, pierces far into the interior. Near Nablus (Shechem), in a beautiful valley between Mt. Gerizim (2849 ft.) on the s. and Mt. Ebal (3077 ft.) on the N., several valleys have their origin. Among them is the Wadi es Shair, which opens out N.W. into the plain in which the ancient city of Samaria (q.v.) was situated, and continues from there to the coast. Another valley opens into the Wadi Fara and thus affords a connection with the valley of the Jordan. To the N. of Samaria the country takes on a new character. The low-lying Plain of Dothan connects the seacoast region with the great Plain of Jezreel (see JEZREEL, PLAIN OF), a triangular-shaped expanse, about 16 mi. across, situated midway between the Jordan R. and the Mediterranean Sea, with an average elevation of about 250 ft. This district is separated from the seacoast plain to the w. by a series of low hills running N.W. from the Plain of Dothan and culminating in the short mountain ridge Mt. Carmel (q.v.) with a maximum elevation of about 1800 ft., which juts out into the Mediterranean Sea in a promontory 556 ft. high. The Jezreel is shut in on the E. by the hilly range Mt. Gilboa (1300 to 1650 ft.) and by the hills near the sites of ancient Shunem and Nain. Between these two ranges the deep valley of Jezreel, all of

The hill range of Mt. Gilboa, west of the Jordan River in Palestine.
Israel Information Services

PALESTINE

which lies below sea level, leads down to the Jordan R. The N.E. corner of the Jezreel opens into another precipitous valley, across which rises Mt. Tabor (1929 ft.).

North of the Jezreel, in lower Galilee (q.v.), the terrain becomes mountainous again. The entire region between Lake Tiberias and the Mediterranean Sea is relatively open. The peaks are less than 2000 ft. above sea level and are for the most part isolated and interspersed with valleys and plains. Two main systems of hills run through lower Galilee. One bounds the Plain of Jezreel on the N., extending from the Kishon R. just opposite Mt. Carmel to Lake Tiberias. North of this first system, extending from the N.W. coast of Lake Tiberias to the Mediterranean coastal plain, is a long, low plain broken into several portions by low hills crossing it from N. to S. The eastern end of the plain as it descends to Lake Tiberias forms the land of Gennesaret, a region of great fertility. The second line of hills, N. of the long plain, completes the hill system of lower Galilee. To the N. upper Galilee consists of a high central plateau with a general elevation of 2000 to 3000 ft. This plateau is narrower in its northern than in its southern portion and is terminated by the Leontes R., which, rising in the Lebanon Mts. in S.W. Syria, makes a sharp turn to the W. and enters the Mediterranean Sea just N. of the ancient city of Tyre, in Lebanon.

Across the valley through which flows the upper courses of the Jordan R. stands Mt. Hermon, the summit of which is 9056 ft. above sea level. From the base of this mountain rise most of the streams that combine to form the Jordan. At the point where these streams converge the valley is from 8 to 10 mi. wide and only a little above sea level. Thereafter it becomes marshy and at length opens into the Waters of Merom. From there the valley narrows, the stream descending rapidly to Lake Tiberias. From the lake to the Dead Sea, a distance of 65 mi., the valley of the Jordan varies from 3 to 14 mi. in width. It is only about 4 mi. wide at the point at which it leaves Lake Tiberias, but broadens to the point at which it joins the valley of Jezreel, 13 mi. below. It narrows once more, but after receiving the waters of the Wadi Zerqa Zarqa', widens steadily until, at Jericho (q.v.), it attains its maximum breadth. On either side of the Jordan valley the ascent to the highlands is generally steep. The western side is broken by many ravines and passes; the eastern side, however, has a more uniform character, being intersected only at long intervals by large streams. The Dead Sea marks the deepest part of the Jordan valley. It has no outlet, and the constant evaporation, together with the saline character of many of the springs that empty into it, make its waters so salty that they are exceedingly bitter in taste and of high specific gravity. In some places the shores are heavily lined with deposits of salt. The Dead Sea is also notable for the petroleum springs below its surface; from these springs come the lumps of bitumen (asphalt) often found floating on the waters. Hence the Dead Sea was known in ancient times as the *Lacus Asphaltites* (Asphalt Lake). The sea is deepest at its northern end (1292 ft. below sea level), the southern portion being quite shallow. It is surrounded by hills rising 3000 to 4000 ft. above its surface, and is one of the hottest regions of the world.

Across the deep, hot valley of the Jordan lies eastern Palestine, which falls physiographically into three regions. From Mt. Hermon to the Yarmuk R., a large stream traversing the eastern plateau and emptying into the Jordan, extinct volcanoes abound, the lava soil rendering the region exceptionally fertile. South of the Yarmuk R. to the Wadi Zerqa Zarqa' and from there to the Arnon R., a total distance of nearly 100 mi., lie the region of Gilead (q.v.) and the Plains of Moab, both of which are coextensive with the Perea of New Testament times. The soil in this vicinity is not as fertile as that found in the region N. of the Yarmuk R., and is consequently less fitted for agriculture. The region has always been noted, however, for its excellent pasturage. The terrain takes the form of a high rolling plateau broken only by large wadis running to the Jordan. Northern Gilead is not as high as southern Gilead and the Plains of Moab, but it is more heavily wooded and better supplied with water. The most southerly portion of Gilead, S. of the Arnon R., the site of the ancient Kingdom of Moab, is even more barren and dry, but is nevertheless suitable for pasturage.

The water supply of Palestine is not abundant. Heavy rains occur during the winter, but the numerous wadis are for the most part dry in the summer months.

Climate. Palestine has two seasons. The rainy or winter season begins in late October. Rain falls more or less continuously until February, when the intensity of the downfall diminishes, permitting the farmers to sow their crops. By May the rains are over and the long hot summer (May to October) begins. The highlands, with a mean annual temperature of 63° F. and a range from 34° F. to 100° F., are dry and healthful. The lowlands are moist and humid. The prevailing winds are from the Mediterranean Sea, N.W. in summer, W. or S.W. in winter. The *sirocco,* a hot

272

The walls and fortifications of the ancient city of Tiberias, on the shore of Lake Tiberias. Israel Information Services

wind carrying clouds of dust from the desert regions to the E. and S., frequently inflicts damage and severe discomfort.

Plants and Animals. The flora of Palestine is remarkably rich and diversified, considering the limited area of the country and the many barren tracts of land. Palestine is the center of three great floral regions, and abounds in Mediterranean flora, Asiatic steppe flora, and tropical flora of Arabia and Egypt. The last-named type is confined to the valleys. Mediterranean flora in Palestine includes date, banana, fig, olive, and almond trees and acacia and azalea bushes. Patches of dense forest cover the mountain slopes N. of Judea. On the lower slopes the trees are deciduous, notably oak, beech, maple, poplar, and mulberry; on the higher slopes are found evergreen forests containing spruce, cypress, juniper, and cedar trees. The fauna of Palestine is also varied, including more than 100 species of mammals and several hundred types of birds. The large wild animals, however, such as the lion, bear, and leopard, are virtually extinct. The most characteristic surviving mammals are the mountain goat and the hyrax, a small, thickset animal with short legs and ears.

HISTORY

The earliest history of Palestine, to the 16th century B.C., is exceedingly obscure, although archeological investigation has produced much material relating to the civilization of the primitive inhabitants. According to ancient Egyptian records, Palestine was originally a part of the land of the Amu, a people dwelling to the northeast of Egypt. The Amu called Palestine *Lotan* or *Ruten,* reserving the name *Kharu* for the southern part of the country and *Amor* or *Amur* for the northern district and the region around what is now Lebanon. Until the 18th century B.C. the dominant power in Palestine, as in all of southwest Asia, was Babylonia (q.v.). This supremacy was destroyed by the incursion of great numbers of Semitic tribesmen from the Arabian Desert (q.v.); *see* SEMITES. Between 1500 and 1450 B.C. Egypt established its overlordship in Palestine. The Tell el-Amarna letters, which make up the correspondence between Ikhnaton (q.v.), King of Egypt, and his father Amenhotep III (*see under* AMENHOTEP), disclose that the common name for Palestine at that time was Canaan and that the language of its people was an earlier form of the tongue known later as Hebrew; *see* CANAAN; CANAANITES; HEBREWS; SEMITIC LANGUAGES. This tongue was spoken not only by the Israelites but also by the Edomites (*see* EDOM), the Moabites (q.v.), and the Phoenicians; *see* PHOENICIA. The Tell el-Amarna letters show further that under the lax rule of Ikhnaton Palestine passed from Egyptian control. The Hittites (q.v.) from the north and the Habiru (an ethnic subdivision of the great Aramean group to which the Israelites belonged) in the central and southern portions then fought to gain possession of the country. This era of conflict was

PALESTINE

ended by the revival of Egyptian supremacy under the XIX Dynasty, the kings of which, Seti I (*see under* SETI) and Ramses II (*see under* RAMSES), drove back the Hittites and once more subjugated Palestine. The succeeding Egyptian dynasty was weak, with the result that Palestine broke up into a number of petty kingdoms.

The Philistines and the Israelites. About this time (1300–1100 B.C.) two peoples of markedly different origin and character sought to make Palestine their home. These peoples were the Philistines and the Israelites. The former acquired dominion over the whole Mediterranean coastal plain; the latter undertook a series of conquests that at length gained them full control of Palestine. The Canaanites appear to have offered little united opposition to the Israelites. The work of conquest was long and gradual, the Israelite tribes being finally settled in the following manner. East of the Jordan R. between the Arnon R. and the Wadi Zerqa Zarqa' the Gadites and Reubenites had their homes; *see* GAD; REUBEN. The Reubenites soon lost their identity, either because they were absorbed by the Gadites, who finally occupied Reubenite territory, or because they drifted further eastward and merged with other tribes near the great Arabian Desert. The western highland from Jerusalem southward constituted the home of the tribes of Judah. Southwest of Judah lay the territory of Simeon. Between Judah and the Plain of Jezreel the country was occupied for the most part by members of the house of Joseph, that is, the tribes of Benjamin northeast of Judah, the tribes of Ephraim in the central portion, and the tribes of Manasseh (qq.v.) in the north. A tiny district northwest of Judah was occupied by the small tribe of Dan (q.v.); a considerable portion of this tribe subsequently migrated to the extreme north near the sources of the Jordan R. In the valley and Plain of Jezreel lay the territory occupied by the tribes of Issachar and the tribes of Zebulun (qq.v.), the former in the east, the latter in the west. Part of southern and all of northern Galilee was inhabited by the tribes of Naphtali (on the east) and of Asher (on the west behind the Phoenician maritime cities of Sidon and Tyre).

About 1020 B.C. the various Israelite tribes were confederated into a kingdom under Saul (q.v.), of the tribe of Benjamin. Saul's successor, David (q.v.), of the tribe of Judah, completed the establishment of Israelite supremacy in Palestine. Under David and his son Solomon (q.v.), Palestine was the home of a free people united under a central government. About 922 B.C. this united kingdom was split into two kingdoms, Israel in the north and Judah in the south. Israel was conquered by Assyria in 722 B.C. The annals of Sargon II, King of Assyria (722–705 B.C.), record that he deported more than 27,000 persons from Israel and sent a number of Arameans into the country from Babylonia. This Aramean colony, subsequently augmented, merged with the remaining Israelites. Thus a mixed population, still essentially Semitic, came to occupy the old Ephraim-Manasseh territory. Galilee was gradually filled with a hybrid Phoenician-Syrian population, which, remained substantially intact until about 100 B.C. The Kingdom of Judah came to an end when Nebuchadnezzar II, King of Babylonia (*see under* NEBUCHADNEZZAR), captured and destroyed Jerusalem in 586 B.C. During the next half century Nabataean Arabs pressed in from the deserts to the east and southeast, occupied much of the old Moabite territory, and, forcing the Edomites from their land, drove them northward into southern Judah, which then became Edomite territory; *see* NABATAEANS. The Jewish exiles who returned to Palestine from Babylonia by permission of Cyrus the Great (q.v.), King of Persia, in 536 B.C. settled only in the northern part of the old Kingdom of Judah.

Under the Persian Empire Palestine was a part of the satrapy, or province, of Syria; *see* PERSIA. The satrapy was subdivided into a number of districts, of which Judah, Phoenicia, and Samaria (q.v.) were administered by separate governors. Through the efforts of the leaders Ezra and Nehemiah (qq.v.) the Judean community was thoroughly consolidated, Jerusalem was fortified, and foreigners were expelled. The inhabitants of Judah constantly encroached on Samaritan territory and gradually extended their frontier toward the northwest. The Samaritans (q.v.) also became more closely united through the founding of the Samaritan religion, based exclusively on the Pentateuch (q.v.), or first five books of the Old Testament and through the building of a temple on Mt. Gerizim; *see* SAMARITAN PENTATEUCH. During the Persian period the language of the Jewish community became assimilated by the Aramaic tongue spoken throughout the region, and Hebrew gradually ceased to be the language of colloquial speech.

Maccabees. The conquest of the Middle East by Alexander III (q.v.), King of Macedonia, known as the Great, introduced Greek influence into Palestine. Samaria was razed and rebuilt as a Macedonian city. In the struggles of Alexander's successors, Palestine came into the possession of Ptolemy I, King of Egypt (*see under* PTOLEMY), and until 197 B.C. was under

The Judaean desert, near Khirbet Qumran, seen from the Qumran Caves, in which the Dead Sea Scrolls were discovered.
UPI

Egyptian control. It then passed to Antiochus III, King of Syria (*see under* ANTIOCHUS). The attempt of Antiochus IV to destroy the Jewish religion in Palestine (168 B.C.) precipitated the great Jewish War of Independence; *see* JEWS; MACCABEES. When the conflict came to an end, a free Judea under the Hasmonaean or Maccabean priest-princes controlled all of southern Palestine from the Jordan R. to the Mediterranean coast. The rest of the country, nominally under the power of Syria, was actually in a state of anarchy. East of the Jordan R. the Nabataean Arabs were in possession of all territory but that occupied by the Greek cities. Under the Hasmonaean rulers John Hyrcanus (*see under* MACCABEES), Aristobulus I (*see under* ARISTOBULUS), and Alexander Jannaeus (*see under* MACCABEES), the Jews subjugated Idumaea (Edom), Samaria, Galilee, and virtually all of the old east Jordanian territory.

Roman Conquest. Quarrels among rival Jewish factions afforded Rome the opportunity of extending its conquests into Palestine. In 63 B.C. the Roman general and statesman Pompey the Great (*see under* POMPEIUS), annexed Syria and Palestine to the Roman Empire. From 63 B.C. until 67 A.D. Palestine was a part of the Roman province of Syria. During most of this time Judea and other districts were administered by Herod the Great (*see under* HEROD) and his successors. The greater part of the country was included in the four districts of Judea, Samaria, Galilee, and Peraea. The territory north of the Wadi Zerqa Zarqaʾ was broken up into minor divisions, such as Gaulanitis, Auranitis, Trachonitis, and Batanaea, administered by tetrarchs, or petty governors. With the outbreak of the Jewish rebellion against Roman rule in 66 A.D., Palestine was detached from Syria and made a separate province under the Roman general and emperor Vespasian (q.v.). The war against Rome ended disastrously for the Jews with the capture and ruin of Jerusalem in 70, the destruction of the Temple (q.v.), and the dissolution of the Jewish state. Thereafter new cities sprang up, fostered by Rome. Another Jewish insurrection against the Romans begun in 132 by Simon Bar Cocheba (q.v.) although at first successful, was finally put down with great bloodshed and devastation three years later. The Roman emperor Hadrian (q.v.) rebuilt Jerusalem, changed its name to Aelia Capitolina, and forbade any Jew to live in it.

Palestine remained an integral part of the Roman Empire, and afterward of the Byzantine Empire, until 614, when Khosrau II, King of Persia (*see under* KHOSRAU) led an invasion. In 628, however, the Byzantine emperor Heraclius (q.v.) utterly defeated Khosrau and expelled him from Palestine. With the advent of Christianity to Palestine it became customary to speak of the country as divided into Palestina Prima (Judea and Samaria), Palestina Secunda (Galilee), and Palestina Tertia (Idumaea and Moab). Each of these districts was subdivided ecclesiastically into bishoprics. The Latin Kingdom of Jerusalem (*see* JERUSALEM, LATIN KINGDOM OF), founded in 1099 and overthrown by Saladin (q.v.), Sultan of Egypt and Syria, in 1187, was merely a passing phase in the history of Palestine, although it left

PALESTINE

its imprint in the form of churches, monasteries, and shrines throughout the land. After the conquest by the Ottoman Turks in 1516, Palestine became a vilayet, or administrative division, of the Turkish province of Syria; see TURKEY: *History: Rise of the Ottoman Empire.*

World War I. In World War I (q.v.) the immediate object of Turkey was to seize the Suez Canal (q.v.) in order to block communications between Great Britain and India. Accordingly, Turkish troops were dispatched to the Sinai Peninsula and Suez. The British garrison of Egypt was thereupon reinforced. Turkish divisions occupied the Sinai Peninsula (belonging to Egypt) from which the British had withdrawn, and early in 1915 launched an attack upon the British positions on the Suez Canal. The British decided to reoccupy the peninsula, an operation requiring a large and well-equipped army. Faced with the problem of maintaining such an army in the desert, the British boldly undertook an extensive engineering program. El Qantara on the Suez Canal was converted into a railroad and water terminus; a broad-gauge railroad was built across the desert; and hundreds of miles of water pipes were laid. In the course of this construction work the British were defeated at Katia, 25 miles E. of the Suez Canal in April, 1916. The Turks were decisively beaten at Romani on Aug. 4, however, and driven back from their stronghold at El 'Arish on the Sinai Peninsula. The British then forced the Turks from Rafal on the Egypt-Palestine frontier, Jan. 9, 1917. They attacked Gaza in March, and again in April, incurring heavy losses but failing to capture the town. General Edmund Henry Hynman Allenby (q.v.), succeeded as British commander in chief; he trained his troops intensively before resuming the offensive against the Turks. On Oct. 27 cavalry was sent into action on the approaches to Gaza in a diversionary feint, a main attack being simultaneously delivered to the left of the Turkish line on the town of Beersheba, which fell on Oct. 31. Gaza was captured on Nov. 7, and Jaffa three days later. Two British columns, one inland and one on the coast, moved northward, driving the Turkish army before them. Ashqelon, Ashdod, and Gath capitulated in quick succession, and by Nov. 25, after a victory at El Maghar, Jerusalem was virtually surrounded. The city was not fired upon, however, and after the negotiation of surrender terms, British forces entered Palestine on Dec. 11, 1917.

British Mandate. In 1922 the League of Nations approved the assignment to Great Britain of the mandate for Palestine. From that time until the establishment of the Jewish State of Israel on May 15, 1948, the conflicting claims of Arabs and Jews resulted in perpetual tension in the Middle East, punctuated by frequent armed clashes. The Arabs maintained that in 1914–15 the British gave pledges to the sharif of Mecca that were in direct contravention of the Balfour Declaration (q.v.) of Nov. 2, 1917. This instrument pledged the British government to the "establishment in Palestine of a national home for the Jewish people". For an account of the rivalry between Arabs and Jews in Palestine and a survey of proposals leading to the establishment of the Jewish homeland, see ISRAEL: *History;* MIDDLE EAST; ZIONISM; UNITED NATIONS: *The Role of the United Nations in Peacekeeping Operations: Middle East.*

PALESTINIAN ARCHEOLOGY, scientific recovery and interpretation of material remains from ancient Palestine. Located strategically between northeastern Africa and western Asia, Palestine was an early site of agriculture and urbanization and the scene of most of the events recorded in the Bible. Accordingly, it is archeologically one of the most thoroughly studied areas of the world. For identification of periods in archeology used below, see the accompanying chart. *See also* ARCHEOLOGY; PALESTINE: *History.*

ARCHEOLOGICAL PERIODS IN PALESTINE

Name	Dates[1]	Characteristics
Paleolithic Age	Ended about 10,000	Rough, chipped stone implements
Mesolithic Age	About 10,000–7000	First flint agricultural implements
Prepottery Neolithic Age	About 7000–5000	Stone implements; first villages
Pottery Neolithic Age	About 5000–3500	First use of pottery
Chalcolithic Age	3500–3200	Stone, pottery, and a few copper implements used
Early Bronze Age	3200–2100	Copper implements; urban culture
Middle Bronze Age	2100–1550	Age of Patriarchs; developed urban culture, fine pottery
Late Bronze Age	1550–1200	Canaanite civilization
Iron I Age	1200–900	Period of the Judges; Philistine culture
Iron II Age	900–587	Period of the monarchy
Persian Period	587–333	Babylonian Captivity; cultural eclipse
Hellenistic Period	333–63	Greek domination and cultural influence
Roman Period	63–325 A.D.	Roman rule
Byzantine Period	325–637	Christian dominance; rule by Byzantine Empire
Arab Period	637–1516	Islamic dominance; Arabic culture
Turkish Period	1516–1918	Turkish rule

[1] Years 10,000 through 63 refer to the pre-Christian era.

PALESTINIAN ARCHEOLOGY

A fresco above the niche for the Torah scrolls, from the synagogue of Dura (present-day Qal'at es Salihiye, Syria), on the Euphrates River. At center is a Torah ark, representing the Temple; at right, the sacrifice of Isaac; and at left, the seven-branched candelabrum.

Frank J. Darmstaedter – Jewish Museum

Excavation Technique. The typical archeological site in Palestine is an artificial mound that has been formed by the successive collapse and rebuilding of a city or cities on approximately the same site. Such a mound, technically described by the word "tell" (Ar. *tell*, "tall"), is composed of a number of strata, or layers, of earth and stone debris. The recognition of the nature of such mounds and of the prospect offered by them for stratigraphic excavation was pioneered in Palestine by the British Egyptologist Sir William Matthew Flinders Petrie (q.v.). Since Petrie did his instrumental work at Tell el-Hesi (ancient Eglon), in 1890, increasingly refined methods of digging and recording have been developed. The more significant innovations include special emphasis on careful architectural recording, encouraged by the American Egyptologist George Andrew Reisner (1867–1942) and the American historical architect Clarence Stanley Fisher (1876–1941), at Samaria (q.v.; modern Sabastiya), in 1908, and important techniques for minute analysis of soil and debris sections introduced by the British archeologist Kathleen Kenyon (1906–   ), again at Samaria, in the 1930's. Current archeological work in Palestine is based on the detailed observation of the relationship between debris sections and the architectural remains, and the careful recording of all finds in relation to this observed stratigraphy.

Research and Discovery. Serious research in Palestinian archeology began with the surface exploration conducted by the American Biblical scholar Edward Robinson (1794–1863) in the 1830's; see BIBLE SCHOLARSHIP: *Biblical Archeology*. Robinson's work resulted in the identification of hundreds of ancient sites. During the middle years of the 19th century discoveries by a number of adventurers and scholars added considerable stimulus to Palestinian research. One such discovery was that of the Moabite Stone (q.v.), found in 1868 by the French Orientalist Charles Clermont-Ganneau (1846–1923). The stone is now in the Louvre (q.v.). In the late 1800's a number of excavations were conducted by the Palestine Exploration Fund (founded by the British in 1865) and the American Exploration Society (founded in 1870), as well as by various individuals. Sir Flinders Petrie was succeeded at Tell el-Hesi by the American archeologist Frederick Jones Bliss (1859–1937). The pottery chronology developed by them made it possible to date excavated materials.

PALESTINIAN ARCHEOLOGY

In 1900 the American Schools of Oriental Research (which subsequently sponsored many archeological excavations and exploratory expeditions) was founded in Jerusalem (the school is now also located at Baghdad). The Deutsche Orient-Gesellschaft (German Oriental Society, founded in 1898) began excavations on Tell es-Sultan, the site of ancient Jericho (q.v.), in 1907. The next year Reisner, sponsored by Harvard University, began his work at Samaria. With staffs trained to record finds properly, these expeditions marked a new period in the history of Palestinian archeology. Although archeological research declined sharply during World War I, numerous excavations were conducted in Palestine in the ensuing period. Between 1929 and 1936, the British archeologist John Garstang (1876–1956) worked in new areas at Jericho. Garstang learned much about the ancient city walls and made the first discovery in Palestine of prepottery levels of Neolithic culture. A joint Samaria expedition (1931–35), under the direction of the British classical scholar and archeologist John Winter Crowfoot (1873–1959), correctly dated the impressive Hellenistic towers at the site to the late 4th century B.C.; *see* GREEK ART AND ARCHITECTURE: *Hellenistic Period*. During this same period, an expedition under the direction of the British archeologist James Leslie Starkey (1895–1938) at Tell ed-Duweir (ancient Lachish) discovered several Hebrew ostraca or inscribed potsherds. These provided a most useful supplement to the growth in understanding of the early Hebrew language (q.v.) and script. Between 1925 and 1939, the Oriental Institute of the University of Chicago undertook a large expedition at Tell el-Mutesellim (ancient Megiddo). The aim of this expedition was to excavate the entire tell layer by layer. Although this goal was not finally realized, the work completed by the expedition members added greatly to the understanding of Palestinian stratigraphy and history. During the same time, the study of pottery remains from Tell Beit Mirsim (ancient Debir) in southern Palestine, excavated (1926–32) by the American Orientalist William Foxwell Albright (1891–   ), provided a vital basis for the correlation of the occupation sequences from all these sites.

This same era also witnessed substantive work in the recovery of the prehistory of the Palestinian area. Between 1929 and 1938 a group of Jesuit fathers excavated a series of small mounds at Teleilat el-Ghassul in the southern Jordan R. valley, and they uncovered remains of a Chalcolithic (New Stone Age) village from the middle of the 4th millennium B.C. These included remnants of polychrome wall frescoes with intricate geometric figures. From 1929 to 1934 the British archeologist Dorothy Annie Elizabeth Garrod (1892–   ) directed seven excavations in prehistoric caves on the southern slopes of Mt. Carmel; *see* CARMEL, MOUNT. Outstanding finds included human skeletal remains more than 100,000 years old giving evidence of the earliest stages of man's evolution.

In the decade 1938–48 little archeological work was done in Palestine. After 1948, however, archeological research resumed in both Jordan and Israel (qq.v.). Israeli archeologists, many with European backgrounds and training, continued work begun earlier at an accelerated pace. Major Israeli excavations include those conducted by the archeologist Yigael Yadin (1917–   ) at Tell el-Qedah (ancient Hazor) in 1955, and at Masada (q.v.), along the western shore of the Dead Sea (q.v.) in 1963–65, as well as that of Yohanan Aharoni and Ruth Amiran at nearby Tell Arod (ancient Arad) between 1964 and 1968. The most important period of Hazor's history belongs to the 2nd millennium B.C. From this era the remains of a substantial Canaanite temple were uncovered; *see* CANAANITES. At Arad two main archeological periods are represented. In the outlying lower city a substantial early Bronze Age settlement was discovered just below the present surface. The citadel area, on the other hand, represents a fortress of the Iron Age contemporary with the kings of Judah (q.v.). More recent work in Israel has involved several American enterprises. A joint Israeli-American team has been working at Ashdod since 1963, and a major effort was begun at Tell Jezer (ancient Gezer) under the auspices of the Hebrew Union College Biblical and Archeological School (Cincinnati, Ohio) in 1964.

In Jordan the Jordanian Department of Antiquities has undertaken excavation projects at Khirbet Mefjir (ancient Gilgal) and at the ancient Nabataean capital, Petra, and has continued to encourage expeditions from abroad. The American Schools of Oriental Research and various other American institutions have conducted major expeditions at such sites as Balatah (ancient Shechem), beginning in 1956; el-Jib (ancient Gibeon), between 1957 and 1964; and et-Tel (ancient Ai), beginning in 1963. The work at Balatah, under the general direction of the American Bible scholar and archeologist George Ernest Wright (1909–   ), currently focuses on Tell er-Ras atop Mt. Gerezim, where the remains of a Samaritan temple and successive Roman temples are being investigated. Efforts of the British School of Archaeology in Jurusalem dur-

Ruins of the ancient city of Gerasa, a major Greco-Roman site in modern Jordan. Above: A triumphal arch built to celebrate the visit of the Roman emperor Hadrian in 129 A.D. Below: The Roman temple dedicated to the goddess Artemis, completed about 150, one of the finest preserved examples of Roman temples in the East.

Arab Information Center

Joe D. Seger

PALESTINIAN ARCHEOLOGY

ing this period focused on Jericho (1952–58) and Jerusalem (1964–67). Both of these projects were directed by the British archeologist Kathleen Kenyon. At Jericho the work done by the British School has clarified many problems of the history of the city back to the 7th millennium B.C.

Cultural History. The sequence of emerging cultures in Palestine is the most clearly documented of that of any area of the world. The oldest evidences of man in Palestine include the Paleolithic remains from the Mt. Carmel caves representing a type intermediate between Neanderthal and *Homo sapiens; see* MAN; MAN, ANCIENT. The succeeding Mesolithic assemblages (called Natufian, after the Wadi en Natuf where they were discovered) from these caves relate to those of similar cultures found throughout the Palestinian area, and most significantly to those in the earliest levels at Jericho. From this latter site, and from the nearby Ghassulian settlements, the transition through the Neolithic and Chalcolithic eras down to the period of great urban development in the early Bronze Age can be clearly traced.

Evidence of early Bronze Age culture can be found in virtually every major Palestinian site. Substantial population increase and developed structures are thus indicated. During the early Bronze Age, pottery techniques improved and attractive painted and incised pottery designs appeared; but this developing urban culture collapsed in the late 3rd millennium, giving way to a period of nomadic transition. City building was resumed again in the early 2nd millennium, during the middle Bronze Age, and continued through the ensuing late Bronze Age period. Remains of these periods give evidence also of the emerging Canaanite culture, which reached its apex in the 14th and 13th centuries B.C. This is reflected in architectural development as well as in examples of domestic utensils, in cultic and artistic objects, and in a smattering of epigraphs in the Canaanite language.

With the transition to the Iron Age about 1200 B.C., the cultural development of the area becomes integral with Biblical history. Against the background provided by growing evidences of architectural levels and other cultural remains, the events of the Israelite conquest, of the steps toward statehood, and of the course of the Hebrew kingdoms down to the Babylonian Captivity in the early 6th century B.C. are thrown into bold relief. In addition, the archeological identification of many of the places mentioned in Biblical accounts has substantially furthered understanding of the geopolitical relationships in Palestine during this era. *See* JEWS.

The following era of Persian domination was a period of cultural eclipse, and only the barest traces of occupation remain as reminders of the scant population left after the Babylonian conquest. This period of cultural eclipse was swiftly terminated, however, with the advent of Greek influences at the end of the 4th century B.C. The towers of Samaria, built at this time, are among the earliest examples of Hellenistic architecture. Later Hellenistic antiquities include wall paintings produced in the city of Mareshah (modern Tell Sandahanna in southern Palestine) in the 3rd century B.C. Mareshah, as it existed in the 2nd century B.C., has been almost entirely recovered. Other evidences of Hellenistic culture have recently been excavated at Gezer and Ashdod.

The first north Arabian civilization, that of the Nabataeans, was near its height just at the turn of the Christian era. Fragments of Nabataean pottery, temple ruins, fortifications, and irrigation reservoirs have been found throughout southern Palestine. The ruins of Petra, situated on the northeastern slope of Jebel Harun in Jordan, include temples, tombs, and other structures carved in the varicolored sandstone cliffs at the site.

Evidences of Roman civilization are apparent throughout the area, especially in Jerusalem and at the coastal sites of Caesarea and Ashquelon. Gerasa (modern Jarash, in Jordan) is the most famous of a group of about ten cities which formed the Decapolis, a confederation in the early Christian era. Gerasa reached its height in the 2nd century A.D. and Roman characteristics predominate among its well-preserved remains. Temples, theaters, colonnaded streets, a forum and a hippodrome have all been uncovered.

After the adoption of Christianity by Emperor Constantine I (q.v.) in the beginning of the 4th century A.D., many pagan temples gave way to church structures. One of the oldest buildings found in Palestine is the church of Julianos in Umm el-Jimal in northern Jordan. Built (before the middle of the 4th century) according to a simple rectangular plan, it contains a semicircular apse (q.v.) at the eastern end.

In recent years archeological research in Palestine has taken serious cognizance of the remains of materials belonging to the Islamic period; *see* ISLAM. In the 7th and 8th centuries a number of beautiful palaces and hunting lodges were built by Arabic Muslims on the fringes of the desert. The excavation of some of these buildings has provided much information about the origins of Muslim architecture, stucco decoration, and painting. It has also provided examples of Muslim sculpture, previously thought to be nonexistent. Large wall paintings at Quesier Amra, Jordan, depicting human figures, animals, and plants indicate that representational arts may well have been used in early Islam. The palace of Hisham at Khirbet Mefjir (ancient Gilgal) contains elegant floor mosaics, one of which portrays a lion, gazelles, and a pomegranate tree. *See* ISLAMIC ART AND ARCHITECTURE. J.D.Se.

PALESTRINA (anc. *Praeneste*), city of Italy, in Latium Region, about 20 miles S.E. of Rome. It is the site of the ruins of the large ancient Roman temple of Fortuna Primigenia, which had a famous oracle. The National Archeological Museum is housed there in the Palazzo Barberini. Pop. (1962), 10,407.

PALESTRINA, Giovanni Pierluigi da (1525?–94), Italian composer of church music, born in the town of Palestrina, southeast of Rome. He studied singing at the Church of Santa Maria Maggiore in Rome beginning about 1537. He

Giovanni Pierluigi da Palestrina — Bettmann Archive

became organist and choir director at the cathedral in Palestrina in 1544, leaving in 1551 to take the position of choirmaster at the Julian Chapel at Saint Peter's in Rome. His next positions were also in Rome, as choirmaster at Saint John Lateran from 1555 to 1560, at Santa Maria Maggiore from 1561 to 1566, and as master of music at a seminary for Jesuits from 1565 to 1571. From 1567 to 1571 he held the secular post of music director at the villa of Ippolito II, Cardinal d'Este (1509–72). In 1571 he returned to the Julian Chapel, where he remained until his death.

Although Palestrina was offered positions in cities other than Rome, he never pursued the offers seriously. Instead he always demanded of prospective non-Roman employers a high salary that was beyond their means. In his music he remained close to the mystical and highly ritualized spirit of the Roman Catholic Church (q.v.). No other composer, in fact, has worked so successfully within the limitations of that religious aesthetic.

The serenity of Palestrina's style arises from several technical sources. His music is vocal; no parts are written specifically for instruments. All the voice parts have a similar character, producing a homogeneous sound. The music is almost always contrapuntal, with simultaneously sounding and equally important melodic lines; *see* COUNTERPOINT. Although Palestrina used only a few chords in any one composition, he altered the manner in which the individual tones of each chord were spaced among the various voice parts. He thus achieved subtle changes while maintaining a general feeling of constancy. In rhythm he avoided the feeling of a strong pulse by allowing each voice part to have its own accent patterns independent of the other parts. He created a sublte pulse by confining dissonant, or unstable, tones to weak beats within a measure and always placing consonant, or stable, tones on strong beats. Finally, his melodic lines unfold in long, gentle curves in which any large leaps upward or downward are balanced by a return to the center of the curve.

Palestrina's religious music includes 102 masses, 250 motets, 35 magnificats, 68 offertories, 45 hymns, and other works. His secular works include many madrigals. Unlike most influential composers, Palestrina was not primarily an innovator in musical technique. Rather, he provided a model for other composers to emulate when they wished to recapture the mystical religious tone that his music exemplifies. *See* RELIGIOUS MUSIC.

PALEY, William (1743–1805), British theologian, clergyman, and philosopher, born in Peterborough, England, and educated at Christ's College, University of Cambridge, where he later lectured. He was ordained in the Church of England (q.v.) in 1767. In 1785 he published his *Principles of Moral and Political Philosophy*, in which he propounds his ethical theory, a form of utilitarianism (q.v.). In 1790 appeared his *Horae Paulinae; or the Truth of the Scripture History of St. Paul . . .* , the aim of which is to prove the historical value of the New Testament. It was followed in 1794 by his *View of the Evidences of Christianity* (2 vol.). In 1802 he published the most popular of all his works, *Natural Theology, or Evidences of the Existence and Attributes of the Deity.*

PALGRAVE, Francis Turner (1824–97), British poet and critic, born in Great Yarmouth, England, and educated at Charterhouse and Balliol College, University of Oxford. He was professor of poetry at Oxford from 1885 to 1895. He was the editor of the *Golden Treasury of English Songs and Lyrics* (1861 and 1897), *Treasury of Sacred Songs* (1889), and *Landscape in Poetry* (1887), a volume of critical essays.

PALI, ancient Indian language, of the Prakrit group, descended from Vedic Aryan; see INDIAN LANGUAGES. It was formerly widespread as the sacred language of Buddhism (q.v.), and is in limited use at the present time in Ceylon, Burma, and Thailand. Pali has no distinctive alphabet; it can be written in Ceylonese, Burmese, or Cambodian script.

Strictly speaking, Pali (Skr. *pali,* "row", "line", "series") refers to the written language, so called because it is applied to a series of sacred texts; spoken Pali was called *Palibhāsā* ("language of the series"). Ancient Pali is divided into two groups, that found in inscriptions and that used in literature, inscriptional Pali being the older. The earliest writings in Pali occur in the inscriptions of the Indian Buddhist king Asoka (q.v.), and date from the third quarter of the 3rd century B.C.; the latest writings date from the 10th century A.D. Pali literature is almost entirely religious. The best-known works are the *Tripitaka,* three collections of rules, doctrines, and analyses pertaining to Buddhism; the *Visuddhi Magga,* a Buddhist treatise by the Indian scholar Buddhaghosa (fl. 5th cent. A.D.); and the *Milindapañha,* a series of questions and answers on Buddhism. A number of historical and grammatical works also exist.

See SANSKRIT LANGUAGE.

PALIMPSEST, manuscript of parchment, papyrus, or other writing material, from which an early text was removed and which was then covered with a second writing. The term, derived from Greek, means "scraped again" and, in its strict sense, applies only to waxen tablets or to vellum books. It is also applied to papyrus manuscripts of ancient writers; writing on papyri could be washed off, somewhat imperfectly, with a sponge, and because the writing on papyri was usually on only one side, the back of the papyrus sheet could be used for a second writing. In the case of books of parchment, which by the 4th century A.D. had become the most popular material for literary works, erasure was necessary for a second use. In the early Middle Ages, the number of books increased and material for making them became scarce because Muslim caliph Omar I (q.v.) cut off the supply of Egyptian papyrus that Europe relied on for manuscript material prior to European paper manufacture, which started in 1150; see PAPER: *History.* In the absence of writing material, numerous early manuscripts of classical authors were used. Sometimes the earlier writing was incompletely erased or scraped away, and an ancient and valuable work of literature can be deciphered. The importance of palimpsest manuscripts is in the ancient works which they preserve and the legibility which the original writing retains. Usually the more ancient writing, being in capitals or uncials is larger than the later writing; see PALEOGRAPHY.

Among the most important Greek palimpsests are the *Fragments of the Gospel of Saint Matthew,* the original writing dating from the 6th century A.D.; and the *Codex Nitriensis,* containing part of the Gospel of Saint Luke, part of Homer's *Iliad,* and the *Elements* of Euclid, all used by a monk as material for a copy of a Syriac treatise. Latin palimpsests include the *Codex Ambrosianus* of the Roman dramatist Titus Maccius Plautus (q.v.) in rustic capitals of the 4th or 5th century A.D., over which were written portions of the Bible in the 9th century, a manuscript of special value because it provides a text of Plautus about 600 years older than any other existing Plautine manuscript; the *De Republica* of Marcus Tullius Cicero (q.v.) over which Saint Augustine (q.v.) wrote his commentary on the Psalms, and the *Institutiones* of the Roman jurist Gaius (110?–180? A.D.), discovered at Verona, Italy, in 1816 by the German historian and statesman Barthold Georg Niebuhr (q.v.). Occasionally a palimpsest was written over twice; a manuscript of the British Museum contains as its original writing the *Annals* of Gaius Granius Licinianus, a writer of the 2nd century A.D., over which was written a grammatical treatise, the third writing being in Syriac.

PALISADES, cliffs of traprock, on the w. bank of the Hudson River (q.v.), in Rockland County, N.Y., and Bergen and Hudson counties, N.J. The cliffs, which vary in height from 350 to 550 ft. above sea level, extend N. about 20 mi. from Jersey City, N.J., to the vicinity of Piermont, N.Y.

PALISADES INTERSTATE PARK, tract of land in New Jersey and New York, consisting of over 50,000 acres along the Palisades (q.v.) on the w. bank of the Hudson R. It includes Bear Mountain (q.v.) and Storm King mountain. *See* NEW JERSEY: *Parks, Forests, and Other Places of Interest;* NEW YORK: *Parks, Forests, and Other Places of Interest.*

PALLADIO, Andrea (1508–80), Italian architect, born in Vicenza, and trained as an architect in Vicenza and Rome. His first important work was a two-storied arcade around the basilica at Vicenza, begun in 1549, in which the composition, proportion, and details were based on Roman architectural design and adapted to the requirements of the era. A distinguishing feature of this arcade and of many of Palladio's later works was an opening, such as a door or window, with an arched top, flanked by two flat-topped openings. This motif became popular as the "Palladian motif", and was widely employed by Renaissance and later architects. Palladio designed many buildings in and near Vicenza. The best known of these are the Barbarano, Chieregati, Tiene, Porto, and Valmarana palaces and the Villa Capri or Villa Rotunda. From about 1560 to 1580 he built a number of churches in Venice, including San Francesco della Vigna, San Giorgio Maggiore, and the church of Il Redentore. His last great work was the Teatro Olimpico, a theater at Vicenza, which was completed after his death. Palladio's work represents the Classisima or Palladian phase of the High Renaissance; *see* ITALIAN ART AND ARCHITECTURE: *High Renaissance.* He was the author of a scientific treatise on architecture, *I Quattro Libri dell' Architettura* (1570; Eng. trans., *The Four Books of Architecture,* 1716), which was translated into many European languages and influenced many later architects. The precise rules and formulas given in the book were widely utilized, especially in England, and were basic in the formation of a Palladian style, adopted by Inigo Jones, Christopher Wren (qq.v.), and other English architects, that preceded and influenced the Georgian style; *see* GEORGIAN ARCHITECTURE.

PALLADIUM, metallic element of the platinum group with at.no. 46, at.wt. 106.4, b.p. over 2700° C. (4892° F.), m.p. 1550° C. (2822° F.), sp.gr. 12$^{20°}$, and symbol Pd. It was discovered in 1804 by the British chemist William Hyde Wollaston (q.v.). The metal occurs in the pure state in platinum ores and in the combined state in Canadian nickel ore; *see* NICKEL; PLATINUM. Palladium is a silvery-white metal with a hardness of 4.8. Like platinum it is ductile, malleable, and resistant to corrosion; it fuses more easily than platinum and can be welded easily. Finely divided palladium is an excellent adsorbent for some gases; it adsorbs 1000 to 3000 times its vol-

The two-story arcade around the basilica in Vicenza, Italy, built by Andrea Palladio in adaptation of the Roman architectural style.   Alinari

PALLADIUM

ume of hydrogen or acetylene gas when heated to 100° C. (212° F.). Palladium is dissolved readily by aqua regia (q.v.). It forms bivalent and quadrivalent compounds and resembles platinum chemically. The chief use of the metal is in the field of communications, where it is used to face electrical contacts in automatic switchgear. It is also used in dentistry, for nonmagnetic springs in clocks and watches, for coating special mirrors, and in jewelry, alloyed with gold, in what is called white gold; see GOLD: *Uses.*

PALLADIUM, in Greek mythology, statue of the goddess Athena (q.v.) holding a shield and a spear. It was believed to have been hurled from Olympus (q.v.) by the god Zeus (q.v.) at the founding of Troy (q.v.). The safety of a city was believed to depend upon the careful preservation of the image in the sanctuary of the goddess. In the tenth year of the Trojan War (q.v.) the Greek heroes Diomedes (q.v.) and Odysseus (*see* ULYSSES) stole the Palladium, thus facilitating the fall of Troy. The Romans, tracing their ancestry from the Trojans, believed that the Palladium, which was kept at Rome in the temple of Vesta, goddess of the hearth, was the Trojan original, and had been brought to Italy by the hero Aeneas (q.v.) after the sack of Troy.

PALLAH ANTELOPE. *See* IMPALA.

PALLAS, one of the planetoids (q.v.), the second to be discovered, first observed by the German astronomer Heinrich Wilhelm Matthäus Olbers (q.v.) in 1802. It revolves about the sun in 1684 days.

PALLAS ATHENA. *See* ATHENA.

PALM, common name for any plant of the family Palmaceae, comprising the order Palmales. The family, which includes about 170 genera and 1500 species, is native to all tropical and subtropical regions of the world. Plants of the Palm family are monocotyledons characterized by a simple stem, a terminal crown of large leaves that are usually pinnate or palmately cleft with deep wedge-shaped notches, and perfect or unisexual flowers. The typical genus of the family is *Areca* (q.v.). In most species the stem is long and undivided; stems of the jupati, buriti, and palmyra palms are sufficiently large and strong to be used for timber. Species of the genus *Chamaerops* have short stems, and the doom palm is unusual in having branched stems. In the rattan palm the stem is exceptionally long and flexible, sometimes reaching a length of 600 ft.; this palm climbs upon other plants by means of hooked spines. Palm leaves have a strong sheathing, and are often a source of fiber. Plants of the genus *Astrocaryum,* among many others, furnish fiber for rope;

leaves of the gebang palm are used for thatching and making baskets and single leaves of the talipot are used for umbrellas and parasols. The enormous leaves of the bussu palm of Central and South America are atypical in being undivided; one or two leaves suffice to cover the entire roof of a native house. Wax is obtained from

Coconut palm, in the Florida Keys. Allan D. Cruickshank – National Audubon Society

the leaves of some species of wax palm, other species produce a resinous wax from the stem. The stem produces a form of starch in species of the sago palm; in species of the genus *Caryota* and other types of jaggery palm the sap is sweet and furnishes palm sugar. The sap of these and related species is used as a refreshing beverage, which sometimes is fermented to make palm wine. The terminal bud of the cabbage palm, or assai, is valued for food and, like the cabbage, is used either cooked or raw.

The fruit of various species of palm range in form from that of the date palm to that of the coconut. The sweet, fleshy part of the date corresponds botanically to the fibrous husk surrounding the shell of the coconut, and the hard stone of the date is homologous with the sweet, oily flesh of the coconut. The seeds of species of oil palm produce palm oil, as in species of the genus Elaeis and of the grugru palm. Fruits of the ivory palm (q.v.) produce vegetable ivory, used in the manufacture of buttons and other small turned or carved products. Many palms produce a variety of products; the gomuti palm, for example, yields rope fiber from the leaves, sago from the pith, and sugar and palm wine from the sap. Species of the genus *Attalea* produce piassava fiber; some species also yield oil from the fruit, called cohune nuts, others produce coquilla nuts, resembling a brown variety of vegetable ivory.

Most palms are ornamental in cultivation, and many of the smaller species are grown as pot or greenhouse plants in cool climates. See separate articles on many of the plants mentioned; see also PALMETTO.

PALMA, city in Spain, and capital of Baleares Province, on the island of Majorca, on the Bay of Palma, an arm of the Mediterranean Sea, about 130 miles S.E. of Barcelona. The chief manufactures are shoes, woolen goods, pottery, crystal and glass, matches, hardware, ship engines, cement, paper, iron, and brewery products. The houses are mostly in Moorish architectural styles; the city itself was captured from the Moors in 1229. It has a Gothic cathedral begun in 1229 and completed in the 17th century, a castle that was once a Moorish palace, a former Spanish royal palace located 400 ft. above the Bay of Palma, and the 13th century San Francisco Church. Pop. (1968 est.) 177,089.

PALMA, name of two Italian painters of the Venetian school.

Jacopo Palma, called IL VECCHIO ("Jacopo the Elder") or PALMA VECCHIO (1480?–1528), born in Serina, near Bergamo. His work was allied in spirit and treatment to that of the Venetian masters Il Giorgione and Titian (qq.v.). His forms were large and ample; his colors rich and warm. "Holy Conversations" is a subject which he painted many times. It shows groupings of figures conversing in a quiet landscape suffused in a golden glow. Noted portraits are those of Francesco Querini (Querini Stampalia Gallery, Venice) and "The Poet" (National Gallery, London). "The Three Sisters", in the Dresden Gallery, is one of his best known works. It is often called "The Three Graces".

Jacopo Palma, called IL GIOVANE ("Jacopo the Younger") or PALMA GIOVANE (1544–1628), the grandnephew of the preceding, born in Venice. Although he utilized characteristically rich Venetian coloring in his work, he was influenced by classical Roman grandeur, and his art, which combined both sources, marked a transition to the decadence of Venetian painting. After the death of the great Venetian painters Titian and Paolo Veronese (qq.v.), Palma was the sole heir of the tradition, and received many important commissions, painting a "Last Judgment" in the hall of the Doges' Palace, and other scenes in the Great Council Hall in Venice.

PALMA, Tomás Estrada (1835–1908), Cuban revolutionist and statesman, born near Bayamo. He joined the Cuban patriot forces in the 1868–78 revolt against the Spanish, and rose to the rank of general. In 1877, after he had been elected president of a Cuban provisional government, he was captured by the Spanish, who imprisoned him for about one year. After his release Palma spent some years in Honduras and then settled in the United States, where he established a school for Latin-Americans at Central Valley, N.Y. In 1895, when a second Cuban revolution began, he was designated minister plenipotentiary for the Republic of Cuba in the U.S. He became the head of a revolutionary junta in New York City, which purchased arms and secured American aid for the insurgents. He was elected the first president of the Cuban Republic in 1901, was re-elected in 1906, but was charged with corruption and forced to resign in the same year.

PALMAS, LAS. See LAS PALMAS.

PALM BEACH, town of Florida, in Palm Beach Co., on an island between the Atlantic Ocean and Lake Worth, opposite the city of West Palm Beach (q.v.), with which it is connected by bridges, and 300 miles S.E. of Jacksonville. Palm Beach is one of the most noted and fashionable winter resorts in the world. The town has facilities for bathing and boating, including a yacht basin on Lake Worth and an extensive public beach. The resident population of the city is increased each winter by a transient population of more than 16,000. Pop. (1960) 6055; (1970) 9086.

PALMER, Alice (Elvira) Freeman (1855–1902), American educator, born in Colesville, N.Y., and educated at the University of Michigan. A dedicated promoter of education for women, she was president of Wellesley College from 1882 to 1887 and dean of women at the University of Chicago from 1892 to 1895. In 1887 she married the American philosopher and Harvard University professor George Herbert Palmer (1842–1933). A bronze bust honoring her contributions is in the Hall of Fame for Great Americans (q.v.).

PALMER, Arnold (1929–   ), American golfer, born in Latrobe, Pa., and educated at Wake Forest College. From 1950 until 1953 Palmer served in the United States Coast Guard. The son of a

PALMER PENINSULA

Arnold Palmer

golf (q.v.) teacher and himself a golfer since the age of three, Palmer won the National Amateur championship of the United States Golf Association in 1954. A few months later he became a professional golfer. Palmer was the only golfer to win the Masters championship at Augusta, Ga., four times, having won in 1958, 1960, 1962, and 1964. He won the British Open championship twice, in 1961 and 1962. He won the U.S. Golf Association Open Tournament in 1960. In 1966 he won the Australian Open championship and the following year took individual honors in World Cup golf in Mexico City. In February, 1971, he won the Bob Hope Desert Classic at Palm Springs, Calif., and, in March, the Florida Citrus Invitational.

PALMER PENINSULA. See ANTARCTIC PENINSULA.

PALMERSTON, 3rd Viscount Henry John Temple (1784–1865), British statesman, born near Romsey, Hampshire, England, and educated at Harrow School and Saint John's College, University of Cambridge. He entered Parliament as a representative of Newtown, on the Isle of Wight, in 1807. Offered the chancellorship of the exchequer in 1809, Palmerston refused, and took, instead, the position of secretary of war, the supervisor of the financial business of the army, where he remained, without cabinet rank, refusing every offer of promotion, until 1827. During this period Palmerston was recognized more as a man of fashion and a writer of satirical poetry than as a political figure. In 1827, however, he became a member of the Tory cabinet formed by Arthur Wellesley, 1st Duke of Wellington (q.v.). In 1828 Palmerston resigned and joined the opposition, becoming foreign secretary of the Whig government formed in 1830, and remained in this post, except for one brief interval, until 1841. Palmerston re-entered the cabinet as foreign secretary under the prime ministership of Lord John Russell (q.v.) in 1846. As foreign secretary, he often acted without consulting the court. He was dismissed in 1851 for expressing his approval of the coup d'etat by which Louis Napoleon became Napoleon III (q.v.), Emperor of France; Palmerston's colleagues and the prime minister did not support Napoleon III. Palmerston became prime minister in 1855. He proposed that Great Britain enter the Crimean War (q.v.) and the success of British forces in that war made him popular as a leader. He held the post of prime minister until his death.

As the leader of British foreign policy, Palmerston obtained the annexation of Hong Kong and the opening of five other Chinese ports by the Treaty of Nanking (1842); he fought the international slave trade (see SLAVERY) and supported British neutrality in the American Civil War. See also GREAT BRITAIN: *History: The Reign of William IV.*

PALMERSTON NORTH, city of New Zealand, in Wellington Provincial District, on North Island, on the Manawatu R., 80 miles N.E. of Wellington. A road and rail hub in a sheep-raising and dairying area, the city manufactures furniture, bricks, apparel, flour, dairy products, and beer. It is the site of Massey Agricultural College and the attached Dairy Research Institute, a teachers' college, and the Grasslands Research Station. The city was settled by Scandinavians in 1871. Pop. (1965) 46,816.

PALMETTO, common name of several species of palms. Cabbage palmetto, *Sabal Palmetto,* is a native of maritime parts of North America, from Florida to North Carolina. It may attain a height of 80 ft. and has a crown of large palmate leaves, the blade being from 1 ft. to 5 ft. in length and width. Other palmettos are Texas palmetto, *S. texana;* Louisiana palmetto, *S. louisiana;* and Saw palmetto, *Serenoa repens;* these are all smaller than the cabbage palmetto.

PALMISTRY, or CHIROMANCY (Gr. *cheir,* "hand"; *manteia,* "divination"), art of characterization and foretelling the future through the study of the palm of the hand. Palmistry was known among the Chaldaeans, Assyrians, Egyptians, and Hebrews, and was recognized by such philosophers as Plato, and Aristotle (qq.v.). Palmistry was seriously practiced and widely accepted during the Middle Ages, and was revived as a serious art during the 19th century, especially in France. Since the turn of the century it has been regarded as a branch of fortunetelling (q.v.), without scientific basis. Palmistry is chiefly concerned with the mounts of the palm, the lines on the mounts, and the lines interlacing the palm. The left hand supposedly reflects inbred and the right hand acquired characteristics. The presence of each mount signifies a certain personality trait and the absence of a particular mount indicates the lack of a corresponding trait. The mount of Jupiter denotes honor and a happy disposition; of Saturn, prudence and therefore success; of Apollo, appreciation of beauty; of Mercury, scientific, industrial, and commercial interests; of Mars, courage; of the Moon, a dreamy disposition; and of Venus, an amorous nature. The four most important lines represent life, intelligence, the heart or sensation, and personal fortune. Markings known as squares, stars, circles, points, triangles, crosses, rings, branches, and islands corroborate or modify by their positions in the palm the deductions made from the mounts and lines.

PALM SPRINGS, city of California, in Riverside Co., about 39 miles S.E. of San Bernardino. A desert resort, the city has some manufacturing. The Joshua Tree National Monument is about 12 mi. to the N.E. The city was founded in 1876 and incorporated in 1938. Pop. (1960) 13,468; (1970) 20,936.

PALM SUNDAY, in Christianity, Sunday before Easter (q.v.), so called from the custom of blessing palms and of carrying the portions of branches in procession, in commemoration of the triumphal entry of Jesus (see JESUS CHRIST) into Jerusalem. The custom may be traced back at least to the 4th century.

PALMYRA, ancient city of Syria, in an oasis on the N. edge of the Syrian Desert, about 150 miles N.E. of Damascus. According to tradition, it was founded by Solomon (q.v.), King of Israel. In the Bible it is called Tadmor (1 Kings 9:18). A prosperous caravan station in the 1st century B.C., Palmyra became a Roman outpost and a major city-state with the Roman empire. Odenathus, Prince of Palmyra (d. 266? A.D.), defeated a Persian army, and when his wife, Zenobia (q.v.), became leader of the East upon the assassination of her husband, she declared her independence from Rome. In 272 Lucius Domitius Aurelian (q.v.), Emperor of Rome, captured Zenobia and razed the city. Of the ancient city, the temple of the Sun (or Baal) and the colonnade, nearly 1 mi. long, originally of some 1500 Corinthian columns, still stand. In modern times, a town, Tadmor, has been built near the ancient city.

PALO ALTO, city of California, in Santa Clara Co., 28 miles S.E. of San Francisco. It is the site of Stanford University (q.v.), established in 1885. Industries include electronics manufacturing, missile development, printing, and publishing. Incorporated as a town in 1894, Palo Alto was chartered as a city in 1909. Pop. (1960) 52,287; (1970) 55,966.

PALO ALTO, BATTLE OF, first battle of the Mexican War (q.v.), fought near present-day Brownsville, Texas, at the southern edge of the State. After the United States had annexed Texas, the American general Zachary Taylor (q.v.) advanced to the Rio Grande, which the U.S. considered the southern border of Texas. The Mexican government considered this Mexican territory, and the Mexican general Mariano Arista (q.v.) crossed the Rio Grande and was defeated in a battle with Taylor's army at Palo Alto on May 8, 1846. The American President James Knox Polk (q.v.) announced that Arista had invaded American territory, and Congress declared war.

PALOMAR OBSERVATORY, formerly MOUNT PALOMAR OBSERVATORY, astronomical observatory located on Mt. Palomar, 135 miles S.E. of Pasadena, Calif. The observatory is owned by the California Institute of Technology (q.v.) and is operated with the Mount Wilson Observatory (q.v.) as a unified research organization. Plans for this observatory were begun in 1928, and in 1949 the 200-in. Hale reflecting telescope and the 48-in. reflecting-refracting Schmidt photographic telescope began operation. The Schmidt telescope can accurately photograph large areas of the sky, and in the first several years of operation it was used to make a photographic atlas of the entire sky visible at Mt. Palomar. The Hale telescope, weighing 530 tons, is not used for visual observation, but for making photographic and photoelectric records of the faintest and most distant objects in the heavens. The 200-in. mirror is a ribbed casting of Pyrex glass, weighing 14½ tons after being ground and polished to a concave parabolic shape. The surface was coated in a high vacuum with a thin film of highly reflective aluminum. Other telescopes at the observatory are an 18-in. Schmidt telescope and a 20-in. photoelectric telescope.

PALOMETA

A 60-in. Cassegrain reflector, which consists of a convex rather than a concave mirror and is analogous in function to a telephoto lens, was dedicated in November, 1970. See TELESCOPE.

PALOMETA. See POMPANO.

PALSY. See PARALYSIS.

PALSY, CEREBRAL. See CEREBRAL PALSY.

PAMIRS, high plateau region of central Asia, extending through the Soviet Union into Afghanistan and China, and forming part of the Pamir-Alai mountain system. Also in the system are the Trans-Alai Range, the Peter the First Range, and Akademiya Nauk Range. The Pamirs has a mean elevation of 13,000 ft.; the highest peaks are Mt. Communism (24,590 ft.) and Mt. Lenin (23,508 ft.). The plateau is desolate and inhabited by nomads who call it the roof of the world. The Pamirs is a connecting link between the Tien Shan, Kunlun, Karakoram, and Hindu Kush (qq.v.) mountain ranges.

PAMLICO SOUND, inlet of the Atlantic Ocean, on the coast of North Carolina. The sound, which is about 80 mi. long and between 10 and 25 mi. wide, is separated from the ocean by long, narrow islands of sand, with narrow passages. The Pamlico and Neuse rivers empty into the sound, which is connected with Albermarle Sound in the N. through Croatan Sound. A thriving fishing industry is carried on here.

PAMPA, city in Texas, and county seat of Gray Co., in the Panhandle prairie region near the North Fork of the Red R., 55 miles N.E. of Amarillo. In an area of oil and gas fields, it is a rail junction and trade center for a region producing wheat, sorghums, cattle, and poultry. Industries include oil and gas refining and the manufacture of oil-field equipment, chemicals, electrical equipment, and textiles. Pop. (1960) 24,664; (1970) 21,726.

PAMPAS, vast treeless plains of Argentina, which rise, almost imperceptibly, from the Atlantic coast to the Andes Mts. The E. portion, known as the Humid Pampas, is one of the most fertile regions in the country. From the Humid Pampa to the Andes Mts. is the Dry Pampa, a less populated region supporting cattle, horses, and sheep. The name "pampas" is sometimes given to level districts of Peru. The term is derived from Peruvian *Pampa* ("plain").

PAMPHYLIA, ancient country on the S. coast of Asia Minor, between Lycia and Cilicia, in what is now Turkey. The inhabitants, a mixed race of aborigines, Cilicians, and Greek colonists, spoke a language which was probably Greek in origin but which was changed through the addition of barbaric elements. Persian domination was followed by conquest of Alexander III (q.v.), King of Macedonia, called the Great in the 4th century B.C. After his death the country was ruled by the Seleucid (q.v.) dynasty. Later becoming part of Pergamum (q.v.), it was bequeathed to the Romans along with the rest of the kingdom by Attalus III (q.v.) in 133 B.C.

PAMPLONA, or PAMPELUNA, city in Spain, and capital of Navarre Province, on a tributary of the Ebro R., 11 miles N.W. of Saragossa. Its industries include sugar milling, wine making, textiles, canning, meat packing, brewing, and tanning. Manufacturing includes firearms, flour, fertilizer, shoes, and candy. Pamplona is noted for a Roman Catholic cathedral, completed in the 14th century and for the feast of San Fermin, which is celebrated each July by running bulls through the streets to the bullring; see EUROPE: *Plate 3.*

History. The known history of Pamplona goes back to 68 B.C., when it was founded, probably by Roman statesman and general Pompey the Great (q.v.). This Basque (q.v.) outpost was repeatedly occupied by the Visigoths (see GOTHS: *Visigoths*) from 476 A.D. and was sacked by Charlemagne (q.v.), King of the Franks, in 778. The Moors (q.v.) captured Pamplona during the 8th century. In 824 the Basque Kingdom of Pamplona was founded. The kingdom was renamed the Kingdom of Navarre (q.v.), and Pamplona remained its capital. Philip II (q.v.), King of Spain, built the city into a major fortress in 1571. It was captured twice during the Peninsular War (see SPAIN: *History*), first by the French in 1808 and later by the British in 1813. Pop. (1965) 124,199.

PAN, in Greek mythology, god of woods, fields, and fertility, the son of Hermes (q.v.), messenger of the gods, and a nymph. Part animal, with the horns, hoofs, and ears of a goat, he was a rollicking deity, the god of the shepherds and the goatherds. A wonderful musician, he accompanied, with his pipe of reeds, the woodland nymphs when they danced. He invented this pipe when the nymph Syrinx (q.v.), whom he was pursuing, was transformed into a bed of reeds to escape him; Pan then took reeds of unequal length and played upon them. The god was always wooing one of the nymphs by playing on his pipes, but was always rejected because of his ugliness. Pan's haunts were the mountains and caves and all wild places, but his favorite spot was Arcady, where he was born. The word panic is supposed to have derived from the fears of travelers who heard the sound of his pipes at night in the wilderness.

PANAMA, republic, forms an S-shaped isthmus linking South America with Central and

PANAMA

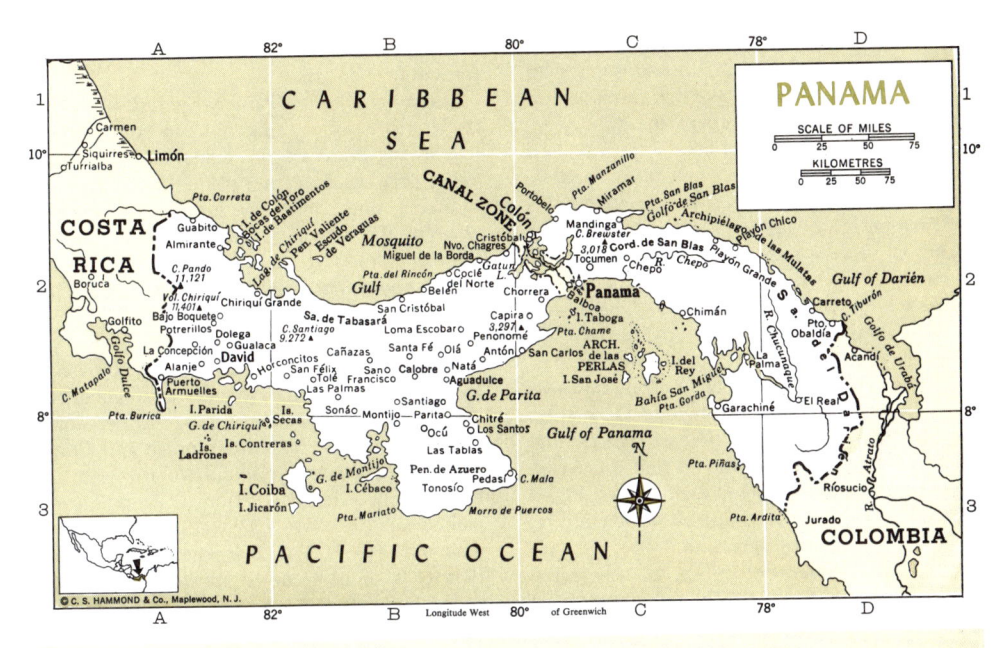

INDEX TO MAP OF PANAMA

Cities and Towns

Aguadulce	B 2
Alanje	A 2
Almirante	A 2
Antón	B 2
Bajo Boquete	A 2
Belén	B 2
Bocas del Toro	A 2
Calobre	B 2
Cañazas	B 2
Capira	B 2
Carreto	D 2
Chepo	C 2
Chimán	C 2
Chiriquí Grande	A 2
Chitré	B 3
Chorrera	C 2
Coclé del Norte	B 2
Colón	C 2
David	A 2
Dolega	A 2
El Real	D 2
Garachiné	C 2
Guabito	A 2
Gualaca	A 2
Horconcitos	A 2
La Concepción	A 2
La Palma	C 2
Las Palmas	B 2
Las Tablas	B 3
Mandinga	C 2
Miguel de la Borda	B 2
Miramar	C 2
Montijo	B 2
Natá	B 2
Ocú	B 3
Olá	B 2
Panamá (capital)	C 2
Parita	B 2
Pedasí	B 3
Penonomé	B 2
Playón Grande	C 2
Portobelo	C 2
Potrerillos	A 2
Puerto Armuelles	A 2
Puerto Obaldía	D 2
San Carlos	C 2
San Cristóbal	B 2
San Félix	B 2
San Francisco	B 2
Santa Fé	B 2
Santiago	B 2
Soná	B 2
Tolé	B 2
Tonosí	B 3

Physical Features

Azuero (pen.)	B 3
Bastimentos (isl.)	B 2
Brewster (mt.)	C 2
Burica (point)	A 2
Cébaco (isl.)	B 3
Chepo (river)	C 2
Chiriquí (gulf)	A 3
Chiriquí (lagoon)	B 2
Chiriquí (volcano)	A 2
Chucunaque (river)	D 2
Coiba (isl.)	A 3
Colón (isl.)	A 2
Darién (mts.)	D 2
Gatun (lake)	B 2
Jicarón (isl.)	A 3
Manzanillo (point)	C 2
Montijo (gulf)	B 3
Mosquitos (gulf)	B 2
Mulatas (arch.)	D 2
Panama (gulf)	C 3
Pando (mt.)	A 2
Parita (gulf)	B 2
Perlas (arch.)	C 2
Puercos, Morro de (prom.)	B 2
Rey (isl.)	C 2
Rincón (point)	B 2
San Blas (gulf)	C 2
San Blas (range)	C 2
San José (isl.)	C 2
San Miguel (bay)	C 2
Santiago (mt.)	B 2
Secas (isls.)	B 3
Tabasará (mts.)	B 2
Taboga (isl.)	C 2
Tiburón (cape)	D 2
Valiente (pen.)	B 2

North America. It is bisected by the Panama Canal Zone (q.v.). The country is bounded on the N. by the Caribbean Sea, on the E. by Colombia, on the S. by the Pacific Ocean, and on the W. by Costa Rica. The respective N. and S. limits are delineated approximately but lat. 7°15′ N. and lat. 9°39′ N.; the respective E. and W. limits by long. 77°15′ W. and long. 83°30′ W. Panama has an extreme length of about 480 mi.; the width varies from 37 to 110 mi. The coastline is 426 mi. long on the Caribbean and 767 mi. on the Pacific; the total area is about 28,575 sq.mi.

THE LAND

Panama is traversed lengthwise by two mountain ranges. The loftier, the Costa Rican range, crosses into Panama from the W.; it averages 5000 ft. in height; its tallest peak, Chiriquí (11,410 ft.), is an extinct volcano. The Darién Mts., which form the lower range, average about 3000 ft. and begin within the country on the Colombian border. The mountains enclose fertile, well-drained valleys and plains.

The region between the two mountain systems consists of hills, ranging from 300 to 1500 ft. high, and valleys. It is thickly matted with forests and tangled undergrowth, and is studded with ridges, crests, and occasional plains and high plateaus. The two mountain ranges are watersheds that give form to some 325 streams emptying into the Pacific and 150 descending to the Caribbean. The largest and most important river, the Tuira, flows into the bay of San Miguel

289

PANAMA

on the Pacific coast. Another large river, the Chagres, rises in central Panama and is dammed at Gatun into an artificial lake that forms an important section of the Panama Canal (q.v.).

Both of the Panamanian coasts are indented by lagoons, bays, and gulfs. The Gulf of Panama, 100 mi. wide, lies on the Pacific side. It contains the Archipelago de las Perlas (Pearl Islands), 116 islands of varying size with a total area of 450 sq.mi.

Climate. Panama has a tropical climate with average annual temperatures ranging from 70° to 90° F. In the interior, at the higher altitudes, the average temperature is 66° F. The rainy season extends from mid-May to mid-December. On the Caribbean coast the average annual rainfall is 117 in., on the Pacific side it is 63 in.

Natural Resources. Panama has developed very few of the natural resources of the country, which are primarily agricultural. By the late 1960's, only a small percentage of the arable land was under cultivation. The rich forests have not been extensively exploited; nor have mineral deposits of manganese, molybdenum, limestone, and copper.

Plants and Animals. The vegetation of Panama differs in variety and abundance according to the amount of local rainfall. The Atlantic side of the country and eastern Panama are covered by tropical rain forests underlaid with luxuriant growths of sedge, tropical flowers, and a variety of wild grasses. The Pacific slopes of the isthmus, because of the drier climate, are covered by a relatively sparse growth of deciduous trees and grassy plains called savannas. More than 2000 varieties of tropical plants flourish throughout the country.

The animal life of Panama includes most of the animal species indigenous to South America; among these are the puma, armadillo, kinkajou, ocelot, anteater, spider and capuchin monkeys, sloth, and deer. Reptiles include the alligator, the crocodile, and a variety of snakes. Vividly colored tropical birds abound, as do ducks and other migratory birds familiar to North America.

THE PEOPLE

About 65 percent of the population is mestizo (persons of mixed Spanish and Indian ancestry); some 15 percent is Negro; about 10 percent is European; and the remainder Indian and Oriental. The population is primarily rural.

Population. The population of Panama (official census 1960) was 1,075,541; United Nations estimated (1969), 1,417,000. Overall population density is about 47 per sq.mi. (U.N. est. 1967). More than half of the population is engaged in subsistence farming in the hinterlands; nearly one third is concentrated in the two largest cities, Colón and Panamá.

Political Divisions and Principal Cities. Panama is divided into nine provinces: Bocas del Toro, Coclé, Colón, Chiriquí, Darién, Herrera, Los Santos, Panamá, and Veraguas.

The capital, Panamá (pop., 1968 est., 373,000), and Colón (64,000) border the Panama Canal, and each is an important commercial and transportation center. David, the third largest city (46,919), is a farming center near the Costa Rican border.

The Cathedral of Panamá, in the most modern residential section of the capital city. **United Nations**

Panamanian youngsters take out a canoe in sheltered waters. UPI

Language and Religion. Spanish is the official and traditional language, and English is widely used. About 95 percent of the population is Roman Catholic. The constitution provides for the separation of church and state, and freedom of religion is guaranteed.

Education. Education is free and compulsory for children between the ages of seven and fifteen. The census of 1960 showed an illiteracy rate of 14 percent of the non-Indian population over ten years of age. In the late 1960's Panama had some 1600 public and private primary schools with a combined enrollment of more than 218,000; some 150 secondary technical schools had an enrollment of 65,000. About 10,000 students attended 2 universities.

Culture. Basically the culture of Panama is a mixture of Spanish, African, Indian, and North American traditions. The dances, music, and celebrations are colorful and gay. During Carnival, the last four days before Lent, a variety of folk customs are discernible. The *tamborito*, danced to handclapping and drums, dates from the 17th century; the *cumbia*, also popular today, is of African origin.

ARCHEOLOGY. The site of Coclé, situated southwest of the Panama Canal near the Gulf of Panamá, has yielded magnificent relics that have been tentatively dated from as early as 800. Gold jewelry, finely cut precious and semiprecious gems set in gold, helmets, and other artifacts originating at Coclé have been discovered as far north as the Yucatán Peninsula, evidence of the value placed on these objects in pre-conquest times. Coclé-style pottery is unique, with its curved-bottom plates and bowls decorated in five and six colors.

THE ECONOMY

The major source of revenue is the rent and payment for services associated with the operation of the canal. In the mid-1960's, the government undertook the expansion of industrial activity and agricultural programs; it sought to establish a network of farm-to-market roads, to develop water and energy resources, to construct warehouse and marketing facilities, to extend supervised agricultural credit, and to encourage new industry. In the late 1960's some 582,000,000 kw hours of electric power were produced annually. In a recent year budget figures were balanced at about $130,000,000.

Agriculture. Only slightly more than 4 percent of the land area is under cultivation. The main

A pre-Columbian gold ornament found in Panama.
El Halcon – El Panama Hilton

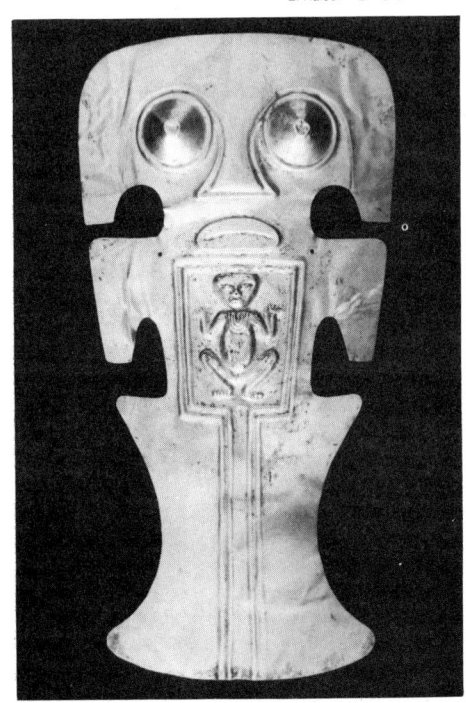

The shrimp industry is one of the most important sources of revenue in Panama. Above: A trawler net is lowered from a fishing vessel. Below: Shrimps are separated according to size, weighed, and distributed in small pails to workers for peeling before packing and freezing.
United Nations

cash crop is bananas, which are grown by an American-owned company and shipped to the United States. Annual production in the late 1960's totaled about 14,000,000 stems. Other leading commercial crops, with production figures, were coffee (12,000 tons), sugarcane (2,000,000 tons), tobacco (2000 tons), and cocoa. Principal food crops grown for local consumption were rice (360,000 tons), corn (210,000 tons), and beans (14,000 tons). Livestock included about 1,000,000 cattle, 168,000 pigs, and 2,700,000 poultry.

Forest and Fishing Industries. Forest products include a variety of woods, notably mahogany. In the late 1960's vast forest reserves were practically untouched because of a lack of transportation facilities in the interior. However, wild stands of castilla rubber trees are being increasingly tapped.

Fishing is a leading industry. The principal catch is shrimp (12,900,275 lb. in the mid-1960's); tuna and snapper are also caught. Pearl fisheries are centered in the Pearl Islands.

Mining and Manufacturing. Gold and silver are mined on a small scale in Santiago. Salt, a major mineral product, is extracted on the Pacific coast. Most manufactured goods, such as cement, cigarettes, shoes, clothing, soaps, canned goods, and alcoholic beverages, are produced for local markets.

Commerce and Trade. The balboa is the basic monetary unit (1 balboa equals U.S.$1; 1970). United States paper money and coinage are legal currency and no exchange control is exercised. The National Bank of Panama is the official bank.

In the late 1960's the chief exports, of which more than 65 percent were shipped to the U.S., were bananas, sugar, coffee, and shrimp. The main imports were fuel, foodstuffs, chemicals, machinery and transport material, and manufactured goods. A continuing negative balance of trade is partially made up by a steady inflow of dollars from the Panama Canal Zone, income from transit trade, tourism, and foreign investments and assistance.

Transportation and Communications. In the late 1960's only one third of the existing 4000 mi. of roads was paved. This included 300 mi. of the Inter-American Highway (q.v.). The rugged, precipitous terrain severely limits inland travel. Of the three railroads in Panama two are U.S.-owned; one operates in conjunction with the Panama Canal and the other is used for the transportation of fruit. The Chiriqui National Railroad is owned and operated by the Panamanian government. Railroad routes total about 425 mi.; most of which is narrow-gauge track.

The Thatcher Ferry Bridge, traversing the canal at the Pacific entrance, unites northern and southern Panama. Panama is connected with Colombia by a ferry service. In the mid-1960's about 700 vessels were registered; most were owned by foreign shipping companies attracted to Panama by low registration fees.

PANAMA

Fifty radio stations and three television stations were operating in the late 1960's. Two of the thirteen daily newspapers are published in English, and a third has an English edition. The combined circulation was more than 148,000.

Labor. The labor force comprises one third of the total population. More than 45 percent of the workers are employed in agriculture, and about 20 percent in services. Of the remainder, some 20 percent are in manufacturing, construction, and commerce; and about 5 percent are employed in the Panama Canal Zone. The country has several trade unions.

GOVERNMENT

Panama is officially a centralized democracy, under a constitution adopted in 1946.

Central Government. The constitution of 1946 organized the government into executive, legislative, and judicial branches. The president is the head of state as well as of the government, and is assisted by a cabinet of eight members. The president and two vice-presidents are elected by direct popular vote for four-year terms. The constitution was suspended in October, 1968, following a military coup (see *History*, below).

HEALTH AND WELFARE. The Social Security Fund, established by the government, offers medical service and hospitalization, as well as maternity care, for disability and old age pensions, and funeral benefits. Social services, including child welfare, social work, housing, and recreation for tuberculosis victims, are provided through other government offices.

Legislature. The unicameral national assembly has forty-two deputies. The deputies are elected on a proportional basis, by direct popular vote, for terms of four years. When the assembly is in recess, some nine months each year, its functions are exercised by a permanent legislative commission of seven members elected by the assembly prior to adjournment.

Political Parties. In the late 1960's the National Liberal, the National Union, and the Christian Democratic parties were the major political groups. Frequently, coalitions of the many splinter groups were formed. These, and all other political parties, were banned in February, 1969.

Local Government. The nine provinces are divided into sixty-three municipal districts; each province is administered by a governor who is appointed by the president. The mayors and councilmen of each district are elected for four-year terms by direct popular vote.

Judiciary. The supreme court is composed of nine justices appointed by the president, a new justice being appointed every two years for a term of eighteen years. The judicial system also includes two superior courts, several circuit courts, and a number of municipal courts.

Defense. Panama is dependent on the U.S. for defense because the country maintains no military forces of its own. The national guard, a police force, with an authorized strength of 4700, is responsible for internal order.

HISTORY

The first European to land on what is now Panama was the Spanish explorer Rodrigo de Bastidas (b. about 1460), who in 1501 went ashore at the site of Porto Bello. A year later the Genoese-born navigator Christopher Columbus (q.v.) touched on the Panamanian coast. In 1508

A Panamanian woman makes an embroidered blouse. Handicrafts are popular items in the important tourist trade of Panama. UPI

PANAMA

Ferdinand V (q.v.), King of Castile assigned lands including Panama to the Spanish explorer Diego de Nicuesa, or Diego de Niuesa (1465–1511). Panama assumed importance in 1513 when Vasca Núñez de Balboa (q.v.) discovered the Pacific.

During the succeeding decades of the 16th century the region was entirely conquered by Spain. In 1718 it became part of the viceroyalty of New Granada; see COLOMBIA: History. The isthmus became the route of nearly all traffic to and from Peru and the neighboring colonies; treasure was shipped to the city of Panamá, taken overland to Porto Bello, and there transferred to galleons bound for Spain. English mariners and buccaneers tried continually during the 16th and 17th centuries to cut the isthmus route, capture its terminals, or seize the shipments. The most notable of these mariners were Sir Francis Drake and Sir Henry Morgan (qq.v.).

Colombian Rule. Panama declared itself independent of Spain in 1821 and voluntarily became a part of Colombia. The union was never firm, however, because of the special position of Panama as an interoceanic trade route. In 1830 discontent with Colombian rule led to the first of a long series of revolts. In the most important of these outbreaks, that of 1840, Panama briefly threw off Colombian rule, but in 1842 Colombia reestablished its authority.

In 1846 the Bidlach treaty between the United States and Colombia gave the U.S. transportation rights across the Panamanian isthmus in return for American recognition of Colombian sovereignty in Panama. During the 1840's the isthmus was used as a land bridge by Americans migrating to Oregon and California from the east coast of the U.S. In 1848 an American company was granted rights to build a railroad across the isthmus; construction, begun in 1850, was completed in 1855. Panama won from Colombia a large measure of self-rule in 1855, and in 1863 a new Colombian constitution gave each of its provinces, including Panama, virtual independence. In 1886, however, direct control by Colombia was restored; subsequently numerous unsuccessful revolts against Colombia took place, partly because of repressive and corrupt rule by Colombian officials and partly because many Panamanians were dissatisfied with the progress of negotiations for the building of a canal across the isthmus.

Independence. On Nov. 8, 1903, when the Colombian legislature failed to ratify a treaty with the U.S. concerning the canal, panama proclaimed its independence and was immediately recognized by the U.S. On Nov. 18, the U.S. and Panama signed a treaty giving the U.S. the right to build the canal and the perpetual right to occupy and control a strip of land on either side. In return the U.S. paid Panama $10,000,000 and agreed to pay $250,000 each year. The U.S. also guaranteed the independence of Panama, and was given the right to intervene in case of military disorder in Panama. Nationalist political factions resented the last-named provision, which became an issue in Panamanian politics.

American Interventionism. In 1904 a constituent assembly drafted the first Panamanian constitution, which provided for a democratically elected government with a president, two vice-presidents, a supreme court, and a unicameral legislature. The Panamanian physician and nationalist leader Manuel Amador Guerrero (1833–1909) was elected the first president of the republic. During the building of the Panama Canal from 1907 to 1914 and for years afterward, American troops repeatedly intervened to maintain peace in Panama. The exigencies of World War I, which Panama entered on the Allied side in April, 1917, intensified U.S. intervention in Panamanian affairs.

The Panama Canal. The opening of the Panama Canal (q.v.), which was put into limited use in 1914 and formally inaugurated in 1920, marked the beginning of a new era of prosperity in Panama. Internal political ferment continued undiminished throughout the 1920's, however, and nationalist agitation against the U.S. increased despite a marked lessening of U.S. military and political activity in Panama.

A revolutionary group headed by Harmodio Arias (1886–1962) seized power in 1931, but the U.S. did not exercise its rights to intervene. Arias was elected president in 1932. Relations between the two countries improved during the next few years. In 1934, when the U.S. devaluated the dollar, Panama refused the cheaper currency as payment of the annual $250,000 fee for the Canal Zone, thus precipitating a sharp controversy. Subsequent negotiations between the two countries resulted in 1936 in settlement of this dispute in favor of Panama, and in a general revision of the 1903 agreement. By the terms of the new treaty, ratified by the U.S. Senate in 1939, the U.S. received the right to send troops into Panamanian territory in an emergency for the purpose of defending the Panama Canal. At the same time, the U.S. surrendered the right to intervene in the internal affairs of Panama, and the U.S. guarantee of Panamanian independence was not renewed. Panama obtained various commercial rights under the provisions of the treaty.

PANAMA CANAL

In 1941 President Arnulfo Arias (1897–), sympathetic to the Axis powers (q.v.), was ousted and exiled. Panama entered World War II on the Allied side in December, 1942. In 1945 Panama became a member of the United Nations. During the war years the economy boomed, partly because a number of U.S. bases were established in the country. All the bases were evacuated in 1948 after the Panamanian legislature rejected a ten-year lease agreement.

Relations with the United States. A treaty of Aug. 23, 1955, between Panama and the U.S. provided that the annual U.S. payment for use of Panamanian territory in the Canal Zone would be increased from $430,000 to $1,930,000. During 1956 opposition groups within the government agitated vigorously for another increase in the canal revenues paid to Panama. Extremists, who demanded nationalization of the canal, were particularly outspoken following nationalization of the Suez Canal by Egypt in July. Throughout 1957 the controversy over canal revenues continued unabated. Many government officials, notably President Ernesto de la Guardia (1904–61), upheld traditional U.S. prerogatives in the Canal Zone and denounced Panamanians favoring nationalization of the canal. Numerous opposition groups affirmed the right of Panama to sovereignty within the Canal Zone, however, and threatened eventual nationalization of the canal. In early November, 1959, mass demonstrations against the U.S. were staged in Panama. United States flags were torn down, U.S. agencies were stoned, and repeated attempts were made to invade the Canal Zone. Riots occurred again in late November, allegedly influenced by Cuban revolutionists.

To allay resentment over U.S. operation of the canal, U.S. President Dwight David Eisenhower (q.v.), in September, ordered the Panamanian flag raised alongside that of the U.S. in the Canal Zone.

Rioting among U.S. and Panamanian students in January, 1964, over the raising of national flags in front of a Balboa school, was quelled by U.S. military forces. The incident led to suspension of diplomatic relations between the U.S. and Panama from Jan. 10 to Apr. 4, and to an acknowledgment by the U.S. that Panamanian grievances warranted review. In elections held on May 10, Marco Aurelio Robles (1906–) was elected president; his supporters won 28 of the 42 national assembly seats, and Robles took office Oct. 1. In 1965 Robles prevented nationalist elements from rioting over the canal issue and opened negotiations with the U.S. on Canal Zone problems. In June, 1967, Panama and the U.S. agreed on three new draft treaties governing the control, defense, and neutrality of the Panama Canal, and the possible construction of a new sea-level canal between the Atlantic and Pacific Oceans. In September, 1970, however, Panama formally rejected three drafts proposed by the U.S. for revising the Panama Canal treaty. In June, 1971, negotiations were begun on a new treaty governing the Canal Zone.

On Oct. 11, 1968, the national guard overthrew President Arnulfo Arias, who had been elected in May and been in office for only two weeks.

A civilian cabinet and provisional president were appointed to hold office until new elections could be held. The real power, however, remained in the hands of the military junta, led by Brigadier General Omar Torrijos Herrara, commander of the national guard. In 1970 major reforms in the banking system were introduced to promote Panama as a major financial center of Latin America. Despite economic gains and relative political stability, the Herrara government continued to restrict and censor severely dissent.

PANAMÁ, city, port, and capital of the Republic of Panama, on the Gulf of Panamá, an arm of the Pacific Ocean, 47 miles S.E. of Colón. The city, the largest in the country, is built on a coral peninsula which juts into the gulf; its harbor is shallow, and the town of Balboa, at the Pacific extremity of the Panama Canal (q.v.), serves as its port. The location of the city at the s. end of the Panama Railroad, which was completed in 1855, and the Panama Canal, finished in 1914, brought prosperity to the city. Industries include the production of beer, shoes, clothing, furniture, bakery goods, and beverages. The city was founded in 1519. Its cathedral, completed in 1776, has twin towers, and domes encased in mother-of-pearl. During the 17th and 18th centuries Panamá was the principal Spanish port on the Pacific Ocean. In 1671 it was captured and destroyed by the English buccaneer Sir Henry Morgan (q.v.), and was later rebuilt on a new site about 5 miles w. of the original site. Pop. (1968 est.) 373,200.

PANAMA CANAL, canal joining the Atlantic and Pacific oceans across the Isthmus of Panama. From the shore of the Atlantic to the shore of the Pacific the canal is slightly more than 40 mi. long, not including the dredged approach channels at either end.

Location and Structure. The approach to the canal from the Atlantic is along 4.5 mi. of dredged channel. The bottom of this channel, which extends due south, is 41 ft. below mean

295

PANAMA CANAL

low-water level and is 500 ft. in width. The canal then proceeds at sea level for 6.9 mi., veering slightly westward before reaching the Gatun Locks. Ships are lifted 85 ft. by these three locks, to the level of Gatun Lake. The lake was formed as a result of the damming of the Chagres R. by the Gatun Dam, which adjoins the locks. The crest of this dam is 1.5 mi. in length and 105 ft. above sea level. The Gatun Locks open directly into one another and are double, as are the other locks, so that one ship can be raised while another is being lowered. All the locks on the canal have a usable length of 1000 ft. and a usable width of 110 ft.

From the Gatun Locks the canal passes through Gatun Lake in a south and southeasterly direction to the mouth of Gaillard Cut (formerly called Culebra Cut), an excavated channel 8.1 mi. long. At the end of the Gaillard Cut is the Pedro Miguel Lock, which has a drop of 31 ft. The lock communicates with Miraflores Lake, which is 55 ft. above the level of the Pacific. The canal passes 1.3 mi. through Miraflores Lake and reaches the two Miraflores Locks. These locks lower ships to Pacific tidewater level. From the Miraflores Locks the canal runs 2.5 mi. to Balboa on the Gulf of Panamá, from which a dredged channel extends approximately 5 mi. out into the bay. In addition to the canal itself, auxiliary works include the Madden Dam on the Chagres R., east of the canal, which provides a reservoir to maintain the level of Gatun Lake during the dry season; breakwaters to protect the channels at either end of the canal; hydroelectric plants at the Gatun and Madden dams; and the Panama Railway that extends 47.6 mi. from Colón at the Atlantic end of the canal to the city of Panamá on the Pacific. Facilities for commercial shipping and naval vessels are located at both ends of the canal.

Early History. Interest in a short route from the Atlantic to the Pacific began with the explorers of Central America early in the 16th century. Hernando Cortes (q.v.), the Spanish conqueror of Mexico, suggested a canal across the Isthmus of Tehuantepec, and other explorers favored canal routes through Nicaragua and Darién. The first project for a canal through the Isthmus of Panamá was initiated by Charles V (q.v.), Holy Roman Emperor, who, in 1523, ordered a survey of the isthmus. The first actual working plan for a canal was drawn up in 1529, but was not submitted to the king. In 1534 a local Spanish official suggested a canal route utilizing the valley of the Chagres R., essentially the route of the present canal. Later, several other canal plans were suggested, but no action was taken.

After the accession of Philip II (q.v.) to the Spanish throne in 1556, the Spanish government abandoned its interest in the canal project, apparently because it was reluctant to incur the enmity of other European powers by assuming control of a short route to Asia. In the early 19th century, the books of the German scientist and traveler Baron Alexander von Humboldt (q.v.) revived interest in the possibility of a canal, and in 1819 the Spanish government formally authorized the construction of a canal and the creation of a company to build it. Nothing came of this effort and within ten years the revolt of the Spanish colonies in the Americas had taken control of possible canal sites out of the hands of the Spanish. From about 1825 the republics of Central America endeavored to interest groups in the United States and Europe in the building of a canal, and the canal became a subject of perennial debate in the United States Congress.

U.S. Interest. The discovery of gold in California in 1848 and the rush of would-be miners stimulated U.S. interest in the possibility of constructing a canal. Various surveys made between 1850 and 1875 indicated that only two canal routes were practical, the route across Panamá and a route across Nicaragua. In 1876 an international company was organized which two years later obtained a concession from the Colombian government to build a canal across the isthmus.

The international company was not successful and in 1880 a French company, the Panama Canal Company, was organized which took over the concession of the earlier company. This organization, under Ferdinand Marie de Lesseps (q.v.), the builder of the Suez Canal, spent eight years in an unavailing attempt to push a sea-level canal across the isthmus, and went bankrupt in 1889. In 1894 the company was reorganized and recommended work on the canal but was limited in its accomplishment by lack of funds.

In the meantime in the U.S., interest in an Atlantic-Pacific canal continued. In 1889 a U.S. company began work on a canal across Nicaragua but succumbed during the depression of 1893. In 1899 the U.S. Congress created an Isthmian Canal Commission to examine the possibilities of a Central American canal and to recommend a route. The commission first decided upon the Nicaraguan route, but reversed its decision in 1902 when the second Panama Canal Company offered its assets to the U.S. at a price of $40,000,000; see HAY-PAUNCEFOTE TREATY. The U.S. government negotiated with the Colombian government to obtain a strip of land 6 mi.

The Miraflores Lock of the Panama Canal is viewed from the Atlantic side as a ship is passing through.
Agence France Presse

wide across the isthmus, but the Colombian senate refused to ratify the treaty embodying this concession. In 1903, however, Panama revolted from Colombia. That same year the U.S. and the new state of Panama signed the Hay-Buneau-Varilla Treaty by which the U.S. guaranteed the independence of Panama and secured a perpetual lease on a 10-mi. strip for the canal. Panama was to be compensated by an initial payment of $10,000,000 and an annuity of $250,000, beginning in 1913. The figure was increased to $430,000 in 1939 and $1,930,000 in 1955. *See* PANAMA: *History: Relations with the United States.*

Construction. In 1905 the Isthmian Canal Commission decided to build a canal with locks rather than a sea-level channel, and this plan was approved by the U.S. Congress the following year. After unsuccessful attempts to obtain satisfactory bids from private contractors, the commission was reorganized and in 1907 President Theodore Roosevelt (q.v.) put the construction work under the direction of the United States Army Corps of Engineers. Colonel George Washington Goethals (q.v.) was named to head the project.

The construction of the canal ranks as one of the greatest engineering works of all time. It was estimated that the canal would be completed in ten years; however, it was in operation by the summer of 1914. The construction of the canal involved not only the excavation of an estimated 175,000,000 cu. yd. of earth but also the sanitation of the entire canal area, which was infested with the mosquitoes that spread yellow fever and malaria. The heavy incidence of these diseases was one of the chief reasons for the failure of the French companies to complete the canal. The sanitation work was undertaken by Colonel William Crawford Gorgas (q.v.) of the U.S. Army Medical Corps, who was named a member of the canal commission in 1907, and was so successful that the diseases were virtually eliminated. An unexpected difficulty in the actual construction of the canal was the prevalence of slides of earth from the banks of the canal, particularly in the Gaillard Cut. The reexcavation of the Panama Canal after such slides added about 25 percent to the estimated amount of earth moved. The final cost of the canal was $366,650,000.

One of the most important recent pieces of construction work is the $20,000,000 Thatcher Ferry Bridge, which spans the Pacific entrance to the canal and provides a vital link in the Pan American Highway (q.v.). This high-level 5425-ft.-long span was dedicated in 1962. The widening of the 8.5-mi.-long Gaillard Cut from 300 ft. to a width of 500 ft. was completed in 1970.

PANAMA CANAL ZONE

Work on the final 3-mi. stretch of the cut was finished in the summer of 1970. Completion of the project, which permits two-way traffic throughout the entire cut, was marked by a ceremony and a symbolic final blast. The widening project will permit, for the first time, two-way passage through the Gaillard Cut.

Statistics. About 434,080 ships passed through the canal from the time of its opening in 1914 to June 30, 1970. Cargo for the same period totaled 2,053,131,634 tons. During the fiscal year 1970–71, 15,348 oceangoing vessels passed through the canal, carrying about 121,000,000 long tons of cargo. Tolls for both oceangoing and smaller vessels totaled $100,566,541. Tolls are levied on the basis of each 100 cu. ft. of space of actual earning capacity, which is the so-called Panama Canal measurement.

PANAMA CANAL ZONE, strip of land and associated water areas crossing the Isthmus of Panama (see PANAMA, ISTHMUS OF), and extending about 5 mi. on either side of the center line of the canal and 3 marine mi. beyond the low-water mark in the Atlantic and Pacific oceans. The zone does not include the cities of Colón and Panamá, which belong to the Republic of Panama. By the terms of the Hay-Bunau-Varilla Treaty concluded on Nov. 18, 1903, Panama granted to the United States in perpetuity the use, occupation, and control of the Canal Zone for the construction, maintenance, operation, sanitation, and protection of the canal. A new treaty, signed on March 2, 1936 (ratified by the U.S. Senate on July 25, 1939), revised and amended the 1903 convention; see PANAMA: *History: Panama Canal.* Under the Panama Canal Act of 1951 the Zone is administered by the Canal Zone Government under a governor appointed by the President of the U.S., with the advice and consent of the Senate. The canal and its related commercial enterprises are operated by the Panama Canal Company, a self-sustaining government corporation. Balboa Heights is the administrative center.

Most of the population is engaged in the operation and maintenance of the canal and the Panama Railroad. The total area of the Canal Zone is 648 sq.mi., including 276 sq.mi. of inland waters. The population of the zone (1970) was 44,198, of whom about 40,000 were U.S. citizens; 15,300 persons, including 4100 Americans, were full-time employees of the Panama Canal Company.

PANAMA CITY, city and port of entry in Florida, and county seat of Bay Co., on Saint Andrew Bay, 7 miles from the Gulf of Mexico, and 95 miles S.E. of Pensacola. It is a fishing center and resort; many fishing, boating, and bathing facilities are nearby. The center of a large lumbering and paper-milling industry started in the 1700's, the city also manufactures soft drinks, food (especially fish) products, marine parts, ice, aluminum products, and concrete. Peat deposits lie in the vicinity. The city is the site of Gulf Coast Junior College (1957), and nearby are a Navy mine laboratory, Tyndall Air Force Base, and Saint Andrew State Park. Settled by British Tories before and during the American Revolution, Saint Andrew, now the western residential end of Panama City, became a base for blockade runners and a salt-producing center in the Civil War. The city was merged with Millville and St. Andrew and incorporated in 1909. Pop. (1960) 33,275; (1970) 32,096.

PANAMA, ISTHMUS OF, connecting link between Central and South America, comprising the independent Republic of Panama and the Canal Zone, belonging to the United States. It is bounded on the N. by the Caribbean Sea and Costa Rica and on the S. by the Gulf of Panamá, the Pacific Ocean, and Colombia.

It is said to have been discovered by Spanish explorer Rodrigo de Bastidas (1460–1526) about 1500, but the first exploration was made in 1502 by the Italian navigator Christopher Columbus (q.v.), who entered what is now Porto Bello and established a colony there. The Spanish explorer Vasco Núñez de Balboa (q.v.), crossed the isthmus to discover the Pacific Ocean on Sept. 26, 1513.

PAN-AMERICAN CONFERENCES. See INTER-AMERICAN CONFERENCES.

PAN-AMERICAN GAMES, quadrennial, amateur sports competitions for athletes from the Western Hemisphere. The games were conceived in 1940, during a meeting of the Pan-American Congress in Buenos Aires, Argentina, as a means of establishing closer bonds among athletes from the Americas.

The first games were to have taken place in Buenos Aires in 1942, but these plans were set aside because of World War II and the games did not begin until 1951 in Buenos Aires. Subsequent games took place in 1955 in Mexico City, Mexico; in 1959 in Chicago, Ill.; in 1963 in São Paulo, Brazil; and in 1967 in Winnipeg, Canada.

The games are conducted by the Pan-American Sports Organization under rules of the International Olympic Committee and of the various international federations that govern individual sports. The number of sports has ranged from 18 to 22, the number of nations from 20 to 28, and the number of athletes from 1600 to 2400.

At the conclusion of the 1951 games Argentina had won 66 gold medals for first places, 20 more than the U.S. Since then, the U.S. has won a majority of the gold medals in each of the games held: 87 of 148 in 1955, 120 of 163 in 1959, 109 of 158 in 1963, and 120 of 171 in 1967.

PAN AMERICAN HIGHWAY, system of highways extending from Alaska through South America. The northern section of the route, beginning in Fairbanks, Alaska, and continuing to the city of Dawson Creek, in British Colombia, Canada, is called the Alcan Highway or Alaska Highway (q.v.). In Mexico and Central America, the segment known as the Inter-American Highway (q.v.) runs from Laredo, Texas, to the city of Panamá, Panama. The Alaska and the Inter-American highways are connected by routes in the United States and Canada. One section of the Pan American Highway remains unfinished: a stretch of approximately 550 mi., mostly jungle, between the city of Panamá and the highway system in Colombia. In 1971 Colombia began a ferry service to transport cars and passengers from Colón, just north of Panamá, to Turbo on the eastern coast of Colombia; the ferry service was established to provide a transportation route until the highway connecting the two countries was completed.

In South America the highway follows the west coast of the continent to Santiago, Chile, turning east across the Andes (q.v.) Mts. to Buenos Aires, Argentina. The Simon Bolivar Highway forms an important northern branch of the highway system, connecting the Atlantic port of La Guaira, near Caracas, Venezuela, with Bogotá, Colombia. From Buenos Aires, the main highway extends up the east coast of South America through Montevideo, Uruguay, to Rio de Janeiro, Brazil. A central branch leads from Buenos Aires to Asunción, Paraguay, where the highway joins a new transverse route. The latter makes possible a coast-to-coast connection from Paranaguá, Brazil, via Asunción and La Paz, Bolivia, to Lima, Peru. Another transverse route will connect Lima and Brasilia, the capital of Brazil. A recent addition to the system is the Bolivariana Highway, extending from Maracaibo, Venezuela, and linking the inner regions of Bolivia, Colombia, Ecuador, Paraguay, and Peru. Other new highways will reach Punta Arenas, Chile, on the Strait of Magellan, and Ushuaia, Argentina, near the southern tip of South America, in Tierra del Fuego.

Since the first Pan American Highway Congress at Buenos Aires in 1925, the U.S. has cooperated with Latin-American countries in planning and building the international highway system. Subsequent congresses have been held every three years to plan the system and to facilitate the movement of international traffic.

PAN-AMERICANISM. See INTER-AMERICAN CONFERENCES; ORGANIZATION OF AMERICAN STATES; PAN-AMERICAN GAMES; PAN AMERICAN HIGHWAY; PAN AMERICAN UNION.

PAN AMERICAN UNION, international organization of the United States and twenty Latin American republics. It was established on April 14, 1890, in accordance with a resolution adopted by the First International Conference of American States for the purpose of promoting peace, friendship, and commerce among the member republics; see INTER-AMERICAN CONFERENCES. April 14 is now celebrated as Pan American Day in those countries. The organization was first called the Commercial Bureau of the American Republics; the present name was adopted in 1910 by a resolution of the fourth inter-American conference. In 1948 the Pact of Bogotá established the Organization of American States (q.v.), known as O.A.S., and designated the Pan American Union as the central organ and general secretariat of the new organization. The governing board of the union became the Council of the Organization of American States.

The Pan American Union, presided over by the secretary-general of the O.A.S., is divided into nine departments, covering economics, social problems, legal matters, cultural affairs, administration, science, technical cooperation, statistics, and public information. The union serves as a permanent secretariat for the O.A.S. council and its various organs. It is also a center for research and for dissemination of information on subjects affecting the interests and welfare of the American nations. Under the amendments to the charter of the O.A.S., which will become effective when two thirds of the O.A.S. member nations ratify them, the name of the union will be changed to General Secretariat of the O.A.S.

Headquarters of the union and the O.A.S. are in the Pan American Union Building in Washington, D.C., donated by the American industrialist and philanthropist Andrew Carnegie (q.v.), who was a delegate to the first inter-American conference. The union also has offices in capital cities of nineteen of the member nations and one office in Europe.

PANATHENAEA, oldest and most famous festival of Athens, celebrated in honor of Athena (q.v.), patron goddess of the city. Ancient writers speak of a Lesser and a Greater Panathenaea, the former held annually, the latter every fourth year. A patriotic as well as a religious festival, the Panathenaea included processions, dances, sacrifices, poetry, recitations, and musical and athletic contests. One of these processions, a march by the people to the temple of Athena, was depicted upon the frieze of the Parthenon (q.v.). See FESTIVALS AND FEASTS: *Ancient Greek Festivals*.

PANAY, U.S.S., river gunboat of the United States Navy which was sunk by Japanese naval aircraft on Dec. 12, 1937, in the Yangtze R., 28 miles N. of Nanking, China, precipitating a diplomatic crisis between Japan and the United States. The incident occurred, five months after the outbreak of the Sino-Japanese War (see CHINA: *History*), despite the fact that the *Panay* was outside the active area of hostilities and flew the U.S. flag. Seventy survivors were rescued by American and British gunboats. Three American tankers were also sunk in the same attack.

Two days later the Japanese government complied in full with a note issued by the U.S. government requesting a full apology for the attack; and full reparations were subsequently made by the Japanese government for loss of lives and property.

PANAY, island in the Republic of the Philippines, the northernmost of the Visayan Islands, about 10 miles N.W. of Negros Island and about 40 miles S.E. of Mindoro Island. The sixth-largest island in the Philippines, Panay is bounded by the Sibuyan Sea on the N., the Visayan Sea on the E., the Sulu Sea on the S., and the Cuyo East Passage on the W. The Panay plain in the E.-central part of the island is the primary agricultural region of Panay; rice and sugar are produced here. Coconuts are grown in the N. and N.E. and corn is planted in the mountainous interior. Fishing, copper mining, sugar processing, and the manufacture of handicrafts, particularly piña or pineapple fiber, are important industries on the island. Panay is comprised of four provinces, Aklan, Antique, Capiz, and Iloilo, which includes neighboring Guimaras I. The cities of Iloilo in the S. and Roxas in the N. are connected by railroad and are the major commercial centers of Panay. The municipality of Panay was the first Spanish settlement on the island. The island, about 95 mi. long and 75 mi. wide, was bombed by the Allies in 1944. Area, 4749 sq.mi.; pop. (1964 est.) 2,015,000.

PANCHATANTRA, oldest extant collection of fables, primarily animal, in Sanskrit literature (q.v.), dating from before 500 A.D. It is believed to be the work of the Indian writer Bidpai (q.v.). The work is composed of five books compiled from Buddhist sources, and was originally intended to educate noblemen and princes to behave in a way consistent with ethical standards.

PANCHEN LAMA. See LAMAISM; TIBET: *People and Religion; History*.

PANCREAS, conglomerate gland lying transversely across the posterior wall of the abdomen, varying in length from 6 to 8 in., having a breadth of about 1½ in., and a thickness of from ½ in. to 1 in. Its usual weight is about 3 oz. The head of the pancreas lies in the concavity of the duodenum. The pancreas has both an exocrine and an endocrine secretion. The exocrine secretion is made up of a number of enzymes which are discharged into the intestine to aid in digestion. The endocrine secretion, insulin (q.v.), is important in the metabolism of sugar in the body; see SUGAR, METABOLISM OF. Insulin is produced in small groups of especially modified glandular cells in the pancreas; these cell groups are known as the islets of Langerhans. The failure of these cells to secrete sufficient amounts of insulin causes diabetes; see DIABETES MELLITIS. In 1968 a team of surgeons at the medical school of the University of Minnesota performed the first pancreas transplants on four diabetics, using the pancreases of cadavers.

Diseases of the pancreas are not common. Hemorrhage in the pancreas and acute pancreatitis are, however, serious conditions, and if not relieved rapidly may cause death. The symptoms are not definite, resembling those of peritonitis or intestinal obstruction. The pancreas of such ruminant animals as calves is a favorite article of food under the name "sweetbread".

See also ENDOCRINE SYSTEM: *Pancreas;* HORMONES: *Hormones in Animals*.

PANDA, common name of a mammal *Ailurus fulgens,* of the raccoon (q.v.) family that lives in bamboo forests at great altitude in the Himalaya

Giant pandas, Ailuropoda melanoleuca

Camera Press – Pix

Mts. Like a large cat in size, it has thick reddish-brown fur, high pointed ears, stout plantigrade limbs, with large, slightly retractile claws, and woolly soles. The bushy tail is almost as long as the body, and has inconspicuous rings of red and yellow. The rare giant panda, *Ailuropoda melanoleuca*, belongs to the same family as the common or lesser panda, but differs widely from it in appearance. A bearlike mammal, the giant panda is white with black markings and has a short tail. It inhabits Tibet and western China.

PANDARUS, in Greek mythology, Lycian who fought as an ally of the Trojans in the Trojan War (q.v.). He was a famous archer, and broke the truce between the Greeks and the Trojans by wounding Menelaus (q.v.), King of Sparta. Pandarus was later slain by the Greek hero Diomedes (q.v.).

PANDIT, Vijaya Lakshmi (1900–), Indian political leader and diplomat, sister of the Indian statesman Jawaharlal Nehru (q.v.), born in Allahabad, and educated at the University of Allahabad. In 1921 she became the wife of the Indian lawyer and nationalist leader Ranjit Sitaram Pandit (1890–1943). In the early 1920's, as a strong partisan of the Indian nationalist leader Mohandas Karamchand Gandhi (q.v.), she joined the civil-disobedience movement against British rule; she subsequently served three terms in prison for her nationalist activities. Active in local politics in Allahabad, in 1937 Mrs. Pandit was elected to the provincial legislature of the United Provinces and designated minister of local self-government and public health. She held the latter post until 1939 and again from 1946 to 1947, the first woman in India to become a minister. Mrs. Pandit was Indian Union ambassador to the U.S.S.R. (1947–49) and ambassador to the United States (1949–51), the first woman ambassador to hold that rank in either country. During this period she also headed the Indian delegation to the United Nations (1946–48; 1952). While a member of the Indian parliament (1952–54) she was chosen president of the U.N. General Assembly (1953). She became Indian high commissioner to Great Britain and served concurrently as ambassador to Ireland (1955–61) and to Spain (1958–61). From 1962 to 1964 she was governor of Maharashtra State, and from 1964 to 1968 she again served in the Indian parliament.

PANDORA, in Greek mythology, first woman on earth, created by the god Hephaestus at the request of the god Zeus (q.v.). Zeus wished to counteract the blessing of fire, which had been stolen from the gods by the Titan Prometheus (q.v.) and given to man. Endowed by the gods with every attribute of beauty and goodness, Pandora was sent to Epimetheus, who was happy to have her for his wife, although he had been warned by his brother Prometheus never to accept anything from Zeus. In bestowing their gifts upon Pandora, the gods had given her a box, warning her never to open it. Her curiosity finally overcame her, however, and she opened the mysterious box, from which flew innumerable plagues for the body and sorrows for the mind. In terror, she tried to shut the box, but only Hope, the one good thing among many evils the box had contained, remained to comfort mankind in his misfortunes. According to another legend, the box contained blessings that would have been preserved for the benefit of mortals if Pandora had not allowed them to escape.

PANGOLIN, or SCALY ANTEATER, common name for several genera that make up the only family, Manidae, in the mammalian order Pholidota. Pangolins, native to Asia and Africa, are brown in color and range in length from about 3 to 5 ft. The animal resembles an enormous pine cone, being almost completely covered with overlapping horny scales. For protection the pangolin rolls up in a ball and raises its scales, which are very sharp on the edges; it may also lash out at an enemy with its tail. The pangolin is toothless but has a long, thin, sticky tongue with which it picks up ants and termites. The front feet have long, rakelike claws adapted for ripping open termite nests.

PANIC, FINANCIAL, in economics, crisis condition, marked by emotional and overpowering alarm, in financial or commercial circles, or in both, leading to a sudden and drastic restriction of credit and great shrinkage in commodity and property prices. A panic usually precipitates a wave of business failures and may be followed by a period of depression; see BUSINESS CYCLE. Financial panics are frequently the result of an undue expansion of bank loans, an overextension of commercial credits, widespread speculation, or unsound governmental fiscal policies.

The panic of 1907, brought on by questionable banking practices and a loss of confidence in the banking system, resulted in the establishment of the Federal Reserve System (q.v.). Widespread changes in stock-market regulation followed the crash in 1929; see EXCHANGE; SECURITIES AND EXCHANGE COMMISSION.

See also BLACK FRIDAY; LAW, JOHN; SOUTH SEA BUBBLE.

PANIPAT, city of the Republic of India, in Haryana State, 53 miles N. of Delhi. Panipat is a rail

301

junction and a center of trade in wool, grains, and cotton. Major industries include wool weaving and spinning and cotton ginning.

History. A city of great antiquity, Panipat is mentioned in the epic *Mahabharata* (q.v.), which recounts events believed to have occurred prior to the 10th century B.C. In later times Panipat was notable as the site of three historic battles. In the first, in 1526, the Mogul chief Baber (q.v.) conquered the forces of Sultan Ibrahim Lodi (d. 1526), the Afghan king of Delhi, thereby laying the foundation for the establishment of the Mogul dynasty in India. In the second battle at Panipat, in 1556, the Mogul emperor Akbar (q.v.), grandson of Baber, crushed an army of the Afghan house that had driven Baber's heirs from the throne, reestablishing the Mogul empire in India. In the third battle, in 1761, the Afghan ruler of Kandahar, Ahmad Shah (q.v.), routed an army of Marathas and Sikhs (qq.v.), and virtually destroyed the power of the Maratha confederacy in India. See INDIA: *History.* Pop. (1961) 67,026.

PANKHURST, Emmeline (1857–1928), British suffragette leader, born in Manchester, England. In 1879 she married the British barrister Dr. Richard Marsden Pankhurst (1839–98), who was involved in various reform movements including the fight for woman suffrage (q.v.). In 1889 Mrs. Pankhurst and her husband helped to found a woman-suffrage society. In 1903 Mrs. Pankhurst founded the Women's Social and Political Union, an organization that attracted worldwide notice for its resourceful militancy for women's suffrage prior to World War I. During her various periods in jail, Mrs. Pankhurst introduced the hunger strike, since used by other activists.

PANKOW, community of East Germany, in the northern part of East Berlin, adjoining the West Berlin border community of Reinickendorf. The surrounding area manufactures electrical equipment and food products. The city was the site of a prison-fortress in which war-crimes trial defendants were held after World War II. It later became the administrative center for the Soviet Zone of Germany. Pop. (1963 est.) 68,785.

PANMUNJOM. See KOREA: *History: Truce at Panmunjom;* KOREAN WAR.

PANNONIA, in ancient history, country bounded on the N. and E. by the Danube R., on the S. by Dalmatia, and on the W. by Noricum and parts of upper Italy, including parts of contemporary Austria, Hungary, and Yugoslavia. It received its name from the Pannonians, a people probably of Illyrian race. Octavian, later the Roman emperor Augustus (q.v.), invaded Pannonia in 35 B.C. As Augustus, he finally subdued the country in 9 B.C. and made it a part of Illyria, which had been conquered by the Romans in 168 B.C. An insurrection in 6 A.D. was suppressed, and the Pannonians moved to the N. part of the region, which in 10 A.D. was made a separate Roman province called Pannonia. Numerous fortresses were erected along its frontiers, military roads were constructed, and Roman colonies and municipalities were established. The province was divided in the beginning of the 2nd century A.D. by the Roman emperor Trajan (q.v.) into Upper Pannonia and Lower Pannonia. At the end of the 4th century A.D. the region was abandoned by Rome, after which it was held successively by the Huns (q.v.), Ostrogoths (*see* GOTHS), Lombards, Avars, and Slavs (qq.v.). The Magyars or Hungarians took possession of the area at the end of the 11th century.

See HUNGARY: *History: Ancient and Medieval History.*

PANSY (from Fr. *pensée,* "thought"), common name applied to the garden plant *Viola tricolor hortensis,* belonging to the violet (q.v.) family. One of the oldest known garden flowers, the pansy is believed to be a descendant of the wild violet, *V. tricolor,* a small perennial native to Europe. The wild plant has small, five-petaled, tricolored flowers, usually purple, blue, and yellow. Present-day strains of the garden plant are cultivated for large-sized flowers, about 3 in. in diameter, with many variations in coloring. Some strains have flowers of a single color; others are parti-colored. In the United States the pansy is grown as an annual. The markings of some varieties of pansy often resemble a human face.

PANTHEISM, mode of speculation that identifies the universe (Gr. *pan,* "all") with God (Gr. *theos*). The thinker may start from an awareness of the full reality of God and then seek to include an awareness of the relationship of the dependent reality of the nondivine to that of God; this position is commonly called acosmic pantheism. Conversely, the thinker may start from an apprehension of the full reality of finite, changing entities and give the name "God" to their all-inclusive unified totality; this is called cosmic pantheism.

The most typical presentations of acosmic pantheism come from the Hindu tradition (*see* HINDUISM), the greatest philosophical exponent of which was the Indian philosopher Sankara (fl. 9th cent. A.D.). The difficulties of acosmism are visible in his system: tendencies to deny the full reality of the changing finite, to deny the reality of evil, to deny the reality of freedom and chance, and to see individual personality as ultimately unreal.

In Western thought, the Dutch philosopher Baruch Spinoza (q.v.) is the greatest exponent of a position that is almost unqualifiedly pantheistic. His view represents an important criticism of the "orthodox" view that God's reality is somehow external to the reality of the world.

In fact, simple equations of "God" and "world" are hard to find in the major writings in philosophy or theology. Usually qualifications abound to cope with such traditional problems as those of the one and the many, good and evil, necessity and accident, and permanence and change. In the contemporary scene, a view termed "panentheism" has been espoused by some philosophers—including the American Charles Hartshorne (1897–)—who seek to overcome at once the paradoxes of pantheism and those of "classical" theism.   E.G.W.

PANTHEON. **1.** A temple dedicated to all the gods. The Pantheon of Rome is the only perfectly preserved edifice of ancient Rome. The great vaulted dome is about 142 ft. in diameter, and the entire structure is lighted through one aperture in the center of the dome. The Pantheon was erected by the Roman statesman Marcus Vipsanius Agrippa (q.v.) in 27 B.C. and was rebuilt by the Roman emperor Hadrian (q.v.) in the 2nd century A.D. In the early 7th century it was consecrated as a church, Santa Maria Rotonda.

2. A building that serves as a mausoleum or memorial for eminent men who have made outstanding contributions to their country. The most famous example is the Church of Sainte Geneviève in Paris, designed in the classical style by the French architect Jacques Germain Soufflot (1713–80) in 1764. It was later secularized, renamed the Pantheon, and used as a temple to honor the great men of France.

PANTHER. See LEOPARD; PUMA.

PANTOMIME, art of dramatic representation without words, by means of attitudes, gestures, facial expressions, and body movements. In the great open theaters of ancient Rome the public could see much better than it could hear, a fact that probably contributed to the popularity of mime or pantomime as a form of acting. The Romans applied the term *pantomimus* to an actor who used rhythmic gesture and various masks to relate mythological or heroic tales; *see* MASK.

Pantomimic elements have always been found in the theater, notably in the Italian commedia dell'arte (q.v.), in which the characters of Harlequin (q.v.), Pantalone, and Columbine were developed. In France and England in the early 18th century the word "pantomime" was applied to a kind of ballet spectacle in which allegorical characters appeared in costume to enact themes from classical mythology. In 18th-century England the harlequinade, in which dancing comics

Marcel Marceau, considered among the greatest of 20th-century pantomimists.   Ronald A. Wilford Assoc. Inc.

burlesqued pantomime ballet, became popular. The noted British harlequin John Rich (1692–1761) is generally credited with establishing the tradition of pantomime shows at Christmastime. English pantomime was further developed by the British pantomimist Joseph Grimaldi (q.v.), who was especially clever at inventing tricks and stage machinery. The current form of English pantomime, based on fairy-tale themes, frequently incorporates elements of the music hall. It is an elaborate spectacle and is no longer wordless.

In the United States, pantomime plays little part in dramatic history, except for *Humpty-Dumpty* (1868), which featured the American actor and pantomimist George Washington Lafayette Fox (1825–77). Early in the 20th century silent motion-picture actors relied entirely, in true pantomimic fashion, upon movement and facial expression to tell their story. Famous contemporary mimes include the British motion-picture actor Charles Spencer Chaplin and the French pantomimist Marcel Marceau (qq.v.).

PAOKI, city of the People's Republic of China, in Shensi Province, on the Wei R., about 100 miles w. of Sian. A road and rail hub on the

Lunghai Railroad, it is the trade center of an agricultural area growing wheat, millet, cotton, and beans. The city has railroad shops and cotton-weaving, paper, flour, and vegetable-oil mills; it also manufactures railroad equipment and tobacco products. Nearby are the Wei, or Paoki, Gorges and the Chapingling waterfalls. The name is also spelled Pao-chi. Pop. (1958 est.) 180,000.

PAOLI, Pasquale di (1725–1807), Corsican patriot, born in Morosaglia. Paoli took part in the early struggles of his country against Genoa. In July, 1755, he was chosen president according to a republican constitution. Under his administration liberal reforms were made. When Genoa sold Corsica to France in 1768, Paoli fought for Corsican independence. After a year of fighting he was defeated by superior French forces at Ponte-Nuovo and he fled to England. In 1791, after the outbreak of the French Revolution, a political amnesty was declared. Paoli was recalled to Corsica and appointed governor. Unsympathetic with the radical trend of the French Revolution, in 1793 Paoli proclaimed Corsican independence. The British helped him defeat the French in 1794, but made Corsica a British protectorate. Instead of allowing Paoli to rule the British appointed a British viceroy, and in 1795 recalled Paoli to England, where he remained. In 1796 the Corsicans drove the British out with French aid.

PAOTING, formerly TSINGYÜAN, city of the People's Republic of China, in Hopei Province, 90 miles s.w. of Peking. It is a trade and railroad center; cotton cloth, pharmaceuticals, and handicrafts are manufactured here. Paoting is the seat of the Hopei Agricultural Institute, founded in 1902. The city dates from the 13th century. As capital of Hopei Province from 1911 to 1956, Paoting was an important administrative center. Pop. (1957 est.) 265,000.

PAOTOW, city of the People's Republic of China, in Inner Mongolian Autonomous Region, on the Hwang Ho R., about 300 miles N.W. of Peking. The city is in an area rich in coke, coal, and pig iron and contains one of the three largest steel-producing plants in China. Major industries include the smelting of pig iron and the production of machinery, textiles, and foodstuffs. Pop. (1957 est.) 400,000.

PAPACY, Roman Catholic system of church government, which theoretically and historically acknowledges the supremacy of the Roman pontiffs. The term is used also for the actual succession of persons and their administration of affairs in the supreme government of the Roman Catholic Church (q.v.). The doctrine of the papacy is that the pope is the successor of Saint Peter (q.v.), the vicar of Christ (see JESUS CHRIST), and the visible head of the Christian Church. See POPE.

PAPAL LEGATE, representative sent by the pope as his envoy to a sovereign, a government, or on a special mission. A *legate a latere* is a cardinal appointed to represent the pope at a specific function, usually one of international importance.

PAPAL STATES, or STATES OF THE CHURCH or PONTIFICAL STATES, territory of Italy formerly under direct temporal rule of the papacy; see POPE; ROMAN CATHOLIC CHURCH. The first papal lands were granted in 754 A.D. by the king of the Franks Pepin the Short to Pope Stephen III. Additions were made by gifts and purchases until the Papal States included nearly the whole of central Italy. Papal control reached its height late in the 12th century under Innocent III. The acquisitions of the papacy were for the most part retained until 1797, when French forces under Napoléon Bonaparte, later Napoleon I, Emperor of France, seized much of the territory. In 1801 Pope Pius VII regained some power, and in 1815 the Congress of Vienna, restored nearly all the territory of the States, under Austrian protection; see VIENNA, CONGRESS OF. The final dissolution of the Papal States came in 1870, when nearly all the territory, including Rome, was annexed to a united Italy by its king, Victor Emmanuel II. The jurisdiction of the pope was confined to the Vatican in which, as a protest against the Italian occupation, each succeeding pope remained a voluntary prisoner until 1929, when the Lateran Treaty (q.v.) recognized the full and independent sovereignty of the Holy See in the Vatican City (q.v.).

See separate articles for the individuals mentioned above.

PAPAW, common name applied to a small tropical and subtropical South American tree, *Carica papaya,* belonging to the Custard Apple family, Annonaceae. The juice of the fruit and the sap of the tree are used to tenderize tough meat. In the United States the name "papaw" is given to *Asimina triloba,* a small tree of the Custard Apple family. See PAPAYA.

PAPAYA, melonlike fruit of a small tree *Carica papaya,* belonging to the Papaw family, Caricaceae, grown widely throughout the tropical world. Indigenous to Central America and Mexico, the wild tree (actually a gigantic herb of tree size), is generally about 6 ft. tall, but under cultivation it may achieve a height of 25 ft. The papaya tree grows straight without branches like the palm and is crowned by large, deep-

Papaya, fruit of the tree
Carica papaya
Molly Adams –
National Audubon Society

lobed leaves. It produces male or female flowers and fruits before the end of the first year. The ripe fruit, which resembles the cantaloupe, is popular as a breakfast food in many warm countries; unripe, it is cooked as a vegetable. The sap of the tree, its leaves, and unripe fruit contain a digestive enzyme, papain, which acts similarly to the enzyme pepsin. Its value was recognized long ago in the tropics, where papaya juice is used as a meat tenderizer. The name "papaw" (q.v.), sometimes used for the papaya tree, is correctly applied to the North American tree, *Asimina triloba,* belonging to the Custard Apple family.

PAPEN, Franz von (1879–1969), German diplomat, born in Werl. He served as the German military attaché in Mexico from 1913 to 1915, when he was transferred to the German embassy in Washington, D.C. Later in 1915 he was recalled to Germany on the demand of Woodrow Wilson (q.v.), President of the United States, who accused him of activities harmful to the neutrality of the U.S. After World War I he became an influential publisher in Germany and was a Catholic Center Party member of the Prussian diet from 1921 to 1932. He was designated chancellor of Germany in May, 1932, but his ultraconservative administration aroused such opposition that he was forced to resign in November of the same year. In the ensuing period he played an important role in the rise to power of Adolf Hitler (q.v.), leader of the National Socialist Party. Hitler made him vice-chancellor in January, 1933. Von Papen was special minister, then ambassador, to Austria between 1934 and 1938. During World War II he served as ambassador to Turkey. He was tried in 1946 as a war criminal but was acquitted because of insufficient evidence; *see* War-Crimes Trials. In February, 1947, a German court sentenced him to eight years in prison, but in 1949 he was released because of his age and ill health. An English translation of his memoirs was published as *Memoirs* in 1953.

PAPER, material in the form of thin sheets manufactured by webbing types of vegetable cellulose fibers. Paper is used for writing and printing, for wrapping and packaging, and for a variety of special purposes ranging from the filtration of precipitates from solutions to the manufacture of certain types of building materials. In 20th-century civilization paper is a basic material, and the development of machinery for its high-speed production has been in a great measure responsible for the increase of literacy and the raising of the educational level of people throughout the world.

Hand Papermaking. The basic process of making paper has not changed in more than 2000 years. The process involves two stages: the breaking up of the raw material in water to form a suspension of individual fibers; and the formation of felted sheets by spreading this suspension on a suitable porous surface, through which excess water can drain.

In making paper by hand the raw material—straw, leaves, bark, rags, or other fibrous material—is placed in a vat or trough and is pounded with a heavy pestle or hammer to separate the fibers. During the first portion of this operation, the material is washed with running water to remove impurities, but after the fibers have been sufficiently broken up they are kept in suspension, and the water in the vat is not changed. At this stage the liquid material, called half stuff, is ready for the actual process of papermaking. The chief tool of the papermaker is the mold, a reinforced sheet of metal mesh having either a square mesh pattern, called a wove pattern; or a pattern of more widely spaced longitudinal wires held together with smaller transverse wires, called a laid pattern. The mold pattern imprints itself on the finished sheet of paper, and thus handmade papers that are not given special finishes are identified as wove or laid papers, depending upon the style of mold used in their making.

The mold is placed inside a removable

305

PAPER

In the manufacture of paper, logs are reduced to chips in seconds in the chipper, whose twelve blades rotate at 4000 revolutions per minute. Hammermill Paper Co.

wooden frame called a deckle, which forms a low rim around its edge. The papermaker dips the mold and deckle into a vat containing the half stuff; when he removes the mold and deckle from the vat, the surface of the mold is coated with a thin film of fiber-water mixture. He then shakes the device forward and backward and from side to side. This shaking has two effects; it distributes the mixture evenly on the surface of the mold and causes the individual fibers to interlock with those adjacent, giving strength to the sheet. While the device is being shaken, much of the water from the mixture drains out through the mold mesh. The device, with its formed sheet of wet paper, is then laid aside until the paper is sufficiently cohesive to permit the removal of the deckle.

After the deckle has been taken from the mold, the mold is turned over and the sheet of paper is laid smoothly on a sheet of woven woolen cloth called a felt. Another felt is laid over the sheet of paper, and the process is repeated; the process of placing the paper between two felts is known as couching. When a number of sheets of paper have been interleaved with felts, the entire pile, called a post, is placed in a hydraulic press and subjected to a pressure of 100 or more tons, expelling most of the water remaining in the paper. The sheets of paper are then separated from the felts, stacked, and pressed. The process of pressing the stack of paper is repeated several times, and each time the stack is built up in a different order with the individual sheets in different positions relative to one another. This procedure is called exchanging, and its repetition improves the surface of the finished paper. The final stage in papermaking is drying. The paper is hung, in groups of four or five sheets, over ropes in a special drying room until its moisture has almost completely evaporated.

Papers that are to be used for writing or printing with ink require additional treatment following drying, because without such treatment the paper would absorb ink and yield fuzzy lines or impressions. The treatment consists of sizing the paper by dipping it into a solution of animal glue, drying the sized paper, and finally finishing the paper by pressing the sheets between sheets of metal or smooth cardboard. The amount of pressing determines the texture of the surface of the paper. Rough-textured papers are pressed lightly for a comparatively short period of time, and smooth-surfaced papers are

Below left: The wood pulp, made by cooking the chips under pressure, undergoes three bleaching and washing stages until it is snow-white. Below right: In blenders, the pulp is mixed with dyestuffs, sizing, and fillers to produce the desired color and characteristics of the paper being manufactured. Hammermill Paper Co.

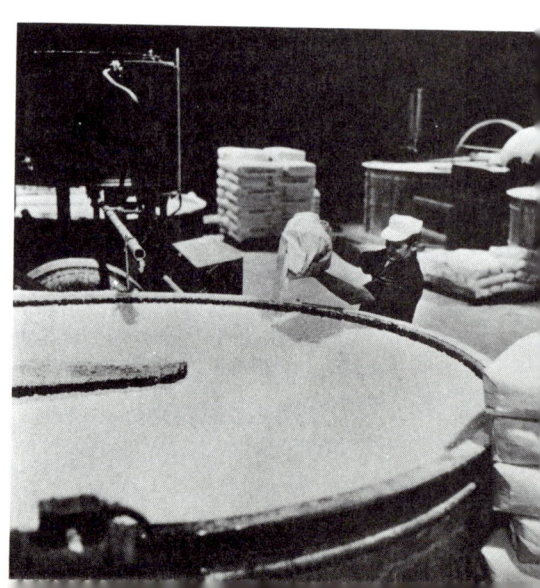

pressed heavily for comparatively long periods.

Machine Papermaking. Although the essential procedures of papermaking by machine are identical with those of hand papermaking, the former process is one of considerably more complexity. The first step in machine papermaking is the preparation of the raw material. The materials chiefly used in modern papermaking are cotton or linen rags and wood pulp. Today more than 95 percent of the paper made is from wood cellulose. For the cheapest grades of paper, such as newsprint, groundwood pulp alone is used; for better grades, chemical wood, pulp, or a mixture of pulp and rag fiber is employed; and for the finest papers, such as the highest grades of writing papers, rag fiber alone is used.

Rags used in the making of paper are first cleaned mechanically to remove dust and foreign matter. Following this cleaning, the rags are cooked in a large rotary boiler. This process involves boiling the rags with lime under steam pressure for a period of several hours. The lime combines with greases and other impurities in the rags to form nonsoluble soaps, which can be washed away in a later process, and at the same time reduces any colored dyes present to colorless compounds. The rags are then transferred to a machine called a beater or Hollander, which is a long tub divided longitudinally so as to form a continuous channel around the tub. In one half of the tub, a horizontal cylinder carrying a series of knives revolves rapidly close to a curved bedplate, which is also provided with knives. The mixture of rags and water passes between the cylinder and the bedplate and the rags are reduced to fibers. In the other half of the tub, a hollow washing cylinder covered with fine mesh screening is so arranged that it scoops water from the tub, leaving the rags and fibers behind. As the mixture of rags and water flows around the beater, the dirt is removed and the rags are gradually macerated until they are finally resolved into individual fibers. The half stuff is then passed through one or more secondary beaters to break up the fibers still further. At this point are added coloring matter, sizing material such as rosin or glue, and fillers such as sulfate of lime or kaolin, which give added weight and body to the finished paper. In many American paper mills the second beater is of the type known as a Jordan engine. This machine consists of a stationary cone fitted with knives mounted outside of a revolving cone also equipped with knives. The fiber material flows between these two sets of knives, and the cones can be adjusted relative to each other with great accuracy to regulate the fineness of the fibers.

Top: After having been refined, the paper stock is placed in centricleaners to remove any remaining impurities. Above: Next, the stock, diluted with more than 99 percent water, flows onto the paper machine, on which a fine-mesh screen weaves and mats the fibers together as the water drains off. During this process the paper travels around more than fifty drying drums, is given a coat of sizing to seal the surface, and passes between steel calender rolls that give it a uniformly smooth surface. Hammermill Paper Co.

The preparation of wood for papermaking is accomplished in two different ways. In the groundwood process, blocks of wood are held against a rapidly revolving grindstone that shreds off short wood fibers from the block. The fibers produced by this process are short and are used only in the production of cheap newsprint and for admixture with other types of wood fiber in the making of paper of high quality. In various chemical-solvent processes, wood chips are treated with solvents that remove res-

307

Top: Throughout the manufacturing process, testing stations control the quality of the paper. Bottom: The finished product is stored in huge rolls, some weighing up to 4 tons. Hammermill Paper Co.

early years of the 19th century. The heart of the Fourdrinier machine is an endless belt of wire mesh which moves horizontally. A flow of watery pulp is spread on the level belt which passes over a number of rolls. A shallow wooden box beneath the belt catches much of the water that drains off during this stage. This water is remixed with the pulp to salvage the fiber contained in it. Spreading of the sheet of wet pulp on the wire belt is limited by rubber deckle straps moving at the sides of the belt. Air suction pumps beneath the belt hasten drying of the paper, and the belt itself is moved from side to side to aid the felting of the fibers. As the paper travels along the belt it passes under a turning cylinder called a dandy roll. The surface of this cylinder is covered with wire mesh or single wires to impart a wove or laid surface to the paper. In addition the surface carries words or patterns worked in wire; the words or patterns are impressed on the paper and appear as watermarks that serve to identify the grade of paper and the maker. In handmade papers the watermark patterns are fixed to the surface of the mold.

Near the far end of the machine, the belt passes through two felt-covered couching rolls. These rolls press still more water out of the web of paper and consolidate the fiber, giving the paper enough strength to continue through the machine without the support of the belt. The function of these rolls is the same as that of the felts used in couching handmade paper. From the couching rolls the paper is carried on a belt of cloth through two sets of smooth metal press rolls. These rolls impart a smooth finish to the upper and lower surface of the paper.

After pressing, the paper is fully formed; it is then carried through a series of heated rolls, which complete the drying. The next step is calendering, pressing between smooth chilled rolls to produce the smooth finish known as machine finish. At the end of the Fourdrinier machine the paper is slit by revolving cutters and wound on reels. The manufacture of the paper is completed by cutting into sheets, unless the paper is to be used on a continuous press that employs rolls of paper. Special papers are given additional treatment. Supercalendered paper is subjected to a further calendering process under great pressure between metal and paper-covered rolls. Coated paper, such as is used for fine half tone reproduction, is sized with clay or glue and calendered. Paper is also made on cylinder machines. Much of the tissue paper manufactured is made on Yankee machines, which have a single steam-heated cylinder for drying.

inous material and lignin from the wood, leaving pure fibers of cellulose. The oldest of the chemical-solvent processes, the soda process, introduced in 1851, employs a solution of caustic soda (sodium hydroxide) as a solvent. The wood is cooked or "digested" in this solution under steam pressure. The fibers produced by this process do not have great strength, but are used in mixtures with other wood fibers. The process most generally employed in the United States is the sulfate process. In this process, the solvent is sodium sulfate or magnesium sulfate.

Most paper today is made on Fourdrinier machines patterned after the first successful paper-making machine, which was developed in the

Equipment used in pulp-making and papermaking is constantly being improved and modernized, and new machines, such as the recent Inverform, are constantly being developed.

Paper Sizes. Paper is usually sold by the ream in sheets of standard sizes. A ream of paper usually contains 480 sheets, but reams of drawing paper and handmade paper contain 472 sheets. Book paper and newsprint for flat-plate printing are sold in reams of 500 sheets and also in perfect reams of 516 sheets. The most common book-paper size is octavo (44 × 66 in.). Newsprint for rotary-press printing comes in rolls of varying sizes; a typical roll of newsprint, as used by large metropolitan newspapers in the U.S., is about 66 in. wide, 26,000 ft. long, and weighs about 1600 lb.

Synthetic-Fiber Paper. It was announced in 1955 that papers had been prepared from nylon, Dacron, and Orlon fibers, and from blends of these fibers with wood pulp; see PLASTICS. Such papers are produced on conventional papermaking machinery and can be made with a wide range of appearances and characteristics, from crisp stock resembling ordinary paper to drapable, fabriclike materials. Because of their unique properties, synthetic-fiber papers have many applications for which ordinary paper is unsuitable, notably as electrical insulation, filtration material in air-conditioning equipment, electrical tapes for sound recording, shoe fabrics, and interlining in clothing.

History. According to tradition, paper was first made in 105 A.D. by Ts'ai Lun (50?–118) a eunuch attached to the Later Han court of the Chinese emperor Ho Ti. The material used was probably the bark of the mulberry tree, and the paper was made on a mold of bamboo strips similar to those still used in certain parts of the Orient; see BAMBOO; MULBERRY. The earliest known paper still in existence dates from approximately 150 A.D. and was made from rags. For approximately 500 years the art of papermaking was confined to China, but in 610 it was introduced into Japan, and about 750 into central Asia. Paper made its appearance in Egypt about 800 but was not manufactured in that country until 900.

The use of paper was introduced into Europe by the Moors and the first papermaking mill was established in Spain about 1150. In succeeding centuries the craft spread to most of the countries of Europe. The introduction of movable type about the middle of the 15th century made book printing practical and greatly stimulated papermaking; see PRINTING. The first paper mill in England was established in 1495, and the first such mill in America in 1690.

The increasing use of paper in the 17th and 18th centuries created shortages of rags, which were the only satisfactory raw material known to European papermakers. As a result many attempts were made to devise substitutes, but none was commercially satisfactory. At the same time attempts were made to reduce the cost of paper by developing a machine that would supplant the hand-molding process in paper manufacture. The first practical machine was made in 1798 by the French inventor Nicholas Louis Robert (1761–1829). Robert's machine was improved by the British stationers and brothers Henry Fourdrinier (1766–1854) and Sealy Fourdrinier (d. 1847), who in 1803 produced the first of the machines that bear their name. The solution of the problem of making paper from cheap raw material was achieved by the introduction of the groundwood process of pulp-making about 1840 and the first of the chemical pulp processes approximately ten years later.

Statistics. In the U.S., which has the largest paper industry in the world, there are about 290 pulp-manufacturing establishments, about 730 primary paper and paperboard plants, and more than 5000 plants for the manufacture of paper and paperboard products. The U.S. produces nearly half of the world's pulp and paper. In the late 1960's well over 50,000,000 tons of paper and paperboard were produced annually in the U.S. The approximate tonnage of the major products each year was: newsprint, 3,200,000 tons; other printing papers and writing papers, 10,000,000 tons; packaging and industrial converting paper, 5,800,000 tons; bleached bristol, 1,000,000 tons; sanitary and other tissue papers, 3,600,000 tons; construction paper and board, 4,400,000 tons; and paperboard, 26,000,000 tons.

See also FIBER: *Vegetable Fibers;* NEWSPAPERS; PALEOGRAPHY; PAPYRUS; PARCHMENT AND VELLUM.

AMERICAN PAPER AND PULP ASSOCIATION

PAPIN, Denis (1647–1712?), French physicist, born in Blois. He studied and practiced medicine briefly in Blois and Paris. He was then influenced by the Dutch mathematician and physicist Christian Huygens (see under HUYGENS) to devote himself to the physical sciences, the field in which he made his most outstanding contributions. While serving as assistant to Huygens and later to the English physicist Robert Boyle (q.v.), he devised numerous improvements in the air pump, invented the condensing pump, and experimented with the transmission of power through the use of air pressure. From 1687 to 1696 he served as professor of mathematics at the University of Marburg (now Philipps University), in West Germany. Papin con-

PAPRIKA

tributed greatly to the development of the steam engine by his use of steam power to drive a piston; see STEAM AND STEAM ENGINEERING. In 1679 he invented a steam digester, equipped with the first safety valve, with which he demonstrated that the boiling point of liquids varies with the amount of atmospheric pressure to which they are exposed. This invention was the forerunner of the contemporary pressure cooker, or autoclave. He also discovered the mechanical principle upon which the siphon (q.v.) is based. Papin was elected a Fellow of the Royal Society of London for Improving Natural Knowledge in 1680.

PAPRIKA, name given to the ripe fruit of the bonnet pepper, *Capsicum tetragonum,* and to the spice prepared from the fruit. The spice is used in cooking for its mildly pungent flavor and for its red color. The chief types are Hungarian paprika, which is made from the pods only, and king's paprika, which is made from seeds, stalks, and pods.

PAPUA, territory of Australia, situated in the s.w. Pacific Ocean, and comprising the s.e. section of the island of New Guinea (q.v.) and the Woodlark, Trobriand, D'Entrecasteaux, and Louisiade island groups. Papua is bounded on the N. by the Territory of New Guinea (see NEW GUINEA, TERRITORY OF); on the N.E. and E. by the Solomon Sea, an arm of the Coral Sea; on the s. by the Coral Sea, the Gulf of Papua, and Torres Strait; and on the w. by the Indonesian province of West Irian (see INDONESIA, REPUBLIC OF). The territory lies between about lat. 2° S. and lat. 12° S. and long. 141° E. and long. 154° E. Port Moresby (q.v.) is the capital and principal town. The total area is 86,100 sq.mi., of which 2775 are on adjacent islands. The population (1966 census) was 606,336; the United Nations estimated (1969) 648,000 including more than 14,500 nonnative inhabitants, chiefly European.

Physical Characteristics. Most of the mainland portion adjoins the Gulf of Papua. The coastline is low-lying and deeply indented by river mouths and by a number of bays including, at the E. extremity, Milne Bay. The interior is mainly a low-lying, swampy plain formed by alluvial action. The chief uplifts are the Owen Stanley Range, in the s.e., and several ranges that delineate most of the boundary with the Territory of New Guinea. Mount Victoria (13,240 ft.) in the Owen Stanley Range is the highest peak in Papua. Other peaks in the range exceed 12,000 ft. in elevation. A number of rivers, all comparatively minor, rise in the range and empty into the Coral Sea. The largest river of Papua, the Fly R., rises in the N.W. and flows about 650 miles s. and then E. to the Gulf of Papua. The Fly R. forms approximately 50 mi. of the boundary with West Irian. The river is about 50 mi. wide at its mouth. It is navigable by small craft for about 500 mi. from its mouth.

CLIMATE. The climate is generally warm and very humid. In the lowlands temperatures range between 70° and 90° F. In the mountainous regions lows of 38° F. have been recorded. Annual rainfall totals nearly 200 in. in the Milne Bay region and about 230 in. at the mouth of the Fly R. Port Moresby, which lies between these two points, is sheltered by the Owen Stanley Range and receives only about 45 in. of rain annually.

PLANTS AND ANIMALS. Sago and mangrove swamps exist along parts of the coast. Farther inland are found tropical rain forest, jungle vegetation, and grassland. Scattered stands of pine trees are found on the mountains, as are deciduous forest and some alpine flora. Plants of economic value include the coconut, sugarcane, banana, sandalwood, rattan, bamboo, ginger, and several species of palm.

The wild animal life of Papua is abundant and varied. Commonly found mammals include the tree kangaroo, wallaby, wild pig, dingo, and varieties of squirrel, rat, bat, and mouse. Numerous species of tropical birds abound, including the bird of paradise. Reptile species, including snakes, lizards, and crocodiles, are numerous. The coastal waters support many species of fish, shellfish, turtles, and other marine fauna.

The Economy. Agriculture is by far the most important economic activity. For the most part it is practiced on a subsistence level by the native population. Taros, sweet potatoes, bananas, and papaws are important crops. Subsistence fishing and hunting are also carried on by the native population. In some semiswamp areas near the coast the sago palm yields a starch that is the staple of the native diet.

Commercial crops are raised on plantations. Labor is provided by natives under contract to work for a specified term during which they are maintained on the plantation. The principal commercial crops and their annual production estimates in the late 1960's were copra (17,950 tons), rubber (6000 tons), cacao (1100 tons), and coffee (275 tons).

Gold and silver are mined in small quantities, and deposits of copper, lead, and zinc are being investigated.

The annual value of imports in the late 1960's was about $56,500,000; exports totaled about $11,000,000. Copra and rubber are the principal exports. The imports are mainly foodstuffs, tobacco, and manufactured goods, including machinery and transport equipment. The bulk of the trade is with Australia.

Internal transportation for the most part is by means of small river craft. Papua has about 2300 mi. of roads and no railroads. Steamship and airline services connect Port Moresby with Australia. Shipping connections exist between Australia and some lesser Papuan ports.

Government. The Territory of New Guinea and Papua together constitute the Territory of Papua and New Guinea, which is administered as a unit by Australia; a resident administrator is appointed by the governor-general of Australia. In May, 1963, the Commonwealth government passed an amendment to the Papua and New Guinea Act of 1949–1964, replacing the legislative council with a house of assembly. The house convened for the first time in 1964. Since 1968 the house has had 94 members; 10 are official members appointed by the governor-general, 69 elected from open electorates, and 15 chosen from regional electorates.

Papua is subdivided into eighteen districts, each headed by a district commissioner. Judicial authority rests in a supreme court with headquarters in Port Moresby. In the mid-1960's effective governmental control extended over about 77 percent of the area of Papua, the rest was under only nominal control.

History. For a discussion of the history, prior to 1883, of the area presently designated as Papua; see NEW GUINEA: *History*. In 1883 the government of Queensland, Australia, annexed this area to prevent an apparently imminent German annexation. The following year Great Britain established the area as part of the protectorate of British New Guinea. Australia assumed administrative responsibility in 1901, and the formal transfer to Australian jurisdiction was effected in 1905. Under Australian administration an educational system was introduced, sanitation was improved, and commercial plantations were established.

In 1942, during World War II, Japanese forces advancing south through the island of New Guinea penetrated to within 35 mi. of Port Moresby. An American and Australian counteroffensive drove the invaders from Papua before the end of January, 1943.

After the war Australia continued its efforts to educate the native population and to develop the economy. The administration developed extensive educational and medical facilities and contributed to the support of those facilities maintained by Christian missions. In 1957 the Netherlands and Australia declared in a joint statement their intention of ultimately granting autonomy, respectively, to Netherlands New Guinea and to the territories of Papua and New Guinea. Netherlands New Guinea, however, was subsequently transferred to Indonesian administration and renamed West Irian. A university was opened in 1966 at Port Moresby. During that same year plans for new tourist facilities were under way and a board was selected to investigate ways of expanding tourism.

PAPYRI, DISCOVERIES OF, archeological finds of ancient documents, usually those inscribed on rolls made from papyrus (q.v.). The first major discoveries occurred in the 18th century. Charred rolls containing writings of the Epicurean philosopher Philodemus were found at Herculaneum, in Italy, in 1752, and some fragments of the *Iliad* of the Greek poet Homer were discovered in Egypt early in the 19th century. Between 1847 and 1856 more fragments of the *Iliad* and several orations of Hyperides (about 390–322 B.C.) were unearthed. Scholars and explorers began an extensive search for Greek papyri in Egypt, and thousands of documents in varying stages of preservation were discovered. Papyri, often in very fragmentary condition, have been excavated at the sites of ancient towns and cities, where they were discarded or lost. Others have been found in ancient tombs, where they were deposited with the bodies of their owners and remained preserved in an almost perfect state. The great majority of these papyri, which date from the 4th century B.C. to the 7th or 8th century A.D., are now in libraries and museums in Europe and the United States.

The papyrus discoveries comprise manuscripts of two general classes: literary works; and documents of an official or private character, such as laws, revenue records, tax lists, business contracts, wills, and personal correspondence. The documents of the second class are of immense value for reconstructing the social and economic history of Egypt under Greek and Roman rule. The discovery of the papyri has had three additional results of great importance: an entire new science, known as papyrology, has been developed to assist scholars in the reading, interpretation, and evaluation of the papyri; the discovery of thousands of written documents extending over a period of a thousand years has revolutionized the study of Greek paleography (q.v.), for many ancient forms of book writing can now be studied, as well as countless individual hands; and modern knowledge of Greek literature has been enriched by the discovery of famous works, in complete or fragmentary form, which had been lost since ancient times. The lit-

PAPYRUS

erary papyri include manuscripts of many works already extant, such as the Homeric epics. The study of such papyri yields valuable clues for the determination of the correct texts of classic Greek writers, but such papyri are less significant than those containing previously unknown works.

Among the more important of these newly discovered works are the *Orations* of Hyperides, the *Mimes* of Herondas, the *Constitution of Athens* of Aristotle, and the *Odes* of Bacchylides. Among the thousands of papyri found at Behnesa, the ancient Oxyrhynchus, by the British paleographers Bernard Pyne Grenfell (1869–1926) and Arthur Surridge Hunt (1871–1934) in 1896 and 1897 were many fragments of lost literary works, such as the *Ichneutæ* of Sophocles. In 1902 a large portion of the *Persæ* of the poet Timotheus was found, important paleographically as the oldest literary papyrus in existence, and in 1905 fragments of several plays of the comic dramatist Menander. Other papyri contain new fragments of the works of well-known poets, such as Corinna, Sappho, and Pindar. More Greek literature is thus extant today than at any time in the past thousand years.

See GREEK LITERATURE. See also separate articles on most of the individuals mentioned above whose birth and death dates are not given.

PAPYRUS, common name applied to *Cyperus papyrus* in the family Cyperaceae. Papyrus, a kind of sedge, grows about 3 ft. to about 10 ft. high and has a woody, aromatic, creeping rhizome. The leaves are long and sharp-keeled, and the upright flowering stems are naked, soft, and triangular in shape. The lower part of the stem is as thick as the arm of a man, and at the top is a compound umbel of numerous drooping spikelets, with a whorl of eight leaves. Papyrus grows in Egypt, Ethiopia, in the Jordan R. valley, and in Sicily. Various parts of the papyrus were used in ancient times for both ornamental and useful purposes, including wreaths for the head, sandals, boxes, boats, and rope. The pith of the stem was boiled and eaten, and its root dried for fuel. The most important use of the plant, however, was in the manufacture of a sort of paper that was the chief writing material of classical antiquity.

The papyrus of the Egyptians was made of slices of the cellular pith laid lengthwise, with other layers laid crosswise on it; the whole was then moistened with water, pressed and dried, and rubbed smooth with ivory or a smooth shell. The sheets of papyrus, varying from about 5 in. by 9 in. to about 9 in. by 15 in., were made into rolls, probably about 20 ft. to 30 ft. in length. The Egyptians wrote on papyrus in regular columns, which in literary prose rarely exceeded 3 in. in width; in poetry the columns were often wider in order to accommodate the length of the verse. The Greeks seem to have known papyrus as early as the beginning of the 5th century B.C., but earliest extant Greek papyrus is believed to be the *Persae* of the poet Timotheus (446?–357? B.C.). The use of papyrus for literary works continued among the Greeks and the Romans to the 4th century A.D., when it was superseded by parchment (*see* PARCHMENT AND VELLUM), but it continued to be used for official and private documents until the 8th or 9th century; *see* PALEOGRAPHY.

The astounding discoveries of large numbers of papyri in Egypt in the past hundred years have brought to light documents invaluable for

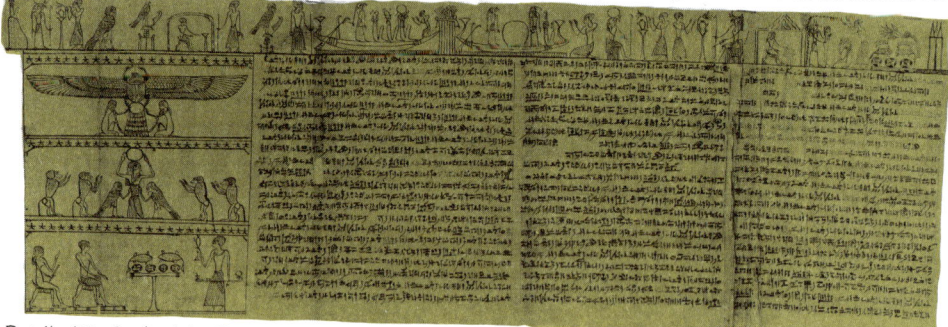

Detail of the Book of the Dead, inscribed on papyrus in the Ptolemaic period (323–30 B.C.).
Metropolitan Museum of Art

the reconstruction of the social and economic history of Hellenistic and Roman Egypt and have restored many important literary works that had been lost. *See* PAPYRI, DISCOVERIES OF; WRITING.

PARABLE, name given originally by Greek rhetoricians to a literary illustration. In the New Testament it signifies a short, fictitious narrative, designed to illuminate a spiritual truth; it has been used similarly by later writers to convey a moral point. *See* FABLE.

PARABOLA, in mathematics, plane curve formed by the intersection of a cone with a plane parallel to a straight line on the slanting surface of the cone; see CONIC SECTIONS. Each point of the curve is equidistant from a fixed point, called the focus, and a fixed straight line, known as the directrix. The parabola is symmetrical about a line passing through the focus and perpendicular to the directrix. For a parabola symmetrical to the *x*-axis, and with its vertex at the origin, the mathematical equation is $y^2 = 2px$, in which *p* is the distance between the focus and the directrix.

The parabola is the curve that would be described by any projectile, such as a bullet or a ball, in the absence of air resistance. Because of air resistance, the curves that projectiles travel in closely approximate true parabolas. Parabolic mirrors consisting of a curved reflector, the cross section of which is a parabola, reflect rays of light from a source at its focus in parallel lines. Such reflectors are used in automobile headlights and all other forms of searchlights. Parabolic mirrors also bring parallel rays of light to a focus without spherical aberration; see OPTICS. This type of reflector is therefore valuable in astronomical telescopes; see TELESCOPE. Parabolic reflectors are used also as antennas in radio astronomy and radar (qq.v.). J.Si.

PARACELSUS, Philippus Aureolus, pen name of THEOPHRASTUS BOMBASTUS VON HOHENHEIM (1493?–1541), Swiss physician and alchemist, born in Einsiedeln, and educated at the University of Basel. He is best known for introducing the use of chemicals into medicine. While studying metallurgy at the mines in Tirol, Austria, he investigated diseases of miners and the possible medicinal properties of metals. Although accused by many of his contemporaries of charlatanism, Paracelsus profoundly influenced the development of medicine. He repudiated the ancient theory of the Greek physician Galen (q.v.) that diseases are caused by excesses or deficiencies of certain body fluids or humors. He identified the characteristics of numerous diseases and attempted to find chemical agents for treating these diseases, thereby founding the science of chemotherapy (q.v.). In 1526 he was appointed professor of medicine and surgery at the University of Basel. Two years later he was forced to resign from this position as a result of his unorthodox teachings. This took place at other universities. Among the English translations of his works is *Four Treatises of Theophrastus von Hohenheim* (1941).

PARACHUTE (Fr. *para*, "preventing", and *chute*, "fall"), large, umbrella-shaped fabric can-

Parachutes carry supplies from U.S. Air Force transport planes to ground troops operating in advanced war zones. U.S. Air Force

opy used to reduce the speed of a person or object falling through the air, and carried as an escape device in aircraft. The use of the parachute was first suggested by the Italian artist and inventor Leonardo da Vinci (q.v.), but the first practical parachute was invented in the 1780's. The French aeronaut Jean Pierre Blanchard (q.v.) dropped a dog equipped with a parachute from a balloon in 1785, and in 1793 claimed to have made the first successful human parachute descent. After this time parachutes became a regular part of the equipment of balloonists, and after World War I were adopted as lifesaving devices for the pilots and passengers of airplanes.

A parachute designed for human use is typically a canopy about 24 ft. in diameter composed of about twenty-five panels, or gores, of nylon or silk. The canopy has a small vent hole in its center that is normally held closed by elastic bands but which expands when the canopy

PARACHUTE

opens, so as to lessen the initial shock of deceleration. So-called shroud lines are sewed into the seams between the panels, passing over the top of the canopy, and are connected at their ends to two metal rings. The parachutist is equipped with a harness of strong webbing which passes over the shoulders, around the body, and between the legs, and this harness, in turn, is attached to the rings.

When not in use the parachute is folded compactly into a canvas container worn by the parachutist. The pack is so arranged that it flies open with the aid of rubber bands and metal springs when a metal closing line called the rip cord is pulled. The parachute is also equipped with a small parachute, which is ejected from the pack when the rip cord is pulled and which pulls the main parachute out of the container.

A parachutist dives, jumps, or steps from the plane and pulls the rip cord after an interval of about three seconds. This interval enables him to fall far enough to ensure that the parachute will be clear of the plane when it opens. Once the parachute opens, the jumper descends at a rate of about 17 ft. per second and strikes the ground with about the same force as if he had jumped freely from a height of 10 ft.

During World War II armies made extensive use of paratroops, or parachute troops, who were often flown behind the enemy lines in transport planes; they were usually landed from low altitudes and their parachutes were arranged to open automatically, as the men jumped, by means of long straps attached to the carrying plane. In the Korean War the United States Air Force also used parachutes to drop heavy equipment, such as tanks, trucks, and field guns. The canopy of a heavy-equipment parachute may measure up to 100 ft. in diameter.

In the conflict in Vietnam, parachute troops have been little used because of the nature of the terrain and the increased use of helicopters, which carry combat troops and their equipment swiftly and in large numbers. The chief uses of parachutes in Vietnam have been for dropping flares at night to expose enemy positions and for dropping supplies to isolated posts where enemy firepower prevents the use of helicopters. See VIETNAM, WAR IN.

The design of parachutes has become increasingly sophisticated; especially designed parachutes control the rate of descent, reduce the effect of winds, and maintain stability according to the weight and shape of the object being carried. Other parachutes, called drogue chutes, are used to decelerate spacecraft, experimental rockets, airplanes, and sports cars. In the late 1960's, sport parachuting, or skydiving (q.v.) increased greatly in popularity.

PARADISE (Gk. *paradeisos,* "garden, orchard, paradise"), term for Eden (q.v.) as the first abode of man or as a symbol for the state of innocence that ended with the Fall and poetic term for Heaven (q.v.), especially in its aspect as a place of bliss. Outside of the Bible, the concept of paradise figures prominently in literature in several Western classics. In *The Divine Comedy* (q.v.) of the Italian poet Dante Alighieri (q.v.), in the final section, the *"Paradiso",* the soul of the poet is guided through heaven. The English poet John Milton (q.v.) uses both the edenic and the heavenly senses of paradise in two related epic poems. His masterpiece *Paradise Lost* deals with the origin of evil (see EVIL, ORIGIN OF) and the resultant expulsion of Adam and Eve (q.v.) from Eden; its companion piece, *Paradise Regained,* is concerned with the entrance of Christ into the heavenly paradise after He has overcome the temptations of Satan (see DEVIL).

PARADISE FISH, small freshwater fish, *Macropodus opercularis,* of the family Anabantidae, which includes also the fighting fish (q.v.), kissing gourami (see GOURAMI), and climbing perch (see CLIMBING FISH). Native to China, the paradise fish has been an aquarium favorite for centuries because of its beauty and fascinating nesting habits. At mating time the male, like most members of this family, blows air bubbles at the water's surface to create a bubble nest for the eggs and the newly hatched young.

PARAFFIN. See PETROLEUM.

PARAGUAY, inland republic of South America, bounded on the N.W. and N. by Bolivia, on the E. by Brazil, and on the S. and S.W. by Argentina. Paraguay lies between about lat. 19°15′ S. and lat. 27°27′ S. and long. 54°16′ W. and long. 62°20′ W. The total area of Paraguay is about 157,042 sq.mi.

THE LAND

The Paraguay R. divides the country into sharply contrasting regions, namely, in the w. the Gran Chaco (q.v.), extending across the border into Bolivia, and in the E., Paraguay proper. The Gran Chaco is part of a low, flat, alluvial plain which extends from Paraguay into Bolivia on the w., Argentina on the S., and Brazil on the E. Grassy plains, swamps, and scrub forests cover the area. Underlying the Gran Chaco is a rock stratum containing salty water unsuitable for drinking and irrigation.

Paraguay proper, known also as the Oriental, consists mainly of the S. extension of the Paraná

The government of Paraguay, with the cooperation of the United Nations Development Program, is providing a modern telecommunication network to facilitate economic development of the country. Shown here is the master control room at the Paraguayan international telephone exchange. United Nations

plateau. This elevation, from 1000 to 2000 ft. high, forms a watershed which gives rise to numerous tributaries of the Paraguay and Paraná rivers. On its w. edge the plateau falls off sharply to a region of fertile grassy foothills extending to the Paraguay R. In the E. the highlands descend gradually toward the Alto Paraná R. The main rivers of Paraguay are the Alto Paraná, the Paraguay, and the Pilcomayo. Lake Ypoá (100 sq.mi.) is the only large inland body of water. Paraguay has many spectacular waterfalls, notably the Guairá Falls (374 ft.).

Climate. The climate is subtropical. At Asunción mean temperatures range from 62.5° F. in July to 80.4° F. in January. In the Chaco and other points to the N. temperatures often reach 100° F. Annual rainfall averages 44 in. in the Asunción area, 32 in. in the Gran Chaco, and 60 in. in the E. forest regions. The Chaco has heavy rainfall in the summer and almost no rain in the winter.

Natural Resources. The primary resource of Paraguay is its fertile soil. It has few mineral resources, of which limestone is the most important.

Plants and Animals. The plants and animals of Paraguay are substantially those of neighboring South American countries. Paraguay proper, where rainfall is heavy, is covered by dense evergreen forests interspersed with a wide variety of tropical grasses, ferns, palms, and exotic flowers. In the Gran Chaco, vegetation is comparatively sparse but includes the red quebracho tree, a rich source of tannin extract. The plains are covered by coarse tropical reeds, grasses, and stunted trees.

The animals of Paraguay include the armadillo, capybara, tapir, jaguar, anteater, wild boar, deer, alligator, and various species of snake. Among the local birds are the toucan, ibis, heron, parrot, black duck, dove, partridge, American ostrich, rhea, and parakeet. Many of these birds exhibit strikingly beautiful plumage.

Soils and Waterpower. Fertile soil covers eastern Paraguay. The soil of the Chaco consists of clay and sand deposited by rivers draining the Andes Mts.; see ANDES. No waterpower sources have been exploited, although their estimated potential is great.

THE PEOPLE

Paraguay has perhaps the most racially homogeneous population in South America. A large majority of the people are of mixed Spanish and Guarani (q.v.) Indian blood. Minority groups include individuals of pure Spanish ancestry, living mainly in Asunción; unassimilated Guarani tribesmen of the E. forest region, and small colonies of immigrants from Japan, Italy, Portugal, Canada, and other countries. The Mennonites, a German-speaking religious sect, form a notable immigrant group. The society is predominantly rural.

Population. The population of Paraguay census (1962) was 1,816,103; the United Nations estimated (1970) 2,379,000. The density is only about 15 persons per sq.mi., one of the lowest in South America. Population is densest in the western Oriental and most sparse in the Chaco.

Political Divisions. Paraguay is divided into sixteen departments: thirteen in the Oriental and three in the Chaco. Asunción (q.v.), the capital, has the rank of a federal district. The departments in the Oriental are Alto Paraná, Amambay, Caaguazú, Caazapá, Central, Concepción, Cordillera, Guairá, Itapúa, Misiones, Ñeembucú, Paraguarí, and San Pedro; in the Chaco the departments are Boquerón, Olimpo, Presidente Hayes. The departments are divided into districts, which comprise municipalities and rural districts.

PARAGUAY

INDEX TO MAP OF PARAGUAY

Departments

Alto Paraná .... E 5
Amambay .... E 4
Boquerón .... B 3
Caaguazú .... E 5
Caazapá .... D 6
Central .... D 5
Concepción .... D 4
Cordillera .... D 5
Distrito Federal .... A 6
Guairá .... D 5
Itapúa .... E 6
Misiones .... D 6
Ñeembucú .... C 6
Olimpo .... C 3
Paraguarí .... D 6
Presidente Hayes .... C 4
San Pedro .... D 5

Cities and Towns

Acahay .... B 7
Alberdi .... D 6
Altos .... B 6
Angelito .... D 4
Angostura .... A 6
Areguá .... B 6
Arroyos y Esteros ...... B 6
Asunción (cap.) .... A 6
Atyrá .... B 6
Ayolas .... D 6
Bahía Negra .... C 3
Ballivián .... B 4
Belén .... D 4
Bella Vista .... D 4
Benjamín Aceval .... D 5
Borja .... C 7
Buena Vista .... E 5
Caacupé .... B 6
Caaguazú .... E 5
Caapucú .... D 6
Caazapá .... D 6
Caballero .... B 6
Cañada Oruro .... A 3
Capiatá .... B 6
Capiitindy .... E 5
Capitán Bado .... E 4
Capitán Meza .... E 6
Caraguatay .... C 6
Carapeguá .... B 6
Carayaó .... C 6
Carmen del Paraná ...... D 6
Carrería .... C 3
Celia .... C 4
Cerrito .... D 6
Cerrito Jara .... C 2
Colonial Mariscal
  López .... E 4
Colonia Presidente
  Franco .... B 6
Concepción .... D 4
Coronel Bogado .... E 6
Coronel Martínez .... C 6
Coronel Oviedo .... C 6
Curuguaty .... E 5
Desmochados .... D 6
Emboscada .... B 6
Encarnación .... E 6
Escobar .... B 6
Esteros .... B 4
Eusebio Ayala .... B 6
Fernando de la Mora .... A 6
Filadelfia .... C 4
Fortín 27 de
  Noviembre .... B 3
Fortín Avalos Sánchez .. B 4
Fortín Ayacucho .... B 2
Fortín Boquerón .... C 4
Fortín Buenos Aires .... B 4
Fortín Carlos Antonio
  López .... C 3
Fortín Coronel Bogado .. C 3
Fortín Coroneles
  Sánchez .... B 2
Fortín Falcón .... B 4
Fortín Florida .... C 3
Fortín Gabino
  Mendoza .... B 3
Fortín Galpón .... C 2
Fortín Garrapatal ...... B 3
Fortín General Aquino .. C 5
Fortín General Bruguez . C 5
Fortín General
  Caballero .... C 5
Fortín General Díaz,
  Boquerón .... B 4
Fortín General Díaz,
  Olimpo .... C 3
Fortín General Pando ... C 2
Fortín Guachalla .... A 4
Fortín Hernandarias .... B 3
Fortín Ingavi .... B 2
Fortín Juan de
  Zalazar .... C 4
Fortín Junín .... B 3
Fortín Linares .... B 4
Fortín Madrejón .... B 3
Fortín Mayor
  Rodríguez .... B 4
Fortín Orihuela .... C 4
Fortín Patria .... C 2
Fortín Presidente
  Ayala .... C 4
Fortín Salto Palmar .... C 5
Fortín Tinfunqué .... B 4
Fortín Toledo .... B 4
Fortín Torres .... C 3
Fortín Valois
  Rivarola .... C 4
Fuerte Olimpo .... D 3
General Aquino .... D 5
General Artigas .... E 6
Guarambaré .... B 6
Guazú-cuá .... D 6
Hohenau .... E 6
Horqueta .... D 4
Humaitá .... C 6
Irala .... E 5
Isla Alta .... D 6
Isla Pucú .... B 6
Isla Umbú .... C 6
Itá .... B 6
Itacurubí de la
  Cordillera .... C 6
Itacurubí del
  Rosario .... D 5
Itakyry .... E 5
Itapé .... C 6
Itauguá .... B 6
Iturbe .... C 7
Jesús .... E 6
Juan de Mena .... D 6
La Esmeralda .... A 4
La Florestal .... C 3
Lambaré .... B 6
Laureles .... D 6
Lima .... D 4
Limpio .... B 6
Loreto .... D 4
Luque .... B 6
Maciel .... D 6
Magariños .... B 4
Maldonado-cué .... D 4
Mariscal
  Estigarribia .... B 4
Mbocayaty .... C 6
Mbuyapey .... D 6
Minas-cué .... C 4
Ñacunday .... E 6
Natalicio Talavera ..... D 5
Neu Halbstadt .... B 4
Nueva Germania .... D 4
Numí .... D 5
Paraguarí .... B 6
Paso Barreto .... D 4
Paso de Patria .... C 6
Pedernal .... D 4
Pedro González .... C 6
Pedro Juan
  Caballero .... E 4
Pilar .... C 6
Pirayú .... B 6
Piribebuy .... B 6
Primavera .... C 5
Primero de Marzo .... B 6
Puerto Adela .... E 5
Puerto Alegre .... A 6
Puerto Antequera .... D 5
Puerto Casado .... C 4
Puerto Colón .... D 4
Puerto Cooper .... C 4
Puerto Esperanza .... C 3
Puerto Fonciere .... D 4
Puerto Galileo .... C 5
Puerto Guaraní .... D 3
Puerto María .... C 5
Puerto Max .... D 4
Puerto Mihanovich ...... C 3
Puerto Palma Chica ..... C 3
Puerto Pinasco .... C 4
Puerto Presidente
  Stroessner .... E 5
Puerto Rosario .... D 5
Puerto Sastre .... D 4
Puerto Ybapobó .... D 4
Puesto Estrella .... B 3
Quiindy .... B 7
Quyquyhó .... D 6
Rojas Silva .... C 4
Roque González .... B 7
Rosario .... D 5
San Antonio,
  Central .... A 6
San Antonio,
  San Pedro .... D 4
San Bernardino .... B 6
San Carlos, Central .... B 6
San Carlos,
  Concepción .... D 4
San Cosme .... D 6
San Estanislao .... D 5
San Florencio .... E 4
San Ignacio .... D 6
San Joaquín .... D 5
San José .... C 6
San Juan Bautista ...... D 6
San Juan Bautista de
  Ñeembucú .... C 6
San Juan Nepomuceno .... E 6
San Lázaro .... D 4
San Lorenzo .... B 6
San Luis de la
  Sierra .... D 4
San Miguel .... D 6
San Pedro .... D 5
San Pedro del
  Paraná .... E 6
San Salvador .... D 4
Santa Elena .... C 6
Santa Luisa .... D 4
Santa María .... D 6
Santa Rosa .... D 6
Santiago .... D 6
Sapucaí .... B 6
Siracuas .... B 3
Sommerfeld .... C 4
Tabaí .... E 6
Tacuara .... C 6
Tacuatí .... D 4
Tacurupucú
  (Hernandarias) .... E 5
Tayí-Caré .... D 5
Tobatí .... B 6
Trinidad .... E 6
Unión .... D 5
Valenzuela .... B 6
Villa Florida .... D 6
Villa Franca .... C 6
Villa Hayes .... A 6
Villa Militar .... C 4
Villa Oliva .... C 5
Villa Sana .... D 4
Villarrica .... C 6
Villazón .... A 3
Villeta .... A 6
Yabebyry .... D 6
Yaguarón .... B 6
Yataity .... C 6
Ybycuí .... B 7
Ybytimí .... B 6
Yegros .... D 6
Ygatimí .... E 5
Yhaty .... C 6
Yhú .... E 5
Ypacaraí .... B 6
Ypané .... A 6
Ypejhú .... E 4
Yuty .... D 6

Physical Features

Acaray (river) .... E 5
Aguaray-guazú (river) .. C 5
Alegre (river) .... C 3
Alto Paraná (river) .... D 6
Amambay, Cord, de
  (mts.) .... D 4
Apa (river) .... D 4
Aquidabán (river) ...... D 4
Capitán Ustarés (hill) . B 2
Cará (mt.) .... D 4
Chaco Boreal (reg.) .... B 4
Chovoreca (hill) .... C 2
Confuso (river) .... C 5
González (river) .... C 4
Gran Chaco (reg.) ...... B 4
Guairá (falls) .... E 5
Guaran (Cap. Ustarés)
  (hill) .... B 2
León (mt.) .... B 3
Mbaracayú (mts.) .... E 4
Monday (river) .... E 5
Monte Lindo (river) .... D 4
Negro (river) .... D 5
Paraguay (river) .... D 5
Pilcomayo (river) ...... C 5
Siete Puntas (river) ... D 4
Tebicuary (river) ...... D 6
Tímane (river) .... C 3
Verá (lagoon) .... B 7
Verde (river) .... C 4
Yacaré (river) .... C 4
Ypané (river) .... D 4
Ypoá (lake) .... B 6

Principal Cities. The chief cities of Paraguay (pop., 1966 est.) are Asunción (380,000), a commercial city and chief port; Encarnación (60,000), a railroad and agricultural center; Concepción (40,000), a river port; and Coronel Oviedo (35,000).

Language and Religion. Paraguay is a bilingual country. Spanish is the official tongue; however, Guarani is commonly spoken by about 90 percent of the people and is used in most folk poems and songs and in books and periodicals. See TUPI-GUARANI.

Roman Catholicism, the official religion, is the faith of the vast majority of Paraguayans. Freedom of worship is extended to other faiths. A number of small Protestant groups exist, of which the Mennonite group is the largest. (See MENNONITE CHURCH).

PARAGUAY

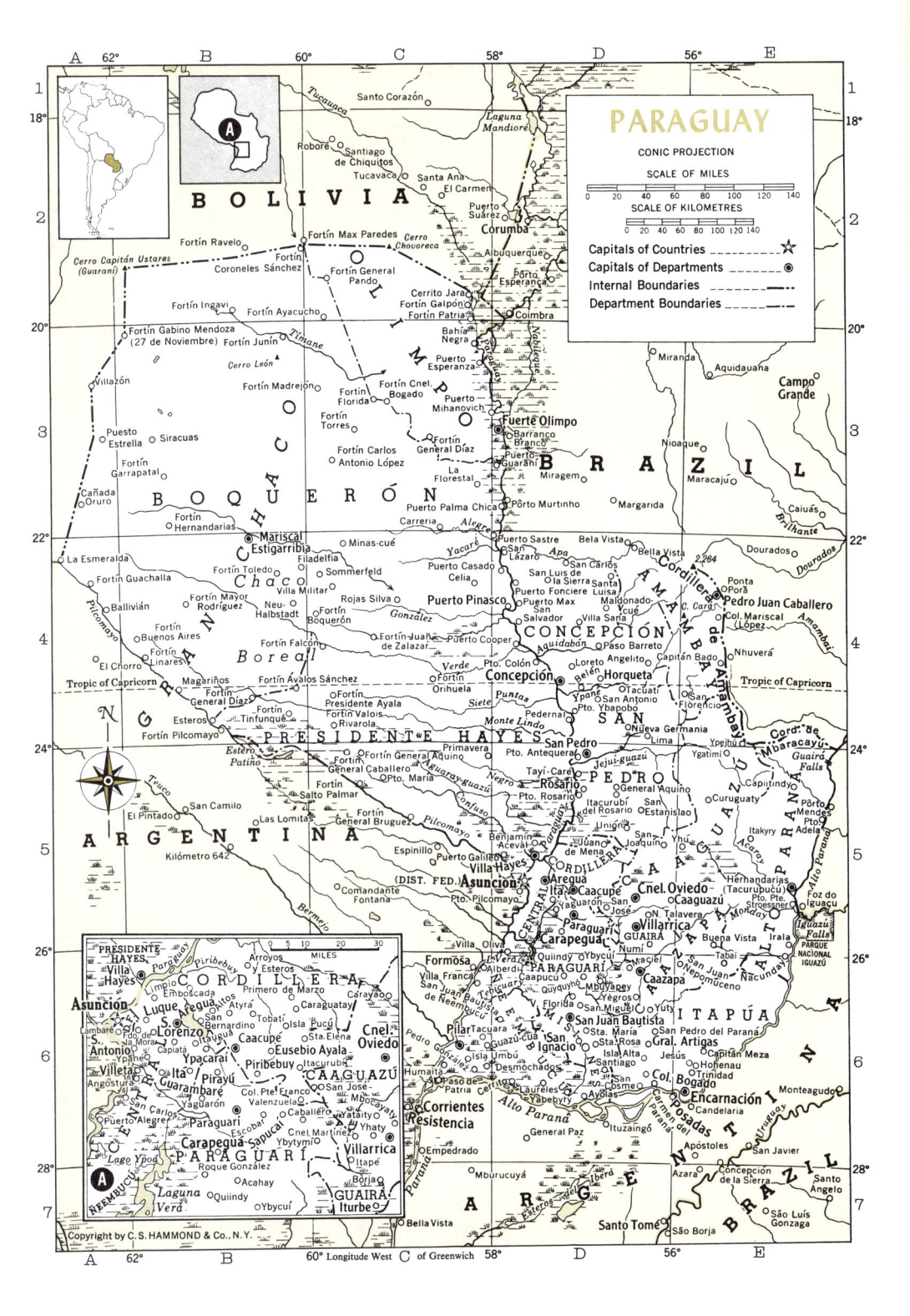

Children and adults work in a community garden.
United Nations

Education. Elementary education is free and nominally compulsory for children from seven to fourteen years of age. The number of schools is inadequate, however, and about thirty-two percent of the population is illiterate. Adult education on the primary level is actively encouraged. In the late 1960's, about 2750 state-run and 220 private primary schools had about 400,000 students in annual attendance and some 12,700 teachers, and about 435 secondary schools had about 4500 teachers and an annual enrollment of about 45,000 students. Paraguay also has private, technical, and vocational schools, and junior colleges. The National University in Asunción has a student enrollment of 5500.

Culture. Paraguayan culture is a blend chiefly of Guaranian and Spanish elements, supplemented by more recent Argentine, German, and Italian influences. The culture of Paraguay has remained isolated and therefore has retained many features introduced in the 16th and 17th centuries by the Spanish conquerors, artisans, and Jesuit missionaries. The Ateneo Paraguayo, a leading cultural center, sponsors art exhibits, lectures, and concerts, and Guarani culture is promoted by the Academy of Guarani Culture, the Indian Association of Paraguay, and the Guarani Theater.

LIBRARIES AND MUSEUMS. Among the notable libraries are the National Archives and American Library of the Godoy Museum, which also houses paintings and historical objects, the library of the Museum of Natural History and Ethnography, and the library of the Paraguayan Scientific Society; all are in Asunción. Important museums in Asunción, in addition to those above, include the National Museum of Fine Arts and the Museum of Military History.

LITERATURE AND MUSIC. Historical and legal writings occupy the leading place in Paraguayan literature; even poetry seldom loses touch with social realities. Among the foremost 20th-century Paraguayan writers are Juan Natalicio Gonzalez and Manuel Ortiz Guerrero. *See* SPANISH-AMERICAN LITERATURE.

From remote times, the Guarani have used primitive wind and percussion instruments, mostly wooden flutes, whistles, rattles, and bells. Guitars and harps, introduced by early Spanish settlers, are basic instruments of contemporary Paraguayan music. One of the oldest forms of Paraguayan popular music is the polka, and ballads and songs preserve much history and tradition. The Guarania, a song with a flowing lyric melody, introduced in the early 20th century, is the first distinctive variation of the Hispanic colonial tradition. Two music schools are in Asunción, in addition to the Asunción Symphony Orchestra and a military band.

ART. Much Paraguayan art uses themes of native folklore and of religion, frequently expressed in church decoration. The earliest well-defined Paraguayan art dates from colonial times when Jesuit and Franciscan missions established art schools. Examples of early art, now extant, in both baroque Spanish and Indian styles, include pediments adorned with figures of saints, pulpits, seats carved in stone, and magnificent wood-carved altarpieces.

Among the greatest names in modern Paraguayan art are the painters Pablo Alborno (1877–   ) and Juan Samudio (1878–1936). The most renowned Paraguayan craft is the production of the very delicate nanduti lace.

THE ECONOMY

The economy of Paraguay is primarily agricultural; the country is severely handicapped, however, by low agricultural output and by lack of easy access to world markets. In a recent year the annual budget showed about $80,000,000 in revenue and about $83,000,000 in expenditures.

Agriculture. The principal industry of Paraguay is farming, but of the 41,500,000 arable acres in the country, only about 1,700,000 are cultivated. In the late 1960's, the annual yield of leading agricultural products, in metric tons, was: Paraguay tea, or yerba maté (15,000); long-staple cotton (30,000); sugarcane (1,100,000); tobacco (20,000); manioc (1,500,000); corn (180,000); and sweet potatoes (130,000).

Livestock breeding is a major agricultural occupation and Paraguay has about 5,600,000 cattle, 600,000 horses, 410,000 sheep, and 625,000 pigs. Meat packing and the preparation of hides are auxiliary industries.

Forest and Fishing Industries. The forest industry is very important in the economy of Paraguay, and its products have represented about 40 percent of the value of all exports in recent years. In the late 1960's annual production tonnage of the most important commercial forest products was tannin (33,000); hardwoods and other timber (275,000); and yaguaraón (355,000), the chief source of petitgrain oil, which is a perfume base. Fishing is negligible.

Mining and Manufacturing. Mining is unimportant in Paraguay. Although deposits of iron, manganese, salt, and other minerals are reported, they are not exploited commercially. Limestone, the only mineral extracted in significant amounts, was used in producing about 28,000 tons of cement annually in the late 1960's.

Manufacturing is confined largely to animal, agricultural, and forestry products, and to domestic consumer goods. Among the more important products are tinned meat and other foodstuffs, textiles, wood products, and chemicals.

Commerce and Trade. The basic unit of national currency is the guaraní (126 guaraníes equal U.S.$1; 1971). The Bank of Paraguay issues currency and controls exchange. Other banks include the Bank of London and South America, the Bank of the Argentine Nation, and the Bank of Brazil.

Import-export traffic is closely regulated by the government and is facilitated by the 1955

Grade-school children armed with gardening tools march off to work on the school farm.   United Nations

treaty of economic union between Paraguay and Argentina. Argentine money circulates freely within Paraguay. In 1970 exports totaled annually about $64,070,000 and imports were slightly lower. Exports included meat products ($13,500,000), lumber ($8,000,000) and quebracho ($2,000,000). Other exports included cotton, tobacco, coffee, hides, and essential oils. The three leading consumers of Paraguayan exports are Argentina, the United States, and Great Britain.

Imports consisted mainly of machinery and motors ($11,000,000), vehicles and accessories ($7,500,000), food, beverages, and tobacco ($6,000,000), and fuel and lubricants ($4,500,000). The three main suppliers of imports are Argentina, the U.S., and West Germany.

Transportation and Communications. For a long time more than 1800 mi. of internal waterways (chiefly the Paraná and Paraguay rivers) have provided the main means of transportation, with most of the boats owned by Argentine interests. In the late 1960's, Paraguay had more than 3800 mi. of roads, with additional roads under construction. Railroads total about 715 mi. International and domestic air service are provided at the airport in Asunción.

Paraguay has about 16,000 state-owned telephones, of which about 15,000 were in Asunción, some 16 radio stations and 165,000 radio receivers, and 3 radio-telegraph companies operating 12 stations. Six daily newspapers are published in Asunción.

Labor. The government has virtually unlimited regulatory authority over trade-union activity. Trade unionists in the late 1960's totaled about 25,000. Nearly all members belonged to some 115 affiliates of the Confederación Paraguaya de

PARAGUAY

Trabajadores (Confederation of Paraguayan Workers), or C.P.T. Of minor importance were the Movimiento Sindicalista Paraguayo, affiliated with the International Federation of Christian Trade Unions, and the Confederación Paraguaya de Trabajadores en el Exilio (Confederation of Paraguayan Workers in Exile), formed in 1959 when the government suppressed a general strike attempted by the C.P.T.

GOVERNMENT

The Republic of Paraguay has a highly centralized government, the structure of which was established by the constitution of 1967. Voting is compulsory for all citizens over eighteen years of age. Government functions are carried out by executive, legislative, and judicial branches.

Central Government. The executive consists of a president who is popularly elected for a five-year term and who may be reelected to a second term. He effectively controls the executive, legislative, and judicial branches of the government, and is assisted by a cabinet of eleven appointees. When the legislature is not in session he has the power to issue decree-laws and to govern through the Council of State, an appointive body made up of cabinet members and other prominent citizens.

The chief executive also appoints the three supreme court members and the magistrates of lower courts. He holds appointive power over the diplomatic corps, the armed forces, the Roman Catholic Church hierarchy, and the civil service. In addition he chooses all commissioners who administer the departments of Paraguay.

HEALTH AND WELFARE. Under the executive branch is the ministry of public health, which administers the public health and welfare program. A system of government insurance guarantees to citizens free medical and burial services, old-age pensions, and payments for absences from work due to illness, accident, or maternity.

Legislature and Judiciary. The constitution provides for a popularly elected legislature consisting of a 60-member chamber of deputies and a 30-member senate. The party polling the largest number of votes in the legislative elections receives two thirds of the seats in each chamber, and the remaining third is divided proportionately among the other contenders.

The judiciary consists of a three-man supreme court of justice, special chambers of appeal for civil and criminal cases, and judges of first instance. Minor cases are heard by justices of the peace.

Political Parties. The most powerful political force in Paraguay is the Asociación Nacional Republicana (National Republican Party), known popularly as the Colorado Party; its policies are ultraconservative. Other parties include the Liberal Party, which is split into the rightist Directorado Revolucionario del Partido Liberal and the leftist Partido Liberal Radical, in addition to the Partido Febrerista Revolucionaria (Febrerista Party), a leftist organization. The Communist Party is barred by law from participation in elections.

Local Government. The regions and departments of Paraguay have no executive, legislative, or judicial autonomy. The central government exercises all executive authority, and each department is run by a government delegate. A municipal board, chosen by direct election, and an executive department manage the municipal governments. A police chief, who is appointed by the national government, governs each rural district.

Defense. The armed forces have long dominated political institutions in Paraguay and are supported by about half the national budget. The personnel of the Paraguayan armed forces number about 13,500 men. Two years of military service is compulsory for all males between the ages of eighteen and twenty.

HISTORY

The aborigines of Paraguay were Indians of various tribes collectively known as Guarani (q.v.) because of their common language. They were very numerous when the country was discovered, probably about 1525, by the Portuguese explorer Alejo García (d. about 1526). During the next few years the Italian navigator Sebastian Cabot (see under CABOT), then in the service of Spain, partly explored the rivers of the country.

Spanish Settlement. In 1537 Spanish adventurers seeking gold established a fort on the Paraguay R., calling it Nuestra Señora de la Asunción. Colonial Paraguay and the territory of present-day Argentina were ruled jointly until 1620, when they became separate dependencies of the viceroyalty of Peru.

Beginning about 1609, the Jesuits (q.v.), working under great hardship, established many missions called *reducciónes,* which were settlements of Indian converts whom the missionaries educated. The communal life on these settlements was similar to the original life of the Indians. Granted almost complete freedom from civil and ecclesiastical local authorities, the Jesuits, through the missions, became the strongest power in the colony. In 1750 Ferdinand VI, King of Spain (see under FERDINAND), by the Treaty of Madrid, ceded Paraguayan territory including

PARAGUAY

seven *reducciónes* to Portugal, and the Jesuits incited a Guarani revolt against the transfer. In 1767 the missionaries were expelled from all of Spanish America, including Paraguay. Soon after the expulsion, the missions were deserted.

In 1776 Spain created the viceroyalty of La Plata, which comprised present-day Argentina, Paraguay, Uruguay, and Bolivia. Paraguay became an unimportant border dependency of Buenos Aires, the capital of the viceroyalty, and sank gradually into relative insignificance until the early 19th century.

Independence. In 1810 Argentina proclaimed its independence of Spain, but Paraguay refused to join it and in the next year proclaimed its own independence on May 14. In 1814 José Gaspar Rodríguez Francia (q.v.) made himself dictator and ruled absolutely until his death in 1840. Fearing that Paraguay might fall prey to stronger Argentina, Francia dictated a policy of national isolation. In the administrative reorganization following the dictator's death, his nephew Carlos Antonio López (1790–1862), became the leading political figure. In 1844 López became president and dictator. He reversed the isolation policy, encouraged commerce, instituted many reforms, and began building a railroad. Under his rule the population of Paraguay rose to more than 1,000,000 persons.

Ruinous War. At his death in 1862 López was succeeded by his son, Francisco Solano López (1827–1870). In 1865, desirous of building an empire for himself, he led the country into a war against an alliance of Argentina, Brazil, and Uruguay. The war devastated Paraguay, and when the death of López in 1870 ended the conflict, more than one half of the population had been killed, the economy had been destroyed, and agricultural activity was at a standstill. Territorial losses exceeded 55,000 sq.mi.; the country was occupied by a Brazilian army until 1876; and the peace treaties imposed heavy indemnities on the country. In 1878 President Rutherford Birchard Hayes (q.v.) of the U.S. was arbiter in the settlement of boundaries between Argentina and Paraguay. Paraguayan history after the war was largely an effort to reconstruct the country. To increase the population, immigration was encouraged and Paraguay established subsidized agricultural colonies.

The 20th Century. The unsettling effects of the war were apparent for many decades, particularly from 1870 to 1912, when no president of Paraguay was able to serve out his full term. Subsequently, periods of political stability alternated with periods of ferment and revolt. The administration (1912–16) of Eduardo Schaerer was relatively enlightened. The country was neutral and prosperous during World War I, and the administrations of Manuel Gondra in 1920–21, Eusebio Ayala from 1921 to 1923 (1875–1942), and Eligio Ayala from 1924 to 1928 were on the whole periods of peace and progress.

WAR WITH BOLIVIA. The border with Bolivia in the Chaco, which had never been formally drawn, was the scene of numerous incidents between 1929 and 1932. In the latter year full-scale war broke out when the area was invaded by Bolivia. An armistice was declared in 1935. In the final settlement, made by an arbitration commission in 1938, Paraguay was given about three quarters (95,313 sq.mi.) of the disputed area.

THE 1940's. The Paraguayan government was then reorganized to permit widespread economic and social reforms. By a new constitution adopted in 1940, the state was given the power to regulate economic activities and the government was highly centralized. Paraguay ended diplomatic relations with Germany, Italy, and Japan in January, 1942, and declared war on Germany and Japan on Feb. 7, 1945. The country became a charter member of the United Nations in 1945.

In 1940 General Higinio Morínigo (1897–   ) made himself president and ruled with enlightened despotism for the next eight years. A coup d'état deposed the dictator in 1948. In September, 1949, after a period of marked political instability, Federico Chaves, army-backed leader of a faction of the dominant Colorado Party, was elected president without opposition.

ECONOMIC CRISIS. In March, 1951, the Chaves regime devaluated the currency in an attempt to check inflation and the loss of gold reserves. The economic crisis was aggravated in 1952 following the abrogation by Argentina, itself the victim of depressed economic conditions, of a barter agreement with Paraguay. During the year legislation granted various benefits to workers. In general elections, held on Feb. 15, 1953, President Federico Chaves was reelected, again without opposition. Chaves imposed wage and price controls in June, 1953, in an effort to check inflation. On May 5, 1954, his government was overthrown by an army-police junta. The electorate on July 11, endorsed General Alfredo Stroessner (1912–   ), commander in chief of the army, who was the banner bearer of the Colorado Party and the only candidate. Paraguay granted asylum in September, 1955, to the deposed Argentine president Juan Domingo Perón (*see under* PERÓN).

Attempts by leftist forces to seize power were put down in 1956 and 1957. A plebiscite in 1958

PARAGUAY

confirmed President Stroessner in office for another five years.

NEW ECONOMIC TIES. In elections for a new congress in 1960, all sixty seats were won by the president's supporters in the Colorado Party. Diplomatic relations with Cuba were severed in December. At the meeting of the Organization of American States (q.v.) in 1962 in Punta del Este, Uruguay, to consider the Cuban question, Paraguay was among the states that favored collective action against the Cuban regime, but such measures were not approved by the two-thirds majority required. In 1963 Stroessner was reelected president, running against the first opposition candidate in a Paraguayan presidential election in thirty years. He enjoyed some popularity in the mid-1960's, partly because of continued economic progress, and continued in power in 1968 after having had the constitution altered the previous year to permit his reelection.

The most significant international development in the late 1960's was the establishment by Paraguay of close economic relations with neighboring countries. In May, 1968, the La Plata Basin Pact was signed by the foreign ministers of Argentina, Bolivia, Brazil, Paraguay, and Uruguay. This agreement, calling for joint development of the La Plata river basin, was expected to stimulate the economy of the entire region and would be of special importance to Paraguay, the least developed nation in the area.

In June, 1971, the chancellors of four neighboring nations and Paraguay met in Asunción for the fourth Cuenca del Plata conference to discuss matters of regional interest.

PARAGUAY, or PARAGUAI, river of central South America, originating in the highlands of Mato Grosso State, W. Brazil, and flowing 1500 miles s. across central Paraguay to join the Paraná River (q.v.) at the N. border of Argentina. It is joined from the w. by two tributaries, the Pilcomayo and Bermejo rivers. Although the river channel is subject to shifts, it is navigable for most of its course. The chief port is Asunción, Paraguay.

PARAGUAY TEA. See MATÉ.

PARAKEET, common name applied to many species of small birds belonging to the family Psittacidae, which also contains the parrot and the macaw (qq.v.). Parakeets are distinguished from other members of the parrot family chiefly by their small size, slender bodies, and long pointed tails. Their plumage is brilliantly colored, and many varieties have been bred for different combinations of green, blue, red, or violet feathers on the face, body, tail, and wings.

Parakeets are easily tamed. With proper training, they learn to speak a few words. They are extremely popular as cage birds and become very affectionate pets.

Most species are tropical in distribution, centered in the Indo-Malayan region. In their native habitat parakeets feed on fruit and seeds. One

A pair of parakeets nest in a coconut shell found in the crotch of a tree in Miami, Fla. UPI

species in universal demand as pets is the grass parakeet, *Melopsittacus undulatus,* which is native to Australia. In the wild state, birds of this species travel in large flocks. They are largely terrestrial in habit, nest in the hollows of trees, and lay three or four eggs in a clutch. The grass parakeet is known also as the budgerigar (q.v.), from an aboriginal Australian word meaning "pretty", and as the zebra parakeet, for the striped pattern on the bird's upper parts.

Other Australian species include the ground parakeet, which inhabits the plains regions. The rose-ringed parakeet, *Palaeornis torquata,* native to India, has a pink band encircling its neck. Another well-known variety is the African parakeet, *P. alexandri,* which may be taught to speak with distinctness. Because birds of this species live in solitary pairs, they are known also as lovebirds.

Parakeets are subject to the virus disease psittacosis (q.v.), which is communicable to man. To prevent epidemics, the Federal government strictly controls the importation of parakeets into the United States.

PARALLAX, in astronomy, such apparent displacement of the actual position of an object in space as would appear if the object were viewed from some other than the standard point; specifically, the difference between the directions of a body from the center of the earth and from a point of observation on the surface. Parallax is measured by the angle, at the object observed, between a line passing through the earth's center and one to the observer; this angle is called the angle of geocentric parallax.

The term geocentric parallax is also applied to the displacement of a heavenly body as a result of its being observed from a point on the surface of the earth instead of from its center. In the case of the moon and nearer planets, the geocentric parallax can be measured by means of simultaneous observations from widely separate points on the surface of the earth.

The determination of the parallax of nearby heavenly bodies is of great importance, for two reasons. It is necessary to refer all astronomical observations to one constant position, the earth's center, that is, to modify the observations so as to make it appear as if they had been made at the earth's center. Also, parallax is the only means of determining accurately the magnitude and distance of the heavenly bodies.

Parallax determination for extremely distant objects, such as the stars, is accomplished by observations made at six-month intervals on the earth's annual orbit. This so-called annual parallax uses the diameter of the earth's orbit, whereas the geocentric parallax uses only the diameter of the earth itself.

PARALYSIS, or PALSY, loss of voluntary movement in a part of the human body, caused by disease or injury anywhere along the motor-nerve path from the brain to the muscle fiber. Paralysis is a symptom, not a disease; therefore, there is no specific causative factor, but it may result from injury, poisoning, infection, hemorrhage, occluded blood vessels, or tumors. Paralysis without organic tissue damage is simulated in cases of hysteria (q.v.), and occasionally paralysis is due to congenital deficiency in motor-nerve development. Permanent paralysis results from extensive damage to nerve cells or to a nerve trunk; severely damaged nerve cells cannot regenerate. Transient or incomplete paralysis, called paresis, may occasionally result from psychogenic conditions (see MENTAL DISORDERS), but more often derives from infections, trauma, or poisons which temporarily suppress motor activity but do not extensively damage nerve cells. Frequently such infections and toxins interfere with impulses from the brain to the muscles at the junction or synapse of neighboring nerve cells. Because most of the motor nerves from either half of the brain supply the opposite side of the body, lesions in one part of the brain usually produce paralyses in the opposite half of the body. Paralysis of one limb is known as monoplegia; paralysis of two limbs on the same side of the body as hemiplegia; paralysis of both lower limbs as paraplegia or diplegia; and paralysis of all four limbs as quadriplegia, or tetraplegia. Paralysis originating in the brain may sometimes be flaccid, that is, the affected muscles may be loose, weak, flabby, and without normal reflexes. More frequently it is spastic, that is, the affected muscles are rigid and the reflexes accentuated. Paralysis originating in a motor nerve of the spinal cord is always spastic; paralysis originating in peripheral nerves or thin ganglion cells is always flaccid. See NERVOUS SYSTEM.

Among well-known paralytic conditions are poliomyelitis, cerebral palsy, and multiple sclerosis (qq.v.). Bell's palsy is a common facial paralysis, generally temporary and produced by such factors as neuritis (q.v.) or infection. Locomotor ataxia is a paralytic condition caused by infestation of the spinal cord and brain with microorganisms which cause syphilis (q.v.). Alcoholic paralysis is caused by degeneration of nerve cells, in the spinal cord or, less often, in the brain, which have been deprived of essential nutrients. The alcoholic substitutes alcohol for food, and the nerve cells cannot survive without vitamin B and other requirements; see ALCOHOLISM; VITAMIN. Parkinson's disease (q.v.) was once classified as a form of paralysis, but the ailment is now recognized as a separate entity.

Temporary paralyses are treated by removing the underlying cause. Permanent paralyses may be ameliorated by appropriate physical therapy and rehabilitation (qq.v.) procedures. Occasionally, suture or graft of injured or severed peripheral nerves may result in restoration of function; see SURGERY: *Modern Surgery: Curative Surgery.*

PARAMAGNETISM. See MAGNETISM: *Theory of Magnets.*

PARAMARIBO, city, seaport, and capital of Surinam, an overseas part of the Netherlands, on the left bank of the Surinam R., 7 miles w. of Marienburg. Paramaribo, the largest city and chief port of Surinam, is noted as a trading and export center for timber, rice, citrus fruits, and bauxite. Major industries include lumber production and food processing. Paramaribo was originally an Indian village. When Surinam became an English colony in 1650, Paramaribo became the capital, a position it has retained since Surinam came under Dutch rule in 1816. Pop. (1967 est.) 123,000.

PARAMECIUM, genus of cilia-bearing protozoans (see PROTOZOA), belonging to the class

PARAMOUNT

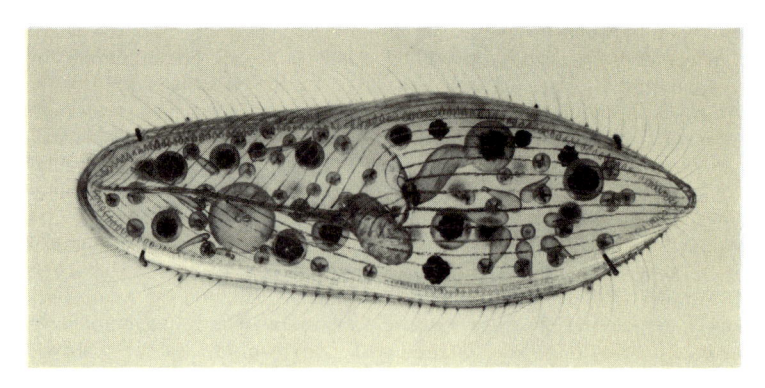

Model of a paramecium.
American Museum of Natural History

Ciliata (see INFUSORIA) and known popularly as slipper animalcules because of their slipperlike shape. Paramecia are one-celled animals, usually less than $1/100$ in. in length. Each organism is covered with minute hairlike projections called cilia, which serve to propel it through the water. In moving forward it follows a spiral path while rotating on its long axis. When an obstacle is encountered, paramecia exhibit the so-called avoiding reaction, which consists of backing away at an angle and starting off in a new direction. Paramecia feed chiefly on bacteria, which are driven into the gullet by the cilia. Two contractile vacuoles, which regulate osmotic pressure, may also be involved in excretion. One large macronucleus is present and one or two small micronuclei lie close beside it. Reproduction is usually asexual, by transverse binary fission, occasionally sexual, by conjugation, and rarely by endomixis, a phenomenon characterized by total nuclear reorganization of individual organisms; see REPRODUCTION.

Paramecia abound in freshwater ponds throughout the world; there is one marine species. They may be cultivated in the laboratory by allowing vegetable matter to stand in water for a few days. The common species *P. caudatum* is used extensively in research and for laboratory demonstrations in elementary biology courses.

PARAMOUNT, city of California, in Los Angeles Co., on the Los Angeles R., adjoining Long Beach on the N., and 10 miles S.E. of Los Angeles. Industries include meat packing, structural prefabricating, and the manufacture of metal and machine products, tools and dies, steel, brass, rubber, wood products, resins, and textile products. The city was incorporated in 1957. Pop. (1960) 27,249; (1970) 34,341.

PARAMUS, borough of New Jersey, in Bergen Co., 6 miles N.E. of Paterson. Although the borough is now a center of large suburban shopping plazas, the truck-farm products it formerly grew earned it the nickname of "Celery Town". Industries include the manufacture of electric and electronic equipment, machine and metal products, industrial equipment, building materials, fixtures, textile products, and photographic equipment. In Paramus are early Dutch buildings, including the Van Emburgh House (1701) and the Old Paramus Church, where the American statesman Aaron Burr (q.v.) was first married, in 1782. Settled in 1666, the borough was incorporated in 1922. Pop. (1970) 29,495.

PARANÁ, city in Argentina, and capital of Entre Ríos Province, on the Río Paraná, opposite Santa Fe, 235 miles N.W. of Buenos Aires. It is a river port important for the transshipment of grains, cattle, fish, and lumber from the surrounding region. The principal industries in the city are the manufacture of cement, furniture, and ceramics. Paraná was founded in 1730, and served as the capital of the Argentine Confederation between 1853 and 1861. Pop. (1969 est.) 111,258.

PARANÁ, river of South America, formed in S.-central Brazil by the confluence of the Rio Grande and Paranaíba R. It flows S.W. and separates Paraná State first from Mato Grosso State and then from Paraguay. The river sweeps westward, forming part of the border between Paraguay and Argentina, to its confluence with the Paraguay R. The Paraná then runs S. and E. through Argentina until it unites with the Uruguay R. to form the Rio de la Plata estuary on the Atlantic Ocean. The river is about 2450 mi. long, of which about 1000 mi. are navigable by large ships. The Paraná, with its confluent rivers, forms one of the largest drainage systems in South America, second only to that of the Amazon R.

PARANOIA. See MENTAL DISORDERS: *Psychoses: Paranoid Psychoses.*

PARAPLEGIA. See PARALYSIS.

PARAPSYCHOLOGY. See PSYCHICAL RESEARCH.

PARASITE, any organism living upon or within another living organism, plant or animal, and

PARASITE

deriving part or all subsistence from the host without supplying anything to the host in return. In most cases, parasites cause damage to or disease of the host. Parasites such as lice, which live on the surface of the host, are known as ectoparasites; parasites, such as threadworms, which live within the body of the host, are known as endoparasites. Some parasites, known as permanent parasites, pass most of their life cycle in or on a host; others, known as temporary parasites, pass only a brief time in or on a host and are free-living for the remainder of the life cycle. Parasites which must subsist on a living host are known as obligate parasites; parasites which may feed either on a living host or on dead matter are known as facultative parasites. Heteroecious parasites, such as the liver fluke, pass different stages of their life cycle in hosts of different species; autoecious parasites, such as the pinworm, pass the parasitic portion of their life cycle in only one host. The scientific study of parasites is known as parasitology.

The Lowest Parasites. Viruses, although not accepted by all present-day biologists as living organisms, are similar to true parasites in method of transmission from host to host and in effects upon plants and animals. Some viruses, called bacteriophages, are parasites that use bacteria as their host. A phage infects a bacterium and produces hundreds of its own offspring. The bacterium eventually bursts and scatters the new phages, which can then infect other bacteria. Several microorganisms named *Rickettsia* (q.v.) are larger than viruses but smaller than most bacteria. They transmit such diseases as typhus, Rocky Mountain spotted fever, tsutsugamushi disease, and trench fever. The *Rickettsia* parasites are carried by arthropods such as lice, fleas, and ticks and enter the bodies of animals through the bites of these vectors.

Parasitic Plants. Most parasites injurious to man are members of the plant kingdom. Bacteria, most of which are parasitic, cause numerous infectious diseases of animals and a number of plant diseases. Fungal parasites produce most plant diseases and several animal diseases; see ANTHRACNOSE; DISEASES OF PLANTS; FUNGI; MILDEW; RUST. All parasitic plants except bacteria and fungi feed on other plants. Seed plants may be partial parasites, deriving some of their food from the host, or total parasites, completely dependent on the host for food. Partial parasites have green leaves, and are capable of synthesizing carbohydrates, proteins, and fats by photosynthesis (q.v.); however, they derive all their water, nitrogen, and mineral salts from the host.

Common examples of such parasites are the painted cup, parasitic on roots, and mistletoe, parasitic on branches. The mistletoe is typical of a group of parasitic plants which never form roots of their own; the seeds of these plants are carried from tree to tree by birds, and develop penetrating outgrowths, known as haustoria, which pierce the host and enter the conducting system. Total parasites have vestigial leaves without chlorophyll, and never have functioning roots. In dodder, the seed germinates in the ground, forming a small root attaching the plant to the soil but deriving no food from the soil; a long, thin, pliable stem grows out above the ground until it contacts a green plant, up which it climbs. Haustoria from the stem of the parasite enter the green plant, and the root attaching the parasite to the ground withers and dies. Branches may develop from the main stem of the parasite and grow along the ground until they reach another green plant. In this manner, one parasitic plant may attack several hosts at the same time. The ultimate in total parasitism is exhibited by certain tropical plants of the family Rafflesiaceae which have neither stems nor leaves. These plants are specific parasites, that is, they grow only on specific species of green plants. The germinated seed sends haustoria directly into the host; the only other organs of the parasite are apetalous flowers, composed of five huge, fleshy sepals which give off the odor of

Hornworm with cocoons of the parasitic braconid wasp.   Jerome Wexler – National Audubon Society

PARATHYROID GLANDS

dead meat. Insects, attracted by this odor, carry the pollen of the parasite from flower to flower.
Parasitic Animals. The most injurious parasitic animals include sporozoans, flukes, threadworms, and insects. These animals may be parasitic in the adult or larval forms or both. Among insects, parasites are themselves often parasitized, a condition called hyperparasitism; see ICHNEUMON FLY. Invertebrate parasites infest both animals and plants. Among the higher animals, lampreys and hagfishes are regularly parasitic upon fishes; bloodsucking bats of the genera *Desmodus, Diphylla,* and *Diaemus,* the true vampire bats of South and Central America, are parasitic particularly on mammals, but also on birds and reptiles. Vampire bats also are a natural reservoir of rabies. For animal parasites of animals lower than man, see BOTFLY; HAIRWORM.

See also articles on most of the common parasitic plants and animals mentioned above.

PARATHYROID GLANDS, group of glandular cell aggregations located in the neck region close to the thyroid gland in lizards, some birds, and most mammals. In man, four such clumps are usually present as distinct, yellowish-brown, encapsulated organs, each about ¼ in. long. The combined weight of these glands is no more than ⅟₅₀ oz. They are located beneath the thyroid gland; one or more of them are occasionally embedded in the thyroid tissue. Sometimes one or more are aberrant in their location and may appear in association with the thymus, or may occur anywhere between the thyroid and thymus gland or even elsewhere in the neck or upper anterior chest. Such glands may be present in addition to four normally placed ones and are known as accessory parathyroid tissue. The parathyroid glands secrete a hormone (q.v.), known as *parathormone,* which controls the concentration of calcium (calcium ion) and phosphorus (phosphate) in the blood. Calcium and phosphorus are normally kept within a narrow range and bear a relationship to each other which the body keeps fairly constant. Parathyroid hormone acts to increase the excretion of phosphorus by the kidneys (which tends to lower blood phosphorus levels) and to increase the rate of resorption of calcium from bone (which tends to raise the level of blood calcium). Deficiency of parathormone, which rarely occurs spontaneously and which is sometimes caused by accidental removal of the parathyroid glands during surgical excision of the thyroid, results in reduction of blood calcium, increase of blood phosphorus, and increased nervous excitability leading to rapid involuntary contractions of the muscles, a condition known as *tetany.* The accessory parathyroid tissue is occasionally sufficient to prevent severe deficiency symptoms when the essential four clumps are removed. Unless accessory tissue is formed or hormone injections are given, parathormone deficiency results in death. Overactivity of the parathyroid glands, occurring in cases of parathyroid tumors or hyperplasia of the normal glands results in decreased blood phosphorus and increased blood calcium; the calcium in the bloodstream is withdrawn from the bones, which become soft as a result. Crystallization of excess calcium excreted in the urine in hyperparathyroidism may cause formation of kidney stones. The calcium may be carried to and deposited in the soft tissues of the body by the bloodstream; deposition of this calcium sometimes interferes with the functions of various organs, particularly the kidneys.　　L.J.V.

PARCAE.　See FATES, THE.

PARCHMENT AND VELLUM, writing materials made from specially prepared skins of animals, usually sheep, calves, or goats. Parchment has been used at least since about 200 B.C.; its name is derived from the ancient Greek city of Pergamum (q.v.), where an especially fine quality of the material was produced. Vellum is a finer-quality parchment made from the skins of kids, lambs, and young calves. The finest vellum is made from the skins of stillborn kids and lambs. It is still used occasionally for formal honorary documents. Parchment or vellum is prepared by cleaning the skin and removing the hairs, scraping and smoothing both sides of the skin, and finally rubbing it with powdered pumice. Coarser parchments made from the skins of older animals are used for drumheads and tambourines. So-called parchment paper, a modern invention, is made by dipping ordinary unsized paper into a solution of two parts concentrated sulfuric acid and one part water for a few seconds and then quickly neutralizing the acid.

PARDO BAZÁN, Emilia (1852–1921), Spanish novelist, born in La Coruña. She introduced into Spanish literature the naturalism (q.v.) expressed by contemporary French writers, and many of her works reflect strongly the influence of the French novelist Émile Zola (q.v.). Her best-known novels are *Los Pazos de Ulloa* ("The Manors of Ulloa," 1886), and *La Madre Naturaleza* ("Mother Nature", 1887). The former, which deals with a decadent noble family in Galicia, is especially noteworthy for its poetic, yet naturalistic, treatment of Galician rural life. With the latter, a sequel to *Los Pazos de Ulloa,* she won universal recognition as the leading exponent of naturalism in Spanish letters. Her other writings include several critical works and a collection of short stories.

PARDON, in law, act by which an individual or class of individuals is freed from the consequences of having committed a breach of the law. Article II, Section 2 of the Constitution of the United States (q.v.) confers on the President "power to grant reprieves and pardons for offences against the United States, except in cases of impeachment". Under most State constitutions this power is exercised by the governor, although in some cases the consent of the legislature or the executive council is required. A number of States have established boards of pardon consisting, as a rule, of certain high executive and judicial officers of the State.

A pardon may be granted either before or after conviction for a crime. It can not, however, apply retroactively to allow one who paid a fine to recover the same, or to allow one who has served a term of imprisonment to obtain compensation for such imprisonment. A pardon may be absolute or conditional. Any condition may be imposed provided it is not impossible, illegal, or immoral. A full pardon effects a remission of the punishment, and generally removes any legal disabilities consequent upon conviction. In most States of the U.S., however, a pardon does not restore to a person convicted of an infamous crime his rights of citizenship, unless such restitution is expressly granted by the pardoning power. See AMNESTY; CRIME; PUNISHMENT; REPRIEVE.

PARDUBICE, city in Czechoslovakia, and capital of Pardubice Province, on the Elbe R., 60 miles E. of Prague. Products manufactured in the city include liquor, radio and telegraph equipment, milling machinery, and shoes. Pardubice is an important horse-breeding and racing center. One of Czechoslovakia's oldest cities, it has a 13th-century church and several well-preserved 16th-century buildings. Pop. (1967 est.) 66,000.

PARÉ, Ambroise (about 1510–90), French surgeon, born in Laval. Between 1536 and 1545 he was in the French army as a military surgeon, serving in the Italian campaigns of Francis I (q.v.), King of France. In 1552 Paré was appointed royal surgeon to King Henry II (*see under* HENRY), and subsequently served in the same position under Henry's successors, Francis II, Charles IX, and Henry III (qq.v.). His most notable contribution was in establishing the use of ligatures for binding arteries to prevent hemorrhage. He did away with the practice of cauterizing wounds with boiling oil, improved the treatment of fractures, and promoted the use of artificial limbs. Paré was the first surgeon to describe his technical work in his native language rather than in Latin; consequently, his writings had a wide influence on both the lay and professional men of his time. His best-known works include *La Méthode de Traicter les Playes* ("Method of Treating Wounds", 1545), and *Deux Livres de Chirurgie* ("Two Books on Surgery", 1573).

PARENT AND CHILD, in law, that branch of the law of domestic relations which determines the legal rights and obligations of fathers or mothers to their children, and of children to their parents. The legal relation is to be distinguished from the natural relation; for example, two persons who have a natural relationship of parent and child may not be legally considered such, as in the case of a parent and an illegitimate child. Conversely, the legal relation may exist although there is no natural relation, as in the case of an adopted child.

At common law in Great Britain and the United States, parents were the legal as well as the natural guardians of their child. They had the right to name the child and were entitled to his custody. As custodians, they could reasonably chastise the child, but for excessive punishment the parents were criminally liable for assault, or for homicide in case of death. At common law the father was deemed entitled to custody of the child in preference to the mother. A parent was not liable for a tort (q.v.) of his child unless its commission was incited or authorized by the parent. A parent could recover damages for torts committed against the child. At common law the parent was not civilly liable to maintain the child, but was criminally responsible if he neglected to do so and, by failure to provide food or clothing, caused the child's injury or death.

The legal relations of parent and child established under the common law have been modified by statute in Great Britain and the U.S. In general such statutes provide that a married woman is a joint guardian of her children with her husband, with equal powers, rights, and duties in regard to them. Either parent has the right to the custody of the children of the marriage, and in the case of divorce or separation the court can award the custody of the child to the parent best qualified and able to care for it. Parents are liable for necessaries furnished by others to their minor children when they neglect or refuse to provide them. A father who fails to support his minor children, legitimate or illegitimate, may be criminally liable. In the U.S., some States permit illegitimate children to in-

PARENTS AND TEACHERS, NATIONAL CONGRESS OF

herit from the mother, and allow the mother to inherit from her illegitimate child. Inheritance from the father is permitted for illegitimate children in some States, if the relationship has been admitted or adjudicated.

PARENTS AND TEACHERS, NATIONAL CONGRESS OF, known also as P.T.A. (abbrev. for Parent-Teachers Association), volunteer organization in the United States devoted to the education, welfare, and protection of children and youths, founded in 1897 in Washington, D.C. Through the cooperative efforts of parents and teachers, the P.T.A. helps to develop a range of programs in home, school, church, and community, including library services, educational television, reading clinics, and legislation for the care and protection of children and youths. The organization is made up of branches in every State, in the District of Columbia, and among schools for American dependents in Europe. Under the authority of the branches, local P.T.A. groups, usually organized in the individual school, plan such programs and activities as the establishment of community child-care centers and recreational areas for youths. Membership in a local unit includes membership in the State branch and in the National Congress. In 1970 about 44,500 local P.T.A. units were in existence, and national P.T.A. memberships totaled almost 10,800,000. Publications include *National Parent-Teacher: The P.T.A. Magazine*. Headquarters is located in Chicago, Ill.

PARENT-TEACHER ASSOCIATION. See PARENTS AND TEACHERS, NATIONAL CONGRESS OF.

PARESIS. See MENTAL DISORDERS: *Psychoses: Organic Psychoses;* SYPHILIS.

PARIAH. See CASTE.

PARÍCUTIN. See VOLCANO.

PARI-MUTUEL. See HORSE RACING, FLAT: *Betting*.

PARIS, city in Texas, and county seat of Lamar Co., in the Red R. valley, about 95 miles N.E. of Dallas. It is the commercial center and shipping point of an area producing cotton, poultry, and dairy products. Among the industrial establishments are cottonseed-oil and flour mills, and factories producing furniture, concrete products, leather goods, and processed food. The city is the site of Paris Junior College, established in 1924. Paris, which was settled in 1841, was originally called Pinhook. It was given its present name in 1844, and was chartered as a city in 1905. Following a disastrous fire in 1916 the city was largely replanned and rebuilt. Pop. (1960) 20,977; (1970) 23,441.

PARIS, capital of France and administrative center of the Paris Department, on the Seine R., about 138 mi. from its mouth. It is the center of a great network of rivers, canals, roads, and railroads. For administrative purposes the city is divided into twenty districts (*arrondissements*). The Seine, which enters Paris in the S.E. at Bercy and leaves it at Passy in the W., divides the city in two and forms the islands of La Cité and Saint Louis, which are both covered with buildings. Pop. (1968) 2,590,771; including suburbs, 9,250,674.

Industry and Trade. Paris is the largest industrial and trade center of France. Large factories are found in the manufacture of machinery, railroad supplies, chemical products, soap, dyes, beer, china, porcelain, and leather. Small workshops, however, predominate in the production of clothing, gold and silver articles, furniture, optical and surgical instruments, toys, paper boxes, steel and aluminum articles, artificial flowers, perfumes, articles of luxury, and gloves. The book-publishing business of France is almost wholly concentrated in Paris. It was among the first cities of the world to introduce large department stores such as the Louvre, the Bon Marché, and Printemps. Banking institutions include the Banque de France, Crédit Foncier, and Crédit Lyonnais.

Communications and Bridges. Several major railroad lines enter Paris, and numerous bus lines and electric tramways give access to its numerous suburbs as well as to other important cities in France. With the demolition of the city walls, the subway system of Paris was extended to the suburbs. A major addition to the underground transit system was completed in 1970.

The Seine is crossed by thirty-two bridges in Paris, the oldest and most famous being the Pont Neuf, begun in 1578. Other well-known bridges include Pont Notre Dame, Pont de la Concorde, Pont d'Austerlitz, Pont d'Iéna, Pont du Carrousel, and Pont Mirabeau.

Streets, Buildings, and Monuments. Among the better-known thoroughfares are the Rue de Rivoli, Rue de la Paix, Rue du Faubourg-St. Honoré, Rue Royale, Avenue de l'Opéra, Boulevard des Italiens, and Boulevard St. Denis. The many squares containing statues and other memorials include the Place de la Concorde, connecting the gardens of the Tuileries (q.v.) with the Champs Elysées and containing the Luxor obelisk; Place du Carrousel with the small Arc de Triomphe; Place de l'Opéra; Place de la Bastille; Place de l'Hôtel de Ville; Place Charles de Gaulle (formerly Place de l'Etoile) with the Arc de Triomphe; Place Vendome; and Champ-de-Mars with the famous Eiffel Tower (q.v.).

The most notable buildings are the Louvre

The Seine is crossed by numerous bridges as it cuts through the heart of the city.   UPI

(q.v.), Palais de Chaillot, Hôtel des Invalides, Palais Royal, Hôtel de Ville, Opéra, Palais de l'Élysée (now the official residence of the president of France), Palais Bourbon (the meeting place of the Chamber of Deputies), and the Palais de Justice.

Among the large number of churches the grandest and most interesting from a historic point of view is the 12th-century cathedral of Notre Dame, which stands on a site on the Île de la Cité. Of nearly equal antiquity is Saint Pierre-de-Montmartre. Other famous churches are Saint Étienne-du-Mont (1517–41); Saint Germain-l'Auxerrois; Sainte Chapelle, built by Louis IX (q.v.), known as Saint Louis, in 1245–48 for the reception of the crown of thorns; Saint Eustache (1532–1637), the largest parish church in Paris; and Saint Sulpice, 1749.

The mammoth Halles Centrales or Central Markets, once located on the north of the river, have been moved to Rungis, in the suburbs of Paris. On the south side of the river are the Sorbonne (q.v.), the center of the famous Latin Quarter, the Panthéon, the palace and gardens of the Luxembourg, and the Boulevard du Montparnasse, frequented by artists and writers.

Paris is well equipped with theaters, chief of which is the Opéra. Other well-known theaters are the Théâtre de la Comédie Française, Opéra Comique, and the Odéon.

The Bohemian life is concentrated in Montmartre, where many places of amusement are found. In this district also is located the Église du Sacré Coeur.

Education. The University of Paris includes the Sorbonne, in addition to such faculties as law, medicine, and sciences; see PARIS, UNIVERSITY OF. Near the Sorbonne is the Collège de France. The École Polytechnique, the School of Medicine and the School of Law, the Observatory, and the Jardin des Plantes are in the same quarter. The main public library, the Bibliothèque Nationale, originated in a small collection of books donated by Louis XI (q.v.). Paris is rich in fine art collections, the chief of which is at the Louvre.

History. The earliest notice of Paris is in the *Commentaries* by the Roman statesman Gaius Julius Caesar (q.v.), who called it Lutetia. In the 4th century it became known as Parisia, or Paris.

In the Middle Ages Paris was divided into three distinct parts: the Cité, on the islands; the Ville, on the right bank; and the Quartier Latin, or University, on the left bank of the river, and on the Montagne St. Geneviève. In 1358 the first of the long series of Paris revolutions broke out. On the accession of Henry IV (q.v.) of Navarre, in 1589, a new era was opened for Paris.

The French Revolution (q.v.) caused a temporary reaction; but the improvement of Paris was recommenced on a new and grander scale under Napoleon I (q.v.), when new quays, bridges, markets, streets, squares, and public gardens were created. In the restoration he spent more than $20,000,000 in twelve years. His downfall arrested progress, and it was reserved for Napoleon III (q.v.) to reconstruct the city. During the Franco-German War (q.v.) Paris was badly damaged by German bombardment, but by 1873 the streets and public places were restored as in the best days of the empire.

In World War I (q.v.) Paris was the objective of the German armies that swept through Bel-

The Arc de Triomphe dominates the Place de l'Etoile, which in 1970 was renamed the Place Charles de Gaulle, in honor of the French statesman Charles de Gaulle. — Trans World Airlines

gium in the fall of 1914 and, although the threat of conquest was averted by the Battle of the Marne (q.v.), to which the garrison of Paris was sent in taxicabs, the city continued to be virtually within the war zone. The government was removed to Bordeaux on Sept. 2, 1914, as a precaution, but returned to Paris four months later. German aircraft bombed Paris in August and October, 1914, and many times in the succeeding years of war. An Allied conference was convened at Paris, March, 1916, for consideration of military affairs, and another one dealing with economic matters was opened the following month. An improved type of German airplane, the Gotha, systematically raided Paris toward the end of 1917, and a long-range gun shelled Paris during 1918. In World War II (q.v.), Paris, only slightly damaged by the war, was occupied by German troops on June 14, 1940, after the government had left the capital and declared it an open city. The liberation of Paris began on Aug. 19, 1944, and the city was officially declared free when General Charles de Gaulle (q.v.) entered it on Aug. 26. It was the seat of two peace conferences in 1946 and, beginning in 1968, of a conference involving the participants in the Vietnam conflict; *see* VIETNAM, WAR IN.

PARIS, also called ALEXANDER, in Greek mythology, son of Priam and Hecuba (qq.v.), King and Queen of Troy. Priam had been warned that the young prince would someday be the ruin of his country and had, therefore, exposed the infant Paris on Mt. Ida. The youth was brought up as a shepherd, and he was tending his sheep when an argument arose between the goddesses Hera, Athena, and Aphrodite (qq.v.) as to who was the most beautiful. The three goddesses approached him asking him to be the judge. Each tried to bribe him, Hera promising to make him ruler of Europe and Asia, Athena to help him lead Troy to victory against the Greeks, and Aphrodite to give him the most beautiful woman in the world. Paris decided in favor of Aphrodite, even though at that time he was in

"Paris and Helen", a painting by the French artist Jacques Louis David (1748–1825). — Bettmann Archive

love with Oenone, a beautiful young nymph. His decision made Hera and Athena bitter enemies of his country and started the chain of events that led to the Trojan War (q.v.).

Forgetting Oenone, Paris went with Aphrodite to the court of Menelaus (q.v.), King of Sparta, whose wife, Helen of Troy (q.v.), was the most beautiful woman in the world. In Menelaus' absence, Paris persuaded Helen to go with him to Troy. In the tenth year of the siege of Troy that followed, Paris and Menelaus met in hand-to-hand combat. Menelaus would easily have been the victor except for the intervention of Aphrodite, who saved Paris by enveloping him in a cloud and carrying him back to Troy. Before the fall of the city, Paris was mortally wounded by the archer Philoctetes (q.v.). Paris then went to Oenone, the nymph he had loved and forgotten, because she had a magic drug that could cure all illness. Oenone had suffered so much she could not bring herself to save Paris, but when he died she killed herself.

PARIS, Comte de, Louis Philippe Albert d'Orléans (1838–94), pretender to the French throne and member of the house of Orléans (q.v.). He was the grandson of Louis Philippe (q.v.), titular king of the French; on the death of his father, Ferdinand, Duc d'Orléans (1810–42), Paris became the heir apparent to the throne. With the deposition of Louis Philippe and the establishment of the Second Republic in 1848, the mother of the young count took him to live abroad; he lived in various parts of Europe and in the United States for twenty-three years. In 1861 he was an officer in the Union Army in the American Civil War, serving on the staff of Union General George Brinton McClellan (q.v.). He returned to France in 1871 and was recognized as the heir to the throne by the Orleanist faction of the French royalists; see BOURBON: *French Bourbons*. The Legitimist faction wished to place on the throne Henri Charles Dieudonne d'Artois, Comte de Chambord (1820–83), the grandson of the last Bourbon king, Charles X (*see under* CHARLES), who had designated him as his successor when forced to abdicate in 1830. In 1873 Paris gave up his claims in favor of Chambord, but on the death of the latter in 1883 both parties, advocating restoration of the monarchy, united behind Paris. Fearing that the Third Republic was being menaced by the Orleanists, the French legislature passed a law in 1886 expelling all direct claimants to the throne from France. Paris spent the rest of his life in exile in England.

PARIS, Matthew (1200?–59), English chronicler and monk. In 1217 he entered the monastery of Saint Albans, in Hertfordshire, where he became official historiographer. Matthew's principal work was the *Chronica Majora*, a chronicle of events from the creation of the world to the year 1259. He later wrote the *Chronica Minora*, an abridgement of his major chronicle with some added material. In 1248 he was sent on a mission to Norway by Pope Innocent IV (d. 1254) to reform the Abbey of Saint Benet Holm, in present-day Trondheim, after which he returned to St. Albans.

PARIS COMMUNE. See COMMUNE OF PARIS, 1871.

PARIS GREEN, poisonous, bright-green powder, used as an insecticide (q.v.) and fungicide and as a green pigment for ships and submarines. It is a double salt containing copper and arsenic in the form of cupric acetate and cupric arsenite, $Cu(C_2H_3O_2)_2 \cdot 3Cu(AsO_2)_2$, formed by boiling arsenious oxide and copper acetate.

PARIS, TREATY OF, name of several important treaties signed at or near Paris, France.

Treaty of Paris, 1763. The Treaty of Paris signed on Feb. 10, 1763, by Great Britain and her adversaries France and Spain ended the Seven Years' War in Europe and the New World phase of the conflict, the French and Indian War in America. For the causative issues and military engagements involved and for the provisions of the treaty, see FRENCH AND INDIAN WAR; SEVEN YEARS' WAR.

Treaty of Paris, 1783. The Treaty of Paris signed on Sept. 3, 1783, by Great Britain and the United States concluded the American Revolution. By its terms, Great Britain recognized her former thirteen colonies as the free and sovereign United States of America. On Sept. 3, 1783, Great Britain also signed separate treaties with France, an ally of the United States, and Spain, an ally of France. See AMERICAN REVOLUTION: *Treaty of Paris*.

Treaties of Paris, 1814 and 1815. From 1799 to 1815 France, under Napoléon Bonaparte, after 1804 Emperor Napoleon I (q.v.), waged a series of wars, called the Napoleonic Wars (q.v.), against various European nations. On March 31, 1814, Napoleon was defeated. The Treaty of Paris, signed on May 30, 1814, by France and her seven allied adversaries, Great Britain, Russia, Austria, Prussia, Sweden, Portugal, and Spain, was a lenient one for the defeated nation. France was allowed to retain all the territory held by her in Europe as of 1792 and was not required to pay an indemnity. Great Britain returned to France all the French colonies except Tobago, Saint Lucas, and Mauritius. The Congress of Vienna was called for the resettlement

PARIS, UNIVERSITY OF

of territories that had been taken by Napoleon in Europe; see VIENNA, CONGRESS OF.

Napoleon returned to France on March 1, 1815, in an attempt to regain power. Defeated at Waterloo, he abdicated a second time. A new peace treaty, actually a treaty of alliance, more stern than the first, was signed at Paris on Nov. 20, 1815, by Great Britain, Austria, Russia, and Prussia. The boundaries of France were reduced to those of 1790. France was made to pay 700,000,000 francs in war damages and to finance an allied occupation army in France for a maximum of five years. The Treaty of 1814, except for provisions not revoked by the Treaty of 1815, was to continue as binding, as were the territorial arrangements of the Congress of Vienna.

Treaty of Paris, 1856. The Treaty of Paris signed on March 30, 1856, ended the Crimean War, a conflict between Turkey, supported by Great Britain, France, and Sardinia, and the Russian Empire. For the important treaty provisions, see CRIMEAN WAR.

Treaty of Paris, 1898. The Treaty of Paris signed on Dec. 10, 1898, and ratified by the United States Senate on Feb. 6, 1899, ended the Spanish-American War. For the terms of the treaty, see SPANISH-AMERICAN WAR.

PARIS, UNIVERSITY OF, one of the oldest institutions of higher learning in Europe, dating from the 12th century and organized around various schools attached to the Cathedral of Notre Dame on the Île de la Cité in the center of the medieval city of Paris. These schools and their teachers were presided over by the bishop of Paris. One of the first of the famous medieval scholars connected with the university was the French philosopher Peter Abelard (q.v.), who was a student of theological dialectic.

Origin. The university itself was recognized formally about the middle of the 12th century, and its first written statutes date from the first decade of the 13th century. It was recognized as a legal corporation in 1211 by Pope Innocent III (see under INNOCENT), who granted it the right to send a proctor as its representative to the papal court. Shortly thereafter the university was divided into four faculties: theology, medicine, canon law, and arts; the last-named body was divided into four so-called nations, composed of both scholars and professors, comprising the French (including Spanish, Italian, and Greek), the Picard (including northeastern European and Netherlandish), the Norman, and the English (including English, Irish, Scottish, German, and French under the English rule). During the 13th and 14th centuries the students of canon law, medicine, and theology were successively placed under the authority of the rector of the university, who was originally the head of the faculty of arts. By the 14th century the university was composed of forty individual colleges, both secular and religious, and was famous throughout Europe as a great center of the study of theology.

The Sorbonne. The Sorbonne, founded in 1256 by the French theologian Robert de Sorbon (1201–74), became the most famous as the main school of the theological faculty. The college was originally intended as a residence hall for needy theological students and was named La Communauté des Pauvres Maîtres Étudiant en Théologie ("The Community of Needy Theological Students"); by the end of the 13th century, however, the name La Sorbonne was applied to the college through popular usage, and it had been organized as a full theological faculty with the power of conferring degrees. It was recognized as a theological school by the pope in 1268. From the 13th to the 16th centuries, the Sorbonne, because of its high standards, was recognized as the outstanding theological school in Europe, particularly in the fields of dogma and canon law. In the 16th and 17th centuries, however, although it continued to exercise great religious and political influence, its conservatism and refusal to permit educational reforms caused its reputation to decline. The creation of the Collège de France in 1530 by King Francis I (q.v.) was undertaken to fight against this conservatism.

From the 16th century until the French Revolution, the University of Paris, like the great English universities of Oxford and Cambridge (qq.v.), existed as a federation of independent colleges under university control. The religious dissensions and civil wars in France during the 16th and 17th centuries contributed to the decline of the university's academic functions at that period and to the increase of its political power. It took a leading part in the persecution of religious dissenters during the Reformation, but its colleges were almost empty at the beginning of the 17th century. In 1793, during the French Revolution, all universities and colleges throughout France were abolished by the National Convention, and not until 1808, when Napoleon I (q.v.), Emperor of France, reorganized the entire French educational system under the University of France, was the University of Paris reopened. At this time the Sorbonne became the seat of the academy of Paris, one of the seventeen educational districts into which the country was divided, and of the university itself;

soon thereafter the faculties of science, literature, law, and medicine, in addition to the faculty of theology which later was abolished, were established at the Sorbonne, as was the university library. In 1896, when French higher education was decentralized, the University of Paris received its present constitution. It is a national institution under the jurisdiction of the ministry of education and is financed by the government.

Current Divisions. The university consists of faculties of law and economics, letters and human sciences, science, medicine, and pharmacy. More than 200 institutes and schools in a wide variety of fields are associated with the university. The École des Hautes Études, the Collège de France, the École des Chartes, the École Normale Supérieure, the École des Beaux-Arts, and other specialized schools, such as those of Oriental languages, decorative arts, engineering, and mines, are administratively independent of the university. Students in such of these schools as give courses coinciding with those of the university receive their degrees from the university itself. The *licence,* the approximate equivalent of an American baccalaureate degree, is awarded after a three- to four-year course of study. The *diplôme d'études supérieures,* the approximate equivalent of an American degree of master, is awarded after an additional year of study. The *doctorat du troisième cycle* requires two years of study beyond the *licence* and the completion of a thesis. The highest degree is the *doctorat d'état,* which requires several years of additional study and the completion of a major and minor thesis. This degree qualifies the recipient to teach at a university and is comparable to an American Ph.D. The library at the Sorbonne contains about 1,500,000 bound volumes. The combined university libraries hold more than 4,500,000 bound volumes, as well as important collections of manuscripts, incunabula, and maps. The oldest archives of the university were transferred to the National Archives in 1794. In 1967–68 the university had an enrollment of 115,000, of whom some 10,000 were students from foreign countries. The faculty numbered about 4450.

J.Ro.

PARITY PRICES, in agriculture. See AGRICULTURE: *Agriculture in the United States.*

PARK, Chung Hee. See KOREA: *History.*

PARK, Mungo (1771–1806), British explorer, born in Foulshiels, Selkirk, Scotland. In 1795 he went to Africa to explore the Niger River (q.v.). Upon arriving in present-day Gambia, he went 200 mi. up the Gambia R. to the trading station of Pisania (now Karantaba), and then traveled east into unexplored territory. He was captured by a local chief but escaped and in 1796 reached the Niger R. at the town of Ségou. He then traveled 80 mi. downstream as far as Silla before his supplies were exhausted. After his return to Great Britain in 1797 Park published an account of his trip in *Travels in the Interior of Africa* (1799). In 1805 he returned to Africa to explore the Niger, from Ségou to the mouth of the river, by canoe. His expedition was attacked at Bussa, however, and Park was drowned. An account of Park's second journey, taken from his journals, was published posthumously in London in 1815.

PARKER, Dorothy (1893–1967), American writer, born DOROTHY ROTHSCHILD in West End, N.J., and educated at the Blessed Sacrament Convent, in New York City. Between 1916 and 1920 she was a drama and literary critic for

Dorothy Parker   Viking Press

the magazines *Vogue* and *Vanity Fair,* in New York City, after which she became a free-lance writer. Among her works are a number of books of verse and volumes of short stories and sketches; her poems and short stories alike are characterized by a style that is often bitingly humorous and sardonic. Her writings are concerned mainly with love and with the frustrations and contradictions of modern life. Her books of verse include *Death and Taxes* (1931) and *Not So Deep as a Well* (1936); among her collections of short stories are *Laments for the Living* (1930), *After Such Pleasures* (1933), and the posthumously published *Constant Reader* (1970), stories she wrote for the *New Yorker* magazine from 1927 to 1933 under the pen name Constant Reader. She was also a co-author of several plays including *Ladies of the Corridor* (1953).

PARKER, Francis Wayland. See EDUCATION IN THE UNITED STATES: *Trends in the 20th Century.*

PARKER, Sir (Horatio) Gilbert (1862–1932), Canadian novelist, born in Camden East, Ontario, and educated at Trinity College, Toronto. He became associate editor of the *Morning Herald,* Sydney, Australia in 1886 and traveled in the East, the South Sea Islands, Europe, Egypt, and Canada. From 1900 to 1918 he was a Conservative member of Parliament for Gravesend. He was created a baronet in 1915 and made a member of the Privy Council in 1916. During the first two years of World War I he had general charge of British publicity in the United States. His best-known book is *The Seats of the Mighty* (1897), a novel of the American Revolution. Other novels are, *The Right of Way* (1901), *The Weavers* (1907), *The World for Sale* (1916), *The Power and the Glory* (1925), and *The Promised Land* (1928).

PARKER, Horatio William (1863–1919), American composer and music teacher, born in Auburndale, Mass., and educated privately and at the Munich Conservatory in Germany. In 1886 he became organist and choirmaster at Saint Andrew's Church, New York City, and two years later assumed similar posts at Trinity Church, Boston, Mass. In 1894 he became professor of music at Yale University, and from 1904 until his death was dean of the Yale Music School. Parker's oratorio *Hora Novissima* (1893) is generally considered his masterpiece. It exemplifies the German musical style that was popular in New England at the time; *see* AMERICAN MUSIC: *The 19th Century.* He twice won prizes amounting to $10,000 each with his operas *Mona* and *Fairyland,* which were completed in 1911 and 1915, respectively, both with librettos by the American playwright Brian Hooker (1880–1946). Among his other works are a number of concert overtures; an oratorio, *The Legend of Saint Christopher* (1896); a number of choral works with orchestra, including *King Trojan* (1885), *The Holy Child* (1890), *A Star Song* (1891), and *The Dream King and His Love* (1893); pieces for piano and organ; songs; and chamber music.

PARKER, Matthew (1504–75), second Protestant archbishop of Canterbury, born in Norwich, England. In 1535 he was appointed chaplain to Queen Anne Boleyn and in 1537 to King Henry VIII (qq.v.). In 1544 he became master of Corpus Christi College, University of Cambridge, and the following year vice-chancellor of the university. At the accession of Elizabeth I (q.v.) Parker was consecrated archbishop of Canterbury and

Matthew Parker

defended the Church against encroachments by the crown. To Parker belongs the credit of originating the revised translation of the Scriptures known as the Bishops' Bible; *see* BIBLE, ENGLISH TRANSLATIONS OF THE. Parker wrote and edited many works, including the *Chronica Majora* by Matthew Paris (q.v.). He also founded the Society of Antiquaries and was its first president, and endowed the University of Cambridge and particularly his own college with many fellowships and scholarships and with a magnificent collection of manuscripts relating to English history.

PARKER, Theodore (1810–60), American preacher and social reformer, born in Lexington, Mass. He was graduated from the divinity school at Harvard University in 1836 and settled the year after as Unitarian minister at West Roxbury (now part of Boston). The naturalistic, or rationalistic, views that separated him from the more conservative portion of the Unitarians first attracted wide notice in a sermon on "The Transient and Permanent in Christianity" (1841); *see* NATURALISM; RATIONALISM. The sermon did not deny the miraculous in Christianity, but men's present need of it; *see* CHRISTIANITY: *Basic Doc-*

trines. He was invited to preach in Boston, and his first important sermons there were gathered into a book, *A Discourse of Matters Pertaining to Religion* (1842), that increased the controversial heat. Many Unitarians wished to expel him formally from their fellowship, and most of the ministers refused to associate with him in church relations. In 1846 the Twenty-Eighth Congregational Society (*see* CONGREGATIONALISM) was formed in Boston, and he became its minister, preaching regularly before large congregations until 1859. *See* UNITARIANISM.

Theodore Parker's Christianity was antisupernatural; his philosophy, intuitional and transcendental (indeed, he was a leader of the New England transcendentalists); *see* TRANSCENDENTALISM. His theology was theistic, affirming God, the moral law, and immortality as certainties of consciousness; *see* CONSCIOUSNESS; IMMORTALITY; THEISM. His conception of Jesus Christ was purely humanitarian, and his criticism of the Bible anticipated the results of more recent orthodox scholarship (*see* BIBLE SCHOLARSHIP). He was one of the most conspicuous leaders of the New England abolitionists (q.v.), and he was active in prison reform.

PARKERSBURG, city in West Virginia, and county seat of Wood Co., on the Ohio R., at the mouth of the Little Kanawha R., 63 miles N. of Charleston. Parkersburg is an important manufacturing center, and the trading center of an area producing oil, natural gas, timber, clay, coal, livestock, and farm products. Industries in the city include the manufacture of oil-field equipment, shovels, glassware, chemicals, porcelain, tiles, plastics, paper boxes, shoes, and rayon. Parkersburg was founded in 1785, incorporated as a town in 1820, and chartered as a city in 1863. Pop. (1960) 44,797; (1970) 44,208.

PARK FOREST, village of Illinois, in Cook and Will counties, 25 miles s.w. of downtown Chicago. A planned community incorporated in 1940, it manufactures chemicals, industrial machinery, and firearms. Pop. (1960) 29,993; (1970) 30,638.

PARKINSON'S DISEASE, slowly progressive disabling ailment marked by increasing stiffness of the muscles and tremor. The disease formerly was called paralysis agitans but the term has been discontinued because true paralysis is lacking. The disease, which occurs in all parts of the world, affects more men than women and is most likely to develop after the age of thirty-five. About 1,000,000 cases are recorded annually in the United States. The disease is neither contagious nor hereditary. The exact cause is not known, but various theories link the disease to infection by an influenza virus, hardening of the arteries of the brain, or toxic chemicals manufactured by the body of the patient. The basal ganglia area, a small center at the base of the brain, is affected. Symptoms include excessive salivation, poor coordination and faulty body balance, tremor, rigidity of muscles, and some shortening of muscles. Shortening of muscles along the front of the neck tends to bend the head and spine forward.

The disease is not fatal, but no cure exists. Symptoms may be relieved by physical therapy and exercise of affected muscles, or injection of supercooled liquids into the brain center involved. Since 1966 a new drug, L-dopa, has been tested in the U.S. A naturally occurring amino acid, L-dopa can relieve many symptoms of Parkinson's disease. A wide range of drugs is also used, including drugs to relax muscles and control tremors, tranquilizers (q.v.), amphetamines, and barbiturates. Curare (q.v.) is sometimes employed as a muscle relaxant. *See also* BRAIN; compare PARALYSIS.

PARKMAN, Francis (1823–93), American historian, born in Boston, Mass. He was graduated from Harvard University in 1844, and afterward studied law for two years. He then traveled in Europe, and returned to explore the American West, living at times among the Sioux and other Indian tribes. The hardships he endured seriously injured his health, yet in spite of this and his defective eyesight, Parkman became an authoritative historical writer on the struggle between France and England for dominance in colonial America.

On one of his journeys he took the overland route from western Missouri to Oregon, and recorded his observations in *The Oregon Trail,* which was published in 1849. In 1851 *The History of the Conspiracy of Pontiac* appeared. His chief works form a connected series, and should be read in the following order: *The Pioneers of France in the New World* (1865); *The Jesuits in North America in the Seventeenth Century* (1867); *The Old Régime in Canada* (1874); *La-Salle and the Discovery of the Great West* (1869); *Count Frontenac and New France under Louis XIV* (1877); *Montcalm and Wolfe* (1884); and *A Half-Century of Conflict* (1892). Besides these works, he published a *Historic Handbook of the Northern Tour* (1885), and numerous articles, many of which advance chapters from his histories, in magazines and other periodicals.

PARK RIDGE, city of Illinois, in Cook Co., 10 miles N.W. of downtown Chicago. The chief industries of the city are printing and the manufacture of transportation, electric, and electronic equipment. Settled in 1853, it was formerly known as Pennyville and Brickton and was incorporated in 1910. Pop. (1960) 32,659; (1970) 42,466.

PARKS, NATIONAL. See NATIONAL PARK SERVICE, and separate entries on many national parks.

PARKS, STATE. See separate articles on the individual States of the United States, section on *Parks, Forests, and Other Places of Interest.*

PARKVILLE-CARNEY, unincorporated area of Maryland, in Baltimore Co., adjoining Baltimore on the northeast and 7 mi. from the city center. It was formed after 1950 by the combination of the former villages of Parkville and Carney. Pop. (1960) 27,236; (1970) 33,897.

PARLIAMENT, supreme legislature of Great Britain, the members of which meet, deliberate, and pass laws in the Houses of Parliament in London; see LEGISLATURE. The word derives from "parlement", meaning "speechmaking", "debate", or "discussion" in Old French, and stemming in its usage from a chronicle reporting that William I the Conqueror (q.v.) had "very deep speech with his Witan", or national council; see WITENAGEMOT. The British Parliament popularly is called the Mother of Parliaments; it is the oldest in existence, and the parliaments of the British dominions and of several other countries are modeled on the British form.

Composition of Parliament. The British Parliament consists of three parts: the Crown, the House of Lords, and the House of Commons. The crown is the traditional and legal source of parliamentary power, and performs certain traditional rituals pertaining to the convening of Parliament and the passage of laws. In actual practice, the crown is without power to alter or influence the promulgation or the content of British legislation.

The House of Lords is composed of peers and, since the Peerage Act of 1963, peeresses, who hold their seats by hereditary right; by creation of the crown; or by virtue of their office as law lords, archbishops, and bishops. The House of Lords is the highest court of appeal in Great Britain and until recently held legislative powers equal to those of the House of Commons. Since the passage of the Parliament Act of 1949, however, the House of Lords has been unable to delay the passage of any legislation for more than one year after it has been passed three times by the lower house.

The House of Commons passes all laws, subject to the delaying power of the upper house; and, through the cabinet ministers, who are chosen from the ranks of the majority party in the House of Commons, as well as from the House of Lords, it directs and supervises the administration of all of the executive agencies of the British government; see CABINET. The membership of the House of Commons, like that of the United States House of Representatives, varies according to the size of the electorate. In a recent year, it was composed of 630 elected members, representing counties and boroughs; until 1948, universities were also represented. Catholic priests, clergymen of the Church of England, ministers of the Scottish Kirk, and English and Scottish peers, unless they have renounced their titles under the 1963 Peerage Act, are all ineligible for election to the House of Commons.

History. The evolution of the British Parliament can be traced to the Witenagemot, which exercised important legislative, administrative, and judicial functions under the Anglo-Saxon kings; it was superseded, after the Norman invasion of England in 1066, by the *curia regis* under William I and his successors. With the granting of the Magna Charta (q.v.) by King John (q.v.) in 1215, the national assembly entered a period of transition. Sentiment favoring elections (q.v.) and national representation became widespread; and, finally, in 1265, Simon de Montfort (q.v.), Earl of Leicester, called an assembly that two knights from every shire and two citizens or burgesses from each of twenty-one cities and boroughs were permitted to attend.

In 1295, King Edward I (q.v.) convened what became known as the Model Parliament, at which four so-called estates were present or represented: the peerage, including the higher clergy, who held baronies of the crown; the knights (see KNIGHT); the burgesses; and the lower clergy. These estates sat separately, though probably in the same hall, and made separate grants of money to the king. In time, the lower clergy ceased to attend Parliament; and the knights and burgesses, perceiving a common interest, drew together. By 1332, the form, if not the powers, of the modern Parliament was established in the existence of two distinct houses: the House of Lords, consisting of the peerage and higher clergy; and the House of Commons, consisting of the knights and burgesses.

The civil conflict known as the Wars of the Roses (q.v.) and the rise of absolutism under the Tudor sovereigns led to the almost complete disintegration of parliamentary power during the next three centuries. The economic and intellectual ferment of the 17th century, however, led to changes instituted by the Long Parliament (q.v.) and by the protectorate of the soldier and

The British Houses of Parliament and Westminster Bridge, London. British Information Services

statesman Oliver Cromwell (*see under* CROMWELL), which made the crown responsible to Parliament, forbade the dissolution of Parliament without its own consent, and initiated the modern period of parliamentary ascendancy. In 1707, the Parliaments of England and Scotland were united into the Parliament of Great Britain, to which Irish representatives were admitted in 1801.

Reform and Voting Rights. The Reform Bill (q.v.) of 1832 shifted the balance of political power from the House of lords to the House of Commons by eliminating fifty-six sparsely inhabited nomination boroughs, popularly called rotten boroughs, the representation of which had formerly been controlled by local peers; *see* BOROUGH. Another feature of the bill was its extension of the franchise to another 500,000 voters; but five-sixths of the adult male population, including most of the working class, still lacked the right to vote.

Several other reform acts have been passed since 1832. The franchise was extended to all householders in 1867; voting by secret ballot was introduced in 1872; a zoning reform in 1884 provided a more equal distribution of parliamentary seats according to population density; agricultural laborers were given the vote in 1885; the Parliamentary Act of 1911 barred interference by the House of Lords in the passage of finance or money bills, and provided a limitation to delay of bills passed by the House of Commons; all men over twenty-one, and all women over thirty were given the vote in 1918; and the Equal Franchise Act of 1928 made age and other conditions for women voters equal to those for men. The Representation of the People Act of 1969 lowered the voting age to eighteen, and the eighteen-year-old voter first cast his ballot in the by-election for Bridgewater on March 12, 1970.

See BALLOT; DEMOCRACY; ENGLAND: *History;* PARLIAMENT, HOUSES OF; REPUBLIC.

PARLIAMENTARY LAW, term used to designate the body of rules and precedents regulating the modes of procedure and course of debate in legislative and other deliberative assemblies. By extension, the term has been applied to the rules governing the procedure and conduct of organizational meetings generally, whether in business, labor, or fraternal organizations. The basic principles of parliamentary law are majority rule, equal rights of all members to participate in the proceedings, protection of the right of the minority to be heard, and orderly consideration of matters brought before the meeting.

Choice of Rules. An organization may adopt as its rules of procedure those of the United States House of Representatives, if applicable, or of a standard reference work on parliamentary law; *see* CONGRESS OF THE UNITED STATES: *The House of Representatives.* A permanent organization may incorporate certain procedural rules in its constitution or bylaws. A long-standing authority in parliamentary procedure, used by

PARLIAMENTARY LAW

many nonlegislative organizations, is *Robert's Rules of Order* (1876, rev. ed. 1915) by the American army engineer Henry Martyn Robert (1837–1923). Robert was also the author of *Parliamentary Practice* (1921) and *Parliamentary Law* (1923). Like most other American parliamentary texts, Robert's procedure is based on the House rules, which in turn derive from British parliamentary law; see PARLIAMENT. Many international bodies, including the Japanese Diet, have procedures based upon British and American parliamentary law; see DIET; JAPAN: *Government*.

Officers. The officers of a deliberative assembly include a presiding officer, who may be called the chairman, speaker, president, or moderator; and a secretary or clerk. The presiding officer, whose office at a meeting is called the chair, must be fair in the exercise of his authority. Because he has the power of recognition, that is, of deciding which member is entitled to speak, he must be impartial and permit the presentation of opposing views. It is his duty to call the meeting to order, to put motions properly made, to preserve order and enforce rules of procedure, and to decide questions of order subject to the right of appeal to the whole assembly. If he is a member of the organization, the presiding officer may participate in debate, but he should relinquish the chair and ask another member to preside temporarily while he does so; and he may vote whenever his vote would be decisive to the result, that is, to make or break a tie.

Procedure. Business is brought before an assembly by a motion, or proposal, of a member, or by the presentation of a resolution. When the motion has been stated, the question of its adoption is considered as pending. While this question or matter is before the assembly, no other business of a different nature can intervene. A motion to adjourn the meeting, however, is always in order, and questions of higher privilege may sometimes intervene. Questions subsidiary to the main question are also in order when they aid in, or result in, the disposition of the main question: thus, motions to table, to postpone to a later time, to refer to committee, to amend, or to postpone indefinitely may be offered, and have precedence in the order listed. Debate on a specific question or issue is in order after that question has been stated by the chair. When debate has ended, or has been closed by motion and vote of members present, the presiding officer rises and puts the debated question to a vote.

The rules of the U.S. House of Representatives require those favoring the motion to indicate their preference by saying together "aye", and those opposing it to say together "no". If the presiding officer is in doubt as to the result of the voice vote, or at the demand of any member, a so-called division, or standing, vote is in order; that is, a vote whereby those in favor of and those opposed to the proposition are alternately asked to stand and be counted. The presiding officer may also appoint tellers to make the count and report the results to him; House rules also provide that one-fifth of a quorum may order that tellers be appointed to make such a count. A specified percentage of the minority of the membership, a figure normally stated in the constitution or by-laws, may order the roll to be called. In such a case the presiding officer directs the secretary or clerk to call the roll, and the vote of each member is recorded and tallied as his name is called. To insure secrecy, a vote by ballot may be held if supported by a majority. In the case of a tie vote, under any voting procedure, the proposition fails.

Committee Work. The work of deliberative bodies is usually prepared by means of committees. These may be standing committees appointed for a definite time; select committees, appointed for a special purpose; or committees of the whole, consisting of the entire assembly. The first person named on a committee is usually the chairman, whose duty it is to call the committee together and preside over its deliberations. A committee may facilitate its task by the appointment of a subcommittee or subcommittees, selected out of its own membership. A committee report is usually made by the chairman, is signed by the members, and is delivered to the clerk. In the case of disagreement among members, a majority and a minority report may be rendered. The report of the majority is considered the report of the committee, and when reviewed by the full assembly may be subject to the usual motions to table, postpone, recommit, or amend before the question is brought up for adoption. An assembly may, by motion, resolve itself into a committee of the whole for consideration of a matter that has been reported from a committee, or of a matter that is under consideration in the full assembly. The assembly may do this in order to consider the matter under procedures specifically established to expedite such consideration. When this is done, the presiding officer appoints another member, who retains the right to vote, to act as chairman. The regular presiding officer then may participate in the deliberations of the committee.

See BALLOT; ELECTIONS; LEGISLATURE.　　L.D.

PARLIAMENT, HOUSES OF, or NEW PALACE OF WESTMINSTER, seat of the British legislature, a great mass of buildings on the east bank of the Thames R. in London, built (1840–60) after plans by Sir Charles Barry (q.v.), on the site of the medieval royal residence, the Palace of Westminster, which was largely destroyed by fire in 1834. The buildings cover an area of 8 acres, and contain 1100 apartments, 100 staircases, and 11 courts. The exterior, in rich late Gothic style, is made impressive by three massive towers: Victoria Tower, 336 ft. high; Middle Tower, 300 ft. high; and Saint Stephen's, or the Clock Tower, 320 ft. high. The latter contains a clock with four dials each 23 ft. in diameter and a great bell, Big Ben, weighing 13½ tons. Among the Houses are the sumptuous House of Peers, House of Commons, Saint Stephen's Hall on the site of Saint Stephen's Chapel, the residence of the Speaker, the libraries, committee rooms, and lobbies connected with the two Houses, and offices. Westminster Hall (begun in 1097) is all that remains of the original palace.

In World War II, the buildings were seriously damaged several times during air raids. The House of Commons was completely destroyed in 1941, and rebuilt in 1950.

PARMA, city of Ohio, in Cuyahoga Co., on Big Creek, adjoining Cleveland on the south. Automobile parts and tools are made. Settled in 1821, it was incorporated as a village in 1924 and as a city in 1931. Pop. (1960) 82,845; (1970) 100,216.

PARMA, city of Italy, in Emilia-Romagna Region, and capital of Parma Province, on the Parma R., 55 miles N.W. of Bologna. The river bisects the city. Parma is crossed also by the Roman road called the Aemilian Way (q.v.). The city is a rail junction and a commercial and agricultural-marketing center. Its best-known manufacture is Parmesan cheese. Other products are tomato paste, sausages, pasta, jam, perfume, canning machinery, fertilizers, glass, furniture, leather goods, and pharmaceuticals.

The Romanesque cathedral (mainly 12th century), the interior of which is decorated with frescoes by the Italian artist Antonio Allegri da Correggio (q.v.), is a major point of interest. The former Farnese palace, or Palazzo della Pilotta, a colossal complex of buildings most of which were built during the 16th and 17th centuries, contains the National Gallery of Parma. Educational institutions include the University of Parma, which developed from a school of arts founded in the 11th century.

Parma was established as a Roman colony in 183 B.C. After a period as an independent commune, Parma came successively under the control of the ruling families of Milan (1346–1500), of the papacy (1512–45), of the Farnese dukes of Parma (1545–1730), and of Spain and, at times, Austria. Following the invasion of Italy in 1796 by Napoléon Bonaparte, later Napoleon I (q.v.), Emperor of France, Parma was annexed to France. In 1815, after the defeat of Napoleon, the Congress of Vienna constituted Parma, Piacenza, and Guastalla a small realm for Napoleon's wife Marie Louise (1791–1847). After her death, Austria-supported princes ruled until, in 1859, Parma was united with the Kingdom of Sardinia. The city was severely bombed in World War II (q.v.). Pop. (1967 est.) 167,998.

PARMENIDES (b. about 514 B.C.), Greek philosopher, considered by many scholars as the greatest member of the Eleatic School (q.v.). He is said to have visited Athens at the age of sixty-five, and on that occasion the philosopher Socrates (q.v.), then a young man, heard him speak. Parmenides expounded his philosophy in verse form, his only surviving work being large fragments of a didactic poem, *On Nature*, demonstrating the reality of Absolute Being, the nonexistence of which Parmenides declared to be inconceivable, but the nature of which, on the other hand, he admitted to be equally inconceivable, inasmuch as it is dissociated from every limitation under which man thinks. Parmenides held that the phenomena of nature are only apparent and due to man's error; they seem to exist, but have no real existence. He also held that reality, True Being, is not known to the senses but is to be found only in reason. This belief makes him a precursor of the idealism of Plato (q.v.). Parmenides' theory that Being cannot arise from Nonbeing, and that Being neither arises nor passes away, was applied to matter by his successors Empedocles and Democritus (qq.v.), who made it the foundation of their materialistic explanations of the universe.

PARMIGIANINO, IL or **PARMIGIANO, IL,** (1503–40), Italian painter, born in Parma. His real name was GIROLAMO FRANCESCO MARIA MAZZUOLI or GIRALOMO FRANCESCO MARIA MAZZOLA. He studied with painter Antonio Allegri da Correggio (q.v.) in Parma and was one of the chief disciples of Correggio's style, which he blended with the style of Roman painter Raphael (q.v.). About 1523 he went to Rome, from which he fled to Bologna in 1527, after the sack of Rome by the armies of Charles V (q.v.), Holy Roman Emperor. In Bologna he painted some of his finest works, including the "Madonna and Child with Saint Margaret and Other Saints" (now in the Academy of Bologna). He returned to Parma in 1531, and began the

PARNAÍBA

"The Vision of Saint Jerome" (about 1527) by Parmigianino.
National Gallery, London

frescoes of the Church of Santa Maria della Steccata, left unfinished at his death. "The Madonna with the Long Neck" (1535?, Uffizi Gallery in Florence) is among his principal works. Also a distinguished portrait painter, and one of the first Italian etchers, he painted studies of the Italian navigators Christopher Columbus and Amerigo Vespucci (qq.v.) and a self-portrait (1524, Kunsthistorisches Museum in Vienna).

PARNAÍBA, formerly PARNAHYBA, river of Brazil. It rises in the Serra das Mangabeiras and flows 750 mi. generally N., forming the border between Maranhão State and Piauí State before reaching the Atlantic Ocean. It enters the Atlantic Ocean through several branches near the city of Parnaíba.

PARNASSIANS, *or* PARNASSIENS, school of French poets founded by Théophile Gautier (q.v.) about 1856. See FRENCH LITERATURE: *Parnassians and Symbolists.*

PARNASSUS, mountain in central Greece, rising to an altitude of 8061 ft. In Greek mythology Parnassus was sacred to the god Apollo (q.v.), whose oracle, Delphi (q.v.), was situated at its base. It was also believed to be a favorite habitation of the Muses (q.v.) and a center of musical and poetic inspiration. Parnassus was also the site of worship of the gods Pan and Dionysus (qq.v.).

PARNELL, Charles Stewart (1846–91), Irish Nationalist leader and statesman, born in Avondale, and educated at Magdalene College, University of Cambridge. In his youth and early adulthood he was comparatively uninterested in politics, but he eventually became a supporter of Isaac Butt (1813–79), the founder of the Irish home-rule movement. In 1875 Parnell was elected to Parliament. During his term of office he pursued a policy of obstructionism, resorting to all-night filibusters to draw attention to the severity of the Irish problem. In 1878 he received the support of the Fenians (q.v.), and became an active opponent of the Irish land laws. In 1879 Parnell was elected president of the newly-founded National Land League. In 1880 he visited the United States, and succeeded in gaining both funds and support for his cause.

In the elections of 1880, Parnell supported the Liberal Party leader, William Ewart Gladstone (q.v.), but when Gladstone sponsored the Land Act, which fell far short of Nationalists' demands, he joined the opposition. At his direction, the Land League planned to commit a number of deliberate violations of the Land Act in order to test it in the courts. In 1881 Parnell encouraged boycott (q.v.) as a means of influencing landlords and land agents. The promulgation of these policies led to the jailing of Parnell and several of his principal followers at Kilmainham Prison, and to the suppression of the League. One of Parnell's first acts after entering prison was the issuance of a manifesto calling upon the Irish peasants not to pay their rents. Soon afterward Parnell and Gladstone reached an agreement known as the Kilmainham Treaty, whereby Parnell abandoned the "No-Rent" policy and urged his followers to avoid physical violence. In return for these compromises he was released. Parnell's peaceful policy was completely shattered, however, by the murder of Lord Frederick Charles Cavendish (1836–82) and Thomas Burke (1829–82), chief secretary and undersecretary for Ireland, respectively, at Phoenix Park, Dublin, in 1882, by the Irish Invincibles, a militant faction of the Fenians. He strongly denounced this act, but was unable to prevent a wave of terrorism which caused the enactment of new coercive legislation. In 1885, when the Gladstone government moved to extend these laws past their scheduled expiration date, Parnell, whose party held the balance of power in Parliament, voted against Gladstone and thus brought about the fall of his ministry.

Parnell's influence among the Irish people and among many of his English supporters began to decline in 1889, when William Henry O'Shea (1840–1905), formerly one of his most devoted lieutenants, filed a suit for divorce charging that Parnell had committed adultery with his wife. No defense was offered, as Parnell and Katherine O'Shea (d. 1921) had indeed been deeply in love for some years; they were married several months after the divorce was granted. The resulting scandal precipitated a split within the Irish Nationalist League (which replaced the dissolved National Land League), with the majority of the members turning against Parnell. From this time until his death, Parnell waged a ceaseless struggle to reunite the Nationalists, but the schism lasted for several years after his death, and was one of the principal factors which delayed the achievement of Irish home rule until after World War I. *See also* IRELAND: *History: The Period of English Supremacy.*

PAROCHIAL SCHOOL EDUCATION, in the United States, schooling offered by a parish or other local body of a religious organization, most typically, elementary or secondary schooling offered by a parish of the Roman Catholic Church (q.v.). The parish is a division of a diocese (q.v.), centered around a single church, and it ordinarily supports a single elementary school. Secondary and special schools may be organized by a single parish, by several parishes, or by a diocese. Pupils pay tuition, and teachers may be members of religious orders or lay teachers employed by the parish or diocese.

Local schools have also been supported by other religious bodies, and private schools of various types have also been provided. Schools similar to the Catholic parochial school have frequently been supported by Lutherans and Jews in recent years.

In the U.S., tax-supported public schools supply education for children between seven and sixteen, or through the secondary level. But, by law, such schools may not teach religious subjects, and parents who wish training in such subjects for their children must provide it outside the public-school system.

Federal Law. The First Amendment to the Constitution of the United States (q.v.) specifically forbids any Federal law "respecting the establishment of religion". Some States have paid sums to parochial schools for textbooks, transportation expenses, and various health-care services for their pupils. In July, 1971, however, State provisions for payment of a portion of teachers' salaries or for instructional aids such as laboratory equipment were declared unconstitutional by the Supreme Court of the United States (q.v.), in a 5-to-4 decision. Federal assistance to parochial schools was also forbidden by this decision, but one-time construction funds for college-level sectarian institutions were not prohibited.

Enrollment. Some 44,000,000 students were enrolled in all elementary and secondary schools in the U.S. in the early 1960's. Of these, about 5,300,000 were attending Catholic schools, and about 1,000,000 students were in other non-tax-supported schools. By 1969–70 enrollment in parochial schools had declined to 4,700,000 of a total enrollment of 51,300,000.

See EDUCATION IN THE UNITED STATES.

PARODY, comic imitation of a serious poem or of some part of it, according to the Greeks in early times. The term has come to be applied also to the comic imitation of any variety of prose, such as history, fiction, or scientific writings.

Parody, like travesty, is a form of burlesque (q.v.). The essence of parody is the treatment of a light theme in the style appropriate to a serious work. Such is "The Nun's Priest's Tale" from *The Canterbury Tales* (q.v.) by the 14th-century English writer Geoffrey Chaucer (q.v.); the hubbub caused by Master Reynard in the widow's household is described in language suggestive of the fall of Troy. The humor lies in the contrast between subject matter and the treatment of it. In travesty the characters of the original are turned to a humorous account by some change in the incidents that results in a debasement of the original theme. In parody the theme and the characters are greatly modified or completely changed, but the style of the original is closely followed in those peculiarities that easily lend themselves to ridicule.

Most famous writers have been parodied, and

PAROLE

those who have written parody include Aristophanes, Alexander Pope, Jonathan Swift, William Makepiece Thackeray, Francis Brett Harte, James Joyce, Sir Max Beerbohm, and Ogden Nash (qq.v.).

PAROLE (Fr., "word" or "promise"), in criminal law (q.v.), pledge of good conduct given by a person convicted of crime (q.v.) as a condition of release from imprisonment before the expiration of the term of confinement. The word parole is also broadly used to denote such a conditional release or period of liberty. Parole is usually granted to a prisoner in recognition of past good conduct, both in prison and earlier. A sentenced criminal may be released on parole before the maximum limit of his term has been reached, either on the expiration of the minimum term or of some other shorter term fixed by statute, on condition of good behavior. The release in such case is not an absolute discharge, such as he receives as a matter of right on the expiration of his full term, but is conditional on the due performance of his pledge. During the parole period he is required to report from time to time to the prison authorities or to a parole agent or parole officer to whose custody he was committed when released. Other stipulations of parole include avoidance of association with known criminals, working in a reputable occupation, and remaining within a certain locality. For a violation of his parole within the time limited, he is liable to be apprehended and returned to prison to serve out his full or maximum term. See also PARDON; PROBATION; REPRIEVE.

PAROL EVIDENCE. See EVIDENCE.

PÁROS, island of Greece, in the Aegean Sea, one of the Cyclades group. It is noted for Parian marble, favored by sculptors since the 6th century B.C. Páros was settled by Ionians and later formed part of the Athenian confederacy. Area, 77 sq.mi. Pop. (1968 est.) 9,000.

PAROTID GLAND. See SALIVARY GLANDS.

PARR, Catherine (1512–48), Queen Consort of England, sixth and last wife of Henry VIII (q.v.), King of England. She was twice widowed before marrying Henry in 1543. She had a restraining effect on his ruthlessness and helped educate and restore to Henry's favor his daughters, the later queens Mary I and Elizabeth I (qq.v.).

PARRAMATTA, city of Australia, in New South Wales, on the Parramatta R., 14 miles N.W. of Sydney. The noted merino-sheep industry of Australia started here, and the city was an early grain port and is now a rail junction. Local manufactures include bicycles, leather and metal products, and woolen textiles. Called the "Cradle of Australia", the city contains many relics of colonial history and is the second-oldest settlement in the country, after Sydney. Points of interest are Elizabeth House, Saint John's Church, the first Government House, the observatory remains in Parramatta Park, and King School (1832), as well as Rosehill Race Course. Settled in 1788 as Rose Hill, the community was laid out in 1791, and the city was chartered in 1938. The name was formerly also spelled Parramata. Pop. (1966) 107,006.

PARRINGTON, Vernon Louis (1871–1929), American educator and literary critic, born in Aurora, Ill., and educated at Harvard University. After teaching at the University of Oklahoma from 1897 to 1908, he became assistant professor of English at the University of Washington in 1908. He became a full professor in 1912 and continued in that capacity until his death. He wrote the three-volume *Main Currents in American Thought* (1927–30). This searching study explores the relations between American writing and the social, economic, and political developments of the country from colonial times to 1920; the first two volumes received the 1928 Pulitzer Prize for history. Parrington also wrote *The Connecticut Wits* (1926).

PARRISH, Maxfield (1870–1966), American painter and illustrator, born in Philadelphia. He studied at the Pennsylvania Academy of Fine Arts and later with the American artist Howard Pyle (q.v.). Parrish became widely known as an illustrator and as a designer of magazine covers. Many of his delicate, romantic studies of streams, forests, and nymphs enjoyed a popular vogue through color reproductions. Among his best-known illustrations are those for *Knickerbocker's History of New York* by the American writer Washington Irving (q.v.). His series of mural paintings illustrating the story of "Old King Cole" is at the Saint Regis-Sheraton Hotel in New York City. Parrish's work is characterized by distinctive, vivid colors, and by a simplified decorative treatment involving the use of flat masses. He was elected a member of the National Academy of Design in 1906.

PARROT, common name for several genera of birds of the family Psittacidae, which includes also the macaw, the cockatoo, and the parakeet. Parrots vary from about 3½ to 20 in. in length and are characterized by a relatively massive hooked bill, a prehensile tongue, and yoke-toed feet, in which the fist and fourth toes are turned backward. The larger parrots, including both tree-dwelling species and the owl parrot, which lives on the ground, may be distinguished from other members of the family by their square

Yellow-headed amazon parrot, Amazona ochrocephala
Molly Adams – National Audubon Society

tails and the predominance of green in their plumage. Among the tree-dwelling group are the parrots popular as cage birds because of their ability to mimic human speech. The smaller parrots, called pygmy parrots, are diminutive types differing from other species in having tail feathers with spinelike tips. The chief areas of distribution of parrots are South America and Africa, but some species occur in Australia, New Zealand, and New Guinea. The diet of parrots generally is restricted to seeds, nuts, and fruit.

Tree-Dwelling Parrots. The forests of South America and Africa abound with medium-sized parrots. These birds live high among the branches and foliage and travel in large flocks. The genus *Amazona* includes the best-known South American parrots: the white-fronted parrot, *A. albifrons,* and the yellow-headed amazon, *A. ochrocephala.* The latter reaches a length of 15 in. and is one of the largest parrots in the genus. The African gray parrot, *Psittacus erithacus,* which may be recognized by its red tail, is the most sought African species because of its readiness to imitate the human voice.

The popularity of parrots as cage birds is equaled only by that of the canary. Besides being facile imitators of sounds, captive parrots seem to respond readily to affectionate treatment such as gentle stroking of the neck and head. Captive parrots are generally long-lived, an African gray parrot reportedly having attained a record age of eighty years.

Because parrots are subject to the virus disease psittacosis (q.v.), which can be transmitted to man, importation of these birds into the United States, as well as domestic breeding, is governed by Federal regulations to prevent the spread of the disease.

PARSIPPANY-TROY HILLS

Ground-Dwelling Parrot. Unlike the tree-dwelling parrots, the owl parrot, *Strigops habroptilus,* is flightless and lives in ground burrows. Although formerly distributed throughout the New Zealand archipelago, the owl parrot currently is limited to North Island, where it forages for tender roots and fruit in shady forest undergrowth. The owl parrot attains an average length of 20 in.

Pygmy Parrots. The pygmy parrots, which average about 3½ in. in length, are limited to the deep forests and mountainous regions of New Guinea and several neighboring islands. The best-known species, the lesser pygmy parrot, *Micropsitta pusio,* is noted for its nesting habits. To meet the competition of overabundant wasps and bees for ideal nesting space, such as tree hollows from which these insects dislodge unprotected small birds, the lesser pygmy parrot builds its nest in cavities drilled into the hills of termites. The latter do not molest its young.

PARROT FEVER. See Psittacosis.

PARSEC, in astronomy, unit of measurement equal to approximately 19,000,000,000,000 mi., or 3.26 light-years. The size of the parsec was fixed by astronomers as equal to the distance between a star having a parallax (q.v.) of one second of arc and the earth.

PARSEES or **PARSIS** (Old Persian *Parsa,* "Persia"), followers of the ancient Persian religion known as Zoroastrianism (q.v.). They are descended from Zoroastrians who fled from Persia in the 7th and 8th centuries A.D. to avoid persecution by Muslim invaders. They now number more than 120,000, of whom the majority live in and around the city of Bombay, India; following tradition, many Indian Parsees are businessmen. A community of some 5000 Parsees exists also in Pakistan, mainly in Karachi.

The Parsees divided into two sects in the 18th century over a calendar disagreement, and almost all present-day Parsees belong to either one of these sects. The religious and ethical literature of the Parsees derives chiefly from the Avesta (q.v.). Their priesthood is hereditary, and they regard fire as purifying and sacred. A fire is kept constantly burning in the main Parsee temples by priests, and prayers and sacrifices are offered before this fire on all festival days. In the past, to avoid defilement, the Parsees left their dead exposed on towers to vultures and other carrion-eating birds, but this practice is no longer widely followed.

PARSIPPANY-TROY HILLS, township of New Jersey, in Morris Co., at the s. end of the Boonton Reservoir on the Rockaway R., 6 miles N.E. of Morristown. The township includes the lake-re-

343

sort communities of Lake Parsippany, Lake Hiawatha, and Rainbow Lakes, the Greystone Park State Hospital, and the villages of Mt. Tabor, Parsippany (or Cobb's Corners), and Rockaway Neck. Manufactures include industrial equipment, ceramic goods, electric and electronic equipment, food products, and pharmaceuticals. The township is the site of a Presbyterian church originally built in 1718, the Benedict House, the Beverwyck Inn, and the county fairgrounds; the Troy Meadows constitute a natural bird refuge. Old Boone Town, a pioneer village, was on the site of the reservoir. Bloomfield College has purchased land for a campus in the township. Pop. (1960) 25,557; (1970) 55,112.

PARSLEY, common name of herbs belonging to the genus *Petroselinum*, in the family Umbelliferae (q.v.); the species are annual or biennial. Parsley is a branching, smooth, and herbaceous plant, with variously pinnated leaves. A variety with curled leaflets is generally preferred, in cooking and as a garnish, to those with plain leaflets. Hamburg parsley is a variety cultivated for its large white carrotlike root. Parsley contains a peculiar gelatinous substance called apiol, which formerly had medicinal uses.

PARSNIP, genus of annual, biennial, and perennial herbs of the Carrot family, Umbelliferae, with carrotlike fleshy roots and pinnate leaves. The common parsnip, *Pastinaca sativa*, native to Europe and northern Asia, is a biennial, with stems 2 to 3 ft. tall and ovate leaflets. The edible white roots are aromatic, mucilaginous, and sweet, but slightly acrid. The parsnip thrives in an open rich soil, but will succeed in clay soils.

PARSONS' CAUSE, in American colonial history, the term applied to a celebrated legal action heard in the court of Hanover County, Va., in 1763. The action arose from the imposition by the legislature of Virginia in 1758 of a law to fix the salaries of the clergy, payable in tobacco, at a flat rate, irrespective of market conditions. George II (q.v.) King of Great Britain, vetoed the law in 1759 and various clergymen brought suit against their vestries for the salaries legally due them for 1758 in terms of the real, rather than fixed, value of tobacco. The best known of these suits was the one brought by a cleric of Hanover County; Patrick Henry (q.v.), then a young, almost unknown lawyer, was engaged as counsel against the clergy. The court decided against the validity of the law of 1758. The jury, influenced by a speech by Henry in which the king's action in overriding the action of the legislature was attacked as tyrannical, returned a verdict of only one penny damages for the clergyman.

PARTHENOGENESIS. *See* REPRODUCTION.

PARTHENON, Doric temple of the goddess of wisdom Athena (q.v.) Parthenos, or Athena "the Virgin", on the Acropolis (q.v.) in Athens, Greece. The greatest masterpiece of ancient Greek architecture, it was erected between 447 and 432 B.C., under the rule of Pericles, the architectural supervision of Ictinus and Callicrates and the sculptural supervision of Phidias (qq.v.). The building is 228 ft. long, 101 ft. wide, and 66 ft. high from the top of the building platform to the gable. Now in ruins, the white Pentelic marble structure stood unchanged until the 6th century A.D., when it was consecrated as a church. In 1456, when the Ottoman Turks captured Athens, a minaret was added and the church was transformed into a mosque. When Athens was taken by the Venetians in 1687, the building was greatly damaged by an explosion which detonated the munitions the Turks had stored there. Many of the remains of the sculpture of the temple were removed in 1791, and these now form part of the British Museum collection; *see* ELGIN MARBLES. A number of the sculptures are in the Louvre Museum and other European museums; others, however, still remain in Athens, both on the Parthenon itself

The Parthenon, on the Acropolis at Athens.

The liquid hydrogen bubble chamber, at Argonne National Laboratory, Chicago, Ill. A typical large-scale facility, the chamber is completely enclosed by magnets, which cause the tracks of high-energy particles to be curved. Argonne National Laboratory

and in museums. In recent years, considerable restoration of the building has been effected.

PARTHIA, ancient empire of Asia, in what are now Iran and Afghanistan. The Parthians were of Scythian descent, and adopted Median dress and Aryan speech; see INDO-EUROPEAN LANGUAGES; MEDIA; SCYTHIANS. They were excellent horsemen, archers, and warriors. In battle, mounted Parthians often discharged their arrows backwards in pretended flight; this is the origin of the phrase "a Parthian shot".

Parthia was subject successively to the Assyrians, Medes, Persians, Macedonians under King Alexander III (q.v.), and Seleucidae. About 250 B.C. the Parthians succeeded in founding an independent kingdom which, during the 1st century B.C., grew into an empire extending from the Euphrates R. to the Indus R. and from the Oxus (now Amu Dar'ya) R. to the Indian Ocean. The main Parthian cities were Seleucia, Ctesiphon, and Hecatompylos. After the middle of the 1st century B.C. Parthia was a rival of Rome, and several wars occurred between the two powers. In 226 A.D. Parthia was conquered by Ardashir I, King of Persia and founder of the Sassanid dynasty (see under ARDASHIR).

PARTICLE DETECTORS, instruments that are used to detect and study fundamental nuclear particles; see ATOM AND ATOMIC THEORY; NUCLEAR ENERGY. These detectors range in complexity from the well-known portable Geiger counter to room-sized spark and bubble chambers; see IONIZATION CHAMBER. Detectors that enable physicists to study high-energy particles by observing the tracks the particles leave behind are called track detectors. Spark and bubble chambers are track detectors, as are the cloud chamber (q.v.) and nuclear emulsions. Nuclear emulsions resemble photographic emulsions but are thicker and not as sensitive to light. A charged particle passing through the emulsion ionizes silver grains along its track. These grains become black when the emulsion is developed and can be studied with a microsocope; see ION; IONIZATION.

The bubble chamber, invented in 1952 by the American physicist Donald A(rthur) Glaser (1926–), is similar in operation to the cloud chamber, which it has largely replaced. In a bubble chamber a liquid is momentarily superheated to a temperature just above its boiling point (q.v.). For an instant the liquid will not boil unless some impurity or disturbance is introduced. High-energy particles provide such a disturbance. Tiny bubbles form along the tracks as these particles pass through the liquid. If a photograph is taken just after the particles have crossed the chamber, these bubbles will make

PARTICLE DETECTORS

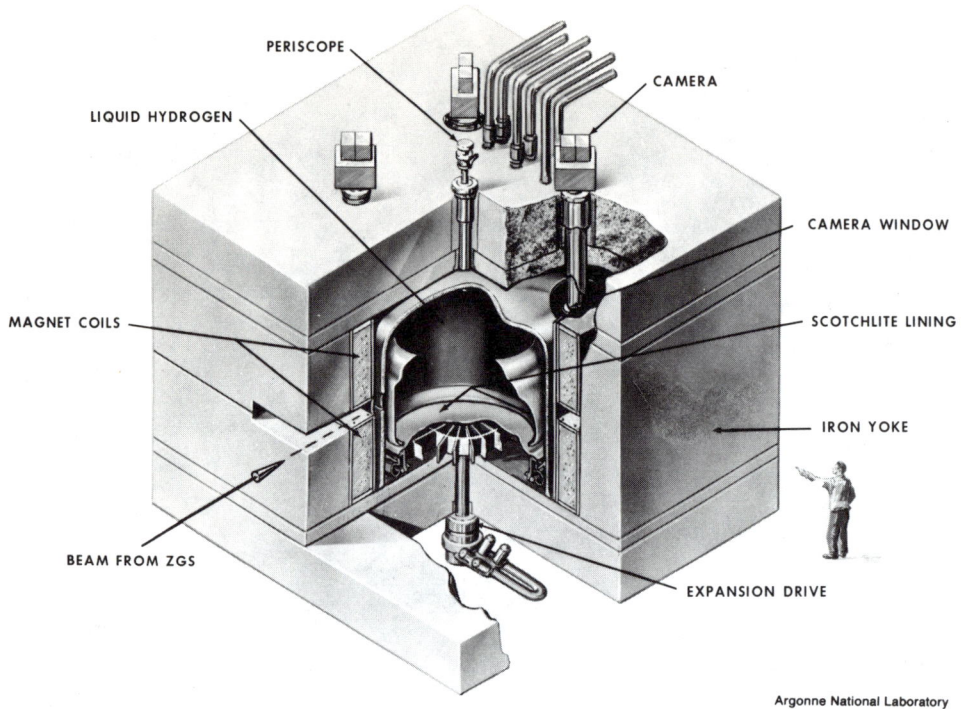

Argonne National Laboratory

Above: Cutaway diagram of a 12-ft. bubble chamber at the Argonne National Laboratory, showing the super-conducting magnet coils surrounding the liquid chamber, the entry point for the high-energy particle beam from the zero-gradient synchrotron (ZGS), and the observation and photographic apparatus. Below: Particle paths in liquid-hydrogen bubble-chamber photograph (left) and line sketch (right) showing the production, by an incoming K^--meson (at 1), of a negatively charged Omega (Ω^-) meson (at 3 in sketch), a neutral K-meson ($K°$, broken line), and a positive K-meson (K^+ at 2). The broken lines in the drawing represent the paths of neutral particles that do not leave tracks. The symbols π^-, $\Xi°$, γ_1, γ_2, $\Lambda°$, and p represent pions, hyperons, and a proton produced by the decay of Ω^-.

Brookhaven National Lab.

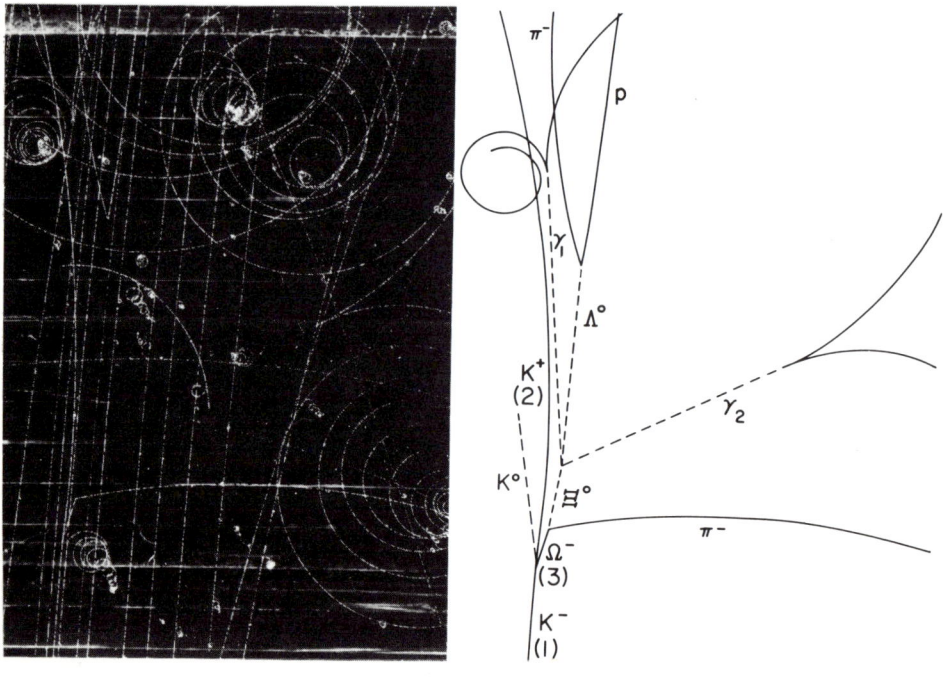

visible the paths of the particles. Because the paths of electrically charged fundamental particles are bent or deflected by a magnetic field, and the amount of deflection depends on the energy of the particle, a bubble chamber placed between the poles of a magnet can be used to measure the energies of the particles; see ENERGY; MAGNETISM. In the future, many bubble chambers will use newly developed superconducting magnets instead of conventional magnets. These new magnets, which operate at very low temperatures approaching absolute zero, are capable of sustaining very high magnetic fields with essentially no consumption of electricity. It is probable that future synchrotrons and other accelerators will also use superconducting magnets to confine beams of particles while they are being accelerated; see ACCELERATORS, PARTICLE; CYCLOTRON. The world's largest bubble chamber, installed in 1963 at Brookhaven National Laboratory (q.v.), is 80 in. long. A bubble chamber 12 ft. in diameter, using a superconducting magnet, was scheduled to be put into operation in the early 1970's at Argonne National Laboratory, Argonne, Ill.

In a spark chamber, oncoming high-energy particles ionize the air or a gas between plates or wire grids that are kept alternately positively and negatively charged. Sparks jump along the paths of ionization, and can be photographed to show particle tracks. In some spark-chamber installations, information on particle tracks is fed directly into electronic computer circuits without the necessity of photography. A spark chamber can be operated very quickly and selectively. The instrument can be set to record particle tracks only when a particle of the type that the researchers want to study is produced in a nuclear reaction. This advantage is important in studies of the rarer particles; spark-chamber pictures, however, lack the resolution and fine detail of bubble-chamber pictures. See also SCINTILLATION COUNTER.   J.T.S.

PARTNERSHIP, in law, term applied to an association of two or more persons who have agreed to combine their labor, property, and skill, or some or all of them, for the purpose of engaging in lawful business and sharing profits and losses between them; in this definition the term business includes every trade, occupation, and profession. The parties forming such an association are known as partners. Partners may adopt a fictitious firm name or use a real family name. In the United States, most States require filing with the county clerk of a certificate of partnership when the firm or association will be doing business under an assumed name. The agreement to form a partnership is known as a partnership contract, the most important provision of which sets out the manner in which profits are to be distributed among the partners.

A partnership can be formed only by contract (q.v.); the Statute of Frauds requires the agreement to be in writing if the term exceeds one year, and failure to comply results in a partnership at will. Any number of persons may contract to form a partnership, and firms of partners may enter into partnership with each other. In most States a corporation (q.v.), however, has no power to enter into a partnership unless such power is expressly given in the corporate charter. New members may not be admitted into an existing partnership unless all partners consent to such admission. The agreement of partnership generally provides for its duration for a definite term of years; if no duration is specified it is said to be a partnership at will, and can be terminated at any time by any of the partners. By agreement of the members, moreover, a partnership may be dissolved or terminated, and the terms of the partnership agreement may be changed or modified at any time. Death or bankruptcy (q.v.) of a partner, the decree of a court because of insanity or misconduct of a partner, and the termination of the period fixed for the duration of the partnership, also operate to effect a dissolution of the partnership.

A partner acts as an agent of the firm in the conduct of its business. His authority to act depends not only on the express powers given him by the partnership agreement, but also on the implied powers resulting from the partnership relation and the character of the business conducted. In the case of a partnership formed to conduct a wholesale or retail business, for example, a partner has implied power to borrow money for trade purposes, to buy on cash or credit, to make contracts and negotiable instruments (q.v.), to hire employees, to pay firm debts and sell or mortgage property (see MORTGAGE) for that purpose, and to receive payment of debts owed the firm. A partner must, however, exercise the highest degree of good faith in all dealings with his partners, must devote his time and attention to the partnership business, and must account to the other partners for any secret profits made in the conduct of the partnership business. The liability of a partner for partnership debts is said to be unlimited, except when he is a limited partner of a limited partnership organized in accordance with the provisions of a State statute permitting such limitation of liability. See also BUSINESS.

PARTRIDGE

PARTRIDGE, common name applied to Eurasian gallinaceous birds belonging to the genus *Perdix* in the family Tetraonidae. The partridge has a short, strong bill, naked at the base; the upper mandible convex, bent down at the tip; the wings and tail short; and the tarsi as well as the toes naked, the tarsi not spurred. The common partridge, *P. perdix,* is the most plentiful of all game birds in Great Britain. On the continent of Europe it is abundant in almost all districts suitable to its habits, from Scandinavia to the Mediterranean, and is found also in northern Africa and in some parts of western Asia.

The red-legged or French partridge, *Alectoris rufa,* is a native of southern Europe and of the Channel Islands. The name is loosely used for the North America ruffed grouse, the Virginian quail, the tinamou, and other birds. In India the term has been borrowed for some more or less similar game birds, especially the chukor. Compare GROUSE.

PARTRIDGEBERRY, common name applied to *Mitchella repens,* belonging to the Madder family, a small trailing evergreen herb with round or oval shining leaves and white fragrant flowers in pairs. The name partridgeberry also refers to the scarlet edible berry that remains on the plant over winter. The berry of the common wintergreen (q.v.) or checkerberry, *Gaultheria procumbens,* is also, less properly, so named. Other names for partridgeberry are twinberry and squawberry.

PASADENA, city of California, in Los Angeles Co., in the foothills of the San Gabriel Mts., 11 miles N.E. of central Los Angeles. Pasadena is a noted winter resort and a residential city. It has an elevation of from 800 to 1200 ft. above sea level, with Mt. Wilson (6666 ft.) and Mt. Lowe (6100 ft.) rising above. It is surrounded by a fruit-growing area, and the industries in the city include the packing and preserving of citrus fruits and the manufacture of furniture, scientific instruments, pottery, and art products. Pasadena is the site of the California Institute of Technology (1891), the Pasadena College of Theatre Arts, Pasadena College, and Pasadena City College. Cultural facilities include the Pasadena Community Playhouse, one of the first and most successful institutions of its kind in the United States, the Grace Nicholson Oriental Art Gallery, and the Busch Gardens (famous for rare plants).

The city is noted for many beautiful flowers, especially roses, and an annual event, held on New Year's Day since 1890, is the festival and floral display known as the Tournament of Roses. The "Street of Christmas Trees", an avenue bordered for more than a mile with Himalayan cedars, or deodars, is illuminated at night for the week preceding the festival. The Rose Bowl, a vast outdoor amphitheater, built in a dry canyon and seating 85,000 persons, is the site of an annual championship intercollegiate football game, also held on New Year's Day.

Pasadena was settled by a group of fruit-growers from Indianapolis, Ind., in 1874, incorporated as a town in 1886, and chartered as a city in 1901. Pop. (1960) 116,407; (1970) 113,327.

PASADENA, city of Texas, in Harris Co., on the Houston Ship Channel, at the mouth of Vince Bayou, adjoining Houston on the east. The surrounding area produces cattle, corn, rice, peanuts, and cotton. Industries include oil refining, paper milling, lumbering, and the manufacture of chemicals and synthetic rubber. Oil and cattle are shipped. San Jacinto College (1901) is in Pasadena, and the monument commemorating the Battle of San Jacinto (q.v.) of the war of Texan independence is 10 miles to the east. Settled in 1892, the city was incorporated in 1928. Pop. (1960) 58,737; (1970) 89,277.

PASCAGOULA, city and port of entry in Mississippi, and county seat of Jackson Co., at the mouth of the Pascagoula R., 20 miles E. of Biloxi. It is a fishing and boat-building center. Manufactures include clothing, fish oil and fish meal. The city is the site of United States dry docks and a United States Coast Guard base; it is also a popular vacation resort. The original settlement grew around the still-existing "Old Spanish Fort", built in 1718. Pop. (1960) 17,155; (1970) 27,264.

PASCAL, Blaise (1623–62), French philosopher and physicist, born in Clermont-Ferrand. His family settled in Paris in 1629. Pascal, under the tutelage of his father, soon proved himself a mathematical prodigy, and at the age of sixteen formulated one of the basic theorems of projective geometry, known as Pascal's theorem and described in his *Essai pour les Coniques* ("Essay on Conics", 1639); *see* GEOMETRY: *Demonstrative Geometry.* In 1642 he invented the first mechanical adding machine; *see* COMPUTER. Pascal proved by experimentation in 1648 that the level of the mercury column in a barometer is determined by an increase or decrease in the surrounding atmospheric pressure rather than by a vacuum, as previously believed. This discovery verified the hypothesis of the Italian physicist Evangelista Torricelli (q.v.) concerning the effect of atmospheric pressure on the equilibrium of liquids. Six years later, in conjunction with the French mathematician Pierre de Fermat (q.v.), Pascal formulated the mathematical theory of probability (q.v.), which has become important in such fields as actuarial, mathematical, and social statistics, and as a fundamental element in the calculations of modern theoretical physics. Pascal's other important scientific contributions include the derivation of Pascal's law or principle, which states that fluids transmit pressures equally in all directions (see FLUID MECHANICS); and his investigations in the geometry of infinitesimals. His methodology reflected

Blaise Pascal   IBM

his emphasis on empirical experimentation as opposed to analytical, a priori methods, and he believed that human progress is perpetuated by the accumulation of scientific discoveries resulting from such experimentation.

Later Life and Works. Pascal espoused Jansenism and in 1654 entered the Jansenist community at Port Royal, where he led a rigorously ascetic life until his death eight years later; see JANSEN, CORNELIS. In 1656 he wrote the famous eighteen *Lettres Provinciales* ("Provincial Letters"), in which he attacked the Jesuits (q.v.) for their attempts to reconcile 16th-century naturalism with orthodox Catholicism. His most positive religious statement appeared in fragmentary form in 1670 as *Apologie de la Religion Chrétienne* ("Apology of the Christian Religion"). In these fragments, that later were incorporated into his major work, he posed the alternatives of potential salvation and eternal damnation, with the implication that only by conversion to Jansenism could salvation be achieved. Pascal asserted that whether salvation was achieved or not, man's ultimate destiny was an afterlife belonging to a supernatural realm which could be only intuitively known. Pascal's final important work was *Pensées sur la Religion et sur Quelques Autres Sujets* ("Thoughts on Religion and on Other Subjects") also published in 1670. In the *Pensées* Pascal attempted to explain and justify the difficulties of human life by the doctrine of original sin, and contended that revelation can be comprehended only by faith, which in turn is justified by revelation. Pascal's writings urging acceptance of the Christian life contain frequent applications of the calculations of probability; he reasoned that the value of eternal happiness is infinite, and that although the probability of gaining such happiness by religion may be small, it is infinitely greater than by any other course of human conduct or belief. A reclassification of the *Pensées*, a careful work begun in 1935 and continued by several scholars, does not reconstruct the *Apologie*, but allows the reader to follow the plan that Pascal himself would have followed.

Evaluation. Pascal was one of the most eminent mathematicians and physicists of his period and one of the greatest mystical writers in Christian literature. His religious works are personal in their speculation upon matters beyond human understanding. He is generally ranked among the finest French polemicists, especially in the *Lettres Provinciales,* a classic in the literature of irony. Pascal's prose style is noted for its originality and, in particular, for its total lack of artifice. He affects his readers by his use of logic and the passionate force of his dialectic.   W.F.

PASCHAL, name of two popes of the medieval Christian Church.

Saint Paschal I (d. 824), pope from 817 to 824. The earliest extant document concerning the temporal possessions of the Roman see dates from his pontificate; issued by Louis I (q.v.), Holy Roman Emperor, it acknowledged the sovereignty of the pope over the Papal States (q.v.).

Paschal II (1050?–1118), original name RANIERI, pope from 1099 to 1118. His administration was marked by conflicts over the question of investiture (q.v.).

PASCO, city in Washington, and county seat of Franklin Co., on the Columbia R., about 76 miles S.E. of Yakima. Pasco is a marketing and shipping area. It is the site of Columbia Basin College, established in 1955. Nearby is the Hanford Works of the Atomic Energy Commission. Pasco was founded in 1884 and incorporated in 1891. Pop. (1960) 14,522; (1970) 13,920.

PASHTO. See PUSHTU.

PASQUEFLOWER. See ANEMONE.

PASSAIC, city of New Jersey, in Passaic Co., on the Passaic R., 8 miles N. of Newark. The city is a

349

PASSAIC

textile center and is also noted for the manufacture of radio and telegraph equipment, railroad cars, rubber, leather, paper products, and chemcals. The site of the present city was first settled by the Dutch in 1678. During the American Revolution it was occupied by both the Americans and the British. Known as Paterson Landing until 1852 it was incorporated as a village in 1869, chartered as a city in 1873, and renamed Passaic in 1874. Pop. (1960) 53,963; (1970) 55,124.

PASSAIC, river of New Jersey, rising near Morristown. It flows about 80 miles S. past Millington, and N.E. to Paterson, where it falls 70 ft., furnishing great water power. It then continues S. and E., past Passaic and Newark, and empties into Newark Bay.

PASSAMAQUODDY, North American Indian tribe of the Abnaki (q.v.) confederacy. Now about 400 members of this tribe live near Passamaquoddy Bay, between Maine and New Brunswick, Canada.

PASSAMAQUODDY BAY, inlet of the Bay of Fundy, between N.E. Maine and S.W. New Brunswick, Canada. It contains several New Brunswick islands; the chief Maine towns on the inlet are Eastport and Lubec. The bay is 30 mi. long and 20 mi. wide at the entrance.

PASSAU, TREATY OF. See AUGSBURG.

PASSENGER PIGEON. See PIGEON.

PASSERIFORMES or **PASSERINES,** largest order of birds, more than half the known species. They are perching birds, and include nightingales, skylarks, and many other songbirds. See BIRD.

PASSIONFLOWER, common name of plants in the genus *Passiflora,* belonging to the family Passifloraceae. The flowers are usually perfect, with generally a five-parted calyx and five-parted corolla; all species have a more or less conspicuous crown of filaments springing from the throat of the tube formed by the base of the calyx and corolla. The species number about 400 and are mostly climbing plants, such as the passion vine, *P. incarnata,* of the southern United States, which sometimes reaches a height of 30 ft. The bell apple or water lemon of the West Indies is the edible fruit of *P. laurifolia.* The giant granadilla, *P. quadrangularis,* is a closely related plant native to Jamaica and South America. The pulp or aril surrounding each seed of the granadilla is used in flavoring drinks and ices.

PASSION PLAY, form of miracle play or, more specifically, mystery play (qq.v.), depicting the suffering, death, and resurrection of Jesus Christ (q.v.). The earliest dramatic representations of the crucifixion, in Latin verse, were given early in the 13th century. One hundred years later passion plays were being performed by amateur players, grouped into societies for the purpose, in both German and French. At the height of their popularity, in the middle of the 15th century, they had developed into elaborate productions requiring three days for performance. During the Renaissance (q.v.) the tradition languished. Of the passion plays performed in modern times, the best known is one dating from 1634, given every ten years by the residents of Oberammergau (q.v.) in the Bavarian Alps. In 1932 some immigrants from Lünen, Germany, presented the first performance of the Black Hills Passion Play in Spearfish, S.Dak. Said to date from 1242, this version is performed annually.

PASSION WEEK, in Christianity, name sometimes given to Holy Week (q.v.), or the week immediately preceding Easter (q.v.). In proper usage, however, Passion Week is the week preceding Holy Week, commencing on Passion Sunday, the fifth Sunday in Lent (q.v.). In the Roman Catholic Church, the more solemn part of Lent begins on Passion Sunday, and during the succeeding fortnight the *Gloria Patri* is omitted from certain portions of the service, and all pictures, crucifixes (see CRUCIFIX), statues, and other sacred representations in a church are veiled.

PASSOVER. See PESACH.

PASSPORT, document of nationality and identity usually granted only to a person who is a national of the issuing country for his identification and protection when traveling abroad. It is also a formal permit authorizing the holder to leave and return to the nation of which he is a subject. Sometimes, a passport must be examined and approved by officials of the foreign state, prior to the holder's legal entry there. The endorsement of a passport by a foreign state is called a visa (q.v.).

The origin of the practice of granting passports grew out of the right of nations to withhold from foreigners the privilege of transit through their territory. The formal permission granted to a foreigner by a government to pass through its territory was a passport. To avoid the inconvenience of this requirement the practice was adopted by which a subject of one government, leaving his country for travel in another, obtained from his government a certificate of citizenship that was accepted by the other government as a passport. This certificate is presented to the foreign government as an identification of the bearer, who, instead of receiving a passport from the foreign government, is given permission to visit the foreign state.

In the United States passports are issued only by the Department of State and only to citizens upon application supported by proof of citizenship and identity. No distinction is made between native-born and naturalized citizens in the granting of passports. A passport for the head of a family may cover his wife and minor children if they are traveling together. A married woman may obtain a passport for herself. In foreign countries a passport may be obtained by native or naturalized citizens of the U.S. from a U.S. diplomatic mission or consular office. In some European nations no subject is allowed to depart from his country without first securing a passport from his government authorizing him to leave the country. There may be a further requirement that the passport be visaed by the consul of the foreign country that the bearer intends to visit. In the U.S. a passport is not necessary for persons temporarily visiting Canada, Bermuda, Mexico, and certain other localities of the Western Hemisphere.

BUREAU OF SECURITY AND CONSULAR AFFAIRS

PASSY, Frédéric (1822–1912), French political economist and statesman, born in Paris. Educated as a lawyer, he gave up law to devote himself to economics and the cause of peace. He founded the International League for Peace in 1867 and served as its general secretary until 1889. At that time Passy joined the British pacifist Sir William Randal Cremer (q.v.) in founding the Interparliamentary Union of Arbitration to promote peace. From 1874 to 1889 he was a member of the Chamber of Deputies of the French legislature. Passy shared the first Nobel Peace Prize with the Swiss philanthropist Jean Henri Dunant (q.v.) in 1901.

PASTE. *See* GLUE.

PASTERNAK, Boris Leonidovich (1890–1960), Soviet poet and author, born in Moscow, and educated at the universities of Moscow and of Marburg, Germany. He studied music during his youth but later turned to writing poetry. His first collection of poems, *Twin in the Clouds* (1914), was marked by the use of symbolist techniques (*see* SYMBOLISTS). It was followed by other collections of poems, including *Above the Barriers* (1917; Eng. trans., 1923), *My Sister, Life* (1922), and *Second Birth* (1932). Although the influence of the symbolist tradition is evident in his work, the poems reveal strong modernistic tendencies, particularly in unusual associations of images and in a philosophical approach to nature and history.

These works established Pasternak as the outstanding poet in the Soviet Union. Communist critics, however, reproached him because his poetry did not follow the preferred patterns of socialist realism, and after 1932 only two collections, *On Early Trains* (1943) and *The Terrestrial Expanse* (1945), were published. He earned his living from his notable translations of various works by the English dramatist and poet William Shakespeare, the German poet Johann Wolfgang von Goethe (qq.v.), and other English and German writers.

Boris Leonidovich Pasternak — Pantheon Books

Pasternak's only novel, *Doctor Zhivago,* completed in 1956, was rejected by Soviet publishers because of its critical approach to Soviet Communism. In 1957 it appeared in an Italian translation and won international acclaim. It has been translated subsequently into many languages and, in 1958, was published in the United States. The novel presents a panoramic view of Russian society in the first quarter of the 20th century. The protagonist, Doctor Zhivago, is an intellectual whose sincerity, religious convictions, and independence of spirit enter into conflict with the theory and practice of the Soviet regime.

Pasternak won and accepted the 1958 Nobel Prize in literature. Both the award and his acceptance were denounced by various Soviet Communist groups, some of which reviled him as a traitor and suggested that he leave the Soviet Union. Announcing publicly his unwillingness to enter exile, he rejected the prize. Among

PASTEUR

his other works are the collection of short stories *Airy Paths* (1925), the autobiographical *Safe Conduct* (1931; Eng. trans., 1958), *I Remember: Sketch for an Autobiography* (1957; Eng. trans., 1959), and the posthumously published unfinished play *The Blind Beauty* (1969; Eng. trans., 1969).

PASTEUR, Louis (1822–95), French chemist and microbiologist, born in Dôle, and educated at the Royal College of Besançon and the École Normale Supérieure in Paris. He served as professor of physics at the University of Dijon in 1848 and at the University of Strasbourg from 1849 to 1854, when he was appointed professor of chemistry and dean of the faculty of sciences at the University of Lille. Pasteur served as director of scientific studies at the École Normale Supérieure in Paris from 1857 to 1867 and also as professor of physics, chemistry, and geology at the École des Beaux Arts from 1863 to 1868. He was professor of chemistry at the Sorbonne from 1867 to 1889, when he became the first director of the Institut Pasteur in Paris and served in this position until his death.

The Role of Microorganisms. Pasteur is recognized as the founder of microbiological sciences, but his first contribution was in organic chemistry. In 1848, while investigating the effects of tartaric acids (*see* TARTARIC ACID) on a ray of polarized light, he discovered that one type of the acid has two isomeric constituents; this discovery laid the basis for modern stereochemistry, the study of spatial arrangements of atoms in molecules; *see* ATOM AND ATOMIC THEORY; OPTICS: *Physical Optics: Polarization of Light.* Pasteur's stereochemical work led to his classical researches on the processes of fermentation (q.v.) and putrefaction in wine, beer, milk, alcohol, and other liquids. He proved that these processes are caused by microorganisms, or germs (*see* GERM), which are not spontaneously generated by the processes themselves as had previously been thought, but are found in air to which the affected substances have been exposed. By demonstrating that the contamination and subsequent putrefaction of many substances is caused by specific organisms in the atmosphere, Pasteur not only made possible the scientific processing of beer, wine, milk, and other perishable products (*see* PASTEURIZATION), but also demonstrated the process of anaerobiosis by which some microorganisms derive energy from reactions that do not make use of oxygen.

Bacterial Diseases. His subsequent investigations of anthrax and rabies (qq.v.), further validated his theories and resulted in the prevention and cure of these and many other diseases in men and animals; *see* BACTERIA; BACTERIOLOGY. Pasteur thus proved the germ theory of disease and founded the science of immunity, considered to be the greatest medical discoveries of all time; *see* DISEASE; IMMUNITY. He had effectively explained why the technique of vaccination (q.v.), introduced by the British physicist Edward Jenner (q.v.) at the end of the 18th century, but never understood, worked. In 1865 Pasteur discovered the bacilli causing silk-worm disease and devised a method of destroying them by eliminating the diseased adult, thereby saving the silk industry in France from extinction. Pasteur next turned his attention to the cause of fowl cholera (q.v.), anthrax, and rabies or hydrophobia, and found that all these diseases were induced by specific microbes, and could be prevented and cured by inoculation with artificially grown cultures of the disease-producing bacilli. After numerous experiments with rabid animals, in 1885 he successfully inoculated a human being with his curative vaccine for hydrophobia. Three years later the Institut Pasteur was established in Paris for the prevention and cure of hydrophobia. It subsequently developed into one of the foremost scientific research organizations in the world, and Pasteur institutes have since been founded in several other countries.

Pasteur's discovery that most diseases are caused by specific microorganisms was applied by the British surgeon and biologist Joseph

Louis Pasteur

Lister (q.v.) in his development of antiseptic surgery by the chemical treatment of septic infections; see INFECTION; SURGERY. Among his many honors, Pasteur was elected to the French Academy of Sciences (1862), the Royal Society of Great Britain (1869), the French Academy of Medicine (1873), and the French Academy (1888).

PASTEURIZATION, process of heating a liquid, particularly milk, to a temperature between 131° F. and 158° F. (55° C. and 70° C.), to destroy harmful bacteria without materially changing the composition, flavor, or nutritive value of the liquid. The process is named after the French chemist Louis Pasteur (q.v.), who devised it in 1865 to inhibit fermentation (q.v.) of wine and milk. Milk is pasteurized by heating at the temperature 145° F. (63° C.) for thirty minutes, rapidly cooling it, and then storing it at a temperature below 50° F. (10° C.). Beer and wine are pasteurized by being heated at about 140° F. (60° C.) for about twenty minutes. A more recent method involves heating at 158° F. for about thirty seconds, and filling the container under sterile conditions.

PASTO, city in Colombia, and capital of Nariño Department, on a plateau of the Andes Mts., 8510 ft. above sea level, 330 miles S.W. of Bogotá. The city is on the Pan American Highway (q.v.) and is an important commercial and communications center for the surrounding agricultural region. Manufactures include furniture, textiles, and processed food. Pasto was founded in 1539, and was one of the last Spanish royalist strongholds in Colombia's struggle for independence from Spain in the second decade of the 19th century. Pop. (1968) 112,876.

PASTORAL POETRY, poetry professing to portray the innocence of shepherd life, according to a specific literary convention. Pastoral poems range from love lyrics to lengthy dramatic works and elaborate elegies; see POETRY. Classical pastoral poetry stemmed from the folk songs and ceremonies that honored the pastoral gods. The earliest extant pastoral poetry, the *Idylls,* was written by the Alexandrine Theocritus in the 3rd century B.C.; he was followed by the Greek poets Bion and Moschus in the 2nd century B.C. The Roman poet Vergil Latinized the mode in his *Bucolics* or *Eclogues* (37 B.C.).

The pastoral eclogue, a dialogue or conversation, often was the means by which, in contrasting simple shepherds in rustic surroundings with the urbane society of a corrupt court or city, the author expressed his moral or philosophical viewpoint. The form was popular with such humanists as the Italian poets Francesco Petrarch and Giovanni Boccaccio. One of the earliest dramatic pastorals is *Orfeo,* by the Italian poet Politian, performed at the court of Mantua about 1471 A.D. Others include *Aminta* (1573) by the Italian poet Torquato Tasso and *Pastor Fido* (1590) by the Italian poet Giovanni Battista Guarini. Nondramatic pastorals of 16th-century Italy include the romance *Arcadia* (1504) by the Italian writer Jacopo Sannazaro. In Portugal and Spain the pastoral flourished during the 16th century in the poems of the Portuguese writer Gil Vicente and the Spanish writers Juan del Encina, Miguel de Cervantes Saavedra, and others. The Spanish poet and novelist Jorge de Montemayor (about 1520–61) influenced later poets with his pastoral novel *Diana* (1559?). Most French pastoral poetry was artificial and was inferior to that of Italy and Spain.

In England *The Shepheardes Calendar* in twelve pastoral eclogues (1579) by the English poet Edmund Spenser formed a model for posterity. The pastoral spirit overflowed into other forms of English literature; into drama with *The Arraignment of Paris* (about 1581) by George Peele and *Sad Shepherd* (1641) by Ben Jonson; into romance with *Arcadia* (1590) by Sir Philip Sidney, and many of the pamphlet stories by Thomas Lodge and Robert Greene; into the sonnet with Lodge's cycle *Phillis* (1593); and above all, into the lyric with innumerable songs and madrigals by the English writers Lodge, Greene, Thomas Campion, Robert Herrick, Andrew Marvell, and others. Several of these are to be found in *England's Helicon* (1600) and other anthologies of the day. Even the master English poet and playwright William Shakespeare used the pastoral conventions, for example, in the comedy *As You Like It* (1600). *The Shepherd's Week* (1714) by the British poet John Gay was brightened by glimpses of genuine country life. Allan Ramsay, another 18th-century British poet, wrote the successful pastoral comedy *The Gentle Shepherd* (1725). From the days of Moschus' *Lament for Bion* the pastoral had been held as an appropriate setting for the funeral elegy. This particular use influenced later British poets, as evidenced in the 17th-century pastoral elegy "Lycidas" by John Milton and in the 19th-century *Adonais* (1821) by Percy Bysshe Shelley and *Thyrsis* (1866) by Matthew Arnold.

See separate article for those poets whose birth and death dates are not given.

PASTURE, plants grown to feed grazing animals and the land on which animals graze. See AGRICULTURE: *Animal Husbandry;* CONSERVATION: *Conservation of Grazing Lands;* GRASSES; GRASSLAND; HAY.

PATAGONIA

PATAGONIA, region of Argentina lying E. of the Andes Mts. and S. of the Río Colorado. It comprises an area of about 300,000 sq.mi., marked by desert plateaus, that includes the E., or Argentine, part of the Tierra del Fuego, an archipelago off the S. tip of South America. Sheep raising is the principal economic activity of Patagonia. The name Patagonia formerly applied to the southernmost portion of the South American continent, including what is now the S. parts of both Argentina and Chile. It was first visited by the Portuguese explorer Ferdinand Magellan (q.v.) in 1520. The region was not settled, however, until after 1880. The final division of Patagonia between Argentina and Chile occurred in 1902.

PATAN, former name of Lalitpur (q.v.), a city in Nepal.

PATENT, in law, the abbreviated term for "letters patent", in its most general sense a document issued by a government conferring some special right or privilege. In the United States the term is now restricted principally to patents for inventions (see INVENTION) granted under Federal statute, although occasionally applied to land patents, or to government grants of a part of the public domain to a private party. The specific attributes of novelty, of the new item for which a patent is sought, are defined as what is known as claims. The grant of a patent for an invention gives the inventor the exclusive privilege of using a specific process, such as the vulcanizing of rubber (q.v.), or of making, using, and selling a specific product or device, such as a machine, for a limited period of time.

History. In America patents for inventions were issued in 1641 by the colonial governments. The first U.S. patent laws were enacted by Congress in 1790 under the authority of Art. I, Sec. 8 of the Constitution, under which Congress is empowered "to promote the progress of science and useful arts by securing for limited times to authors and inventors the exclusive rights to their respective writings and discoveries"; see CONSTITUTION OF THE UNITED STATES. The Patent Act of 1790 was administered by a board or commission composed of the secretary of state, the secretary of war, and the attorney general of the U.S. The Act of Feb. 21, 1793, superseded the Act of 1790 and provided a registration system by which the granting of patents became a purely clerical function. This Act caused much trouble from the start and the many evils that arose under it culminated in the passage of the Act of July 4, 1836, the basis of the present patent system in the U.S. Since that time many legislative enactments have modified the original patent law. The most important of these is the Act of July 8, 1870, and subsequently the Act of July 19, 1952, which revised and codified the patent laws, and which, with amendments, constitutes the patent law in force at the present time. A superintendent of patents under the secretary of state administered the patent law from 1802 to 1836, when the office of commissioner of patents was created. In 1849 the Patent Office became a part of the Department of the Interior; it was transferred by executive order of the President to the Department of Commerce in 1925.

Purpose. In the U.S. the law provides that a patent may be granted to any person for the invention or discovery of any new and useful art, machine, manufacture, or composition of matter, or any new and useful improvement thereto; for the invention or asexual reproduction of any distinct and new variety of plant, other than a tuber-propagated plant; or for any new, original, and ornamental design for an article of manufacture. A patent is granted only upon a filed application complete in all respects, upon payment of the fees, and only after a determination that the disclosure is complete and the invention is new and useful.

The patent is issued in the name of the U.S., under the seal of the Patent Office. It consists of a short title, together with a printed copy of the specification and claims, a patent number, and a grant to the patentee, his heirs and assigns, for a period of seventeen years. In the case of design patents the period of the patent is $3\frac{1}{2}$, 7, or 14 years, as the applicant may, in his application, elect. Every patent must be applied for by the actual inventor, and if two or more parties make an invention jointly they must apply jointly. If the inventor dies or becomes insane before making application, his legal representative or guardian is permitted to do so. Patents may be transferred from one party to another by assignment in writing, the assignment being recorded in the Patent Office.

Once a patent is granted it is out of the jurisdiction of the Patent Office, and matters of infringement, the scope of the patent, or any other questions that arise out of the grant are within the original jurisdiction of the U.S. district courts. Infringement consists of wrongfully making, using, or selling a patented invention. The law requires the marking of patented articles with the patent number; failure to do so will prevent the recovery of damages (q.v.) for infringement, unless the patentee can prove that due notice of such infringement was given to the person charged with infringing the patent, who continued after such notice to make or sell the patented product. The remedy for an infringement is an action for damages, or for a restraining injunction (q.v.), or both. It is customary for the manufacturer of an item, for which a patent is sought, to mark the product "patent pending" or "patent applied for"; such notice to the public affords an opportunity to others who may claim to have invented the same product to institute proceedings, called "interference proceedings" in the Patent Office to determine the originality of the claim of the applicant.

In general, a patent affords protection against infringement only within the jurisdiction of the government by which it is issued, and it is therefore necessary to take out a patent in every country in which protection is desired. Patent statutes have been enacted in a majority of the civilized countries of the world, and there exists an International Convention for the Protection of Industrial Property, originated in 1883 and since revised.

Printed copies of U.S. patents may be purchased from the Patent Office in Washington; photostatic copies of foreign patents may also be obtained upon payment of the required fees, as nearly complete sets of the patents of many foreign countries are available in the Patent Office library. A copyright (q.v.) is not a patent, because it applies to literary and other works. Copyrights of labels or prints used on or for advertising and merchandise were registered with the Patent Office until that function was transferred to the Copyright Office by a law passed in 1939.

PATER, Walter Horatio (1839–94), British essayist and critic, born in London, England, and educated at the University of Oxford. Except for his visits to the Continent and a short residence in London, he spent his life at Oxford. He concentrated on interpreting to his age the humanist spirit of the Renaissance (q.v.) in art and literature through the historical novel, the story, and, mainly, the essay. His attention to the elaborate, exquisite sentence revealed his preoccupation with perfecting the form of prose style without neglecting depth of subject matter; he is remembered primarily as an innovator in aesthetics. Pater's works include *Studies in the History of the Renaissance* (1873) and the autobiographical *The Child in the House* (1894).

PATERSON, city in New Jersey, and county seat of Passaic Co., on the Passaic R., 12 miles N. of Newark. The Great Falls in the Passaic R. at Paterson have a drop of about 70 ft., furnishing abundant hydroelectric power for the industries of the city. Paterson is the third-largest city of New Jersey and is an important manufacturing center. It was called "The Silk City" before silk production was superseded in the last half of the 20th century by the manufacture of rayon and other synthetic fabrics. Textile products, machinery, fabricated metals, transportation equipment, metal and rubber goods, plastics, furniture, clothing, chemicals, and processed food are made here. A public library designed by the American architect Henry Bacon (q.v.) is in Paterson and Paterson State College (founded in 1855) is in nearby Wayne.

Paterson was founded in 1791 when the area around the falls was chosen as the site for an industrial city by members of the Society for Establishing Useful Manufactures, a group encouraged by United States Secretary of the Treasury Alexander Hamilton (q.v.) to foster industry in the new nation. By 1870 half the silk manufactured in the U.S. was made in the city. Paterson was incorporated as a town in 1831. The *Sandusky,* the first steam locomotive produced in Paterson, was built in 1837, and for the remainder of the century the town was noted for the manufacture of locomotives. In 1851 Paterson was chartered as a city. Pop. (1960) 143,663; (1970) 144,824.

PATHOLOGY, branch of medicine dealing with abnormalities, or diseases, their nature, causes, symptoms, transmission, and particularly, their progress. General pathology deals with disease or morbid processes in general, and special pathology with particular diseases. Pathology is also divided as to internal and external, and into medical and surgical investigations. Historically, humoral pathology was based on the theory that all diseases were due to the disordered condition of the humors and fluids of the body, while cellular pathology dealt with the action of cells in the healthy and diseased functions of the body. Mostly unknown before 1850, pathology made huge strides through the employment of X-ray techniques, blood chemistry, biopsy, virology, and bacteriophagy. Today it embraces the subdisciplines of bacteriology, immunology, histology, morbid anatomy, hematology, and chemical pathology. *See also* ANATOMY: *Microsopic Anatomy;* BACTERIA; BACTERIOLOGY; BIOCHEMISTRY; BIOPSY; CYTOLOGY; DISEASE; HISTOLOGY; IMMUNITY; MEDICINE: *Modern Medicine;* PHYSIOLOGY; X RAY: *Applications of X Rays.*

PATIALA, city of the Republic of India, in Haryana State, on the E. branch of the Sirhind Canal, 125 miles N.W. of New Delhi. A trade center in an area growing grains, sugarcane, and cotton, the city manufactures metal handicrafts, hardware, electric goods, textiles, shoes, and flour. It is the site of several palaces of the former maharajah, the King Edward Memorial, an old fort housing a museum, several temples of note, sports facilities, and a government clinical-research laboratory. Educational institutions include Mahendra College, Yavindra College, the Bikram College of Commerce, a college for women, a medical college, a state college of education, and the Thapar Institute of Engineering and Technology, all affiliated with Punjab University. The city was capital of the princely State of Patiala from 1763 to 1948, and of the Patiala and East Punjab States Union from 1948 to 1956. Pop. (1965 est.) 137,094.

PATNA, city in the Republic of India, and capital of Bihar State, on the Ganges R., 300 miles N.W. of Calcutta. It is a trade center for an agricultural area producing rice, grains, sesame, linseed, and sugarcane. Notable features of the city include a mosque built in 1499, Patna Museum, and the University of Patna, founded in 1917. Patna also houses a Sikh temple and is a sacred city for Sikhs (q.v.); their last guru, Govind Singh (1666–1708), was born here.

Patna was settled in the 6th century B.C. as Pataliputra. In the 3rd century B.C. the city became the imperial capital of the Indian ruler Asoka (q.v.). Patna deteriorated after 400 A.D., but some of its former greatness was restored in the 16th century. The Moguls made it the seat of the viceroy of Bihar and a leading trading center; see INDIA: *History: The Mogul Empire.* In 1763 the British seized Patna after a struggle with the nawab of Bengal. Patna was made capital of Bihar and Orissa Province in 1912 and capital of Bihar State in 1935. Pop. (1969 est.) 449,471.

PATON, Alan Stewart (1903–), South African writer and social reformer, born in Pietermaritzburg, and educated at the University of Natal. He entered the teaching profession in 1925. During the ensuing decade he developed a keen interest in the social and racial problems of South Africa. From 1935 to 1948 he was principal of the Diepkloof Reformatory for delinquent boys near Johannesburg, where he introduced many enlightened reforms. Paton received great critical and popular acclaim for his first published novel, *Cry, The Beloved Country* (1948), which is distinguished for its compassionate treatment of those caught up in the racial conflicts of South Africa. The work was translated into many languages. It was made into an opera, *Lost in the Stars* (1949), with music by the German-American composer Kurt Weill (q.v.) and, under the original title, into a motion picture (1952). His second novel, *Too Late the Phalarope* (1953), and short stories, *Tales from a Troubled Land* (1961), also dealt with racial tensions in present-day South African society. In 1955 he published *The Land and People of South Africa* (rev. ed., 1964), a nonfiction work, and in 1968 *The Long View*, which deals with apartheid. Paton was a founder and president of the Liberal Party of South Africa, which challenged the practice of apartheid.

PÁTRAI or **PATRAS,** city and port in Greece, and administrative center of the region of Pelopónnisos, on the Gulf of Pátrai, 81 miles N.W. of Corinth. Pátrai is one of the largest cities in Greece, and a commercial and industrial center. Major industries include food processing, shipbuilding, and the manufacture of textiles, bricks, and tiles. Chief exports are currants, wine, olive oil, citrus fruits, and sheepskins. Founded by the ancient Greeks, Pátrai was one of the twelve cities of the second Achaean League (q.v.). The city passed to Roman control in the 2nd century B.C., becoming a prosperous port and commercial center. It was also an early center of Christianity. For a short time in the 15th century the city was held by Venice but then it passed to the Turks. Except for a second brief period of Venetian rule from 1687 to 1715, the Turks controlled Pátrai until 1828, near the end of the Greek War of Independence. During the war, however, the city was completely destroyed by the Turks; it was rebuilt in 1829 as a modern city in a rectangular pattern. Pop. (1968 est.) 96,000.

PATRAS. See PÁTRAI.

PATRIARCH, in the hierarchy of the Christian Church, a bishop of high degree; see BISHOP; CHRISTIAN CHURCH, HISTORY OF THE. The patriarchs of present-day Christianity are found particularly in the Orthodox Church (q.v.), but some bishops of special authority in the Roman Catholic Church (q.v.) are also known as patriarchs. *See also* POPE.

PATRIARCHS, in Biblical history, the leaders of the Hebrews of the period before Moses (qq.v.), the great lawgiver. As listed in the book of Genesis (q.v.), the traditional patriarchs are Abraham, Isaac, Jacob (qq.v.), and Jacob's sons, the leaders of the twelve tribes of Israel. The patriarchs would seem to have been active in the middle of the Bronze Age, about the first half of the 2nd millennium B.C. See JEWS.

PATRIARCHY, in sociology and anthropology, system of social organization in which descent is traced through the male line and all children bear the name of the father or belong to his clan. The system is often associated with inheritance, in the male line, of material goods and social prerogatives; see PRIMOGENITURE. The social organization of the ancient Hebrews, as described in the Old Testament, was strongly patriarchal; and patriarchy still exists among nomadic peoples today, particularly in the Arabian Desert and the steppes of central Asia. The family and clan organization of the ancient Greeks and Romans was also patriarchal, as was the family and social organization of Europe during the Middle Ages. Many residues of this earlier patriarchy, such as the inheritance of the family name through the male line, still persist in modern Western society, but exclusive male inheritance of property and other patriarchal features are gradually disappearing. Compare MATRIARCHY.

PATRICIANS, members of Roman gentes (see GENS), or citizen families, of which the Roman people originally consisted, and their descendants by blood and adoption. Originally the patricians are said to have been a Sabine (see SABINES) race that conquered a Ligurian (see LIGURIA) people already established on the site of Rome; according to this theory the plebs (q.v.), who made up the other element of the free Roman populace, were the conquered Ligurians and had a family organization less highly developed than that of the conquering Sabines. All political and religious offices were reserved to the patricians, and intermarriage with plebs was forbidden. A long struggle between the two orders, beginning in the 6th century B.C., ended in the attainment by the plebs of political equality and the establishment of a new aristocracy of *nobiles* made up of ruling families of both classes. From 300 B.C. the old political distinctions between patricians and plebs had no real meaning, except that patricians were ineligible for the tribunate (see TRIBUNE) or the council of the plebs. Under Constantine I (q.v.), the Roman emperor, in the 4th century A.D., *patricius* became a personal title, not hereditary, and conferred very high honor and privileges.

PATRICK, Saint (389?–461?), called "the Apostle of Ireland", Christian prelate. His birthplace is uncertain, but was probably in southwestern Britain; his British name was Succat. At sixteen years of age he was carried off by Irish marauders and passed his captivity as a herdsman near the mountain Slemish in County Antrim (as tradition has it) or in County Connacht. The young herdsman saw visions in which he was urged to escape, and after six years of slavery he did so, to the northern coast of Gaul (now France). Ordained a priest, possibly by Saint Germanus (378–448), at Auxerre, he returned to Ireland. Patrick was appointed, sometime after 431, successor to Saint Palladius, first bishop of Ireland.

A bell that traditionally belonged to Saint Patrick is preserved in the Shrine of Saint Patrick, National Museum, Dublin, Ireland.   Irish Tourist Board

Patrick concentrated on the west and north of Ireland. It is possible that he visited Rome and returned with relics. His reported use of the shamrock (q.v.) as an illustration of the Trinity (q.v.) led to its being regarded as the Irish national symbol. A strange chant of his, called the Lorica, is preserved in the *Liber Hymnorum* ("Book of Hymns"), and what purports to have been a handbell he used during Mass is shown in the Museum of Science and Art, Dublin. His traditional feast day is March 17.

PATRISTIC LITERATURE. See FATHERS OF THE CHURCH.

PATROCLUS, in Greek mythology, dearest friend of the hero Achilles (q.v.), whom he accompanied to the Trojan War (q.v.). In the tenth year of the conflict Achilles withdrew his troops, the Myrmidons (q.v.), from combat because of a quarrel with Agamemnon (q.v.), commander of the Greek forces. Without Achilles, the Greeks began to lose to the Trojans. Finally, as the Trojans began to burn the Greek ships, Patroclus persuaded Achilles to allow him to lead the Myrmidons to the rescue. Clad in Achilles' armor, Patroclus led the Greeks to victory, forcing the Trojans back to the walls of their city. In his moment of splendor, however, Patroclus was slain by the Trojan commander Hector (q.v.). To avenge his friend's death, Achilles rejoined the battle and killed Hector. See ILIAD.

357

PATRONS OF HUSBANDRY

PATRONS OF HUSBANDRY. See NATIONAL GRANGE.

PATROONS, proprietors of feudal estates, called patroonships, established under old Dutch grants in New Netherland, the present-day States of New York and New Jersey; see FEUDALISM. In 1629 the Dutch West India Company (q.v.) granted tracts of land to any of its members who would establish a colony of fifty persons on that land within four years. The holders of these tracts were called patroons, and they were granted important manorial privileges. The patroon held his land in perpetuity and leased it to tenants. Usually the tenant's expenses were so great that he was in debt to the patroon and therefore bound to his service. Because of Indian raids and lack of proper management by the patroons and the Dutch West India Company, almost all the patroonships failed. They were intended to encourage settlement in New Netherland but, in fact, delayed it. The English took possession of New Netherland in 1664 and continued the patroonships, with some modifications, until the early 19th century. Antirent riots in 1839 resulted in the abolishment of most of the old feudal obligations, and the patroons soon sold their estates to their tenants.

PATTI, Adelina (1843–1919), Italian-American coloratura soprano, born in Madrid, Spain, of Italian parents, and raised and trained in singing in New York City. She made her first concert appearance at the age of seven. Her formal operatic debut took place in New York City in 1859. Her London debut, made in 1861 as Amina in *La Sonnambula* ("The Sleepwalker", 1831) by the Italian composer Vincenzo Bellini (q.v.), won her recognition as one of the greatest singers of her day. Patti's voice had an extremely wide compass, a pure, bell-like quality, and remarkable flexibility and evenness. Her popularity was ascribed to the beauty of her voice and her technical skill; she was not noted as an actress. Patti's repertory comprised more than thirty roles, her most famous ones being in operas by the Italian composers Bellini, Gaetano Donizetti, and Giuseppe Verdi (qq.v.). She was especially praised for her interpretation of the role of Rosina in *Il Barbiere di Siviglia* ("The Barber of Seville", 1816) by the Italian composer Gioacchino Antonio Rossini (q.v.). After about 1895 Patti confined herself almost entirely to concert work. She officially retired in 1906 but actually made her final appearance in 1914, when she was seventy-one.

PATTON, George Smith (1885–1945), American army officer, born in San Gabriel, Calif., and educated at the United States Military Academy. Upon his graduation in 1909, he was commissioned a second lieutenant; he advanced in rank to full general by 1945. He served as aide-de-camp to the American general John Joseph Pershing (q.v.) on Pershing's expedition to Mexico in 1917. In France during World War I, Patton established a tank training school and commanded a tank brigade. In 1942 and 1943, during World War II, he commanded United States forces in Morocco, Tunisia, and Sicily. Early in 1944 he was given command of the Third Army. Controversial throughout the war for his personal flamboyance, outspokenness, uncompromising standards, and aggressive combat strategy, he played a key role in the headlong Allied armored thrust to Germany after D-Day.

In the summer of 1944 the Third Army broke through the German defenses in the Normandy campaign and advanced rapidly across France; in March, 1945, it crossed the Rhine R. into Germany and also moved toward Austria. After the war Patton served as military governor of Bavaria but because of criticism of his lenient policy toward the former enemy, he was relieved of the post. He was named head of the Fifteenth Army late in 1945, shortly before he was fatally injured in a traffic accident. In 1970 a motion picture entitled *Patton: A Salute to a Rebel* portrayed Patton's war career.

PAU, town in France, and capital of Pyrenees-Atlantiques Department, about 500 miles S. of Paris. Pau, built on a steep hill overlooking the Gave de Pau valley, is a well-known tourist center and a gateway to the Pyrenees. Pau's commercial interests include the production of petrochemicals from the abundant local supply of natural gas. Other industries include the manufacture of electronic equipment, paper products, pharmaceuticals, and furniture. Pau was the capital of the viscounty of Béarn and the residence of the kings of Navarre. Henry IV, King of France, and Charles XIV John (qq.v.), King of Sweden and Norway, were born in Pau. Pop. (1968) 74,005.

PAUL, Saint (about 3–65 A.D.), Christian missionary and theologian, called Apostle (q.v.) to the Gentiles, born a Jew and a Roman citizen in Tarsus (now in Turkey) and known originally by his Jewish name, Saul. Educated as a Pharisee (see PHARISEES), he was converted to Christianity (q.v.) through a vision of Christ during a journey from Jerusalem (q.v.) to Damascus (Acts 9:1–19, 22:5–16, 26:12–18). The remainder of his life was spent in preaching and organizing the early Church (see CHRISTIAN CHURCH, HISTORY OF THE), mainly through writings addressed to churches founded during his three great missionary journeys. The first took him from Antioch (now Antâkya, Turkey) to Cyprus and several cities in Galatia (now part of Turkey); the second, from Jerusalem through cities in Syria and Asia Minor to Macedonia (now part of Greece), where he visited Philippi, Thessalonica (now Salonika) Athens, and Corinth (q.v.); the third, to many of these cities again and to Ephesus (q.v.), where he spent two years.

Eventually imprisoned in Jerusalem after disturbances caused by Jewish enemies, he spent the rest of his life in confinement. His trial before Porcius Festus (d. about 62 A.D.), Roman governor of Judea, led to an appeal to the emperor Nero (q.v.) and further imprisonment in Rome, where the emperor may have put him to death.

Saint Paul formulated the language and systematized the doctrines of Christian theology; see THEOLOGY. He was the founder of many flourishing churches and one of the greatest of moral and spiritual teachers. His epistles, many of which survive in the New Testament, deal with theology, discipline, and church procedure; see COLOSSIANS; CORINTHIANS; EPHESIANS; GALATIANS; HEBREWS; PHILEMON; PHILIPPIANS; ROMANS; THESSALONIANS; TIMOTHY AND TITUS. His feast day, with that of Saint Peter (q.v.), is June 29: in Anglican churches, his feast is celebrated on Jan. 25, commemorating his conversion at Damascus.

PAUL, name of six popes of the Roman Catholic Church, the most important of whom were the following.

Paul III (1468–1549), original name ALESSANDRO FARNESE, pope from 1534 to 1549, born in Canino, Italy. An extremely able statesman and member of the powerful Farnese (q.v.) family, he was influential in the politics of Western Europe. He initiated many church reforms.

Paul IV (1476–1559), name GIOVANNI PIETRO CARAFFA, pope from 1555 to 1559, born in Naples, Italy. He enforced the observance of all clerical duties and enacted laws for the maintenance of public morality. He established church censorship, was the first to issue a full *Index Librorum Prohibitorum* (Index of Prohibited Books), and completed the organization of the Roman Inquisition (*see* INQUISITION).

Paul V (1552–1621), original name CAMILLO BORGHESE, pope from 1605 to 1621, born in Rome. His pontificate was marked by his conflict with Venice. The original ground of dispute was the question of immunity of the clergy to jurisdiction by civil courts. The clergy demanded to be tried by ecclesiastical tribunals alone; the Republic of Venice refused to recognize the exemption of the clergy from civil jurisdiction. The dispute was finally decided in 1607 by Henry IV (q.v.), King of France, against the ecclesiastical claims.

Paul VI, (1897–   ), original name GIOVANNI BATISTA MONTINI, elected pope in 1963, born in Concesio, Italy. He studied in Brescia and Rome, receiving degrees in civil and canon law, theology, and philosophy. Ordained in 1920, he served as an attaché of the nunciature in Warsaw, Poland (1923), and as spiritual adviser and moderator of the Roman group of the Italian Catholic Federation of Universities (1923–33). He became a clerk in the Vatican Secretariat of State (1933), undersecretary to the papal secretary of state (1936), Vatican substitute secretary of state (1944), and pro-secretary of state for ordinary affairs (1952). In 1954 he was consecrated archbishop of Milan, and in 1958, was made a cardinal. He succeeded John XXIII (*see under* JOHN) as supreme pontiff, and presided over Vatican Council II beginning with its second session; *see* VATICAN COUNCILS. In 1964, Pope Paul visited the Holy Land, the present-day countries of Jordan and Israel (qq.v.). During this visit he met with Benedictos (1892–   ), the Greek Orthodox patriarch of Jerusalem, in the first meeting between the head of

Pope Paul VI arrives by jet airliner at Kampala, Uganda, in July, 1969. His visit to Africa was the first to be made by a reigning pontiff. UPI

PAUL

the Roman Catholic Church and an Eastern Orthodox patriarch since 1438. In 1965 he and Athenagoras I (1886–   ), Greek Orthodox ecumenical patriarch of Constantinople, nullified the mutual excommunications of the Eastern and Western Churches of 1054; see CHRISTIAN CHURCH, HISTORY OF THE.

Paul VI has been active in extending the concern of the Vatican to Roman Catholics outside Europe. He traveled to the United States in 1965, to Colombia in 1968, to Uganda in 1969, and to various Asian countries, including the Republic of the Philippines, in 1970. He conferred with the head of the Anglican Communion, Arthur Michael Ramsey (1904–   ), the archbishop of Canterbury, in 1966 and with Athenagoras I on several occasions. In all of these travels and encounters, he was either the first pope to travel to the given area, or the first head of the Roman Catholic Church to attempt such systematic rapproachment with other Christian bodies. Among secular leaders with whom the pope has had meetings were also Communist leaders such as President Nikolai V. Podgorny (1903–   ) of the Soviet Union in 1967 and President Tito (q.v.) of Yugoslavia in 1971.

The pope was also the first to work with an advisory body set up on the basis of the principle of collegiality announced at Vatican Council II. The Synod of Bishops, in regular biannual meetings, discusses problems of interest to the Roman Catholic Church throughout the world. The first such meeting was held in 1967.

Among Paul's more important encyclicals were his decision to increase the use of the vernacular in parts of the Mass (1963) and his reaffirmations of the traditional church bans on priestly matrimony (1967) and artificial birth control (1968).   T.M.H.

PAUL I (1901–64), King of Greece (1947–64), youngest son of Constantine I, King of Greece (see under CONSTANTINE), born in Athens, and educated at the Greek Naval Academy. After completing his studies he served in the Royal Hellenic Navy. He became heir presumptive to the throne on the accession, in 1922, of his brother as King George II (q.v.). Between 1924, when the monarchy was abolished, and 1935, when it was restored, Paul lived in exile, mainly in the United States, England, and Italy. After his return to Greece, he became a commander in the Greek navy and later served on the general staff of the army. In 1938 he married Princess Frederika (1917–   ), daughter of the duke of Brunswick. During most of World War II, when Greece was under German occupation, Paul was with the Greek government-in-exile in London and Cairo. From Cairo he broadcast messages to the Greek people. He returned to Greece in 1946, following a plebiscite that approved the return of the monarchy, and succeeded to the throne in 1947, upon the death of George II. In 1949 government forces under Paul were victorious over the Communist insurgents who had begun fighting for control of the country during World War II. In 1964 Paul was succeeded by his only son, who ruled as Constantine II.

PAULDING, James Kirke (1778–1860), American writer and naval official, born near Tarrytown, N.Y. He was a friend of the American writer Washington Irving (q.v.) and wrote a portion of the satirical periodical *Salmagundi*. During the War of 1812 he published the *Diverting History of John Bull and Brother Jonathan*; and in 1815 a more serious work, *The United States and England*, which gained him an appointment on the Board of Naval Commissioners. Paulding wrote several historical novels, many short stories, a popularly written *Life of Washington* (1835), and *Slavery in the United States* (1836). From 1838 to 1841 he was secretary of the navy under United States President Martin Van Buren (q.v.).

PAULI, Wolfgang (1900–58), Austro-American physicist, born in Vienna, and educated at the University of Munich. He taught physics at the universities of Göttingen (1921–22), Copenhagen (1922–23), and Hamburg (1923–28) and was professor of theoretical physics at the Federal Institute of Technology, Zürich, from 1928 to 1935. Pauli served as visiting professor at the Institute for Advanced Study at Princeton, N.J. (1935–36, 1940–45, 1949–50, and 1954).

Pauli is best known for his definition in 1923 of the exclusion principle (q.v.), named after him, which states that only two electrons can occupy the same energy level (that is, have the same quantum numbers) simultaneously in an atom; see ATOM AND ATOMIC THEORY; QANTUM MECHANICS; QUANTUM THEORY. His hypothesis in 1931 of the existence of the subatomic particle, the neutrino (q.v.), was a fundamental contribution to the development of meson theory; see MESON. He was awarded the 1945 Nobel Prize in physics and became a naturalized American citizen the following year.

PAULICIANS, in Christian Church history, heretical sect in the East, with a basis in ethical dualism (q.v.) and growing probably out of opposition to the hierarchical structure of the Church; see HERSEY. Their founder was Constantine of Mananalis (fl. 7th cent.), who established his first congregation in Armenia (q.v.) about

660. He was put to death by order of the Byzantine emperor Constantine IV (648–85), but the sect lived on. In the 9th century they allied themselves with the Saracens (q.v.) against the Byzantine Empire and reached their peak strength. Though defeated decisively by the Byzantine emperor Basil I (see under BASIL) in 872, they remained a military power, notably in Thrace (now in Bulgaria), during the next century. The sect fused there with the Bogomils (q.v.), who survived into the 15th century, and some present-day Armenian sects may be derived from the Paulicians. The sect rejected, in addition to Church hierarchy, the Old Testament and parts of the New Testament, as well as the sacraments of Baptism, the Lord's Supper (qq.v.), and Marriage; see SACRAMENT. Paulicians were iconoclasts; see ICONOCLASM.

PAULING, Linus (1901–   ), American chemist and physicist, born in Portland, Oreg., and educated at Oregon State College and the California Institute of Technology. He taught chemistry at the California Institute of Technology from 1922 to 1964. He was research professor at the Center for the Study of Democratic Institutions, Santa Barbara, from 1963 to 1967, and became professor of chemistry at the University of California at San Diego in 1967. Pauling is known for his investigations of molecular structure, the nature of chemical bonds in compounds, and the application of quantum mechanics (q.v.) to chemical problems. He successfully determined the crystal structure of molecules by using X-ray-diffraction analysis (see X RAY), and discovered the atomic structure of a number of proteins including hemoglobin (q.v.).

Pauling was awarded the 1954 Nobel Prize in chemistry. An outspoken critic of war and of the testing of nuclear weapons, he was also awarded the 1962 Nobel Peace Prize, and thus became the second person ever to win two Nobel prizes; the first was the Polish-French physicist and chemist Maria Sklodowska Curie (see under CURIE).

Among other books, Pauling wrote *General Chemistry* (1947), *No More War!* (1958), and *Vitamin C and the Common Cold* (1970).

PAULISTS, common designation of members of the Society of Missionary Priests of Saint Paul the Apostle, a society founded in New York in 1858 by the American Roman Catholic clergyman Isaac Thomas Hecker (q.v.) and other priests who therefore were dispensed from their vows as Redemptorists (q.v.) by Pope Pius IX (see under PIUS). The Paulists devote themselves especially to mission preaching. They were the first to carry on systematic movement efforts to extend their faith among the non-Catholics of America. They have establishments in the United States, Canada, and the Republic of South Africa. In 1922 they took charge of the Church of Santa Susanna, in Rome, which is maintained for American residents and visitors. They are active in Newman clubs, direct information centers, operate the Paulist-Newman Press, and publish a monthly magazine, *Catholic World.*

PAUNCEFOTE, Julian, 1st Baron Pauncefote. See HAY-PAUNCEFOTE TREATY.

PAUSANIAS (d. 470? B.C.), Spartan regent and general, the nephew of Leonidas I, King of Sparta (see under LEONIDAS). Pausanias was regent for Leonidas' son about 480 B.C. He commanded the Greek army in the Battle of Plataea (479 B.C.), in which the Persians were totally routed from Greece, and their leader Mardonius (fl. 5th century B.C.), slain. Soon thereafter Pausanias, in command of the combined Greek fleets, secured most of Cyprus and captured Byzantium. His adoption of Persian ways aroused suspicion among his fellow Greeks, and he was recalled to Sparta where he was accused of trea-

Linus Pauling (right) is congratulated by Soviet physicist Dmitry V. Skobeltsyn (1892–   ), who presented him with the International Lenin Peace Prize in a ceremony in Washington, D.C., in 1970.   UPI

son, but acquitted in 475. Thought to have entered into treasonable negotiations with the Persian king Xerxes II (q.v.), about 470, Pausanias was again recalled to Sparta, where a scheme to overthrow the Spartan government was uncovered. He was forced to seek refuge on the Spartan Acropolis in the temple of the goddess Athena (q.v.). The Spartans blocked up the entrance and allowed him to starve before bringing him outside to die.

PAUSANIAS (2nd cent. A.D.), Greek historian, traveler, and geographer, probably a native of Lydia in Asia Minor. He traveled in Greece, Macedonia, and parts of Asia and Africa, and wrote a major work, *Hellados Periegesis*, which describes Greece and gives a detailed account of the monuments of art and of the legends connected with them. Pausanias used earlier writings as historical and legendary source material. His work, however, represents observations made during personal travel and investigation, and its general accuracy has been confirmed by archeological discoveries in modern times. Although his book has little literary merit, it is a valuable source for historical information on the topography, monuments, and local cults of ancient Greece. Written apparently as a guidebook for travelers, it has become, for modern Greek archeologists, an important guide to the location and interpretation of ancient sites.

PAVANE, type of 16th-century court dance of Spanish or Italian origin, performed by couples clothed in ceremonial dress. The pavane was often played by woodwind instruments at weddings and ceremonial feasts. After the dance went out of fashion in the late 16th century, pavanes continued to be written by composers of art music, especially by the English keyboard composers John Bull (1562?–1628), John Dowland (1563–1626), Orlando Gibbons (1583–1625), and William Byrd (q.v.). For 18th-century composers it was the forerunner of the sarabande movement of the suite (q.v.). A popular modern composition that captures the solemn tone of this dance is *Pavane pour une Infante Défunte* ("Pavane for a Dead Princess", 1899) by the French composer Maurice Joseph Ravel (q.v.).

PAVIA (anc. *Ticinum*), city of Italy, in Lombardy Region, and capital of Pavia Province, on the Ticino R. 2 mi. above its confluence with the Po R., 21 miles s. of Milan. It is an industrial center specializing in the manufacture of sewing machines, agricultural machinery, toys, synthetic fibers, and processed foods. It is also a market for agricultural products, especially cereals and rice. The most famous landmark is the Certosa, a monastery founded by the Carthusians (q.v.) in 1396, which contains an extensive art collection of the Lombards (q.v.).

A municipality of the ancient Roman Empire, Pavia was occupied successively by the Goths, the Byzantines, and the Lombards, who made it their capital. Late in the 11th century it became an independent commune. At various times thereafter Pavia was controlled by the powerful Visconti family and by Spain, France, and Austria. Pop. (1961) 73,503.

PAVIA, UNIVERSITY OF, coeducational autonomous institution of higher learning, located in Pavia, Italy, and supported by the national government. The university was founded in 1361 by Galeazzo II Visconti, Duke of Milan (1320–78), received a charter the same year from Charles IV, Holy Roman Emperor (*see under* CHARLES), and was recognized in 1389 by Pope Boniface IX (*see under* BONIFACE). Prior to this a liberal arts school, founded in the 9th century, and a school of law, established in the 10th century, had existed in Pavia. The university is organized into the following faculties: jurisprudence, political science, economics and commerce, letters and philosophy, medicine, science, and pharmacy. The degree of *laurea*, entitling the recipient to the honorific *dottore*, is awarded by all faculties after a four- to six-year course of study. The *laurea* is approximately equivalent to an American degree of master. Post-*laurea* studies are offered by most faculties and lead to a higher specialized diploma after an additional period of study, normally two years in length. The library contains 388,000 bound volumes. In 1968–69 the student body numbered about 8500 and the faculty, about 355.

PAVLOV, Ivan Petrovich (1849–1936), Russian physiologist, born in Ryazan (now in the Russian S.F.S.R.), and educated at the University of Saint Petersburg (now Leningrad A. A. Zhdanov State University) and at the former Military Medical Academy, St. Petersburg (now Leningrad). From 1884 to 1886 he studied in Breslau and Leipzig, Germany. Before the Russian Revolution (q.v.), Pavlov was director of the department of physiology at the Institute of Experimental Medicine (now part of the Academy of Medical Sciences of the U.S.S.R.), St. Petersburg, and professor of medicine at the Military Medical Academy. In spite of his opposition to Communism, Pavlov was allowed to remain in the U.S.S.R. and continued his research in a laboratory built by the Soviet government in 1935. Pavlov is noted for his pioneer work in the physiology of the heart, nervous system, and digestion (qq.v.). His most famous experiments, begun in 1889, demonstrated the conditioned and unconditioned reflexes (see REFLEX) in dogs, and had an influence on the development of physiologically oriented behaviorist theories of psychology (q.v.) during the early years of the 20th century; see PSYCHOLOGY, EXPERIMENTAL. His work on the physiology of the digestive glands won him the 1904 Nobel Prize in medicine and physiology. His major work is *Conditioned Reflexes* (1926; Eng. trans., 1927).

PAVLOVA, Anna (1882–1931), Russian ballerina, born in Saint Petersburg (now Leningrad), and trained at the Imperial Ballet School. She made her debut in 1899 in St. Petersburg, and by 1906 she was the prima ballerina at the Marinsky Theater there. Her most famous role was as the swan in *Le Cygne* ("The Dying Swan", 1905), a solo dance created for her by the Russian choreographer Michel Fokine (q.v.). Pavlova began touring Europe in 1907, and appeared in Paris two years later as a member of the Ballets Russes, a company organized by the Russian ballet producer Sergei Diaghilev (q.v.). In 1910 she made her American debut with the Russian dancer Mikhail Mordkin (1881–1944) at the Metropolitan Opera House in New York City. She founded her own ballet company in 1911, and until 1925 when she retired, she performed extensively throughout the world. In addition to her success in *Le Cygne*, she also gained international fame for her roles in *Les Syphildes* and *Coppélia*. Pavlova is known as a great classical ballerina. See BALLET: *20th Century*.

PAWNBROKING, in law, business conducted by a pawnbroker, a person who lends money, to be repaid within a given period, on the pledge or pawn of personal property other than negotiable paper and negotiable instruments (q.v.). Loans can be made by a pawnbroker only on articles that can be delivered over to his possession and custody by the person requesting the loan. In the United States pawnbrokers do business under State regulations and municipal ordinances. The State regulations usually provide for a license, a bond, the rates of interest (q.v.) to be charged, and methods of disposition of unredeemed property. Interest charges are regulated in most of the States, generally under either of two systems: (1) an interest rate varying according to the size of the loan; (2) a uniform rate, irrespective of the amount of the loan. In the latter case extra charges are usually permitted to cover the cost of handling small loans. Municipal ordinances often place pawnshops under police supervision, providing for daily inspection or daily reports. The pawnbroker has the legal right to retain the articles pledged until the loan is repaid; if repayment is not made within the specified time, he may sell the articles and reimburse himself from the proceeds; such merchandise is usually sold to the public or to dealers at auctions. The borrower has the right to redeem his property at any time before sale takes place.

PAWNEE, tribe of North American Indians who formerly lived in what is now Nebraska,

Ivan Petrovich Pavlov — World Health Organization

Anna Pavlova — Wide World

PAWTUCKET

having migrated from the region that is present-day Texas. The Pawnee surrendered their land south of the Platte R. in Nebraska by treaty in the 1830's. Their number was greatly diminished by exposure to various illnesses of the white man, by the attacks of their hereditary enemies, the Sioux (q.v.), and by their removal to a reservation in Oklahoma in 1876. The Pawnee, although known as fierce warriors to the Sioux, were friendly to the white man, often serving as scouts in expeditions.

PAWTUCKET, city of Rhode Island, in Providence Co., on both sides of the Blackstone R., at Pawtucket Falls, 4 miles N.E. of Providence. It is an important textile center. Printing and the manufacture of machinery, electrical equipment, food products, and metals are other important industries. A 16-ft. man-made channel connects the Blackstone R. with Narragansett Bay; the 50-ft. falls on the w. side of the river provide abundant waterpower to this manufacturing city. Among the noteworthy features are the Sayles Memorial Library erected between 1899 and 1902 and the Narragansett Racetrack. The site of the city was deeded to Roger Williams (q.v.), the English Puritan clergyman who founded the colony of Rhode Island in 1638, and the first settlement was made about 1670. In 1790 the English-born American industrialist Samuel Slater (1768–1835), erected here the first water-powered cotton manufacturing plant in the United States. The mill he built in 1793 has been preserved as a museum. The city was chartered in 1885. Pop. (1960) 81,001; (1970) 76,984.

PAYNE, John Howard (1791–1852), American playwright and actor, born in New York City, and educated at Union College. He was a successful actor and he wrote about sixty plays, chiefly translations and adaptations. His best-known works are *Brutus, or, The Fall of Tarquin* (1818), a verse tragedy, and *Charles II, or, The Merry Monarch* (1824), a comedy. He also wrote the libretto of the opera *Clari, or, The Maid of Milan* (1823), which contains the famous song "Home, Sweet Home". The music was written by the British composer Sir Henry Rowley Bishop (q.v.). Although Payne was a popular and successful playwright, he spent much of his life trying to escape from his creditors. In 1842 he was appointed American consul in Tunis, where he died. See AMERICAN MUSIC: *European Influences.*

PAYSANDÚ, city in Uruguay, and capital of Paysandú Department on the Uruguay R., about 220 miles N.W. of Montevideo. It is a busy river port for oceangoing ships, and contains meat-packing plants, tanneries, and flour mills. Pop. (1967 est.) 60,000.

PAZ, LA. See LA PAZ.

PEA, common name of herbs, trees, and shrubs in the Legume family, Leguminosae, especially herbs of the genus *Pisum.* The family, which includes about 500 genera and 12,000 species growing all over the world, includes such plants as alfalfa, clover, locust, lupine, peanut, soybean, vetch (qq.v.), and sweet pea (see LATHYRUS). Two varieties of *Pisum sativum* are widely cultivated for their seeds (peas): the common, or garden, pea and the field pea, var. *arvense.* Garden peas are of two main types, having smooth or wrinkled seeds. Those with smooth seeds are earlier and hardier, but the wrinkled varieties are sweeter. Some varieties have edible pods that are eaten in much the same manner as green beans. These are grown to a considerable extent in Europe but are not popular in the United States. Varieties of both the field pea and the garden pea are innumerable. Peas are cultivated to a considerable extent as a field crop in the northern U.S. and Canada, and both the grain and straw are used in feeding stock. The plant withstands light frosts and may therefore be grown as early in spring as the ground can be worked. Semidwarf varieties are preferred for field culture, since the crop is more easily harvested.

PEABODY, city of Massachusetts, in Essex Co., 13 miles N.E. of Boston. It is an important center for tanning and finishing leather and sheepskin. Principal manufactures are leather goods, particularly shoes, leather finishes, tanning machinery, and gelatin. The site of the present city was settled in the 1630's. It was incorporated as the town of South Danvers in 1855. The name was changed to Peabody in 1868 to honor a distinguished resident, the American banker and philanthropist George Peabody (q.v.), who here founded the Peabody Institute (1852). The city of Peabody was incorporated in 1916. Pop. (1960) 32,202; (1970) 48,080.

PEABODY, George (1795–1869), American businessman and philanthropist, born in South Danvers (now Peabody), Mass. From 1815 to 1837 he was a partner in a wholesale dry goods firm in Baltimore, Md. He then settled in London, England, where he established the banking and brokerage firm of George Peabody and Company and amassed a considerable fortune. Peabody is best known for his numerous benefactions in the field of American education. He donated $250,000 to his native town for the establishment of the Peabody Institute, which maintains a free library and offers lecture

PEACE CORPS

courses; $150,000 to Yale University for the establishment of the Peabody Museum of Natural History and Natural Sciences; an equal amount to Harvard University for the establishment of the Peabody Museum of Archaeology and Ethnology; $1,500,000 to the city of Baltimore, Md., for the establishment of the Peabody Institute, which maintains a conservatory of music, an art gallery, and a free library and offers lecture courses; and $3,500,000 for the establishment of the Peabody Education Fund to advance education in the South. From the last-named came the funds to establish what was later called the George Peabody College for Teachers, in Nashville, Tenn. His other philanthropies include a gift of $2,500,000 to the city of London, for the construction of moderate-rent tenement houses to replace slum dwellings. See also FOUNDATION.

PEABODY EDUCATION FUND. See PEABODY, GEORGE.

PEACE, river of Canada, formed by the joining of the Finlay and Parsnip rivers in central British Columbia. It flows E. through the Rocky Mts. to Alberta, to the town of Peace River, N. to Fort Vermilion, and E. to the outlet of Lake Athabasca, where it joins the Slave R. The Peace R. is part of the more than 2000-mi.-long MacKenzie River (q.v.) system of western Canada. The Peace R. is about 1050 mi. long.

PEACE CONFERENCE, HAGUE. See HAGUE CONFERENCES.

PEACE CORPS, originally agency of the United States Department of State, created by Executive Order in 1961, and transferred to ACTION, an independent agency, in 1971. The Peace Corps was intended to promote world peace and friendship by training those Americans who apply to perform social and humanitarian service overseas. The volunteers who are accepted, trained, and assigned help people of young or underdeveloped countries meet their needs for trained manpower and seek to further better mutual understanding between the American people and government and the nation served. Each corpsman serves for a two-year term. The organization, with national headquarters in Washington, D.C., is headed by the director of ACTION, appointed by the President with the consent of the United States Senate.

Requirements for a Peace Corps volunteer are that he be a United States citizen, be at least eighteen years of age, and have not more than four dependents under eighteen. Of the more than 8000 volunteers, in 1971, approximately one half teach, one fourth work in rural and urban community development projects, and one fifth are in health and agriculture programs.

A Peace Corps nurse works with child patients at a hospital in Tegucigalpa, Honduras. Richey – Peace Corps

About 300 different job skills are utilized in the corps. In the late-1960's volunteers were working in sixty-one countries throughout the agency's four main geographical regions: sub-Saharan African Region (A.R.); East Asia and the Pacific Region (E.A.P.); Latin America (L.A.R.); and North Africa, the Near East, and South Asia (N.A.N.E.S.A.).

The Peace Corps recognizes that the work of the volunteers should satisfy the most pressing needs of developing countries. For example, in Africa, where 85 percent of the people work on the land, Peace Corps programming is shifting from secondary education to agriculture and related rural programs. In India, where the shortage of food is acute, the emphasis is on poultry production, nutrition, vegetable gardening, and family planning.

In recent years reduced recruitment by the Peace Corps, in part because of budget cutbacks, has been attributed to a growing awareness of American youth that serious domestic and foreign problems exist. In 1968 campaigns to recruit more nonwhite applicants from minority groups and to accept and transport married technicians with their families were instituted. Other industrialized nations, such as Canada, Great Britain, and Sweden, have organizations similar in purpose to the Peace Corps.

PEACH

PEACH, common name of deciduous or chard trees of the species *Prunus persica*, of the Rose family, Rosaceae, and of the fruits of these trees. The species, which is believed by botanists to be native to China, is cultivated throughout warm temperate and subtropical regions of the world. In the peach fruit the stone is covered with a fleshy substance that is juicy, melting, and of the finest flavor when matured and mellowed. The peach tree, like the almond, is of moderate height, more or less spreading, according to variety, deciduous, and, when left to itself, deep-rooted. The popular division of fruit varieties into clingstones and freestones is by no means accurate. These two classes merge in different varieties, and even the same variety may be freestone and clingstone in different seasons. The nearly 300 varieties of peaches grown in America have been classified in five races, each with outstanding characteristics, ripening season, and uses. The nectarine (q.v.) is a variety of peach.

The peach is not a long-lived tree, seldom living thirty years, and the life of a commerical orchard is usually seven to nine years. The principal peach-growing States are California, South Carolina, and New Jersey. Peaches are shipped from Texas for the early market, and they are grown commercially in many other States. The canning of peaches is an important industry. In the late 1960's approximately 35,900,000 cases were canned each year in the United States. During the same period about 75,000,000 bu. of peaches were harvested annually in the U.S., with a farm value of almost $185,000,000. World production totals about 100,000,000 bu. annually.

PEACOCK, name popularly applied to birds of the genus *Pavo*, including two species: the common peacock, *P. cristatus*, and the Javanese peacock, *P. muticus*. The male peacock is noted for his resplendent train of long upper tail coverts, which he raises and spreads in strutting. The feathers are generally iridescent green and gold and are ornamented with eyelike markings of a rich color, known as peacock blue. The same blue also appears on the head, neck, breast, and crest of the common peacock; in the male Javanese peacock the head, neck, and underparts are green. The female of both species has no train and lacks the spectacular coloring of the male. Peacocks build their nests on the ground or in the low branches of trees. The birds subsist on an omnivorous diet of worms, insects, small snakes, and seeds. Peacocks are now common in most parts of the world. Few eggs are laid, however, in the colder climates as the young seem unable to survive the harsh weather conditions. White varieties of peacocks are produced on farms by selective breeding. The peacock is regarded as sacred by various Indian castes and was made the emblem of certain classic divinities in antiquity.

PEACOCK, Thomas Love (1785–1866), British novelist and poet, born in Weymouth, England. A friend of the British poet Percy Bysshe Shelley (*see under* SHELLEY), he was Shelley's executor and provided much material for a biography of the poet, *Memoirs of Shelley with Shelley's Letters to Peacock*. The publication of *Headlong Hall* (1816) established Peacock's literary reputation. *Nightmare Abbey* (1818), a satire of the Romantic movement in England, is his best-known work. Peacock was an employee of the British East India Company from 1819 to 1856, during which time he published two historical romances, *Maid Marian* (1822) and *The Misfortunes of Elfin* (1829), and the satiric *Crochet Castle* (1831). Almost thirty years after *Crochet Castle* he published his last novel, *Gryll Grange* (1860). In most of Peacock's works the characters, many of them caricatures of famous men of the time, reveal themselves through incidental dialogue at social gatherings. Peacock's novels often contain drinking songs and poems written by him.

PEALE, Charles Willson (1741–1827), American painter, born in Queen Annes County, Md. In 1765, after having given up his business as a saddler, he went to Boston, where he studied with the American painter John Singleton Copley (q.v.). The following year he was sent abroad by some wealthy citizens to study with the American artist Benjamin West (q.v.) in London, where he also practiced miniature painting and mezzotint engraving. In 1769 he returned to the United States. He settled in Philadelphia, painting many portraits of the American statesman George Washington (q.v.) and of other distinguished men of the period. He served on political committees, including the General Assembly of Philadelphia, and was a captain in the American Revolution (q.v.). Peale was also interested in natural science and in 1784 established Peale's Museum, consisting of objects of natural history and portraits. In 1801, the artist excavated a mastodon skeleton in New York State, restoring it for his museum, which was moved to Independence Hall, Philadelphia, the following year. Peale was instrumental in founding the Pennsylvania Academy of the Fine Arts in 1805, and exhibited there regularly. Peale's portraits were executed in the formal traditions of English painting, with characteristic land-

"The Peale Family" by Charles Willson Peale (painted between 1772 and 1809).
New York Historical Society

scape backgrounds and emphasis on the social distinction of the sitter. His reputation rests mainly on his studies of Washington, of which he made seven from life and more than fifty from memory. Examples of his work are in the Brooklyn Museum and the Metropolitan Museum of Art, New York City; at Princeton University, Princeton, N.J.; and in the National Gallery, Washington, D.C. Peale also was a skilled silversmith and taxidermist; his inventions include false teeth and a velocipede.

PEALE, Norman Vincent (1898–   ), American clergyman and author, born in Bowersville, Ohio. He was educated at Ohio Wesleyan University where he received his A.B. degree (1920); he received the degrees of master of arts and bachelor of sacred theology from Boston University in 1924. Ordained a minister of the Methodist Episcopal Church in 1922, he served pastorates in Berkeley, R.I. (1922–24), Brooklyn, N.Y. (1924–27), and Syracuse, N.Y. (1927–32). In 1932 he became pastor of the Marble Collegiate Reformed Church in New York City, and since then he has gained distinction for his sermons, on a positive approach to modern living, which are regularly broadcast over the radio. From 1965 to 1969 he was president of the Protestant Council of the City of New York, and from 1969 to 1970 he was president of the Reformed Church in America. His books, which are widely read, include *The Power of Positive Thinking* (1952), *The Tough-Minded Optimist* (1962), and *Enthusiasm Makes the Difference* (1967). His newspaper column "Confident Living" is nationally syndicated.

PEANUT, common name of an annual warm-season legume, *Arachis hypogaea,* originally grown in South America. Plants grow up to 2½ ft. tall and spread 3 to 4 ft. The peanut is remarkable in that, after fertilization of the flower, the elongated receptacle, called the peg, grows downward from the base of the flower stalk to bury the ovary tip in the soil, where the fruit or pod develops. Four commercial types are grown in the United States: Spanish, Valencia, Runner, and Virginia. Size of pod and seed distinguish the Virginia and Runner; both have varieties with upright, intermediate or spreading habit of growth. Spanish and Valencia types grow upright.

To meet the industrial and food demands for peanuts, the growers in the U.S. produce over 2,500,000,000 lb. each year. Georgia, the largest American producer, grows over one third of this total. The leading peanut-producing countries in order of production are India, the People's Republic of China, Nigeria, the U.S. and Senegal. In the U.S., peanuts are grown primarily for food; in other countries principally for edible oil.   R.O.H.

PEAR, common name applied to about 20 species of trees, especially *Pyrus communis* and *P. pyrifolia,* in the same genus as the apple, and belonging to the Rose family. The name is also applied to their fruit. The common pear, *P. communis,* is native to Europe; the Chinese sand pear, *P. pyrifolia,* is native to the Orient; both species are extensively cultivated for their fruit in cool, humid, temperate regions throughout the world. Under cultivation, standard pear trees attain heights of from 20 to 30 ft., with trunks 1 ft. or more in diameter. The leaves are oval and simple, and unlike those of the apple, are smooth and glossy. The white flowers, which are borne in umbels, have five sepals, five petals, many stamens, and a single pistil. The

PEAR

fruit is a pome, juicier than the apple, and varying from apple-shaped to teardrop-shaped. Among different varieties, the thin skin varies in color from light yellow through red and brown. The thick flesh, in which the seeds are embedded, varies in flavor among different varieties; in young, unripe common pears, and in young and mature Chinese sand pears, the flesh contains numerous gritty cells called stone cells. Pears are gathered from the trees before they are completely ripe and are allowed to ripen in storage; cold retards ripening, and heat speeds it. Pears are eaten fresh and canned. Pears contain about 16 percent carbohydrate and negligible amounts of fat and protein. They are good sources of the B-complex vitamins and also contain vitamin C; in addition they contain small amounts of phosphorus and iodine.

Commerical pear production in the United States averages about 29,000,000 bu. annually. The best American pear-growing districts are in California, Washington, and Oregon, and to a lesser degree in the northern U.S. from New England to the Great Lakes. Pears are grown extensively in home orchards in the U.S. Most pear varieties may be grown in either standard or dwarf sizes. Dwarf pears are propagated by grafting (q.v.) a pear scion on a quince stock. Angoulême, Elizabeth, Louis Bonne, and Deal pears are desirable dessert varieties usually cultivated as dwarfs. Anjou, Boussoc, and Tyson pears are about equally good in either standard or dwarf sizes. Bosc, Washington, and Dix pears are usually grown as dwarfs by a type of grafting called double working, in which stocks are grafted onto stocks that have previously been dwarfed by grafting on quince. Bartlett, Seckel, and Doyenné pears are usually grown in standard sizes.

Several plants that are not related to the pear but which produce pear-shaped fruits are commonly called pears; see AVOCADO; PRICKLY PEAR.

PEA RIDGE NATIONAL MILITARY PARK. See NATIONAL PARK SERVICE.

PEARL, lustrous concretion produced by certain bivalve mollusks (see MOLLUSCA) and valued as a gem. Pearls consist almost entirely of nacre, which is the substance forming the inner layers of the mollusk shells. Nacre, known as mother-of-pearl (q.v.), is composed chiefly of aragonite crystals. The pearl is an abnormal growth resulting from the invasion of the body of the mollusk by a minute particle of foreign matter, such as a fine grain of sand. The particle acts as an irritant in the mollusk and becomes coated with layer upon layer of nacreous material. Both marine and freshwater mollusks produce pearls, but the most valuable varieties originate in the pearl oyster of the Persian Gulf.

The most highly prized pearls are spherical. When a pearl that has been cut from the shell presents a hemispherical surface, it is sometimes called a bouton pearl. If a solid pearl has an irregular shape, having grown over a rough object, it is known as a baroque pearl. In the jewelry trade, pearls are commonly known as pear, bell, or drop, according to the shape. Pearl coloration varies widely, the most prized shades being white, black, rose, and cream.

One of the important marine-pearl fisheries on the American continent is that of Baja California, the central point being at La Paz. Other fisheries are located on the Pearl Islands near the coast of Nicaragua, in the Gulf of Panamá, in the South Sea Islands, in the West Indies, and along the coasts of India, Ceylon, the Persian Gulf, Japan, western Central America, and Mexico. In Australian waters pearls are fished on the coast of Western Australia and of Queensland, and in Torres Strait.

River pearls are produced by freshwater mussels in various parts of the world. China is the principal trader in river pearls.

Natural, spherical pearls have been cultured successfully since 1920. In this process a mother-of-pearl bead, from three quarters to nine tenths of the diameter of the desired prod-

Cultured pearls are studied for quality by buyers at a pearl auction in Atami, Japan. UPI

PEARL HARBOR

Smoke billows from a ship set afire during the Japanese attack on Pearl Harbor, Dec. 7, 1941. U.S. Army

uct, is introduced into the pearl oyster. Over a period of years the oyster deposits layers of nacre around the bead. Cultured pearls are not easily distinguished from genuine pearls except by an expert. The technique of producing spherical cultured pearls was developed in Japan, and the culturing of pearls is a major Japanese industry. Artificial pearls, in contrast to cultured pearls, are entirely man-made largely of glass; *see* GEM, ARTIFICIAL.

PEARL, river rising in Mississippi near Jackson, and flowing s.w. to Lake Borgne, an arm of the Gulf of Mexico. The river, about 485 mi. long, forms part of the border between Mississippi and Louisiana; it is navigable to Bogalusa, La. In Louisiana it passes through Honey Island Swamp, a refuge for pirates in the 19th century.

PEARL HARBOR, inlet of the State of Hawaii, on the s. shore of the island of Oahu, 6 miles w. of Honolulu, the site of one of the principal naval bases of the United States. In 1887 the U.S. government received from the Hawaiian government the right to maintain a repair and coaling station for ships here, as well as exclusive use of the inlet. Surveys of the harbor were made in 1887 and 1897, but improvements were not begun until after the annexation of the Hawaiian Islands by the U.S. in 1898. In 1911 the work of dredging a wide channel from the sea, across the sandbar and coral reef at the mouth of the harbor, was completed. The channel is about 35 ft. deep, and the harbor has a maximum depth of 50 to 60 ft., making the piers, docks, and other installations on the shores of the harbor available to the largest naval vessels.

World War II. Early in the morning of Dec. 7, 1941, while negotiations between American and Japanese diplomats for the preservation of peace were still in progress at Washington, D.C., Japanese submarines and carrier-based planes attacked the U.S. Pacific fleet, the bulk of which was at anchor or in drydock at Pearl Harbor. Nearby military and naval airfields were also attacked by the Japanese planes. Eight American battleships and ten other naval vessels were sunk or badly damaged, almost 200 American aircraft were destroyed, and approximately 3000 naval and military personnel were killed or wounded. The attack marked the entrance of Japan into World War II on the side of Germany and Italy. The following day, Dec. 8, the U.S. declared war on Japan, and, following declarations

369

PEARL HARBOR

of war on the U.S. by the Axis powers, on Dec. 11 the U.S. formally declared war on Germany and Italy. See WORLD WAR II: *The Japanese Attack.*

Investigations. Soon after the attack U.S. President Franklin Delano Roosevelt (q.v.) appointed a commission of inquiry to determine whether negligence by the army and navy had been a contributory factor to the success of the Japanese raid on Pearl Harbor. The commission, consisting of army and navy officers, was headed by Justice Owen Josephus Roberts (q.v.) of the Supreme Court. The report of the commission, made public on Jan. 24, 1942, found the naval and army commanders of the Hawaiian area, Rear Admiral Husband Edward Kimmel (1882–1968) and Major General Walter Campbell Short (1880–1949), guilty of "derelictions of duty" and "errors of judgment"; the two men were subsequently retired. The findings and the action against the officers did not end the heated controversy over responsibility for the disaster at Pearl Harbor. Other inquiries were made at later dates, including investigations by army and navy boards. Reports by the military boards made public after the end of the war, on Aug. 29, 1945, differed in their conclusions. Congress, in an effort to make a definitive disposition of the controversy, decided on a full, public investigation by a joint committee of members of both houses.

The bipartisan committee headed by Senator, later Vice-President, Alben William Barkley (q.v.) opened its investigation on Nov. 15, 1945. Testimony from many people, including U.S. General George Catlett Marshall (q.v.), reviewed all known information about the attack on Pearl Harbor and made public for the first time such important and relevant facts as the success of the U.S. in breaking the highest Japanese secret code before Dec. 7, 1941. The committee reported on July 20, 1946. It rejected allegations made against the Roosevelt government, praised Roosevelt and other administration leaders for their efforts to avert war, and held Japan guilty of an "unprovoked act of aggression". It placed the chief blame for the disaster at Pearl Harbor on General Short and Admiral Kimmel, who, however, were declared to be guilty only of errors of judgment, and not of derelictions of duty. The report also censured administration officials for not paying enough attention to intelligence indicating the interest of the Japanese government in Pearl Harbor; criticized the army and navy for their failure "to effect a state of readiness [at Pearl Harbor] commensurate with the realization that war was at hand"; and blamed the Army War Plans Division for not being aware that Hawaii had not been sufficiently alerted. Recommendations made by the report included unification of the armed forces of the U.S., which went into effect the following year. See DEFENSE, DEPARTMENT OF.

PEARSON, Lester Bowles (1897–   ), Canadian statesman, born in Newtonbrook, Ontario, and educated at the University of Toronto and the University of Oxford. In 1928 he joined the Canadian Department of External Affairs as first secretary. His foreign assignments took him to London, England, as first secretary in the office of the High Commissioner for Canada (1935–41); and to Washington, D.C., as minister-counselor, minister, and ambassador (1942–45). He returned to Canada in 1946 and became undersecretary of state for external affairs; in 1948 he was named secretary of state for external affairs. He early advanced proposals for a Western alliance, which culminated in the formation of the North Atlantic Treaty Organization (q.v.). A member of the Canadian delegation to the United Nations from 1948 to 1957, Pearson was president of the 7th U.N. General Assembly (1952–53).

Pearson was awarded the 1957 Nobel Peace Prize for his formulation of international policy in the post-World War II period, especially for his plan that led to the establishment of a U.N. emergency force in the Suez Canal area in 1956. In 1958 he was selected to lead the Liberal Party of Canada. In the elections of 1963 the Liberal Party won a majority, and Pearson became prime minister. He retired in April, 1968, and was succeeded by Pierre Elliott Trudeau (1921–   ), who had served as minister of justice in the Pearson cabinet. Later in 1968 Pearson was appointed to head a commission sponsored by the International Bank for Reconstruction and Development (q.v.) to review and chart the future of economic aid to undeveloped countries. Among his writings is *Peace in the Family of Man* (1969), a collection of lectures on international relations.

PEARY, Robert Edwin (1856–1920), American explorer, born in Cresson, Pa., and educated at Bowdoin College. In 1861 he became a civil engineer in the United States Navy; in this capacity he participated in the Nicaragua Canal Survey in 1884–85 and made an exploration into Greenland in 1886. He led further expeditions to Greenland in 1891–92 and from 1893 to 1895. He proved Greenland was an island rather than a continent and that the Greenland ice cap extended no farther north than lat. 82° N. and he contributed to scientific knowledge of Eskimo

Robert Edwin Peary — Granger Collection

ethnology and of glacial formation. Between 1898 and 1902 Peary engaged in surveys in Greenland. In 1902 and in 1905–06 he made unsuccessful attempts to reach the North Pole, coming within 174 mi. of his goal on the latter trip.

On July 17, 1908, Peary led another expedition to the Pole and on April 6, 1909, he and a small party consisting of his Negro assistant Matthew A. Henson (1867–1955) and four Eskimos reached their target. On September 6, 1909, the day he announced his achievement, Peary learned that the discovery of the Pole had been claimed five days previously by the American explorer and surgeon Frederick Albert Cook (q.v.). Examination by experts established that the doctor's claim was false; Peary's records were accepted as genuine. In 1911, the year Peary retired, Congress recognized his discovery as unimpeachable, and he was given the rank of rear admiral before his retirement. His books include *The North Pole* (1910) and *Secrets of Polar Travel* (1917).

See also ARCTIC, THE: *Exploration of the Arctic Regions.*

PEASANTS' REVOLT. See TYLER'S REBELLION.

PEASANTS' WAR, in German history, revolt from 1524 to 1526 of the peasantry and the lower classes of the towns against their feudal overlords. It was caused by the growing economic, religious, and judicial oppression to which the lower classes of Germany were subjected by the nobles and clergy. Fighting between peasants and retainers of the nobles broke out in 1524 in Stühlingen, near what is now the Swiss canton of Schaffhausen, and the insurrection rapidly spread over much of central, western, and southern Germany except Bavaria; it also was strong in Austria. In 1525 the peasants formulated their demands, which included the right to choose their own ministers, the abolition of serfdom, the right to fish and kill wild game, the abolition of a number of kinds of feudal dues, and the guarantee of fair treatment in courts presided over by the feudal nobles. The revolt was particularly violent in Thuringia, where it was made a religious issue by the sect of Anabaptists (q.v.), headed by the German religious leader Thomas Münzer (1489?–1525). Münzer was successful in overthrowing the feudal regime and in maintaining for a time a community of peasants in which all property was commonly owned; in 1525, however, he was decisively defeated and executed. By the end of 1525, after fighting in which both sides committed atrocities and thousands were killed, the nobles in the Swabian League (q.v.) succeeded in putting down the rebellion everywhere in Germany; the revolt continued into the following year in Austria. The peasants of Germany won no concessions by their revolt; in Austria the nobles abolished a few of the evils that brought it about. Paradoxically, the opposition of the German religious reformer Martin Luther (q.v.), whose principles were adopted by the dissatisfied peasants and lent inspiration to the revolt, contributed to the defeat of the peasants. Luther had been sympathetic with their aspirations, but was adamantly against their armed revolt.

PEAT, compact, dark brown organic material with high carbon content, built up by the partial decay and carbonization of vegetation in the acid water of bogs. In the Northern Hemisphere peat-forming vegetation consists mostly of mosses of the genus *Sphagnum*. Salt peat is a kind of peat that develops in salt marshes from the partially decayed portions of such plants as the cordgrasses (species of *Spartina*). The formation of peat represents the first stage in the transformation of vegetation into coal (q.v.). Peat bogs are distributed throughout the world; extensive deposits are found in the northern United States, in Canada, Newfoundland, the Soviet Union, the Scandinavian countries, England, and Ireland. Dried peat, often compressed in the form of briquettes, is used in many European countries, particularly Ireland, as a fuel, although it cannot compete commercially with coal because of its large content of water and ash. Peat and commercial preparations of par-

PEAT MOSS

tially decayed vegetable matter that are also called peat have excellent moisture-retaining qualities and are used as mulching and soil-improving material for plants; see MULCH.

PEAT MOSS. See SPHAGNUM.

PECAN, common name of a species of hickory, *Carya illinoensis*, belonging to the Walnut family; the name is applied also to its edible fruit, a nut enclosed in the fleshy ripened hypanthium. The tree, which grows 75 to 100 ft. high, is native to North America; it grows in river bottoms from Iowa and Indiana southwest into Texas and Mexico, and is now grown commercially in a number of southeastern States and in California. The pecan has not proved commercially successful north of latitude 40°. Pecans grow on nearly all soils, but for nut production a sandy loam soil with a clay subsoil has proved most satisfactory in the Southern States.

The nuts have a rounded oblong shape and vary in weight from 25 to 100 to the pound. The varieties called paper shells are considered most desirable. Texas, Oklahoma, Louisiana, Mississippi, Georgia, and Florida furnish the bulk of commercial nut.

PECCARY, common name applied to two mammals belonging to the family Tayassuidae. Peccaries, which are native to the Western Hemisphere from Texas to Paraguay, are dark gray or black, nocturnal animals that run in herds. The collared peccary, *Tayassu tajacu*, has a white, collarlike stripe about its neck. The white-lipped peccary, *Tayassu pecari*, has white cheeks and whitish lips. Both species have three-toed hind feet.

PECHORA, river of the Soviet Union, in the Russian S.F.S.R., rising on the w. slopes of the Ural Mts. and flowing generally northward into Pechora Bay, an arm of Barents Sea. The river, 1110 mi. long, flows primarily through wooded regions, forming a 20-mi. wide delta at the port of Nar'Yan-Mar. In its course the Pechora drains an area of more than 125,000 sq.mi. Most of the river is navigable in spring and autumn, the high-water seasons. Major tributaries include the Ilyich, Usa, Shchugor, and Izhma rivers.

PECOS, river of New Mexico and Texas, rising in the Sangre de Cristo Mts. in north-central N.Mex., and flowing 926 miles s.e. to join the Rio Grande in Val Verde County, Texas. The Pecos R. drains an area of more than 25,000 sq.mi. and is an important source of irrigation.

PECOS NATIONAL MONUMENT, area of historic interest in New Mexico, near Santa Fe, containing the ruins of an early Pueblo Indian village and two Spanish missions. See NATIONAL PARK SERVICE.

PÉCS, city in Hungary, and capital of Baranya County, at the foot of the Mecsek Mts., about 110 miles s.w. of Budapest, and about 20 miles N. of the border with Yugoslavia. Pécs is an industrial city deriving its economic significance primarily from neighboring coal mines. Pottery, leather goods, and machine tools are manufactured here. In addition, Pécs is a commerical center for the wine and tobacco produced in the surrounding region. The University of Pécs, founded in 1922, occupies the site of the first university in Hungary, established in 1367. Among the principal buildings in the city are an 11th-century Romanesque cathedral and two Turkish mosques that are now used as churches. Pécs was the site of the ancient Roman settlement of Sopianae. In 1009 A.D. it became a Roman Catholic bishopric. From 1543 to 1686 the city was held by the Turks. German miners came to Pécs in the 18th century to work the coal mines. The population was further enlarged by migrations from rural Hungary late in the 19th century. Pop. (1969 est.) 139,000.

PECTEN. See SCALLOP.

PECTINS, group of complex carbohydrate de-

The reconstructed skeleton of a peccary dating from the Ice Age, some 17,000 years ago, and a sketch (top) of its appearance in life. The fossil remains, found in Kentucky in 1967, are in the Smithsonian Institution in Washington, D.C.   UPI

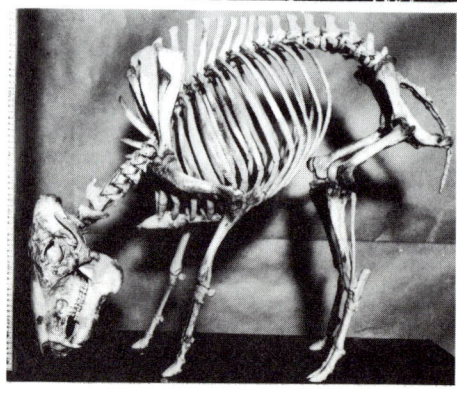

372

rivatives produced in plants. Pectins are white, amorphous substances, that yield a viscous solution with water; when combined in the proper proportions with sugar and acids, they form a gelatinous substance that is the thickening agent in fruit jellies. Commercial pectin, obtained from apples or lemons, is used in preparing jelly from fruits, such as gooseberries, which are deficient in pectin.

PEDIATRICS, branch of medicine that comprises the care and treatment of the diseases of childhood. Pediatrics was not recognized as a separate branch of medicine until the beginning of the 20th century. Like geriatrics (q.v.), which is the branch of medicine dealing with the care and treatment of the aged, pediatrics has since become a specialty that embraces all of the fields of medicine, as these fields apply to children. See separate articles on diseases common to children. *See also* CHILD PSYCHOLOGY; MATERNAL AND CHILD WELFARE.

PEDRARIAS *or* **PEDRARIAS DÁVILA,** in full PEDRO ARIAS DE ÁVILA (1440?–1531), Spanish soldier and colonial administrator, born near Segovia. In 1514 he was sent to the Spanish colony at Darien (now Panama) to take over the governorship from the Spanish explorer Vasco Núñez de Balboa (q.v.). Pedrarias and Balboa quarreled, and in 1517 Pedrarias charged Balboa with sedition and had him tried and executed, an act that contributed to Pedrarias' reputation as a ruthless administrator. Two years later Pedrarias founded a settlement on the site of the present city of Panamá (q.v.). In 1522 he sent the Spanish soldier and explorer Francisco Fernández de Córdoba (1475–1526) to assume the governorship of Nicaragua; Córdoba led a revolt against him in 1525, but was captured and executed in the following year. Pedrarias was transferred to the governorship of Nicaragua in 1526, and served there until his death. His best-known act during this period was to aid the Spanish explorers Francisco Pizarro and Diego de Almagro (qq.v.) for their expedition to Peru in 1530, although he is known to have hindered later explorations by the two men.

PEDRO I (1798–1834), Emperor of Brazil (1822–31) and as Pedro IV, King of Portugal (1826), second son of John VI (q.v.), King of Portugal, born in Lisbon, Portugal. To escape from a French invasion of Portugal Pedro and his parents fled to Brazil in 1807. In 1821, when his father returned to Portugal, Pedro became prince regent of Brazil. The following year, he proclaimed Brazilian independence and was crowned emperor of Brazil. The constitution he promulgated remained effective from 1824 to 1889, when the Brazilian Empire was dissolved; *see* BRAZIL: *History.* Proclaimed king of Portugal, in 1826, he granted Portugal a constitution before abdicating that same year in favor of his daughter Maria II (1819–53). Pedro's arbitrary rule and his involvement in the internal affairs of Portugal caused his popularity to wane in Brazil. Abdicating in 1831, he returned to Portugal, where he successfully supported Maria, reinstating her to the Portuguese throne from which she had been usurped in 1828 by her uncle, the regent Miguel (1802–66).

PEDRO II (1825–91), Emperor of Brazil (1831–89), son and successor of Pedro I (q.v.), Emperor of Brazil, born in Rio de Janeiro. Pedro was distinguished for his learning and scholarly tastes. His enlightened reign, which was marked by cultural and civic progress, including the abolition of slavery in 1888, lasted until the demand for a republic culminated in the revolution of Nov. 15, 1889. Pedro was compelled to abdicate and retired to Paris. *See* BRAZIL: *History.*

PEDRO EL CRUEL *or* **PETER THE CRUEL** (1334–69), King of Castile and León (1350–69), the son of King Alfonso XI (*see under* ALFONSO), born in Burgos. Pedro owes his sobriquet "the cruel" to his ready use of murder and execution to eliminate his political opponents, including, reportedly, several of his ambitious half-brothers. His principal conflict was with his older half-brother, Henry, later Henry II (q.v.), King of Castille and León, who also claimed the throne. Henry enlisted the aid of France, which in 1365 sent troops through Spain under the command of the famous French military leader Bertrand Du Guesclin (q.v.). Overthrown, Pedro left the country and requested aid from England, at that time engaged in fighting the Hundred Years' War (q.v.) with France; England sent an army commanded by the Prince of Wales, the great general Edward (q.v.), known as the Black Prince. The forces of Pedro and Edward defeated those of Henry, the French, and other allies at Nájera in 1367 and Henry fled to France. Political differences between Pedro and Edward resulted in the withdrawal of Edward and his army from Spain. Henry then hastened back into Spain and with Du Guesclin's help engaged Pedro and his supporters in a civil war. Pedro was defeated and killed at Campo de Montiel in 1369; Henry assumed the throne.

PEEKSKILL, city of New York, in Westchester Co., on the E. bank of the Hudson R., 41 miles N. of New York City. Peekskill is an industrial city in a dairying region; chief manufactures are machinery, food products, including yeasts and alcohol, and clothing. The city, also a shopping center, is the site of the Peekskill Military Academy and Saint Mary's School for Girls. A few miles N.W. of the city is the Bear Mountain Bridge, leading to Bear Mountain (q.v.) in Palisades Interstate Park on the opposite side of the Hudson R. Peekskill is named for a Dutch navigator Jan Peek who operated a trading post here from 1667 to 1677. During the American Revolution it was an important post of the Continental Army; in 1777 it was burned by British troops. Peekskill was incorporated as a village in 1816 and chartered as a city in 1940. Pop. (1960) 18,737; (1970) 18,881.

PEEL, Sir Robert (1788–1850), British statesman, born near Bury, Lancashire, England, and educated at Harrow School and the University of Oxford. He entered the House of Commons in 1809, and in 1811 he became a cabinet member as undersecretary for war and for the colonies. From 1812 to 1818, as chief secretary for Ireland, he suppressed Irish agitation for increased freedom for Roman Catholics. In 1822 he reentered the cabinet as home secretary. He distinguished himself in this post through a series of penal reforms and especially, in 1829, by reorganizing the London metropolitan police force, thereafter called "bobbies", after his first name. Although he had successfully opposed a Catholic emancipation bill in 1817, Peel later recognized the explosiveness of the Irish situation. He introduced and carried through the Catholic Emancipation Act (q.v.) of 1829, granting Roman Catholics political equality.

In 1834–35 peel was prime minister for four months. During the next six years, he established the Conservative Party (q.v.) as a major political force by attracting such men as the later prime ministers Benjamin Disraeli and William Ewart Gladstone (qq.v.). In the general elections of 1841, the Conservatives gained a majority and Peel formed the first Conservative ministry. Peel's ministry was notable for introducing an income tax and for revising the British banking laws. Most important, he reversed his earlier opposition to free trade (q.v.) and urged repeal of the Corn Laws (q.v.). Although repeal was approved in 1846, the controversy over the measure was so great that Peel was forced to resign. He continued to serve in Parliament until his death four years later.

PEELE, George. See DRAMA: *National Drama: England.*

PEGASUS, northern constellation, situated southeast of Andromeda (q.v.). The three brightest stars of Pegasus, α Pegasi, or Markab, β Pegasi, or Scheat, and γ Pegasi, or Algenib, form a square with α Andromedae, called the square of Pegasus. The constellation is usually seen upside down in the sky, with only the head, neck, and front half of the animal represented by the stars.

PEGASUS, in Greek mythology, winged horse, son of Poseidon (q.v.), god of the sea, and the Gorgon (q.v.) Medusa. Pegasus sprang from Medusa's neck when she was killed by the hero Perseus (q.v.). Shortly after its birth, the magic steed struck the ground on Mt. Helicon, and on the spot a spring, later sacred to the Muses and believed to be a source for poetic inspiration, began to flow. All longed in vain to catch and tame the creature, and this became the dominating desire of Bellerophon (q.v.), Prince of Corinth. On the advice of a seer, Bellerophon spent a night in the temple of the goddess Athena (q.v.). As he slept, the goddess appeared to him with a golden bridle and told him that it would enable him to capture Pegasus. When Bellerophon awoke, he found the golden bridle beside him and, with it, easily captured and tamed the winged horse. Pegasus thereafter proved to be a great help to Bellerophon and aided the hero in his adventures against the Amazons and the Chimaera (qq.v.). Bellerophon was overcome by his own pride, however. When he attempted to fly to the top of Olympus (q.v.) to join the gods the wise horse threw him, leaving Bellerophon to wander disconsolately about, hated by the gods. Pegasus himself found shelter in the Olympian stalls, and was entrusted by the god Zeus (q.v.) with bringing him his lightning and thunderbolts.

PEGMATITE, variety of natural mineral formation containing holocrystalline (wholly crystallized) rocks that are in part very coarse-grained. The major constituents of pegmatite include minerals typically found in ordinary igneous rocks. Extreme textural variations, especially in grain size, are characteristic. Pegmatite is widely distributed in the crust of the earth but is found especially in older mountain chains, where it is restricted essentially to those surface areas in which igneous and metamorphic rocks are prevalent. Minerals containing the elements boron, beryllium, and lithium are abundant in some pegmatites. Other pegmatites contain commercial quantities of feldspar, mica, and gem-grade tourmaline. It has been speculated that the minerals formed as the molten earth mass cooled from 700° C. (1292° F.) to 250° C. (482° F.).

PEGU, city of Burma, in Pegu Division, on the Pegu R., 46 miles N.E. of Rangoon. The city is a rail junction in an area of rice production, and spur lines extend to teak forests in the nearby Pegu Yoma Mts. A former major river port, the city still has an important fishing industry. Pottery and bronze statuettes are manufactured. Pegu is a Buddhist pilgrimage center and contains many outstanding pagodas, including the Kyaikpun, Magazedi, Shwegugale, and Shwemawdaw, as well as the Shwethalyaung, or Reclining Buddha, built in 994. Ruins of walls and palaces can be seen, and nearby to the N.E. is the site of the ancient city of Hanthawaddy. Founded in 573 by Mon people, the community became the capital of the powerful Talaing kingdom in the 13th century. It succeeded Toungoo as capital of a united Burmese kingdom until 1635. Destroyed in 1757 and rebuilt, it served as capital of British, or Lower, Burma from 1852 to 1862. Pop. (1953) 47,378.

PÉGUY, Charles Pierre. see Dreyfus Affair.

PEIPING. See Peking.

PEIPUS, LAKE, lake of the Soviet Union, between the Russian S.F.S.R. and the Estonia S.S.R. Lake Peipus is connected on the s. with Lake Pskoff by a long, narrow channel. The area of Lake Peipus is about 1360 sq.mi. and the depth varies from 30 to 50 ft. The lake is drained on the N. by the Narva R., which flows into the Gulf of Finland. Lake Peipus is navigable for about eight months of the year and fishing is a major industry in the area. On the frozen lake the Russian hero Alexander Nevski (q.v.) defeated the Livonian knights in 1242.

PEIRCE, name of a family of American scholars who made important contributions to the fields of science, mathematics, and philosophy. Among the more important members of the family are the following.

Benjamin Peirce (1809–80), mathematician and philosopher, born in Salem, Mass. He graduated from Harvard University in 1829 and was appointed a tutor there in 1831; from 1833 until his death he was a professor, first of mathematics and natural history and later of mathematics and astronomy. From 1849 to 1867 he was consulting astronomer of the *American Ephemeris and Nautical Almanac,* and between 1867 and 1874 he was superintendent of the United States Coast Survey. The astronomical observatory at Harvard was established largely through his efforts. He is best known for his computations of the perturbations of the planets Uranus and Neptune and for his research on the rings of Saturn. His written works include *A System of Analytic Mechanics* (1855), *Linear Associative Algebra* (1870), and *Ideality in the Physical Sciences* (1881).

Charles Sanders Peirce (1839–1914), philosopher and physicist, son of Benjamin, born in Cambridge, Mass., and educated at Harvard University. In 1861 Peirce was appointed to the U.S. Coast Survey. Between 1864 and 1884 he lectured intermittently on logic and philosophy at Johns Hopkins and Harvard universities, and in 1877 he became the first American representative to the International Geodetic Congress.

In 1861 Peirce began a series of experiments with pendulums that contributed greatly to the determination of the density and shape of the earth and an investigation of the measurement of light waves. In 1867 he turned his attention to the system of logic created by the British logician and mathematician George Boole (q.v.). Peirce occupied himself with extending and transforming Boolean algebra (q.v.) until 1885.

He is best known for his philosophical system, later called pragmatism (q.v.). According to Peirce's pragmatic philosophy, no object or concept possesses inherent validity or importance. Its significance lies only in the practical effects resulting from its use or application. The "truth" of an idea or object, therefore, can be measured by empirical investigation of its usefulness. The concept was expanded by the American philosophers William James and John Dewey (qq.v.), and profoundly influenced modern philosophical and sociological thought. Peirce's works include *Photometric Researches* (1878) and *Studies in Logic* (1883). His major essays appear in *Chance, Love, and Logic,* published posthumously in 1923.

PEKALONGAN, city of Indonesia, in Central Java Province, on the island of Java, on the Java Sea, 210 miles s.e. of Djakarta. A fort here dates from 1753. One of the five chief ports of central Java, it ships chiefly sugar; the surrounding area also grows rice, tea, and rubber. There is a noted batik production in the city, which also has sugar and textile mills and tobacco processing plants. Pop. (1961) 102,380.

PEKIN, city in Illinois, and county seat of Tazewell County, on the Illinois R., 10 miles s.w. of Peoria. In a rich agricultural and coal-mining area, Pekin is a shipping point for grain, corn, coal, and manufactured products. The principal industries are distilling and the manufacture of corn products, paper board and containers, tractors and tractor parts, automotive parts, and chemicals. Machine tooling and the processing of foods and nonferrous metals are also important. As a young lawyer, United States President Abraham Lincoln (q.v.) argued many cases at the old courthouse in the city. Pekin was settled in 1829 and incorporated in 1839. Pop. (1960) 28,146; (1970) 31,375.

PEKING, formerly PEIPING, city and capital of the People's Republic of China, 90 miles N.E. of

PEKING

the Gulf of Po Hai and 527 miles s.w. of Mukden. Peking is the showplace of the Communist nation and is continuously undergoing change and embellishment. It is the center of rail transport, connecting major cities of China as well as North Korea, the Mongolian People's Republic, and the Soviet Union. Growing industries of the city include publishing and printing and the production of textiles, canned goods, automobiles, iron, steel, and agricultural and industrial machinery. Peking serves as the intellectual, political, and cultural center of the People's Republic of China. Among its institutions of higher learning are the Peking University (founded in 1898), the Union Medical College, the Peking Library, and the National Academy.

Layout of the City. Peking is a walled and moated city, built on a sloping, sandy plain about 12 miles w. of the Pai R. The city consists of two parts, the Inner City, or Tatar City, originally the residence of the imperial family; and the Outer City, or Chinese City, built for the populace.

The Inner City, built between 1409 and 1420, is a square enclosure on the N. It is surrounded by a brick-faced earth and concrete wall, about 15 mi. long and 50 ft. high, with nine gates. Directly inside the walls is the Legation Quarter, which houses the foreign embassies; the Peking University; the Peking observatory; and many temples. The Inner City contains two major areas. One is the Imperial City, surrounded by a towered, red-plastered wall about 6 mi. long and presently containing government offices, temples, gardens, and palaces. Almost 2 mi. within the Imperial City is the innermost enclosure, the Forbidden City, which contains the Museum of the Chinese Revolution and the Peking Library. Here also is the Imperial Palace, in front of which rallies are often held. The Forbidden City, nearly 1 sq.mi. in area, is surrounded by pink-washed walls and a moat 120 ft. wide.

The Outer City adjoins the Inner City on the s., sharing 4 mi. of its wall and three of its gates. The Outer City was built between 1553 and 1564. It is oblong in shape and is surrounded by a wall about 14 mi. in length. On the E. side of the roadway leading to the main entrance of the Inner City is an enclosure, more than 1 sq.mi. in size, containing the Temple of Heaven, a group of religious structures at which, during the Chinese Empire, the emperor worshiped at stated periods. On the w. side is the Temple of Agriculture. Both temples are situated in spacious grounds and are among the most famous and most beautiful examples of Chinese architecture. The commercial section, and the most congested quarter of Peking, is the N. part of the Outer City. The s. part is extensively farmed.

Outside the walls of Peking, on the E., N., and w. sides, are temples at which the emperor was required to worship during the summer solstice and vernal equinox. To the N.W. are tombs of most of the emperors of the Ming dynasty (1368–1644). These tombs are approachable through a long avenue of marble lions, unicorns, camels, elephants, and horses. The ruins of the former imperial summer palace, destroyed in 1860, are 9 mi. to the N.W. Nearby is the newer palace, built in 1889.

History. Ancient Chinese records witness that a city existed approximately on the site of Peking as early as the Chou dynasty (1122 or 1027–256 B.C.). The city was a frontier outpost under successive imperial dynasties. In 937 A.D. the Khitan Tatars (q.v.), who had conquered part of northern China, made it one of their capitals. They named it Nanking ("Southern Capital") and rebuilt it as an imperial city. In 1153, ruled by the Kin dynasty of the Tatars of the Golden Horde, the city became Chung-tu ("Middle Capital"), between present Mukden in the north and Kai Feng in the south. The Mongol conqueror Genghis Khan (q.v.) captured the city in 1215 and in 1264 his grandson Kublai Khan (q.v.) made it the capital of the vast Mongol Empire, giving it the Mongolian name of Khanbalik. It is also referred to as Cambaluc, as it was called in the writings of the Venetian traveler Marco Polo (q.v.), who served with Kublai Khan for many years. Under the descendants of Kublai, the city remained the imperial capital until 1368, when, after a successful revolt against the Mongols, the Ming dynasty established their capital at present Nanking. In 1421 the Ming emperor Yung Lo (1359–1424) moved his capital to the northern city; his court was established in an area somewhat to the south of the Mongol center. He named the capital Peking ("Northern Capital") and build the wall that still surrounds the city. After their conquest of China in the 17th century, the Manchu dynasty (1648–1912), the last of the Chinese dynasties, moved their court from Mukden to Peking. The Manchu emperors built many of the famous structures of the city. After the Chinese revolution of 1911 Peking was made the republican capital. The capital was removed to Nanking in 1928 and Peking was then renamed Peiping, its name under the first three Ming emperors.

On July 7, 1937, Japanese troops opened fire on the Chinese army at the Marco Polo Bridge in a Peking suburb, marking the beginning of the undeclared Sino-Japanese War (1937–38).

The Temple of Heaven, in the Outer City of Peking.
UPI

The city was taken on July 29 and on Dec. 14, as Peking, became the capital of all of Japanese-controlled northern China. Peking was one of the principal centers of Japanese activity in China until the Japanese garrison, on Oct. 10, 1945, surrendered it to the Chinese army, when it again became known as Peiping. During the civil strife in China following World War II the Chinese Communists launched an all-out offensive against the Nationalist forces in Peiping. After prolonged attack, the city surrendered to the Communist forces on Jan. 22, 1949. Later that year the Communists renamed the city Peking and made it the capital of the newly established People's Republic of China. In 1953 the territorial extent of the city was increased to a total of about 3400 sq.mi. Pop. (1957) 4,010,000.

PEKINGESE, breed of toy dog that originated in China in about the 8th century A.D. The Pekingese has a broad, massive skull, flat between the ears; a short, flat, black nose; a short, wrinkled muzzle; large, lustrous, dark eyes; heart-shaped ears; a long, soft coat; a thick mane that forms a ruff about the neck; bowed forelegs; and a tail that is set high. It can be found in a variety of colors; the most frequent are fawn, black, red, and parti-colored. The weight varies from about six to fourteen pounds. In general the animal is characterized by courage, dignified bearing, good temper, and considerable stamina. The Pekingese was the pet of the Chinese aristocracy, particularly in the Imperial household, and for a long time was regarded as a sacred animal in China. The dog was first brought to the Occident in the late 19th century when British military officers took to England four specimens they found during the looting of the Imperial Palace, Peking, by British troops in 1860. The animal is today a popular pet in the United States.

PEKING MAN. See MAN, ANCIENT: *Pithocanthropines.*

PELAGIANISM, in Christian theology, heresy (q.v.) advanced by the followers of Pelagius (360?–420?), probably a British monk. The heresy was condemned by councils of the Church in the 5th and 6th centuries, and it had largely disappeared by the end of the 6th century. In the attempt to vindicate human freedom and responsibility, the Pelagians denied original sin, confined grace (qq.v.), to forgiveness, asserted that man's will unaided by divine grace is capable of spiritual good, and maintained that Adam's fall involved only himself; see ADAM AND EVE; FREE WILL.

PELAGIC ZONE. See ANIMALS, GEOGRAPHIC DISTRIBUTION OF: *Saltwater Animals.*

PELARGONIUM

PELARGONIUM, genus of more than 250 species of the family Geraniaceae. The plant has showy flowers of various shades of red and white and is widely grown in gardens and in pots in the United States and Europe. The genus *Pelargonium* is commonly confused with the genus *Geranium* of the same family, the term geranium being frequently used as the common name of certain species of *Pelargonium*. Four distinct groups of Pelargonium are recognized, of which the Martha Washington, *P. domesticum,* has the largest and showiest flowers. The zonal (fancy-leaved) geranium is probably the most popular of the groups. Species in the zonal group include the variegated forms which commonly have leaves of green and white. The miniature and semidwarf *Pelargonium* are grown for their large flowers and very small leaves. The fourth group, the scented-leaved geraniums, includes more than 200 varieties, among which are the lemon, nutmeg, cinnamon, apple, and rose, and geraniums. The peppermint geranium, *P. tomentosum,* grows to 5 ft., with four to twenty white flowers in a cluster.

PELASGIANS, name applied to the very early inhabitants of ancient Greece. In the epic poems of the Greek poet Homer (q.v.), the Pelasgians are mentioned as the inhabitants of several locations in Greece including the ancient city of Dodona in eastern Epirus, southeastern Thrace, Argos, the Pelopónnisos, and Crete. Later writers placed them in Asia Minor. Some modern scholars regard them as the pre-Indo-European inhabitants of Greece, originally from eastern Thessaly in the northern part of the country; others regard them as the common ancestors of the Greeks and the Italians. In more recent years the term "Pelasgian" has been employed to designate the builders of the so-called Cyclopean architecture; *see* MYCENAEAN ART AND ARCHITECTURE. Some scholars believe that the Pelasgians were responsible for the development of the Mycenaean civilization; this theory, however, has not won general acceptance.

PELECYPODA. *See* BIVALVE.

PELÉE, MONT, volcano on the island of Martinique, French West Indies (qq.v.), rising to about 4800 ft. It became famous after it erupted on May 8, 1902, destroying the city of Saint-Pierre (q.v.), and causing the death of about 30,000 people in the city and the surrounding area. Saint-Pierre had only one survivor. Earlier eruptions took place in 1792 and 1851.

PELEUS, in Greek mythology, King of the Myrmidons (q.v.) in Thessaly, the son of Aeacus (q.v.), King of Aegina. He took part in the hunt for the Calydonian boar (*see* MELEAGER) and the journey of the Argonauts (q.v.) in search of the Golden Fleece (q.v.), but he is especially famed for his marriage to Thetis (q.v.), one of the Nereids (q.v.), who was destined to bear a son mightier than his father. Although Zeus (q.v.), father of the gods, loved Thetis, he wished her married to a mortal because of this prophecy. Aided by the gods, Peleus lay in wait for Thetis by the shore, and in spite of her transformations into fire, water, and wild beasts, held her fast until she returned to her original form. The marriage was attended by all the gods, with the exception of Eris, goddess of discord and strife, who, enraged at being excluded, threw into the gathering a golden apple inscribed "To the Most Beautiful". The award of the apple to Aphrodite (q.v.), goddess of love, by the Trojan prince Paris (q.v.) led to the Trojan War (q.v.). By Thetis, Peleus was the father of the famous Greek hero and warrior Achilles (q.v.). Peleus outlived both his son and his grandson Neoptolemus (q.v.), and was finally taken by Thetis to dwell among the Nereids.

PELHAM-HOLLES, Thomas, 1st Duke of Newcastle (1693–1768), British statesman, educated at the University of Cambridge. In 1711 he inherited the estates but not the title of his uncle John Holles, Duke of Newcastle (*see* NEWCASTLE), and adopted his name. Pelham-Holles vigorously supported George I (q.v.), first British king of the house of Hanover, and aided him during the rebellion of the Jacobites (q.v.) in 1715. In the same year he was created duke of Newcastle upon Tyne. He was an active member of the Whig Party (*see* WHIG), serving under the British kings George II and George III (qq.v.), as secretary of state from 1724 to 1754 and as prime minister from 1754 to 1756 and again from 1757 to 1762. In 1756 he was awarded the additional title of 1st duke of Newcastle-under-Lyme by George II.

PELIAS, in Greek mythology, son of Poseidon (q.v.), god of the sea. Pelias usurped the throne of Iolcus from his uncle Aeson, who fled into exile after sending his young son, Jason (q.v.), the rightful heir to the throne, to a place of safety. When Jason was grown he came boldly back to claim the throne from his wicked cousin. Pelias had been warned by an oracle that he would die at the hands of a kinsman and that he should beware of anyone who came wearing a single sandal. When Jason appeared with one foot bare, though otherwise well dressed, Pelias realized at once who the stranger was. Jason told him that he could keep all the riches he had taken, but that he must relinquish the throne. Pretending to comply, Pelias asked

Jason first to bring him the Golden Fleece (q.v.) from Colchis, a mission he believed to be impossible. With the aid of the sorceress Medea (q.v.), however, Jason accomplished the dangerous and difficult task. When he and Medea returned to Pelias with the Golden Fleece, they found that the wicked king had forced Jason's father to kill himself and that his mother had died of grief. To avenge their deaths, Jason once more appealed to Medea for help. Medea then cunningly contrived the death of Pelias by convincing his devoted daughters that they could make him young again by killing him and boiling his flesh with magic herbs. After Pelias thus met his death at the hands of his own daughters, Jason and Medea fled to Corinth.

PELICAN, common name applied to six species of large birds of the genus *Pelecanus*, comprising the family Pelecanidae. Pelicans have a very long, large, flattened bill, the upper mandible terminated by a strong hook that curves over the tip of the lower one. Beneath the lower mandible a great pouch of naked skin is appended. The tongue is very short and almost rudimentary. The face and throat are naked, the wings of moderate length and the tail rounded.

Pelicans are widely distributed over most of the warm regions, frequenting the shores of the seas, lakes, and rivers, and feeding chiefly on fish. They hover over the water and plunge upon their prey when it appears. They then store the catch in their pouch, from which they can bring it out at leisure either for their own eating or to feed their young.

Pelican, genus Pelecanus   UPI

The American white pelican, *P. erythrorhynchos*, which lives in the western part of the United States, is distinguished by its black wing tips. In the brown pelican, *P. occidentalis*, the head and neck are white and the wings and underside are dark. An eastern and a western subspecies of the brown pelican are recognized in the U.S. The white pelican, *P. onocrotalus*, found in southeastern Europe, Asia, and Africa is as large as a swan and appears white, slightly tinged with flesh color. The rufous-necked pelican, *P. fuscus*, abounds in the West Indies and in many parts of America. The other Old World species inhabits southern Europe, Africa, and southern Asia south to Australia.

PELLAGRA, dietary-deficiency disease resulting from inadequate intake or absorption of niacin, one of the components of the B-complex vitamins. The disease was first described (1735) by the Spanish physician Gaspar Casal (1679–1759), soon after the introduction of corn into Spain, but it was the American physician Joseph Goldberger (q.v.) who showed that the disease was due to vitamin deficiency. Common throughout the world, pellagra is especially prevalent in the Mediterranean countries, Central America, and the southern portion of the United States, although its incidence in this country is very low today due to fortification of processed wheat with vitamin B. The disease mainly afflicts those whose diet lack proteins, particularly those whose diet is principally corn, and sometimes occurs in people with gastrointestinal diseases due to poor absorption of vitamins. See VITAMIN: *Vitamin-B Complex.*

The symptoms of the disease appear gradually, affecting primarily the skin, the digestive tract, and the nervous system, but the disease often begins with weakness, lassitude, insomnia, and weight loss. Exposed skin on the neck, hands, arms, feet, and legs, particularly after exposure to sunlight, becomes rough, reddened, and scaly, and painful mouth lesions develop, with inflammation and soreness of the tongue. The gastrointestinal disturbances consist of loss of appetite, indigestion, and diarrhea; nervous system involvement appears later in the course of the disease and includes such symptoms as headache, vertigo, generalized aches, muscular tremors, and mental disturbances, including nervousness, depression, confusion, apathy, and even delerium.

Present-day treatment includes the administration of niacin and the other B-complex vitamins as well, since patients with pellagra usually have other deficiencies. A daily diet of adequate amounts of milk, lean meat, eggs, and fresh vegetables is imperative for cure and prevention of the disease. L.J.V.

PELOPIA. See Aegisthus; Atreus; Thyestes.

PELOPIDAS (d. 364 B.C.), Theban general and patriot. In 382 B.C. he was driven from Thebes by the oligarchic party, which was supported by the Spartans. He took refuge at Athens, but returned in 379 B.C., taking possession of the citadel, and establishing a democratic form of government. His Sacred Band of Theban youth contributed largely to the victory of the Theban general Epaminondas (q.v.) over the Spartans at Leuctra in 371 B.C. In the expedition of the Thebans against the Thessalian tyrant Alexander of Pherae (r. 369–358 B.C.) in 358 B.C., Pelopidas was taken prisoner, but was rescued by Epaminondas the following year. He was then sent to Susa, as ambassador from Thebes to the Persians. In 364 B.C. he defeated Alexander of Pherae at the Battle of Cynoscephalae, but was himself killed in action.

PELOPONNESIAN WAR. See Greece: *History: Ancient Greece: The Ascendancy of Athens.*

PELOPÓNNISOS or **PELOPONNESUS.** See Greece; Pelops.

PELOPS, in Greek mythology, son of Tantalus (q.v.). When he was a child his father killed him and attempted to serve his boiled flesh to the gods at a banquet. The gods realized the nature of the meal, punished Tantalus, and restored Pelops to life. The goddess Demeter, distracted by loss of her daughter Persephone (qq.v.), had eaten the flesh of the left shoulder. When the body was put together again the shoulder was replaced with one made of ivory. Pelops later won the hand of Princess Hippodamia by winning a chariot race from her father King Oenomaus of Pisa. Unknown to Pelops, the princess had bribed the charioteer Myrtilus to remove the linchpins from Oenomaus' chariot. Later Pelops quarreled with Myrtilus and hurled him into the sea. Before he drowned, the charioteer cursed Pelops, but the curse had no apparent effect during Pelops' lifetime. The Peloponnisos Peninsula of southern Greece is named in his honor. See Atreus, House of.

PELOTA. See Jai Alai.

PELOTAS, city of Brazil, in Rio Grande do Sul State, 26 miles N.W. of Rio Grande. It has a considerable export trade in hides, dried beef, wool, and timber. The leading industries are meat packing, flour milling, and tanning. Pop. (1968 est.) 208,672.

PELVIS, lower part of the trunk of the body, bounded at the front and on either side by the hipbone, and at the back by the sacrum and the coccyx, the lowest part of the spinal column;

see Hip; Sacroiliac Joint. The hipbone is composed of three separate bones: the ilium, the ischium or lower part of the hipbone, and the pubis, the central pubic bone that unites with the ischium at either side. In early life, the three bones are separate, but in the late teens or early twenties they unite to form a single structure called the innominate bone. At the lower end of

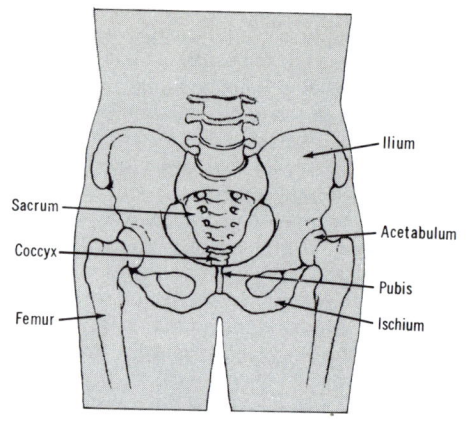

Diagram of the human pelvis.

the hipbone is a cup-shaped depression called the acetabulum in which the femur (q.v.), or thighbone, rotates. The pelvis thus acts as a unit in all bodily movements. The weight of the trunk is transferred from the spine through the sacrum and then through the hipbone to the thighbone and the lower extremities. Conversely, all forces acting on the lower limbs are transmitted to the trunk by the same route.

The cavity formed by the pelvic bones contains the lower portion of the intestines and rectum, the urinary bladder, and the internal organs of reproduction; see Bladder; Intestine. In females, the pelvis is rounder and wider than in men and the bones are lighter, reflecting the greater capacity required for expansion of the uterus in pregnancy and the emergence of the fetus in childbirth; see Gestation.

PEMATANGSIANTAR, city of Indonesia, in North Sumatra Province, on the island of Sumatra, 50 miles S.E. of Medan. It is the terminus of a railroad from Medan and a trade center for a plantation area growing rice, rubber, tea, tobacco, fibers, and oil palms. The development of the area occurred mainly after 1900. Pop. (1961) 114,870.

PEMBA, coral island of Tanzania, in the Indian Ocean, 25 miles N.E. of Zanzibar. It is 42 mi. long and 14 mi. wide, with an area of 380 sq.mi. It was a British protectorate from 1890 to 1964, when it became a part of Tanzania. The chief town is Chake Chake. Cloves, coconuts, and copra are the chief exports. Pop. (1967) 164,243.

PEMMICAN, North American Indian food preparation, consisting of the lean portions of venison, buffalo, or beef dried in the sun or wind, and then pounded into a paste, mixed with melted fat, tightly pressed into cakes, and packed into parfleche (rawhide) cases. Pemmican is now commercially manufactured for hunters and explorers.

PEN, instrument for writing with a fluid ink. When the ancient Egyptians wrote on papyrus or parchment (qq.v.), they used pens made from sharpened and split reeds. Quill pens, made from the wing feathers of geese and crows, are known to have been used for writing as early as the 7th century A.D. The quill was the most important writing instrument until the development of the steel pen in the 19th century.

Metal Pens. A barrel pen, a pen point and a rolled metal barrel on a wooden holder, was first made in 1780 by Samuel Harrison, a locksmith in Birmingham England. The first patent in Great Britain for steel pens was issued in 1803 to Byran Donkin (1768–1855), a British inventor. By the 1830's, the British pen makers Joseph Gillott (1799–1873) and Sir Josiah Mason (1795–1881) were making steel pens by machine, thereby enabling them to be sold cheaply and to become articles of common use. In the United States the first mechanically manufactured pens were made in New York in 1858.

Although the modern steel pen is inexpensive, sixteen different processes are involved in its manufacture, including annealing, polishing, rolling, shaping, curving, hardening, tempering, and slitting. Pens may also be made of silver, platinum, aluminum, bronze, or vulcanite. Swedish steel is commonly used by U.S. pen makers. The gold-point pen, which is incorrodable in ink, was first manufactured in Birmingham, England, and later in the U.S. in 1836. Pens that must be dipped into an inkwell are no longer used for everyday purposes; they are used mostly for ink drawing and hand lettering.

Fountain Pens. The fountain pen eliminates dipping and redipping the pen, because a reservoir in the barrel of the pen supplies ink by capillary action as required (the action of temperature and air-pressure changes). Fountain pens were manufactured in England as early as 1835, but because they were relatively unreliable did not come into general use until improvements were made some decades later. In these early fountain pens devices to control the flow of ink from the barrel included tubes, springs, and valves; however, in all these the flow of ink was irregular. In 1884 a patent was granted to the American inventor and manufacturer Lewis Edson Waterman (1837–1901) for an automatic underfeed pen in which a rubber bar with a groove in its surface and three fine slits at the base enabled the ink to flow freely on demand by capillary action. In the modern fountain pen, which is based on this principle, air is admitted to take the place of the ink that is used. With these improvements in design and, therefore, reliability, fountain pens increased in general use, especially beginning in the 1920's.

The stylographic pen, like the fountain pen, has a reservoir to hold the ink, but instead of an ordinary pen point it has a hollow tubular point containing a needle. The needle releases the ink when pressed on the paper. This type of pen is used by draftsmen for making lines of precise width.

Ball-Point Pens. In the ball-point pen the ink has more viscosity than ordinary fountain-pen ink; release of this ink to the paper is controlled by a small metal ball at the tip of the pen which revolves as the pen is moved across the paper. The ball-point pen was first marketed in the U.S. in 1945, but the early ones did not write well. With many improvements in the ink and in design, ball-point pens are being used increasingly in place of fountain pens. In 1965 more than three out of four pens sold in the U.S. were ball-points.

Soft-tip pens and felt-tip pens have also become popular. Soft-tip pens consist of fine nylon or other synthetic fibers drawn into a point and fastened securely to the barrel of the pen. The tips are flexible and produce strokes of varying thickness. Felt-tipped pens are made of hard-packed fibrous or fluorocarbon substances shaped into a rounded or flat tip. Felt-tip pens are typically used as marking pens and may include a variety of colored and fluorescent inks.

PENANCE, performance of some specific act of mortification, voluntarily undertaken, as an expression of sorrow for and satisfaction for sin (q.v.). Specifically, in Christianity, it is the discipline or act of reparation or austerity imposed by the priest after sacramental confession (see CONFESSION) and forming an integral part of the sacrament (q.v.) of Penance. In the Roman Catholic and Greek Churches it ranks as one of seven sacraments; see ROMAN CATHOLIC CHURCH; ORTHODOX CHURCH. The Anglicans (see CHURCH OF ENGLAND) consider it one of the lesser sacraments. The sacrament of Penance consists of contrition, confession, and satisfaction, or penance, on the part of the penitent, and of absolution (q.v.) on the part of the confessor.

PENANG

Under certain circumstances Penance as a sacrament becomes an obligation. In the Anglican churches Penance is a matter of private devotion.

Penance is also a disciplinary punishment inflicted by an ecclesiastical court for a spiritual offense.

PENANG, State of Malaysia, comprised of Penang Island in the Strait of Malacca, 2 to 10 mi. off the w. coast of the Malay Peninsula, and the former Province Wellesley on the Malay Peninsula opposite Penang Island. The capital of the State is the port of Penang (pop. in 1957, 234,930), on the Penang Island of the same name. Rubber, cultivated on plantations, is the chief product of the State. Other agricultural products include rice, coconuts, coffee, spices, and a wide variety of tropical fruits. Poultry, hogs, cattle, and buffaloes are raised. Fishing is an important industry. Abundant deposits of tin exist but are not extensively mined.

The first British settlement in the Malay Peninsula was established on Penang Island in 1786, by the English East India Company; see EAST INDIA COMPANY. Province Wellesley was acquired in 1798, and was incorporated with Penang Island as a single administrative unit in 1800. In 1826 the enlarged settlement of Penang was united with the settlements of Malacca and Singapore under a single British colonial governor; and in 1867 the three settlements became a crown colony with the name of the Straits Settlements. In 1946 Penang became a member of the Malayan Union, which was superseded in 1948 by the Federation of Malaya, and in 1963 became part of Malaysia. Area, 399 sq.mi.; pop. (1967 est.) 761,194.

PENATES, in Roman mythology, gods of the storeroom, who were worshiped, along with the Lares (q.v.), in every home as protectors of the house. They were often represented as dancing, holding a drinking horn as a symbol of prosperity. The Penates were also worshiped publicly as special protectors of the community and the state.

PENCIL, implement for writing or drawing; specifically, a cylinder of wood, plastic, or metal, containing a mineral, commonly graphite, for making marks. In ancient times pencils employed metallic lead as the marking material. Although the instrument remains widely known as a lead pencil, modern pencils are actually made of graphite, or plumbago, which contains no lead whatever in its composition, but is in reality almost pure carbon. In 1969 approximately 13,500,000 gross of pencils were sold in the United States.

History. The use of metallic lead for marking is of ancient origin. The Roman scholar Pliny (q.v.) refers to the use of lead for making lines on papyrus (q.v.), and the Spanish adventurer Hernando Cortes (q.v.) in 1520 found the Aztec (q.v.) using lead crayons. From 1564 the plumbago from the Borrowdale mines in Cumberland, England, furnished the coloring material in the best pencils. These mines have been exhausted since 1850. Graphite is now mined at Passau, West Germany, and in Norway, New Zealand, Mexico, and various parts of the U.S. The mine containing the purest graphite yet discovered is located at Ticonderoga, in New York State. It yields a product that is 99.9 percent pure carbon.

In 1795 the French chemist Nicolas Jacques Conté (1755–1805) invented a process that consisted of thoroughly mixing the black lead with clay and water, cutting the squeezed mass into strips, and baking; in this condition it was marketed. The first manufacturer of lead pencils in the U.S. was William Monroe, of Concord, Mass. Monroe, in 1812, invented a process by which, after pulverizing and mixing the material, he encased it in cedar holders. Another pioneer in the industry was the American inventor Joseph Dixon (1799–1869), and in 1849 the German manufacturers Johann Lothar von Faber (1817–96) and Eberhard Faber (1823–79), whose family had established a factory in Nuremberg, Germany, in 1761, established a factory in the U.S.

Methods of Manufacture. The familiar lead pencil of everyday use consists of a round or polygonal stick of graphite mixed with clay, surrounded by a cedar case. The graphite is first reduced to an impalpable powder by grinding. Water is then added and the substance is run through mixers in a fluid state, the proper amount of finely powdered clay being put into the mixture and thoroughly blended with it. A little lampblack is sometimes added to the composition to increase the blackness. The more clay used, the harder will be the pencil. After thorough mixing the mass is placed in filter presses to exclude the water and reduce the mixture to a doughy consistency. The material is next passed through dies consisting of successive plates with holes of varying diameter. Great pressure is used, causing the mixture to ooze forth in doughy strings. The final dies are of the same diameter as the finished lead. The graphite in this form is straightened, cut into 3-ft. lengths, and allowed to dry. It is next cut into the 7 in. pieces of required length. These pieces are packed in crucibles and burned for several hours, to extract the moisture.

The leads are usually encased in the wood before it is shaped into a pencil. Little slabs of cedar, two to eight pencils wide, are passed through a machine that cuts out semicircular grooves the diameter of the lead. Into the grooves in one of these slabs the leads are laid and another grooved slab is glued to it, thus completely encasing the graphite. The slabs are now passed through machines that divide them into pencils, with their sides shaped in hexagonal or in curved form. After polishing, varnishing, and stamping, all performed by machinery, the pencils are ready for shipment.

Colored Pencils. Colored pencils are made of chalk, clay, or wax, mixed with coloring pigments, the nature of which does not permit their being calcined like black pencils. They may be encased in wood like ordinary pencils, or simply wrapped in paper. Toward the close of the 19th century a process was invented by which both black and colored pencils were encased in paper instead of wood. A sheet of paper cut for a part of its width into strips about $\frac{1}{4}$ in. wide is wrapped around the lead to form a case of the usual thickness. The surface is painted. When the pencil point wears down too close to the paper it is sharpened, that is, more lead is exposed, by simply unwinding one of the narrow strips of paper.

Mechanical Pencil. A mechanical pencil is a slender cylinder, usually made out of metal or plastic, that dispenses thin sticks of graphite, called leads. The lead is inserted into the cylinder against a movable rod that can be adjusted so as to push out and expose part of the lead for use and afterward to withdraw it. The mechanical pencil was first patented in 1879. For the past twenty years, U.S. manufacturers have produced from 40,000,000 to 70,000,000 mechanical pencils annually.

PENDLETON, city in Oregon, and county seat of Umatilla Co., on the Umatilla R., 217 miles E. of Portland. Transportation facilities include railroads and a municipal airport. The city is the trading and distributing center of a vast wheat-growing area, which is also noted for the production of livestock and timber. Among the industrial establishments in Pendleton are flour mills, canneries, woolen mills, lumber mills, and factories manufacturing furniture and leather goods. The headquarters of the Umatilla National Forest are in Pendleton, and the Umatilla Indian Agency is 5 miles E. of the city. Pendleton is famous for its annual cattle roundup. The city was founded in 1869 and incorporated in 1880. It is on the historic Oregon Trail (q.v.). Pop. (1960) 14,434; (1970) 13,197.

PENDULUM, body or weight suspended from a fixed horizontal axis so as to swing along a path called an arc under the influence of gravity; *see* GRAVITATION. The most elementary type of pendulum is a small weight, called a bob, at the end of a fine thread. This is called a simple pendulum, and is the type used to regulate clockwork and other machinery, in which a weight is attached to the bottom of a rod. If such a pendulum is free-swinging and its path is not confined to one vertical plane, it is called a rotary or spherical pendulum.

The principle of the pendulum was discovered by the Italian astronomer, mathematician, and physicist Galileo Galilei (q.v.), who established that the period for the swing or oscillation, also called vibration (q.v.), of a pendulum remains the same, no matter how long its arc or amplitude. This phenomenon is called isochronism, and Galileo noted its possible applications in timekeeping. Because of the role played by gravity, however, the period of a pendulum is related to geographical location, and the period changes if the pendulum is moved from one location to another. The period, for example, will be greater on a mountain than at sea level. Thus the pendulum can be used to determine accurately the local acceleration (q.v.) of gravity, which varies as a function of latitude and el-

A Foucault pendulum in the General Assembly Building, New York City. The gold-plated sphere, 12 in. in diameter, swings by a single wire over a raised metal ring, its plane shifting slowly in a clockwise direction, thus giving visual proof of the rotation of the earth.
United Nations

PENELOPE

evation. Pendulums of various types have also been useful for engineering and astronomical measurement.

Compensation Pendulum. The simple pendulum, used for timekeeping, is accurate as a regulator, if the proper length of the rod is preserved. It was found, however, that in winter clocks went too fast, and at midsummer too slow, because cold shortened the metallic rod and heat lengthened it. A refinement was made to ensure uniform length, and accurate timekeeping, by the use of compensation pendulums. The two common types of compensation pendulum are the mercurial pendulum and the gridiron pendulum. The mercurial pendulum carries a glass cylinder almost full of mercury. This cylinder is proportional in quantity to the weight of the pendulum, and when the latter expands downward because of heat, the change is counterbalanced by the upward expansion of the mercury in the cylinder. The gridiron pendulum is composed of a series of upright metal bars, usually of steel and copper, having different compositions and therefore different coefficients of thermal expansion. If the relative lengths of these bars are carefully adjusted, no change of temperature will materially affect the timekeeping property of the pendulum.

Other Pendulums. Pendulums are also used in various scientific instruments, the more complex pendulums including the bifilar pendulum, the Foucault pendulum, and the torsion pendulum. Fifilar pendulums employ two strings or wires, and have been used to record the irregular rotation (q.v.) of the earth and to detect earthquakes; see SEISMOGRAPH. In 1851 the French physicist Jean Bernard Léon Foucault (q.v.) used the pendulum to demonstrate the rotation of the earth. Foucault suspended a 62-lb. iron ball on a 220-ft. wire over a circular enclosure, and demonstrated that the earth turns in relation to the arc of the pendulum. This shift in the path of the pendulum is most pronounced at the North Pole, and decreases with latitude. Such a rotary pendulum is today known as a Foucault pendulum.

The so-called torsion pendulum, which vibrates by twisting back and forth rather than swinging, consists of a vertical wire that becomes a spring when it is wound, but is technically not a pendulum because it does not function gravitationally; see TORSION. Pendulums have also been used in the science of ballistics (q.v.) to measure the momentum of projectiles.

See CLOCKS AND WATCHES; EQUILIBRIUM.

PENELOPE, in Greek mythology, daughter of Icarius, King of Sparta, wife of Odysseus (see ULYSSES), King of Ithaca, and mother of Telemachus (q.v.), Although her husband was gone for more than twenty years during and after the Trojan War (q.v.), Penelope never doubted that he would return and remained faithful to him. She was wooed by many suitors, however, and they devoured and wasted Odysseus' property. Unwilling to choose one of the suitors as a husband, Penelope kept their advances in check under the pretext of completing a shroud, which she was weaving for Laertes, her father-in-law. Each night she unraveled the work she completed during the day, and by this means avoided having to choose a husband. Finally, betrayed by a maid, Penelope was compelled to finish the work. The suitors were preparing to force a decision when Odysseus returned in disguise, killed them, and revealed his identity to his faithful wife. See ODYSSEY.

PENGHU ISLANDS *or* **PESCADORES.** See TAIWAN.

PENGPU, city of the People's Republic of China, in Anhwei Province, on the Hwai R., about 100 miles N.W. of Nanking. A rail junction and grain-trading center, it is reached by large junks on the river and has plants engaged in light industry. The name is also spelled Peng-pu and was formerly Pang-fou. Pop. (1958 est.) 330,000.

PENGUIN, flightless, aquatic bird of the Southern Hemisphere, comprising the order Sphenisciformes. The name "penguin" originally was applied to the now extinct great auk of the North Atlantic, a large, flightless, black-and-white bird with an upright stance. Similar flightless birds were discovered subsequently in the Southern Hemisphere, and they also were called penguin, a name that is now restricted exclusively to these birds.

Physical Appearance. Most penguins have a white breast and a black back and head. Many species exhibit red, orange, or yellow patches on the head and neck. Because their short legs are placed far back on their bodies, penguins assume an upright posture. Their flipperlike wings are short and mostly black in color.

Penguins are grouped into seventeen species and six genera, most of which are found in Antarctica and on subantarctic islands. Some species are native to the coasts of Australia, South Africa, and South America, and two species range into the tropical latitudes.

The largest species are the king penguin, *Aptenodytes patagonica,* from 36 to 38 in. in height, and the emperor penguin, *A. forsteri,* which may attain a height of 48 in. Both species of the *Aptenodytes* genus are found on the antarctic ice barrier. The king penguin is also found in Tierra del Fuego and on eight islands in the Southern Hemisphere. The smallest penguin is the little blue penguin, eudyptula minor, of Australia and New Zealand; its height is 16 in. or less. Unlike most species, the king, emperor, and little penguins have blue-gray backs. Another distinguishing feature of the king and emperor penguins is the presence of bright reddish or pinkish shields on the sides of their mandibles and large orange or yellow patches on the sides of their necks.

The royal penguin, Eudyptes schlegeli, the rock hopper, E. crestatus, the yellow-eyed penguin, Megadyptes antipodes, the macaroni penguin, E. chrysolophus, and the erect-crested penguin, E. sclarteri, are distinguished by yellowish feather crests on their heads. Members of the Eudyptes genus inhabit the antarctic waters south of New Zealand and Tasmania and range northward along the east coast of South America and to Tristan da Cunha, an island in the s. Atlantic Ocean. The gentoo penguin, Pygoscelis papua, and the Adélie penguin, P. adeliae, are representative of the genus found in Antarctica and in the South Shetland, South Orkney, and South Sandwich islands. The jackass penguin, Spheniscus demersus, is found off the coasts of South Africa. Two members of the Spheniscus genus have tropical habitats; the Galápagos penguin, S. mendiculus, is found on the Galápagos Islands and the Peruvian penguin, S. humboldti, inhabits the west coast of South America.

Although their flippers bear little resemblance to the wings of most birds, penguins are believed to have descended from flying ancestors.

Emperor penguins, Aptenodytes forsteri   U.S. Navy

Penguins do not have specific feather tracts, as do most birds, but are covered almost uniformly with small, scalelike feathers. Whereas most birds shed their feathers and grow new ones during a relatively long period of the year, penguins molt all of their feathers and, in some species, even shed the shields from the beak within a very short space of time. A molting penguin has a swollen, disheveled appearance; it loses its feathers in huge patches as new feathers appear. During the molting period, which may last several weeks, the penguin does not enter the water to feed.

Mobility and Survival. Penguins usually walk or hop and toboggan along on their breasts, pushing with wings and feet. They swim with great speed and agility. The flippers are their sole means of propulsion; the feet are trailed behind or used in steering. Some species progress by porpoising, which is swimming underwater some distance, emerging in a graceful arc to take a fresh breath, and submerging again. Penguins feed on fish, cuttlefish, crustaceans, and other small sea animals. In captivity the king and emperor penguins normally do not learn to pick up their own food, and after they have been taught to feed by strenuous forced feeding, must be fed by hand each day.

The ability to withstand intense cold is one of the penguin's greatest assets. Most penguins have rather small feet, wings, and heads; the relatively little surface area in comparison to the bird's volume results in excellent heat conservation. In addition to helpful proportions, many penguins have a thick insulating layer of fat

385

PENGUIN

under the skin. Some species are better equipped for cold weather than others. The emperor penguin, which may weigh 60 to 70 lb., appears to be the best equipped of all.

Penguins are gregarious birds and are found in flocks even at sea. On land the colonies often number in the hundreds of thousands. Although the birds have suffered greatly at the hands of man, who has slaughtered great numbers for their blubber and, more recently, for their skins, the inaccessibility of the Antarctic Region helped preserve the group. Natural enemies of the penguin include leopard seals, killer whales, and, in the case of young chicks and eggs, skuas.

Breeding. The greatest concentrations of penguins are seen in rookeries where the birds gather to breed. Several species of penguin may be found nesting in a single rookery, but usually the species are well segregated. At the mating season the penguins of the Antarctic Region appear along desolate, ice-bound, or rocky coasts and hop, jump, waddle, and toboggan toward favored breeding sites. In many of these areas smooth paths have been worn over hard rock formations by countless generations; the birds use precisely the same paths as their antecedents to approach the rookery. Often the paths seem to be the most circuitous and difficult routes to the rookery, and in some cases the sites are located many miles from the ocean. More northern species may be resident in the area of the rookery. The emperor penguin breeds in one of the world's most inhospitable regions during one of the coldest periods of the year, laying and incubating its eggs in temperatures as low as $-80°$ F.

Like most birds, penguins indulge in strange postural displays and calls in the process of finding mates within their own species. The gentoo penguin raises his flippers and calls or bows in a manner peculiar to the gentoo; the jackass penguin bows, shakes his head, and brays in a characteristic jackasslike call attractive to females of that species; and the courtship display and clear trumpeting of the king penguin are specific among the kings. Birds of the same genus are more likely to have similar courtship displays than less closely related penguins.

Penguins vary in their nesting methods, and some species build no nests at all. The Peruvian and jackass penguins prefer a sheltered retreat, such as a burrow, and utilize sticks and other debris to form the nest. Others, such as the Adélies, incubate their eggs in the open on nests formed of stones or sticks. King and emperor penguins build no nests; in these species the bird holds its single egg in the tops of its feet, hunching down over it so that a fold of abdominal skin covers and warms the egg.

Most species of penguin lay a clutch of two eggs, which are white or greenish in color. Incubation periods vary according to species. King penguin eggs require more than fifty days of incubation before hatching, whereas jackass eggs hatch in thirty-two to thirty-six days.

In general, both sexes incubate the eggs and feed the young. The male Adélie penguin may incubate the eggs for the first two weeks, and during this period the female returns to the sea to feed and bathe. The male fasts during her absence. Actually, a male Adélie may fast for six weeks, or while the nesting territory is established and defended, and courtship takes place, the eggs are laid, and he incubates the eggs. When the female takes over incubation, the male goes to the distant sea to feed and, within an amazingly short period, he restores his reservoir of fat and returns to the rookery with food for the young soon due to hatch. Both parents share responsibility for feeding the young penguins. All species of penguin do not undergo such strenuous fast periods during the breeding period as do the Adélies; many nest in areas where the birds can make several trips daily to the sea for food.

Most penguin chicks are covered with a sooty-gray down at hatching, although some have a pattern of soft grays and whites. Chicks of certain species remain confined to the burrow or nest through the entire nesting period, during which they are fed by their parents. Among other species the chicks, after reaching a stage of development in which they do not require constant care from the parents, are grouped in areas called nurseries. There they wait while the parents hunt for food. On their parents' return parents and chicks recognize each other in a group often numbering thousands. In some cases there ensues a feeding chase in which the chick leaves the nursery to chase one of its food-laden parents. The parent finally stops and regurgitates partially digested food for the chick. After a young penguin has shed the last vestiges of its down and is arrayed in its first plumage, it enters the sea to fend for itself. W.C.

PENICILLIN, antibiotic derived from the mold *Penicillium notatum; see* ANTIBIOTIC; BACTERIA; BACTERIOLOGY. The action of this antibiotic was first observed in 1929 by the British bacteriologist Sir Alexander Fleming but it was ten years later that pencillin was concentrated and studied by the British biochemist Ernst Boris Chain, the British pathologist Sir Howard Walter Florey (qq.v.), and other scientists.

Penicillin acts both by killing bacteria and by inhibiting their growth. It does not kill organisms in the resting stage but only those which are growing and reproducing. Although the action of the drug is not fully understood, it is believed to inhibit the metabolism of bacteria during development. Penicillin is effective against a wide range of disease-bearing microorganisms,

A colony of the green mold Penicillium chrysogenum, *a mutant form of which produces almost all of the world's commercial penicillin. The beads of liquid on the surface of the colony contain measurable quantities of the antibiotic.* Chas. Pfizer & Co., Inc.

including pneumococci, staphylococci, streptococci, gonococci, meningococci, the clostridium of tetanus, and the syphilis spirochete. The drug has been successfully employed to treat such deadly diseases as subacute bacterial endocarditis, septicemia, and gas gangrene, and also syphilis, gonorrhea, scarlet fever, and osteomyelitis. It has been particularly useful in the treatment of patients who have unfavorable reactions to the sulfa drugs or who are suffering from infections caused by strains of bacteria which have developed immunity to sulfa drugs; see CHEMOTHERAPY; SULFA DRUGS. Toxic symptoms produced by penicillin are limited largely to allergic reactions; the latter may be determined by scratch tests before administration of the drug.

Penicillin is manufactured in quantity under conditions as precisely controlled as those of any research laboratory. The large vats containing culture medium are sterilized, agitated, and maintained at the proper temperature. After two days of fermentation, the culture broth is filtered and undergoes a long series of concentration processes including adsorption (q.v.), repeated extractions with solvents, and centrifuging (see CENTRIFUGE). The final product, usually in the form of a sodium salt, is frozen and vacuum dried to a colorless, crystalline powder.

Semisynthetic Penicillin. Despite the effectiveness displayed by penicillin in curing a wide range of diseases, infections caused by certain strains of staphylococci could not be cured by the antibiotic as a result of the ability of the organism to produce an enzyme, penicillinase, capable of destroying the antibiotic. In addition, enterococci and many gram-negative bacilli known to cause respiratory and urinary-tract infections were found to be intrinsically resistant to the action of penicillin. Chemical modification of penicillin, although long considered as a possible means of making it more effective against these organisms, became feasible after a portion of the penicillin molecule, the cyclic moiety or nucleus, was isolated in pure form from fermentation broths. Appropriate chemical treatment of this biologically-produced compound resulted recently in formation of a number of so-called semisynthetic penicillins. The most important of these are Methicillin and Ampicillin, the former remarkably effective against penicillinase-producing staphylococci and the latter not only active against all organisms normally killed by penicillin, but also inhibiting enterococci and most gram-negative bacilli.

The strength and dosage of penicillin are measured in terms of international units. Each of these units is equal to .0006 g of the crystalline fraction of penicillin called penicillin G. In the early days of penicillin therapy, the drug was administered every 3 hr. in small doses. Subsequent therapy consisted of large doses suspended in oil, which released the penicillin slowly into the blood stream. In general usage in the 1950's was a compound called procaine penicillin which remained effective for as long as 3 days. Another compound of penicillin, known as bicillin, produces protracted blood levels of penicillin for 3 weeks following the administration of 1,250,000 units. It is particularly valuable in the treatment of syphilis.

See also separate articles on most of the diseases mentioned in this article.

S.A.W. & K.E.P.

PENINSULAR CAMPAIGN, military campaign of the American Civil War, fought from April to July, 1862. At the request of the Union general George Brinton McClellan, President Abraham

Lincoln (qq.v.) agreed that an attempt should be made to capture Richmond, Va., the Confederate capital. On April 4, a Union force of 112,000 men set out from Fort Monroe at the eastern end of the peninsula formed by the York and James rivers. Almost immediately the army met strong resistance at Yorktown and was forced to undertake a month-long siege before the town fell; see YORKTOWN, SIEGE OF. McClellan then continued his advance on Richmond, but his indecision combined with bad weather and lack of reinforcements delayed him. The Union advance was halted at the Battle of Fair Oaks and Seven Pines, fought on May 31–June 1, about 6 miles E. of Richmond. The Confederate general Joseph Eggleston Johnston (q.v.), commanding nearly 42,000 troops, was severely wounded in the battle and replaced by General Robert E. Lee (see under LEE). The turning point of the campaign was reached in the Seven Days' Battle (q.v.) fought between June 25 and July 1, in which the Confederate forces suffered the greater losses, but were able, because of Lee's adroit maneuvering, to force McClellan to retreat. Several stubborn battles, including the battles of Savage's Station, Frayser's Farm, and Malvern Hill, were fought in the course of the retreat, but McClellan was able to lead his troops back to the James R., where he gained the support of gunboats of the Union navy. The campaign was a failure, however, and the Union army was forced to abandon the attempt to take Richmond. The Confederate success in saving the capital gave a new impetus to the Southern war effort. See CIVIL WAR, THE AMERICAN.

PENINSULAR WAR. See NAPOLEONIC WARS: *Anti-Napoleonic Nationalism;* SPAIN: *History; The Bourbon Dynasty: Peninsular War.*

PENITENTIAL PSALMS, seven of the Psalms (q.v.), so called as being specially suitable for the repentant sinner. They formerly were prescribed for recitation by the priests on certain days, and they are still used liturgically in the Church of England (q.v.); see BOOK OF COMMON PRAYER. The Penitential Psalms are Psalms 6, 32, 38, 51, 102, 130, and 143, according to the Authorized (King James) Version, which correspond with 6, 31, 37, 50, 101, 129, and 142 of the Vulgate (q.v.); see BIBLE, ENGLISH TRANSLATIONS OF THE. These Psalms have been set apart from a very early period, and their special qualities are referred to by the Christian writer, teacher, and theologian Origen (q.v.).

PENKI, city of the People's Republic of China, in Liaoning Province, 50 miles S.E. of Mukden. A rail junction, it is the second-largest center for the production of iron and steel in Manchuria and also produces cement. Coal, iron, and alunite are mined within the municipal limits, which cover 2000 sq.mi. Industrialization of the area was begun by the Japanese in 1915. In 1952 the city limits were greatly extended to include the mining areas. The name is also spelled Pench'i. Pop. (1958 est.) 449,000.

PENN, William (1644–1718), English Quaker and the founder of the colony of Pennsylvania, the son of Admiral William Penn (1621–70), born in London, and educated at Christ Church, University of Oxford. While at Oxford he was converted to Quakerism; see FRIENDS, SOCIETY OF. In 1666 his father sent him to Ireland to look after his estates in County Cork. In Ireland his religious convictions brought him into conflict with the authorities and he was imprisoned. On his return to England, Penn began work on a religious tract, *The Sandy Foundation Shaken* (1688); the tract was published without a license and Penn was jailed in the Tower of London (q.v.). During his imprisonment he wrote his most famous book, *No Cross, No Crown,* and *Innocency with Her Open Eyes* (1669), a vindication of himself that contributed to his liberation. In 1671 he was sent to Newgate prison for six months. There he wrote four treatises; one of them, *The Great Cause of Liberty of Conscience,* is a defense of the doctrine of toleration.

In 1681 he obtained from the crown, in payment for a debt owed to his father, a grant of territory in North America. Penn, with several friends, sailed for America in September, 1682, and in October held his famous interview with the Indian tribes. He planned and named the city of Philadelphia, and for two years governed the colony wisely and well.

Toward the end of the reign of Charles II (q.v.), King of England, Penn returned to England in order to aid persecuted Quakers there. After the accession of William III (q.v.), King of England and Ireland, Penn was twice accused of treason, and of corresponding with the exiled monarch, but was acquitted. In 1699 he paid a second visit to Pennsylvania where his presence was required to restore peace and order after the aribtrary behavior of his deputy. Penn's acomplishments during this visit included the suppression of piracy, the granting of a charter to Philadelphia, and the issuance of the Charter of Privileges, a quarantee of religious freedom. He departed for England late in 1701, leaving the management of his affairs to an agent whose manipulations virtually ruined Penn. See PENNSYLVANIA: *History.*

PENNACOOK, confederation of North American Indian tribes of Algonquian (q.v.) stock who

PENNSYLVANIA

inhabited, in colonial times, the Merrimack basin and parts of Massachusetts, New Hampshire, and Maine. During the wars between Britain and France in America, the Pennacook sided at first with the British, but later joined the French. Their capital was at Amoskeag, the modern Manchester, New Hampshire. About 1676 they emigrated to Canada and the West. The Pennacook language was similar to that of the Penobscot (q.v.).

PENNANT. See FLAG.

PENNELL, Joseph (1857–1926), American etcher, lithographer, and author, born in Philadelphia, Pa., and trained at the Pennsylvania Academy of Fine Arts and the Pennsylvania School of Industrial Art. During long periods of residence in London he was greatly influenced by the American painter and etcher James Abbott McNeill Whistler (q.v.). At first an illustrator of books and publishing his works in literary magazines, Pennell settled in New York City in 1917 and became a teacher of the graphic arts at the Art Students League. His simple and direct drawings, etchings, and lithographs, chiefly of architectural landscape subjects, were widely acclaimed. Numerous examples are included in many European and American art collections, including the Uffizi Gallery, Florence; the British Museum, London; and the Library of Congress, Washington, D.C. His principal writings are *Pen Drawing and Pen Draughtsmen* (1889), *Modern Illustration* (1895), *Pictures of the Panama Canal* (1912), and *The Adventures of an Illustrator* (1925).

PENNEY, James Cash (1875–1971), American merchant. He developed the chain of department stores known as J. C. Penney Company. See CHAIN STORES.

PENN HILLS, township of Pennsylvania, in Allegheny Co., on the Allegheny R., adjoining Pittsburg on the N.E. Communities within the township include North Bessemer, Universal, Lincoln Park, Ritzland, Penn Rose, Rodi, Laketon Heights, Sandy Creek, Haffey, Gascola, and Nadine. The name of the township was changed from Penn in 1958. Pop. (1960) 51,512; (1970) 62,886.

PENNINE ALPS. See ALPS: *Swiss Alps.*

PENNINE CHAIN, extensive range of hills of Great Britain, in N. England, extending in a general southerly direction from the Cheviot Hills on the S. border of Scotland to the Midland Plain of England. In the N.W., the Eden Valley separates the Pennine Chain from the region known as the Lake District. In the S., the chain is broken by the Aire R., which traverses it in a general N.W. to S.E. direction, forming the Aire Gap. The Pennine Chain covers parts of Northumberland, Cumberland, Westmoreland, Lancashire, Yorkshire, Derbyshire, and Cheshire; the S. foothills extend into Nottinghamshire and Staffordshire. The highest point, Cross Fell, is 2930 ft. above sea level.

PENNSAUKEN, township of New Jersey, in Camden Co., adjoining Camden on the N.E., and bordered by the Delaware R., Pennsauken Creek, and the Cooper R. Included in the township are the communities of Delair, Morrisville, East Pennsauken, Jordantown, Delaware Gardens, North Pennsville, and Fish House. Manufactured products include textiles and apparel, food products, electronic equipment, glass products, mineral wool, asphalt, steel and plastic products, chemicals, and tools. Pop. (1960) 33,771; (1970) 36,394.

PENNSYLVANIA, one of the Middle Atlantic States of the United States, bounded on the N. by Lake Erie and New York; on the E. by the Delaware R.; on the S. by Maryland, West Virginia, and Delaware; and on the W. by West Virginia and Ohio. Pennsylvania is rectangular in shape, measuring about 312 mi. from E. to W. and about 158 mi. from N. to S.

Area (33rd State in rank)	45,333 sq. mi.
Land	45,045 sq. mi.
Inland water	288 sq. mi.
Population	(1970, 3rd in rank) 11,793,909
	(1960, 3rd in rank) 11,319,366
	(1950) 10,498,012
Altitude	sea level to 3213 ft.
Capital	Harrisburg (1970) 68,061
Largest city	Philadelphia (1970) 1,948,609
Entered Union (2nd of original 13)	Dec. 12, 1787
Nickname	The Keystone State
Motto	Virtue, Liberty, and Independence
Flower	mountain laurel
Bird	ruffed grouse

THE LAND

Nearly all of the physiographic features that are common to the eastern U.S. are found in Pennsylvania. The S.E. portion of the State falls within the province of the Piedmont Lowlands, which slope upward from the valley of the Delaware R. to a maximum elevation of about 500 ft. along the base of the Blue Mts. These mountains delineate the S.E. limits of the next physiographic division of the State, the Appalachian Ridge and Valley, which extends from New York to the Maryland boundary in a general N.E. and S.W. direction. This region consists of a series of parallel mountain ranges and narrow valleys. Adjoining the appalachian Valley on the W. and extending to the W. border is the Allegheny Plateau. This region contains the highest elevations in Pennsylvania, including Negro Mt., or Mt. Davis (3213 ft.), the highest summit. The area is dissected by numerous valleys and precipitous gorges. Steep slopes predominate, but gently

The Cathedral of Learning, center of academic activities at the University of Pittsburgh. Bethlehem Steel Corp.

sloping or level plateau remnants are found throughout the area. The lowest point in Pennsylvania is sea level, on the Delaware R. The mean elevation of the State is 1100 ft.

Rivers and Lakes. The Delaware R. forms the entire E. boundary with New Jersey and New York. The Schuylkill R. flows into the Delaware at Philadelphia. The Susquehanna R., in the east-central part of the State, flows generally S. into Maryland. The Juniata R., in the south-central area, flows E. into the Susquehanna. The main rivers in the W. are the Allegheny and Monongahela rivers, which meet at Pittsburgh to form the Ohio R. Pennsylvania has numerous lakes and ponds, the largest of which is Lake Wallenpaupack, in the N.E. Man-made lakes include Allegheny Reservoir on the Allegheny R., and Pymatuning and Shenango River reservoirs on the Shenango R.

Climate. Pennsylvania has a generally humid continental type of climate, but the various sections are markedly affected by topographic differences. In the S.E. coastal plain and Piedmont Plateau, summers are long and hot, and winters are comparatively mild. Annual precipitation averages from 38 to 46 in.; snowfall averages 30 in. In the ridge and valley area of the central part of the State, both the extremes and the daily range of temperatures increase, and both rainfall and snowfall are greater. The Allegheny Plateau, to the W. and N., has a continental climate, with changeable temperatures and more rain and snow, with means of 41 in. and 54 in. respectively. The relatively small Lake Erie plain enjoys the moderating effect of the lake water, having an earlier spring and a later fall; rainfall totals about 34 in. and snowfall 54 in. per year. The average annual number of days with measurable precipitation varies from 117 at Philadelphia to 135 at Scranton, 146 at Pittsburgh, and 153 at Erie. Hurricanes occur infrequently in the E., and thunderstorms throughout the State are responsible for most of the summer rainfall.

Climate	Erie	Philadelphia	Pittsburgh
Normal temperatures (in °F.)			
January maximum	34.0	40.3	40.4
January minimum	20.5	24.3	26.2
July maximum	80.1	85.9	85.4
July minimum	62.0	65.2	66.1
Annual	48.7	53.5	53.9
Normal precipitation (in inches)			
Wettest month	3.67	4.63	3.95
Driest month	2.32	2.78	2.31
Annual	37.50	42.48	36.87
Latest frost	April 20	March 30	April 16
Earliest frost	Nov. 7	Nov. 17	Nov. 3
Mean number of days between latest and earliest frosts	200	232	200

Plants and Animals. Among the principal trees of Pennsylvania are yellow poplar, spruce, white pine, birch, hemlock, hickory, black walnut, oak, elm, ash, maple, and sycamore. Flowering shrubs, including rhododendron, redbud, mountain laurel, and dogwood, grow in many parts of the State. White-tailed deer, black bear, beaver, rabbit, squirrel, raccoon, and woodchuck are found in the forested regions of Pennsylvania. The many species of songbirds include oriole, eastern meadowlark, bobolink, and cardinal; game birds such as the woodcock, wild turkey, ring-necked pheasant, bobwhite quail, Canada goose, and various ducks are found. The lakes and streams are inhabited by trout, perch, pickerel, muskellunge, catfish, bass, and other species of fish.

Parks, Forests, and Other Places of Interest. Independence National Historical Park (q.v.) in Philadelphia preserves buildings and areas associated with the American Revolution, including Independence Hall. Fort Necessity National Battlefield (q.v.), near Uniontown, commemorates the opening battle (1754) of the French and Indian War (q.v.). Gettysburg National Military Park and Gettysburg National Cemetery mark the pivotal battle of the Civil War and the site of President Abraham Lincoln's Gettysburg Ad-

PENNSYLVANIA

INDEX TO MAP OF PENNSYLVANIA

Cities and Towns

Abington	M 5	Cheltenham	M 5	Ferndale	E 5	Latrobe	D 5
Akron	K 5	Chester	L 7	Fleetwood	L 5	Laureldale	L 5
Aldan	M 7	Cheswick	C 6	Flemington	G 3	Laurel Gardens	B 6
Allquippa	B 4	Churchill	C 7	Folcroft	M 7	Lawrence Park	C 1
Allentown ⊙	L 4	Clairton	C 7	Folsom	M 7	Lebanon ⊙	K 5
Allison Park	C 4	Clarion ⊙	D 3	Ford City	D 4	Leechburg	C 4
Altoona	F 4	Clarks Summit	L 3	Forest City	L 2	Leetsdale	B 4
Ambler	M 5	Claysburg	F 5	Forest Hills	C 7	Lehighton	L 4
Ambridge	B 4	Clearfield ⊙	F 3	Forty Fort	L 3	Lemont	G 4
Andalusia	N 5	Clifton Heights	M 7	Fountain Hill	L 4	Lemoyne	J 5
Annville	J 5	Clymer	E 4	Fox Chapel	C 6	Lester	M 7
Apollo	C 4	Coaldale	L 4	Frackville	K 4	Levittown	N 5
Archbald	M 2	Coatesville	L 5	Franklin ⊙	C 3	Lewisburg ⊙	J 4
Ardmore	M 6	Collegeville	M 5	Freedom	B 4	Lewistown ⊙	G 4
Arnold	C 4	Collingdale	N 7	Freeland	L 3	Liberty	C 7
Ashland	K 4	Columbia	K 5	Freemansburg	M 4	Library	B 7
Ashley	L 3	Colwyn	N 7	Freeport	C 4	Ligonier	D 5
Aspinwall	C 6	Connellsville	C 5	Galeton	G 2	Lincoln	C 7
Athens	K 2	Conshohocken	M 5	Gallitzin	E 4	Lincoln University	L 6
Avalon	B 6	Conway	B 4	Garden View	H 3	Linglestown	J 5
Avoca	L 3	Conyngham	K 3	Geistown	E 5	Linntown	J 4
Baden	B 4	Coopersburg	M 5	Gettysburg ⊙	H 6	Linwood	L 7
Bala-Cynwyd	N 6	Coplay	L 4	Girard	B 2	Lititz	K 5
Baldwin	B 7	Coraopolis	B 4	Girardville	K 4	Littlestown	H 6
Bangor	M 4	Cornwall	K 5	Glassport	C 7	Lock Haven ⊙	H 3
Barnesboro	E 4	Corry	C 2	Glen Lyon	K 3	Loretto	E 4
Beaver ⊙	B 4	Coudersport ⊙	G 2	Glenolden	M 7	Lower Burrell	C 4
Beaver Falls	B 4	Crafton	B 7	Glen Rock	J 6	Loyalhanna	D 5
Bedford ⊙	F 5	Cresson	E 5	Glenshaw	C 6	Luzerne	L 3
Bellefonte ⊙	G 4	Cressona	K 4	Glenside	M 5	Lykens	J 4
Bellevue	B 6	Crum Lynne	M 7	Grapeville	C 5	Lyndora	B 4
Bellwood	F 4	Cuddy	B 5	Greencastle	G 6	Mahanoy City	K 4
Ben Avon	B 6	Curwensville	E 4	Greensburg ⊙	D 5	Malvern	L 5
Bentleyville	B 5	Dale	E 5	Greentree	B 7	Manchester	J 5
Berwick	K 3	Dallas	K 3	Greenville	B 3	Manheim	K 5
Berwyn	L 5	Dallastown	J 6	Grove City	B 3	Manor	C 5
Bethel Park	B 7	Danville ⊙	J 4	Hamburg	L 4	Mansfield	H 2
Bethlehem	M 4	Darby	M 7	Hanover	J 6	Marcus Hook	L 7
Birdsboro	L 5	Delmont	D 5	Harmarville	C 6	Marietta	J 5
Blairsville	D 5	Denver	K 5	Harrisburg (cap.) ⊙	H 5	Martinsburg	F 5
Blakely	L 2	Derry	D 5	Harveys Lake	K 3	Marysville	H 5
Bloomfield (New Bloomfield) ⊙	H 5	Dickson City	L 3	Hastings	E 4	Masontown	C 6
Bloomsburg ⊙	J 3	Donora	C 5	Hatboro	M 5	Matamoras	N 3
Blossburg	H 2	Dormont	B 7	Hatfield	M 5	Mauch Chunk (Jim Thorpe) ⊙	L 4
Boiling Springs	H 5	Downingtown	L 5	Haverford	M 6	Mayfield	L 2
Boothwyn	L 7	Doylestown ⊙	M 5	Havertown	M 6	McAdoo	L 4
Boston	C 7	Dravosburg	C 7	Hazleton	L 4	McConnellsburg ⊙	F 6
Boswell	E 5	Drexel Hill	M 6	Heidelberg	B 7	McDonald	B 5
Boyertown	L 5	DuBois	E 3	Hellam	J 6	McKeesport	C 7
Brackenridge	C 4	Dunbar	C 6	Hellertown	M 4	McKees Rocks	B 7
Braddock	C 7	Duncannon	H 5	Hershey	J 5	McSherrystown	H 6
Bradford	E 2	Duncansville	F 5	Highland Park	H 4	Meadow Lands	B 5
Brentwood	B 7	Dunmore	L 3	High Spire	J 5	Meadville ⊙	B 2
Bridgeport	M 5	Duquesne	C 7	Hollidaysburg ⊙	F 5	Mechanicsburg	H 5
Bridgeville	B 5	Duryea	L 3	Homer City	D 4	Media ⊙	L 7
Bristol (borough)	N 5	East Berwick	K 3	Homestead	B 7	Mercer ⊙	B 3
Bristol (urban township)	N 5	East Conemaugh	E 5	Honesdale ⊙	M 2	Mercersburg	G 6
Brockway	E 3	East Faxon	J 3	Hopwood	C 6	Merion Station	M 6
Brookhaven	M 7	East Greenville	L 5	Houston	B 5	Meyersdale	E 6
Brookville ⊙	D 3	East Lansdowne	M 7	Hughesville	J 3	Middleburg ⊙	H 4
Broomall	M 6	Easton ⊙	M 4	Hummelstown	J 5	Middletown	J 5
Broughton	B 7	East Petersburg	K 5	Huntingdon ⊙	G 5	Midland	A 4
Brownsville	C 5	East Stroudsburg	M 4	Imperial	B 5	Mifflinburg	H 4
Bryn Mawr	M 5	East Washington	B 5	Indiana ⊙	D 4	Mifflintown ⊙	H 4
Burgettstown	A 5	Ebensburg ⊙	E 5	Industry	B 4	Milford ⊙	N 3
Burnham	H 4	Economy	B 4	Ingram	B 7	Millersburg	J 4
Butler ⊙	C 4	Eddington	N 5	Irwin	C 5	Millersville	K 6
California	C 5	Eddystone	M 7	Jeannette	C 5	Mill Hall	G 3
Cambridge Springs	C 2	Edgewood	B 7	Jefferson	M 5	Millvale	B 7
Camp Hill	H 5	Edgeworth	B 4	Jenkintown	M 5	Milmont Park	M 7
Canonsburg	B 5	Edinboro	B 2	Jermyn	L 2	Milroy	G 4
Canton	J 2	Elizabeth	C 5	Jersey Shore	H 3	Milton	J 3
Carbondale	L 2	Elizabethtown	J 5	Jim Thorpe ⊙	L 4	Minersville	K 4
Carlisle ⊙	H 5	Elizabethville	J 4	Johnsonburg	E 3	Mohnton	L 5
Carnegie	B 7	Elkland	H 1	Johnstown	D 5	Monaca	B 4
Carrolltown	E 4	Ellwood City	B 4	Kane	E 2	Monessen	C 5
Castle Shannon	B 7	Emmaus	M 4	Kearsarge	B 1	Monongahela	B 5
Catasauqua	M 4	Emporium ⊙	F 2	Kenhorst	L 5	Monroeville	C 7
Catawissa	K 4	Emsworth	B 6	Kennett Square	L 6	Mont Alto	G 6
Cecil	B 5	Enola	J 5	Kingston	K 3	Montgomery	H 3
Centerville	B 6	Ephrata	K 5	Kittanning ⊙	D 4	Montoursville	J 3
Central City	E 5	Erie ⊙	B 1	Kulpmont	J 4	Montrose ⊙	L 2
Chalfont	M 5	Espy	J 3	Kutztown	L 5	Moosic	L 3
Chambersburg ⊙	G 6	Essington	M 7	Lake City	B 1	Morrisville	N 5
Charleroi	C 5	Etna	B 6	Lancaster ⊙	K 5	Morton	M 7
Chatwood	L 6	Evans City	B 4	Landisville	K 5	Mount Carmel	K 4
		Everett	F 5	Langhorne	N 5	Mount Holly Springs	H 5
		Fairchance	C 6	Lansdale	M 5	Mount Joy	K 5
		Fairless Hills	N 5	Lansdowne	M 7	Mount Lebanon	B 7
		Fairview	B 1	Lansford	L 4	Mount Oliver	B 7
		Farrell	A 3	Laporte ⊙	K 3		
		Fayetteville	G 6	Larimer	C 5		

⊙ County seat.

Continued on page 394

PENNSYLVANIA

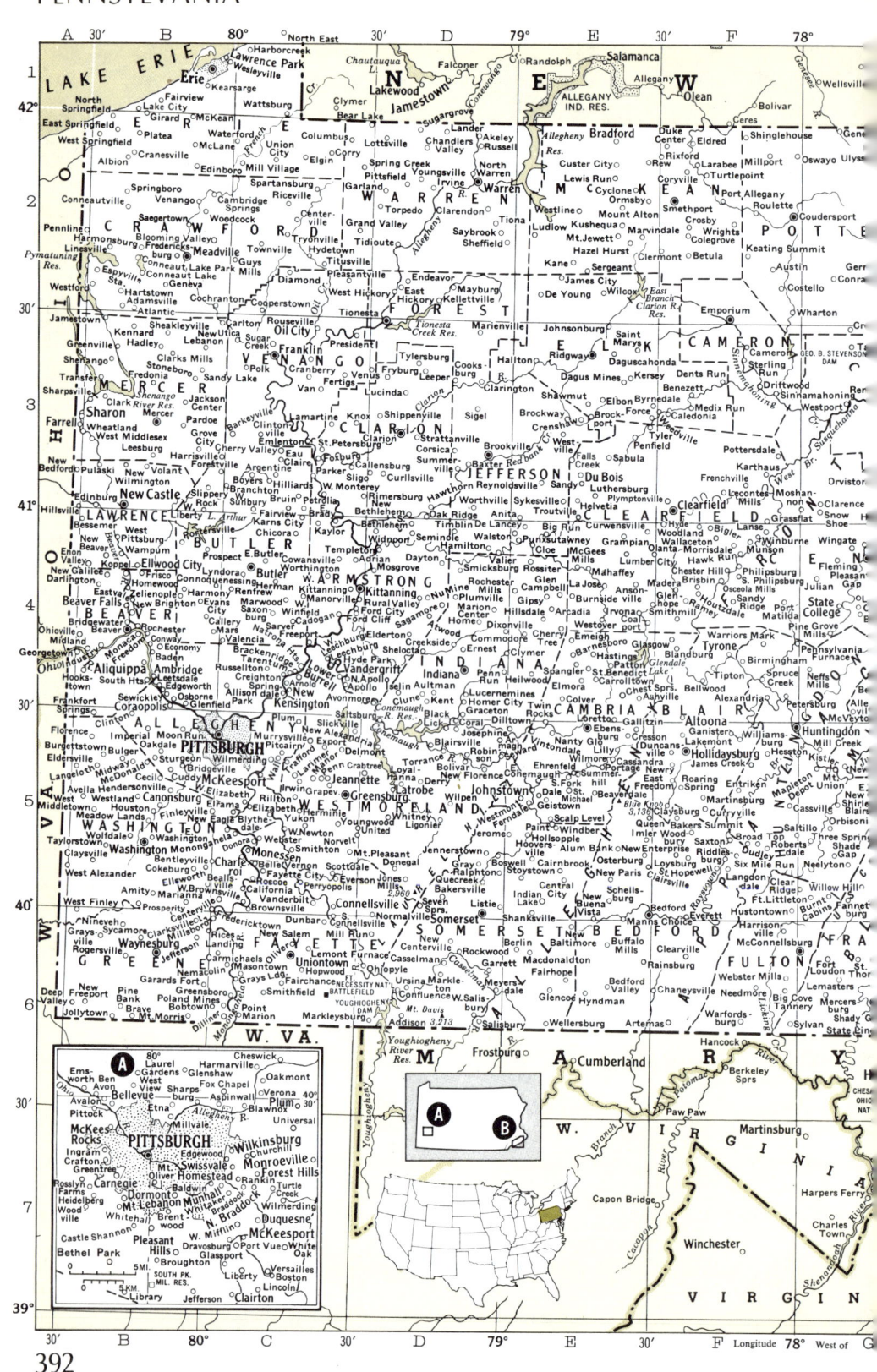

PENNSYLVANIA

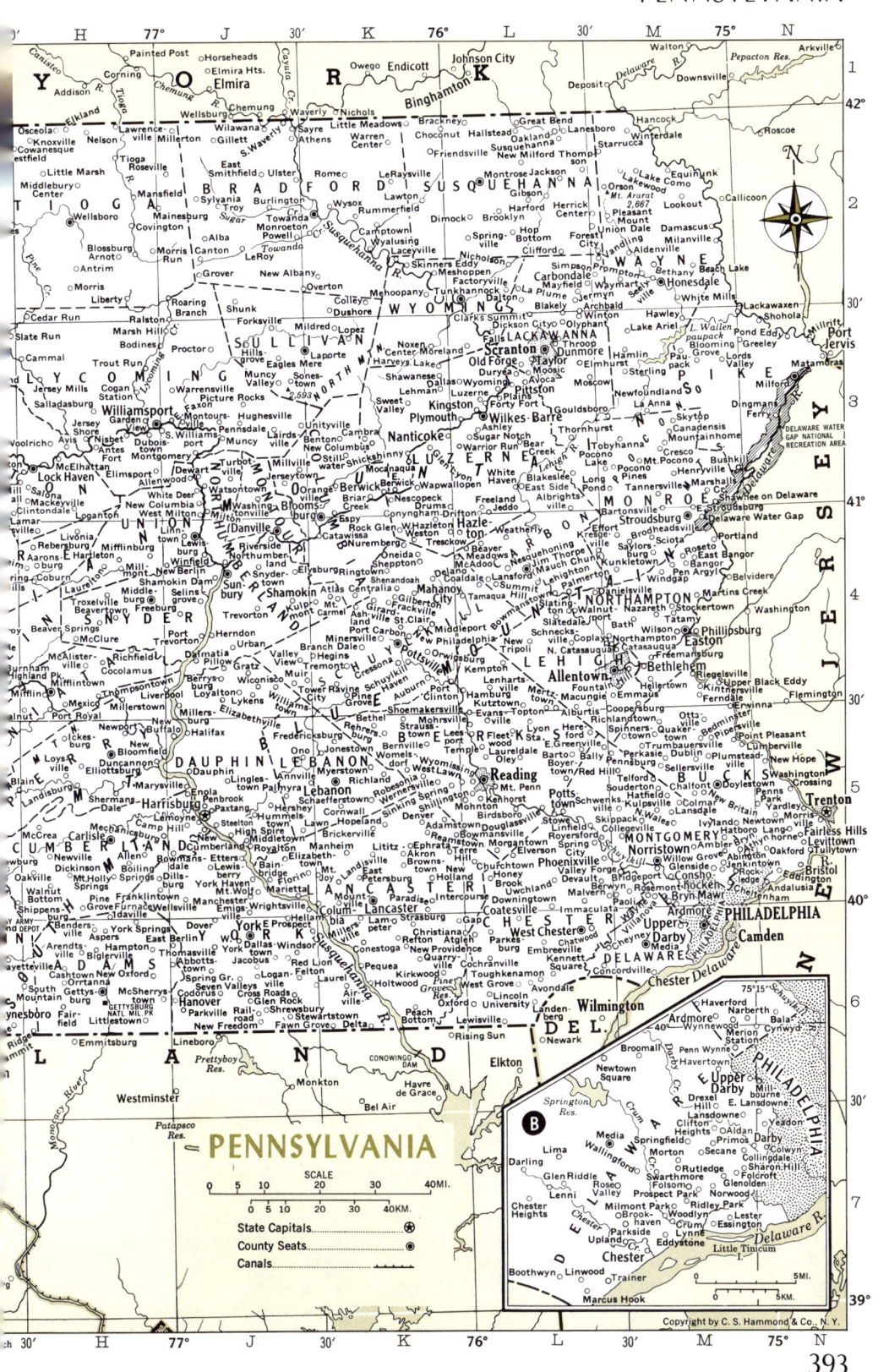

PENNSYLVANIA

Index to Map of Pennsylvania — Continued from page 391

Mount Penn ....L 5	Point Marion ....C 6	Sugarcreek ....C 3	Wilmerding ....C 7
Mount Pleasant ......D 5	Polk ....C 3	Sugar Notch ....L 3	Wilson ....M 4
Mount Pocono ....M 3	Portage ....E 5	Summit Hill ....L 4	Windber ....E 5
Mount Union ....G 5	Port Allegany ....F 2	Sunbury ⊙ ....J 4	Windgap ....M 4
Mount Wolf ....J 5	Port Carbon ....K 4	Susquehanna ....L 2	Winton ....M 3
Muncy ....J 3	Port Vue ....C 7	Swarthmore ....M 7	Wolfdale ....B 5
Munhall ....C 7	Pottstown ....L 5	Swissvale ....C 7	Womelsdorf ....K 5
Murrysville ....C 5	Pottsville ⊙ ....K 4	Sykesville ....E 3	Woodlyn ....M 7
Myerstown ....K 5	Primos ....M 7	Tamaqua ....L 4	Wrightsville ....J 5
Nanticoke ....K 3	Prospect Park ....M 7	Tarentum ....C 4	Wynnewood ....M 6
Nanty Glo ....E 5	Punxsutawney ......E 4	Taylor ....L 3	Wyoming ....L 3
Narberth ....M 6	Quakertown ....M 5	Telford ....M 5	Wyomissing ....K 5
Natrona Heights ....C 4	Quarryville ....K 6	Temple ....L 5	Yardley ....N 5
Nazareth ....M 4	Rankin ....C 7	Throop ....L 3	Yeadon ....N 7
Nescopeck ....K 3	Reading ⊙ ....L 5	Tionesta ⊙ ....C 2	Yeagertown ....G 4
Nesquehoning ......L 4	Red Lion ....J 6	Titusville ....C 2	York ⊙ ....J 6
New Bloomfield ⊙ ..H 5	Renovo ....G 3	Topton ....L 5	Youngsville ....D 2
New Brighton ......B 4	Reynoldsville ....D 3	Toughkenamon ......L 6	Youngwood ....D 5
New Britain ....M 5	Ridgway ....E 3	Towanda ⊙ ....J 2	Zelienople ....B 4
New Castle ⊙ .....B 3	Ridley Park ....M 7	Tower City ....J 4	
New Cumberland ...J 5	Riverside ....J 4	Trafford ....C 5	**Physical Features**
New Eagle ....B 5	Roaring Spring ......F 5	Trainer ....L 7	Allegheny (res.) .....E 2
New Holland ....K 5	Robesonia ....K 5	Tremont ....K 4	Allegheny (riv.) .....D 2
New Kensington ....C 4	Rochester ....B 4	Trevorton ....J 4	Appalachian (mts.) ..H 4
New Philadelphia ...K 4	Rockledge ....M 5	Troy ....J 2	Ararat (mt.) ....M 2
Newport ....H 5	Rosemont ....M 5	Tullytown ....N 5	Arthur (lake) ....B 4
New Salem (Delmont) .D 5	Roseto ....M 4	Tunkhannock ⊙ ....L 2	Beaver (riv.) ....B 4
Newtown ....N 5	Rouzerville ....G 6	Turtle Creek ....C 7	Blue (mt.) ....G 5
Newtown Square ...L 6	Royersford ....L 5	Tyrone ....F 4	Casselman (riv.) ....D 6
Newville ....H 5	Russellton ....C 4	Union City ....C 2	Clarion (riv.) ....D 3
New Wilmington ...B 3	Saegertown ....B 2	Uniontown ⊙ ....C 6	Conemaugh (riv.) ...D 5
Norristown ⊙ ......M 5	Saint Clair ....K 4	Universal ....C 7	Conewango (creek) ..D 1
Northampton ....M 4	Saint Marys ....E 3	Upland ....L 7	Crum (creek) ....M 7
North Apollo ....D 4	Sandy ....E 3	Upper Darby ....M 6	Darby (creek) ....M 6
North Braddock ....C 7	Sayre ....K 2	Valley Forge ....L 5	Davis (mt.) ....D 6
North Catasauqua ..L 4	Scalp Level ....E 5	Valley View ....J 4	Delaware (riv.) ......N 3
North East ....C 1	Schnecksville ....L 4	Vandergrift ....D 4	Delaware Water Gap Nat'l
Northumberland ....J 4	Schuylkill Haven ....K 4	Verona ....C 6	Recreation Area ..N 3
North Wales ....M 5	Scottdale ....C 5	Versailles ....C 7	Erie (lake) ....B 1
Norvelt ....C 5	Scranton ⊙ ....L 3	Villanova ....M 6	Fort Necessity Nat'l
Norwood ....M 7	Secane ....M 7	Wall ....C 5	Battlefield ....C 6
Oakdale ....B 5	Selinsgrove ....J 4	Wallingford ....L 7	French (creek) ......C 2
Oakford ....N 5	Sellersville ....M 5	Walnutport ....L 4	Gettysburg Nat'l Mil.
Oak Lane ....M 5	Sewickley ....B 4	Warren ⊙ ....D 2	Park ....H 6
Oakmont ....C 6	Shamokin ....J 4	Washington ⊙ ......B 5	Glendale (lake) .....F 4
Ohioville ....B 4	Shamokin Dam ....J 4	Waterford ....B 2	Juniata (riv.) ....G 5
Oil City ....C 3	Sharon ....B 3	Watsontown ....J 3	Laurel Hill (mt.) ....D 5
Old Forge ....L 3	Sharon Hill ....N 7	Wayne ....M 6	Lehigh (riv.) ....L 3
Oliver ....C 6	Sharpsburg ....B 6	Waynesboro ....G 6	Letterkenny Army
Olyphant ....L 3	Sharpsville ....A 3	Waynesburg ⊙ .....B 6	Depot ....G 6
Orwigsburg ....K 4	Sheffield ....D 2	Weatherly ....L 4	Licking (creek) ......F 6
Osceola Mills ......F 4	Shenandoah ....K 4	Wellsboro ⊙ ....H 2	Little Tinicum (isl.) .M 7
Oxford ....K 6	Shickshinny ....K 3	Wernersville ....K 5	Lycoming (creek) ...H 3
Palmerton ....L 4	Shillington ....K 5	Wesleyville ....C 1	Monongahela (riv.) ..C 6
Palmyra ....J 5	Shinglehouse ....F 2	West Brownsville ...C 5	North (mt.) ....K 3
Paoli ....M 5	Shippensburg ....H 5	West Chester ⊙ ....L 6	Ohio (riv.) ....A 4
Parkesburg ....L 6	Shoemakersville ....K 4	Westfield ....H 2	Oil (creek) ....C 2
Parkside ....M 7	Shrewsbury ....J 6	West Grove ....L 6	Pine (creek) ....H 2
Parkville ....J 6	Simpson ....L 2	West Hazleton .....K 4	Pine Grove (res.) ...K 6
Patton ....E 4	Sinking Spring ......K 5	West Lawn ....K 5	Pocono (mts.) ......M 3
Paxtang ....J 5	Slatington ....L 4	West Leechburg ....C 4	Pymatuning (res.) ...A 2
Pen Argyl ....M 4	Slippery Rock ......B 3	West Middlesex ....B 3	Redbank (creek) ....E 3
Penbrook ....J 5	Smethport ⊙ ....F 2	West Mifflin ....C 7	Schuylkill (riv.) .....M 5
Pennsburg ....M 5	Somerset ⊙ ....D 6	Westmont ....D 5	Shenango River (res.) .B 3
Penn Wynne ....M 6	Souderton ....M 5	West Newton ....C 5	Sinnemahoning
Perkasie ....M 5	South Connellsville ..C 6	West View ....B 6	(creek) ....F 3
Perryopolis ....C 6	South Fork ....E 5	West York ....J 6	South (mt.) ....H 6
Philadelphia ⊙ .....N 6	South Waverly ......J 2	Wheatland ....B 3	South Park Military
Philipsburg ....F 4	South Williamsport ..J 3	Whitaker ....C 7	Res. ....B 7
Phoenixville ....L 5	Spangler ....E 4	Whitehall ....B 7	Springton (res.) .....L 6
Pine Grove ....K 4	Spring City ....L 5	White Haven ....L 3	Sugar (creek) ....J 2
Pitcairn ....C 7	Springdale ....C 4	White Oak ....C 7	Susquehanna (riv.) ..K 6
Pittsburgh ⊙ ....B 7	Springfield ....M 7	Wiconisco ....J 4	Tioga (riv.) ....H 1
Pittston ....L 3	Spring Grove ....J 6	Wilkes-Barre ⊙ .....L 3	Tionesta Creek (res.) .D 3
Plains ....L 3	State College ....G 4	Wilkinsburg ....C 7	Towanda (creek) ....J 2
Pleasant Gap ....G 4	Steelton ....J 5	Williamsburg ....F 5	Tuscarora (mt.) .....G 5
Pleasant Hills ......B 7	Stowe ....L 5	Williamsport ⊙ .....H 3	Wallenpaupack (lake) .M 3
Plum ....C 5	Strasburg ....K 6	Williamstown ....J 4	Youghiogheny River
Plymouth ....K 3	Stroudsburg ⊙ .....M 4	Willow Grove ......M 5	(res.) ....D 6

dress; see GETTYSBURG, BATTLE OF. The Gloria Dei National Historic Site, or Old Swedes' Church, in Philadelphia, is the second-oldest Swedish church in the U.S.; the present structure was built about 1700. Hopewell Village National Historic Site (q.v.), in French Creek State Park, near Reading, is an excellent example of an 18th-century iron-making village. Allegheny Portage Railroad National Historic Site, near Johnstown, commemorating the 36-mi. inclined-plane railroad that lifted cargoes of canalboats over the Allegheny Mts., was authorized in 1964. The Johnstown Flood National Memorial, established in 1964, memorializes the flood (1889)

Views of rural Pennsylvania. Above: A farm near Bedford. Right: Children in the family buggy wait outside a country store in the Amish country of Pennsylvania.

Standard Oil Co. (N.J.)

PENNSYLVANIA

caused by the failure of the South Fork Dam on the Conemaugh R. A scenic area along the Delaware R. (partly in Delaware) was authorized in 1965 as the Delaware Gap National Recreation Area. The one national forest in Pennsylvania is Allegheny National Forest, near Bradford; its 470,000 acres contain rivers, lakes, and virgin timber stands in plateau country. Pennsylvania maintains more than 125 State parks. Among the outstanding components of the system are Valley Forge State Park, near Norristown; Lawrence State Park, in Erie; Caledonia State Park, near Gettysburg; Cook Forest State Park on the Clarion R.; French Creek State Park, near Reading; and Raccoon Creek State Park, near Pittsburgh. The Hawk Mt. Bird Sanctuary, near Hamburg, is a refuge for birds of prey.

Sports. The numerous rivers, limestone streams, and lakes of Pennsylvania offer excellent fishing. Among the species found are black bass, muskellunge, walleye and northern pike, bluegill, eastern chain pickerel, four varieties of trout, and a run of shad on the Delaware R. in the spring. Game animals and birds hunted are white-tailed deer, black bear, snowshoe hare, cottontail rabbit, gray and fox squirrels, wild turkey, bobwhite quail, ring-necked pheasant, and ruffed grouse. More than a dozen ski areas operate in Pennsylvania between December and April. They include Big Boulder, near Split Rock; Laurel Mt., at Ligonier; Hidden Valley, near Somerset; and Seven Springs, at Donegal.

THE PEOPLE

According to the 1970 decennial census, the population of Pennsylvania was 11,793,909, an increase of 4.2 percent over the 1960 population. The urban segment comprised 8,430,410 persons, 71.5 percent of the total, compared with 71.6 percent in 1960. The rural segment comprised 3,363,499 persons, 28.5 percent of the total, compared with 28.4 percent in 1960. Ethnically, the 1970 population was distributed as follows: white persons, 10,737,732, nonwhites, 1,056,177, including 1,016,514 Negroes, 7053 Chinese, 5461 Japanese, 5533 Indians, 4560 Filipinos, and others. The percentage of native-born residents in 1960 was 94.7; of foreign-born, 5.3. The major countries of origin of the foreign-born, in order of rank, were Poland, Germany, and Great Britain. The 1970 population density averaged 262.3 per sq.mi., compared with 251.4 in 1960.

The chief cities are Harrisburg, the capital and eighth-largest city, a governmental, service, and manufacturing center; and, in order of population, Philadelphia, a transportation, shipping, manufacturing, and educational center, noted for its role in U.S. history; Pittsburg, a major steel and iron and river shipping center; Erie, a port on Lake Erie and a manufacturing and commercial center; Allentown, a commercial and industrial center in a farming region; Scranton, center of diversified industries; Reading, a trading and manufacturing center; and Bethlehem, a manufacturing, educational, and musical center.

Education. The public-school system of Pennsylvania was established in 1790. Education is free and compulsory for all children between the ages of eight and seventeen.

ELEMENTARY AND SECONDARY SCHOOLS. In the mid-1960's public elementary schools numbered about 3700 and public secondary schools, about 1050. Enrollment was about 1,227,000 in elementary and about 894,000 in secondary schools. Teachers in the public-school system numbered about 46,025 in elementary and about 49,550 in secondary schools. In the mid-1960's private institutions included about 1300 elementary schools with some 541,700 students, and about 325 secondary schools with some 128,700 students. Teachers in private institutions numbered about 20,175.

UNIVERSITIES AND COLLEGES. In the mid-1960's Pennsylvania had 137 institutions of higher education, 117 of which were private. University and college enrollment was about 273,800. Public institutions include Indiana University of Pennsylvania, Community College of Philadelphia, and thirteen State colleges. A number of publicly supported community colleges have developed in recent years. The University of Pennsylvania, Pennsylvania State University, the University of Pittsburgh (qq.v.), and Temple University receive both public and private support. Private institutions include Bryn Mawr College, Carnegie–Mellon University, Dickinson College, Drexel Institute of Technology, Franklin and Marshall College, Lafayette College, Lehigh University, Swarthmore College, Allegheny College, Beaver College, Bucknell University, Cedar Crest College, Duquesne University, Gannon College, Gettysburg College, Haverford College, Juniata College, Lincoln University, Lycoming College, Marywood College, Muhlenberg College, Saint Joseph's College, Susquehanna University, Ursinus College, Villanova University, and Washington and Jefferson College. For dates of establishment see separate articles on many colleges mentioned in this article.

LIBRARIES AND MUSEUMS. Pennsylvania has some 350 libraries, of which the largest are the Free Library of Philadelphia, with more than 2,000,000 volumes, including many special collections; the Carnegie Library of Pittsburgh, with about 1,750,000 volumes; and the Pennsylvania State

Coal barges on the Ohio River near Pittsburgh.
Standard Oil Co. (N.J.)

University Library, with more than 1,000,000 volumes. Special libraries include the Pennsylvania State Library, in Harrisburg, with 500,000 volumes, and, in Philadelphia, the Historical Society of Pennsylvania, with 500,000 volumes and more than 4,000,000 manuscripts, and the American Philosophical Society Library, with 125,000 volumes and 500,000 manuscripts.

Among cultural institutions in Philadelphia are the Fels Planetarium; the Philadelphia Museum of Art; the Pennsylvania Academy of Fine Arts, oldest museum in the nation, founded in 1805; and the Academy of Natural Sciences of Philadelphia. The Carnegie Museum and Art Gallery and the Buhl Planetarium and Institute of Popular Science are both in Pittsburgh. The Barnes Collection Foundation, in Montgomery County, has a collection of 1000 art masterpieces of several centuries.

THE ECONOMY

Pennsylvania has a highly diversified economy. Manufacturing is the most important source of employment, representing about 36 percent of a total of 4,130,000 employed workers. This is followed by employment in service functions, 27 percent; wholesale and retail trade, 16 percent; transportation and communication, 6 percent; and construction, 6 percent. The primary activities of agriculture, mining, and forestry are declining as sources of employment; agriculture now employs about 2 percent and mining a little over 1 percent of employed persons.

The economy of Pennsylvania is experiencing a period of dynamic change, which is primarily a response to the evolution from activities based on primary functions to those of a secondary and tertiary nature. Pennsylvania was richly endowed with natural resources, and the State economy of the 18th and 19th centuries was based on the development of primary wealth in soils, minerals, and timber. In the 20th century the primary activities of mining, agriculture, and lumbering have declined greatly as sources of employment. As late as 1930 the landscape of Pennsylvania was characterized by dispersed rural farmsteads, small service centers, and fairly compact cities fringed with limited suburban growth. By the 1960's the metropolitan areas were dominant, with great suburban concentrations, and the small service centers had greatly declined. With the development of a highly complex industrial society in Pennsylvania, economic activities are increasingly concentrated into a few major regions.

According to the latest available statistics, Pennsylvania has some 434,000 kw of developed hydroelectric power; an estimated 3,300,000 kw of undeveloped waterpower remains for future development. Total production of electrical power is more than 55,000,000,000 kw.

Manufacturing. Manufacturing is concentrated in the s.e. and s.w. sections of Pennsylvania. Although the s.e. lacks most raw materials and important energy sources, highly diversified

397

In an open-hearth steel mill, workmen skim slag from the tops of ingot molds. Jones & Laughlin Steel Corp.

manufacturing has developed, based on the large local and regional market, a large and highly skilled labor supply, available capital, long traditions of manufacturing, and a well-developed transportation network. The s.w. region is noted for its heavy iron and steel industry, attracted by large coal reserves.

According to the most recent Census of Manufactures (1968), production workers totaled 1,137,000 the largest groups being employed in primary-metals industries and the manufacture of apparel, electrical equipment, and machinery other than electrical. About 40 percent were employed in the Standard Metropolitan Statistical Area (q.v.) of Philadelphia, and half of these worked in the city itself. Other important manufacturing centers were the S.M.S.A.'s of Pittsburgh and Allentown-Bethlehem-Easton. The value added by manufacture (*see* VALUE) in the largest industries totaled $3,579,800,000 for primary metals, $2,049,500,000 for electrical equipment, $1,942,200,000 for machinery other than electrical, and $1,640,700,000 for food and kindred products. Apparel manufacture, although ranking second in employment, ranked eighth in value added at $1,062,500,000. According to the most recent published figures, the value added by all manufacturing in Pennsylvania in 1968 was $20,509,000,000.

Agriculture. Pennsylvania has highly diversified agriculture. Principal commodities include dairy products, cattle, eggs, and corn. Among major crops, besides corn, are apples, hay, tobacco, wheat, and oats. In the late 1960's, the State ranked fourth in production of eggs. Farms numbered about 73,000 in 1970, totaling some 10,585,000 acres and averaging 145 acres each. Cash income from crops, livestock, and government payments in 1970 was $1,044,000,000.

Mining and Minerals. The mineral resources of Pennsylvania include coal, cement, stone, clays, iron ore, petroleum, and natural gas. In 1968, according to the latest available statistics, mineral production was valued at $904,000,000 annually, representing more than 4.4 percent of the U.S. total. Pennsylvania ranked first in production of stone, anthracite, cobalt, and coke; second in bituminous coal, lime, cement, and pyrites; and third in peat and tripoli. Mineral production was reported in all counties, the leaders being Northampton, Luzerne, and Cambria counties. Clay was produced in thirty-two counties, notably Lawrence, Clearfield, and Armstrong. Northampton led the eight cement-producing counties; and leading stone-producing counties were Northampton, Montgomery, Adams, Lawrence, Bucks, and York counties. Major producers of anthracite coal were Luzerne, Schuylkill, Northumberland, and Lackawanna counties; and of bituminous coal, Washington, Greene, Cambria, and Clearfield counties. The proved reserves of crude oil in 1970 were 54,740,000 bbl., and indicated additional reserves were 32,770,000 bbl.

Forestry. The forest land of Pennsylvania consists predominantly of hardwoods. The forest land, primarily under private ownership, comprises some 15,200,000 acres. It produces a net annual cut of sawtimber of some 573,000,000 bd.ft.

Transportation. The first railroads in Pennsylvania were coal tramways, such as Thomas Lieper's Tramway (1809), later abandoned. The first steam railroad was the Delaware & Hudson Canal Co., inaugurated in October, 1829, now the Delaware & Hudson Railroad. The State is served by ten Class 1 railroads, including the Penn-Central Co. and the Reading Co., with a total of about 8900 mi. of track. Rural and municipal roads totaled 112,858 mi. in 1967. Highways of the Federally aided Interstate Highway System totaled 1581 mi. in 1968; Federally aided primary and secondary roads totaled 22,105 mi. Airports numbered about 465 in the mid-1960's, and eleven airlines provided trunk and local service in 1967. The commercially navigable waterways are the Allegheny and Monongahela rivers, which join to form the Ohio R.; and, in the E., the Delaware and Schuylkill rivers.

Communications. The first newspaper in Pennsylvania was the *American Weekly Mer-*

cury, founded in Philadelphia in 1719. An important early paper was the *Pennsylvania Gazette,* founded in 1728, also in Philadelphia, and purchased in 1729 by Benjamin Franklin. The State in 1967 had 113 daily newspapers, 12 Sunday papers, 254 weeklies, and 5 Negro papers, 1 daily and 4 weekly. One of the last-named, the Pittsburgh *Courier,* is said to be the largest Negro publication in the world. Among the leading papers were the Philadelphia *Bulletin, Inquirer,* and *News,* and the Pittsburgh *Press* and *Post-Gazette.* Of some 165 am and 110 FM (12 educational) radio stations, among the earliest were KQV (1919) and KDKA (1920), both in Pittsburgh. Television stations numbered thirty-four, of which four were devoted to educational programming.

GOVERNMENT

Pennsylvania is governed under the constitution of 1873, as amended. Executive authority is vested in a governor, a lieutenant goveror, an auditor general, and a treasurer, all elected for four-year terms. Directly under the control of the governor are departments, boards, and commissions. Legislative authority is exercised by the Senate, with 50 members elected for four-year terms; and the House of Representatives, with 203 members elected for two-year terms. The legislature meets annually. The judicial system includes a seven-member supreme court, a superior court, common pleas courts, and various lesser and special courts. The State is divided into sixty-seven counties.

Pennsylvania is represented in the United States Congress by two Senators and twenty-seven Representatives.

Voting Qualifications. Suffrage is extended generally to U.S. citizens eighteen years of age who have resided one year in the State and sixty days in the election district.

HISTORY

Ownership of the region comprising present-day Pennsylvania was claimed by the Dutch, Swedes, and English during the early 17th century. Beginning in 1614 the Dutch, who based their claims to the territory on the exploratory voyage (1609) of the English navigator Henry Hudson (q.v.), established trading posts along the Delaware R. In 1643 a party of Swedes founded the first permanent settlement within the territory, which was named New Sweden. The settlement, called New Gottenburg, was situated on Tinicum Island, near the site of modern Chester. Another settlement, called Upland, was shortly founded on the last-named site by the Swedes. These settlements and similar Swedish activities in what is now Delaware (q.v.) aroused profound hostility among the Dutch. In 1655 Peter Stuyvesant, (q.v.), governor of New Netherland, led an expedition against the Swedes and imposed Dutch control over New Sweden. Dutch authority was in turn terminated when, in 1664, an English expedition seized New Netherland, known thereafter as New York. The settlements along the Delaware R. remained under the jurisdiction of New York for nearly two decades.

English Settlement. In 1681, William Penn (q.v.), a prominent English Quaker (*see* FRIENDS, SOCIETY OF), obtained from Charles II (q.v.), King

The Liberty Bell, in Independence Hall, Philadelphia.
Philadelphia Convention & Visitors Bureau

of England, a grant of the territory west of the Delaware between the 40th and 43rd parallels of N. latitude, including a portion of Delaware (q.v.). Penn named the territory Pennsylvania (Penn's Woods) in honor of his father, and appointed his kinsman William Markham (1635?–1704) deputy governor. Markham proceeded to Pennsylvania and selected the site of Philadelphia (City of Brotherly Love). Penn arrived at Upland, which he subsequently renamed Chester, on Oct. 27, 1682. A few days later he concluded peace treaties with the Indians. In December, 1682, he submitted a plan of government to the first general assembly. The assembly approved the plan, which contained provisions ensuring universal suffrage and religious tolerance. During the next two years more than 3000 colonists, chiefly Quakers and Ger-

A stone post marks a point on the Mason and Dixon Line, south of Greencastle, Pa., the southern boundary line of Pennsylvania.
Standard Oil Co. (N.J.)

mans from the Palatinate, settled in Pennsylvania. Penn returned to England in 1684, and during his absence the colony was torn by political and religious strife. In 1692 William III (q.v.), King of England, assumed control of the colony, placing it under the jurisdiction of New York. Pennsylvania was returned to Penn's proprietorship in the following year. In 1696 Penn authorized a more liberal constitution, and in 1701, during his final visit to the colony, he granted a charter of privileges that further liberalized the government.

The population of Pennsylvania increased steadily during the early decades of the 18th century. Large numbers of Scotch-Irish settlers and Germans arrived in the colony during this period. As the newcomers pushed westward, the Indians became increasingly restless; see FRENCH AND INDIAN WAR. Hostilities with the Indians continued until after 1764. Meanwhile, in 1753, Connecticut (q.v.) laid claim to a tract of land along the Susquehanna R. Settlers from Connecticut occupied the tract, precipitating a dispute that culminated in serious bloodshed (see WYOMING VALLEY). Throughout most of the 18th century Pennsylvania was involved in boundary disputes with neighboring colonies, including Maryland, Delaware, and New York.

Pennsylvania figured significantly in the events leading to the American Revolution (q.v.). In 1766 Benjamin Franklin (q.v.), then the agent of the colony in Great Britain, vigorously opposed the Stamp Act (q.v.) before the House of Commons. In July, 1774, a provincial congress convened at Philadelphia and elected delegates to the first Continental Congress (q.v.). This body met in Philadelphia in the following September. After the Declaration of Independence, proprietary government was terminated in Pennsylvania. A provincial convention approved a State constitution on Sept. 28, 1776. The State made major contributions to the war effort against Great Britain, and eastern Pennsylvania was the scene of a number of decisive engagements; see BRANDYWINE, BATTLE OF THE; GERMANTOWN, BATTLE OF.

Statehood. A new State constitution was adopted in 1790. In 1794 the farmers of western Pennsylvania, climaxing a protest movement against Federal excise taxes on grain spirits, engaged in riotous demonstrations against the government. The disturbances, known in history as the Whiskey Rebellion (q.v.), were quickly quelled. Numerous internal improvements, including the construction of canals and railways, greatly stimulated industrial and agricultural progress in the State during the first half of the 19th century.

The people of Pennsylvania were overwhelmingly antislavery in sentiment during the controversy that led to the American Civil War. After President Abraham Lincoln (q.v.) called for troops on April 15, 1861, soldiers from Pennsylvania were the first to arrive in Washington. The State furnished twenty-five regiments for the Union armies before the end of the month. Confederate forces invaded Pennsylvania on several occasions during the war. The last of these invasions ended in a disastrous Confederate defeat at Gettysburg. See CIVIL WAR, THE AMERICAN; GETTYSBURG, BATTLE OF.

The period following the war was marked by tremendous industrial expansion in Pennsylvania, particularly in the coal, steel, and oil industries. Recurring industrial strife, with widespread strikes, violent disorders, and martial law, was one of the outstanding features of the period.

Politics. In national politics a majority of the voters of Pennsylvania have voted for the Presidental candidates of the Republican Party in every election from 1860 through 1908. Theo-

PENNSYLVANIA, UNIVERSITY OF

dore Roosevelt (q.v.), candidate of the Progressive Party, received a plurality of the votes of the State in 1912. The Republican Presidential candidates were victorious in Pennsylvania from 1916 until 1936, when the Democratic incumbent Franklin Delano Roosevelt (q.v.) carried the State. Roosevelt was victorious in the next two elections, but in 1948, 1952, and 1956 Pennsylvania voted Republican. In 1960 and 1964 the State voted Democratic. In 1968 Pennsylvania gave the Democratic candidate, Hubert H. Humphrey (q.v.), 2,259,403 votes and the Republican candidate, Richard M. Nixon (q.v.) 2,090,017 votes. E.W.M.

PENNSYLVANIA DUTCH, or PENNSYLVANIA GERMAN, High German dialect, first brought to the United States by German emigrants to Pennsylvania after 1683. These came from the Lower Rhine provinces, Bavaria, and Saxony. Because of their rural life and the segregation of their religious communities, the emigrants long kept their High German unmixed with English. Although none were from the Netherlands they were called "Dutch" by other non-German-speaking colonists who mispronounced the word *Deutsche* ("German").

Consisting first of Mennonites and later of the Amish, a strict Mennonite sect, Dunkers, Moravians, and other religious groups, the Pennsylvania Dutch came to America mainly to obtain religious freedom; see MENNONITE CHURCH; CHURCH OF THE BRETHREN; MORAVIAN CHURCH. Many of the Pennsylvania Dutch still cling to traditional religious customs. The Amish, for example, reject automobiles, tractors, radios, and telephones, and still dress in the black or brown homespun that has caused them to be nicknamed the plain people. Noted for their industriousness and thrift, most Pennsylvania Dutch live on beautifully tended farms, which almost always feature a red barn painted with so-called hex signs. Lancaster, Northampton, Berks, and York counties have the largest Pennsylvania Dutch populations.

PENNSYLVANIAN PERIOD, later geologic time unit of the Carboniferous Period of the Paleozoic Era (qq.v.). It followed the Mississippian Period and preceded the Permian Period (qq.v.), ending about 270,000,000 years ago. The rock strata of the Pennsylvanian Period contain the coal strata of the Appalachian and Mississippi valley systems. See GEOLOGY, HISTORICAL; PALEONTOLOGY.

PENNSYLVANIA STATE UNIVERSITY, THE, coeducational State-controlled land-grant institution (see LAND-GRANT COLLEGES) of higher learning, located in University Park, Pa., founded in 1855, and opened in 1859 as the Farmer's High School. The university was known as the Agricultural College of Pennsylvania from 1862 to 1874 and from 1874 to 1953, when the present name was adopted, as Pennsylvania State College. Twenty-one Pennsylvania State Commonwealth institutions throughout the State are affiliated with the university. The University Park campus is located on 4550 acres, largely devoted to agricultural experiments. Divisions include colleges of liberal arts, arts and architecture, science, agriculture, earth and mineral sciences, engineering, business administration, education, health and physical education, human development, a graduate school, and a school of journalism. The degrees of associate, bachelor, master, and doctor are granted. The university operates on a four-term year. In 1968 the university libraries housed more than 875,000 catalogued volumes. In 1968 students numbered 43,612, the faculty, about 5680, and the endowment of the university was approximately $517,000.

PENNSYLVANIA, UNIVERSITY OF, coeducational privately controlled institution of higher learning benefiting from State aid, situated in Philadelphia, Pa., and founded in 1740, under the auspices of the followers of the British evangelist George Whitefield (q.v.) as a charity school. From 1779 to 1791 it was called the University of the State of Pennsylvania; its present name was adopted in the latter year. The university was the first North American institution of higher learning to establish schools and departments of medicine (1765), botany (1768), business (1881), research medicine (1910), and graduate medicine (1919); it also established the first university hospital (1874) and psychological clinic (1896).

The present divisions within the university include the college of arts and sciences, the Towne School of Civil and Mechanical Engineering, the Moore School of Electrical Engineering, the Wharton School of Finance and Commerce, the college of liberal arts for women, and schools of law, dentistry, medicine, nursing, allied medical professions, fine arts, education, veterinary medicine, metallurgical engineering, chemical engineering, social work, communications, and graduate studies. The degrees of bachelor, master, and doctor are granted. Under government contract, the university engages in nuclear research at the Brookhaven National Laboratory (q.v.). In 1968 the university library housed more than 2,000,000 bound volumes. In 1968 students numbered 17,707 and the faculty, 4518; the endowment was about $150,000,000.

PENOBSCOT

PENOBSCOT, North American Indian tribe of Algonquian (q.v.) stock, formerly dwelling around the Penobscot R. in Maine. During the wars between Britain and France in America, the Penobscot usually sided with the French, but made peace with the British in 1749. During the American Revolution the Indians again opposed the British, and subsequently settled on an island in Penobscot R. near Old Town, Maine.

PENOBSCOT, largest river of Maine. The West Branch rises near the border with Canada, and flows E. and S.E., receives the East Branch or Seboeis R., and flows S.W. into Penobscot Bay, an inlet of the Atlantic Ocean. The river, 350 mi. long, is navigable for large vessels to Bangor, 60 mi. from its mouth. The chief trade is in pulpwood and petroleum products.

PENOLOGY, branch of the science of criminology (q.v.), concerned with the methods of punishment and correction of criminals and the prevention of crime (q.v.).

History. The earliest known form of punishment for crime was execution of the criminal, a practice which in modern times, has steadily decreased; see CAPITAL PUNISHMENT. A later important form of forcible repression of crime is that of transportation or the establishment of penal colonies, geographically isolated, to which criminals were removed; see, for example, DEVIL'S ISLAND. A third and still later form is the prison (q.v.).

The development of modern theories of punishment of the criminal, embodied in codes of criminal law (q.v.) that give primary consideration to reform of the individual, dates from the writings of the 18th-century Italian jurist Cesare Bonesana Beccaria (q.v.). Beccaria argued against the imposition of harsh and unjust penalties, and suggested that the function of a penalty for each crime should be to outweigh sufficiently the assumed advantages of the specific crime. Later writers emphasized that punishment should take into consideration mitigating circumstances and the different degrees of legal and moral responsibility of the criminal, as in crimes committed by children and insane persons. The subsequent development of the concepts of parole, probation (qq.v.), the indeterminate sentence, and the institution of juvenile courts (see JUVENILE COURT) and reformatories (q.v.) demonstrate the increasing emphasis on rehabilitation as opposed to punishment imposed exclusively as a deterrent of crime.

Modern Correction Methods rehabilitation of convicted persons today is attempted with various corrective procedures, including experiments with early releases as an incentive for prisoners to learn a trade. In both Federal and State prison systems, so-called halfway houses have been used as transitional residential centers for prisoners prior to release together with work-release programs that enable internees to work during the day in local communities. Increased emphasis has been placed on constructive practices, such as reliance on the assistance of community volunteers in the probation and parole procedures, and the establishment of prison- and community-based organizations to facilitate the successful reintegration of the prisoner into society.

Among the major handicaps faced by offenders in their attempts to earn a legitimate livelihood is an inadequate education. An important aspect of the correctional process today, therefore, is the establishment of training and career-development programs within the Federal and State prison systems, both for the supervisory staff (to enable them to assist in the rehabilitation process) and the inmates. The key programs are aimed at teaching all inmates to read at least at the sixth-grade level; to enable more ambitious inmates to proceed to a high-school equivalency certificate and even college studies upon release; and to provide skills in vocational trades that will assure maximum opportunities for continued employment. Another major program is directed at the rehabilitation of narcotics addicts; see DRUGS, ADDICTION TO.

Penologists today emphasize the necessity for the modernization of outmoded penal institutions. Basic to such reforms, however, penologists point out it is essential that offenders are brought to trial speedily and trials concluded without undue delay. See also PUNISHMENT.

PENSACOLA, city and port of entry in Florida, and county seat of Escambia Co., on Pensacola Bay, an arm of the Gulf of Mexico, 50 miles S.E. of Mobile, Ala. Transportation facilities include railroads and a municipal airport; the city contains one of the finest natural harbors in the United States. Santa Rosa Island, about 50 mi. in length, protects the harbor from storms on the gulf, with which the harbor is connected by a channel 32 ft. deep. Pensacola is a leading fishing port, the trading center of an extensive area, including parts of Alabama, Georgia, Mississippi, and Louisiana, the site of a large naval aviation training school, and a popular summer and winter vacation resort. Important industries are the manufacture of wood products, paper, chemicals, acrylic fiber, and nylon fiber. Facilities for recreation provided at Pensacola include numerous fine bathing beaches, fishing

PENTECOSTAL CHURCHES

piers, and yacht basins. Among the points of interest in the city and vicinity are the ruins of the old Spanish forts of San Carlos and Barrancas, built in the 1780's.

History. In 1540 the site of the city served as a supply base for the Spanish explorer Hernando de Soto (q.v.). A group of Spanish colonists established a settlement there in 1559, but abandoned it two years later. The first permanent settlement was made in 1596. Pensacola was captured by the French in 1719, returned to Spain in 1723, and ceded to Great Britain in 1763. After passing again to the Spanish in 1781 the city, together with the rest of Florida, became part of the U.S. in 1821. It was the capital of Florida until 1822 and was chartered as a city in 1824. During the American Civil War the navy yard at Pensacola was seized by Confederate forces, but they were unable to dislodge the Union troops from Fort Pickens on Santa Rosa Island; in 1862 the Confederates evacuated the city. Pop. (1960) 56,752; (1970) 59,507.

PENSION PLANS. See WELFARE AND PENSION PLANS.

PENTAGON, any polygon or structure having five sides. In geometry, pentagons are characterized as being equilateral, equiangular, or regular when both sides and angles are equal. A familiar pentagonal object is the home plate used in baseball (q.v.). In Arlington, Va., the five-sided headquarters building of the United States Department of Defense is known as the Pentagon. Completed in 1943, it covers an area of 29 acres and is the largest office building in the world. The name Pentagon is also popularly applied to the Department of Defense itself; see DEFENSE, DEPARTMENT OF.

PENTATEUCH (Gr. *penta*, "five"; *teuch*, "book"), collectively, first five books of the Old Testament, that is, Genesis, Exodus, Leviticus, Numbers, and Deuteronomy (qq.v.). The term was used by the Christian theologian Origen (q.v.) to denote what the Jews of his time called "the Five-Fifths of Torah (teaching)", "Pentateuch" being the translation of the Hebrew term for this concept; see TORAH. The Torah is the holiest and most beloved of the sacred writings of the Jews. "The five books of Moses", as a designation of the Pentateuch, first was used in the Western Church by Saint Jerome (q.v.) and the Christian theologian Tyrranius Rufinus (345?–410). The Mosaic authorship of the work is not directly affirmed in the books, but it became tacitly accepted by Christian orthodoxy. The Pentateuch includes various textual strata of writings, notably those known as Yahvist (or J) and Elohist (or E), which refer to God (q.v.), as Yahweh and Elohim (q.v.), respectively; see JEHOVAH. The Hebrew priest and reformer Ezra (q.v.), whose work is associated with another textual component of the Pentateuch known as the Priestly stratum (or P), gave impetus to observance of the regulations of the Pentateuch. See BIBLE: *The Growth of the Bible*; MOSES; PRAYER, JEWISH.

S.Sa.

PENTATHLON, contest of five exercises, namely, jumping, running, wrestling, throwing the discus, and hurling the spear, which in the ancient Greek games (see OLYMPIAN GAMES) occurred between the same contestants on the same day. The contestant who won three events was considered the victor. In the modern Olympic games (q.v.), the pentathlon comprises cross-country running, horseback riding over obstacles, swimming, pistol shooting, and fencing. The contest is won by the contestant who achieves the greatest number of points.

PENTECOST (Gr. *pentēcostē*, "fiftieth"), name of a religious festival.

In Christianity, the seventh Sunday after Easter, q.v.), commemorating the descent of the Holy Ghost (q.v.) upon the Apostles (see APOSTLE) celebrating the ancient Jewish feast of Shabuoth (Acts 2:1–4). Pentecost is one of the great festivals (see FESTIVALS AND FEASTS: *Christian Festivals*) of the Christian year, and it was chosen as one of the times for the administration of the sacrament of Baptism (qq.v.).

In the Roman Catholic Church (q.v.) it is celebrated as Pentecost; in the Church of England (q.v.) and other Anglican churches as Whitsunday, in allusion to the white robes in which the newly baptized were clad. For a discussion of the Jewish holiday, see SHABUOTH.

PENTECOSTAL CHURCHES, large and varied group of revivalistic religious bodies characterized by belief in the experience of holiness or Christian perfection; see HOLINESS CHURCHES. This perfection is climaxed by an "infilling of the Holy Spirit", as evidenced by "speaking in tongues" (ecstatic utterances frequently unintelligible to listeners) as the Apostles did (Acts 2:1–13) on the day of Pentecost (q.v.). The theology of Pentecostalism, which is drawn principally from Methodist and Baptist tenets, is usually fundamentalist; see BAPTISTS; FUNDAMENTALISM; METHODISM. No one body of doctrine is universally accepted by all groups. Certain beliefs are held in common, however, such as the premillennial Second Advent of Christ (q.v.) and the imminence of that Second Coming. Uncontrolled emotional behavior often accompanies the speaking in tongues, and many groups practice divine healing. Baptism (q.v.), usually by

403

immersion, and the Lord's Supper (q.v.) are the two sacraments observed.

Pentecostal denominations are found in every State of the United States and are widespread abroad as well. In the U.S. most Pentecostal churches had their beginnings in the revival movement in the Negro Holiness Church in Los Angeles in 1906. A minority of them can be traced back to the "Latter Rain" revival movement led by A. J. Tomlinson (d. 1943), an American Bible Society salesman who founded the Church of God in 1903. The first schism occurred in 1917. In the years following, the Pentecostal movement split into several independent groups. Tomlinson's Church of God survives in two divisions, one, the Church of God of Prophecy, with nearly 75,000 members in the U.S. in the late 1960's and with international headquarters in the old city of Jerusalem (now in Israeli-occupied Jordan). The second is based in Cleveland, Tenn., and in the late 1960's had 221,000 members in about 3730 churches. In addition to the many smaller Pentecostal churches, found mainly in the South, West, and Middle West, there are hundreds of small storefront congregations in the U.S. Some of the larger bodies belong to the Pentecostal World Conference, an international fellowship with no fixed headquarters. *See also* ASSEMBLIES OF GOD.

PENTODE. *See* ELECTRONICS: *Pentodes.*

PENTSTEMON, genus of plants belonging to the Figwort family, consisting of herbaceous or shrubby species, mostly yielding beautiful flowers. With the exception of one species in northeastern Asia and one in South America, the genus is restricted to North America, primarily in open woods and grasslands.

PENZA, city of the Soviet Union, in the Russian S.F.S.R., and capital of Penza Oblast, on the Sura R., 350 miles S.E. of Moscow. A rail junction and industrial center, the city has sawmills, tanneries, and food-processing plants. It also manufactures paper, business machines, metal products, agricultural equipment, aircraft parts, textiles, watches, apparel, tools, cement, bicycles, matches, and flour. The surrounding region, part of the black-earth belt, produces grains, potatoes, fruit, sugar beets, hemp, livestock, and timber. Penza is the site of industrial and teachers' colleges and of regional and agricultural museums. Founded as a frontier fortress in the 1660's, the city was chartered in 1682 and developed mainly in the 18th century. Pop. (1970) 374,000.

PEONAGE, system of servitude, formerly common in Latin America, particularly in the area now comprising Mexico. Historically peonage evolved from the 16th-century *encomienda* system, by which the Spanish conquistadors were given proprietary rights over the Indians on the feudal estates granted to them by the Spanish king, and from the later *repartimiento* or assessment system; under the latter system Indian laborers were required to work part of each year for the colonial government. In the 19th century, after the nations of Latin America achieved independence, debt peonage was instituted and became the basis of the economic system. The peon, in debt to his employer for both money and supplies, was bound to labor in the mines or plantations until the debt was paid. Often the debt was so exaggerated that the peonage had to be handed down from generation to generation; but in the 20th century laws prohibiting such servitude were passed.

In the United States before the American Civil War, forms of peonage existed among Mexicans and Indians of the New Mexico and Arizona territories, and in the South it was experienced by poor Negroes and Whites. After the Civil War and the adoption of the Thirteenth Amendment to the Constitution of the United States (q.v.), which prohibits involuntary servitude except as punishment, several Southern States passed individual peonage laws. At this time the practice of leasing prisoners to independent contractors as members of chain gangs was begun. By this practice, the convicts, their legs shackled to prevent escape, were connected to one another by a continuous chain and forced to work in the fields and mines as well as road building. In 1910 the Supreme Court of the United States (q.v.) declared State laws permitting such practices unconstitutional.

Sharecropping, a system of peonage, was popular in the southeastern U.S. from the end of the Civil War until widespread mechanization of the production of cotton and tobacco rendered the system unprofitable. By this system, the sharecropper and his family provide their labor in return for a share in the profits from the crop they produce. The owner of the land provides not only land but equipment, animals, seed, and living accommodations as well.

PEONY, common name for plants constituting the genus *Paeonia* of the Crowfoot family, Ranunculaceae, having large showy flowers composed of five leafy herbaceous sepals, five to ten petals, numerous stamens, and two to five carpels, each with numerous round, black, shiny seeds. The leaves are compound, the leaflets variously and irregularly divided. The fibers of the root are often thickened and tuberous. Peony species are large herbaceous perennials,

Peonies, genus Paeonia
F. E. Westlake –
National Audubon Society

or, rarely, half-shrubby plants, native to Europe, Asia, and northwestern America. Because of the beauty of their flowers, some species are cultivated, particularly the common peony, *P. officinalis,* a native of the mountain woods of southern Europe, with carmine or blood-red flowers. A variety with double flowers is common. The white peony, *P. albiflora,* is another favorite garden species. The mountain peony, *P. moutan,* in favorable circumstances may attain large size and a height of 12 ft. It is propagated by cuttings and also by grafting (q.v.). The roots of most of the peonies have a nauseous smell when fresh. Those of the common peony were in high repute among the ancients as an antispasmodic, but their medicinal properties are now disregarded.

PEOPLE'S PARTY or **POPULIST PARTY,** in United States history, political party formed by the members of various organizations of workers and farmers at a national convention held in Cincinnati, Ohio, in 1891. The formation of this party marked the culminating stage in the development of agrarian and labor movements, centering chiefly in the Middle West, which began shortly after the American Civil War. These movements had led during the 1870's to the formation of such organizations as the National Grange, Greenback Party, Greenback-Labor Party, Farmers' Alliance, Knights of Labor, and American Federation of Labor. The attempts of these organizations to ameliorate the depressed economic condition of their members had been only moderately successful; the People's Party, which drew most of its membership from these organizations, represented a new and stronger attempt by the workers and farmers to achieve a dominating influence in American politics.

At the time of the formation of the People's Party, the farmers were suffering high transportation costs and low prices for their produce, high prices for the manufactured goods and machinery they required, and mounting indebtedness to merchants and banks. Labor was faced with low wages, long hours, and high commodity prices. Both groups viewed the policy of the Federal government of monetary deflation as one of the chief causes of their difficulties; hence, the main planks in the platform formulated at the founding convention of the People's Party called for such inflationary measures as the free coinage of silver and the issuance of large amounts of paper currency. Other demands included the abolition of the national banking system, nationalization of the means of transportation and communication, the institution of a graduated income tax, direct popular election of U.S. Senators, and the adoption of referendum. These demands were renewed at the national convention of the People's Party, held in Omaha, Nebr., in 1892. The powerful 1892 platform was written by one of the founders and leaders of the People's Party, Ignatius Donnelly (1831–1901), the American writer and politician from Minnesota. The Civil War general James Baird Weaver (1833–1912) was then nominated for the Presidency. In the election later that year, Weaver received 1,029,846 popular and 22 electoral votes, and several Populist candidates were elected to Congress.

A large number of Populists attended the Democratic Party convention held at Saint Louis, Mo., in 1896, and succeeded in capturing the convention and in securing the nomination of the lawyer and political leader William Jennings Bryan (q.v.), an avowed supporter of the Populist program, for the Presidency. Bryan received 176 electoral votes, but lost the election

PEORIA

to the Republican candidate William McKinley (q.v.) by a margin of 609,687 popular votes. In the following year the People's Party split into two factions over the question of whether to continue to support the Democrats; the two factions held separate conventions in 1900, the pro-Democrats renominating Bryan, and the anti-Democrats nominating the financier Wharton Barker (1846–1921). Bryan, campaigning on the platform of opposition to the imperialist policies of the Federal government that had caused the Spanish-American War (q.v.) of 1898–99, was again defeated by McKinley, while Barker received comparatively little popular support. A reconciliation was later effected between the two factions, and in 1904 the Populists nominated an independent candidate, the lawyer Thomas Edward Watson (1856–1922), who polled 117,183 votes. Thereafter the influence of the People's Party declined rapidly; the party disappeared soon after the Presidential elections of 1908. *See also* POPULISM.

PEORIA, city and port of entry in Illinois, and county seat of Peoria Co., on the Illinois R., about midway between Chicago and Saint Louis, Mo. It is served by railroads and by river steamers traversing inland waterways from the Great Lakes to the Gulf of Mexico, and maintains a municipal airport. Peoria is the second-largest city in the State, and because of its transportation facilities and location in the heart of a rich agricultural and coal-mining region, it is a leading shipping, distributing, and trading center. In addition, Peoria has varied industrial establishments producing tractors, earth-moving equipment, fencing and wire products, diesel engines, and food products and beverages.

Peoria is the site of Bradley University, established in 1896, and of a United States Department of Agriculture research laboratory. The municipal park system covers 1640 acres, and on the opposite bank of the Illinois R. is Fort Creve Coeur State Monument, containing the site of Fort Crève Coeur, built by the French explorer Robert Cavelier, Sieur de La Salle (q.v.) in 1680. To the s.w. of Peoria is the unincorporated community of West Peoria (pop. 1970, 6873), and across the Illinois R., to the s.e., is the city of East Peoria (pop. 1960, 12,310; 1970, 18,455), which was incorporated in 1919.

History. The city area was first settled by the French about 1711 and the settlement remained French until 1812. In 1813 Fort Clark was built on the site by Federal troops as protection against marauding Indians. Peoria was incorporated as a town in 1835 and chartered as a city in 1845. Pop. (1960) 103,162; (1970) 126,963.

PEPIN *or* **PEPPIN** (Fr. *Pépin*; Ger. *Pippin*) name of several Frankish kings of Aquitaine, mayors of the palace of Austrasia, and one king of Italy.

Pepin the Elder *or* **Pepin of Landen** (d. 639?), mayor of the palace of Austrasia, the eastern portion of the kingdom of the Franks. He was one of the earliest rulers of the Carolingian (q.v.) dynasty, the second dynasty of Frankish kings.

Pepin of Herstal (d. 714), mayor of the palace of Austrasia and the grandson of Pepin the Elder. He ruled Austrasia from about 680. In 687 he extended the Carolingian rule to Neustria and Burgundy, although the Merovingian (q.v.) dynasty retained nominal control of the three portions of the Frankish kingdom. He was succeeded by his son Charles Martel (q.v.).

Pepin the Short *or* **Pépin le Bref** (about 714–68), mayor of the palace of Austrasia and King of the Franks (751–68), the son of the Frankish ruler Charles Martel, and the grandson of Pepin of Herstal. He was mayor of the palace during the reign of Childeric III (r. 741–51), the last of the Merovingian dynasty of kings. In 751, Pepin deposed Childeric, and thus became the first king of the Carolingian dynasty. He was crowned king by Pope Stephen II (III) in 754; *see under* STEPHEN. When the pope was threatened by the Lombards (q.v.) of northern Italy, Pepin led an army into that region, and defeated (754–55) them. He ceded to the pope territory that included Ravenna and other cities. This grant, called the Donation of Pepin, laid the foundation for the Papal States (q.v.). Pepin enlarged his own kingdom by capturing Aquitaine, or Aquitania (q.v.). He was succeeded by his sons Carloman (751–71) and Charlemagne (q.v.) who briefly ruled as joint kings.

Pepin (d. 810), King of Italy (781–810), the son of Charlemagne (q.v.), King of the Franks and Emperor of the West, and the grandson of Pepin the Short. Pepin aided his father in conquering the Avars (q.v.) in central Europe in 795 and 796.

Pepin I (d. 838), King of Aquitaine (817–38), the son of Louis I (q.v.), Holy Roman Emperor, and great nephew of Pepin. Pepin, dissatisfied with the terms of imperial succession set forth by his father, joined in the uprisings of 830 and 833 that briefly deposed Louis. Pepin was succeeded as king of Aquitaine by his youngest brother Charles the Bald, later Charles II (q.v.), Holy Roman Emperor.

Pepin II (d. 870?), King of Aquitaine (838–64), the son of Pepin I. After the death of his father, Pepin was elected king by the Aquitanians although the province had been inherited by Charles the Bald. From 843 when the treaty of

Verdun reaffirmed Charles' authority until 864 when he was defeated and deposed by Charles, Pepin was engaged in war with Charles. It is believed that Pepin died in prison.

PEPPER, common name applied to plants of the genus *Piper,* belonging to the family Piperaceae. Plants of this genus have solitary spikes in the axils of the leaves, and almost perfect flowers. The most important species is common or black pepper, *P. nigrum,* native to Indonesia, cultivated also in many tropical countries. It bears small, green berries that turn red when

Leaves and berries of black pepper, Piper nigrum
U.S. Dept. of Agriculture

ripe. These berries yield both the black pepper and the white pepper used as condiments. Black pepper is prepared from berries that are gathered before they are ripe and dried in the sun. The milder white pepper is made from seeds of the ripe berries. The betel pepper, *P. betle,* yields betel leaves, which are wrapped around betel nuts and chewed throughout much of the Orient; see BETEL.

The name "pepper" is popularly given to substances with a pungency resembling that of pepper, although they come from very different plants. Thus, cayenne pepper is produced from the species *Capsicum* (q.v.), and pimento (q.v.), or Jamaica pepper, from the species *Eugenia.*

PEPPERELL, Sir William (1696–1759), American merchant, statesman, and soldier, born in Kittery Point, Mass. (now in Maine). Largely self-educated, he was appointed chief justice of Massachusetts in 1730, where he served on the governor's council from 1727 to 1759. In 1734 he inherited the bulk of his father's estate and became one of the richest men in New England. His experience as a colonel in the Massachusetts militia led to his command, in 1745, during King George's War (q.v.), of a colonial land and sea force that captured the French stronghold at Louisburg on Cape Breton, in present-day Nova Scotia. He was made a baronet the following year, the first native American to be so honored. In 1754, during the French and Indian War (q.v.), he raised a regiment of 1000 men and commanded the military forces of Massachusetts. After 1756 he served as acting governor of Massachusetts. He was commissioned a lieutenant general shortly before his death.

PEPPERMINT. *See* MINT.

PEPPER TREE, slender evergreen tree in the genus *Schinus,* of the Cashew family, Anarcardiaceae, native to South America and grown in the western United States. The California pepper tree, *S. molle,* also known as the Peruvian mastic, is cultivated as a street ornamental and reaches 20 to 30 ft. It gets its name from its pinkish acrid-smelling berries and is not related to the pepper (q.v.) plant. It has drooping branches that bear yellowish-white flowers, and the delicate, featherlike leaves secrete a milky oil that quickly evaporates. The smaller Brazilian pepper tree, *S. terebinthifolius,* about 15 ft. in height, has a poisonous, allergenic resin and pollen; *see* PLANTS, POISONOUS.

PEPSIN. *See* DIGESTION.

PEPYS, Samuel (1633–1703), English diarist and public official, born in London and educated at the University of Cambridge. He is chiefly remembered for his *Diary,* which was first published in 1825. The *Diary,* which is invaluable as a record of the court and times of Charles II (q.v.), King of England, was begun on Jan. 1, 1660, and was continued for about nine years, when defective eyesight caused Pepys to abandon the work. His only other writing of importance is his *Memoires Relating to the State of the Royal Navy* (1690).

PEQUOT, warlike North American Indian tribe of the Algonquian (q.v.) linguistic stock, formerly occupying the coast region of eastern Connecticut from the Rhode Island border westward to beyond the Thames. They were a branch of the Mohegan (q.v.).

PERCENTAGE, expression in hundredths of a fraction (q.v.) of a whole number. Usually represented by the symbol %, percentage computations are commonly used today in finance and industry to calculate interest rates, costs, prices, profits, losses, discounts, and commissions, by the government to determine taxation, and by scientists to evaluate data.

To find percentage of a number, for example 20 percent of 40, it is necessary to change 20 to a common fraction ($\frac{20}{100}$) or to a decimal (.20), and then to multiply this figure with the whole (40), thus

$$\frac{20}{100} \times 40 = 8; \text{ or } .20 \times 40 = 8.$$

See DECIMAL SYSTEM; FRACTION.

To calculate the percentage relationship of one number (4) to another (16), the former should be divided by the latter, thus

$$4 \div 16 = .25, \text{ or } 25 \text{ percent}.$$

If it is known that a number such as 8 is 5 percent of the principal number, the principal can be discovered by dividing 8 by .05, thus giving 160. See ARITHMETIC; STATISTICS.

PERCEPTION. See PSYCHOLOGY: *Perception*; PSYCHOLOGY, EXPERIMENTAL: *Perception*.

PERCH, common name of a genus of spiny-finned or acanthopterous freshwater fish, belonging to the members of the family Percidae. The perch are carnivorous fish frequenting the freshwaters and coasts of temperate and tropical regions. The European perch, *Perca fluviatilis*, is widely distributed in lakes, ponds, and rivers in Europe, northern Asia, and Britain. In North America it is replaced by the yellow perch, *Perca flavescens*. Both species are of a greenish-brown color above and golden yellow on the underparts, with six or seven indistinct dark bands on the back. In length it measures about 12 in., but the European perch is slightly larger on the average. The perch feeds on smaller fishes, insects, and worms. In spring the fish lays its eggs in long strings, the number of eggs in one spawn sometimes exceeding 40,000.

PERCUSSION INSTRUMENTS. See MUSICAL INSTRUMENTS: *Percussion Instruments*.

PERCY, Sir Henry, known as HOTSPUR (1366–1403) English military leader, eldest son of Henry Percy, 1st Earl of Northumberland (1342–1408). Knighted in 1377 by Edward III (q.v.), King of England, Percy shortly began that service on the Scottish border in which he won his greatest fame, and about 1393 became governor of Bordeaux, in France. He was killed at the Battle of Shrewsbury after he had revolted against Henry IV (q.v.), King of England.

PERCY, Thomas (1729–1811), British poet and antiquary, born in Bridgnorth, and educated at the University of Oxford. In 1769 he became chaplain to George III (q.v.), King of Great Britain, and in 1782 bishop of Dromore, in Ireland. He became famous as the editor of *Reliques of Ancient English Poetry* (3 vol., 1765), a collection of English and Scottish ballads. As a poet he was best known for "The Hermit of Warkworth" and the ballad "O Nanny, Wilt Thou Gang with Me?". Percy was honored by a group of scholars who gave his name to the Percy Society (1840–52) for the publication of old ballads.

PEREIRA, city in Colombia, and capital of Risaralda Department, on the Otún R., in the western foothills of the Cordillera Central, 25 miles S.W. of Manizales. A rail and road hub, it is a market center for an area producing coffee, livestock, sugarcane, fruit, cacao, and corn. Manufactures include processed coffee, food products, textiles, mineral water, cigars, and paper. Founded in 1863 and formerly located in Caldas Department, the city became capital of the new Risaralda Department in 1967. Pop. (1964) 147,487.

PERENNIALS. See GARDENING: *Beds and Borders*.

PÉREZ GALDÓS, Benito (1843–1920), Spanish novelist and playwright, born at Las Palmas in the Canary Islands, and educated in law at the University of Madrid. He is the author of five series of historical novels, a total of forty-six volumes with the general title *Episodios Nacionales* ("National Episodes", 1873–79 and 1897–1912). They are distinguished for their careful documentation and vivid re-creation of Spanish history. His outstanding novels of Spanish society include *Fortunata y Jacinta* ("Fortunata and Jacinta", 1886–87). Pérez Galdós is the author also of novels dealing with contemporary social and religious problems, including *Doña Perfecta* (1876; Eng. trans., 1880) and *Marianela* (1878; Eng. trans., 1883); and of a number of plays, including *La Loca de la Casa* ("The Madwoman in the House", 1893), *Electra* (1900), and *Mariucha* (1903). He is considered one of the greatest authors of Spain.

PERFECTIONISTS, name adopted by the American reformer John Humphrey Noyes (q.v.) and his early followers; it was based upon a verse in Matthew, "Be ye therefore perfect, even as your Father which is in heaven is perfect" (5:48). Their first settlement was at Putney, Vt. Noyes' views were expressed in a paper, *The Perfectionist*. The sect held that Christ (*see* JESUS CHRIST) had returned to earth before the end of the Apostolic Age (*see* APOSTLE), and that His work of saving Christians from the necessity of sin (q.v.) was complete. In the Perfectionists' community all possessions were held in common, and a system of communism (q.v.) gradually was worked out, involving the institution of "complex marriage", a form of group marriage or controlled polygamy. The community was broken up in 1847. Members who held together founded the Oneida Community (q.v.).

PERFUMERY, substances that give off agreeable odors. Perfumes may be divided into two general classes: natural perfumes and artificial or synthetic perfumes. Natural perfumes are of animal or vegetable origin; artificial perfumes are chemical compounds that resemble natural perfumes in their odor. Artificial perfumes are also of two general classes. In one the compounds that produce the perfume in nature have been discovered and then reproduced synthetically, as with vanillin. In the other, only the odor of the natural perfume is imitated in a substance that is itself unlike the substance whose odor it possesses, as with artificial musk.

The four principal animal perfumes are musk, civet, ambergris, and castor. Musk is the dried secretion of the preputial follicles of the musk deer. A similar substance is secreted by the musk ox, muskrat, and the Florida alligator. Civet is secreted by the *Viverra zibetha,* the civet cat, an animal of African origin. Civet is found in a double pouch under the tail, from which it is taken from the living, caged animal, two or three times a week. Ambergris, a biliary secretion of the spermaceti whale, is supposed to be produced by a diseased condition of the organs. It is found floating on the sea. Castor is a glandular secretion of the beaver. When fresh it is semiliquid; it is prepared for commerce by drying in smoke. Animal perfumes are valuable for the permanence that their presence imparts to the more evanescent vegetable odors.

The odor of plants may be found in the leaves, as in sage, thyme, and mint; in the bark, as in cinnamon and cassia; in the wood, as in cedar and sandalwood; in the flower petals, as in the rose and violet; in the seeds, as in anise and caraway; in the roots, as in the orris; in the fruit rind, as in the orange; or it may be secreted in the form of resinous gum from the tree itself, as in camphor and myrrh.

The center of the natural perfumery industry has for many years been in Grasse, France. The culture of flowers for perfumery is carried on also in Turkey, Bulgaria, India, and Syria. İstanbul and Edirne, in Turkey, are especially noted for the production of attar of roses. *See also* COSMETICS.

PERGAMUM, PERGAMON, *or* PERGAMOS, ancient city of Asia Minor, in Mysia (now Turkey), and later capital of the kingdom of Pergamum. The city acquired prominence when the Macedonian general Lysimachus (about 355–281 B.C.) chose its acropolis as a stronghold for his treasures, which he entrusted to the governor of Pergamum Philetaeros (r. 283–278 B.C.). Upon the death of Lysimachus in 281 B.C., Philetaeros became the ruler of Mysia and Troas. His nephew Eumenes I (r. 263–241 B.C.), developed the resources and prosperity of the kingdom. Eumenes' cousin and successor Attalus I Soter (*see under* ATTALUS), who reigned from 241 to 197 B.C., became master of northwestern Asia Minor through his victories over the Gauls and the Syrian king Antiochus III (*see under* ANTIOCHUS), and his policy of allying himself with the distant power of Rome. Attalus made his capital the center of the artistic and literary life of Asia. Eumenes II (r. 197–160? B.C.), son of Attalus I, continued the Roman policy of his father and brought the greater part of Asia Minor under his sway. To his reign belong the altar of Zeus and the development of the great library, founded by his father, where a group of distinguished scholars established a school of grammatical study in opposition to the scholars of the Alexandrian Library (q.v.). The prosperity and power of Pergamum continued under Attalus II Philadelphus, who reigned from about 160 to 138 B.C., and Attalus III Philometor, who reigned from 138 to 133 B.C.; the last-named ruler, having no heirs, bequeathed his kingdom to the Romans. Under Roman control, Pergamum remained one of the chief cities of Asia Minor, being the capital of the province of Asia. The ruins of the ancient city surround the modern town, called Bergama, and are noted for their splendor. They include ruins of a Roman theater, an amphitheater, and a circus.

PERGOLESI, Giovanni Battista *or* **PERGOLESE, Giovanni Battista** (1710–36), Italian composer, born in Iesi, near Ancona, and educated at the conservatory in Naples. His first important work, the oratorio *La Conversione di San Guglielmo d'Aquitania* ("The Conversion of Saint William of Aquitaine"), was composed in 1731. Two years later appeared *La Serva Padrona* ("The Maid as Mistress"), a comic opera now generally considered his masterpiece, which gained him universal fame and became a model for short comic operas up to the time of the Italian composer Gioacchino Antonio Rossini (q.v.). In 1734 Pergolesi was appointed choirmaster of the Church of Loreto, but his delicate health forced him to retire to Pozzuoli, where he died two years later of tuberculosis. The works of his last two years include a *Stabat Mater,* considered his finest work for chorus and orchestra. Among Pergolesi's other compositions are a large body of church music, a violin concerto, and chamber music. Pergolesi's tuneful and clearly phrased melodies contributed to the formation of the preclassic style in music; see MUSIC: *History*.

PERIANTH. See FLOWER: *Parts of a Flower*.

PERICARDITIS, inflammatory disease of the heart (q.v.) in which the pericardium is thickened and roughened. It is most likely to develop during an attack of rheumatic fever, but may also arise in other conditions, such as Bright's disease. Toxemic pericarditis is almost invariably the result of a primary infectious disease elsewhere in the body.

PERICARP. See FRUIT: *Structure of Fruit*.

PERICLES (about 495–429 B.C.), Athenian statesman. He was so influential in Athenian history that the period of his power is called the Age of Pericles. His father was the Athenian commander Xanthippus (fl. 5th cent.), victor over the Persians at Mycale in 479 B.C. Pericles was especially influenced by two of his teachers, the Athenian Sophist and master of music Damon (fl. 5th cent.), and the Ionian philosopher Anaxagoras (q.v.). To their teaching Pericles undoubtedly owed his independence of thought and freedom from superstition. Throughout his life he was conspicuous for his dignity and aloofness, but his eloquence, sagacity, uprightness, and patriotism won recognition from a majority of his fellow Athenians. Among his intimate friends were such outstanding Greeks as the dramatist Sophocles, the historian Herodotus, the sculptor Phidias, and the Sophist Protagoras, and his mistress was the Greek adventuress Aspasia (qq.v.).

Political Leadership. In Athenian politics Pericles sought to enable all citizens to take an active part in the government. Payment of citizens for their services to the state was introduced, and members of the council were chosen by lot from the entire body of Athenians. His foreign policy was based on a desire to extend the power and influence of Athens as widely as possible over the other Greek city-states. Under the Delian League (q.v.), which had been established after the defeat of the Persians, the Athenians created a great naval empire, and embraced, as equal or subject allies, nearly all the larger islands of the Aegean Sea and many cities to the north. The two chief opponents of Pericles were the Athenian statesman Cimon and the historian Thucydides (qq.v.). When these aristocratic leaders were ostracized (*see* OSTRACISM), Pericles became the undisputed leader of Athens and for fifteen years was annually elected to the office of general. He made Athens supreme at the expense of the subject city-states. With the great wealth that came into the Athenian treasury Pericles restored the temples destroyed by the Persians, and erected many new buildings. This program provided employment for the poorer citizens and made Athens the most magnificent city of the ancient world. Among the most splendid of the new structures was the Parthenon (q.v.).

Under Pericles' leadership Athens became a great center of literature and art. The cultural and political supremacy of Athens aroused the jealousy of the other Greek city-states, especially of Sparta, long the bitter rival of Athens. The cities feared the imperialistic schemes of Pericles and sought to overthrow Athenian domination. In 431 B.C. the Peloponnesian War began. Pericles summoned the country residents of Attica within the walls of Athens and allowed the Peloponnesian army to ravage the country districts. The following year a plague broke out in the overcrowded city. The people, exposed to suffering and death, felt great resentment against Pericles. He was deposed from office, tried, and fined for misuse of public funds, but was soon reinstated. He died shortly thereafter.

PERIDOT. See OLIVINE.

PERIDOTITE, coarse-grained, igneous rock composed of dark-colored minerals, chiefly pyroxene (*see* PYROXENES), olivine (q.v.), and hornblende. Magnetite, chromite, ilmenite, and garnet (qq.v.) are often associated with peridotites. Various types of peridotite are: pyroxenite, a variety composed almost entirely of pyroxene; hornblendite, a rare variety composed almost entirely of hornblende; serpentine, a variety composed almost entirely of olivine that has altered completely; and kimberlite, a variety containing diamond (q.v.).

PÉRIGUEUX, city in France, and capital of Dordogne Department, on the Isle R., 79 miles N.E. of Bordeaux. The city has long been known for the production of goose liver and truffle pâtés. Other industries include the manufacture of tobacco products, leather goods, and chemicals. In the city are the Cathedral of Saint Front, which dates from 1120, and the ruins of an ancient Roman amphitheater. Pop. (1962) 41,134.

PERIM, barren island of Southern Yemen, in Bab el Mandeb, a strait connecting the Red Sea and the Gulf of Aden, 97 miles w. of Aden. It has an area of about 5 sq.mi. The British occupied the island from 1851 to 1967 and used it as a coaling station.

PERIOD. See GEOLOGY, HISTORICAL.

PERIODICALS, publications issued at regular intervals. They usually are placed in a class apart from another major form of serial publication, newspapers (q.v.). Most newspapers are issued

PERIODICALS

daily on cheap paper and have relatively large, unbound pages; periodicals, in turn, generally appear on finer paper, with smaller pages bound inexpensively, and at intervals longer than a day (weekly, biweekly, monthly, quarterly, even annually). Also, taken as a whole, periodicals feature, often exclusively, material of special interest to particular audiences. The contents of periodicals are often unrelated or only vaguely linked to news and tend to contain summaries or analyses and commentaries when dealing with the news.

HISTORY.
The earliest forebears of the contemporary periodical were European digests and journals of the 17th and 18th centuries, such as the French *Journal des Sçavans* (founded in 1665 and subsequently titled *Journal des Savants*), and the English *Philosophical Transactions of the Royal Society of London* (1665). These were essentially collections of summaries (later essays) on developments in art, literature, philosophy, and science; the most famous of them, perhaps, were the British essay periodicals *The Tatler* (1709–11), *The Spectator* (1711–12, 1714), *The Rambler* (1750–52), and *The Bee* (1759); see ESSAY. Among the contributors to such magazines were the essayists Sir Richard Steele, Joseph Addison, and Charles Lamb (qq.v.).

The first periodical of the modern general type, devoted to a miscellany of reading entertainment, was the English *The Gentleman's Magazine* (1731–1907) founded by the English printer and journalist Edward Cave (1691–1754). Cave's magazine, which contained reports of political debates, essays, stories, and poems, was widely influential, serving, for example, as the model for the first true American periodicals, *General Magazine and Historical Chronicle* and *American Magazine*. Both first appeared in Philadelphia, in January, 1741, as rival publications, and both proved unsuccessful: the former was founded by the American printer Andrew Bradford (1686–1742) and the latter by the American statesman and scientist Benjamin Franklin (q.v.).

Monthly or quarterly reviews, usually partisan in politics, and with articles contributed by eminent authors and politicians, were introduced in Great Britain early in the 19th century. Of these, three became outstanding: the *Edinburgh Review* (1802–1929), which was founded in support of the Whig Party, and the *Quarterly Review* (1809), and *Blackwood's Magazine* (1817), both of which supported Tory (q.v.) policies. To all three, the Scottish author Sir Walter Scott (q.v.) contributed reviews and poetry.

Popular weeklies and monthlies, some illustrated and selling for as little as sixpence and twopence per issue, made their appearance in Britain in the second quarter of the 19th century. The *Mirror* (1822–49), a twopenny illustrated magazine; *Chamber's Journal* (1832); *Fraser's Magazine* (1830–82); and the *Cornhill Magazine* (1860–1939) were among the leading popular periodicals of this time. The *Cornhill* at first edited by William Makepeace Thackeray (q.v.), was the first sixpenny monthly to publish fiction regularly in serial form; these serials included novels by such authors as Anthony Trollope (q.v.).

The first modern British illustrated magazines appeared during the middle and latter part of the 19th century. The more successful included the weekly *Illustrated London News* (1842) and the monthly *English Illustrated Magazine* (1883–1913). Other important British periodicals dating from the second half of the 19th century include the *Fortnightly Review* (1865–1950; issued monthly after 1866), the *Contemporary Review* (1866), and the *Nineteenth Century* (1877; retitled *Twentieth Century* in 1950).

Periodicals in America. Only sixteen periodicals were published in America before the American Revolution. About a hundred periodicals, most of them short-lived, were issued in the last quarter of the 18th century. By the middle of the 19th century, however, 600 periodicals of various types were being printed in the United States. Many of these periodicals, patterning themselves after English monthlies and quarterlies, were miscellanies intended for general audiences and featuring essays on the arts, history, and politics. There was also an increase in periodicals for special audiences, including monthlies and weeklies for women and children, such as *Godey's Lady's Book* (1830–98), vastly influential in setting fasions in manners, clothing, and taste, and *Youth's Companion* (1827–1929); religious journals appealing to the antislavery and temperance movements; monthly and quarterly literary reviews, such as *Graham's Magazine* (1826–58), the *Southern Literary Messenger* (1834–64), *Knickerbocker Magazine* (1833–65), and *The Dial* (1840–44), which were edited by famous men of letters; and family magazines, such as the *Saturday Evening Post* (1821–1969), which was revived as a quarterly in 1971.

Improvements in techniques of illustration and printing (qq.v.) introduced a new era, especially in the publication of general magazines, during the late 19th century. The number, variety, and readership of periodicals increased enormously, as more Americans became edu-

411

PERIODICALS

cated and Federal laws were passed that provided inexpensive mailing rates. *Harpers New Monthly Magazine* (1850; afterward renamed *Harper's Magazine*), with many woodcut illustrations, a greater number of pages, and serials by popular English authors, led the revolution. Rival illustrated monthlies soon followed, among them, *Scribner's Monthly* (begun in 1870), afterward issued as the *Century* (1881–1930), and *Scribner's Magazine* (1887–1939). Another leading periodical begun in this period, but published from the start without illustrations, was the literary magazine *Atlantic Monthly* (1857).

Toward the end of the 19th century in the U.S., a second revolutionary development, the printing of quality illustrated monthlies at less than half the price of their earlier counterparts, set the stage for the widespread establishment in the 20th century of mass-circulation national magazines. Outstanding cheaper illustrated periodicals founded in the 19th century included *Cosmopolitan* (1886), *McClure's Magazine* (1893–1933), and *Munsey's Magazine* (1889–1929). Notable U.S. periodicals of this time, currently surviving, are *Harper's Bazaar* (1867), *McCall's Magazine* (1873), *Ladies' Home Journal* (1883), *Good Housekeeping* (1885), and *Vogue* (1832).

Also about the turn of the century, a number of periodicals began the practice of "muckraking", a term of the time describing their manner of exposing supposedly corrupt practices in government and business, with considerable effect on the American political and social scene. These magazines particularly flourished in the decade between 1902 and 1912. Among the most influential were *McClure's*, *Munsey's*, *Everybody's Magazine* (1899–1929), *Arena* (1889–1909), *Frank Leslie's Popular Monthly* (1876; retitled *American Magazine,* 1906–56), and the weekly *Collier's* (1883–1957).

20th-Century Periodicals. The 20th century saw the introduction of several magazines that represented more sophisticated literary tastes, and that protested literary censorship and the remnants of Victorian morality. Among these were the *Smart Set* (1900–30) and the *American Mercury* (1924–51), particularly under the editorship of Henry Louis Mencken and George Jean Nathan (qq.v.). General magazines with large circulations were published more frequently, a trend accentuated by the founding of the pocket-sized *Reader's Digest* (1922). Since the 1950's, this magazine, composed of condensed versions of books and articles from other publications, has had a monthly circulation of over 20,000,000, including numerous foreign-language editions in countries throughout the world.

Two other significant developments, dating from the 1920's and 1930's, were the establishment of weekly news reviews, such as *Time* (1923), *Newsweek* (1933), and *U.S. News* (1933; later retitled *U.S. News and World Report*), and the founding of such weekly and biweekly photo-illustrated magazines as *Life* (1936) and *Look* (1937–71). Both types have since been imitated world-wide.

The 1930's and 1940's were years marked by large increases in circulations of periodicals for children, such as *Boy's Life* (first issued in 1912 as the voice of the Boy Scouts of America); the comics (q.v.) also first developed enormous circulations at this time.

Meanwhile, through much of the first half of the 20th century, the so-called "little magazines" contributed substantially to the growth of American literature. Typically small in format, featuring experimental writing of limited audience appeal, such "little magazines" as *Poetry* (1912), the *Sewanee Review* (1892; strictly literary only after 1940), and the *Kenyon Review* (1939–70) introduced many important new authors to their readers. Larger audiences were reached with the establishment of more general literary and opinion magazines, notably the *Saturday Review of Literature* (1924; since 1952 called *Saturday Review*), the *New Yorker* (1935), the liberal Catholic *Commonweal* (1924), and the Jewish-oriented *Commentary* (1945); the liberal *Partisan Review* (1934) and *Reporter* (1949–68); and the conservative *National Review* (1955).

Periodicals for readers with special interests, mostly persons in a particular business and trade, and in areas of technical, scientific or other professional fields, also increased in number as well as in sales after World War II. This class of magazine is most inclusive, covering almost all house organs, university magazines, journals of various professional and scientific societies, and magazines that give semitechnical information and advice. *Scientific American* (1845), *Popular Science Monthly* (1872), and *Popular Mechanics* (1902) are among the best known. Certain periodicals, for example, *Art in America* (1913), *American Heritage* (1954), *Horizon (1958), Holiday (1954), National Geographic Magazine* (1888), and *Sports Illustrated* (1954), appeared in attractive soft- or hard-cover formats during the 1950's and 1960's. Such magazines, devoted to such relatively broad special interest fields as art, history, travel, and sports, are usually profusely illustrated with striking photographs and reproductions in both color and black and white. They represent, in physical appearance, the current high point in periodical publication.

PERIODIC LAW, in chemistry, law stating that many of the physical and chemical properties of the elements tend to recur in a systematic manner with increasing atomic number. Progressing from the lightest to the heaviest atoms, certain properties of the elements approximate those of precursors at regular intervals of two, eight, eighteen, and thirty-two. For example, the second element (helium) is similar in its chemical behavior to the tenth (neon), and also to the eighteenth (argon), the thirty-sixth (krypton), the fifty-fourth (xenon), and the eighty-sixth (radon). Elements 29 (copper), 47 (silver), and 79 (gold) are all exceptionally good conductors of electricity. The chemical family called the halogens, composed of elements 9 (fluorine), 17 (chlorine), 35 (bromine), 53 (iodine), and 85 (Astatine), is an extremely reactive family. See ATOM AND ATOMIC THEORY: *Periodic Table.*

Historical Development. As a result of discoveries that firmly established the atomic theory of matter in the first quarter of the 19th century, it became possible to determine the relative weights of atoms of the then known elements. The development of electrochemistry (q.v.) by the British chemists Sir Humphry Davy and Michael Faraday (qq.v.) during this period led to the discovery of many additional elements. By 1829 a sufficient number of elements had been discovered to permit the German chemist Johann Wolfgang Döbereiner (1780–1849) to observe that certain elements with closely similar properties occur in groups of three, or triads, such as chlorine, bromine, and iodine; calcium, strontium, and barium; sulfur, selenium, and tellurium; and iron, cobalt, and manganese. However, the limited number of elements then known and the confusion existing concerning the distinction between atomic and molecular weights made it impossible for chemists to grasp the significance of the Döbereiner triads.

The development of the spectroscope in 1859 by the German physicists Robert Wilhelm Bunsen and Gustav Robert Kirchhoff (qq.v.) made possible the discovery of many more elements; see SPECTRUM: *Chemical Analysis.* In 1860, at the first international chemical congress ever held, the Italian chemist Stanislao Cannizzaro (q.v.) clarified the fact that some of the elements, for example, oxygen, have molecules containing two atoms. This realization finally made it possible to achieve a self-consistent listing of the elements.

These developments gave new impetus to the attempt to reveal interrelationships among the properties of the elements. In 1864 the British chemist John A. R. Newlands (1837–98) listed the elements in the order of increasing atomic weights and noted that a given set of properties recurs at every eighth place. He named this periodic repetition the law of octaves, by analogy with the musical scales. This discovery by Newlands failed to impress his contemporaries, probably because the observed periodicity was limited only to a small number of the known elements.

The periodic law stating that the properties of all the elements are periodic functions of their atomic weights was developed independently by two chemists, in 1869 by the Russian Dmitri Mendeleev and in 1870 by the German Lothar Meyer (qq.v.). The key to the success of their efforts was the realization that previous attempts had failed because a number of elements were as yet undiscovered, and that vacant places must be left for such elements in the classification. Thus, although no element then known had an atomic weight between those of calcium and titanium, to preserve the periodicity of similar properties it was necessary to leave a vacant place between these two elements. This place in the periodic table soon was assigned to the element scandium (discovered in 1879), which has properties justifying its position in the sequence. The discovery of scandium proved to be one of a series of dramatic verifications of the predictions based on the periodic law.

Validation of the law accelerated the development of inorganic chemistry; indeed, the law systematized that science and served as an invaluable guide in the search for the remaining undiscovered elements.

The periodic law has undergone two principal elaborations since its original formulation by Mendeleev and Meyer. The first revision involved its extension to include a whole new family of elements, the existence of which was completely unsuspected in the 19th century. This group comprised the inert gases (q.v.), such as argon, helium, and neon, discovered in the atmosphere between 1895 and 1900 by the British chemists John William Strutt, 3rd Baron Rayleigh and Sir William Ramsay (qq.v.). The second development was the interpretation of the cause of the periodicity of the elements in terms of the Bohr theory (1913) of the electronic structure of the atom. See ATOM AND ATOMIC THEORY: *Bohr Atom.*

PERIODIC LAW

Periodic Table. The periodic law is most commonly expressed in chemistry in the form of a periodic table, or chart.

SHORT-FORM TABLE. The so-called short-form periodic table, based on Mendeleev's table, with subsequent emendations and additions, is still in widespread use. In this table the elements are arranged in seven horizontal rows called the periods, in order of increasing atomic weights, and in nine vertical columns, called the groups. The first period, containing two elements, hydrogen and helium, and the next two periods, each containing eight elements, are called the short periods. The remaining periods, called the long periods, contain eighteen elements, as in periods 4 and 5, or thirty-two elements, as in period 6. The long period 7, which includes the actinide series containing the transuranium elements, has been filled in recently by the synthesis of radioactive nuclei through element 103, lawrencium; see TRANSURANIUM ELEMENTS.

All the elements within a single group bear a considerable familial resemblance to each other and, in general, differ markedly from elements in other groups. Thus, the elements of Group I are metals with a chemical valence (q.v.) of +1; Group VIIb contains nonmetals, and its members frequently show valences of −1 in their compounds. Hydrogen, the first member of Group I, is, in many respects, unique among the elements. It could, with justification, also be placed at the top of Group VIIb, because certain of its properties resemble those of members of the latter group. Each of the groups from I to VII inclusive is subdivided on the basis of chemical properties into two subgroups, designated by the symbols a and b. For example, although the members of Group Ia (the alkali metals lithium, sodium, potassium, rubidium, cesium, and francium) have certain marked similarities to the Group Ib elements (copper, silver, and gold), these two groups differ markedly in certain other chemical properties, for example, reactivity, thus justifying the division into two subgroups.

In the periodic classification the rare gases, which in most cases are completely unreactive (valence = 0), are interposed between highly reactive metals with a valence of +1 on one side, and highly reactive nonmetals of valence −1 on the other side. This phenomenon led to the theory that the periodicity of properties results from the arrangement of electrons in shells about the atomic nucleus. According to that theory, the rare gases are normally inert because their electron shells are completely filled; other elements, therefore, may have some shells that are only partially filled, and their chemical reactivities involve the electrons in these incomplete shells. Thus, all the elements that occupy a position in the table preceding that of an inert gas have one electron less than the number necessary for completed shells, and show a valence of −1, corresponding to the gain of one electron in reactions. Elements in the group following the inert gases in the table have one electron in excess of the completed shell structure and in reactions can lose that electron, thereby showing a valence of +1. An analysis of the periodic table, based on this theory, indicates that the first electron shell may contain a maximum of two electrons, the second builds up to a maximum of eight, the third to eighteen, and so on. The total number of elements in any one period corresponds to the number of electrons required to achieve a stable configuration. The distinction between the a and b subgroups likewise may be explained on the basis of the electron-shell theory. Both subgroups have the same degree of incompleteness in the outermost shell but differ from each other with respect to the structures of the underlying shells. This picture still provides a good description of chemical bonding. However, it is now known that compounds of the rare gases krypton, xenon, and radon can be made. This is because atoms in a compound can share more than the number of electrons in a completed valence shell when an electron is promoted from one shell to another. See ATOM AND ATOMIC THEORY; RARE GASES.

With the advent of the quantum theory (q.v.) and its application to atomic structure by the Danish physicist Niels Bohr (q.v.) and others, all the detailed features of the periodic table have found a ready explanation. Every electron is characterized by four quantum numbers that designate its orbital motion in space. By means of the selection rules governing these quantum numbers and the exclusion principle (q.v.), of Wolfgang Pauli (q.v.), which states that two electrons in the same atom cannot have all four quantum numbers the same, it is possible to determine theoretically the maximum number of electrons required to complete each shell, confirming the conclusions inferred from the periodic table.

Further development of the quantum theory demonstrated why some elements have only one incomplete shell (namely, the outermost or valence shell), whereas others may have incomplete underlying shells as well. In the latter category is the group of elements known as the rare earths, which are so similar in properties that

PERIODIC LAW

Periodic table of the chemical elements.

GROUP\PERIOD	Ia	IIa	IIIa	IVa	Va	VIa	VIIa	VIII			Ib	IIb	IIIb	IVb	Vb	VIb	VIIb	O
1	1 H																	2 He
2	3 Li	4 Be											5 B	6 C	7 N	8 O	9 F	10 Ne
3	11 Na	12 Mg											13 Al	14 Si	15 P	16 S	17 Cl	18 Ar
4	19 K	20 Ca	21 Sc	22 Ti	23 V	24 Cr	25 Mn	26 Fe	27 Co	28 Ni	29 Cu	30 Zn	31 Ga	32 Ge	33 As	34 Se	35 Br	36 Kr
5	37 Rb	38 Sr	39 Y	40 Zr	41 Nb	42 Mo	43 Tc	44 Ru	45 Rh	46 Pd	47 Ag	48 Cd	49 In	50 Sn	51 Sb	52 Te	53 I	54 Xe
6	55 Cs	56 Ba	57 La*	72 Hf	73 Ta	74 W	75 Re	76 Os	77 Ir	78 Pt	79 Au	80 Hg	81 Tl	82 Pb	83 Bi	84 Po	85 At	86 Rn
7	87 Fr	88 Ra	89 Ac**															

*Lanthanides

58 Ce	59 Pr	60 Nd	61 Pm	62 Sm	63 Eu	64 Gd	65 Tb	66 Dy	67 Ho	68 Er	69 Tm	70 Yb	71 Lu

**Actinides

90 Th	91 Pa	92 U	93 Np	94 Pu	95 Am (243)	96 Cm	97 Bk	98 Cf	99 Es	100 Fm	101 Md	102 No	103 Lw

PERIOSTEUM

Mendeleev had to assign all fourteen to a single place in his table. The rare-earth group is called the lanthanide series. The actinide series, comprising all the elements from actinium through the transuranium elements, constitutes a second rare-earth series. The concept of the actinide series was first proposed in 1944 by the American chemist Glenn T. Seaborg (q.v.). Until the discovery of the transuranium elements, the three elements thorium, protactinium, and uranium had been placed respectively under the elements hafnium, tantalum, and tungsten.

LONG-FORM TABLE. The application of the quantum theory of atomic structure to the periodic law has led to the redesign of the periodic table in the so-called long form, which emphasizes this electronic interpretation.

In this table, each period corresponds to the building up of a new electronic shell. Elements directly in line with each other have strictly analogous electronic structures. The beginning and end of a long period represent the addition of electrons in a valence shell; in the central portion the number of electrons in an underlying shell increases.

The periodic law has been found to correlate a great many different properties of the elements, including such physical properties as melting and boiling points, densities, crystal structures, hardness, electrical conductivity, heat capacity, and thermal conductivity, and such chemical properties as reactivity, acidity or basicity, valence, polarity, and solubility. See ELEMENTS, CHEMICALS; see also ISOTOPE.   S.Z.L.

PERIOSTEUM, tough, fibrous membrane which surrounds each bone (q.v.). It is highly vascular and is the means by which the outer layers of the shafts and the greater part of the spongy portions of the bones are supplied with blood. It consists of an outer or fibrous layer and an inner or osteogenetic layer. The inner layer is very vascular and contains many protoplasmic cells called osteoblasts. Numerous experiments show that the formation of bone is essentially due to the action of the periosteum and that, by transplanting detached portions of periosteum into muscular or other tissues, bony tissue is generated in those parts. It appears to be the curative agent in the case of bone breakage. In most cases in which the periosteum has become detached in consequence of a wound or of disease, the exposed bone perishes (except in the instance of the skull, which derives most of its nutrient matter from the dura mater, actually the periosteum of the inner surface of the skull). Inflammation of the periosteum results in a condition known as periostitis.

PERIPATETIC PHILOSOPHY, name applied to the philosophy of the school of Aristotle (q.v.). The name may have been derived from Aristotle's custom of walking about (*peripatein*) while lecturing, or from the *peripatos* ("covered walk") of the Lyceum, the parklike area outside Athens, where he lectured. Aristotle's followers developed certain points of his logic and metaphysics, but were more concerned with the study of nature and the popularization of the study of ethics. Many of them spent their time arranging and explaining the writings of Aristotle. The most prominent Peripatetic philosophers were Theophrastus of Lesbos (q.v.), a friend of Aristotle as well as cofounder, of the school and famed for his *Characters,* a series of sketches; Eudemus of Rhodes (fl. 4th cent. B.C.), interested mainly in the ethical aspects of Aristotelianism; Strato of Lampsacus (fl. 3rd cent. B.C.), who championed mechanism in nature and denied the existence of a transcendent deity; and Andronicus of Rhodes (fl. 1st cent. B.C.), who edited many of Aristotle's works. The later Peripatetics leaned toward eclecticism and borrowed heavily from Stoicism (qq.v.).   J.D.C.

PERISCOPE, optical instrument for conducting observations from a concealed or protected position. A simple periscope (*see* Figs. 1 & 2) consists essentially of reflecting mirrors or prisms at opposite ends of a tube with the reflecting surfaces parallel and at 45° angle with the tube's axis; *see* MIRROR; PRISM. The so-called field or

An officer of a U.S. Navy nuclear-powered submarine stands by the periscope of his vessel.   U.S. Navy

PERISCOPE

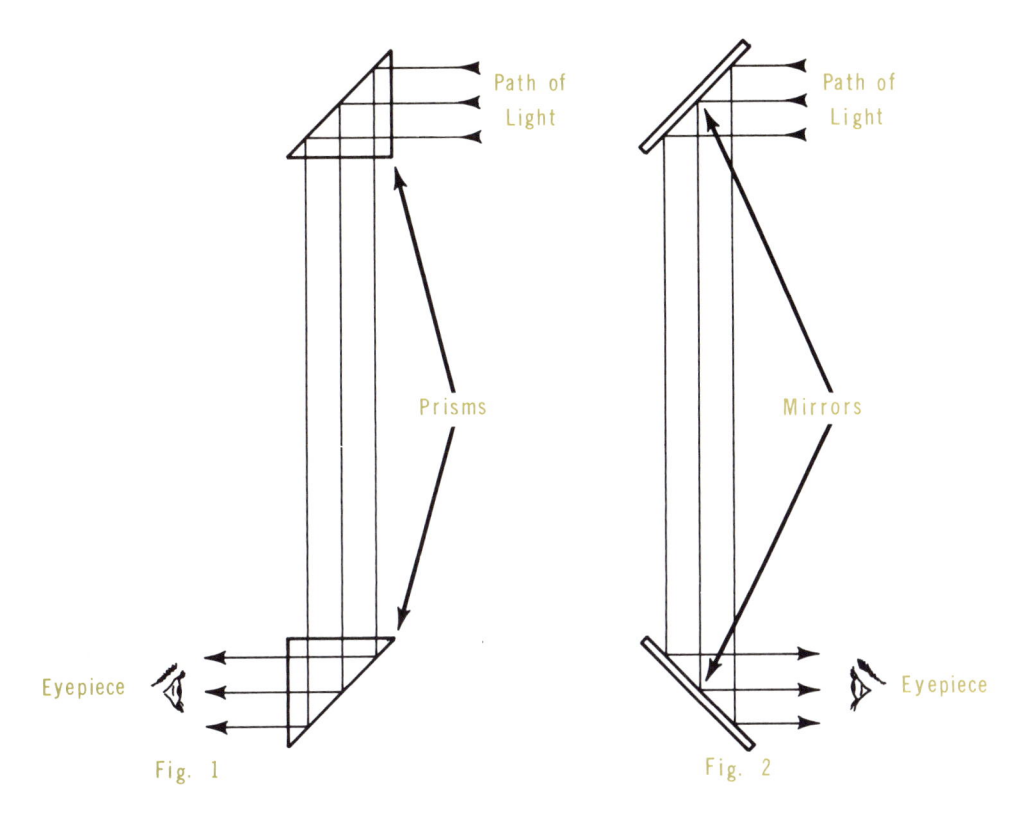

Path of Light

Path of Light

Prisms

Mirrors

Eyepiece

Eyepiece

Fig. 1

Fig. 2

Simple periscopes. Fig. 1. Field or tank prism periscope. Fig. 2. Rear-sighting mirror periscope, producing an inverted image. Right: View through a submarine periscope of the VP-16 Spangle 8 reconnaissance aircraft.

PERITONEUM

tank periscope has been commonly used in trenches, behind parapets and earthworks, and in tanks to provide protected vision for the user. The submarine periscope is a larger and more complex instrument. It consists of reflecting prisms at top and bottom of the vertical periscope tube, with two telescopes and several lenses between them, and an eyepiece at the lower end; see TELESCOPE. The submarine periscope is contained in a strong, thick casing tube, 4 to 6 in. in diameter, which is sufficiently rigid to stand the pressure of the water at great depths. The only part of the outer tube which turns is the head, and this is attached to the inner tube. The observer stands at the lower end of the inner tube, which he can turn by means of a lever or a crank and gearing. The field of a simple periscope is small, but several recent improvements have extended it somewhat. The magnification of distant objects is from 1.5 to 6 diameters. See OPTICS: *Geometrical Optics;* SUBMARINE.

Periscopes are also used as viewing devices in military aircraft, in nuclear-physics laboratories to observe radioactive reactions, and in particle accelerators; see ACCELERATORS, PARTICLE.

PERITONEUM, serous membrane in the abdominal cavity. It consists of two layers, a parietal one lining the walls of the cavity and a visceral one closely investing the majority of the abdominal organs, and mooring them firmly in position. Between the two layers there is provision for a space, the peritoneal cavity; in the male this is closed, while in the female there is a direct communication between the sac and the Fallopian tubes (q.v.) to enable the ova to reach the cavity of the uterus.

Various folds of peritoneum pass between the different viscera and the enclosing walls; thus there are double folds connecting the stomach with the liver and with the transverse colon and spleen. Similarly there are folds binding the small and large intestine (mesenteries) to the posterior wall, and finally a third group of folds (ligaments) connecting other viscera (including liver, bladder, and uterus) with the abdominal or pelvic walls. The greater omentum, or abdominal apron, hangs downward from the lower edge of the stomach, covering the intestines.

Although the functions of the peritoneum are chiefly mechanical—diminishing friction and mooring the viscera—the membrane also possesses marked secretory and absorptive powers. See also PERITONITIS.

PERITONITIS, inflammation of the membrane that lines the abdominal cavity and the organs contained therein. Peritonitis may be local, involving only one specific area, or, more often, general, involving the entire cavity. Peritonitis is most often an acute illness, caused by introduction of infection from a perforation of the bowel such as a ruptured appendix or diverticulum. The intestinal contents then spill into the cavity. The disease is also caused by introduction of chemically irritating material such as stomach acid from a perforated ulcer or bile from a rupture of the gall bladder or laceration of the liver. Localized peritonitis most often occurs in the pelvis from an infected fallopian tube or a ruptured ovarian cyst. Occasionally peritonitis may occur from the rupture of an abscess and pus spills into the abdominal cavity. This sometimes follows surgery inside the bowel with leaking from the site of closure, or from a stab wound through the abdominal wall. Occasionally peritonitis may occur from inflammation of the peritoneal membrane in a variety of disorders such as kidney failure, rheumatic fever, and systemic lupus erythematosis.

Peritonitis is usually an acute disease, but occasionally may be chronic, particularly in such chronic diseases as tuberculosis. Peritonitis usually develops after the onset of the symptoms of whatever is causing it. The principal symptom is severe abdominal pain, much aggravated by any motion. The abdomen usually is very tender and rigid, and when the doctor presses down and suddenly releases his hand there is sudden sharp pain. The patient often has nausea and vomiting, and usually is feverish. As the disease progresses the fever and pulse rate climb and often shock sets in. Untreated cases of acute peritonitis are often fatal. Treatment is directed at the underlying cause. In addition, intravenous fluids and antibiotics are given.

PERIWINKLE, common name applied to gastropods of the genus *Littorina,* represented by several species found on the coast of Great Britain. The common periwinkle, *L. littorea,* is abundant between tidemarks on the rocks and is often collected and used for food. Periwinkles crawl about under water, but usually remain passive when left uncovered by the tide. They feed on microscopic algae and diatoms (qq.v.) and are often useful in keeping beds of young oysters from being smothered. The edible species produce eggs that develop outside the maternal body, but in *L. saxatilis,* which is usually common nearer high-water mark, the young are hatched and have a hard shell before they leave the mother. See GASTROPODA.

PERIWINKLE, common name applied to herbs of the genus *Vinca,* belonging to the Dogbane

Periwinkle, Vinca rosea
Arthur W. Ambler – National Audubon Society

family. The leaves are opposite and evergreen; the flowers grow singly or in pairs from the axils of the leaves. The lesser periwinkle, *V. minor*, is a native of many parts of Europe, growing in woods and thickets. The greater periwinkle, *V. major*, which has much larger flowers and ovatocordate, or egg-shaped, leaves, is a native of the south of Europe. Both species have spread from cultivation.

PERJURY, in criminal law, willful false statement made under oath with respect to a material matter, either in a legal proceeding, as by a witness at a trial (qq.v.) or in matters in which an oath is authorized or required by law, as in an affidavit (q.v.) affecting title to property (q.v.). To constitute perjury in a legal proceeding it is not necessary that the offender know the statement would affect the determination of the case in which it is uttered; it is sufficient if the statement might have affected such a proceeding. A misstatement by a witness, made through inadvertence or mistake, does not, however, constitute perjury. A violation of a promissory oath, as for example, the oath by a judge that he will perform the duties of his office, does not warrant prosecution for perjury.

In most States of the United States perjury is a misdemeanor; in others it is a felony (qq.v.). Corroboration of the falsity of the statement is necessary to convict an offender; perjury cannot be proved by the statement of a single witness. Willfully procuring another person to commit perjury constitutes the crime of subornation of perjury. Any attempt to suborn, although unsuccessful, is also a criminal offense.

PERKIN, Sir William Henry (1838–1907), British chemist, born in London, England, and educated at the Royal College of Chemistry. In 1856, in the course of experiments aimed at the synthesis of quinine, he oxidized aniline (q.v.) and obtained the earliest synthetic dye, aniline purple or mauve. With his father and brother, Perkin set up a factory for the commercial production of mauve, thus founding the great aniline-dye industry; *see* DYESTUFFS. Perkin also developed synthetically other dyes, such as alizarin, and flavoring substances, such as coumarin. The Perkin reaction in organic synthesis is a method devised by him in 1878 for preparing unsaturated fatty acids. He was awarded the Royal medal of the Royal Society in 1879, and was knighted in 1906.

PERKINS, Frances (1882–1965), American sociologist, born in Boston, Mass., and educated at Mt. Holyoke College, the University of Pennsylvania, and Columbia University. She was a member of the New York State Industrial Board from 1923 to 1926 and its chairman from 1926 to 1929; in 1929 Governor Franklin Delano Roosevelt (q.v.) of New York appointed her State industrial commissioner. Soon after Roosevelt's election to the Presidency in 1932, Frances Perkins was designated United States secretary of labor, the first woman member of a cabinet. She subsequently became one of the most important executors of Roosevelt's New Deal (q.v.) program; her consistent defense of the interests of labor, and her advocacy of social-security, unemployment-compensation, minimum-wage and maximum-hour, and child-welfare legislation gained her the strong support of labor unions and of workers generally. She resigned the secretaryship in June, 1945, and in the following year was appointed a member of the United States Civil Service Commission, with which she served until 1952. Her writings include *A Plan for Maternity Care* (1918) and *The Roosevelt I Knew* (1946).

PERKINS, Maxwell E(varts) (1884–1947), American editor, born in New York City, and educated at Harvard University. He began his career as a reporter on the New York *Times* (1907–10). In 1911 he moved to Charles Scribner's Sons, a New York publishing house, and became a book editor. Subsequently, he became director of Scribner's editorial department and a vice-president of the firm in 1932. Perkins owed his

PERM'

reputation chiefly to his ability to discover or assist American authors in their early writing careers. Conrad Aiken, Erskine Caldwell, F. Scott Fitzgerald, Ernest Hemingway, Ring Lardner, and John P. Marquand (qq.v.) were some of the writers he sponsored. He is best known, however, for his association and friendship with the American novelist Thomas Wolfe (q.v.), with whom he worked closely in editing and rewriting of his original manuscripts.

PERM', formerly MOLOTOV, city of the Soviet Union, in the Russian S.F.S.R., and capital of Perm' Oblast, on the Kama R. at the w. base of the Ural Mts., about 250 mi. E. of Kirov. It is a leading transportation and industrial center, where electricity, chemicals and petrochemicals, ships, river boats, aircraft, machinery, and various fabricated metal products are manufactured. The city is the site of a university, several professional and technical colleges, and other cultural institutions. The surrounding area is rich in mineral resources.

The site of the city was settled in ancient times by Permiaks, a people of the Finno-Ugric stock. In 1568 Russian traders established themselves, and in 1781 the city was chartered as Perm' and made the capital of the oblast. Perm' merged with Molotovo in 1938 and the name Molotov was adopted two years later. In 1957 the city and oblast were renamed Perm'. Pop. (1970) 850,000.

PERMAFROST, perennially frozen ground. Vast tracts of permafrost lie across Canada, Alaska, northern Europe and Asia, and Antarctica. Greenland is almost totally covered with permafrost. Pockets of permafrost are found as far south as the 50th parallel in Canada and the 45th parallel in Siberia. Clues to the age of the permafrost of Northern Hemisphere lie in the numerous discoveries of mammoth (q.v.) remains embedded in frozen ground. Mammoths became extinct about 10,000 to 15,000 years ago, coincident with the end of the most recent ice age. See FROST.

PERMANENT COURT OF ARBITRATION, panel of arbitrators established by the Convention for the Pacific Settlement of International Disputes, signed by twenty-four nations at the first international peace conference at The Hague, the Netherlands, in 1899; see HAGUE CONFERENCES. The panel was set up to facilitate the arbitration of international disputes; see ARBITRATION: *International Arbitration*. Under the convention, each of the contracting nations was permitted to select as many as four arbitrators who were listed as members of the court, and served for six years. The names of the members were kept on record, and disputing nations had access to the list to choose a tribunal of arbitrators to settle their differences. The court has never met as a body, and is permanent only in so far as a panel exists from which arbitrators can be chosen.

Before World War I the court participated in the settlement of fifteen cases, among which were the North Atlantic Coast Fisheries Arbitration between the United States and Great Britain; the Preferential Claims Arbitration between Great Britain, Italy, Germany, and Venezuela; and the Casablanca Deserters Arbitration between Germany and France. After World War I, most nations came to believe that arbitration was not a satisfactory means of settling disputes, and the court was utilized less often. The example and reputation of the court was, however, influential in the decision to create the Permanent Court of International Justice in 1921. See INTERNATIONAL COURT OF JUSTICE.

PERMANENT COURT OF INTERNATIONAL JUSTICE. See INTERNATIONAL COURT OF JUSTICE.

PERMIAN PERIOD, last division of geologic time in the Paleozoic Era, following the Carboniferous Period and preceding the Triassic Period of the Mesozoic Era (qq.v.). It began about 270,000,000 years ago and ended about 45,000,000 years later. The name Permian was first applied to formations of rocks in what is now Perm' Oblast in the Soviet Union by British geologist Sir Roderick Impey Murchison (q.v.) in 1841. The Permian was a transitional period, marked by mountain building, changes in climate, and the disappearance of the interior water basins of the North American continent. Some glaciation took place in the Southern Hemisphere and possibly in the northeastern area of the United States. The Appalachian and Ural mountains completed their development during this period.

The rocks laid down in the Permian Period include sandy shales, sandstones, and thin limestones in West Virginia, Pennsylvania, and Ohio. Salt and gypsum were deposited in an area now comprising Texas, Oklahoma, Kansas, and Nebraska, and marine limestones and sandstones in western Texas and southeastern New Mexico. "Red beds" of sandstone and shale, indicating arid conditions, are characteristic of North American and European Permian deposits.

Flora and Fauna. The elevation of continents and the disappearance of inland seas changed the climate of Permian times. Arid conditions are believed to be responsible for the disappearance of some plants that were common in the moist Carboniferous Period. Some types of ferns and conifers were hardier, however, and continued to exist into the Mesozoic Era, although plants were generally smaller than in previous periods. Some marine animals died out, notably the trilobites. More modern forms of marine animals predominated, reptiles increased in number and range, and insects changed considerably. See GEOLOGY, HISTORICAL; PALEONTOLOGY.

PERMUTATIONS AND COMBINATIONS, in mathematics, certain arrangements of objects or elements. A combination is a selection of objects or elements, with or without repetition, from a given set of objects or elements, without regard to their order. For example, the letters a, b, c can be combined six ways without repetition, namely, a, b, c, ab, ac, bc, abc. With repetition, these letters determine the set of combinations of three letters each, or 3-combinations, as follows: abb, acc, aab, bcc, aac, bbc, aaa, bbb, ccc. In a combination, a rearrangement of the elements (abb, bab) is not considered a separate group. A permutation is a selection or arrangement of objects or elements, with or without repetition, with regard to the order of the elements; that is, a rearrangement of the elements (ab, ba) is considered a distinct grouping. Thus, the set of all 2-permutations determined by a, b, c is ab, ba, ac, ca, bc, cb, aa, bb, cc.

Various formulas are used to find out how many combinations or permutations of a specified type are determined by a given set of elements. The number of r-combinations, without repetition, determined by n distinct elements, is given by the formula:

$$C_r^n = \binom{n}{r} = n(n-1)(n-2)\ldots(n-r+1)/r!,$$

in which $r! = 1 \times 2 \times 3 \times \ldots \times r$. The number of r-permutations, without repetition, determined by n distinct elements is given by the formula:

$$P_r^n = (n)_r = n(n-1)(n-2)\ldots(n-r+1).$$

For example, three committee men (in any order) can be selected from a group of fifteen men in

$$\binom{15}{3} = 15 \times 14 \times 13/1 \times 2 \times 3 = 455$$

combinations. Or, a president, vice president, and secretary can be elected by a club with fifteen members in $(15)_3 = 15 \times 14 \times 13 = 2730$ ways (permutations).

The number of r-combinations, with or without repetition, determined by n distinct elements is given by:

$$\binom{n+r-1}{n-1} = \binom{n+r-1}{r}$$
$$= (n+r-1)(n+r-2)\ldots n/r!.$$

The number of r-permutations, with or without repetition, determined by n distinct elements is n^r. For example, three identical prizes are to be awarded to students in a class of fifteen, and a student may receive more than one prize. The prizes can be awarded in

$$\binom{15+3-1}{3} = 17 \times 16 \times 15/1 \times 2 \times 3 = 680$$

ways. Or, if in the above example the prizes are not identical, the prizes can be awarded in $15^3 = 3375$ ways.

Two further formulas that are useful in working with permutations and combinations are as follows: r identical objects can be distributed among n distinct boxes in

$$\binom{n+r-1}{n-1}$$

ways; and a set of $n = n_1 + n_2 + \ldots + n_k$ objects, of which n_1 are alike, n_2 are alike, ..., n_k are alike, can be arranged in $n!/n_1! n_2! \ldots n_k!$ ways. For example, the six letters of the word "banana" can be arranged in $6!/1! 3! 2! = 60$ ways.

The formulas given are only a few that are used in the study of permutations and combinations, but a very large number of problems may be solved with them.   J.Si.

PERNAMBUCO. See RECIFE.

PERNIK, city of Bulgaria, in Sofia Province, on the Struma R., 15 miles s.w. of Sofia. A road and rail junction and coal-mining center in the Pernik Basin since 1891, the city is in an area containing many lignite mines and iron smelters. Industries include the manufacture of machinery, briquettes, electrical equipment, and glass. Ruins of a Byzantine fortress are located here. From 1944 to the 1960's the city was called Dimitrovo. Pop. (1965) 75,844.

PERÓN, name of two Argentine political leaders who were husband and wife.

Juan Domingo Perón (1895–   ), born in Lobos, and educated at the National Military Academy. Commissioned a lieutenant in the army of Argentina in 1913, he rose through grades to general of the army in 1950. In 1941 he was a member of a military junta, known as the colonels, that seized control of the Argentine government. He served the junta successively as secretary of labor and social welfare, minister of war, and vice-president.

In 1945 Perón succeeded in gaining the support of organized labor for the government and was elected president. During his term of office, the Argentine government grew increasingly totalitarian and the trade unions were converted into a militant nationalist organization. Perón was reelected in 1951, but Argentine prosperity and stability steadily decreased. At the same time censorship, repression, and anticlericalism were employed by the government to gain political advantage until in 1955 Perón was ousted by a military coup. In the same year he was excommunicated by the Roman Catholic Church. He went into exile, first in Paraguay and eventually in Spain. Peronism remained a political force in Argentina, however, and his followers made frequent attempts to revive it.

Eva de Perón (1919–52), born MARIA EVA DUARTE in Los Toldos. At the age of sixteen she left school and moved to Buenos Aires, where she rapidly gained popular acclaim as a radio and motion-picture actress. In 1945, shortly before his election as president, she married Juan Perón. The Maria Eva Duarte de Perón Welfare Foundation, which she founded in 1947, raised and distributed millions of dollars annually. Through this organization and her work with the poor, referred to as the *descamisados*, or shirtless ones, and the labor unions, she acquired great political influence, which she deftly wielded in her husband's behalf. In 1951 she was expected to run as the Peronist candidate for the vice-presidency, but illness and some opposition within the army caused her to withdraw. Her death, shortly after her husband's second inauguration, was followed by a period of public mourning.

PERPENDICULAR, style of Gothic architecture in England that succeeded the Decorated style (qq.v.). It prevailed from about the end of the 14th century to the middle of the 16th century, and was thus contemporary with the Flamboyant (q.v.) style in France. The lines of the window tracery are chiefly vertical, and the mullions are frequently crossed by transoms or horizontal bars. The moldings are usually thin and hard.

PERPIGNAN, city in France, and capital of Pyrénées-Orientales Department, on the Tête R., 5 miles w. of the Mediterranean Sea, and 35 miles s. of Narbonne. It commands the passes of the E. Pyrenees. The city is an important center for trade in fruits, olives, and wines and also has brickworks. It is the site of the Gothic Cathedral of Saint Jean and the castle of the kings of Majorca. Perpignan was the capital of the Spanish Kingdom of Majorca until 1642, when it became capital of the ancient French province of Roussillon between Languedoc and the Pyrenees. Pop. (1962 est.) 83,025.

PERRAULT, Charles (1628–1703), French writer, born in Paris, and educated at the Collège de Beauvais and at Orléans. He practiced law for a time in Paris and was secretary to the French statesman Jean Colbert (q.v.), from about 1664 until Colbert's death in 1683; after that time Perrault devoted himself to a literary career. His poem "Siècle de Louis le Grand" ("The Age of Louis XIV", 1687), in which he argued that the arts and sciences had come to their full flowering in 17th century France, touched off a literary controversy in which his point of view was opposed by those who considered the culture of the ancient Greeks and Romans superior to that of France. In this dispute Perrault's principal opponent was the French poet and critic Nicolas Boileau-Despréaux (q.v.). Perrault is best remembered, however, for the eighteen fairy tales that he set down, from oral tradition, in his collection *Stories or Tales from Olden Times* (1697), also called *Mother Goose Tales.*

See CHILDREN'S LITERATURE: *The 17th and 18th Centuries.*

PERRIN, Jean Baptiste (1870–1942), French physicist and chemist, born in Lille, and educated at the École Normale Superieure, Paris. He was professor of physical chemistry at the Faculty of Sciences from 1910 until 1940. He is known for his work on the structure of matter, particularly for his investigation of cathode rays and Brownian movement of particles. He was awarded the 1926 Nobel Prize in physics for his work on the discontinuous structure of matter. His works include *Traité de Chimie Physique* ("Dissertation on Physical Chemistry", 1903), *Les Atomes* (1913; Eng. trans., *Atoms,* 1923), and *Les Éléments de la Physique* ("The Elements of Physics", 1930).

PERRY, name of two American naval officers who were brothers.

Oliver Hazard Perry (1785–1819), born in South Kingstown, R.I. He joined the United States Navy as a midshipman at the age of fourteen. When the War of 1812 (q.v.) broke out he was placed in command of a flotilla of gunboats and in 1813 ordered to Sackets Harbor, N.Y. for service under the American naval officer Commodore Isaac Chauncey (1772–1840). In March of the same year, Perry undertook the equipping of a fleet for service on Lake Erie and distinguishing himself during the attack that resulted in the capture of Fort George. On

The first landing of Americans in Japan, under the command of Matthew Calbraith Perry. Library of Congress

September 10, he defeated the British in the Battle of Lake Erie off Put-in-Bay, Ohio; see ERIE, BATTLE OF LAKE. The whole of Lake Erie was put under American control, and Perry was able to assist the American forces under General William Henry Harrison (q.v.) in the operations culminating in the Battle of the Thames. Perry later served in the Mediterranean; he died of yellow fever while cruising in the West Indies. See NATIONAL PARK SERVICE: *Perry's Victory and International Peace Memorial National Monument.*

Matthew Calbraith Perry (1794–1858), born in Newport, R.I. He began his naval career as midshipman at the age of fifteen, advanced to the rank of lieutenant in 1813, and to commander in 1826. Subsequently he served from 1826 to 1830 in the naval recruiting service and made significant innovations in the training of seamen; he devised the first system of naval apprenticeships. One of the first Americans to realize the importance of steam power in naval operations, he supervised the construction at the Brooklyn Navy Yard of the first naval steamship, the *Fulton.* Upon its completion in 1837 he took command of the ship with the rank of captain. He was promoted to the rank of commodore in 1842. From 1843 to 1844 he led the African squadron against the slave trade and in 1846–47 commanded the Gulf squadron during the Mexican War.

In 1852 Perry was assigned the task of establishing diplomatic contact with Japan, a country that had been closed to foreigners since the 17th century. On July 8, 1853, he led a squadron of four ships into Tokyo Bay and presented representatives of the emperor with the text of a proposed commercial and friendship treaty. To give the reluctant Japanese court time to consider the offer, he then sailed for China. With an even more powerful fleet, he returned to Tokyo in February, 1854, for the Japanese answer. The treaty, which was signed on March 31, 1854, provided that humane treatment be extended to sailors shipwrecked in Japanese territory, that American ships be permitted to buy coal in Japan, and that the Japanese ports of Shimoda and Hakodate be opened to American commerce. Perry's mission ended the period of Japanese isolation and enabled Japan to develop into a modern nation. Perry's personal journal, *The Japan Expedition 1852–1854* was first published in 1969.

PERRY, Ralph Barton (1876–1957), American philosopher, born in Poultney, Vt., and educated at Princeton and Harvard universities. He was a follower of the American philosopher and psychologist William James (*see under* JAMES). From 1899 Perry taught philosophy at various American colleges and universities, principally at Harvard, at which he was a faculty member from 1902 until his retirement as professor emeritus in 1946. Among his writings are *The Approach to Philosophy* (1905), *General Theory of Value* (1926), *The Thought and Character of William James* (2 vol., 1935; Pulitzer Prize, 1936), *Shall Not Perish from the Earth* (1940), *One World in the Making* (1945), *Characteristically American* (1949), *The Citizen Decides* (1951), *Realms of Value* (1954), and *Humanity of Men* (1956).

PERSE, Saint-John. See LÉGER, ALEXIS SAINT-LÉGER.

PERSEPHONE, in Greek mythology, daughter of Zeus, father of the gods, and of Demeter (qq.v.), goddess of the earth and of agriculture. Hades (q.v.), god of the underworld, fell in love with Persephone and wished to marry her. Although Zeus gave his consent, Demeter was unwilling. Hades, therefore, seized the maiden as she was gathering flowers and carried her off to his realm. As Demeter wandered over the world in search of her lost daughter, the earth grew desolate. All vegetation died, and famine devastated the land. Finally Zeus sent Hermes (q.v.), the messenger of the gods, to bring Persephone back to her mother. Before Hades would let her go, he asked her to eat a pomegranate seed, the food of the dead. She was thus compelled to return to the underworld for one third of the year, but was allowed to spend the remainder of the year with Demeter. As both the goddess of the dead and the goddess of the fertility of the earth, Persephone was a personification of the revival of nature in spring. The famous Eleusinian Mysteries (q.v.) were held in honor of Persephone and her mother; see also MYSTERIES, CLASSIC. Proserpine (q.v.) was the Latin counterpart of Persephone.

PERSEPOLIS, city of ancient Persia, situated about 35 mi. N.E. of Shiraz. It was used chiefly as a ceremonial capital, the administrative capitals being in cities that were better located. A vast series of ruins is all that now remains of the city beautified by the Persian kings Darius I (*see under* DARIUS), Xerxes I (q.v.), and Artaxerxes I (d. 425 B.C.). Three groups of ruins are chiefly distinguishable: first, the Forty Pillars, with the Mountain of the Tombs; second, Naksh-i-Rustam, with its tombs; and third, the building called the Haram of Jamshíd. The most important is the first group, situated on a vast terrace of cyclopean masonry at the foot of a mountain range. On its central platform are the so-called Great Hall of Xerxes; the Palace of Xerxes, and the Palace of Darius.

The ascent from the plain to the great northern platform is formed by two double flights of stairs. Portals still standing on this platform bear figures of animals 15 ft. high, closely resembling the Assyrian bulls of Nineveh. See PERSIAN ART AND ARCHITECTURE.

PERSEUS, northern constellation, situated between Taurus and Cassiopeia (qq.v.). The brightest star is α Persei, or Algenib. The constellation contains a pair of star clusters, called the double cluster of Perseus, and Algol, which is the best known of the eclipsing stars.

PERSEUS, in Greek mythology, slayer of the Gorgon (q.v.) Medusa, the son of Zeus, father of the gods, and of Danaë (qq.v.), daughter of Acrisius, King of Argos. Warned that he would be killed by his grandson, Acrisius locked mother and child in a chest and cast them into the sea. They drifted to the island of Seriphus, where they were rescued and where Perseus grew to manhood. Polydectes, King of Seriphus, fell in love with Danaë, and, fearing that Perseus might interfere with his plans, sent him to procure the head of Medusa, a monster whose glance turned men to stone. Aided by Hermes (q.v.), messenger of the gods, Perseus made his way to the Gray Women, three old hags, who shared one eye between them. Perseus took their eye and refused to return it until they gave him directions for reaching the nymphs of the north. From the nymphs he received winged sandals, a magic wallet that would always be the right size for whatever was put into it, and a cap to make him invisible. Well equipped with these magic possessions, and with a sword from Hermes that could never be bent or broken and a shield from the goddess Athena (q.v.) in which he could see a reflection of the Gorgon and thus avoid being turned to stone, Perseus found Medusa and killed her. Invisible in his cap, he was able to escape the wrath of her sisters and with her head in the wallet flew on his winged sandals toward home. As he was passing Ethiopia, he rescued the Princess Andromeda (q.v.) as she was about to be sacrificed to a sea monster, and took her with him as his wife. At Seriphus he freed his mother from the violence of Polydectes by using Medusa's head to turn the king and his followers to stone. Perseus, his wife, and his mother then returned to Greece, where Perseus accidentally killed his grandfather Acrisius with a discus, thus fulfilling the prophecy. According to one legend, Perseus went to Asia, where his son Perses ruled over the Persians, who were said to derive their name from him.

PERSHING, John Joseph (1860–1948), American army officer, born in Linn County, Mo., and educated at the United States Military Academy. He served in the Apache campaign in 1886, the Sioux campaign in 1890–91, in Cuba in 1898, and in the Philippines from 1899 to 1903. In 1916 during the Mexican War (q.v.), he headed a punitive expedition into Mexico in pursuit of the bandit Pancho Villa (*see* VILLA, FRANCISCO), who had committed depredations in American territory. In September of that year, Pershing was made a major general.

When the United States entered World War I in April, 1917, Pershing was appointed commander in chief of the American Expeditionary Force in France, and conducted its operations with great success. In October of that year he was made a full general. Pershing preserved the unity of the American army, in spite of pressure to divide it among other Allied forces. The success of the Americans at Saint-Mihiel, France, greatly stimulated the Allied morale. When the

General John Joseph Pershing (left) confers with Marshal Joseph Joffre of France in 1918. UPI

armistice came, Pershing was almost in sight of his goal, Sedan. His contribution to the Allied victory was widely acknowledged, and in September, 1919, he was made general of the armies of the U.S., a rank only he has held.

Pershing was appointed chief of staff of the United States Army in 1921, and entered on the unprecedented task of combining into one organization the Regular Army, the National Guard, and the Permanent Reserves. After his retirement on Sept. 12, 1924, he served as head of a commission supervising American war memorials in France. Pershing's memoirs, *My Experiences in the World War,* appeared in 1931.

PERSIA, former name of the southwestern Asian kingdom now called Iran. The following article comprises an account of the history of Persia from ancient times until 1935. For information on the geography, population, climate, flora and fauna, natural resources, economy, transportation and communication systems, and government of present-day Iran, as well as Iranian history since 1935, *see* IRAN.

The First Empire. The Iranian plateau was settled about 1500 B.C. by Aryan tribes, the most important of which were the Medes, who occupied the N.W. portion, and the Persians, who emigrated from Parsua, a land W. of Lake Urmia, into the southern region of the plateau, which they named Parsamash or Parsumash. The first prominent leader of the Persians was the warrior chief Hakhamanish or Achaemenes (fl. 7th

PERSIA

century B.C.). The Persians were dominated by the Medes until the accession to the Persian throne in 558 B.C. of Cyrus, afterward known as Cyrus the Great (q.v.). He overthrew the Medean rulers, conquered the kingdoms of Lydia and Babylonia (qq.v.) in 546 and 539 respectively, and established the Persian Empire as the preeminent power of the world. His son and successor Cambyses II (*see under* CAMBYSES) extended the Persian realm even further by conquering the Egyptians in 525. Darius I (*see under* DARIUS), who ascended the throne in 521, pushed the Persian borders as far eastward as the Indus River, had a canal constructed from the Nile to the Red Sea, and reorganized the entire Empire, earning the title "Darius the Great". From 499 to 493 he engaged in crushing a revolt of the Ionian Greeks living under Persian rule in Asia, and then launched a punitive campaign against the European Greeks for supporting the rebels. His forces were disastrously defeated by the Greeks at the historic Battle of Marathon (q.v.) in 490. Darius died while preparing a new expedition against the Greeks; his son and successor Xerxes I (q.v.) attempted to fulfill his plan but met defeat in the great sea Battle of Salamis (q.v.) in 480, and in two successive land battles in the following year. See GREECE: *History.*

The forays of Xerxes were the last notable attempt at expansion of the Persian Empire. During the reign of Artaxerxes I, called Longimanus (r. 464–424 B.C.), the second son of Xerxes, the Egyptians revolted, aided by the Greeks; although the revolt was finally suppressed in 446, it signalized the first major assault against, and the beginning of the decline of the Persian Empire.

Alexander the Great and the Seleucids. Many revolts took place in the next century; the final blow was struck by Alexander III (q.v.), King of Macedonia, called the Great, who added the Persian Empire to his own Mediterranean realm by defeating the troops of Darius III in a series of battles between 334 and 331. Alexander effected a temporary integration of the Persians into his empire by enlisting large numbers of Persian soldiers in his armies, and by causing all of his high officers, who were Macedonians, to wed Persian wives. His death in 323 was followed by a long struggle among his generals for the Persian throne. The victor in this contest was Seleucus I (*see under* SELEUCIDAE), who, after conquering the rich kingdom of Babylon in 312, annexed thereto all of the former Persian realm as far east as the Indus R., as well as Syria and Asia Minor, and founded the Seleucid dynasty.

For more than five centuries thereafter, Persia

425

PERSIA

remained a subordinate unit within this great realm, which, after the overthrow of the Seleucids in the 2nd century B.C., became the Parthian Empire; see PARTHIA.

The Sassanians. In 226 A.D., Ardashir I (see under ARDASHIR), a Persian vassal-king, rebelled against the Parthians, defeated them in the Battle of Hormuz, and founded a new Persian dynasty, that of the Sassanidae or Sassanians. He then conquered several minor, neighboring kingdoms, invaded India, levying heavy tribute from the rulers of the Punjab, and conquered Armenia. A particularly significant accomplishment of his reign was the establishment of Zoroastrianism (q.v.) as the official religion of Persia. Ardashir was succeeded in 240 A.D. by his son Shapur I (r. 241-72), who waged two successive wars against the Roman Empire, conquering territories in Mesopotamia and Syria, and a large area in Asia Minor. Between 260 and 263 he lost his conquests to Odenathus, Prince of Palmyra (d. 266?), and ally of Rome. War with Rome was renewed by Narses (r. 293-302); his army was almost annihilated by Roman forces in 297, and he was compelled to conclude peace terms whereby the western boundary of Persia was moved from the Euphrates R. to the Tigris R. (qq.v.), and much additional territory was lost. Shapur II, King of Persia (r. 309-79), regained the lost territories, however, in three successive wars with the Romans.

The next ruler of note was Yazdegerd I, who reigned in peace from 399 to 420; he at first allowed the Persian Christians freedom of worship and may even have contemplated becoming a Christian himself, but he later returned to the Zoroastrianism of his forebears and launched a four-year campaign of ruthless persecution against the Christians. The persecution was continued by his son and successor Bahram V (r. 420-40), who declared war on Rome in 420. The Romans defeated Bahram in 422; by the terms of the peace treaty the Romans promised toleration for the Zoroastrians within their realm in return for similar treatment of Christians in Persia. Two years later, at the Council of Dad-Ishu, the Eastern Church declared its independence of the Western Church.

Near the end of the 5th century a new enemy, the barbaric Ephthalites or "White Huns", attacked Persia; they defeated the Persian king Firuz II (r. 457-84) in 483 and for some years thereafter exacted heavy tribute. In the same year Nestorianism (see NESTORIANS) was made the official faith of the Persian Christians. Kavadh I (r. 485-531) favored the communistic teachings of Mazdak (fl. 5th cent.), a Zoroastrian high priest, and in 498 was deposed by his orthodox brother Zamasp. With the aid of the Ephthalites, Kavadh was restored to the throne in 501. He fought two inconclusive wars against Rome, and in 523 withdrew his support of Mazdak and caused a great massacre of his followers. His son and successor Khosrau I (see under KHOSRAU), in two wars with the Byzantine emperor Justinian I (q.v.), extended his sway to the Black Sea and the Caucasus, becoming the most powerful of all Sassanian kings. He reformed the administration of the empire and restored Zoroastrianism as the state religion. His grandson Khosrau II reigned from 590 to 628; in 602 he began a long war against the Byzantine Empire and by 616 had conquered almost all of southwestern Asia and Egypt. Further expansion was prevented by the Byzantine Emperor Heraclius (q.v.), who between 622 and 627 drove the Persians back within their original borders. The last of the Sassanian kings was Yazdegerd III (d. 651), during whose reign (632-41) the Arabs invaded Persia, destroyed all resistance, gradually replaced Zoroastrianism with Mohammedanism, and incorporated Persia into the Caliphate; see CALIPH.

Turks and Mongols. During the ensuing eight centuries, Persia was dominated successively by the Turkish dynasty of the Seljuks (q.v.), by the Mongols under Genghis Khan, by Tamerlane and his Mongol hordes, and finally by the Turkomans (qq.v.). The rule of the last-named dynasty was overthrown by Ismail I (1486-1524), who claimed descent from Ali (q.v.), the fourth caliph. He was regarded as a saint by the Persians, and proclaimed himself shah, marking the founding of the Safawid dynasty (1502-1736), and the establishment of the Shi'ite doctrine as the official Persian religion (see SHI'ITES). His reign was marked by the beginning of a conflict with Turkey that lasted more than a century and led to the capture of Baghdad in 1623 by Shah Abbas I (q.v.), greatest of the Safawid rulers. The reign of Abbas is also notable for the commencement of trade with the English East India Company; see EAST INDIA COMPANY. The century following his reign was one of steady decline, which culminated in 1722 in the conquest of Persia by an Afghan army under Mir Mahmud, and in the downfall of the Safawids.

European Intervention. Two years later Russia and Turkey, taking advantage of the confusion within Persia, concluded an agreement for its dismemberment. Within those provinces not seized by these two powers, a Persian national army was formed under a warrior chief who drove out the Afghans in 1730 and became shah

PERSIA

Alexander the Great and the dying Darius III, ruler of the Persian Empire (from a manuscript of the Jami alta-warikh, *by the Arabic historian Rashīd al-Dīn, 1250–1318).*

in 1736 as Nadir Shah (1688–1747). Two years later he invaded India, capturing and sacking Delhi in 1739. Russia had meanwhile evacuated its Persian conquests, and Nadir later succeeded in freeing Persia from all foreign occupation by driving out the Turks. His death was followed by a long period of relative anarchy, which ended in 1794 when Agha Mohammed Khan (1720–97) proclaimed himself shah and founded the Kajar dynasty. His brief reign was notable chiefly for numerous acts of wholesale cruelty against his enemies. He was succeeded in 1797 by his nephew Fath Ali (1762?–1835), shah (1797–1835), during whose reign the British were allowed to extend their influence over Persian trade and finances.

The 19th and early 20th centuries were marked by the struggle between Britain and Russia for hegemony in Persia. The British warred against and defeated the Persians in 1856–57, and compelled the Persians to evacuate Afghanistan and to recognize its independence. During the 1880's the Russians gradually established a sphere of influence in northern Persia, and Britain gained control in the Persian Gulf area. Between 1900 and 1902 the Russian government made substantial loans to Persia, receiving as security all Persian customs receipts except those of the Gulf ports. In 1901 the British were granted a sixty-year concession to exploit the petroleum resources of Persia.

The rise of foreign influence in Persia and the weakness and corruption of the Persian rulers led early in the 20th century to the development of a nationalist movement that demanded the establishment of a constitutional government. In 1906 the reigning shah, Muzaffar-ed-Din (1853–1907), was forced by popular demand to convoke the first *majlis* ("national assembly"), which drew up a liberal constitution. His son and successor, Mohammed Ali (1872–1925), attempted to destroy the constitutional movement by force, but was defeated and deposed; his twelve-year-old son was placed on the throne as Ahmed Shah (1898–1930), and a regency was set up. In 1911 the American financier William Morgan Shuster (1877–1960) arrived in Persia at the invitation of the majlis, and was given full power to reorganize the national finances. His reforms were, however, frustrated by the hostility of Russia; Shuster was dismissed, and Russian power subsequently became dominant in Persia.

During World War I Persia was neutral, but was the scene of several battles between the British and Russian allies and the Turks. In 1919 Persia signed an agreement whereby Britain was to exercise controlling influence in Persian af-

PERSIAN ART AND ARCHITECTURE

fairs, but the majlis refused to ratify it. Two years later the British began a withdrawal of their forces from Persia. Soon afterward, Riza Shah Pahlavi (*see under* PAHLAVI), commander of a Persian Cossack force, established a new independent Persian government, with himself as minister of war. He became prime minister in 1923 and two years later was elected shah by the National Assembly, which had deposed Ahmed Shah, last of the Kajar dynasty. During his reign the judiciary was modernized, transportation and communication facilities were improved, and a broad program of Westernization was begun. On March 21, 1935, the Persian government changed the official name of the country to Iran (q.v.). *See also* PERSIAN ART AND ARCHITECTURE; PERSIAN LANGUAGE AND LITERATURE.

PERSIAN ART AND ARCHITECTURE, term used to describe the traditional culture of the modern country of Iran. In a strict sense it should apply only to the historic periods, because before that time non-Indo-European-speaking peoples formed the main population of the country. The Persians themselves only appear in historical records for the first time in the 9th century B.C. In 1935 the name of the country was changed for political reasons to Iran, and many writers now substitute the term Iranian for the older use of Persian. Popular usage, however, still refers to all of the various stages of cultural development on the Iranian plateau from the seventh millennium B.C. to the present as Persian. In this long history, ceramics and bronze working formed the chief art works of the prehistoric period while architecture and sculpture predominated during the period of the first two Persian empires (6th century B.C. to 7th century A.D.). After the Arab conquest and the introduction of Islam (q.v.) in the 7th century A.D., sculpture was little practiced but architecture flourished. Painting became a major art in the period from the 13th to the 17th century. Under the present Pahlavi dynasty (*see under* PAHLAVI) these ancient crafts are being revived with traditional forms combined with Western technology and contemporary materials to form new styles that are distinctively Iranian.

Architecture. Prehistoric architecture in Iran remains little known but has gradually begun to come to light since World War II. Among the earliest examples are a number of small houses of packed mud and mud brick found at several Neolithic sites in western Iran: Tepe Ali Kosh, Tepe Guran, Ganj Dareh Tepe, and Hajji Firuz Tepe. These sites show that small villages made up of one-room houses and other storage structures were already established along the western border of the country by 6000 B.C. Excavations at Tal-i Bakun, near Persepolis, and Tal-i Iblis and Tepe Yahya, near Kerman, show that by 4000 B.C. buildings with a number of rooms were being erected and grouped into villages or small towns. All of these structures indicate that the traditional building techniques using packed mud and sun-dried mud brick had already been invented.

At Shahr-i Sokhta in Seistan an elaborate Bronze Age palace of about 2500 B.C. is currently being excavated. The plans of these structures show a steady growth in complexity ending with the establishment of important commercial centers on the plateau.

At the end of the second millennium, the Iranian tribal groups, including the Medes and Persians, spread over the plateau and displaced or absorbed the indigenous inhabitants. The architecture and minor craft art of this Iron Age period, which immediately preceded the founding of the Persian Empire by Cyrus the Great (q.v.), have now been brought to light by excavations near Kangavar (Godin Tepe and Babajan Tepe), near Hamadan (Nush-i Jan Tepe), and at Zendan-i Suleiman and Tepe Hasanlu in northwestern Iran. These sites reveal for the first time a tradition of building that uses large columnar halls as a central feature. The columns were of wood set on stone slabs while the buildings themselves were of uncut stone and mud-brick construction. Stairways and terraces along with other features form the prototypes for later developments in the imperial architecture of Pasargadae and Persepolis. The buildings at Nush-i Jan Tepe and Godin Tepe are almost certainly Median in origin and are the first structures excavated belonging to the Medes. These new discoveries confirm the generalized descriptions of battlements and palaces found in the literary sources, especially of the Greek historian Herodotus (q.v.).

The first great development of ancient Persian architecture took place under the Persian Empire of the Achaemenid dynasty, which ruled from about 550 to 331 B.C. Remains of Achaemenian architecture are numerous, the earliest being ruins at Pasargadae, the capital city of Cyrus the Great. These ruins include two palaces, a sacred precinct, a citadel, a tower, and the tomb of Cyrus. The palaces were set in walled gardens and contained central columnar halls, the largest of which was 111 ft. in length. The proportions of the principal rooms varied from square to rectangular; all were lighted by a clerestory. Walls were constructed of mud brick; foundations, doorways, columns, and

Onion-shaped domes and soaring archways of the mosques of Isfahan, the former capital of Persia, sparkle with many-hued tiles.
Marc Riboud – UNESCO

dadoes along the walls were of stone. Columns were capped with stone blocks carved to represent the conjoined forequarters of horses or lions with horns. The roof was flat and was probably made of wood. The sacred precinct consisted of a walled court containing two altars and a rectangular stepped platform. The tower was a tall rectangular structure built of yellow limestone; a contrasting black limestone was used for the doorway and two tiers of blind windows. The tomb of Cyrus was a small stone building with gables placed on a stepped platform. The surrounding columns were placed there during recent Islamic times.

Darius I (*see under* DARIUS) built a new capital at Persepolis, to which additions were made by Xerxes I (q.v.) and Artaxerxes I (r. 464–424 B.C.). Three vast terraces were hewn and leveled out of the rocky site, and on them mud-brick and stone buildings, similar to those at Pasargadae, were erected. The buildings at Persepolis differed from those at Pasargadae in that the columnar halls were square; walls were broken by windows and windowlike niches of stone, and the stone dado was not applied; doorways bore a quarter-round cornice ornamented with a petal motif, probably of Egyptian origin; column shafts were fluted rather than plain, the bases and caps were ornamented with floral decorations, and the termination of the column, called the impost block, took the form of naturalistically rendered forequarters of bulls or bulls with wings. These buildings had ceilings of cedarwood, carried on heavy balks or beams which rested on the stone impost blocks at the tops of the columns.

Other remains of Achaemenian architecture exist at Susa, where Darius I built a large palace, which was subsequently rebuilt by Artaxerxes II (r. 404–359 B.C.). Royal architecture under the Achaemenides also included tombs cut in solid rock, of which the best-known examples are those at Naqshah Rostam near Persepolis. Little is known of the popular building practices of the period, but archeologists believe that the ordinary dwelling house was made of mud-brick.

PERSIAN ART AND ARCHITECTURE

After the conquest of Persia by Alexander III (q.v.), King of Macedonia, called the Great in 331 B.C. and the assumption of power by the Seleucid dynasty, the architecture of the country followed the styles common to the Greek world; see GREEK ART AND ARCHITECTURE. The great Greek-style Temple of Anāhita at Kangavar is currently undergoing excavation by the Archeological Service of Iran with a view to eventual restoration. The temple had been destroyed by a severe earthquake in antiquity.

Subsequently, under the Parthian Arsacid dynasty, which lasted from about 250 B.C. to 226 A.D., a small number of buildings were constructed in native Persian style. The most notable monument of this period is a palace at Hatra (now Al Hadhr, Iraq), dating from the 1st or 2nd century A.D., and exemplifying the use of the barrel vault on a grand scale. The vaults, heavy walls, and small rooms of this palace indicate a continuation of earlier Assyrian and Babylonian tradition.

A great renaissance in architecture took place under the Sassanid dynasty which ruled Persia from 226 A.D. until the Islamic conquest in 651 A.D. Construction was radically different from that of the Achaemenian period. Walls were built of burnt brick or small stones bound with mortar; barrel vaults were used to span rooms and corridors; and domes were erected over the large halls. The principal features of the plan of the palaces at Persepolis were adopted, but the various rooms were enclosed within a single building. Thus the same building incorporated a public audience hall, a smaller private audience hall, and a complex of lesser rooms. Remains of the major monuments of Sassanian architecture include the ruins of domed palaces at Firuzabad, Girra, and Sarvestan, and the vast vaulted hall at Ctesiphon. The large site of Bishapur is currently being systematically excavated by the Archeological Service of Iran. Palace sites have also been excavated at Qais, Hira, and Damghan. Other ruins include bridges at Dizful and Shushtar, and a number of small temples built for the worship of fire at various locales.

After the Arab conquest, Persia became part of the Islamic world, and the mosque became the major building type in Persian architecture; see ISLAMIC ART AND ARCHITECTURE. The established style of vaulted construction was continued; common features were the pointed arch, the ogee arch, and the dome on circular drum. Outstanding examples of early Islamic Persian architecture include the Mosque of Baghdad built in 764 A.D., the Great Mosque at Samarra erected in 847 A.D., and the early-10th-century mosque at Nayin. The Mongols destroyed much of the early Islamic architecture in Persia, but after their conquest of Baghdad in 1258, building was resumed according to Persian traditions. Subsequently, a number of the most notable buildings in the history of Persian architecture were erected. They include the Great Mosque at Veramin, built in 1322; the Mosque of the Imam Riza at Meshad-i-Murghab, erected in 1418; and the Blue Mosque at Tabriz, the mausoleums of the Mongol conqueror Tamerlane (q.v.) and his family at Samarkand, the Royal Mosque at Meshad-i-Murghab, and the vast madrasahs, or mosque schools, at Samarkand, all of the 15th century.

Under the Safawid dynasty from 1502 to 1736, a vast number of mosques, palaces, tombs, and other structures were built. Common features in the mosques were onion-shaped domes on drums, barrel-vaulted porches, and pairs of towering minarets. A striking decoration was the corbel, a projection of stone or wood from the face of a wall, used in rows and tiers. These corbels, arranged to appear as series of intersecting miniature arches, are usually called stalactite corbels. Color was an important part of the architecture of this period, and the surfaces of the buildings were covered with ceramic tiles in glowing blue, green, yellow, and red. The most notable Safawid buildings were constructed at Isfahan (q.v.), the capital at that period. The city, laid out in broad avenues, gardens, and canals, contained palaces, mosques, baths, bazaars, and caravansaries in great numbers.

Since the 18th century, the architectural styles of Western Europe have been adopted in increasing degree in Iran. At the same time, traditional forms have remained vital, and often the native and imported elements have been combined in the same building. In recent times, particularly in the cities, unadorned steel and concrete structures, similar to those seen in all civilized parts of the modern world, have been built as dwellings, public buildings, and factories.

Sculpture. In the first great period of Persian art, during the reign of the Achaemenides, sculpture was practiced on a monumental scale. About 515 B.C., Darius I had a vast relief and inscription carved upon a cliff at Behistun. The relief shows him triumphing over his enemies as the god Ahura Mazda looks on. The carving was derived in plan and detail from Assyrian models, but the naturalistic treatment of the drapery and the eyes was original. At Persepolis, sculpture was an important adjunct to the architecture. In addition to the sculptured animal capitals on

PERSIAN ART AND ARCHITECTURE

Metropolitan Museum of Art – Rogers Fund

Metropolitan Museum of Art – Fletcher Fund

Examples of the pottery and metalwork of Persia. Above, left: Bronze incense burner in the shape of an imaginary animal, from the 12th century. Above, right: Ewer of bronze, dating from the Sassanian period (226–651). Right: Earthenware bowl with overglaze decoration, from the 13th century.

Metropolitan Museum of Art – Rogers Fund

431

PERSIAN ART AND ARCHITECTURE

the columns, which were a dominant feature of the interiors of the buildings, friezes representing lions were set on the exterior cornices. Door jambs were carved with reliefs of the king, and staircases were decorated with friezes of royal guards and tribute bearers carved in low relief. The main gateway to the city was flanked by a pair of huge bulls with human heads.

The decoration of the palace at Susa consisted of stone reliefs in the style of those at Persepolis, and panels of enameled bricks in blue, green, white, and yellow. The use of glazed bricks continued a tradition which was first established in Assyria and Babylonia. The glazed brick panels at Susa portrayed soldiers, winged bulls, sphinxes, and griffins. The best known of these panels comprise the Frieze of Archers, now in the Louvre Museum, Paris. Achaemenian sculpture in relief is further exemplified at Naqshah Rostam, where four royal tombs were hewn out of the rock. At each tomb the face of the cliff was carved to represent the façade of a palace; above the palace, figures support a dais on which the king stands worshiping the gods.

After the conquest of Persia by Alexander the Great, Greek or Hellenistic influence was predominant in the arts of Persia. Examples include fragments of bronze sculpture found at Shami, and the Parthian sculptural reliefs at Behistun. The second great period of Persian art began

"King Khusrau Seated upon His Throne", probably by the 16th-century artist Mahmud Muzahib.
Metropolitan Museum of Art – Gift of Alexander Smith Cochran

Persian Art. Plate 1. A magnificent prayer rug of the 19th century from northern Persia. The art of rug weaving dates from the 3rd- to 7th-century Sassanid dynasty.

Metropolitan Museum of Art

Persian Art. Plate 2. The art of pottery in Persia dates to prehistoric times. Left: A 17th-century A.D. ceramic bottle with a silver stopper. Below: A 15th-century glazed bowl, decorated in green and turquoise.

Metropolitan Museum of Art

PERSIAN ART AND ARCHITECTURE

with the reign of the Sassanid dynasty in 226 A.D. A single example of sculpture in the round has survived from this period: a colossal standing figure of a king near Bishapur. A few statuettes have also survived, but the characteristic sculptural work, as in Achaemenian times, was the relief cut in rock. The best-known examples are colossal reliefs at Naqshah Rostam portraying the Persian kings Ardashir I (see under ARDASHIR) and Shapur I (241–272 A.D.) mounted on horses. A similar equestrian relief at Taq-i-Bustan represents another Persian king of this dynasty Khosrau II (see under KHOSRAU). Following the Sassanian period, sculpture ceased to exist as a major art.

Painting. Painting in fresco and the illumination of manuscripts (see ILLUMINATED MANUSCRIPTS) were practiced in Persia at least as early as the Sassanian period, but only fragments of the work have survived. Manuscripts of the Koran in the Arabic Kufic script were executed on parchment rolls at Basra and Al Kufa at the end of the 7th century. These manuscripts did not contain painted scenes, but depended for their effect on the beauty of the calligraphy. Ornamental calligraphy was widely practiced in the 8th and 9th centuries. Painting and illumination became important elements in the decoration of manuscripts in the 9th century. With the introduction in the 10th century of paper for the making of books, the forms and varieties of religious and secular books increased greatly.

In the 12th century, a school of painting at Baghdad became known for its manuscripts of scientific works, fables, and anecdotes, illustrated with miniature paintings. In the 13th century the influence of Chinese landscape painting, introduced after the Mongols came to power in Persia, became apparent. Paintings of stories, legends, and historical events, often occupying whole pages and pairs of pages, illustrated books devoted to poems and world histories. The text was usually written in Persian rather than Arabic at this time. In the 14th century Baghdad and Tabriz were the main centers for painting. Subsequently, Samarkand, Bukhara, and Herat also became important centers. In general the paintings were composed of figure paintings and of landscapes of jagged rocks, single trees, and little streams bordered by flowers. At the beginning of the 14th century the backgrounds of the paintings were usually red; later they were more often blue, and at the end of the century gold backgrounds became common.

The best-known Persian miniature painter was Behzad (about 1450–about 1520), the greatest artist of the end of the Mongol and the beginning of the Safawid periods. He was head of the academy of painting and calligraphy at Herat until 1506, when he went to Tabriz and became the royal librarian. Behzad's paintings are characterized by rich color and realism in figures and landscapes. He differentiated the figures in group scenes, and his portraits were strongly individual. Many painters studied with him, including the celebrated artists Mirak (about 1475–1545) and Sultan Mohammed (fl. 1st half of the 16th cent.), and his style was imitated throughout Persia, Turkestan, and India. Among the few extant manuscripts illustrated by Behzad are the History of Tamerlane (1467), now in the Princeton University Library, and the Fruit Garden (1487), a book of poems now in the Egyptian Library, Cairo.

Portrait painting became an important art form during the 16th century. One of the most distinguished portraitists was Ali Riza Abbasi (fl. 1598–1643), who delineated his figures with sparing but expressive brush strokes. Most of his paintings represented single figures, but he also painted realistic group scenes of pilgrims and dervishes. In the late 16th century and in the 17th century, monochrome ink drawings brightened with touches of red and gold replaced the jewel-like polychrome paintings of the earlier manuscripts. After the 17th century, Persian artists copied European paintings and engravings, and the native traditions declined. Paintings of conventional Persian themes on lacquer became a handicraft industry in the 19th century, and the lacquerware was exported in large quantities to Western Europe. This industry is still flourishing at the present time. Modern imitations of 16th century miniature paintings are also common, but no contemporary national style of painting has emerged.

Pottery, Metalwork, and Weaving. The earliest examples of minor artwork in Persia date to the late seventh millennium B.C. and consist of animal and human female figures fashioned in clay. The female figurines, found at Tepe Sarab near Kermanshah, are complex objects made of many small pieces fitted together on small dowels. The thighs and breasts of the figures are exaggerated, and the heads are reduced to small pegs. In contrast to the highly stylized and abstracted human figures are quantities of animal figurines done in a very natural style.

The second great development in prehistoric art occurs during the fourth millennium when a variety of painted pottery styles appeared on the plateau. The vessels are usually red or buff in color and are covered with animal figures,

PERSIAN ART AND ARCHITECTURE

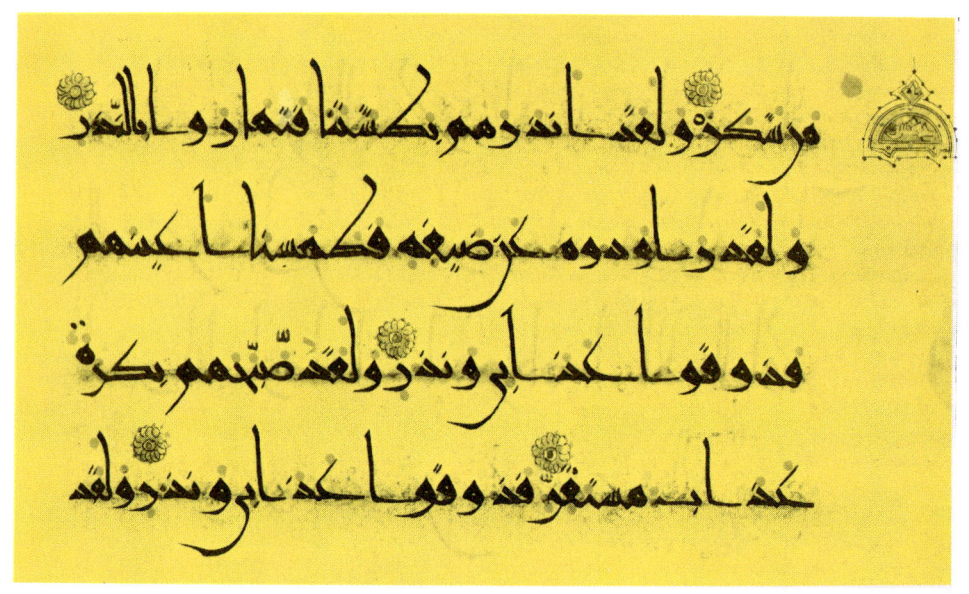

A folio from the Koran, written in Kufic calligraphy in black on light brown glazed paper, 11th to 12th century. Metropolitan Museum of Art - Rogers Fund

often goats, painted in black. The pottery is found alongside small objects like stamp seals and small instruments of copper such as pins and chisels. During the third millennium burnished gray pottery was manufactured in northeastern Persia along with a great amount of cast copper objects such as axes, decorated pins, figurines, and so on. Painted pottery continued to be made in other parts of the country except in northern Azerbaijan where black and gray burnished wares appeared, decorated in many instances with geometric patterns excised into the surface and then filled with a white paste. About 1300 B.C. gray burnished pottery appeared over the whole of the north, perhaps originating from the northeast, and probably associated with the spreading Indo-Iranian tribes. Around 800 B.C. painting again revived with elaborate geometric patterns, horses, bulls, and human figures represented.

Beginning at the end of the second millennium and continuing to the middle first millennium there was a great florescence of bronze casting along the southern Caspian mountain zone and in Luristan. Harness trappings, horse bits, axes, and votive objects were made in large quantities and reflected a complex animal style created by combining parts of animals and fantastic creatures in various combinations.

Luxurious works of minor art were produced during the Achaemenian period, including ornaments and vessels of gold and silver, stone vases, and engraved gems. An extensive collection of these objects, called the "Treasure of the Oxus", is exhibited at the British Museum, London.

Sassanian metalwork was highly developed, the most usual objects being shallow silver cups and large bronze ewers, engraved and worked in repoussé. The commonest themes were court scenes, hunters, animals, birds, and stylized plants. The largest collection of these vessels is in the Hermitage Museum, Leningrad; other examples are in museums in Paris, London, and New York.

Silk weaving was a flourishing industry under the Sassanid dynasty. The designs, consisting of symmetrical animal, plant, and hunter patterns framed in medallions, were imitated throughout the Middle East and also in medieval Europe. Even after the Arab conquest, Sassanian silks and metalware continued to be manufactured, and Sassanian designs strongly influenced artists in Byzantium to the west and as far as Chinese Turkestan to the east. Techniques of weaving, metalwork, and pottery, developed during the Sassanian period, were practiced throughout subsequent Persian history. The weaving of rugs, for which Persia has been especially noted, was encouraged by the Sassanids and has continued to be an important artistic skill until the present time. For a discussion of Persian rugs, see RUGS, ORIENTAL. R.H.D.

PERSIAN GULF, arm of the Arabian Sea, between the Arabian Peninsula on the s.w. and Iran

Aerial view of a port installation at Ras Tanura on the Persian Gulf in Saudi Arabia.
Arabian American Oil Co.

on the N.E. The gulf extends N.W. about 600 mi. from the Strait of Hormuz to Shatt-al-Arab, a river formed by the confluence of the Tigris and Euphrates rivers (qq.v.). The gulf is connected to the Arabian Sea by the Strait of Hormuz and the Gulf of Oman. The Persian Gulf varies in width from 29 mi. to 230 mi. The area is about 90,000 sq.mi. and the greatest depth is about 300 ft. The chief islands in the gulf are Qishm and Bahrain. Large banks of pearl-producing mollusks are found on the Arabian shore. The Union of Arab Emirates, Ras al Khaimah, Saudi Arabia, Qatar, and Kuwait are on the S.W. shore; Iraq is on the N. tip, and Iran is on the N.E. shore.

The principal ports on the Persian Gulf are Al Kuwait, in Kuwait; Basra, in Iraq; and Abadan and Bushire, in Iran. The first three, which lie within 100 mi. of each other at the N.W. end of the gulf, are assuming new prominence as centers for the shipment of oil from the Middle East. On Bahrain Island are oil installations, and a large airport that was an important stopover point on Allied flights between Egypt and India during World War II.

PERSIAN GULF STATES, ten sheikhdoms on the Arabian shore of the Persian Gulf. They include the independent sheikhdoms of Bahrain, Kuwait, Qatar, the six former Trucial States of Abu Dhabi, 'Ajman, Dubai, Fujairah, Sharjah, and Umm al Qaiwain that form the Union of Arab Emirates, and Ras al Khaimah. *See* BAHRAIN; KUWAIT; QATAR; UNION OF ARAB EMIRATES.

The Perpetual Maritime Truce, the culmination of many short-term maritime-truce agreements, was signed in 1853 by Great Britain and the principal sheikhs of the area, which was known as the Pirate Coast. In 1892 these states, according to the exclusive agreement, agreed not to relinquish any territory or enter into relationships with foreign governments except with British consent. Subsequently, similar treaties were entered into by other sheikhdoms of the region including Kuwait which became independent in 1914.

In January, 1968, the British government declared the intention of withdrawing all British military forces from areas east of the Suez Canal, including the Persian Gulf States, by the end of 1971. Fearing the exposure of their territories to the rivalries of Saudi Arabia and Iran and the revolutionary aims of some Arab states, the other nine rulers formed the Federation of Gulf Emirates in October, 1969. The federation did not succeed, however, and the states sought independence in 1971. Bahrain became independent in August, Qatar in September, and six of the Trucial States in December. The status of Ras al Khaimah remained undecided.

PERSIAN LAMB. *See* FUR: *Classification: Sheep and Horses.*

PERSIAN LANGUAGE AND LITERATURE, language of the present-day kingdom of Iran, formerly Persia (qq.v.), and the literature, which dates back more than 1000 years. Persian is a member of the Iranian family of languages, which together with Indian languages form the Indo-Iranian branch of the Indo-European language (q.v.); *see* INDIAN LANGUAGES; INDO-IRANIAN LANGUAGES.

Language. Three phases may be distinguished in the development of Iranian languages; Old, Middle, and Modern. Old Iranian is represented by Avestan and Old Persian. Avestan is the language of Avesta, a collection of hymns, homilies, religious law, myths and legends that form the sacred scriptures of Zoroastrianism (q.v.). The Gathas, a group of religious poems that are the oldest part of the Avesta, were composed by the Persian prophet Zoroaster (q.v.) in metrical form sometime before the 6th century B.C. Aves-

PERSIAN LANGUAGE AND LITERATURE

tan, an Eastern Iranian language, died out centuries before the advent of Islam (q.v.).

Old Persian is recorded in the inscriptions of the Persian kings of the Achaemenid family (about 550–330 B.C.), notably Darius I (see under DARIUS) and Xerxes I (q.v.), in a cuneiform script. The Bistun rock inscription of Darius I near Hamadan (ancient Ecbatana), which relates the events of the coming to power of Darius I, the extent of his vast empire, and his admonitions to his successors, is one of the principal inscriptions in Old Persian, and one of the great documents of antiquity. Old Persian and Avestan, like Greek and Latin, are highly inflected languages and have close affinity with the Sanskrit language (q.v.).

Middle Iranian is represented by Middle Persian, Parthian, Sogdian, Saka, Bactrian, and Khwarazmian. Parthian, the language of the Arsacid kings (about 250 B.C.–226 A.D.), is known chiefly through the inscriptions of early Sassanian kings (226–651 A.D.) as well as the Manichaean writings. Parthian declined during the Sassanian hegemony, but influenced Persian during the long period of Arsacid rule. See PERSIA. Sogdian was the native language of Sogdiana, a northeastern province of Persia, which figured the cities of Samarkand (q.v.) and Bukhara among its centers. Secular and religious (Buddhist and Christian) Sogdian writings exist, mostly from the early centuries of the Christian era. Saka, also known as Khotanese, is documented by a considerable amount of writing, mainly Buddhist, from the Iranian community which had settled in Khotan, east of the Pamir region, now in China. Bactrian, only recently discovered, was spoken in Bactria (q.v.) and is recorded chiefly on Kushan inscriptions found in Afghanistan. Khwarazmian continued at least into the 11th century. It was spoken in the ancient kingdom of Khwarezm, east of the Caspian Sea. The main documents in Khwarazmian are from the post-Islamic period and await further clarification.

Middle Persian, though a continuation of Old Persian, has much simpler grammar than the latter, but is written in an ambiguous script with multivalent letters, adopted from Aramaic; see ARAM. Middle Persian was the language of the Sassanians and its literature has wide range, including Zoroastrian writings, Sassanian inscriptions, and Manichaean works written in a form of Syriac alphabet. Much of Middle Persian literature, particularly works on history, government, and ethics, was translated into Arabic and enriched Arabic literature; see ARABIC LANGUAGE AND LITERATURE. The bulk of Middle Persian writing, which had distinct Zoroastrian connotations, however, was eventually lost during Islamic times.

Middle Persian evolved into Modern Persian, which has been the official and cultural language of Persia for the past twelve centuries since the Arab conquest in the 7th century. It is written in an enlarged Arabic script, and has absorbed a vast Arabic vocabulary.

Literature. Persian language has produced one of the world's major literatures. A principal characteristic of this literature is the preponderance of poetry, a major Persian art.

The first poems in Modern Persian were written in the 9th century. With the establishment of local dynasties in Persia in that century, Persian literature found enthusiastic and generous royal patrons. The Samanid dynasty (892–999), championed a cultural rebirth in Persia, and in their courts flourished a host of able poets such as Rudaki (d. 954), considered the father of Persian poetry. It was also under the Samanids that the preeminent Persian poet Firdausi (q.v.), composed the bulk of his *Shāh-Namāh*, or *Book of Kings*, the Persian national epic. The courts of the Ghaznavids (977–1186) and the Seljuks (1038–1194) followed the tradition of the Samanids in patronizing Persian poetry, and during both dynasties a number of brilliant panegyrists flourished.

Persian poetry excels in two genres, epic and lyric. The *Shāh-Namāh*, a monumental work of some 60,000 lines which deals with the legendary and factual history of Persia from the beginning to the fall of the Sassanian Empire (651 A.D.), is a prime example of epic poetry. The *Shāh-Namāh* is one of the two great epics produced in the East, the other one being the *Mahabharata* of ancient India. Apart from its poetical distinction, the *Shāh-Namāh* has reinforced the sense of national identity in Persia.

The lyric poetry, chiefly expressed in the form of the ghazel, is of a tender and passionate nature and very often imbued with mystical sentiments. The three outstanding Persian poets in this genre are Saadi, Hafiz (qq.v.), and Jalal-uddin Rumi (1207–73). With Hafiz's subtlety of thought, depth of sentiment and inimitable craftsmanship, Persian poetry reached its zenith, and its creative vitality began to weaken after him. The 15th-century Persian poet and mystic Jami (q.v.) is generally considered the last of the great classical poets. In India, however, Persian poetry flourished at the courts of the Muslim rulers and produced a vast treasury of Persian poems; see INDIA: *History*.

Although many Persian poets used the ruba 'i

form of short poem, usually in epigrammatic style, the greatest master of this art was the mathematician, astronomer, and poet Omar Khayyam (q.v.), whose apparent hedonism is inspired by melancholy skepticism.

The prose literature of Persia, somewhat overshadowed by the poetry, includes stories, fables, popular romances, and also works on history, government, ethics, and mysticism, which are generally written in a literary idiom. Among the chief prose works in Persian may be mentioned *Qabusnameh* ("Mirror of Princes") by the 11th-century writer Kai Kavus; *Kalileh va Demneh,* a book of fables by the 12th-century writer Nasrallah; and Saadi's *Golestan,* a book of wit, wisdom and humor, written in elegant and rhymed prose. Persian prose assumed a florid style from about the 12th century and does not regain its former simplicity until about the middle of the 19th century when a return to the style of the earlier masters followed the similar development in poetry in the 18th century.

The modern movement in Persian literature began about the turn of the 20th century and deepened with the quickening of social changes caused largely by the impact of the West. Persian literature adopted the novel, the short story, and the play as new genres. Pioneer work in short story writing was done by M. A. Jamalzadeh (1897–   ), Sadiq Hidayat (1903–51), and Buzurg Alavi (1908–   ). The most significant writer of contemporary Iran was Hidayat whose cynical, morbid, but highly effective works deeply influenced the younger generation of Persian writers. Major fiction writers of Iran are Sadiq Chubak (1916–   ), Jalal Ali Ahmad (1923–69), and M. A. Afghani (1925–   ).

The modern school of Persian poetry was greatly influenced by Nima Yushij (1895–1959), an avant-garde poet of independence, insight and artistic integrity, who almost completely broke with the traditional form and imagery of Persian poetry, and includes N. Naderpour (1929–   ), A. Bamdad (1925–   ), F. Farrokhzad (1935–67), and M. Omid (1928–   ).

Traditional Persian drama consisted chiefly of passion plays centering on the life of the shi'ite martyrs; see SHI'ITES. Plays in the Western sense had their beginnings in Persian in the 19th century. Of the modern Persian playwrights one might mention Malcolm Khan (1833–1908), a satirical playwright, Beyza'i (1938–   ), and Sa'edi (1936–   ), a versatile and able satirist.

PERSIAN WARS. *See* GREECE: *History: The Persian Wars.*

PERSIMMON, name for trees of the genus *Diospyros,* belonging to the Ebony family, and

Persimmon, Diospyros virginiana   John H. Gerard – National Audubon Society

for their edible fruit. The common persimmon, *D. virginiana,* is native to the eastern United States, growing wild from Connecticut and Iowa, south to Florida and Texas; it grows from 30 to 50 ft. in height and has oblong leaves and unisexual flowers. The fruit, which is a berry 1 to 2 in. in diameter, is extremely astringent before it ripens; when ripe it is sweet and palatable. The persimmon tree yields a heavy, hard, close-grained wood, that is used extensively for shuttles and bobbins in the textile industry and for golf-club heads and other sports equipment. The Japanese persimmon, *D. kaki,* is cultivated in the warm sections of the U.S., particularly in California, for its popular large fruit, resembling a pale tomato in appearance.

PERSIUS, in full AULUS PERSIUS FLACCUS (34–62 A.D.), Roman poet, born of a distinguished family in Etruria. As a young man he came under the influence of the Roman Stoic philosopher Lucius Annaeus Cornutus (fl. 1st cent.). Persius wrote fastidiously and sparingly, leaving at his death six brief but noted satires. These have been called sermons on Stoic texts, as they deal with the importance of being earnest, the nature of true religion, the correct use of wealth, and the nature of freedom. The poem on false taste in poetry is considered his best. Although he imitates and quotes the satires of the Roman satirist and poet Horace (q.v.), he lacks Horace's genial humor and knowledge of the world. Persius is remarkable for the stern-

PERSONALITY

ness with which he censured the immorality of his day, contrasting it with the old Roman austerity and with the Stoic ideal of virtue. He was himself said to be a man of exemplary character, modest, gentle, and virtuous.

PERSONALITY, organized behavior revealed by individual traits or characteristics. An individual may be characterized as introverted, anxious, and aggressive by psychologists who specialize in personality assessment; another may be regarded as autonomous, ascendant, and curious. Other branches of psychology are concerned with the sensory apparatus or patterns of response; the psychology of personality considers the organism as a whole and consistency of individual traits.

PERSONALITY DEVELOPMENT

The factors that shape personality are constitutional determinants, childhood conditioning, and social and cultural traditions in the group to which an individual belongs.

Constitutional Determinants. The American psychologist William Herbert Sheldon (1899–) attempted to relate body types to personality. Investigators generally agreed on the classification of body types as round, square, and linear, and some investigators found a high relationship between these physical measurements and personality. Later scientific studies, however, undertaken with more rigorous standards questioned such correlation.

Childhood Environment. The pioneer hypotheses regarding the development of personality evolved by the Austrian psychoanalyst Sigmund Freud (q.v.) stressed the importance of the child's early experiences in the formation of the adult personality. Such factors as gratification or frustration at certain stages of psychosexual development and the resolution of the Oedipus conflict are considered significant; see PSYCHOANALYSIS: *Theory of Psychoanalysis.* Studies of childhood experience suggest that the role of parents is crucial in the formation of the child's personality and his adult psychological health. Case histories of individuals with personality disorders reveal a high frequency of parental mismanagement, either by overindulgence, negligence, or rejection. Research attempting to relate the numbers of brothers and sisters or the birth order of the individual to personality traits has been inconclusive.

Social and Cultural Determinants. Some authorities emphasize the role of social and cultural traditions in personality development. In describing the behavior of members of two New Guinea tribes, the American anthropologist Margaret Mead (q.v.) demonstrated this relationship. Although the tribes are of the same racial stock and live in the same area, one group is peaceful, friendly, and cooperative, whereas the other is assertive, hostile, and competitive. Such differences indicate the profound effect of cultural factors on personality in primitive societies.

Although individuals reared in a primitive culture share common experiences to a greater degree than those in modern social organizations, attempts have been made to discover national characteristics in more complex societies. For example, the Japanese are regarded as compulsively neat; the Germans are viewed as unusually respectful of authority. Citizens of the United States are considered to show exceptional devotion to mechanical conveniences and devices.

CONSISTENCY OF PERSONALITY

Many investigators hold that the traits of an individual are typically related to one another and that individuals of a given character show great consistency in such groupings. Although the concept of the organization of traits is of ancient origin, it was popularized by the Austrian psychiatrist Alfred Adler (q.v.), who termed the individual's behavior his "style of life". One example of the consistency of personality is the cluster of traits that form the so-called authoritarian personality. Its characteristics include conventionalism, toughness, cynicism, and aspiration to dominance, are related to individual beliefs and attitudes, and sometimes include racial bias and a highly conservative outlook.

Although many groups of traits have been described, every person possesses an individuality different from those of his fellows. The American psychologist Gordon Willard Allport (1897–1967) believed that this uniqueness could never be captured by bare descriptions of personality traits.

ASSESSMENT OF PERSONALITY

Individual traits may be determined by (1) the judgment of experts and (2) personality tests. Persons concerned with assessment of personality long have relied on judgments based on individual interviews. Personality tests have a shorter history. Although most standardized tests measure intelligence, many assess personality. Direct tests do not conceal from the subject the traits being measured; indirect tests conceal the traits under examination. Examples of direct tests are those designed to reveal a specific tendency; typical of indirect tests are those in which the individual describes what he sees in an inkblot or creates a story based on a chosen picture.

Tests may be scored mechanically by comparison with established norms or intuitively by experienced judges. The two methods may be combined to evaluate a new personality test. When the Manifest Anxiety Scale was proposed by the American psychologist Janet A. Taylor in the early 1950's, the close correlation between the scores of those taking the test and the objective judgment of experts as to the amount of anxiety shown by the subjects led to its adoption. Tests are used to assess relatively few traits in groups of individuals; clinical judgment is utilized in the intensive analysis of individuals. See PSYCHOLOGICAL TESTING; see also GRAPHOLOGY.

Various types of mental and physical disabilities that give their names to the type of personality involved are discussed in this encyclopedia. For information on the personalities described as alcoholic, neurotic, psychopathic, psychotic, psychosomatic, and schizophrenic, see ALCOHOLISM; MENTAL DISORDERS; MENTAL HEALTH; PSYCHIATRY; PSYCHOANALYSIS; PSYCHOSOMATIC MEDICINE; for the treatment of personality disorders, see PSYCHOTHERAPY.

PERSPECTIVE DRAWING. See DRAWING: *Perspective Drawing.*

PERTH, Great Britain, county of central Scotland, bordered on the N. by Inverness and Aberdeen counties, on the E. by Angus County, on the S. by Fife, Kinross, Clackmannan, and Stirling counties, and on the W. by Argyll County. The terrain is extremely mountainous, particularly in the N. and W. portions, which are traversed by the Grampians (q.v.). Approximately fifty peaks in Perth are more than 3000 ft. in elevation. The outstanding summits are Ben Lawers (3986 ft.), Ben More (3845 ft.), Ben Lui (3708 ft.), and Ben Vorlich (3225 ft.). Numerous streams, including the Tay River (q.v.), the longest river in Scotland, drain the county. The Firth of Tay, which receives the estuary of the Tay R., is an arm of the North Sea (q.v.). Among other notable features of the terrain is the large number of lakes. The largest, Loch Tay (14½ mi. long), is in the central section of the county. Extensive tracts, particularly in the E. and S.E., are cultivated. Fruit growing and sheep raising are the chief agrarian industries. The leading field crops are oats, turnips, and potatoes. Manufacturing industries include bleaching, dyeing, and the manufacture of cotton, linen, woolen, and jute textiles. Perth (q.v.) is the county town. Area, excluding water surface, 2493.4 sq.mi.; pop. (1969 est.) 124,199.

PERTH, city in Australia, and capital of Western Australia State, on the Swan R., about 12 miles N.E. of Fremantle. The city is an important railway junction and the chief commercial and cultural center of the State. Products of the city include clothing, furniture, sandalwood oil, and flour. Noteworthy buildings include two cathedrals, Government House, and the buildings of the University of Western Australia (founded 1911). Perth was settled in 1829 and chartered as a city in 1856. The discovery of gold in the vicinity in the early 1890's helped in the growth of the city. Pop. (1966) 96,223.

PERTH, Great Britain, burgh and county town of Perth County, Scotland, on the Tay R., about 32 miles N.W. of Edinburgh. Three bridges span the Tay at Perth. The burgh is the commercial center of a fertile agricultural region. The industries include dyeing, bleaching, and the manufacture of linen and wool. The principal historic landmark in Perth is the Church of Saint John the Baptist, the nave and transept of which date from the early 13th century. John Knox (q.v.) preached his famous sermon against idolatry at the church in 1559. Noteworthy modern edifices include Saint Ninian's Episcopal Cathedral, the Sandeman Public Library, and the Perthshire Natural History Museum.

History. Perth became a royal burgh in 1210. During the initial phases of the Scottish wars of independence, the burgh was held by the English, but Robert Bruce (q.v.), King of Scotland, captured it in 1311. Edward III (q.v.), King of England, regained Perth in 1335, but lost it in 1339. James I (q.v.), King of Scotland, was murdered here in 1437. Pop. (1969 est.) 41,654.

PERTH AMBOY, city and port of entry of New Jersey, in Middlesex Co., on Raritan Bay, at the mouth of the Raritan R., about 15 miles S. of Newark. It is served by railroad and the harbor, equipped with dry docks and shipyards, is the site of extensive shipping activity. Deposits of fire clay are found in the vicinity. The major industry is copper refining. Other industries include oil refining, food packing, and the manufacture of chemicals and paint, ceramic ware, wire cable and clothing.

History. The site of the city formed part of a tract of land purchased from the Indians in 1651. The first settlers, mostly Scottish Dissenters, arrived in 1685. In 1686 Perth Amboy was made capital of East Jersey and retained that status until 1702; see NEW JERSEY: *History.* It became the first incorporated city in New Jersey in 1718. In 1776, during the American Revolution, William Franklin (q.v.), the last royal governor of New Jersey, was captured in Perth Amboy. Pop. (1960) 38,007; (1970) 38,798.

PERTURBATIONS, in physical astronomy, disturbances produced in the simple elliptic motion of one heavenly body about another by the

PERU

action of a third body or by the nonsphericity of the principal body. For any given position of the moon with reference to the earth and sun, the difference of the accelerating effects of the sun on the earth and moon is a disturbing force. This force causes the perturbations of the orbit of the moon, which are the most important and among the most considerable in the solar system.

Special perturbations are produced in orbits of comets, asteroids, and artificial satellites. A comet orbit is perturbed by larger heavenly bodies, which cause the shape of the orbit to change gradually from parabolic to elliptical and alter the time required to complete an orbit. No perturbations are observed in the sun or planets near the path of a comet. By measuring the orbital deviations, astronomers are able to calculate the mass of the comet. The same laws apply to artificial satellites.

The study of perturbations has helped establish an understanding of the system of planets. A search for causes of unexplained perturbations in the orbit of the planet Uranus led to the discovery of the planet Neptune. Deviations in the orbit of Neptune stimulated, in turn, a search for another planet, resulting in the discovery of Pluto.

See ASTRONOMY.

PERU, city in Indiana, and county seat of Miami Co., on the Wabash R., about 55 miles s.w. of Fort Wayne. It is a trade and shipping center for a rich agricultural area. Manufactures include electrical equipment, paper products, and furniture. Peru was formerly known as the winter headquarters for many of the leading circuses. Nearby is Virgil Grissom Air Force Base. Founded in 1826, Peru was incorporated as a town in 1848 and chartered as a city in 1867. Pop. (1960) 14,453; (1970) 14,139.

PERU, third largest country in South America, bounded on the N. by Ecuador and Colombia, on the E. by Brazil and Bolivia, on the s. by Chile, and on the w. by the Pacific Ocean. The country is situated between lat. 0°10′ S. and lat. 18°30′ S. and between long. 68°40′ W. and long. 81°10′ W. The area of the country, including several offshore islands, is about 500,000 sq.mi.

THE LAND

Peru may be divided into three main topographical regions, namely the coastal plain, the sierra, and the montaña.

The coastal plain is a semiarid, elongated stretch of land extending the entire length of the country and averaging from 40 to 100 mi. in width. The plain has most of the cities and industries of Peru, but few adequate harbors.

Parallel to and lying E. of the coastal plain is the sierra, an upland region with towering mountain ranges of the Andes (q.v.), lofty plateaus, and deep gorges and valleys. The main range is the Cordillera Occidental; other ranges include the Cordillera Oriental, the Cordillera Central, and a number of lesser chains. The sierra, which comprises 30 percent of the land area, traverses the country from S.E. to N.W. and varies in width from 250 mi. in the s. to 150 mi. in the N.; the average height is 12,000 ft. Some of the highest peaks in the world are located in the various sierran cordilleras and plateaus, notably Huascarán (22,205 ft.), the highest peak in Peru. Earthquakes occur often in the sierra.

On the E. the sierra slopes downward to a vast, wet, tropical plain extending to the Brazilian border and forming part of the Amazon River basin. The forested sierran slopes and the tropical plain collectively are designated the montaña. The montaña varies in width from 400 to 500 mi. and constitutes more than 60 percent of the Peruvian land area; it is covered with thick tropical forests in the w. and with dense tropical vegetation in the center and E. As a result, the region remains largely unexplored and undeveloped.

Peru has three main drainage systems. One comprises about fifty torrential streams that rise in the sierra and descend steeply to the coastal plain. Another comprises the tributaries of the Amazon R. In the third the principal feature is Lake Titicaca (q.v.), which drains into Lake Poopó in Bolivia through the Desaguadero R.

Three rivers, the Napo, the Tigre, and the Pastaza, rise in Ecuador and flow into Peru. The latter two streams are tributaries of the Marañón R., and the Napo empties into the Amazon R. The border between Peru and Colombia is delineated by the Putumayo R.

Climate. The climate of Peru varies widely, ranging from tropical in the montaña to arctic in the highest mountains of the Andes.

In the coastal plain the temperature is normally equable, averaging about 68° F. throughout the year and varying seasonally by approximately 14° F. The coastal climate in comparable latitudes is 10° F. below the average because of the cooling effect of the offshore current known as the Peru Current, or Humboldt Current. The coast receives less than 2 in. of rain each year, largely because the cordilleras precipitate most of the rain carried by the trade winds. Mist-laden clouds, however, known as the *guara*, shroud many of the western slopes of the sierra from June to October, providing enough moisture to support grasslands.

PERU

In the sierra the temperature ranges seasonally from about 20° to 70 ° F. Rainfall is usually scanty, but in some localities heavy rains fall from October to April. In Cuzco, in the southern sierra, annual rainfall averages 32 in.

The montaña region is extremely hot and humid. The prevailing easterlies blowing across that region gather moisture that is later precipitated on the E. Andean slopes. Annual rainfall in some districts often averages 150 in. Most of this rain eventually drains back to the montaña.

Natural Resources. Mineral deposits, the primary resource in Peru, include petroleum, found on the N.W. coast and in the Amazon basin; copper in S. Peru; and substantial deposits of silver, iron ore, gold, lead, and zinc, all found throughout the cordilleras. Also important are the forests, especially the stands of cedar, oak, and mahogany.

Plants and Animals. The plant life of the three main geographical regions varies widely. The vast, fertile montaña contains a rich profusion of trees, plants, and jungle vines, including mahogany, cedar, rubber, and cinchona trees, sarsaparilla and vanilla plants, and a variety of exotic tropical flowers. The rugged sierra supports a relatively sparse plant life. Sierra vegetation is largely xerophytic; that is, adapted to survival on a restricted supply of water. Such growths include mesquite, cactus, scrub and fodder grasses, and eucalyptus plants. The dry, sandy reaches of the coastal plain support mainly desert vegetation, such as shrubs, grasses, and tuberous plants.

The wildlife of Peru is limited in number and variety. The coastal plain and offshore islands support gulls and terns and some albatrosses, but little other wildlife except lizards, insects,

Scenes of Peru. View through an old church belfry in Arequipa.
Canadian Pacific Ry.

PERU

INDEX TO MAP OF PERU

Departments

Amazonas . . . . B 4
Ancash . . . . C 6
Apurímac . . . . E 9
Arequipa . . . . E 9
Ayacucho . . . . E 8
Cajamarca . . . . B 5
Callao . . . . C 7
Cuzco . . . . E 8
Huancavelica . . . . . . D 8
Huánuco . . . . D 6
Ica . . . . D 9
Junín . . . . E 7
La Libertad . . . . B 5
Lambayeque . . . . A 5
Lima . . . . C 7
Loreto . . . . D 4
Madre de Dios . . . . . F 7
Moquegua . . . . F 10
Pasco . . . . E 7
Piura . . . . A 4
Puno . . . . F 9
San Martín . . . . C 5
Tacna . . . . F 10
Tumbes . . . . A 3

Cities and Towns

Abancay . . . . E 8
Acarí . . . . D 9
Acobamba . . . . D 8
Acomayo (Cuzco) . . . F 8
Acomayo (Huánuco) . D 6
Aija . . . . C 6
Alca . . . . E 9
Andahuaylas . . . . . . E 8
Andamarca . . . . E 7
Anta . . . . E 8
Antabamba . . . . E 9
Aplao . . . . E 10
Arequipa . . . . F 10
Ascope . . . . B 5
Atalaya . . . . E 7
Atico . . . . E 10
Ayabaca . . . . B 4
Ayacucho . . . . E 8
Ayaviri . . . . F 9
Azángaro . . . . G 9
Bagua . . . . B 4
Balsapuerto . . . . C 4
Barranca (Lima) . . . . B 7
Barranca (Loreto) . . . C 4
Bartra Nuevo . . . . . . D 3
Bayóvar . . . . A 4
Bolívar . . . . C 5
Bretaña . . . . D 4
Caballococha . . . . . . F 4
Cabana . . . . C 6
Cahuapanas . . . . C 4
Cailloma . . . . F 9
Cajabamba . . . . B 5
Cajacay . . . . C 7
Cajamarca . . . . B 5
Cajatambo . . . . C 7
Calca . . . . F 8
Callalli . . . . F 9
Callao . . . . C 8
Camaná . . . . E 10
Candarave . . . . G 10
Capachica . . . . G 9
Carás . . . . C 6
Carhuás . . . . C 6
Carumas . . . . F 10
Cascas . . . . B 5
Casma . . . . B 6
Castilla . . . . A 4
Catacaos . . . . A 4
Celendín . . . . C 5
Cerro de Pasco . . . . . D 7
Chachapoyas . . . . . . C 5
Chala . . . . D 9
Chalhuanca . . . . E 9
Chancay . . . . C 7
Chepén . . . . B 5
Chiclayo . . . . B 5
Chilca (Pucusana) . . . C 8

Chimbote . . . . B 6
Chincha Alta . . . . . . C 8
Chiquián . . . . C 7
Chirinos . . . . B 4
Chivay . . . . F 9
Chorrillos . . . . C 8
Chosica . . . . C 7
Chota . . . . B 5
Chulucanas . . . . A 4
Chupaca . . . . D 8
Chuquibamba . . . . . . E 9
Chuquibambilla . . . . E 8
Cojata . . . . G 9
Colasay . . . . B 4
Colcamar . . . . B 5
Contamana . . . . D 5
Coracora . . . . E 9
Cordova . . . . D 9
Corongo . . . . C 6
Cotahuasi . . . . E 9
Cutervo . . . . B 5
Cuzco . . . . F 8
Echarate . . . . E 8
Ferreñafe . . . . B 5
Fitzcarrald . . . . E 8
Francisco de Orellana . E 3
Guadalupe . . . . D 8
Güeppí . . . . D 2
Huacho . . . . C 7
Huacrachuco . . . . . . C 6
Hualla . . . . E 8
Huamachuco . . . . . . C 5
Huancabamba . . . . . B 4
Huancané . . . . G 9
Huancapi . . . . D 8
Huancavelica . . . . . . D 8
Huancayo . . . . D 8
Huanta . . . . D 8
Huánuco . . . . D 6
Huaral . . . . C 7
Huaráz . . . . C 6
Huariaca . . . . E 7
Huarmey . . . . B 7
Huarochirí . . . . C 8
Huaylas . . . . B 6
Ica . . . . D 9
Ilave . . . . G 10
Ilo . . . . F 10
Inambari . . . . G 8
Iñapari . . . . G 7
Iparia . . . . D 6
Iquitos . . . . E 3
Jaén . . . . B 4
Jauja . . . . E 7
Jayanca . . . . A 5
Jeberos . . . . C 4
Juanjuí . . . . C 5
Juli . . . . G 10
Juliaca . . . . F 9
Jumbilla . . . . C 4
Junín . . . . E 7
La Huaca . . . . A 4
La Jalca . . . . C 5
La Joya . . . . F 10
La Oroya . . . . C 7
La Unión . . . . C 6
Lagunas . . . . D 4
Lamas . . . . C 5
Lambayeque . . . . A 5
Lampa . . . . F 9
Lamud . . . . B 5
Lanlacuni Bajo . . . . . F 8
Las Piedras . . . . G 8
Lima (cap.) . . . . C 7
Limbani . . . . G 9
Lircay . . . . D 8
Llata . . . . C 6
Locumba . . . . F 10
Lomas . . . . D 9
Machupicchu
  (Machu-Picchu) . . . E 8
Macusani . . . . F 9
Madre de Dios . . . . . F 8
Máncora . . . . A 4
Marcapata . . . . F 8
Marcona . . . . D 9
Margos . . . . C 7

Masisea . . . . D 6
Matarani . . . . E 10
Matucana . . . . C 7
Mazán . . . . E 3
Miraflores . . . . E 10
Mishagua . . . . E 7
Moho . . . . G 9
Mollendo . . . . E 10
Monsefú . . . . A 5
Moquegua . . . . F 10
Morococha . . . . C 7
Motupe . . . . B 5
Moyobamba . . . . C 5
Nauta . . . . E 4
Nazca . . . . D 9
Negritos . . . . A 4
Nuñoa . . . . F 9
Ocoña . . . . E 10
Ollachea . . . . F 8
Ollantaytambo . . . . . E 8
Olmos . . . . B 4
Omate . . . . F 10
Orellana . . . . D 5
Otuzco . . . . B 5
Oyón . . . . C 7
Pacasmayo . . . . A 5
Pachiza . . . . C 5
Paiján . . . . B 5
Paita . . . . A 4
Palpa . . . . D 9
Pampachiri . . . . E 9
Pampacolca . . . . E 9
Pampas . . . . D 8
Parinari . . . . D 4
Paruro . . . . E 8
Pataz . . . . C 5
Paucartambo . . . . . . F 8
Pevas . . . . F 3
Picota . . . . C 5
Pimentel . . . . A 5
Pisco . . . . C 8
Piura . . . . A 4
Pizacoma . . . . G 10
Pomabamba . . . . C 6
Pozuzo . . . . E 7
Pucusana (Chilca) . . . C 8
Puerto Alianza . . . . . C 4
Puerto América . . . . C 4
Puerto Arturo . . . . . . E 2
Puerto Bermúdez . . . E 7
Puerto Chicama . . . . A 5
Puerto José Pardo . . . C 3
Puerto Leguía . . . . . . F 8
Puerto Maldonado . . G 8
Puerto Ocopa . . . . . . E 7
Puerto Pardo . . . . . . E 6
Puerto Portillo . . . . . E 6
Puerto Samanco . . . . B 6
Puerto Victoria . . . . . D 6
Puno . . . . F 9
Punta de Bombón . . . E 10
Puquio . . . . E 9
Quillabamba . . . . . . E 8
Recuay . . . . C 6
Requena . . . . E 4
Rioja . . . . C 5
Salaverry . . . . B 6
San José de Sisa . . . . C 5
San Miguel . . . . B 5
San Pedro de Lloc . . . A 5
Sana . . . . B 5
Sandia . . . . G 9
Santa . . . . B 6
Santa Cruz . . . . D 4
Santa Isabel de
  Sihuas . . . . E 10
Santa María de Nanay . E 3
Santiago de Chuco . . B 6
Santo Tomás . . . . . . F 9
Saquena . . . . E 4
Satipo . . . . E 7
Sayán . . . . C 7
Sechura . . . . A 4
Sicuani . . . . F 9
Sihuas . . . . B 6
Sullana . . . . A 4
Supe . . . . C 7

Tacna . . . . F 11
Talara . . . . A 4
Tambo Grande . . . . . A 4
Tamshiyacu . . . . E 4
Tarapoto . . . . C 5
Tarata . . . . G 10
Tayabamba . . . . C 6
Tingo María . . . . C 6
Tocache Nuevo . . . . . C 6
Torata . . . . F 10
Trujillo . . . . B 6
Tumbes . . . . A 3
Ubinas . . . . F 10
Uchiza . . . . C 6
Urcos . . . . F 8
Urubamba . . . . E 8
Vinchos . . . . D 8
Virú . . . . B 6
Yambrasbamba . . . . . C 4
Yanaoca . . . . F 9
Yauri . . . . F 9
Yauyos . . . . D 8
Yunguyo . . . . G 10
Yurimaguas . . . . D 4
Zarumilla . . . . A 3
Zorritos . . . . A 3

Physical Features

Aguaytía (river) . . . . . D 6
Aguja (pt.) . . . . A 4
Amazon (river) . . . . . E 3
Andes (mts.) . . . . E 9
Apurímac (river) . . . . E 8
Azángaro (river) . . . . F 9
Azul (mts.) . . . . D 6
Blanco (river) . . . . . . E 5
Cañete (river) . . . . . . C 8
Casma (river) . . . . . . B 6
Chira (river) . . . . A 4
Cóndor (mts.) . . . . . . B 4
Coropuna, Nudo (mt.) . E 9
Corrientes (river) . . . D 3
Ferrol (penín.) . . . . . . B 6
Grande (river) . . . . . . D 9
Guañape (isls.) . . . . . B 6
Huallaga (river) . . . . C 4
Huascarán (mt.) . . . . . C 6
Junín (lake) . . . . E 7
Lachay (pt.) . . . . C 7
Lobos de Afuera (isls.) . A 5
Lobos de Tierra (isl.) . A 5
Madre de Dios (river) . F 8
Mantaro (river) . . . . . D 8
Marañón (river) . . . . D 4
Mayo (river) . . . . C 5
Misti, El (mt.) . . . . . . F 9
Morona (river) . . . . . C 3
Nanay (river) . . . . . . D 3
Napo (river) . . . . E 3
Nermete (pt.) . . . . . . A 4
Occidental (mts.) . . . . E 9
Ocoña (river) . . . . . . E 10
Oriental (mts.) . . . . . F 9
Pachitea (river) . . . . . D 6
Paita (bay) . . . . A 4
Pampas (river) . . . . . D 8
Paracas (penín.) . . . . . C 8
Pastaza (river) . . . . . C 4
Perené (river) . . . . . . E 7
Piedras (river) . . . . . G 7
Pisco (river) . . . . D 8
Purus (river) . . . . F 7
San Lorenzo (isl.) . . . C 8
San Nicolás (bay) . . . D 9
Santa (river) . . . . B 6
Santiago (river) . . . . . C 3
Sechura (bay) . . . . . . A 4
Tapiche (river) . . . . . D 5
Tigre (river) . . . . D 3
Titicaca (lake) . . . . . . G 9
Tumbes (river) . . . . . A 3
Ucayali (river) . . . . . E 4
Urubamba (river) . . . E 7
Vilcanota (mt.) . . . . . F 9
Vítor (river) . . . . F 11
Yavarí (river) . . . . . . F 4
Yavero (river) . . . . . . E 8

444

PERU

PERU

tarantulas, and scorpions. Peruvian ocean waters abound in haddock, sole, mackerel, smelt, flounder, lobster, shrimp, and other marine species. In the sierra are found the llama, alpaca, vicuña, chinchilla, and huanaco. Birds of the region include the giant condor, robin, phoebe, flycatcher, finch, partridge, duck, and goose. Lake Titicaca and other sierran bodies of water teem with fish. Animals of the tropical montaña include the jaguar, cougar, armadillo, peccary, tapir, anteater, several dozen species of monkey, alligator, turtle, and a variety of snakes and insects; among the birds are the parrot, the flamingo, and other tropical species.

Waterpower. The development of the great power potential of the rivers of Peru has been slow until recent years. Large-scale irrigation and power systems, under construction in the late 1960's, were to greatly increase the nation's supply of electric power. Hydroelectric power production in this period totaled some 3,121,000,000 kw hours annually.

THE PEOPLE

Nearly 90 percent of the population is Indian and mestizo; the remainder comprises mostly persons of European, Chinese, Japanese, and Negro descent. The population is primarily rural.

A popular Pacific Ocean beach resort near Lima. UPI

Population. The population of Peru (census 1961) was 10,364,620; the United Nations estimate (1970) 13,586,000. The overall population density is about 26 per sq.mi. (U.N. est. 1969). The distribution is uneven, with about 50 percent of the people inhabiting the sierra region, and about 40 percent inhabiting the coastal plain. About 25 percent of the people live in cities of 25,000 or more; the majority live in towns and villages of less than 300 persons.

Political Divisions. For administrative purposes the country is divided into twenty-four departments which are subdivided into provinces. *See* Table on page 449.

Principal Cities. The largest city in Peru is Lima (pop., 1969 est., 2,415,700), the capital. Other important cities include Callao (321,700), the chief seaport on Callao Bay; Arequipa (187,400), an industrial center; Trujillo (149,500), a commercial center; Chiclayo (134,100), in the sugar district; and Cuzco (105,400), once the capital of the Inca Empire, now famous for its ruins.

Language and Religion. Spanish is the official language of Peru and is spoken by 65 percent of the people. Aymará and Quechua (qq.v.) are the principal languages of the native Indians.

The overwhelming majority of Peruvians are Roman Catholics. In accordance with a law passed in 1915, Roman Catholicism is the estab-

Totora reeds dry in the sun on the shore of Lake Titicaca, the highest navigable lake in the world. The Indians of Peru use totora reeds to weave fishing boats strong enough to withstand the severe storms that strike the lake.

Peru. Plate 1.

Pictures Plates 1 and 2, United Nations

A conveyor carries anchovies to be processed into fishmeal in a plant at the newly developed port of Pisco, in the shelter of Paracas Peninsula. The waters off Pisco provide rich anchovy-fishing grounds.

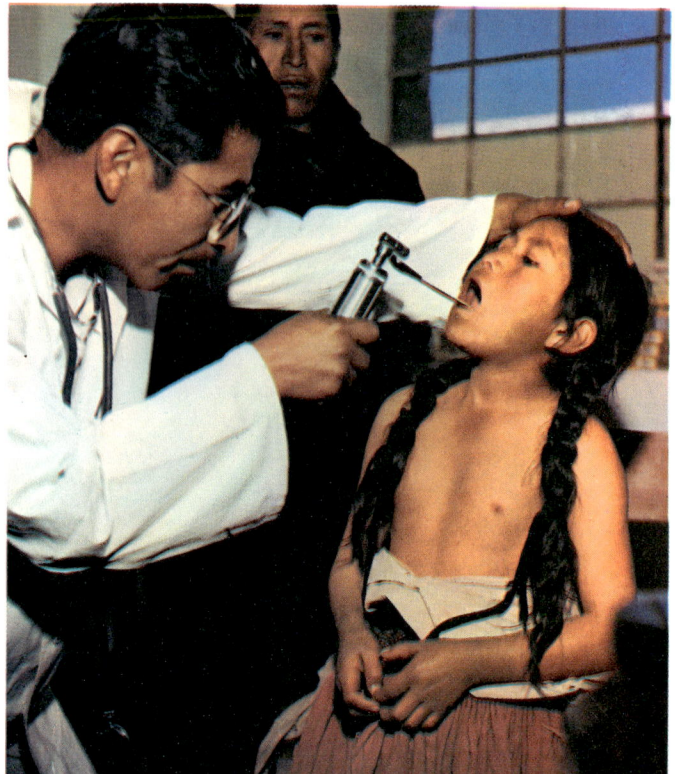

Peru. Plate 2. Left: An Indian girl has her throat examined during a medical check-up. Health care is brought to the Andean Indians by visiting doctors who staff village health centers. Below: Indian women of an Andean village chop straw to be mixed with clay while their husbands do heavier work in construction of a schoolhouse.

PERU

POLITICAL DIVISIONS OF PERU

Department	Capital	Area (sq. mi.)	Population (est.)
Amazonas	Chachapoyas	13,947	148,200
Ancash	Huarás	14,705	662,200
Apurímac	Abancay	8,189	314,600
Arequipa	Arequipa	21,952	452,400
Ayacucho	Ayacucho	18,190	449,000
Cajamarca	Cajamarca	12,541	877,400
Callao (province with constitutional rank of department)	Callao	14	266,700
Cuzco	Cuzco	55,731	693,300
Huancavelica	Huancavelica	8,300	336,600
Huánuco	Huánuco	15,430	389,100
Ica	Ica	9,799	302,500
Junín	Trujillo	22,820	612,300
La Libertad	Huancayo	10,209	680,700
Lambayeque	Chiclayo	4,615	407,300
Lima	Lima	15,052	2,526,000
Loreto	Iquitos	119,301	471,900
Madre de Dios	Puerto Maldonado	58,842	194,400
Moquegua	Moquegua	5,550	59,600
Pasco	Cerro de Pasco	8,438	167,800
Piura	Piura	15,239	786,000
Puno	Puno	26,140	776,900
San Martín	Moyobamba	17,452	194,400
Tacna	Tacna	4,922	78,400
Tumbes	Tumbes	1,591	68,300

lished religion of the country. Other religions are tolerated, and small numbers of Protestants, Jews, and Muslims live in Peru. By law, the only form of religious instruction permitted in either public or private schools is Roman Catholic.

Education. The literacy rate has increased substantially in recent years as a result of greater emphasis on education. According to the latest figures, the adult literate population rose from 42 percent in 1940 to more than 60 percent in the late 1960's.

ELEMENTARY AND SECONDARY SCHOOLS. Public elementary education is free and compulsory for all children between the ages of seven and sixteen. In the late 1960's Peru had about 15,000 public and private elementary schools, supported wholly or in part by the state; enrollment totaled about 2,200,000. About 260 public, 420 private, and 305 religious academies on the secondary level with a total enrollment of about 500,000 were also in operation.

Specialized courses in farming, industrial, and commercial techniques are offered at approximately 400 private and public institutions with a combined enrollment of about 45,000. Other educational facilities include about 60 rural Indian schools and 30 teacher-training institutes.

UNIVERSITIES AND COLLEGES. Peru has eight state universities, the most notable of which is the National University of San Marcos in Lima (founded 1551). The Catholic University of Lima and the national universities of Arequipa, Cuzco, and Trujillo are among the noteworthy

A workman drives llamas carrying petroleum products to a mine miles from the nearest road.
Standard Oil Co. (N.J.)

449

An Indian mother and child from the Amazon area of eastern Peru.   UPI

institutions of higher education. The combined annual enrollment at the university level in the late 1960's was about 64,500.

Culture. The Indian heritage of Peru is one of the richest in South America. Although Spain gave Peru its language, religion, and rulers, the highly developed civilization of the Inca has left its traces throughout Peruvian culture; see INCA. Archeological excavations have uncovered monumental Indian remains. Architecture of the Spanish colonial period is a fusion of Spanish and Indian forms known as the Creole style. In art today, the "indigenist" school pointedly interprets 20th century Peru in an Indian mode. The Indian pentatonic musical scale is still used today, as are ancient instruments such as conchshells, flutes, ocarina, and panpipes; see LATIN-AMERICAN MUSIC; SPANISH-AMERICAN LITERATURE.

The descendants of the Quechua and Aymará Indians populate the Andean highlands. Many still do not speak Spanish and have preserved the customs and folklore of their ancestors. Along the coast and in the highland cities, the Europeans, mestizos, Negroes, and Orientals live in a modern Western style. In vivid contrast to these settlements are the jungles of eastern Peru, the home of Indian tribes so isolated that their life style resembles that of their ancestors 500 years ago.

LIBRARIES AND MUSEUMS. The most important libraries are located in the larger cities and are affiliated with the major universities. Within the various libraries of the National University of San Marcos can be found more than 100,000 volumes.

Museums throughout the country display the art and archeology indigenous to Peru. Thirteen museums are situated in Lima, as well as the City Hall, which contains a full record of every official act in the capital since its founding.

ARCHEOLOGY. Peru is dotted with archeological sites of the many advanced cultures that once flourished on its territory. Explorations and excavations have uncovered the three outstanding archeological zones of Chavín de Huántar, Tiahuanacu, and the Inca ruins in the Cuzco area. See PERUVIAN ARCHEOLOGY.

THE ECONOMY

The economy is primarily agricultural; about 4,700,000 acres are under cultivation. Large-scale irrigation and power schemes are being undertaken partly to increase the acreage available for farming. In the mid-1960's about 4,000,000,000 kw hours of power were produced annually. The mining and fishing industries are becoming increasingly important. The economy relies heavily on the export of raw materials, chiefly farm products, fish meal, and minerals, to create an exchange surplus for importing machinery and manufactured goods. In 1970 the budget es-

In a "sewing machine city" in a market area of Lima, hundreds of workers make shoes and other leather goods.   UPI

450

A paper factory at Paramonga.   W. R. Grace & Co.

timates showed revenues and expenditures balanced at about $982,000,000.

Agriculture. About 62 percent of the population is engaged in farming. Most of the coastal area (30 percent of all farming) is devoted to the raising of export crops; on the montaña (10 percent) and the sierra (60 percent) are grown crops for local consumption. The chief agricultural products, together with the approximate annual yield (in tons) in the late 1960's, were cotton (400,000), sugar (864,000), rice (320,000), wheat (160,000), coffee (76,000), and cocoa (2020).

The livestock population includes about 3825 cattle, 16,110,000 sheep, 3,950,000 goats, 925,400 horses and mules, 28,000,000 poultry, and more than 1,500,000 pigs. Llamas, sheep, and vicuñas provide valuable wools, hides, and skins.

Forest and Fishing. The fishing and guano (q.v.) industries are important to the economy, and comprise a sizable portion of the exports. The fishing industry underwent a remarkable expansion after World War II; the catch now exceeds 9,500,000 tons annually. About 96 percent of the catch is anchovies, used for making fish meal, a product in which Peru leads the world. Each year about 200,000 tons of guano are gathered from the offshore islands for use as fertilizer.

The forests of Peru cover about 62 percent of the land surface, but have not been significantly exploited. Forest products include balsa lumber and balata gum, rubber, and a variety of medicinal plants. Notable among the latter is the cinchona plant, from which quinine is derived.

Mining. The extractive industries figure significantly in the Peruvian economy. Copper is the most important mineral mined; new deposits in s. Peru have recently been developed. In the late 1960's, the chief minerals mined, and the approximate annual output in tons, were copper (194,000), lead (160,000), zinc (285,000), iron ore (8,600,000), and silver (1100).

Petroleum production totaled about 20,000,000 barrels and natural gas production about 2,500,000 cu.yd. annually.

Manufacturing. In 1959 the Industrial Promotion Law was passed as a means of encouraging local enterprise. The most important industry is textile manufacture; 345 concerns had an annual production in the late 1960's valued at about $58,500,000. Other important manufactures, and annual output, include fish meal (1,400,000 tons), cement (1,200,000 tons), and oil and fuel products (17,000,000 barrels). The first iron and steel mills were opened in Chimbote in 1958; products include pig iron, wire rods, and galvanized roofing sheets.

PERU

Commerce and Trade. The unit of currency is the sol (26.8 soles equal U.S.$1; 1971).

The Banco Central de Reserva del Perú is the central bank and bank of issue. All banking operations are under the jurisdiction of the superintendent of banks.

Exports are more diversified in Peru than in most South American countries. The principal export, in the late 1960's was fish and fish products (mostly fish meal), which represented more than 25 percent of total exports. The three other main exports are copper (17 percent), cotton (7 percent), sugar (7 percent), and coffee (4 percent). The chief markets for Peruvian exports, by value, are the United States (42 percent), the Netherlands (9 percent), Great Britain (9 percent), and Belgium (8 percent). The total value of exports in the late 1960's was more than $866,000,000 annually.

The leading imports include machinery and vehicles, foodstuffs, textiles, dyes and paints, iron and steel products, electrical appliances, and chemicals. The total value of imports in the late 1960's was about $630,000,000 annually.

Transportation. The national system of railroads, highways, and airports has been expanded considerably since World War II. Combined highways total about 28,000 mi.; less than half of the roads are hard surfaced. One section of the Pan-American Highway (q.v.) traverses Peru from Ecuador to Chile, covering a distance of about 2000 mi. Peru also has about 2000 mi. of railroads. One trans-Andean line, the Callao-Huancayo, ascends to 15,693 ft. above sea level, the highest point reached by any standard-gauge line in the world. The most notable waterway is the Amazon R., which is navigable by ship from the Atlantic Ocean to Iquitos in Peru, a distance of some 2300 mi. Lake Titicaca also serves as a waterway. A growing network of domestic and foreign airlines facilitates travel within the country and to all parts of the world.

Communications. The telephone system, which is privately owned, has more than 165,000 instruments. Lima is connected by radio-telephone circuits with all distant towns. The country is connected with Chile by three submarine telegraph cables; and one such cable connects Peru with all South American countries to the N. The country has about 150 broadcasting stations and almost 25 television stations.

Labor. Nearly half of the labor force is engaged in agriculture. The next largest sectors are services and government (17 percent), manufacturing (13 percent), commerce (7 percent), and mining (3 percent); all other industries total 10 percent. Half of the economically active population is under 24 years of age.

Although a number of independent unions exist, the main labor group is the Confederación de Trabajadores del Perú (Peruvian Confederation of Labor), with about 500,000 members.

GOVERNMENT

Until 1968 Peru was a constitutional republic and the government was based on the constitution of 1933 as amended. In 1968 a military coup resulted in the setting up of a military junta and the suspension of the constitution. Under the new regime Peru is a highly centralized republic controlled by an executive with great powers.

Voting is compulsory for both men and women between the ages of twenty-one and sixty.

Central Government. According to the suspended constitution of 1933, executive authority is vested in a president and two vice-presidents, each of whom is popularly elected to a six-year term. The president may not serve two successive terms in office. The Peruvian executive dominates the legislative and judicial branches of government. The constitution grants the executive the right to suspend temporarily all democratic guarantees, including those relating to freedom of speech, labor, and the press. Important presidential prerogatives include the power to appoint a prime minister and a twelve-man cabinet, to nominate candidates for high church offices, and to appoint supreme court justices with the approval of Congress. In addition, the executive dictates Peruvian foreign policy and chooses, directly or indirectly, all major government officials.

HEALTH AND WELFARE. The ministry of public health and social welfare is responsible for the administration of all health and welfare services. The government has made strides in the reduction of epidemic diseases and the improvement of sanitation and medical facilities. Peru, however, needs more extensive medical services; and such illnesses as venereal diseases, typhoid, dysentery, and smallpox still pose serious problems. In the late 1960's the country had only one doctor for every 18,000 persons outside of the Lima-Callao area.

Under the social-security program as authorized by the constitution, social insurance is compulsory, and is contributed to by employers, employees, and the government. Benefits cover sickness, disability, and old age.

Legislature. By terms of the constitution the legislative function is performed by a congress consisting of a senate with 45 members and a chamber of deputies with 140 members. The congress convenes each year on July 28 and remains in session for four months. Members of the congress are popularly elected to six-year terms; elections are staggered to permit a biennial turnover of one third of the membership. All senators and deputies must be native-born citizens.

Political Parties. Peru has four major political parties. The American Popular Revolutionary Alliance (APRA), formed in 1924, is a prolabor, pro-Indian group. APRA was outlawed several times, but was legalized in 1956. The Partido Acción Popular (Popular Action Party) and the Partido Demócrata Cristiana (Christian Democratic Party) formed the government coalition of 1963–68. The Unión Nacional Odriísta (U.N.O.) is a social-reform party allied to APRA. The Communist Party is an illegal body.

Local Government. Each of the twenty-four departments is governed by a prefect; and each of the 148 provinces by a subprefect. Prefects and subprefects are appointed by the central government. A governor presides over each municipality. Every district capital and provincial capital is governed by a municipal council which is elected by direct popular vote.

Judiciary. The supreme court, at Lima, consists of 11 judges and 4 fiscals. The judicature also comprises 19 superior courts, with 156 judges and 42 fiscals. The country does not use juries.

Defense. A two-year term of conscription is compulsory for all male citizens between the ages of twenty and twenty-five. The defense system includes an army, navy, and air force, with a total strength of 52,000, and a national police force of about 18,000.

HISTORY

Little is known of the history of the region comprising present-day Peru before the rise of the Inca. The earlier settlers were peoples unrelated to the Inca, who in about 1000 B.C. began to migrate south from Mexico and Central America. Some aspects of the history and culture of the pre-Inca Indian peoples have been determined

Fishing is a major industry along the 1400-mi. coastline of Peru. UPI

from the surviving examples of their art and architecture.

Inca Empire. The Inca, sometimes called "peoples of the sun", were originally a warlike tribe living in a semiarid region of the southern sierra. From 1100 to 1300 the Inca moved north into the fertile Cuzco valley. From this base they subsequently overran a number of neighboring lands. By 1500 the empire of the Inca stretched from the Pacific Ocean east to the sources of the Paraguay and Amazon rivers and from the region of modern Quito in Ecuador south to the Maule R. in Chile. This vast empire was a theocracy, organized along socialistic lines and ruled by an Inca, or emperor, who was worshiped as a divinity. Because the Inca realm contained extensive deposits of gold and silver, it became in the early 16th century a natural target of Spanish imperial ambitions in the New World.

Spanish Rule. In 1532 the Spanish soldier and adventurer Francisco Pizarro (q.v.) landed in Peru with a force of about 180 men. By guile and by force of arms Pizarro made the Inca Empire a Spanish possession. In 1535 Pizarro founded on the banks of the Rimac R. the Peruvian capital city of Ciudad de los Reyes (Sp., "City of the Kings"), renamed Lima. Subsequently disputes over jurisdictional powers broke out among the Spanish conquerors, or conquistadors, and in 1541 a member of one of the conflicting Spanish factions assassinated Pizarro in Lima.

In 1542 a Spanish imperial council promulgated statutes, called "New Laws for the Indies", which were designed to put a stop to cruelties inflicted upon the Indians. In the same year Spain created the viceroyalty of Peru, which comprised all of Spanish South America and Panama, except what is now Venezuela.

The first Spanish viceroy arrived in Peru in 1544 and attempted to enforce the New Laws, but the conquistadors rebelled and, in 1546, killed the viceroy. Although the rebellion was crushed by Spanish government forces in 1548, the New Laws were never put into effect.

In 1569 the Spanish colonial administrator Francisco de Toledo (1515?–84) arrived in Peru. During the ensuing fourteen years he established a highly effective, although harshly repressive, system of government. Toledo's method of administration consisted of a major government of Spanish officials ruling through a minor government made up of Indians who dealt directly with the native population. The system was oppressive but workable and lasted for almost 200 years.

Revolts for Independence. In 1780 a force of 60,000 Indians revolted against Spanish rule under the leadership of the Peruvian patriot José Gabriel Condorcanqui (1742–81), who adopted the name of an ancestor, the Inca Tupac Amaru. Although initially successful, the uprising was crushed in 1781, and Condorcanqui was tortured and executed, as were thousands of his fellow revolutionaries. Another revolt was similarly put down in 1814. Subsequently, however, opposition to imperial rule grew throughout Spanish South America. The opposition was led largely by so-called Creoles, that is, persons of Spanish descent born in South America. The Creoles, who were usually of humble parentage, long resented having a status inferior to that of the ruling minorities.

19th Century. Making common cause with various dissident native elements, the Creoles led an independence movement that in the first decades of the 19th century brought independence to what are now Paraguay (1811), Chile (1818), and Colombia (1821).

In September, 1820, the Argentine soldier and patriot José de San Martín (q.v.), who had defeated the Spanish forces in Chile, landed an invasion army at the seaport of Pisco, Peru. On July 12, 1821, Martín's forces entered Lima, which had been abandoned by Spanish troops. Peruvian independence was proclaimed formally on July 28, 1821. The struggle against the Spanish was continued later by the Venezuelan revolutionary hero Simón Bolívar (q.v.), who entered Peru with his armies on Sept. 21, 1822. In the battles of Junín on Aug. 6, 1824, and Ayacucho on Dec. 9, 1824, Bolívar's forces routed the Spanish. In the fifty years following the liberation the country was ruled by quasi-dictators and wracked by a succession of civil and foreign wars. In 1827 a revolutionary junta drew up a provisional constitution (adopted formally in 1828), and chose as president General José Lamar (1778–1830). Lamar, however, was deposed in 1829 because of an ill-fated invasion into neighboring territory.

A particularly notable president was the mestizo Ramón Castilla (1797–1867) who, during his two terms in office (1845–51 and 1855–62), initiated many important reforms, including the abolition of Negro slavery, the construction of railroads and telegraph facilities, and the adoption in 1860 of a liberal constitution.

In 1864 Peru and Spain became involved in war because Spain had seized the Chincha Islands off the coast of Peru. Ecuador, Bolivia, and Chile aided Peru, and in May, 1866, after the defeat of Spanish land and naval forces, the fighting ceased. Spain later relinquished the islands and in 1879 signed a treaty that constituted its first formal recognition of Peruvian sovereignty.

Peru was badly defeated by Chile in a conflict (1879–83) known as the War of the Pacific (see CHILE: *History*). The war severely depleted Peruvian financial reserves and placed subsequent relations between the two countries under a continuing strain. For the next twenty-five years Peru was ruled by a succession of dictators, mainly of military background.

Early 20th Century. In 1908 a program of economic reform was instituted by President Augusto Leguía y Salcedo (q.v.). After his first term (1908–12) Leguía traveled in Great Britain and the U.S., where he learned modern methods of banking and finance, which he later applied in Peru, and made many friends in the business community. He regained the presidency in 1919 by means of a military coup, and ruled as virtual dictator until 1930, when he was ousted by a revolutionary group. In 1929 the tense relations between Chile and Peru were ended by a treaty that in part provided for a territorial settlement; see TACNA-ARICA DISPUTE.

On April 9, 1933, a new constitution was adopted. Later in April President Leguía's successor, Luis Sánchez Cerro (1889–1933), was assassinated. The next chief executive was General Óscar Raimundo Benavides (1876–1945). Benavides, who took office in 1933, followed the new pattern of harsh political rule combined with marked economic advances. Manuel Prado y Ugarteche (1889–   ), who succeeded Benavides in 1939, was forced, however, to make a number of concessions to powerful reform sentiment fostered largely by the American Popular Revolutionary Alliance (APRA).

During World War II Peru gave limited support to the Allied cause, breaking off relations with the Axis powers (q.v.) in January, 1942, and declaring war against Germany and Japan in February, 1945. In 1945 Peru became a charter member of the United Nations.

POST-WAR REFORMS. In 1945 a coalition of liberal and leftist parties, including the APRA, elected as president José Luis Bustamante y Rivero (1894–   ). Bustamante instituted numerous liberal reforms; civil rights and freedom of the press were strengthened, and certain dictatorial powers of the president were abolished by constitutional amendment. In October, 1948, however, rightist revolutionary leaders unseated Bustamante, seized the government, and outlawed the APRA. On July 2, 1950, Manuel A. Odría (1897–   ), the leader of the 1948 coup d'état, was elected president. Odría's chief opponent was denied a place on the ballot.

On Feb. 22, 1952, Peru and the U.S. signed a mutual military-assistance agreement. In addition to strengthening Peruvian defenses by this and other military means, the Odría administration initiated a large public-works program. In August, 1953, Peru and Brazil concluded a series of economic and cultural pacts providing for closer cooperation between the two countries.

By August, 1953, Peru, Chile, and Ecuador had extended their claims to territorial waters to 200 mi. off the mainland. The decision brought sharp protests from the U.S., as many U.S. fishing vessels were operating in South American waters.

In the presidential elections of June, 1956, Manuel Prado y Ugarteche was again victorious and was inaugurated on July 28, 1956. Prado immediately effected sweeping liberal reforms.

The 1960's. Strikes and riots, occasioned by economic instability marked by a runaway inflation, began in 1957 and continued into 1959. To help stabilize the economy, the government, in August, 1959, introduced a comprehensive program of restricting the outflow of dollars and encouraging domestic industries through various means, including facilitating the importation of capital goods. By May, 1960, the economy had improved greatly, and foreign capital flowed into the country in the form of loans and development contracts.

On Oct. 12, 1960, the government won approval of its policy of gradual nationalization of most of the country's oil-production facilities. Peru severed diplomatic relations with Cuba on Dec. 30.

In the presidential elections of 1962 no candidate received the necessary one third of the votes, and a military junta took control; General Ricardo Pio Perez Godoy (1905–   ) was installed as president in July.

The junta deposed Perez Godoy in March, 1963; three months later Fernando Belaúnde Terry (1913–   ) was elected president. During the second half of his administration, political opposition grew, and increasing inflation resulted in devaluation of the currency in September, 1967, following eight years of stability.

Military Rule. A long dispute over the claims of the International Petroleum Company (I.P.C.), a subsidiary of the Standard Oil Company of New Jersey, in the operation of the rich La Brea y Pariñas oil fields resulted, in August, 1968, in a settlement drawn up by the Belaúnde government. Widespread disapproval of this settlement forced the resignation of the cabinet on Oct. 1, and on Oct. 3 a bloodless coup resulted in the suspension of the constitution and the establishment of a military junta headed by General Juan Velasco Alvarado (1910–), army chief of staff and president of the joint chiefs of staff. A referendum on the adoption of a new constitution was promised, but no date was set for it. Relations with the U.S. became strained when the new government expropriated the interests of the I.P.C. Relations deteriorated still further in February, 1969, when the Peruvian Navy attacked two American fishing vessels off the Peruvian coast, claiming they were violating Peru's right to offshore waters within 200 mi. of the mainland. The governments of the two countries were driven to set up conferences to resolve their differences. Also in February Peru established diplomatic relations and signed a bilateral trade agreement with the Soviet Union.

Despite the differences with the U.S., American relief supplies were quickly sent following an Andean earthquake in May, 1970, which killed about 50,000 persons and left about 600,000 persons homeless. Mrs. Richard Nixon, wife of the American President, delivered two planeloads of supplies.

As Peru entered the 1970's the military government showed itself dedicated to a program of radical reform of the social economic system of the country. Among the major actions were the seizure of extensive foreign-owned ranch lands, the imposition of price controls on major food items, and a sweeping land-reform law designed to break the economic power of the landowning class that has dominated Peru for centuries.

In 1971 U.S. relations with Peru deteriorated noticeably. In January the government took over a copper concession held by a U.S. firm, and the State Department announced that, since 1966, 18 tuna boats had been seized and their owners fined by Peru. In June Congress cut sugar quotas from five countries, one of them Peru. In September President Allende of Chile was received in Lima where he received a pledge of moral support for ideological pluralism.

PERU CURRENT. See Ocean and Oceanography: *Ocean Currents;* Peru: *The Land: Climate.*

PERUGIA (anc. *Perusia*), city of Italy, in Umbria Region, and capital of Perugia Province, 85 miles N. of Rome. The city lies in a picturesque highland region, more than 1500 ft. above sea level, between the Tiber R. and Lake Trasimeno. It is a market for agricultural products and livestock. Manufactures include chocolate candy, pasta, and other foodstuffs, textiles, ceramics, glassware, furniture, pharmaceuticals, and metal goods.

One of the oldest cities in Italy, Perugia contains walls constructed when it was one of the confederated cities of Etruria (q.v.). The city has many medieval and Renaissance structures, including the circular Church of Sant'Angelo (5th cent.), the Church of San Pietro (10th cent.), which has a notable art collection, the Palazzo dei Priori (begun in the 13th cent.), the large Basilica of San Domenico (14th cent.; rebuilt 17th cent.), and the Oratory of San Bernardino (15th cent.), which has a sculptured Renaissance facade. Outstanding museums include the National Archeological Museum of Umbria and the National Gallery of Umbria. The National Gallery, in the Palazzo dei Priori, contains work by the masters of central Italy from the primitives to the 16th century. Perugia has a university, founded in the 13th century, and a special university for foreigners, founded in 1925.

History. Perugia belonged to an Etruscan confederacy (*see* Etruria: *Political and Economic Structure*) when it fell under Roman rule in 309 B.C. It was destroyed and rebuilt twice during the next nine centuries. In the 9th century it became a possession of the popes, but subsequently achieved independence. About the middle of the 16th century it was incorporated into the Papal States (q.v.). In 1861 it became part of the Kingdom of Italy. During World War II, the city was occupied by the British in June 1944. Pop. (1968) 124,123.

PERUGIA, UNIVERSITY OF, coeducational autonomous institution of higher learning, located in Perugia, Italy, and supported by the national government. The university was founded in 1308 by Pope Clement V (*see under* Clement). Prior to this a 13th-century liberal arts school had existed in Perugia. The university is organized into the following faculties: jurisprudence, letters and philosophy, political science, medicine, pharmacy, agrarian science, veterinary medicine, natural and biological science, and education. The degree of *laurea,* entitling the recipient to the honorific *dottore,* is awarded by all faculties after a four- to six-year course of study. The *laurea* is approximately equivalent to an American master's degree. Post-*laurea* studies are offered by most faculties and lead to a higher specialized diploma after an additional period of study, normally two years in length. In 1968–69 the student body numbered about 10,700 and the faculty, about 90 professors.

PERUGINO, IL, real name PIETRO VANNUCCI (about 1446–1523?), Italian painter, born in Città della Pieve, Umbria. Perugino, also called Pier della Pieve, studied painting with the Florentine sculptor and painter Andrea del Verrocchio (q.v.), and may also have worked with the Italian painter Piero della Francesca (q.v.). Few of his early works have survived. One example, dated 1478, is a fresco representing Saint Sebastian in the Church of Castel Cerqueto near Perugia. From 1479 to 1482 Perugino worked in Rome, painting a series of frescoes in the Sistine Chapel (q.v.) of the Vatican. These works included his earliest extant major work, "Christ Giving the Keys to Saint Peter". Perugino lived in Florence from 1486 to 1499, making a number of trips to Perugia, the city from which his name is derived, and Rome. His works of this period include the "Madonna with Saints and Angels" (1493), now in the Louvre, Paris; and his celebrated "Pietà" (1495), in the Pitti Palace, Florence. Between 1499 and 1500 at Perugia he decorated the audience hall of the bankers' guild, the Cambio, with extensive frescoes depicting allegorical and sacred subjects. Among his pupils at about this time was the Italian painter Raphael (q.v.). One of the best of Perugino's later works is an elaborate altarpiece painted between 1512 and 1517 for the Church of Sant'-Agostino, Perugia. In 1523 he painted a fresco representing "The Adoration of the Shepherds", thought to be his last work, and now in the National Gallery, London. Among other works by Perugino are "The Marriage of the Virgin" (about 1503–04), in the museum at Caen, France, a painting that served as the model for Raphael's "Sposalizio"; "Combat of Love and Chastity" (1505), in the Louvre; and "Virgin between Saint Jerome and Saint Francis" (1507), in the National Gallery, London.

PERUTZ, Max Ferdinand (1914–   ), Austrian-British chemist, born in Vienna, and educated at the universities of Vienna and Cambridge. In 1947 he was named chairman of the laboratory of molecular biology of the medical research council, a high-level government agency located at Cambridge. Perutz shared the 1962 Nobel Prize in chemistry with an associate, the British biophysicist John Cowdery Kendrew (q.v.). By the use of crystallography, the bombardment of a molecule with X rays, Perutz was able to determine the molecular structure of hemoglobin (q.v.), a substance found in red blood cells.

PERUVIAN ARCHEOLOGY, study of the remains of the ancient cultures of the peoples of Peru and of neighboring regions, including Ecuador, Bolivia, and Chile.

The most important, and one of the earliest cultures of the northern highlands of Peru was that of Chavin. The archeological site of Chavín de Huántar, near Huarás, may have been the center for the culture, but its influence was felt from the most northern to the southern coast of Peru. The Chavin culture had its beginnings as early as 800 B.C. and continued until approximately 200 B.C.

Toward the close of the Chavin culture and during the next millennium, the northern coast of Peru came under the influence of the Mochica culture. Our knowledge of the Mochica comes largely from their pottery. By 700 A.D. the Mochica culture had collapsed, largely because of their struggles with the Wari people, whose culture subsequently had considerable influence on the northern area. The next important culture in the northern area was the Chimu. The Chimu had their capital at Chan Chan, near Trujillo, and their culture persisted until the time of the Inca Empire; see INCA.

Contemporary with the Mochica culture in the north were the Paracas and Nazca cultures, located on the southern coast of Peru. Like the Mochica, both cultures are best known through their pottery.

In the southern highlands of Peru and in the region of Bolivia near Lake Titicaca (q.v.) the most important culture during the 4th to 10th centuries was that of Tiahuanacu (q.v.). This was a pan-Andean culture that had a wide influence over a large part of Peru and Bolivia, as well as over areas in Chile and Argentina. The great ceremonial center of the Tiahuanacu culture was located southeast of Lake Titicaca.

In the period beginning about 1100 A.D., the Inca occupied the area around the site of Tiahuanacu and adopted Cuzco as their capital. Their empire, which extended from Quito in north-central Ecuador to the Maule R. in Chile, was destroyed by the Spanish conquerors in 1533. Subsequently, the native Peruvian traditions continued to determine in large part the forms of the folk arts practiced in the former Inca territories, and vestiges of the ancient Inca culture are still to be seen today in the arts of the Indians of those regions.

Architecture. The ruins of the three great archeological zones of Chavín de Huántar, Tiahuanacu, and the Inca ruins in the Cuzco area attest to the great accomplishments that the pre-Columbian architects reached in stone. Working only with bronze and stone tools, they carved colossal blocks of stone and fitted them together, for the most part without mortar, to form the walls of vast temples, palaces, and entire cities.

The site of Chavín de Huántar is dominated by an imposing structure, the so-called Castillo, mostly of granite, next to a sunken court. Projecting from the 50-ft.-high walls of the Castillo

PERUVIAN ARCHEOLOGY

are carved heads that combine feline and serpentine features. The stelae are carved in a unique style of bas-relief, a famous example of which is the Stela Raimondi, now in the National Museum of Archeology and Anthropology in Lima, Peru.

The coastal peoples, comprising the Nazca, Mochica, Chimu, and numerous other smaller cultures, constructed their buildings of sun-baked clay. Surviving ruins of coastal architecture include enormous terraced pyramids, such as those at Moche near Trujillo, Peru. These pyramids, built over graves in some instances, were surmounted by shrines or temples and served as mortuary monuments. Some of the walls of these structures were painted with designs in polychrome fresco. Among the Chimu people, in particular, clay architecture was developed to a high degree. Outstanding among the remains of Chimu architecture are series of long walls at Chan Chan, which are decorated with patterns derived from textile designs. Other important archeological sites of adobe, or sun-dried clay, along the southern coast of Peru are Pachacamac and Tambo Colorado, near Lima; and Cajamarquilla, near Huarás.

The Inca adopted the masonry techniques of the Tiahuanacu, and also became highly skilled in building tremendous architectural works in stone. Buildings were roofed in thatch carried on beams. Exteriors were generally plain and severe, ornamentation being limited to series of niches breaking the surface of walls and occasional angular and symmetrical carvings in low relief, marking such prominent features as doorways. The monumental effect of the architecture was achieved by the massiveness of the construction and the smooth fitting of the blocks. Inca architectural and engineering skill, readily apparent in the ruins of their buildings, was also applied to stone terracing; this terracing was constructed to keep the soil of farms, perched on the slopes of the Andes, from washing away. Hundreds of miles of these stone terraces still exist throughout the former Inca regions. The Inca also built a vast network of stone roads connecting all parts of their empire.

Among the most notable remains of Inca architecture are those at Machu Picchu, near Cuzco, and in Cuzco and its environs. Machu Picchu, rediscovered in the 20th century by the American explorer Hiram Bingham (q.v.), was a great city built of granite and comprising numerous temples, palaces, terraces, stairways, baths, and fountains. At Cuzco, the Temple of the Sun, often considered to have been one of the most imposing edifices in Peru, stood among a great number of lesser temples, palace buildings, and other structures. The great treasures of these buildings were all taken by the Spanish conquerors. The royal family and dignitaries were usually buried in temple buildings. Mummification was practiced by both the mountain and coastal peoples; see EMBALMING.

Pottery. Among the artifacts of ancient Peru, ceramic objects constitute the most important

The ruins of an ancient Peruvian fortress rise above Cuzco.

Standard Oil Co. (N.J.)

PERUVIAN ARCHEOLOGY

Cooper Union Museum —
Purchased in memory of Georgiana L. McClellan

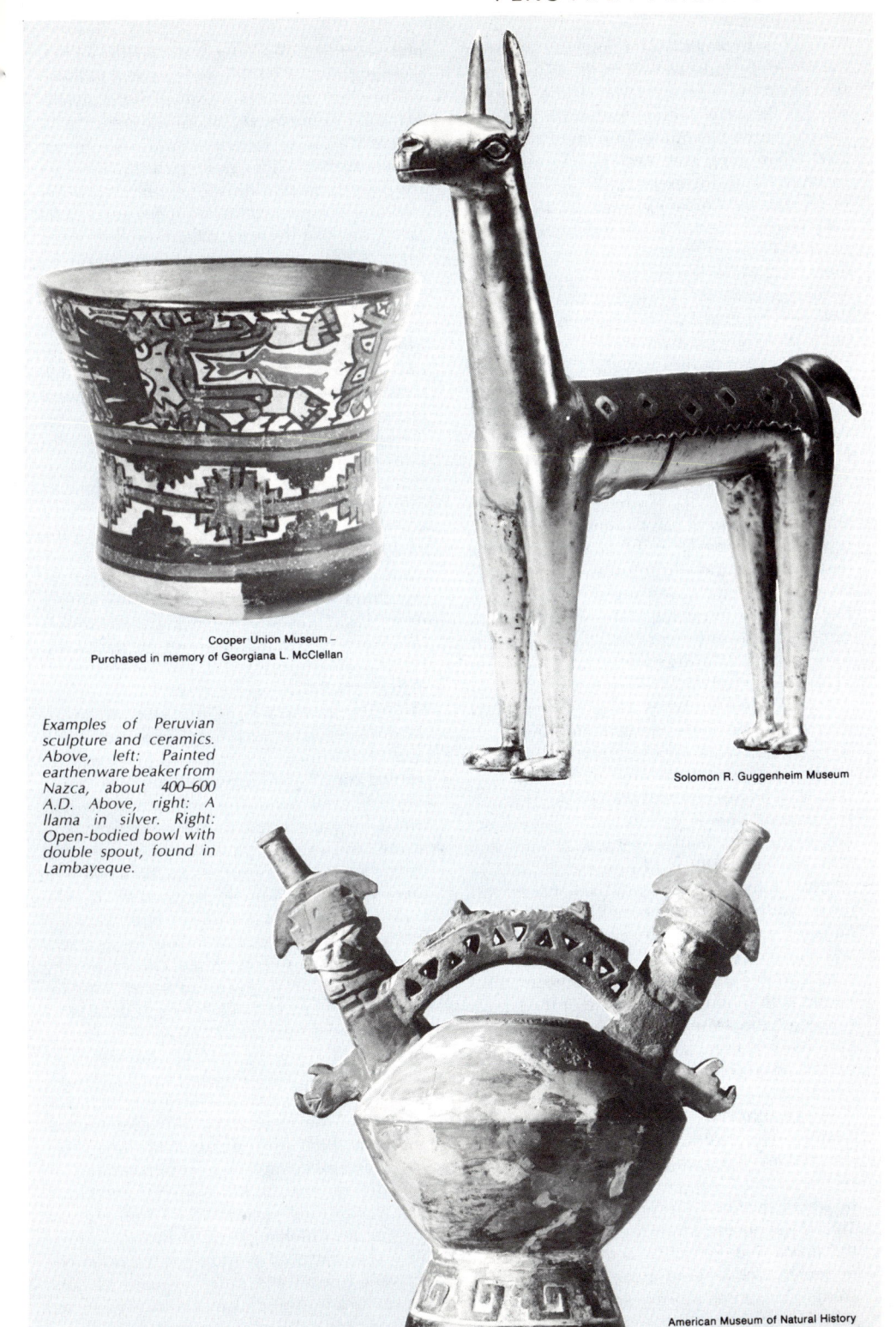

Solomon R. Guggenheim Museum

Examples of Peruvian sculpture and ceramics. Above, left: Painted earthenware beaker from Nazca, about 400–600 A.D. Above, right: A llama in silver. Right: Open-bodied bowl with double spout, found in Lambayeque.

American Museum of Natural History

459

PERUVIAN ARCHEOLOGY

body of archeological data, and the dating of the various periods is based on the styles of pottery found in successive layers at the principal sites of Peruvian culture. Radiocarbon dating has placed the beginnings of pottery as early as 1800 B.C. in Peru; (see ARCHEOLOGY: *Methods*). Much earlier dating exists, however, for pottery of Equador and Colombia, and more archeological research is needed before a definitive chronology of Peruvian pottery sequences can be established. One of the first pan-Peruvian cultural sequences in ceramics is that of Chavín. Chavín pottery is typified by the depiction of a feline deity, a design used on their stone carvings, metalwork, and textiles as well.

Elaborate burials of important persons in the coastal deserts of southern Peru have given the world a wealth of pottery from the earliest of times. Both the Nazca and Paracas pottery is highly painted in polychrome designs of yellow, violet, and blue on a white, red, or black ground. For the most part designs are geometric, or of stylized animals or birds, although some designs include people and scenes of everyday life. The rock-type desert region in this area is the site of an intriguing archeological puzzle: stones of different colors are arranged in the form of large animals, spirals, and geometrical figures recognizable only from the air.

Coastal pottery reaches a high degree of refinement in the shape, design, and thinness of some of the wares. Mochica pottery from the northern coast of Peru is famous for designs depicting all phases of life of the people. This pottery presents one of the best archeological records of the dress, deities, methods of work, and other manners of living of a people.

In the southern highlands, Tiahuanacan pottery is typified by the use of both geometric and human forms, in colors of yellow, white, black, and gray on a red base.

Inca pottery also bears designs of geometrical figures with subdued colors. One of the typical shapes of the vessels, originated by the Inca, consists of a swelling body terminating at the bottom in a point and at the top in a neck, which flares out at the mouth of the vase.

See also POTTERY.

Textiles, Stonework, and Metalwork. Peruvian textiles rank with pottery in excellence of technique and design and are often considered to be among the finest ever produced in the world. Thread was obtained from the wool of the llama, the alpaca, and the vicuña, and the colors most frequently used were red, green, brown, and blue. Designs comprised series of stylized representations of pumas, birds, fish, and men; occasionally, plant and flower motifs were also employed. Numerous garments, girdles, and pouches, found in graves where they were preserved by the dryness of the soil, exemplify virtually all the known techniques of weaving. Tapestry weaves are common in Tiahuanacan textiles. Late Nazcan examples are usually embroidered in elaborate polychrome designs. Late Chimu textiles frequently are double-faced, showing the same pattern on both sides. Many other types of weaving were applied in the making of textiles in the various periods of Peruvian culture.

The Peruvian peoples manufactured stone axes, mortars, and vessels, which were brought to a high polish, probably with the use of stone tools alone. Gold, silver, and copper were known from the earliest times, and were worked by hammering and casting. The Inca smelted metal in furnaces and wrought elaborate metal vases, cups, and personal ornaments such as bracelets and collars. One of the most fanciful uses for metal in Inca times was the creation of entire gardens of simulated flowers made of precious metals. In the coastal regions, metallurgy was also practiced from the earliest periods, and numerous hammered metal vessels have been discovered in graves on the plains.

See also ARCHEOLOGY.

PERUVIAN BARK. See CINCHONA.

PERUZZI, Baldassare (1481–1536), Italian architect and painter, born near Siena, and trained as a painter there and in Rome. In Rome, he studied Roman antiquities, particularly architecture, and came under the influence of the Italian painter Raphael and the Italian architect Bramante (qq.v.). He himself soon achieved distinction with his frescoes in the Church of Santa Maria della Pace. He designed a villa, now known as the Villa Farnesina, built between 1509 and 1511, that became famous for its graceful proportions and its fresco decorations by Raphael and his followers. Peruzzi was appointed architect of Saint Peter's Basilica (q.v.) by Pope Leo X (*see under* LEO) in 1520. During the sack of Rome in 1527 by the armies of Charles V (q.v.), Holy Roman Emperor, Peruzzi fled to Siena, where he was made city architect. He directed the construction of the Sienese fortifications, built the Palazzo Polini and other works, and executed a number of paintings.

Peruzzi returned to Rome in 1532 and began his architectural masterpiece, the Palazzo Massimi alle Colonne (1535). The palace is notable for its balanced proportions, its restrained yet varied detail and ornament, and its bold, convex facade. These elements, much admired by other Renaissance architects, foreshadowed the later baroque (q.v.) style; see ITALIAN ART AND ARCHITECTURE: *Architecture.*

PESACH or **PASSOVER,** important Jewish festival commemorating the exodus of the Israelites from Egypt and their safe flight across the Red Sea; see FESTIVALS AND FEASTS: *Jewish Festivals;* PRAYER, JEWISH. This flight, described in the book of Exodus (q.v.) was led by the Hebrew lawgiver Moses (q.v.); see JEWS: *The Hebrews in Canaan.*

The festival derives its name (Heb. *pesaḥ,* "passing over" or "protection"), from the instructions given to Moses by God (Exod. 12:3–17). In order to encourage the Egyptians to allow the Israelites to leave Egypt, God intends to "smite all the firstborn . . . both man and beast" in the land. To protect themselves, the Israelites are told to mark their dwellings with lamb's blood so that God can identify and thus pass over them. The celebration of the holiday begins after sundown on the fourteenth day of Nisan, the first month of the Jewish ecclesiastical year, about the time of the vernal equinox; see ECLIPTIC. In accordance with rabbinic law (see HALAKAH; RABBI), Jews living outside the limits of ancient Palestine (see DIASPORA) celebrate the holiday for eight days and partake of a ceremonial meal, known as the Seder, on the first two nights. The Seder consists of prescribed foods, each of which symbolizes some aspect of the ordeal undergone by the Israelites during their enslavement in Egypt. For example, horseradish signifies the bitterness of the experience, and a mixture of chopped nuts and apples in wine symbolizes the building mortar used by the Israelites in their forced labor. During the Seder the narrative of the exodus is recounted and prayers of thanksgiving are offered up to God for His loving protection. The readings, songs, and prayers of the Seder are contained in the Haggada (q.v.), copies of which are available for all at the table. Jews living within the limits of ancient Palestine celebrate Passover for seven days, conducting a Seder only on the first night. Throughout the holiday the Orthodox Jew must abstain from eating leavened bread, substituting unleavened bread, usually in the form of matzoth. These matzoth recall the unleavened bread eaten by the Israelites during their flight because they had no time to prepare raised bread. Orthodox Jewish tradition prescribes that during Pesach meals be prepared and served using sets of utensils and dishes reserved strictly for that festival. *See also* EASTER.

S.L.

PESARO (anc. *Pisaurum*), city of Italy, in Marche Region, and capital of Pesaro e Urbino Province, on the Adriatic Sea, about 20 miles N.E. of Urbino. The city is a popular bathing resort, a fishing port, and a commercial center with trade in agricultural products. Majolica pottery is the best-known manufacture of the city. Other manufactures include machinery and textiles. Among its historic buildings are several churches dating from the 13th and 14th centuries, including the Church of San Franceso and the former Church of San Domenico, and a number of 15th-century structures, including the fortress of Rocca Costanza and the Villa Imperiale. The civil museum, containing a rare pottery collection, and the Oliveriana Library are noteworthy. Pesaro has a school of music which was endowed by the Italian composer Gioacchino Antonio Rossini (q.v.), a native of the city.

Founded by the Romans, Pesaro passed successively to the Goths, Byzantines, and Franks. After 1631 it was under papal control except during the Napoleonic era. In 1860 it was incorporated into the Kingdom of Italy. Pop. (1960) 47,185.

PESCADORES *or* **PENGHU ISLANDS.** See TAIWAN.

PESCARA, city and port of Italy, in Abruzzi Region, and capital of Pescara Province, on the Adriatic Sea at the mouth of the Pescara R., 95 miles N.E. of Rome. It is a seaside resort as well as a road and rail junction. The surrounding area produces grains, vegetables, olives, grapes, livestock, asphalt, and oil. The city refines sulfur and manufactures metal products, glass, furniture, woolen textiles, cement, dyes, liquor, macaroni, scales, and soap. Pescara is the birthplace of the Italian poet-patriot Gabriele d'Annunzio (q.v.). Called Aternum (or Ostia Aterni) by the Romans, who took it in 214 B.C. Pop. (1961) 81,697.

PESHAWAR, city of Pakistan, in West Pakistan Province, about 10 miles E. of the entrance to the Khyber Pass (q.v.) and 235 miles N.W. of Lahore. The city is a flourishing commercial center and the traditional terminus of caravans from Afghanistan. Industries include handicrafts and the manufacture of silk and cotton textiles. Peshawar University was established here in 1950. Also in the city is Peshawar Museum which houses important collections of sculpture of the ancient Gandhara civilization; see INDIAN ART AND ARCHITECTURE: *Sculpture.*

An ancient trading center known as Purushapure, the city's strategic location near the pass made it the target for successive invaders of the Indian subcontinent. In the early 19th century Peshawar fell under the control of the Sikhs (q.v.), and in the mid-19th century it was captured by the British. Peshawar served as capital of the former North-West Frontier Province of Pakistan until 1955. Pop. (1969 est.) 296,000.

PESSIMISM, doctrine that reality, life, and the world are evil rather than good. Pessimism generally takes one of two forms: that of an entrenched negative state of mind or permanent expectation of the worst under all circumstances, and that of a philosophical system. The former instance may arise, depending on the temperament of the individual, from the reaction of a person to the difference between the world as it is and the world as it could be. The existence of evil and the link between suffering and sin have been dwelt upon since ancient times; one example is the ancient Hebrew book of Job (q.v.).

In the 19th century, pessimism was elaborated into a system of philosophy by the German philosophers Arthur Schopenhauer (q.v.) and his successor Eduard von Hartmann (1842–1906). Each saw life in this world as rooted in misery, pain, and endless struggle. An unqualified pessimism encompasses the idea that all the ends and aims of life are illusory. The opposite doctrine of pessimism is optimism (q.v.), which applauds the world as it is and embraces the feeling of hope.

PESTALOZZI, Johann Heinrich (1746–1827), Swiss educational reformer, born in Zürich, and educated at the University of Zürich. In 1775, influenced by the works of the French philosopher Jean Jacques Rousseau (q.v.), he began his experiments in education by opening a school for the children of the poor on his estate near Zürich. After five years the project was abandoned for lack of funds. For the next twenty years he remained on the estate, formulating his theories and writing two books, *Abendstunde eines Einsiedlers* (1781; Eng. trans., *The Evening Hours of a Hermit*, 1912), a series of aphoristic observations on education and life; and *Lienhard und Gertrud* (4 vol., 1781–85; Eng. trans., *Leonard and Gertrude*, 1801), a didactic novel expounding his theories on social reform through education.

In 1798 Pestalozzi established a school for orphans at Stans; it failed after a few months. In 1799 he opened a school at Burgdorf, moving it in 1805 to Yverdon. This school, attended by pupils from all over Europe, survived for twenty years as a testing ground for the Pestalozzian system, in which the child is guided to learn through practice and observation and through the natural employment of his senses.

Pestalozzi stresses the individuality of the child and the necessity for teachers to be taught how to develop rather than to try to implant knowledge. In time, his ideas influenced the elementary-school systems of the Western world, particularly in the area of teacher training. Among his later books are *Wie Gertrud ihre Kinder lehrt* ("How Gertrude Teaches Her Children", 1801), an epistolary educational tract; and the autobiographical *Schwanengesang* ("Swansong", 1826). Much of Pestalozzi's work appeared in English translation in *Collected Educational Writings of Pestalozzi* (1912). See EDUCATION: *The 19th Century and the Rise of National School Systems*.

PESTICIDE. See AGRICULTURAL CHEMISTRY.
PESTILENCE. See PLAGUE.
PETAH TIQWA, city of Israel, in the Central District, on the Plain of Sharon near the Hayarqon R., 7 miles N.E. of Tel Aviv-Jaffa. The city is in a region of citrus orchards, vineyards, and limestone quarries. The varied industries include textile and paper milling, food canning, distilling, and the manufacture of chemicals, electrical equipment, machinery, metal and rubber products, furniture, asbestos cement, and pharmaceuticals.

A stone arch found within the city is dedicated to the philanthropist Edmond Baron de Rothschild (*see under* ROTHSCHILD), who gave badly needed financial support to the early settlement there. Nearby to the N.E. is the site of Antipatris, the Biblical Aphek, founded by the king of Judaea Herod the Great (q.v.). Petah Tiqwa was founded in 1878 as the first modern Jewish agricultural settlement in Palestine. The name is also spelled Petah Tiqva and Petah Tikva. Pop. (1961) 58,700.

PÉTAIN, Henri Philippe (1856–1951), French soldier, born in Cauchy-à-la-Tour, and educated at the military academy at Saint-Cyr and L'École Supérieure de Guerre, or army war college, in Paris. At the outbreak of World War I, Pétain, then a colonel, was made a brigadier general. In 1916 he became a national hero when he halted the German advance in the Battle of Verdun and then drove the invaders back; see VERDUN, BATTLE OF. Pétain was appointed chief of the general staff in April, 1917, and commander in chief of the French armies the following month. In March, 1918, Pétain became head of the French army operations under the supreme Allied commander, Marshal Ferdinand Foch (q.v.). On Nov. 21, 1918, following the armistice of Nov. 11, Pétain was made a marshal of France. From 1920 to 1930 he was vice-president of the advisory military body called the Superior Council of War; in 1925 he went to Morocco to direct the French campaign against the rebellion of the Riffian

Marshal Henri Philippe Pétain appears in court in Paris in 1945 to face charges of conspiring with Germany to destroy the French republic.
UPI

tribesmen led by the Moorish chief Abd-el-Krim (q.v.). In 1934 Pétain was minister of war, and in 1939–40 he was the French ambassador to Spain.

Following the German invasion of France in 1940, Pétain was recalled to active military service as adviser to the minister of war. On June 16, 1940, he succeeded Paul Reynaud (1878–1966) as premier of France and soon afterward he asked the German dictator Adolf Hitler for an armistice, which was concluded on June 22, 1940; see also COMPIÈGNE. On July 2, with the consent of the Germans, he established his government in Vichy in central France, and on July 10 he assumed the title of chief of state, ruling thereafter with dictatorial powers over that portion of France not directly under German control. Pétain's regime, often called the Vichy government, became notorious for its collaboration with the Germans, particularly after April, 1942, when the French politician Pierre Laval (q.v.) became premier. After the Allies landed in France in 1944, Pétain went to Germany and then to Switzerland. He returned to France after the war to stand trial for treason. On Aug. 15, 1945, he was found guilty of intelligence with the enemy and was sentenced to death. The death sentence, however, was accompanied by a recommendation for clemency, and Charles André Joseph Marie de Gaulle (q.v.), then provisional head of the French government, commuted Pétain's sentence to life imprisonment, and he was moved to Ile d'Yew, an island off Britany. See FRANCE: *History; World War II; Vichy Government and Resistance: Post-War Governments.*

PETAL, in botany. *See* FLOWER.

PETALUMA, city of California, in Sonoma Co., at the head of navigation on the Petaluma Creek, 35 miles N.W. of San Francisco. It is one of the leading poultry-raising centers in the United States and contains one of the largest poultry hatcheries in the world. Dairying is also important. The manufactures include poultry equipment, oil burners, fertilizers, twine and paper boxes, and the processing of dairy products. Petaluma was founded by Mexican colonists in 1833, laid out in 1852 and incorporated as a town in 1858 and as a city in 1911. Pop. (1960) 14,035; (1970) 24,870.

PETER, two books of the New Testament (*see* BIBLE), in the King James Version, THE FIRST EPISTLE GENERAL OF PETER, and THE SECOND EPISTLE GENERAL OF PETER. The two letters of Peter are among the seven Epistles of the New Testament designated as Catholic by the early Church because they are addressed to Christians generally, instead of to particular churches. The first Epistle of Peter is addressed "to the strangers scattered throughout Pontus, Galatia, Cappadocia, Asia, and Bithynia" (1 Pet. 1:1); that is, to Christians living in Roman provinces in the northern part of Asia Minor (q.v.). The second Epistle of Peter is addressed "to them that have obtained . . . precious faith with us through the righteousness of God and our Saviour Jesus Christ" (2 Pet. 1:1); that is, to all Christians. Ecclesiastical tradition has attributed both Epistles to Saint Peter (q.v.), but chiefly on the basis of internal evidence many modern scholars have questioned St. Peter's authorship of the first Epistle, and most

PETER

have doubted his authorship of the second Epistle.

First Epistle. The first Epistle claims to be from "Peter, an apostle of Jesus Christ" (1:1), "a witness of the sufferings of Christ" (5:1), "by Silvanus, a faithful brother" (5:12). It is written in excellent Greek, apparently reflects a knowledge of certain Epistles of Saint Paul (q.v.), and accurately cites the Greek Septuagint (q.v.), instead of the Hebrew text of the Old Testament. Largely for these reasons, many scholars today are reluctant to believe that St. Peter, Palestinian fisherman, could have written it. They propose that it was written by a Roman Christian who, following a widely accepted ancient literary convention of pseudonymously ascribing new works to venerated figures of the past, credited his work to St. Peter. Scholars who today accept St. Peter's authorship hold that Silvanus (Silas), a traveling companion of St. Paul, actually might have written the letter for the Apostle. If St. Peter was the author (either by himself or "by Silvanus"), the Epistle probably dates from 64–65 A.D., or just after persecution of Christians began in Rome under the emperor Nero (q.v.). If the author is unknown, then the persecution referred to in 4:12–19 and 5:9 probably was the more general one that occurred under the emperor Domitian (q.v.) in 81–96 A.D.; and the Epistle would date from about 96 A.D. The place of composition is commonly believed to have been Rome, chiefly because of the phrase "the church that is at Babylon . . . saluteth you" (5:13), "Babylon" being an apocalyptic name for Rome; see APOCALYPTIC WRITINGS. Some scholars have proposed that the Epistle may actually have been composed in the ancient city of Babylon (q.v.).

The First Epistle General of Peter was written to newly converted Christians to encourage them to rejoice and to persevere in their faith in spite of persecution and other hardships. The readers are told of their spiritual rebirth "unto a lively hope by the resurrection of Jesus Christ" (1:3) and exhorted, therefore, to live in a manner worthy of "the grace that is to be brought . . . at the revelation of Jesus Christ" (1:13); that is, at the Second Advent of Christ (q.v.). Servants (slaves) specifically are exhorted to show obedience, in imitation of Jesus' example (2:18–25), and Christian women married to non-Christians are also urged to "be in subjection to your own husbands; that, if any obey not the word, they also may without the word be won by the conversation of their wives" (3:1). All must lead loving, holy lives, and not fear to suffer even unjustly; for so Jesus "once suffered for sins, the just for the unjust, that he might bring us to God" (3:18). Those who would disobey, who would do evil, who would not love one another, are warned that "the end of all things is at hand" (4:7), and that "the time is come that judgment must begin at the house of God" (4:17). The instructional portion of the Epistle concludes with several exhortations. Special significance was attached by the early Church to passages in this Epistle believed to refer to Christ's preaching in the underworld between the times of His crucifixion and His resurrection; see HELL. These passages (3:19–21, 4:6) provided the scriptural basis for the Christian doctrine of Jesus' descent into Hell; see CREEDS.

Second Epistle. The Second Epistle General of Peter claims to be from "Simon Peter, a servant and an apostle of Jesus Christ" (2 Pet. 1:1); an eyewitness to Christ's Transfiguration (1:18); a "brother" of St. Paul (3:15); and the author of 1 Peter (3:1). Peter's authorship, however, was questioned by the early Church, and it is now doubted by most scholars on the basis of internal and external evidence. Furthermore, 2 Peter incorporates virtually all of the Epistle of Jude (q.v.), and shows a knowledge of a collection of St. Paul's Epistles (3:15–16), and of their Gnostic misinterpreters; see GNOSTICISM. Peter could not have known these things. Therefore, most modern scholars have suggested 2 Peter was written by an unknown person, perhaps a disciple of St. Peter, some time in the 2nd century. (Some Catholic and conservative Protestant scholars continue to defend St. Peter's authorship.) The Epistle has been accepted as canonical since the 4th century; see BIBLE, CANON OF THE.

The second Epistle of Peter was written to strengthen the Christian belief in the Second Advent of Christ, a hope that had been attacked and ridiculed as ill-founded, since it was believed imminent but had not come to pass, in the heretical teachings of the Gnostics. The Epistle may be divided into three main sections, each making up a single chapter. In the first section the readers are reminded of God's "exceeding great and precious promises", which have been given to them through Christ. They must, however, lead truly Christian lives in addition to believing in these promises, to gain an "entrance . . . into the everlasting kingdom of our Lord and Saviour Jesus Christ". Finally, the readers should remember always that their Christian beliefs are not "cunningly devised fables" but are based on Apostolic (see APOSTLE) testimony to Jesus' power and glory, and on divinely inspired prophecies in the Old Testament. An attack on "false teachers . . . who privily . . .

bring in damnable heresies" and a condemnation of their lustful, brutish nature constitute the second main section. The portions of the Epistle of Jude incorporated in 2 Peter are found in this section. In the third section the "scoffers" are refuted, and "the day of the Lord" is reaffirmed. Christians should not lose faith though it may seem to them that "the day of God, wherein the heavens being on fire shall be dissolved and the elements shall melt with fervent heat" has been long delayed; for God's sense of time is not man's, and He is "longsuffering . . . not willing that any should perish, but that all should come to repentance".

PETER, Saint, *or* SIMON PETER (d. 67?), in Christianity, one of the twelve Apostles (*see* APOSTLE), a native of Bethsaida (now in Israel), a village near the Sea of Galilee (now Lake Tiberias). His principal name, Peter, is the Greek translation of that given him (John 1:42) by Jesus (*see* JESUS CHRIST); Cephas is the Grecian form of the Aramaic *kepha*, "rock" or "stone".

When Jesus began his ministry, Peter was living at Capernaum (q.v.), on the Sea of Galilee, where he and his brother Andrew (q.v.) shared a house. Jesus called them both to abandon their fishing trade to become "fishers of men" (Matt. 4:18–22). According to the Gospels (*see* GOSPEL) he was regarded by Jesus with particular affection, though he denied being a follower of Jesus at the time of His arrest (Matt. 26:69–75). In the Acts of the Apostles (q.v.), Peter is described as the prime influence in the election of a successor to the betrayer of Christ, Judas Iscariot (q.v.; Acts 1:15–26), and he was spokesman on the day of Pentecost (q.v.; Acts 2:14–41). With John (*see* JOHN THE EVANGELIST) he was sent from Jerusalem to the Samaritan converts (*see* SAMARITANS) that they might receive the Holy Ghost (q.v.). Although he was the first to baptize a Gentile convert (Acts 10:47–48), he later fell into disagreement with Saint Paul (q.v.) at Antioch (now Antâkya, Turkey), about the role of Gentiles in the Church. Peter took a prominent part in the first council (q.v.) of the Church, at Jerusalem. According to tradition he died in Rome during the persecutions of the Christians under Roman Emperor Nero (q.v.), which, if accurate, would place the time of his death in the year 64.

The feast day of St. Peter, and that of St. Paul, is June 29.

The true leader of the Church after Pentecost, Peter was noted for his miracles (*see* MIRACLE) and his devotion to Christ. The authorship of the two New Testament Epistles bearing his name is uncertain; *see* books of PETER. *See also* CHRISTIAN CHURCH, HISTORY OF THE; PAPACY; POPE.

PETER, name of a number of European rulers. Brief accounts of less important monarchs are included in this article under the names of the countries that they ruled. The more important monarchs are described in separate biographical articles, to which the reader is referred below.

The English name *Peter* appears as *Petar* in Yugoslav and *Pëtr* in Russian. *See also* PEDRO.

BYZANTINE EMPIRE

Peter of Courtenay (d. 1217), Latin Emperor of Constantinople (1216–17), grandson of Louis VI (q.v.), King of France. Peter joined Philip II (q.v.), King of France, on the Third Crusade and fought at the Battle of Bouvines (q.v.) in 1214; *see* CRUSADES. Peter married Yolande (d. after 1219), the sister of Henry of Flanders (q.v.), Latin Emperor of Constantinople, and in 1216 when Henry died, leaving no male heir, Peter was chosen to succeed him. After his consecration as emperor at Rome in 1217, Peter set out to conquer the Adriatic port of Durazzo or Durrës, from the Greek despot of Epirus (q.v.), who captured and imprisoned him. Yolande ruled as regent from 1217 to 1219 for their son Robert of Courtenay (d. 1228).

RUSSIA

Peter I (1672–1725). *See* PETER I, known as PETER THE GREAT, Czar of Russia.

Peter II (1715–30), Emperor of Russia (1727–30), son of Czarevitch Alexis Petrovich (1690–1718), and grandson of Emperor Peter I (q.v.) by his first wife, born in Saint Petersburg (now LENINGRAD). Peter succeeded Empress Catherine I (*see under* CATHERINE), Peter I's second wife. Peter II died of smallpox shortly before he was to be married.

Peter III (1728–62), Emperor of Russia (1762), grandson of Peter I, and husband of Catherine, later Empress Catherine II, born in Kiel, Germany. In 1741, after the death of his father, he was adopted by his aunt, Empress Elizabeth Petrovna (q.v.). On his accession in 1762, Russia was at war with Prussia, whose ruler, Frederick II (q.v.), known as Frederick the Great, Peter so greatly admired that he quickly concluded a peace treaty. He thereby sacrificed all the advantages Russia had gained during the Seven Years' War (q.v.), and antagonized many Russian nobles. The nobles, aided by Catherine, Peter's wife and successor, deposed him on July 8, 1762. He abdicated the following day in favor of Catherine, and was murdered on July 17.

SERBIA

Peter I Karageorgevich (1844–1921), King of Serbia (1903–21), son of Alexander Karageorgevich, Prince of Serbia (1806–85), born in Bel-

PETER

grade, and educated in Paris. Peter lived with his father in exile from 1858 to 1903. During this period he fought on the French side in the Franco-German War (q.v.) of 1870–71 and commanded a corps in the revolt of Bosnia against Turkey in 1875. Following the assassinations in 1903 of the Serbian monarchs Alexander I Obrenovich (1876–1903) and Draga (1867–1903), Peter was elected king. His reign was marked by liberal reforms, alliance with Russia, friendship for France, and a decrease of Austrian influence in Serbia. Because of ill health Peter, in 1914, surrendered his governmental duties to his son, Crown Prince Alexander, later Alexander I (q.v.), King of Yugoslavia. In acknowledgment of the territorial gains made by Serbia after World War I, in 1918 Peter, although in retirement, received the title of King of the Serbs, Croats, and Slovenes.

YUGOSLAVIA

Peter II (1923–70), King of Yugoslavia (1934–45), son of Alexander I (q.v.), King of Yugoslavia, and grandson of Peter I Karageorgevich, King of Serbia, born in Belgrade. Peter succeeded to the throne under the regency of his uncle, Prince Paul (1893–   ), after his father's assassination in 1934. In 1941, during World War II (q.v.), the Yugoslavs ousted the pro-Axis administration of the regent. Peter assumed full control and brought his kingdom into the war on the Allied side, whereupon the Germans invaded Yugoslavia. Peter fled to Great Britain, where he established a Yugoslav government in exile. In 1945, at the end of the war, Yugoslavia became a Communist republic and Peter remained in exile.

PETER I, known as PETER THE GREAT (1672–1725), Czar of Russia (1682–1725) and Emperor of Russia (1721–25), son of Czar Alexis I Mikhailovich (q.v.), born in Moscow. Peter was taught in early childhood by private tutors; later, he taught himself technical and mechanical arts, especially in relation to military and naval science. From 1682 to 1689, under the regency of his half-sister Sophia Alekseevna (1657–1704), Peter shared the throne with his older half-brother Ivan V (q.v.). In 1689 Peter's partisans at court overthrew Sophia and installed Peter as sole ruler.

During his reign Russia emerged as a great European power, in part because of his introduction of many Western European scientific, technological, cultural, and political conceptions and practices. In 1696, after creating the Russian navy, Peter captured from the Turks the important fortress of Azov, which commanded the Sea of Azov and gave Russia access to the Black Sea (q.v.). In an effort to secure allies among the European powers against the Turks, Peter, in 1696, accompanied a diplomatic mission that he sent to the principal capitals of Western Europe; thus he was the first Russian leader to journey beyond the borders of his country. During his travels Peter induced about 900 artisans, craftsmen, technical advisers, and other experts to

Peter the Great — Bettmann Archive

emigrate to Russia. Later he sent many young Russians abroad to learn Western crafts and trades.

On his return to Moscow in 1698 Peter, determined to gain control of the eastern part of the Baltic Sea, began military preparations for an attack on Sweden. During the Northern War (1700–21) that ensued, he won one of the greatest military victories in Russian history at the Battle of Poltava in 1709. By the terms of the Treaty of Nystadt (1721) that concluded the war, Russia won a considerable area of the Baltic littoral, later called the Baltic Provinces. Through Peter's efforts, the Russo-Chinese border was established, and commercial relations between the two countries were initiated. In 1703, during the war, Peter founded Saint Petersburg (now Leningrad) as a "window to Europe" and made it the capital.

Peter was proclaimed emperor in 1721 and thus established the Russian Empire. He introduced such internal reforms as abolition of the power of the boyars, or aristocrats, and the subordination of those nobles and of the church to the throne; the encouragement of industry, trade, and education; and the reorganization of the administrative apparatus of the state to make it more modern and efficient. During Peter's reign the Russian alphabet was simplified, Arabic numerals were introduced, the first newspaper in the Russian language was published, schools were founded, and the Academy of Sciences was augmented.

Under Peter, Russia became a regimented state. His police-state philosophy was based on the conviction that, just as he spent his life unceasingly in service for the state, so his subjects, whose welfare was his object, should discharge their obligation to the state. Both his reforms and his swift, often cruel, reprisals for infractions of his regulations made indelible impressions upon Russian life. See also RUSSIA: *History*.

PETER THE GREAT, See PETER I.

PETER THE HERMIT, known also as PETER OF AMIENS (about 1050–1115), apostle of the First Crusade (*see* CRUSADES: *First Crusade*), a native of Amiens, France. He is said to have served as a soldier, to have become a hermit, and in 1093 to have made a pilgrimage to Palestine, although he was unable to reach the Holy City. In 1095 he began the campaign that was to leave a mark on history, preaching the Crusade throughout central and northern France. In 1096 he led a group of Crusaders to Constantinople (now Istanbul, Turkey) and over to Asia Minor, where they were destroyed by the Ottoman Turks while he was away trying to get help. He then joined a band of Crusaders under the French nobleman Godfrey of Bouillon (q.v.) in the conquest of Jerusalem in 1099. Many historians believe that Peter the Hermit was only one of several who preached the First Crusade and that his importance has been greatly exaggerated.

PETERBORO, mill town of New Hampshire, in Hillsboro Co. on the Contoocook R. between Keene and Nashua. The town produces textiles, electrical equipment, and ball bearings. Peterboro, also famous as a resort town, is well known as the site of the MacDowell Colony, a center for writers, musicians, and artists, planned by, and named after the American musician Edward MacDowell (q.v.). In 1833 the first tax-subsidized free library in the United States was established here. Pop. (1970) 3,807.

PETERBOROUGH, city of Canada, in Ontario, Province, and county seat of Peterborough Co., on the Otonabee R., about 75 miles N.E. of Toronto. Hydroelectric power is supplied by the falls of the Otonabee R., about 10 mi. above the city. Principal manufactures are electrical equipment, watches and clocks, food products, canoes, and outboard motors. The city is a port of entry and is served by inland water carriers operating to Lake Ontario, several highways, and railroads. Founded in 1825, Peterborough was incorporated as a town in 1850 and as a city in 1905. Pop. (1966) 56,177.

PETERBOROUGH, Great Britain, municipal borough in Huntingdon and Peterborough County, England, on the Nene R., about 76 miles N. of London. Peterborough is an important railway center, with an extensive trade in coal and agricultural products. The chief industrial establishments are railway repair shops and plants engaged in the manufacture of bricks, tiles, diesel engines, and the refining of beet sugar. The principal point of interest in the city is the cathedral, built between 1117 and 1528, revealing all stages of traditional architecture from early Norman to Perpendicular; *see* ARCHITECTURE.

Medeshamstede, on the site of present-day Peterborough, developed around a Benedictine monastery built in 655. The town was destroyed by the Danes in 870 and was rebuilt in the 10th century and renamed Peterboro. The town became a borough in the 12th century and the seat of a bishopric in 1541. Peterborough was the county seat of the administrative county of the Soke of Peterborough in Northamptonshire until 1965 when the Soke merged with Huntingdon County; *see* HUNTINGDON AND PETERBORO. Pop. (1969 est.) 66,800.

PETERBOROUGH, SOKE OF. See HUNTINGDON AND PETERBOROUGH.

PETER PAN, title character of a fantasy play for children by the Scottish writer Sir James Matthew Barrie (q.v.), first produced in 1904. *See also* CHILDREN'S LITERATURE: *The 19th and Early 20th Centuries.*

PETERSBURG, city of Virginia, in Dinwiddie Co., at the head of navigation on the Appomattox R., about 20 miles S. of Richmond. Petersburg is a port of entry. Several railroads serve the city, and it is an important market center for tobacco. Industrial establishments include factories manufacturing cigarettes and other tobacco products, luggage, powder and chemicals, optical goods, synthetic fibers, clothing, paperboard, lumber, and furniture. Petersburg is the site of Virginia State College, established in 1882.

Places of historical interest in and near the city include several houses and taverns dating from the colonial period; Bristol Parish Church, or Blandford Church, built about 1735, and now a memorial to the Confederate dead; and Petersburg National Battlefield, covering about 2731 acres, and containing the battle sites of the

PETER'S PENCE

Petersburg campaign (1864–65) of the American Civil War, which prefaced the surrender of the Army of Northern Virginia by General Robert E. Lee (see under LEE) to Union general Ulysses Simpson Grant; see CIVIL WAR, THE AMERICAN. Centre Hill Mansion Museum, built about 1823, and Saint Paul's Episcopal Church, completed in 1856, are also of historic interest.

A fort was built on the site of the present city in about 1646. It developed into a frontier trading post and along with two other villages was incorporated as a town in 1784. During the American Revolution, the town was occupied by British soldiers for a brief period of time in 1781. During the Civil War, the city suffered a ten-month siege before capitulating on April 3, 1865. Petersburg was chartered as a city in 1850. Pop. (1960) 36,750; (1970) 36,103.

PETER'S PENCE, financial offering to the pope, formerly exacted as tribute. It was a tax on individual households in Anglo-Saxon England, in the reign of Alfred the Great (q.v.), King of the West Saxons. It may have originated up to a century earlier, however, in a payment made by Offa, King of Mercia (r. 759–96), to Pope Adrian I (see under ADRIAN). The tax, also called Romescot (M. Eng. *scot*, "payment" or "one's share of a payment"), continued to be paid at intervals until the Reformation (q.v.), when it was abolished (1534), along with much larger payments to the papacy, by King Henry VIII (q.v.). Traces of a similar payment appear in medieval Denmark, Sweden, Norway, and Iceland, and it may have existed as a tax distinct from feudal tribute in Hungary, Poland, and lands near them. The tribute ceased at the Reformation in all these lands, too. In the 1860's, however, Pope Pius IX (see under PIUS) revived Peter's Pence as a voluntary contribution to the papacy from dioceses throughout the world.

PÉTION, Alexandre Sabès (1770–1818), Haitian general and politician, born in Port-au-Prince, and educated at a military school in Paris. He joined the troops of the Haitian revolutionist Pierre Dominique Toussaint L'Ouverture (q.v.) in 1791 and participated in the expulsion of the British and Spanish from Haiti in 1798; see HISPANIOLA. In 1799 he joined the Haitian general André Rigaud (1761–1811) in a civil war against Toussaint L'Ouverture. They were defeated and Pétion fled to France. In 1802 he returned to Haiti with a French military force led by the French officer General Charles Victor Emmanuel Leclerc (1772–1802), who had been sent by Napoleon I (q.v.), later Emperor of the French, to conquer the island. After the French had been defeated and expelled by the Haitian leader Jean Jacques Dessalines (q.v.), Pétion served under Dessalines. Two years after the latter declared himself emperor of Haiti in 1804, however, Pétion joined the Haitian revolutionist Henri Christophe (q.v.) in a conspiracy against Dessalines, and Dessalines was assassinated. In 1807 Pétion set up an independent republic in southern and western Haiti of which he was chosen president for life. He divided the land from confiscated French plantations among the Haitian peasants. At the same time Christophe had established a kingdom in the north, proclaiming himself King Henri I. Claiming sovereignty over all Haiti, in 1811 he launched an unsuccessful war to depose Pétion that lasted until Pétion's death.

PETIT, Roland (1924–), French dancer and choreographer, born in Villemomble, a suburb of Paris. Petit studied at the ballet school of the Paris Opera and in 1945 became chief choreographer and premier danseur of Les Ballets des Champs-Élysées. Three years later he organized his own company, Les Ballets de Paris de Roland Petit. It toured the United States in 1949–50 and 1950–51, disbanding when Petit stayed in Hollywood to do the choreography for the film *Hans Christian Andersen* (1952). Petit organized other troupes, including two that appeared in the United States (1953; 1958) and another that appeared at Expo '67, a world's fair in Montréal.

Noted for his highly dramatic, sophisticated style, Petit borrowed freely from modern dance, classic ballet, pantomime, and the music hall. Among his notable ballets are *Le Jeune Homme et la Mort* ("The Young Man and Death", 1946), *Les Forains* ("The Traveling Players", 1948), *Carmen* (1949), and *Paradise Lost* (1967). In 1954 he married the star of several of his ballets, Renée Jeanmaire (q.v.). Petit was director of the Paris Opera Ballet in 1970.

PETITION OF RIGHT, in English history, title of a petition addressed to Charles I (q.v.), King of England, by Parliament in 1628. Parliament demanded that the king desist from levying taxes without its consent, that he cease billeting soldiers and sailors in the homes of private citizens and proclaiming martial law in time of peace, and that no subject be imprisoned without cause shown. After some attempts to circumvent these demands, Charles was obliged to assent to the petition.

PETIT JURY. See JURY.

PETIT LARCENY. See LARCENY.

PETIT MAL. See EPILEPSY.

PETŐFI, Sándor, original name SÁNDOR PETROVICS (1823–49), Hungarian poet, born in

Kiskőrös in the county of Pest. He became successively an actor and a soldier. His first poem, published in 1842, was followed in 1844 by a volume that secured his fame as a poet. In 1848 he identified himself with the Hungarian revolutionary cause, writing numerous popular war poems, including "Rise, Magyar" (1848), which became the Hungarian national anthem. He died in battle at Segesvár (now Sighişoara, Rumania). His poetry, dealing in a clear, direct style with the themes of love and patriotism and revealing the intense feelings and convictions of the author, began a new epoch in Hungarian literature. His long epic about peasant life in Hungary, *János the Hero* (1845; Eng. trans., 1866), is considered his best poem.

PETRA, ancient city of Arabia, in what is now Jordan, immediately E. of the village of Wadi Musa. The stronghold and treasure city of the Nabataeans, an Arab people, Petra is referred to as Sela in the Bible (2 Kings 14:7). The city of rock was situated in the land of Edom (q.v.) between the Dead Sea and the Gulf of 'Aqaba, near the points of intersection of great caravan routes from Gaza on the Mediterranean Sea, from Damascus, from Elath on the Red Sea, and from the Persian Gulf. From the 4th century B.C. until the 2nd century A.D., Petra was the capital of the Nabataean kingdom. The Romans conquered it in 106 A.D. and made it part of the Roman province of Arabia Petraea. The city continued to flourish in the 2nd and 3rd centuries, but later, when the rival city of Palmyra took away most of Petra's trade, the importance of Petra declined. It was conquered by the Muslims in the 7th century and captured by the Crusaders in the 12th century; gradually it fell into ruins.

The site of the ancient city was rediscovered in 1812 by the Swiss traveler Johann Ludwig Burckhardt (1784–1817). An impregnable fortress, conspicuous both for its great natural beauty and for the magnificence of its monuments, it is approached by a chasm, or ravine, which in some places is only 12 ft. wide and has towering rocky walls. Along this ravine are the ancient ruins shaped out of the walls of solid rock, the most famous of which include the Khaznah, a temple also known as the treasury of Pharaoh, and a semicircular theater capable of seating about 3000 spectators. All along the face of the pink rocks that overlook the valley are rows of tombs hewn out of the solid stone. The ruins of Petra bear eloquent testimony to its former power, wealth, and culture.

PETRARCH, Francesco (It. *Francesco Petrarca,* originally FRANCESCO PETRACCO (1304–74), Italian poet and humanist, born in Arezzo. Until he was eight years old, his family lived in Tuscany, then in 1312 they moved to Avignon, France. In 1326, after the death of his father, Petrarch, who had been studying law at Bologna, returned to Avignon, where he took minor orders in the church about 1330. It was on Good Friday in 1327 that he first saw Laura (probably Laure de Noves, 1308?–48), a Frenchwoman whose name he was to immortalize in his lyrics, and who inspired him with a passion that has become proverbial for its constancy and purity.

During a lifetime spent principally in the service of the church and the Visconti family, the poet traveled widely; he went to France, the Low Countries, and Germany (about 1333), to Rome (1337), and to Parma, Italy, Vaucluse, near Avignon, and Naples, Italy (in the 1340's). At Florence, Italy, in 1350, he met the Italian poet Giovanni Boccaccio (q.v.), with whom he had previously corresponded. From 1353 to 1374 Petrarch remained in Italy, in Milan, for eight years, and from 1361 to 1374 in Padua, Venice, and Arquà, the town in which he died. Possibly as a result of his travels, he developed a strong belief in the role of a unified Italy as the cultural heir of the Roman Empire.

Petrarch wrote in Latin and in Italian. His Latin works include "Africa" (1338–42), an epic poem about the Roman conqueror Publius Cornelius Scipio Africanus (*see under* SCIPIO), and *De Viris Illustribus* ("Concerning Famous Men", about 1338), a series of biographies. Also in Latin are his eclogues and epistles in verse; the dialogue *Secretum* (1343; Eng. trans., *Petrarch's Secret,* 1911); and the treatise *De Vita Solitaria* (1346–56; Eng. trans., *Solitary Life,* 1924). His vast collection of letters is important for its historical and biographical details. Yet his most famous work is the collection of Italian verses, the *Rime in Vita e Morta di Madonna Laura* ("Verses on the Life and Death of My Lady Laura", after 1327). Better known as *Canzoniere* or "Songbook", it has been translated into English as *Petrarch's Sonnets* (1931). The Songbook's sonnets and odes, almost all inspired by his unrequited passion for Laura, express the character of the man and the reality of a strong sentiment. His last work was a series of allegorical poems about Laura written in Latin, *I Trionfi* (1352–74; Eng. trans., *The Triumphs of Petrarch,* 1962).

Petrarch is considered by many to be the first modern poet, and his perfection of the sonnet form later influenced such English poets as Geoffrey Chaucer, William Shakespeare, and Edmund Spenser (qq.v.). Made poet laureate by the senate of Rome in 1341, Petrarch was highly respected in his lifetime. His wide knowledge of the classical authors and his restoration of the classical Latin language earned him his reputation as the first great humanist. But his use of Italian as a literary language also made him possibly the first modern man of letters.

See ITALIAN LITERATURE: *14th Century.*

PETREL, common name applied to any small or medium-sized sea bird in the family Procellariidae, which also includes the fulmar and shearwater (qq.v.). The true petrels, of which there are about fifty species, are long-winged birds of powerful flight; the tail is broad and short; the hind toe is vestigial; the claws are narrow and pointed; the bill is short and slender; and the tubelike nostrils are set close together. The true petrels are often confused with the stormy petrels that constitute the family Hydrobatidae.

PETRIE, Sir Flinders, in full WILLIAM MATTHEW FLINDERS PETRIE (1853–1942), British archeologist and Egyptologist, born in Charlton, kent, and educated privately. He was professor of Egyptology at the University of London from 1892 to 1933. From 1875 to 1880 he excavated sites in Great Britain, including the prehistoric monument Stonehenge (q.v.). His archeological research in Egypt began in 1881 with excavations at the pyramids of Giza (q.v.). He conducted diggings at the great temple in Tanis (1884), at the Greek city of Naucratis (1885), and in the Fayum region (1888–90). From 1927 to 1938 he conducted excavations in Palestine notably at the ancient city of Lachish (now Tell ed Duweir, Israel). His early excavations revealed that ancient Greek colonies had existed in Egypt. Petrie suggested a chronological scheme, based on a type sequence of pottery, whereby the evolution of a culture could be traced. Although subsequent scholars have developed more effective chronologies, he was the first to devise such a method. In 1894 he founded what became the British School of Archaeology in Egypt. Among his writings is *Seventy Years in Archaeology* (1931).

PETRIFIED FOREST NATIONAL PARK, region of natural interest in Arizona, about 20 miles E. of Holbrook, on the Painted Desert. It contains six separate "forests" of petrified coniferous tree trunks, lying on the ground, and countless chips of petrified wood. Some of the trunks are 6 ft. in diameter and exceed 100 ft. in length. One arched log forms a natural bridge, called the Agate Bridge, with a span of 40 ft. According to authorities, the trees originally grew during the Triassic Period (q.v.); killed by natural processes, the logs were buried by sediment and penetrated by underground waters rich in silica.

Gradually the wood fibers were replaced by the silica deposits and the logs were converted into stone. The brilliant coloring on the petrified logs is considered the result of staining by iron oxide. Later the sediment covering was removed by the elements, bringing most of the logs into view. See NATIONAL PARK SERVICE.

PETROCHEMICALS, chemical derivatives obtained from natural gas or petroleum; *see* GAS: *Natural Gas;* PETROLEUM: *Refining.*

PETROLATUM, odorless, tasteless, greasy substance obtained as the residue from petroleum (q.v.) after the lighter and more volatile components have been boiled off. The purified residue is obtained in the form of a yellowish or decolorized semisolid, known as petroleum jelly, or by various trademark names, such as Vaseline, and in the form of a faintly yellow liquid, known as mineral oil. The semisolid form is used as an unguent and as a base for pharmaceutical ointments; the liquid form is used in the preparation of nasal sprays and as a laxative.

PETROLEUM, or CRUDE OIL, naturally occurring oily, bituminous liquid, composed of various organic chemicals. It is found in large quantities below the surface of the earth in many parts of the world, and is used as fuel and as a raw material in the chemical industry. Chemically all petroleum consists principally of hydrocarbons (q.v.), although a few sulfur-containing and oxygen-containing compounds are usually present; the sulfur content varies from about 0.1 percent to about 5 percent. Physically petroleum is a liquid containing gaseous, liquid, and solid elements. The consistency of petroleum varies from liquid as thin as kerosine to liquid so thick that it will barely pour. Small quantities of gaseous compounds are usually dissolved in the liquid; when large quantities of gaseous compounds are present, the petroleum deposit is associated with a deposit of natural gas; *see* GAS: *Natural Gas.*

Three broad classes of crude petroleum exist, namely the paraffin types, the asphaltic types, and the mixed-base types. The paraffin types are composed of molecules in which the number of hydrogen atoms is always two more than twice the number of carbon atoms. The characteristic molecules in the asphaltic types are naphthenes, composed of twice as many hydrogen atoms as carbon atoms. In the mixed-base group are found both paraffin hydrocarbons and naphthenes. See also ASPHALT; NAPHTHA.

History. Petroleum deposits, which have come to the surface of the earth through the operation of natural forces, have been known to mankind for thousands of years. Such surface depos-

The first commercial oil well in the world, near Titusville, Pa. In the foreground, in top hat, is Edwin L. Drake, who conceived the idea of drilling for oil and built the primitive rig in 1859. Drake Well Museum

its include bituminous lakes; petroleum seepages coating the surfaces of rivers; and escaping inflammable natural gas, notably in the Baku Peninsula, U.S.S.R., forming so-called eternal fires. Such substances were occasionally used as fuels. By the middle of the 19th century liquid fuels were being regularly manufactured by the distillation of petroleum, asphalt, or bituminous shale. In 1859, in Titusville, Pa., a retired railroad conductor named Edwin Laurentine Drake (1819–80) drilled the first well for the specific purpose of bringing liquid petroleum to the surface.

For many years men had been seeking a safe, effective burning illuminant, easier to obtain and less expensive than whale oils; *see* WHALING. In 1850 the British industrial chemist James Young (1811–83) obtained a patent for the manufacture of paraffin and an intermediate crude oil from bituminous coal. By distillation of this oil he obtained a naphtha, the coal-oil kerosine, and basic material for lubricants and wax.

Kerosine proved a formidable competitor for whale oil. Coal-oil manufacturers soon began to establish plants near coal sources, and by 1858 in the United States alone twenty-three manufacturers were licensed to use Young's process. Some coal-oil manufacturers who experimented with crude oil obtained from seepages and salt wells were so pleased with kerosine obtained from it that they began to seek out sources of natural petroleum. Hence, the Drake well had an established market for its oil.

Drake's discovery touched off an oil boom. Thousands of wells were drilled in western Pennsylvania; the State produced in 1859 about 2000 barrels (bl) of oil, each containing 42 gal. By 1869 oil production in Pennsylvania had climbed to over 4,000,000 bl annually.

Discovery of oil in other States followed quickly. Oil was discovered in Ohio in 1860, in California in 1861, in Colorado in 1862, and in Kentucky in 1867. Illinois and Indiana joined these oilproducing States in 1886 and 1888, respectively. Kansas began to produce significant amounts of oil in 1900. The discovery of the Spindletop oil pool, near Beaumont, Texas, in 1901 established Texas as the most prolific oil-producing State. Large-scale oil production began in Oklahoma in 1907.

Virtually all the oil produced in the 19th century was used to meet the demand for kerosine, lubricants, and wax. Gasoline (q.v.) was considered a nuisance and was run off into the rivers because no market for the product existed until the development of the internal-combustion engine (q.v.) in the early 1900's. In 1900 about 8000 automobiles were in use, and ten years later the number had risen to 458,000. By 1914 nearly 1,664,000 automobiles utilizing gasoline as fuel were in operation in the U.S., and gasoline was rapidly overtaking kerosine as the most

PETROLEUM

important product made by the oil industry. With the outbreak of World War I, demands for gasoline gave further impetus to gasoline production.

The economies of technologically advanced countries, notably the U.S., Great Britain, Germany, the Soviet Union, and other European countries, were modified to take advantage of the convenience and efficiency of gasoline and diesel engines using petroleum fuel. Continued production of petroleum products became essential to the economies and military establishments of these nations. Hence, the production of petroleum was accelerated greatly. Daily oil production in the U.S. climbed from 3,500,000 bl in 1939 to 4,700,000 in 1945. Annual production during this period averaged 1,500,000,000 bl. As a result of newly discovered deposits, reserves of crude oil rose from 18,500,000,000 bl in 1939 to 20,800,000,000 bl in 1945. Although the oil industry showed a severe decline in the years 1942–43, during the war period as a whole, the rate of growth remained constant and began to increase again by 1944. Wartime demand for oil was so intense that existing wells were operated above the maximum efficiency rate of production, thus depleting the oil reserves. Consequently, a large-scale program of oil-well drilling was undertaken in the postwar years. In the early 1960's about 45,000 wells were drilled per year, compared to 27,717 in 1939. By the late 1960's, about 33,000 oil wells were drilled per year, but in 1971 only about 25,750 were drilled.

Origin. Petroleum was formed millions of years ago, but the exact process of its formation is unknown. It is found only in beds of ancient seas, many of which are now thousands of feet below dry land. A widely accepted theory holds that petroleum was formed from dead plants and animals which settled to the sea bottoms. Some of this matter was carried from the land, along with clay and sand, to the seas by ancient rivers; and some of the matter was marine life, mostly microscopic in size, but occurring in vast quantities. These organic materials were subjected to tremendous pressures at the sea bottom. The pressures generated high temperatures, and heat, together with the action of bacteria, is thought to have converted the organic matter into petroleum, which is therefore called a fossil fuel.

High pressure and heat were also responsible for the cementing together of loose particles to form sedimentary rocks (q.v.) such as shales, sandstones, and limestones. Some of these sedimentary rocks, such as sandstones and limestones, were porous enough to permit oil and gas to penetrate; some rocks retained oil between the sand grains and others such as shales were nonporous, so that oil accumulated when it reached this type of impervious rock.

Petroleum deposits are found in geologic structures such as structural traps, faults, and stratigraphic traps; see GEOLOGY. The simplest form of structural trap is the anticline, a dome structure formed by the upfolding of rock, in which oil, gas, and salt water may be found. Oil may be trapped also in a fault, a deep fracture in which the shearing of the earth's crust shifts the porous oil-bearing strata upward or downward, blocking the oil off against an impervious rock layer. In a stratigraphic trap containing oil, the oil-bearing layer is inclined upward and gradually thins or is pinched out between two impervious layers.

Oil Prospecting. The oil geologist seeks out regions where oil is most likely to be found in abundance. This is determined by the use of aerial surveys in areas with favorable surface indications, of geological maps, and occasionally of data from wells drilled in the area. The geologist seeks sedimentary basins with large accumulations of marine sediments laid down under favorable conditions, on the floors of ancient seas. Sometimes small bore holes may be drilled into the bedrock with a core drill. The drill cuttings are examined for fossil evidence of the approximate age of the underlying rock formations, and for clues to the possible presence of petroleum.

GEOPHYSICAL INSTRUMENTS. After a likely site is discovered, geophysical means are employed to locate geological structures that may contain oil or gas. The instruments used by the geophysicist are the gravimeter, the magnetometer, and the seismograph (q.v.); see GEOPHYSICS.

The gravimeter measures differences in the pull of gravity at the surface of the earth. Geological oil-bearing structures, such as salt domes, anticlines, and faults, cause slight local variations in the force of gravity. These variations disclose the possible presence of oil below the surface of the earth. The magnetometer indicates minute variations in the magnetic field of the earth, caused by different subsurface formations. Varying magnetic intensities over a wide area may be recorded by a recently developed type of magnetometer, which is trailed by a cable from a surveying plane. The seismograph, devised originally to record earthquakes, is an important instrument in present-day prospecting for subsurface structures which may contain oil or natural gas. It detects shock waves caused by a dynamite blast that are reflected back by rock formations. Soft formations reflect weakly on the recording film, and hard formations make larger jogs. By noting the time elapsed between the blast and the return of the shock waves, it is possible to calculate the depth of the formations. Since its adoption for oil prospecting in the mid-1920's, millions of acres of land in the U.S. have been mapped by means of this instrument.

These three geophysical instruments can be used to locate such structures as salt domes, anticlines, and faults, but no scientific instrument currently in use provides any definitive clue to the location of a stratigraphic trap. Such traps may be located only by exhaustive geological study. The eastern Texas oil field, which is the largest in the U.S., is a stratigraphic trap.

Oil Wells. Although prospecting devices can locate some geological structures which may contain petroleum deposits, none indicates the actual presence of petroleum.

DRILLING. The only method of determining the location of oil and gas deposits is drilling, a highly speculative venture even after adequate prospecting. In wildcatting, that is, drilling in virgin territory, the odds are eight to one that the well will prove to be a dry hole. If the well does produce, the financial rewards may not be great. Only about one in fifty wells drilled will exploit a high-yield field with recoverable reserves that represent a large profit on the capital invested; it may take twenty years to recover those reserves.

Most oil wells in the U.S. are drilled by the rotary method, which was invented in 1860. The first rotary drill patent was issued in 1889. In rotary drilling an augerlike bit is fastened to a series of connected steel pipes known as drill pipe. A high derrick supports the drilling mechanism, and power is supplied usually by a steam engine, but sometimes by an internal-combustion engine or an electric motor. As the drill pipe rotates, the bit bores a hole similar to that bored by a carpenter's bit. Drill cuttings are lifted continually to the surface by a circulating-fluid system driven by a pump.

Another drilling method, known as churn drilling, is less commonly in use in the U.S. at present. This method uses an up-and-down motion instead of a rotary motion. The heavy drilling tool, supported by a derrick, is raised by a power-driven cable and allowed to drop, crumbling the rocky formations in its path. The drill cuttings, which are suspended in water, are bailed from the well.

Rotary drilling is capable of producing the deepest wells. Although a number of wells have

A giant portable rig drills for oil in 137 ft. of water in the Gulf of Mexico. Cities Service Co.

been drilled in the U.S. to depths exceeding 20,000 ft., only a few of such depth have proved to be producing wells.

Not all wells are drilled to be producers. Some wells, called service wells, are drilled for injecting water or gas into an underground formation in order to maintain the reservoir pressure or to increase it.

WELL PRODUCTIVITY. The life of a producing well has several phases, known as the flush, settled, stripper, and secondary-recovery periods of production. A flush well flows as a result of natural-gas or water pressure, which forces the oil to the surface. A settled well no longer has sufficient drive, or reservoir pressure, to force the oil upward, so that the oil must be pumped to the surface. A stripper well is in the last stages of its

473

As a pipeline is laid, the pipe is given a corrosion-resistant coating before being lowered into the trench.
Northern Illinois Gas Co.

producing life and yields less than 10 bl per day with pumping. Over 66 percent of the producing wells in the U.S. are strippers. Secondary-recovery wells are those in which adequate reservoir pressure is artificially produced. To bolster reservoir pressure, service wells are drilled to permit natural gas or water to be pumped back into the oil reservoir, creating the pressure required to force the oil to well bores, from which it is pumped to the surface. Of the 25,750 wells drilled in 1971, about 11,600 were oil producers, 3800 were gas producers, and 10,350 were dry holes. Total footage drilled for these wells came to about 125,350,000 ft.

OFFSHORE DRILLING. Tidelands oil deposits, among the most impressive potential resources, figure very significantly in present-day exploration and drilling. Although offshore drilling was begun in 1938 in the Gulf of Mexico, most of the drilling took place after World War II, mainly off the coast of Louisiana but also along the Texas and California coastlines.

Nearly 2200 wells were drilled offshore between 1938 and 1957. About 85 percent of these wells were completed after the settlement in 1953 of the dispute between the Federal and State governments over title to the tidelands area. The dispute was settled by legislation granting to the States ownership of the offshore lands within limits ranging from 3 mi. to 3 leagues off the coast. Title to land beyond these limits was vested in the Federal government. Precise definition of these limits, however, is still disputed.

Offshore-drilling operations initially were conducted from fixed platforms in shallow waters. Subsequently, as operators ventured farther offshore, they built self-contained, permanent platforms large enough to house personnel and supplies, and to furnish space for the drilling rig and auxiliary machinery. Such a platform may be used for the drilling of a dozen or more wells. Another method of offshore drilling uses a small platform and a floating tender, which carries equipment and furnishes accommodations for the drilling crew. In still another method a mobile platform and a submersible barge are used. It is estimated that during the late 1960's almost half of the exploratory wells in the world were drilled from mobile platforms and submersible barges, which can drill in waters ranging from 40 to 100 ft. in depth.

Industry Regulation. Lack of knowledge concerning the behavior of underground oil reservoirs and the proper methods of conservation led to great waste in the early days of oil production. Because of the erroneous belief that restriction of the rate of flow would damage productivity, wells were allowed to flow freely, with a resultant reduction of reservoir pressure and entrapment of much of the oil underground. Gas was flared or blown off into the air, and gushers soaked the ground with downpours of crude oil. After producing at high rates for a very brief period, the early wells entered a long

PETROLEUM

period of low productivity, followed by an even longer period during which expensive pumping was required to recover the oil. In addition, oil was produced long before it was needed and stored in pits hastily dug and diked, so that leakage, evaporation, and fire took a heavy toll.

Knowledge of oil conservation was so meager in the early days of the oil industry that only the most flagrant displays of waste were prohibited by legislation. In 1878 Pennsylvania enacted a law requiring the plugging of abandoned wells in order to keep fresh water from infiltrating into oil-bearing rock. The use of casing, that is, lining the hole with steel pipe, to prevent infiltration of water-bearing sands through the walls of the well was required by Kansas in 1892 and by Texas in 1899. The blowing of natural gas and burning it in open flares was prohibited by law in Indiana in 1891, and Kentucky, Texas, Kansas, Utah, and Ohio soon enacted similar laws.

Prospecting for oil. Below: A seismic truck is used to help select likely sites for drilling for petroleum. The truck sends shock waves deep into the earth from a confined explosion in a detonation chamber. The waves bounce off underground rock formations and are reflected back to the surface, where they are recorded and analyzed. Bottom: A driller inspects the bit on a rig.

Sinclair Oil Corp.

Standard Oil Co. (N.J.)

PETROLEUM

Recognition of the need for oil conservation arose as a result of the glut in oil production that followed the discovery and development, during the period from 1925 to 1930, of vast new oil fields in Texas and Oklahoma. Neither State had adequate control laws, and by 1931 the oil industry was plagued with more oil than could be transported or consumed. The price of oil fell steadily. In 1935 an oil code, called the Interstate Compact to Conserve Oil and Gas, was established on a temporary basis under the administration of the National Recovery Administration (N.R.A.).

A conservation step of far-reaching importance was the establishment by Congress in 1935 of the Interstate Oil Compact Commission. Currently supported by twenty-nine States, including Alaska, the commission functions to conserve oil and gas by the prevention of physical waste. Some States regulate both the drilling of wells and the drawing of petroleum from producing wells, limiting producers to a specified number of barrels per day from each well. Such regulation is designed to counter the tendency of competing companies to overexploit their own wells by recovering a maximum amount of oil before the reservoir stops producing. This type of competition results in rapid depletion of the reservoir pressure with entrapment of much of the oil underground.

Transportation. The transportation of petroleum is a significant factor in the U.S. economy. In terms of tonnage the amount carried compares with that of bituminous coal. An average of more than 560,000,000 gal. of petroleum products are delivered and consumed daily in the U.S. Crude oil and petroleum products are transported at some stage of delivery by pipelines, tankers or barges, railroad tank cars, and tank trucks.

A drilling crew moves another length of pipe into position as the bit drives deeper into earth.
Michigan Consolidated Gas Co.

PETROLEUM

Pipelines, known as gathering lines, move the crude oil from the lease tanks in the oil fields to the trunk pipelines, which carry it directly to refineries or to storage tanks, from which it may be pumped into tankers for delivery to refineries along the eastern seaboard. The refineries deliver in tanks, trucks, or by means of product pipelines to consumer markets such petroleum products as gasoline, kerosine, and fuel oil for diesel engines and domestic heating.

The U.S. has about 209,500 mi. of pipeline. Gathering and trunk pipelines carrying crude oil account for about 70 percent of the total mileage. The remainder consists of product pipelines. The railroads handle less volume than the product pipelines but more than the trucking industry. Tankers transport one third of the total tonnage produced by the petroleum industry.

Refining. An oil refinery is essentially a complex still in which crude oil is heated so that various fractions are progressively vaporized; see DISTILLATION. The resulting vapors, drawn off and recondensed, form the lighter petroleum products, that is, gases, gasoline, kerosine and heating oil. The heavier fractions, used for heavy lubricating oil and residual fuel oils, are drawn from the bottom of the still after the lighter fractions have been evaporated.

To increase the yield of gasoline, heavier fractions may be converted by means of either a thermal or catalytic process called cracking (q.v.). In thermal cracking, some of the heavier components of crude oil are subjected to high temperatures and pressures that split the hydrocarbon molecules apart. The catalytic cracking process involves the use of a catalyst in conjunction with heat and pressure.

More recently developed processes, such as hydrogenation, hydroforming, polymerization, and alkylation, modify completely the chemical structure of the petroleum molecules; polymerization and alkylation have been in use since the 1940's. These processes produce gasoline and other substances which have the desired physical properties, notably boiling point for gasoline and viscosity for oil. The substances also have desirable chemical properties, including high antiknock rating and lack of gum-forming tendencies.

The fractions produced by distillation of petroleum are given various names, which are not accurately defined. In more or less definite order, the first fractions are the gaseous hydrocarbons, methane, and ethane, which are used in chemical manufacture and as refinery fuel. The highly volatile liquids or easily condensed gases, propane, butane, and pentane are also used in chemical manufacture and may be sold as bottled gas. A low-boiling fraction containing principally pentane and hexane is sometimes used as a solvent under the name of petroleum ether.

The most important fraction is gasoline, which generally boils in the range 100° F. (38° C.) to 400° F. (204° C.). The amount of gasoline obtained from each barrel of crude oil has been increased greatly through improved refining techniques. In 1918 only about 26 bl of gasoline were derived from every 100 bl of crude oil refined, compared to the present-day yield of almost 45 bl of gasoline from the same amount of crude oil. Commercial gasoline used as fuel in automobiles and airplanes consists of a mixture of products; they include gasoline obtained by distilling crude oil, natural gasoline condensed out of natural gas, cracked gasoline, and other compounds, each of which contributes to the octane rating and other properties of the fuel. Gasoline varies greatly in volatility and properties. In the U.S., for example, gasoline sold to motorists in winter contains more of the low-boiling constituents in order to permit easy starting of automobile engines in cold weather; gasoline sold in the summer contains less of such low-boiling constituents, in order to prevent vapor lock. The term "naphtha" is sometimes used synonymously with gasoline; but the term "special naphtha" is often applied, by the U.S. Bureau of Mines, to a fraction intermediate between gasoline and kerosine.

Kerosine generally boils in the range 400° F. (204° C.) to 600° F. (316° C.). The next fractions below kerosine are called gas oil and fuel oil. The light-fuel-oil category includes domestic heating oils, diesel fuel, tractor fuel, spray oils, insecticides, smudge oil, absorption oils, and gas oils. Gas oil was used formerly as an enricher for manufactured gas, which has been largely supplanted by natural gas; it is currently used primarily as cracking stock from which cracked gasoline and other products are obtained. The remainder of the fuel-oil fraction, heavy fuel oil, is used as fuel in the refinery or is sold as bunker oil, an inexpensive fuel.

The next fraction is lubricating oil; nearly all crude oils have some lubricating stocks among the heavier fractions. To prepare commercial lubricating oils, these fractions are redistilled into light, medium, and heavy grades. Many of the lubricants intended for special uses require further processing. Of about 2400 products produced by refineries, the large majority is in the lubricants category, including oils and greases.

PETROLEUM

An oil company scientist at work on a project to manufacture protein from petroleum.
Esso Research and Engineering Co.

The next fraction is a semisolid called petrolatum (q.v.), widely known by the trademark name Vaseline; still heavier fractions are asphalt and wax. When a batch of petroleum is distilled, producing these successive fractions, a nonvolatile portion remains in the still at the end of the run; this portion consists almost wholly of carbon, and is called petroleum coke.

Just as liquid petroleum contains some gases in solution, natural gas may contain liquids such as gasoline in vapor state. This gasoline is extracted by cooling, by absorption in oil, or by absorption on charcoal or silica gel, forming natural gasoline or casinghead gasoline. Natural gasoline is frequently mixed with refinery gasoline without further processing.

Both crude oil and natural gas are the base stock from which many petrochemicals are obtained. These petrochemicals, which are sold to the chemical industry, account for about 2 percent of the volume produced by the petroleum industry.

Researchers in the U.S. and Europe are beginning to synthesize fats, carbohydrates, and proteins from oil and petroleum products, using certain strains of bacteria and yeast in the process. Petroleum-based proteins are produced as a tasteless, bland, white powder or flour costing less than the equivalent amount of skim-milk powder. In the Soviet Union and Nigeria the petroleum flour is being used increasingly to feed livestock.

The Petroleum Industry. The consumption of petroleum products in the U.S. received its greatest impetus from the increasing use of automobiles during and after World War I, and the acceptance by industry and public utilities of heavy fuel oils for driving steam generators. Domestic demand represented about 2,500,000 bl daily in 1929, twice as much as the daily consumption during the first year of the war.

Another sharp increase in domestic demand occurred after World War II. That increase was followed by a record rise in imports of crude oil from the Middle East. In 1957, as a result of the crisis involving the Suez Canal (q.v.), voluntary quotas established by the petroleum industry prevented further increases in oil imports.

RESERVES. It was estimated in the early 1970's that proved reserves of crude oil in the U.S. totaled almost 39,000,000,000 bl. The oil reserves in the six major oil-producing countries of the Middle East were estimated at 260,000,000,000 bl during the same period. One of these countries, Kuwait, a sheikhdom about the size of Connecticut, had oil reserves estimated at 70,000,000,000 bl, and Saudi Arabia had reserves of about 77,000,000,000 bl. The important South American oil-producing country Venezuela had reserves of about 15,500,000,000 bl.

PRODUCTION. Although its oil reserves are well below those of the Middle East, the U.S. leads the world in production. (1970, 4,129,604,000 bl).

This lead, however, is shrinking; in 1946 the U.S. produced 63 percent of the total world output, compared to only about 24 percent in the late 1960's. Other important oil-producing nations in the late 1960's were the Soviet Union, which accounts for 16 percent of world production; Venezuela, 9.4 percent; Saudi Arabia, 7.4 percent; Iran, 7.4 percent; Libya, 6.8 percent; Kuwait, 6.3 percent; Iraq, 3.4 percent; and Canada, 2.7 percent. World production of crude oil during that period averaged more than 14,000,000,000 bl annually.

Pollution and Conservation. A great deal of concern has recently been expressed by public officials, health officers, and conservationists in many industrialized nations about pollution of the environment caused by petroleum and its refined products. Several major accidents at sea involving mammoth oil tankers prompted international discussions about the contamination of the coastline and pollution of the sea by massive oil spills and the resulting harmful effects on ocean environment by both the crude-petroleum spills and the chemicals used to dissipate them; see ECOLOGY; OCEAN AND OCEANOGRAPHY; WATER POLLUTION. Another pollution problem caused by oil was the discharge of waste oil products into the sewage systems and rivers by industrial plants and motor vehicles. Conservationists also voiced disapproval of the construction of major oil pipelines for their deleterious impact on the ecology of the surrounding region.

The largest and probably most harmful source of air pollution (q.v.), particularly in heavily populated metropolitan areas such as New York City and Los Angeles, Calif., was found to come from the exhaust emissions, of the 100,000,000 gasoline-driven motor vehicles registered in the U.S. Steps were being taken by Federal, State, and local governments to prevent the ill effects of such discharges consisting mainly of carbon monoxide and nitrogen oxides. The production of more refined gasoline and the development of an internal-combustion engine of lesser polluting potency, was being encouraged as well as the development of electric and steam-driven automobiles; see AUTOMOBILE.

PETROLOGY. See GEOLOGY: *Petrology.*

PETRONIUS, Gaius, in full GAIUS PETRONIUS ARBITER (d. about 66), Roman writer. Petronius was referred to as "Arbiter Elegantiae" ("judge of elegance") by the Roman historian Cornelius Tacitus (q.v.). Because of his feeling for luxury and elegance, he planned many of the entertainments at the court of the Roman emperor Nero (q.v.). Petronius also served as proconsul of Bithynia, and later consul. His influence with Nero aroused the jealousy of the Roman politician Ofonius Tigellinus (d. 69), another of Nero's favorites, who brought false accusations against him; these aroused Nero's anger, and Petronius, realizing that his death was inevitable, committed suicide at Cumae. Before his death he is said to have written and dispatched to Nero a paper containing an account of the tyrant's vices.

Petronius is generally believed to have been the author of a remarkable work of fiction, a satirical romance titled *Satyricon* (about 60). Parts of the fifteenth and sixteenth books have survived, and the best-known English translation of the fragments dates from 1694. The *Satyricon* is memorable as the earliest example in European literature of the picaresque novel (q.v.), and is the prototype of such 18th-century novels as *The Adventures of Gil Blas of Santillane* (1715–35; Eng. trans., 1749) by the French author Alain René Lesage and *Roderick Random* (1748) by the British novelist Tobias George Smollett (qq.v.). The *Satyricon* is a unique, often extremely bawdy, description of life in the 1st century of the Christian era. Although the narrator speaks in the best Latin of the Silver Age (*see* LATIN LITERATURE: *The Silver Age*) the work is especially valuable for the colloquialisms and solecisms in the speeches of many of the characters. The most famous episode of the fragmentary work is *Trimalchio's Banquet,* a realistic description of a banquet given by an ostentatious newly rich freedman. The *Satyricon* was the basis of a motion picture by the Italian director Federico Fellini (q.v.) in 1969.

PETROPAVLOVSK, city of the Soviet Union, in Kazakh S.S.R., and capital of North Kazhakhstan Oblast, on the Ishim R., about 175 miles w. of Omsk. The city is served by a railway and is an important commercial center, with an extensive trade in livestock and agricultural products. Flour milling, tanning, meat packing, canning, and the manufacture of agricultural machinery are leading industries. Pop. (1970 est.) 173,000.

PETRÓPOLIS, city of Brazil, in Rio de Janeiro State, about 30 miles N. of the city of Rio de Janeiro. The city is a popular health and summer resort. It is named in honor of Pedro II (q.v.), Emperor of Brazil, for whom it was a favorite summer residence. Pop. (1960) 93,849.

PETROVGRAD. See ZRENJANIN.

PETROZAVODSK, city of the Soviet Union, in the Russian S.F.S.R., and capital of the Karelian A.S.S.R., on the w. shore of Lake Onega, about 175 miles N.E. of Leningrad. Substantial deposits of iron ore are located in the vicinity as well as a vast timber wealth and numerous sawmills; the manufacture of pig iron, machinery, furniture, paper, skis, and other timber products are important industries of the city. Pop. (1970) 185,000.

PETTY, name of a family of British statesmen. See under LANSDOWNE.

PETTY LARCENY. See LARCENY.

PETUNIA, genus of perennial herbs belonging to the Nightshade family. The genus, which

Petunia, genus Petunia

J. D. Spillane – National Audubon Society

PEWTER

Pewter. English and Dutch pieces from the 18th and 19th centuries. — Metropolitan Museum of Art

contains more than twenty-five species, is native to South America, chiefly Argentina and southern Brazil, is naturalized in Central America and Mexico, and is widely cultivated for its showy flowers. The leaves are alternate; the slender stems are weak, causing the plants to sprawl. Petunia flowers, which are usually solitary, have five sepals, five petals, five stamens, and a solitary pistil. The corolla is usually funnel-shaped. The fruit is a two-celled, many-seeded capsule. The common petunia cultivated as a bedding plant in gardens in the United States is *P. hybrida,* a hybrid between two Argentine species: *P. axillaris,* with white flowers, and *P. violacea,* with violet flowers. This plant is popular for use in window boxes, because its stems droop over the sides; varieties used for this purpose are called balcony petunias. Many strains of the common petunia have been developed by horticulturists, including plants with red, pink, purple, or parti-colored flowers. Fringed flowers, double flowers, and flowers reaching a diameter of over 5 in. have been produced on petunia plants by careful breeding. Newer dwarf varieties with stronger stems, growing as a low mound, are popular as edging plants for garden borders.

PEWTER, any of several alloys consisting principally of tin and lead, formerly used extensively for making domestic and religious utensils, vessels, and decorative objects. The term is also applied to objects made of the alloy, most specifically to pewter tankards or mugs. The common form of pewter consists of four parts of tin to one of lead, frequently combined with small amounts of antimony, copper, and bismuth (qq.v.) to produce a more durable alloy (qq.v.). It is a relatively soft, bluish gray metal, similar in appearance to tin. Pewter was used throughout Europe from the Middle Ages to the end of the 18th century in the form of communion vessels and plates, altar furniture, flagons, tankards, and household objects of various kinds. The production of pewter reached its height in England during the Elizabethan period, but declined throughout Europe during the 19th century. In America pewter was used primarily for the manufacture of domestic utensils and was particularly popular from about 1750 to 1850. Because of the poisonous properties of its lead and antimony content (see LEAD: *Lead Poisoning*), pewter has largely been replaced in domestic utensils and vessels by other alloys, although it still is prized by antique collectors.

PEYOTE or **MESCAL,** common names for a small, spineless, turnip-shaped cactus, *Lophophora williamsii,* native to Mexico and the southwestern United States. The grayish, mushroom-shaped tops, called peyote or mescal buttons, yield nine alkaloids, of which mescaline is the principal active agent. The dried buttons are eaten, brewed into a tea, or powdered and packaged in capsules. The mescaline in these preparations alters perception, producing vivid color hallucinations, inaccurate estimation of time, and a feeling of anxiety. It is not known to be habit forming, but use of impure or large doses can have toxic effects, such as nausea and depressed breathing. Peyote has been used since pre-Columbian times by American Indians in their religious rites; the practice has been incorporated into their modern Christian ceremonies. Mescaline has been used experimentally in investigations of schizophrenia and other psychoses.

See PSYCHEDELIC DRUGS.